THE
CROWN
GUIDE
TO THE
WORLD'S
GREAT
PLAYS

THE CROWN GUIDE TO THE WORLD'S GREAT PLAYS

From Ancient Greece to Modern Times

REVISED, UPDATED EDITION

by Joseph T. Shipley

CROWN PUBLISHERS, INC.
New York

To Shirley,
who with me for half a century
has seen most of these plays

Published by Crown Publishers, Inc.,
One Park Avenue, New York, New York 10016, and
simultaneously in Canada by
General Publishing Company Limited
Manufactured in the United States of America
Library of Congress Cataloging in Publication Data
Shipley, Joseph Twadell, 1893–
The Crown guide to the world's great plays.
Rev. ed. of: Guide to great plays. 1956.
Includes index.
1. Drama—Stories, plots, etc. 2. Drama—History and
criticism. 3. Theater—History. I. Shipley, Joseph
Twadell, 1893–   Guide to great plays. II. Title.
PN6112.5.S45   1984   809.2   83-27211
ISBN 0-517-55392-9

10 9 8 7 6 5 4 3 2 1
First Revised and Updated Edition

Preface to the Second Edition

SINCE THE PUBLICATION of the *Guide to Great Plays* in 1956, new types of drama have appeared. The work of the "angry young men" has sparked upon the scene; plays without plot have rambled across the stages; the absurdists have indulged their fantasies, finding no meaning in life; dramas have striven to bypass the checks and restraints of the intellect in order to drive directly at the basic human feelings.

Revivals of the classics have of course continued, their frequency indicating which plays seem to have relevance to the time. A few older plays have here been added; some were left out of the first edition by pressure of space; some have grown, in the years since, to seem more significant than when first produced. On the other hand, a number of plays in the first edition do not appear in this one. It seemed appropriate, in the first work of this kind, to include all the ancient Greek and Roman plays extant. This gesture to our great predecessors having been made, it seems now fitting to include only those that have to their credit more than the accident of survival.

The definition of *great* is of course subjective, and flexible. A lengthily popular play, as with a record run, while perhaps not intrinsically great, has been at least a "great success" and may call for inclusion on the grounds of history. After its time, such a play may well be omitted; thus, *Abie's Irish Rose* is absent from these pages. Similarly, *The Mousetrap,* at this writing in its thirty-second continuous year on the London stage, hence included in this edition, will in all probability be dropped by whoever prepares such a book as this for the twenty-first century, when I too shall have dropped from circulation.

And inevitably, other plays that seemed significant in their day, "great" in one or another aspect of their writing or production, will have lapsed to less estimation in the coursing of the years. A play may have been temporarily a *succès de scandale,* social, political, or sexual, as were *Tobacco Road, Waiting for Lefty, The Captive*; these also have lapsed, as may, from the present volume, *Five-Finger Exercise; Accidental Death of an Anarchist; No Sex Please, We're British.* I have also decided, in this volume, not to include one-act plays.

I was first taken to the theatre, to see *The Mikado,* when I was six years old. I was fortunate in having an uncle able to secure free seats for me all through my teens. I have been a professional reviewer of the New York theatre since 1918, and for many years have also covered plays in Paris and London. I have thus seen many of the plays in this volume at their premieres and most of the older ones in revivals, sometimes several times. I have seen Hamlets, beginning with Sarah Bernhardt. I have seen every Gilbert and Sullivan company in New York in this century. I still feel that the theatre is the most rewarding form of public art.

In addition to the critics on both sides of the Atlantic whom I quote, I wish to express special thanks to Dorothy Swerdlove, director of the Theatre Collection of the New York Public Library at Lincoln Center, whose thoughtfulness and kindness in laying out material, with many suggestions of sources, greatly facilitated my research. Of her large staff, Messrs. Roderick Bladel, Jonathan Chappell, Richard C. Lynch, and Daniel C. Patri also evinced continuing interest and extended special help through the many hours during which I drew from this fullest reservoir of information regarding the living theatre. Nothing like it exists in London or Paris. Dorothy Swerdlove and her predecessors, George Freedley and Paul Myers, have created a constantly growing treasure store of theatre material, of which New York can justly be proud.

Other professional critics and experienced theatre folk have been consulted before I chose or rejected plays, but final responsibility is of course my own. I trust that the great body of plays herein will seem representative of the richest dramatic accomplishment in world theatre.

JOSEPH T. SHIPLEY

London and New York, 1984

Note

ALL PLAYS are arranged under the names of their authors, who are listed alphabetically. A few by unknown authors follow these. An index of titles appears at the end of the book. An asterisk (*) in the text indicates a cross-reference to the play or author thus marked.

List of Abbreviations of Organizations

ACT • American Conservatory Theatre, San Francisco.

ACSTA • American Center for Stanislavsky Theatre Art, New York.

ANTA • American National Theatre and Academy. The Guild Theatre, New York, opening April 13, 1935, with Helen Hayes in *Caesar and Cleopatra,* was renamed the Anta Theatre in 1950, for productions of ANTA, but since 1957 has been open for commercial use. In 1982 it was renamed the Virginia, by Jujamcyn, a new firm buying theatres and producing plays, to vie with the Shuberts and the Niederlanders. *Jujamcyn* is an acrostic telescope of Judy, James, and Cynthia, children of James H. Binger and Virginia McKnight Binger, who combine the wealth of Minnesota Mining and Manufacturing and the Honeywell Corp.

APA • Association of Producing Artists, founded in 1961 by Ellis Rabb. In 1964 this became APA-Phoenix, merging with the Phoenix Theatre, founded in 1953 by T. Edward Hambledon and Norris Houghton. This association ended in 1969; since then Phoenix has again been producing on its own, in 1976 adopting the policy of presenting only new plays. It has headquarters at the Ann Arbor University of Michigan and plays annually in several cities, including New York.

ASOLO • State Theatre of Florida, at Sarasota. The Asolo Theatre began in 1798, opening in the medieval castle of queen Catherine Carnaro, in the little town of Asolo, Italy, twenty miles northwest of Venice. For a time it was the home theatre of Eleonora Duse. In 1949 it was transplanted to the Ringling Museum in Sarasota, where, in 1960, with modern equipment, it was taken over by what grew into the Asolo State Theatre Company.

BAM • Brooklyn Academy of Music, New York. Home of the Chelsea Theatre and many theatrical and musical events.

CIRCLE IN THE SQUARE • So named because first at a theatre-in-the-round at Sheridan Square, Greenwich Village, New York. It was founded in 1951 by Theodore Mann. In 1972 it added an annual season on Broadway.

CRC • Circle Repertory Company, New York. Founded 1969. Lucille Lortel, whose Greenwich Village Theatre de Lys was noted for its ventures, is on the board.

CSC • Classic Stage Company. New York. Founded 1967. In 1983 it changed its name to City Stage Company. Presented the two parts of Goethe's *Faust*.

ELT • Equity Library Theatre, New York. Founded in 1943 by Sam Jaffe and George Freedley; producing only revivals, long free, hoping to reach a new young public while providing a showcase for young professionals in the various fields of the theatrical arts. Since 1961 ELT has been presenting plays at the Master Theatre in the Roerich Museum on Riverside Drive, New York. Its usual annual program is four musicals and four straight shows. At the Lincoln Center Library are nine new workshop productions called ELT Informals.

FRINGE • Applied originally to the scores of activities in small houses or open squares in Edinburgh, during but not of the major offerings of its annual festival, the term *fringe* came also to be loosely applied to the smaller theatrical houses, groups, and offerings outside of the commercial sections of the London theatre. *See* OffBway.

IASTA • Institute for Advanced Studies in the Theatrical Arts, New York. Presented plays with directors invited from abroad.

LOOM • Light Opera of Manhattan. Home of the American Savoyards, imaginatively directed by William Mount-Burke. Founded in 1968, specializing in the works of Gilbert and Sullivan, though from 1975 adding a few other light operas to the repertory. On East Seventy-fourth Street, New York.

NSC • New Shakespeare Company, founded 1962 by David Conville, especially for the Open Air Theatre in Regents Park, London. (Conville has directed *Love's Labor's Lost* in Germany and, in 1980, *A Midsummer Night's Dream* in Turkish in Istanbul.) The Open Air Theatre has a most attractive outdoor setting. In front, a level greensward, where quick scenery, if necessary, can set a room. To audience left, a road wide enough for a car. Right, a rising footpath past the slant entrance to a high cave, on into a grove. Back center, a path up a steep hill in a woodland, flanked, some thirty feet back, by the door of a wooden fort or castle, of which a balcony can be glimpsed through the treetops. At the twentieth anniversary performances, the Queen planted a tree.

   This is an ideal setting for much of Shakespeare—though on an August afternoon in 1983 I saw NSC's first musical, *Bashville,* music by Denis King, lyrics and adaptation by Benny Green, from *The Admirable Bashville* (1901) by Bernard Shaw, itself adapted by Shaw from his novel *Cashel Byron's Profession* (1886). The musical, like Shaw's play, is a romp in which, among many amusing and some bloody incidents, prizefighter Cashel Byron in "Byronic" mood (the word is his) finds himself bound in mutual love with the wealthy lady Lydia Carew. The King of Zulu, for no apparent reason arriving with his bare-limbed spear-wielding warriors, after their dance and song, "Black Man's Burden," sits on a high throne to watch the prize ring, where Byron batters his opponent. The defeated man takes a surprise revenge (offstage), beating Cashel with bare fists, so that he comes in bloody, but unbowed, to the great distress of the lady. At the end, Cashel himself is distressed by the arrival of his mother, a bedizened and formidable woman of no uncertain background, who nonetheless reveals that her son is actually, if I may use the term, "of gentle blood," and thus a fit match for the lady. Hailing one of her worshipping valets, Bashville, as fated for physical success, Cashel and Lydia cement their union. They were excellently played by Peter Woodward and Christine Collier.

Shaw was long fond of boxing. Champion James J. Corbett at Daly's, 1906, enacted Cashel Byron. Champion Gene Tunney and his wife were good friends of the Shaws; Tunney said that he learned how to ride a punch from Cashel Byron. *The Admirable Bashville* was played at the London Imperial, June 7, 1903, with Henrietta Watson as Lydia and Ben Webster as Cashel. C. Aubrey Smith, as a policeman, was dressed to resemble Shaw. There was a revival at His Majesty's, January 26, 1909, with Webster and Marie Löhr.

About his play, which is in blank verse, Shaw wrote, in 1909, that he had produced "a masterpiece to show that I had the Shakespearean technique at my fingers' ends if I chose to use it. . . . I may say that I am childishly fond of blank verse, and that my idea of happiness in a regenerated world is to write Elizabethan plays and rehearse them every day. . . . The euphemism and extravagance of the lines do not go beyond the ordinary practice of Shakespeare. I have occasionally patched in actual Shakespearean lines to show that the patches are never noticeable; they fit imperceptibly into my own stuff." Part of the fun (in both play and musical) comes from detecting such Shakespearean "patches." Starting with Lydia's impossibly pompous soliloquy that opens the play, Shaw's blank verse is, as he himself proclaims, "irresistibly ridiculous."

With fresh songs, including "Fancy Free," "One Pair of Hands," "A Gentleman's True to His Code," and "Take the Road to the Ring," *Bashville* is a constantly amusing flight of fancy about a fighter and the lady who joins his love. The Shakespeare out-of-door productions are also delightful.

NT • National Theatre of Great Britain, on the south bank of the River Thames, London. Its one building, opened by the Queen on October 25, 1976, houses three theatres: the 1,160-seat Olivier, with an open stage; the 890-seat Lyttleton, with an adjustable proscenium stage; and the rectangular Cottesloe, where 400 can watch.

NYSF • New York Shakespeare Festival. In 1954 Joseph Papp organized a Shakespeare workshop in a Lower East Side church basement. In 1956 he began offering Shakespeare free in the city parks; since 1962 the Delacorte Theatre has housed the annual free summer shows in Central Park. In 1964 its Mobile Theatre began touring city parks and playgrounds. In 1967 it took over the old Astor Library on downtown Lafayette Street, as the Public Theatre, opening with *Hair.* * Several of the productions have gone from the five playhouses in the Public up to Broadway, where at this writing *A Chorus Line* and *The Pirates of Penzance* * are still running, the latter also a current hit in London. *A Chorus Line,* opening quietly at the Public on May 21, 1975, moved to the Shubert that July; it took the Pulitzer Prize and danced along until it attained the longest run in Broadway history, moving as I write toward its 3,500th performance (see *Grease* *). Opening at the London Drury Lane, July 22, 1976, it ran for three years. It has played in 185 American cities, and has had ten companies touring abroad. Its story is novel in musical comedy: various members of the chorus tell how—often despite their parents—they came to choose this career. Conceived and choreographed by Michael Bennett, the book was written by James Kirkwood and Nicholas Dante, with music by Marvin Hamlisch, lyrics by Edward Kleban. While other musicals have been more sparkling or more spectacular, in sheer popularity *A Chorus Line* is unsurpassed.

Papp's most recent activity, with the consent of both the British and the American Actors' Equity, has been to organize a mutual international exchange. The London Royal Court Theatre sends him one of its plays, cast and all; he sends them one of his. This trade began on December 26, 1982, with the coming to the Public of the London production of *Top Girls,* by Caryl Churchill: a curious piece in which Pope Joan, Patient Griselda (from the olden tale), Dull Gret (from the Breughel painting), Isobel Bird (Victorian explorer), and Lady Nijo (Japanese geisha) sit at a banquet table and talk their hearts out. (Pope Joan, in medieval anticlerical legend, donned monastic habits to be near Friar Faldo; being clever and obedient, she was elected in 855 to succeed Pope Leo IV—and gave birth during the enthronement ceremony.) Transferred to the Royal Court, June 23, 1983, was *Buried Inside Extra,* by Thomas Babe, showing the final day of a newspaper, whose editor for twenty years has kept a liaison with a colleague; his wife turns up to confront them; an atomic bomb is ticking away in the building. Both plays are mentioned here only as the start of what one hopes will prove a fruitful international cooperation between the Royal Court Theatre, noted for its avant-garde ventures, and Joseph Papp, noted for his initiative, drive, and taste attuned to the desires of the young generation of viewers and aspirants in the theatre.

OFFBWAY, OFFOFFBWAY • Not part of the commercial theatre, which runs from about Times Square (Forty-second Street) to Lincoln Center (Sixty-fifth Street) on or near Broadway, New York. The distinction between OffBway and OffOffBway is elastic, but in the main the second group has fewer, if any, Equity members and is both more amateurish and more sporadic. *The Scene* of May 1977 lists 25 London Fringe houses and 288 OffOffBway, with addresses and occasional descriptions.

PHOENIX • *See* APA.

RADA • Royal Academy of Dramatic Art, London. The goal of most English youth who aspire to the stage, but not quite so *de rigueur* as the Paris Conservatoire, which is virtually prerequisite to work at the French State theatres.

ROUNDABOUT • Founded 1965 by Gene Feist, on West Twenty-sixth Street, New York, and since 1974 also on West Twenty-third Street, presents annual series of new plays and modern classics.

RSC • Royal Shakespeare Company of England, producing mainly Shakespeare but also classics and some new plays. It has two houses at Stratford-upon-Avon. In London it produced mainly at the Aldwych until 1982, when it moved to the large new Barbican Center, built on land devastated by the Luftwaffe in World War II, near London's Roman Wall and the Church of St. Giles Cripplegate, where Milton is buried. In the center the RSC has a 200-seat pit, for experimental work, as well as the main 1,200-seat Barbican

Theatre. As I write, the RSC is showing its production of *All's Well That Ends Well** in New York.

SOHO • London: district around Shaftesbury Avenue, center of theatres, film studios, and night life. New York: named after the London district, but actually an acrostic of *So*uth of *Ho*uston Street, below Greenwich Village, Manhattan, where, after the mid-twentieth century, artists began to rent empty lofts, and OffOffBway productions were offered.

STRAW HAT CIRCUIT • In the mid-years of the twentieth century, when summer theatres were sprouting all over the land, special companies were formed, usually with a musical or light comedy, with which they toured what came to be called the straw hat circuit. Thus, a summer theatre could fill its schedule without the trouble and expense of organizing its own productions.

THE SUPPLIANTS   *Aeschylus*

This is the earliest extant Greek drama, the first of the seven plays by
Aeschylus (525–455 B.C.) that have survived (almost ninety were apparently written). The worthy scion of a distinguished Athenian family,
Aeschylus used the tales of the Greek gods and heroes as the spearheads of
his searching inquiries into basic human problems.

Drama during Aeschylus' early days was a matter of ritual. Aeschylus was
in large measure responsible for its theatrical growth. Although *The Suppliants,* produced about 492 B.C., has the originally religious chorus of fifty
members to serve as its protagonist, there is also a distinct player, second to
the leader of the chorus. If, moreover, as Aristotle says, it was Sophocles that
introduced the third actor into the drama, Aeschylus in his trilogy the
Oresteia was prompt to make use of the added player.

At annual contests, the Greek dramatists presented three serious plays
and one satyr-play, all four usually based on a single theme. Thus, *The
Suppliants* is one play, the first of a trilogy. The other two, *The Egyptians* and
The Daughters of Danaus, have been lost, so that it is impossible to say how
Aeschylus fully developed his theme.

A number of mystical, religious interpretations of the drama have been put
forth, but basically *The Suppliants* is a story of love and freedom. The fifty
daughters of Danaus, having fled their native Egypt for Argos, the home of
their ancestress, Io, beg protection against the fifty sons of Aegyptus. Pel-
asgus, King of Argos, is thus confronted with the problem: shall he grant the
privilege of sanctuary, so highly esteemed by the Athenians, to the daughters
of Danaus, at the possible cost of war? Or shall he refuse that privilege,
perhaps to find the altars of the gods polluted with blood? After some
hesitation, he offers them sanctuary and refuses to turn them over to the
herald of Aegyptus. The play opens with the prayer of the chorus of Danaids
to the benevolent Zeus and ends with the hope that he will continue to favor
them, "for the hands of thy saving are sure."

The Egyptians probably carried the story on through the eventual success
of the sons of Aegyptus, to the enforced marriage of the maidens, whom their
father Danaus commanded to kill their husbands on their wedding night.
Only one daughter, Hypermnestra, in love with Lynceus, spared her husband
on that fatal night. In the third play, *The Daughters of Danaus,* Hypermnestra was probably brought to trial, and defended by Aphrodite, thus
manifesting Aeschylus' belief in the universal power and the claims of love.

Some of the most violent dramatic conflicts in *The Suppliants* arise when

1

the herald of Aegyptus and his cohort seek to capture the fifty maidens. Their Egyptian costumes are themselves striking, the dark masks contrasting with white robes traced with formal patterns in gold. The lines of the herald are sung alternately with those of the daughters of Danaus, during "a frenzied symbolic dance." The Chorus, as Gilbert Murray has described it, is "pursued by a hideous rabble of negroid slaves from Egypt, led by a brutal Herald. The effect is somewhat dreamlike: the virgin pursued by the ravisher, the white girl pursued by something black and dreadful, the Greek woman—or, as we should say, the English woman—pursued by a creature of foreign speech." The impact of such choral scenes on the Athenian audience can hardly be recaptured today.

Even in the corrupt text of *The Suppliants* that has come down to us, the language is rich yet simple. It has been compared in magnificence to certain passages of Isaiah. In simplicity of movement and beauty of form, this earliest European drama sets a standard that every subsequent period has found it hard to equal.

THE PERSIANS   *Aeschylus*

Written in 472 B.C., this is the only surviving Greek tragedy that deals with an actual historical situation, as opposed to the legendary or mythological themes of the other dramas. Dealing with a battle in which Aeschylus himself had fought and in which the very existence of his city was at stake, the play depicts the enemy of Athens without rancor. The Persians are vigorous human beings who maintain their dignity even in defeat. As Gilbert Murray has remarked, "There is no hatred of them, no remotest suggestion of what we now call 'war propaganda.'"

The great conflict between the Greeks and the Persians is presented by Aeschylus to the Athenians from the Persian point of view. The glory of Athens is made manifest only in the Persian picture of the significance and the enormity of their defeat.

The action of *The Persians* takes place in Susa, the capital of the Persian Empire, in 480 B.C., the year of the battle of Salamis. Atossa, the widow of Darius and mother of Xerxes, awaits word of her son's victory. A messenger brings news of disastrous losses on land and sea. The ghost of Darius joins in Atossa's lamentation; then Xerxes himself appears, crushed by the blow that has stricken his host and his farthest hopes.

The ordinarily trite consideration that pride goeth before a fall is turned in *The Persians* to a pondering of basic ethical concepts in the Greek drama; great or prolonged prosperity breeds satiety (koros), leads to pride, boastfulness, insolence (hybris) and thence to ruin (ate). Aeschylus' ethical fervor is combined with an intense patriotism. A panegyric could be no more inspiring than the description the Persian messenger gives of the great battle of Salamis; it is perhaps the most famous passage in all Greek poetry. Thus, *The Persians* accomplishes the unique feat of awakening sorrow for the defeated foe together with respect for the righteous victor.

The choregus (patron who paid the expenses) of *The Persians* was the great Athenian lover of democracy, Pericles. In 472 B.C. the play won first prize.

The Persians was performed at the Sorbonne, Paris, in 1936. During the same year, Eva Sikelianos worked on a production for the American Federal Theatre project, and in 1939 she helped dancer Ted Shawn with a "visible song" arrangement of the opening chorus of the play at Lee, Massachusetts. A version by Gilbert Murray was broadcast in England in 1939. In beauty, dignity, and moral power, *The Persians* is one of the great dramas of the world.

PROMETHEUS BOUND   *Aeschylus*

In the trilogy of which *Prometheus Bound* is the one surviving play, Aeschylus ponders one of the most perplexing problems of all time—the existence of evil in the world. If the divine power of the universe is accepted as both omnipotent and benevolent, the problem is indeed a complex one. Seeking a solution, Jews and Christians look upon the serpent, which led Adam and Eve to eat of the fruit of the tree of knowledge, as an instrument of the powers of darkness, and upon Lucifer, the light-bearer, as a fallen angel.

Prometheus, "the fore-thinker," (as was probably shown in the lost first play of the trilogy, *Prometheus the Fire-Bearer*), taught man the use of fire. But Aeschylus, veering from his usual concept, in *Prometheus Bound* depicts Zeus as a jealous tyrant, who punishes Prometheus for having brought that knowledge to man. The Biblical story offers a parallel to that of Aeschylus: "And the Lord God said, Behold, the man is become as one of us, to know good and evil; and now, lest he put forth his hand, and take also of the tree of life, and eat, and live forever: Therefore the Lord God sent him forth from the Garden of Eden" (*Genesis* 3, 22–23). Prometheus, however, by possession of a secret regarding the future of Zeus, is able to secure his freedom, as was probably depicted in the last play of the trilogy, *Prometheus Unbound*.

The portrayal of Prometheus as the "suffering servant" and stricken benefactor of mankind brought Aeschylus before the city magistrates on charges of impious disrespect to the gods. Alexander Harvey in *The Freeman* (January 31, 1923) surmised that in summoning Aeschylus the magistrates discerned political satire in *Prometheus Bound*: "Io, transformed into a heifer, stands in the Aeschylus scene for the young lady with whom the politician newly in power in Athens is hopelessly infatuated. This politician is referred to in the play only as Zeus, precisely as the wife of that politician becomes Hera or Juno for stage purposes, Prometheus being the candidate for office, whose defeat led inevitably to his ostracism. The situation is so familiar to a student of ancient Athenian politics that the names of all the parties in the case—with the exception of the heifer—might be gleaned from a somewhat casual perusal of any history of Greece." The trilogy was written about 465 B.C.

Aeschylus' full estimate of Prometheus, of course, is lost with the other plays of the trilogy. Shelley sought to reconstruct *Prometheus Unbound* in 1819, writing a version in which Demogorgon, the all-pervading spirit and primal power of the universe, takes form as the child of Zeus and Thetis. He hurls Zeus over the battlements of heaven, and Prometheus is unbound by Heracles to introduce on the earth a reign of love, freedom, and peace based on individual self-control.

The Aeschylean conclusion of *Prometheus Unbound,* however, if we reconstruct the lost play aright, would show Zeus, on learning from Prometheus that "the son of Thetis will be greater than his father," abandoning his intention of marrying Thetis. And Prometheus, for revealing his secret, would be set free. What is important, here, is that Zeus is the first god to be pictured as learning from experience. Aeschylus offers the concept of the perfectibility of god. And if man is made in god's image . . .

Prometheus Bound has little external action, for, after Prometheus is borne onto the stage at the opening of the play, he remains chained to a rock throughout the rest of the drama. Inwardly, however, the play is anything but calm. "It seethes," as John Mason Brown phrased it, "with a defiance that reaches beyond the limits of earthly challenge and involves the very elements themselves." The fact that all the characters save Io are super-human adds to the weight of its mighty issues. In lofty language of great poetic beauty, Prometheus bears his torture with quiet resolution. His endurance, as well as his thought, challenges the evil of the world, however highly placed the evil-doer.

"I have been reading *Prometheus Bound*," Gerald Manley Hopkins once wrote to E. H. Coleridge. "It is immensely superior to anything else of Aeschylus I have read . . . It is really full of splendid poetry; when you read it, read with it Shelley's *Prometheus Unbound,* which is as fine or finer, perhaps a little fantastic though." Despite his supernatural characters, Aeschylus is never fantastic; his spirit is noble yet wholly down on earth.

Among the English translations of *Prometheus Bound* are the dignified 1899 version by Paul Elmer More and the more vibrant one by Edith Hamilton, which was staged in New York in 1930. William Vaughn Moody wrote a play on the theme entitled *The Fire Bringer,* 1904. Recent performances of Aeschylus' play in Greek have been given at Syracuse, Sicily, 1921; Delphi, 1927; Bath, England, 1932; and in the United States at Randolph-Macon College, 1934, and at Wellesley College, 1936. American performances in English include one at New York University, 1930, and another at Yale, 1939.

The beauty, power, and pertinence of Aeschylus' protest against tyranny, even when divine, remain bright and challenging to our time. Foe of the traditional, Aeschylus was, nevertheless, steadfast in his quest of the ideal.

ORESTEIA   *Aeschylus*

Oresteia is the only trilogy of which all three plays have come down to us from ancient Greece. Aeschylus' last work, and by contemporary repute his best, *Oresteia* won first prize in the contest of 458 B.C. Its three plays are certainly the most dramatic and most majestic of his extant dramas. In them we see most fully the pattern of Aeschylus' thought, turned upon the topical problem of public justice as opposed to the private blood-feud.

Oresteia tells of the curse on the house of Atreus, as it works its tragic doom even unto the third generation, when there is promise of final release. The curse was laid upon the house long before Aeschylus takes up the story, when bitter blood was spilled between Atreus and his brother Thyestes. The sons of Atreus, Menelaus and Agamemnon, King of Argos, however, lived in peace until Menelaus' wife, Helen, was snatched by Paris of Troy and the Greeks rallied to avenge the deed. Warned that the Trojans could be defeated only if Iphigenia, daughter of Agamemnon and Clytemnestra, were offered to the gods, Agamemnon reluctantly consents to her sacrifice. During the ten-year siege of Troy, Clytemnestra broods over the killing of her daughter and grows to hate her husband. She takes as her lover Aegisthus, son of Thyestes and therefore bitter enemy of Agamemnon. Together, they plot the murder of the king, should he return from the Trojan War. He comes, and they kill him. His return and murder are the story of *Agamemnon*.

The second play of the trilogy, *The Choephori (The Libation Bearers),* named after the chorus that goes with Electra to Agamemnon's tomb, is the story of the return of Agamemnon's son, Orestes, who with his sister Electra avenges the murder of his father by slaying Aegisthus and Clytemnestra.

The Furies (Eumenides) gather about Orestes, symbols of his tortured conscience.

The third play, *The Eumenides,* tells of Orestes' pursuit by the Furies. Enanguished by their unrelenting chase, Orestes appeals to Apollo, is tried by the goddess Athena and a jury of twelve Athenians, and is declared free from guilt of blood. The curse of the house of Atreus is spent.

The tragic story of the house of Atreus has attracted many playwrights. Euripides left us two *Iphigenia** plays, an *Orestes,** and an *Electra.* Better known in present-day translations and revivals is Sophocles' *Electra*.* The Roman Naevius wrote an *Iphigenia* in the third century B.C. Seneca's *Agamemnon* (about A.D. 60) is one of his weakest tragedies. Erasmus translated a version of the story in 1524; Racine's *Iphigenie* was first produced at the French court in 1674; and the Englishman John Dennis wrote a version in 1700. Shortly after this, the Italian Apostolo Zeno, court poet to the Holy Roman Emperor Charles VI, presented a musical version, the most successful of his sixty operas; Gluck's opera on the theme was first heard in 1774. Goethe's first prose draft was written in 1779; he finished the work in 1787, three years before Schiller's version. Jean Moréas wrote a French version in 1903, and in 1941 the German Gerhardt Hauptmann's play vividly contrasted the calm of Iphigenia with the passion of Electra.

Among the many versions or adaptations of *Agamemnon* after that of Seneca are one by James Thomson, poet of *The Seasons,* and another by Count Vittorio Alfieri*. The latter also wrote an *Orestes,* following the Italian Rucelli of the fifteenth century. Voltaire's *Oreste* appeared in 1750.

Most popular of the episodes in the tragedy, in ancient as in recent times, has been the story of Electra. It was in the French version by Jolyot de Crébillion (1709) that Adrienne Lecouvreur made her debut at the Comédie-Française in 1727. Modern treatments of the theme have been made in various lands: a violent version by Hofmannsthal* in German, 1874, on which the opera by Richard Strauss is based; one by the Spanish Benito Pérez Galdós, 1901, from an anti-clerical point of view; one by the French Alfred Poizat, 1907; one—with modern and trivial images—by Jean Giraudoux* in 1937; and still another, an existential drama called *The Flies,** by Jean-Paul Sartre. In addition, there is Eugene O'Neill's trilogy *Mourning Becomes Electra,** with its gloomy American setting during the War Between the States. The entire trilogy was condensed into three scenes in the dramatic version of the poem *The Tower Beyond Tragedy* (1925) by Robinson Jeffers.

In his trilogy, Aeschylus sought with profound thought to combine concepts of divine and human justice. Early in *Agamemnon* he sets the theme in the chorus: Zeus, the one god, "that name of many names," has so ordered the world that "Men shall learn wisdom, through affliction schooled." Throughout *Agamemnon* and *The Choephori,* the hideous course of that affliction unfolds as crime breeds vengeful crime. And in *The Eumenides,* Athena charges the jury at Orestes' trial: "Thou shalt do no unjust thing . . . Let no man live uncurbed by law, nor curbed by tyranny." Aeschylus gives scope to Athenian pride; for Athena tells the court it is to continue dealing justice thereafter, thus assigning ancient origin and divine sanction to the Areopagus, the court which the Athenians properly regarded as the cornerstone of their state.

The jury trying Orestes is evenly divided, as indeed justice in this case must be, for Orestes is traditionally right in avenging the murder of his father, but cruelly wrong in slaying his mother. Athena then tempers justice with mercy and sets Orestes free. Here is Aeschylus' richest thought on the problem of good and evil. It aproaches the Christian view: Man, by forces within and circumstances without, is driven against his will to evil, to be redeemed by something less akin to justice than to love. Even the Furies (Erinyes) are changed by Athena into goddesses of grace, while the Athenians rejoice in the glory of the justice of their great city. (The word *Eumenides,* which was used by the Greeks as a euphemism for the Furies, literally means daughters of grace.) Thus out of the tragic pattern of life, as it rises to its peak, suffers, and sinks to death, Aeschylus derives a basic moral order.

The trilogy is marked by its simplicity; to our Shakespeare-trained minds, it seems almost barren of imagery. It is free from figures such as Shakespeare loved to weave, elaborated for sheer delight in the beauty of their image and sound. Rarely indeed—the *London Times* (September 25, 1948) found Clytemnestra's picture of a wife's anxiety over her husband at war a rare exception—does "the sheer intensity and completeness of the poet's insight almost outrun his immediate dramatic purpose." The drive of the emotions is unbroken, and direct.

The plays of the trilogy have had recent performances. The first American production of *Agamemnon* was at Harvard University in 1906. It had a powerful effect. Other performances have been at Chapel Hill, North Carolina, in 1929; at the University of California, Los Angeles, in 1932; and, along with *The Choephori,* at Ogunquit, Maine, in 1937. *Agamemnon* was staged in London in 1934 and 1936. *The Choephori* was given in New York in 1908 and in Los Angeles in 1933. Los Angeles saw *The Eumenides* in 1934; New York, in 1942.

After 2,400 years, the power, beauty, and nobility of the work of Aeschylus are still deeply felt. In his own time, too, his plays were highly valued. Aristophanes, in *The Frogs,** has Dionysus go down to Hades to bring back Euripides and, for the good of Greece—after some gentle satire and weighing of their virtues—return with Aeschylus instead.

Aeschylus was particularly skillful in his portraits of women. Clytemnestra is pictured masterfully. The *London Times* (June 18, 1934) reminded us that she "is not merely a bad woman who has had an adulterous intrigue during her husband's absence, and resorts to murder in order to cover her tracks. She is above all an outraged mother, whose whole being is concentrated on avenging her murdered daughter. And although throughout the play the sympathy of the audience is meant to be against her, Aeschylus was careful not to depict her as a vulgar murderess or an inhuman monster. And at the end of the play, though her hatred against her murdered husband is by no means exhausted, she is more and more overcome by the fear that in her vengeance she is after all merely the instrument of the Doom that broods over the House of Atreus."

Even more pitifully drawn is Cassandra, daughter of the King of Troy. Brought to Greece a prisoner by Agamemnon, she is cursed with the power of foreseeing the future but not being believed. She cries out upon Agamemnon's blind approach to his doom, then goes to her own death beside him.

In *The Choephori* there is an equally revealing portrait of Electra, an instrument of vengeance yet a heart-wrung woman. With sensitive reticence, Aeschylus lets us see no more of Electra, once her brother has advanced to the killings. And Orestes himself, having slain Aegisthus, hesitates before his mother. He has to be reminded of his vow before he can lift his sword against her.

The dramaturgic skill of Aeschylus is shown in the opposition of his characters. Agamemnon's pride, for example, prevents his understanding the veiled warning of the chorus on his return. He accepts Clytemnestra's excessive show of welcome and walks the crimson carpet she has spread as if he were a god. Thus the Queen's hypocrisy easily outmatches his astuteness, as her double-edged words press with sharp irony upon the audience. But in the next scene, Clytemnestra loses her grasp on power before the calm and silent Cassandra, who knows the fate in store for all. Not until Clytemnestra has rushed away in futile fury does Cassandra speak. Then in sorrow and dignity she goes to her doom. Through such opposition pathos and irony are deepened to plumb the soul.

A new use of the chorus can be traced to *Oresteia*. The chorus of *The Eumenides* is as active as in earlier dramas. Resting, at first, while Orestes seeks refuge at the innermost altar of Apollo, the Furies murmur at the summons of Clytemnestra's ghost. They gather force and fierceness until they move like baying hounds upon the trail of Orestes. Horribly masked, in weird and ghoulish round, they weave a terror with their dancing, and the glee of their closing in on their victim is beyond the capture of words. When these Furies first appeared in the Athenian theatre, we are told, women fainted and babes were prematurely born. In the two other dramas of the trilogy, however, the chorus takes a different role. Its figures are less partici- pants than spectators. They guide and share the emotions of the audience, responding to events as beholders would respond. Thus they draw the au- dience into the drama with a profound effectiveness.

In this greatest work of the earliest known dramatist lies the secret of great theatrical art: the spectator become participant. Each of us, looking at any other mortal in our daily span, might say "There, but for the grace of God, go I." The theatre extends no such withholding grace; it absorbs us into its spell so that, in its problems and its passions, "There go I!"

UNCLE TOM'S CABIN   *George L. Aiken*

In 1851 Gamaliel Bailey, editor of the *National Era,* a weekly published in Washington, D.C., wrote Harriet Beecher Stowe (1811–1896): "My dear Mrs. Stowe—I enclose a $100 bill. Please send me a story—anything you choose." The result of that letter was *Uncle Tom; or Life Among the Lowly.* Like its own character Topsy, the story "just growed"; it appeared in book form as *Uncle Tom's Cabin* in 1852.

In response to a request from Asa Hutchinson, a friend, for permission to dramatize the story, Mrs. Stowe replied: "If the barrier which now keeps young people of Christian families from theatrical entertainments is once broken down by the introduction of respectable and moral plays, they will then be open to all the temptations of those who are not such, as there will be, as the world now is, five bad plays to one good. However specious may be the idea of reforming dramatic entertainments, I fear that it is wholly imprac- ticable, and, as a friend to you, should hope that you would not run the risk of so dangerous an experiment. The world is not good enough yet for it to succeed."

However, since Mrs. Stowe had not reserved the dramatic rights to *Uncle Tom's Cabin,* unauthorized productions sprang up on all sides. The version written by George L. Aiken (1830–1876) for actor-producer George C. Howard was the first to reach the stage. Opening in Troy, New York, on September 27, 1852, this version (it ended with the death of little Eva) ran for over a hundred nights. Aiken, then aged twenty-two, was a member of the company; his payment for the dramatization was a gold watch. He played the role of George Harris. Mrs. Howard played Topsy and her daughter Cordelia played little Eva. No one wanted to play the oily fellow who introduces himself with the remark: "I am a lawyer, and my name is Marks"; this role, finally thrust upon young Frank Aiken, brother of the playwright, became one of the most famous comedy parts on the American stage.

During the run in Troy, a sequel was added to the play, showing Uncle Tom's life as a slave on Legree's plantation. With this version, the company repeated its success in Albany and in Boston. In the latter city a rival version, already on stage when the Aikens and the Howards arrived, ran for 103 performances.

The editor of the *Atlantic Monthly* took Mrs. Stowe to see the play—the first theatrical "entertainment" she had ever attended. "We entered privately," he reported, "she being well muffled . . . I never saw such delight upon a human face as she displayed when she first comprehended the full power of Mrs. Howard's Topsy. She scarcely spoke during the evening, but her expression was eloquent, smiles and tears succeeding each other through the whole . . . Drawn along by the threads of her own romance, and inexperienced in the deceptions of the theatre, she could not have been keenly sensible of the faults of the piece or the shortcomings of the actors . . . The Eliza of the evening was a reasonably good actress and skipped over the floating ice of the Ohio River with frantic agility. The Uncle Tom was rather stolid—such a man as I have seen preaching among the Negroes when I lived in Kentucky."

On August 23, 1852, another version, by Charles W. Taylor, strangely omitting Eva and Topsy, opened at Purdy's National Theatre in New York and ran for but eleven nights. The Aiken version, however, played at the same theatre, at a higher admission price, and with three performances daily, for over a year. The poet William Cullen Bryant and the actor Edwin Forrest were among those that wept at Cordelia Howard's characterization of Eva. Mrs. Howard played Topsy continuously for thirty-five years, and G. C. German, the Uncle Tom of the original cast, acted no other part during the rest of his life.

Since popular sentiment in New York in 1853 was generally anti-abolitionist, the local press was cold toward the play. An editorial in the *New York Herald* ended with the following admonition: "We would advise all concerned to drop the play of *Uncle Tom's Cabin* at once and forever. The thing is in bad taste—is not according to good faith to the Constitution and is calculated, if persisted in, to become a firebrand of the most dangerous character to the peace of the country." The play remained popular, and within a decade the country was torn by civil war. The stage version of *Uncle Tom's Cabin,* even more than Mrs. Stowe's book, helped to solidify Northern sentiment against slavery. It pressed home the moral issue and prepared the people for the War Between the States.

There have been some twenty different stage versions of *Uncle Tom's Cabin,* all fairly closely following the plot of the novel. When financial straits force the kindly Shelbys to sell their slaves, the mulatto Eliza, rather than be separated from her baby, runs away with it into the snowstorm. Bloodhounds follow close upon their trail, but she carries the babe out into the ice of the Ohio River, leaping from floe to floe until safe on the northern shore. Uncle Tom is sold to a trader, but George Shelby promises to redeem him. While sailing down the Mississippi, Tom saves little Eva, whose father, St. Clare, buys him. Tom lives happily with them and Eva's playmate, the lively Negro girl Topsy, until the frail Eva dies, and St. Clare is stabbed to death. Tom is then bought at auction by the brutal planter Simon Legree, who hates him for his independent spirit. Legree demands: "Ain't you mine, body and soul?" Tom replies that his soul is God's, and Legree has him savagely flogged. The lawyer Marks now confronts Legree with evidence of his having killed St. Clare; Legree fights, and Marks shoots him. Tom's old master, Shelby, arrives as Tom is dying, and vows to work for the freedom of the slaves.

This story was invariably supplemented with Negro plantation scenes, songs and dances, and with many spectacular effects—the famous crossing of the river on the ice was followed by a fight on the edge of a cliff between Eliza's husband, George Harris, and the slave-dealer pursuing her, until the Quaker Phineas Fletcher heaves the slave-dealer into the torrent below; and always there came the final vision of little Eva in heaven, her outstretched arms blessing her father and her beloved Uncle Tom.

As early as 1853 there were three dramatizations of *Uncle Tom's Cabin* playing at one time in London, and two in Paris. In February 1862, four companies opened in New York within a single week; the Old Bowery version had horses as well as hounds chasing Eliza. Jubilee singers added to the show became a popular feature. For fifty-seven consecutive years, ten to twenty Uncle Tom companies were on continuous tour of the United States, and three to five in Great Britain. Some of the companies were beneath even small town tolerance; one western paper reviewed an *Uncle Tom* show with the remark: "The cast gave the bloodhounds poor support."

In the 1880's, the first attempts were made to show the play in the South. In Georgia, the actors fled as the scenery was smashed. In Kentucky, a law was enacted forbidding performances of the play. By now, however, *Uncle Tom's Cabin* had been shown in Texas, Arkansas, Louisiana, Missouri, and Mississippi. A Soviet Russian production of 1949 pictured the United States as the land of lynchings; Uncle Tom, accordingly, was not flogged to death, but hanged.

The Aiken version of *Uncle Tom's Cabin,* by far the most frequently played, was revised in 1933 by A. E. Thomas for the Players' Club annual revival. Otis Skinner, who made his stage debut in Philadelphia in 1877 as Uncle Tom, played the same role in this revival. Lois Shore played Eva; Fay Bainter, Topsy; Ernest Glendenning, St. Clare. Also in the cast were Cecilia Loftus, Minnie Dupree, Gene Lockhart, Thomas Chalmers, and Pedro de Cordoba. The production glowed with surprising lustre. Richard Lockridge warned: "Several of the big scenes will get you if you don't watch out . . . The slave-market scene, for example, is stirring drama in which the violent taking of sides is unavoidable . . . It is not only authentic Americana; it is in its own rights a pretty grand evening." The *New York Herald-Tribune* reported that the blasé audience came to scoff but "remained to sniffle as the bright spirit of little Eva was exhaled, and Uncle Tom suffered his sable martyrdom . . . The Players make the old prejudiced and hateful show an exciting entertainment."

Uncle Tom's Cabin, which John Mason Brown has called "the greatest grease-paint curiosity of all time," helped make American history. Its record of performances is unparalleled in the annals of the theatre.

During the Depression, the Department of Public Works presented *Uncle Tom's Cabin* on portable stages, as at Coentes Slip, where 3,000 hard-boiled seamen hissed the slave-driving villains in angry earnest.

In 1951 the play became a short ballet, *The Small House of Uncle Thomas,* introduced in the musical of Siam, *The King and I.* Luigi F. Trecati made it an opera, *La Capanna dello Zio Tom,* in 1954.

The woman President Lincoln greeted as "the little lady who started this big war" moved Harry Birdoff in 1948 to write *The World's Greatest Hit;* he produced a version of the play in 1975.

Note that the term of scorn, "Uncle Tom Nigger," for a black obsequious to whites, is a misnomer: in both book and play, Uncle Tom loved little Eva and was dear to her family, but he steadfastly refused to reveal the hiding place of the runaway slaves and was whipped to death for his refusal.

THE GREEKS HAD A WORD FOR IT   *Zoe Akins*

This frisky but completely un-Hellenic comedy is a lively picture of women who live by the sale of their loveliness. Three Broadway Loreleis have put their lures together. The play has little progressive plot but deftly intertwines the squabbles, rivalries, treacheries, small talk, and final fidelity of the tramp trio.

Polaire, southern and lazy, is a scarlet sister with a soul attuned to music and a yen for higher things. Schatze is a thrifty fleshpot, half hausfrau, half concubine. Jean is a callous gold digger, with a strip complex that she indulges three times in the evening. Jean's good looks twice slip her into arms that had reached toward the more languorous and pretentious Polaire. The second of these opportunities offers marriage to a boring billionaire, an opportunity to go live with him "on an expensive island covered with quail." After a final quarrel Jean spins around, jilts the moneyman, and joins the other two on a jaunt to seek new skies and lies in Paris.

Opening in New York at the Sam Harris Theatre, September 25, 1920, Muriel Kirkland, Veree Teasdale, and Dorothy Hall played Polaire, Jean, and Schatze. The public was delighted, but the critical reception was mixed. Percy Hammond called the play "all phony, excepting its characters, its speech, and its acting. Miss Akins, one regretfully suspects, is not a dramatist." Hammond's exceptions would suffice a good many dramatists; but his final remark was roundly challenged by Arthur Pollack: "Any new play by Zoe Akins is an event, since she is one of the most intelligent and least easily satisfied of American dramatists."

The Greeks Had a Word for It kept running in New York for three years. It toured the country in 1935. It was very popular in the summer theatre: in 1940, Libby Holman headed one company; Madge Evans, Betty Furness, and Diana Barrymore a second; and Helen Twelvetrees, Elaine Barrie, and Zella Russell a third.

In London, *The Greeks Had a Word for It* was produced in 1934 and revived in 1936. W. A. Darlington (*London Telegraph,* November 23, 1934) called it "a hard-boiled play for hard-boiled people . . . They do unforgivable things to one another and then forgive one another with the undiscriminating readiness of those who have good hearts but no morals." The *London Times* (March 13, 1936) declared that the play "appeals to that form of sophistication which is unconnected with intelligence."

There is, however, a keen intelligence in the picturing of these three differently delightful lights-o'-love and in the deft management of their very natural relationships with one another and with those necessary evils, their gentleman friends. Good times—and more leisure than we perhaps today desire to spend—give blossom to such passionflowers; *The Greeks Had a Word for It* emphials their fragrance before the inevitable swift withering on the stalk.

The word the Greeks had for it is *hetaera.*

THE WEAVER OF SEGOVIA   *Ruiz de Alarcón*

The fervent honesty and integrity of Juan Ruiz de Alarcón y Mendoza (1581?–1639) won the respect of even his enemies. Lope de Vega*, who earlier had gone to prison for creating a disturbance during a performance of one of Alarcón's plays, in his poem "The Laurel of Apollo," 1630, declared that Alarcón "joins genius with virtue."

Writing in seventeenth-century Spain, Alarcón was naturally drawn to a drama centering on the *pundonor* (point of honor). His most vivid such play is *The Weaver of Segovia,* 1628, with an intricate plot as clear as it is exciting to follow on the stage.

"A man of honor insulted is a wounded bull," says Don Fernando Remirez in the play. His father had been ruined and executed through the machinations of the Marquis Suero Pelaez, and Fernando himself was forced to flee. Disguised as a weaver in Segovia, Fernando finds the Marquis's son, Count Don Juan, trying to force himself upon Teodora, Fernando's love. Imprisoned for opposing the Count, Fernando escapes. He becomes a bandit, but in one great battle saves the King's forces from the Moors and destroys his own enemies. The dying Marquis confesses, and the family of Don Fernando is restored to its honor and proud place.

Alarcón's persons are vivid and ring true. Most human, perhaps, is the cowardly rascal Chichon, alternating his alliance with Fernando or the Count as favors and fortune tempt.

The action of the play is swift and violent. Fernando has a friend wound him in jail, so that he'll be sent to the hospital, whence escape is easier. Held prisoner in a tavern, he stands against a candle to burn the rope binding his wrists, then snatches a traveler's sword to beat down opposition. Fights against odds are frequent, to the last triumphant moment when, his true name revealed and his honor cleared, Don Fernando kneels before his king.

Even in the swift and violent action, Alarcón sustains the artistry that makes his work seem natural. He avoids the florid figures, the extravagant conceits, popular in his day. He maintains his careful and sure hand, his—as critic Alfonso Reyes listed—"cleverness as an observer; the serenity and intimacy of certain conversations; his touch, never exaggerated, in defining characters; his faith in reason as the sole standard of life; his respect for appointed station in all orders of human life."

The Weaver of Segovia was twice translated into French in the nineteenth century. Alphonse Royer, whose version appeared in 1865, in his preface stated: "Vengeance is tasted in deep draughts; as it is based upon a just cause, it rises almost to the heights of virtue. Watching its heroic realization, the spectator feels drawn to the heroic outlaw by a resistless sympathy."

In his lighter plays, Alarcón created the Spanish comedy of manners. In *The Weaver of Segovia* he followed an established pattern, the melodrama of the *pundonor* and revenge; but he gave to the old formula a freshness and a sympathetic surge of real humanity that are still valid and moving today.

WHO'S AFRAID OF VIRGINIA WOOLF?   *Edward Albee*

Before and after *Who's Afraid of Virginia Woolf* (1962) Edward Albee (b. 1928; adopted from a foundling home at the age of two weeks) wrote a number of plays: first *The Zoo Story* (it premiered in German in West Berlin, 1959), a one-act play set on a park bench where two strangers meet, and the young rebel Jerry provokes the middle-aged bourgeois Peter into killing him. *Tiny Alice* (1964), with John Gielgud, won the Pulitzer Prize, but ran only four months; it continued an anti-feminine bias as well as a picture of society in decay—emphasized also in *Box* and *Quotations from Chairman Mao Tse-Tung,* plays presented monotonously together in 1968. In *Box,* no one is onstage; we hear a recorded lecture from an unseen source.

The most vehement and controversial of Albee's plays, *Who's Afraid of Virginia Woolf?* won the award of the New York Drama Critics' Circle and the Tony; when it was not given the Pulitzer Prize, the two Pulitzer drama advisers resigned. Its title, we are told, springs from the fact that the copyright holder of "Who's Afraid of the Big Bad Wolf?" demanded an exorbitant sum. The two women in the play are so drawn that some critics felt they should have been men, and indeed in Amsterdam the play was presented with an all-male cast, "as was the original intention."

The first act is titled "Fun and Games." In it George, a professor of history, and his wife, Martha, daughter of the college president, have brought home, after a faculty meeting, the younger Nick, a biologist, and his wife, Honey. Argumentative Martha at once pours insults on George, who she had hoped would succeed to her father's post. Vehement quarreling continues through Act II, called "Walpurgisnacht;" we discover that Nick had married Honey during a false pregnancy. Honey becomes incompetently drunk. Baldly, with George in semi-agreement, Martha leads Nick upstairs, to make love. In the last act, "The Exorcism," George announces the death of the imaginary son he and Martha had "begotten" as a sort of foil for their fencing. The lovemaking upstairs has been a fiasco; Nick takes the maudlin Honey home, and the other couple find a transitory truce as the curtain closes them in.

Opening in New York on October 13, 1962, the play ran for 664 performances at the Billy Rose. In the evenings, Uta Hagen played Martha; Arthur Hill, George; Melinda Dillon, Honey; George Grizzard, Nick. At matinees, the roles were played by Kate Reid (then Elaine Stritch); Shepperd Strudwick; Abba Petrides (followed by Rochelle Oliver, then Eileen Fulton); and Bill Berger. Uta Hagen and Arthur Hill were in the London production of 1964. Of this, Harold Hobson in the *Times* said it "has an intensity, a demoniac misery, a ferocious humour, an ability to rend and tear and crucify to a degree unfamiliar in the English theatre. No English dramatist could be as sick as this, or as clever, or at the end . . . so unjustifiably optimistic." The Lord Chamberlain laid hands upon the script: in the production, *scrotum* becomes *privacies; balls* becomes *bowels*; and every exclamatory *Jesus* and *Christ* was omitted. On the contrary (as Ingrid Bergman told Ben Gazzara, during his New York run in the play with Colleen Dewhurst, at the Martin Beck in 1976), in the 1964 Paris production, directed by Ingrid's husband, Lars Schneider, the swearing was longer, louder, and rougher, because of the feud between actress Madeleine Robinson and her stage husband, Raymond Gerome: she accused him of trying to "steal the limelight" from her; he sued her for libel. The play ran in Paris for over a year.

In 1970 there was a Chicago company with Eileen Herlie and James Broderick. The motion picture version starred Elizabeth Taylor and Richard Burton. The Italian production was directed by Franco Zeffirelli. In 1980 Elaine May and Mike Nichols took the play on a U.S. tour. (In 1963 a play by David Starkweather, *So Who's Afraid of Edward Albee?*, a wild fantasy about verbal abuse, lust, attempted rape, and literary criticism, ran for sixteen performances in New York and the next year briefly in Paris, with little dramatic power.)

After the London 1981 revival at the NT the critics drew wider significance from the play. Robert Cushman in *The Observer* pointed out that the two characters do not hate each other so much as they hate themselves: George, for his weakness in marrying the president's daughter as a step toward advancement, and for his inability to move ahead on his own energy and merit; Martha, for her misjudgment of George and her boredom at having lapsed into the routine pattern of a professor's wife. John Barber in *The Telegraph* found English opportunity to flay the overgrown onetime colony, the United States, first to break away from the motherland: "The effect of the play was gorgon-like. It turned to stone the hearts of the middle class, who flocked to it and gleefully identified the characters with their neighbors. Thoughtful members of the audience, looking for a more substantial metaphor, came up with a variety of them; the homosexual life (it was rumoured that all the characters should be played by men); the ferocity of children's play (the first act was indeed entitled "Fun and Games"); the confrontation of past and future (George teaches history, his guest is a geneticist); and the history of the United States, ending with the destruction of the American dream . . . It is not for nothing that Albee gives them the names of President (George) Washington and his wife (Martha). Through its fury of invective, the play stands as an indictment of the barrenness, the immorality, and the greed in American society."

To most, the situation is too individual to harbor such wide implications; but the play has a pugnacious power that leaves no character untorn and no spectator unaffected.

Magazine comments are likely to be more measured than newspaper reviews. Three thoughtful writers make a sort of progression in regard to Albee's plays. First, Harold Clurman in *The Nation,* October 27, 1962: "I do not object to Albee's being 'morbid,' for, as conspicuously healthy William James said, 'Morbid-mindedness ranges over a wider scale of experience than healthy-mindedness.' What I do object to in his play is that its disease has become something of a brilliant formula, as slick and automatic as a happy entertainment for the trade. The right to pessimism has to be earned within the artistic terms one sets up; the pessimism and rage of *Who's Afraid of Virginia Woolf?* are immature. Immaturity coupled with a commanding deftness is dangerous."

In the *New Republic,* January 23, 1965, Robert Brustein turned to *Tiny Alice*: "A hoax is being perpetrated, no doubt of that; but is it intentional or not? . . . *Tiny Alice* is a much more ambitious work than the usual variety of *camp*; but it shares the same ambiguity of motive. For while some of Albee's obscurity is pure playfulness, designed to con the spectator into looking for nonexistent meanings, some is obviously there for the sake of a sham profundity in which the author apparently believes."

Finally, in the *Hudson Review,* winter 1966–1967, John Simon sums up the playwright's movement: "Albee is progressing. *Who's Afraid of Virginia Woolf?* was about the emptiness that surrounds and threatens to swallow our relationships; *Tiny Alice* was about the void lurking behind our deepest beliefs; now, *A Delicate Balance* is about the nothingness, the bare nothingness of it all—it is a play about nothing." Let's hope there'll be more from Albee.

SAUL   *Count Vittorio Alfieri*

This is the best play by Count Vittorio Alfieri (1749–1803), one of Italy's finest dramatists. In a severe style, suited to the patriarchal age it depicts, it moves with dramatic grandeur through the last days of the mad King Saul.

Taken from the First Book of Samuel, in the Bible, the story begins with the submission of David to King Saul. A fugitive, David plans to surrender while Saul's son, Jonathan, and his daughter, Michal, David's wife, try to dispel from the King's heart the suspicion and hatred of David that his uncle,

Abner, has planted there. When David, by showing a piece of cloth cut from the robe Saul had worn in the Cave of En-gedi, proves that he had once had Saul in his power and spared him, the King once more receives David into his favor. Together, they plan a campaign against the Philistines.

Roused again by Abner, Saul appears in a spell of madness. David sings and soothes the King, but when his song grows warlike, the King rages against him. David flees; the battle plans are changed; and the Philistines, victorious, kill Jonathan. As Abner spirits Michal away to safety, Saul, in quiet majesty, rather than surrender kills himself.

Alfieri's tragedy *Saul,* published in 1777, has been universally acclaimed. The playwright himself, in dedicating *Saul* to Abbot Tommaso Valperga, said that "perhaps wrongly, I am singularly pleased" with the play. His judgment was not wrong. Matthew Arnold, however, spoke of the play's "narrow elevation" and called Alfieri a "noble-minded, deeply interesting man, but a monotonous poet." Mme. de Staël found "a superb use of lyric poetry" in *Saul.* Schlegel felt that among Alfieri's works the play was "favorably distinguished from the rest by a certain Oriental splendor, and the lyrical sublimity with which the troubled mind of Saul finds utterance." Emiliani Giudici believed that "in Alfieri art once more achieved the faultless purity of its proper character: Greek tragedy reached the same height in the Italian's *Saul* that it touched in the Greek's *Prometheus,* the two dramas that are perhaps the most gigantic creations of any literature."

A dignity animates the characters of *Saul* and their actions. Although their station in life may be as high as it is unique, their motives and their emotions are understood and shared by the beholders. Even Saul, whom Alfred Bates called "perhaps the only heroic madman in classical drama," stays within the bounds of human sympathy. At the end of the play, his sanity returned, Alfieri's Saul is a pitiable figure. Shorn of power, surrounded by enemies, he nevertheless defies defeat and challenges the fear of death in a reaffirmation of the will, the dignity, and the stature of man. From such a stand rises the exaltation born of tragedy.

The basic theme of *Saul* is one to which Alfieri turned again and again: the staunch defying tyranny. While *Saul* was less immediately pertinent to Alfieri's compatriots than others of his plays, they felt in it the fervor of Alfieri's drive against oppression.

A version of the play by André Gide was produced at the Vieux Colombier, Paris, in 1922, with Jacques Copeau. The role of Saul was a favorite with the great actor Salvini.

The *Christian Science Monitor* said of a comparatively poor production of the play: "One feels in some particularly audacious and vigorous scenes a truly Shakespearean breath. All the work is filled with the sober force of the classics. The style is lucid and harmonious. And if—apart from certain scenes which reach an intensely pathetic grandeur—one does not feel much emotion, at least one is constantly and acutely interested, owing to the incomparable literary qualities of *Saul.*"

After writing *Saul,* Alfieri himself said, "Here I lay down the buskin forever."

THE LADY FROM ALFÁQUEQUE   *Alvarez Quintero Brothers*

Liveliest of the Quintero brothers' longer plays is the two-act comedy *La Consulesa (The Lady from Alfáqueque),* written in 1914. Produced in London in 1928 and again in 1933, in New York by the Civic Repertory Theatre with

Alma Kruger in 1929, and widely performed in Europe, this play, more than any other of their some 200 plays, has made the Quintero brothers internationally known.

It is a delightful comedy of a woman in a big city who cannot forget the small town that was her childhood home. Doña Fernandita, wife of a wealthy Madrid manufacturer, idolizes everything and everybody, the almond cakes, the saints, the poor relations, from her home town Alfáqueque. As a result, a constant stream of guests makes her home a minor bedlam, a pleasant but constantly chaotic, crowded household, over which her adoring and tolerant husband watches with amused and greatly abused patience. One day a poet, Felipe Rivas, arrives from Alfáqueque. Fainting from the worries of a secret danger, he stays on, heartily welcomed by Doña Fernandita. Exercising the prerogative of the poet, he makes love to three of the girls. When Doña Fernandita discovers that he is not really from Alfáqueque, and that the danger threatening him is the danger of having to work, she finally admits that she has been imposed upon. As she gathers strength to tell Felipe to leave, he launches into a new poem on the glories of Alfáqueque. Her anger smooths to rapture, as her husband looks on with reasonable doubt, and the curtain falls.

While the play neatly captures the local atmosphere, with the idiosyncrasies of an overpolite Spanish gentleman and a ubiquitous but befuddled priest, it has wider implications even in these figures, as well as in its portrayal of poor relatives. It suggests, without malice but with quiet understanding, that differences in conduct and outlook between dependents and those who are financially and socially secure are to be expected and accepted. Equally universal is the play's basic theme. As pointed out by the *New York Herald Tribune* (January 20, 1929), Doña Fernandita could be any American small town woman whose husband's work holds her in Manhattan.

Shrewd, but unfailingly amusing, this delightful play does not always use new materials, but it lends the old a warmth of humor and a zest for life. Its externals are but slightly heightened for drama, its essence is widely true. Reported the *Boston Transcript* (May 16, 1929): "The Quinteros' humor, again, eschews current modes, being as far from wise-cracking as it is from buffoonery . . . unpretentious, honest, good-natured, made from foibles and idiosyncrasies as the pleasing part they are in the common lot . . . They neither gird at Doña Fernandita nor guy her. They are content to smile, wonder, sigh, and look the other way. Don Pascual, who makes the best of his wife and her infirmity after this fashion, is their spokesman. For them, a hint is better than italics. How grown-up they are, how wide-minded and honest-minded, too, how good tempered as well! Americans need them and their works, not only for two hours' pleasure in the theatre but also for mental and moral good." *The Lady from Alfáqueque,* their most mellow work, is a heart-warming and heart-lifting comedy. In plays to which Joaquin contributed lightness and gay wit and Serafin the more philosophic view, they combined realistic externals with an inner content that makes their work a pattern of delight.

THE ARCADIANS   *Mark Ambient*

Here is a fresh and lively combination of what theatre-folk call the "girlie show" and the gay fantasy of an amusing story. Mark Ambient (1860–1937) co-authored it with fellow-Englishman A. M. Thompson (1861–1948).

The play opens in an Arcadian dell, where maids and youths enjoy primal innocence and a care-free happiness. Their curiosity is aroused by reports of a country, England by name, where the truth is not always told, where the inhabitants have found an ingenious substitute called the lie. Their wonder is satisfied when James Smith, a middle-aged Londoner, descends upon Arcady from a balloon. Finding that they have little liking for Smith's lies, the Arcadians dip him in a well, from which he comes forth a truth-telling young man. The Arcadians then christen him Simplicitas.

Successful with Smith, the Arcadians resolve to cure his countrymen of the lying habit. They journey to England, where they visit the Askwood Race Track and set up the Arcadian Restaurant. Eventually, they decide to return to Arcadia before they too become liars. They leave the English to their fate.

In the second act, at the race track, there are two contrasting choruses: the diaphanously clad but innocent maids of Arcady; and the sophisticated ladies in Directoire gowns who come to Ascot ("Askwood") to watch the races and the men. This contrast, not of the sexes, but rather of the awareness of sex, is delightfully effective.

Mrs. James Smith is at the races too, enjoying the country and a brisk flirtation, little knowing that her husband is the handsome young "stranger" nearby. Eileen Cavanagh is also there; her sweetheart Jack Meadows has all his money on an entry. The Arcadians, understanding animal talk, know which horse the horses have decided will win. Simplicitas rides him. Thus girlies and gags join in amusing situations.

The music by Lionel Monckton and Howard Talbot is tuneful and pleasant; the lyrics, fresh and clever. Among the more popular songs from the play are "The Pipes of Pan," "Since the Days Before the Flood," "The Dear Little Girl With a Bit of a Brogue," "Charming Weather."

The Arcadians opened in London on April 28, 1909, with Frank Moulan (of Gilbert and Sullivan fame) as Simplicitas-Smith and Julia Sanderson as Eileen. It ran for 809 performances. "It is long since anything on the light opera stage of London has been seen that can be compared for prettiness, cleverness, and melody to *The Arcadians*," reported *The Times*. During the following season, the play repeated its London success in New York.

With a swirl of Arcadian nymphs and the sweep of English ladies, this delightful play gives a fanciful approach to the eternal problem of truth-telling and to the eternal mystery and mastery of sex. The play was revived again in London in 1956, and again, successfully in Exeter in 1984.

ELIZABETH THE QUEEN   *Maxwell Anderson*

Originally entitled *Elizabeth and Essex,* this drama in verse by Maxwell Anderson (1887–1959) made its bow in a brilliant production by the Theatre Guild in New York on November 3, 1930, with Lynn Fontanne as Elizabeth and Alfred Lunt as Lord Essex. In 1932 it was again produced in New York, with Mildred Natwick and Vincent Price, and it has been revived somewhere in the country almost every year. In 1941, it was recorded on disc for the blind by Mady Christians and Wesley Addy.

The play is written in a crisp prose that alternates with a loose blank verse. At times, as in the banter between the court ladies and the fool in Act II, Scene 3, the patter and the puns of its prose are a rather obvious and consequently dull imitation of such effects in Elizabethan plays. The essential theme of the play, however, is presented in strong, dramatic terms and, in usually vigorous prose or swift if uninspired verse, it moves with speed and power.

Elizabeth is torn between her indomitable will, her need to hold her power, and her love for Essex. Aging, she desperately loves the gallant young Essex, and he loves Elizabeth. But Essex, too, suffers the need for power. He wishes to share the throne as Elizabeth's equal. Loved by the people, but snared by his enemies, Raleigh and Cecil, into a command in Ireland where all English expeditions fail, Essex returns to capture London and the palace. By promising to share the throne, Elizabeth tricks him into dismissing his guard, whereupon she has him arrested and taken to the Tower. The stubbornness of both Elizabeth and Essex leads thence to his execution.

Maxwell Anderson slipped a number of interesting literary references into the play. Much, for example, is made of a performance of Shakespeare's *Richard II,** given supposedly in support of Essex' rebellion, since it portrays the deposition of Richard; later, when the Queen hopes that Essex will sue for pardon, the players attempt to distract her with scenes of her favorite character, Falstaff.

Despite such allusions to the period of the play, and despite the date of its events (1601), the psychological responses and complexities of the characters are essentially of our own time.

The power of the characterization of Elizabeth and Essex is felt despite the language of the play rather than because of it. The fateful spur to power pricks within the individual; and the intensity, as reading reveals, is in the play itself. The critics, however, inclined to attribute it wholly to the performers. Thus the *New York World* (November 4, 1930) concluded: "By far the most remarkable feature . . . is the playing of the Queen by Lynn Fontanne." John Mason Brown went further: "The Lunts outdistanced not only the material with which they were working but all of those who stand near them on the stage . . . they converted what threatened to be a very much beruffed and cross-gartered adventure into a high-voltage and exciting evening in the theatre."

Elizabeth the Queen certainly provides a challenge to great actors. In 1966 Judith Anderson played the Queen; Donald Davis, Essex, at the City Center, New York.

MARY OF SCOTLAND   *Maxwell Anderson*

Beginning with a sweep of Puritan prose and surging into vigorous verse, *Mary of Scotland* is another play in which Maxwell Anderson vividly dramatizes history, depicting the six sad years that begin with the return of Mary from France in 1561, and end with her imprisonment by Queen Elizabeth of England in 1567.

Although Puritan John Knox abominates his Catholic Queen and her Scottish lords fear her frailty, Queen Elizabeth hates her as a young and beautiful rival to the throne. At the end of the play, Mary becomes aware that the critical events of her career—her marriage to Darnley, the murder of her secretary Rizzio, the murder of Darnley, her marriage to Bothwell, the rebellion, the truce—were all the results of traps deliberately set by Elizabeth for her own particular ends.

In having Elizabeth visit the imprisoned Mary at the close of the play, Anderson forges history to his dramatic purpose, creating a great scene wherein the crafty, plausible, but indomitable Elizabeth of England meets the meek, yet proud and undaunted Mary, Queen of Scots. Mary has the one shaft in her quiver to sink into Elizabeth's heart, for Elizabeth, politically victorious over Mary, has been a hater, a schemer, a liar, and a barren woman—while her victim has known a rich life, with love and its fruition, a child.

The simple power of the verse of *Mary of Scotland* places it among Anderson's best writings. It was originally presented in New York on November 27, 1933 (it ran for 248 performances), with a superb cast including Helen Hayes as Mary, Philip Merivale as Bothwell, and Helen Menken as Elizabeth. Katharine Hepburn later played Mary in the motion picture version.

If the scales of history are tipped to attract the sympathy of the audience, the playwright's enthusiasm rather than his honesty is at fault. As emphasized by Brooks Atkinson in his review of this play, Anderson "has not always succeeded on the stage, but he has never failed in integrity." Atkinson, indeed, gave *Mary of Scotland* his fullest praise: "This is the drama of heroes . . . a drama that is streaked with greatness. It has restored the English language to its high estate as an instrument of lustrous beauty"; and in his Sunday "second thoughts" he called the play "one of the finest pieces of writing in the collected works of the American Drama."

In *Mary of Scotland,* Anderson deals more with individuals than with ideas. The characters of the play are not there to set in contrast ideals or theories of government so much as to portray the struggle of two women, two rulers, for power.

The story of Mary of Scotland has attracted other writers. John Drinkwater wrote *Mary Stuart,* which opened in New York at the Ritz in 1921, with Clare Eames as Mary, Charles Waldman as Darnley; it went to the London Everyman in 1922. More classical was *Maria Stuart,* by Johann Schiller, 1800; see his *The Robbers.**

An absurdist story of *Mary and the Executioner,* by Wolfgang Hildesheimer, was presented in New York at the Public, February 11, 1981, with the audience seated in the dungeon. The play combines slapstick and sex, in the current fashion. There is a fight over Mary's jewel box; the maid gives Mary her final hairdo while raising her own skirt for an amorous approach from the rear. Mary strokes the executioner's blade; she strokes her dogs, not noticing that they've been killed and stuffed. When she is blindfolded, the maids steal her earrings; to her cry "Farewell, you thieves and robbers" they retort, "Farewell, you slave driver." The audience notices an attendant making a homosexual approach to the young assistant executioner—and life descends from the tragedy of monarchal days to the brutal and absurdist farce of our own time, in which many deride all values.

VALLEY FORGE   *Maxwell Anderson*

This play is especially interesting as a twentieth-century view of the eighteenth century. If, as has often been said, history offers a lesson to our day, it is no less true that we see the past through our own eyes.

Valley Forge portrays the American Revolutionary forces during the dreary winter of 1778, when their fortune was at its lowest ebb, when Washington had to fight not only the British, but the double-dealing war-weary among the colonists; the Congress, with its petty disputes, indecisions, and delays; the impatient among the merchant class, whose business had been damaged by the war; the homesick and the deserters among his worn-out, rag-wrapped men; and the fierce winter's cold. Earlier histories, borne on the surge of rugged individualism in the United States, showed Washington as the dominant leader, who by the power of his personality and iron will held together the shriveling remnants of his half-starved and half-frozen forces. But Anderson's *Valley Forge,* with the mass-impetus and emphasis of our time, shows a discouraged, defeated General, who meets with the British Lord Howe in a shack on a Delaware River island in order to seek terms of surrender; a General who is reproached by the rank and file (the proletariat!) of his men and who, through their determination (mass-pressure!), is brought to a new resolve. We behold not the leader rallying his men, but the men inspiriting their commander. Thus does the twentieth century interpret the eighteenth.

Valley Forge opened at the Guild Theatre on December 10, 1934, with Philip Merivale as Washington and Margalo Gillmore as Mary Philipse, the charming lady who accompanied Howe and brought to Washington word of the French alliance. It played fifty-eight performances.

Arthur Pollock called *Valley Forge* "as articulate as lightning and made eloquent by liquid language that is often liquid fire." The play, however, rather haphazardly shifts from prose to an irregular, often prosaic verse.

Estimates of this work differ greatly. Brooks Atkinson, for example, said: "Formal English seems better suited to English and Scottish courts than it does to the ragamuffins of a cruel Valley Forge winter . . . It is hard to worship a great character in the theatre without slopping over. To tell the truth, *Valley Forge* gives a splash or two."

John Anderson (no relative of Maxwell) was very much impressed. He called the play "a noble work, its author's full-seasoned best, a play stirring with passionate eloquence and majestic drama, at the deep roots of American history . . . something that he can be proud of, and something that we, the inheritors of this rediscovered Valley Forge, can be grateful for as history, entertainment, and, if it please you, warning."

WINTERSET   *Maxwell Anderson*

This is Maxwell Anderson's finest drama and one of the few great American tragedies. It offers an imagined aftermath of the Sacco-Vanzetti case, which had furnished Anderson the theme of his *Gods of the Lightning*.

Mio, the son of one of the two executed men, hopes to clear his father of the judgment against him. Judge Gaunt, who had handed down the verdict, cracks beneath the pressure of conscience. He and Mio are drawn to the home of one Garth, a witness to the murder for which the two men were condemned but who had never been called to testify. The real killer, Trock, watches Garth and, in order to keep himself clear, kills Mio; and Mio's sweetheart, Mirianne, dies with him.

No one who saw *Winterset* during its New York run will forget the grim setting designed by Jo Mielziner: a slum district beside a river where tenement wall and natural rock rise to the great loom of a bridge. The cheerless basement of a tenement with pipes running outside its walls, a large steam-pipe crossing low on the stage—a rat-hole where cowards and killers might hide, but where the poorest could look toward the bridge, and dream. The vividness of the setting was matched by the acting of Eduardo Ciannelli as Trock, Margo as Mirianne, Richard Bennett as Judge Gaunt, and Burgess Meredith as Mio.

The play opened in New York, September 25, 1935, and toured the country for five years. It had the distinction of winning the first award of the New York Drama Critics' Circle. Margo and Burgess Meredith starred in the motion picture version of the play in 1936, and it was presented in New York, 1945, by Equity Library.

Looking back upon a wrong committed by a previous generation, *Winterset* saw beyond the immediate facts of that wrong into the larger issues of faith, justice, and integrity. When the sin of their father is visited upon the sons and daughters of *Winterset,* Anderson achieves, not the flare of indignation that was his *Gods of the Lightning,* but the even flame of steadfastness and truth. Even his verse is ennobled by the depth and fullness of his perception. His language is at his simplest, most effective, and most beautiful.

Brooks Atkinson, in his first review of the play, said, "There are moments when the verse seems superfluous or ostentatious," but he retracted after reading the play: "I called the final lines 'formal and prolix.' They are not. They are as hard and cutting as emerald dust and a fair token of the philosophy and style of a fine American drama . . . By comparison with *Winterset,* journeyman drama has a pettiness that is almost contemptible . . . *Winterset* ought to be, not an incident, but an event, in the theatre."

The critics, as is usual in the case of Anderson, met *Winterset* with divided opinions. Percy Hammond called it "a murky drama." John Anderson commented: "Maxwell Anderson has stirred the embers of a poet's wrath . . . [the play] achieves one superlative scene in the second act and leaves the rest of the evening lost in articulate emptiness." The scene he singled out is that in which the gangster, the judge, and the executed man's son together come face to face with the truth. Robert Garland was disappointed: "*Winterset* isn't the fine play it set out to be. Instead, it is a murder melodrama in masquerade, a gun-and-gangster thriller with poetic aspirations."

The action of the play draws its title from the time symbolically chosen for its happenings. There is the chill of remembered cold in *Winterset;* but after it comes the warmth of love, even of exaltation.

Other performances include: 1952, ELT; 1959, Yale; February 9, 1966, Jan Hus OffBway for thirty performances; a tour of New York City parks in 1968, in Spanish, by the Puerto Rican Traveling Theatre Co.

HIGH TOR   *Maxwell Anderson*

A combination of melodrama and farce, of Hudson River legend and contemporary satire, of smiling surface and serious depth, *High Tor* is the most delightful of Maxwell Anderson's plays. It is, as Brooks Atkinson declared, "the gustiest fantasy in the American drama."

High Tor is a crag looming 832 feet above the Hudson River, along the Palisades below the town of Haverstraw. The owner, Van Van Dorn, a young American who loves the mountain for its beauty, refuses to sell it to a crushed-stone firm. Mixed in the tangle of the play are two local politicians trying to swindle the lad out of the property, three fellows who have robbed a bank in nearby Nanuet, a company of Dutch sailors waiting for Henry Hudson to come back for them, a philosophical old Indian, a maiden of today, and a young seventeenth-century lass, Lise. The Dutch sailors stuff the two rascal politicians into a steam shovel and hoist them up for a night. Van falls in love with the wraith Lise but at the end of the play, in a return to reality, he sells the crag and with the modern maid, Judith, goes west toward fresher mountains.

The end of the play may seem a surrender. Indeed the *New York Daily News* spoke of the "unbelievably shallow conclusion" that Anderson had embodied in the last words of the Indian, "Nothing is made by men but makes, in the end, good ruins." The *News* overlooked an earlier reflection by the Indian on the olden days: "Then, as now, the young braves were for keeping what was ours, whatever it cost in blood. And they did try, but when they'd paid their blood, and still must sell, the price was always less than what it was before their blood was paid."

The dialogue is for the most part spirited, amusing, and imaginative. Atkinson, after the opening night, thought some of the verse "too lyric to be dramatic," but upon reading *High Tor,* he declared: "My admiration, especially for the verse, has on the whole increased."

Following their wont, the critics disagreed sharply over the play. After its world premiere in Cleveland on December 29, 1936, *Variety* with its usual elegance said that the play delivered "another kick in the pants for the machine age—without arriving at any definite attitude, and without gripping the listener . . . Very little danger is there, of his new one copping any sort of prize, except a medal for being the season's most confusing play." But after *High Tor* opened in New York, on January 9, 1937, with Burgess Meredith, Peggy Ashcroft, and John Drew Colt, it won the New York Drama Critics' Circle award.

Nonetheless, New York opinion was divided. Richard Watts considered *High Tor* one of Anderson's "strongest and most arresting plays." But John Anderson found the play's fantasy disappointing: "In dramatic poetry especially, there must be a complete unity, maintained against all intrusion, and held surely against dramatic irrelevance. *High Tor* repeatedly breaks its own spell by a clash of moods, and since the mood here is the chief thing, I found the illusion in fragments . . . It would be a fine bubble if it didn't have a pinhole in it." In direct disagreement, John Mason Brown declared: "One false step, one lapse into the mundane, the heavy-handed, or the conventional, and its enchantment would vanish. But vanish it does not. Because, even while it is dealing with a spell cast upon those who are brought together one stormy night on a haunted mountain up the Hudson, *High Tor* succeeds in casting a spell of its own. It is a magic spell which finds Mr. Anderson doing the best, most creative and original work of his distinguished career."

Maxwell Anderson had his home on South Mountain Road in the shadow of High Tor. The nearby Nanuet bank really had been robbed. Anderson's neighbor, William A. Caldwell, commenting on the play in the New Jersey *Bergen County Evening Record,* said, "I will swear I can call the two politicians by name. Can it be that Maxwell Anderson is busting a first-rate scandal story on the New York stage instead of in the local gazettes?" The owner of most of High Tor, Elmer Van Orden, who holds the deed by grant of George III, after seeing the play, swore that he'd never sell the mountain. Thus the Hudson's High Tor may remain a lift of beauty in the Palisades, as Maxwell Anderson's *High Tor* remains a lift of beauty in the American drama.

High Tor has frequently been produced by community and college theatres. While recognizing the inevitable advance of the industrial age, it plays upon nostalgia with light humor and tearful fantasy; and it discloses the spirit of man unbound by the chains of the material world.

JOAN OF LORRAINE   *Maxwell Anderson*

Within a year of his major fiasco, *Truckline Café,* Maxwell Anderson achieved a success with *Joan of Lorraine.* However, when the play opened in New York on November 18, 1946, the crowds that overflowed the lobby were not there to see what sort of dramatic challenge Anderson was bringing to his critics; they were attracted by the glamour of movie star Ingrid Bergman as St. Joan.

Miss Bergman was cast in the play as the actress Mary Grey assigned the title role in a production of Joan of Arc. On an almost bare stage, the action of the play takes place at rehearsal scenes. In the play depicted, a compromise between Joan and the politicians of her day seems unnatural to the modern actress who is to play Joan. In fact, rehearsals are stopped as she and the director discuss the matter of the compromise. At one point, the actress is about to quit the play. Finally, however, in the middle of a scene, she awakens to the realization that life demands a compromise on non-essentials if the living are to hold steadfast to basic ideals.

To many, Anderson seemed to base his play on a truism; George Jean Nathan went so far as to say that Anderson "enjoys all the attributes of a profound thinker save profundity." The fact remains, however, that in many fields of thought and action today, precisely this issue of compromise is being fought; and many highly placed persons could use the lesson learned by the actress Mary Grey while playing Joan.

The sneer many today bestow upon the word *compromise* suggests—if it does not demonstrate—that the theme of *Joan of Lorraine* is both vital and timely. Beyond the issue of compromise the play also presses home the idea that all men live by faith, despite the fact that the articles of their faith cannot be verified. Faith nourishes itself to strengthen humankind.

An excellent cast helped assure the play's success. Ingrid Bergman was supported by Sam Wanamaker in the dual role of the director of the rehearsed play and the Inquisitor within that play. Other performers included Romney Brent as the Dauphin, and Joanna Roos.

Once again the critics were divided. "Like all Mr. Anderson's dramas, this one is sincere," said Brooks Atkinson. "Unlike some of them, it is written in excellent prose; and it is informal, like an intelligent discussion among people of high principle who are seriously wondering about sublime problems. Toward the end it seems, perhaps, to be overwritten and to be groping among abstractions, words taking precedence over ideas. But that does not alter the general impression that Mr. Anderson has written an engrossing play that is variously poignant, rhapsodic, and genial, and much above the common level of the theatre."

Somewhat less cordial, Richard Watts admired Ingrid Bergman's acting but found the play "by no means completely satisfactory or successful . . . Where *St. Joan** soared, *Joan of Lorraine* remains pedestrian . . . The plot device does not greatly help dramatically . . ." Significantly, the modern framework was omitted from the motion picture version of 1948, in which Ingrid Bergman again played Joan; only the story of Joan of Arc was presented.

George Jean Nathan, as urbane as ever, drew a number of devastating comparisons in his review of the play: "The impression one gains from it is of a Readers' Theatre performance of Percy MacKaye's *Joan of Arc* directed by a second cousin of Pirandello and interrupted from time to time by some old patent medicine doctor faith and hope messages from Mr. Anderson and with a popular screen actress as ballyhoo. In essaying the Maid of Orleans theme, Mr. Anderson plainly accepted a pretty difficult challenge. It is not surprising that, from any viewpoint a bit loftier than that identified with Broadway, he has not succeeded, except at the box-office, which is seldom disturbingly critical. The list of his silent challengers is too formidable. Shakespeare has outpoetized him; Schiller has outfelt him; Barbier has outdramatized him: Twain has outwitted him; Shaw has outthought him; even MacKaye has outwritten him."

Against such adverse opinions, Robert Garland was all praise: "The theatre is itself again . . . a heady mixture of drama and melodrama, bitterness and beauty, romance and reality, belief and disbelief"; and Arthur Pollock called *Joan of Lorraine* one of Anderson's best: it "has sunshine in it . . . the clearest and the warmest treatment that the Joan of Arc story has enjoyed in the theatre."

What makes *Joan of Lorraine* an outstanding play is the way it presses an old theme to a modern problem, the way in which it presents the argument over the compromises made by Joan on minor things, and her firm resolve, unto death, on a major issue. By her faith, Joan answers the practical, material demands of our time. Yet the play makes clear that compromise has its place in the practical but not in the spiritual world. Through its dramatized answer to an eternal problem, *Joan of Lorraine* gives good measure of the three hoped-for-rewards of the theatre: entertainment, enlightenment, exaltation.

In 1953 Ingrid Bergman toured Europe in Honegger's concert-opera *Joan of Arc at the Stake*; she played this for her first London appearance, in 1954; in 1955 in Sweden. *Joan of Lorraine* was shown OffBway (Lenox Hill) in 1955.

In addition to Anderson and Shaw, in 1953 Anouilh's *L'Alouette* was presented in Paris; as *The Lark,* London saw it open May 15, 1955, translated by Christopher Fry*, with Dorothy Tutin, directed by Peter Brook, for 109 performances. It ends before the Maid's burning, with preparations for the coronation of the King at Rheims. At the questioning of the judges, Joan recalls her humble birth and her sure spotting of the real king amid the anonymous crowd at Avignon. Anouilh pictures her as unassuming, but firm in the assurance of her divine mission. The play gave a lift to the French at a time when the country needed inspiriting after its sorry activity in World War II.

A less happy adaptation by Lillian Hellman, with Julie Harris, was shown in Boston and New York in 1955, and revived in Chicago in 1981.

Joseph Wood Krutch, in his book *American Drama Since 1918,* discussed the poetry of Anderson's eleven poetic dramas: "His verse found ready comprehension in part because it did not, like so much modern poetry, require a familiarity with a modern tradition of which four-fifths of the theatergoing public is completely ignorant. It has at least the primary virtue of dramatic verse inasmuch as it is easily speakable and easily understood when spoken."

ANATHEMA   *Leonid N. Andreyev*

The gloom and despair that marked the life of Andreyev (1871–1919)—he attempted suicide three times—pervades this play, the greatest of the dramas of this Russian playwright.

In the prologue, Anathema sits at heaven's gate, demanding knowledge. What kind of god, he asks, has created this kind of world? Denied an answer, he goes to live with the saintly David Leizer, a Jew who gives everything—his love, his toil, and the 4,000,000 rubles left him by a brother in America—to the poor. David wishes to do good quietly, unobserved, but the people seek him out and worship him. When his wealth is used up, however, the mob turns on him and stones him. In the epilogue, Anathema, again at the Gate, is told that "David has his immortality," to which he replies that in David's name men will be murderers.

Originally produced in Andreyev's native land, *Anathema* was suppressed after thirty-seven performances for giving too favorable a picture of the Jews. As has been pointed out by translator Herman Bernstein, Andreyev attributed to David "the qualities of Christ and subordinated them to the Russian Jew . . . For this, he was accused of blasphemy. He was excommunicated, and his play was suppressed by the Holy Synod. At a special ceremony, presided over by Archbishop Germogen of Kiev, black candles were lighted, and the play was anathematized."

In New York, *Anathema* was presented in Yiddish, opening on November 25, 1910. The *New York Tribune* —the only English-language paper to review it—said that it was "universal in interest, rich in poetic symbolism, and profound in philosophical conception."

Enacted again in Yiddish, February 7, 1923, with Maurice Schwartz as Anathema and Muni Weisenfreund (later known as Paul Muni) as David, the play was most favorably received. The *New York Times* spoke of "Andreyev's tremendous tragedy" as "a spectacle notable for poignance, vehemence, and color."

As a result of the hearty reception given the Jewish production, *Anathema* was brought to Broadway on April 10, 1923, in a translation by Herman Bernstein. A mixed welcome followed. "What to a Russian audience," said John Corbin, "is profound philosophy set forth in luminous symbols, seemed to an American audience pompous vaporings—a meaningless story enveloped in turgid verbosity." The *New York Sun* called David Leizer "a doddering old fool who ought to have gone to heaven years before the play started." J. Ranken Towse, however, observed that "there can be no question of its descriptive or imaginative power."

Although *anathema* has come to mean an accursed person or thing, the word literally meant consecrated, devoted. The play pictures Anathema as relentlessly dedicated to the quest of knowledge—whereas most men, as Andreyev sees them, will deny or destroy truth for wealth and power. Andreyev felt that *Anathema* was his masterpiece. It combines realism with allegory, and drives home the idea that, despite the sense of doom, man ever batters at the barriers of ignorance, hate, and greed.

HE WHO GETS SLAPPED   *Leonid N. Andreyev*

This is the greatest of Andreyev's studies of the tortured soul. It is the story of a gentleman called "He" who comes to live among circus folk. Given the part of a clown, he endures an inordinate amount of slapping. The wiser and more beautiful his words, the more the public laughs when he is slapped.

All is not well inside the circus world. The bare-back rider, Consuelo, whom everybody loves, is to be sold by her father to the wealthy Baron Regnard. As the time for the wedding approaches, Consuelo becomes frightened; "He," who has also come to love her, shares a fatal dose of poison with Consuelo, and at her death the Baron commits suicide. Thus, Andreyev tells us that even in the world of make-believe there is no escape from the doom of human weakness.

Written in 1914, the play was produced by the Theatre Guild in New York in 1922, and ran for 182 performances. In the cast were Helen Westley, Margalo Gillmore, Richard Bennett, and Louis Calvert. The play was well received. Alexander Woollcott called it "alive in its every moment, and abrim with color and beauty." The play was revived in New York in 1944 by Equity Library and again in 1946 by the Theatre Guild with Stella Adler and Dennis King in the cast. Of the latter production, Louis Kronenberger observed that the first half had "a tingling, hopped-up excitement, a highwire exhibition of the emotions ... After that, everything started to crumble. The falsity remained, without the lure." Many critics found in the play "much that is exciting, and much that will arouse the softer sentiments."

Tyrone Guthrie directed a London production which *Theatre World* (August 1947) considered "an outstanding piece of theatre." Harold Hobson, in the *London Sunday Times* (June 17, 1947), gave special credit to the production: "The stage is never still: clowns and conjurers, in yellow tinselled garments, lion-tamers and jockeys, dart continually across it." Mr. Hobson felt, however, that the play, at the end, "dissolves into the shadow of a shade" because Andreyev "does not seem to make up his mind whether this is an abdication or a release, whether the Prince ("He") is a coward or a philosopher. The play wanders directionless, and the Prince, who started by being a real, if mysterious, figure, ends only as a vague abstraction of the world's resignation from responsibility."

The original New York production provided a noteworthy instance of "slapping" in the experience of the Negro author, Claude McKay, who attended the play with artist William Gropper. McKay recorded the experience in the *Liberator* (May 1922): "The stubs were handed to Gropper and we started towards the orchestra. But the usher, with a look of quizzical amazement on his face, stopped us. Snatching the stubs from Gropper and muttering something about seeing the manager, he left us wondering and bewildered. In a moment he returned, with the manager. "The—wrong date," the manager stammered, and taking the stubs marked 'Orchestra,' he hurried off to the box-office, returning with others marked 'Balcony' . . . I had come to see a tragic farce, and I found myself unwillingly the hero of one. He who got slapped was I. As always in the world-embracing Anglo-Saxon circus, the intelligence, the sensibilities, of the black clown were slapped without mercy." It is pleasant to note that the "Anglo-Saxon" reaction to this incident did much to end racial discrimination in the New York theatre.

But Claude McKay also struck a sharp blow at the despair portrayed by Andreyev. "Dear Leonid Andreyev," he wrote, "if you had only risen out of your introspective Nihilistic despair to create the clown in the circus of hell, the clown slapped on every side by the devil's red-hot tongs, yet growing wiser, stronger, and firmer in purposeful determination, seeking no refuge in suicide, but bearing it out to the bitter end, you might have touched me." In taking the path to death, however, "He" and the girl, like Antigone and Oedipus of Greek drama, maintain against life's overpowering evil the upright stand of human dignity. *He Who Gets Slapped* remains a continuing challenge, both to performers and to intelligent audiences.

In 1956 the opera *Pantaloon,* with music by Robert Ward and libretto by Bernard Stambler, gave *He Who Gets Slapped* a happy ending. It was heard in New York at the Actors' Playhouse in 1956; at the City Center, 1959; at Long Island University in 1974.

London saw the play in 1958 and (Hampstead Theatre Club) 1964. In the United States, ELT 1967; Yale, San Francisco, and OffBway, 1979. The play was filmed in 1974.

A musical of the play, book by Larry Arrick, music and lyrics by Barbara Damashek, was tried out (and found wanting) at Stamford, Conn., in 1977, with humans playing the animals, with lion taming and stunts, in a circus ring.

VOYAGEUR SANS BAGAGE   *Jean Anouilh*

Jean Anouilh (b. 1910), said British director Peter Brook, "is a poet but not a poet of words; he is a poet of words-acted, of scenes-set, of players performing." Stephen Spender added: "The plays of Anouilh seem to have more poetry of the theatre in them than anything a contemporary poet has yet put in metrical lines upon the page."

A lively illustration of the Anouilh style is his first success in Paris, *Voyageur sans Bagage,* 1937. "Gaston" is a living "unknown soldier"; he has suffered from amnesia since the war. After seventeen years, a new psychiatrist makes his story public; at once four hundred families claim him. Narrowing the possibilities to six, the Duchess Dupont-Defort, aunt of the psychiatrist, takes him to the home of the Renauds, the most aristocratic claimants.

Valentine Renaud is overjoyed; she pleads with Gaston: "Our entire life, with our fine moral code and our precious freedom, consists ultimately in accepting ourselves as we are . . . You are about to become a man again, with everything that entails in the way of failures and blemishes—and moments of happiness. Accept yourself—and accept me, Jacques." As the woman, if he acknowledges the relationship, would be his brother's wife, and as a no-longer-maidservant also looks forward to renewing an affair, "Jacques-Gaston" prefers another family.

Meanwhile, the other five selected claimants have arrived. Among them are a young boy from England, with his guardian; he needs a relative for rights of succession. There are no other relatives to burden Gaston with memories; they know—says Gaston—that he has a scar below his left shoulder blade (where Valentine said she had once scratched him in a fit of jealousy); and Gaston arranges to slip away with the boy, without seeing the Renauds again.

In one way or another, main characters in plays of Anouilh say no. Gaston has said no to binding memories, which would predetermine him; he is thus left free to follow his own pattern.

The play was translated by Lucienne Hill in 1959 as *Traveler Without Luggage*. Translated by John Whiting, it was shown in Birmingham in 1971, then moved to a good run in London. In the 1964 ANTA Theatre production in New York, Ben Gazzara played Gaston; Nancy Wickwire, his would-be sister-in-law Valentine. Some hint may be surmised that he recognizes the Renauds as his true relatives; but this is part of Anouilh's frequent guessing game. Thus, Howard Taubman in the *New York Times* said that the play "whets the curiosity and holds the interest. As an intellectual conceit it ends with an ironic flourish. . . In Robert Lewis' silken staging it moves smoothly through its chiseled obligatory encounters, pausing to smile at its glinting humors, to shudder at its bursts of theatricalism, and to chuckle lightly at its detached irony . . . expertly composed encounters, shading from genre comedy to loyal, tormented affection, to unbending pride, to demanding passion . . . Such craftsmanship is a pleasure in itself." The picture of a man taking advantage of his situation to fashion his own future makes *Voyageur sans Bagage* a further and continuing pleasure.

L'INVITATION AU CHÂTEAU (RING   *Jean Anouilh*
AROUND THE MOON)

The most popular of Anouilh's plays is *L'Invitation au Château*, 1947, which had 333 performances in Paris, with music by Francis Poulenc. Anouilh listed it as one of his *pièces roses*; his *pièces noires* include *Antigone* and *The Lark*. In an adaptation by Christopher Fry* called *Ring Around the Moon*, the play ran over a year at the London Globe, opening January 26, 1950. This version came to New York's Martin Beck, November 23, 1950, and was performed by college or other amateur groups every year at least until 1972 (for example, 1955, San José, Swarthmore, University of Texas, University of Illinois, Vassar). Also ELT 1960; 1963, a national tour directed by Eva Le Gallienne; 1968, with Flora Robson and Isobel Jeans.

The story has complicated but never confusing tangles. The shy and sensitive Frederick loves a lively heiress, who is in love with his twin brother, the more aggressive Hugo. To cure Frederick, Hugo invites a beautiful dancer to the fabulous ball at the Auverne Château, arranged by the formidable patrician Mme. Desmermortes, wise and witty and mischievous, who presides benignly from her wheelchair. The dancer succeeds in turning Frederick from the heiress, but loses her own heart to him. Hugo, having heard that the heiress's father is broke, pops the question while tripping a burlesque tango with her—to learn, after he's accepted, that the father is wealthier than ever. At one point the bewildered butler exclaims: "I feel like a beetle in bedlam!" But it's an attractive bedlam, which ends with a proper coupling for bedlock.

Christopher Fry's translation, said Brooks Atkinson, "is beautifully done, with spirit, humor, and loveliness . . . the play has a sensuous quality that is wholly enchanting." In the New York production, Lucile Watson played the dominating lady in the wheelchair; Oscar Karlweiss, the millionaire; Denholm Elliott played both the twin brothers. Usually one actor plays both twins, as in New Orleans, 1958, and Melbourne, Australia, 1977–1978.

George Jean Nathan (*Journal-American,* December 11, 1950) used his review to discuss "the four shapes of twindrama" from Plautus through Shakespeare to Anouilh. *L'Invitation au Château* is a neat variation; which holds amused attention to the end.

THE WALTZ OF THE TOREADORS   *Jean Anouilh*

Increasingly Anouilh added sly mockery and subtler variation to his use of theatrical devices, with a modern sophisticated turn and always deft characterization. Thus, in *The Waltz of the Toreadors,* 1956, the aging General, still lecherous in spirit, however weak in the flesh, is at once amusing and somehow pathetic.

General St. Pé is tied to his wife, Emilie, who has taken to her bed to tighten her hold on him. He is visited by Mlle. Ghislaine de Ste-Euverte, with whom seventeen years before he had danced to the "Waltz of the Toreadors"; they had loved platonically ever since. Now she appears with two love letters Emilie had written to Dr. Bonfant—Emilie's physician and friend of the General's—and she demands that he leave Emilie. Both women "attempt" suicide. Ghislaine is consoled by the General's virginal secretary, Gaston; they go off and consummate their love. Meanwhile, the General's two daughters also "attempt" suicide—swimming as far as they can, then swimming back—for love of Gaston. But now, as Gaston's mother has died, Father Ambrose is free to announce the truth: Gaston is the son of a dressmaker—and the General. After surprise, general embracing. And Gaston is free to marry Ghislaine.

The General puts his arm about the waist of the new maid, Pamela:

"Do you mind?"
"No, sir, but what will Madame say?"
"Madame will say nothing so long as you don't tell her. That's a good girl. It's nicer like this, don't you think? Not that it means anything, but still, one feels less lonely in the dark."

They go into the garden, to the music of the "Waltz of the Toreadors." The General has found a way of contented survival.

BECKET   *Jean Anouilh*

Becket, by Jean Anouilh, tells the story already made known by Tennyson* and T. S. Eliot,* but it would hardly be used, as theirs are, for playing on the anniversary of the archbishop's martyrdom. It opens, indeed, with Henry naked in Canterbury Cathedral, awaiting the monks with their penitential lashes. And the shade of Becket appears to the King, who wonders at his friend's rigidity; he had been pliant "in all save the honor of the realm." Becket responds that he had been pliant too, "in all save the honor of God." But in the remainder of the play, which flows back through their friendly years, we find them jolly together, Becket a hunting and whoring companion, prodding Henry on. Becket dares to draw sword against a Norman knight who laid hands upon his sister. Becket teaches Henry how to use a fork, that new refinement, which Henry tries on his rude Normans. But when Thomas à Becket unwillingly accepts appointment as Archbishop of Canterbury (1162), all is changed; defending the rights of the Church against the King's power, he moves inevitably to his death at the hands of four knights of King Henry, 1170. Becket was canonized in 1172; Chaucer's characters in *The Canterbury Tales* are the most famous of the many groups that went on pilgrimage to his shrine, until Henry VIII plundered it and expunged Saint Becket's name from the English church calendar.

Translated by Lucienne Hill, Anouilh's *Becket* opened in New York at the St. James, October 5, 1960, for 193 performances, with Anthony Quinn as Henry and Laurence Olivier as Becket, returning on May 8, 1961, for 24 more with Olivier as Henry and Arthur Kennedy as Becket. There were forty persons listed in the cast, plus assorted soldiers, servants, and monks.

Howard Taubman in the *New York Times* (October 6, 1960) said: "The eye is diverted and the mind stimulated. But the heart is not often stirred . . . There are some impressive scenes, humorous, derisive, colorful, and eloquent." Walter Kerr, in the *Herald Tribune,* found the play "fluid, unfocused but fascinating . . . Two of the most important scenes take place on horseback, one against a pleasant summer backdrop of slender trees, one against a landscape that is dour with frost . . . Both stars—and they really are stars—are riding the horses rather better than they are the play . . . Mr. Quinn (as King Henry) seems perfectly at home in nearly every century as he eyes an available wench and asks 'Shall we take her with us, or have her sent?'"

The Anouilh *Becket* opened for ten days beginning Ash Wednesday, February 16, 1983, at St. Bart's OffOffBway. Of the three tellings of Becket's story, Anouilh's is the most humorous and lively, up to the fatal rupture of the opposed loyalties of church and state.

THE DYBBUK   *S. Ansky*

Stimulated by the Dreyfus case while living in Paris, S. Ansky (Solomon Z. Rappaport, 1863-1920) began to explore Jewish folklore. He was struck by the legend of the *dybbuk,* the spirit of a dead person which enters another's body when its work is incomplete. He wrote a first version of *The Dybbuk,* called *Between Two Worlds,* in 1914, in which he contrasted the other-world of love with this world of reality.

As developed ten years later in *The Dybbuk,* the spirit of Chanan, who dies when his love for Leah is thwarted, enters into Leah's body, so that when her family prepares a rich match for her, the spirit of Chanan cries out against another bridegroom. When the rabbi exorcises the *dybbuk,* Leah falls dead and, completing the work of the *dybbuk,* rejoins her beloved Chanan.

In the play, the fight for personal happiness on the part of Leah and Chanan is balanced against the patriarchal authority of the rabbi, "the eternal tree of the House of David." As Ansky himself put it, "The play is, of course, a realistic one about mystical people . . . Both Chanan and Leah—and also the rabbi—are right, and furthermore are justified in their struggle."

The Dybbuk was written in Russian in 1917, at the suggestion of Stanislavski of the Moscow Art Theatre. Banned by the censor, it was translated into Yiddish and rehearsed by the Vilna Troupe, but it was again suppressed. Chaim Nachman Bialik, the greatest Hebrew poet of our age, made a Hebrew adaptation, which was also banned. Ansky, however, liked the Hebrew version so much that he retranslated it into Yiddish, in which form the play had its world premiere in Warsaw in 1920. It has become the main piece in the repertory of the famous Habima Players, formerly of Moscow, now of Tel-Aviv.

In 1921 *The Dybbuk* was produced at New York's Yiddish Art Theatre. An English version, by Henry G. Alsberg and Winifred Katzin, directed by David Vardi of the Habima Players, was given at the Neighborhood Playhouse in 1925. With Mary Ellis as Leah, supported by Albert Carroll and Dorothy Sands, the latter production moved uptown to Broadway in 1926. During 1926, the play was also revived in Yiddish and presented in New York by the visiting Habima Players. In 1927, New York's Second Avenue saw a Yiddish version with marionettes. A motion picture production was made in 1938. Among the more recent New York revivals of the play are an Equity Library production in English in 1947, and the Hebrew version again by the visiting Habima Players in 1948. An operatic version by Lodovico Rocco made its bow at La Scala in Milan on March 24, 1934, and in New York in 1936; another, by David Tamkin, composed in 1931, had its world premiere at the New York City Center on October 4, 1951.

Most comments on all the versions stress the play less than the production. Thus Richard Watts said of the 1926 English version: "It probably would seem to the alien spectator little better than superstitious drivel but for the perfect staging." Alexander Woollcott declared that no other production of the season could "compare in moving and memorable beauty with *The Dybbuk*"; but Brooks Atkinson found that the muted tones and mysterious movements of the cast in the third act "seem somewhat tedious, and the audience begins to emerge from the spell."

Of the Habima production in Hebrew, opinions have differed. In 1926 Alan Dale insisted that its players had an utter disregard for all the essentials of the theatre; "They were crudely true and blatantly droll . . . I was not gripped or held absorbed. Nor was my imagination touched for an instant." Gilbert W. Gabriel said: "One is terribly aware of its power, of the huge energy of this conception; but one cannot love it, hold it close." The eerie dance of the beggars at the wedding feast was termed by Brooks Atkinson "one of the theatre's immortal creations."

The significance of the play was aptly expressed by its English adapter, Henry G. Alsberg: "*The Dybbuk* attempts to give the quintessence of the Jewish ghetto, to fix forever the intense reality of the religious life and beliefs of the Jewish masses, just at the moment when the inroads of modern civilization were driving this life and these beliefs out of existence." The inroads of modern war, and the horrors of genocide, have now more completely made *The Dybbuk* an evocative picture of a vanished past.

In a Hebrew translation by the great poet Bialik, *The Dybbuk* was shown in London, 1965. With English adaptation and direction by John Hirsch, it toured Canada in 1974 and played in Los Angeles in 1975. In a new translation by Nira Rafalowicz and Joseph Chaikin, it was presented in New York by Joseph Papp in 1977.

THE BREASTS OF TIRESIAS   *Guillaume Apollinaire*

Born in Italy, Guillaume Apollinaire (G. de Kosovitski, 1880–1918), of Polish origin, lived in Paris from 1898. In 1903 he wrote *Les Mamelles de Tirésias,* adding a prologue and a new ending in 1916, for its production in Paris, June 24, 1917. "To characterize my drama," he said, "I have coined the word *surrealist.*" In translation by Louis Simpson, the play had its British premiere, April 13, 1965, with Rosamund Dickson as Thérèse-Tiresias. In 1967 and again in 1968, it was presented OffOffBway at the Calvary Church (Park Avenue South) in a translation by Robert Goss, stressing the seriousness underlying the balloonistic farce. In 1972 it was presented as an opera, with music by Francis Poulenc, set on the Riviera in 1971, with Goss's "eminently singable" translation.

According to legend, Tiresias was a Theban who saw two snakes copulating, killed the female, and was transformed into a woman. Zeus and Hera asked him which sex derives greater pleasure in making love; when he told them the woman's pleasure was ten times the man's, Hera in anger turned him back into a man—and blinded him. Thereupon Zeus gave him the gift of prophecy, and Hera—the woman has the last word—said he would never be believed. Tiresias was visited by Odysseus in Hades (we learn from Homer's *Odyssey*) to find out how to get home to Ithaca. He is a character in Sophocles' *Antigone** and *Oedipus Tyrannus** and in Euripides' *Bacchae** and *Phoenissae.** Tennyson (as also Swinburne) has a poem on Tiresias, but based on a different turn of the myth: that Athene blinded him because he had seen her bathing:

> *Henceforth be blind for thou hast seen too much,*
> *And speak the truth that no man will believe.*

In the Prologue, Apollinaire says: "The theatre is no more the life it interprets than a wheel is a leg . . . In the war [this is 1916] guns fired so high that they put out the stars. The unknown captain who always saves us cried: 'It's high time to rekindle them!'" So Apollinaire would light the inner stars: let the French make new children; let the theatre take new ways. The Prologue ends: "O Public, be the inextinguishable torch of the new fire."

The play takes place in Zanzibar: "The scene is in Zanzibar as the Seine is in Paris." (*Zanzibar* is also a game played with three dice, which are used in the stage decor.) It opens with Thérèse rebelling against the female's role; she wants to be all the things a man can be—lawyer, doctor, mathematician, philosopher. She opens her blouse: her breasts pop up—two balloons, which she bursts with a light—and she tosses balls from her bosom to the audience, while she sprouts mustache and beard. Her husband enters; she tells him that henceforth she is a man, Tiresias; and she forces him to exchange clothes.

Rhymes and puns abound. "The power of language is offered as a substitute for dramatic coherence and impact," says Anna Balakian, who gives seven pithy columns to surrealism in *The Reader's Encyclopedia of World Drama,* 1969. A gendarme wants to make love to the husband, now dressed in his wife's garments. While female voices offstage cry, "No more children!" Tiresias fills the stage with his offspring, 40,049 in a single day. A fortune-teller enters, prophesying that only the fertile will inherit the earth. The husband offers her a pipe; she removes her tinsel finery—and is Thérèse. Her husband says she's as flat as a pancake, and offers her balloons and balls. She releases the balloons—"Fly away, birds of my weakness"—and tosses the balls to the audience. They all sing:

> Come now, sing both morn and night.
> Scratch yourself whenever you itch.
> Love the black—or else the white—
> It's much more fun when they can switch.
> It's enough for you to keep this insight in sight.

The curtain falls.

Surrealism has no better illustration than this play by the man that coined the word.

THE GREEN GODDESS   *William Archer*

As a London critic, William Archer (1856–1924) helped clear the stage for the drama of realism. His translation (1880) of *The Pillars of Society** introduced Ibsen to the English theatre. As a playwright, however, Archer is remembered for his romantic melodrama of smooth-fingered Oriental intrigue, *The Green Goddess.*

With a keen sense of dramatic situation, the critic-turned-playwright wove his plot. Dr. Basil Traherne, Major Anthony Crespin, and the latter's wife, Lucilla, whose plane has made a forced landing in the almost inaccessible territory of the Rajah of Rukh, are a troubled triangle. The Major is a suspicious dipsomaniac; his wife and the doctor are in love. The suave Rajah, a Cambridge graduate sporting a monocle and a long cigarette-holder, courteously informs them that, when the English execute some of his tribesmen on the morrow, they must also die. "The priests," he says, "demand the sacrifice of the white goats" to their Green Goddess. He can perhaps persuade them to spare the lady, if she will enter his harem.

Deftly and swiftly the story moves on: The Rajah, who has a wireless set, tests his "guests" by having his man Watkins send a message: "The Lady has come to terms, will enter His Highness' household." Crespin, who is an operator, gives not a blink. Later, the party gags Watkins, heaves him out of the tower, starts to broadcast for help, when the Rajah enters and shoots Crespin. Did his calls get through? Next morning, as the sacrifice is to begin, a British plane arrives, and Lucilla and Dr. Traherne are free to return "to civili—to India."

It is Crespin who, when they first meet the Rajah, thus expresses their hope of escape. The Rajah responds: "To civilization, you were going to say? Why hesitate, my dear sir? We know very well that we are barbarians. We are quite reconciled to the fact. We have had some five thousand years to accustom ourselves to it. This sword is a barbarous weapon compared with your revolver; but it was worn by my ancestors when yours were daubing themselves blue and picking up a precarious livelihood in the woods.—But Madam is standing up all this time. Watkins, what are you thinking of? Some cushions!" Such a mixture of civilized urbanity and pagan ruthlessness led the *London Times,* after the London opening (September 6, 1923, for 416 performances), to call *The Green Goddess* "a thrilling melodrama with all the old situations and all the newest embellishments; a play which is not only thrilling but also 'amusing' in the best sense of the term, with its literary allusions, its picture of Oriental savagery veneered with Occidental culture, its cocktails and its Perrier Jouet 1906." Mischievously, several of the London papers exclaimed, "It isn't Ibsen!"

The Green Goddess had its premiere in Philadelphia, December 16, 1920; the *Philadelphia Inquirer* called it "a superb and horrible cameo of a human devil with exquisite manners." The play opened in New York January 18, 1921, and had a run of 440 performances. The *New York Mail* labelled it "one of the most fascinating melodramas—intelligent and, if you like, refined, but also a bully show"; and the *New York Star* (January 26) recognized it as "a well constructed piece of dramatic writing . . . The interest is cumulative, the suspense thoroughly justified by the stage proceedings, and there is not a wasted line or situation . . . written deftly, economically, and to excellent purpose."

In addition to the fascinating portrait of the Rajah of Rukh, as suave a villain as ever bowed before a fair heroine, there is a neat sketch of his valet Watkins, a cockney with a criminal record and a grudge against all English gentlemen, such as those now fallen into the Rajah's hands. The servant's mean cruelty, and his master's gentle ruthlessness, make stirring contrast to the English composure of the captured three.

George Arliss, in America and England, gave one of his most rounded portrayals as the Rajah of Rukh. The play has been very popular. Cyril Maude broadcast in it, in 1936; and Orson Welles, in 1939, toured in a twenty-minute condensation of it, which the *Hartford Courant* (February 15, 1939) characterized as "indubitably melodrama at its peak of perfection." *The Green Goddess* is indeed, with polished villain and brave heroine, an outstanding example of the melodrama of the bestial claw in the velvet glove.

SERJEANT MUSGRAVE'S DANCE   *John Arden*

An ironic, black-humor transposition of *The Recruiting Officer* * is *Serjeant Musgrave's Dance,* by John Arden (b. 1930), which attained only twenty-eight performances at the London Royal Court in 1959, but won critical acclaim for its fresh use of language and the manner of presentation of its anti-war idea. Dame Peggy Ashcroft, protesting the cool reception, called it "my most exciting experience in the theatre since I saw the Berliner Ensemble in *Mother Courage.* *" Directed by Peter Brook, it was a failure in Paris in 1963; but was successful in London in 1965; also in 1972, in a version by John McGrath called *Serjeant Musgrave Dances On,* with hecklers set among the audience, which was held at gunpoint.

A group of soldiers comes to a mining town in the north of England, in the 1880's. The miners at first mistrust them as strikebreakers. They turn out to be deserters, whom Serjeant Musgrave has gathered. He exhibits a box of bones, all that's left of a boy from that town, killed during the occupation of a foreign town. In reprisal, five natives were killed; now, says the serjeant, "with the inexorable arithmetic of military logic," twenty-five in authority must die, to press home the spiraling horrors of war. It is for this purpose that he has come, to recruit volunteers.

Unfortunately, the dragoons sweep in, clad in their blood-red uniforms, and with this return of "law and order" the miners confusedly dance. Arden explains the color symbolism: "Black is for death, and for the coal miners; Red is for murder, and for the soldier's coat the collier puts on to escape his black."

The play is not one-sided pacifist propaganda; arguments for and against are given equal force. The characters are not mouthpieces of a point of view, but complicated and confused—like most of us, on this subject—or, at best, perplexed human beings.

Among American productions: 1965–1966, Arena Stage, Washington, D.C.; 1965, Theatre de Lys, OffBway, with John Colicos "a mad martinet on the side of the angels"; 1967, Ann Arbor, University of Michigan; 1968, Tyrone Guthrie Theatre, Minneapolis.

Of the play, John Arden observed: "I think that many of us must at some time have felt an overpowering urge to match some particularly outrageous piece of violence with an even greater and more outrageous retaliation." With prose, free verse, and song intertwined, Arden has fashioned a flexible and effective movement, with a vivid and "explosive invasion of the extraordinary and disruptive into the normal and fairly orderly." There is a stir in the attitudes of the miners that carries itself into the audience, along with the recognition that no important problem in the world today has all the right on one side.

Ed Marvish, new owner of the refurbished Old Vic, home of the NT before it moved to its Thames-side triple quarters, has listed his openings: *Serjeant Musgrave's Dance,* set for May 23, 1984, for six weeks, with Albert Finney.

THE SUPPOSES   *Lodovico Ariosto*

An attentive student of the Latin classics, Ariosto (1474–1531) wrote several plays in imitation of the comedies of Plautus. They were widely hailed, being the first comedies that, in lively verse, presented to Italy the swift intrigues and amusing incidents that were the substance of Roman drama.

Most effective of Ariosto's comedies, and the most influential in passing along the Roman comic tradition, is *The Supposes,* written in 1503. It is in plot a typical Roman intrigue of mistaken identity, and in spirit a genially satiric character-gallery drawn from the Ferrara of Ariosto's day. The story is a complicated one. Erostrato, come to Ferrara to study, falls in love with Polinesta, daughter of the wealthy merchant Damon. To enter her household, Erostrato changes name and place with his servant Dulipo. Helped by the usual bawdy Nurse, he gains access to the maiden and, revealing his identity, wins her heart. Meanwhile, Polinesta's father wants her to wed a wealthy old Doctor of Laws, Cleander. The false Erostrato (the servant), appearing as Cleander's rival, brings a false father with him. Erostrato's real father, Philogano, meanwhile arrives. Suspecting false play, he hires a lawyer—none other than Cleander!—to ferret out the truth for him. The merchant sees his "servant" with his daughter and imprisons him; Erostrato's danger leads Dulipo to confess the impostures. Further complications end with the marriage of the loving couple. This story became the subplot of Shakespeare's *The Taming of the Shrew.*

With considerable incidental comedy, the play is really a satire, directed against doctors, and against customs-house officials, who, in those days of active trade among the Italian city-states, had many opportunities for profitable irregularity.

A prose version of *The Supposes* enacted during the 1509 carnival at Ferrara proved instantly popular. The version in verse was staged for Pope Leo X in 1519; and with many minor changes, it was printed in 1542. Within a quarter of a century, it had been adapted in French by Jean de la Taille and in English by George Gascoigne (1525–1577). Gascoigne's *The Supposes* was produced at Gray's Inn Court in 1566. It is in vigorous prose; although it lacks some of the polish and the gaiety of Ariosto's play, it affects the alliteration and other verbal devices of the Euphuistic style.

Though the plot is largely an amalgam of Terence's *The Eunuch** and Plautus' *The Captives,** the Italian of Ariosto's *Gli Suppositi* has a distinctive quality of its own. "Everywhere in these lively scenes," said R. Warrick Bond in *Early Plays From the Italian* (1911), "we feel the working of the same gay fancy; we find the same constructive imagination, as enabled Shakespeare to transmute and vivify the materials he found. The initial information is given without artificiality . . . The admirably natural action evolves with rapidity and smoothness . . . The absence of love scenes is partly a heritage from Latin comedy, which excluded respectable girls from the stage, partly a consequence of Italian custom, which discouraged their appearance in the street."

The Supposes is in essence a lively interfusion of the earliest elements of the drama.

THE ACHARNIANS   *Aristophanes*

Written about 425 B.C., *The Acharnians* satirizes the war policy of the Athenians and especially the leader of the war party, Cleon.

After the death (429 B.C.) of Pericles, who had started the Peloponnesian War "over three hussies," political power was shrewdly wielded by Cleon, whose war policy was cowardly, mean, and cruel. At his orders, the population of Megara was systematically starved; and in 427, at his insistence, the death of all males in the rebelling city of Mytilene was ordered, along with the enslavement of the women and children. The order was revoked, but similar ones, later in the War, were not. As a result of his attack on Cleon in *The Babylonians,* Aristophanes was brought before the City Council. The charges against him were dismissed, and the next year his comedy *The Acharnians* was produced.

The chorus of Acharnian charcoal-burners in Athens was a timely choice for the play. During the Spartan invasion of Attica, Acharnae was overrun and her citizens forced into Athens for shelter. The play portrays the Acharnian Dicaeopolis ("honest citizen") who, when he finds that even the god Amphitheus ("the god on both sides") is manhandled by the police for advocating peace, decides to negotiate a private peace of his own. Arrested for treason by the Acharnians, he successfully defends himself; and while the general, Lamachus, dolefully dresses for battle, Dicaeopolis prepares for festive and feminine joy.

The plot of the play, as of a modern musical comedy, gives but scant measure of its worth. The Old Comedies were gaily costumed and played with music and merriment. *The Acharnians* is representative of the pattern they followed; in fact, if all the other comedies had been lost, we should still, from this one, know the general nature of the Old Comedy. It opens with a "bright idea" (in *The Acharnians,* Dicaeopolis' decision to sue for a private peace); a debate follows, interrupted by occasional lyrics and frequent comic questions or remarks. Always, however, the "bright idea" triumphs. Then comes a long speech by the leader of the chorus (with choral comment), the *parabasis,* in which the theme of the play is discussed seriously, and counsel offered to the Athenians. The end of the *parabasis,* the *pnigos* (choker), was spoken as rapidly as possible, much like the "patter-song" of a Gilbert and Sullivan musical, a modern art form close to the Aristophanic comedy. From this point on, the structure of the play is looser. There is usually a series of episodes— bawdy, slapstick, uproarious—showing how the "bright idea" works out in practice and ending with the *comos,* or gay revel with wine, women, song, and the *gamos,* the union of the sexes. Thus in one play are mingled beautiful lyric poetry, serious political satire and advice on the issues of the day, and broadest farce.

At a time when Athens was in the midst of a life-and-death war, with Cleon dictating Athenian policy, Aristophanes included the following words in the *parabasis* of *The Acharnians*: "I scoff at Cleon's tricks and plotting; honesty and justice shall fight my cause; never will you find me a political poltroon, a prostitute to the highest bidder."

Incidental political satire is evident throughout the play. Dicaeopolis is given samples of three kinds of peace-treaty, which he tastes like wine. He rejects the five-year truce; it would merely provide time to recoup losses and rush along in an armament race. Likewise, he rejects the ten-year truce; it would be used for cementing alliances and finding new allies. He welcomes and ratifies the truce of thirty years, both on sea and on land, with its aroma of nectar and its glad message of "Go whither you will"—unbarred by hostile hand or iron curtain. Beneath the swift and bawdy comedy the ruin of war is shown when a starved Megarian puts up his daughters for sale, pretending that they are sows.

Aristophanes shoots straight shafts of satire at many Athenian figures, especially at the tragic dramatist Euripides*. Throughout the very years when Aristophanes was urging the people toward peace, Euripides wrote play after play exalting the glory of the martial spirit of Athens.

The Acharnians won first prize at the Lenaean Festival in 425 B.C.; two older and already famous playwrights, Cratinus and Eupolis, took second and third place.

The first American production of *The Acharnians,* in Greek, was given at the University of Pennsylvania on May 15, 1886. The *New York Times,* the day before, declared: "The humanity of today has no interest in the person-ages of the comedies of Aristophanes or in the events they deal with . . ." On May 17, however, the *Times* retracted: "It is an excellent example of the poet's liveliest style, and the text is pure and comparatively easy to master. The performance, contrary to the expectations of many, was remarkably bright and entertaining . . ." The production was brought to New York in November, when the *Times* (November 14, 1886) reported: "The action of the comedy is brisk and amusing, and much of its wit is easily understood ages after the great comic poet's death."

Still using the ancient Greek tongue, but in modern dress, with comic policemen and a messenger on bicycle, a performance was given at Bradfield College, England, in March 1930. Finally presented in English by the Balliol Players, *The Acharnians* proved, according to the *London Times* (July 8, 1938), "almost as topical in A.D. 1938 as it was in 425 B.C. . . . At the close one felt that a sense of humor can do as much to end a war as to win it." *The Acharnians* is a rapid flow of tumbling comedy and keen satire, still pertinent and still alive.

In London, 1977, the Greek Art Theatre put on a modern version of *The Acharnians,* in full fun, with straw beards, false noses, pumpkin masks. In the *parabasis,* seventeen young Greeks removed their masks and directly addressed the audience. Soon bobbly-breasted ladies and men with phalluses at all stages of tumescence were doing a conga up and down the aisles. A typical Greek comedy would end with a wedding feast that was a simulated orgy. The *London Observer* said that the play "crosses Walt Disney with a bit of Zorba, shadow puppetry with mime, drag, Monty Python . . . Peace means feasting, dancing, and uncomplicated screwing . . . There's fair touch of *Hair* here." *Hair** has far to go to equal the slick work of Aristophanes.

THE CLOUDS   *Aristophanes*

In *The Clouds* Aristophanes turned from politics to education, to attack the Sophists who were then spreading their ideas throughout Greece, especially to attack the newly developed art of pleading, that made "the worse cause seem the better." With characteristic courage, Aristophanes singled out Socrates, the most prominent of the new teachers. But he also foisted upon Socrates all the extreme practices of the school, of which the Socrates of history was in no wise guilty.

So potent was the influence of *The Clouds* that Plato in "The Apology" pointed out that, when on trial for his life in 399 B.C., Socrates found it harder to dispel the picture of him that the Athenians knew from *The Clouds* than to answer the specific charges leveled against him. Robert Browning, in his *Aristophanes' Apology,* took pains to picture the playwright as attacking not the individual but the school.

The extant version of *The Clouds* is a revised one, often read but never performed in ancient times. Made about 421 B.C., it contains a reference to Cleon's death, which occurred in 422. In *The Knights,* Aristophanes had dismissed the playwright Cratinus as outmoded, bidding him go sit among the spectators. To Aristophanes' chagrin, the very next year Cratinus took first prize with his *Wine Flagon.* Ameipsias took second place with his *Konnos,* which also attacked Socrates. *The Clouds,* over the audience's heads, had to be content with last place. In the *parabasis* of the revised version, Aristophanes rebukes the "unrefined" public for not preferring his play, which, he points out, turned from lewd and low comedy to deal with higher things.

To treat of the "higher things," Aristophanes introduces a chorus of clouds; "their unsubstantial mistiness," as Henry Ten Eyck Perry indicated in *Masters of Dramatic Comedy* (1939), is "a good symbol for the practical weakness of abstract reasoning." Socrates himself is suspended in a basket, because the earth's moisture sucks the intellect dry: "I could not have searched out celestial matters," says Socrates, "without suspending judgment, and infusing my subtle spirit with the kindred air." Thus hanging aloft, he does all his thinking in the clouds.

The play opens with Strepsiades ("son of a twister") in debt. He hits upon the bright idea of having his son study with Socrates, to learn to out-argue the creditors. Just Discourse and Unjust Discourse present their advantages; Strepsiades chooses the latter, as the way to confute the laws. But when his son emerges from the school and uses the lessons, he does so not to save Strepsiades, but to justify thrashing him. Thereupon Strepsiades sees what a fool he has been to trust the new education, and sets fire to Socrates' Think-Shop.

Aristophanes' attack on Socrates is shrewdly advanced and captures the philosopher's physical peculiarities—his refusal to wear sandals, his need of a haircut, his dislike of hot baths—in order to carry along the more serious charges. The fire in the finale doubtless struck a note of actuality in the contemporary audience, for there had been physical attacks upon the Sophists in various parts of Greece, as well as in southern Italy, where a mob had burned the Pythagorean school at Croton.

"It had required courage to attack Cleon," observed Henry Ten Eyck Perry, "but it took skill to oppose Socrates, and perhaps partially as a result of the difference in the caliber of their subjects, *The Clouds* is a much richer and more intricate piece of work than either *The Acharnians* * or *The Knights.*" In structure, the play is more like a tragedy (therefore, more like the New Comedy) than a typical Old Comedy play, i.e., instead of being divided into two sections by a long *parabasis,* it moves more directly in a single drive to the climax. In other respects, too, *The Clouds* shows Aristophanes' power. The songs of the chorus are among the most beautiful lyrics in Greek literature. The metrical forms are effectively varied with the thought; Just Discourse, for example, speaks in dignified, rolling anapests, while Unjust Discourse flaunts his pretensions in pert iambics.

The scenic arrangement of *The Clouds,* while simple, was undoubtedly effective. Thornton Wilder in the *New York Times* (February 13, 1938) referred to it in defending the devices of his play *Our Town:** "In its healthiest ages the theatre has always exhibited the least scenery."

The Clouds was a favorite among Aristophanes' plays in earlier times; 127 manuscripts of the comedy survive from Byzantium and medieval Italy. (This number is exceeded only by the 148 of *Plutus.*)

The Clouds was performed in Greek at Oxford, England, in 1905 and 1938. It was also presented in Greek at Swarthmore College, Pennsylvania, in 1939. Of a performance at Williams College, Massachusetts, in June 1933, Clayton Hamilton wrote: "It is always interesting to be reminded at first hand that the human sense of humor has altered very little in the last 2500 years . . . Its satirical exposition of the topsy-turvy mental means by which an upstart younger generation may be taught to confute its conservative elders by ingenious argumentative devices, is not at all inapplicable to conditions on many of our college campuses at the present time . . . It still excels in comic force a majority of the timely products of these more journalistic days."

In translation by William Arrowsmith, *The Clouds* was presented in 1952 at Catholic University, Washington, D.C. Socrates was given the lines "Sophistry tastes good like philosophy should."

On the English scene, London saw the play in 1957, and there was a performance in Greek at Cambridge in 1962.

PEACE   *Aristophanes*

One of the happiest, warmest, and most exuberant of the comedies of Aristophanes is his *Peace,* which was written after reverses on both sides of the war and the death of two leaders, Cleon of Athens and Brasidas of Sparta, had renewed negotiations. The Spartan ambassadors probably attended the Great Dionysia of 421 B.C., in which *Peace* won second prize (*The Tradies* of Eupolis was first; *The Clansmen* of Leucon, third). Prospects of a rapid end of the war were bright, and within the year, the treaty of peace was signed.

The hopeful mood of Athens is captured in the play's story. Trygaeus (the "vine man") carefully rears a dung-beetle, until it is strong enough to bear him to Olympus to beg Peace of Zeus. He learns from Hermes that the angry Zeus has pitched Peace into a well, leaving the Hellenic world in charge of the god of war. Persuading Hermes to help him and his chorus of husbandmen, Trygaeus brings Peace back to earth. He also brings Opora, goddess of harvests, for himself, and Theoria, mistress of festivals, for the Athenian Senate. The play ends as the wedding feast is being prepared.

The delightfully playful quality of *Peace* bubbles out in all sorts of romping. Astride the beetle, Trygaeus plans to use his phallus as a rudder, in case of need. He tells the audience that from heaven they looked like rascals; from earth, the same, only bigger. Striving to extricate Peace from the well, the men work, as Eugene O'Neill, Jr. has phrased it, "with great enthusiasm and greater inefficiency. The difficulties are delightfully Hellenic; the Boeotians are only pretending; Lamachus is in the way; the Argives laugh at the others while they try to profit from their troubles; the Megarians are trying hard, but are too undernourished to be of much use; some of the Greeks are pulling one way and some another."

When Trygaeus gets back to earth with the three beautiful women, humor turns to love making and festive sports. The chorus sings: "What I love is to drink with good comrades in the corner by the fire when good dry wood, cut at the height of the summer, is crackling; it is to cook pease on the coals and beechnuts among the embers; it is to kiss our pretty Thracian while my wife is at the bath." With good-humored anticipation, the amorous delights quicken the home-bound warriors.

With the same warm good humor, Aristophanes touches upon more serious concerns. In the *parabasis,* he reminds the audience (by quoting four lines from *The Wasps*) that he has never attacked women or obscure persons, but only the very greatest. He then changes immediately to a jesting tone, asking not only the peace-loving to give him victory in the dramatic contest, but also the bald, for he is one of them: "Do not grudge the prize to the poet whose talent shines as bright as his own bare skull!" (Aristophanes was then twenty-four years old). When Peace comes to earth, Aristophanes pictures the great dismay of those whose interests are promoted by war. First, the diviners and oracle-mongers, who profit from bad times, seek a share in the festivities, while at the same time they proclaim that the bonds of peace must be broken. (History soon showed their words were sadly true.) Then come the war profiteers, the manufacturers of weapons, breastplates, trumpets, shields. They bewail the coming of peace, and try to sell their surplus supplies, which (as is the case with government equipment today) go for odd sums for odd uses: the helmet crests for table dusters; the spears to split into vine-props; the breastplates and helmets for less public purposes. Combining scatological and erotic humor, good-natured satire and fantastic fable, *Peace* is the merriest of the comedies of Aristophanes.

A French version, 1932, of *Peace* by François Porché was performed in England in 1936, without enthusiastic reception. In the United States the students of Swarthmore and Haverford colleges combined to present the Greek play in May 1941. The necessities of bowdlerization for public perform-ances would remove much of the play's sparkle; but *Peace* shows Aristophanes in his lightest and liveliest mood.

In 1967 *Peace* was performed at Harvard University (Cambridge, Mass.). In 1968, translated by Timothy Reynolds, with music by Al Car-mines, it was performed at Carmines' Greenwich Village church; and again by Roundabout in 1969. This was an irreverent minstrel-showy ver-sion with Greek slaves, whites in blackface, moseying along as in planta-tion days, pouring the "essences" of the Greek states into a toilet basin, flushed with a cacophony of piano and drums. The "essence" of Athens was in red, white, and blue.

In 1969 a version was presented at Cambridge University, England. It was so deliberately crude that the university treasurer refused to endorse it and the students staged it themselves. Amid its bawdry, it reminded us that Peace is as "a sweet wine, violets by a spring, and the taste of olives." Greek desideranda.

Coming to London on its way to the Edinburgh Festival of 1970, the Deutsches Theater staged *Der Frieden (Peace)*, which came to the OffBway Barbizon Plaza in 1972.

THE BIRDS   *Aristophanes*

In the stress of a disastrous war, Athens in 414 B.C. tightened her belt and her temper. Rebellion and sacrilege were followed by widespread persecution. Direct criticism of persons and events was dangerous; it was a time to dream. During that year, Aristophanes wrote *The Birds,* a brilliant flight of the imagination. Rich, mellow and mischievous, the play was awarded second prize at the contests of that year; it is today generally considered Aristophanes' best work.

In *The Birds,* Peisthetaerus, ("Plausible") seeking a happier land, gets the bright idea of persuading the birds to establish their rule. Strategically placed between heaven and earth, they could dictate both to the gods and to mortals. The delighted birds at once erect the great wall of their new city of Cloud-Cuckooland. The Athenians, hearing of the new state, quick to seek fresh fields for exploitation and eager to acquire the advantages of wings, come ten thousand strong to colonize the land. Peisthetaerus drives them away as pests. Meanwhile the gods, barred from contact with the earth and starving for want of sacrifices, send Poseidon, Heracles and Triballus to treat with the birds. Peisthetaerus cajoles and bribes Heracles into awarding him the hand of Basileia ("Sovereignty"). The play ends with the celebration of their union.

On this fanciful framework Aristophanes wove some of his finest poetry, and some of his freshest fooling. The lyric song of the nightingale (lines 209– 259) is among the greatest in Greek poetry, and the *parabasis* of the chorus of birds, with its recurring call, *tiotiotiotiotinx,* is delicate and charming. When the chorus addresses the judges, it promises them all sorts of benefits if they award the play the prize, but warns them that if they do not, they had better protect their heads with metal discs, such as are placed over statues, for the birds will befoul them when they go abroad.

Aristophanes makes the impossible quite plausible. When word comes that the great wall of Cloud-Cuckooland is built, no one wonders at the speed. Instead, the birds boast that they have raised it all by themselves, without human aid; and in the preposterous details of the construction—thirty thousand cranes from Libya brought the stones; plovers bore up the water; the geese used their web-feet as spades—the absurdity of the whole is at once heightened and slipped beyond the barriers of incredulity. Guards are posted and beacons burned, to intercept the messengers of the gods.

Among those that come to enjoy the benefits of the new city—those whom Peisthetaerus drives away—are a poet who seeks inspiration in the clouds; a geometer who plans to lay out the city scientifically; a dealer who hopes to sell the new laws for the city; an informer who thinks wings will help him in his trade; and a tax-supervisor from Athens.

While Aristophanes lays about him with a vigorous hand, it should be noted that he does not repudiate democracy; he denounces those that seek personal profit from its institutions.

In Goethe's youthful drama, *The Birds, After Aristophanes,* 1778, Hopeful and Truefriend look for a Utopia in the clouds; but, once winged, they are borne on a burlesque extravagance far from Aristophanes.

Recent adaptations of *The Birds* include a notable one in French by Fernand Nozieres in 1911. In English, *The Birds* was produced at Berkeley, California, and Mt. Vernon, Iowa, in 1934; at Bar Harbor, Maine, in 1935; at East Hampton, Long Island, in 1936. Donald Oenslager made a series of designs (some of them were reproduced in *Theatre Arts,* June 1929) for a version of *The Birds* set in the airplane age, with Peisthetaerus as a go-getter flying off with the birds, in the finale, to conquer the universe. A deft English adaptation by Walter Kerr was presented at Yale University in May 1952.

The Birds is the last play of Aristophanes in which there is a fully developed *parabasis,* i.e., the long ode of the chorus that divides the drama. Translating this, Swinburne called Aristophanes "the half divine humorist in whose incomparable genius the highest qualities of Rabelais were fused and harmonized with the supremest gifts of Shelley." We seldom, today, think of a dramatist as a lyric poet; but, in the blending of free-ranging humor and high-soaring verse, there is no one that comes within a thousand starry twinkles of Aristophanes.

A 1959 production of *The Birds,* its politics still pertinent, was banned by the Greek government. It was shown in Greek in London, at the RSC (Aldwych), April 12, 1965, in the World Theatre Season. Translated by William Arrowsmith in modern slang, it opened at Ypsilanti, Mich., June 29, 1966, for forty performances. Of a pretty girl bird: "Holy Zeus, what a hunk of stuff!" Of one with a long beak: "Go get yourself a nose job." Bert Lahr played Peisthetaerus. The New York Actors' Studio used (mainly) this version in 1972, and ELT in 1978.

With book and lyrics by Kenneth Cavender and music by Stanley Silverman, *The Birds* came to Lincoln Center, New York, in 1969. In 1971 the opera *Des Oiseaux,* by Serge Ouaknine and Costas Ferris, came from Paris to London. In 1975 a musical by Lawrence Raab and Jonathan Simon was presented at the University of Michigan.

We have lost the Greek music, but no one except the team of Gilbert and Sullivan comes near to the riotous, romping, right-minded Aristophanes. A 1983 production at the OffOffBway Greek Theatre reminded us this was the 2,397th anniversary of *The Birds.*

LYSISTRATA   *Aristophanes*

This is the most modern of Aristophanes' comedies. Produced in 411 B.C., when Athens was on the verge of ruin in the Peloponnesian War, the play urges a pan-Hellenic peace and offers a unique means to achieve it.

Lysistrata, leader of Athenian women, persuades the fair sex of Greece to adopt her proposal to refuse themselves to their husbands until the men make peace. With the help of Lampito, a husky damsel from Sparta, she holds the frailer women to the line. Sex-starvation proves too much for the men, and the play ends with peace and marital joy.

No other of Aristophanes' comedies is so unified and so logically presented. The women are neatly portrayed: a few are stern and immovable, untouched by the men's sore desire; but the majority, especially the sweet Kalonike, find excuses to leave the Acropolis for their husband's embraces. Only the arrival of Cinesias, his phallus upreared to symbolize the men's impatient need, saves the situation. Lysistrata sends Cinesias' wife, Myrrhine, to gather strength from her husband's need of her. Myrrhine teases and tempts him, until he will have peace at any price. When the Spartan Herald and the Athenian Magistrate, in fact all the men, gather together, with swords down, but with their lances of flesh tipped high, to humble their war-time hates so that they may tumble their peace-won mates, they make one of the funniest scenes the theatre has ever beheld. For its "mad indecencies," said August Wilhelm Schlegel a century ago, *Lysistrata* "is in such bad repute that we must mention it lightly and rapidly, just as we would tread over hot embers."

In all of *Lysistrata*—and, for that matter, in all of Aristophanes—the fun with sex is frank, but never suggestive. Moreover, it is put to good use. The sexagenarians of the chorus, no less than the sex-agonized soldiers, point the phallus of nature at the follies of war. And for all the hearty laughter, "no Greek poet," as Henry Ten Eyck Perry emphasized, "not even Sophocles, has more tenderly dealt with maidenhood's soft season" than Aristophanes in this play.

Lysistrata expresses a most unusual fairmindedness considering the desperate straits of Athens in 411 B.C. Its author sees no special breed of evil in the enemies of Athens. Among the Athenians, however, Peisander, who had fomented a briefly successful rebellion, is accused of favoring the war because it covers his thieveries. The Spartan woman, Lampito, states, "No doubt we shall persuade our husbands to conclude a fair and honest peace; but there is the Athenian populace: how are we to cure these folk of their warlike frenzy?", to which Lysistrata replies, "Have no fear; we undertake to make our own people listen to reason."

It is recorded that a pupil of Melanchthon, at Basel in 1532, read Aristophanes in order to contrast his obscenities with the purity of the Christian Church, in which connection it may be suggested that whereas to the pagan Greek woman was beauty to behold and love to enjoy, the fig-leaf after the Garden of Eden made Christian woman a secret and a sin. The delights of the Greek, as mirrored in Aristophanes, may be pagan, but they are not perverse.

The first effective revival of *Lysistrata* in recent times was produced by Maurice Donnay in Paris in 1892. The best was probably the production of the Moscow Art Theatre, in a version by Dmitry Smolin, 1923, which was brought to New York in 1925. Of the latter, Brooks Atkinson (December 14, 1925) said that it wrought "the organization of all the theatrical arts, vocal, scenic, and plastic, into a perfect projection."

The Moscow Art version was adapted in English by Gilbert Seldes. Opening in Philadelphia, it reached New York on June 5, 1930, for a run of 252 performances, followed by a long tour. The cast included Violet Kemble Cooper, Ernest Truex, Miriam Hopkins, Eric Dressler, Hope Emerson, and Sydney Greenstreet. In 1935, the Maurice Donnay version was presented in New York as an *Ode to a Grecian Urge*; the production was as heavy-handed as its title. Fay Bainter appeared in the Seldes version in 1931; Nance O'Neil, in 1933; the Coburns, in 1935. Westport, Connecticut, saw the play in 1936 and 1937, and again in 1948 in "modernized" version with June Havoc. The Federal Theatre presented an "African version" in Seattle in 1938; an all-Negro cast brought the play to New York again in 1946. George Jean Nathan remarked that the Seldes adaptation "apparently has been dirtied up." Robert Garland declared, "Fall flat it does, right on its double-entendre. Sex is made actually uninteresting." Aristophanes, however, survives all such perversion of his work.

The Seldes translation of *Lysistrata,* published with superb drawings by Picasso, is lively, and makes a good theatre production. More literal translation does perhaps fuller justice to the Greek, which has qualities of universal portent that o'erleap the comedy, demonstrating that laughter can open wide the door to truth.

Lysistrata is the most frequently revived of Aristophanes' comedies (pronounced for Broadway *Lysistra' ta,* instead of the Greek *Lysis' trata*). There was a Gilbert Seldes adaptation in New York in 1956. A Dudley Fitts adaptation, with Joan Greenwood, directed by Minos Volonakis, was shown in London, 1958, and New York at the Phoenix in 1959. It romped along with pie-throwing, pratfalls, and cooch dances. A John Lewin adaptation in Boston, 1968, was lively, poetic, and obscene. In the same year, Hunter College, New York, presented the play "hippified," with dancing by José Limón. The 1970 OffBway adaptation by Darrel de Chaby used modern clothes or none. The play was performed at Syracuse, N.Y., in 1970, with the slogan "Make Love, Not War." Melina Mercouri played Lysistrata at New York's Brooks Atkinson, 1972, in adaptation by Michael Cacoyannis, with music by Peter Link. There was an ELT production in 1982.

A musical, *The Happiest Girl in the World,* from *Lysistrata* with touches of Bulfinch's *Mythology,* book by Fred Saidy and Henry Meyers, and lyrics set by E. Y. Harburg to the music of Offenbach, came to the Martin Beck, New York, for ninety-six performances. Cyril Ritchard played a variety of roles, from Pluto to the Pied Piper of Hamelin. Aristophanes survives.

THESMOPHORIAZUSAE   *Aristophanes*

Written in 411 B.C., *Thesmophoriazusae* (The Women at the Festival of Demeter) is one of the freshest and most frolicsome of Aristophanes' comedies. A farcical attack upon the work of Euripides,* it is constructed much like a modern play, with a plot that moves gaily and speedily to a climax.

If it were not for the limited appeal of its subject, the play would undoubtedly be Aristophanes' most popular drama today.

The play pictures a gathering of the Athenian women to celebrate the Eleusinian mysteries at the festival of Demeter, goddess of fruitfulness, from which all men are barred. Warned that the women plan to punish him for showing only the evil-doers of their sex in his plays, Euripides has the bright idea of persuading his father-in-law, Mnesilochus, to go to the festival disguised as a woman in order to see whether he can defend Euripides against their charges. The manner in which Mnesilochus is detected by the women and the various attempts made by Euripides to rescue him are highly comic. At the end, Euripides makes peace with the women, promising not to reveal their pranks to their husbands when the men come back from the war.

Throughout the play shafts of satire are constantly directed against Euripides, or against his young disciple, the playwright Agathon. Euripides' frequent use of stage machinery, the prettiness of his dialogue, the emphasis he places upon devices rather than fundamentals, his supposed concern for dramatic effectiveness instead of spiritual depth or poetic beauty, all are given attention. When Euripides swears to come to the rescue of his father-in-law if necessary, the old man tells him to keep in mind that it's the heart and not the tongue that swore—thus recalling the line in *Hippolytus** by which Euripides had shocked the Athenians: when Hippolytus threatens to repudiate an oath, he says, "It was the tongue that swore, and not the heart."

The heaviest of the charges against Euripides concerns his many portraits of women in the excesses of love: of women whirled into adultery or deception; of women attempting to rid themselves of illegitimate children, or kidnapping to conceal their sterility. Such matters may have entered superficially into the great themes of Aeschylus and Sophocles; but, Aristophanes charges, with Euripides they are the groundwork of his dramatic structure and the chief subject of his studies.

At the festival in the *Thesmophoriazusae,* Aristophanes draws double humor from his charges. In the first place, the women do not deny the evil attributed to them; they merely call for punishment of Euripides for revealing it. Nor does Mnesilochus, in defense, deny Euripides' attack; instead, he lists many more evil actions of women, declaring that they should be grateful to Euripides for not having mentioned these. Thus Aristophanes flays both the Athenian women and the playwright.

Once Mnesilochus is caught, he casts about for ways to escape the women's clutches. He tries half a dozen different ways, each taken from a drama by Euripides.

The deftness of the allusions and quotations, the neatness with which episodes from Euripides are fitted to the situation of his father-in-law in the *Thesmophoriazusae,* must have kept the Athenians engulfed in waves of laughter. Beneath what seems a purely aesthetic concern, Aristophanes was aware of the implications that Euripides' work held for the welfare of the state; he makes this abundantly clear in his next play, *The Frogs.**

Thesmophoriazusae was acted in New York, 1955; at Oxford, 1956; in London, 1958. An OffBway adaptation by Ed Wode in 1969 stressed the shrill cries of the women.

THE FROGS   *Aristophanes*

During the six years between Aristophanes' previous two plays and *The Frogs,* Athens had recalled from exile the great leader Alcibiades. He did not enter the city, however, until after four years of naval successes. Then, with the loss of an engagement with the Spartan Lysander, the fickle Athenian government sent him into exile once more.

Written during these crucial years of the Peloponnesian War, and shortly after the death in 406 B.C. of both Sophocles and Euripides, *The Frogs* combines patriotic fervor with its satire. It opens with Dionysus, the god of tragedy as well as of wine, waiting before the battle of Arginusae, reading Euripides' play *Andromeda.* Impelled to bring Euripides back from the underworld, Dionysus, disguised as Heracles (the only one that ever drew a mortal back from Hades), with his servant Xanthias enters the underworld. Ferried across the lake of the dead by Charon, Dionysus finds the newly arrived Euripides disputing with Aeschylus the throne of tragedy. A trial is held, in which each tragic dramatist points to the flaws of the other's work and recites the virtues of his own. None can decide between them save that, when scales are brought, Aeschylus' verses outweigh Euripides'. Dionysus determines to select the one "whose advice may guide the city true." He returns from Hades with Aeschylus. Thus, against the realism, the reason, and the sophistry of his day, Aristophanes urges a return to the dignity, the valour, and the integrity that had brought glory to his city.

Incidental political references are made throughout the play. Several, for instance, stress the fact that, in the recent battles, slaves that had volunteered for military service were given their freedom, while many true Athenians were still ostracized or exiled. This point is further pressed in the *parabasis,* the main choral ode, in which Aristophanes vigorously pleads that, in view of the crisis, Athens should forgive and recall her exiles. His exhortation so stirred the Athenians that, by public demand, the play received the unprecedented tribute of an immediate second performance, at which Aristophanes was presented with an olive wreath from Athena's sacred tree on the Acropolis.

The literary references in the play, however, are much more fully developed. Aristophanes repeats earlier charges he had made against Euripides, especially those of *Thesmophoriazusae;** but he develops and adds to them. In addition to attacking Euripides' realistic, even colloquial and undignified, style, he accuses him of immorality and sophistry. In a final blow, when Euripides reminds Dionysus that the god has sworn to take him back to earth, Dionysus replies with the fateful words from Euripides' own *Hippolytus,** "Only my tongue has sworn."

Although Aristophanes makes no effort to be fair when balancing Aeschylus against Euripides, by no means does he leave the earlier dramatist unscathed. After giving some examples of Aeschylus' high-flown phrases, his pompous and straining compounds, which make Euripides cry out, "Let us at least use the language of men!", the great length of Aeschylus' choral odes and his frequent undramatic silences are attacked. Aristophanes presents Aeschylus, however, with dignity and poise; Euripides, with a quick ease that verges upon impudence.

It is Euripides, nevertheless, that gives the answer that the ages have echoed. When Aeschylus challenges him to tell on what grounds a poet should be admired, Euripides responds: "If his art is true, and his counsel sound, and if he brings help to the nation, by making men better in some respect." Aristophanes—as indeed all his works show—was not unaware of the poet's duty to entertain, but his immediate purpose in *The Frogs* joined him with Euripides, whose plays rang with patriotic fervor. Aristophanes knew that, beyond the rouse of a crisis, Athens had need of the dignity, the sense of honor, for which Aeschylus stood firm.

In recent years, *The Frogs* has been produced in many parts of the world: in 1936 at Missoula, Montana; in 1936 and 1937 in England; in 1938 in Minnesota (Winona State Teachers' College), with names changed to those of modern politicians and dictators; in 1940; in New South Wales. Of the 1936 English performance, the *London Times* (March 4) commented: "After twenty-three centuries this comedy does still win the laughter of all spectators, and that not only in its more boisterous moments. The audience naturally and properly revelled in the broad humour of the earlier scenes . . . The schools of Aeschylus and Euripides will always have their disciples, and it might be a profitable exercise for a satirist of today to set contemporary dramatists on the stage in an imitation of *The Frogs*."

In an interesting anticipation of modern economics, Aristophanes in the *parabasis* of *The Frogs* compares the *Kaloikagathoi* (the noble young aristocrats) to the good coins of old, driven out of circulation by the bad new ones.

In America, *The Frogs* has developed a tradition at Yale University. In the early 1890's the Greek students (perhaps after Dionysiac festivals) would sing, under the professors' windows, the refrain of the chorus of frogs that is sung while Dionysus crosses the underworld lake: the cry has been incorporated into the Yale cheer—"Bre-ke-ke-kex, co-ax, co-ax!" Monty Woolley staged a production of the play at Yale in 1921, with Stephen Vincent Benét handling the choruses. Some bright classicist, more recently, noticed that in the swimming pool of the new Yale gymnasium the seats rise round as in the Greek Theatre, while at one end the wall has three doors and benches beyond a platform. Consequently, in November 1941, an aquatic production of *The Frogs* was given there, with floats and underwater lights, with a surprisingly effective movement. John O'Reilly reported, in the *New York Herald Tribune*: "Aristophanes was the Rodgers and Hart of his day. His slang was more than pungent and his choruses were snappy . . . The undergraduate translation of the work of this ancient satirist is hot . . . When Bacchus and his faithful slave, Xanthias, are being paddled across the River Styx by Charon, with the Yale swimming team in froggy headdress swimming figures about the boat and croaking 'Bre-ke-ke-kex, co-ax, co-ax,' it creates a spectacle that would make Billy Rose turn an envious shade of batrachian green."

Those that read or see *The Frogs* with some knowledge of the desperate military and pig-headed political situation of Athens when the play was produced, recognize the courage and wisdom of Aristophanes. Even without such knowledge, his playfulness and his power—his unique combination of slapstick, serious satire, bawdry and beauty—shine through.

At Oxford, 1958, the adaptation of *The Frogs* by Dudley Fitts was "sinewy, flexible, whether wielding the stiletto of satire or the burnt-poker-and-sausage of low comedy." There was a 1960 production at the State University of Iowa, and one adapted by Peter Arnott at the University of Michigan. London saw the play in Greek in 1967.

In 1974 a new version came to New York, book by Burt Shevelove (who had directed at the Yale swimming pool), music and lyrics by Stephen Sondheim. "The Time is the Present, the Place is Ancient Greece." The duel in the play is not Aeschylus versus Euripides, but Shakespeare versus Shaw—with mention of O'Neill, Pirandello, and "that big trouble-maker, Brecht." When Shakespeare is announced as victor, Pluto says: "Take Shaw, and I'll throw in Ibsen."

ECCLESIAZUSAE   *Aristophanes*

In 404 B.C., the year after Aristophanes' *The Frogs,* * Athens surrendered to Sparta and the walls of the city were thrown down. The government of Athens changed hands several times until Thrasybulus, exiled in 404 by the Thirty Tyrants, overcame them in 403, re-established the Athenian democracy and offered amnesty to all Athenians in exile. During these tumultuous years, all sorts of political expedients were considered, if not tried. "Love of novelty," says Chremes (the ordinary citizen) in *Ecclesiazusae,* "and disdain for tradition are our ruling principles."

It was in this atmosphere that Aristophanes presented his *Ecclesiazusae (Women In Parliament),* a travesty of the communistic ideas of the period, with women in control. Men having made such a mess of the world, Praxagora communes with her lamp as the play opens, why shouldn't she do better? She gets the bright idea of having the women of Athens, disguised as men, slip into the Assembly early and vote power into their own hands. "Let us save the ship of state," she cries, "which nobody now seems able to sail or to row." When Chremes hears that the women are to be given the reins of government, he exclaims, "That's the only thing we haven't tried!"

Thus the women gain political power. Although their speeches praise their conservatism, in action, they at once set up a communist system. All property is to be turned over to the state, and the women and children are to be held in common. If children do not know who their parents are, Praxagora argues, they will respect all their elders.

The rest of the play shows the "bright idea" in practice. As might be expected, the citizens are less eager to give their wealth to the state than to enjoy the free banquets which the women have substituted for the law courts. Free love brings other complications. To be fair, it is ruled that no man may enjoy a young woman until her elders have first been satisfied. There is a most amusing scene in which a girl has her lover snatched away by three successively older and uglier hags. Despite such minor troubles, however, life seems to move joyously, as the final chorus moves to the great feast. Yet deftly the bubble is pricked, when the sumptuous spread of the public banquet is announced, by the suggestion that each citizen bring his own portion of soup.

The *Ecclesiazusae* was the first play presented in the contest of 392 B.C.; there is no record of the judges' decision. Its continuing timeliness is shown by the fact that, in a New York 1954 performance, 130 lines were cut, lest, it was protested, the play seem pro-Communist.

We do not know what Aristophanes wrote during the thirteen years after *The Frogs,* but in several ways the *Ecclesiazusae* marks a transition to a newer style of comedy. It retains the bawdry of the early plays, with occasional thrusts of political satire, and its general spirit recalls the revolt of the women in *Lysistrata** and the travesty on utopian ideas in *The Birds.** But its form has changed. Most of the play is in a new meter (iambic trimeter); and there is no central choral ode (*parabasis*), only a dance. The chorus, indeed, has dwindled in importance; it has no entrance song, and it is long offstage. The play more closely approximates the latter-day five-act structure. Its setting is typical of the New Comedy: a city street, backed by a row of houses. Even the names of the characters begin to show a change: 'Praxagora' is, as in the earlier plays, an invented name, meaning 'active in the market place'; but Chremes was a common name among the citizens of Athens—the first such name to be used by Aristophanes. The fourth century, indeed, brought new masters and new devices; the great days of Greek tragedy and of the Old Comedy had passed.

The *Ecclesiazusae* should not be left without mention of the glorious dish to which the citizens address themselves in the final banquet—the longest word in any Indo-European tongue: *lepadotemachoselachogaleo-kranioleipsanodrimypotrimmatosilphiotyromelitokatakechymenokichlepikos-syphophattoperisteralektryonoptokephaliokinklopeleiolagoiosiraiobaphetrag-alopterygon.* This more-than-a-mouthful includes, as Oates and O'Neill note in *The Complete Greek Drama* (1938) "limpets, slices of salt fish, thornbacks, whistle-fishes, cornel-berries, a remoulade of leftover brains seasoned with silphium and cheese, thrushes basted with honey, blackbirds, ringdoves, squabs, chickens, fried mullets, wagtails, rockpigeons, hare, and wings ground up in new wine that has been boiled down."

No successor has succeeded in boiling down the essence of Aristophanes. In many little touches of humor, in deft darts of satire, as well as in over-all conception and execution, Aristophanes is in full and unique command of the comic vein in the *Ecclesiazusae.*

Oxford saw *The Parliament of Women* in 1965. An OffBway version by Ed Wode in 1970 was modernized as a satire on the "new woman" and fem lib.

PLUTUS   *Aristophanes*

This is the last extant work of Aristophanes. We know, however, that he later wrote two more comedies, which were produced by his son, Araros. One of these, *Cocalus,* seems to have set the pattern followed by Menander* and other writers of the New Comedy.

Athens in 388 B.C. was in the midst of distressing times. Material and moral poverty was widespread. No one dared to attack the leaders as Aristophanes had done in his earlier works. The comedies in the contest of that year disguised contemporary issues in mythological terms. Aristophanes took as his subject Plutus, the god of wealth. The play marks a shift from political to economic concern.

Chremylus, a citizen of Athens, upon asking the oracle how his son might grow successful without becoming a scoundrel, is told to follow the first man he sees when he leaves the temple. That man, raggedy, old, and blind, turns out to be none other than the god Plutus. Chremylus conceives the bright idea of curing Plutus of his blindness, so that he can look about and reward honest men with his wealth. Poverty appears, to argue that she too is of value to mankind; but Chremylus will have none of her. His slave, Cario, leads Plutus to the temple of Asclepius to have his sight restored. An amusing account is given by Cario of his night in the temple. The rest of the play follows the usual Old Comedy pattern, showing the consequences of the bright idea. A threadbare, just man is rewarded. An informer is bereft of his trade. An old woman loses a gigolo, for he no longer needs her cash. Hermes, god of thieves, likewise starves for lack of sacrifices; he takes a job, in his capacity as god of games, at the great games Plutus inaugurates. The play ends with a procession moving to install Plutus on the Acropolis. Indeed, Athens had sore need of his resources.

There is much fun in *Plutus,* but only mild satire. When the blind Plutus remarks that it is a long time since he has seen a good man, the slave, Cario, looking over the audience, says: "That's not surprising. I, who have clear eyes, can't see a single one." Chremylus declares that "whatever is dazzling, beautiful, or charming in the eyes of mankind" depends on wealth; and when Poverty recites her benefits to mankind, it is not Plutus, but the citizen Chremylus that answers her. Poverty argues that, "Modesty dwells with me, and insolence with Riches," and that the desire for wealth distorts the thinking of the citizens. When Poverty leaves, she prophesies, "One day you will recall me," but she does not reappear in the play.

Plutus, like the *Ecclesiazusae,* * is a mingling of the old style and the new. The chorus is reduced virtually to a group that dances between the episodes of the action; and although the gods are involved in the story, the humans are neither heroes nor kings, but ordinary citizens concerned with domestic affairs. The impudent, confidential slave, a stock figure of later Greek and Roman comedy (first suggested by Xanthias in *The Frogs* *) is fully developed in the figure of Cario.

The general nature of the mild satire in *Plutus,* and the universal appeal of the story, made it through Byzantine and medieval times the most popular of all Aristophanes' plays. No fewer than 148 manuscripts of *Plutus* survive, over twenty more than of the next in popularity, *The Clouds.* * Altogether, Aristophanes illuminated Athenian society; when Dionysius, tyrant of Syracuse, wanted to learn more about Athens, Plato sent him the plays of Aristophanes.

Plutus was performed in Paris, in 1938, in a version by Simone Jollivet. Pierre Audiat in *Paris-Soir* (February 1938) declared: "Plutus was not alone; Taste accompanied him . . . The first act is, in itself, a perfect masterpiece . . . What! Already, in the fourth century before our era, Aristophanes made that subtle criticism of wealth in society! With very broad comic effects, he put across the nicest nuances. He saw the role of poverty—not to be confused with misery—in the social body; he saw that leveling by wealth would destroy all ties of solidarity between the members; he set the ideal to attain: that wealth enter the dwellings only of honest folk. And he said this neatly, strongly, without pedantry, without preachy-preachy, in the midst of sharp laughter and salty wit." This French version picked up and realized Poverty's prophecy of her return: at the end, it effected a union of Plutus and Poverty in a city where only workers thrive.

The old Greek plays reveal that the social panaceas of our time are no novelties fresh-sprung from the brow of Karl Marx; their virtues and their weaknesses alike were shrewdly foreseen two dozen centuries ago. It is not merely the proffered panaceas, but human nature, in which their virtues and their weaknesses are rooted, that Aristophanes gently but shrewdly holds for our smiles in *Plutus.*

The play opened August 20, 1963, for four performances at New York's East River Park.

ALIAS JIMMY VALENTINE   *Paul Armstrong*

Alias Jimmy Valentine, the most popular of a long line of American plays dealing with "honest crooks," is a dramatization of *A Retrieved Reformation,* a short story by O. Henry (William Sidney Porter, 1862–1910), who himself served a term in prison for embezzlement and, like his hero, lived "straight" thereafter. Some see a resemblance to "Johnny the Gent," a real person, John Wood, who went to Yale, but spent forty-two of his eighty-four years in prison. The story was dramatized by Paul Armstrong (1869–1915).

When Lee Randall, alias Jimmy Valentine, secures a pardon from Sing Sing, the authorities prophesy that he will soon return, and his pals prepare plans for the next bank robbery. Jimmy is their expert cracksman. But during his journey toward safety after a "job" in Massachusetts, Jimmy looks into the eyes of Rose Lane, and becomes an honest man. He gets a respectable job in a bank, and he keeps company with Rose. Detective Doyle in the meantime has traced Jimmy to the bank, and is watching there—when Rose's little sister, Kitty, gets locked in the great bank safe. It has a time lock; the girl seems doomed. Everyone stands helplessly by; Rose looks despairingly at her hero. Jimmy's love overcomes his regard for safety; he sets to work with accomplished hands, and frees the collapsing Kitty. He then turns past the uncomprehending Rose to the detective he has spied watching; but Doyle says, "I guess she needs you more than Massachusetts, Jimmy," and walks away.

Alias Jimmy Valentine opened in New York on January 18, 1910, with H. B. Warner as Jimmy; Laurette Taylor first gained attention in the role of Rose. In March it was presented at a special matinee by an all-child cast. In London, 1910, Gerald du Maurier played Jimmy, with Alexandra Carlisle and Guy Standing. Bert Lytell starred in the 1920 film; in the 1929 film William Haines played Jimmy and Lionel Barrymore, Detective Doyle.

A New York production of *Alias Jimmy Valentine* opening December 8, 1921, starred Otto Kruger, with Margalo Gillmore and Mary Boland. The *New York Herald* called it "the best of all dramas that deal with the underworld." Jimmy is pardoned at the beginning and forgiven at the end, but the play, the *New York World* noted, "is sentenced to serve a long term . . . It almost caused seasoned first-nighters to die of heart failure because of the tense strain of its exciting last act." Why doesn't a producer step forward? Joe Papp, where are you?

THE AUTOMOBILE GRAVEYARD   *Fernando Arrabal*

The plays of Fernando Arrabal (b. 1933 in Spain; writes in French) combine innocence and cruelty, in absurdist style. His most striking play is *Le Cemetière des Voitures* (Paris, 1958), translated by Barbara Wright as *The Car Cemetery,* 1962; by Richard Howard as *The Automobile Graveyard,* 1961. It progresses on three levels, of cackling comedy, of religious passion, of the absurdity of life.

On the stage, people living in junked cars in an auto dump are tended by a decorous-seeming servant, Milos; they honk for service, he provides breakfast in bed; and by the friendly promiscuous Dila, who has a good-night kiss for every "gentleman." The occupants speak behind the curtained car doors, urinate, copulate; in Car Three, a son is born. Lasca, an athletic elderly woman, is training young Trissodo; he and she constantly cross the stage, exercising with grotesque acrobatics, she indefatigable, he worn out and ultimately collapsing.

Emanou, a trumpeter aged thirty-three (Christ's final age; Emanuel in Hebrew means "God is within me"); Topé, a clarinetist; and Fodère, a saxophonist—dumb and reminiscent of Harpo Marx—nightly play for the poor. We hear the poor offstage, howling for the musicians, then dancing to rock 'n' roll. Emanou has learned by heart: "When we are good we feel a great inner joy, born of the peace of spirit that is revealed to us when we see that we resemble the ideal man." He was born in a stable, and worked for a while with his father, a carpenter. When Dila says she wants to be good, he says she's good already: doesn't she give of herself to all who desire her?

The two athletes don police uniforms, and when Topé gives Emanou a kiss, they arrest Emanou, dragging him offstage, to the loud laughter of those in the cars. Fodère by gestures dissociates himself from Emanou. (We recognize Judas, and perhaps remember that Peter "denied" Christ thrice before cockcrow.)

Groans and a beating are heard outside; then Emanou is wheeled in, stretched out on a motorcycle as though crucified on a cross. Dila sponges the sweat from Emanou's brow, then rings a bell in every car. The couple in Car Three comment that the infant is "sleeping like a little angel." Now Lasca and Trissodo come in, again dressed as athletes; she wears his number, 456, and he marks time while she moves on the double: 1, 2; 1, 2; 1, 2—as the curtain falls on the absurdist passion of Christ in a grotesque landscape of squalor in a mainly insensitive world.

The play had only eight performances after it opened on November 13, 1961, at the 41st Street Theatre, New York—which is perhaps par for absurdist drama. But the threefold presentation of *The Automobile Graveyard* makes high sense in the realm of the absurd.

The play was triplicated at Dijon in 1966 by the Argentinian director Victor Garcia, as *Orison, The Two Executioners, The Solemn Communion.* These playlets combine the fashionable features of the absurd: the pollution, physical and moral, of the modern age; the filthy desolation amid which wretched people pretend to live as in a grand hotel (see also Tennessee Williams' *Camino Real*);* and a perversion of the religious "mystery" of olden ritual.

THE GOD OF VENGEANCE   *Sholem Asch*

Novelist on biblical themes and dramatist of Jewish life, Sholem Asch (1880–1957) is best known in the theatre for this study of a ghetto brothel keeper.

Presented first in Yiddish in 1907, *The God of Vengeance* swept rapidly all over Europe. Reinhardt produced it in Berlin, 1910, with Rudolph Schildkraut. A production in English, also starring Schildkraut, opened at the Provincetown Playhouse, New York, December 20, 1922, with Morris Carnovsky and Sam Jaffe, and was moved to Broadway on January 21, 1923. After 133 performances, it was interrupted by the police and declared by the judge to be a desecration of "the sacred scrolls of the Torah." An English production in London in 1923 and a Yiddish production there by the Vilna troupe in 1926 were also closed. The play was presented without interference in Germany, Austria, Poland, Russia, France, Holland, Norway, Sweden, and for a whole season, in 1916, in Italy.

The play pictures the sins of the father being visited. Yekel (Yankel) Shapshowitch, married to a former prostitute, maintains a brothel in the basement of his home. He is, nevertheless, a pious, God-fearing man. He commissions a scribe to copy the Torah and he hopes to marry his daughter,

Rifkele, to a rabbinical student. But Rifkele is debauched by Manka, one of the women downstairs, whose lover plans to use the girl in a rival house. Tortured by her father to reveal what has happened, Rifkele cries "I am my mother's daughter!" Yekel, in disappointment and fury, defies and denies his God. He drives his wife and his daughter back to the brothel, and is left a lonely, desolate man. The God of the Jews has exacted his pound of flesh.

"The love between the two girls," Asch has explained, "is not only an erotic one. It is the unconscious mother-love of which they are deprived . . . I also wanted to bring out the innocent, longing for sin, and the sinful, dreaming of purity. Manka, overweighed with sin, loves the clean soul of Rifkele; and Rifkele, the innocent young girl, longs to stay near the door of such a woman as Manka, and listen within." The picture of brothel life, and of Rifkele's curiosity and temptation, is so real as to grip the emotions with both pity and horror.

The play provoked a sharp division of opinion in the press. "We know there are sewers and cess pools," reported the *New York Telegraph* (December 31, 1922). "Indeed, they are very necessary components of everyday life; but the theatre is scarcely the place for their representation." Most of the reviewers defended the play. The *New York Sun* (December 20) claimed that "in spite of two episodes such as we have never before seen on the stage, [the play] is, in our opinion, a highly moral drama."

Some of the papers managed to turn from defense to analysis. The *London Jewish Chronicle* (May 28, 1926) said that Asch "plumbs 'lower depths' than Gorki,* is as harrowing as Andreyev*—by simpler means." And although it described the play as "ugly, sordid, and repellent beyond any other play that has yet been presented on the contemporary English-speaking stage," the *New York Call* (December 21, 1922) said that *The God of Vengeance* is nonetheless a powerful, realistic study of humanity in its most degraded form, expressed with that fierce vitality which is one of the characteristics of Yiddish drama . . . It has an unmistakable Oriental quality in its religious and ethical mood, in its sexual standards, and in the lyric beauty that gleams now and again out of the muck and filth of debased human life."

Asch meant only the surface of his play to be individualized. "Call Yekel John and instead of the Holy Scroll place in his hand the crucifix," he said, "and the play will then be as much Christian as it is now Jewish." Bernard Shaw presents a Christian brothel-owner in *Mrs. Warren's Profession;* * but he is concerned chiefly with the economic aspects of the problem, whereas Asch lays bare the tortured soul of a male counterpart of Mrs. Warren. *The God of Vengeance* strikes deep to the core of environmental influence and ethical concern, and its brothel setting gives a sensational spur to its intrinsic dramatic power. It was produced OffBway in 1974.

CHU CHIN CHOW   *Oscar Asche*

By turning the successful pantomime *The Forty Thieves** into an extravaganza with music by Frederick Norton, Oscar Asche (English, 1871–1936) achieved in *Chu Chin Chow* a delightful spectacle and gorgeous musical drama. Opening in London, August 31, 1916, in the midst of World War I, *Chu Chin Chow* attained the longest run of any musical on the London stage, 2,238 performances. *Chu Chin Chow* has several times been revived in London: 1929, 1935–1936, 1940, and 1941. The New York production, which opened on October 22, 1917, with Tyrone Power, Florence Reed, Henry F. Dixey, ran for 208 performances. Marjorie Wood and Lionel Braham went on the road with it in 1919; and a film was made in 1934 with Fritz Kortner and Anna May Wong.

Chu Chin Chow, a giant of malign and inhuman visage, his robe ablaze with embroidered dragons, and his fingers tipped with silvered talons like those of a bird of prey, is really Abu Hassan, the leader of the forty thieves. Ali Baba and the other characters of the tale all appear as the play moves through the familiar story from the *Arabian Nights*. Ali's son, called Nur-al-Huda, is in love with the slave girl, Marjanah.

Among the picturesque scenes that adorn the extravaganza are the feast of a thousand candles in a moonlit orchard and the dance of the jewels, which come to life as Ali Baba uncovers them in the robbers' cave.

Observed the *St. Louis Post-Dispatch* (December 2, 1919): "Raptures of color and sound, ecstasies of youth and beauty, and since man is so constituted as to find esthetic joy in evil, transports of grossness and monstrosity—these are the pagan beatitudes of the senses that burn with a devouring flame throughout that stupendous embodiment of romance, *Chu Chin Chow*."

The plot upon which *Chu Chin Chow* is built, with the drowning of the forty thieves in their jars of oil, is of course, as the *Toronto Star* (April 29, 1919) reminds us, "a rather grim and gory story, but nevertheless human." The play naturally stresses the love between Ali's son and the slave girl, who discovers the thieves hiding in the jars. Among the songs are the vigorous "We Are the Robbers of the Woods," the traditional song of the cobbler; the sentimental and very popular "Any Time Is Kissing Time," and a rousing love chant of the wild women of the desert.

The artistic director of the Metropolitan Opera House, Giulio Gatti-Casazza, called *Chu Chin Chow* "truly a beautiful spectacle, spirited and full of action, charming in its fantasy, a delight to eye and ear." And Enrico Caruso called it "one of the most artistic and most absorbing entertainments I have ever attended." With a lavishness that both London and New York have since surrendered to Hollywood, *Chu Chin Chow* remains the most successful of the spectacular musical comedies, a surpassing capture of Oriental color, fiery passion, and tender romance.

The New York production of *Chu Chin Chow* moved from the Manhattan Opera House to the Century, doubling its delights with a cast of three hundred, and an Oriental Fashion Show with forty mannequins. Jascha Heifetz declared: "It is really more beautiful than anything I have seen in all my travels." Motion-picture director David W. Griffiths, who saw it five times in London, thought its beauty unsurpassable, then said of the Century show: "You have surpassed even that."

MR. POIRIER'S SON-IN-LAW   *Emile Augier*

The early plays of this French playwright (1820–1899) were written in verse. Later, Augier turned to prose dramas exalting the virtues of middle class life. In his day the old nobility of France was being absorbed into the ranks of the prosperous bourgeoisie. Without being blind to the faults of the newly rich, Augier in a number of "thesis plays" examined the interrelationship of the aristocrat and the bourgeois. His best play, one that Francisque Sarcey said will always remain a classic, is *Mr. Poirier's Son-in-Law (Le Gendre de M. Poirier),* 1854, a dramatization, with Jules Sandeau (1811–1883) of Sandeau's novel *Sacs et Parchemins.*

Old Poirier, in the hope that his money will bring him a peerage, has married his daughter to a ruined marquis, Gaston de Presles. The Marquis ignores his wife, however, to pay attention to the frivolous Mme. de Montjoy, only to get himself financially entangled. When his wife saves his honor for a second time, the Marquis awakens to the fact that he loves her; the better qualities of both aristocrat and bourgeois are brought to the fore. At the end of the play, Poirier's ambitions are sheared, but the union of his daughter and the Marquis promises sound growth for France.

The role of Poirier was a favorite of Coquelin's, and until 1914 the play was highly popular in France. Frequently performed in the United States by French groups and classes, it was presented there professionally in 1904 by Cazelle's French company, and in 1918 by the Vieux Colombier. The *New York Dramatic Mirror* (November 12, 1904) commented on "the play's red blood of human passions and backbone of truth to life." In 1927, the dramatist Jacques Deval* expressed the general French opinion, that *Le Gendre de M. Poirier* "has not lost anything of its freshness, nor of its humor and emotion."

Mr. Poirier's Son-in-Law is a "well-made play," a type that later degenerated into expertly but mechanically contrived potboilers. In Augier and Sandeau's drama, the situation is real, the characters are natural, the feelings humanly warm. Born of a contemporary social problem in France, the play strikes to the heart of human nature everywhere. Produced constantly in French, Augier's deft comedy, in adaptation by Ida Lublenski, was shown in New York in 1956.

ABSURD PERSON SINGULAR   *Alan Ayckbourn*

Alan Ayckbourn (b. 1939) is artistic director of the 250-seat Theatre-in-the-Round at Scarborough, an English summer holiday town, where his plays have premiered. The little theatre can accommodate—and afford—no more than six players. The title *Absurd Person Singular* is one Ayckbourn liked for a play he never completed; its present application implies that in each of us lurks a cluster of absurdities. The play is an excellent example of black farce: broad comedy over tragic spirits. It opened in Scarborough in June 1972 and came to London on June 4, 1973, with Richard Briers as Sidney Hopcroft; Bridget Turner, his wife, Jane; David Burke as Geoffrey Jackson; Anna Calder-Marshall, his wife, Eva; Michael Aldwidge as Ronald Brewster-Wright; Sheila Hancock, his wife, Marion. At the Criterion, then from September 30, 1974, at the Vaudeville, it ran for 973 performances. In the fall of 1975 Ayckbourn had five plays running in London's West End. After playing at the Kennedy Center in Washington, D.C., *Absurd Person Singular* opened at the New York Music Box on May 20, 1974, for 592 performances, with Larry Bryden as Sidney; Carola Shelley, June; Tony Roberts, Geoffrey; Sandy Dennis, Eva; Richard Kiley, then Fritz Weaver, Ronald; Geraldine Page, Marion. Among other productions have been Melbourne, 1975; Alberta, Canada, 1976; Seattle, Wash.; Austin, Texas, and the Bristol Old Vic, 1977; ACT, 1978; Des Moines, 1981.

The action takes place in three kitchens, on Christmas of three successive years. Last Christmas is in the scrupulously clean kitchen of the Hopcrofts. Sidney is a young real estate man and architect on the make; June is a fastidious, even fussy housewife, now flustered because they expect important guests, the successful architect Jackson and the well-to-do banker Brewster-Wright. Whenever the inner door opens, conversation is heard, including the voices of the never seen Potters. Whatever can, goes amiss; and snobbish Marion Brewster-Wright sniffs at the upstart couple. Jane, dressing for the rain, rushes out to buy tonic; she's forgotten her key, and has to return past all the guests in the dining room, who do not recognize her. On her discomfiture and despair the curtain falls.

Act II: this Christmas, at the Jacksons', Geoffrey has told Eva they'd best break up; in the untidy kitchen she writes a suicide note, and sticks her head in the oven. Entering, Jane says she'd love to clean the oven for her, and pulls her out. Geoffrey helps Eva down from the windowsill as she's planning to jump. Trying to tie a rope, she pulls down the chandelier, and as Ronald is fixing it, tipsy Marion comes in and turns on the light; Ronald gets a shock. They wrap him in the dirty laundry from the hamper. Eva begins to sing: "On the first day of Christmas my true love sent to me . . ." As the others join in, Geoffrey goes to the door and says: "Through here, doctor; please hurry," and the curtain falls.

Act III: next Christmas, in the large Victorian kitchen of the Brewster-Wrights. Eva is helping Ronald; the heating doesn't work; they are cold. Marion is upstairs, drunk. Geoffrey's work is failing; the ceiling of his last project fell in. As Marion tipsily comes down, the Hopcrofts ring the bell. He is now quite successful, and the banker could use his business. Embarrassed, they turn out the lights; but the Harpers come in through the kitchen door, laden with presents. They insist on playing a game, a variety of Musical Chairs called Musical Dancing, with forfeits. Ronald has to hold a spoon in his mouth, balancing a pear on it. Tipsy Marion must gulp a glass of gin in one swallow. As they swirl with the forfeits, Sidney cries, "Dance! Dance!" and the curtain falls on a topsy-turvy world.

As the *London Times Literary Supplement* stated: "Mr. Ayckbourn uses farce to illuminate small nooks of human desolation." Robert Cushman in *The Observer,* July 8, 1973, developed the point: "He has taken the textbook maxim that the true mother of farce is desperation and extended it to its logical limit." His forte, said Benedict Nightingale in the *New Statesman,* "is the wry portrayal of unattractive characters"—wryly too like ourselves.

After the New York production, Jack Kroll in *Newsweek* commented: "In this three-Christmas shot the six characters carom off each other, changing their social and personal fortunes in the process. The pushy parvenu land-developer moves up, the conservative Bank of England type fizzes out, the failed architect moves down, all accompanied by their wives—the obsessive house-cleaner, the blowzy alcoholic, the cheated-on pill-popper"—who, incidentally, spends the whole second act trying to kill herself, without uttering a single word. As Walter Kerr observed: "She can't even get her damned suicide note written; others keep appropriating it to sketch necessary household repair work on its back. High madness has taken over; humor has risked its outer limits. Ferociously Eva nails her note to the kitchen table. Laughter has been nailed, too: a spike is driven right throught its heart, where its noise is heartiest. *Absurd Person Singular* has one of the funniest second acts I have ever seen, and death is the joke." The action is farcical; within it, tragic lives are laid bare.

THE NORMAN CONQUESTS   *Alan Ayckbourn*

This trilogy deserves mention, if only for its organization. The three full-length plays deal with the same six characters through the same period of time, a sextet that Norman tangles on the verge of sex. The plays are extraordinary, said John Barber in the *Sunday Telegraph* (August 2, 1974), "on three counts. First, they dovetail so ingeniously; each is complete, but the others fill in what is happening elsewhere in the house. Second, they are marvellously funny. And third, they are profound. The comedy is based on the sharpest comprehension of character." Clive Barnes in *New York* said that Ayckbourn "likes to write plays as if they were jig-saw puzzles."

Table Manners takes place in the dining room; *Living Together* in the living room; *Round and Round the Garden* on the terrace. In all three plays Norman, married to Ruth, is planning affairs with his two sisters-in-law. Sarah, who is married to dull real estate agent Reg, is tempted to slip away for a weekend with Norman; Annie, who is being courted by the prosaic veterinarian Tom, confesses to Sarah that she has already once succumbed to Norman's lure. When Tom finally proposes, Annie puts him off "At least until I've had a chance to—go away somewhere. And think about it." We know her "going away" would be with Norman. But at the end, when Norman smiles smugly, along with the three women, each in turn silently leaves. Bewildered, then hurt and indignant, Norman expostulates: "I only wanted to make you happy!"—and on the vista of unhappiness the curtain falls. J. W. Lambert in the *Sunday Times* (London) said that "there is an elemental pain shivering darkly through the uproarious comedy of manners."

Opening at the London Globe on August 1, 1974, the three plays moved to the Apollo on December 1, 1975, for a total of 672 performances. In Los Angeles they opened on January 10, 1975, then went to New York's Morosco, December 7, 1975, for 68 performances. In London the cast was: Reg, Mark Kingston; Sarah, Penelope Keith; Ruth, Bridget Turner; Norman, Tom Courtenay; Annie, Felicity Kendal; Tom, Michael Gambon. In New York, in the same order: Barrie Nelson; Estelle Parsons; Carole Shelley (from May 19 Elaine Hyman); Richard Benjamin; Paula Prentiss; Ken Howard (from February 10 Dore Murray).

Walter Kerr, his heading "Hail the Conquering Ayckbourn" carrying along the play's allusive title, commented; "In any household there are three or four plays going on all the time, interlocking, overlapping, arriving perhaps at the same joint catastrophes but creating room by room and half-hour by half-hour, their separate happy or horrendous ambiances. God and Mr. Ayckbourn can see everything and, whatever God does about it, Mr. Ayckbourn laughs. So will you." But behind the laughter *Sunt lacrymae rerum*: tears are at the heart of mortal things.

In Ayckbourn's most recent experiment, at Scarborough 1982–1983, *Intimate Exchanges,* two performers (Lavinia Bertram and Robin Herford) enact ten characters who try out various couplings and dreams of couplings—will the diffident young chairman of the school board of governors seduce the dissatisfied wife of the headmaster?—and what new relationship will try the next "exchange"? Ayckbourn has readied sixteen variations to be separately performed, shown in Greenwich and London (Ambassadors), August 1984.

THE CHINESE PRIME MINISTER   *Enid Bagnold*

> *Grow old along with me,*
> *The best is yet to be,*
> *The last of life, for which the first was made.*

These lines of browning reflect the old Chinese attitude, that age is a high point, not a descent. And "She," a great actress who at seventy decides to retire from the stage, looks around for something fresh to do—like meeting a Chinese Prime Minister, B.C.!

"She" has two grown sons. The younger, Oliver, is separated from his wife, the promiscuous Roxane. The elder son, Tarver, is possessed by the dominating Alice, who wants what she wants, and she wants him. (She wears "whatever is anti-uniform when the play is produced.") But Alice also wants Red Gus Risko, a champion boxer, who'd taken her home when she was sick in a pub. The boxer, however, meets Roxane, and they fall for each other; as a result, he loses his match.

"She" meanwhile, surprisingly, phones for her husband, Sir Gregory, aged seventy-nine, away for twenty years, managing oil as adviser to the Sheik of Mwelta. (The hundred-year-old butler, Bent, disapproving, seems twice to die; but holds his duty first, and recovers.) "She" thinks of going back to the Sheikdom with her husband, but on his sudden recall—they've found more oil—he opens his arms wide; "She" hands him his umbrella; he kisses the hand that proffered it, and goes. Oliver goes with him.

"She" is still seeking herself: "Thirty authors—or thirty lovers—have made thirty women of me." As Alice pours tea, Bent says to "She": "I am glad that you are back. You were meant to be a single woman. And I'm glad for Sir Gregory. Women of individuality—are damned uncomfortable for men." Alice announces she's going to have a baby; and "She" looks within herself for her Chinese Prime Minister.

The play, by Enid Bagnold (1889–1981), had its world premiere in Toronto on October 20, 1963, came to Boston with Margaret Leighton, December 16, 1963, then to the Royale, New York, January 2, 1964, for 109 performances. It was played at the London Globe, May 20, 1965, by Edith Evans in her fiftieth year of stardom, in a superbly sensitive portrayal, the play being, said the *Financial Times,* "a hymn to old age." The *Express* said: "While little actually happens to Miss Bagnold's characters in their once-fashionable London drawing-room, she makes them talk magnificently." Bernard Levin analyzed the play's power: "composed of warmth and grace and intelligence, and language that serves the half-forgotten purpose of delineating human beings and putting them in communication with one another . . . explores in a gentle, witty, and observant way areas of life and thought that have for too long been left unexplored on our stage."

"God is very kind, because when beauty fades, he dims the sight." (We may remember that the great Queen Elizabeth allowed no mirrors in her castles for her last twenty years.) The Chinese Prime Minister, though we but imagine him in the play, is a reminder of the respect due to age, in a play— said Elliot Norton on the Boston opening—"laced with bright, sudden humors." We laugh with, not at, the aging.

DRACULA   *John L. Balderston*

Chief among the fiendish fancies of European folklore is the vampire, whose like is found in many parts of the world. The vampire is a lost soul, a living corpse, which comes from its burial ground and drinks the blood of the living. It sleeps in its grave by day, seeking prey by night; anyone bitten and thus dying becomes a vampire in turn. The main home of the legend is Transylvania; in eighteenth-century Hungary there was a Count Draco who supposedly was the most notorious "historical" vampire. In a novel by Bram Stoker he became Count Dracula, and as such he came into the drama, most lastingly in *Dracula,* 1927, by John L. Balderston and Hamilton Deane.

The play opens in Dr. Seward's sanatorium in Purley, England. The doctor's daughter, Lucy, despite transfusions, is growing paler and fainter. Her fiancé, Harker, is in despair. The doctor appeals to a learned friend, Abraham van Helsing; and Count Dracula, who has come from Transylvania to Carfax, a ruined mansion nearby, offers his assistance.

Lucy's friend Mina had died in the same fashion. Both girls have two tiny bite-marks on the throat; van Helsing tells them this is a vampire's sign. Renfield, a patient of the doctor's, eating flies and bloated spiders, is clearly in the vampire's power. Lucy grows more and more to welcome Dracula's coming. He soon no longer dissembles, but defies them. Meanwhile, reports come of a woman tempting children with chocolates; the dead Mina is now a vampire in her turn.

With howling dogs and flying bats, with Lucy's nurse hypnotized to remove precautions, Dracula, who can appear and disappear at will, through windows, sliding panels or trapdoors, grows more triumphant—until the three men front him with a holy Host. They bar his way with crosses; they try to hold him past dawn; on the stroke he vanishes. But Renfield slips through the panel, and the others follow him to a vault near Carfax, where Dracula lies in earth brought from his 500-year-old grave in Transylvania. Van Helsing holds a stake over Dracula's heart, and with a prayer Harker hammers it home.

Final comfort is offered to the audience: "A word of reassurance. When you get home tonight and the lights have been turned out and you are afraid to look behind the curtains and you dread to see a face appear at the window—why, just pull yourself together and remember that after all, *there are such things.*" Final curtain.

Dracula, opening at the London Little, February 14, 1927, had 391 performances. At the Fulton, New York, from October 5, 1927, it attained 261, with Bela Lugosi playing Dracula. Uncounted productions have persisted. Among them: 1972, Asolo; 1974, Stratford and London, and, directed by Crane Johnson with four rotating casts, over twenty-three weeks OffBway; also at Berkeley, California, a musical, book by Douglas Johnson, music by John Aschenbrenner. Opening October 20, 1977, at New York's Martin Beck, the play attained 925 performances. In London, December 1, 1978, a musical by and directed by Pip Simmons, said Bernard Levin, "alternates between the bizarre and the boring." In the same year four companies toured with the play in the United States, including the Balderston version, opening at Los Angeles, September 9, 1978, for 56 performances. The Kabuki star Matumoto Koshiro IX, of a long line of masters, played *The Passion of Dracula* in Japanese in Tokyo. *Dracula* was played in Manitoba in 1980; by the London Young Vic in 1981. In the cinema, I mention only *The Son of Dracula,* Anthony Alucard (Dracula backward), of 1943, and in 1972 both *Blacula* and *Scream, Blacula, Scream!.* An oddity, 1983, at the OffOffBway Prometheus, was Fred Fondren's brief fantasy *Sherlock Holmes Embattles Count Dracula.* The legend, half believed by many, still sends shivers down the stiffest spine.

A London BBC production of the Balderston version, June 25, 1983—with Frank Langella as a suave, alluring Dracula until he flaunts his eerie power, Donald Pleasance as Harker, and Laurence Olivier as Van Helsing—was recorded as the twenty-third London retelling of the story since the horrifying 1931 Bela Lugosi as the fiendish Count. And on July 9, 1983, BBC brought back the Bela Lugosi performance.

THE BLACK CROOK   *Charles M. Barras*

Theatrical history turned a distinctly new page when *The Black Crook* opened at Niblo's Garden in New York in September 12, 1866. Originally planned as "an original magical and spectacular drama," the play was elaborately transformed into a song and dance musical, with beauteous ladies in tights or ballet costumes doing the first high kicking the *New York Times'* critic had ever seen. It started the trail that led past Lydia Thompson, Pauline Markham, Billy Watson's *Beef Trust,* to the increasing nudity of the burlesque show, the fan, bubble, or dove dances of Sally Rand, to Gypsy Rose

Lee, Margie Hart, and the other ecdysiasts, artists of the strip-tease.

Though the trail would probably have been blazed in any event, its start with *The Black Crook* was burned into history. Jarret and Palmer had imported a ballet troupe for the opera *La Biche au Bois* at the N.Y. Academy of Music. From London, Paris, Berlin, Milan, the loveliest of feminine beauties were summoned, including Rita Sangelli, Betty Regal, Da Rosa, Paglieri, and fourteen-year-old premiere danseuse Mlle. Marie Bonfanti. But the Academy of Music burned down.

William Wheatley, preparing Barras' play for Niblo's Garden, sniffed a bargain, and bought the dancing girls. For all practical purposes he used Barras' script as "a clothesline on which to hang pretty dresses"—thus leaving the young ladies the more displayed. Barras was given an extra $1500 as consolation for clear miss-handling of his plot. At a total cost (then deemed tremendous) of $50,000, the play was opened and ran sixteen months, into January 1868. It grossed $1,100,000. (A musical based on this fire-story, *The Girl in Pink Tights,* ran in New York in 1954.)

New York City, aburst with profiteers from the Civil War, was ready for such lavish display. Barras' plot, in truth, gave opportunities for many contrasting colors. Hertzog, "the black crook," makes a pact with the devil: he can live through every year in which he tempts a soul to Satan. The humble painter Rodophe looks like an easy victim, for Count Wolfenstein has fallen in love with Rodophe's sweetheart Amina, and locked Rodophe in a dungeon cell. Freed by Hertzog, Rodophe swears bloody vengeance. But he kills a serpent as it is about to snare a dove, and the dove is the Fairy Queen Stalacta. The Queen, of course, warns Rodophe, and with her aid, the Count is killed. Thus Hertzog, with no soul to offer the devil, is borne off to hell, and the lovers are reunited.

The play offered countless opportunities both for the mechanical effects and "transformations" in which the age delighted, and for dances of grotesque demons and delicate fairy maidens. Act I ended with a demon incantation in a wild glen, a phantasmagoria of horrors rising to tempestuous power. The finale of Act III showed the demons invading Queen Stalacta's lakelovely grotto. And at the close, as the *New York Tribune* (September 17, 1866) raved: "All that gold, silver, and gems and lights and women's beauty can contribute to fascinate the eye and charm the senses is gathered up in this gorgeous spectacle." No lovers ever had more elaborate glory to grace their union. The presentation lasted from 7:45 p.m. to 1:15 a.m.

The play swept the city into a storm. The *New York World* (September 17, 1866) declared; "As a drama *The Black Crook* is a pretentious boast; that is, what little is left of it, for it is known that nothing but the name and a few dreary 'carpenter's scenes' have survived the stage manager's process of stuffing it with pageant and gorgeously spectacular transformations . . . It would have been wiser to have presented the *Colored Crook* as a pantomime, not that the players are professional pantomimists, but they could certainly express their sentiments of heroic virtue and hopeful revenge quite as satisfactorily by dumb show as they do now by Bowery word of mouth . . . During the two hundred and odd years of its existence New York has never enjoyed the presence of so beautiful, varied, efficient, facile, graceful, and thoroughly captivating a corps de ballet." Joseph Whitton, treasurer of Niblo's Garden in 1866, looking back thirty years later, remarked: "I have said nothing of the literary merits of the *Crook* for the best of reasons: it had none. This, however, is no serious fault."

Shortly after the play's opening the city's clergymen rose up in arms; their Sunday sermons merely increased the week-day attendance at the play.

James Gordon Bennett railed against it in editorial after editorial of his *New York Herald*. There is a suspicion, however, that his was a roundabout friendly gesture. The continuing abuse the *Herald* poured upon *The Black Crook* certainly kept the play in the public mind. A sample: "Nothing in any other Christian country, or in modern times, has approached the indecent and demoralizing exhibition at Wheatley's theatre in this city . . . Let all husbands and parents and guardians who value the morals of their wives, their daughters, and their wards, bear a watchful eye on their charges, and keep them from the walks of Niblo's Garden during the reign of *The Black Crook*." Ladies who went to the play wore long veils, as their respectable sisters of Queen Elizabeth's days wore masks.

Popular discussion kept the play going for 475 performances, with occasional "embellishments," duly reviewed. In May 1867 a grand-ballroom scene was added. Although Marie Bonfanti continued to be the star of the ballet, other dancers were added to the cast—among them Mme. Billon, an agile man ("Mexico alone can equal M. Van Hamme in the number and variety of his revolutions"), and a baby ballet ("a march of intricate military evolutions performed by over a hundred youngsters, varying in height from 35 to 45 inches") led by la petite Ravel, aged four.

In 1869, not long after its first run, *The Black Crook* was revived. Still the play remained hidden by the grottos and lakes and demon dens of the gorgeous scenery, and by "the bewildering forest of female legs." Kate Santley and Jennie Lee rose to fame in it in 1871. There were other New York productions about every second year till the century's end. Through the country, *The Black Crook* played almost continuously until 1909, the longest road run of any musical. Christopher Morley and his boonfellows produced it in 1929, with ballets arranged by Agnes de Mille, as part of their Hoboken laugh-at-the-old-plays exhibit; the superior, sophisticated laughter was muted by the production's beauty. It was done more simply, by the Federal Theatre in Los Angeles, in 1936.

As a literate drama, *The Black Crook* makes no claim; it remains a clothesline (now somewhat frayed) on which to hang such beauties as an enterprising director may assemble. Its original production will be remembered primarily because it brought the first surge of burlesque, with toss of skirts and spin of tights and lift of lissome legs, onto the American stage. As *The Black Crook*'s producers, Jarret and Palmer, discerned: "Legs are staple articles and will never go out of fashion while the world lasts." Recent theatrical ventures (see *Hair**) have shown that exposure of the remainder of the female body can also attract spectators, more concerned with visual than with intellectual delights.

A reminiscent production of *The Black Crook* was given as part of the entertainment on the new luxurious Mississippi Showboat in 1977, as it made its leisurely course down the Ohio and the Mississippi rivers to New Orleans, with its bid for passengers with time and money to spare. (TV is in the lounge.)

RABELAIS, ETC.   *Barrault, etc.*

There has been a tendency, in recent years, to turn into a musical extravaganza a noted work, or the life and work, of a well-known figure. Several lively plays of the sort are here discussed, chronologically by their origin.

I. François Rabelais (1494?–1553). The "absurdists" who imagine their viewpoint is new may know little more than the name of the French contemporary of Shakespeare who was forerunner and master of them all. The writer Leon Daudet said, "Rabelais is an author to be drunk, to be savoured by the palate. He is best enjoyed aloud, for his is the acme of the spoken style." That bawdy madness with satiric undertones was put on the Paris stage in 1968—*Rabelais,* a survey of the man and his works—by Jean Louis Barrault, noted French actor and director. Translated by Robert Baldic, it came to the Old Vic in London in 1969, to the City Center of New York in 1970, to Los Angeles and Berkeley; to Berlin, Brussels, Rome.

The printed version has a Prologue in which the Orator, from a stage in the form of a cross, lists discoveries, disasters, crimes—constantly interrupting with the query: "Rabelais' time, or our own?" Onstage there is a different Prologue: nine actors enter around a cross; each speaks a different quotation. (The first speaker lights a huge match, as though to set fire to the pile of books onstage.)

"Society is a sort of prison full of sinners, in which order has to be maintained by force.—Luther."

"A free man finds his rule of conduct in his sense of honor.—Rabelais."

"Fear is the foundation of religion.—Calvin."

"Fear and slavery pervert human nature.—Rabelais."

"There is not a single drop of good in us, and we have no cause to hold ourselves in the slightest regard.—Calvin."

"Yes, we have: some people have a wonderful gaiety born of a contempt for the quirks of fate.—Rabelais. For want of a better name, we call it joy.—Michelet."

"God sees nothing in such people but filth and corruption. They are hateful in His sight. He rejects them utterly.—Calvin."

"I am a man, and nothing human is alien to me. I have all men's vices and all men's virtues. I understand them, and taking them upon myself, I am ready to excuse them and forgive them.—Terence."

"Seize hold of life, for life is health.—Rabelais."

The play presents a topsy-turvy world of romping youth, which knows no moral codes or verbal inhibitions. There are hippies in shake-and-jerk sessions; mini-dolls in see-through tops; giant codpieces, stylized sex. Friar Jean's crucifix darts to his foe's posterior. The mood shifts from poetic to sinister, from mock solemnity to slapstick farce. The language—often Rabelais' own—is pierced with puns, pricked with bawdry, tumbled with spoonerisms (*folle à la messe; molle à la fesse*). There is praise of "the herb Pantagruelion," namely hemp, which gives us a lift in hashish, or in the hangman's noose. Hans Carvel has his dream of the ring, the wearing of which will give him assurance of his wife's fidelity:

> Hans woke, and his hand was pressed
> In passion's nest;
> And then Hans ruefully knew
> His dream was true.

Beginning with Grandgousier and Garamelle in modern dress, who "meet, embrace, and engage in the divine combat," then put on their stage costumes (lively-colored, grotesque), the play mimes the birth of Gargantua; the newborn babe cries, "Drink! Drink!" We watch Gargantua grow; at one time he appears as a huge balloon, over fifteen feet high. He determines that the best cleanser after defecation is the neck of a downy goose. (Medieval) medicine and (humanist) education are laughed aside. The great war with King Pirochole, whose bakers had refused to cook cakes for Grandgousier's shepherds, is won with the help of Friar Jean, upon whom Grandgousier bestows the region of Thelême, where he sets up the Abbey, with its motto: Do as you will.

The birth of Pantagruel is blended with the vicissitudes that beset Rabelais himself. Pantagruel and Panurge take ship; they meet a vessel with a cargo of sheep, one of which Panurge buys and throws overboard—and all the rest, in their usual game of Follow-the-Leader, leap after it and drown. After other mockeries of human folly, at the temple of the Holy Bottle and the cry of "Trink!" everyone dances (a modern dance of wild swirling) until Panurge falls to the ground—and, in the present, Panurge rises as Rabelais and speaks that writer's actual last words: "I go to seek a great perhaps . . . Ring down the curtain, the farce is over."

The freedom of the Reformation, through the laughter of Rabelais, challenges the more solemn but more heedless "shackle-breaking" of our permissive days, as everything from hovel to palace, from holiness to phallus, is exalted—and pricked down again, in this capture of the world's most exuberant mockery of the pretensions of man, and affirmation of the essential joy of living. As Baudelaire expressed it, "Get you drunk; on wine, on poetry, or on virtue. But get you drunk."

II. Miguel de Cervantes Saavedra (1547–1616). The story of "the knight of the woeful countenance," Don Quixote de la Mancha, was dramatized in English as early as 1694, when Thomas D'Orfey wrote the first of three parts of his Comical History of Don Quixote. A 1933 film, Don Quixote, with music by Jacques Iberts, starred Feodor Chaliapin and George Robes; among its many showings was one in New York, April 1983. The most recent dramatization of scenes from the book, by Richard Curtis and John Rettallack, was presented in April and May 1983 by the Actors' Touring Company of London as part of the "Britain Salutes New York" festival. The great success, however—with book by Dale Wasserman, music (operatic, with arias, trios, recitative, etc.) by Mitch Leigh, and lyrics by Joe Darion, directed by Albert Marre, with choreography by Jack Cole—began when Man of La Mancha had a trial run in East Haddam, Conn., beginning April 24, 1965. It moved, unheralded, to ANTA, Washington Square, New York, on November 22, then up to the Martin Beck Theatre and on . . . and on (Lincoln Center's Beaumont, June 22, 1972) for 2,328 performances. Among those who played Don Quixote were Richard Kiley, José Ferrer, and David Atkinson (on tour through 1967). It has been played in forty-five countries, in twenty-two languages. London in 1968–1972. With Patrice Munsell as Aldonza-Dulcinea in summer theatre, Latham, N.Y. In 1969 the producers planned to use, in the New York showing, stars in the play from other lands: Jacques Brel, France and Belgium; Gideon Singer, Israel; Josef Meinrod, Austria; Charles West, Australia; Somegoro Ichikawa Matsumoto (Koshira IX, who starred in it in Kyoto and Osaka, the latter in 1982), Japan. Only in Spain, Cervantes' own country, was the play a flop. In New York Sancho Panza was played by Irving Jacobson; Aldonza, by Joan Diener.

The play begins with the author, Cervantes, in the Inquisition jail in Seville. He is held for trial by the other prisoners, who crawl into his underground cell from a door twenty feet above the stage. In self-defense, he asks permission to tell his story. He thus becomes Don Quixote; he takes the tavern whore, Aldonza, to be his lady Dulcinea. The story moves on its roundabout way, past the windmills, which he takes to be his enemies, with his man Sancho Panza shaking his head and uttering proverbs. Among the songs, most attractive are "Dulcinea" and especially "The Impossible Dream." At the end, when Don Quixote dies, Cervantes goes on living. (He still does.)

The Russian Mikail Bulgakov (see Molière) wrote a *Don Quixote* in 1940. In 1974 Asolo produced *Don Quixote of La Mancha,* by Arthur Fauquez, in its Theatre for Young People. Mention should be made of the Cervantes Festival in Guanajuata, Mexico, which at its tenth annual presentation, in 1982, had music, dance, and drama groups from twenty-one countries. The festival began with, and still highlights, skits from the Cervantes story, with Don Quixote always the butt, and Sancho Panza the shrewd commentator and profiteer. One deeper note: offered the governorship of the island of Barataria, Sancho is overjoyed, but explains: "I don't know my a.b.cs, but I can make the mark that comes before them" (the sign of the cross). "Excellent!" cries the Duke; "That is all one needs to know, to make a good governor." The surface satire is obvious; thought may move to a deeper truth. (W. S. Gilbert bowed to Cervantes when he moved all the characters in *The Gondoliers* to the island of Barataria for the second act.) The short, potbellied Sancho is well named, *panza* being Spanish for *paunch.*

On June 18, 1982, the NT (Olivier) presented *Don Quixote* by Keith Dewhurst, with twenty-four brief episodes from Cervantes' story. Rosinante, the knight's steed, was a tricycle with a large front wheel and a stylized head (curved rod with tassels); Sancho's donkey was a smaller one; the "Yanguesan Carriers" rolled in on bicycles. There were acrobatics and lively tomfoolery, with accordant loud music, but the performances were disappointing, with Paul Scofield as the sorrowful knight and a not-so-bouncy Tony Haygarth as his reluctant but faithful squire. The play ran in repertory for the season; but it was *The Man of La Mancha* that the *London Times* said "had earth and sky and splendor."

III. Voltaire (1694–1778; b. François Marie Arouet). Voltaire's *Candide* has been tried upon the stage several times. At the Odéon, Paris, in 1923, an adaptation by Clement Vautel and Leo Marches, with Robert Arnoux as Candide, using marionettes, was presented briefly. In New York in 1945, for a version with book and lyrics by George Foss and music by Jack Shore, an all-black cast was contemplated, but the project was dropped. Opening December 1, 1956, with book by Lillian Hellman, music by Leonard Bernstein, and lyrics by Richard Wilbur, John Latouche, and Dorothy Parker, was *Candide* at the Martin Beck, New York; it was directed by Tyrone Guthrie. Robert Rounseville played Candide; Barbara Cook, Cunegonde; Max Adrian, Dr. Pangloss. Brooks Atkinson wrote: "Since Voltaire was a brilliant writer, it is only right that his *Candide* should turn out to be a brilliant satire." Walter Kerr countered: "Three of the most talented people our theatre possesses—Lillian Hellman, Leonard Bernstein, Tyrone Guthrie—have joined hands to transform Voltaire's *Candide* into a really spectacular disaster." The public agreed with Kerr; the musical lasted but seventy-three performances.

This version was seen in London in 1959, with Lillian Hellman "assisted by Michael Stewart"; it had Denis Quilly as Candide, Mary Costa as Cunegonde, and Laurence Naismith as Dr. Pangloss. It belongs, said the *London Times* (May 3, 1959), "to that simple school of humorists who desolatingly believe that you have only to pronounce words like rape or whore to cause an audience to laugh ... written as though the authors' sole acquaintance with civilisation had been gained from the subtitles of second-feature French films." In April 1971 there came to the Public Theatre in New York a "totally disastrous" production by the Organic Theatre of Chicago, "the entire enterprise on the level of washroom graffiti." With the Leonard Bernstein music but a new book by Michael Stewart and Sheldon Patinkin and with an added Narrator, *Candide* was played by the Civic Light Opera Company in Los Angeles, with a tour to San Francisco and Washington, D.C.

Finally (on the principle of "if at first you don't succeed"—rarely practiced on Broadway), still with the Bernstein music, book by Hugh Wheeler, Stephen Sondheim replacing Dorothy Parker with lyrics, and now directed by Harold Prince, *Candide* opened December 11, 1973, at BAM, for 48 performances, then moved to Broadway for 149 more. Lewis J. Stadler played Voltaire and Dr. Pangloss; Mark Baker, Candide; Maureen Brennan, Cunegonde. In 1978 this version was performed at Stratford, Ontario, directed by Lotfi Mansouri, director of the Canadian Opera Company, with Edward Evanko as Candide and Loralyn Tomlin as Cunegonde. Richard Eder reported in the *Times* that it "still rambles aimlessly . . . unified mainly by some good music by Leonard Bernstein as well as some that sounds as if he had dictated it to his secretary." In 1980 there was an OffBroadway adaptation of Voltaire's *Candide,* written and directed by Arthur Reel.

In the Wheeler version, onstage, on platforms around the theatre and up and down the aisles, Candide and his ever-optimistic this-is-the-best-of-all-possible-worlds tutor Dr. Pangloss pursue their worldwide search for Cunegonde and happiness. Candide, illegitimate son of the sister of Baron Thunder-ten-Tronkh, has been exiled from his native Westphalia for being caught kissing the Baron's daughter Cunegonde—who, loving Candide, seeks to follow him. She is raped (in the play) not by a Bulgarian, but by a Bulgarian regiment. She is kept by a Jew, then by an Inquisitor, whom Candide slays. Shipwrecked off Portugal, blamed for the Lisbon earthquake, robbed in Cadiz, they take ship for Paraguay. Candide is captured by Indians, finds wealth in El Dorado, then loses it. From Buenos Aires he goes to Bordeaux to Paris to Portsmouth to Venice to Constantinople. On this last trip Dr. Pangloss and Cunegonde's brother, thought dead, turn up as galley slaves. Somehow surviving, Candide takes Cunegonde home to Westphalia, where he buys a farm, having decided that the best thing one can do is to "cultivate one's own garden." The blue bird of happiness, as Maeterlinck turns the figure, awaits us at home. Meanwhile, we have had a jaunt helter-skelter around a world fraught with evil and peril; perhaps we have learned that "the best of all possible worlds" must be built within oneself. Thus, what Lytton Strachey said of Voltaire's work is retained in the musical: "Perhaps the most wonderful thing about *Candide* is that it contains, after all, something more than mere pessimism; it contains a positive doctrine as well. Voltaire's common sense withers the ideal, but it remains common sense. *Il faut cultiver notre jardin* is his final word—"one of the few pieces of practical wisdom ever uttered by a philosopher."

IV. Charles Dickens (1812–1870). Dickens grew at once popular when in 1836 he introduced Sam Weller in *The Pickwick Papers.* The next year, readers waited eagerly for the instalments of *Oliver Twist.* This novel won over a dozen dramatizations in the nineteenth century (for example, adapted by and with Joseph Jefferson, 1860; with Fanny Davenport, 1895). In 1912 it was played by Wilton Lackaye and Constance Collier.

In 1960 it was turned into the musical *Oliver,* book, lyrics, and music by Lionel Bart, which, directed by Peter Coe, opened at the London New, then moved in June to the Albery and ran for 2,618 performances, with a revival in December 1977. It came to the Imperial, New York, on January 6, 1963, attaining 774 performances.

The play follows the story closely. When Oliver in the workhouse has the temerity to ask for more gruel, his sycophantic mates mock as the aghast Mr. Bumble devises fit punishment. (Then the boys sing a wishful dream song, "Food, Glorious Food!") Oliver is sold for five pounds to a coffin maker. The lad of thirteen looks lugubrious in a mourner's high hat. Punished by confinement in a coffin, Oliver runs away. Through the London streets the Artful Dodger leads him to Fagin's Thieves' Kitchen, where he is given lessons on how to pick a pocket. Watching while the Dodger picks Mr. Brownlow's pocket, Oliver runs and is knocked out by a Bow Street Runner.

Brownlow takes the lad to his fine home, where he wakes to the pleasant sound of the London street cries. Bill Sykes, Fagin's enforcer, recaptures Oliver; when Nancy, one of Fagin's girls, befriends Oliver, Sykes kills her. Chased over rooftops, with Oliver as a shield, Sykes is shot. Oliver returns to Brownlow. Fagin, his gang dispersed, walks along across the London bridge toward daybreak.

With lively songs, as "Pick a Pocket or Two" and "I'll do Anything," the play no doubt sent many back to the consummate storyteller, Dickens, whom one tale cannot confine. It was raves again at the New York Mark Hellinger, April 7, 1984, directed by Peter Coe.

Dickens' next novel had a more varied conversion to the theater. Adaptations of *Nicholas Nickleby* appeared even before its serialization was complete. Edward Sterling in 1839 wrote *Dotheboys Hall,* produced at the London Adelphi Theatre with an ending Sterling invented; he added a sequel, *The Fortunes of Smikes,* in 1840. Dickens wrote the fellow into a late chapter of his novel, as "a literary gentleman who has dramatized in his time 247 novels, as fast as they came out." He likened the adapter to a pickpocket, save that "the legislature has a regard for pocket-handkerchiefs, and leaves men's brains (except when they are knocked out by violence) to take care of themselves." Dickens' popularity and his protest helped to have the first English copyright law passed, in 1842.

In the story Nicholas and Smikes, a dull-witted lad he rescues from Squeer's school, Dotheboys Hall, join the Crummles Theatrical Company, for which Nicholas also adapts plays. Dickens' interest in the theatre—he was himself an ardent amateur actor, and from 1847 to 1852 managed a company that toured England—added to the resentment any author would feel at having his work stolen and mangled.

Among the numerous adaptations of *Nicholas Nickleby* is that of George Fawcett in 1875, popular on both sides of the Atlantic. Joseph Jefferson was among those who played Newman Foggs, the clerk of Nicholas' uncle, who helps clear Nicholas of his uncle's charge that he is a thief. In 1958 came an adaptation by Kenneth McMillan, of the Dickens Fellowship of Toronto. In Glasgow in 1969 and on tour in England in 1970 was a version by Caryl Brahms and Ned Dherrin. In 1975 a musical version by Arthur Schwartz was announced as "undergoing revisions." But the most widely touted adaptation, eight and a half hours long, is that by David Edgar, with music and lyrics by Stephen Oliver, directed by Trevor Nunn and John Caird in London for the RSC in 1980. The play might be seen on two successive nights, or straight through, with a break for a bite, on Wednesdays and Saturdays, matinee and evening. Roger Rees played Nicholas.

The Edgar version, "a cultural folk opera wallowing in pathos"—which one must refrain from deeming bathos—has Nicholas run the gamut from poverty to wealth, from desperate days at the aptly named Dotheboys Hall, through the efforts of his miserly uncle Ralph to have him jailed, on until his love for Madeline Bray (for a while penniless and pressed to marry a penniless pal of Ralph's, a fellow-miser Arthur Gride, until a stolen will the misers have hidden, recovered in the nick o' time, proves her very rich), abetted by the Cheeryble brothers, attains its happy goal. The righteous are rewarded, the villains sink to a deservedly wretched end.

Edgar, however, added a less happy note not in Dickens (whose work actually improved social conditions in English life). For at the close, Edgar has Nicholas cradle in his arms a shabby youngster resembling poor Smikes, Squeer's victim, and look across the footlights with bitterness and suppressed anger, as though our generation too will repeat the old evils . . . as slowly the lights grow dim.

The mood of the production ranged from clearest caricature to roughest realism. Most of the scenic effects were swiftly fashioned on an almost bare stage. Thus, when Nicholas sets out for Dotheboys Hall, a few chairs are set together, and the guard tootles his horn. Yet there does come across a vivid picture of the crowding life, and the sharp variation of fortune, in good Queen Victoria's murky days.

Tickets for the 1981 New York production were $100; there were (despite mixed reviews) packed houses for all the scheduled fifty-five performances. And "the original cast of 39, playing 150 parts in 315 costume changes" was announced as the first major drama on the new (1982) Channel Four of British Television, with Germany and the United States to follow. On January 3, 1982, the day the New York run ended, a full-page advertisement in the *Times* announced that, for a mere $300, one could buy a video cassette of the play and see and hear it in one's own home.

Dickens was a superb storyteller, whose sentimental tales floated his fame on rivers of tears. They have not ceased to flow.

V. Phineas Taylor Barnum (1810–1891). The Hasty Pudding Club of Harvard seems the first to have turned to the legendary P. T. Barnum for a drama; in 1920 it put on a skit called *Barnum Was Right*—"There's one born every minute." (With no connection save the title, *There's One Born Every Minute* was a 1942 motion picture, in which Elizabeth Taylor, aged ten, made her film debut.) *Humbug, the Art of Barnum* was a 1973 book by Neil Harris. *Barnum and Bailey's Clown Songbook* was issued back in 1887, but the musical *Barnum*, 1980, ends when Phineas T. suggests the partnership that grew from the "side show" that once was the main attraction to the three-ring circus that still makes annual tours of the United States. As a boy, in Decorah, Iowa, I earned free admission by carrying water for the elephants.

Barnum was tried as a musical twice before the third swing made a hit. In 1961 New York saw a version with book by Romeo Muller, music by Milton Kaye, lyrics by Edward Heyman. On February 29, 1964 (Toronto, April 22), came one with book by Edward Chodorov, music by Marian Grude and Raymond Jessel. Then, on April 3, 1980, at the St. James Theatre, New York, with book by Mark Bramble, music by Cy Coleman, lyrics by Michael Stewart, Jim Dale played through forty-five years of the life of America's most famous showman. He sang while walking the tightrope across the stage to his waiting lady; he led a troupe of acrobats, who kept tumbling around. He rode a unicycle; he jumped from a trampoline to an upper box onstage. He displayed Tom Thumb; he dallied amorously—as contrast to his formal wife, who frowned on his horseplay—with the Swedish Nightingale, Jenny Lind, as he moved on his long up-and-down pathway from his "Museum" to the greatest show on earth. The plot is feeble. Jack Kroll in *Newsweek* called the play "humdrum humbug, even though the hum is loud and the drum is deafening."

The play opened in April 1981 in Paris, directed in a circus ring by Yves Mourousi, with Jean-Luc Moreau as Barnum, and trapeze experts from the

French National Circus School. Two months later—in the first play from Broadway to be shown in Paris before London—Michael Crawford played Barnum, with Marianne Tatum, as Jenny Lind, entering high on a gigantic platter. Outside the London theatre cavorted a clown on stilts; everywhere clowns clowned amid the gathering audience. Michael Crawford was voted "actor of the year." Barnum was still running at the London Palladium in 1983. In the fall of 1981 the play toured Australia. Stacy Keach played Barnum in the 1981 American tour, starting in New Orleans.

The stars underwent hard training for the Barnum role. An understudy, called to play Barnum one night, fell and started over several times, before he completed the tightwire walk across stage. The circus atmosphere does much to make up for the flaccid story; but those who agree with Jack Kroll that the book is "a prostrate pachyderm of prosaic pomposity" may follow the sign Barnum always put up when the sideshow was crowded: "This way to the egress."

VI. T(homas) S(tearns) Eliot (1888–1965). Eliot's verses in *Old Possum's Book of Practical Cats* (1939) seem an odd source for a musical comedy, but the mewsic of Andrew Lloyd Webber, and the ingenious staging of Trevor Nunn, made *Cats,* when it opened at the New London Theatre, May 11, 1981, at once the hit of the season. On entering, the audience saw an enormous fantastic dump heap; soon this revolved (carrying along a section of the orchestra seats) and became the background of a large bare stage, with a high platform and trampoline on one side; on the other, stairs running high into the balcony—and cats all over. Before and during the play cats prance up the aisles, in their various ways snarling or smiling at the audience, and cats' eyes blink all over heaven. The cats, to be sure, are humans, in varied skins, on two feet but with arms maneuvering like forepaws, as they strut or skitter across the stage to swift choreography by Gillian Lynne, in a series of disconnected danced episodes, such as the tempestuous "Jellicle Ball," to the words of the Eliot verses. Director Nunn wrote some connecting material.

Judi Dench was scheduled, but snapped an Achilles tendon, so Elaine Page played Grizabella, a tarty cat who "haunts the grimy road of Tottenham Court." Wayne Sleep, of the Royal Ballet, cavorted as Mistoffolus the Magician cat; Paul Nicholas swaggered as Rum Tum Tugger, a rock 'n' roll tomcat. The cat-as-cat-can tomfoolery would be hard to catalog, but the very novelty of the cat-cast and its operations—leaping onto the scene via trampoline, coming up the aisles to charm or threaten spectators nearby, some in the finale rising to heaven on a giant tire—gripped the attention of every catawampus that would like to see a cat amount to more than a mousetrap. *Cats* won the London 1981 award as Musical of the Year. Opening at New York's Winter Garden, October 16, 1982, it won seven Tony awards, including Best Musical. But whoa! Walter Kerr in the *New York Times* felt that the total effect of all the cat stir was "to inflate [Eliot's verses] beyond all reason, beyond such meaning as they possess. The strain after a false significance puts us under a strain as well, the strain—and it is a futile one—of trying to make verses and visuals (together with music) match. The cats' meow, too pranked and too persistent, makes us yearn for silence. More and more," Kerr concludes, "we are making our theatrical mountains out of less and less solid rock."

Cats do not need rock for their climbing. As I write, the play is running catlike on in both cities, with the slogan "Now and Forever, Cats." T. S. Eliot in the beyond must be wearing a Cheshire-cat smile.

VII. Perhaps I should add mention of *The Three Musketeers,* by and directed by Eberle Thomas, based on the book (1844) and play of Alexandre

Dumas père, which had its world premiere at Asolo in 1981. Its thirteen scenes, mainly in 1628, range from a small-town vicarage to the convent of the Carmelites, the cabinet of Cardinal Richelieu, and the antechamber of Queen Anne, wife of Louis XIII. The play features, of course, the famous trio, Athos, Porthos, and Aramis, with the Gascon daredevil who joins them, D'Artagnan, liltingly played by James Hunt, in a swirl of swashbuckling opposition to the Queen's soldiers and the conniving Cardinal's guardsmen, as fun and derring-do interflow in swift and delightful rouse.

THE LITTLE MINISTER   *James M. Barrie*

When James Matthew Barrie (1860–1937), beloved Scotch writer, visited New York, Charles Frohman was seeking a play for Maude Adams. With considerable change, *The Little Minister,* one of Barrie's early novels of Scotch life, was dramatized, and Lady Babbie, the wild gypsy with red rowans in her hair, came to the stage of the Empire Theatre, September 27, 1897, to give Maude Adams her first starring role.

The play tells of the capture of Gavin Dishart, young Presbyterian minister in the narrow and suspicious village of Thrums, by the vivacious and wayward Babbie. Dressed as a gypsy, Babbie is in the woods to warn the striking handloom weavers that the soldiers are coming for them; Gavin is there to see that the weavers do not resist the law. Before the soldiers, Babbie declares she is Gavin's wife. To protect her, he remains silent, and by Scotch law they are wed. They meet again at Lord Rintoul's, where the Lord's daughter, Lady Babbie, claims Gavin, while her suitors swear Gavin is wed to a gypsy girl. The offended congregation is reconciled, and the suitors are foiled, as they learn that the gypsy girl and the Lady are one.

The *New York Dramatic Mirror* (October 2, 1897) found *The Little Minister* "at times prosy and inactive, and it frequently verges upon incoherence. Miss Adams . . . gave life, color, and rare delicacy to the highly improbable Lady Babbie." The play was better received in London, where it opened on November 6, with Cyril Maude and Winifred Emery. The *London Graphic* (November 13, 1897) praised Barrie's "removing what was merely episodical, giving to his story a compactness which it did not have before, and concentrating the interest upon its real dramatic feature, which is the development and final triumph of the love of the Little Minister for his wild and wayward temptress." Bernard Shaw, who had seen the Shakespeare play the night before, reported: "*The Little Minister* is a much happier play than *The Tempest.* * Mr. Barrie has no impulse to throw his adaptation of a popular novel at the public head with a sarcastic title [*As You Like It* *], because he has written the novel himself, and thoroughly enjoys it . . . The popular stage, which was a prison to Shakespeare's genius, is a playground to Mr. Barrie's . . . He has apparently no eye for human character; but he has a keen sense of human qualities, and he produces highly popular assortments of them." Barrie's combination of nine-tenths fun and one-tenth sentiment struck Shaw as most toothsome; he felt that *The Little Minister* "has every prospect of running into the next century."

It ran, in London, for over 200 performances. In the United States, Maude Adams played Lady Babbie frequently until 1916. In 1925, Ruth Chatterton revived the role, with Ralph Forbes (her husband in the play as in life) and J. M. Kerrigan. Heywood Broun commented (March 23, 1925): "There is something of genius in writing of Prince Charming and making that same prince assume the habiliments of a young Presbyterian parson." Stark Young made some reservations, finding "the mood thin though arch and the situation forced and squeezed a trifle dry for every sweet or whimsical effect possible to it. On the other hand, there are spots full of the old [sic] Barrie savour, and motivations, like that of the elders and kirk members and their devotion to the young minister, that are lovable and delightful."

The generation that remembers Maude Adams continues to love the gypsy lady; but to every generation *The Little Minister* brings the tender stir, the universal quickening of hopefulness and ardor, the wild rouse of woodland freedom from urban restraints, the joy of love and make-believe, of misunderstanding and making up, that curl in the heart of romance.

There was a musical attempt at *The Little Minister,* called *Wild Grows the Heather,* in England in 1956; but, with the social message, the gypsy lass who turns out to be a noble lady, and the prim but love-won minister, the play still holds the promise of a madcap magical musical.

THE ADMIRABLE CRICHTON   *James M. Barrie*

In this play the humor and charm of Barrie take on the savor of satire as the claims of equality and rank are examined. Barrie called the play "a fantasy," but its roots are spread through loam of truth.

Believing in "the equality of man," Lord Loam has his three daughters join with the servants in monthly teas, to the equal discomfort of both and the disgust of Crichton, the butler, who insists that "social inequalities are right because they are natural." On a cruise around the world, Lord Loam and his daughters, with one maid, Tweeny, and Crichton, are wrecked on an uninhabited island. As they dwell there for some time, natural inequalities make the competent Crichton their leader. Lady Mary, the most self-reliant of the ladies, is about to enjoy the privilege of being his bride when a ship is sighted; Lady Mary wants to stay on the island, but Crichton sounds the signal and reverts to his butler's role.

Elaborately produced in London by Charles Frohman, directed by Dion Boucicault, *The Admirable Crichton* won great success, with H. B. Irving as Crichton, supported by Henry Kemble, Gerald du Maurier, Irene Vanbrugh (Lady Mary), Sybil Carlisle, Muriel Beaumont, and Pattie Browne. The English press reacted pleasantly to the picture of a butler better than his lord. Said the *London Times* (November 18, 1902), "It is a bewildering and amusing piece of topsy-turvydom, but it all comes out all right when they return to Lord Loam's house in London in the last act."

The play came to New York a year later, November 17, 1903, with most of the English cast, but with William Gillette as Crichton. Democratic America received it with delight. The *New York Dramatic Mirror* suggested that the plot resembled that of Sydney Rosenfeld's *A Modern Crusoe,* 1900, itself like Ludwig Fulda's *Robinson's Island,* both of which are serious sociological problem plays, remote from Barrie's light touch and mellow mood. The theme of Barrie's play was earlier touched in Gilbert's *The Gondoliers.* *

There have been many revivals of *The Admirable Crichton.* It was put on film in 1921 as *Male and Female,* with Gloria Swanson; a talking version, *We're Not Dressing,* was produced in 1934. Among recent revivals on the stage was one in 1931 with Walter Hampden, Fay Bainter, Herbert Druce, Ernest Glendinning, Estelle Winwood, and Effie Shannon.

At the time of the latter revival, Brooks Atkinson (March 10, 1931) observed: "If there is anything priceless in Barrie it is the dainty allusiveness of his writing . . . He can catch all the emotion in the world in a buoyant phrase." Robert Garland dissented: "The occasion was gala and, if I may say so, dull . . . the whimsey scarcely worth retelling in these hard-boiled post-war days." To which William Allen White's words are fitly counter-poised: "Barrie is one of the few living dramatists who can dramatize the thesis that man on this planet is, on the whole, with his many foibles, a noble creature, following out through many zig-zags the unchartable purpose of God; and who with that thesis can be gay and lovely and charitable and never dull."

With light humor, amusing story, and deft character portrayal, the play tilts a warning finger to those that accept without question the proffered social panacea that would level all folk in assumed equality.

Among the many recent performances of *The Admirable Crichton*: 1955, Boston University; 1960, Pilochry Festival; 1976, Ontario; 1977, Greenwich, Conn.; 1978 and again 1979, OffBway (Hudson Guild); 1979, London; 1980–1981, New Haven. With book and lyrics by Herbert Kretzmer, music by David Lee, *Our Man Crichton* opened at the London Shaftesbury, December 2, 1964.

Barrie borrowed his title from Sir Thomas Urquhart, who spoke of James "the admirable" Crichton (1560–1585), a Scottish scholar, traveler, and swordsman.

PETER PAN   *James M. Barrie*

This play, Barrie's most successful, is the story of the boy who wouldn't grow up. It will never grow old.

Peter Pan drops in on the Darling children. In spite of the efforts of their nurse, the dog Nana, he teaches Wendy and her brothers to fly. They soar with him to Never-Never Land, where Wendy becomes the mother of the lost children who live underground and in the hollow trunks of trees. Adventures with Indians and pirates follow. The pirate chief, Captain Hook, is followed by a crocodile that, having devoured the Captain's hand, seeks the remainder of his meal; but the ticking of a clock the crocodile has swallowed always warns the Captain. There is desperate war between the children and the pirates. Peter's friend, the fairy Tinker Bell—visible only as a dancing light—swallows the poison Hook has prepared for Peter. To save her life, Peter appeals to the audience: Do you believe in fairies? and as the audience applauds Tinker Bell's light grows bright again. Peter leads his forces onto the pirate ship, and the desperados walk the plank. Wendy goes home, promising always to return, for the spring cleaning, to Peter's house in the tree-top in Never-Never Land.

When Barrie wrote *Peter Pan* in 1904, he took it to Beerbohm Tree, whom he visualized as Captain Hook. Tree at once warned Frohman: "Barrie has gone out of his mind. I am sorry to say it; but you ought to know it. He's just read me a play. He's going to read it to you, so I am warning you. I know I have not gone woozy in my mind, because I have tested myself since hearing the play. But Barrie must be mad. He has written four acts all about fairies, children, and Indians running through the most incoherent story you ever listened to; and what do you suppose? The last act is to be set on top of trees!" Later, Tree said he'd probably be known to posterity as the man that had refused *Peter Pan*.

Both in London, and in New York, the play was an instant success. Maude Adams will always be associated with the title role, which she played again and again, although many others have essayed it: Cecilia Loftus in 1906, Ann Harding in 1923, Marilyn Miller in 1924, Eva Le Gallienne in 1928, and Betty Bronson in a movie version in 1924. J. Edward Bromberg is one of many that have endeared to audiences the part of Nana, the dog-nurse; he played the part in 1928–1929.

Young and old alike respond to the appeal of *Peter Pan*. Those who maintain—as many do—that it is a children's play, the *Boston Transcript* chided (May 8, 1929): "Fools and slow of heart! It is middle age's own tragicomedy—the faint, far memories of boyhood and girlhood blown back in the bright breeze of Barrie's imagination." Percy Hammond made the same point on November 7, 1927: "*Peter Pan* is as young as it was eighteen years ago—but I am not." The *New York Times* (January 2, 1916) made the point more precisely: "*Peter Pan* is not children at play, but an old man smiling—and smiling a little sadly—as he watches children at play."

"And if there be anybody," said the reviewer of London's *King* (January 14, 1905) "who can sit through the performance without an occasional tear, I can only wish for him that he may some day have children of his own, and will then understand why in the first and last scenes so many eyes around him were moist and so many throats felt in them the lump that a tender emotion brings."

Tenderness is in the play, but deeper things are there as well. Charles Frohman, Maude Adams' producer and close friend, spoke as his last words as the *Lusitania* went down, Peter Pan's words in the mermaid scene when he too expected to drown: "To die must be an awfully big adventure."

Peter Pan came back to New York, April 24, 1950, with music and songs by Leonard Bernstein. Jean Arthur played Peter; and Boris Karloff, both Wendy's father and Captain Hook (Ernest Lawford played both roles in New York in 1905). Jean Arthur played Peter ingratiatingly, with pert mischief; but Karloff burlesqued the Pirate as though he were playing Gilbert and Sullivan instead of Barrie. Bernstein's music, on the other hand, improperly approached the sentimentality the rest of the production strained to avoid. For those that could not remember Maude Adams, the quality of Jean Arthur's work gave validity to this interpretation of Peter. The production attained 321 performances, a record for the play. Mary Martin appeared in a musical version in 1954.

Playful and alive, tenderly gay with undertones of pathos, reaching through fantasy to the truths that time must cull, *Peter Pan* (approached only by Maeterlinck's *The Blue Bird* *) captures the essential child each of us hopes to hold throughout our days. Small wonder that it is produced in London every Christmastide.

Peter Pan has missed few Christmas revivals in London. The spectacular 1972 Christmas production was directed by Robert Helpmann, with Dorothy Tutin as Peter and Eric Porter as Captain Hook; Helpmann directed it again in 1975. The 1972 Liverpool Christmas revival went on a twenty-four-week national tour.

In New York, opening at the Lunt-Fontanne on September 6, 1978, Sandy Duncan literally soared as Peter Pan through 578 performances, a new record.

With Maude Adams as Peter, December 21, 1915, Ruth Gordon made her Broadway debut. Sir Gerald du Maurier was the first Captain Hook.

WHAT EVERY WOMAN KNOWS   *James M. Barrie*

In life's intertangling of the sexes, Bernard Shaw saw woman as the huntress, love being but a disguise for the "life-force" that must find continuance; Barrie, on the other hand, emphasized the tender and tolerant, protective mother-feeling of a loving wife. Barrie's attitude was most fully developed in *What Every Woman Knows*.

When John Shand breaks into the Wylie house in this play, he does so in search of learning, not money. The Wylies have the best library in their little Scotch town. They also have the unmarried Maggie. Catching John in unlawful entry, the Wylies bargain with him: they will put him through law school if he will marry Maggie. The bargain kept, Shand goes on to Parliament, becoming a popular leader. When he is attracted to Lady Sybil Lazenby while Maggie is away from him, Shand discovers how much his success has hinged upon Maggie, whose sense of humor gives sparkle to the ideas of her intelligent and hard-working but humorless husband. Shand manages to see the irony and humor of the situation, and the way is cleared for the happiness of John and Maggie.

What Every Woman Knows opened in London in September 1908, with Hilda Trevelyan (Maggie), Gerald du Maurier (John), Lillah McCarthy, Edmund Gwenn, and Mrs. Beerbohm Tree. It was an immediate success. The play came as a Christmas present to Broadway on December 23, 1908, with Maude Adams and Richard Bennett. It has since been continuously popular. Maggie has been played by Helen Hayes (1926, 1938); Frances Starr (1931); Pauline Lord (1931); and Muriel Kirkland (1942). In 1946 the American Repertory Theatre revived the play, with June Duprez (Maggie), Richard Waring (John), Ernest Truex, Philip Bourneuf, Walter Hampden, and Eva Le Gallienne. It was filmed in 1921 with Lois Wilson and Conrad Nagel, and again in 1934.

Of the Broadway premiere, the *New York Dramatic Mirror* (January 2, 1909) commented: "What every woman knows is that Eve was made not from Adam's rib but from his funny-bone . . . Perhaps it is not his best play, but it is as good as any of the others, no matter how paradoxical that may sound. And the role of Maggie was made for Maude Adams."

Critics have expressed curious ideas as to Barrie's intent in writing *What Every Woman Knows*. Freedley and Reeves said in *A History of the Theatre* (1941): "The thesis that every prominent man is a fool and that an intelligent wife must struggle to prevent his learning it, is distinctly depressing." (Freedley apologized in part by calling the play, after the 1946 revival, "the most delightful Scottish comedy of them all.") And Alexander Woollcott (April 14, 1926) said that the play was written "in support of Barrie's favorite conviction that all women have the wisdom of the serpent and that all men are but lummoxes." As a matter of fact, John Shand is both hard working and intelligent; he has both ambition and drive, together with a recognition of his potentialities. What he lacks is a sense of humor, the ability to stand off and look and laugh at himself—which Maggie manages to supply. That a woman can twist a man around her little finger is another matter, and, as Shaw and Barrie agree, a common masculine susceptibility.

There abide in *What Every Woman Knows* the quintessential qualities of Barrie. It has satire, "tenderized" by humor; it has charm, and the author's love of life; it has understanding without malice, understanding that humbles a man without lessening his dignity; it has a rippling and ripening of character; and it has a swift and easy flow of plot. The Wylies in the play are alarmed at what a Scot may do with £300 of education; Barrie shows what a mind of understanding and a heart of love can do—which is indeed what every woman knows.

Helen Hayes in the play, September 1954, opened the new Huntington Hartford Theatre in Hollywood, "possibly the most beautiful theatre in America." The theatre was adorned by the actress, and the play. It was in the London Old Vic repertory, December 4, 1960. It came from Guilford to London in 1967 with Maggie Smith as Maggie and Fay Compton as Lady Sybil. At the

London Albery, November 28, 1974, Dorothy Tutin played Maggie; Peter Egan, John. The play was shown by Roundabout, 1974–1975.

DEAR BRUTUS   *James M. Barrie*

One of the most enchanting, as well as enchanted, of Barrie's plays, *Dear Brutus* took London by storm. It opened on October 17, 1917, with Gerald du Maurier, and ran for 365 performances. Among its many revivals, one in 1941 (124 performances) starred John Gielgud. The New York opening, December 23, 1918, not only was a similar triumph for William Gillette, but it awakened American theatregoers to the charm of a young actress, playing Margaret, by the name of Helen Hayes.

The title of the play, and its theme, are drawn from two lines of Shakespeare's *Julius Caesar**: "The fault, dear Brutus, is not in our stars, But in ourselves, that we are underlings." This idea is emphasized by a character in the play, who says: "Fate is something outside us. What really plays the dickens with us is something in ourselves. Something that makes us go on doing the same sort of fool things, however many chances we get."

The characters of the play are weekend guests of Mr. Lob—another name for the elfin Puck, whose many pranks include the transmogrifications in Shakespeare's *A Midsummer Night's Dream.** In *Dear Brutus,* the dream is on Midsummer Eve.

The garden behind Lob's house becomes a wood. As his guests wander there, we see that it is the "Wood of What Might Have Been," where each guest is given the chance to relive a basic situation in his life, the circumstances of which are shifted or changed in scale. The philanderer Purdie, for example, relives the time that his wife Mabel had caught him kissing Joanna, but, in the woods, he is married to Joanna and trying to tempt Mabel to a kiss.

But there is one change for the better. Dearth, the unhappily married artist, in the woodland meets his dream-daughter, Margaret. We see her as a girl about seventeen, in short green skirt and soft green cap, tossing beechnuts about, while her father works at his easel. All of Barrie's magic lifts that tender scene. It is bright with the love of father and child, a love that reaches out to the unhappy woman they meet in the wood, who in the life outside is Mrs. Dearth, to give her of its bounty. And outside the wood, the dream of love continues to hold its power, sending the artist and his wife off together, richer, happier, reconciled.

Although New York reviewers are inclined to shy from the sentimental, *Dear Brutus* swept down their guards. The *New York Times* declared: "'Sentimental Tommy' has found the way to dramatize character and fate in terms that illuminate our minds as inevitably as they delight our risibilities and our nether regions of the heart." But highest praise went to the Margaret scene; the *Times* said it "has all the spiritual comprehension and the wistful beauty in affection of Barrie at his best."

Dear Brutus is deservedly a favorite play with college and community groups. It was played in England during the Blitz. On January 28, 1941, just as Joanna pushed Purdie away, with a warning "Listen!" and he responded, "I think I hear someone!" the air-raid sirens shrilled overhead. A wave of laughter swept the audience and the cast.

At every performance of *Dear Brutus,* there are softer overtones, as each in the audience relives his cherished or regretted hour and, caught in the drama's spell, resolves to bring his later days nearer to the brighter aspects of What Might Have Been.

The peculiar genius of Barrie as playwright, says James Agate in his review of this play in *At Half-Past Eight* (1923), "consists in his bringing from the back of his mind the simple things which lie behind the mind of the spectator. They are the things which, but for the twist of kindly laughter, would be unbearable." The secret of *Dear Brutus* is that it induces surrender. If you yield to its woodland magic and to its tender mood, criticism withdraws as you shape your own fancies, with the genial if somewhat cynical help of Mr. Lob. Less captured, more captious, critics still recognize that *Dear Brutus* works with the same power as brings to tender spirits the spell of *Peter Pan.** Barrie, like Peter—for those that have walked with fairies—is youth, eternal youth.

Dear Brutus was played in 1955 at the Washington, D.C., Arts Club. After the 1972 Pitlochry Festival revival, *Stage and Television Today* spoke of "Barrie's sheer theatrical craftsmanship which still thrills, penetrates, and often disturbs . . . The passing years cannot write off Barrie's strange flair for touching the tenderest spots in the psyche."

Further revivals include one at Oxford, 1973, and one OffBway (The Troupe) in 1981.

LA VIE DE BOHEME   *Théodore Barrière*

The most famous stories of bohemian life in Paris are those of Henri Murger, contained in his *Scènes de la vie de Bohème* (1847). Working with Murger, Théodore Barrière (French, 1823–1877) based *La Vie de Bohème (The Bohemian Life)*, 1849, on Murger's tales. The play was an instant success.

It was adapted in English by Dion Boucicault* under the title *Mimi* (the title also of a 1935 film version with Douglas Fairbanks and Gertrude Lawrence). In 1896, Clyde Fitch* in the United States wrote his drama *Bohemia*, with Henry Miller, Viola Allen, and William Faversham in the cast; in this version the happy Mimi is restored to health at the end. Two operatic versions entitled *La Bohème* have also been written. The one by Ruggiero Leoncavallo was first played in Venice in 1897; the other, with book by Giacosa and Illica, and music by Giacomo Puccini, first played in Turin in February 1896, is one of the most popular of Italian operas.

Mimi is the sweetheart of Rudolph, the poet, one of the four boon companions leading a happy-go-lucky life in a garret in the Parisian Latin Quarter, about 1830. Rather than marry a woman he does not love, Rudolph has turned from his family and a fortune; he is happier in gay poverty with his friends. Marcel, the painter, is in love with Musette, a lively lass who leads on the wealthy Alcindoro, then leaves him with the dinner bills. Schaunard, a musician whose frequently erring wife constantly returns to him, and Colline, half philosopher, half dreamer, complete the quartet. But Mimi, who is sickly, watches Rudolph lured by one of the girls of the Quarter; she thinks he has abandoned her, and pines away. Rudolph returns to his one true love, and the despairing and ecstatic Mimi dies in his arms.

La Vie de Bohème, in its many versions, was invariably a success. The *New York Sun* said that the Clyde Fitch adaptation roused "a great deal of laughter on account of its scintillant wit and characteristic good humor, and there was still more of undemonstrative appreciation of its lifelike aspects." However, the sweet savoring of sadness in the story, the love and the anguish, together with the irresponsible ways of the artists, deepen in mood with music. Among the best-liked moments of song are the first act solo "They

Call Me Mimi" and the succeeding duet "O Lovely Maiden" (O soave fanciulla!). It is chiefly as Puccini's *La Bohème* that Barrière's play and Murger's story are constantly heard around the world today.

HOLIDAY   *Philip Barry*

The problem pricked by Barry (1896-1949) in *Paris Bound* (1927) is more deeply probed in *Holiday,* a distinctly witty play which opened on November 26, 1928, in New York, with Hope Williams and Donald Ogden Stewart, and ran for 229 performances. It has been played frequently around the country. It was produced in New York by Equity Library in 1945.

Two attitudes toward life are contrasted in *Holiday.* The young lawyer Johnny Case, engaged to Julia Seton of the wealthy Setons, as the play opens, meets and startles her family by announcing that he intends to retire (on some oil deal profits) to enjoy life while young. In ten years or so, after he has tasted life, he says, he may settle down to work. Julia sides with her conservative father, who thinks Johnny is crazy, but Linda Seton and her ebrious brother Ned understand Johnny's point of view. It becomes apparent that Julia has no deep love for Johnny Case; and when, the engagement broken, Johnny boards an ocean liner, it is Linda that ships aboard with him.

"A mad, mad gambol!" said reviewer Robert Coleman. "It tells a serious story in as light-hearted a fashion as e'er a serious story has been told . . . intimate, gay, irresponsible, effective." Barry succeeded in combining a swiftly moving and absorbing story of emotional conflict with a sharp opposition of two points of view regarding the social and ethical problem involved. "In the sparkling new piece at the Plymouth," Robert Garland held, "there is a great moral lesson . . . the old fight between spirit and matter. Old whines in new bottles, as it were." Barry has, said Gilbert Gabriel, "the gift of blowing big, gay bubbles which break right under your nose into cool, stinging little truths."

The dialogue of *Holiday* has the merit of speed, with a colloquial freshness that does not depend upon current slang; hence it has lasting virtue. It appealed only partially, however, to St. John Ervine, visiting from England, who wrote for the *New York World* (November 27, 1928) that "the dialogue, mostly composed of abrupt, brief sentences, varies oddly in its quality, and is full of unexpected sparkles followed by stretches of lustreless stuff." To Americans, it seemed more valid. Representative praise and a good analysis were combined in the *Boston Transcript* (April 5, 1929): "Even when the playwright is most fertile in his own devices, it seems in character with the speaking personage, the moment in the play, the social, even the scenic, background. Throughout, with allowance for the two or three outsiders (as it were) who must be foils, it is a quick-flowing banter, here nonsensical, there comic, now serio-comic, again darting in and then darting out for self-revelation; palaver when it is frailest; wisdom or feeling when for an instant it shows its muscle. A speech of this day and no other; of a social class and environment; devised and conducted to convey trait, thought, faith, and emotion through a brightly glittering yet semi-transparent envelope. A speech of speeches for the theatre, since it incessantly beguiles audiences; as often as not he also entraps them into something near belief."

Holiday makes its persons seem natural human beings; they are not mere mouthpieces of a point of view. The question it poses, of the opposition of material ambition to artistic appreciation and enjoyment of life, grows important because the lives of its persons are entangled in the answers.

Cleanly, humanly, wittily, the alternatives of long drudging and early joying are set in *Holiday*.

The play had a musical version in 1968, with book by Bert Shevelove and seventeen thitherto unpublished songs of Cole Porter. In 1973-1974 Phoenix played *Holiday* at the Ethel Barrymore in New York and on tour: 1978, Hartford; 1979 (Phoenix again) and Chicago; 1980, Los Angeles with Maurice Evans and Sally Kellerman.

HOTEL UNIVERSE   *Philip Barry*

The problem of the "lost generation," drained of faith and of zest for life by World War I and its disillusioning aftermath, is viewed through the various needs and bafflements of an assorted group of persons in Philip Barry's *Hotel Universe*. Gathered on the terrace of a house in the south of France, and living, or so they feel, "on borrowed time," these half-dozen intelligent folk, self-critical and aware of Freud, fight through to the promise of a readjustment of their lives. Some of Barry's writing in *Hotel Universe* is too tangential to grasp easily, but much of it is at his brilliant best.

The gathering at the home of Stephen Field and his daughter, Ann, is a varied one, though all in it feel that life has been drained of any purpose. Norman Rose is there, in love with music and with Alice Kendall, but entangled in the responsibilities of his wealth. There, too, are Tom and Hope Ames; he, tortured with a sense of sin since he turned away from a planned priesthood; she, so much a mother that she forgets she is Tom's wife. Lily Malone, the dancer daughter of a ham actor that she idolized, is there, plagued with the fear of her own insufficiency. "You can have my public," she says to Ann, "if you'll give me your heart." Ann Field alone needs no defense of dreams or bitter words. She has always given rather than sought. She is troubled, nevertheless, over Pat Farley, who had once loved Ann, but later wooed another girl, who committed suicide.

With slanting satire and gibe, with playful banter that may flare into angry quarrel, these young folks thrust at themselves through one another. Lily shows a scar where she had pressed a razor-blade across her wrist. "That's right, Actress," says Pat, "do your stuff. God's out front tonight." Lily responds: "Will you tell the Kind Gentleman I enjoyed his little piece, but found no part in it for me?" Into their despair comes old Stephen Field, a physicist who has made his peace with the three worlds: the temporal world of daily motion, the inner world of constant adjustment, and the ultimate timeless world where all things find their place. With a mystic psychanalytic drive, Stephen becomes to these tortured folk a piece of their past they can relive, through which they break free of their fears to find strength to face the future. When Stephen slumps, unseen, but stricken unto death, in his great chair, Pat and Ann beside him look forward to a life they will share.

Hotel Universe opened in New York, April 14, 1930, with Ruth Gordon, Glenn Anders, Franchot Tone, Earl Larimore and Morris Carnovsky. London saw it in 1932. It has had many productions in the United States. It was given in New York by Equity Library in 1947 and at Boston College in August 1949.

The critics were not single-minded as to Barry's success in carrying over its theme. Richard Lockridge (April 21, 1930) said: "*Hotel Universe* is a play of philosophy, and its philosophy is not very clear. But it is a great deal more than that. It is an adventure among strange dreams; an equilibrium established between stranger forces ... It is a brave adventure in the country beyond the moon. There are flickering moments when from this adventure there comes back the music of unearthly trumpets." The *Boston Transcript* (May 27, 1930) declared that Barry equipped his characters with "minds that work quickly, if not too deeply; with lips that open readily to darts of humor, jets of capricious fancy, thrusts of wit, intimate and therefore piercing gibes." London felt that the adjustments at the end of the play weakened its power. "It is extremely easy," remarked the *London Times* (November 16, 1932) "with the assistance of ghosts or marvels to present an exciting situation, but it is extremely difficult to round it off without disappointment . . ." (Played without break in New York, the continuous action of *Hotel Universe* was given one intermission in London.) The end, though it lessens the tension—as endings should—is the inevitable result of the play's movements.

The persons of *Hotel Universe* are natural, alive; they have problems, and out of their problems rises the basic thought of the play. "Mr. Barry never forgets," said Arthur Hobson Quinn in the *New York Herald-Tribune* (May 25, 1930), "that drama proceeds primarily not through ideas but rather through emotions. Indeed, my one criticism of the play lies in the fact that our sympathies are so strongly enlisted in the joys and sorrows of the characters that there is a certain strain after two hours from the very intensity of our interest." That interest, however, is not merely held by the play, it is quickened with a rouse of the emotions and kindled by thought. There is reward in the sense of fulfillment when the death of Stephen is counterpoised in the rebirth of Pat. There is a measure of awe, too, in the recognition that we ourselves are passing patrons of the *Hotel Universe*. Perhaps not fully enlightened, we are nonetheless lighted up, by Barry's play.

Eleanor Flexner, in *American Playwrights* (1938), pointed out that Barry "deals for the most part with the individual's revolt against conventional pressure for social conformity and the attempts to force him into a pattern of behavior to which he is inimical. Most frequently his antagonist is 'business' and everything it stands for: its goal, its way of life, its hostility to originality and individuality." W. David Sievers, in *Freud on Broadway* (1955), observed: "No other American playwright was able to transmute the raw elements of unconscious life into a work of art so delicate, so subtly ingratiating, and so fresh in form." If these are criteria of greatness, *Hotel Universe* belongs among the great plays.

THE ANIMAL KINGDOM   *Philip Barry*

Several of Barry's plays seem to defend the conventional moral values of married life. In *The Animal Kingdom,* however, he reverses the accepted roles of the wife and the mistress, showing that his ethical concern goes beneath legal codes to attain more fundamental standards of conduct.

Set among the wealthy sophisticates of suburban Connecticut, *The Animal Kingdom* tells the story of Tom Collier, playboy, aesthete, publisher, who, after living for three years with the tasteful Daisy Sage, marries, as the play opens, beautiful Cecilia Henry. Cecilia tries to keep Tom to a practical path. It takes Tom somewhat over a year to recognize that his wife is using her physical appeal to make him betray his aesthetic ideals for mundane advantages. Once his eyes can break from Cecilia's beauty to look at her soul, Tom goes back to his true mate, Daisy.

In this play Barry again interests us in a personal problem, with warm, engaging humans, beyond whom the basic issues of the play are shadowed. Even Cecilia is a natural woman, not at all unlike many we see about us.

Especially lifelike is the portrait of Richard Regan, Tom's ex-prizefighter butler and friend. Cecilia urges Tom to fire Regan, who does not fit into the formal home she plans; while Regan, unable to stand the stuffy atmosphere of Cecilia's home, tries to summon courage to tell Tom he's quitting. At the end, the two leave Cecilia together.

The Animal Kingdom opened in New York on January 12, 1932, with Ilka Chase and Leslie Howard, and ran for 183 performances. Ann Harding and Myrna Loy appeared with Howard in the film. In 1937, John Barrymore played a radio version. There have been numerous productions of the play, about the country. The critics received The Animal Kingdom warmly. "Discussing the integrity of a group of cultivated moderns," said Brooks Atkinson (January 13, 1932), "Mr. Barry has preserved his own integrity as an artist and a believer, and illuminated his thesis with splendor . . . The Animal Kingdom brings great loveliness into the theatre." John Mason Brown commented: "The conflict between 'Business' and 'Art'—or, if you will, Money and Self-Expression, or Society and Personal Freedom—has long been a skirmish that has interested Mr. Barry. But never has Mr. Barry stated it more skillfully or more poignantly than in The Animal Kingdom . . . Mr. Barry is the most genteel, the most 'knowing' and sophisticated of our dramatists."

Barry's dialogue flows with a sparkle, yet seems always to belong to the speakers. The wiles of Cecilia to woo Tom from his past are natural and defensible, until, almost imperceptibly, they become her wiles to dictate his future. The one aspect of the play not clearly motivated is the marriage itself. Why, one asks, after three years with Daisy Sage, should Tom have turned to Cecilia Henry? His turning shows the sheer force of physical beauty, for the world of material pleasures—"the animal kingdom"—wherein Cecilia loved to graze, held no lure for Tom. The Animal Kingdom bears the shape of an irresponsible, light-hearted and light-headed triangle play, save that its points are sharp and, this time, in the triangle, the wife is base.

Among revivals of The Animal Kingdom: 1974, East Hampton, Long Island; 1977, San Francisco; 1978, Stamford, Conn., winning a rave review from Clive Barnes.

THE WIZARD OF OZ   L. Frank Baum

When Lyman Frank Baum (American, 1856-1919) wrote the story The Wonderful Wizard of Oz, he and his illustrator, William W. Denslow, had to raise the money for its publication in 1900. Since then some 9,000,000 copies of that fanciful book and its fourteen sequels have been sold. The movies took over the story in 1938, producing it in technicolor with Judy Garland, Bert Lahr, Ray Bolger, Jack Haley and Frank Morgan. Dramatizations have been played in community and school theatres all over the country. With music by Paul Tietjens, The Wizard of Oz, "a musical extravaganza," opened in Chicago, June 16, 1902. In New York this production made its debut on January 20, 1903; there it ran for 306 performances and was revived on November 8, 1904.

The familiar story begins with a cyclone that carries Dorothy Gale's house from Kansas to the Kingdom of Oz. Among the Munchkins who inhabit Oz, the Good Fairy grants Dorothy two wishes; one she wastes, but with the other she brings the strawman Scarecrow to life. With the Scarecrow and the Cowardly Lion, she sets forth for the Emerald City, hoping that the Tin

Woodsman, who has oiled his joints and joined the party, will have his heart restored by the Wizard and that the Scarecrow will be given brains. The lion, taking them on his back, leaps the unbridgeable chasm into the city. There they discover that the wizard, Sir Wyley Gyle, is a fraud. They journey on to Dreamland, whence Dorothy is returned to her Kansas home, while the others settle down to live happily ever after.

The staging of Julian Mitchell made the original production of *The Wizard of Oz* superbly memorable. It opened with a wild storm of swirling lights and shadows. When the travelers fall asleep in a poppy field and the good witch sends a frost to make the poppies droop and the sleepers wake, each poppy flower becomes a radiant girl. The dances in the production were numerous and varied. "There are evolutions," said the *New York Mail and Express* (January 21, 1903), "by marching women to remind us of *The Black Crook,** and the same women are displayed in pantomimic choruses in the modern Mitchell manner."

The dialogue of the play is lively, and often funny. The *Mail and Express* asserted: "Not since the burlesque of Lydia Thompson's time have we had so many puns in a play—and most of them so apt as to be worth making." Moreover, there are hilarious bits of comic action, such as the burlesque of football by the Scarecrow and the Tin Woodsman—played originally by the excellent team of David C. Montgomery and Fred A. Stone. To say that the new piece is a hit, commented the *New York Dramatic Mirror* (January 31, 1903), "is putting it mildly. There is enough material in it to make three or four ordinary musical comedies, and it is staged with a lavishness that is simply stunning. As a production, *The Wizard of Oz* has never been excelled in its class in this city."

With music and merriment, fantasy and spectacle, gay antics and lively dancing, colorful scenes and odd costumes, *The Wizard of Oz,* like the best Walt Disney films of a later day, gives a good measure of frolicsome and wholesome fun to the warm in spirit of every age.

There have been numerous revivals of *The Wizard of Oz,* as in 1973, at the University of Tennessee, and for Christmas at the New York Public Library. Adapted with lyrics by Jim Eiler and music by Eiler and Jeanne Bargy, it was played at Adelphi University in 1976. Based on the Judy Garland–Ray Bolger–Bert Lahr movie was the 1973 musical by Harold Arlen, lyrics by E. Y. Harburg, often revived, as at Queens College (New York) in 1980. Off Off Bway, *Twister,* a version by Pat Staten, ran briefly in 1981, with Cotton (Dorothy) in a treehouse when the cyclone swooped on.

On January 5, 1975, with book by William F. Brown and music and lyrics by Charlie Smalls, an all-black adaptation, *The Wiz,* opened at the Majestic (New York), then moved to the Broadway, to run for 1,672 performances, sending out two national companies. This was played at a more feverish pace than the original. Dee Dee Bridgewater played the fairy godmother; Mabel King, the mammoth wicked witch; Stephanie Mills was Dorothy, with companions Ted Ross (later Ken Prymus) as the Cowardly Lion, Hinton Battle as the Scarecrow Strawman, and Tiger Haynes (then Ben Harney) as the Tinman. André de Shields was the Wiz. Funky monkeys romped all over the stage. The Yellow Brick Road to the home of the Wiz was played by a man.

This came to Toronto in 1978; in Sheffield, England, 1980, Calena Duncan played Dorothy. *The Wiz* was set going by a special splurging publicity campaign of $100,000 by Twentieth Century-Fox; it shouted and splashed its way to success, but it lacked the freshness and almost innocent gaiety of the good old *Wizard of Oz.*

GRAND HOTEL   *Vicki Baum*

The best-selling novel of Vicki Baum (Austrian, 1898-1960) proved equally successful as a play. Produced by Max Reinhardt in Berlin, 1929, as *Menschen im Hotel (People in the Hotel)*, it was seen on 146 European stages before it opened in New York, November 13, 1930, as *Grand Hotel,* for a run of fifty-nine weeks, before spending twenty-one weeks on tour. The play is a deft dramatic integration of individual lives into the constant stir of the changing population at a city hotel, where beside unwitting figures, tragedies are enacted, farces played, fortunes squabbled, trifles expanded, profundities probed, and the wraiths of joy feverishly pursued; where tomorrow a stranger tosses in another's last night's bed.

Vicki Baum weaves the lives of the principals of her story with the thread of time. Almost as powerfully as in *Macbeth**—both plays will reward study in this regard—*Grand Hotel* drives destiny implacably on; its every character must meet a deadline.

An outwardly respectable baron is compelled to raise money for a gang. He enters a Russian dancer's room to steal her jewels. When she returns unexpectedly, he pretends to be infatuated, and she falls in love. Touched, he confesses and returns her jewels, making his need for money still more desperate. The dancer herself is only too conscious of the passage of time. Her current tour threatens to be her last. She is fading, as it was put by J. T. Grein in the *Illustrated London News,* November 28, 1931: "worn out by work and excitement, tired, neurotic, sick of life until her sudden infatuation for that newcomer brought her a dream of rejuvenation, and, for a brief spell, magnetized the sere and yellow into fresh blossoming." She is always late for rehearsal, always being hurried by her frenzied manager.

Especially pressed for time is Preysing, an industrialist who has to swing a gigantic deal. A telegram brings news that his terms are refused; in an emergency conference, he lies about the telegram and forces through the deal. But he must take a plane to England to make good his lie. This presses a decision upon his stenographer, Flaemmchen ("Sparklet"), whom he wants to take along as his mistress. Although she has a soft spot for Kringelein, she decides to go.

Kringelein is, of all the hotel's guests, the most conscious of time. A petty clerk in one of Preysing's plants, he has been warned by the doctor that he has but a month to live, and he has come to the city for a final fling. Preysing takes Flaemmchen to his room, 170, where they find the Baron, plundering; in the ensuing struggle Preysing shoots the Baron. He is led away, and Kringelein is left with Flaemmchen, in the brief illusion of happiness.

A newcomer asks for a large room with bath; he is assigned 170. A couple returning to this, their honeymoon hotel, for their silver wedding anniversary, comment on its quiet, peaceful atmosphere, as the curtain falls.

The play has had scintillating productions. For Reinhardt, Oskar Karlweiss and Sybille Binder starred. In London, September 1931, Raymond Massey directed an adaptation by Edward Knoblock, with Lyn Harding, Ivor Barnard, Ursula Jeans, and Elena Miramova.

In New York, in translation by William A. Drake, the cast included Siegfried Rumann (Preysing), Henry Hull (Baron), Hortense Alden (Flaemmchen), Eugenie Leontovich, Albert V. Dekker, and Sam Jaffe. In the motion picture version were Greta Garbo, Joan Crawford, John and Lionel Barrymore, Wallace Beery, Ferdinand Gottschalk, and Frank Conroy. In Philadelphia the play and the film were shown at the same time, both to packed houses.

In the New York production, Sam Jaffe as the tenderly wistful Kringelein gave the finest performance of his sensitive career. Eugenie Leontovich, as the dancer, drew an entire column of praise from Richard Lockridge, with two paragraphs for her yielding kiss, one of those rare achievements, Lockridge felt, that present "the physical love scene that shows itself partly as a symbol; that is beautiful and cruel and an end in itself." John Mason Brown acclaimed the play as "the kind of adventure that restores the theatre to its high estate." At the London opening James Agate, in three words, called it a triumph: *"Veni, vidi, Vicki!"*

Grand Hotel attains distinction of several sorts. It is a model of speedy action, driving on with the tideless torrent of time; it presents a series of neatly drawn character studies, catching each person in a moment of hang-fire decision; and it weaves the several lives into one multiplex pattern. Its persons and their problems pass swiftly through the Grand Hotel of life. Insignificant and little known beyond the narrow borders of their concerns, they are the sort that, like us that watch them, make up the world.

THE DAUGHTER OF THE REGIMENT   *Jean François Alfred Bayard*

Opera buffa in two acts. *The Daughter of the Regiment* is one of the liveliest of light operas. The book is by Jean François Alfred Bayard (French, 1796-1853) and Jules H. Vernoy; the music is by Gaetano Donizetti (Italian, 1797-1848).

Set in the Swiss Tyrol in 1815, the play centers around a foundling, Marie, who has grown up as the adopted child of the 21st Regiment of Napoleon's Grand Army. Sulpice, the Sergeant that found her, objects to her love for Tonio, a Tyrolean peasant; but finally Tonio is accepted into the company. Then, however, the Marchioness of Birkenfeld comes to claim Marie as her niece. In the castle, where the Marchioness admits that Marie is her own child, "the daughter of the regiment" feels hemmed in, chafing at the lessons a young lady must take. To her great joy, the soldiers come, with Tonio now a captain. At Marie's plea the Marchioness relents and the young lovers are reunited.

The Daughter of the Regiment is one of the few musicals of its kind that is still played. It was first performed in Paris, February 11, 1840; in New Orleans for its American premiere, March 7, 1843; in New York, in September of that year. London first saw the play, in English, December 2, 1847, and there was a Command Performance for Queen Victoria, November 8, 1893. Among those that have sung the role of Marie are Jenny Lind, Adelina Patti, Frieda Hempel, Luisa Tetrazzini, and Lily Pons.

The play tells its story in warmly human terms, pleasantly expanded through the music. It is "a delightful work," commented Pitts Sanborn in the *New York World-Telegram* (December 30, 1940), "melodious, sprightly, admirable in its relishing verve. The Metropolitan presented it with such dash and drollery, and Lily Pons as the vivandiere was so utterly delightful, that no doubt is possible about its being one of the season's hits." The play retains, said the *New York Times* (February 2, 1941) "the secret of the earthy antic that is broad, without losing the warm human undertone that makes comedy endearing." *The Daughter of the Regiment,* in its appealing story, lively music, and friendly warmth, remains deservedly a favorite among light operas.

THE BARBER OF SEVILLE   *Pierre Beaumarchais*

Set in Spain, but thoroughly French in spirit, *The Barber of Seville* was a potent dramatic instrument in rousing the middle-class against the aristocracy, for the imminent French Revolution. The play survives as an amusing comedy and as a light opera.

Pierre Augustin Caron (1732-1799)—he called himself Beaumarchais— was a bourgeois French liberal. He began work as a clockmaker, then turned to commercial affairs (he financed the purchase of supplies for the American colonies, for which he was never repaid). As musical instructor to the daughters of Louis XV, he had opportunity to observe the extravagance and heedlessness of the nobles. In 1767 he wrote a lively domestic comedy, *Eugénie,* a tale of Eugénie's love of, seduction by, and eventual marriage to Lord Clarendon. His next play was a failure. Then, the five-act *Barber of Seville,* after a year's ban by the King, opened at the Théâtre Français on February 23, 1775. The play fell flat; but Beaumarchais condensed and rearranged it, and it became a lasting hit. Marie Antoinette acted Rosine in 1785, inviting the author to watch her performance with the royal guests.

The play was made into a motion picture in 1914 and 1947. Although there are occasional revivals of Beaumarchais' comedy, it is best known in this country as Rossini's comic opera (Gioacchino Antonio Rossini, Italian, 1792-1868). This opera was first performed in Rome in 1816; London in 1818; New York, in English, in 1819. It opened in 1853 at both the Broadway Theatre and Niblo's Garden in New York. Marcella Sembrich sang it, first at the Metropolitan Opera House, December 15, 1883. It is the only one of Rossini's operas that has held a continuous place in repertory. The play itself is frequently performed by college and little theatre groups; it was produced in New York in 1939, in French, by Le Théâtre des Quatre Saisons.

The Barber of Seville pictures the devices by which Rosine (Rosina in the opera) evades the advances of her amorous old guardian Bartholo, and succeeds in marrying her beloved young Lindoro, who turns out to be the Count Almaviva. The lively episodes of the story are swept into constant interest by the barber, Figaro, who fusses about, imagines himself indispensable, gives vitality to the play, and serves as an amusing but forceful vehicle of Beaumarchais' satire against aristocrats. As Austin Dobson has said, Figaro is "perpetually witty, inexhaustibly ingenious, perennially gay . . . the irrepressible mouthpiece of the popular voice, the cynical and incorrigible laugher . . . who opposes to rank, prescription, and prerogative, nothing but his indomitable audacity or his sublime indifference." Figaro is not merely the best incarnation of the stock theatrical character, the intriguing servant, in the tradition of Menander,* Plautus,* and Molière;* he is a typical French bourgeois, with the Revolution already in his heart, but laughter always bubbling as his first line of attack. His gay, irrepressible spirits, refusing to take the aristocrats at their own evaluation as a superior breed, helped rouse the citizens that on July 14, 1789, stormed the Bastille.

"Simple in plot," Brander Matthews has said, "ingenious in incident, brisk in dialogue, broadly effective in character-drawing, *The Barber of Seville* is the most famous French comedy of the eighteenth century—with the single exception of its successor from the same pen." Even in the twentieth century, with its revolutionary appeal tamed by the march of history, *The Barber of Seville* is a lively presentation of character and a gay theatrical romp.

The play, translated by John Wood, was revived at Bath in 1960, in America at Asolo in 1962. In Paris, the 1966 revival by Jean-Louis Barrault was most enthusiastically received; it was brought to London (in French) in 1968. Translated by James Ringo into current slang, it was performed OffBway (Pennygate) in 1972.

THE MARRIAGE OF FIGARO   *Pierre Beaumarchais*

Written about 1776, *The Marriage of Figaro* was at once banned by Louis XVI. "The King does not want *The Marriage of Figaro* played," Beaumarchais declared, "therefore it shall be played." It achieved quite a vogue through readings at the homes of nobles. A private performance, arranged for June 13, 1783, was stopped by the King after the audience had assembled. It was finally released, and performed to great acclaim at the Comédie-Française, April 27, 1784. Three persons were killed in the crush to see the play. After an original run of seventy-five nights, *The Marriage of Figaro* continued to be a great favorite. It was played by Coquelin (first in 1861), and revived in Russia by Stanislavsky. But, like Beaumarchais' other great comedy, *The Marriage of Figaro* is best known as a comic opera. With music by Wolfgang Amadeus Mozart (Austrian, 1756-1791), it had its premiere in Vienna on May 1, 1786; in New York at the Metropolitan Opera House, 1895.

The factotum Figaro of *The Barber of Seville** has become the center of intrigue in *The Marriage of Figaro,* as Count Almaviva, though now married to Rosine, covets Figaro's fiancée Susanne, and tries to thrust Figaro into the arms of his aging housekeeper, Marceline. A rendezvous with the Count is made for Susanne, which Rosine intends to keep; complicated misunderstandings and surprises ensue; Marceline turns out to be Figaro's mother; and all ends happily.

As the central figure, Figaro even more shrewdly than in the earlier play sends flaming darts of satire against the abuses of the times, in the spirit of the impending revolution. Brander Matthews called the play "as adroit as its predecessor, and the hits at the times are sharper and swifter and more frequent."

Figaro is both a wit and a buffoon. Buffeted by the Count on every pretext, he bounces up again, buoyant, irrepressible, indestructibly alive. The servant is superior to the master in everything except social status. Figaro is an individualized figure in a long tradition, stemming from the shrewd slave of ancient Greek comedy, here, as occasionally in earlier times, fraught with social implications. Comic sense and courage peered together from the searching eyes of Beaumarchais, creating in Figaro one of the world's great comic characters, fit fellow to Falstaff or Pantagruel. The Mozart opera, which had its Paris premiere on March 20, 1793, is now in virtually every operatic repertoire.

The play, adapted by Jacques Barzun, was shown at the Carnegie College of Fine Arts in 1961. Jean Piat played Figaro at the Comédie Française in 1963. The John Wood English version was shown in Farnham, England, 1968. In 1973 *Figaro* was played in Vienna.

Although the play had been given a short run at London's Covent Garden in 1785, what was called "the first ever major London performance" came in John Wells' translation at the NT (Old Vic) in 1974, to great acclaim. Clive Barnes, who had crossed back over the Atlantic, pointed out that the play "celebrates freedom at a time when freedom was not always celebrated." As opera or as play, the public continues to celebrate *The Marriage of Figaro*.

THE KNIGHT OF THE BURNING PESTLE   *Francis Beaumont*

The best plays of Francis Beaumont (English, 1584-1616) were written in collaboration with John Fletcher (1579-1625). Most amusing among them is the riotous farce *The Knight of the Burning Pestle*. Written some two years after *Don Quixote* (published in 1605), it followed the Spanish novel in its burlesque of the romance of chivalry, popular and excessive in that day.

With swiftly humorous prose, lively song, and a blank verse that is at times vigorous, at times deliberately prinked and panoplied with figures, *The Knight of the Burning Pestle* moves tumultuously on three levels of action. The Induction, like the Induction of *The Taming of the Shrew*,* serves to introduce two actors onto the stage among the gay bloods of the audience seated there. The actors represent a London grocer and his wife. The grocer protests against the play about to be performed, *The London Merchant*, crying that there have been enough attacks on citizens from the stage. If they can't put on a better play, at least let them put a grocer into this one. They can't spare any actors? All right, his apprentice, Ralph, will play the part. Ralph comes on stage, spouts a few lines from Shakespeare's *Henry IV*, is given a costume, and carries on. Throughout the play, the grocer and his wife comment upon the course of the action, and upon Ralph's performance.

The romantic comedy *The London Merchant*, save for the interruptions, runs the familiar course from thwarted love to happy ending. In addition to its action, there is the mock-heroic extravaganza, encouraged by the grocer's wife, in which Ralph, as the Knight of the Burning Pestle, rejects the Princess of Moldavia for a cobbler's maid in Milk Street. This story constantly interrupts the original plot, though actually linked with it only at occasional and minor points. Through Knight Ralph (with Squire and Dwarf) there is considerable satire of the military fervor then aflame in London and kindled by such dramas as Heywood's *Four Prentices of London* and Kyd's *Spanish Tragedy*,* which is parodied in the final blank verse of the Beaumont-Fletcher play. Finally, there is the direct, realistic satire of the merchant-grocer and his assertive wife.

The overstrained romanticism and heroics then popular made the first audiences unsympathetic to *The Knight of the Burning Pestle*. When the play was printed in 1613, the dedication admitted that "the world, for want of judgment, or not understanding the privy mask of irony about it (which showed it was no offspring of any vulgar brain) utterly rejected it." Gradually, however, the play grew in popularity. It was presented in 1635; during the Restoration, Nell Gwynne performed in it. Up to the nineteenth century, indeed, it shared in the general popularity of the Beaumont and Fletcher plays, which were performed more frequently than Shakespeare's; as Dryden said in 1668, "two of theirs being acted through the year for one of Shakespeare's or Jonson's."

Recent revivals of *The Knight of the Burning Pestle* include two in London: 1920, with Noel Coward; 1932, at the Old Vic, with Sybil Thorndike and Ralph Richardson. In the United States, there have been many productions; among them, at Pasadena, 1929; Missoula (University of Montana), 1936; OffBway, New York, 1938 and 1954. Poland saw the play in 1949.

In reviewing the 1920 London production, the *Christian Science Monitor*'s correspondent objected to the style in which Ralph was acted: "Beaumont and

Fletcher intended him to take himself as seriously as the Knight of La Mancha, of whom he is almost certainly a reflection. But Noel Coward plays the part with his tongue patently in his cheek. The scene with the Princess of Moldavia, in particular, is rendered as sheer farce." The Old Vic production was wiser, as noted in the *London Times* (January 5, 1932): "Much of *The Knight of the Burning Pestle* is remarkably similar, both in spirit and in shape, or lack of it, to a present-day review . . . The Old Vic Company have brought all their graces and ability to the task of making the inner play in *The Knight of the Burning Pestle* appear as bad as possible. With the gallant help of Miss Thorndike as the Citizen's Wife, the result is an evening of most spirited slapstick."

The 1635 edition of the play indicates the authors' purpose, "to move inward delight, not outward lightness; and to breed (if it might be) soft smiling, not loud laughing; knowing it, to the wise, to be as great pleasure to hear counsel mixed with wit, as to the foolish, to have sport mingled with rudeness." In the last words of the play, the grocer's wife (anticipating Gilbert's *The Pirates of Penzance**) begs sympathy for Ralph because he is an orphan. But the doubly fathered comedy *The Knight of the Burning Pestle,* still lustily amusing, has held well over the years; in it, Beaumont and Fletcher looked keenly and kindly into the extravagances of both romantic pretension and middle-class assurance.

The play has recently been shown on both sides of the ocean. In England: 1960, an open-air romp at Stratford-upon-Avon. In 1969 in London, directed by Michael Bogdanov, it overflowed into the audience. 1976, Greenwich; 1981, RSC, again Bogdanov. In America: 1964 at the outdoor Oregon Shakespeare Festival (at Ashland), with the caution: "Bring blankets." In 1970 OffBway, *The Worlde It Runs on Love,* book by Jerry Devine, lyrics by P. F. Webster, music by Alan Friedman, was "loosely based" on *The Knight of the Burning Pestle.* In 1981, Marymount, OffBway.

THE MAID'S TRAGEDY   *Francis Beaumont*

The fierce passions and cruel lusts that sear *The Maid's Tragedy* make it the most powerful tragedy of the two playwrights, Francis Beaumont and John Fletcher, whose works are almost unanimously accorded second place to Shakespeare's in Elizabethan drama and in popularity outranked Shakespeare's for over two centuries. Adapted as *The Bridal* (London, June 6, 1837) by James Sheridan Knowles, the story maintained its popular hold; Macready revived it constantly for twenty years. In New York City, when Macready opened in the play with Charlotte Cushman on December 6, 1843, *The Spirit of the Times* (December 9) reported that "the whole performance gave entire satisfaction."

The play begins with an arranged marriage. The King of Rhodes has his mistress Evadne wed the young courtier Amintor, who at the King's bidding relinquishes his own beloved Aspatia. After a lively nuptial Masque, Evadne scornfully tells her husband that he is but a cloak for the King. But Melantius, Evadne's brother and Amintor's friend, discovers the situation and so awakens Evadne to the debasement of her lot that she takes upon herself the task of revenge. With equal scorn, she now reproaches the King with his lust and slays him. Before the tangled passions can be cleared, Evadne dies by her own hand and Aspatia in disguise is slain by Amintor, who with remorseful love joins her in death.

The scene in which Evadne reveals the true conditions of their marriage to the unsuspecting Amintor is full of pathos and horror. The happy lover comes to the nuptial bed, where Evadne halts him. "The dreadful intensity of the dialogue," said J. St. Loe Strachey in his introduction to the *Mermaid Series,* "the hollow grace and gentleness of Amintor's earlier phrases, the frenzied weakness of his utterance as the scene proceeds; the brutal scorn and still more brutal pity of Evadne, as she tortures her husband before she lets him hear the shameful story she had never meant to hide, blister the heart, and leave the fancy seared and deadened."

There is irony, next morning, in the gay mockery of the couple's friends, and double irony in the anxiety of the King, who now begins to doubt whether Evadne has been true to him. The cup of degradation runs over. Aspatia alone is not bespattered, despite the scorn of Amintor. As Charles Lamb has said: "While we pity her, we respect her, and she descends without degradation. So much true poetry and passion can do to confer dignity upon subjects that do not seem capable of it."

Samuel Pepys thought *The Maid's Tragedy* too sad and melancholy. Charles II had other thoughts; the play was banned in his reign, until Waller wrote a new fifth act, in rhyme, keeping the king alive.

In various adaptions, *The Maid's Tragedy* was revived up to the mid-nineteenth century; and, in cut versions of the original, in 1904 and 1908, in London. The full version, including the mythological masque, was given in London in 1921, with Sybil Thorndike as Evadne. *The Stage* (November 17, 1921) remarked: "One can easily understand why, apart from its lofty and beautiful language, it has engaged the attention of so many prominent actors and actresses ever since its inception. It is full of splendid acting parts, and one is always finding emotion treading on the heels of real or potential tragedy, as in the finely written Quarrel Scene between Melantius and Amintor . . . In spite of much gore and many coarse expressions characteristic of the period, its main effect is eminently moral and uplifting . . . The performance of Miss Sybil Thorndike as Evadne must have been very near the poet's ideal. In the earlier scenes, before remorse or fear comes, this king's concubine was that most tragic of all things, a human being with a dead soul; and Miss Thorndike, with her flinty, smirking demeanor and joyless laughter, made one feel its deadness." Speaking of the same production, the *Christian Science Monitor* (December 27, 1921) said, "It is an extremely well-constructed stage play, teeming with intensely dramatic situations, affording excellent acting opportunities, and decorated with poetry that gives scope to the elocutionist as well as to the player."

With the advent of the Stuarts, the flowering of drama under Elizabeth, though still in gorgeous blossom, began to show the overbrightness and profusion of incipient decay. The audience, habituated to horror, as it were defied the dramatist to shock its jaded senses; situations and characters were framed rather to startle than to ring true. "Both the beauty and the latent decadence of this new style," said Allardyce Nicoll, "are to be traced in *The Maid's Tragedy* . . . the temper of the blank verse, which seems, in its vague rhythm and frenzy, premonitory of the dramatic decay to come." It is also, of course, and legitimately, premonitory of the degeneration and death of the figures within the play.

The emotions in *The Maid's Tragedy,* though pressed for sensation, stem naturally from the situations, to make a fiercely surging drama, with dialogue attuned to passion's drive and the grim and fateful, tortured ends of lust.

I find a note in Samuel Pepys' *Diary* that he sucked a shilling's worth of oranges while enjoying *The Maid's Tragedy*. It seemed "curiously modern" (without fruit) when directed by Bernard Miles at the London Mermaid, February 6, 1964.

James Russell Lowell summed up the qualities of the two playwrights: "In spite of all their coarseness, there is a delicacy, a sensibility, an air of romance, and above all a grace, in their best work, that make them forever attractive to the young, and to all those who have learned to grow old amiably."

PHILASTER   *Francis Beaumont*

The Story of *Philaster; or, Love Lies a-Bleeding* (1608) is complicated with romantic intrigue. Arethusa, daughter of the King of Calabria, is in love with Philaster, heir to the throne of Sicily; but her father pledges her, and the kingdom, to Pharamond, Prince of Spain. Pharamond dallies with Megrá, a vain and envious lady of the court, who accuses Arethusa of misconduct with Philaster's page, Bellario. Misunderstandings lead to almost tragic consequences before Bellario is revealed as a woman—the Lady Euphrasia, who in love of Philaster had taken service with him—and Philaster and Arethusa are happily united.

The page, Bellario, said Charles Lamb, "must have been extremely popular. For many years after the date of Philaster's first exhibition on the stage, scarce a play can be found without one of these women pages in it, following in the train of some pre-engaged lover, calling on the gods to bless her happy rival (his mistress) whom no doubt she secretly curses in her heart, giving rise to many pretty *équivoques* by the way on the confusion of sex, and either made happy at last by some surprising turn of fate, or dismissed with the joint pity of the lovers and the audience."

The succession of swift events makes Philaster lively entertainment; its romantic mood was popular for a century and a half.

In one important respect, *Philaster* is unique among plays of its time. Many contemporary dramas, using faraway settings to ward off the censor, make reference to the politics of the day; audiences were quick to transfer the events from Muscovy or Thule to their own England. In such plays, shown exclusively for court and for the gentlefolk, the collective commoners are scorned; "the hydra-headed multitude" is pictured as an ignorant, fickle rabble. *Philaster* is the one exception. Throughout the play, we hear high praise of "the abused people, who, like to raging torrents, shall swell high." The common people—their resemblance to the Londoners stressed by their being called more than once by a London street cry: "Dear countrymen what-ye-lacks"—are the play's hero.

The boldness of this treatment seems the greater when we note that in the period 1604-1612 James I of England several times sought to arrange a marriage between Prince Henry and the Spanish Infanta, hoping to bolster his own power through the prestige and the absolutism of Philip III of Spain. As *Philaster* phrases it, the king "labors to bring in the power of a foreign nation to awe his own with." Such parallels endowed the play with an intensity of contemporaneous concern.

Philaster has as many, and as swift, changes of mood as the sea in autumn, with something of the ocean's turbulent and deep romantic beauty. In addition, it is the one play of its period—the first English drama—to present the common people as the champions and instruments of freedom.

WAITING FOR GODOT   *Samuel Beckett*

Written first in French, by James Joyce's one-time secretary Samuel Beckett (b. 1906), *En Attendant Godot* opened at the Théâtre de Babylone in Paris, 1952, and ran for more than four hundred performances. Translated by the author, *Waiting for Godot* has puzzled theatregoers. Brooks Atkinson (his first phrase borrowed from Churchill) called it "a mystery wrapped in an enigma. *Waiting for Godot* is all feeling. Perhaps that's why it is puzzling and convincing at the same time." He neglected to mention of what he was convinced. And that's the crux of the matter. That's how, as John McClain put it in the *Journal-American*: "To some it is one of the most profound and amusing plays ever written; to others, it is a practical joke played by author Samuel Beckett on a gullible, pseudo-intellectual public."

On a stage bare except for a leafless tree, two tramps, dressed in ragged baggy trousers as in the old burlesque, wait in boredom, passing the time (which, they observe, would have passed anyway) waiting for Godot, whose appearance will, apparently, solve all their problems—or at least put an end to their waiting. A boy comes, on each day of the play, to assure them that Godot will come—tomorrow. In the second act, the second day, the tree has sprouted two leaves.

In one production, reversing the symbolism, there were two leaves on the tree in the first act, fallen in the second. In the first New York production, 1956, Michael Meyerberg used an all-white cast; in his next, 1957, an all-black one. I am reminded of the jingle that ends Apollinaire's *Les Mamelles de Tiresias**: work it which way you will, it is equally meaningful—or meaningless; like life.

Estragon, Gogo for short, is short and stubby; Vladimir, Didi for short, is tall and skinny. The two tramps are further differentiated. As Whitney Bolton in the *Telegraph* pointed out: "Didi is nicely decayed and rather touching, a lean and wand-like Didi who is a proper mentor and guide for the shiftless and utterly lost Gogo." Didi has stinking breath, Gogo has stinking feet. Didi goes offstage to perform a physiological function; Gogo, watching, cries, "Encore!" (I don't find that in the printed version, but onstage Bert Lahr delightedly called, "Encore!") The Lord Chamberlain (British censor until this function was abolished in 1968) ordered several changes in the play; for *arse, farted,* and *the clap,* London heard *backside, belched,* and *warts.*

After a while a wealthy businessman, Pozzo, comes in, with a whip and a slave, Lucky, whom he guides by a rope around the neck. Toward the end of the act Lucky delivers a long pseudo-philosophical absurdist speech, which begins: "Given the existence as uttered forth in the public works of Puncher and Wattmann of a personal god quaquaquaqua outside time without extension who from the heights of divine apathia divine athambia divine aphasia loves us dearly with some exceptions . . ." and ends: "in a word I resume alas alas abandoned unfinished the skull the skull in Connemara in spite of the tennis the skul⌐ alas the stones Cunard . . . tennis . . . the stones . . . so calm . . . Cunard . . . unfinished." On their later reappearance, Pozzo is blind; Lucky, still roped, is dumb.

Save for the absurdist pomposity of Lucky's one long speech, the conversation stumbles repetitively on at a subliterate level. The play thus sets itself in what has been called anti-drama, with its devaluation of the word; the dialogue is diminished in importance, and the director raised. Of the play's 11,953 words, 9,754 are of one syllable; 1,779, of two syllables. Of the remaining 420 words, 192 are in the deliberate nonsense of Lucky's speech.

The two tramps engage in a stichomythic bandying battle of words: "Sewer-rat!" "Curate!" "Cretin!"—which Gogo wins by crying, "Critic!" At the end of each act, the tramps say, "Let's go"—and do not move, as the curtain slowly falls.

The French critic Pierre Paul Auger headed his comment, "Waiting For Nothing?" The action in the play's two acts was summed up as a "double bill: Waiting for Godot; More waiting for Godot." In one speech of Estragon the author unwittingly, or mockingly, indulges in self-criticism: "Nothing happens, nobody comes, nobody goes; it's awful."

London saw the play in 1955. The American production of the play in 1956, at Coconut Grove, Florida, came to the Golden Theatre, New York, April 19, 1956, for 89 performances, with Bert Lahr as Estragon; E. G. Marshall, Vladimir; Alvin Epstein, Lucky; Kurt Kasznar, Pozzo; directed by Herbert Berghof. And the vogue was on. Among other productions were one in 1971 in the original French at the Barbizon Plaza, New York, and the same year one in English OffBway for 136 performances; London, 1970-1971, and at the Royal Court Theatre in 1976. In German, 1976, in West Berlin and Munich, directed by Beckett. In New York, 1977, Roundabout; 1978, BAM. Also 1978 in French at the Comédie Française. In 1980 the French NT of Strasbourg set the play on an urban street corner, made the two tramps a man and his wife, and added a homosexual couple. In London, it was revived by the Young Vic in 1982, to poor notices.

Those who admire *Waiting for Godot* see in it humanity's plight, adrift in a meaningless world. It is a portrait, says the Dramatists Play Service's 1981-1982 *Catalogue*, "of the dogged resilience of man's spirit in the face of little hope." It embodies, says Wallace Fowlie in the 1969 *Reader's Encyclopedia of World Drama,* "Beckett's comment on man's absurd hope and the absurd insignificance of man." Somehow one thinks that it might be more representative of mankind if the lousy tramps, the blind master and the dumb slave, were balanced by at least a glimpse of such humans as, shall I say, deaf Beethoven and blind Milton. Val Gielgud, brother of the actor, expressed the unadulatory view in a letter of July 18, 1971, in answer to a comment of the *London Times* critic: "Mr. Hobson takes exception to the 'fact'—for which, incidentally, he provides no proof—that Sir John Gielgud harmed the contemporary theatre by advising Sir Alec Guinness and Sir Ralph Richardson not to accept engagements in *Waiting for Godot.* It may be news to Mr. Hobson that quite a number of intelligent people, apart from actors of distinction, to this day regard *Waiting for Godot* as a pretentious bore, just as they regard the Theatre of Non-Communication as a contradiction in terms."

In 1966 the Montenegran Miodrag Bulatović (b. 1930) wrote a three-act play, *Godot Has Come.* I saw the world premiere in Dusseldorf, where it won more curtain calls than any of the plays of Ionesco,* which had their premieres at the same theatre. It has been played elsewhere in Europe; but the other characters are the same as in Beckett's play, and although Beckett himself said he didn't care, it has not been produced in America because of the threat of a suit for copyright infringement. It has a more specific, clearer, and more potent story than the Beckett play. Godot has come; he is an itinerant baker. Bread is the physical staff of life; this baker seeks to provide the spiritual staff of life, a thing essential to man's well-being, called peace. He finds the world not ready for him, and leaves, with the promise of a second coming when mankind is mature. The play was shown at the Edinburgh Festival in 1971.

Godot Has Come makes an interesting suggestion, but there is a more promising thought intrinsic in Beckett's play. Asked who Godot is, he replied: "If I knew, I would have told you in the play." Perhaps he winked mentally; but it is the faculty of a genius to be building better than he knew. Remember that Beckett is bilingual. *God* is not a French word, but *ot* (pronounced *oh*) is a French suffix, diminutive, belittling. Look first at *pierre. Pierre* is French for Peter, but it also means *rock.* In the Bible (Matthew; the pun holds in the original Aramaic) Jesus says to Simon: "Thou art Peter, and upon this rock I will build my church." Saint Peter was "petrified" into the Vatican. *Pierrot* means *little Peter,* the pantomime figure linked with Columbine; but it also— *c'est un pierrot*—means *simpleton, a fool—absurd.* Similarly, *Godot* is the diminished hint of God, the inkling of divinity that awaits us all, that in the play is promised for tomorrow. And if tomorrow never comes, by the same token it is always to be: the eternal promise.

> Hope springs eternal in the human breast;
> Man never is, but always to be *blest.*

The Eternal Promise: a fair description of God. Godot comes as a baker— Didi is there as a bum—but it is the Prince of Peace for whose promised return we are waiting. And lousy Gogo and stinking Didi have the same right to the promise as Beethoven deaf, as Milton blind. Even as you and I.

Absurd? There is nothing new in the absurdists. In the early third century Tertullian gave us the thought: *Credo quia absurdum*: I believe because it is absurd. Nonsense? The devout Chesterton declared that those who say "faith is nonsense" may find the thought returning to them in the form that "nonsense is faith." Therefore laugh. God should be welcomed with laughter. Not the cynical, sneering laughter of the world-weary, world-rejecting man, but the bright, shining laughter of the innocent, accepting child. In the face of the future, we are simpletons all. Let us laugh while waiting for God-ot . . . It is perhaps for such intimations that in 1969 Samuel Beckett was awarded the Nobel Prize.

There seems always an extra fillip when a play leaves alternatives for the audience to choose (the Lady or the Tiger?). In *The Guardsman,** did she know all along or only at the last moment? In *Traveler Without Baggage,** did he knowingly reject his true family? This extra stimulation is intensified when the question is more general and more basic: do the apparent absurdity and emptiness of *Waiting for Godot* imply the same of all life? The absurdist plays seem to dance an adagio on the brink of significance; they picture man trying to stand erect on what he hopes is solid earth, beside a great void of meaning. Beckett's play, empty of clear meaning, has challenged many thoughts.

Another, quite different play, but also consisting mainly of waiting, is *The Connection,* 1959, by the American Jack Gelber (b. 1932). A group of hippies in a city pad wait for their drug dealer. The talk is aimless, with increasing anxiety as time stretches; jazz music makes rhythmic counterpart to their words. In Act II, the dealer arrives; we see them each in the toilet getting the dose; the pad owner suffers from an overdose; the curtain falls. Robert Brustein in the *New Republic* (September 28, 1959) stated that Gelber "avoids the overintellectualization of human behavior which informs the work of Beckett, Ionesco* and Genet* . . . the most striking thing about this work is its Spartan honesty." Not Spartan brevity; but a sense that one is looking on at an actual drug scene.

There is, in *The Connection,* no pressure of the social problem of drug addiction. Any question arises outside, apart from, the play. With *Waiting for Godot,* on the contrary, the question is implicit in the play. Hence, although, unlike Atkinson, we are not convinced, we are convicted: we have been made guilty of perplexity, and we are condemned to ponder. The sensitive are likely to find this a restless world, a sobering, if not a fearsome, world, in which we are waiting for God-ot.

LA PARISIENNE   *Henri Becque*

The position of Henri Becque (French, 1837-1899) in French drama is a matter of dispute. Freedley and Reeves in *A History of the Theatre,* 1941, include him among "the names associated with naturalism." However, S. A. Rhodes, in *A History of Modern Drama,* 1947, separates him from the naturalists. Becque himself said: "I have never had a great liking for assassins, hysterical and alcoholic characters, and for those martyrs of heredity and victims of evolution." He is quiet in his effects, slipping in a trenchant phrase quite unobtrusively, reaching his climaxes without hubbub and to-do. At the same time, his plays are constructed without orthodox pattern; and, while they do not slice life through the viscera, they do present, in naturalistic phrasing, "a slice of life." As a pioneer of the new movement in the drama, Becque unquestionably stands clear. His *Les Corbeaux (The Ravens;* translated as *The Vultures)* inaugurated the modern social drama, and his *La Parisienne* is the first of the modern triangle comedies.

The Vultures, 1877, was rejected by seven producers, and its first run, at the Comédie Française in 1882, consisted of three performances before tumultuous audiences. Equally unattractive to producers, but much more favored of the public, was *La Parisienne,* presented at the Renaissance Theatre in 1885. It is famed in France as the outstanding example of *comédie rosse* (gay light comedy masking a bitter irony and cynical realism). *La Parisienne* was again presented at the Comédie Française in 1890 and later by Antoine at the Théâtre Libre, with Réjane. New York saw *La Parisienne* in French in 1904 with Réjane and in 1924 with Mme. Simone. London saw the play, January 29, 1934, and again in 1943, in an English version called *A Woman of This World,* by Ashley Dukes. *La Parisienne* was a great success all over Europe, especially in Italy. The Ashley Dukes version, now called *Parisienne,* was revived in New York for two weeks opening July 24, 1950, with Faye Emerson, Francis Lederer, and Romney Brent, in a sadly dated production.

La Parisienne is not a triangle play in the usual sense. Clotilde Du Mesnil manages her adulterous life with a strict regard for propriety and for the well-being of her quite happy husband. She discards her lover Lafont when the dismissal helps her husband to a better social and financial position and also keeps Clotilde herself from being too readily taken for granted by her lover. Later, when young Simpson is beginning to weary of Clotilde's somewhat demanding ways and carefully preserved charms, she is ready to yield to Lafont's feelings and accept him as lover once more. But all the time, the interests and reputation and happiness of M. Du Mesnil are thoroughly safeguarded.

The brilliant dialogue of Becque calls for a simple naturalness in the performance. There is never any build-up to an effect, yet the impact when it comes seems most natural, springing neatly from the character and the action.

Despite Clotilde's delicious and malicious pleasure in her own adroitness, she is completely at ease only with her husband. With him, the guards are lowered; the battle of the sexes has its truce. They are good friends. To M. Du Mesnil, her friend, if not to M. Du Mesnil, her husband, Clotilde is always loyal. She deceives him as a woman, but remains a clever and competent helpmeet.

La Parisienne has been most favorably reviewed. Desmond McCarthy, after the 1943 London production, with Michael Redgrave as Lafont, declared that the play "can be enjoyed as much by those who do not reflect as by those who do, which is equivalent to saying that it is first-rate comedy." The New York Globe (November 19, 1904) stated: "It moves briskly and surely. It is adroitly dovetailed, yet not a joint is visible. The dialogue has a dry crispness that points its wit with bright suggestion. The insight into character is of the keenest, yet the traits that it discovers are set with the lightest of hands in the clear, dry light of sane, witty, sometimes sardonic, truth." One of the earliest, La Parisienne is also one of the best, of the modern French comedies of sex.

In 1946 Redgrave repeated his performance. In 1950 there was a production at Bucks County, Pa., and an adaptation by Ashley Dukes at the Fulton (New York), repeated OffBway in 1959; in 1954 a more stilted version by Jacques Barzun had also been shown OffBway. Edwige Feuillère brought her French performance of Clotilde from Paris to London in 1957. In 1959 in Berlin the play was set to music by Paul Burkhard with lyrics by Fridolin Tschudi. On August 7, 1981, Geraldine Page presented a version, A Woman of Paris, at Adelphi University. The combination of courtesan and concerned wife in Clotilde keeps La Parisienne engaging.

JACOB'S DREAM   Richard Beer-Hoffmann

Out of the "Young Vienna" group, Richard Beer-Hoffmann (Austrian, 1866-1945) was moved by an intense concern for his Jewish people. His best play, Jacob's Dream, 1918, reconstructs a story from Genesis of the constant trials and holy mission of the Jews. A second play of a projected trilogy, Young David, 1933, shows the testing of the future king of Israel, and continues the mood of exhaltation, and high destiny.

Jacob's Dream pictures Esau, the elder son, selling his birthright, and Jacob by trickery winning his father Isaac's blessing. It continues through Jacob's dream, his wrestling with the angel of the Lord (in the play he wrestles Semal, Satan), his change of name from Jacob to Israel ("prince prevailing with God"), with the prophesy of eternal woe but eternal life.

A highly stylized production of Jacob's Dream was given in New York, January 3, 1927, in a Hebrew version by the Habimah Players. The scenery rose at weird angles; the actors wore grotesque make-up and used extravagant gestures; lurid flashes of lightning broke through inhuman noises echoing from the wings.

The people in the play, especially Esau and his Hittite wives, are rude and primitive; Jacob alone is gentle and pensive, as though the burden of the future were his own. The play, said the Boston Transcript (April 3, 1928), "is the expression of a nation, a scattered, sometimes driven and fugitive nation, but nonetheless a nation very powerful in its leavening influence upon all the nations of the world . . . The satisfaction in wealth of Ahalibama, the lust of power of Basmath [Esau's wives] are overspread with spiritual exaltation and exultation: the race goes on."

There is a power of poetry in *Jacob's Dream,* as well as the almost naïve directness of the medieval Latin church plays. It is, said the *New York Evening World* (January 4, 1927), "as touching as the sincerest of lyric operas and as picturesque as the dream of an imaginative child . . .beautiful lines of the dialogue, with their vigorous simplicity, shedding sidelights on traits that are never-changing fundamentals of human nature . . . the text of the play has the sweep of true genius." Present events have not belied the olden prophecy, of which *Jacob's Dream* is a moving and beautiful reiteration in the drama.

THE QUARE FELLOW   *Brendan Behan*

Brendan Behan (1923-1964) joined the IRA in 1937, and was twice sent to Borstal by the English, in 1939 for three years; in 1942 for fourteen years, of which he served six. (Borstal, a reformatory for "juvenile adults," was established in Rochester, Kent, in 1901; the Borstal system, developed in 1908, is now employed in four other prisons in England.) In 1955 Behan wrote *The Quare Fellow,* which, with his assistance, director Joan Littlewood revised, tightening the structure and "eliminating the sentimental passages." The play was produced at the Stratford East London workshop, May 24, 1956, and moved to the Comedy, July 24.

The play is set in Borstal Prison the night before an execution; the condemned man had killed his brother with an axe. Prisoners and warders are, each in his personal way, tense with expectation. The sentence of Silvertop, who killed his wife, is commuted to life imprisonment; appalled at the prospect, he tries to hang himself in his cell. The daily routine, nonetheless, goes on.

A lad from the Islands finds comfort in talking Gaelic with a warder. Two old lags, Dunlavin and Neighbor, know all the dodges of prison life, including how to bamboozle Healey, the visitor from the charitable society, into promising to take care of them on their release. The young prisoners pass time watching the women hanging out their wash in the women's yard. The hangman, as usual, is not known as such; he is an amiable-looking Englishman whom the locals assume to be some sort of commercial traveler.

The picture is unfolded in a mood of deep compassion, of all-embracing humanity. Harold Hobson in the *Sunday Times* emphasized the sense of ritual that emerges from the play. The dialogue is in a vivid Irish tongue. Behan is preparing a funeral for us, but it is an Irish wake, with not only prayer but laughter and lively drinking: to sing as well as to wail and weep and ponder. "The quare fellow" is Irish slang for the condemned man, whom we do not see.

The play was well received. José Quintero directed it for the Circle in the Square, New York, in 1958. It played in Dublin at the Abbey Theatre, 1956, 1960, 1968; Philadelphia, 1961; Bremen State Theater, 1964; Bristol Old Vic, 1965. Despite the author's statement: "I have a total irreverence for anything connected with society except that which makes the roads safer, the food cheaper, the old men and women warmer in winter, happier in summer," it is clear that he has a warming concern for all of us fellow-sufferers in life.

THE HOSTAGE   *Brendan Behan*

After *The Quare Fellow,* Joan Littlewood coaxed *The Hostage (An Giall)* out of Brendan Behan, and produced it in London in 1958. The *Sunday Times* said the play "seemed to project, in its medley of jokes and songs, some humane sense of the world's injustice." It proved more popular than his earlier play, though it was occasionally banned in the United States and Canada. Among its productions were: Sheridan Square, OffBway, December 12, 1961, for 545 performances; Phoenix, 1964–1965; ELT, 1967, and a national tour the same year; 1969, Philadelphia, Harvard, Asolo, and by ACT in San Francisco. At a 1970 production in Greenwich, England, "the play's humanity and verve seem larger than in Joan Littlewood's production a decade ago." London saw the Littlewood production again in 1972. OffOffBway, 1976; New Haven (Long Wharf), 1983.

The hostage is an eighteen-year-old British soldier, Leslie, who will be executed if the death sentence of an IRA member for killing a British policeman is carried out. He is being held in a brothel run by a mad Englishman turned Irish, which is full of eccentric lodgers and whores, who "brawl, sing, jig, and poke free-for-all fun at life," one patron "skittering about in the nude."

Leslie and the innocent Teresa, just out of a convent school, fall in love. He sings, "There's no place on earth like the world." The two agree, before marriage, to see whether they fit each other. They jump into bed. As the lights dim for them, they spotlight Miss Gilchrist, a gospel-singing social worker—whose innocent song has bawdy overtones. Informed by two of the boarders, the police raid the brothel; the startled Leslie is shot. As Teresa weeps over his corpse, it sits up and sings:

> *The bells of hell go tingaling aling*
> *For you but not for me,*
> *O death where is thy stingaling aling*
> *O grave, thy victory?*
> *If you meet the undertaker*
> *Or the young man from the Pru,*
> *Get a pint of what's left over.*
> *Now I'll say goodbye to you.*

As he falls back, the curtain falls. Without much plot, Brendan Behan has made us deeply and compassionately aware of the sorry lot of many mortals.

THE SECOND MAN   *S. N. Behrman*

There is, in each of us, a second self that observes and appraises all we do. That self, in the play of Samuel Nathaniel Behrman (American, 1893-1973), is the "second man"; a cynical, rather unemotional fellow, with shrugging acceptance of the smoother ways of living.

Clark Storey, a suave but not yet noted novelist, thinks of marrying the wealthy and tolerant widow Mrs. Kendall Frayne. He is besieged, however, by the determined young Monica Grey, whom he calls "a Tennysonian ingenue with a Freudian patter." Monica is so determined to save Clark from a mercenary marriage that she claims he is the father of her unborn child. When the earnest scientist Austin Lowe, who loves Monica, goes gunning for Clark, Monica hastily confesses her lie. Disillusioned in her novelist hero, she opens her heart to Austin, and Clark is freed from financial pressure as he makes the wealthy widow happy.

The Second Man opened in New York on April 11, 1927, with the Lunts and Margalo Gillmore, and ran for 109 performances. Opening in London on January 24, 1928, it had 109 performances there, too. Among revivals: ELT, December 1946; Barter Theatre, Va., September 1978; and twice OffOffBway: by the Joseph Jefferson Theatre, June 1977, and the Soho Rep, January 1980.

"Over the opus," said the *New Yorker,* April 23, 1927, "is set the image of a wise, small Eros grown just a little cross-eyed from the long, rapt contemplation of both Beauty and Bank Accounts." Behrman, said Brooks Atkinson in the *Times,* "is adroit in his anatomizing of human emotions and delightful in his dialogue." Later, the *Times* added: "For pace and hilarity, Behrman's first comedy is still his most successful."

The Second Man is a cynical, scintillating piece. Its shallowness lies not in Behrman's treatment of the story but in the motives of the characters themselves. They are neatly but mercilessly displayed by a fine-grained and polished intelligence, which knows how to evoke our emotion with our laughter.

BRIEF MOMENT   *S. N. Behrman*

In *Brief Moment* S. N. Behrman further exploited his intellectual vein, fashioning a skeleton of plot upon which flesh of sharp dialogue and keen epigram grows. The play affords, as the *Herald-Tribune* remarked, "that rarest of Broadway curiosities, intellectual pleasure for its own sake . . . the fun coming not so much from the exciting things the characters do as from the exciting things they think and say." By presenting several contrasted types in the play, Behrman strikes effectively from every corner.

Several men form a patterned periphery to the charms of the beautiful nightclub star Abby Fane. She turns down the racketeer Manny Walsh and the attractive polo player Cass Worthing to marry a wealthy Park Avenue Hamlet, Roderick Dean. Bored and blasé, Roderick finds in Abby a freshness and vitality unspoiled by the trappings of culture; but in half a year Abby has become all that Roderick hates. Aping the society to which she is unaccustomed, Abby begins a flirtation with Cass. Her Hamlet husband tells her to go off with Cass if she wants to; and it is the racketeer who finally knocks down the polo player Cass. Abby comes to her senses, to recognize that she and Roderick complement each other, and they decide to make a fresh start.

In New York, November 9, 1931, for 129 performances, Alexander Woollcott gave amusing bulk to the role of Roderick's friend Harold Sigrist, who, largely recumbent, from the vantage of a nest of pillows exudes witticisms. Among frequent performances: Robert Garland in 1933 played the obese sybarite Sigrist; Betty Furness played Abby at Westport in 1955. The subtlety of Behrman's intellect and the freshness of his wit shape dialogue that wins interest over and above the story, to give distinction to *Brief Moment.*

NO TIME FOR COMEDY   *S. N. Behrman*

In the World, as it moved toward the year 1939, the slick society that was Behrman's forte seemed to him a vacuous impertinence amid portentous world affairs. Hence he said, "Why not dramatize my own dilemma, write a comedy on the impossibility of writing comedy?" The result is a triangle play with sociological trimmings.

No Time For Comedy is both a comedy and an examination of the comic dramatist in serious times. The author in the play, Gaylord Easterbrook, has written many star comic parts for his wife, Linda. Now, having fallen under the spell of Amanda Smith, a romantic woman who deems herself most understanding, he is urged to fight for immortality and Loyalist Spain. Linda, failing to wean her husband away—his natural sympathy for the underdog combines with Amanda's appeal—as a last resort throws him into Amanda's arms. Philo Smith, Amanda's banker husband, tries to console Linda; but Philo has no feeling for the underdog. Linda, watching her husband pack, is inspired: Why not dramatize their problem? Easterbrook, caught in the spell, thinks it a good idea for a play, but how can they end it? Amanda calls; it is time for her and Easterbrook to leave. He hangs up on her; and that is the ending.

The ending is an effective turn. As Harold Hobson, writing from London, said in the *Christian Science Monitor* (April 19, 1941): "Every artist must sympathize with Gaylord Easterbrook's quandary. The play, therefore, is both topical and serious in theme, though in characters and story it is reminiscent of most of the brittle drawing-room comedies that have been written since Noel Coward* first showed how profitable it is to present worthless people doing worthless things . . . It is evident that the only satisfactory ending to the play can be Easterbrook's recognition of the fact that his essay in the portentous is nothing more than a sham, running clean contrary to the bent of his abilities."

Philo Smith calls his wife "a Lorelei with an intellectual patter"; but it is clear that the two wives embody, if they do not symbolize, two attitudes toward the urgent world. Amanda presses for embattled partisanship: Recognize the right, then fight for it. Linda eases toward the continuance of things that are good: You have a proper job in the world, why let enemies interrupt it? Since Linda holds Easterbrook at the end, reviewer Richard Watts could say (April 23, 1939): "There is no more persuasive advocate of the gospel of urbane liberalism than Mr. S. N. Behrman. His prose style is so graceful, his wit so sprightly, his mind so tolerant and his viewpoint so modest that he becomes the most winning of the drama's counselors . . . The play of his ideas is so mellow and bantering and he is so clearly bent upon saving the gracious amenities of life in a world determined to destroy them—." But Harold Hobson pointed out that Behrman's play but skates the surface of the problem: "The idea that tragedy is a more seriously significant form of art than comedy is a delusion. . . . It is folly to abandon culture when culture is one of the things that make civilization worth while. And I can assure Mr. Behrman that an audience whose individual members have been bombed quite as much as is comfortable did not in the least find his comedy out of place or inappropriate." Easterbrook should continue to write comedy not merely because that's his forte, but because such plays have a worthy place in the world.

No Time for Comedy opened in New York, April 17, 1939, with Laurence Olivier, Margalo Gillmore, and Katharine Cornell in her first modern comedy role. It ran for 185 performances, with 261 more on tour. London saw the play March 27, 1941, with Diana Wynyard and Rex Harrison, for 348 performances. The play's announced background, of the author "profoundly affected" by the tendencies of the times, affected the reviewers. Thus *Time* (May 1, 1939) declared that Behrman "too often makes sex a mere come-on for ideas, none of which he accepts. He is a kind of ideological window-shopper." *No Time for Comedy,* despite the author's preliminary protest, skates over the thin ice of political and social ideas, but plunges with delight into the perfumed pool of sex. The play was revived at Princeton in 1978.

THE HEART OF MARYLAND   *David Belasco*

The shrewd showman David Belasco (American, 1854-1931) capped a sentimental melodrama of the War Between the States with a rousing climax characteristic of the sensational thriller, to create the most popular of the dramas of "the blue and the gray," *The Heart of Maryland.* Opening in Washington, October 9, 1895, and in New York, October 22, with Maurice Barrymore and Mrs. Leslie Carter, the play was showered with superlatives. *The Heart of Maryland,* said the *New York Dispatch* (October 27) "is beyond doubt the most perfect and carefully constructed dramatic work that Mr. Belasco has yet brought forward." The *Sun* called it "the best war play of them all"; and the *Dramatic News* (October 29) considered it "the greatest American play up to this time." The play was revived annually through 1902, and was frequently played throughout the United States until the World War took the theatre from the War Between the States.

The romance runs through a typical Civil War tale of divided families. General Hugh Kendrick is in command of the Confederate forces with headquarters at "the Lilacs," the Maryland home of the Calverts; his son Alan is a Cavalry Colonel of the Union Army. Alan, in love with Maryland Calvert, a loyal Southerner, comes disguised as a Confederate officer in hope of meeting her. Maryland's brother, a true-blue Union man, trying to carry Confederate plans to Alan, is mortally wounded, and sends his sister in his stead. Unwittingly Maryland betrays Alan to Southern Col. Fulton Thorpe, and General Kendrick condemns his captured son to death. The General is killed in battle and Thorpe, now in command, promises to spare Alan if Maryland will sign a statement that she has betrayed the Southern cause; but when Thorpe seeks to embrace her, Maryland stabs him and frees Alan. The dying Thorpe orders the alarm bell sounded, for pursuit of Alan. Maryland dashes up the stairs to the belfry and reaches the bell just in time to catch desperate hold of the moving tongue; she hangs onto it as it swings back and forth, high in the misty night; her hands are bruised and bloodied, but the bell is silenced and her beloved saved.

With dialogue more terse, direct, and simple than was usual with Belasco, *The Heart of Maryland* conveyed a vivid sense of war-torn spirits, on both sides greatly daring for what they deemed the right. "Here was a drama without horses or boisterous guns," Vance Thompson pointed out in the *New York Commercial Advertiser.* "And yet so convincing was it that the characters moved as in the blown smoke of a battlefield . . . An admirable play, absolute in its unity of impression, a synthesis of war . . . a well-made play, at bottom a melodrama, but lit with romance and informed with the subtle realism not of fact but of mood. Nothing of its kind could be better done." The strength and beauty of the play, observed the *New York World* (October 27, 1895), "are not limited to the clearly drawn characters. The minor touches are sure and faithful indications of a keen study of human nature. They give balance and finish to stage pictures of splendid breadth." James Huneker epitomized the praises in the *Morning Advertiser:* "The thrills relieved each other in squads last night. Every war play I have ever seen was here in some form or other . . . but the synthesis was the work of the master hand."

The tremendously rousing climax of *The Heart of Maryland,* as the audience well knew, was suggested by the poem of Rosa Hartwick Thorpe,

Curfew Must Not Ring Tonight, written in 1882 and long a favorite for recitation.

The one adverse criticism the play received appeared in the *Illustrated American* of November 11, 1895: "The introduction of the device is so obviously artificial, its employment is so forced, so patent is it that the play was built around the incident instead of the incident's growing out of the action that, despite its admitted theatric qualities, it loses most of its dramatic effect." Although Charles Frederic Nirdlinger in this review challenged the "ignorant or careless or venal or intimidated criticism that proclaims such a piece . . . to be a master-work," his protest remained a lonely one (though to us his point bears considerable merit); and *The Heart of Maryland,* along with William Gillette's *Secret Service** and Bronson Howard's *Shenandoah,** is one of the best three mixtures of sentiment and melodrama that strove to bring the intertwining conflicts of the Civil War to life upon the stage. Mordecai Gorelik in *New Theatres for Old* (1941) discussed Belasco's "colorful plays produced with meticulous realism . . . Belasco's melodramas had an admixture of sweetness and light in a blend to which, it was likely, he had a unique claim. If any social criticism remained, it was reduced to a whisper."

MADAME BUTTERFLY   *David Belasco*

In January 1898 *Century* magazine published a short story by John Luther Long (1861-1927) entitled "Madame Butterfly." David Belasco received a letter from a stranger, suggesting that he dramatize the story. Belasco read *Madame Butterfly,* discharged his reader for having cast it aside, and in two weeks completed the play.

Madame Butterfly, with Blanche Bates, opened in New York, March 5, 1900; in London, April 28. It was excellently received in both cities. The staging was especially praised; in particular, the lighting of one scene held the audience enthralled through fourteen minutes of silence onstage, as the heroine awaits her love until dark fades to dawn. Giacomo Puccini (Italian, 1858-1924) saw the Belasco play in London and, with Italian book by Illica and Giacosa, fashioned the story into an opera. In two acts, opening February 17, 1904, at La Scala in Milan, the opera was hooted off the stage. The whole of Belasco's play was in Puccini's second act. Puccini added prior details, then made a third act by dropping the curtain for the night watch. In three acts, *Madame Butterfly* was tried again at Brescia, May 28, 1904, and was a success. Opening in Washington, D. C., in October 1906, the opera came to New York, November 12, 1906, and played forty-nine times in seven weeks. Puccini was in New York for the Metropolitan performance of February 11, 1907, with Farrar, Caruso, Scotti, and Homer.

Madame Butterfly tells the story of Cho-Cho-San (Madame Butterfly) and the American naval lieutenant, Pinkerton. Finding himself stationed for some time at Nagasaki, Pinkerton contracts a "Japanese marriage" with Cho-Cho-San, which leaves him free, the broker assures him, whenever he wishes. Cho-Cho-San, however, loves him and, defying the curses of her uncle, an old bonze (native priest), she renounces her religion, to be forever his. (This much is the first act of Puccini's opera; the second act begins three years later—when Belasco's play starts.)

Pinkerton, with his American bride, returns to Japan. He asks the American consul, Sharpless, to break the news to Cho-Cho-San. She has had a baby boy, named Trouble (when her husband returns to her, the child's name is to be changed to Joy) and has refused Japanese offers of marriage, confident that she will be happy when Pinkerton returns. Sharpless is too touched by Cho-Cho-San's joy at word of Pinkerton's return to give her the bitter news. Night comes; the child, then the maid, fall asleep; Cho-Cho-San keeps watch. Next morning, she consents to rest a little, to look her best when Pinkerton comes. He arrives but, on learning of her devotion, leaves while Cho-Cho-San is still asleep. She comes out in time to hear Pinkerton's American wife offer to take care of the child. Grasping the situation, Cho-Cho-San drapes her son in the American flag, and commits hara-kiri.

Belasco's play made a deep impression. "It is rarely," said the *New York Dramatic Mirror* (March 17, 1900) "that theatregoers are privileged to witness so exquisitely artistic a performance . . . the pathetic story is told with unusual artistic skill. There is no pretense of theatricalism, or of unnecessary comedy . . . a gem of the purest water." In London, *The Mail* (April 30, 1900) called *Madame Butterfly* "very weird and strange and beautiful . . . treated in such deliberate and fantastic fashion that the glamour and power of it have an effect of aloofness and strangeness, that mask the real horror of the tragedy; while its pathos and its pitifulness are not lost, it has nothing of brutality . . . one of the most pathetic little plays imaginable."

Belasco, in addition to the imaginative staging, added a few pathetic touches to Long's account, such as Cho-Cho-San's blindfolding of the baby before committing suicide, and having her errant lover return, for her to fall dying into his arms. She kills herself with her father's ceremonial sword, which bears the words: "To die with honor when one cannot live with honor."

Belasco's play was revived, again with Blanche Bates, in 1914, in a benefit performance. It was successful, although by that time it had been largely supplanted by Puccini's opera, which the *New York Sun* (October 20, 1913) called "the most popular opera in America today." *Madame Butterfly* has indeed been widely sung: by Geraldine Farrar; by Grace Moore (also over radio, 1937); by Gladys Swarthout, who also sang in a film version in 1937. The play was first filmed in 1915; and Sylvia Sidney was in a 1932 film. The Japanese Tamaki Misera was famous as Madame Butterfly in the United States, 1915-1930; the opera was played in Japanese in Tokyo, in 1937. It was withdrawn from the repertoire of the New York Metropolitan Opera House after December 7, 1941, until January 1946. Licia Albanese, who made a spectacular debut at the Metropolitan in 1940, as Cho-Cho-San, sang the role for her tenth anniversary with the Metropolitan in 1950.

The music of *Madame Butterfly* flows almost uninterruptedly with Japanese melody. In the first act "Evening is falling," a calm duet of Cho-Cho-San and Pinkerton, grows to the passion of "O Night of rapture!" In the second act the "letter scene" is followed by a delightful "Flower duet" as Cho-Cho-San and Suzuki decorate the house for the returning Pinkerton. The last act opens with a "vigil theme," as Cho-Cho-San waits for the dawn in a scene that marks a high point of the Belasco drama.

Both the opera and the drama have been very well presented, with "the seven veils of cloud-capped Fujiyama and a wealth of picturesque Oriental devices" in what the *London Times* (July 14, 1905) called "a rare and perfect use of local colour." The sentimental plot of *Madame Butterfly* seems to current taste, however, less suited to straight drama than to opera. The music, with its charming sense of the faraway, helps distance not only the story but the emotions involved in it, so that it becomes a touching dream-play, with sadness and beauty intermingled in a story of a love in which the simple faith and dignity of Cho-Cho-San prefer, to the lingering futility of wretched days, the sharp clean stroke of death.

THE BONDS OF INTEREST　　　　　　　　　　　*Jacinto Benavente*

While most of the plays of Jacinto Benavente y Martinez (1866-1954) present, with a skeptical yet tolerant optimism, the society of his native Madrid, the dramas that have won him international recognition are those that turn from the comedy of manners to a more universal, emotional range of the drama. Although most of Benavente's plays, of which there are more than a hundred, are satiric studies of upperclass life in Madrid (his lifelong home), his masterpiece, *The Bonds of Interest*, 1907, is an unlocalized fantasy. As Crispin points out in the Prologue, it is "a little play of puppets, impossible in theme, without any reality at all."

Crispin is the traditional shrewd and trickful servant who devises schemes that seem always to grow more tangled but that carry his master Leander through to triumph at the end. After Crispin's lies establish the credit of himself and the penniless Leander, the two men live in luxury and manoeuvre so that Leander may win the purse of Silvia, daughter of the wealthy but suspicious and niggardly Polichinelle. With the help of the imposing, though impoverished, Dona Sirena and her maid Columbine, the match is well advanced.

Two obstacles, however, arise: Leander falls in love with Silvia, and his creditors storm him. Unwilling to deceive the maiden he loves, Leander tells her of his true state. Meanwhile Crispin points out to the creditors that the only way they can be paid is for Leander to marry Silvia. They turn upon Polichinelle and—they will be paid. Crispin leaves the happy pair, with a warning to Leander that "the bonds of love are as nothing to the bonds of interest."

What lifts the *Bonds of Interest* beyond the banality of a retold puppet-story is its combination of kindliness and keen, satiric observation. The play, said Brooks Atkinson (October 15, 1929) "is commedia dell' arte in spirit, but it is also the work of the sardonic, pointed Jacinto Benavente." The figures, named as puppets, have human traits; Benavente implacably notes and exposes their frailties. He shows both the good and the bad side of his characters; let him who lacks the latter stand as judge.

The Bonds of Interest was presented in New York in 1919 as the first play of the newly organized Theatre Guild, with Helen Westley, Dudley Digges, and Augustin Duncan. In 1929 it was revived by Walter Hampden; it has intermittently found favor among amateurs.

Rivaling *The Bonds of Interest*, in the minds of some critics, is Benavente's *The Evil Doers of Good*, 1905, which, by satirizing the complacent, super-ficial, smugly parading good folk, defends the ideal of moral tolerance. These two plays, with *The Passion Flower*,* were instrumental in establishing Benavente's reputation outside of Spain. He was awarded the Nobel Prize in 1922.

The translator of *The Bonds of Interest*, John Garrett Underhill, observed that "the comedy is so deft and so facile that it is easy to pass its significance by. What the playwright sets out to say is that every man has within him two irreconcilable selves, the good and the bad, the generous and the base, the Dr. Jekyll and Mr. Hyde." This thought is coated, in *The Bonds of Interest*, with smiling comedy and playful romance; through a puppet foreground, it gives a view of the underlying traits of human nature.

The play was revived OffBway in 1958, with Peter Falk as Crispin. It was produced in New York in 1961 by Circle in the Square, and in Spanish at Columbia University in 1964.

At the close of the play, Silvia addresses the audience: "You have seen how these puppets have been moved by plain and obvious strings, like men and women in the farces of our lives—strings that were their interests, their passions, and all the illusions and petty miseries of their states . . . But into the hearts of all, there descends sometimes from heaven the invisible thread of love, which makes these men and women almost divine . . . and whispers to us still that this farce is not entirely a farce, that there is something noble, something in our lives that is true and that is eternal, and that shall not close when the farce of life shall close."

THE PASSION FLOWER   *Jacinto Benavente*

Apart from the general tone and type of Benavente's plays, *La Malquerida* (translated as *The Passion Flower*) brought him international repute and with *The Bonds of Interest** helped win him the Nobel Prize in 1922.

The Passion Flower, in a superb Castillian atmosphere, is a gripping tragedy of peasant life, of the proud Spanish folk whose passions are a religion, quite as their religion is a passion with them. In the play, the widow Raimunda has remarried, but her daughter Acacia never calls Esteban "Father." Acacia breaks off her engagement with Norbert, and on the eve of her marriage to Faustino, Faustino is killed. A smouldering sense of guilt flashes into flame when Acacia, bidden to embrace Esteban as a father, finds herself held in his arms as a lover. Acacia's servant Rugio, who killed Faustino, frees Norbert from suspicion of the crime, by talking in his cups. Raimunda then accuses her husband of helping Acacia in the murder; arrested, he shoots his wife, bringing death to the only one in the family guiltless in thought and deed.

Written in 1913, *The Passion Flower* became a success all over Europe. It opened in New York, with Nance O'Neil, on January 13, 1920, and ran for 144 performances. Miss O'Neil and Leslie Banks acted in it in London in 1926. The play is a deeply moving picture of suppressed desires; at first unrecognized, love masquerades as hate, then boils fiercely as will battles emotion, until the passions explode to wreck the family. Two well-meaning persons and an innocent one are drowned in passion's flood.

The melodramatic aspects of this story are subdued by the simplicity of its setting and the restraint of its presentation. As the *Boston Transcript* stated (October 10, 1921), the story "unfolds gradually but inevitably, as solid tragedy must do . . . Since Benavente has brought to it so many ripened qualities of mind it must hold for many a day a high place in modern drama." Engrossing, carrying the audience somberly in its sway, *The Passion Flower* has a blood-red beauty in its grim revelation of tortured souls.

INVITATION TO THE VOYAGE   *Jean-Jacques Bernard*

Jean-Jacques Bernard (1888-1972) is the son of Tristan Bernard, French author of many light comedies. Early in his career he turned from the usual modes of drama to create what has been called "the theatre of silence." He seeks, said Thomas H. Dickinson in *Continental Plays* (1935) "to give voice to the unspoken, to dramatize the intangible overtones of experience." Perhaps it would be more accurate to call his "the theatre of reticence." For, as *Le Théâtre* (March 2, 1924) pointed out, "in actual life one keeps intimate concerns within oneself, talks of daily banalities, reveals moods and feelings by imponderables—an intonation, a gesture, a pause. Thus his characters reveal their preoccupations while speaking of other things. A subtle art, in which the smallest detail takes on a suggestive value."

In the *London Observer* (January 12, 1930) Harold Hobson described Bernard's approach: "Into the full-throated theatre of France, with its resonant past and its grand tradition of virtuosity in declamation, comes M. Bernard, as quiet as a mouse. It is a pensive mouse that strays into that historic cage of lions, a mouse with an ear for all the whisperings of the troubled spirit and with a mind to ponder them before the hand recreates them in his own terms of muted scene and dim suggestion . . . There is uncanny cleverness in his ability to reveal the seething tumult of suppressed eruption by showing only the tremors on the surface-soil."

Some critics feel that Bernard's best play is *Martine,* 1922, a sensitive study of a country girl enticed by a city charmer. However, his most widely popular play, and the one that most fully exhibits his rare and sensitive touch, is *Invitation to the Voyage.*

Invitation to the Voyage—the title is that of a poem by Baudelaire—opened in Paris, February 15, 1924, in five scenes, and was revived there in four scenes, October 17, 1926. It was translated as *Glamour* in 1927, and played in London in 1930 as *Illusion.* In New York, it was played, as *L'Invitation au Voyage,* by Eva Le Gallienne, October 4, 1928. London saw it again, under its French title, in 1937 and 1948. Though its delicacy and subtlety make it difficult to present, *Invitation to the Voyage* is a delightful and touching, and widely played picture of a woman waking from a wistful dream.

The action, if it can be called such, involves the family of Olivier Mailly, well-to-do manufacturer of hobnails, in the Vosges. Into the Mailly home comes Philippe Valbeille, to spend a few days at the factory before setting off for the Argentine. We do not see Philippe at all, throughout the play. Offstage, he plays tennis with Olivier's daughter Jacqueline, he gives Olivier's wife Marie-Louise a volume of Baudelaire's poems, and he departs. For two years, Marie-Louise is in love with the idea of distant places, and the man that has gone there. When he returns, she has dinner with him. His conversation is more banal, more filled with financial figures and industrial concerns, than her husband's, and Marie-Louise hurries thankfully back to her husband and home.

The deftness of the drama was well described by the *London Times* (February 4, 1947): "This piece not only dispenses with a hero, but for story dares to give us no more than the tracing of a day-dream inspired in the mind of an ineffectual woman by a perfectly commonplace young man whom we are never permitted to see. Marie-Louise has all the domestic blessings—a pleasant house in delightful country, an affectionate husband, a charming child; but real people and real things have never been a part of her inner life. It is the departure of Philippe for Argentina which suddenly invests his figure with the strangeness and beauty of lands unvisited, and during the two years of his stay abroad he is the most wonderful thing that has ever happened to Marie-Louise. But he returns, she goes to meet him, and instantly recognizes the commonplace creature who utterly failed to solicit her imagination when he lived in her house. With dialogue exquisitely apt for the purpose, brilliantly glancing and never explicit, the author chronicles the progress of this romantic illusion. He shows how its ending influences the woman's attitude to those about her. We may suspect that the change is but temporary and that the same kind of romance will soon come to her again, but she has served to make exciting drama of a day dream and to give the life of an introvert palpitating theatrical reality."

The portrayal of the husband matches in sensitivity that of the wife. He is the more intelligent. Indeed, according to *Stage* (April 22, 1948), "if her husband had beaten her, betrayed her, or been anything but understanding and kind, the whole thing would never have happened." Or, once it had begun, only his patience could have helped it to this end. For three of the play's five scenes, there is no mention of Marie-Louise's love for Philippe. Yet the birth of love and the longing it inspires, the almost fevered eagerness and the agony that grow with it, are subtly conveyed. Olivier divines his wife's love, and he, too, follows its course, with gathering jealousy and anxiety—all without an explicit word between them. Nor is any confession needed for Marie-Louise's repentance and Olivier's pardon. Understanding and faith of husband and wife have been enriched. And it is unlikely that Marie-Louise will slip from Olivier again, for she has had her voyage.

The characters in *Invitation to the Voyage* are natural, well-rounded, finely drawn human beings. Although the play is, as the *New York American* (October 5, 1928) said, "utterly devoid of action, as the regular playgoer comes to know it, *L'Invitation au Voyage* carries and sustains, once it swings into rhythm, a suspense that relaxes only with the final curtain. . . . It is drama that is poignant and real and that dominates its audience until the final denouement." It is a rich, rare, sensitive dramatic capture of a wish-fantasy; by its unveiling of the inexpressive, it has widened the resources of the theatre.

Bernard neatly brings Marie's thoughts home through music. At the play's opening Marie-Louise is at the piano, playing a Chopin nocturne. While Philippe is away, and she dreams of him, she plays Dupare's music to Baudelaire's poem "Invitation to the Voyage." At the play's close, she sits down and plays the Chopin nocturne as the curtain slowly falls.

MARTINE   *Jean-Jacques Bernard*

On a shady bank beneath an apple tree, Julien comes upon Martine, a farmer's girl in the little French village of Grandchin. They talk, and love sparks them. He's back from the war, and on his way to his grandmother, Mme. Vervan—who has invited his fiancée, Jeanne, for a few days. To Martine Julien says:

> *I'll wield the sickle, and the curving scythe,*
> *And grass or corn that falls beneath my stroke*
> *Shall in the day of harvest fill your barn.*

She asks what that is; it's from the poet Chenier: "I must teach you to love those things. No one ever has. It's not your fault." But when Jeanne and Julien look upon the same field, and he starts to quote, Jeanne picks up the words after him, and goes on. Jeanne and Julien marry. Jeanne is very friendly with Martine, who manages to hide her love. The perceptive Mme. Vervan tells Martine she must marry Alfred, who loves her, and arranges the match. The grandmother dies; the couple sell the house and move away. He's a journalist in Paris; they go out of Martine's life.

Martine opened at the Paris Théâtre des Mathurins, May 9, 1922; in translation by John Leslie Frith, at the London Gate, December 4, 1929, and the Ambassador's, May 22, 1933. It was played at the New School (New York) in 1934; in Boston, March 27, 1940; at the Hedgerow, Pa., 1944; and at the Club OffOffBway in February 1958.

The play won unanimous critical praise. The *London Era,* December 11, 1929: "Only a great dramatist could have left so vivid, so poignant an impression of the inarticulate girl and given her so little to say . . . One knows that she will go on feeding the animals, bearing Alfred's children, and living each year for All Soul's Day, the day she will remember." James Agate added: "The author has something to say, and says it with extraordinary delicacy, point, and finish . . . not a play for the vulgar, who will see nothing in it, but for the connoisseur of craftsmanship." A tender, touching play.

THE STRONGER SEX   *Tristan Bernard*

The story of the ironically entitled *The Stronger Sex,* by Tristan Bernard, father of Jean-Jacques, centers upon George Soubre, middle-aged and wealthy, living happily with his wife, Bertha. Their daughter has a governess, Clara. Chavarus, a wealthy friend of George's, tells him there's been gossip about his "affair" with the governess. George laughs, but feels it his duty to inform Clara—and the affair starts. She grows more clinging and bossy. Her new employer is an architect, going to Biarritz for the summer. On Clara's plaint, George cancels his summer plans, and rents a place at Biarritz. Then the architect's firm changes plans; they are going to Dinard. Chavarus tell his troubled friend George he must break it off; *he* will speak to Clara. He does; she weeps; and Chavarus goes off with Bertha, leaving George to adjust his mistress and his family.

The play opened at the Théâtre de Gymnase, April 12, 1917; again on January 12, 1927, and April 20, 1932, with Signoret playing George in all three productions. Bernard had originally called the play *La Volonté de l'homme (Man's Will),* but changed it to *Le Sexe Forte* as a "spiritual reply" to Edouard Bourdet's *Le Sex Faible,* then playing.

The Strong(er) Sex is an ironic picture of how events may sweep a man from his intentions. The French critic François Porche has marked Tristan Bernard's place in the theatre: "He is a French classic . . . His observation of mankind radiates around a central idea. His men are full of good will, but what we thus label has no bearing on the actual *will.* They ask nothing better than to behave well, but, that's it! they do not. They are not bad, but weak. His theatre, like the earth, is peopled with folks who do not fully understand why things happen to them, or rather, how they could have done what nevertheless they have done. It is peopled also—as the world, yes, yes, America included—with timid folk. Soubre, you may say, is a fool (*niais*). Not at all. He's quite intelligent. Almost as much as you, dear reader. Check the text, and you'll see how he is *fin, nuancé,* how well he reasons, how well he speaks!"

Thus Bernard deftly displays how one thing leads to another, and step by step we walk an unintended way.

THE THIEF   *Henry Bernstein*

The "brutal drama" has no more powerful playwright than Henry Bernstein (French, 1876-1953). Accomplished architect of dramatic situations, he tightens the passions in the angry snarl that summons a scène à faire, then raises the emotions to such a storm that the spectators are tied to their seats by an inner intensity. Usually, there is the strewn wreckage of the storm in the calm of the final scene. In *The Thief,* as Jean Toulet is quoted by S. A.

Rhodes, in *A History of Modern Drama* (1947), Bernstein "dissects the human heart with a kitchen knife."

The plot of *The Thief,* 1906, is novel, neat, and gripping. A young couple, Richard and Marie-Louise Voysin, are guests at the Lagardes' chateau. Twenty thousand francs are stolen. The detective names the nineteen-year-old Fernand Lagardes, who, admitting his guilt, is ordered by his father to Brazil. But Richard finds 6,000 francs in his wife's letter-case. Also aware that her undergarments are of choicest quality, he accuses her of the theft. Relentlessly he beats upon her, until she confesses that she has been stealing to buy pretty things with which to hold his love. Richard's mind now whips to a jealous fury: Why did Fernand confess? The boy, in love with Marie-Louise, was shielding her. Marie convinces Richard that this was but the boy's infatuation. She confesses her theft to the Lagardes, and the young couple, instead of Fernand, leaves France for Brazil.

The intensity of these situations is hard to convey off the stage. The second act takes place in the Voysins' room, with but the two there. Subtly the husband's suspicions are gathered, swiftly they are roused, ruthlessly he questions, and superbly the wife rallies in her own defense. *The Thief* holds a warning, said Dorothy Dix, when the *New York Journal* published the play (February 1908), "a warning for every foolish husband who admires good clothes on other women, but doesn't put them on his own wife." Bernstein, according to the *New York Sun* (October 20, 1907), "is more than masterful and direct. He is vehement with a well-nigh irresistible vehemence." He can write, the *Boston Transcript* concurred (October 13, 1908), "an eminently dramatic narrative and then fling it across the footlights with such vigor and speed that the spectator who would hold judicially aloof is caught willy-nilly into it . . . Pace, power and mechanism are no less the qualities of his plays than they are of a Mercedes or a Fiat . . . He could hold his audience impaled on an interrogation point, like an excited butterfly on a pin, whenever he would." So highly wrought were the players themselves that during the 1907 New York run of *The Thief,* during its tremendous second act, Daniel Frohman used to signal from his studio over the Lyceum Theatre stage, when his wife Margaret Illington grew overemotional, playing Marie-Louise to Kyrle Bellew's Richard.

While Bernstein is ever ready to display power, he can also command subtlety. After his wife's confession, Richard calls Fernand over, intending to scold the boy. The shamefaced but plucky Fernand comes, and Richard bids him: "Say goodbye to her." Marie-Louise ends her talk with Fernand: "Goodbye, my friend, my brother."

The Thief was a great success in Paris. It opened in New York, October 19, 1907, for a run of 281 performances. It was, the *London Mirror* (January 8, 1908) said, "the most discussed play in London," where it opened November 21, 1907, with Irene Vanbrugh, and ran for 186 performances. The English version calls the couple Mr. and Mrs. Richard Chelford; the boy, Harry. Alice Brady and Lionel Atwill played *The Thief* in New York for 83 performances, opening April 22, 1927.

The action of the play takes place within twenty-four hours. The theft has already occurred when the curtain goes up; we watch only the crisis, which bludgeons our sensibilities, as with a swift surge of passion *The Thief* makes drama out of situations that drive uncomfortably home. The characters are not deeply probed, but they are truly seen; the story is plausible, straightforward, and pile-driver strong.

JUDITH   *Henry Bernstein*

The *Book of Judith* has provided the story of many plays. It remains the finest and most astonishingly vivid and convincing in all that wonderful story-budget known as the *Apocrypha*.

"The mountains shall be drunk with blood, and I will fill their fields with the dead," said Nabuchodnosor. And the Assyrians come down like a wolf on the fold; their huge army of more than 170,000 footmen sweep across helpless lands until they are stopped by the hardy little hill tribe of Israelites at the town of Bethulia. Seizing the springs at the bottom of the hills, the invaders sit, carefree, confident, to starve out the defenders. With the threat of drought and starvation, however, the beautiful widow Judith doffs her mourning, bedecks herself, and descends with her handmaid to the enemy camp. There she rouses the lust of the Assyrian leader, Holofernes. Getting him drunk, with his own falchion she hacks off his head, and carries it back in triumph, to the glory of her people and her God.

Among the plays based on this story are versions by Lorenzo Giudetti (Italian, 1621); Johann Gottfried Gregori (in German, for the Russian Czar Alexis, 1674); Christian Friedrich Hebbel (German, 1839); Gedaliah Belloi (Yiddish, 1870); Thomas Bailey Aldrich (American, *Judith of Bethuliah,* 1907); T. Sturge Moore (English, 1911); Anton H. Tommsarre (Estonian, 1921); Henry Bernstein (French, 1922); Emil Nikolaus Reznicek (Czech, *Holfornes,* 1923); René Morax (French Swiss, 1925; as an opera with music by Honegger, 1926); and Jean Giraudoux (French, 1936).

The earliest versions merely dramatized the biblical story. Hebbel, however, whose drama is largely a succession of lively pictures, offered a complicated psychological study of Judith. Having heard of the sexual prowess of Holofernes, Judith, teased and tempted, persuades herself that she can save her people by testing it. In Holofernes' tent, she recognizes that her motives are personal, not heroic; and she kills Holofernes because her integrity is besmirched. A counterpart to this explanation of Judith's motives was planned for a drama, never written, by the Russian Chekhov,* who saw Judith as going forth to kill Holofernes, then falling in love with him.

The opera of Morax, presented at Monte Carlo, February 13, 1926, with Mary Garden in Chicago, January 27, 1927, by action and music, according to the *Boston Transcript* (February 5, 1927) stressed "the brutish savagery of the animal who, straining the woman to his breast, assures her at the same moment of his inflexible determination to deliver her city to the flames and put her people to the sword." Yet it showed Judith unhappy at the end: "I yield my life to God, so that I may forget." Still another interpretation of Judith's conduct came from Giraudoux; in his play, Judith finds Holofernes a charming and accomplished man; she freely becomes his mistress, finally killing him because she refuses to be no more than a passing fancy in his life. Closest to the Bible, of recent versions, Moore's *Judith,* acted by Lillah McCarthy in London, 1916, showed the widow's reluctance to kill, her horror at the task she somehow was inspired to undertake, and her final desperate deed rising as much from frenzy at her ritual defilement as from a driving patriotism.

Most powerfully dramatic of all versions is the *Judith* of Henry Bernstein. Staged by Antoine, with sets by Soudekine and costumes by Leon Bakst and with the role of Judith acted by Mme. Simone, *Judith* at its Paris premiere, October 11, 1922, offered tense drama and a superb spectacle of Oriental lavishness and lust. Bernstein's version depicts Judith as a naturally frigid woman. Surprising her lustful maid Ada in the arms of a man, Judith questions her with excited curiosity, recognizing that she herself has never known passion. In roused curiosity and a mingling of hope and patriotism, she approaches Holofernes. He divines her purpose; but they both fall in love. Holofernes offers Judith his sword; she offers him her self. In revulsion, next morning, she slays the man. Back in Bethulia, Judith realizes that she has been truly smitten with love. She goes forth to the mountain where Holofernes' head is spiked, and—while at her feet an enamoured captain of her people kills himself for vain desire—Judith mourns the lover and foe whom she has slain.

Bernstein's treatment of the Judith story is, as the *New York Clipper* (November 8, 1922) remarked, "more symbolical and philosophical than usual with him, but he still has the splendidly gripping themes that have helped to make his fame." Robert de Flers, reporting from Paris in the *Boston Transcript* (December 2, 1922) observed that Bernstein's Judith "appears so vivid that for a time we take her as one of our contemporaries." Of the vivid scene in which Holofernes senses Judith's intent and she fears torture, Flers said: "This tremendous scene, profound in its sudden shifts, its voluptuous premonitions, its violent theatrics, making a life-like bit of psychological research applied to two souls reacting upon each other, is a masterpiece."

Bernstein's *Judith* is not only a vivid historical drama but also a living portrait of a complex, intense, magnificent woman.

THE BARRETTS OF WIMPOLE STREET   *Rudolf Besier*

One of the most famous of romances, the wooing of Elizabeth Barrett by the young Robert Browning, is the subject of *The Barretts of Wimpole Street,* by Rudolf Besier (English, 1878-1942). The play discloses the cloistered, almost imprisoned life of the Barretts, while Browning shakes the bars to free Elizabeth from the influence of a sadistic father. Before Browning's coming, her one friend had been her dog, Flush. There is little plot to the play, but it includes the first visit of the famous poet with his invalid admirer, the expression of their love, and the gathering strength and resolution of Elizabeth to marry Browning and flee her dusk-held domicile. Around the lovers, the other Barretts chafe and brood.

The play is written with a rich sense of human integrity that well befits its subject. It has, as John Mason Brown said (February 10, 1931), "a dignity that in no way detracts from the quality of one of the great romances in English literature, even if it does not succeed in capturing its full fine, frenzied nature. It gains immeasurably, too, in both its character and style, from the skillful and frequent use that Mr. Besier has made of actual lines from those almost daily letters that passed between Browning and Elizabeth Barrett when she was still an invalid—and a prisoner—under her warped father's domination at 50 Wimpole Street."

The father, indeed, is the most considerable figure in the drama. Thus, the *New York World* (February 10, 1931) called the play "a curious mixture of charming recapture of the love of two famous poets and of the kind of deep-dyed, all-wool hiss-the-villain melodrama that one expects in plays about cruel sex-starved, half-incestuous old farmers in the backwoods of New England. It is a father and daughter play, a study of fantastic parental tyranny and jealousy, with Robert Browning almost incidental, an impetuous, spirited, human, and normal figure who rushes in to make mad love to a lady he has barely seen." The *New York Herald-Tribune* attempted to belittle the plot: "It is a story based on the eternal verities of the triangle composed of the wicked Dragon, the gallant Knight, and the beautiful Lady in distress." But the story is really more complex, as the *Outlook* (February 25, 1931) observed: "Along with considerable brains and a dominating personality, the father, Edward Moulton-Barrett, is distinguished by hypocrisy and marked incestuous tendencies. He bullies or makes thinly veiled love to the members of his family."

Perhaps the grisly nature of Mr. Barrett discouraged American producers. *The Barretts of Wimpole Street* had its premiere at the Malvern Festival, August 18, 1930, and opened in London, September 23, for a run of 529 performances. Yet in the United States, twenty-seven managers or stars rejected it before Katharine Cornell made it her first venture as actress-manager. It opened in New York, February 9, 1931, for 370 performances. On tour, a storm and flood blocked the company's way to Seattle, Washington, on Christmas Eve, 1933; the audience waited, and at 4 a.m. stood and cheered the troupe for a great performance. During World War II, *The Barretts of Wimpole Street* was shown to many appreciative G.I's in the European theatre of military operations. In 1945 Margalo Gillmore and Patricia Collinge wrote a book—the title was the same as that of the play—telling the story of the G.I. tour. The play has also been produced in Copenhagen, Stockholm, Oslo, Vienna, Budapest, and Australia.

The Barretts of Wimpole Street was Katharine Cornell's greatest success. She revived it in New York with Brian Aherne, March 26, 1945. A modernized musical, *The Barretts and Mr. Browning,* book and lyrics by Ronald Miller, music by Ron Grainer, was briefly tried in London, October 1964.

In Besier's play, when Edward Barrett is handed Elizabeth's farewell letter by her sister Henrietta (whose courtship by Captain Cook Barrett had vainly tried to prevent), he turns to one of his sons: "Octavius, her dog must be destroyed at once." Henrietta tries vainly to control the triumph in her voice as she turns to Barrett and says: "In her letter to me, Ba writes she has taken Flush with her." The dog, a cocker spaniel, appeared faithfully in every performance of the play.

THE BURNT FLOWER-BED   *Ugo Betti*

Ugo Betti (1892-1953), a judge in the Italian high court, wrote thirteen plays from 1941 to 1953, picturing man's fatal disregard of God, but of sinners redeemed—often as they are dying—after an anguished existential search for identity and responsibility. His plays may be seen as a democratic balance to the work of the Communist Dario Fo.* Thus, in *Corruption in the Palace of Justice,* 1949, the President of the Court, the Chief Justice, and Judge Cust, nominated to succeed the President, all in turn confess their relations with the notorious racketeer whose suicide is being investigated. Best-known of Betti's plays is *L'Aiulo bruciata (The Burnt Flower-Bed),* 1953, directed by Peter Hall at the London Arts Theatre, September 9, 1955.

Giovanni, deposed leader of the recent revolution, is visited in his mountain retreat near the border by a committee, which includes Nicola, who has succeeded him but is now weak and ill. They tell him he must lead the group to meet the committee from the other side of the border, to arrange peace. Nicola dies, after revealing to his nurse Rosa that her father had been killed by his own countrymen to create an incident, and that it is their intention now to do the same with Giovanni. Learning this, Giovanni tells them that his fifteen-year-old son's suicide (by leaping from a window into the flower bed below) had been in despair at a world they had made into a "blighted flower-bed." The conspirators Tomaso and Raniero admit to having killed Nicola; but they tell Giovanni he has no alternative.

Dawn comes; it is time to meet the committee. Rosa protests: "I don't believe people want to kill. They are in a dream . . . All that is needed is to warn them, to wake them." She goes to the door—and takes the shots intended for Giovanni. With Rosa in his arms, Giovanni, now followed quietly by the others, goes out to meet the committee. Perhaps there will be peace.

The Burnt Flower-Bed was tried out by the Theatre Guild in Westport, Conn., in 1960, with Eric Portman and Signe Hasso, but withdrawn. In a new adaptation by Henry Denker, with Claude Rains, it came to New York in 1963, toured the United States through 1965, and came back to New York (as *The Burned Flower-Bed*) in 1967, with Claude Rains and Leueen MacGrath. It was shown in Ann Arbor, Mich., in 1968; at New York's Roundabout, July 2, 1974, for forty-eight performances, with Paul Sparer and Jane White; in 1980 in Teaneck, N.J., and again in New York. Among Betti's twenty-seven plays, ranging through naturalism, symbolism, expressionism, and farce, *The Burnt Flower-Bed* is the most vivid and searching picture of the distorted and violent search for peace. The playwright's basic quest, however, is caught in the final word of his 1935 *Landslide at North Station,* as the courtroom spectators gradually recognize their own greed and guilt, and the judge states that the world's great need is for "compassion."

DAME NATURE   *André Birabeau*

At once searching and tender, smiling and serious, Birabeau's drama of adolescent love, *Dame Nature,* is, as *L'Illustration* (February 22, 1936) suggested, when the play was produced at the Theatre de l'Oeuvre (February 13), "as if Daphnis and Chloë, as if Paul and Virginia had had a child."

The story is simple, but novel. Leonie Perrot, left to her own resources at fifteen, runs a little stationery shop near the school where Paul, about the same age, is a pupil. Paul's parents make home a hell for him. Despising one another, they live together "for the child's sake." Unwittingly, they neglect and mistreat him, for he is the symbol of their bondage. Paul and Leonie console one another. When they learn that they are to have a child, they are bewildered, but Paul accepts his responsibilities with adult and loving earnestness. The parents, at first, are aghast. But, as Arthur Pollock remarked (October 4, 1938), the urgency "teaches the children a great deal, and they are happy. It teaches the parents even more, and they are happy too."

The play moves constantly through touching, ironic, or amusing situations. The doctor who tells Leonie she is to have a child insists on seeing the prospective father; from the anteroom comes an anxious, bewildered boy of fourteen! The wondering reaction of the children to the phenomenon of childbirth moves to a gathering of resolve and resources for the emergency. There is a poignant scene in which, absorbed in a miniature shooting gallery, Paul suddenly remembers his beloved Leonie's state.

Paul's mother is a vain woman. Wishing to be thought still young, she keeps Paul in short pants; he's just too big for them. There is a ridiculous, at once absurd and poignant, children's Christmas party, at which Paul is manipulating a Punch-and-Judy show for his playmates when a friend brings word that he's a father.

Things happen to Paul's parents, too. When the mother, on a first indignant impulse, goes to see Leonie, she thinks the girl is having an affair with her husband. Aghast at the truth, she turns to her husband. The discovery of the spiritual innocence of Leonie and Paul reawakens the decency of the older couple. Watching Paul help Leonie in the store, they surreptitiously slip money into the cash register—and love slips back into their hearts.

With Gallic wit and Gallic delicacy, Birabeau keeps the tender sentiments from growing sentimental. Granted the situation, he unfolds its consequences with psychological insight and truth. "He handles most ingeniously," said *L'Illustration* (February 22, 1936) "the shiftings of this comedy that might easily have become a problem play and that remains from beginning to end freshly innocent, when it might easily have become scabrous."

Dame Nature, in an adaptation by Patricia Collinge, was produced at Westport, Connecticut, in the summer of 1938, with great success. It was then brought to New York, September 26, 1938, by the Theatre Guild, with Lois Hall and Montgomery Clift as the children, Jessie Royce Landis and Onslow Stevens as the parents. Arthur Pollock called the play "all tenderness." The *New York World-Telegram* headed its review (September 27): "Poignant moments and humor mingle." The general New York reception was, however, but half-hearted; the adaptation dragged in the second act, and the brightness, lightness, good taste, and delicacy of the original were, as John Mason Brown moderately phrased it, "rendered into wooden English." In the original, *Dame Nature* is superbly entertaining; and in the picture it gives of spiritual awakening in a crisis, it is exalting, too.

PAMPELMOUSSE   *André Birabeau*

The rash of ardent American plays on racial prejudice, especially on discrimination against the Negro, gives piquancy to Birabeau's deft handling of the subject, in *Pampelmousse.* He presents the problem as it arises among children; and there is delight in watching the honesty and the directness with which the children face the issues, as contrasted with the roundabout, shame-faced evasions or downright prejudices of their elders. A pampelmousse (small grapefruit), explains the author, resembles "a slightly bitter orange or a somewhat sweet lemon, and my play has at once that bitterness and that sweet."

The setting for the theme is ingenious. In a small French town, where slander is quick-tongued, the engineer Guillaume Monfavet is taken seriously ill. His wife discovers that Monfavet has been supporting an illegitimate son. She feels it her duty to send for the boy, so that he can say his last farewells to his father. Her brother brings the boy. Monfavet recovers, but the eight-year-old child is there. A black, the child was born to Monfavet during his three years' work, away from his family, in the Congo.

Noel, or Pampelmousse, as they call the black child, becomes a problem. The legitimate children are at once shocked and delighted. The two mothers-in-law of the Monfavets are horrified. The neighbors buzz, intrigued. The boy himself is a superb study in hurt pride, grim resolution, hatred breaking down before good treatment, and growing normal understanding and love. Jean Pierre (age 16), Catherine, and younger Patrick Monfavet decide to vote whether to accept Pampelmousse as a brother. As they hesitate, he asks whether he may vote, too; when they say yes, he votes No! Whereupon, at once and unanimously, they overrule him and take him in.

The children grow fond of Noel. When the question of sending him back to school arises, they work on their paternal grandmother until she consents to keep the child. Then a neighbor comes in, and it becomes clear to the Monfavets that the town gossips, having seen Mme. Monfavet's bachelor brother bring the child, have decided that Noel is the result of a bachelor indiscretion. The elders jump at this way out of the scandal, and the children are just as happy, for Noel will be a neighbor, even though living with their paternal grandmother.

When *Pampelmousse* was first produced in Paris, 1937, a few papers cried scandal. The French Colonial Minister went to see the play, and praised it. So did most of the press, to judge by excerpts appearing in *La Petite Illustration,* July 31, 1937. *La Republique* held that Birabeau "marvelously understands the language of youth." *Correspondence Havas* reported that the play "brings to the surface troubled aspects of the human soul." *L'Ami du peuple* summed up the play's double power: "It is not only a gay comedy, one of the most irresistibly amusing, rich in laugh-compelling comments and insinuations that we have seen in a long time; it is also a comedy in which, suddenly and effortlessly, the tone elevates, and deep feeling springs, as easily as the humor, from the comic situation."

The American adaptation of *Pampelmousse* did scant justice to the subtlety and poignancy of the play. As *Little Dark Horse,* with Cecilia (Cissy) Loftus, Lily Cahill, and Walter Slezak, after a summer tryout it came to New York, November 16, 1941, to be buffeted by the reviewers. Brooks Atkinson insisted it was presented as "a comedy for guffawing . . . the huge joke of passing an unwelcome child from one person to another and trying to get him out of sight." George Freedley protested that "miscegenation may be funny to the French, but it is not a laughing matter in this country." *Little Dark Horse* unfortunately gave us no ground for judging how laughter might purge our emotions on the subject. The American version ends with Pampelmousse sent back to school and obscurity, instead of being admitted to the family—however obliquely, in smiling French acceptance of reality—as one of the Monfavets.

Through its laughter, Birabeau's *Pampelmousse* faces clearly and realistically what may at best be called an awkward situation; and, clear-eyed, it shows that, left to themselves, children can teach their elders how to deal with discrimination, how to accept all humans for their own human values. To exhibit this, with a tender portrait of young Noel; to snare all the humor in the embarrassed elders, and all the poignancy and nobility in the entangled youngsters, and thus to create a play at once comic and cosmic in appeal, is the achievement of Birabeau in *Pampelmousse.*

THE RED MILL   *Henry M. Blossom*

With book by Henry M. Blossom (American, 1866-1919) and music by Victor Herbert (American, born in Dublin, 1859-1924), *The Red Mill* is a continuously popular musical comedy. David Montgomery and Fred Stone, whose first success was in *The Wizard of Oz,** carried the new musical in New York to 318 performances, beginning September 24, 1906. It ran for four months in Chicago. Revived in New York, October 16, 1945, with Fred's daughter, Dorothy Stone, and with Michael O'Shea and Eddie Foy, Jr., as the two American tourists, it had a run of 531 performances. It remains a favorite with amateurs and light opera companies. The *New York Herald* stated that "no musical on the American stage has approached it in popularity."

The play is set in Holland. Con Kidder and Kid Conner, American tourists, are working out what they owe for board by acting as interpreter and waiter at the Red Mill Inn. Meanwhile, they help Gretchen, the daughter of innkeeper Jan, to escape marrying the old governor and to elope with Captain Van Damm. They disguise themselves as organ-grinders and as detectives (Sherlock Holmes and Watson), finally rescuing Gretchen, who has been locked up, by lifting her out on the great circling wings of the mill.

Many lively songs grace *The Red Mill,* among them "Every Day is Ladies' Day for Me," "Go While the Going is Good," "Moonbeams," "In Old New York," "The Isle of Our Dreams," and "Because You're You." The organ-grinders, with their monkey, sing the well-known "Good-a-bye John." The 1906 production had a "Dago Duet" and a "Coon Quartet," omitted in more race-conscious 1945. There was plenty, as the *New York Times* (September 25, 1906) observed, "to cheer the heart, delight the eye, charm the ear, tickle the fancy, and wreathe the face in smiles." After eighty years, the verdict has not changed. More recent productions include one with Pat O'Brien in Meadowbrook, N.J., in 1964; and. with updated book and more lyrics by Frederick S. Roffman, OffOffBway by the Bel Canto Opera in 1978 and 1979.

Even the comedy continues to justify the enthusiasm for the show. As the *New York Herald* said: "*The Red Mill* has a story and a plot that permit comedy to ooze through the entire action without once descending to horseplay or vulgarity," and, said the *Post*: "You couldn't for the life of you laugh in the wrong place, although you laughed the whole play through." *The Red Mill* has not been copied to satiety; and with its music and gay atmosphere it remains excellent theatrical fare.

A MAN FOR ALL SEASONS   *Robert Bolt*

The title of *A Man for All Seasons,* by Robert Bolt (b. 1924), is taken from an exercise book of 1520, *Vulgaria,* by Robert Whittington, which gives sentences of topical interest for translation into Latin. One such set discusses Sir Thomas More: "More is a man of an angel's wit and singular learning: I know not his fellow. For where is the man of that gentleness, lowliness, and affability? And as time requireth, a man of marvellous mirth and pastimes; as sometimes of as sad gravity: a man for all seasons."

The play begins with a man who introduces himself as a "Common Man" and reflects that "the 16th century is the Century of the Common Man—like all the other centuries." As he talks, he puts on the livery of Sir Thomas More's butler, and tastes Sir Thomas More's wine. He introduces the other characters as they come on, and assumes other minor roles: boatman, jailer, executioner—and continues commenting on events to the audience, an ironic and witty chorus to the play.

The story is the well-known one of Sir Thomas More, against his will appointed Lord Chancellor by Henry VIII, but preserving a core of conscience not even the King can break—"man's soul is his self"—and, on refusing to uphold the King's religious supremacy, beheaded in 1535. His comment to Cardinal Wolsey may well be in our minds today: "When statesmen forget their own private conscience for the sake of their public duties . . . they lead the country by a short route to chaos."

More is presented as a pleasant man, affectionate to his wife and daughter, but steadfast in his selfhood, expressing his fundamental stand with a wry humor even when he knows it leads to his doomed fall: "What matters to me is not whether it is true or not, but that I believe it to be true; or, rather, not that I *believe* it, but that *I* believe it. I trust I make myself obscure?" Grimly he has advised young Richard Rich: "Be a teacher," thus to withdraw from the sycophants and proffered bribes and royal demands of public office, into which More himself "was commanded."

A Man for All Seasons opened in London, July 1960, and ran for 315 performances, with a glittering, headstrong, restless King, played by Keith Baxter. Paul Scofield played More; George Rose, the Common Man. In New York, opening November 22, 1961, it ran for 637 performances, and won the Critics' Circle award. The *Post* commented: "We are so accustomed to seeing Henry VIII as a gross and vulgar figure with a Holbein beard that it is illuminating to see him as a slender young man with some of his youthful idealism left, a pride in the music he has composed, and a trace of human warmth." But there is also present the relentless will, that must have its way, that ultimately gave him six wives and made him head of the Church of England.

Scofield, in his first American appearance, enriched the stage with the nobility of Sir Thomas More (made a saint in 1935). The Common Man was neatly caught (with an echo of Shakespeare) in the *Daily News:* "He is still with us; he is, in fact, ourselves, whose consciences are more apt to make cowards than heroes of us all." The Common Man encourages his peers: "It isn't difficult to stay alive, friends—just don't make trouble."

Revivals include: Bristol Old Vic, 1962; Honolulu, 1963; New York, 1964; Asolo, 1966; a national tour, 1968-1969, and again 1970; Worthing, England, and Boston, Mass., 1974; Melbourne, 1962 and 1981; London, St. George's, 1983.

The Oscar-winning film of 1966 starred Paul Scofield, Robert Shaw, Orson Welles, Wendy Hiller, Susannah York, Vanessa Redgrave, and Leo McKern. There is much to enjoy, and much to ponder, in *A Man for All Seasons.*

LONDON ASSURANCE   *Dion Boucicault*

Dion Boucicault (originally Bourcicault, Irish, 1822-1890) was eighteen when, under the pseudonym Leo Moreton, he wrote a play called *Out of Town.* Mme. (Lucia Elizabeth Bartalozzi) Vestris accepted it for her theatre and changed the name to *London Assurance.* With some alterations by John Brougham, the play opened in London, March 4, 1841, with Mme. Vestris and her husband, Charles James Mathews. It was the first in a long line of Boucicault successes.

Boucicault came to the United States in 1853. He helped bring about the passage of copyright laws to protect performances of plays; he also inaugurated the sending out of road companies instead of single stars. He wrote over 140 plays, some of them adapted from the French, and he acted in some of them. Although without great literary distinction, most of his plays are superbly constructed, with effective climaxes.

The story of *London Assurance* sets two generations of city blades as rivals for a sweet blossom of the country. Fashionable and polished Sir Harcourt Courtly and his son Charles both love Grace, the niece of Squire Harkaway of Oak Hall, Gloucestershire. While Lady Gay Spanker diverts the old man, young Courtly wins the lovely maiden and her £20,000 a year. Befuddlement and fun are provided by Lady Spanker's absurdly dull husband, by lawyer Mark Meddle, and by the town blade, Dazzle, who manages to live like an idle gentleman on close to nothing a year.

London Assurance was continuously popular throughout the nineteenth century. In an 1856 production, with E. A. Sothern as Sir Harcourt, Mrs.

John Hoey as Lady Gay, Agnes Robertson as Grace, Boucicault played Dazzle. At her theatre, Laura Keane starred in the play in 1858, with E. A. Sothern, and Louisa Nesbit as Lady Gay. The London revival of January 6, 1872, ran for 165 performances; that of the Bancrofts, March 31, 1877, for 110. King George V chose the play for an all-star production, June 27, 1913, headed by Herbert Beerbohm Tree and Irene Vanbrugh, as a benefit for his Actors' Pension Fund. It played at the London Criterion in 1890, the year Boucicault died.

New York saw the play on October 11, 1841, and many times since. Ethel Colt played it at the Vanderbilt, February 19, 1937. Updated and directed by Ronald Eyre, it starred Donald Sinden and Judi Dench as Grace and Elizabeth Spriggs as Lady Gay in London, June 23, 1970; it went on to Toronto, Detroit, and Washington, and reached New York's Palace on December 5, 1974.

The *Boston Advertiser* (May 7, 1897) said that the play was "as new and fresh as though its time-seamed old visage had never before been seen upon the boards . . . The comedy brims with action and perpetual motion; its plot is faultlessly brilliant in ingenuity and in interest." The *New York Sun* (April 4, 1905) hailed "Boucicault's ever ancient and perennial young theatre piece." A score of years later, the *New York Post* (February 19, 1935) spoke of the play's "undeniable charm." Thirty-five years on, the *London Observer* (April 9, 1972) stated: "In Ronald Eyre's RSC production, the box of tricks emerges as something magical." Harold Hobson went further: "Judi Dench's formidably unusual heroine looks as innocent as a bowl of cream, and as powerfully self-protective as a bed of nettles. Elizabeth Spriggs' Lady Gay Spanker, a great woman to hounds, takes all her flirtatious fences with enthusiastic relish: her eyes sparkle, her teeth glitter, and she hurls her legs about as if she were throwing the hammer over a five-barred gate. This exhilarating performance is matched by Donald Sinden's Sir Harcourt, who resembles Oscar Wilde simultaneously playing George IV and the Apollo Belvedere . . . Long discarded as absurd, *London Assurance* returned to the Aldwych to gain, after more than a hundred years, its considerable revenge."

Someone has observed that the difference between a drama and a melodrama is that in a drama the heroine throws the villain over; in a melodrama she throws him over a cliff. *London Assurance* is as smiling as the rolling English hills; it remains lively and laughable, still effective theatrical stock.

THE STREETS OF LONDON   *Dion Boucicault*

The nineteenth century spate of melodrama with rousing theatrical effects reached its full spring flood with Boucicault's *The Sidewalks of New York*. Based on the French melodrama *Les Pauvres de Paris (The Poor of Paris)*, 1856, by Edouard Brisebarre and Eugène Nus, Boucicault's play replaced the maudlin and moralizing sentimentality of the French with a vigorous sweep of action.

The play opened in New York, December 9, 1857, with E. A. Sothern. It was also enacted under the title *The Poor of New York*. In both versions the setting and characters were made wholly American; the panic of 1857 was introduced, along with the vivid spectacle of a blazing building, with a real fire engine and horses clanging onto the stage.

Since the copyright of plays did not hold across the English Channel or across the Atlantic, with its title changed to *The Poor of London* and with appropriate changes of characters and locale, Boucicault's play was rushed over to England, where two translations of *Les Pauvres de Paris (Fraud and Its Victims* and *Pride and Poverty)* were already playing, in 1858. Boucicault's drama was revived in London under the title *The Streets of London,* August 1, 1864. It then ran for 209 performances, and by all indications—if one counts other transmogrifications and motion picture versions—it has been played somewhere ever since. In London, with changes by W. A. Darlington, it was revived again on December 20, 1932, for 158 performances, and again in 1943. In New York, as *The Streets of New York, or Poverty is No Crime,* it was played in 1931 with Rollo Peters, A. P. Kaye, Romney Brent, and Dorothy Gish; in May 1951 it was revived by the Henry Street Playhouse on Grand Street.

In its various manifestations, *The Streets of London* tells of the plight of the widow Fairweather and her two children Lucy and Paul, after the dying Captain Fairweather has been swindled of £20,000 by the scoundrelly banker Bloodgood. The Hon. Mark Livingstone, also rendered penniless, can refurbish himself by marrying Bloodgood's heartless, mercenary, and title-hungry daughter, Alida. But seeing Lucy, barefoot in the snow, selling flowers in front of the Opera House, Mark falls in love with her, and love, as the audience hopes, works to its triumph. The widow Fairweather in desperation tries to dismiss the family troubles with charcoal fumes; the fire brigade clangs to the rescue; and Bloodgood and his clerk Badger wrestle in the flames until the clerk jumps through the window with the receipt for the Captain's £20,000. Then Mark's wedding with Alida is interrupted; the foiled fury Alida is replaced by the gentle Lucy; the wretched Bloodgood, forgiven because of his love for his daughter, leaves to lead "a better life"; and young Paul Fairweather beseeches the audience, if their hearts have been touched, not to forget the poor of London.

Not to be outdone in theatrical thrills, Augustin Daly offered in New York, August 12, 1867, a melodrama entitled *Under the Gaslight; or Life and Love in These Times,* in which Laura Courtland was thrown from a pier (in later productions, a high tower) into a river, and the one-armed veteran Snorkey, tied by the villain to a railroad track, was rescued by Laura from beneath the cowcatcher of the approaching train. Daly patented this train effect, but before he could open the show in England, April 20, 1868, to protect his patent there, a new version of Charles Selby's old melodrama *London by Night; or The Dark Side of the Great City* opened, with its hero tied to the track before an onrushing train. In September 1868, the same device was used in Miss Hazlewood's *London by Gaslight;* and in Boucicault's *After Dark, a Tale of London Life* of the same year, the rescuer breaks through a cellar wall as the victim lies in the London underground.

Well into the twentieth century, such melodramas were the rage throughout England and the United States. From their price of admission, they came to be known as the "ten-twent'-thirt' melodramas," and they gave more than their money's worth of thrills.

It became fashionable during the second quarter of the twentieth century to present burlesque revivals of the ten-twent'-thirt' melodrama, often in beer-gardens, with old-time songs and vaudeville skits between the acts and the audience loudly hissing the double-dyed, handle-bar-moustachioed villain. Some of the plays lent themselves to this treatment, but the better ones turned the tables upon their producers, and evoked anew the olden spell of vivid melodrama. This was especially the case with Boucicault's

The Streets of London. When the play was revived in Australia, the *Sydney Herald* (September 4, 1937) reported, "The audience took it seriously." If this seems provincial, hearken to the reaction of theatre-wise London to a revival of January 1943. The *Daily Express* declared: "By the end it was the actual melodrama, rather than the parody of it, that moved the audience." The *Sunday Referee* added: "It lives still, as any authentic work of art must ... *The Streets of London* is grand entertainment." Finally, the *Spectator* said: "From the technical point of view, the play is an amazingly strong piece of work ... brilliant entertainment."

Deftly constructed, with theatrical effects of breath-taking power, *The Streets of London* is one of the first, and one of the greatest, of the many-sided, heart-wringing, spine-tingling spectacular ten-twenty-thirty melodramas, which for a century made popular theatrical fare.

Opening January 21, 1962, a musical version called *The Banker's Daughter,* book and lyrics by Edward Eliscu, music by Sol Kaplan, ran at the OffBway Jan Hus for 68 performances. Opening October 29, 1963, at the OffBway Maidman, *The Streets of New York,* with book and lyrics by Barry Alan Grael and music by Richard B. Chodosh, attained 318 performances. In 1970 it was presented (guess where!) as *The Streets of Liverpool.* In 1980 the play was at the OffBway Soho; the same year, at Westport, Conn., Lilian Gish was in the audience. London saw *The Streets of London* on October 29, 1980, with lyrics by Ian Barnett and music by Gary Carpenter, and it is likely to turn up again, anytime, anywhere.

Daly's *Under the Gaslight* also proved tenacious of audiences. It was revived in 1961 in Detroit, with olio songs and dances between the acts; in 1967 at ELT, with music and lyrics by Norman Dean. The Lambs (New York) staged it in 1970. In 1973 it was presented OffBway, with songs of Stephen Foster. In 1979, the OffOffBway Theatre Ensemble set the locale as an 1890 Brooklyn Negro community.

THE OCTOROON   *Dion Boucicault*

In the tense days preceding the Civil War, it was inevitable that melodrama should take up the subject of miscegenation. The best of the early plays on this theme is Boucicault's *The Octoroon; or, Life in Louisiana,* which opened in New York, December 6, 1859, with Joseph Jefferson playing the Indian, Wah-No-Tee. London saw the play open on November 18, 1861, and again on February 10, 1868. It was revived in this country frequently until 1910, and sporadically since, with productions in 1929, 1930, 1932, and one by the Federal Theatre in 1936. What seemed a bold subject for the theatre in 1859 was still deemed daring ninety years later, when it was presented in the movie *Pinky.*

Boucicault's play, indeed, brought editorial fire from the press. The abolitionist *New York Tribune* (December 7, 1859) took the drama as occasion for a fulmination against slave civilization: "The love—the impossible love of a high-souled generous young man, for one damned among woman, though lovely, feminine, and with all the eternities of love glowing in the gentlest of bosoms—because out of eight parts of her nature one was derived from African blood—gives rise to a tragic drama, with some tremendous scenes in it—some of which would grind to the last trituration of shame and horror the barbarism that claims supremacy of the Government of this country, from the head of the White House down to the tide-water—down to below low water mark." The *New York Herald,* on the other hand, suggested that the inflammatory subject of slavery were best avoided on the stage; to which Boucicault (December 5, 1859) made answer: "I believe the drama to be a proper and very effective instrument to use in the dissection of all social matters . . . It is by such means that the drama can be elevated into the social importance it deserves to enjoy. Therefore I have involved in *The Octoroon* sketches of slave life, truthful I know, and I hope gentle and kind." Boucicault withdrew as stage manager of the play shortly after the New York run began, saying that his life was in danger if he continued.

The octoroon is Zoe, a handsome girl on the Peyton Plantation of Terrebonne in Louisiana. Salem Scudder, from New England, manages the plantation, but even his shrewdness cannot save it from the Peytons' apparent lack of concern; all is to be sold. Actually, Jacob McCloskey has killed the Negro boy Paul and stolen, from the mail pouch Paul carried, the letter from the London bank with Peyton money to save the plantation. McCloskey lusts after Zoe, who is loved by George Peyton, but to whom she denies herself because her one drop of colored blood in every eight "creates a chasm between us as wide as your love and as deep as my despair." George could save the plantation by marrying rich Dora Sunnyside; instead, he tells her of his love for Zoe. Sunnyside buys in the plantation, but McCloskey keeps bidding for Zoe, and finally gets her for $25,000.

Melodramatic action and theatrical effects now crowd into the play. Zoe, to escape McCloskey's loathed embrace, takes poison. But her death is avenged. The plate in Scudder's camera is developed—McCloskey had knocked it over while struggling to overcome Paul—and the picture shows the crime. To avoid arrest, McCloskey sets the cotton-boat *Magnolia* on fire, then leaps into the water. But the Indian Wah-No-Tee, who "with an air of primitive ritual" had gathered up the dead Paul and his belongings, tracks down the murderer McCloskey to a duel of death in the swamps.

The Octoroon was the first play to make use of the camera trick—the accidentally exposed plate that exposes the villain. Its melodramatic devices and action drive steadily along; and it presents a problem that has lost none of its timeliness. In England, the ending was altered: Zoe hears of McCloskey's guilt soon enough to keep her from taking the poison; and she marries George.

The power of the play has held throughout the years. In 1893 the *Boston Transcript* (May 23) declared: "Its action is swift, its color vivid, its dialogue catchy: the galleries are enraptured, the parquet good-humoredly entertained; the revival, a popular success." In 1929, the *Transcript* (January 23) said: "The audience was as sympathetic and as serious as though sitting before the trial of Mary Dugan, A.D. 1928." The *New York Times* called *The Octoroon* "a piece packed with dynamite when it was first produced, just before the Civil War, and still tingling with perfectly sound theatrical thrills."

The characters, even in minor parts, are vividly etched. *The Octoroon* is melodrama that trembles on the somber brink of tragedy.

There was an ELT performance in 1949. On January 27, 1961, it opened at the New York Phoenix for forty-five performances, directed by Stuart Vaughan. John Mason Brown, calling it a sort of American *Cherry Orchard,* said the play possessed "a vitality absent from the current plays."

THE COLLEEN BAWN   *Dion Boucicault*

One of the most popular melodramas of the nineteenth century, *The Colleen Bawn; or, The Brides of Garryowen,* was the first play to dwarf the art of the actor through the use of mechanical devices and the resources of the stage. It must have been immensely thrilling that night in New York, March 29, 1860, when the blarney boy Myles-na-Cappaleen first dived to the underwater entrance of the cave where he hid his illicit distillery and swam up again with the supposedly murdered heroine Eily in his arms.

The play was popular all over the United States until World War I. The Irish Repertory Players revived it in New York in 1933. It was made into a film called *The Lily of Killarney* in 1929, and another called *The Bride of the Lake* in 1934.

The Colleen Bawn opened in London, September 10, 1860, for a run of 165 performances. Bell's *Life in London* recorded that on February 2, 1861, "Her Majesty and the Court went to the Adelphi Theatre to see that wonderful piece of dramatic and sensational vitality, *The Colleen Bawn.*" Bernard Shaw, who saw a revival of the play, January 25, 1896, complained that the use of real water in the rescue scene destroyed the illusion, and chuckled over the two players' taking their bows sopping wet; yet he found *The Colleen Bawn* "far superior to the average modern melodrama." The play was adapted in French, October 17, 1861, as *Le Lac de Glenaston,* by Adolphe d'Ennery, whose *The Two Orphans* the English borrowed with equal alacrity. There was an English burlesque of the play, *The Cooleen Drawn,* by H. J. Byron in 1862; another called *Eily O'Connor* opened at Wallach's Theatre in New York the same year.

Laura Keene had asked Boucicault for a play. He wrote her that he had it; sent her some Irish melodies to be scored and some Killarney scenes for the sets; and the first act went into rehearsal while he was writing the second. The play was scarce a week in the writing. What fired Boucicault were the dramatic possibilities of a novel *The Collegians* (1829) by Gerald Griffin. Based on a true story that had earlier been dramatized in *Eily O'Connor, or, The Foster Brother* by J. Egerton Wilks and presented in London, July 23, 1831, with Ellen Tree, *The Colleen Bawn* (which is Irish for the "white maiden") depicts the distress and final happiness of Hardress Cregan of the Irish gentry and the peasant girl Eily to whom he is secretly married. For family reasons, Cregan is pressed to marry the heiress Anne Chute. His foster brother, Danny Mann, learning of the secret match and misunderstanding Cregan's desire, gets Eily into a boat and leaves her unconscious in the cave that the high tide fills. Told that Eily has killed herself, Cregan consents to the marriage with Anne. In the meantime Danny, dying, confesses his deed. He is overheard by Cregan's enemy Carrigan, and at the wedding Cregan is arrested for Eily's murder. Then, as the *New York Tribune* put it (March 30, 1860), Eily herself arrives, "in a state of serious objection to the marriage of her husband to another woman." Eily and Cregan are joyfully rejoined, and there is an old lover for Anne to fall back on. "These are the main features of the story," said the *Tribune,* "about which are grouped many minor incidents of interest, which all add to the beauty of the play, and make it one of the most intensely interesting of melodramas."

In the actual case of 1820 on which the play is based, a man named Scanlan, who had secretly married Eily O'Connor, of Garryowen, a suburb of Limerick, tired of her, killed her, and threw her body into the Shannon River. The horses drawing Scanlan to the gallows balked, refusing to cross Shannon Bridge, a "manifestation of the abhorrence of heaven at the crime." Boucicault shifted the crime so as to leave Scanlan (Cregan in the novel and the play) innocent and still in love with Eily; and he turned the river scene into vivid theatrical action by introducing Myles' dive (Boucicault played Myles) and rescue of the unconscious Eily. Laura Keene originally played Anne Chute, wearing a green riding habit; Frances Starr, 1905 and later, in a huge feathered hat, with riding whip. Thus the finery of high life was contrasted with the picturesqueness and humor of the peasant folk. "Unlike the conventional Irish play," said the *Boston Herald* (March 14, 1905), "Boucicault's appeals to every class of theatregoer, to each succeeding generation, and will do so as long as wit, humor, pathos, and dramatic interest attract people to the theatre." The play is livened with songs, too.

On the eve of its seventieth birthday, the *Boston Herald* (June 10, 1929) called *The Colleen Bawn* "a play of perennial popularity"; the *Transcript* said: "Plentiful and diversified are the incidents of the play—comic, pathetic, sentimental, homely, what you will—as changeful as an Irish day of sun and shower." With its spectacular water scene and the steady drive of its varied action, *The Colleen Bawn* is deservedly one of the most popular of all romantic melodramas. Among the play's pleasant songs is "The Pretty Girl Milking Her Cow," and the one by Cregan that gives the play its name:

> *The girl I love is beautiful, and soft-eyed like the dawn;*
> *She comes from Garryowen, and she's called the Colleen Bawn.*

RIP VAN WINKLE   *Dion Boucicault*

Performances of *Rip Van Winkle* are literally innumerable; even the various versions of the play are beyond accurate count. The story first appeared in *The Sketch Book* of Washington Irving in 1819. It is the story everyone knows, of happy-go-lucky, luckless Rip, who, henpecked by his wife, Gretchen, seeks refuge with his dog in the Kaatskill Mountains, and there comes upon the old crew of Hendrick Hudson playing at ninepins, sips some of their liquor, and falls asleep for twenty years.

The first production of Rip's tale seems to have been in Cincinnati in 1826. There was another there in 1829, and one in Philadelphia. In 1830, James H. Hackett played Rip in New York, in a version "altered from a piece written and produced in London." Hackett kept on playing the part and altering the play. In 1849 his company took on a new man in the role of the innkeeper, one Jefferson (Joseph Jefferson 4th, 1829-1905). Ten years later, Joe Jefferson appeared in his own version of *Rip Van Winkle*. It failed, but Jefferson struggled along with the play for five years, when Dion Boucicault wrote a new version for him. This opened in London, September 4, 1865, and ran for 172 nights. It opened in New York, September 3, 1866, and for the rest of his life Jefferson acted Rip. In Chicago, just before he retired, Jefferson, comfortably tucked into the forest floor, actually fell asleep one night onstage. The curtain rose; and all was silent, until from the gallery someone cried: "Do we have to wait for the whole twenty years?" The prompter pinched "Rip," and his waking groan this time was real. When Joe Jefferson withdrew from the stage, his son continued for some years the role of Rip.

Although Joe Jefferson and Rip Van Winkle today seem almost one figure, the actor in his time had many rivals. In the 1870's, indeed, both McKee Rankin and Robert McWade were thought by many to be superior in the role. Each performer sought new turns of phrase or bits of business.

Thus, while Jefferson merely mentioned his dog Schneider, McWade had an actual dog onstage. Coming into the woods, he tied the dog to a sapling; twenty years later, the skeleton of a dog was shown high on a tree that had grown in the middle in the meantime. The waking Rip looked around, spied the skeleton, and said ruefully, "Ah, Schneider, you barked up the wrong tree that time!"

In the Boucicault version, Rip, on his return, finds his wife remarried. In the version used by Beerbohm Tree (1900) Gretchen was a more pleasant figure. It was not her shrewishness that drove Rip to drink, but his drinking that set her to complaining; she refused to marry the eager Diedrich (who wanted the land even more than the lady), and on Rip's return he found a wife with open arms.

When Cyril Maude played Rip in 1911, after his sleep Rip was so covered with leaves—his beard and the moss grown one—that he seemed truly a part of the forest floor. He is, truly, in the groundwork of the American theatre.

Rip Van Winkle has also attracted composers. In 1855, an opera on the story by the American George F. Bristow ran for a month in New York. In 1881, *Rip Van Winkle,* to music by Robert Planquette, played in Paris; in 1882 in London for 323 performances; then in New York. This version was given a modern dress in 1933, with Rip as a radio announcer, put to sleep by bootleg gin; the election returns after the Revolution are broadcast to the village. Franco Leoni's version was heard in London in 1897, with book by Edgar B. Smith; the *Illustrated London News* (September 25, 1897) protested: "Imagine a skirt-dance in the Catskill Mountains!" Although there was a children's version by Edward Manning in 1932, the musical form of *Rip Van Winkle* that has best endured is the one by Reginald De Koven (1920), which still finds almost annual revival among operatic troupes.

The Dion Boucicault version remains the most popular, partly because it was endeared to a theatre generation by the acting of Joseph Jefferson. Boucicault managed to make Rip appealingly human. What in Irving is a mere, though interesting, legend, is made a calamity befalling a weak but not wholly unworthy man. As William Winter, in his book *Joseph Jefferson,* declared: "There is no trickery in the charm . . . Rip Van Winkle's goodness exists as an oak exists . . . Howsoever he may drift, he cannot drift away from human affection. Weakness was never punished with more sorrowful misfortune than his. Dear to us for what he is, he becomes dearer still for what he suffers and (in the acting of Jefferson) for the manner in which he suffers it." Eleanor Farjeon, in her Foreword to *Rip Van Winkle: The Autobiography of Joseph Jefferson* (1950), quoted a friend visiting America: "In this land of short memories I find two names which are remembered by everybody—George Washington and Joseph Jefferson."

When Jefferson, as Rip returning from his long slumber, was told that Rip was no more, he used to say, sadly, "So poor Rip is gone," and point to heaven; a villager pulled at his hand until it pointed down. The audience knew better; a tender affection has kept *Rip Van Winkle* among the elect.

Of course, when Rip came back to town from his slumber, he rubbed his eyes again: what he had known as "The George III" he now saw as "The George Washington Inn."

The 1953 production, with music by Erwin McArthur, book and lyrics by Morton Da Costa, was at least the seventh musical version of the play.

Among recent productions of *Rip Van Winkle:* OffBway, 1957; Midland Texas summer theatre, 1964; the Joe Jefferson Theatre Co. at Sunnyside,

New York, with a visit to Irving's home in Tarrytown, 1974—repeated 1975 and 1976.

The American Bicentennial in 1975 naturally included *Rip* at Kennedy Center, Washington; and in 1976 Anthony Quayle played Rip in Philadelphia. Joe Jefferson died in 1905.

THE SHAUGRAUN   *Dion Boucicault*

A "shaugraun" is a "merry rogue," such as Boucicault himself has been pictured; and Conn O'Kelly, the shaugraun of his favorite play, was Boucicault's favorite role. Conn is a lovable rascal, a blarney boy, "the soul of every fair, the life of every funeral, the first fiddle at all the weddings and patterns in the parish." He is also a revolutionist in the Irish uprising, who wins his love despite his politics.

The Shaugraun depicts the wild romp of Conn's, as he goes about in the ragged red coat, kit on his back, that became known all over the English and the American stage. Conn bounds in and out of cabin windows, scales prison walls, leaps over church ruins, with nimble wit and laughing careless courage. He helps the Irish gentleman, Robert, against the English officer, Molyneux, a fine fellow himself, though he must do his duty. After Conn attends the wake for his own (feigned) death, he revives to do battle with a pair of ruffians, and tricks the English soldiers into firing the two shots at night that mark the signal for their own doom.

Opening in New York, November 14, 1874, *The Shaugraun* ran for 143 performances. F. B. Chatterton tried to put it on at the Adelphi, London— British law did not then protect a play if it were first produced abroad—but the actors Mr. and Mrs. J. C. Williamson refused to perform it when they learned that Boucicault wanted to appear in it himself. He opened in London, September 4, 1875, and had a run of 119 performances.

The play provided one of Boucicault's best roles, and was frequently revived after the turn of the century. In one New York revival, the then sheriff Al Smith and state senator Jimmy Walker played the villain and the hero of the play.

The chief virtue of *The Shaugraun* lies in the character of Conn. His genial ways and irrepressible good humor make him a mixture of Rip Van Winkle and Robin Hood, a sort of Irish Tyl Eulenspiegel, a picaresque rascal with love of his country in his heart.

The Shaugraun was given a lively revival at the Abbey Theatre, Dublin, in 1968 and 1970, and taken to the London Aldwych both times. When the hired mourners at the wake help themselves to a drink, the corpse reaches out for the bottle.

THE PRIVATE LIFE OF THE MASTER RACE   *Bertolt Brecht*

The best known plays of Bertolt Brecht (Eugen Berthold Friedrich Brecht, German, 1898-1956) are avowedly *Lehrstücke,* propaganda plays. In most of his works, Brecht has drawn upon earlier writers, shaping their ideas to contemporary use. With Erwin Piscator, Brecht was a founder of the "epic theatre," which used the stage as an instrument of education for the masses. Piscator was the director of plays; Brecht, the poet-adapter. Their most original contribution was perhaps the mingling of realistic and expressionistic modes to picture portions of contemporary civilization. Their sort of dramatized harangue gave birth, during the American Federal

Theatre years, to *The Living Newspaper* (see *Hoopla!**). Brecht developed it in *The Private Life of the Master Race.*

Written in the United States, *the Private Life of the Master Race* had its world premiere in Berkeley, California, June 7, 1945. New York saw it on June 12, with Albert and Else Basserman, and Clarence Derwent. The play, in seventeen scenes, is a documentary of events from 1933 to 1938, showing how the Nazis took over Germany. In New York performance, the scenes were cut to nine. They vary in length and in satiric power. Some are scarcely more than swift "black-outs," for example, the scene in the prison yard, with the prisoners walking silently in two opposite circles: Two bakers exchange words each time they pass: "What did they get you for? Look out!" Next round, the answer: "For not putting bran in the bread. And you?" Next round: "For putting bran in the bread!" Curtain. Three scenes are outstanding. In one, a radio announcer tries to praise his sponsor's product, working against three uncooperative guests on the air; in another, a venal judge is shown seeking an acceptable pretext to justify his decision; and in the third, an informer is ironically portrayed, with psychological overtones.

The *New York Times* (December 17, 1944) said of the published play, that "except for a few aridities suggesting the schoolroom rather than the barricades, the play is intensely dramatic." The call to the barricades, however, is the core of the work, which does not pose a problem or present a conflict. It is a call to arms. "To prevent any sentimental identification with his characters, Brecht changes them with every scene; the only constant prop is a panzer which rumbles offstage and occasionally appears, holding twelve chalk-faced soldiers. This is not for unity but for 'interruptions' calculated to jolt the average audience out of its habits." The audience must not sit back and watch; it must join the crusade. Such was the aim of epic theatre, which was most moving to those already at one with the playwright's motives. Hence *The New Masses* praised Brecht for "social analysis done with the keenest psychological perceptions, a broad historical grasp, a deep poetic vision, a subtle dramatic sense."

Among the other plays of Brecht, four call for brief mention. His *Mother,* based on Gorki's novel (1907), a picture of Russia during the rebellion of 1905, was vividly produced by Piscator in Berlin; but the English version, which opened in New York, November 19, 1935, was an overstrained, hyperemotional kindergarten for Communists.

Most successful of Brecht's plays, all through Europe, was his version of Gay's *The Beggar's Opera,** produced as *Dreigroschenoper* (*Three Penny Opera*), 1928. Although Eric and Maya Bentley felt that this play "summed up a whole epoch in European culture," American opinion was highly critical.

In 1947, the Experimental Theatre in New York put aside its contemplated production of a study of Galileo, *Lamp at Midnight,* by Barrie Stavis,* for another play by Brecht, *Galileo,* which Charles Laughton had translated and, opening July 30, 1947, had acted in Los Angeles. In New York (December 7, 1947) *Galileo* was revealed as an episodic piece, with a coarse, calculating scientist, fond of the fleshpots, an unscrupulous sensualist. The translation destroyed Brecht's poetry; but the picture of Galileo as a victim of economic determinism and gluttonous desires is in the original.

In *Galileo,* propaganda was incidental. It was even less important to *The Good Woman of Setzuan,** which Brecht set in China. John Gassner in his *Masters of the Drama* (1945) said that in *The Good Woman of Setzuan*

Brecht, "the ablest German poet, reaches the peak of his dramatic powers." With an Oriental leisureliness and a supernatural story, the play seeks universal significance.

Peter Lorre once declared that "Brecht is the poet of our generation and to my mind its greatest writer." Despite the enthusiasm of admirers, he has done little that today seems to qualify him for such high praise. His ideas are obvious; his pace pedestrian. The most swift-moving and really dramatic of his works of *The Private Life of the Master Race.* There was a London revival in 1979.

MOTHER COURAGE   *Bertolt Brecht*

Mother Courage (and Her Children), 1941, is Brecht's picture of a born survivor. Mother Courage plods painfully but ruthlessly along, caring only for her day-to-day continuance. We first see her with her mute daughter, Katrin, and her two sons, following the Swedish army in part of the Thirty Years' War, 1624-1636, pulling her mobile canteen. When her first son is executed, Mother Courage, to protect herself, pretends not to know the corpse. For a time peace threatens to break out, but she consoles herself with the thought that the Pope and other rulers will see to it that there always is a war. The second son, looting, is shot. Mute Katrin, drumming to alert the town, is killed by the approaching soldiers. Mother Courage hitches herself to the wagon and plods on. The only time she ever moaned was when truce threatened to kill, not the family, but her business. She took not the slightest interest in politics, but one can read the "rather red than dead" beneath Brecht's Marxian lines.

In addition to being a vogue, the play offers an almost single and theatrical role to an actress, and it has had many productions. Among them: 1949, Berliner Ensemble in East Berlin, with Brecht's wife, Helene Weigel; 1954, Paris, directed by Brecht (*En France la gloire de Brecht commence*); 1955, London, with and directed by Joan Littlewood; 1956, the Berliner Ensemble at the London Palace; 1958, London, translation by Eric Bentley, American champion of Brecht; March 28, 1963, Martin Beck (New York), directed by Jerome Robbins, with the "too charming" Anne Bancroft; May 12, 1965, the first Brecht at the NT (Old Vic), with Madge Ryan, and lyrics by W. H. Auden; November 16, 1967, Billy Rose (New York), eleven performances in Yiddish; 1975, Tyrone Guthrie Theatre, Minneapolis, in current slang; 1975, New Jersey, audience sat on floor and platform with the play around and among them; 1980, Stoke-on-Trent, England; 1982, London, with Margaret Robertson.

In New York, 1980, came a version by Ntozake Shange, set in the U.S. post–Civil War period, with Mother Courage a freed slave. It stressed the "responsibilities all whites must accept for the machinations of the Capitalist state." By contrast, the May 13, 1965, *New York Daily News* said that *Mother Courage* is "not a play so much as a tract, anti-war, anti-religion, anti-Establishment, anti-man."

Brecht for a time became the cynosure of the leftists, both the Communists and the loose liberals, not to mention the great host of non-thinkers always ready to jump on the bandwagon. For a more restrained consideration, with word of his *Galileo,* see *Lamp at Midnight.** For his *Three-Penny Opera,* see *The Beggar's Opera;** for *The Caucasian Chalk Circle* and *The Good Woman of Setzuan,* see *The Circle of Chalk.** See Marlowe's *Edward II.**

THE RED ROBE   *Eugène Brieux*

This play has an astounding theatrical force as it moves relentlessly to picture the perversion of justice by ambition. "Had I been an English citizen," said its author, Eugène Brieux (1858-1932), "instead of writing a play against the abuse of justice by a judge, I might have had to illustrate the same abuse by a lawyer." In the United States, the protagonist might well be a district attorney.

The story of the play centers on a simple French peasant, Etchepars, who is accused of murder. Ambitious for the red robe of a judge, Mouzon and Vagret do their best to convict him. Vagret, regaining his integrity, withdraws; but Mouzon presses on. To discredit the testimony of Etchepars' wife, Yanetta, he discloses a scandalous episode of her early life, which her husband did not know. As a result, when Etchepars repulses her, Yanetta kills Mouzon.

When the play was presented in Paris, 1900, the star Réjane ironically suggested the title *La Robe Rouge,* saying that people would come to the theatre expecting excitement over a new dress. The play, however, carried its own excitement. In New York, it was performed in German at the Irving Place Theatre in 1902; and by Réjane and a French company in 1904. The latter production provoked the *New York Dramatic Mirror* (November 14, 1904) to say: "Justice is free, but it costs a lot to get it." The first American production in English opened in Yonkers on January 14, 1920, and was called *The Letter of the Law.* It came to New York on February 23, with Lionel Barrymore, Clarence Derwent, and Louis Wolheim. The report from Yonkers called the play "tiresome and full of sermons," but when it reached New York, the critics were impressed. Heywood Broun said that the fundamental complaint "holds true of American law, and probably of Patagonian law as well." Burns Mantle said that the play exposed "relentlessly the prosecution that becomes the persecution of the poor." The *New York World* called it "a potent example of the good use to which the dramatic stage can be put when it raises its voice against social wrong."The *Telegram* declared: "The play delivers its message in the terms of extraordinarily effective acting drama . . . It employs real persons, in whose fate you share, and sets them in situations of dramatic power and pathos. The dramatist who can do this is entitled to all the sociology he likes."

The Red Robe discloses the manner in which unscrupulous men in legal posts can bring ruin upon a family. It is considered by many to be Brieux' finest drama, although less notorious than his *Les Avariés,* 1901 (*Damaged Goods*), a study of the physical consequences of syphilis and of the dread and secrecy smudged across the disease, which was a succès de scandale in many countries.

Though changing times have lessened the interest of his plays, Brieux himself did not lose interest in the "social and moralizing" drama. In 1925, he offered a prize of 30,000 francs for such a play. Of the several hundred manuscripts submitted, none was found acceptable. The later social dramatists were more concerned with picturing the general collapse of standards, the loss of ideals, the disintegration of society. The dramas of Brieux remain vivid, melodramatic studies of social abuses and social evils, of which each age must find and cure its own. Brieux was chiefly concerned, however, not with the specific social evil, but with the basic human attitude that permits such an evil to grow. Of the continuing dangers to justice in the ambitious designs of its supposed guardians, *The Red Robe* is a stirring dramatic picture.

DANTON'S DEATH   *Georg Büchner*

The twenty-two-year-old Georg Büchner (German, 1813-1837), fired by
the French Revolution, wrote the play *Danton's Death*, which more than any
other captures the hopes and fury and disappointment of that tremendous
time. "I felt myself crushed down," Büchner declared, "under the ghastly
fatalism of history. I find a horrible sameness in all human nature, and in
men's relationships to one inevitable power. Individuals are so much foam
on a wave, greatness the sheerest accident, the strength of genius a puppet
play—a child's struggle against an iron law—the greatest of us all can only
recognize it; to control it is impossible. *Must* is the cursed word to which
human beings are born." In such a mood, in order to finance his escape from
arrest for political plotting, Büchner wrote *Danton's Death* in 1835—
stealthily, on his father's surgical table, in spite of paternal prohibitions
and fulminations. The play was finished in a fortnight; but the police came
before the money, and Büchner fled.

In twelve swift scenes—anticipating the technique of the expressionists—
the play evokes the spirit of Revolutionary days, as Robespierre and St. Just
set the crowds aflame and the more moderate Danton and the poet Desmoulins go to their death. (Danton was arrested March 31, 1794, and
executed April 5.) The fiery Robespierre is the essence of revolutionary zeal;
Danton is the calmer advocate of bourgeois reform. One of the two must fall;
and in passionate times, invariably the calmer individuals succumb to the
hungry mob. *Danton's Death* fills the theatre with the fickle, lurid, terrifying cyclone of the Revolution, the surging blood-drunk mob, and sets in
contrast to this scenes of individual action: Danton with his young wife;
Desmoulins and Danton reflecting upon the cruelty of the times; the husband beating his wife—(onlookers side with the wife until diverted to
attack a young man who uses a handkerchief and therefore must be an
aristocrat); the lamenting Lucile Desmoulins who, when the tumbrils carry
her beloved to the guillotine, cries "Vive le roi!" and thus invites her doom.
The most striking scenes of all are those of Robespierre's inciting of the
Convention, and of the defense of Desmoulins and Danton.

The play forms a prodigious spectacle, with torrential mob scenes,
drunken brawling on the street, bellowing and gathering frenzy at the
Convention, surging passions at the trial. "I doubt if any stage in this
country has ever before witnessed anything so impressive," said R. Dana
Skinner in the *Commonweal* (January 4, 1928), "so moving, or so filled with
magnificent vitality, as the scene in the Convention during the trial of
Danton."

The single-eyed fanatic, Robespierre, embodies the basic heartlessness of
the humanitarian doctrinaire. But love and beauty persist, evoked by the
two women beloved of Danton and of Desmoulins who, though not prominent
in the play, give a splendid, almost romantic quality to the hard historical
realism. Tempestuous passion, pathos, human integrity, and poetic beauty
surge to tragic exaltation in Büchner's masterpiece.

Danton's Death was not acted for some sixty years. The People's Free
Theatre presented it in Berlin in the 1890's; Munich saw it in 1913; Rein-
hardt directed it in Berlin in 1919. Reinhardt's production came to New
York, December 20, 1927, with Vladimir Sokoloff (Robespierre), Paul
Hartmann (Danton), Arnold Korff, Lili Darvas, Tilly Losch, Harald
Kreutzberg, and Herman Thimig. There were forty-seven named roles on
the program, and hordes of soldiers, revolutionaries, citizens screaming for

blood. In the Convention and trial scenes, voices called out from all parts of the theatre to carry the audience deep into the drama's mood. "It is a landmark in European drama," said Gilbert W. Gabriel, "a play apart from the spectacle it affords. Its many swift, short scenes may hurl themselves up to a pitch of clamor, the free-handed illusion of a world gone mad . . . but the writing of each of these scenes has a weight, a terror or a beauty, of its own."

A Mercury Theatre production in 1938, staged by Orson Welles, who played St. Just, added one effective device, a backdrop of a thousand masks. These little faces, said the *New Yorker* (November 12, 1938) were "illuminated with such hellish ingenuity that, as death draws nearer for Danton and his friends, they come to look like skulls, have a macabre effect, suggesting the millions grimly watching and waiting all over France." However, the crowding masks and the constricted stage of the Welles production gave it a static quality alien to the surge and swell of Büchner's drama. "Welles reduced it," said Freedley and Reeves in their *History of the Theatre* (1941) "to a series of soliloquies delivered in the manner of arias."

A version of *Danton's Death* by Stephen Spender and Goronwy Rees, presented in England in 1939, captured, according to the *London Times* (March 24), "much of the poetry, the tempestuous passion, and the pathos of Büchner's masterpiece." An opera was made of *Danton's Death* by Nikolai Lopatnikoff in 1933; another, by Gottfried von Einem, was played at the Salzburg Festival in 1947.

More episodic, less spun in one connected story than Romain Rolland's *Danton,** which was also presented by Reinhardt, Büchner's *Danton's Death* is not merely a forerunner of the episodic expressionist drama, but a vivid and turbulent masterpiece, picturing men who carry into the teeth of Revolution, and hold against the gnashing of mob violence, the calm and lofty assertion of human dignity and measured values.

The play retains its force. It was presented in Berlin in 1939 to foster Hitler-worship. The star Jean Vilar played Robespierre in Paris in 1953 and again in 1959. Opening October 21, 1965, in translation by Herbert Blau, it was the first play at New York's Lincoln Center (Beaumont), with ninety-six performances. On April 30, 1983, it was opened by the CSC OffBway, with Noble Shropshire as Robespierre and Tom Spiller as Danton.

> Danton: Men are epicures, coarse or fine. Christ was the finest.
> Robespierre: He redeemed them with His blood; I redeem them with
>   their own.

Of the NT (Olivier) production, July 24, 1982, directed by Peter Gill, the *Times* said: "Nothing in the English repertoire of the 18th or 19th century can match the interest, beauty, and power of *Danton's Death*." Robert Cushman in the *Observer* detailed: "On a set by Alison Chitty of constantly reforming wooden slabs he transports us from brothel to courtroom to guillotine. Every character is allowed his say, and takes it lucidly; while no director is better than Mr. Gill in the instant collection or dispersal of crowds. He gets fine central performances from Brian Cox's Danton, a bull who thinks, and John Normington's Robespierre, a machine who feels." The play "captures a movement of history."

WOZZECK   *Georg Büchner*

At his death in 1837 Georg Büchner left unfinished a succession of scenes he called *Wozzeck* (*Woyzeck*). In an expressionistic pattern later followed by

Georg Kaiser,* *Wozzeck* presents the story of a poor ex-soldier, a serf whom emancipation has torn from the soil, and who lives from hand to mouth. A certain rough tenderness holds him to his mistress and their child, to support whom he sells himself as a guinea pig to a medical crank. Marie seeks relief from drudgery with a drum-major, whose boasts, along with jibes of the doctor and a captain, make Wozzeck aware of her infidelity. He slits her throat and throws the knife in a pond; then, for fear that it will be recovered, goes in after it and is drowned. The play ends with the little boy riding his hobby-horse, with no grasp at all of what is happening around, even though the other children shout to him that his mother is dead.

Wozzeck was presented in Berlin in 1928, and elsewhere in Germany; the significance of the play lies in what one sees beyond the characters. Kurt List, in the *New Leader* (May 14, 1941), declared that *Wozzeck* "more and more has come to be the keynote of modern times." This uprooted serf symbolizes our social dislocation in a senseless world. In the captain is manifest the power of the petty bureaucrat; in the drum-major, the complacent vanity of the stupid male; and in the doctor, the wanton cruelty of the so-called scientific mind, in the name of humanity and the quest of immortality growing inhumane and deadly. In the disorderly existence in which he can divine no purpose, Wozzeck stumbles around.

Wozzeck had its London premiere, December 22, 1951. The *New Chronicle* called it "an astonishing work, a solitary masterpiece . . . One leaves the theater incredibly moved."

The mood in which Wozzeck's ideas are conveyed is one of melodramatic violence: "a sketchy expressionism, the brute force, the free rein of passion . . . atmosphere of sheer terror." This mood is at once organized, conveyed, and rendered bearable by the music of Alban Berg (Austrian, 1885-1935), who in the years before 1921 converted *Wozzeck* into an opera. It is the first full-length opera to make extensive use of atonality and other devices of modern music; it introduces symphonic elements and employs ballet technique. The opera was first heard in Berlin on December 14, 1925; in Prague, 1926; Leningrad, 1927; New York, 1931—in New York, and at the Salzburg Festival, in 1951. Harold Taubman, in the *New York Times* of August 26, 1951, said that "the terrible and purging impact . . . of *Wozzeck* would haunt the audience for days to come." Expressionistic in form, slantwise in allusiveness, *Wozzeck* reaches across a century as a bitter commentary on the cruelty and confused helplessness of modern times.

When the opera came to the Metropolitan Opera in New York in 1959, the music was dismissed: It "sounds as if the orchestra were tuning up all evening." Such dissonance now meets a more accustomed ear.

The play has continued to arouse audiences. It was shown in London, 1958, 1959, and (Covent Garden) 1960. At the Edinburgh Festival, 1973, the dead on the floor tattoo with their heels to the accelerating drumbeat. At the London Open Stage, 1973, avant-garde director Charles Marowitz had the drum-major mount Marie like a mating horse, while Wozzek played the showman's monkey. In 1976 Joseph Papp produced the play at his New York Public Theatre.

RICHELIEU   *Edward Bulwer-Lytton*

A five-act play written in blank verse, *Richelieu* is a resounding political melodrama. It was a prime favorite of the nineteenth-century theatre, when the stage with its huge projecting "apron" favored the rhetorical star. In

Richelieu, William Macready found one of his most successful roles; Edwin Booth was at his best as the wily Cardinal; and, according to *The Season* (January 14, 1871, looking back ten years), "he who saw Edwin Forrest play Bulwer's *Richelieu* saw the very perfection of the actor's art."

The play deals with the plot of the Count of Baradas and the Duke of Orleans to destroy Cardinal Richelieu (1585-1642) and make Louis XIII of France their puppet. Baradas and the King both covet Richelieu's ward, Julie, but the Cardinal gives her to the Chevalier de Mauprat, who thereupon shifts his allegiance to the Cardinal. After difficulties and dangers, Richelieu reveals to the King the intrigues of Baradas and Orleans, who are then banished.

The 1839 preface to *Richelieu* acknowledged that a scene in the fifth act was drawn from *The Fifth of March* by Alfred de Vigny, but *The Season* (date above) charged that most of the story was drawn from *A Tale of Romance,* by G. P. R. James. Bulwer-Lytton has, however, merely followed history. Macready, who had already produced Bulwer-Lytton's *The Lady of Lyons,* objected to the interpretation of Richelieu: "Bulwer has made the character particularly difficult by its inconsistency: he has made him resort to low jest, which outrages one's notions of the ideal of Cardinal Richelieu, with all his vanity and suppleness and craft." Bulwer-Lytton, however, had made the Cardinal human; he persuaded Macready to read the play to the company, which was enthusiastic.

London saw the play with Macready and Helen Faucit, March 7, 1839, and thereafter almost yearly, down the century. Edwin Booth played Richelieu from 1861 to 1882. On his Cincinnati opening, Booth was too drunk to play; his manager's plea saved him from critical castigation; and the next night he scored a blazing triumph. Henry Irving carried Richelieu along, from a run of 114 performances opening September 20, 1873, with revivals as late as 1904. His 1873 success prompted the burlesque *Richelieu Re-Dressed,* by Robert Reece, which opened October 27, 1873, for 110 performances.

The American premiere of *Richelieu* was in Philadelphia, the farewell performance of actor Harrington, May 13, 1839; in the same year, September 24, Edwin Forrest gave a munificent production, with costumes and sets of Paris in 1641, costing the then considerable sum of $600. Among others who have included *Richelieu* in their repertory are Lawrence Barrett, Robert Mantell, from 1904, and Walter Hampden, who acted in a three-act adaptation by Arthur Goodrich, December 25, 1929, and on to 1940. Henry Irving alternated *Richelieu, Hamlet,** and *Macbeth,** so much that many began to think all three plays were by Shakespeare.

Out of performances of *Richelieu* grew the most disastrous rivalry in theatre history. William Macready, after creating the role in London, played it in 1843 at the Park Theatre in New York. The American actor Edwin Forrest followed him in the same theatre in the same play. Most of the critics favored Macready; the rivalry was born. Two years later Forrest, visiting England, was booed and hissed by the London audience. He had his revenge in Edinburgh when, watching a performance of *Hamlet,* he himself hissed at the way Macready as Hamlet fluttered about Ophelia and did a "fancy dance" with his handkerchief in the play scene. Again in America in 1848-1849, Macready was scheduled to play Macbeth at the Astor Place Theatre. On May 7, in the surge of anti-British feeling, he was so bombarded with hisses, howls, and more solid objects that the performance could not continue. Ned Buntline, creator of Buffalo Bill, was one of the anti-

British instigators of the riot. Urged by Washington Irving and others to try again, Macready raised the curtain on May 10, 1849. There was another riot; the militia interfered; and when the theatre and the street outside were cleared, there were left lying thirty-six wounded and twenty-two dead.

Richelieu, though the dialogue is in a rhetorical blank verse now out of fashion, retains its forcefulness. The *New York Telegram* (December 26, 1929) found "a lively gusto throughout the play." Two of its lines are widely known: "The pen is mightier than the sword" and "In the lexicon of youth . . . there is no such word as fail." The play affords a still striking and emotionally sustained portrait of Cardinal Richelieu and of the tempestuous times he helped to mold.

THE LADY OF LYONS   *Edward Bulwer-Lytton*

Edward George Earle Lytton Bulwer-Lytton, First Baron Lytton of Knebworth (1803-1873), wrote his best novels *Eugene Aram,* 1832; *The Last Days of Pompeii,* 1834; *Rienzi,* 1838) and his only plays (*The Lady of Lyons, Richelieu, Money*) while serving in Parliament.

His first play opened in London, with Macready and Helen Faucit, February 15, 1838. Bulwer-Lytton in the Parliament that afternoon delivered one of his best speeches, on the extension of the franchise. He went directly to the theatre, where *The Lady of Lyons* was being presented anonymously. In the lobby, he asked an earlier-arrived member of the House how the play was going, and received answer: "All very well, for that sort of thing." When at final curtain the play received an ovation, Bulwer remarked: "All very well, for that sort of thing."

The idea for *The Lady of Lyons* was drawn from "The History of Perou; or, The Bellows Mender," a story taken from the French and related in a travel book by Helen Maria Williams, already dramatized unsuccessfully as *The Bellows Mender.* Macready first presented Bulwer-Lytton's play as *The Adventurer;* after its success, the authorship was acknowledged, and the title changed to *The Lady of Lyons; or, Love and Pride.*

The story covers the years 1795 to 1798. Pauline Deschapelles, proud daughter of a merchant of Lyons, is sought in marriage by many men. One that she rejects, the *ci-devant* Marquis de Beauséant, vengefully persuades the son of the former Deschapelles gardener, Claude Melnotte, to claim noble birth and woo her. As the Prince of Como, the accomplished Claude wins her hand. They are married; then he, ashamed of the trickery, discloses himself and offers to help Pauline annul the marriage. This proof of his devotion clinches her love.

Claude joins Napoleon's army. Under another name, he wins the rank of colonel and grows rich. Returning to Lyons incognito after two years, he finds Pauline on the brink of marriage to Beauséant, to save her father from bankruptcy. By "the Colonel," who comes as a friend of Claude, she sends despairing word of her true love. Claude thereupon takes her in his husbandly arms, and all is well.

The Lady of Lyons was constantly revived throughout the nineteenth century. Charlotte Cushman, beginning in 1838, varied her role, playing Pauline, the widow Melnotte, and even the male Claude. Others in the play were Mr. and Mrs. Charles Kean, 1842; Sam Phelps, 1844; Barry Sullivan with Helen Faucit, 1853; Laura Keene, 1853; Adelaide Neilson, 1872; Mr. and Mrs. Kendal, 1875; Ellen Terry, 1875, and with Henry Irving, 1879; Lily Langtry, 1886; J. Forbes Robertson, 1888 and a score of years after.

In New York, *The Lady of Lyons* had its premiere with Edwin Forrest, May 14, 1838. In it Mrs. Mowatt (the author of *Fashion*) made her debut in 1845. Edgar Allan Poe, who saw her in it several times, thought the play almost perfect, its one flaw being Pauline's readiness to remarry without making sure of her first husband's fate. The play was a favorite with Dickens. Actors made their names in it; when John Lester played Claude in New York in 1875, young ladies wore the tricolor in their bonnets; as with a movie star today, they set his picture in their choicest frames, and sent their beaux to Wallack's Theatre to study a lover's ways.

Montrose J. Moses in *Theatre Magazine,* November 1905, said: "There has perhaps never been a play more adversely criticized than *The Lady of Lyons,* yet we always turn to it with a certain sentimental satisfaction . . . there is no play that is more lavish with its situations." Despite these words, encomiums are far more frequent than dispraise. Thus, in the *London Times,* October 25, 1845: "*The Lady of Lyons* is a play that contains all the elements of popularity. It is admirably constructed; the course of its incidents never appears to outrage probability, in a dramatic point of view; the emotions of its characters are natural ones, and a culminating interest keeps its action from ever flagging." And the *Boston Transcript,* half a century later (May 27, 1902), declared: "It still interests, arouses, excites, and enthuses."

There is no question that, to our ears, the language of *The Lady of Lyons* is both stilted and extravagant. Yet in and for its period, it was unquestionably a powerful drama. In the larger scale of time, the play must still be recognized as valid and tender in its emotions, and surging in its dramatic drive.

MONEY   *Edward Bulwer-Lytton*

The play *Money,* first presented at the Haymarket, December 8, 1840, was one of the most popular dramas for the rest of the century. The title brings it promptly to everyone's attention.

In the play, Alfred Evelyn, whom an inheritance from a faraway relative brought suddenly from poverty to wealth, finds himself surrounded by new friends. Among them is the pretentious Sir John Vesey, who puts on a proud and wealthy front while maneuvering to have Evelyn marry his daughter Gloriana. Evelyn loves the simple country girl Clara. As *The Spirit of the Times* (January 16, 1841) put it: "The bitter lessons of dependence, and the mistakes they have generated, cling to him in the new world he enters, but the strength of a better nature triumphs. He tests and exposes his fashionable friends by affecting to be ruined at play, and re-unites himself to a gentle and earnest girl (very beautifully played by Miss Helen Faucit) from whom the errors of both his poverty and his wealth had unhappily separated him."

The paper more analytically continued: "With a singular and marked variety of incident and character, it has an impressive unity of purpose." Instead of random gags, or wit in anyone's mouth, as in the plays of Oscar Wilde, "There is not a ridiculous turn of expression, a touch of wit, or a thrust of pungent satire, that could be transferred to any other person without an obvious falsification of the character."

The play, as was the current fashion, exemplified in Dickens, gives aptronyms to the minor figures: the lawyer Mr. Sharp; the gambler Mr. Dudley (to his fellow-players "deadly") Smooth. Seeking the wealthy

Evelyn's patronage, there are brief appearances—cut from some revivals—
of Tabouret the jeweler, McStucco the architect, Kite the horse dealer,
Crimson the portrait painter, Grab the publisher, Patent the coach builder.
Mentioned but unseen in the play are the Radical Mr. Squab and the
Conservative Mr. Calm, as well as the more naturally named and neatly
revealed defeated candidate: "Mr. Popkins is in despair—not for himself—
but for the country! What *will* become of the COUNTRY!"

When William Macready accepted the manuscript of *Money,* he prepared
for its production with meticulous care, learning picquet so that he'd seem
natural in the important gambling scene. The play was an instant hit, with
Macready as Evelyn, Strickland as Vesey, Wrench as Captain Dudley
Smooth, Helen Faucit as Clara. Benjamin Webster as Graves and Miss P.
Horton as Gloriana were also in the June 13, 1848, Haymarket revival with
Charles Kean. Among other nineteenth-century productions were that of
Barry Sullivan as Evelyn, May 5, 1869, inaugurating his management of
the London Holborn; and the Forbes Robertson Evelyn, with John Hare as
Vesey, at the Garrick, May 21, 1894, which made considerable cuts but "with
the old wine in new bottles" offered "a very pleasant beverage to the public."

Lester Wallack (né John Johnstone) acted Evelyn for some years in the
1880's at Wallack's Theatre, New York.

In the twentieth century the play was for a time neglected. It was revived
at the Malvern Festival, England, August 1931. It was given a special
Actors' Fund Benefit performance at the New York New Amsterdam with
an all-star cast including Basil Sydney, Frances Starr, June Walker,
Miriam Hopkins. From November 23, 1979 to December 16, it was presented by the Meat and Potatoes Company OffOff Bway. In England again it
opened at the Stratford Other Place in November 1981. At the new Bar-
bizan Pit in London, June 22, 1982, Paul Shelley played Evelyn, John
Burgess, Vesey. Recent productions still find vitality in this presentation of
the eternal problem of money. As Evelyn exclaims when his fair-weather
friends turn from him in his pretended poverty: "I am the same man. Vice
and Virtue are written in one language: Failure and Success." *Plus ça
change, plus c'est la même chose.*

THE BOHEMIAN GIRL   *Alfred Bunn*

One of the most popular of romantic operas is *The Bohemian Girl,* by
Alfred Bunn (English, 1796?-1860), music by Michael William Balfe (Irish,
1806-1870). Opening in London, November 27, 1843, it ran for almost a
year. The original company repeated its triumph in New York, November
25, 1844, taking trade from the rival Italian Opera Company. For over ten
years *The Bohemian Girl* was the musical favorite of the United States,
inaugurating a vogue of gypsy festivals and gypsy styles. In 1933 Roy
Cropper sang in a production with gypsy dances by Albertina Rasch, and
whirlwind Arab acrobats in the scene of the Pressburg Fair. In 1943 and
1944, the centenary years, there were productions in many cities from
Dallas to Dublin.

The play was also an immediate success all over Europe. Balfe conducted
it in Vienna in 1851. It was presented in Italian, *La Zingara,* in Paris, 1869,
and Balfe was given the Cross of the Legion of Honor by Napoleon III.

There was a burlesque, *The Bohemian G'yurl,* by H. J. Byron*, 1877, in
which the Count's wife elopes with the gypsy leader. A burlesque film, with
Laurel and Hardy, was screened in 1936.

The opera opens in the eighteenth century on the estate of Count Arnheim, Governor of Pressburg. A Polish refugee, Thaddeus, escapes from the forces of the Count, aided by Devilshoof, leader of the gypsies, who carries with him the Count's daughter, Arline. Twelve years pass; Arline, raised among the gypsies, is guarded and loved by Thaddeus. Despite the jealousy of the gypsy Queen, they have a gypsy wedding. But at the Pressburg fair the Queen gives Arline a stolen medallion; Arline is arrested and brought before the Count. Her story leads to his recognizing her as his daughter. Thaddeus slips in to see her at the Count's home; amid the guests the gypsy Queen discloses him, thinking to disgrace Arline. When Thaddeus reveals that he is a Polish noble, and the Count accepts him as a son-in-law, the Queen tries to shoot Arline. Devilshoof interposes; in the struggle the weapon goes off and kills the Queen.

The Bohemian Girl is crowded (*New York Post,* July 28, 1933) "with some of the loveliest and most beloved melodies ever written for the light opera stage." Perhaps the most beloved song in all operetta is Arline's awakening: "I dreamt that I dwelt in marble halls." With the magical freshness that such melodies preserve," reported the *Post,* "when all that surrounded their beginnings has faded, they moved last night's audience just as they must have the one at Drury Lane when they were first sung nearly a century ago."

More popular now on the road than in metropolitan areas, *The Bohemian Girl* continues to appeal because of the charm of its music, the pleasant movement of its story, and the fact that its characters still seem thoroughly alive.

OUR BOYS   *Henry James Byron*

Our Boys, by Henry James Byron (1834-1884), was the first English play to achieve a run of over 1,000 performances. Opening on January 16, 1875, *Our Boys* ran until April 19, 1879, when, though still popular, it closed to make way for a sequel, *Our Girls,* having surpassed all earlier successes with an unbroken run of 1,362 performances. Among its several revivals, that of February 6, 1884, had 263 performances; that of September 14, 1892, 137. New York saw *Our Boys* September 18, 1875, and frequently thereafter until the early years of this century. In 1907, when a production was given in Italian, the *New York Dramatic Mirror* (April 13), noted that *Our Boys* had been played by nearly every amateur organization in this country and in England.

The story of the play has the appeal of love triumphing over parental opposition. It contrasts wealth in the country with city deprivation. Act I is laid at the home of Perkyn Middlewick, a retired and wealthy cheesemonger and butterman. Balanced against this rough but good-hearted self-made man is Sir Geoffrey Champneys, aristocratic heir of a long line of baronets, whose home in the charming countryside is the scene of the second act. Talbot, the baronet's son, is in love with Mary Melrose, who is poor. His friend Charles, son of the butterman, is in love with Violet Melrose, who is rich, and who scorns the uncultured Perkyn. Both boys are forbidden to marry their choices. The third act finds them in Mrs. Patcham's London garret, earning a precarious living at literary work. Here they are visited by the girls, and by their fathers. Their independence and their constancy win them forgiveness and love.

Our Boys has considerable, if to us somewhat obvious, humor. The two fathers are neatly contrasted: the aristocrat, haughty and formal; the businessman, bluff and jovial, uneducated but as wholesome as the products of his dairies. He is, like many characters from Shakespeare on, a bit of a Malaprop, who hurls his "ultapomatum" at his son. Both fathers are strict, yet basically decent and desirous of serving the best interests of their sons. *Our Boys* is a play without villains.

The play was critically well received in both London and New York. In London, the *Illustrated Sporting and Dramatic News* (January 23, 1875) said: "The excessive humour of the dialogue overpowers all critical consideration of the improbability of the characters and principal incidents . . . Those who go to the theatre for real enjoyment, to have a good laugh and to revel in witticisms poured forth without stint at every instant, cannot possibly do better than occupy places at this theatre during the performance of *Our Boys.*" The *New York Tribune* (September 20, 1875) called the play "fresh and charming . . . for at least two-thirds of the way genuine comedy, and it is, all the way, a delightful piece of literary and dramatic work."

The wit seems too purely verbal today; the characters not probed as dramatists since have learned to probe them. *Our Boys'* wholesome and elemental humor made it the first play of a thousand and one nights on the British stage. A musical by Bob Harris was tried in Farnham, England, December 23, 1963, but lacks the spell.

THE WONDER-WORKING MAGICIAN   *Pedro Calderón*

After an apparently wild youth, Pedro Calderón de la Barca (Spanish, 1600-1681) became attached to the court and was commissioned to write spectacular plays—in which the mechanic and the scenic designer outvied the dramatist—for the theatre of Philip IV of Spain at Buen Retiro. He was knighted for his *The Three Oldest Wonders* in 1636. Although ordained a priest in 1651, at the King's wish he continued writing plays. More and more of his 120 plays, however, were *autos sacramentales,* allegories of the mystery of the Eucharist. Calderón wrote his last secular play at the age of eighty-one, and was at work upon an *auto* when he died.

Calderón wrote plays of many types—palace comedies, historical plays, symbolic dramas (such as *The Wonder-Working Magician,* 1637, of which Shelley made a free translation), plays on the theme of jealousy, *pundonor* (point of honor) plays, cloak-and-sword dramas, and the *autos,* in which he was unrivalled. In every type, he proved himself an exquisite poet, sometimes extravagantly baroque, sometimes refreshingly direct and simple, admirably skilled in dramatic technique and full of the spirit of the devout, patriotic, chivalrous, artificial society of his time.

Calderón's most powerful play, rich in character development through tense dramatic conflict, is *The Wonder-Working Magician,* in which he presents the temptations and martyrdoms of Saint Cyprian and Saint Justina, who were put to death by the Governor of Antioch in A.D. 290. The scholar Cyprian falls in love with the poor Justina, a Christian maid whom Lelius, son of the Governor, also loves. When Cyprian is rejected by Justina, the devil disguised as a magician promises him the maid in return for his soul. The piety of the maid, however, protects her against the devil's wiles, although Lelius is led to believe her wanton. A simulacrum of the maid, conjured up by the devil, turns into a skeleton beneath Cyprian's gaze. The Governor, disliking the influence he thinks Justina has upon his son, orders the Christians arrested, and the maiden slain. Cyprian confesses, and goes to martyrdom by her side.

The main mood of the play is one of human goodness struggling against the temptations to which the flesh is heir. With cascades of rhetoric, elaborate diction and stage device, with strict observance of the rules of decorum, are combined a devout spirit and an inner simplicity of faith that sustain the power of *The Wonder-Working Magician* and through it sum up its age.

THE MAYOR OF ZALAMEA   *Pedro Calderón*

El Alcalde de Zalamea (The Mayor of Zalamea), c. 1650, is written with a simplicity that contrasts sharply with the flowery rhetoric of Calderón's cloak-and-sword dramas and with the elaborate and majestic structure of his religious works. Like many others of his time, he freely adapted and revised plays of earlier dramatists, including some by his rival Lope de Vega;* and from a rapid improvisation of Lope's came the finished masterpiece that is *The Mayor of Zalamea*. Freest of all Calderón's plays from farfetched symbols and high-heaped figures, *The Mayor of Zalamea* is a sober and realistic problem play. A tale of seduction lightly undertaken but dearly paid, it is pertinent today because the center of its action lies in conflict between civil and military authorities such as may recently have occurred in many parts of the world.

A proud and prosperous man of humble birth, the farmer Pedro Crespo has civil authority in a town through which the army is passing. When his daughter Isabel is ravished by an hidalgo captain, Don Alvaro, Crespo maintains that however loyal to his country a man may be, his honor is his own. He therefore arrests, then executes, the captain. King Philip II, passing through, checks further trouble by commending the mayor's action. Thus in Spain, the heart of conservative morality and monarchic devotion, a liberal thought took root: the notion that the *pundonor* (point of honor) applies not only to nobles but to all honest men.

The vigor of *The Mayor of Zalamea*, its straightforward and courageous drive, can still be felt. It was presented in Milwaukee in 1903; in New York in German in 1907; in Chicago in 1917, with Leo Dietrichstein as the Mayor; and again in New York, for one English performance by the Readers' Theatre, January 27, 1946. Arthur Pollock then called it "a fluent, vivid, wise drama." James Fitzmaurice-Kelly, in the *Encyclopedia Britannica,* referred to the play as "one of the greatest tragedies in Spanish literature"; and the playwright Benavente* has declared that "had Calderón written no more than *The Mayor of Zalamea* and *Life Is a Dream,* he would still be accounted one of the master dramatists of the world."

The first two acts of *The Mayor of Zalamea* present a pleasing picture of life in a Spanish country town, upon which the irruption of the troops breaks harshly. In the play, with simple dignity and forcefulness, Calderón probed deeply into a moral problem entangled in a political situation of continuing concern.

A new translation by Adrian Mitchell, close to the original, with rough rhymes and insistent rhythms, was effectively produced at the NT (Cottesloe), December 8, 1981. Michael Bryant played the Mayor; Daniel Massey, Don Alvaro; and the quality of the play was brilliantly maintained. The NT sent this production, directed by Michael Bogdanov, to the first Denver World Theatre Festival, July 1982.

The most popular of Calderón's mysteries, raising questions of reason and free will, balancing the forces of evil with the Divine Mercy, was *Life Is a Dream* (1635); its characters include Shadow, Earth, Air, Fire, and Water, the Prince of Darkness, and the Light of Grace. The Roy Campbell translation was shown January 26, 1958, at Oxford; in February 1967 at Leeds, England; and in 1962 OffBway. In 1964 at the OffBway Astor, it was shown on alternate nights in Spanish and in English. Adapted and directed by Maria Irene Fornes, it was performed OffBway (West 42d Street Little Theatre Row) in 1981, the three hundredth anniversary of Calderón's death. It was in the RSC repertory in 1984.

CALIGULA   *Albert Camus*

Albert Camus (French, 1913-1960) in 1935 organized a little theatre of students and factory workers in Algiers, for whom in 1938 he wrote *Caligula.* Interrupted by World War II, during which Camus worked for the Underground, the play was produced in Paris in 1945, with Gerard Philipe as the Emperor, and ran for two years. Camus added a philosophical basis to the material from Suetonius' *Lives of the Twelve Caesars;* then for twenty years he continued writing new versions, drawing ideas from *The Myth of Sisyphus,* 1942. In 1952, he was awarded the Nobel Prize.

The play pictures "the passion for the impossible," a development of Camus' need for clarity and reason in the face of the unreasonable silence of the universe. Solitary, man must endeavor to be free. Caligula, after the death of his sister-mistress, Drusilla, chose freedom as a career of motiveless cruelty. He kills a patrician's son; at a banquet he takes another's wife into an adjoining room to make love. He summons the leader of the patrician conspirators, Chearea, who boldly declares that he refuses to live in a world that pushes absurdity to its logical conclusion, who demands a world of security and happiness. Caligula tells him that logic and security do not go together; but he spares the man.

Caligula sets a poetry contest: subject, Death; time limit, one minute. The patricians scribble till the whistle blows. But Caligula's mood has changed; he dresses as Venus, and demands their worship.

Fronting his mirror, the Emperor states: "There is no understanding Fate; therefore I choose to play Fate." The conspirators crowd in. Caligula cries: "My freedom is not the right one." He shatters the mirror and calls defiantly, "I am still alive," as he dies.

Adapted by Justin O'Brien, *Caligula* was presented at the 59th Street Theatre OffBway, opening February 16, 1960, for thirty-eight performances, with Kenneth Haigh as the Emperor; in London, 1962, with Haigh, Colleen Dewhurst, and Philip Bourneuf. Again in London, 1964 and 1966, it was termed "all-absorbing, with unremitting and undeviating intelligence, with a nimble yet chilling wit." Further revivals include Washington, D.C., 1968; London, 1970, by Le Tréteau de Paris, in French; 1972, at Yale, and by La Mama OffBway; and in April 1978 at New Rochelle College, N.Y., with Caligula (said Richard Eder in the *Times*) capering like "a degenerate transvestite." Out of this tragedy of the intelligence, *Caligula* through the exaltation of evil poses a basic and never finally answered question.

R. U. R.   *Karel Capek*

After his first play, a lyrical comedy entitled *The Robber,* 1920, Karel Capek (Czechoslovakian, 1890-1938) wrote the full-bodied melodrama,

R. U. R., which has driven sharply home the thought that man may become slave to the machine.

The play introduces Russum's Universal Robots, mechanical men manufactured wholesale for every purpose—male robots for factory, farm, and battlefield; female robots as shop clerks, typists, and maids. The robots are designed to do nothing but relieve humans of all toil, until Helena Glory, President of the Humanitarian League, persuades their creator, Dr. Gall, to "better" the condition of the robots by giving them nerves and feelings. Almost their first feeling is one of hatred for their maker, man. Rising in rebellion, they wipe out the entire human race, save the mason Alquist. With the formula for their manufacture destroyed by the disappointed Helena, Alquist tells them he can do nothing to continue their species without dissecting one of them. A robotess is chosen but when a robot volunteers in her place, Alquist sees the love agleam in their eyes and knows he is not needed.

Opening in Prague in 1921, *R. U. R.* came to New York on October 9, 1922, for 184 performances, with Basil Sydney, Helen Westley, and Louis Calvert. It opened in London, March 24, 1923, for 126 performances, with Basil Rathbone and Frances Carson, and was revived in New York in 1930 and 1942. During the latter year, it was also played by marionettes. The play has been very popular in college and community theatres; there were three OffBway productions in 1935.

The critics were highly enthusiastic in their reception of *R. U. R.* The *Illustrated Sporting and Dramatic News* (May 26, 1923) said of the London production, "In the last act, when the audience and one feeble old man on the stage are the only humans left alive, and the stage is filled with swaggering, Prussianized robots, we feel almost nervous as to our own safety." Heywood Broun was even more moved after the New York premiere: "Against a bloody sky the audience sees the head of the Robot leader as he climbs up the balcony, and then more and more sweep into the room and exterminate the feeble garrison. Not more than ten or twelve actors clad in the uniform blue of the Robots actually enter the room, but the director has managed to create the effect that millions are on the move. The movement is quite the most terrifying one we have ever known in the theatre." Years later, when Capek was dead and Europe overrun by mechanized men, Broun said (December 27, 1938), "I remember it still as one of the most frightening experiences I have ever seen in a theatre." Alexander Woollcott called the play a "Murderous social satire." The *New York Sun* (October 10, 1922) called *R. U. R.* "a supermelodrama, of action plus ideas."

When he observes the havoc wrought by the robots, the sole human survivor, Alquist, recalls that there are prayers against drought, against most natural disasters and human diseases, and wonders why there has never been a prayer against progress. (The present writer supplied one in the *Folio*, 1926.) But Capek, wiser than his mason, did not attack progress; he levelled his satire against mechanization, against the soulless growth of instruments of power; and out of a cataclysm that obliterates civilization (such as our split-atom age fears from another war) Capek saw the regeneration of the human spirit. The double prophecy of doom and resurrection gives *R. U. R.* power and persisting appeal.

Among recent revivals of the play: London, 1962; Pitlochry Festival, Scotland, 1969; Hollywood (Masquers' Club), 1981. The last words of the play are spoken by the remaining human, as he watches the tender couple of robots walk away: "Adam, Eve."

THE INSECT COMEDY   *Karel Capek*

"A bug-eye view of the human race" was presented by the Capek brothers in *The Insect Comedy*, 1921 (also translated as *The Insect Play, And So Ad Infinitum* and *The World We Live In*), an ingenious satire à la Gulliver, through the behavior of insects exposing the foibles of man. Karel Capek, novelist and playwright, wrote the drama with his brother, the novelist and painter, Joseph (1887-1945).

The action of the play begins with a human wanderer, a broken-down student left stranded by World War I, who falls asleep, watching an insect. As he dreams, the world of insects takes on human size and human speech. Butterflies, in trifling dalliance, fight for the favors of a poet. Beetles, rolling a monster ball of dung, hoard their pile and steal it. A cricket, fatuously proud, cricks over his hungry brood until it is devoured. Brown and yellow ants, totalitarian both, whip up their industry for war, and when the leader of the victorious yellow ants cries, "I am Ruler of the world," the indignant human tramples him down.

Throughout all this insect activity, there is a chrysalis on stage, to which something tremendous is to happen. From it is born a Mayfly, which, after some late moths promise it eternal life, flutters and falls dead. Exhausted, the human being joins the troop of death.

After a brilliant success in Europe, the play opened in New York as *The World We Live In,* with a cast of two hundred, on October 31, 1922. Adapted by Owen Davis, with verses by Louis Untermeyer, it was, according to Alan Dale, received "with crescendo interest by a fascinated audience." The *New York Times* somewhat caustically commented that "somewhere these butterflies, beetles, and ants must have been contaminated by the example of rather degenerate humans . . . a travesty conceived in the spirit of the wartime pacifist and the peacetime hater of progress. "Alexander Woollcott called it "as bitter and despondent and resentful a play as this city has seen in our time . . . far and away the handsomest and most ambitious project of all Brady's adventuring in the theatre . . . a thrilling and magnificent spectacle."

The size of the cast and the complexity of the production have kept the number of revivals to a minimum, but the play was seen again in New York in 1948.

London accorded *The Insect Play* an even heartier reception than New York. An adaptation by Nigel Playfair and Clifford Bax from a translation by Paul Selver opened, May 5, 1923, with Claude Rains, John Gielgud, Marie O'Neill, and Elsa Lanchester. There were revivals in 1936 and 1938; the latter included Joyce Redman as Mrs. Cricket. James Agate in the *London Times* (June 28, 1936) quoted his own earlier praise of the play, adding that "with the possible exception of *Everyman,* the allegory in this play fits better than in any other that I know . . . But the play has a good deal more than satire. It attains in the character of Chrysalis to both beauty and pathos . . . Let not the normal playgoer be afraid of this piece, which is just as highbrow as he likes to make it, and is intensely amusing and arresting throughout."

The insect world, as seen in the play, is one of incessant struggle, savage and heartless competition. It depicts life as less a progress of living than a postponement of dying. Only here and there, among the most ephemeral of creatures, are there moments of hope and wonder, or of quickly dispelled impulses of happiness. The Capeks, nevertheless, have made the play continuously absorbing. In it we watch the pompous, cunning, and ruthless actions of the insects until we are carried along with them. Their application to human life is an intellectual exercise that comes after the emotional flow of the drama itself.

The 1948 revival at the New York City Center included José Ferrer, George Coulouris, and Paula Laurence. It was OffOffBway in 1976 (Park Avenue Presbyterian Church) and 1978 (Soho Rep). A 1966 version by the Czech National Theatre in London used modern human clothes; with ingenious slanting mirrors over the Aldwych stage, it gave the audience a double view, so that, for example, the butterflies (as Harold Hobson said), "which on the ground look rather like beefy Czechs waving pieces of colored tulle become graceful and poetic." James Agate added: "In the third act more sense is talked in twenty minutes than the peace-mongers and war-mongers have mastered in the past twenty years." The play was shown in 1971 in Toronto.

THE MAKROPOULOS SECRET   *Karel Capek*

Those who are familiar with Bernard Shaw's *Back to Methusaleh** will find quite a different consideration of longevity in Karel Capek's *The Makropoulos Secret*, 1922. Capek's aged ones do not achieve the indefinite prolongation of life that results in the "intellectual ecstasy" of Shaw's ancients. In their three-hundred-year spells of renewal, they do not even attain the widsom and earnestness of purpose that animate Shaw's tricentenarians. *The Makropoulos Secret*, indeed, dramatizes the thought that we should be content with one life span as it is.

In Capek's play, complications in the law courts reveal that Emilia Marti, a Viennese opera singer, is really Ellena Makrops, born in the sixteenth century. Her father, a Greek alchemist at the court of Emperor Rudolph, had found a formula for longevity, which requires renewal every three centuries. His daughter has stayed young, as Ellena MacGregor, as Eugenie Montez, and now as Emilia Marti, achieving new careers with her successive regenerations. Life, to her, is a round of love affairs, with an ever-widening edge of boredom that grows to disgust and then to horror when her own son Gregor and then her great-great-grandson Janek unwittingly fall in love with her. When they discover the truth, Janek kills himself, and his sweetheart Kristina destroys the formula. Emilia is quite content to have her centuries end.

The Makropoulos Secret, the *New Yorker* observed (February 6, 1926), presents "as weird and engrossing a theme as six nightmares and twenty-seven love affairs can conjure." The *London Observer* (July 13, 1930) said that it "makes strangeness palpable."

The *London Times* (September 13, 1931), however, regretted the gradual lapse of years into weary boredom: "After immensities of leading up, the thing led up to turns out to be almost nothing at all . . . at the end, the play has only allayed curiosity without satisfying the mind." Contrasting Capek with Shaw, the *Times* did not allow the Czech playwright the privilege of his own purpose. In *Back to Methusaleh*, Shaw shows a longer life leading to wisdom. Capek, on the other hand, inquires into what longevity can mean to us. Be content with your allotted span, he concludes: With agelessness such values as good and bad, such feelings as faith and hope, lose their meaning; endurance becomes a fully foreseen, drab, changeless span of boredom: Happiness requires change and hinges upon uncertainty. The boredom in

The Makropoulos Secret, however, does not tinge the audience, whether it prefers Shaw's ascetic optimism or Capek's view of banal years.

The play was shown by the Phoenix, opening in New York, November 26, 1957, with Eileen Herlie, adapted and directed by Tyrone Guthrie. An opera by Leoš Janáček, *The Makropulos Affair* (1925), was shown at the Holland Festival, 1958; Sadlers Wells, London, 1964; San Francisco Opera, 1966; Philharmonic Hall, New York, 1967, with soprano Maralin Niska as the 342-year-old Emilia, showing, Harriet Jonson reported in the *Post,* November 2, 1970, "not only the scars of her body caused by her past lovers, but her seductive bare back and behind in the bargain."

SHADOW AND SUBSTANCE   *Paul Vincent Carroll*

The problems of faith—of rigid adherence and tolerant acceptance—are pressed to dramatic intensity in the plays of Paul Vincent Carroll (1900-1968), Irish-born schoolmaster of Glasgow, Scotland. His *Things That Are Caesar's,* 1932, written with Teresa Deevey, centered the two attitudes in the Hardy family; with a bigoted mother and a free-thinking father, the daughter tries to work out her own happiness. The play won the Abbey Theatre Prize.

Shadow and Substance, 1934, sets a similar opposition in the household of the Very Reverend Thomas Canon Skerritt, whose brilliant mind and acid wit have to be attuned to the small minds of the townsfolk of whom he is the spiritual mentor. A young and crusading schoolmaster has written a book against intolerant rigidity, which, issued anonymously, enrages the town. The Canon, upon learning that schoolmaster Dermot Francis O'Flingsley is the author of the work, discharges him. A naïve serving maid, Brigid, has the sympathy of Dermot in her belief that she has talked with St. Brigid, while the Canon, whom she loves equally well, sternly bids her to dismiss the thought. When the townsfolk learn that Dermot is the author of the book that has scandalized them, Brigid, running to save him from their wrath, is hit by a rock and killed. Dermot and the Canon are left to ponder the excesses of virtue, as the sacrifice of the maid breaks through the Canon's intellectual shield.

Carroll's portraits of the schoolmaster and the Canon are superb. Especially the latter is drawn with sympathy, with understanding of his devotion, and of the submission of his fine intellect to the simple station where the Lord has posted him. The Canon's faith is intellectual rather than emotional, his view of life is almost aesthetic rather than ethical. He says: "Catholicism rests on a classical, almost abstract love of God rather than the frothy swirl of emotionalism." Brigid, who loves him, says: "His pride would need the tears of a hundred just men and the soul of a child to soften it." Her soul sufficed.

The beauty and power of *Shadow and Substance* were at once recognized. The play was a hit in Dublin, where it opened on January 25, 1937. In New York it opened on January 26, 1938, with Sir Cedric Hardwicke, Sara Allgood, and Julie Haydon, and ran for 274 performances, winning the Drama Critics' Circle Award as the best foreign play of the year. London saw it on May 25, 1943. It has been shown widely in the United States. On its New York opening, John Andersen declared: "No play that has come this way in many a long lost night has filled a theatre with such passionate eloquence, such probing power, and such spiritual beauty." *Stage* (February 1938) stated: "The tragedy—which leaves the Canon at last facing his icy abstractions alone, sees her happily dead with her faith unscarred—builds grandly, in the hands of a true playwright and prophet."

Shadow and Substance, reminding us that a great drama may soar without consent of sex, is built upon natural persons, earnest and honest in their different sorts. It is a drama that probes deeply into the ways by which goodness itself may engender evil and examines the opposition of dogmatic austerity to the emotional necessities of the heart.

When the play was shown in New York, opening November 1959, the part of Brigid was played by the author's daughter, Helen Carroll.

THE WHITE STEED   *Paul Vincent Carroll*

The White Steed, 1938, more specifically presses the problem of the letter and the spirit, the strict and the tolerant, than Paul Vincent Carroll's earlier plays. Its title is taken from the old Irish legend of Ossian, son of Finn, who was borne by the lovely goddess Niam to the land of eternal youth, where he dwelled with her for three hundred years. When he returned to earth, he found no heroes—only little black-haired men. Trying to show them how the olden warriors met their tasks, Ossian slipped from his white steed, touched the earth, and crumbled into dust.

In the play, a dreaming, liberal woman returns from England, to find the Irish oppressed and ignorant, dominated by selfish, rapacious masters. She hoists a schoolmaster on the "white steed" of her zeal to bring reform. His rebellious impulses are clouded by drink, and opposed both by young Father Shaughnessy, who pins the hope for the world on laws and their strict observance and by old Canon Matt Lavelle, who is paralyzed below the waist, but tolerant and forgiving. When the priest organizes a vigilante committee the Canon asserts himself, to establish the simpler ways of kindly faith.

Presented in New York, January 10, 1939, with Barry Fitzgerald and Jessica Tandy, *The White Steed* ran for 136 performances, and became the second Carroll play to win the Drama Critics' Circle award. London saw the play with Wendy Hiller.

While it is more limited in its appeal than *Shadow and Substance,** The White Steed* again reveals Carroll's ability to penetrate his characters and portray their soul-struggles. His problems rise out of contrasted natures, both good, opposed neither in starting-point nor in goal, yet by temperament driven to methods that clash. *The White Steed* "is a play of bone and sinew" said *Variety* (January 18, 1939), "of passion and tenderness, tears and laughter. It is timely yet timeless, earthy yet exalted. It electrifies the mind and enkindles the heart."

Combining realism with beauty, the play has at times a homely humor that keeps it close to the Irish soil and a lilting poetry and spiritual surge that lift it to the Irish heavens. Carroll, said Brooks Atkinson (January 11, 1939) "straps winged words to his white steed and trails flaming phrases through the empyrean." That the world has shriveled to a waste land, from the golden days of yore, is no new notion; *The White Steed,* quite the contrary, rings with affirmation of the worth of the present-day world, of the value of simple faith and a gentle heart. It brings such assurance with beauty and dramatic power.

A BOLD STROKE FOR A WIFE   *Mrs. Centlivre*

Mrs. (Susannah Freeman) Centlivre (English, 1667?-1723), wife of the cook to Queen Anne, wrote eighteen plays, one of which, *The Wonder! A*

Woman Keeps a Secret, 1714, provided Garrick with one of his most suc-cessful roles; and two—*The Busybody,* 1709, and *A Bold Stroke for a Wife,* 1718—have characters whose names have added words to the language.

A Bold Stroke for a Wife involves a pair of lovers, Colonel Fainall and Anne Lovely. Anne's guardian is the Quaker Obadiah Prim. To win his consent, the Colonel pretends to be "the quaking preacher," Simon Pure. After all is settled, "the real Simon Pure" arrives.

This play was presented in London, February 3, 1718; and it was the first professional production in New York, at the Nassau Theatre, November 9, 1750. Although its plot is in the usual vein of Restoration comedy, the play was at first not very favorably received for, in spirit, it was already ap-proaching the sentimental comedy of the later eighteenth century. Instead of suggestive situations and cynical lines, with wit so singly sexed that it can hardly be said to have a double-meaning, *A Bold Stroke for a Wife* relies upon more innocent complications and a dialogue in which the sparkle of erotic wit is replaced by a milder but warmer gleam of humor. Consequently, after but few revivals over a period of sixty years, *A Bold Stroke for a Wife* became quite popular in the 1780's and 1790's, when sentimental drama held the English stage.

One sign of the play's popularity was the production (February 25, 1783) of *A Bold Stroke for a Husband,* by Mrs. Hannah (Parkhouse) Cowley (1743-1809). This showed Donna Olivia acting as a termagant to drive away her persistent suitors. Her maid, Minette, impersonates Olivia to interview Don Julio, and he becomes the successful wooer of Olivia. The sentimental mood is at its height in this artificial comedy. It was played in New York, at the John Street Theatre, May 19, 1794; and by Fanny Davenport in 1872. An unfortunate musical was made of it, called *Miss Leasing Lady,* in London, 1979.

A Bold Stroke for A Wife looks ahead to the sentimental comedy of the later eighteenth century. It is not mawkish, but mellows its artificial story with the glow of natural feeling, and a rich element of Simon Pure charm.

ALL FOOLS   *George Chapman*

Next to Ben Jonson,* George Chapman (English, 1559-1634), is the most learned and most erratic of the Elizabethan dramatists. Within one play, he rises to great heights and sinks to extravagant bathos. His first play, *The Blind Beggar of Alexandria,* 1596, is faulty to excess. "Of all the English play-writers," said Charles Lamb, "Chapman perhaps approaches nearest to Shakespeare in the descriptive and didactic, in passages which are less purely dramatic . . . In himself he had an eye to see and a soul to embrace all forms . . . I have often thought that the vulgar misconception of Shake-speare, as of a wild irregular genius 'in whom great faults are compensated by great beauties,' would be really true, applied to Chapman."

Chapman's present-day fame rests largely on Keats' sonnet in praise of his translation of Homer (*The Iliad,* in 14-syllable rhyming lines, 1611; *The Odyssey,* in heroic couplets, 1615). Of his plays, two comedies, and four tragedies on French themes, are powerful enough to be still rewarding.

All Fools, 1599, is Chapman's best comedy. More than any other of his plays, it follows an ingenious plot (drawn from the *Heautontimoroumenos** of Terence) to a fit climax. The play is a realistic satire; it shows the influence of Ben Jonson, both in its pervasive cynicism and in its portrayal of the characters, who are less individuals than personifications of humours.

The main movement of *All Fools* is in the intrigue centered on the vain and dictatorial knight Gostanzo, who believes that his spendthrift son, Valerio, secretly married to Gratiana, is a paragon of bachelor virtue. Gostanzo's friend, Marc Antonio, has two sons: the elder, Fortunio, is in love with Gostanzo's daughter, Bellonora; his brother, Rinaldo, is a gay young blade, who seeks "to win renown by gulling." Rinaldo tells Gostanzo that Fortunio has married Gratiana. As a result Gostanzo is led unwittingly to give sanction to the wedding of both his son and his daughter.

The comedy was played in 1599 under the title *The World Runs on Wheels;* it was presented before King James as *All Fools But the Fool.* Much of the bustle of the turbulent and colorful Elizabethan age is caught in this lively comedy.

EASTWARD HOE   *George Chapman*

As Swinburne has said of *Eastward Hoe,* "In no other play of the time do we get such a true taste of the old city life, so often turned to ridicule by playwrights of less good humour, or feel about us such a familiar air of ancient London as blows through every scene." The play was written by George Chapman in collaboration with Ben Jonson and John Marston. The title is drawn from the cries of the boatmen on the Thames.

Eastward Hoe, 1605, tells of the efforts of Sir Petronel Flash to dodge his debts and—beguiling the vain and ambitious Gertrude with tales of a nonexistent estate eastward in England—to escape with her wealth to Virginia. Caught in a storm on the Thames, he is brought back and his ruse discovered. Nevertheless, he and Gertrude seek to make a match of it.

The value of the work lies in its ripe display of characters. A. H. Bullen has said: "Of the merits of *Eastward Hoe* it would be difficult to speak too highly. To any who are in need of a pill to purge melancholy this racy old comedy may be safely commended."

The play was popular for a century. In 1685 Nahum Tate combined it with Jonson's *The Devil is an Ass* to make his own farce, *The Cuckold's Haven.* In 1751 Garrick revived it as *The Prentices.* From it Hogarth drew the idea for his prints, the *Industrious* and the *Idle Prentice.* Then the play lapsed from the stage. There was a production at Cambridge, Massachusetts, in 1903; another at Columbia University, New York, in 1947, which showed that *Eastward Hoe* is still richly entertaining.

For a time, the play sent its authors to prison. Accounts vary as to just what in *Eastward Hoe* displeased the new king (James I, crowned 1603) and his Scottish followers. There are references to the now proverbial canniness and thrift of the Scot; it is said that one of the actors imitated the King's brogue. The influx of Scots friends and followers of James was undoubtedly resented by the Londoners; in one passage (Act III, iii, lines 40-47), speaking of the advantages of Virginia, Seagull wishes the Scots would all go there: "For my part I would a hundred thousand of 'hem were there, for we are all one countrymen now, ye know; and we should find ten times more comfort of them there than we do here." This passage is not in the later quartos, nor in the version James himself laughed at when he saw the play in 1614. But in 1605, on complaint of the newly created knight Sir James Graham, the authors were sent to prison and were sentenced to have their ears and noses cropped. Again, accounts vary. Some say all three spent some time in jail. Others say Marston, who really wrote the lines in question, escaped punishment. Jonson, in his later conversations with Drummond of Hawthornden, declared that Chapman and Marston were arrested, and that he voluntarily associated himself with them in the jail. At any rate, the plea of powerful patrons soon brought them forth unscathed. At a dinner Jonson gave to celebrate their release, his mother showed the poison she had secured for her son and herself if he were disgraced by ear lopping . . . The triple collaboration made *Eastward Hoe* a genial yet searching picture of London ways and characters.

Another reason for the imprisonment may well have been the line alluding to the King's device of increasing his funds by selling preferment: "I ken the man weel; he's one of my forty-pound knights." Indeed, everyone seems to be engaged in cheating or cuckolding everyone else. Of course, in America, as Flash puts it, "the chamber-pots are made of gold."

The Mermaid Theatre, London, is a stone's throw from Puddle Dock, where Flash embarked. And there were revivals of the play at the Mermaid in 1953 and 1962. Also at the Mermaid, July 7, 1981, a musical version by Eder and Robert Chetwyn, music by Nick Briat, lyrics by Howard Schuman, ran briefly. It omits Gertrude's footman named Hamlet, with the allusion to Shakespeare's play on his first entrance: "Sfoot, Hamlet are you mad?"

HARVEY   *Mary Chase*

Those that have had no personal experience with a pooka will meet one most amusingly in *Harvey,* and will come almost to believe that they see the invisible six-foot-one-and-a-half-inch rabbit that has become the boon companion of Elwood P. Dowd. A fellow who notes that the sober persons of the world are also inclined to be dyspeptic, grouchy, mean, and generally intolerant and unendurable, Elwood prefers to be pie-eyed, good-natured, and happy. In his ebrious hours, he becomes attached to the big pooka, Harvey, who accompanies him everywhere. His deeply concerned but somewhat silly sister, Veta Louise Simmons (whose daughter intensifies her mother's quality) thinks Elwood might be better off in a sanitarium; but signals are switched and it is Veta who is confined. By the time she is released, she too is making eyes at Harvey.

Harvey, written by Mary Chase (American, b. 1907), was at first called *The White Rabbit;* then it was decided to call the white rabbit Harvey. Boston liked the play when it opened there, October 17, 1944. *The Post* called it "a mad, sweet, and soundly sane comedy of a mild, sweet screwball who was kind, gentle, polite and comical." *Harvey* came to New York, November 1, 1944, took the Pulitzer Prize in its six-foot-one-and-a-half-inch stride, and went on for 1,775 performances. Elwood was played by Frank Fay (then by James Stewart, Joe E. Brown, James Dunn, Jack Buchanan, the play's producer Brock Pemberton, and Bert Wheeler). Elwood's sister Veta was, for the most part, played by the superbly competent Josephine Hull. Harvey remained blandly invisible, but, as Robert Coleman said (June 7, 1948), "continues to give a marvelous performance. That is probably because the world's most famous Pooka becomes a creation of every member of the audience."

The press bubbled over with praise of *Harvey.* Robert Garland, for instance, called it "stage sorcery at its whimsical best, with gaiety, gusto, and guts." Even George Jean Nathan announced that "The Nathan Fife and Drum Corps parades today in honor of Mary Chase's *Harvey* . . . an evening of intelligent laughter."

There is good fun in the play from the efforts of Elwood's associates, at first to convince him that Harvey does not exist, then, gradually, to get a glimpse of the creature. There are amusing caricatures of psychiatrists and more usual citizens. There is, basically, the pleasure many folks derive from the spectacle of someone who, though possessed of the failings to which mankind is prone, is fundamentally good and ultimately triumphant. *Harvey* is a modern transmogrification of *Rip Van Winkle*.* But one should not take the play as a prescription.

Among the numerous revivals of the inimitable *Harvey*: a 1951 Negro Touring Company; 1955 at the Paper Mill, N.J., with Joe E. Brown; 1967, ANTA (New York) for seventy-nine performances; 1970, Phoenix, with James Stewart (who also took along Harvey in the film) and Helen Hayes; 1971, Phoenix, touring with Gig Young and Shirley Booth; 1975, London, with James Stewart. Harvey still hops around.

George Jean Nathan, who was fond of tracing an idea to however remote a source, called *Harvey* "an extended paraphrase of the old burlesque skit wherein the inebriated low comedian is told that he is sitting opposite a great big luscious blonde and drinking champagne and wherein he thereupon for the next ten minutes accepts the delusion as fact and has himself a wonderful time, embroidered with the Pirandello theory of the superiority of illusion to reality." O'Neill's *The Iceman Cometh** argues that man requires illusion.

THE SEA GULL   *Anton P. Chekhov*

Anton P. Chekhov's grandfather was a Russian serf who saved enough to buy his family's freedom. Anton's father struggled unsuccessfully to make a living; Anton (1860-1904), while studying medicine, helped support the family by writing short stories for humorous periodicals. Later, he turned to the writing of brief dramatic sketches.

In all his work, Chekhov manifests deep sympathy for the peasant and the poor, combined with keen observation of the various levels of society into which his work as a physician gave him intimate entry. "As a doctor," he said, "I have tried to diagnose the illnesses of the soul." As for his writings, he observed, "I have no doubt that the study of the medical sciences has had an important influence on my literary work: they have considerably widened the range of my observation, and enriched me with knowledge, the true value of which to me, as a writer, can be understood only by one that is himself a doctor . . . I do not belong to those fiction writers that take a negative attitude toward science; nor would I belong to the order of those that arrive at everything by their own wits."

When *The Sea Gull* opened on October 17, 1896, at the Alexandrinski Imperial Theatre in St. Petersburg, the audience, familiar with the comic skits Chekhov had written previously, laughed at the wrong moments. On December 17, 1898, the two-months-old Moscow Art Theatre presented *The Sea Gull*, and the Moscow Art and Chekhov soared to fame together. In the cast were Stanislavski (Trigorin), Meyerhold (Treplev, the young poet), Olga Knipper, whom Chekhov later married (Irina), and Roxanova (Nina). So important was the production in the history of the new group, that the emblem of the Moscow Art Theatre has, ever since, been a sea gull.

In the play, the sea gull is a symbol of the restless young Nina, who turns from the devoted love of the young dreamer and poet, Konstantin Treplev, to run off with the older writer Trigorin. After two years, the bored Trigorin returns to his earlier mistress, the fading actress Irina, Treplev's mother. Treplev, as an artist, has meanwhile abandoned the quest of new forms, in order to set down, direct, the outpourings of his soul. These outpourings, he would again dedicate to Nina; but she joins a traveling theatrical company, and Treplev kills himself.

Over this story hangs a fog of frustration, a sense of lives frittered away. The actress Irina lives on the glamorized memory of a second-rate past. Trigorin is drawn to Nina because she worships in him the things he'd have liked to be, but is not, the true success he has been too smug a drifter to achieve. Each of the persons in the play is a study in wasted potentiality. Such a tone-quality is best shadowed forth in moments of silence, and as Kenneth Tynan remarked in *He That Plays the King* (1950), Chekhov applied in the drama his observation that the normal condition of man is not "one of endlessly reshuffled conversation, but dead quiet . . . By exploiting this mood of stage silence, Chekhov immeasurably magnified the importance of speech. For him action is the interval between pauses; for other playwrights pauses are the intervals between actions. All the big battles in Chekhov are fought in the silences between the lines." It is in silence that intimacies ripen, that confidences—and decisions—prepare.

The Sea Gull has been given superb productions in English as well as in Russian. The best in London—James Agate called it "endlessly beautiful"—opened May 20, 1936, with Edith Evans as Irina, Peggy Ashcroft as Nina, John Gielgud as Trigorin, Stephen Haggard as Treplev, and Leon Quartermaine. The *London Times* (May 21, 1936) declared: "*The Sea Gull* is among the supreme masterpieces in the theatre, having, particularly in the first and second acts, a fluidity and ease that by their perfection make the heart turn over. To these qualities are added, as the play advances, a terrible insight into human weakness that has created the scene of Nina's clinging to her unwilling lover, and the superb pity that enabled Chekhov to reach, without strain, the tragic climax of the last act." It opened again in London, November 16, 1949.

New York has seen four outstanding presentations of the play: the Washington Square Players (May 22, 1916), with Helen Westley (Irina), Mary Morris (Nina), and Roland Young (Trigorin); a Bulgakov production (April 8, 1929) with Dorothy Sands, Barbara Bulgakova, and Walter Abel; the Civic Repertory (September 16, 1929) with Merle Maddern, Josephine Hutchinson, Jacob Ben-Ami, and Eva Le Gallienne; and the Theatre Guild, opening March 28, 1938, with Lynn Fontanne, Uta Hagen, Alfred Lunt, Richard Whorf, and Margaret Webster. Equity Library revived the play, April 3, 1945.

Brooks Atkinson said of *The Sea Gull* (April 9, 1929): "It is written in words of sheer light; it illuminates everything it touches." On September 17, 1929, he called the Constance Garnett translation "a strange, sombre, infinitely sympathetic sweep of truth." The Lunts used a version by Stark Young which brought the play nearer to the directness and simplicity of diction of the original. On March 29, 1938, Atkinson spoke of "lines which echo mortality . . . pure expression, limpid and translucent . . . the tragedy of indifference."

Chekhov's deep sympathy wells in *The Sea Gull,* but it does not cloud his comprehension of heartbreak and futility. He can mix farce with tragedy, and, out of laughter at our follies, distill tears for our fate. Somehow, from the very mire of despair, his clear vision and his compassion rise to a gathering hope. The melancholy of *The Sea Gull,* though not heroic, does not fling but somehow wafts a challenge. Out of the picture of depression, an exaltation wells.

Chekhov has been presented by innumerable college and community theatres, with constant revival at the Moscow Art Theatre and other professional companies. To name a few, for *The Sea Gull*: New York: 1954, with Judith Evelyn and Sam Jaffe; 1962, Rosemary Harris; Roundabout, 1973-1974. London: 1960, translated by J. P. Davis, with Judith Anderson; 1964, translated by Ann Jellico, with Vanessa Redgrave; Moscow Art in 1970 and 1976, in Russian; Oxford Repertory Company, directed by Mike Alfreds, voted the "best revival of the year."

UNCLE VANYA   *Anton P. Chekhov*

Chekhov's play *Ivanov,* 1887, spoiled by the censor and the actors, was not given proper performance until the Moscow Art Theatre produced it in October 1904, after Chekhov had died. His play, *The Wood Demon,* 1888, closed after six performances; it pictures a poet dreaming over the growth of the forest and the future flourishing of the land. In the mood of the first of these plays, and with ideas of the second, Chekhov in 1897 wrote his second great drama, *Uncle Vanya.*

The play depicts the lives of a group on the estate of a retired professor, Alexander Serebryakov, a pompous fellow who has returned, with his young second wife, Yelena, to write his masterpiece. His daughter by his first wife (Sonya), his first wife's mother, and her brother (Uncle Vanya) grow increasingly unable to endure the professor's assumption of superiority. Finally Uncle Vanya takes two shots at the professor, misses, and life resumes its weary way around the seasons.

Played in the smaller cities during 1898, *Uncle Vanya* was offered to the Imperial Maly Theatre in Moscow. When the management demanded revision, Chekhov gave the play to the Moscow Art Theatre, where it opened, October 26, 1899, with Stanislavski as the cynical looker-on Dr. Astrov. In 1924 the Moscow Art Theatre played *Uncle Vanya* during its New York season. It was produced in New York in English in 1927; also in 1929 with Morris Carnovsky; in 1930 with Lillian Gish, Walter Connolly, Osgood Perkins, Joanna Roos, Eugene Powers, Kate Mayhew, and Eduardo Ciannelli; and in May 1946, by the Old Vic Company, with Ralph Richardson, Lawrence Olivier, Mary Leighton and Joyce Redman.

Speaking of *Uncle Vanya,* Chekhov said: "The whole meaning and drama of man lies in internal and not external phenomena." To capture such meaning demands performance. As Granville Barker has observed, the printed play is like an opera libretto; the acting supplies the music, creates the mood. Prince Mirsky pictured the play as a symphony, in "the orchestration of parts . . . the resultant mood is achieved by the complex interaction of human voices."

Uncle Vanya has been called "a gloomy essay in stagnation"; it is rather a picture of well-meaning muddlers imposed upon by mediocre men with a sense of self-importance. "An extremely unhappy affair," said the *London Times* (December 19, 1935), after a broadcast of the play, "and Vanya himself writes its epitaph in his superb answer to the comment that the day is fine and not too warm. 'A fine day,' says Uncle Vanya, 'to hang oneself.' Had Uncle Vanya attempted to hang himself he would almost certainly have failed, for everybody in this play is doomed to fail in the simplest tasks they undertake. Doomed is the word, for what could so easily bear an uncomfortable resemblance to burlesque is turned by Chekhov's genius into a truly tragic story of people thwarted and broken by their sensitiveness and their perception of their own thwarted potentialities." Even the decent persons are dull, yet Chekhov spreads over their dullness the quiet glow of genius. James Agate saw the play as "an embroidery upon the theme of apprenticeship to sorrow."

Some knowledge of the Russian temperament is requisite to a full understanding of the play. As the *London Times* (February 6, 1937) said, "The English tendency is to treat the attempt [to shoot the Professor] and the wild quarrel that precedes it as extravagant farce, for the plain reason that only in farces do Englishmen so wildly express their feelings as these Russians do in this scene." It was probably a failure to take this difference of temperament into account that led the *New Yorker* (May 25, 1946) to say that *Uncle Vanya* seems at times "a deliberate and wicked parody of all Russian drama."

No other of Chekhov's four great plays has won such divided opinions as *Uncle Vanya*. The *New York Times* (April 16, 1930) called it "the least interesting of Chekhov's major dramas"; on the same day the *New York World* declared it "the finest of Chekhov's plays; Chekhov's plays, at least four of them, are the finest plays of this century; and Jed Harris' production of *Uncle Vanya* is the best Chekhov that America has seen in a language it can understand." This judgment was affirmed by James Agate in *At Half Past Eight* (1923), where he called the play "quite perfect. I shall never know exactly 'what it means,' but then I do not know that I hunger for that knowledge. It is, and that suffices."

Tuberculosis kept Chekhov from seeing *Uncle Vanya* in Moscow; and in May 1900, the Moscow Art Theatre went to Chekhov's home in Yalta to enact the play for him. On that visit, Gorki* saw the play, and was drawn to write for the theatre.

The dramas of Chekhov and Gorki best suit the "Stanislavski system," the quest of which is a "psychological realism" that bids the actor seek "self-justification" for his every action and prescribes "improvisation" in which the actor pretends to be the character in many situations not in the play, so as to grow more fully into the personality. For a play such as *Uncle Vanya* shows the everyday situations of ordinary folks; the initial genius of the author demands the rounded cooperation of the actor and of the theatre for full realization of the emotional impact and the mood. In *Uncle Vanya* the characters look forward to a time when, lengthily, they may rest; yet Chekhov suggests what the English poet Milton stated: They also serve who only stand and wait. *Uncle Vanya* is the drama of man's lifelong waiting. When *The Wood Demon,* the first version of *Uncle Vanya,* was played in London, Harold Hobson (*Times,* September 2, 1973) called it "the more joyous play. There is in it much of that uneventful summer sunshine that makes the heart ache with its happiness, and the nerves almost break with the tension of unrecognized desires. In the first act there occurs one of Chekhov's most marvellous moments ... A hawk unexpectedly flies through the skies, and suddenly, for no reason suggested or discussed, the gaiety of an outdoor luncheon party is for a few seconds halted, and then as unexplainedly renewed. The audience is stilled by a sense of wonder." This version was also done by BAM in 1974.

Among the performances of *Uncle Vanya*: England: Bristol, 1955, with Eric Porter and Moira Shearer; Chichester Festival, 1962, to London in 1963, with Dame Sybil Thorndike, Laurence Olivier, Michael Redgrave, Max Adrian, Joan Plowright, Rosemary Harris, Fay Compton; 1970, Royal Court, with Paul Scofield (whom some deemed off-key); 1982, both at the

NT (Lyttleton), directed by Michael Bogdanov, and at the Haymarket with Donald Sinden, universally praised. America: CSC, 1968, 1969, Los Angeles, directed by Harold Clurman; New York OffBway (Cherry Lane), fifty performances, 1971, also Roundabout; 1973, in lively translation by Albert Todd, at the Circle in the Square, directed by Mike Nichols, with Nicol Williamson, George C. Scott, Cathleen Nesbitt, and Lillian Gish (who had seen it in 1930) playing a maid. In 1978, Seattle Repertory and Stratford, Ontario, with Peter O'Toole, thence to Kennedy Center, Washington; 1980, Stamford, Conn.

THE THREE SISTERS   *Anton P. Chekhov*

Perhaps the pressures created by Chekhov's own confinement in the country gave impetus to his depiction of the boredom and frustration of small town life. In *The Three Sisters,* 1900, the reiterant desire to go to Moscow, to Moscow, is coupled with a greater faith in the future than in the earlier plays; at least it gives the feeling that this life, not alone the life hereafter, bears some hope.

The three sisters of the play want to break away from their petty provincial lives to join in the gaiety and activity of the great city. The eldest, Olga Prozorov, is an old maid school-teacher who hates her work and whose life outside the school is barren. Masha is married to a commonplace man; she has a brief affair with Battery Commander Vershinin. Irina, the youngest, works in a telegraph office; she is engaged, but her fiancé is killed in a duel, leaving her to lapse into drudgery. Their brother Andrey, of whose help they have high hopes, secretly mortgages their property and marries a country girl, Natasha. "Coming coyly into the Prozorov family," said Lewis Nichols (December 22, 1942), "she eventually is a vixen and a harridan, driving them off and at the end in violent control of their lives." With their hopes of escape gone, the three sisters find purpose only in work, until—some time—life's deeper purpose will be revealed.

The Three Sisters opened January 31, 1901, at the Moscow Art Theatre with Olga Knipper (who in May 1901 married Chekhov) as Masha. It was an instant success, and has since been the most frequently performed of Chekhov's plays. The Moscow Art Theatre production was given in New York, 1923, with five members of the original cast. The Civic Repertory Theatre, with Eva Le Gallienne, Beatrice Terry, and Rose Hobart, presented the play in 1926 and for six years thereafter. The American Laboratory Theatre produced it in 1929 and 1930. London saw it at the Old Vic in 1935; in 1938 with John Gielgud, Peggy Ashcroft, Michael Redgrave, and Leon Quartermaine, and in 1951, with Ralph Richardson, Diana Churchill, Celia Johnson, Margaret Leighton, and Renée Asherson. It has been seen all over the United States, and is constantly revived. Of the first performance in English, Gilbert W. Gabriel said (October 27, 1926): "Out of the nineteenth century no wiser nor more sensitive drama was anywhere born."

The best American production of *The Three Sisters* opened December 21, 1942, with Katharine Cornell (Masha), Judith Anderson (Olga), Gertrude Musgrove (Irina), Ruth Gordon (Natasha), Dennis King (Vershinin), and Edmund Gwenn (the philosophical doctor). Lewis Kronenberger stated: "One of the finest plays in the modern theatre was received last night with one of the most notable casts in living memory." Its director, Guthrie McClintic, was wise in not letting his wife (Katharine Cornell) see the script until she had heard it read aloud. Judith Anderson, upon reading the play, said that it didn't amount to much, and the sisters were obviously crazy, but she'd go along with the others; but, listening to a scene in rehearsal, she was moved to tears. The greatness of the play is fully illuminated by a great production. Robert Coleman said (December 22, 1942): "Like a big, sluggish river, it is not very exciting of itself to watch. But impelled by exciting acting, it can become a fearsome, potent force to see."

After the Russian Revolution, *The Three Sisters* was acclaimed as a herald of that storm. In the play Irina's fiancé, the Baron, who has never worked, exclaims: "The time is at hand, an avalanche is moving down upon us, a mighty clearing storm which is coming, is already near and will soon blow the laziness, the indifference, the distaste for work, the rotten boredom, out of our society. I shall work, and in another twenty-five or thirty years every one will have to work. Every one!" Imagine how Soviet audiences cheer those words till the rafters ring!

Moving quietly, with rich comic moments nonetheless steeped in pathos, where tragedy lapses into a sense of futile drift, and hope digs its spurs into cloud-flanks of despair, *The Three Sisters* at once films our eyes with tears and brightens them with vision. Through the Prozorov family we share the frustrations and the enduring courage of the world.

English performances of *The Three Sisters* include a tour, 1976, with the *Sea Gull*; 1978, the RSC at the Edinburgh Festival, brought back in 1979 to Stratford-upon-Avon; and two earlier adaptations in London: 1965 by Randall Jarrell, with Kim Stanley and Luther Adler; 1966, by Tyrone Guthrie and Leonid Kipnis. In America: adapted by Stark Young, 1955 and 1959 OffBway. At the New York Morosco opening, June 22, 1964, for 119 performances—Brooks Atkinson called the production "as fragile and beautiful as the writing"; 1969, ANTA Theatre; 1976, Stratford, Ontario, with Maggie Smith; 1977, BAM with Rosemary Harris; 1978, Springfield, Mass.; 1981, OffOffBway. In 1969 CRC gave two forms, one straight, one experimental.

THE CHERRY ORCHARD   *Anton P. Chekhov*

Developed more quietly than his other plays, as Chekhov smilingly pointed out, his masterpiece, *The Cherry Orchard,* 1903, has "not a shot in it" as it depicts futile, wasteful aristocracy incapable of managing affairs, allowing control to pass into more competent hands. "All Russia is our orchard," cries the student in the play, giving symbolic meaning to its title. When the aristocratic Madame Ranevsky, together with her fussy brother whose plans evaporate into words and her amiable but ineffectual daughters, must leave their estate, a practical middle-class merchant, whose grandfather (like Chekhov's own) had been a serf, buys the cherry orchard. He plans to have the trees cut down in order to make way for suburban homes. With the house locked and the old servant, unnoticed, left behind to die, "Life," as the servant says, "has slipped by, as though I hadn't lived." The final curtain falls as strokes of the axe are heard in the orchard. A new life, a new world, is to begin on the morrow.

Chekhov felt the throbbing of an enwombed new day. While writing *The Cherry Orchard,* he said that the new play would be "something entirely different, something cheerful and strong. We have outlived the gray dawdle." Scarcely a year passed before the abortive revolution of 1905, and twelve years later came the complete overturning of Russian life.

The Cherry Orchard opened at the Moscow Art Theatre on Chekhov's birthday, January 17, 1904. It was forbidden by the censor in 1906. After 1917, however, it became, along with Gorki's *The Lower Depths*,* the most popular play in Soviet Russia. A gala performance was given by the Moscow Art Theatre on January 17, 1944, at which time Eva Le Gallienne and Joseph Schildkraut were performing the play in New York. Miss Le Gallienne had first played it in 1928, with Alla Nazimova; it was also played in New York in Yiddish during that year. The Moscow Art Company performed it in the United States in 1923-1924, to a total of 244 performances, the Chekhov record in the United States.

Ward Morehouse was apparently not impressed by the Le Gallienne production. He called *The Cherry Orchard* (January 26, 1944) "a play of inaction . . . crowded with pauses, sighs, chuckles, and irrelevancies. There is incessant prattling by minor characters." Robert Garland felt the deeper impact of the play: "It is, fundamentally, one of the most skilfully contrived and most heart-breaking comedies in the modern theatre."

Gorki has said that Chekhov portrays "the tragedy of life's trivialities." Beyond such tragedy, however, there is in the play the ruthless inevitability of the coarse, but competent new order, which wipes away the refinements of the order that has fallen into decay. Lopahin, the practical neighbor of *The Cherry Orchard*, is indeed the boor the aristocrats find him to be, but he is no treacherous villain. At first, he tries to help the aristocrats to save themselves. It is not until their heedless impracticality and fluttering incompetence make disaster imminent, that he steps in to direct events and to steer their benefits in his own complacent direction. Perhaps Chekhov intended to show in that complacence the first signs of the new order's own decay. The Soviet audience may not like such an interpretation, but there are touches in *The Cherry Orchard* of continuing prophecy. "The old order changeth, yielding place to new"; and the sadness, the inevitability, the hopefulness, and the consequent disappointments of the flux of time have no more poignant dramatic expression than in *The Cherry Orchard*.

The play was produced in Los Angeles, June 6, 1950, with Eugenie Leontovich and Charles Laughton. On March 29, 1950, an adaptation by Joshua Logan, which transposed the Russia of *The Cherry Orchard* to the United States of *The Wisteria Trees* on a southern plantation about 1890, opened in New York with Helen Hayes. In spite of Logan's serious efforts as both adapter and director, most of the changes he made either melodramatize or romanticize the starker work of Chekhov so that they lessen the irony and weaken the calm, implacable movement that gives power to *The Cherry Orchard*.

The Cherry Orchard has been the most frequently performed Chekhov play. Here are just a few productions. England: December 1961, with Sir John Gielgud, Dame Peggy Ashcroft, Judy Dench and Dorothy Tutin at the Aldwych; 1978, NT (Olivier), directed by Peter Hall, with Dorothy Tutin, Albert Finney, and Ralph Richardson as the old servant, Firs. The 1981 direction of Peter Brook made Madame Ranevsky a glamorous woman who needed solicitous care, of practical helplessness but generosity of spirit. Mel Gussow said in the *New York Times*: "Paradoxically, this revival of a well-known classic became one of the most original events of the season."

The London Roundhouse production of 1982 led the *Telegraph* (August 15, 1982) to quote Stanislavski: "The play has all the tenderness of a flower. Break its stem and the flower dies, its odor vanishes"—and to add: "In Mike Alfred's Oxford Playhouse production, the flower has not merely had its stem broken, it has been trampled under foot."

America: After Joshua Logan's "Southern Fried Chicken" adaptation of 1950, Chekhov returns: 1962, New York OffBway (Theatre 4), sixty-one performances; Asolo, 1967, again in 1978; 1968, Phoenix, directed by Eva Le Gallienne, with Uta Hagen and Donald Moffat, thirty-eight performances; 1977, New York's Beaumont with the Rumanian director Andrei Serban—followed by the Canadian Festival of 1980, directed by Rabu Penciulescu, who had taught Serban. Of the 1973 New York production with (and despite) Constance Cummings, the *Herald Tribune* (John Walker, June 2, 1973) called "Michael Blakemore's production . . . Chekhov with laughs: bouquets of flowers unexpectedly disintegrate, chairs collapse at inconvenient moments, and conjuring tricks go wrong. There were even moments when I expected that Dennis Quilley's eager, thrusting Lopahin, the serf turned squire, might lose his trousers and his precarious dignity, or that a couple of custard pies would come sailing out of the wings." This aberration left Chekhov to more serious performers, such as Colleen Dewhurst, 1980, at Williamstown, Mass. There was an OffOffBway production in 1982; and *The Cherry Orchard* will long endure those fateful blows of the axe.

MAGIC   *G. K. Chesterton*

Although Gilbert Keith Chesterton (English, 1874-1936) did not become a Catholic until 1922, his interest in religious forces and problems was earlier made manifest in such essays as *The Defendant,* 1901, and *Heretics,* 1905. His one play, *Magic,* which opened in London, November 7, 1913, is hinged upon supernatural forces.

Magic is an oddly delightful play. Patricia, niece of a duke, encounters and is attracted to a stranger in the Duke's garden. She is disappointed to learn that he is the conjurer hired for their entertainment. But after the conjurer, who believes in the supernatural and cannot explain his "tricks," demonstrates his talents and his faith before her agnostic young brother, an unsure clergyman, and the Duke, she is ready to go away with him. The conjurer, however, tries to dissuade her. He tells her of his mother's hardships, after she had married a wandering fiddler. "She might have worn pearls," he points out, "by consenting to be a rational person." Patricia retorts, "She might have grown pearls by consenting to be an oyster." And she holds her man.

The play ran for 168 performances in London, 1913-1914; it was revived there in 1923, 1925, and 1942. New York saw the play in February 1917, in 1929, and in 1942 with Julie Haydon and Eddie Dowling.

In London, William Archer, writing in the *Star,* November 8, 1913, said that the play "must be seen by everybody." The *Graphic* found it "a magical masterpiece in thought and feeling. It is elusive and wonderfully suggestive. It is touched at times with the eloquence of high poetry, and so, of course, it is tremendously emotional." The *Illustrated London News* (November 15, 1913) thought the play showed Chesterton at his best: "His buoyant personality makes itself felt, his wit gives delight, his freakishness and his mysticism alike obtain expression . . . Quaint, bewildering, argumentative, grotesque as is his story of the way in which a belief in fairy lore permeated a fussy duke's household, it is told in something of a dramatic fashion; it is developed through action and clash of character; it does really present a conflict of wills and standpoints, and this culminates in a climax immensely exciting and bordering on the horrible."

New York received the play favorably, but more calmly. Heywood Broun, himself not yet a Catholic, called it (February 13, 1917) "the eloquent expression of a revolt against the materialistic conception of the universe," adding that Chesterton "writes with such charm as to make even asceticism seem attractive." Twenty-five years later, John Mason Brown (September 30, 1942) called *Magic* "a remarkable tour-de-force."

Quietly, but with a gentle growth to deep power, *Magic* is a dramatic suggestion that science is less than the sum of human understanding, that the course of love, of life itself, remains a divine mystery. There were several productions of the play in England in 1974, the centenary of Chesterton's birth.

THE MASK AND THE FACE   *Luigi Chiarelli*

Among the many plays of Luigi Chiarelli (Italian, 1885–1947) *The Mask and the Face* has justly achieved international fame. It inaugurated the "grotesque" school of drama in which the spiritual upheaval of the First World War found bitter or wry expression.

The Mask and the Face is an attack upon those social fetishes which are intended to simplify and sweeten life but actually complicate and distort its movement. The strict and rigidly formal Count Paolo Grazia, finding his wife Savina unfaithful, has not the heart to do "the proper thing" and slay her. Instead, he sends her secretly abroad and "confesses" to having drowned her. At the trial, his lawyer produces a man who testifies to Savina's profligacy; and the jury absolves Paolo. The women of the city then pester him with such admiring and amorous attention that he resolves to call Savina back in order to rid himself of them. Meanwhile a body found in a lake is erroneously identified as Savina's. Paolo must attend the funeral, during which Savina arrives. Honored as a murderer, Paolo is now in danger of being arrested as a fraud. As the *London Times* (April 13, 1934) observed: "Life is a burden to him until she returns. After that it is a nightmare—but, fortunately, exposure reduces him to laughter, a relief he has never known before; and he who has once laughed, the dramatist seems to say, is safe for eternity." Loving and laughing, Paolo and Savina slip away during the funeral, suggesting, as did Barrie at the end of *What Every Woman Knows,** that while there is laughter there is hope.

The "grotesque" element in *The Mask and the Face* is not obtrusive. It takes shape in the novel action of the avenging husband and in some of the sharply satiric situations. At the funeral, for example, Chiarelli builds drama on the irony of Paolo's real feelings and the mask of sorrow he must assume; and in a scene where Savina faces the man who has denounced her at the trial, further irony rises through our learning that she really had never been unfaithful to her husband. Through such moments the play grows, as Domenico Vittorini declared in *A History of Modern Drama* (1947), into "an intriguing, strong, and impressive drama." The last act, especially, is a gem of comic invention.

Chiarelli wrote some half-dozen routine plays before *The Mask and the Face* and several afterwards in which the "grotesque" technique is more apparent. The best of the latter is *The Ladder of Silk,* 1917, a satire of political ambition, in which the aims of the earnest, honest Roberto are contrasted with the ambitions of the vain, shallow, but shining dancer Désiré, who rises to the rank of minister. Désiré makes a fluent address, grandiloquent of liberty and justice; the crowd applauds, and out of ingrained habit Désiré goes into his dance.

The Mask and the Face opened in Rome, May 31, 1916. London saw it in a version by Chester B. Fernald on February 5, 1924; again May 27, 1924, with Leslie Banks as the lawyer, for 232 performances. Fernald changed most of the men's names: Count Paolo became Count Mario. He also quickened the action at the end of the play: Savina hears her own funeral services; Mario is not allowed to confess, his friends saying to do so would ruin his career; Savina appears and dumbfounds the women who have been making eyes at Mario; the funeral procession still waits as the curtain falls. This ending scants the transformation of the husband, but it snaps along the action. The *London Sunday Pictorial* called Fernald's version "one of the most nearly perfect comedies of our times." A closer adaptation, by Somerset Maugham, was also presented in London, in 1934 and 1946. New York saw the play September 10, 1924, with William Faversham; again, in the Maugham version, May 8, 1933, with Judith Anderson and Humphrey Bogart.

The play was most favorably reviewed. *The Boston Transcript* (November 11, 1925) spoke of its "nimble and witty handling of a brilliantly original plot" whose characters are "sparingly but unmistakably individualized in the give and take of drawing-room conversation." *The Stage* (June 1933) said that Chiarelli seems able to "grab a word and give it the precise emphasis that will carry it through the house like a shot of electricity."

Despite the favorable reviews, *The Mask and the Face* was not a success with the American public. "It springs," according to the *New York Herald Tribune* (May 7, 1933) "from an intellectual milieu already rather overripe." Which is one way of saying that Europe takes the problems of marital fidelity more seriously than the United States: To the sophisticated American playgoer, Paolo seems to be making a mountain out of a Venus-mound. *The Mask and the Face,* nevertheless, is a striking and dramatic satire on convention and reality. With considerable incidental comedy, it moves warm characters through intense concerns.

KIND LADY   *Edward Chodorov*

One of the most thrilling psychological melodramas is that of the "kind lady," kidnapped in her own home, which Edward Chodorov (American. b. 1911) wrought from the story *The Silver Mask* by Hugh Walpole. Tried out in 1934 at Southampton, Long Island, and in the summer theatre with Effie Shannon, *Kind Lady* came to the Booth Theatre in New York on April 23, 1935, with Grace George and Henry Daniell, for 102 performances. The play continued on the road until it returned to New York, again with Grace George, in 1940. It still finds frequent revival about the land.

In a prologue, the door of Mary Herries' house is opened to a banker. The play is the story he hears, and the epilogue shows what he does about it. In the play Mary, a kindly lady, who lives, in lonely old-maidenhood, befriends a street beggar on Christmas Eve. The beggar's wife appears and falls ill, and the doctor forbids her to leave the house. The intruders impose upon the lady; when she makes a desperate effort to expel them, they circle and close around her in silence. She then recognizes—as does the audience—that she is prisoner in her own house. This heart-catching discovery brings down the curtain of Act One. The invading family begin to sell the valuable paintings in the house, and seek to break the lady's willpower, in order to gain control of her wealth. They announce to her few friends that she has gone on a long trip; they permit her to have contacts only with one or two outsiders, whom they warn to expect a crazy story. The outsiders consider her insane; indeed, her kidnappers impress upon her that she is insane. When a representative comes from the bank, the lady finds herself alone with him. Will he too think she is insane? The audience—and the kidnappers—wait to learn. They learn that he gives credence to her story and effects her release.

The situation is ingenious and excellently developed. "We thought we'd better bring Aggie with us," says the beggar's wife, introducing an inquisitive and kleptomaniac child, who is one of three characters that speak scarcely a word, but who, by their sinister and silent actions, add to the foreboding terror of the play. Few figures in melodrama have been subjected to such mental torture as the "kind lady." Moving gracefully into her riper years, half-trusting, half-fearful of life, generous, yet ashamed of her impulses—manifestly naïve, seemingly weak—when the criminals reveal their purpose, she staunchly holds the fortress of her soul.

After the New York premiere, Arthur Pollock (April 24, 1935) reported that "the things that happen thrill to the last degree." John Anderson was afraid that the play would "drive sweet old ladies to going around the town on Christmas Eve kicking handsome young beggars in the face, and jerking the whiskers off the sidewalk Santa Clauses."

Brooks Atkinson (September 4) found the play, in the 1940 revival, "just as tingling now as it was in 1935, when it first began to tighten nerves in this vicinity, and Miss George is playing it with greater sensitivity and skill." Combining a natural sympathy for virtue in distress with a plausible situation, *Kind Lady* is a quietly terrifying play, one of the stage's best psychological melodramas.

It was played in New York in 1952, with Sylvia Sidney, and in 1972 at the Henry Street Playhouse, OffBway.

MY SISTER EILEEN   *Jerome Chodorov*

One of the gayest stories of life in New York's Greenwich Village is *My Sister Eileen,* by Joseph Fields (1895–1966) and Jerome Chodorov (b. 1911, brother of Edward*) from the novel by Ruth McKenny (1910–1972). Ruth tells of the days when she and her sister Eileen came from a small Ohio town to seek life and shining success in the Big City. It came to the New York Biltmore, December 26, 1940, for 864 performances. (The real Eileen was killed in an automobile accident on the West Coast just before the Broadway opening.)

The girls find a basement studio in the Village, with a concerned landlord, Appopolous, who knows he is a genius as a painter, and an interested unemployed football player who lives upstairs. There is a big curtainless window fronting the street above, which, said John Anderson in the *Journal,* "Lets in the noise, the rowdies, the Peeping Toms, and all the gusty and gaudy transience of Greenwich Village: soda jerker, drunken reporter, romantic magazinist, and six cadets of the Brazilian navy."

Ruth wants to be a writer; Eileen is aiming at the stage. Among the complications that add to the audience-enjoyed confusion is the fact that a busy prostitute had recently been doing business at that address. In the play, of course, the girls make good, careerwise and manwise.

In the first production Morris Carnovsky played the landlord; Shirley Booth, Ruth; Jo Ann Sayers, Eileen. Philip Loeb was the landlord in Chicago, where the play, opening 1941, ran for eight months; in 1947, he and Shirley Booth performed at Bucks County, Pa. The play toured widely (eight weeks in Boston) in the 1940's and 1950's. Rosalind Russell was in the film.

From *My Sister Eileen, Wonderful Town,* with music by Leonard Bernstein, lyrics by Betty Comden and Adolph Green, came to the Winter Garden on February 25, 1953, for 559 performances, with Rosalind Russell as Ruth returning to Broadway after twenty-two Hollywood years. Edie Adams played Eileen. There was enlivening music, especially in the swirling conga in a subway car and along the Village street with the Brazilian navy boys.

Among the numerous revivals: 1954 at the New York Shubert, with Carol Channing, Betty Gillett, George Gaynes; 1955 in London, the British cast lacking the vim of the Americans; New York City Center, 1958, with Nancy Walker as Ruth; Jo Sullivan, Eileen; and Peter Cookson; City Center again, May 17, 1967, with Elaine Stritch as Ruth and Betsy von Furstenberg; and again February 3, 1968, with Kaye Ballard as Ruth and Jacquelyn McKeever. "This is New York for the fun of it," and Fun City is indeed a *Wonderful Town.*

THE MOUSETRAP   *Agatha Christie*

Perhaps the most successful writer of mystery stories and plays is Agatha Christie (Agatha Mary Clarissa Miller, 1890–1976), and the longest-running play in all history is her mystery drama *The Mousetrap.* Written first as a radio play for Queen Mary's eighty-sixth birthday, it was called *Three Blind Mice.* Transformed into a full-length play, *The Mousetrap,* it opened at the Ambassador Theatre, London on November 15, 1952, and has been running ever since. Richard Attenborough was the first Detective-Sergeant Trotter and Sheila Sim the Mollie Ralston. (*The Mousetrap,* some may recall, is the name given by Hamlet to *The Murder of Gonzago,* slightly altered "to catch the conscience of the King," when King Claudius asks him: "What do you call the play?") Agatha Christie's mystery has been played in more than forty countries and translated into twenty-two languages. The cast in London is changed every year, to keep the playing fresh. (When the play opened Agatha Christie's grandson, Matthew Prichard, became eight; as his birthday present, she gave him all the royalties the play might earn.)

The curtain rises on a dark stage; the jingle "Three Blind Mice" is playing. There is a scream; the radio announces the death of a woman at 24 Culver Street, Paddington. The lights come on in Monkswell Manor, which Mollie and Giles Ralston, wed just a year, have opened as a country guest house. Through the snow, guests arrive: a young architect, named after Sir Christopher Wren; a bossy woman, Mrs. Boyle; a military man, Major Metcalf; a self-assured younger woman, Miss Caswell; and a foreigner whose car has overturned in a snowdrift. Detective-Sergeant Trotter phones; he's coming, and he arrives on skis—with a notebook containing two addresses: 24 Culver Street, Paddington, and Monkswell Manor.

We learn that, years before, two boys and a girl had been sent by the court to a home on a farm, where one of the boys died from persistent ill-treatment and criminal neglect. The farmer died in prison; his wife was the woman strangled on Culver Street, to the tune of "Three Blind Mice." Then Mrs. Boyle is strangled; she was the judge that sent the children to the farm.

Trotter asks the others to repeat their actions at the time of Mrs. Boyle's strangling. Then he accuses Mollie; she was the teacher to whom the dead boy had written for help. (Down with pneumonia, she'd read the letter after the boy had died.) Alone with Mollie, Trotter whistles "Three Blind Mice," and moves to strangle her—then the Major and Miss Caswell come in. She calls Trotter "Georgie;" she is the farm girl, his sister, come back from Majorca hoping to find him; he is the surviving boy, seeking revenge; she recognized him from his habit of twirling his hair. Major Metcalf had been suspicious of Trotter all along: "I knew he wasn't a policeman; you see, Mrs. Ralston, I am a policeman."

Giles and Mollie Ralston had been suspicious of each other; each had been to London without telling the other—to buy an anniversary present. Now the Major exclaims: "Mrs. Ralston! There's a terrible smell of burning from the kitchen." Mollie cries out, "Oh! My pie!" and rushes to save it as the curtain falls.

The *London Evening Standard* exclaimed: "What a wily mistress of criminal ceremonies Agatha Christie is! She is like a perfect hostess serving hemlock at a cocktail party." The *Sunday Times* emphasized her fairness: "There is none of this hiding of facts in Mrs. Christie. It is this honesty of procedure that puts her so high."

American critics and audiences were less enthusiastic. The play's first American production was at the Washington Arena Stage in 1955; its longest run was OffBroadway (Maidman Theatre, November 5, 1960) for three months; though there were also OffBway productions in 1957, 1975, 1976, and 1977; Palm Beach, Denver, and Seattle in 1976; Springfield, Mass., and Buffalo, 1979. John Barber reported in the *London Telegraph,* September 27, 1982, that he had seen performance 1 and also performance 12,403; he said the story has "unique facets" and "I think it could run forever."

The *London Ambassador,* October 18, 1978, presented *Who Killed Agatha Christie?* by Tudor Gates. The victim turns out to be a gay theatre critic.

Dame Agatha Christie is known worldwide for her ingenious plots, keeping more persons under suspicion for longer than most mystery writers can manage. And, while Hamlet's mousetrap will outlast it, no other play has approached the continuous run of *The Mousetrap* of Agatha Christie.

THE TIDINGS BROUGHT TO MARY   *Paul Claudel*

This tender and touching drama—its original title was *L'Annonce faite à Marie*—by Paul Claudel (French, 1868–1955), is a breath of quiet beauty in a straining world. A modern mystery, a nativity play, it has its climax on the Christmas Day when Joan of Arc crowns the French king at Rheims Cathedral, when concerns of the world—the pressures and pains, the passions and bitter distractions of life—fade into the great symbol of mankind's eternal rebirth.

In the play, the saintly Violaine in compassion kisses Pierre de Craon, the great builder of churches, who has become a leper. She contracts the disease, and her jealous sister, Mara, marries Jacques, the former fiancé of the now blind and ostracized Violaine. On Christmas Day the compassionate and saintly Violaine restores to life her weeping sister's child. As simple as the soil are the characters of the drama: the peasant mother, who is left alone at the end of the play; and the father with a Crusader's fervor.

The Tidings Brought to Mary was presented in Paris in 1912 and has been frequently revived. The Theatre Guild presented it in New York on Christmas Day, 1922; Montreal saw it in English in 1939; New York viewed it in French in 1942. In Montreal, *Le Devoir* (April 1, 1939) commented that "even translated, Claudel continues great" in spite of the loss of "that savour of the word, that rhythm of the style, that breath which overturns syntax and sings like nature herself, who does not always follow our rules." *Les Nouvelles Littéraires,* Paris (June 20, 1946) expressed the view that the play "is in every respect one of the rare French works of this half-century, which can be listed among the masterpieces of the world theatre. It stands at the peak of Claudel's dramatic art."

Deftly suggested, beyond the immediate story of the play, are the stir of a military cavalcade, the rapt dedication of Joan of Arc, and the infinite implications of man's redemption. "It is only the unseen," said Heywood Broun, "that can ever be utterly convincing. It is curious that the theatre, which began in the church, has for the most part forgotten this vital fact, upon which all religion is founded." *The Tidings Brought to Mary* recaptured that early, devoted fusion of theatre and church, inducing an exaltation akin to worship.

Something of the deep effect of this quiet play is conveyed by the words of Stark Young (January 10, 1923): "Miss Jeanne de Casalis and Miss Mary Fowler, in the scene where the child is brought to life, really succeed in creating an ecstatic moment. And Miss Helen Westley, as the woman who has borne the burden of the lives around her and, when she is grown dry and empty, is abandoned by her husband and children for their separate pilgrimages, has something about her that is like the picture of his mother Dürer drew, something like an old and worn and exhausted bitter soil, like blood and ashes mingled . . . And as Claudel's play draws to an end we know what the tidings are: that a child is born to men, a perpetual renewal of life among men through beauty and passion and the mystical power of thought. And we see in the play the objects and the actions and the life around them become one; and the bread these people break is not only bread but all life; and all life is included and renewed in the bread." Beauty takes dramatic form in the love of man that wells through *The Tidings Brought to Mary.*

ORPHEUS   *Jean Cocteau*

Jean Cocteau (French, 1889–1963) was at the forefront of every experimental artistic movement of his time, as in his surrealist film *The Blood of a Poet,* 1932. For his play *Orphée,* 1925, Cocteau took opium to get the name Heurtebise (windbreaker) for the glazier he introduced into the play, a role he himself enacted.

The play, in thirteen scenes, mixes fantasy with the Greek legend of Orpheus and Eurydice. Eurydice is enamored of Heurtebise, and breaks the window daily to draw him to her. But she is jealous of Orpheus' favorite horse, for which Heurtebise brings poison—which Eurydice unwittingly licks, and dies. Death, an elegantly garbed and beautiful woman, comes for her through the window, with two assistants in surgeons' uniforms. Orpheus seeks her, but Death withdraws. The horse, with power of speech, assures Orpheus: *M*adame *E*urydice *r*eviendra *d*es *e*nfers (Madame Eurydice will come back from hell); but it shows its own jealousy in the initial letters. The Bacchantes are ready to kill Orpheus; their leader Aglaonice, recognizing the horse's acrostic (*merde*: shit), sees also that Orpheus does not resist, dying to rejoin Eurydice. Heurtebise sets Orpheus' severed head on a mirror, from which it talks to the police. They ask his name; he answers: "Jean Cocteau." The police carry off his head as they search for Heurtebise. Orpheus and Eurydice rejoin in heaven, where he thanks God, who saved Eurydice, who "killed the Devil in the shape of a horse, and saved me because I adore poetry and Thou art poetry. Amen."

In 1926 the avant-garde Pitoeff company took *Orphée* on a European tour. *Orpheus* was shown at Yale in 1935; in London in 1937; at the Provincetown Playhouse in Greenwich Village, New York, 1945. An adaptation by Charles Wildman opened with Judith Malina at the New York Living Theatre, September 30, 1954. In 1956 an adaptation by George Montgomery played in Cambridge, Mass. Another, by the radical director Jerzy Grotowski, opened in Warsaw, 1959, and came to London in 1978, with Death a crippled androgyne holding an umbrella, Eurydice an acrobat, Orpheus playing not a lyre but an accordion.

Cocteau, like Baudelaire, saw beauty as lethal. As to God: "It is not necessary to understand; it is necessary only to believe." As with all good drama, *Orpheus* imposes the temporary suspension of disbelief.

THE INFERNAL MACHINE   *Jean Cocteau*

In 1928, Cocteau wrote the familiar story by Sophocles, *Oedipus Rex,* * as a libretto for an opera by Igor Stravinsky. In 1934 he reshaped the legend as *The Infernal Machine.*

Act I, "The Ghost," has a voice summarizing the story, declaring the plot "one of the most perfect machines devised by the infernal gods for the mathematical destruction of a mortal." And we see the ghost of the slain King Laius (killed by his unwitting son, Oedipus) trying vainly to warn his wife Jocasta and the high priest Tiresias, of what is to be.

Act II, "The Sphinx," shows Oedipus overcome by the Sphinx; but she falls in love with him, tells him the answer to her riddle—and dies. Her riddle, which a comer must guess, or be killed by her, is: "What is it that goes on four legs in the morning, on two legs at noon, and on three in the evening?" The answer: man, who crawls as a babe, walks erect as an adult, and in his darkening hours needs a cane. Odysseus bears off her body, and goes happily to be a king.

Act III, "The Wedding Night," shows the old Jocasta with a young husband. She sees his pierced foot and recalls the prophecy, but does not mention (recognize?) that she is his mother. She massages her wrinkled cheeks while the sated Oedipus sleeps.

Act IV, *Oedipus Rex.*" A voice states that Oedipus has ruled for seventeen years. A messenger from Corinth unwittingly makes them all recognize the incestuous relationship. Jocasta hangs herself with her scarf; Oedipus blinds himself with her brooch. As Antigone leads her blind father away, Tiresias says: "Now they belong to the people, to poets, to glory." The new King, Creon, says: "You mean to dishonor, shame." Tiresias: "Who knows?"

The play was well received. In Paris, 1934, directed by Louis Jouvet, Cocteau himself was "the Voice"; Jean-Pierre Aumont, Oedipus; Marthe Regnier, Jocasta; Pierre Renoir, Tiresias. The French author Colette called the close of the play "one of the greatest scenes in French drama." The same year the play was performed at Harvard; in 1937 at the Gate Theatre, Dublin, and directed at Vassar College by John Houseman, who declared: "with a mixture of perversity and magic it transforms Sophocles' tragedy of swift, inexorable horror into a tense, nervous psychological drama."

Later productions include one in Paris, 1954, with Jeanne Moreau as the Sphinx; Jean Marais, Oedipus; and as Jocasta the Rumanian Elvire Popescu, for whom Cocteau had written the part. Also 1954, Club Theatre

OffBway, with Leslie Woods and Alan Shayne; 1959, the Phoenix, adapted by Albert Bernel, with June Havoc, John Kerr, Jacob Ben-Ami, and Philip Bourneuf. In 1973, the Experiment Laboratory, Boston; Soho Repertory OffBway, 1976; Meat and Potatoes Co. OffOffBway, 1977.

With what the *Christian Science Monitor* called a reversal of Cocteau's usual attitude, "new subtlety masking a flippancy," young companies seem to prefer the Cocteau transformation to Sophocles' overpowering masterpiece.

SEVEN KEYS TO BALDPATE   *George Michael Cohan*

A staunch American and a great man of the theatre, was George M. Cohan (1878–1942). He came on the stage early, in *Peck's Bad Boy* (1890); then he toured in vaudeville in "The Four Cohans," with his father and mother and sister Josephine. He wrote, produced, and performed in many plays and musicals. A deft and shrewd craftsman, with a light finger on the theatregoer's pulse, Cohan wrote, in *Seven Keys to Baldpate,* the most popular and the best murder mystery farce.

Based on a novel by Earl Derr Biggers, *Seven Keys to Baldpate* pictures the tough time had by William Hallowell Magee in winning a bet. On a stormy night, caretaker Elijah Quimby lets Magee into a lonely house on top of Baldpate Mountain where, Magee has wagered, he will write a play in twenty-four hours. Quimby assures Magee that his is the only key to the house. Nevertheless, Magee is interrupted by a gang of thieves, a murderer, a pretty reporter (Mary Nolan), and a policeman who wants to slip off to Canada with the thieves' loot. Many thrilling and amusing complications sweep through the storm upon the much-tried Magee. Finally the owner of the house appears and informs Magee that all these persons were sent by his friend Bentley to create a disturbance in order to prevent Magee from winning the bet. Mary, however, is real, Magee responds; he's found her, the rest doesn't matter. And the curtain falls. Then Magee comes out with a manuscript. He phones Bentley: He's won the bet. All these events and creatures are the invented story of Magee's play, *Seven Keys to Baldpate.* Over the phone he says: "The critics? I don't care a darn about the critics. This is the stuff the public wants." And the curtain falls.

Driving to Hartford for the premiere (September 15, 1913) of *Seven Keys to Baldpate,* Cohan and the star, Wallace Eddinger, were injured in an automobile accident; Cohan, with a broken collar-bone, took over the star's part. The play came to New York, September 22, to run 320 performances. Clayton Hamilton stated in *Vogue* (November 1, 1913): "The material is trivial, and the cleverest of craftsmanship was required to develop it into the very successful entertainment that is now crowding the Astor Theatre."

London saw *Seven Keys to Baldpate,* September 12, 1914. In the United States, the play is a constantly revived favorite. It was chosen, in 1935, for the Players' annual revival, with Cohan as Magee, Zita Johann as Mary, Josephine Hull, Walter Hampden, James T. Powers, and Ernest Glendinning. "A song and dance man and Yankeedoodler," said H. I. Brock in the *New York Times* (May 19, 1935), "had written a mystery piece that was so good a satire on all the other mystery pieces that it was about the best mystery piece of them all." Charles Darnton called the proceedings "the wildest fun that has run riot on the stage in ages." More recently, Magee was enacted (June 9, 1948) by William Gaxton.

The lively and absurd events of *Seven Keys to Baldpate,* having little connection with reality, have not grown dim with time. The characters are not rounded; they are there only for the story. Yet this gather-all of mystery tricks turned farcical, remains a highly amusing sample of what "the public wants." The "seven keys," still popular in college theatre groups, were amusingly turned at Providence, R. I., in 1975, and at the Ogunquit, Maine, summer theatre in 1977.

THE DOUBLE DEALER　　　　　　　　　　　　　　　*William Congreve*

Turning from law to literature, William Congreve (English, 1670–1729) found himself in one year the author of two successful comedies and launched on the brief career that set him supreme among playwrights that depict the narrow world of gallantry and society intrigue.

More highly polished and with even sharper darts of wit and satire than *The Old Bachelor,* its predecessor, *The Double Dealer* opened in London with Mrs. Bracegirdle in November 1693. Although it was considered by many to be too sharp in its satire of fashionable society, Queen Mary's request for a Command Performance set the seal of royal approval on the play. Dryden, with Commendatory Verses, put his weight on the play's side.

Maskwell is the double-dealer in the play. He covets Cynthia, daughter of Sir Paul Plyant, who is engaged to Mellefont, nephew and heir of Lord Touchwood, whose wife covets Mellefont. While pretending to be Mellefont's friend, Maskwell tells Plyant that Mellefont is intriguing with Lady Plyant and also manages to have the suspicious Touchwood find Mellefont in Lady Touchwood's chamber. With Mellefont thus disgraced. Lord Touchwood informs his wife that Maskwell is to wed Cynthia. When Lady Touchwood reproaches Maskwell for this treachery, however, Lord Touchwood overhears. All is straightened out, and Mellefont and Cynthia are united.

Maskwell has been played by Thomas Sheridan and Basil Sydney. Lady Froth, "a great coquette . . . pretender to poetry, wit, and learning" was played by Kitty Clive. Peg Woffington played Lady Plyant, "insolvent to her husband, and easy to any pretender." There is some incongruity in the violence of Lady Touchwood's amorous desire for Mellefont amidst the more artificial intrigues of Brisk and Careless and the Froths and the Plyants. But the wit, the crackling dialogue of dalliance, and the satiric thrust are evident throughout. After the 1916 London revival, the *Pall Mall Gazette* noted that "the richness of its satire and the music of its dialogue are still pungent and pleasing." The *Daily Chronicle* remarked: "Here the English comedy reaches its highest perfection, a perfection from which even the genius of Sheridan and Goldsmith is a decline . . . According to modern standards, all the ladies are lax and all the gentlemen loose. But actually Congreve suffers neither virtue nor vice upon the stage . . . Congreve's wit is all headwork. There is never a heartbeat in all his comic theatre."

The Double Dealer is a heady draught of sparkling drama, a relentless set of portraits of pleasure-bound gallants and especially of luxurious ladies, in the dreg-depths of a dissolute society.

The play went from the 1959 Edinburgh Festival to London, with Ursula Jeans and Miles Mallison. It was shown by the NT (Olivier) in 1978.

LOVE FOR LOVE　　　　　　　　　　　　　　　　　*William Congreve*

Resentful of the treatment they were receiving at the Drury Lane Theatre, several of its stars built the Lincoln's Inn Fields Theatre. They opened it on April 29, 1695, with Congreve's *Love For Love.* The play was so successful that the actors gave the dramatist a share in the theatre; he was to write a play a year for them. Actually, however, he wrote but two more dramas.

Love For Love is another complicated intrigue of amours. Sir Sampson Legend, exasperated by the expensive ways of his son Valentine, will pay Valentine's debts only if he signs over his inheritance to Ben, his younger brother. Valentine signs the preliminary bond, then feigns madness to avoid signing the final conveyance. Wealthy Angelica, who has been keeping Valentine at arm's length, woos Sir Sampson into a marriage proposal and gets Valentine's bond. Despite his frivolous ways, life means nothing to Valentine without Angelica. When he hears of her engagement to his father, he reaches for the conveyance to sign, whereupon Angelica destroys the bond and confesses her love for Valentine.

The incidental action of the other characters in the play adds much to its lively movement. Ben, a plainspoken man of the sea, is intended by his father to marry Miss Prue, "a silly awkward country girl" eager to learn what love is all about. Tattle, "a half-witted beau, vain of his amours, yet valuing himself for secrecy"—the descriptions are Congreve's—is always on the brink of teaching Prue, and always interrupted; he hurries off to marry the rich Angelica, but (on a plan arranged by Valentine's servant, Jeremy) finds himself wed to Mrs. Frail, whose virtue is no stronger than her name. Prue's father, Foresight, "an illiterate old fellow, peevish and positive," prides himself on being a proper astrologer. The figure of Foresight "was then common," said Johnson; "Dryden calculated nativities; both Cromwell and King William had their lucky days." The elegance and the brilliant wit of *Love For Love* are thus balanced by elements of farce rising from these varied figures.

Every period has liked *Love For Love.* The *Tatler* and the *Spectator* gave it frequent praise, the latter (No. 189) calling it "one of the finest comedies that ever appeared upon the English stage." The play's wit shines in "a gorgeous blaze which dazzles us almost to blindness," said Macaulay, who also praised "the constant movement, the effervescence of animal spirits" in the play. William Hazlitt said that the play presents the highest model of comic dialogue: "Every sentence is replete with sense and satire, conveyed in the most polished and pointed terms. Every page represents a shower of brilliant conceits, is a tissue of epigrams in prose, is a new triumph of wit."

Love For Love has also been continuously popular on stage. A recent London production, opening April 8, 1943, with John Gielgud, Leslie Banks, and Leon Quartermaine, attained 471 performances. A New York production of 1925 was directed by Robert Edmond Jones, who also supervised the Players' annual revival production of *Love For Love,* which opened June 3, 1940, with Dorothy Gish, Peggy Wood, Violet Heming, Cornelia Otis Skinner, Dudley Digges, Bobby Clark, and Romney Brent, and Walter Hampden speaking the Prologue. A production with John Gielgud opened May 26, 1947. In the summer of 1936 Eva Le Gallienne was in a Westport, Connecticut, production with Dennis King, Rex O'Malley, and Van Heflin, using a version in which lines from Congreve's *The Way of the World* * were inserted.

In London, when *Love For Love* was given as a benefit for Betterton, the *Tatler* (April 12, 1709) said that its reception "gives an undeniable instance, that the true relish for manly entertainments and rational pleasures is not wholly lost." Two centuries later, in New York, *Time* (June 9, 1947) commented: ". . . where most Restoration writers were gross, Congreve was graceful. His people air their low thoughts in high language; his scandalmongers are witty; his sluts have style." John Mason Brown (June 14,

1947) said the play is written "by as superlative a stylist as ever employed prose in the form of dialogue."

The pretended madness of Valentine is usually burlesqued. It roused Gielgud, as Harold Hobson noted in the *Christian Science Monitor* (July 3, 1943) "to a magnificent frenzy of mockery of all the similar scenes in Shakespeare," including Gielgud's own work as Hamlet. But Gielgud found deeper moments too; particularly, the one where Valentine, forsaking his pretended madness, asks Angelica to own her love for him and she repels him. The power of this passage was well caught by John Hobart in the *San Francisco Chronicle* (November 11, 1945): The scene lasted "for only a minute or two, but during it Gielgud held us under a spell. For here, in the midst of Vanity Fair, with its cynicism and insincerity, its protocol of wit, its preoccupation with appetite, was an honest man, speaking his most private thoughts, and who, ironically, was to be repulsed. By the sheer magic of his acting, Gielgud suddenly made us understand that this unobtrusive scene was the great climax to which the whole play had been leading—the exposure of an honest heart. And *Love For Love* then brushed, as all great comedies must, against tragedy—just for the one poignant, passing moment, before it returned to its high, heartless Restoration ways."

Along with such constant praise, *Love For Love* has been continually attacked on the score of immorality. Congreve himself came off second best in his reply to Jeremy Collier's *Short View of the Profaneness and Immorality of the English Stage* (1698). Lamb defended Congreve's works from the charge of immorality, but, says Harold Hobson, "hardly secured an acquittal." The play's fine ladies, Hobson avers, "are brilliant, for they are decked with jewels, but they are unwashed." It might, of course, be stated that it is usually wrong to accredit (or besmirch) an author with his characters' failings. Congreve in *Humour in Comedy* declared: "If anything does appear comical or ridiculous in a woman, I think it is little more than an acquired folly or an affectation. We may call them the weaker sex, but I think the true reason is because our follies are stronger and our faults are more prevailing." He does not spare the weaker sex in his plays; his purpose is to display, not to defend them. *Love For Love,* as the *New York Times* (June 30, 1936) remarked, is "full of what Dr. Johnson called 'gay remarks and unexpected answers' . . . the flashing stuff of his great artifice, carrying its modish sin with delicate balance and wicked wit."

Valentine calls after the lawyer whom his pretended madness sends scurrying: "Ha! You need not run so fast, honesty will not overtake you." Those that enjoy brilliance of wit, sharp satire deftly poised and bull's-eye-darted, will be overtaken with delight at *Love For Love.*

It entered the NT repertory in 1965, with Laurence Olivier, Lynn Redgrave, Miles Mallison, Joyce Redman, and John Stride. It was played in America at Asolo in 1971, and by the Phoenix at the Helen Hayes, New York, 1974–1975.

THE WAY OF THE WORLD   *William Congreve*

Paradoxically, *The Way of the World,* 1700, the greatest of William Congreve's plays, was so poorly received that the author resolved, and kept his resolve, to write no more for the theatre. Despite the best efforts of the stars Thomas Betterton and Ann Bracegirdle, the scintillating wit of the play—"There is as much bullion in it," said Pope, "as would serve to lace fifty modern comedies"—was too much for its early audiences. Congreve wrote it at the age of thirty, and lived for thirty years more without writing another line for the theatre.

The Way of the World was later recognized as a great play. It opened at the new Covent Garden Theatre on December 7, 1732, and has been played more than any other English comedy since. Swinburne has called it "the unequalled and unapproached masterpiece of English comedy," and Edmund Gosse considered it "the best written, the most dazzling, the most intellectually accomplished of all English comedies."

The increasing emphasis on morals produced a decline in the stage popularity of Congreve's plays, although all five he wrote were produced, in bowdlerized versions, in 1776. Productions were few through the Victorian regime.

London saw *The Way of the World* in 1942 with Godfrey Tearle, Edith Evans, and Peggy Ashcroft; New York saw it in 1924, 1925, 1927, 1931, and 1954. The 1931 production, by the Players' Club, engaged Walter Hampden, Fay Bainter, Dorothy Stickney, Cora Witherspoon, Ernest Cossart, and Moffat Johnson. A sparkling production was given at the Johns Hopkins Playhouse, Baltimore, in November 1949.

The Way of the World shows how Mirabell and Lady Millamant manage to achieve matrimony despite the jealous obstruction of Millamant's aunt and guardian, Lady Wishfort. Intrigue and cozenage form the substructure upon which Congreve's wit and worldly wisdom coruscate and cascade. As William Hazlitt has said: "The style of Congreve is inimitable, nay, perfect. It is the highest model of comic dialogue . . . The fire of artful raillery is nowhere else so well kept up." Note that the comedy intended by Congreve is not the humorous variety, warm with emotion, light with animal spirits, as in Shakespeare; it is the crackling of the intellect, the sparkling of wit, as in Molière. In this vein, as Voltaire estimated, "Congreve raised the glory of comedy to a greater height than any English writer before or since."

The Way of the World is no romantic comedy like the spring-tide sunny dramas of Shakespeare, but a play of wit like the glint of sun on a lake of ice, where expert skaters cut fancy figures, and slide more lightly where the ice is thin. Objection has been made to the morals of Congreve's characters—though they are more exemplary than those of most contemporary dramatists—but such objections were routed by Charles Lamb: "I feel the better always for the perusal of one of Congreve's comedies. I am the gayer at least for it; and I could never connect those sports of a witty fancy in any shape with any result to be drawn from them to imitation in real life . . . The Fainalls and the Mirabells, the Dorimants and the Lady Touchwoods, in their own sphere, do not affend my moral sense; in fact, they do not appeal to it at all . . . They have got out of Christendom into the land—what shall I call it?—of cuckoldry, the Utopia of gallantry, where pleasure is duty, and manners perfect freedom. No good person can be justly offended as a spectator, because no good person suffers on the stage . . . No peace of families is violated, because no family ties exist among them . . . No deep affections are disquieted, no holy wedlock bands are snapped asunder, for affection's depth and wedded faith are not of the growth of that soil." There is profound observation in Lamb's words, for, while tragedy shows the dire consequence of violating ethical and social laws, comedy, like love itself, laughs at such locks.

Millamant is a truly rich creation. While she is self-designed in elegance, refinement, wit, and high assurance, the tapping toe of a woman genuinely in love peeps beneath the petticoat of her artifice. Millamant, observed

Leigh Hunt, "pushes the confident playfulness of a coquette to the verge of what is pleasing; but her animal spirits and good nature secure her. You feel that her airs will give way by and by to a genuine tenderness; and meanwhile some of them are exquisite in their affected superiority to circumstances."

The *Manchester Guardian* called the 1924 London production "the choicest and most piquant thing the English theatre has done this year." Percy Hammond disagreed sharply; looking around on opening night (June 1, 1931) of the Players' Club revival, he announced: "During intermission I counted twelve persons in the stalls who can write better comedies than *The Way of the World* . . . Mr. Congreve's corpse." Allardyce Nicoll walked middle ground: "Congreve is the perfect stylist, but he is by no means perfect in his plot construction or his truth to character. For a *bon mot* he will sacrifice both the one and the other . . . The precision and balance of the prose are exquisite."

Most critics today would still deem quite moderate the judgment of the *London Chronicle,* after a Drury Lane performance of November 14, 1758: *The Way of the World* is "a comedy which for poignancy of wit, delicacy of humor, regularity of conduct, propriety of manners, and continuity of character, may (if ever work might) be reckoned a finished piece." Behind the froth of recherché clothes, the tapping of snuffboxes, the powdering of curly wigs, the high fantastic fashioning of amours, *The Way of the World* has vitality enough to quicken audiences, as Lady Wishfort says, "to all futurity."

A touch of that "futurity": London, 1956, with Margaret Rutherford, Kay Hammond, and John Clements (who also directed); 1958, a musical version briefly at Bath; 1962, Asolo; 1966, Pitlochry Festival; London, 1969 and (NT) 1970; Edinburgh Festival, 1973. (In that year, retiring from the *London Sunday Times,* Harold Hobson was knighted—the first knight created for distinction in a career as drama critic.)

THE GREEN PASTURES   *Marc Connelly*

Out of the simple picture of man's earliest days that a southern pickaninny might conceive, Marc Connelly (Marcus Cook, American, 1890–1980) fashioned *The Green Pastures,* which surged into the hearts of all beholders. Alexander Woollcott in the *Ladies' Home Journal* (September 1935) called it "the finest achievement of the American theatre in the hundred years during which there has been one worth considering."

Starting in the Louisiana Sunday School of the Reverend Deshee, *The Green Pastures* moves through seventeen scenes of biblical times, after a fish-fry in heaven, with Gabriel smoking "ten cent seegars." In that scene, the jubilant singing of spirituals is suddenly hushed by the most awesome entrance cue in the history of the theatre: "Gangway!" the Angel Gabriel cries, "Gangway for de Lawd God Jehovah!"

De Lawd leaves the angels' fish-fry to create Adam and Eve. He then follows humanity on its uneven course—driving off Cain; rescuing Noah when crap-shooting revelers and revilers are left to drown; leading Moses, after a Minstrel Show magic competition with the Egyptian high priests, along the road to the promised land; putting into the trumpets of Joshua the compelling rhythm that seems the Negro's heritage today; sweeping wrath upon the Harlem cabarets of ancient Babylon; and finally moving on to another angelic fish-fry at which, after looking along the course of creation, the Lord of Wrath envisages the Crucifixion and knows that he must also be the Lord of Mercy. When He thunders upon erring and sinful humanity, however, it is man's Job-like faith in God that restores God's faith in man.

Attempting to explain the deep appeal of *The Green Pastures,* John Mason Brown spoke of its moving simplicity; Alexander Woollcott, of its innocence. "Perhaps those whom it most readily moves to tears" said Woollcott, "are people who are crying in the dark and cold, weeping for something their world has lost." The author himself remarked that what touched him, while writing the play, was the way "these untutored black Christians have adapted the contents of the Bible to the consistency of their everyday lives ... with terrific spiritual hunger and the greatest humility." Their picture, at times garish, at times is fraught with the simple wonder of the dawn.

An equal humility, and a great daring, must have animated Marc Connelly. He succeeded in being both colloquial and reverent in bringing the actions of the Lord—even when He "passes a miracle"—to the level of comprehension of the simplest human.

For all its warm reception, *The Green Pastures* had no easy road. No Broadway producer would touch the play; the subject seemed anathema. It was finally backed by a Wall Street man new to Broadway. Then came the problem of finding someone to play de Lawd. Broadway and Harlem casting agencies were at a loss. Connelly remarked that he must come "from heaven"—when in walked sixty-five-year-old Richard Berry Harrison. Born in Canada of runaway slaves, Harrison had never been on the stage, but had long wandered, as bell-hop, porter, itinerant elocutionist. Assured by his bishop that it was all right to enact the part, Harrison accepted. He made a simple, magnificent figure of de Lawd, a cross between a benign pastor and a paternal plantation owner, with flashes of majesty. As he was making up for the 1,657th performance, Harrison fell ill: "Hold me up, Charlie," he pleaded; "the world needs this play at this time." He was buried beneath a blanket of 1,657 roses.

The Green Pastures opened in New York, February 26, 1930, and had a run of 557 performances. It returned to New York, after a country-wide tour, in 1935. In some places, however, the play was forbidden. In Philadelphia and Washington, the law against child actors was invoked. One Willmoore Kendall, a blind preacher of Miami, Oklahoma, reminded his congregation that de Lawd was not God, but "the Afro-American's anthropomorphic personification of God." From the *London Daily Mail* came the indignant protest of J. H. Barton: "How any creature can dare to personate and caricature our ineffable Holy God passes understanding. That the actor is not struck dead is only another of the multitudinous proofs that God is long-suffering and plenteous in goodness and mercy." London, where representation of deity onstage is forbidden, banned *The Green Pastures* as sacrilegious; Russia banned it as too religious, "too servile in its démodé piety."

In Europe, the play was produced only in Sweden. In the Stockholm production, after the cleaning women had mopped and dusted Jehovah's office—where Gabriel's trumpet of Doomsday hangs enticingly on a hatpeg—one of the women picked up her bucket and nonchalantly flew out of the window. These charwomen wore dust-jackets over their wings in the New York revival that opened March 15, 1951, with William Marshall as de Lawd. The play was warmly welcomed by the reviewers; but an earnestness in our lives, with many plays and motion pictures attacking discrimination, made the childlike conception of biblical days, with its sinner-or-saint morality, seem too blandly condescending. In another few decades, it may again seem like a timeless legend.

Marc Connelly drew *The Green Pastures* from sketches by Roark Bradford, which had been collected as *Old Man Adam an' His Chillun* (1928). The Sunday School prologue is Connelly's addition. Robert Garland, with parallel passages, showed that much of the play's language was taken directly from the book; Brooks Atkinson analyzed the nature of Connelly's changes and came to the conclusion that "all that is so inexplicably transfiguring about *The Green Pastures* is Mr. Connelly's personal contribution."

Those that have seen *The Green Pastures* are likely to agree with Alexander Woollcott that it is "an experience which will thereafter be a part of their lives as long as they live." In its simplicity and reverence, even through the pictures of innocent fish-fry jollity and of guilty Babylonian revels, *The Green Pastures* captures the primal wonder of man about the upward march of living.

The 1930 Swedish production was played by whites, as was the one in Frankfurt in 1958. The play was finally allowed in London in 1963.

Attitudes toward *The Green Pastures* have varied widely. Heywood Broun (*The Nation,* April 9, 1930) said that Connelly "*has taken black loam and breathed upon it.* There is nothing in the book that lays hands upon my spine as does the march of the Children on the road to the Promised Land." Harold Clurman, conversely (*The New Republic,* April 16, 1951), stated: "I find no trace of moral sentiment here, only the pseudo-religiosity of the Easter pageant in the larger movie-houses—far more skillful and entertaining, of course, but only a little less hypocritical." Later presentations of Bible story are discussed with *Jesus Christ Superstar.* *

THE CID   *Pierre Corneille*

The greatest play of the first great French tragic dramatist, Pierre Corneille (1606–1684), *Le Cid* was written in 1636 after the Spanish play, *The Youthful Exploits of the Cid,* by Guillen de Castro y Bello (1569–1631). It deals with the problem of love and honor (the Spanish *pundonor*) in the career of "the Cid" (from the Arabic *Sayyid,* Lord), the Spanish hero Don Rodrigue Diaz de Bivat, who died in 1099 and whose beloved, Ximena (Chimène), entered a convent in 1102. The play is centered on the climactic moment of their lives when, despite his love for Chimène, the Cid challenges and kills her father to avenge an insult to his own father. Thereupon, despite her love of the Cid and despite his great victory over the Moors, Chimène is obliged by honor to bring about his death. A compromise, however, develops in the form of a duel: Chimène says she will wed whoever slays Rodrigue; the King says she shall wed whoever wins. Don Sancho, who loves her, is killed by Don Rodrigue, whom she loves. The King grants her a year to mourn her father, before they marry.

Corneille did not merely repeat the time-worn formula of the struggle between love and honor in *The Cid.* His hero is bent upon the pursuit of glory, which love, joined with honor, impels him to seek. "The originality of the analysis of passion in *The Cid,*" said Octave Nadal in *Love in the Works of Corneille* (1948), "springs from this discovery: love and honor do not enter into conflict; they conspire together." The conflict lies between the quest of glory and the drive of love.

The Cid marked the peak of Corneille's rebellion against the literary domination of Cardinal Richelieu, who imposed the "law" of the dramatic unities upon the playwrights of the time. Corneille had first been attracted to the theatre when Mondory's troupe visited Rouen, where Corneille was practicing law. He wrote the comedy *Mélite,* which Mondory produced in Paris in 1629. Richelieu, under whose sponsorship the French Academy was coming into being, insisted upon observance of the three unities—of time, of place, and of action—and Corneille, to show his distaste for these, wrote another comedy, *Clitandre,* 1632, "obeying all the rules of the drama, but having nothing in it." Richelieu then hit upon the notion of assigning five authors, each to write one act of a play; Corneille accepted one such assignment. Refusing a second, he wrote *The Cid.*

Playing through the opening days of the year 1637, *The Cid* raised a storm of controversy. France was then at war with Spain. Since the Queen was Spanish, Richelieu, leader of the war party, did not dare openly oppose the play. He had, however, made stringent regulations against duelling, and in the play Rodrigue fights two duels within twenty-four hours. But *The Cid* was praised by the King, and presented three times at court. Three hundred years later (when *The Cid* was presented via radio in 1938) Burns Mantle called it "the first smash hit in the history of French drama."

In 1637, however, friends of the Cardinal protested vigorously. Over a score of poems and pamphlets carried on the controversy. Most influential was the *Observations on "The Cid,"* by the brother of Mlle. de Scudéry, Georges, which charged the play with being undignified in subject, with showing poor judgment, with breaking the rules, and with having many faulty verses. Georges appealed to the newly formed Academy, and Richelieu ordered Corneille to submit to the Academy's judgment. In 1638, *The Opinions of the French Academy on the Tragicomedy "The Cid"* condemned both its subject and its denouement. Corneille was vanquished. He dedicated his next play, *Horace,* 1639, to Cardinal Richelieu and was elected to the Academy.

Polyeucte, produced in 1642, also stands against time. A picture of the Christian Polyeucte whose martyrdom effects the conversion of his wife Pauline, it was long played at the Comédie-Française, annually, before and after Lent. *Les Nouvelles Littéraires* said of it (March 4, 1937): "Here the great man finds his place again, first. The Father. To him we owe all, including Racine, Molière, Victor Hugo, Claudel. He has been subject to eclipses; but the periods indifferent to him condemned themselves . . . For Sarcey, Polyeucte is a man who sacrifices his woman. One might say that he sacrifices woman."

In *Polyeucte,* as in *The Cid,* there is a transmutation of the usual concept of love; love becomes part of a deeper drive. As the *London Times* (December 4, 1948) observed: "In *Polyeucte* there is an apparent conflict between the claims of Divine and human love; but for Polyeucte human love is the first step toward sanctity and sacrifice. It is only by choosing Divine love that a proper value is placed on human love, and the reconciliation of opposing claims produces the moral transformation that is common to the characters of all Corneille's greatest plays."

Increasingly, however, it became clear that Corneille's work did not accord with the spirit of his time. Unfortunately, he seems to have been convinced by his critics; he tried to write what was wanted. He failed. And he watched himself being superseded by dramatists more attuned to the age, especially by Racine.*

Corneille's works have been divided into four periods: that of spontaneous creation, of *The Cid*; that in which he repented and was taken into the

Academy; that of gallant historical romances—*Pompée,* 1643, and other plays exhibiting the "tender reasonableness" and the artificial style of the day; and that of his doomed rivalry with Racine. These periods mark a steady descent in his talent; his gifts never found fuller expression than in *The Cid.*

As late as 1660 Corneille was still apologizing for the "irregularities" in *The Cid.* He altered the opening and the ending, to make it seem that Chimène did not intend to marry Rodrigue. Productions since have wisely returned to the original version.

The drama of Corneille, as in *The Cid,* does not stir the audience to pity or horror, but rather quickens its awareness of the heroic, the assertion of individual integrity in the face of disaster. Thus, in his first tragedy, *Medea,* 1635, when, after losing her husband and killing her sons, Medea is asked what she has left, she replies "Moi, dis-je, et c'est assez!"—"Myself, I say, and that is enough!" The audience grows exalted in contemplation of such greatness as transcends doom. But the appeal of the tragedies is thus directed to the intelligence more than to the emotions. The heart may be touched, but the mind is uplifted.

In his concept of human dignity, Corneille is "sublime without ever losing elegance." He may lack the pellucid regularity of Racine, but he has complete command over all the appropriate resources of the language. As Edith Hamilton said in *Theatre Arts* (August 1937): "The power of definite and complete expression is the very heart of Corneille's drama. He is not only able to put into words all that he has in mind; he depends almost wholly upon words for his interest. There is practically no action in his plays. What the actors do is to talk to, or, rather, to argue with each other. It is excellent argument if Corneille's premises are granted, admirably logical, sharp-cut, maintaining an astonishing degree of intensity." The eloquence of the speeches, the dignity and grandeur of the rhetoric, the sweetness and power of the versification, and the validity of the characters, give *The Cid* commanding stature.

Corneille's characters and their motives approach the complexity of life more than those of any other dramatist save Shakespeare. For dramatic effectiveness, emotional power, and psychological insight, the two interviews of Chimène and Rodrigue are twin peaks of the drama; but throughout, their relationship is marked by the most subtle interplay. This is traced in some detail in Lacy Lockert's introduction to his translations from Corneille, and he notes: "Jules Lemaitre has cleverly observed that they often express not the sentiments which they have, but those which they think they ought to have; that they are conscious of the noble figure they cut, each in the other's eyes, and that they want to compel each other's admiration and prove themselves worthy of being loved; that constantly in all their anguish they thus are, after a fashion, making love to each other: it is a very delicate and beautiful touch."

The Cid was produced in English as early as January 26, 1637, in a translation by Joseph Rutter. Samuel Pepys saw a production of this version some time later, when its style was outmoded in English verse, and he wrote in his *Diary,* December 1, 1662: "I saw *The Valiant Cid* acted, a play which I have read with great delight, but it is a most dull thing acted, which I never understood before: there being no pleasure in it though done by Betterton and by Yanthe and another fine wench."

Colley Cibber's version of *The Cid,* called *The Heroick Daughter,* opened November 28, 1712, with Mrs. Oldfield, and was revived several times. Its printed preface (1718), which praised the influence of Richard Steele in the theatre but slighted Joseph Addison, precipitated a controversy; Mist's *Journal* (October 31, 1719) sneered at it, saying that Cibber "very modestly confesses he has infinitely outdone the French original."

The French have always been receptive to *The Cid*; it has remained a favorite in French repertoire. As the *London Times* remarked (November 9, 1924): "There are Frenchmen who have gone every year of their lives to hear *The Cid*." In 1907, director André Antoine, at the Odéon in Paris, gave a "facsimile" of the original performance.

The great French tragedian Mounet-Sully brought *The Cid* to the United States in March 1894; it was presented at Hunter College, New York City, in October 1936. A new translation of the play (with five others of Corneille's) by Lacy Lockert was published in 1952.

On the occasion of a Comédie-Française production in London, the *Times* (May 31, 1934) said: "In his preface to *The Cid* Voltaire observes that Corneille was the first writer, after the deplorable attempts of the Spanish and English theatres, whose tragedies were sufficiently regular to move the audience to tears. And, of course, he was more or less right. Nothing but perfect regularity could save those sustained and purely artificial conflicts of love and honor, of public and private duty, which seem to have been constructed for the express purpose of matching the formal antitheses of rhetorical verse." What gives *The Cid* power is the pressure of its romantic subject upon its mainly classical form.

Recent productions of *The Cid* have been mainly in French, as by the Théâtre National Populaire in New York, 1958; the Comédie Française in London, 1961; and a Canadian tour in 1979. The play was shown in English at the OffBway Bouerie Lane in 1978. It always continues to impress.

BOUBOUROCHE   *Georges Courteline*

Boubouroche has been called the most touching farce, with wistful overtones, about an unfaithful woman and a gullible lover. Written by Georges Courteline (Georges Victor-Marcel Moinaux, French, 1858–1929), it was shown first at the Paris Théâtre Libre in 1892, entering the Comédie Française in 1910 and still in its repertoire.

Boubouroche, playing cards in a café, dictates to his partner, Potasse, how to play. They lose, but Boubouroche pays for the drinks as the winners leave. Potasse calls him a patsy.

In her apartment, meanwhile, Adèle has been talking contemptuously with her lover André of the simpleton Boubouroche, who supports her. Twice the bell rings; André hides; it's the wrong apartment. The third time, it's Boubouroche.

For, when the others have left the café, an old man reading the paper at another table comes over, and tells Boubouroche that for eight years he's been living in the apartment adjoining Adèle's, and knows of her constant unfaithfulness. "You're a cuckold! Your health!" They clink glasses, and drink.

When Boubouroche enters her apartment, she is enraged; he apologizes, but she insists that he search around. As she opens the closet door, the wind blows out the lamp, so that a candle within reveals the intruder. André comes out, calm, and refuses to leave until Boubouroche promises not to hurt Adèle. Then he quietly combs and brushes his hair—"Good night, Madame. Good night, Sir"—and goes. Boubouroche is dejected, but Adèle rails at him; she has been faithful for eight years, and he can't trust her because there's a man in her closet? "It's not my secret. But for the sake of our love . . . Do you want me to go that far? One word, and I'll tell you all." Boubouroche responds: "What kind of man do you take me for? Other people's secrets have nothing to do with me." They kiss and make up.

In the doorway, meeting the talkative old man, Boubouroche grabs him angrily: "My sweet little Adèle is a tramp, eh? Let me tell you you're an old goat. That's what you are. You're a patsy." He starts to beat the old man as the curtain falls.

Boubouroche was presented by the Theatre Guild at the Garrick, New York, November 28, 1921, and by Max Reinhardt in Vienna, 1925. It was filmed in French with André Berley and Madeleine Renaud. OffOffBway, it was shown by the Masterworks, and by Theatre-in-a-Courthouse, in 1971. Amusing in itself, it is a reminder that behind every farce there lurks a tragedy.

TONIGHT AT 8:30   *Noel Coward*

Nine sketches by Noel Coward (Sir Noel Pierce, 1899–1973), usually presented in three groups on successive evenings, are joined in the theatre under the title of this play. Directed and acted by the author, with Gertrude Lawrence, they were successful in London in the spring of 1936, acclaimed in Boston in the fall, and achieved a triumph on their opening in New York on November 24, 1936, with a run of 118 performances.

In 1937, the sketches were presented in San Francisco with a cast including Helen Chandler, Estelle Winwood, Bramwell Fletcher, Mary Astor, Claud Allister, and Carol Stone. Individual sketches from the group have been frequently performed in little theatres. Six of them were presented again in New York in two groups, opening February 20, 1948, with Gertrude Lawrence, and with Noel Coward directing but not playing a part. Independent though the pieces are, they are all character sketches, mainly of persons reflected from various facets of English life.

1. *Hands Across the Sea,* a masterpiece of organized irrelevance, pictures visitors to the witless Lady Maureen, just back from a trip around the world. She mistakes the couple that had entertained her at Malaya for a couple she had met at Penang. With a scramble of persons and phone calls and flying tangents of conversation, including a stranger whose errand is never ascertained, the piece tells no story but is a superbly satiric picture of flighty folk and their social irresponsibility.

2. *Fumed Oak* is a caustic picture of lower-middle-class Cockney life. Henry Gow, long dominated by his bossy mother-in-law, his nagging wife, and his adenoidal daughter, reveals that he has been secretly saving; in a swirl of petty triumph, he leaves his family. In this brief sketch, Coward achieves a searing picture of a lower-middle-class family—marred only by a sense that the author despises what he depicts.

3. *Shadow Play,* a danced and crooned episode, shows Simon telling Victoria that their rapture cannot last. An overdose of sleeping powder brings memories through delirium, and they decide to try all over again. This is a semi-satiric, sentimental trifle, deftly done.

4. *Family Album* presents a Victorian family, gathered in 1860 for the reading of their father's will. A few drinks break down their reticences and pretenses—"To hell with father!"—and we discover that the youngest daughter, who has given years of care to the old man, has destroyed a will in

which he left everything to a mistress. The faithful butler, who had witnessed the destroyed will, stands by the family. Ironic and comical, the sketch is a picture which sympathy and satire, blending, make both poignant and absurd.

5. *The Astonished Heart.* After twelve years of happy married life, a successful psychiatrist is lured by his wife's former schoolmate, who is piqued by his indifference. When she wins him, she stops the affair. Though he loves his wife, his body—or his vanity—requires the other woman; rebuffed, the psychiatrist jumps out of a window. Lightly moving, these characters suggest troubled depths.

6. *Red Peppers* is a rowdy, gusty picture of a cheap variety team, a married pair of ham vaudevillians, who act together onstage, but quarrel offstage, while hoping for a better billing in the theatres out of town. This is the most uproarious and richly comic sketch of the group.

7. *Ways and Means* shows an extravagant, impecunious, and incurably silly couple, talking in bed, wondering how to avoid eviction from their rooms in the Villa Zephyre on the Côte d'Azure, when a theft happily provides the wherewithal for continuing their inane existence. The complete emptiness of the couple's life is revealed beneath the swift movement and easy laughter.

8. *Still Life,* one of the more serious sketches, shows the final rendezvous of a man and woman—each married—who have been meeting in a railway refreshment room. Recognizing that continuance would be too sordid, they decide to part; ironically the gushing of a garrulous friend interrupts their last farewell. This sketch contains the best character drawing, the most sympathetic figures, and the mellowest writing of the group.

9. *We Were Dancing* is another frail piece set to music. A man and a woman meet at the Country Club at Samolo, Malaysia; they dance; they fall in love. The woman asks her husband to release her. The three talk through the night, and in the light of morning all is as it was before. With the dawn comes the yawn. The sentiment and the satire battle in the audience's mind and heart.

On the first presentation of these playlets, the critics found them of uneven merit. James Agate in the *London Times* said of *Hands Across the Sea*: "Every second of this admirable skit is not only perfect theatre but first-class satire." He objected, however, to the determined respectability of Coward's middle-class characters, as opposed to the determined irrespectability of the "Mayfairies." W. A. Darlington of the *London Telegraph* declared that in *Fumed Oak* Coward "reveals a new power of seeing simple ordinary humanity for what it is . . ." While Agate called *Shadow Play* "a revue number interminably spun out," Darlington felt that "the theme is handled with great delicacy."

The New York critics were more receptive, as the papers of November 25, 1936, attest. Brooks Atkinson called *Fumed Oak* "a little masterpiece of sour-puss dramaturgy." John Anderson deemed *Hands Across the Sea* "hilariously malevolent." Robert Coleman said that *The Astonished Heart* showed "an iceberg heaving over a volcano." The works as a whole, John Mason Brown characterized as "vaudeville sketches of a kind that you used to dream of seeing, but never saw, when vaudeville was in its heyday." And Richard Watts called Noel Coward "one of the great figures of the modern theatre."

The revival in 1948 did not fare so well. It ran for but twenty-six performances, and found the critics unenthusiastic. George Freedley, it is true, called the sketches "still as delightful as ever." But Atkinson—exempting *Red Peppers* and *Fumed Oak*—exclaimed: "Don't look now, but 12 years have disappeared. Although Gertrude Lawrence is a superwoman, she cannot restore a world that has been lost." And John Chapman found the occasion "like trying to get a bang from the leftovers of an Elsa Maxwell party which I'd never been to."

Louis Kronenberger gives a fuller analysis: "Mr. Coward himself is so very important a symbol of our time, so very successful and clever a writer for our age, that it somehow seems one's duty to try to account for one's distaste. We can be sure only of his satiric perceptions, never of his sense of values. We cannot be sure, for instance, whether he regards the hard-up couple in *Ways and Means* as unspeakable, or merely unfortunate . . . Yet he is enough in the line of the Congreves to make us wonder why he merely emerges as the most gifted jack-of-all-trash of our age. His very versatility—his sorties into the sentimental and fantastic and melodramatic—explain it a little; your true master of social comedy keeps his gifts in a cool dry place, and his eye consistently on the object. Coward, too, I suppose, always keeps his eye on the object; but the object is always his audience: he's first and last and always a showman. That is his real vulgarity—a vulgarity of intentions. Hence we are happiest with him when he is writing pure fantasy or farce, a *Blithe Spirit** or a crazy ditty; when there is no possible meaning, when there is only an effect."

To the supercilious, all things are superficial. Noel Coward may, as some of his critics aver, enjoy the society he is satirizing. Precisely! For the best satire—not savage, but sunny and supple and searching—is based on the excesses of those we love. With the deftness of a chef with an onion, Noel Coward peels off the outer layers of the persons he presents and usually finds material enough to flavor a goodly dish; and sometimes, at the end, there is what remains when one has peeled an onion—tears. The sketches comprising *Tonight at 8:30* are a permanent picture of a fading society.

The sketches continue popular. In London, 1970, for ninety-five performances, the play was called *Tonight at 8*; there in 1981 it was again *Tonight at 8:30*. New York saw the show OffBway in 1967 and 1976; Phoenix in 1975 played it also at East Hampton, Long Island, for the summer.

Sketch 3, at the London Lyric, 1981, called *Shadow Line,* ends with a mood that brings to mind the last lines of Paul Geraldy's book of verses, *You and Me,* when the separating lovers decide to stay; quoted in *Private Lives.**

BLITHE SPIRIT   *Noel Coward*

A light-hearted mixture of fantasy and mirth, *Blithe Spirit,* the first play to present an astral bigamist, was literally a howling success. Opening in London during World War II (July 2, 1941), it ran for 1,997 performances, while three other companies toured England. It came to New York on November 5, 1941, with Clifton Webb, Peggy Wood, Mildred Natwick (as the medium), and Leonora Corbett (her American debut), and in spite of Pearl Harbor the play ran for 657 performances. It has been played frequently around the country; in 1949 at Syracuse, it was presented as a bawdy Restoration farce.

The play pictures the plight of Charles Condomine, novelist, widower, and husband. He permits the bicycle-riding medium, Mme. Arcati, to hold a seance at his house; and behold, his seven-years-dead wife Elvira materializes and refuses to leave. As she is visible only to Charles and the audience (and later to the mediumistic maid), the living wife, Ruth, is naturally hard to convince that Elvira has returned. Both wives are jealous to such a degree that Charles is relieved when an accident makes him twice a widower. Happily he prepares to sail abroad. As he jestingly bids the two wraiths a gay goodbye, toppling vases and falling pictures show that now both women are haunting him.

"So deft is Noel Coward's writing," said *Life* (December 8, 1941)," and so skillfully does he skim the thin, slick ice of his inventions, that *Blithe Spirit* emerges as the most amusing bauble on the United States stage." John Anderson declared that the theatre where *Blithe Spirit* was showing was "just the place to die laughing," but he would be a hardy ghost that would care to face those cunning and mischief-making females. Nevertheless the antics of the wraiths are amusing to watch; their early rivalry, Charles trying to play them one against the other, and their final joining to plague their single man, make delightful theatre.

The play, said John Mason Brown, "is as audacious in its subject matter as it is expert in its treatment. In it Mr. Coward turns death into the merriest of merry topics and the dear departed into the gayest of gay companions . . . Just when you would swear that his theme is bound to become as tedious as a coloratura's solo concert, Mr. Coward changes the register, and by doing so gives his performance a new lease on life. He does this effortlessly, with infinite suavity, with a perfect control of his materials, with an eagle's eye for what is unsuspected or unexplored in a situation, and with all those side-splitting irrelevancies which are so much to the point and add so to the delights of Mr. Coward's writing when it is at its best. If his play lacks body, remember that it deals with shades. But its spirit is of the blithest." Just as *Arsenic and Old Lace** makes a farce of murder, *Blithe Spirit* turns the return of the dead into gay comedy.

Revivals in London include: 1964, with Beatrice Lillie and Tammy Grimes; opening July 23, 1970, for 204 performances; June 24, 1976, NT (Lyttleton, then the Olivier), with Elizabeth Spriggs as the medium. In America: New York, 1964; summer at Ogunquit, Maine, 1970; Tammy Grimes as Elvira, Illinois, 1972; Omaha, 1978. In November 1979 a musical, *High Spirits,* by Hugh Martin and Timothy Gray, was tried at Westport, Conn.

In his autobiography *Future Indefinite* (1954), Coward stated: "I shall ever be grateful for the almost psychic gift that enabled me to write *Blithe Spirit* in five days during one of the darkest years of the War. It fell into my mind and onto the manuscript. Six weeks later it was produced and ran for four and a half years . . . Beyond a few typographical errors I made no corrections, and only two lines of the script were ultimately cut." The author and uncounted audiences have been in blithe spirits with the play.

PRIVATE LIVES   *Noel Coward*

Fans of Noel Coward are likely to consider *Private Lives* his best comedy, though the lives are hardly private. The story is quite clear.

Two adjoining suites of a good hotel in Deauville share a balcony. On it Amanda and Elyot Chase, just divorced and on new honeymoons, come together with Elyot's new wife, Sybil, and Amanda's new husband, Victor Prynne. Faced with the assorted tangle, the two divorced ones prefer each other, deem it love renewed, and slip away. Home, the old boredom reasserts itself. Tenderness lapses to irritation; a quarrel ensues; Amanda dumps a bouquet, water and all, on Elyot's head; thumped pillows extend the violence—and the indignant husband and wondering bride break in. At the morning confrontation, Elyot suavely turns aside the angry Victor; in frustrated annoyance the two new ones shout at each other, and as the slanging match continues, Elyot takes Amanda by the hand and they slip away, silent and unnoticed, to freedom.

What happens on the morrow? Never ask. The curtain falls; the comedy is over. Enjoy the pranks. Coward is a shrewd performer.

There comes to mind the deft French poet and playwright Paul Geraldy, who almost earns entrance to these pages. His book of verse, *You and Me,* is a lover's monologue of the ups and downs of an attachment. It ends:

> *You can't go in this weather . . . Well then, stay!*
> *Yes, stay, dear. We will try to fix things up.*
> *You can never tell. Our hearts have drifted away,*
> *But lips can taste anew of the olden cup.*

> *We'll do our best. We'll be good. You see,*
> *Habit does clutch at one. So you'd*
> *Better sit down. Renew your ennui,*
> *And near you I'll resume my solitude.*

When Noel Coward himself played Elyot in 1930, Gertrude Lawrence's Amanda showed resourcefulness; here was a willing lady who still could take care of herself. But with all her sweetness and beauty, Elizabeth Taylor's 1983 Amanda is no more brainy than her fluttery successor. Her difference is that she's unconventional; she's ready to be Elyot's mistress, so long as she can be his. Nor is Richard Burton as the supercilious Elyot better than young Victor; he is "a man of the world," superior through his own sense of superiority, able to make Victor uncomfortable, as a sincere man is apt to be on encountering one who is essentially a playboy. "Each man kills the thing he loves," said Oscar Wilde. "The coward does it with a kiss." Noel Coward makes us oblivious of the eventual doom, while we enjoy the spectacle of the embracing.

Private Lives opened at the London Phoenix, September 24, 1930, with Noel Coward and Gertrude Lawrence, for 101 performances; at the New York Times Square, January 27, 1931, for 256. The October 31, 1944, opening at the London Apollo ran on for 716 performances; from the Queens, September 21, 1972, it moved to the Globe, July 2, 1973, for 517. The *London Times* wondered whether, with Laurence Olivier and Adrienne Allen (Mrs. Raymond Massey), "so far from being a badly dated relic, it wasn't in fact the funniest play to have adorned the English theatre this century." In New York, December 4, 1969, it had 204 performances. The Taylor Theatre Group, although sold out for its opening in Boston and at the Lunt-Fontanne opening, April 28, 1983, for its scheduled 120 performances, lost some of the lustre. The *Times* felt that, of Elizabeth Taylor, "It is only when she stares out over the vast reaches of the theatre that her eyes reveal a hint of sparkle: what she sees then is a full house." (Burton got remarried; Elizabeth Taylor fell sick; the revival closed.)

At Coward's death in 1973, theatre historian Allardyce Nicoll called him "a true master in that realm of comedy which exists purely to give us delight." Coward himself believed that the best of his plays "mirrored, without overexaggeration, a certain section of the social life of the times." *Private Lives* justifies that claim.

THE MAGNIFICENT CUCKOLD   *Fernand Crommelynck*

Born of a theatrical family, Fernand Crommelynck (Belgian, 1888–1970) took to writing plays when he was eighteen (1906). He was on the stage until 1921, when he was set free for writing by the swift success of what he called "a lyrical farce"—his masterpiece *Le Cocu magnifique (The Magnificent Cuckold)*.

A grand rouse of irony and biting satire, with Roman candles of colorful dialogue and flaming pinwheels of figurative speech, *The Magnificent Cuckold* depicts the pride, then the suspicion and jealousy, of a possessive husband who drives his wife to the very infidelities he fears. The husband, Bruno, struggles between the vanity of having his wife Stella coveted, and himself envied by all men, and the vanity of having her as his exclusive prize. He compels Stella to exhibit her charms to his cousin Petrus. Detecting a glint of desire in the man's eyes, Bruno needs assurance of his wife's fidelity; he deliberately exposes her to temptation. A sort of second self of Bruno, Estrugo, constantly baits Bruno's jealousy and renews the prick of suspicion, until in his mind a phantasmagoria of his wife's indiscretions develops to a point where tragedy mingles with farce: A line of impatient lovers awaits outside her door, kept in order by a policeman and entertained by circus acts. Then, in a touching balcony scene, Bruno himself approaches his wife, disguised; she recognizes him and accepts his advances, whereupon he, misunderstanding, reveals himself and casts her off. Wishing to be faithful, she is driven to unfaithfulness, fleeing from her plagued and plaguing husband with a herdsman.

The Magnificent Cuckold is at once madly swirling and realistic. It externalizes the inner movements of the spirit in a way that suggests the odd turns and intense drives of expressionism. The play was given an interesting "constructional" (also called "constructivist") setting by L. F. Popova, which has become the model for other productions. Two platforms on the stage, with stairs leading up to them, are connected by a plank; the skeleton of a house stands behind the right-hand platform, and off to the left are the great wings of a windmill. American designer Albert Johnson made sets for the play, but it has not yet had professional performance in the United States. In 1932, a London performance was directed by Theodore Komisarjevsky, with George Hayes and Peggy Ashcroft. It was performed at Yale in 1981.

In Rabelaisian rouse and swift, tumultuous satire, *The Magnificent Cuckold* exposes individual weakness and suggests universal ills: Is it not the same fear that in the field of international affairs, for instance, brings on armament races and suspicions and consequent conflicts, the very disasters nations are seeking to avert? The world is a cuckold that works toward its own betrayal.

The cuckold became a frequent figure in the drama during the twenties, a symbol of the betrayal of the hopes of man. In 1922, Paris saw *Dardamelle, or The Cuckold,* a play by Emile Mazaud. More grim is *Hinkemann (Crippleman),* written by Ernst Toller;* this tragedy, with symbolic significance, combined the themes of the cuckold and the castrate.

Two of Crommelynck's later plays continue the mood and, to some degree, the wider implications of *The Magnificent Cuckold. Corinne* (1929), a mixture of symbolism and romance, pictures a girl who would rather die than see her dream of life polluted by reality. A more important work, *A Woman With Too Small a Heart* (1934) is a searing satire on cold efficiency. With effective byplay and radiating fancy, Crommelynck develops an intensity in his plays and wraps an enveloping atmosphere of meaning around their stories, to lift what might seem surface comedies of sex to the level of dramas of man's deepest problems.

A CHINESE HONEYMOON   *George Dance*

Among the musicals that set their story in the romantic land of the golden dragon, outstanding is *A Chinese Honeymoon,* by George Dance (English, 1858–1932), with music by Howard Talbot (1865–1928). With colorful sets and costumes, it opened in London, October 16, 1899; on its revival, October 5, 1901, it ran for 1,075 performances. In New York, opening June 2, 1902, it reached 404.

The plot, ingeniously sustained and consistently amusing, is a springboard for Gilbertian fun and folly. At Ylang Ylang, Tom Hatherton is in love with the singing girl Soo-Soo, who is really the niece of the Emperor Hang Chow. Tom's uncle, Mr. Pineapple, a stockholder who has married his typist, is there with his bride for a Chinese honeymoon. He meets an old flame, Mrs. Brown, who has come with her parrot to assume the duties of the official "mother-in-law" to the Emperor. A law in this musical-comedy China, that any couple caught kissing must marry within six hours, tangles Pineapple with Soo-Soo and Mrs. Pineapple with the Emperor. When the tangles are unsnarled, Tom has his princess, and the Emperor finds himself marrying the lovesick waitress Fi-Fi.

Among the gay songs of the play is the title sextet. "There's Nothing Like a little Pat" won amused laughter. Fi-Fi sings a lively lyric, "Martha spanks the grand pianner"; of her singing "I want to be a lidy, and ride in a coach and four" the *London Graphic* (October 7, 1901) exclaimed: "A moment like this is worth all the tomfoolery in the world." There is goodly store of foolery, as well as colorful and playful romance, in *A Chinese Honeymoon.*

COSI FAN TUTTE   *Lorenzo Da Ponte*

This comic opera (known in English as *Everybody's Doing It* or *The School For Lovers)* is a gay and lively play of amorous intrigue. The book is by Lorenzo Da Ponte (Italian, 1749–1838, born a Jew as Emanuele Conegliano, baptized a Catholic by the bishop whose name he took, migrated to the United States in 1805). The music which sparkles through the whole play was written by Mozart.

Cosi Fan Tutte was presented in a command performance before Emperor Josef II of Austria on January 26, 1790. It has been very popular in opera repertory and with light opera groups. The story, set mainly in Naples, centers upon cynical Don Alfonso's wager with Fernando and Gratiano, that their sweethearts, the sisters Dorabella and Isidora, are accessible to other suitors. Pretending to be called away to war, the two men disguise themselves as foreigners and woo the fair but fickle ladies; then they discard their disguise and rebuke the faithless ones. Don Alfonso, his wager won, assures the men that a little harmless flirtation is not only harmless, but quite the vogue—"everybody's doing it"—and the lovers are reconciled.

A lively factor of the fun is the sisters' maid, Despina. Made part of the plot, she introduces the "foreign gentlemen." Disguised as a doctor, she revives the men when the girls' early obduracy drives them to "suicide"; disguised as a notary, she prepares the marriage contracts when the girls decide to yield. There is an unusually swift swirl of comic action in the play, a crescendo that rises to its peak when Fernando and Gratiano, returning from the "war," dash out in chase of the "foreigners," and come in again using the manners and accents they had assumed when in disguise.

A variant form of *Cosi Fan Tutte,* used especially in English, pictures Dorabella and Isidora as seeing through the disguises of their lovers and leading them on to punish them for their presumption. This at once makes them less fickle and more sympathetic to the conventional conscience, and adds a suggestion of such irony as is more deeply sprung in *The Guardsman,* by Ferenc Molnar,* which leaves wholly unanswered the question as to whether the succumbing lady saw through a similar disguise. The best English version is by Ruth and Thomas Martin.

The press has constantly praised *Cosi Fan Tutte.* In the *New York Times* (March 7, 1924) Deems Taylor took especial note of the decor by Joseph Urban. In London, the *Times* (April 25, 1930) declared: "We are transported at once into a world of fantasy, where anything may happen." It is a gay, gracious, ingratiating world of make-believe. With music that charms as it carries the playful mood of the story, *Cosi Fan Tutte* is a delightful dalliance of drama.

It remains in operatic repertory. It might be mentioned that the New York Metropolitan Opera House 1952 production, with Patrice Munsell as Despina, was directed by the noted actor Alfred Lunt.

ICEBOUND   *Owen Davis*

Out of the ten-twenty-thirty-cent theatre of lurid melodramas, with a hundred plays such as *The Gambler's Daughter* and *Nellie the Beautiful Cloak Model*—at least one play on Broadway every season for thirty-seven years—Owen Davis (American, 1874–1956) made a long detour to the realistic theatre, with authentic and understanding pictures of American country life. The first of these was *The Detour,* opening August 23, 1921, which led the *New York Telegram* to declare: "The tradition that Mr. Davis is not a dramatist but a play factory has been demolished."

Encouraged by the reception of *The Detour,* Owen Davis tried another play of the same sort—this time set in New England. Opening in New York, February 10, 1923, *Icebound* ran for 171 performances and won the Pulitzer Prize.

According to the author, "Few serious attempts have been made in the direction of a genre comedy of this locality. Here I have tried, at least, to draw a true picture of these people, and I am of their blood, born of generations of Northern Maine small town folk, and brought up among them." The characters in *Icebound* seem hewn of that stern and rockbound coast.

The Jordan family are waiting for Mother Jordan to die so they can share the inheritance. They include the crusty old shopkeeper, Henry; his oppressive wife, Emma, and Nettie, her daughter by an earlier marriage; the forlorn old maid, Ella; and a poor relative, Jane Crosby, who is Mother Jordan's companion, and whom they plan to send packing as soon as the old lady dies. The youngest son, ne'er-do-well Ben Jordan, returns, sent for by

Jane at his dying mother's wish. Ben had fled years before to escape an arson charge; he seems as dissolute and opinionated as ever; he is quarreling with Henry when their mother dies.

Mother Jordan leaves everything to Jane Crosby, who takes a shine to Ben. She buys a new dress to impress him, and hopes to reform him. Nettie, however, puts on the new dress and swirls it into Ben's embrace; but the thought that he may go to jail scares her off. Jane, having persuaded those concerned to drop the arson charge, announces that she is leaving and turning over the farm and all the inheritance to Ben, as his mother would have wished when he proved worthy. Ben proves that he is worthy by asking Jane to marry him.

The whole Jordan family is, the *New York Tribune* said (February 12, 1923), "a bickering, unlovely lot, from Henry, the hypocritical smalltown storekeeper, to young Nettie, who is cattish and shows omens of sex." In the play, Ben remarks that the Jordans were "half froze before we was born."

Icebound has been played quite frequently about the country; in 1936, Owen Davis, Jr., played Ben. The play manifests the skill in construction that kept pace swift and interest tense through a hundred lurid melodramas, together with a capture of character—vivid, biting, clear as pond ice—grown out of close acquaintance and dramatic power.

The most recent revival is by the OffOffBway Meat and Potatoes Co., 1981.

THE SHOEMAKER'S HOLIDAY   *Thomas Dekker*

The Shoemaker's Holiday, by Thomas Dekker (English, 1570?–1632?), was the first dramatic presentation of the rising spirit of personal independence, the forerunner of democracy, in England. In it, apprentices hold to their rights against arrogant nobles; a shoemaker becomes Lord Mayor of London, and talks on familiar terms with the King. That such an attitude was in high vogue may be seen in the fact that the premiere of the play was a Command Performance before Queen Elizabeth, on Christmas, 1599.

There is less concern with the plot than with the activity of Simon Eyre, master of "the gentle craft" of shoemaking and of his lively journeymen, and more interest in the picture of faithful Jane than in the main love story. Jane, the wife of the lame journeyman Ralph, refuses Hammon's advances and his gold. Dekker himself, in a dedicatory note to "all good fellows, professors of the gentle craft," stated the argument of the play: "Sir Hugh Lacy, Earl of Lincoln, had a young gentleman of his own name, his near kinsman, that loved the Lord Mayor's daughter of London; to prevent and cross which love, the Earl caused his kinsman to be sent Colonel of a company into France: who resigned his place to another gentleman his friend, and came disguised like a Dutch shoemaker to the house of Simon Eyre in Tower Street, who served the Mayor and his household with shoes: the merriments that passed in Eyre's house, his coming to be Mayor of London, Lacy's getting his love, and other accidents, with two merry Threemen's songs. Take all in good worth that is well intended, for nothing is purposed but mirth; mirth lengtheneth long life, which, with all other blessings, I heartily wish you. Farewell!"

The Shoemaker's Holiday is Dekker's earliest extant play. Acted in 1599 as *The Gentle Craft,* it was published under its present title in 1600. Its technique is as good as Dekker ever achieved; its philosophy is simple and homely: "A pound of care pays not a dram of debt." Dekker's genuine enthusiasm for the simple aspects of London life is contagious, as his experience of London ways was intimate. The comedy, said Ernest Rhys, "is indeed the most perfect presentation of the brightness and social interest of the everyday Elizabethan life which is to be found in the English drama . . . The craftsman's life, merging in the citizen's, is the end and all of the play; the King himself is but a shadow of social eminence compared with the Lord Mayor. Simon Eyre, the shoemaker, jolliest, most exuberant of all comedy types, is the very incarnation of the hearty English character on its prosperous workaday side."

Simon Eyre is a figure out of history; as is mentioned in the fifth act, he built Leadenhall in London in 1419 and became Lord Mayor in 1445. The real Simon Eyre was a draper, but, since Leadenhall, in Dekker's day, was used as a leather market, it was natural to picture him as a shoemaker.

The Shoemaker's Holiday was sure to appeal to its audience, said Charles Dudley Warner, "especially the pit, where the tradesmen and artisans with their wives applauded, and, noisiest of all, the apprentices showed their satisfaction: here they saw themselves and their masters brought on the stage, somewhat idealized, but still full of frolic and good nature." That the play still appeals to its audience has been made manifest by numerous revivals, especially in college theatres, and by a lively professional production of the Mercury Theatre, with Orson Welles, in New York, which opened on New Year's night, 1938. Sidney B. Whipple's comment emphasized the idea of democracy: "It is the puissant Earl of Lincoln who, attempting to meddle with the right of a 'young, fair, and virtuous maid' to marry his kinsman, is confounded in the final scene." John Mason Brown stressed the sheer fun of the production: "For all its baffling complexities of plot and subplot, the play in which they caper continues to be what its author would have saluted, and we gladly welcome, as 'fine, tickling sport' . . . Theirs is a philosophy of joy. Hum, let's be merry whiles we are young; old age, sack, and sugar will steal upon us, ere we be aware . . . It is the gayest and most unblushing excursion into Elizabethan low comedy which contemporary playgoers have been privileged to enjoy." The natural humor of *The Shoemaker's Holiday* has kept its flavor fresh along the years.

London revivals include: The NT at the Old Vic, 1962, 1964, 1965; National Youth Theatre, 1971; Crucible Theatre Co., 1972; NT (Olivier), opening June 19, 1981, with Alfred Lynch as Simon Eyre. In America, a version with book and lyrics by Ted Berger, music by Mel Marvin, ran for two weeks in Paramus, N.J., 1966, then at the West Side YMCA OffOffBway, opening March 3, 1967. The mirth that "lengtheneth long life" still romps along the play.

SATIROMASTIX   *Thomas Dekker*

In the Elizabethan War of the Theatres, Ben Jonson hurried his satire *The Poetaster** to put it on stage before the attack he had heard Dekker was preparing. Although Dekker and Jonson, in 1599 and 1600, had collaborated in the writing of two plays, Jonson's love of the classics and his precise, methodical workmanship were in such sharp contrast to Dekker's romantic tendencies and slipshod habits that Dekker could be persuaded to enter the lists, in behalf of Marston and his friends, against the satiric, "humorous" poet. Taking a romantic play which was then in the writing, Dekker added an extensive satirical element, and called the mixture *Satiromastix (Satire's Scourge); or, The Untrussing of the Humorous Poet*. Allardyce Nicoll called this, of all the War of the Theatres plays, "easily the wittiest and most entertaining." It was presented privately by the Children of Paules and publicly by the Lord Chamberlain's company in 1601, and first printed the year following.

Into *Satiromastix*, Dekker brought many of the characters from Jonson's *The Poetaster*; Horace (Jonson); Crispinus (Marston); Demetrius (Dekker himself); Captain Tucca; Asinius Lupus. Most of the abuse of Jonson comes from the coarse mouth of the swaggering Captain Tucca, whom Dekker made an amusingly exaggerated burlesque of Jonson's own Tucca, the liveliest figure in *The Poetaster*. In *Satiromastix*, the Captain alludes to Jonson's work in his stepfather's brickyard—"poor lyme and hayre rascall"; "foul-fisted Morter-treader"—and even makes reference to Jonson's narrow escape from hanging after a duel. He mocks Jonson for his shabby clothes; Jonson set the pattern for this in *The Poetaster*, taunting both Crispinus and Demetrius with their defective doublet and ravelled satin sleeves— though more nobly Horace in *The Poetaster* chides Augustus Caesar for a glancing mention of his lack of wealth.

Who the chief victim of Dekker's satire is, Captain Tucca leaves the audience no need of guessing. In addition to frequently quoting or parodying *The Poetaster*, he addresses Horace as Asper and as Criticus, both names Jonson had used for himself in his own plays, and he complains: "A Gentleman or an honest citizen shall not sit in your penniebench Theatres, with his Squirrel by his side cracking nuts; nor sneak into a Tavern with his Mermaid, but he shall be satyrd and epigramd upon, and his humour must run upo' the stage: you'll have Every Gentleman in's humour and Every Gentleman out on's humour." Identification could hardly be pinned more clearly upon Jonson.

At the end of the play's satire, King William Rufus of England, at whose court the action takes place, delivers Horace over to Crispinus for punishment. Horace is given an oath to take, analogous to the palinode in *Cynthia's Revels* * and the oath of Crispinus and Demetrius in *The Poetaster*; then punishment such as Crispinus' emetic is pondered. Horace is finally tossed in a blanket and crowned with a crown of thorns.

Perhaps, in 1609, when writing, in *The Gull's Horn-Book*, the satiric chapter on *How a Gallant should behave himself in a Playhouse*, Dekker looked back laughingly upon these matters, remembering how Jonson had laughed at Crispinus' (Marston's) kinky hair and "little legs"; for in this chapter Dekker wrote: "Now Sir, if the writer be a fellow that hath either epigrammed you, or hath had a flirt with your mistress, or hath brought either your feather, or your red beard, or your little legs etc. on the stage, you shall disgrace him worse than by tossing him in a blanket, or giving him the bastinado in a Tavern, if in the middle of his play you rise with a screwd and discontented face from your stool to be gone." Doubtless friends of the playwrights took such steps in the War of the Theatres.

The attack upon Jonson quite overbalances the original story of Dekker's play, which deals with the marriage of Sir Walter Terill to Caelestina at William Rufus' court, and with Caelestina's taking what she thinks is poison but turns out to be a sleeping potion, to escape the unwanted advances of the King.

Dekker's attack upon Jonson, however, is gentle, almost amiable; it does not emulate the sharpness and arrogance of Jonson's words. Demetrius, in *Satiromastix*, admires the good qualities of Horace. No lasting enmity resulted from the dramatic exchange of fire. Dekker was in reality scarcely more than an amused bystander, who joined the fight for the fun. When it was over, all were friends again. In 1604, Jonson collaborated with Marston and Chapman in the writing of *Eastward Hoe,** for which all three spent some time in the King's gaol; and later that year, Marston dedicated his drama *The Malcontent* to Jonson. It should be noted, however, that, in 1619, Jonson told Drummond of Hawthornden that Dekker was a knave.

In dismissing the disputants in the play, King William Rufus says: "True poets are with art and nature crowned." The genial Dekker gives ample evidence in *Satiromastix* that he is graced with such a double crown.

THE WITCH OF EDMONTON   *Thomas Dekker*

Throughout the seventeenth century, the belief in witches ebbed, then rose to fury. In New England, twenty-four persons were killed as witches; another half hundred were tortured until they "confessed." In old England, pamphlets frequently appeared, detailing the misdeeds of one who had sold her soul to the Devil, with the story of her detection and dire punishment this side of Hell. One such pamphlet, about Elizabeth Sawyer of Islington, executed in 1621 for witchcraft, is the basis of the best of the dramas on such subjects, *The Witch of Edmonton,* 1623 (performed at court), by Thomas Dekker, William Rowley, and John Ford.

The share of each of the three authors is hard to determine, as all seem to have made suggestions throughout. The character of Sir Arthur is usually attributed to Ford. The rustics and clowns, and Mother Sawyer herself, are considered Dekker's creation. Swinburne, contrasting the "poignant simplicity of Dekker" with the "majestic energy of Ford," sees in these figures Dekker's "intimate and familiar sense of wretchedness, his great and gentle spirit of compassion for the poor and suffering with whom his lot in life was so often cast, in prison and out."

Mother Sawyer's story runs through the play, scarcely touching the main plot. She is so plagued by her neighbors that, to win revenge, she gives suck to the Devil in the guise of a dog; after much mischief, she is led off to execution. It is her dog that barks Frank Thorney to his bloody deed.

Frank Thorney marries his fellow-servant Winifred, not knowing that their master, Sir Arthur Clarington, has seduced the girl, then fobbed her off on him. To secure his inheritance, Frank keeps the marriage secret; then, to please his father, he goes through another ceremony with Susan Carter. He rids himself of Susan, throwing the blame for her killing on the suitors of Susan and her sister; but, his guilt exposed, he is led to execution.

The portrait of Mother Sawyer is most sympathetically drawn, her persecution by her neighbors made vivid, so that we can understand her coming to make the Devil's bargain of which she is accused. She is, as Lamb says, "the plain traditional old woman witch of our ancestors; poor, deformed, and ignorant . . ." When at court Sir Arthur flings the word "Witch!" at her, she turns it back upon many in higher estate: "the court witches, blowing fires / To burn men's souls in sensual hot desires"; the city housewives, spendthrifts, gadabouts, scolds,

> *who can turn*
> *Their husbands' wares, whole standing shops of wares,*
> *To sumptuous tables, gardens of stolen sin,*
> *In one year wasting what scarce twenty win—*

the fleecing lawyer; the gentleman that seduces a trusting maid, "with golden hooks flung at her chastity"—and here Sir Arthur is so closely touched that he the more fiercely demands Mother Sawyer's destruction.

Among revivals of *The Witch of Edmonton* was one at the London Old Vic, December 9, 1936, with Edith Evans. Of an 1820 production the *London Times* said: "Of all witches that walk the ground, and know not the use of broomsticks, she of Edmonton bears off the bell." In 1936 the *Times* said the play "is stamped with sympathy for the outcast and suffering, and is able to see always two sides of the human picture—even when the picture is of a villain or a witch . . . through all its violence, there is perceptible the warmth and gentleness of the dramatist's mind." A London Mermaid revival, November 21, 1962, with Ruby Head, won further praise in the *Times*: "a richly absorbing piece of work . . . a magnificent speech on the humanity of witches, which markedly recalls Shylock's defence of the Jews." The *Stage* (November 29, 1962) went on: "The grave, serious moments came from Ford; there is the comedy of Cuddy Banks from Rowley; Dekker supplies the down-to-earth, everyday strokes of character and colouring. The blend works. The play works, too." There was an August 29, 1980, revival at the Jean Cocteau Repertory, OffOffBway. When it entered the RSC repertory in 1982, the *London Times* called it "utterly fascinating."

The melodrama of the main plot is kept within the limits of probability through the naturalness of the characters, especially Susan, who welcomes death when Frank confesses his bigamy. But it is as a sympathetic, dramatic portrait of the causes and consequences of "witchcraft," among the simple folk bewitched by the belief, that *The Witch of Edmonton* rises to distinction.

The play sympathetically widens the outcast's lot by drawing the rest of us in:

> All life is but a wandering to find home;
> When we are gone, we're there.

Some viewers have seen *The Crucible,* by Arthur Miller,* as an attack upon Senator McCarthy's "witch-hunt" days; but of course there were many Communists, and by the twentieth century there were few witches.

A TASTE OF HONEY   *Shelagh Delaney*

At seventeen Shelagh Delaney, an usher in a Lancaster theatre, saw Terence Rattigan's slick *Variations on a Theme*, and in rebellion went home and wrote her own play, about a lonely Lancaster lass of eighteen, *A Taste of Honey*. (In the Bible, Samuel 14:43, Jonathan, not having heard the King's command that no food be touched that day, when brought before his father, King Saul, stated: "I did but taste a little honey with the tip of the rod that was in my hand and, lo, I must die.") And indeed, the play pictures a sorry cluster of unhappy beings: a woman of cheerful indifference and easy virtue; her current lover, a faithless sot; her daughter, a lonely virgin for one act only; a silken-smooth black sailor who casually makes love to the daughter and blithely sails away; and a young homosexual, Geoffrey, who moves in and takes care of the pregnant girl. "With all their reprehensibility," said George Oppenheimer, "there is something tender and pitiful about them, especially Josephine, whose mother wastes so much love on worthless men and has none for her, and Geoffrey, who wants so desperately to love her as a normal man should, but, unhappily, has neither the normalcy nor the manhood."

Events in the play run on with the apparent irrelevancy of everyday living. It is when her mother goes off with her new lover that Josephine succumbs to the Black's blandishments. The homosexual finds peace in sewing clothes for the baby, preparing the cradle, establishing order in the slovenly flat. As Josephine's confinement nears, back bustles her mother with gifts and loud words of maternal affection, and sends the young homosexual—who had even proposed marriage, to bring respectability to the issue—packing. Then, learning the father's color, she goes out to find consolation at the corner bar. Her comforting words to her daughter are "It's your own life—ruin it in your own way. I've certainly supervised my own downfall." Josephine, alone, cries out in the first pang of her delivery, as the curtain mercilessly falls.

Opening in Stratford, England, in 1958, *A Taste of Honey* was reworked at Joan Littlewood's Workshop. Then London Criterion and Wyndham's, 1959; in 1960, Bristol Old Vic. The New York Lyceum, October 4, 1960, then the Booth, with Joan Plowright as Josephine; Angela Lansbury, then Hermione Baddeley, as the mother; 376 performances. In 1975, at the Young Vic, London; 1978, 1979, OffOffBway. An "ode to misery," it was revived by Roundabout, April 28, 1981, still displaying and evoking deep compassion for the persons warped and wracked by their own human weaknesses.

TOVARICH   *Jacques Deval*

Tovarich, by Jacques Deval (J. Boularan, French, 1890–1972), is the most amusing play about the Russian nobility that sought survival in post-revolutionary days.

Several years after the Revolution, Prince Mikhail Alexandrovitch and the Grand Duchess Tatiana Petrovna are living in happy poverty in a shabby Parisian hotel. In the Banque de France they hold four billion francs, entrusted to them by the late Czar, to be spent for Russia's good. Quixotically, they refuse to use it for themselves.

They take jobs as butler and maid with a wealthy banker, Dupont. He and his wife are snobs; the Russians bewilder them, but fascinate their children, a girl of eighteen and a son of twenty. Then, at a party, Russian commissar Gorotchenko recognizes the two. They too recognize him, as their torturer; but he knows they have the Czar's funds.

In the kitchen, Gorotchenko reminds the Prince and the Grand Duchess that as Governor of the prison he had permitted their escape; she promises that when they return to a proper Russia she'll have his eyes burned out and the sockets filled with Siberian salt. But the Commissar says his appeal to France for money has been denied; he's trying to sell some Russian oil fields to an international combine; but unless money is found to manufacture tractors for the Ukraine and the Ural, five million peasants will starve to death. To save his country and his people, Mikhail signs over the four billion francs.

Mikhail: We are the Russia of yesterday. You are the Russia of today. But I seriously suspect that none of us will have a logical place in the Russia of tomorrow. And now I'm late with the lemonade.

Gorotchenko: Goodbye, Imperial Highness!

Tatiana: Goodbye, Tovarich!

The two emigrés plan to go to South America, but, egged on by the children, the Duponts ask them to stay.

In Paris, opening in 1933, *Tovarich* attained 800 performances. Hitler, after checking Deval for Semitic origins, saw the play three times. Beginning in London, April 19, 1935, it ran for a year, with Sir Cedric Hardwicke and Eugenio Leontovich. Robert Sherwood* adapted it for the New York Plymouth, Ocotober 15, 1936, directed by Gilbert Miller, with John Halliday and Marta Abba as the Russian nobles, Cecil Humphreys as the Commissar, and Ernest Lawford and James E Truex. It ran for 356 performances. Sherwood said: "It departs from the accepted formula only in the final scene, which was written on Jacques Deval's cuff . . . When I first read the play it got me, and I was induced to make my one and only adaptation."

Tovarich (Comrade) remains an amusing and touching picture of adaptation to the new conditions imposed by a revolution upon those who have escaped its ruthless hands.

ABRAHAM LINCOLN   *John Drinkwater*

Great men of history are a constant lure to playwrights; yet it is exceedingly difficult to compress the surge of a lengthy and eventful career into the compact form of an evening's drama. In most cases, the famous figure becomes little more than a wax-museum exhibit, an effigy in an historical tableau, a mouthpiece of the author's ideals, or a fellow whom the author labels, say, Lincoln, but who for significance and vitality might just as well be called John Doe. Of the many plays that have been written about the United States' most beloved President, two rise to lasting worth: *Abe Lincoln in Illinois,** by the American Robert E. Sherwood; and the English John Drinkwater's *Abraham Lincoln.*

John Drinkwater (1882-1937) was director of the Birmingham Repertory Theatre, and for it pondered an historical play. As he tells the story in the *Pictorial Review* (December, 1920), "The choice was made as objectively as though Lincoln had been a Pharaoh or an Alexander of old. . . . My aim had been toward the essential and universal qualities of Lincoln; and upon the dramatic presentation of these the play must stand or fall."

Abraham Lincoln proved of considerable interest to many audiences. After its Birmingham premiere, October 12, 1918, the play went to London, where it opened on February 19, 1919, for a run of 466 performances and reopened, August 6, 1921, for 173 more. The first New York production came December 15, 1919, and ran for 311 performances. The play is still quite popular everywhere. Walter Hampden played in it in 1939; the King and Queen of England watched a performance in 1940; it was a hit in Japan in 1946. Alexander Woollcott called it "a moving, exciting, and forever memorable experience." President Hoover declared: "I never enjoyed a play more in my life."

Inevitably episodic, *Abraham Lincoln* shows its hero in six significant situations: First; amid homely surroundings, notified of his nomination and accepting it in dedication to the cause of justice: Second, in the grim and painful decision to hold Fort Sumter and to deny secession: Third, in an interview with two women, a war profiteer's wife who cries for bloody vengeance and a widow whose son has been killed in the War, when in shining tolerance he stands (almost alone in history) with Christ, as one who loved his enemies: Fourth, in a challenge to his Cabinet and the issuance of the Emancipation Proclamation: Fifth, at the moment of Lee's capitulation and the chivalrous terms of "Unconditional Surrender" Grant: and finally, in the box at Ford's Theatre, April 14, 1865, when he was assassinated.

Throughout this pageant, Drinkwater keeps Lincoln within the human mold by countless homely touches: the English ambassador finds the President busy blacking his boots; Grant's orderly comes upon him asleep, stretched across two chairs in the General's headquarters. Drinkwater's Lincoln is a sad and weary man, called by destiny, and unwillingly come, to play a decisive role in the movement of his country toward the realization of its ideals.

On both sides of the ocean, reviewers agreed as to the merit of the play. Kenneth Macgowan (December 16, 1919) exclaimed: "The thrill of the theatre—the surge of history—the lift of the creative imagination: these three things made a rare and exciting evening ... The appeal of John Drinkwater's creation goes beyond the appeal of Lincoln himself, great as that is ... the language of *Abraham Lincoln* is the language of the Bible— strong, simple, true." James Agate in the *London Times* (March 18, 1943) looked back to the first performance he had seen, in 1921, and declared that then "Quite suddenly I 'got' Lincoln in the way people 'get' religion."

The lofty nobility of Lincoln, coupled with his simple humanity, is drawn with power and passion through the well chosen and finely wrought episodes of Drinkwater's play.

A Japanese production of 1975(?) used a prologue, with a large map, to explain the relevant circumstances of American history.

ALL FOR LOVE   *John Dryden*

John Dryden (English, 1631-1700) began writing plays quite in the Restoration mood of licentious wit and bawdry. From about 1670, he wrote a play a year for some fifteen years.

Dryden's first play in blank verse, and his best play, is a version of the story of Antony and Cleopatra, *All For Love, or The World Well Lost.* Observing the unities of time, place, and action, more exactly "than perhaps the English theatre requires," Dryden concentrated on the final days of the fated lovers, when Antony is besieged in Alexandria by Octavius Caesar. Starting at the point Shakespeare reached in Act IV, Dryden reduced the speaking parts from thirty-four to ten and the scenes from forty-two to one for each of the five acts. Dryden concentrated also on the all-encompassing love of the doomed couple, in contrast to Shakespeare, who in *Antony and Cleopatra** set in conflict the urge of private love and the drive of public power, with Antony's disaster hung upon his failure to choose between his personal feelings and his political career. In Dryden's drama, the disaster springs from the tortured jealousy of Antony's all-consuming love. Antony's general Ventidius, his friend Dolabella, and his wife Octavia have persuaded him to leave Cleopatra and join in friendship with Octavius, when a gust of suspicion that Dolabella will succeed him with Cleopatra flings him back into the Egyptian's open arms.

Cleopatra is likewise wholly enamoured of her Roman. She is bemused in love beyond resourcefuness, incapable of the wiles and lures wherewith Shakespeare shows "the gypsy of the Nile" seeking to win and hold her

Antony. In Dryden, it is love complete, love the conqueror; and all for love. A false report of Cleopatra's death fells Antony on his sword. Cleopatra comes to him as he dies, and sets the asp upon her soft arm, that had often held her Antony.

Without the majestic sweep of Shakespeare's, Dryden's play has a soft, sweet power of its own. Shakespeare's tragedy has largely supplanted Dryden's on the stage. When Dryden's was presented, however, opening May 27, 1946, by Equity Library (the first New York production since 1797), George Freedley said that it "plays astonishingly well ... makes an extremely interesting performance on the stage." Another revival opened at Fordham University on December 6, 1951, "to complete the cycle," it was smilingly announced, represented on Broadway by the Oliviers' alternating productions of *Antony and Cleopatra** and *Caesar and Cleopatra.**

There rises from *Antony and Cleopatra* a sympathetic flow of emotion, and an impulse of respect, for two great persons torn between their passion and their thrones; out of *All For Love* wells a deeper spring of sadness and of pity for two great lovers whom the wide concerns of empire condemn to die for love.

Recent productions include one opening April 4, 1958, in the gardens of New College, Oxford, then moving to the open air at Stratford-upon-Avon, with Cleopatra's barge on the river. The play was shown in 1964 at Southern Connecticut State College. Shown at the Edinburgh Festival in 1977 with Barbara Jefford and John Turner, the play went on to the London Old Vic with Dorothy Tutin and Alex McCowen, then, 1978, on tour.

> *And let our parting be as gently made*
> *As other loves begin*

THE MAN WITH A LOAD OF MISCHIEF   *Ashley Dukes*

Ashley Dukes (English, 1885-1959) had a varied career in the theatre. He is well known as a critic. He was, since 1933, manager of the little, experimental Mercury Theatre where T. S. Eliot's *Murder In the Cathedral** was produced. He adapted a number of plays from the German and the French, including *The Machine Wreckers* and *The Man Who Married a Dumb Wife*. Of his several original dramas, only the first, the romantic comedy *The Man With a Load of Mischief,* has lasting merit.

The Man With a Load of Mischief pictures a swift idyll of a stormy night on the Bath-to-London road, these many years ago. A beautiful lady, once a famous Covent Garden singer, now the mistress of a prince, is running from that prince and from a nobleman who also desires her. The noble libertine, rejected, and lecherous in his cups, sets on his valet, Charles, to woo the lady. Charles, who had heard her sing years before and had always adored her, turns out to be a manly, self-respecting, understanding fellow, and as the prince arrives the lady goes off with the man. The noble finds consolation with the maid.

This simple story takes its title from the sign of the roadside inn where the lady takes refuge from the storm, a sign that shows a portly old amorous baron bearing a ribald young blonde upon his back. There is little substance to the drama; it is fetching but conventional, entertaining but sentimental. Its value lies in its delicacy and its neat style.

The Man With a Load of Mischief opened in London, December 7, 1924, and was revived there June 16, 1925 for a run of 261 performances and was played again in 1933 and 1942. New York saw the play, October 26, 1925, with Ruth Chatterton; Westport, Connecticut, in 1932 with Jane Cowl. The *New York World* (October 27, 1925) called it a "sedately indecorous and beautifully written romance," and Arthur Pollock said it is "a comedy wise as well as delicate." The *London Times* (September 24, 1933) also praised the play, discerning that "this lovely little romance of the Regency has a sense of style and a distinction that are missing from most modern plays."

So delicate is the drawing, so fine-spun the sentiment, that the subtle satire may be missed. The picture of the nobleman, addicted to fleshly pursuits, wholly unobservant of his valet Charles' true worth, gives a fuller flavor of independence to Charles' quiet poise and self-respecting love. The movement toward the assertion of human worth regardless of title and station, however, establishes a sound core of dignity within the polished gallantry and dukely dastardry and romantic rouse of the delicate and charming comedy, *The Man With a Load of Mischief.*

There were two productions of the play in London the same season, one opening August, one December, 1968. A version with music by John Clifton, book by Ben Tarver, opened in New York, November 1966, for 241 performances.

THE TOWER OF NESLE   *Alexandre Dumas, père*

Henri III and his Court, 1829, by Alexandre Dumas père (1802-1870) was the first French romantic drama.

Dumas' second, and most successful, romantic melodrama was *The Tower of Nesle,* in which Mlle. Georges (Marguerite Josephine Weimer) appeared in 1832. It is based upon actual scandalous incidents in French history, involving the wives of three French kings, brothers all: Louis X (King, 1314-1316), Philip V (1316-1322), and Charles IV (1322-1328). The wife of the first; the licentious Marguerite of Burgundy, chose her lover each day, enjoyed her amours by night in the Tower of Nesle, and let the waters of the Seine cover the favored one before sunrise. She was strangled by order of her husband. Associated with her in these amorous and lethal enterprises were her two sisters-in-law.

Dumas' play, *The Tower of Nesle,* is built mainly upon a duel of wits between Marguerite and a captain who, with incriminating papers scrawled with her secrets, forces his way to the prime ministership, until his overweening ambition tumbles them all.

The Tower of Nesle remains a melodramatic favorite of the French theatre. It is, indeed, a vivid and still stageable piece, the forerunner of a host of less literate plays, which degenerated into the "ten-twenty-thirty" melodrama of our grandfathers. When Dumas' drama was presented in Chicago in 1927, directed by Whitford Kane at the Goodman Theatre, the *Chicago Journal* (October 10) said "It is gratifying to report that the Dumas piece, for all its demands, is better than anything the Goodmanites have previously done."

In Paris, Robert Kemp reported of a revival, in *Bravo* (October 1930): "The newest play? Undoubtedly *The Tower of Nesle,* of which, in twenty months, we'll observe the centenary. What a delight to find in it so much innocence, life, ridiculous and charming passion! It's the history of our grandparents of 1832, ardent, candid, childlike, thunderous." When it was made into a motion picture, in 1937, *La Critique cinématographique* called the play "a strong, powerful work, masterfully constructed, and spun of steel, for it has preserved its attractive qualities through the generations." In 1938, Richard Le Gallienne, writing from Paris for the *New York Sun* (August 27), said that *"The Tower of Nesle,* produced at the Porte Saint Martin Theatre May 29, 1832, has never stopped running in some Paris theatre since, a record that no other playwright has ever matched."

Dumas turned from plays to novels; he is best known for his two romances published in 1844: *The Three Musketeers,* and *The Count of Monte Cristo.* We are told that his many sprawling romances were written with a staff of "ghosts," but his earlier plays were singly and carefully constructed. The complicated intrigue of the plot is skillfully carried to a strong climax. The characters are seen on the surface only, but—especially in *The Tower of Nesle*—they are dynamic, and they drive toward their goals with an energy of mind and will that still gives power to the play, one of the vivid melodramas of the romantic stage.

The "queens" of the day played their roles with bare breasts. François Villon refers to the story in his best-known and superbly translated ballad:

> *And where is the Queen who willed whilere*
> *That Buridan, tied in a sack, should go*
> *Floating down Seine from the tower-stair:*
> *Where are the snows of yester-year?*

CAMILLE   *Alexandre Dumas, fils*

The greatest 'tear-jerker' of all time is this drama of the lady of the camellias, the Parisian courtesan Marguerite Gautier, who gives up the young man she loves, Armand Duval, at his father's plea. Only as she is dying from tuberculosis does Armand learn that Marguerite really still loves him; he rejoins her, and she breathes her last in his arms.

Alexandre Dumas, fils (French, 1824-1895) based his novel *La Dame aux camélias* (Camille) on the actual story of Alphonsine du Plessis. While waiting penniless, in a Marseilles tavern, for a remittance from the generous but often pinched Dumas père, Alexandre within three weeks turned the novel into a dramatic pot-boiler. Surprised when its performance was forbidden by the censor, Dumas left France. When Emperor Napoleon III removed the ban, Dumas was even more surprised at the play's immediate and sensational success. Opening on February 2, 1852, it played for the then unprecedented run of over 100 performances. *Camille* has been played by many stars: by Sarah Bernhardt in France and on several American tours; by Eleanora Duse, who opened her American tour with it in 1893; by Jessie Bonstelle, Margaret Anglin (with Henry Miller), Nance O'Neil, Olga Nethersole, Helena Modjeska (with Maurice Barrymore), and by Forbes Robertson (in England in a version by James Mortimer called *Heartsease*), Margaret Anglin, Eva Le Gallienne in 1931 and 1935, Lillian Gish in 1932, and Jane Cowl (with Rollo Peters) in 1933. In addition, there have been several motion picture versions of the play, one with Norma Talmadge. In 1917 Ethel Barrymore acted in a version that vainly strove to "modernize" the drama, introducing a prologue in which Duval goes to an auction of Marguerite Gautier's effects after her death; he spends the night in her room, and the play is his vision as he relives those days in retrospect.

Of the social attitude behind the play, Brooks Atkinson said in *The Civic Repertory Magazine* (March 1931): "If life was ever like that, life must have been terrible. Of all the cant, hypocrisy, and purple-plush punctilio the *Camille* school of ethics is the most despicable. What a genius these folks had for muddling human relationships and inventing bogus crises out of whole cloth!" This, however, he added, "has no bearing upon such theatrical fustian as *Camille. Camille* is festive . . . With such people, dressed in costumes that delight the eye, gaiety is no more than common civility; and it dispels a good deal of the tedium that plucks at the fringe of such verbose plays as *Camille*." As for Eva Le Gallienne's performance as Camille, Atkinson was quite ecstatic.

Percy Hammond (1922) liked Lillian Gish even more: "I have seen two dozen Camilles, ranging from Barrymore to Bernhardt—some of them chill, some of them passionate—but they all left me with eyes undimmed, excepting Miss Gish and Duse." Miss Gish herself said of her revival: "We went up into the attic of the theatre and took out of its treasure chest—tenderly, I hope—one of its loveliest pieces."

Henry James, in the year of Dumas' death, looked back to earlier impressions: "Written at twenty-five, *La Dame aux camélias* remains in its combination of freshness and form, of the feeling of the springtime of life and the sense of the conditions of the theatre, a singular, an astonishing production. The author has had no time to part with his illusions, but has had full opportunity to master the most difficult of the arts. Consecrated as he was to this mastery, he never afterwards showed greater adroitness in keeping his knowledge and his naïveté from spoiling each other. The play has been blown about the world at a fearful rate, but it has never lost its happy juvenility, a charm that nothing can vulgarize. It is all champagne and tears—fresh perversity, fresh credulity, fresh passion, fresh pain."

William Winter, who made *Camille* the chief weapon in his attack on realism in the theatre, preferring its theatrical effects to the bare bones and dirty crusts of current thesis plays, wistfully recalled the Camille of Madame Modjeska as "faultless in delicacy and superb in completeness."

Those familiar with the opera will recognize that the story of *Camille* is told in *La Traviata (The Castaway)*, by Francesco M. Piavé, with music by Giuseppi Verdi, which opened in Venice in 1853 and in New York in 1856 (later, at the Metropolitan Opera House with Marcella Sembrich and at the Academy of Music with Adelina Patti, both in 1883). The operatic version calls the heroine Violetta Valery; the hero, Alfredo Germont; it moves the story from nineteenth-century Paris to the days of Louis XIV. Otherwise, it follows the play very closely. A failure on its first production, *La Traviata* scored a distinct success in revised form a year later; it holds today a high place in any repertoire of Italian opera.

Camille holds a similarly high place in the theatre. Sentimental rather than sublime, it is one of the first, as well as one of the greatest, of the plays that have drawn women "to enjoy a good cry" in the theatre. Yet for all its sadness, as Willa Cather aptly sums it up, "it is always April" when *Camille* is played.

The name of the play, *Camille,* was of course chosen from the flower, its full title being *The Lady of the Camellias,* and in her merry days Marguerite always wore one—white for twenty-five days a month, and red for five.

Dumas was of colored blood; it's said that, when black coachmen were the vogue in Paris, he had his father drive his carriage; and it has also been said that he first conceived of Camille as a sepian charmer.

French revivals of the play are uncounted. Among those in English: 1947, Los Angeles, an all-black production, with music by Serge Walter; 1951, ELT. Los Angeles and San Francisco, 1974 (and OffBway, 1980), an adaptation by Charles Ludlam, who played Marguerite. He added puns, literary and stage allusions (to Greta Garbo, to Mae West), and drag-show mannerisms. In 1978 there was also an all-male cast on tour. The OffBway Theatre Ensemble opened a more agreeable production, July 3, 1980.

Guy Endore, discussing Dumas fils in *King of Paris,* 1956, stated: "His influence on succeeding dramatists and in the formation of the whole Ibsen school of play-writing is part of the history of literature." *Camille* plays no small part in the history of the stage, especially in its appeal to an actress.

BROADWAY   *Philip Dunning*

This play remains significant for its full dramatic capture of the false glamour of the prohibition era in New York. As Alexander Woollcott said: "Of all the scores of plays that shuffled in endless procession along Broadway in the year of grace 1926, the one which most perfectly caught the accent of the city's voice was this play named after the great Midway itself, this taut and telling and tingling cartoon. . . . The theatre is at its best when it is journalistic, when it makes its fable and its parable out of the life streaming down its own street, when the pageant on its stage is just a cartoon and a criticism of the land and the day lying across the sill of the stage door. So journalistic is *Broadway* that . . . its manuscript could scarcely have been delivered through the ordinary snail-paced channels. It must have come in over the ticker."

Philip Dunning (1890-1968), who wrote the play with George Abbott (b. 1887), and who peddled it for three years before Jed Harris produced it, said that he was "casting a challenge to the so-called silver screen . . . I set out then to write a play of continuous action occurring in a background that adhered to its prototype in real life with utter fidelity. As an indication of the pace at which the action moves, there is the fact that in the three acts of *Broadway* there are more than three hundred entrances and exits."

In its summer tryout at Atlantic City, the play was called *The Roaring Forties* (the New York night-club and theatre district stretches from Fortieth to Fifty-second Street). It opened in New York at the Broadhurst Theatre on September 16, 1926, as *Broadway,* and caught on like wildfire. Never before did a drama gross a million dollars in thirty-seven weeks. (It cost but $9,000 to produce.) *Broadway* ran in New York for three years, while it was being played elsewhere by ten other companies, four of them abroad.

St. John Ervine called the English production "very crude, very direct, and very real." The *London Mail* said, "Much of it seems exceedingly vulgar; and no revue producer has dared undress his chorus to the extent of the girls supposed to represent the cabaret troupe." The English Lord Chamberlain, in truth, ordered some changes. He deleted about 30 percent of the profanity, changed "God!" to "Gee!" and subdued "Make your hands behave!" to "Stop!"

Two movements are intertwined in *Broadway*. There is the melodramatic rivalry of the gangsters, with Steve Crandall as big boss of the bootlegging racket; and there is the sentimental story of sweet Billie Moore, of the chorus at the Paradise Night Club, and her sweetheart, the hoofer Roy Lane. Steve, however, also has designs on Billie, and when the gangster shoots an uptown rival, somehow the police find Roy holding the murder gun. Things look bad for Billie and Roy; but when the uptown gangster's girl friend shoots Steve, the lovers are free to hope for happier days on Broadway.

Some critics were not sure of the play's appeal. Brooks Atkinson observed that it often has "the illusion of motion even when it is not progressing at all," but he felt that it was on the whole a "firmly packed melodrama." Alan Dale insisted that "this ingenious chatter of Broadway has nothing at all to interest anybody but the residents of near-Forty-second street." The *New York Telegram* concurred with Dale. However, the play's stage history, including wide production among college groups, and "little" and summer theatres, shows that the rest of the country thrilled to the picture of life on the Gay White Way.

The play was twice converted into a motion picture: in 1929, with Lee Tracy and Sylvia Field; in 1942, with Pat O'Brien, Janet Blair, and George Raft (who played the part of "George Raft, the hoofer"). A new stage version, *Broadway 1941*, was attempted by Philip Dunning, with a shift from bootlegging to labor racketeering. *Variety* called the new version "antiquated by the host of gangster shows and (especially) pictures that followed and improved on it." The original remains, however, the best melodramatic picture of the "roaring twenties" along New York's "roaring Forties."

Among continuing revivals of *Broadway*: 1961, OffBway (Neighborhood Playhouse); 1964, summer, Skowhegan, Maine; 1975, Barter Theatre, Va.; 1977, the Berkshire Festival, then Boston; 1978, with updated references, OffBway; 1979, Washington University.

As further indication of the swift movement, typical of the continuous flow of the Great White Way, it may be mentioned that there is no scene in the play over four minutes long.

THE VISIT   *Friedrich Dürrenmatt*

The black comedy *The Visit* (1957) by Friedrich Dürrenmatt (Swiss, b. 1921) is a searing picture of the power of greed. Claire Zachanassian, wealthiest woman in the world, returns to her native town of Güllon. Welcomed heartily by the townsfolk, she stuns them by promising to bestow a fortune upon them—if they will kill their fellow-citizen Alfred Ill (Anton Schill in the English adaptation).

She enters in a sedan chair borne by two American thugs. With her are two blind eunuchs, a grim shaven-headed butler, a caged black panther, and an empty coffin. Nonchalantly she nods: "No, take the train away; I don't want it anymore."

We learn that when she was a maiden of seventeen, Alfred Ill had seduced her. The two eunuchs are men whom, for his trial, Ill had bribed to state that they had made love to her. The butler is the magistrate whose words had driven her away in disgrace. To Alfred, she had been his "kitten"; he had been her "black panther."

The townsfolk, at first revolted at her proposition, begin to look askance at Alfred, until finally, in a great crowding, they surround him, and when they clear away he is lying on the ground. The doctor says: "Heart failure";

the mayor: "He died of joy." The coffin has its corpse. John McClain in the *Journal-American* pointed out that in the play "a little item called the soul seemed to be missing."

(Claire's name, Zachanassian, seems to be a telescoping of the names of three Near-Eastern multimillionaires: Zacharoff, Onassis, Galbenkian.)

In 1957-1958 Alfred Lunt and Lynn Fontanne, with Eric Porter, directed by Peter Brook, took the play on a tour of Great Britain and Ireland; then it came to the New York Globe, freshly renovated and renamed the Lunt-Fontanne, May 5, 1958, for 189 performances. In 1959 it won the Molière Prize in Paris. The Peter Brook production opened the new Royalty Theatre in London, June 23, 1960. The play was revived in 1968 by Asolo and ELT, and in 1973 by the Phoenix in Ann Arbor, Philadelphia, and New York (Barrymore Theatre), with Rachel Roberts and John McMartin, directed by Harold Prince. An opera, *Besuch der Alten Dame (Visit of the Old Lady)*, with music by Gottfried von Einem to Dürrenmatt's libretto, was sung in Vienna in May 1971, then in Zurich; in San Francisco, October 28, 1972. In the film version were Ingrid Bergman and Anthony Quinn.

Richard Watts, Jr., said of the play (May 4, 1958): "It is surely one of the most savage dramatic studies of greed since Ben Jonson's *Volpone.** " Walter Kerr in the *Herald Tribune* felt that "the very brutality with which it is dramatized gives it a stinging theatrical life . . . the flesh crawls; the play moves of its own astonishing power." Brooks Atkinson was perhaps ironic in his remark that "Village democracy finally demands the death of Anton Schill, since village democracy is concerned with the good of the greatest number of people." Atkinson notes that Dürrenmatt "writes with wit and humor when he is setting his snares. But he writes with cold fury when he gets to the core of his theme."

The author himself has said: "*The Visit* is the story of something that happened somewhere in Central Europe, written by someone who does not dissociate himself from these people and who is not sure he would have acted differently himself." George Oppenheimer in *Newsday* made a comparison: "It is in this compassion and in the clarity with which he illumines his various moods and moves that Dürrenmatt differs from those disciples of despair, such as Sartre,* Ionesco,* and Samuel Beckett.* Their words sound like incoherent whimpers compared to the loud clear shout of Mr. Dürrenmatt's anger . . . as chilling as anything I have experienced in the theatre."

In a country where millions are offered in lotteries, in lotto games, in newspaper or TV teasings, the lure of wealth makes *The Visit* a grim indictment of everyman's neighbor.

THE PHYSICISTS   *Friedrich Dürrenmatt*

A theme frequent in fiction—as in the novels of John Creasey with his Dr. Palfrey—and on television, of a mad scientist or megalomaniac multi-millionaire with a secret superweapon with which to control or destroy the world, naturally would find expression on the stage. Least "comic strip" or melodramatic and most intelligent of such dramas is Dürrenmatt's *The Physicists* (also *The Nuclear Scientists*), 1962.

When the curtain rises, a nurse is lying dead in the drawing room of a private sanatorium. During the intermission, a second strangled nurse is laid on the open stage. They are the victims of three mad scientists, who call themselves Newton, Einstein, and Mobius, with whom King Solomon talks daily. (Newton and Einstein need no note. August Ferdinand Mobius, 1790-1868, is perhaps best known for the Mobius strip: take a slip of paper, perhaps an inch wide and a foot or so long, twist it once and join the two ends, and you'll discover that it has only one side and one edge.)

It turns out that the two scientists are not mad, "Mobius" is the scientist whose discoveries can shake the world. "Newton" is a western scientist trying to lure him to the West; "Einstein" is a counterspy, trying to lure Mobius to the East. Mobius will have neither of them; it's better for genius to wipe itself out of mankind's memory before mankind wipes itself out. They argue: "We physicists must take back our knowledge." "What once is thought can never be unthought." Scientific advance cannot be stopped; mankind must learn to make proper use of its new resources. The world must find a balance between its scientists and its politicians.

Mobius tells them he cannot trust the rulers of today; he has destroyed his papers. The Director of the sanatorium, Fräulein Dr. Mathilde von Zahnd, smiles; she had recorded the papers before they were destroyed; the three madmen are her patients (prisoners); *she* will take power over the earth. The men turn to the audience, identify themselves: Albert Einstein; Isaac Newton; Solomon!—and go to their rooms.

The Physicists opened in Zurich, February 21, 1962. *Variety* reported: "It's a cinch to become an international hit." Paris next. Then, at the end of 1962 at the London Aldwych, the RSC alternated it with *King Lear,* with Michael Horden (Newton), Alan Webb (Einstein), and Cyril Cusak (Mobius), directed by Peter Brook, who also directed the New York Martin Beck production, opening October 13, 1964, for fifty-five performances with (in the roles as listed above) Hume Cronyn, George Voskovec, Robert Shaw; and Jessica Tandy as Fräulein von Zahnd. Its American premiere had been at the Washington National, September 22, 1964, when Richard L. Coe in the *Washington Post* called it "an absorbing dark comedy . . . a play of beguiling theatricality and surprise . . . bitter originality." As I say, common in fiction, new onstage.

There were revivals: in Manchester, England, 1964; Houston, Texas, 1967; Asolo, 1970; OffBway (Ethical Culture) opening March 6, 1975; Princeton, N.J., 1977. When it came to Washington, December 15, 1981— the first play in the joint J. F. Kennedy-CBS series—with Irene Worth, George Grizzard, Len Cariou, and Brian Bedford, there were in the audience four Nobel Laureates in Physics. Roger L. Stevens, chairman of the Kennedy Center, called it with demure pride "the greatest play written in this century."

Kenneth Tynan in the *Observer* (London, January 3, 1963) declared: "Eagerly abetted by Mr. Brook, Dürrenmatt plays on our nerves and through them reaches our brains, using the techniques of detective fiction to convey an apocalyptic message . . . Beneath the Arctic cap of the argument there simmers a passionate concern for human life." Norman Nadel in the *World Telegram* (October 14, 1964) stated: "It takes a play like *The Physicists*—and, believe me, there aren't many like it—to remind us what an adventure of spirit and mind the theatre can be . . . The play grows in fascinating complications, confounding its audience even while it is progressively clarifying itself . . . It considers the fate of mankind in a world where, as one physicist says: 'Our knowledge is dangerous; our discoveries are lethal.'" Walter Kerr demurred: "*The Physicists* does not so much dramatize its debate as postpone it with bizarre performing tricks."

Despite the corpses of the nurses, the play lacks the direct violence and the displayed sex that make for popularity today; but it is an "adventure of the mind" in the theatre that should attract college and community groups as long as its problem continues to plague mankind.

THE GREAT GALEOTO   *José Echegaray y Eizaguirre*

Until he was forty-two, José Echegaray y Eizaguirre (Spanish, 1832-1916) grew through a career as a scientist and a statesman. In 1874 he wrote two plays; their success encouraged him to devote himself to the theatre. Altogether, he wrote some sixty-five plays. He is best known for *el gran Galeoto* (translated as *The Great Galeoto*, 1895).

The play is dedicated to "everybody," and *everybody* is its theme. It presents the effects of surmise and suspicion, of the whispered word of gossip in the world. Around Ernest, secretary and adopted son of Julian, and Julian's wife Teodora, false rumor rises, until a duel is fought, Julian dies, and the false suspicion of the world thrusts the innocent two into each other's arms. That which started as a lie grew in power until perforce it became the truth.

Galeoto is the book in which Paolo and Francesca were reading on the fateful day whereof Dante tells; Galeoto (Galahad) it was that brought together Launcelot and Guinevere. Throughout Italy and Spain, Galeoto is the name used for a go-between; in the play, Galeoto is the world's gossip that unites the lovers.

Echegaray, said Benito Pérez Galdós, "broke up worn-out forms and imbued the actor's art with a new strength and new resources." His novelty, however, was in large part a return to the past; and, in 1904, when he shared the Nobel Prize with the Provençal poet Frédéric Mistral, the new generation of Spanish writers protested against the award. Echegaray, with modern themes and sharp juxtapositions and stark conflicts, returned to the forms of the romantic drama and managed even to set into his modern considerations the old ideals of chivalry and conjugal honor.

Such ideals are manifested in several of Echegaray's dramas, of which the best known, after *The Great Galeoto,* are *The Son of Don Juan,* 1892, and *Mariana,* 1892.

The Great Galeoto was produced in Chicago on October 22, 1906. The *Chicago Sun* praised its depiction of the power of gossip: "The lifting of an eyebrow, the unfathered innuendo, an intimation that all the world would disclaim having made: these accomplish everything—inspire doubt, fan doubt to flaming hate, pillage a man's peace of mind, blast the fair name of his house, his wife, his friend." In a lecture at the time, William N. Guthrie exclaimed, of the Galeoto, the gossip that is go-between: "Prodigious hero! Enormous central personage! Titanic conception! For here a whole city is your hero, every man and woman in the community your central personage and—most amazing stroke—your hero never appears upon the scene."

The version of *The Great Galeoto* presented in New York as *The World and His Wife* on November 2, 1908, was adapted by Charles Nirdlinger and starred William Faversham as Ernest, with Julie Opp as Teodora. The *New York Dramatic Mirror* (November 14, 1908) called it "a marvel of play building . . . remarkable construction that makes the succession of comparatively commonplace incidents lead inevitably to the conclusion." *The World and His Wife* has been frequently revived by college and little theatre groups: 1911, 1914, 1927, 1934, 1939.

The *Boston Herald* (January 11, 1927) said that it "plays stirringly, with scarcely a moment that is dull."

Echegaray is content to make his characters clearly drawn and baldly opposed types; his passions spring from principles and may remain as abstract; his dialogue is less natural than rhetorical, less welling from the heart than lilted by the mind. From such characteristics, however, grows an intense dramatic effect. *The Great Galeoto* electrified Madrid; its author revitalized the theatre of Spain and broadened the local stage once more to the status of world theatre.

MURDER IN THE CATHEDRAL   *T. S. Eliot*

In this verse play about Archbishop Becket of Canterbury, poet Thomas Stearns Eliot (English; born in U. S.; 1888-1965) presents a very different aspect of the story from that pictured in the drama *Becket,** by Tennyson. Eliot's play deals with the motives behind the Archbishop's martyrdom and brings the issues involved in that twelfth-century struggle into focus in the twentieth century.

The play is in two parts, with an interlude of the Archbishop's Christmas sermon of 1170. It has a chorus of Canterbury women who speak some of Eliot's finest poetry and link the high ritual of the high people with the common life of the day. The chorus opens Part One, which presents Becket returning from his seven years' exile. (For his story, see *Becket.**) In Part Two, the Archbishop defies four knights and is slain. The four knights then step forward; in prose now and, said Eliot, "quite aware that they are addressing an audience of people living 800 years after they themselves are dead," each tries to justify his deed, so that through this defense we discern that the forces that create martyrs and saints are still at work in the world. The priests have the last word—a prayer for mercy.

Murder in the Cathedral is a chronicle of Becket's torture of mind and agony of spirit. All the other characters are merely labeled, "Priest," "Knight," "Tempter." Save in the knights' words at the close, Becket's soul is the one concern. He is tempted in various ways: by worldly pleasure and temporal delights; by power and prestige, as he ponders turning over the king to the ambitious barons. The greatest temptation of all is martyrdom, the urge to do the right thing for the wrong reason, to sacrifice himself, not because he has "lost his will to the will of God," but out of pride. By resisting the temptation of sainthood, Becket proves himself saintly.

Murder in the Cathedral runs swiftly, in easy verse, with many words of Anglo-Saxon origin; the verse itself recalls the Anglo-Saxon in its use of stresses, alliteration, and assonance. Eliot in writing the play wished to avoid Shakespearean echoes, and kept the versification of *Everyman** in mind. John Anderson (March 21, 1936) called the result "the finest dramatic poetry written in our time." Particularly in the passage where Becket makes his decision, where his nature finds true expression in complete surrender to God's will, does the poetry rise in simple yet solemn nobility and power.

The play was first shown at the Canterbury Festival in June 1935. It came to London, November 1, 1935, for a run of 180 performances, and reopened October 30, 1936, for 154 more, and was played there again in 1937 and 1947. In the United States, *Murder in the Cathedral* was shown at Yale University, December 20, 1935; in New York, March 30, 1936, and again in 1937. It has also been widely shown around the country.

Reviewers have found the play not only literate but dramatic. "A tragedy of the first distinction," said the *London Times* (November 2, 1935). "Its mode is the original dramatic mode of ritual; its theme is the theme out of which drama itself, and some would say even religion, first grew—the story of the priest-king who is slain for his people . . . The one great play by a contemporary dramatist now to be seen in England."

In America, Brooks Atkinson (March 21, 1936) declared: "For exaltation, for earthly terror and spiritual submission, *Murder in the Cathedral* is drama restored to its high estate"; and Howard Barnes found that "it testifies eloquently to the compelling power of poetry wrought to significant stage terms . . . a fervent and moving drama with moments of majestic beauty."

Eliot is a practicing advocate of the use of verse in drama. In the narrative portions of a play, however, he said in 1949: "The verse should be unnoticeable . . . Here the purpose of the verse should be to operate upon the auditor unconsciously so that he shall think and feel in the rhythms imposed by the poet without being aware of what these rhythms are doing. All the time these rhythms should be preparing the audience for the moments of intensity when the emotion of the character in the play may be supposed to lift him from his ordinary discourse—until the audience feels, not that the actors are speaking verse, but that the characters of the play have been lifted up into poetry." The application of this procedure in plays of contemporary significance, however, reveals its drawbacks. The demands of neither poetry nor drama are satisfied in Eliot's *The Family Reunion,* 1939, which shadows forth Orestes and the Furies of Aeschylus* with a group in a north-of-England mansion, or in his *The Cocktail Party* (originally *One-Eyed Reilly*), 1949, which has remote resemblances, Eliot has told us, to Euripedes' *Alcestis.* * Especially is this true of *The Cocktail Party;* obvious though earnest in its ethical implications and muddled in its symbolism, this play is one, as John Mason Brown observed, that "everyone seems to understand until asked to explain it."

In spite of the current spate of plays in prose and the frequent flatness of plays in verse, the greatest dramas have had their beauty and power enhanced by the poetry of their expression. In *Murder in the Cathedral,* Eliot's fervor and his theme meet in harmonious fusion, showing that great poetic drama is not limited to treasures of the past, but can be a constant and a contemporary vitalizing force.

Murder in the Cathedral has been played frequently in churches. Also, in England: Edinburgh Festival, 1961; Pitlochry Festival, 1965; Guilford, 1967; London RSC, opening September 9, 1972, fifty-three performances in repertory. In America: Stratford, Conn., thirty-one performances from June 19, 1966; 1970, Emanuel Church, Boston; 1971, Central Presbyterian Church, New York; 1976, New York Lincoln Center (Juilliard) and Church of the Heavenly Rest.

Bonamy Dobrée, in the *Sewanee Review,* Winter 1959, made an interesting point: "What most critics of T. S. Eliot's plays seem to ignore is that he is writing a new kind of drama . Whereas most plays appeal to the passions—pity, terror, the glamour of love—or to the intellect, or would stir our zeal for political reform, his plays are based on an appeal to the conscience, or consciousness of self. Here is this person, he says in effect, guilty of this or that; how far are you, dear spectator, in the like case? . . . In all the plays about conscience, from Sophocles to Ibsen, we are detached spectators . . . Here, however, we are forced to ask ourselves: 'Have I never run away from myself? Have I never tried to blot out incidents from my past?'" Thus in a great play the grace of God is spared: There go I.

There was a revival of *The Family Reunion* by Phoenix, 1958-1959, with Lillian Gish, Florence Reed, and Fritz Weaver. See also *Cats.**

THE POLISH JEW (THE BELLS)   *Erckmann-Chatrian*

Erckmann-Chatrian (French: Emile Erckmann, 1822-1899; Alexandre Chatrian, 1826-1890) collaborated on numerous novels, most of which are historical. Their one memorable drama, *The Polish Jew,* 1869, is a gripping story. It has a superb acting part in the role of a prosperous innkeeper, the mayor of an Alsatian town, who is haunted by an old crime. Long popular on the French stage, where it was first played by Benoit Constant Coquelin (Ainé), *The Polish Jew* was turned into an opera in 1900, with book by Henri Cain and Pierre Gheusi and music by Camille Erlanger. Almost immediately after the play's French premiere, two English versions were produced. The first, opening in London, November 13, 1871, was F. C. Burnand's *Paul Zeyers,* or *The Dream of Retribution.* The second, opening there November 25, 1871, put on in desperation when the Lyceum Theatre was in sore straits, gave Henry Irving his first great triumph and a role to which he repeatedly returned for thirty years; it was the Leopold Lewis (1828-1890) melodrama *The Bells.* In New York, James W. Wallack played Mathias in *The Bells* in 1872-1873, according to the *Oxford Companion to the Theatre* (1951), "most terrifyingly."

The story opens on Christmas Eve, 1833, in a little town of Alsace. The innkeeper and Mayor, Mathias, respected by all, the wealthiest man of the town, is about to marry his only child, Annette, to Christian, a sergeant of police. As the talk goes round, Christian is told of a mystery unsolved for fifteen years: A Polish Jew came to the inn to buy grain and thumped his money-bag on the table; the next day, his horse and his coat were found in the snow beneath the bridge. As this story is being told, a Jew enters and tosses his money-bag on the table. Mathias shrieks and falls in a fit. Fearful for his health, he hastens the wedding. When he counts out Annette's dowry, the clinking of the coins seems to him the jingling of sleigh bells. Terrified, he dreams that he is on trial for having murdered the Jew and disposed of the body in a lime-kiln, and that he is forced to re-enact the crime. In the dream, the executioner approaches. . . . The wedding guests find Mathias dead, and give sad testimony of their high regard for an honest Mayor.

Coquelin played Mathias as a murderer without remorse or fear; Henry Irving, once the arrival of the second Jew betrays Mathias to the audience, played the part as though pursued by fear of detection and by remorse. When Irving celebrated the twenty-fifth anniversary of the role, the *London Observer* (November 26, 1896) hailed it as "a great day in the history of stage triumphs." As late as 1901, the *New York Tribune* could still say, "His performance is unique, and it remains unapproached and unapproachable." H. B. Irving, in 1909, enacted his father's role. The play was popular in the repertoire of Butler Davenport's Free Theatre in New York.

The Bells is a great, perhaps the greatest, "one-part" melodrama; but it is morbid, shrewdly built to break upon the spectator's nervous excitability. The *New York World* (April 14, 1926) exclaimed: "He must have been an actor that could make *The Bells* ring true!" But the play sought no ring of truth, it sought to shock. In plays of this sort, the question of truth does not trouble the audience; they come not to be taught but to be moved. The *New*

York Tribune (April 14, 1926) called *The Bells* a "drama of continuous thrills." The *London Times* (October 5, 1933), of a revival with Martin Harvey, declared: "The scenes of the eve-of-the-wedding party and of the ghostly trial are those that engross us most. But all through the evening we are sufficiently intent upon Mathias not to be worried by the stilted, old-fashioned dialogue, and to ask only those questions which the story intentionally suggests as we listen to the sound of the ghostly bells." Theatre-wise folk may find *The Bells* crude; but the ringing reaches below reason to grislier depths in us all, as the justly famous melodrama shows conscience bringing its own retribution, as the unrecognized murderer shrinks in horror to his doom.

Henry Irving stated that "for many reasons, *The Bells* is a play that those interested in the drama as an art should not fail to see." The play was presented in London, using lyrics from Lord Byron, in 1955, the fiftieth anniversary of Irving's death. It remained frequent in Butler Davenport's repertory until his death in 1958. It was played at Bath and at Oxford in 1959; and in London, 1968, it was adapted and directed by Marius Goring, who played Mathias. The old-time melodrama still sends shivers along the spine.

THE MAN OF MODE   *George Etherege*

Sir George Etherege (1635-1691) set a new fashion in English comedy. His first play, *The Comical Revenge; or, Love in a Tub,* 1664, was the first Restoration prose comedy, though the serious portions are in heroic couplets. In its lively, realistic, roustabout comic scenes, the play established a pattern followed by William Congreve,* Richard Sheridan,* and especially Oliver Goldsmith in *She Stoops to Conquer.**

The best of Etherege's plays is *The Man of Mode; or Sir Fopling Flutter,* which held the stage for over a century. A production of February 24, 1728, included in the cast Mr. and Mrs. Colley Cibber, Wilks, Oldfield, and Mrs. Barton Booth. Horace Walpole in his *Thoughts on Comedy* (1775) observed: "*The Man of Mode* shines as our first genteel comedy; the touches are natural and delicate, and never overcharged . . . almost the best comedy we have."

The Man of Mode presents society at the height of jeweled coquetry, with the code that conceals emotion under epigram and polish or insolent carelessness. The chief character, Dorimant, is a portrait of Lord Rochester. Around him statelily move, in coiled intrigue, Sir Fopling Flutter, full of the latest Parisian plums of fashion and wit; the poet Bellair; together with Harriet—quite a match for Dorimant—and the other ladies whose amorous fencing with the gallants, on mutual quest of gaiety, must suffice for plot. As with Congreve, wit and dalliance take the place of story.

The Man of Mode opened with Mr. and Mrs. Betterton, March 11, 1676; Dryden had written an epilogue for it, and the King was in the audience. Although surpassed by later comedies in the field, it has sparkling dialogue, and its character drawing is as keen as it is shrewdly aimed.

The play was shown at Asolo in 1960. The RSC Aldwych production, in repertory opening September 13, 1971, announced "the last recorded production, 1766, Covent Garden." With Alan Howard as Dorimant and John Wood as Sir Fopling Flutter, it justified revival.

ALCESTIS   *Euripides*

The lives of the three great Greek tragic dramatists span the period of Athens' glory. Aeschylus* fought in the battle of Salamis, which drove back the Persians and inaugurated Athens' proudest and most triumphant period; young Sophocles* led the chorus in the paean of praise at the games celebrating that victory; and Euripides was born on the island of Salamis on the day the battle was fought. Euripides' first extant play, *Alcestis,* was produced in the year (438 B.C.) that marked the completion of the most perfect building of Greek architecture, the temple of the virgin Athene, the Parthenon, "glory of the Acropolis." Although Euripides left Athens in 408 for the court of the King of Macedon, he and Sophocles died within a year, just before the utter defeat of Athens in the Peloponnesian War. Sophocles dressed his actors and chorus in mourning on the news that Euripides had died.

Throughout Greece, not in Athens alone, Euripides was held as the foremost dramatist. He was somewhat unpopular, personally, during his lifetime, but his fame grew rapidly after his death. Of his eighty-eight plays, only five won first prizes (one posthumously), but through the fourth century before Christ he was far more popular than either Aeschylus or Sophocles. As a result, more of his plays—a total of nineteen—have been preserved.

Euripides (480-406 B.C.) was the most "modern" of the three great playwrights. Sophocles, who was in friendly rivalry with Euripides for many years, declared that he himself pictured men as they should be; Euripides, as they are. The legendary demigods and heroes of Greek literature became in Euripides' plays great figures on the human level, where their emotions and motives were examined. In many situations, Euripides restudied basic ethical problems, treating them more realistically than did the other dramatists. His realism was carried over to costumes as well; over a half-dozen plays of Euripides in which the chief characters wore rags are mentioned by the comic dramatist Aristophanes in *The Acharnians.**

Euripides also played more upon the emotions of the audience, seeking not so much the exaltation of tragedy as the arousal of pity, even to the point of sentimentality. Quintilian praised him for his power of pleading and debate. Longinus remarked, in the third century after Christ: "Euripides is most assiduous in giving the utmost tragic effect to these two emotions— fits of love, and madness. Herein he succeeds more, perhaps, than in any other respects, although he is daring enough to invade all the other regions of the imagination."

In the actual construction of his plays, also, Euripides strove to approximate the pattern of life. He often pushed the chorus casually aside, treating it as no more than a lyric interlude. His dialogue is natural, conversational. While he was capable of great poetry, he seldom launched into lofty flights during the action of the drama. His entrances are deftly and naturally managed; in *The Suppliants,** for example, two characters come in talking; in *Iphigenia in Aulis,** a Messenger rushes in interrupting a conversation. Thus, in all aspects of the drama, Euripides came closer than Aeschylus and Sophocles to the modern realistic spirit.

Finally, in his emphasis on contemplation, his sharing of the aristocratic disdain of public life that developed in Athens, Euripides exhibited that indifference to earthly affairs which led Athens to lose its dominant place among the city states of Greece. "Blessed is he that has attained scientific knowledge," Euripides declared, "*that seeks not the troubles of citizenship, nor rushes into unjust deeds, but contemplates the ageless order of immortal nature, how it is constituted and when and why."*

Euripides' first play, *Daughters of Pelias,* an episode of the Medea* story, won him third prize, the last place among plays chosen for presentation. *Alcestis* won him second place in the contest of 438 B.C., in which Sophocles took first place.

Euripides used the olden myth of Admetus and Alcestis to illuminate human character. The intent of the *Alcestis* is to study the effect of his weaknesses on an otherwise good man. It has been prophesied that Admetus, King of Thessaly, must soon die—unless, Apollo adds, someone will volunteer to die in his place. His aged father refuses to volunteer. Admetus' wife, Alcestis, offers herself as the sacrifice: "How could a woman show her husband greater honor, than to wish to die in his place?" Alcestis dies; but Heracles, grateful for Admetus' hospitality, fights with Death and restores Alcestis to her remorseful husband. It is the gentleness, the softness of Admetus that wins Apollo to grant the boon of life, and wins Heracles to bring back Alcestis. The same softness, however, leads the King to accept his wife's sacrifice, and to agree to marry the masked woman Heracles brings in, even before he knows it is his true wife come home. The whole picture of the man, of his weaknesses and their recognition, is natural and appealing.

Juvenal, in the second century after Christ, mentioned a performance of *Alcestis.* In modern times, the play has had many adaptations. French versions include those by P. Quinault, 1674, and Lagrange-Chancel, 1694. Handel composed music for it in 1727; Gluck made it an opera, 1762-1764. Wieland wrote a German version in 1773-1774, followed by a series of articles in which he stated that he preferred his own work to Euripides', which drew a fierce attack from Goethe, *Gods, Heroes, and Wieland.* Ducis wrote a French version in 1778; Alfieri, an Italian in 1798; Herder, another in German in 1802. Browning told the story in *Balaustion's Adventure,* 1871, suggesting that King Admetus accepted Alcestis' sacrifice not because he was a cowardly egotist but for the sake of his people; this conception was followed by the German Hugo von Hofmannsthal, who in *Alkestis,* 1911, pictured a brooding, introspective king, his "reason whirled by passion into dreamland." William Morris includes the story in his *Earthly Paradise* (1868-1870).

English versions of the *Alcestis,* too, have been fairly frequent. One by Blanche Shoemaker Wagstaff was presented in New York in 1910. Edith Wynne Matthison and Charles Rann Kennedy opened the Melbrook Theatre with *Alcestis* in 1922. The Gilbert Murray version was enacted at the Carnegie Institute of Technology in 1935; Horace Gregory called it "a veritable text of what to avoid in adaptation of Greek verse into English." Of a 1936 version by Dudley Fitts and Robert Fitzgerald, Gregory remarked: "The entire play is given a masculine quality that all other versions lack . . . I believe a performance would be extraordinarily successful." His words were proved true by a production at Cambridge, Massachusetts, in 1938. Richard Aldington also made a translation, in prose, in 1930.

Ruskin said that the *Alcestis* sums up "the central idea of all Greek drama." It exemplifies Aristotle's conception of the tragic hero, who through the flaws in his character brings misfortunes upon himself. It is a searching study of natural human emotions and deeds, with both Admetus and Alcestis effectively and sympathetically drawn. Despite the many versions since his day, Euripides' *Alcestis* remains the most successful dramatization of the story.

The Fitts-Fitzgerald translation was used in Dublin, 1948, and at the New York Provincetown, 1955. The Lattimore version was used at Vassar College, 1968; in London, 1972; OffBway (Cubiculo), 1973, and New York City Repertory, 1974. In London, 1958, a version of Irish vernacular dramatized the material Euripides narrates.

Gluck's opera *Alcestis,* in lively translation by John Gutman, was sung at the Metropolitan Opera House, 1960, with Eileen Farrell. A cynical version of the legend, *Alcestis Comes Back,* by A. M. Swinarski, adapted by Anthony P. Swift, ran for a week OffBway in April 1962.

MEDEA   *Euripides*

The tetralogy of Euripides that included *Medea* fell into last place in the contest of 431 B.C., in which the victor was Euphorion, son of Aeschylus, with Sophocles second. *Medea,* the first play of the tetralogy, was followed by *Philoctetes, Dictys,* and the satyr-play *The Reapers.* Since then *Medea* has become one of the most popular plays of all ancient drama.

Medea is the most powerful example of the truth of the adage, Hell hath no fury like a woman scorned. More interested in women than other contemporary dramatists, Euripides in this play had the problem of making Medea's awful revenge seem probable. Jason, for whom Medea had betrayed her family and abandoned her native land, in order to improve his state puts Medea aside and marries the daughter of Creon, King of Corinth. Medea alternately rages and broods over her lot. Then she poisons Creon and his daughter. She allows Jason to live, but in order to drive him to the last brink of helpless grief she kills the two young boys, his sons—and hers.

Despite all this desperate slaughter, Euripides by many subtle touches keeps Medea natural. In her, fully developed in the drama for the first time, we watch the conflict of a divided soul, as love and jealousy contend. She holds her children close, in fierce maternal love, as though to protect them from the thoughts that are gathering within her. She is balanced against a base and calculating Jason, who takes all Medea's help as his due, and then grows contemptuously abrupt with her. From the cold, scheming, and specious arguments of Jason, Medea's passion grows more torrid, and when she slays her children we can understand her action even as we shudder in horror of the deed. Hence we feel no basic injustice when the dragon-drawn chariot, in the upper air, bears Medea and the boys' bodies safely away, leaving Jason in anguish on the ground.

Medea is also the first independent woman roundly drawn in the drama. She utters the first dramatic protest against woman's lot:

> *Men say we women lead a sheltered life*
> *At home, while they face death amid the spears.*
> *The fools! I'd rather stand in the battle line*
> *Thrice, than once bear a child.*

This cry is heard faintly in the dramas of Nicholas Rowe, *The Fair Penitent,* 1703, and *Jane Shore,** 1714, but it does not sound clear again until Ibsen's *A Doll's House,** 1879—2,300 years after *Medea.*

Euripides' *Medea* appeared in the first year of the Peloponnesian War, when Athens hated Corinth and therefore rejoiced that the Corinthian royal family met death in the play. The theme became very popular; a dozen later Greek and Roman playwrights used the story. Seneca's version removed all sympathy from Medea; it excused Jason's marriage as part of his desire to get the best he could for Medea and his children in a strange country; it made Medea a cold-blooded murderess, and started the tradition that turned her into the most notorious cruel witch of the ancient world. But she became a famous figure; there are representations of Medea on the walls of Herculaneum and Pompeii, and Julius Caesar paid a great price for a painting of her. King Alexander the Great of Macedon often quoted *Medea*; his own mother, put aside for a Cleopatra (not Caesar's and Antony's), killed his father, Philip (336 B.C.). The Roman Brutus, dying at Philippi (42 B.C.), uttered his cry for vengeance in words from *Medea*: "God, be not blind to him that caused these things!" The Roman Emperor Caracalla, just before his assassination (A.D. 217), quoted the lines that close the play:

> *In many a way is the gods' will wrought;*
> *For things deemed sure, they bring to nought,*
> *And things none dreamed of, they dispose.*
> *Even such, this story's close.*

With the same words, Euripides ended four other dramas: *Alcestis,* Helen, The Bacchantes,* Andromache.**

With his mastery of theatrical effect and his psychological insight, Euripides was the most discussed of ancient dramatists. His original and striking remarks were often quoted; but his rationalism and his rhetoric were frequently attacked. Among the comic playwrights (as in Aristophanes' *The Frogs**), it was as usual to deride Euripides "as to throw nuts to the spectators or to rob Heracles of his meal."

Written about A.D. 60, *Medea* is one of Seneca's most effective tragedies. Politics no longer interfering, he shifts the sympathy somewhat toward Jason; the fact that Jason plans to have the children stay in Corinth gives color to his claim that he is really abandoning Medea for the children's sake. Seneca's version, on the other hand, heightens the spectacle of horror. Medea kills one of the children onstage, before the audience; she kills the other on the roof as not only the audience but also Jason watch; then she flings their bodies down to their distraught father. Though too gruesome for modern presentation, Seneca's tragedy has a stateliness within its horror.

The power of the story of Medea carries over into modern versions and productions. French playwrights on the subject include de la Peruse, 1553, Corneille, 1634, Longepierre, 1694, Pellegrin, 1713, and Legouvé, 1849. An English version by Glover (at Drury Lane, London, 1767) makes Medea temporarily insane when she kills the children; Creon is slain by the Corinthians; Jason, abandoning his bride, turns back to Medea and provides a happy ending. Samuel Johnson wrote a burlesque translation of a chorus of *Medea*, in the Gray's *Elegy* stanza. He also, as F. L. Lucas pointed out, "produced a serious version of the same passage which, although the modern reader will not find it easy to distinguish from the comic one, had the distinction of being copied out, together with the original Greek—over 220 words in all—in a circle an inch and a half in diameter, by Porson the great Euripidean critic." In Lessing's tragedy *Miss Sarah Sampson*, 1775, the deserted mistress cries "See in me a new Medea!" as she poisons her rival. William Morris tells the story in his poem *The Life and Death of Jason* (1867).

A modern handling of the theme is Maxwell Anderson's *The Wingless Victory,* a tragedy of the African Oparre who, having saved the life of a Yankee sea-captain (as Medea saved Jason's) goes back with him to New England, where, finding herself estranged and abandoned, she kills their children.

The story of *Medea* finds a vehement modern objector in James Agate. In *At Half Past Eight,* 1923, Agate grants "the exquisiteness of Professor Murray's translation," but he fails to find nobility in hate. "The only pity in the *Medea* is expressed by the Chorus, a boring lot of young women feebly enlarging upon what has gone before like a poor parson marring a good text . . . I cannot find tragic interest in monstrosity. Strip the *Medea* of its poetic clothing, and only the monstrous remains . . . Medea, we feel, deserved more than she got. That cruelty turned her into a vile thing is not the fault of cruelty, but of the degenerative metal upon which it was exercised. Medea was essentially not noble, but base, That she should go gadding about Pallas' plain in a golden chariot is, to an English mind, scarcely a fitting reward. What propriety was here to the Greek mind I can but guess; watching the play in the English theatre of today, I care nothing for such fiddle-faddle. We have outgrown these two big emotions. Opera is their sphere, with Strauss to make divine hash of them." Fortunately, stripped of its poetry, *Medea* does not exist. Shelley anticipated and in part answered Agate, in his Note to *The Cenci,** where he states that the pleasure in the poetry mitigates the pain of the moral deformity. Beyond this, what comes upon most spectators of an outstanding production of *Medea* is not a calculation of the deserts of the crazed, rejected wife, but an awesome contemplation of the tremendous power of human passion, of the two sides of the coin of love-and-hate that—more than any golden mintage—rules the world.

Of recent American performances of Euripides' *Medea,* Margaret Anglin's was outstanding. *The Brooklyn Eagle* (February 21, 1918) declared: "Margaret Anglin is probably the greatest actress on our stage today . . . playing the part with a tigerish ferocity that is simply appalling." Margaret Anglin alternated the *Medea* with Sophocles' *Electra;** Clayton Hamilton in *Vogue* (April 1, 1918) contrasted the two: "It would be easy enough to argue that Sophocles, in his *Electra,* has surpassed, in sheer dramatic power, the appeal that was subsequently made by Euripides, in the *Medea.* But this traditional and scholarly adjudication would be divorced from the verdict of the contemporary public. There can scarcely be a doubt that the New York theatregoing public prefers the *Medea.*" The preference may have come because revenge involving matricide is less easily understood, and less frequent, than jealousy that sacrifices the children to hurt the hated spouse. The public was deeply stirred by Margaret Anglin.

Other productions of the *Medea,* vivid but less notable, came in 1919 and in 1920 with Ellen van Volkenberg in the Gilbert Murray translation. In the same translation, another production was given in 1944, when George Freedley (February 21) held out a staff to a project then going the rounds: "Gilbert Murray's somewhat stilted acting version did little to make the evening a happy one . . . a knowing producer would certainly try to enlist Judith Anderson." In 1946, Robinson Jeffers' version of *Medea* was dedicated to Judith Anderson; on October 20, 1947, she opened in the role, and in the second outstanding *Medea* production of our time took New York by storm.

"Perhaps *Medea* was never fully created until Miss Anderson breathed immortal fire into it last evening," raved Brooks Atkinson. "For theatric force, human passion, female ferocity," said Louis Kronenberger, "*Medea* stands virtually alone." Judith Anderson won the Drama League award for the best performance of the year. She enacted the part, opening September 12, at the 1951 Berlin Festival, where Maria Fein opened September 26 in the Grillparzer German version of the story. "A superlative performance by Judith Anderson is the chief distinction of *Medea*," said Howard Barnes, preserving enough detachment to recognize that, save for the flame and flow of her work, the New York 1947 production was "more declamatory than melodramatic." In truth, the Robinson Jeffers version of the play alters parts, does not capture the Greek spirit, and exaggerates Medea's horror to the point of hysteria.

In 1946, also, Jean Anouilh wrote a French modernization of *Medea*, making the tortured queen a foul-mouthed Russian gypsy who, at the end, burns in her own caravan, like the victim in a sordid and cheap sex crime story.

The *Medea* of Euripides, in spite of the faults of translations and the folly of adapters, burns with an intensity of truth and tortured souls that time has not weakened.

Recent productions of *Medea* have been too many to set down. Among them: the 1962 production in Moscow with Yevgenia Kozyowa was hailed as "the greatest performance of the age"; the chorus was masked, and at peaks of intensity great masks were held before Jason and Medea. In Greenwich, England, 1970, adapted and directed by David Thompson, "horror broods over even the stabs of humor." In 1959 at Howard University, adapted by the black poet Countee Cullen, set in South Africa, 1870. A version combining Euripides and Seneca, at OffBway (La Mama), 1972, 1974, also 1982, with masks and candles. New York Circle in the Square, 1972, with Irene Papas, in colloquial English (to Jason: "You lump of evil"; Jason to Medea: "You're obsessed with sex"). OffOffBway, 1974, a bare-breasted Medea, yet with constant emphasis on her role as mother and wife. Stratford, Ontario, 1978, adapted by Larry Fineberg, with a black Medea in modern dress, with no chorus; it struck a high pitch of intensity through all the fifty unrelenting minutes of the play.

New York, 1982: John Gielgud, Dennis King, Florence Reed, with a "rare and riveting" Zoe Caldwell as Medea; Judith Anderson, who thirty-five years before had played Medea, now won a rave review from Walter Kerr (*Times*, May 16, 1982) as the Nurse. There were nineteen more productions between 1955 and 1981.

Perhaps it should be stressed that Medea comes from an alien Oriental world to the Apollonian rational life of Greece, for which she feels ill-disguised contempt. "When she settles herself in a deceptively domestic grouping," Walter Kerr points out, "it is to mock the image she creates. Spreading out before her the golden cloak that will become a gift to Jason's new bride and that will promptly burn that bride alive, Miss Caldwell slyly purrs that 'There is nothing like this in the world—at least in the Western world.'"

Franz Grillparzer (Austrian, 1791-1872) told the Medea story most fully, in his 1820 trilogy, *The Golden Fleece*, which includes the one-act *The Guest-Friend*, the four-act *The Argonauts*, and the five-act *Medea*. It begins with Jason, leading the Argonauts in quest of the Golden Fleece, meeting Medea, the sorceress of Colchis, who helps him win the Fleece. At Corinth, as the last play shows, Jason casts her aside to marry the King's daughter, and she wreaks gruesome vengeance. The poetry of Grillparzer gives the story at once the flush of living blood and the coolness of classic marble.

There was an English translation of *The Golden Fleece* by Arthur Burkhardt in 1942. At the 1983 Edinburgh Festival (The Traverse, Fringe), translated and directed by Barney Simon, Grillparzer's *Medea* was presented, with Yvonne Bryceland as the discarded proud woman "Freezing the blood." Too late the repenting anguished hero cries: "Give me back the Jason that I was!"

Medea shows the flame of a universal feeling at its most blasting heat.

HIPPOLYTUS   *Euripides*

In *Hippolytus,* 428 B.C., Euripides shows the consequences of violating the golden mean of the Greeks: nothing too much. Since Hippolytus has too much disdain for love, Aphrodite punishes him by putting into the breast of his young step-mother, Phaedra, an overpowering passion for the young man. The play makes a searching and dramatic study of the interactions of three persons—Theseus, his young bride Phaedra, and Hippolytus, his son by the Amazon queen—caught in the first full-scale dramatization of the "eternal triangle."

The subject attracted Euripides. *Hippolytus* is his second attempt at the subject; it may be, indeed, a revision of his earlier, lost, *Hippolytus Veiled.* Never in ancient times were the vagaries of the "tender passion" more carefully analyzed, more subtly shown. When Phaedra becomes aware of her love for Hippolytus, she fights against it, even fasting for three days to destroy her desire. It is not Phaedra, but her Nurse, that first mentions Hippolytus' name; it is the Nurse, urging Phaedra to action and swearing Hippolytus to silence, that tells him of Phaedra's love. When Hippolytus rejects her, Phaedra hangs herself, leaving a note accusing her step-son. Hippolytus, saying "With my tongue I swore it, never with my heart," goes to break his oath of silence and tell Theseus the truth; at the crucial moment, however, he remains silent, and preserves Phaedra's secret and good name. When Hippolytus is dying, under his father's curse, the goddess Artemis tells Theseus the truth. Hippolytus, less disdainful now, recognizes that the greatest sufferer of the three is the doubly bereft Theseus, who remains alive. The first triangle in the theatre is a tragic one.

The power of love is vividly pictured by the Nurse: "Cypris goes to and fro in the heavens; she is upon the wave of the deep; and from her all things arise. She it is who sows and scatters love, whose children all we on earth confess ourselves to be." This first dramatic flowering of romantic love is a distinct contribution of Euripides. "The buoyant romance of the lost *Andromeda,*" said F. L. Lucas, "with its rescue of the heroine from the sea-monster at dawn by the young hero, to whom she cries with a strange anticipation of the very words of Miranda to Ferdinand in *The Tempest,* 'Take me, O stranger, as thou wilt, for maid or bride or slave of thine,' the jealousy of Medea, the dark, unhappy loves of Phaedra and Stheneboea, the perverse passions of Canace and Pasiphae—all these were treatments of a theme which, hackneyed today, was then a fiercely criticized innovation on the stage. 'None knows of a woman in love in any play of mine,' is the boast of Aeschylus in the *Frogs** of Aristophanes, as he denounces Euripides on this very ground; but since Euripides there has lived not one great dramatist who could make the same disclaimer."

The effect of these first dramatic pictures of love must have been great indeed. Thus Lucian, in the second century after Christ, tells that, late one spring, after a troupe of strolling players had performed Euripides' *Andromeda* at Abdera in Thrace, the citizens neglected their work, roving through the meadows and groves, singing a song from the play, "O Love, high Lord both over gods and men!" until the winds of autumn cooled them back to sanity. Even allowing for the exaggeration of Lucian's satire, we must recognize the strong appeal of the new theme of "romantic" love.

The deep respect of the Athenian audience for an oath made one line in *Hippolytus* notorious. When Hippolytus threatens to tell his father the truth, averring "With my tongue I swore it, never with my heart," the audience booed. Euripides was perhaps raising the question whether to break an oath secured under false pretenses was a violation of Greek morality; notice that the young man, when the time comes, keeps his word though it means his death. Yet Aristophanes in no less than three plays (*The Acharnians,** *The Frogs,** *The Thesmophoriazusae* *) attacked Euripides for the line, and Cicero made comment upon the equivocaton.

In most later versions of the story, emphasis is shifted from Hippolytus to Phaedra. Seneca's play *Phaedra,* about A.D. 60, one of the Roman's best, makes several changes. The gods Euripides introduces (Aphrodite at the beginning, her chaste rival Artemis at the end) are omitted, as is also the strong scene between Hippolytus and his father. But Seneca made three important additions that humanize the motivation in the drama. He presented a scene between Phaedra and Hippolytus, in which she herself tells him her love; effectively her embarrassment and shame are shown as Hippolytus at first fails to understand her; the scene is rich in pathos. Then Phaedra, in person, denounces Hippolytus to Theseus. Only when Hippolytus' mangled remains are brought in does she break down, confess the truth, and kill herself.

Racine's French *Phèdre,* 1677, combines elements of the Greek and the Roman drama; retaining the three episodes of Seneca just mentioned, it adds a new motive. Hippolyte rejects Phèdre not from chastity, but because he is himself in love; this adds jealousy to Phèdre's gathered wrath. She is the utter victim of her passion: "C'est Vénus toute entière à sa proie attachée." The French play *Phèdre and Hippolyte,* 1677, by Nicolas Pradon, written in competition with Racine, was proclaimed by Racine's enemies as a better play than *Phèdre*; the consequent controversy in verse is known as the War of the Sonnets. Pradon's play—as also the highly praised English *Phaedra and Hippolytus,* 1708, by Edmund Smith—is now neglected; but Racine's *Phèdre* is by many considered his masterpiece. The part of Phèdre, first played by Marie Champmeslé, was played also by Adrienne Lecouvreur, Marie Dumesnil, and Rachel. Sarah Bernhardt deemed Phèdre one of her richest roles. The play is Racine's most moving and most enduring drama of passion and undying love. It was presented in an English version by Bernard Grebanier, at the Dramatic Workshop, New York, in February and March 1953, revealing beauty and moving power.

D'Annunzio's Italian *Fedra,* 1909, is, in fervid style, exaggeratedly romantic.

There have been a number of modern productions of *Hippolytus.* About 1858, Julia Ward Howe wrote a version for Charlotte Cushman and Edwin Booth, but the manager's wife coveted the role of Phaedra and the version was not produced until Margaret Anglin took it over in 1911. In 1935 the play was presented at the Old Vic, in London; in 1936, in the Gilbert Murray translation, at the Carnegie Institute of Technology; and in 1937 at Albright College, Pennsylvania. In 1950, Rex Warner made another English translation of the play.

What was called a "free adaptation" of Euripides' *Hippolytus* by Leighton Rollins was presented by the Experimental Theatre of the American National Theatre and Academy in New York in 1948. In reviewing that production, Brooks Atkinson declared that "*Hippolytus* reveals the gods and their earthly victims in a series of sadistic relationships requiring the services of a licensed psychiatrist. Living in a fantasy world of primitive taboos, the characters of ancient Greek tragedies can certainly get into some harrowing dilemmas . . . Hippolytus is framed by gods whose code of ethics conforms to the most enlightened practices of modern gangsters, although the gods, of course, speak finer verse." It is obvious that Rollins' "free adaptation" conveyed no sense at all of Euripides' use of the gods as symbols of natural forces.

A heart empty of love will have other torments. Excess of love, excess of continence, alike bring train of evil. Its psychological study makes the *Hippolytus*—in spite of the interference of the gods, who are no less symbolic than the three witches in *Macbeth*—one of the most modern in spirit of the ancient Greek dramas.

There have been numerous recent productions of *Hippolytus*. Among them, in England: Oxford, 1955. Hampstead Theatre Club, 1965, with "the idiom of John Osborne and Edward Albee." Cambridge, 1968. Stratford-upon-Avon, 1978. London Warehouse, 1979, on a platform, the actors sitting at the side when not performing; the David Rudkin adaptation made Hippolytus "a saintly prig." In the United States: Chicago, 1960; adapted by Leighton Rollins; OffOffBway (Pillar Players), 1966; also 1967 (Rising Sun), adapted by Stephen Bush, and 1972, adapted by Leslie Ann May.

Racine's *Phèdre* has been even more popular. When Alfred de Musset heard Rachel at her high moment, he swooned. Hearing Marie Bell in French in London, March 7, 1960, Harold Hobson glowed: "Even the supremacy of Shakespeare was a little bit shaken, and France took on a new glory." In English, London heard Margaret Rawlings, November 10, 1957; also *Phèdre* in 1959, the 320th anniversary of Racine's birth. Cambridge, May 2, 1963.

The translation of Robert Lowell was heard December 3, 1964, at Wesleyan University, with Vera Zorina; at Oxford, England, 1966, the *Times* reporting: "In place of the formal chastity of the French, Lowell gives us a romantic abandon and a lusciousness of metaphor that succeed surprisingly well." The Lowell version was used by Diana Sands in 1967, and at Mineola, Long Island, summer of 1968. From IASTA it moved on February 10, 1966, to OffBway Greenwich Mews for 100 performances.

Phèdre contains, said Lytton Strachey, "one of the most finished and beautiful, and at the same time one of the most overwhelming studies of passion in the literature of the world . . . The ruined queen, at the culmination of her passion, her remorse, and her despair, sees in a vision Hell opening to receive her, and the appalling shade of her father Minos dispensing his unutterable doom. The creator of this magnificent passage, in which the imaginative grandeur of the loftiest poetry and the supreme force of dramatic emotion are mingled in a perfect whole, has a right to walk beside Sophocles in the high places of eternity."

ANDROMACHE   *Euripides*

Euripides' *Andromache,* 426 B.C., was first presented, not at Athens, but probably at the court of the King of the Molossians, whose favor Athens was seeking at the beginning of the Peloponnesian War; the king traced his ancestry back to Achilles through Andromache's son, Molossus.

Though she gives the play its name, Andromache drops from sight midway; the contemporary situation seemed more important to Euripides than any unity of plot. In the first part of the play, the lives of Andromache and her son, Molossus, are threatened. Andromache, Hector's widow, has been borne off as a slave to the son of Achilles, Neoptolemus (also called Pyrrhus); Molossus is their child. But Pyrrhus is married to Hermione, daughter of Menelaus, who in jealousy would slay Andromache and Molossus. Menelaus seizes them, but they are saved by the intervention of old Peleus, Achilles' father. At this point, Euripides' hatred of Sparta, rival of Athens in the Peloponnesian War, shifts the play's movement. Orestes, nephew of Menelaus of Sparta, comes in. He kills Pyrrhus, and goes off with Hermione. The play ends when the goddess Thetis descends "from the machine" and declares (as the witch shows of Banquo, in *Macbeth**) that Molossus shall be father of a long line of kings.

Hatred of Sparta is doubly emphasized in *Andromache.* It is pressed in the irony of the fact that the house of Achilles, who was sacrificed to win the Trojan War, is destroyed by the house of the Spartan Menelaus, which had caused the war and gained most by it. More directly, hate pours with the words of Andromache to Menelaus: "O citizens of Sparta, abhorred by all men, ye tricky schemers, masters of falsehood, contrivers of evil plots, with crooked minds and devious devices and never an honest thought, it is unjust that ye should thrive in Hellas."

Euripides' venom against the Spartans led him to vilify even the god Apollo, whose Delphic oracle had promised aid and victory to Sparta in the war. He also attacked the comparative freedom of Spartan women (although in *Medea** he had, conversely, condemned the conservatism of Athens), robing Spartan Hermione in garments to reveal charms that decorum would allow but to be surmised. Euripides' characterizations were also influenced by the political intentions of the play. Andromache is a loftyminded figure, who retains her queenly dignity even when she is snatched away to be slain; Hermione, on the other hand, is both vain and cowardly; and her father Menelaus, as not in Homer, is treacherous, craven, and cruel.

Andromache has not been among Euripides' most popular plays. Racine wrote a French version, *Andromaque,* which was produced November 17, 1667. By bringing in Pyrrhus, who does not apear in Euripides' play, Racine gave his drama greater coherence. Racine, in fact, made numerous inner changes, altering the psychology so that his characters move with the restraint and dignity of seventeenth-century French courtiers. Of the chain of thwarted lovers—Orestes loves Hermione who loves Pyrrhus who loves Andromache—Racine made the women more subtle and altered the ending: Andromache, though still devoted to her late husband Hector, is not untouched by the love of so powerful and renowned a warrior as Pyrrhus; yet she marries him only to save the life of her son and plans to kill herself thereafter. The jealous Hermione makes the suicide unnecessary; she sends Orestes to kill Pyrrhus, then, railing at him for having obeyed, she kills herself over Pyrrhus' body. Orestes goes mad.

The beauties of Racine's play are, in the main, untranslatable; they are matters of balance not merely in the plot but in the verse structure, within the speech, within the sentence, within the phrase. The pellucid quality of the diction, the serenity of the rhythm, almost belie the emotional intensity, so that persons reading the play in translation may feel that Racine is cold. He is controlled, but intensely emotional.

An English adaptation of Racine's *Andromaque* was made by Ambrose Phillips in *The Distressed Mother,* 1712; Mrs. Siddons played in it. Junius Brutus Booth played Orestes in the French version in New Orleans in 1828. The Gilbert Murray translation of Euripides' *Andromache* was presented in London in 1901; a French translation of Euripides was performed in Paris in 1912 and in 1917.

In her performances of Racine's *Andromaque,* Rachel always played Hermione; Sarah Bernhardt always chose Andromaque. When "the divine Sarah" visited England, the *London Graphic* (July 5, 1879) indicated why she preferred that role: "Its attributes are rather tenderness and pathos than strong passion; but it is probably for this very reason chosen by Mlle. Bernhardt, whose outbursts of fury have always a strained and exaggerated air; whereas her tender, pathetic utterances are exquisitely soft and moving . . ."

Racine's *Andromaque* is a great and unified drama of characters under emotional stress; Euripides' *Andromache,* a vivid dramatic portrayal of the tensions and involvements that persisted, beyond the legendary battles, in Euripides' own battle-scarred Greece.

Euripides' play was shown in Paris in 1970, the characters borne by servitors, like statues, with apertures for their arms and faces.

Racine's play, translated by John Edmunds, was shown in London, February 2, 1972. From the Edinburgh Fringe it came to London in November 1978, with a happy ending. In French, John-Louis Barrault, as Orestes, brought it to the London Aldwych, March 22, 1965, as at the New York City Center, February 28, 1964.

A grand condensation of nine classical plays, called *The Greeks,* translated by Kenneth Cavender, adapted by him and John Barton, was produced by the RSC in 1980 (lasting some eleven hours, with two breaks for meals). Condensed, this came in 1981 to the Williamstown Festival; then, with only *Andromache* omitted, to the Hartford Stage Company in 1982. The plays were arranged in three groups: THE WAR: *Iphigenia in Aulis* (Euripides); *Achilles,* shaped from Homer: *Andromache* (Euripides); *The Trojan Women* (Euripides); THE MURDERS: *Hecuba* (Euripides); *Agamemnon* (Aeschylus); *Electra* (Sophocles); THE GODS: *Helen; Orestes; Iphigenia in Tauris* (all Euripides).

This wide-ranging spread permitted varying views of some figures; thus Clytemnestra is first shown as a deceived mother and humiliated wife; then as the lustful villain of *Electra.* The choruses are all of women, who lament a world in which the men bring war and devastation. The translation was colloquial, losing much of the poetry. The attempt, moreover, to capture nine tragic climaxes within one long presentation inevitably diminished the effect of each. *The Greeks* may serve as a condensed conspectus of a great field of ancient myth, but hardly does justice to the art of the earliest, still among the greatest, of the world's tragic dramatists.

HECUBA   *Euripides*

One of the three most popular of Euripides' dramas in ancient times (along with *Orestes* and *The Phoenician Women*), *Hecuba,* 424? B.C., was much read during the Middle Ages and later continued popular in France. The hapless Queen of Troy was well enough known to Elizabethan England for Shakespeare to have Hamlet bid the Players "Say on: come to Hecuba" and to marvel at the actor's real tears over the Queen's fate: "What's Hecuba to him, or he to Hecuba, That he should weep for her?"

Hecuba has drawn tears from uncounted audiences as Euripides shows her meeting misfortune proudly as a queen. Two blows fall upon her in the play. The first strikes grievously at Hecuba's heart, but was to be expected among the horrors of the fall of Troy; her daughter Polyxena is sacrificed in memory of the Greek hero Achilles. The second blow comes from the unexpected treachery of a friend. When the Trojan War was but a threat Hecuba sent her youngest son, Polydorus, to the friendly King Polymestor of Thrace, with ample gold. With the defeat of the Trojans, Polymestor slew the young prince and appropriated his wealth. Learning of this treacherous deed, Hecuba's wild grief changes to a cold fury; she plans and carries through the killing of King Polymestor's two children and the blinding of the King.

The character of Hecuba is presented with sympathy and understanding as Euripides pictures the overpowering emotions of the mother, seventeen of whose nineteen children are dead, and the hardening of her feeling into a bitterness and resolve that coldly wreak her vengeance. At the end of the play, the Greek Agamemnon, judging between Queen Hecuba and King Polymestor, declares that the Thracian king has been properly punished for his treachery. The blinded King thereupon prophesies the death of Hecuba's last child, Cassandra, a slave in Agamemnon's train, and the same fate for the conquering Agamemnon.

The ghost of Polydorus, Hecuba's son, opens the play, announcing the fate of the characters. Passed along in the dramas of Seneca, this ghost was the forerunner of the many apparitions that thronged the theatre—the ghost of Hamlet's father, the visions of Macbeth, and in the minor plays of horror the wraiths that rushed forth in very battalions—until they were (for a season!) laughed away by the ancestors stepping from their picture frames in Gilbert's *Ruddigore.**

Some critics have felt that the hearing of Hecuba and Polymestor before Agamemnon takes disproportionate space in the play. The development of this scene is doubtless a reflection of the interest Athenians at the time took in oratory and argument.

The writing of *Hecuba* is brilliant throughout, with many epigrams and passages of moving beauty. Commenting on a performance of the play in Greek at Holy Cross College in June 1926, the *Boston Transcript* praised Euripides' "craft and masterdom as playwright, fervor and splendor as poet ... Winged often are the free-rhythmed speeches, many-voiced, of the chorus ... World without end, sound and sight remain potent in the theatre. Out of *Hecuba* and Euripides, they span these three and twenty centuries— alien tongue but eye and ear still holden."

Hecuba was presented in 1916, as part of Sarah Bernhardt's New York repertoire. A new translation, by H. B. Lister, was published in 1940. In beauty of expression, pungency of thought, and capture of character, *Hecuba* still holds a high place among the world's great dramas.

Recent revivals in Greek include: 1955, New York, Katina Paxinou of the Greek National Theatre, in Athens, 1957; in London and New York, 1966. At the tenth annual Cervantes Festival, Guanjuato, Mexico, 1982, Jennie Angelidou of the State Theatre of North Greece, to an open-air audience of

5,000, which (I observed)) maintained complete silence and involved attention throughout.

In English: 1959 at the University of Texas and OffOffBway (Open Eye). In 1967 the London Mermaid played successively *Hecuba, Electra, Orestes,* and *Iphigenia in Aulis.*

CYCLOPS   *Euripides*

The *Cyclops,* 423? B.C., is the one extant satyr play. In the dramatic contests of the fifth century before Christ, the tragic poets were expected to present a tetralogy, three tragedies followed by a satyr play. The latter, if we may take the *Cyclops* as representative, was a travesty of the theme handled seriously in the tragedies. It was much shorter than the serious dramas; the *Cyclops* has but 709 lines. (Sophocles' *Oedipus at Colonus* is longest, with 1,770 lines.) Basically, the satyr play was perhaps closest to the early religious dance drama. The dramatic contests were held at the Great Dionysia festival, in March, and the chorus of the satyr play consisted of satyrs; Silenus (son of Pan and foster-father of Dionysus, god of wine and revelry) was always a character, and Silenus and the chorus wore phalluses, as in the old Dionysiac fertility rites.

Euripides, in the *Cyclops,* burlesques the story of Odysseus and the Cyclops Polyphemus, as told in Book Nine of Homer's *Odyssey.* Arriving before the Cyclops' cave in Mount Aetna, Odysseus in exchange for wine buys cheese and sheep from Silenus, who is Polyphemus' slave. The Cyclops surprises Odysseus and his men, and pens them in his cave. There, Polyphemus eats two of Odysseus' companions, gets drunk on Odysseus' wine, and is blinded by Odysseus. The cowardly satyrs, who had refused to help Odysseus, now mislead the blind Cyclops, who bumps his head against the rocks while Odysseus and his men escape.

Save for its brevity, the satyr play has the form of the tragedies: five sections separated by choral songs. The structure and the plot development are very simple; the language is lively with colloquial and slang expressions that were not used in tragedy. Odysseus, however, maintains his dignity, both in action and in speech; indeed, his sobriety and earnestness seem deliberately poised against the ribaldry of the others, to make their tipsy revelry more amusing. Drunken Polyphemus, for example, wants to make love to the drunken Silenus.

The *Cyclops,* however, is not all ribaldry and slapstick; Euripides' satire plays upon more than the old legend. It has Polyphemus laugh with scorn at mortals that wage war over one indecent woman. And the leader of the chorus inquires about Helen, upon the fall of Troy: "After capturing your blooming prize, were you all in turn her lovers? For she likes variety in husbands." Through Polyphemus, Euripides looks with no friendly eye upon those persons that worship "the belly, the greatest of deities." And he has Odysseus point out the misfortunes, the widespread sorrow, that the Trojan War brought, not to the defeated Trojans, but to the conquering Greeks.

[In the name that Odysseus gives the Cyclops, James Joyce found a searching symbol. "My name is No-man," says Odysseus, so that the Cyclops will not recognize his real name; but, in the Greek, this is not a far-fetched change: the name that *Odysseus* gives is *Odys.* This, said James Joyce (in a conversation), prefigures the situation of the artist. The artist must always give all of himself. If he tries to withhold any part of himself, it is inevitably the god (the *Zeus*) in him that is sloughed, and no man (*Odys*) indeed that remains!]

Euripides' *Cyclops* is an amusing travesty, scarcely more than a skit, but quite actable. The French comedian Coquelin enjoyed playing Silenus. The ancient Greeks, after the deep emotional drive of the tragedies, must have had high hilarity with the satyr play.

By coincidence, there were three English productions of *Cyclops* in 1957: Chicago, adapted by Ivor Rogers; William and Mary College, adapted by C. O. Burgess; Amherst College, adapted by Robert Bagg.

HERACLES   *Euripides*

The *Heracles,* 422? B.C., is one of Euripides' most effective dramatic studies of the growth of character through suffering. The hero, Heracles, King of Thebes, returns from his labors to find his wife, Megara, and their sons about to be slain by the usurper Lycas. Heracles kills Lycas, but the gods set a madness upon him, so that he also kills his wife and their children. When the madness is lifted, Heracles at first would kill himself, but recognizing that suicide is the coward's evasion, he decides to endure whatever fate may send. On this note of high resolve, the tragedy ends.

Seneca's Latin version of the drama, *Mad Hercules,* about A.D. 60, emphasizes the Stoic qualities of the hero, making a number of minor changes from the Greek. Most effective is Seneca's leaving Hercules, after he awakens from his madness, uninformed about the murders: he sees the blood on his own arrows and thus becomes aware of his gullt. On the whole, however, Seneca's formal construction lacks the emotional appeal of Euripides' drama.

Opinions of Euripides' *Heracles* vary considerably. Some critics place the play much later in Euripides' life because it pictures the evils of old age, but no poet would advance such an argument. The play emphasizes the friendship of the Athenians and the Dorians, as did other plays written near the beginning of the Peloponnesian War.

On the ground that the two movements in the play—Heracles' triumph and Heracles' downfall—are not well-knit, other critics consider the play inferior, but the theme of the play is the very change of circumstance that overtakes Heracles, and his reaction to it. The French nineteenth-century critic Henry Patin declared that *Heracles* "comes near to being the most pathetic and the most lofty" of all Euripides' dramas. At the end of the nineteenth century, the English critic A. W. Verrall said; "For power, for truth, for poignancy, for depth of penetration into the nature and history of man, this picture of the Hellenic hero may be matched against anything in art."

The English poet, Robert Browning, paid the play high tribute. In his poem *Aristophanes' Apology* (1875), in which he discusses the Greek dramatists, he said, "Accordingly I read the perfect piece," and follows this line with his own translation of Euripides' *Heracles.* The last line of the *Apology* is "Glory to God!—who saves Euripides!"

Browning's words might serve as our last on *Heracles,* save that Heracles' own words in the play serve as a guide both for individuals and for nations, not only of his time but of our own: "Whoever prefers wealth or power to the possession of good friends, thinketh amiss."

Of an Archibald MacLeish adaptation, New York, 1967, Karl Shapiro wrote in the *Times* (August 6, 1967): "In a time when kindergarten drama such as *MacBird!** is acclaimed by the organized 'avant garde,' a play like *Herakles* will probably be passed over or damned with faint praise. That would be a pity . . . MacLeish draws from the tangle of the myths and cults of Hercules the parable of the anti-humanist modern—the scientist who brags that he shall conquer death itself, even at the risk of exterminating life." Heracles is still most pertinent.

THE TROJAN WOMEN   *Euripides*

In all literature there is no picture of the devastation and the sorrow wrought by war more moving than Euripides' *Troades* (*The Trojan Women*), written in 415 B.C. It is the "mightiest of all mighty denunciations of war," said John Mason Brown, when the Edith Hamilton translation was produced in New York in 1938, "which Euripides wrote 2,350 years ago and which even now (perhaps we should say, especially now) is as timely as if it had been written yesterday."

Although the play probably cost Euripides his Athenian citizenship, as Brown pointed out, it won him the gratitude of the world: "None of the many dramatists who have excoriated the savagery and waste of war in the theatre's long history has faced its miseries so fearlessly, or stated them in such simple, moving, and eternal terms as did this ever-prodding Greek . . . This is why his tragedy speaks so poignantly to us who are thinking neither of Troy nor a plundered island, but of Shanghai, Madrid, and the future's cloudy skyline. His drama is ageless in its beauty, its brutality, its majesty . . . It is realism of the finest, most enduring sort because it is a picture, at once accurate and dateless, of the human spirit in agony."

In 416 B.C. the Athenians swarmed upon the island of Melos, which was trying to preserve its neutrality in the Peloponnesian War (427-404 B.C.). In a surge of totalitarian hate, the Athenians killed all the men on the island, and ravished all the women and children into slavery. No one made public protest. But within the year, while the same leaders were planning a similar drive upon Sicily, Euripides produced *The Trojan Women*.

A pageant of sorrow, *The Trojan Women* pictures the rapine and destruction and enslavement that followed upon the fall of Troy. Young Astyanax, son of Hector and Andromache, is snatched from his mother's arms and hurled from the Trojan walls. The women of Troy, watching their sons and husbands die, hearing the topless towers of Ilium crash and crumble in the smoke and dust, are borne away to slavery. Distraught, Trojan Cassandra foretells the doom of the Grecian house of Atreus. Greek Menelaus, recapturing his wife Helen, finds his victory hollow in his heart. Emptiness, and the presage of doom, thus perch upon the victor as upon the vanquished.

In *The Trojan Women*, Euripides has none of the shining belief in Athenian ideals that marks his earlier political plays. The justice of democratic Athens has been belied by the events of the Peloponnesian War. A hopeless grief rises out of the murky doom. All man can do—as the Trojan women show, when, led by Queen Hecuba, they move to the Greek ships—is to meet his fate with dignity and courage. It is the pulse of such steadfast courage in heavy misfortune that adds to the pathos and poignancy of *The Trojan Women*, the exaltation that springs from tragedy.

The choice of such a subject, which thrust upon the Athenians a reminder of their own crimes, helps explain why Euripides was not popular in his own day, in his own city. When it was first presented, the tetralogy of which *The Trojan Women*, the sole survivor, was the third play (with *Alexander;*

Palamedes; and the satyr-play *Sisyphus*) won only second place. Yet the power of the play could not be withstood. When he beheld *The Trojan Women,* Alexander of Pheras (who died in 359 B.C.) left the theatre in the middle of the play; but he sent word to the actor that he left not because of the performance, but because he did not wish men to see him weeping for Hecuba when he had, dry-eyed, watched many of his own victims. (The power of the drama persisted through the ages; remember Hamlet's comment on the Player: "What's Hecuba to him, or he to Hecuba, that he should weep for her!") The scene of the killing of the young Astyanax, Gilbert Murray has said, "is probably the most harrowing in Greek literature."

In other ways, too, Euripides seems to have pressed the story home to his own people. Twice he emphasized that the Trojan War was started over a woman; first the allusive Cassandra says that "one woman's beauty made their myriads fall"; then, more bluntly, the leader of the chorus of women cries: "O ill-starred Troy! For one alien woman, one abhorrèd kiss, how are thy hosts undone!" Gossip in Euripides' day had it that the Athenian Pericles precipitated the Peloponnesian War over two sluts belonging to his mistress Aspasia . . . Shortly after the presentation of *The Trojan Women,* Euripides left Athens. He was sheltered at the court of King Archelaus of Macedon, and his later plays, (The *Bacchantes; Iphigenia in Aulis,* etc.) were produced in Athens by his son.

Seneca's Latin version of *The Trojan Women,* about A.D. 60, is his finest tragedy. In its picture of the horror and futility of war, the insolence of the victors—with the irony of their own imminent disasters—the play reaches depths of emotion, and the formal Latin rhetoric achieves the exaltation of poetry. The occasional lyric songs have a rich beauty and pathos, especially the one in which the old Trojan mother, pointing out to her child a distant cloud of smoke, tells him that this is the only sign by which to know their home.

A German version of Euripides' *The Trojan Women,* by Franz Werfel,* 1913, was hailed by critic Wolfgang Paulson as "a milestone in the history of the expressionist theatre." New York, however, has been content to view the play in less contorted guise. In the Gilbert Murray translation, Euripides' play was produced by Granville Barker in 1915; it was enacted again in 1923, with, according to the *New York Times* (November 9, 1923), "a painfully timely significance since the late armistice . . . a directness and fulness of effect." The same translation was used in 1941, when Margaret Webster staged the play and played Andromache; Walter Slezak, Dame May Whitty (Hecuba), Johanna Roos, and Tamara Geva (Helen) were in the cast, and the conquering soldiers wore Nazi uniforms. In the meantime, Edith Hamilton's translation, 1937, was used in a January 1938 New York production: Atkinson found it "much sharper and crisper" than "Gilbert Murray's otiose and Victorian rhymed translation." In April 1938, the Federal Theatre presented a version by Philip H. Davis of Vassar College.

As Euripides wrote the play, however, and in an adequate translation, *The Trojan Women* contains exquisitely poignant lyrics—the words of Hecuba beginning "Lo, I have seen the open hand of God" approach the sublime—and in its presentation of the horrid aftermath of war has had few equals in the drama, and has still to be surpassed.

In the sensitive translation by Edith Hamilton, *The Trojan Women* was produced OffBway (Circle in the Square), opening December 23, 1963, for six hundred performances, and again September 3, 1965, for forty more. In translation by Neil Curry it was played in London, October 1964. The same year a version in French by Jean-Paul Sartre, with contemporary references, was produced in Paris. This, Englished by Ronald Duncan, came to the Edinburgh Festival, May 29, 1966, with Flora Robson as Helen and Diana Churchill as Hecuba and Leader of the Chorus.

IPHIGENIA IN TAURIS *Euripides*

The suggestion has been made that *Iphigenia in Tauris*, 414? B.C., is an early example of "escape" literature, that Euripides, discouraged by the turn of events in the Peloponnesian War and by the decline of Athens' idealism under the strain of her many losses, deliberately sought to forget the present in exciting adventure of far-off times. After a production of *Iphigenia in Tauris* by Mr. and Mrs. Coburn, the *New York Dramatic Mirror* (August 6, 1913) said: "Had it been written today—and, indeed, it might have been—it would come under the head of thriller. Stripped of its classical mysticisms, it could well be an intrigue of the Italian Renaissance, and as to its emotions—well, it is the same old human nature."

In this play Euripides uses a variant episode of the Trojan legend. Both Aeschylus and Sophocles picture Iphigenia as sacrificed at Aulis so that the Greeks could win the Trojan War. According to Euripides' version, Iphigenia was spirited away from the sacrificial altar by the goddess Artemis. When the play opens, she is serving as priestess of Artemis' temple in Tauris, held there by Thoas, King of the Taurians. An inhospitable people, the Taurians sacrifice to the goddess all strangers that come to their land.

And now, on his wanderings, still at times driven mad by the Furies that have tormented him since he killed his mother, Iphigenia's brother Orestes comes to Tauris, accompanied by his faithful friend Pylades. Captured and held to be sacrificed, Orestes and Pylades are questioned by Iphigenia; Orestes begs that he be killed and his friend spared; and in what Aristotle called the best "recognition scene" in all the Greek drama, Iphigenia and her brother learn each other's identity. King Thoas comes to watch the sacrifice. Iphigenia tells him the strangers are polluted with matricidal blood; the goddess must be cleansed. While the King watches, Iphigenia leads the goddess' statue forth from the temple, followed by Orestes and Pylades. When word comes to King Thoas that they have all taken ship and fled from Tauris, the goddess Athena comes "from the machine" to tell Thoas who the strangers are and forbid his pursuit.

The play did not require the final descent of the goddess; apparently Euripides introduced it purely for its spectacular effect. For *Iphigenia in Tauris* is built for the story interest, with a straight and swift dramatic drive, and less psychological concern than is usual in Euripides.

On the stage the play is unquestionably vivid. Voltaire, who saw a performance when he was eighteen, declared that it gave him his first impetus toward writing tragedy. Goethe took part in a production of his prose *Iphigenie auf Tauris* at the court of Ettersburg in 1779. In 1780, Goethe rewrote the play in iambics, and during his trip to Italy in 1787, he gave the play its final shape. Still in iambics, it took on some of the calmer beauty of Greek tragedy. It presents less action but more character study than Euripides' play, is indeed Goethe's psychological masterpiece in the drama. Goethe changed the ending, having Iphigenie escape not by tricking the Taurian King, but by telling him the true story and trusting to his better nature, which her own candor and trust help to bring into play. Goethe's drama was translated into Finnish by Elino Leino; and in modern Greek it was acted in New York by Marika Cotopoulis in 1930. F. L. Lucas has said of Goethe's version: "Reading the two plays together, one is struck by the greater nobility of the German, the greater grace and truth of the Greek . . ."

The Gilbert Murray translation, the most effective to date, was presented by Harley Granville-Barker in 1915 in the Yale Bowl and in the College of the City of New York stadium with a cast including Lillah McCarthy (Iphigenia), Ian Maclaren (Orestes), Lionel Braham (Thoas), Claude Raines, Philip Merivale, and Alma Kruger. In 1932 and 1935, there were productions at the University of North Carolina.

In Aristotle's discussion of dramaturgy he mentions *Iphigenia in Tauris* favorably no less than five times. For sheer story interest, it is perhaps the most vivid of the Greek dramas.

The Goethe version was played in Zurich, 1955, and in English at the OffBway Jan Hus, June 10, 1959. A Witter Bynner translation went on tour after Columbia University in 1936.

Lillah McCarthy played the Gilbert Murray translation at the London Haymarket in 1932. The play was shown, opening October 22, 1964, at London's Royal (Stratford East).

Opening November 21, 1967, at the OffBway Circle in the Square, a translation by Minos Volanakos ran for 232 performances.

ORESTES   *Euripides*

Full of dramatic incident, surging with swift emotion to tragic heights, *Orestes,* 408 B.C., was deservedly one of the most popular of Euripides' dramas. Along with his *Hecuba** and *The Phoenician Women,* it was the most frequently read during the Middle Ages, and since then, though not frequently performed, it has retained its high repute. A. W. Verrall has called it "one of the triumphs of the stage, which may still be described as supreme of its kind . . . For excitement, for play of emotion, for progression and climax of horror, achieved by natural means and without strain upon the realities of life, it has few rivals in the repertory of the world."

The story of *Orestes* is one of the few of Euripides in which the descent of the god from the top of the theatre is used not merely for the spectacular effect, but as the essential device to resolve the conflict in the drama and to produce a happy ending. There is enough else in the play that is spectacular. It opens in Argos, a week after Orestes has killed his mother and her lover. Orestes, ravaged with spells of madness, is watched over by his sister Electra. Menelaus refuses to shelter him from the citizens, who pass upon Orestes and Electra sentence of death by their own hands. With the help of his friend Pylades, Orestes seeks to seize Helen, back from Troy; when she slips away, they take her daughter by Menelaus, Hermione. While Menelaus watches impotently from below, Pylades and Orestes hold Hermione on the roof of the palace, up which soar flames enkindled by Electra. Amidst the flames Apollo appears, and orders them to cease their struggles. He bids Orestes wed Hermione, Pylades wed Electra, Menelaus return to rule Sparta; Helen, he transports to dwell among the gods. The play ends, like *Iphigenia in Tauris** and *The Phoenician Women,** with the chorus, as it files out, uttering a prayer for victory in the dramatic contest.

The critic Aristophanes of Byzantium, in the third century B.C., commented on the remarkable power of *Orestes* when performed, despite the fact that every character in the play is evil. Pylades, though partially redeemed because he is acting not in self-interest but for friendship's sake, suggests the killing of Helen. Menelaus, the Spartan king, is ungenerous, forgetful of former benefits, and cowardly; Aristotle, indeed, mentions him, as pictured in *Orestes,* as an instance of "unnecessary baseness."

Swift and stimulating in its picture of the frenzied Orestes, the play gives us the most vivid study of an abnormal psychological state in the ancient drama. Of the opening scene, in which Electra watches while Orestes wakes, the French critic Henri Patin remarked: "This scene, in its sentiment, language, arrangement of the dialogue, and grouping of the different ideas, is an epitome of the Greek tragic genius, for the study of which it is almost, in itself, sufficient."

In the legendary material of this drama Euripides has built one of his most moving plays.

Orestes, adapted by William Arrowsmith, was shown at the University of Texas, 1961. In 1967, adapted by Jack Lindsay at the London Mermaid, Menelaus appeared as a German cavalry officer, Orestes "a bully-boy with a flick-knife, alternately blubbering and sniveling." And at the Berkeley University of California, directed by John Cage, Orestes was a hippie in red jeans; there were film clips of the war in Vietnam, of the U.S. Capitol in flames; Pylades seemed a Hell's Angel on a motorbike. There was a more sober adaptation by Gregory Rozakis at the OffBway Cubiculo, 1970 and 1973.

IPHIGENIA IN AULIS   *Euripides*

In Euripides' *Iphigenia in Aulis,* 407? B.C., which the French critic Henri Patin has called "the most perfect of his plays," the old legendary material is translated into a romantic story with human, natural characters. The well-motivated actions carry swiftly along in a plot that could be used today.

Aeschylus and Sophocles, as well as Euripides, have told the story of Iphigenia, the daughter of Agamemnon and Clytemnestra, who, on the island of Aulis, was given in sacrifice by her father so that the Greeks might have safe journey to Troy. All three playwrights have Agamemnon lure Iphigenia to the island by sending word that she is to be married to Achilles. From that point, Euripides adds dramatic device after device, all flowing naturally from the initial situation. He has Agamemnon, the father, repent and write a letter home, telling Clytemnestra not to bring the girl. But the suspicious Menelaus, burning for revenge for his wife Helen's going to Troy, waylays the messenger. Not only Iphigenia, but her mother Clytemnestra comes to Aulis. When Clytemnestra greets Achilles as her son-in-law, he is dumb-founded, and the deceit of Agamemnon is disclosed. Then Clytemnestra bursts out in fury against her husband Agamemnon, reminding him of his murder of her former husband and child (a fact not found in Homer) and confessing that her marriage to him was a forced and hateful one. Achilles, too, is wroth. In his anger at being made a pawn of Agamemnon's deceit, he comes to defend Iphigenia against those ready to sacrifice her. At this turn of events, Iphigenia proves her loyalty and courage; since the safety of the Greeks depends upon the sacrifice, she is ready to die for her country. As the priest strikes, the spectators see on the altar, instead of Iphigenia, a wild doe of the hills. The gods have taken the noble Iphigenia to abide with them.

The natural movement of the characters in the play is supported by sound portraiture. Iphigenia is one of the loveliest maids in the Greek drama. Devoted to her father, she runs to embrace him, happy with thought of her marriage to the great hero. In sharp contrast is her despair when she learns that Achilles was but a decoy to lure her to the island. She is noble in her final resolve and dignified in her dying. Achilles is natural, too. Ready to fight the whole army to save Iphigenia, he does not, however, stand in the way of her duty—perhaps he even is relieved—when she determines to give herself to the sacrifice. Clytemnestra, the doting mother, then the domineering wife, is just the sort of person that could murder her mate. Agamemnon, on the other hand, is just the sort of man one might wish to murder: good-natured, well-meaning, but desirous of praise and power and too weak-willed to oppose the wishes of the mob. Menelaus, the Spartan— here pictured when Sparta was winning the war against Athens—is the only consistently scoundrelly figure, but even he is given natural motives, so that his actions are understandable. The gallery of human figures, sharply etched, in *Iphigenia in Aulis,* is unmatched elsewhere in the Greek drama.

Euripides also makes effective use of dramatic irony, as in Agamemnon's mortification and secret shame when Clytemnestra and Iphigenia, newly come to Aulis, rejoice in the approaching marriage, and he knows that his daughter is doomed.

Numerous writers have pointed out the similarity of Iphigenia's death to Abraham's sacrifice-offering of his son Isaac, and also to Jephtha's sacrifice of his daughter, in the *Bible.*

Unfinished at Euripides' death, *Iphigenia in Aulis* was presented by his son at the contest in Athens in 405 B.C. In the trilogy with *The Bacchantes,** it won first prize. In the modern period, it was translated by Erasmus in 1524; made into a French play, *Iphigénie,* by Racine in 1674, one of his best; and into an opera by Gluck just a hundred years later. Schiller translated *Iphigenia in Aulis* in 1788; while working on it, he declared: "Often the execution is such that no poet could better it; but at times his tediousness spoils my enjoyment and my labor." Of the creator of *Iphigenia in Aulis,* Goethe exclaimed: "Have all the nations of the world possessed a dramatist worthy to hand him his slippers? . . . Over the scenes of Hellas and its primitive body of legends, he sails and swims like a cannon-ball in a sea of quicksilver and cannot sink even if he tried."

Euripides, however, can soar, as those who saw Margaret Anglin as Iphigenia in New York in 1921 will remember. The play revealed its persisting power in a revival at Columbia University in November 1950. In dramatic movement, in character portrayal, in thoughtful phrase and liquid style, Euripides' *Iphigenia in Aulis* soars in surpassing beauty.

Euripides' two Iphigenia plays were reworked by Doug Dyer as a rock musical (music by Peter Link, lyrics loosely from Euripides), as *The Wedding of Iphigenia* and *Iphigenia in Concert,* with a rock chorus of twelve women. Opening OffBway December 16, 1971, it ran for 139 performances. The chorus commented on the play as it proceeded.

Iphigenia in Aulis was performed by the OffBway Circle in the Square November 21, 1967, with Irene Pappas, directed by Michael Cacoyannis; Clive Barnes called it "one of the highlights of the season." At Waterford, Conn., 1966, it was played in sign language, with offstage narration for the hearing. A London 1971 production rattled tambourines and banged kettledrums. The Roundhouse 1975 production went from Flushing Meadow,

New York, to OffBway; directed by Yanni Simonides, it used music by George Prideaux played on ancient Greek instruments.

THE BACCHANTES   *Euripides*

About 407 B.C. Euripides accepted the invitation of King Archelaus of Macedonia, at whose court he lived for the year until his death (at the fangs of Archelaus's hunting dogs, legend says). In Macedon, Euripides probably saw some of the orgiastic rites of the worship of Dionysus. His spirit, already heavy with disillusion at Athens' conduct in the Peloponnesian War, found in those religious excesses further cause for sombre brooding over human nature. His play *Bacchae (The Bacchantes)* pictures the consequences of the frenzied, often hysterical, celebration of the feast of the god of wine.

The Bacchantes (Dionysus is the Greek name of the Roman Bacchus) pictures the coming of Dionysus to impress his worship on Thebes. The old men welcome him, but young King Pentheus considers his worship harmful to the state and binds the god. Laughing Dionysus sets the women into ritual ecstasy on the hilltops; he slips his bonds, hypnotizes Pentheus into dressing as a woman so that he may behold the "mysteries"; and off in the hills the maddened celebrants, the bacchantes in their reveling frenzy, leap upon and destroy Pentheus their king. Pentheus' own mother Agave, thinking she has killed a lion, bears back Pentheus' head with rejoicing song— then gradually she recovers from her Bacchic fury to recognize her son's severed head in her hands. The god has paid the city for its neglect of him.

The attitude of Euripides toward religion cannot be grasped from *The Bacchantes,* especially as portions of it (including part of a climactic speech by Dionysus) are lost; but the dramatist seems to be emphasizing the danger of excess, the need of faith. There are no other extant plays based on this theme—but one line of a play, *Pentheus,* by Aeschylus. There are, however, many other signs of Athenian interest in the wilder and more emotional aspects of the worship of the wine-god in Dionysiac frenzy. Countless vases and jars of the period show maenads with drums; young Dionysus is laughing among them, and Silenus constantly leers. About 420 B.C. a temple to Dionysus was erected in Athens near the theatre where the dramatic contests were held as part of the festival of the Great Dionysia; on the temple wall is a painting of Pentheus' punishment for opposing the god.

Many critics have considered *The Bacchantes* one of the most tragic of dramas. The scene in which the frenzied Agave, coming to her senses, finds herself holding the head of her own son whom she has killed is so terrible that modern audiences would protect themselves from its impact by denying its credibility. Yet even that horror comes home to us. R. P. Winnington-Ingram observed in 1948 that "the play has an immediate relevance to the worship of Dionysus in Greece, being a priceless document for the history of Greek religion. At the next remove it is relevant to all emotional forms of religion in all ages, and particularly to those that manifest the power of the group. But similar manifestations occur in connexion with objects not specifically religious, and so the scope of the play is widened to include the phenomena of group emotion in all social and political life." Robert Graves found the relevance of the actions in *The Bacchantes* more deeply imbedded in our souls: "This tearing apart of the young man by the Bacchantes may seem far removed from modern life, but the archives of morbid pathology are filled with such stories . . . An English or American woman in a nervous breakdown of sexual origin will often instinctively reproduce in faithful and disgusting detail much of the ancient Dionysian ritual. I have witnessed it myself in helpless terror." Euripides anticipated Freud by 2,500 years.

The Bacchantes was presented after Euripides' death by his son. When the dramatist died, Aristophanes in *The Frogs** declared: "His works have perished with him." Two months later, in the Great Dionysia of 405 B.C., Euripides' trilogy won first prize with *Iphigenia in Aulis** and *The Bacchantes.*

In the ancient world, *The Bacchantes* was very popular. When invited to Syracuse as tutor to Dionysius the Younger, the philosopher Plato refused a purple robe Dionysius offered him, quoting from *The Bacchantes* a line (836) objecting to effeminacy; whereupon Aristippus took the robe, quoting from the same play (lines 316-317) a remark that true worth is not easily corrupted. Plato was dismissed.

In 53 B.C., *The Bacchantes* was being performed by strolling Greek players before King Artavasdes of Armenia and King Orodes of Parthia, when Parthian horsemen rode in with the head of Crassus (with Caesar and Pompey, member of the first Roman triumvirate). The actor playing Agave, Jason of Tralles, took the actual head of Crassus and used it for the head of Pentheus in the play.

For elements other than its horrid press of emotion, *The Bacchantes* is outstanding. The two old men, Cadmus, grandsire of Pentheus, and the prophet Tiresias, are excellently drawn; and there is a vivid portrait of Pentheus himself, who opposes the Dionysiac cult for the good of his people, but gradually is drawn under the hypnotic spell of the god. The actual poetry of *The Bacchantes,* furthermore, is of surpassing beauty—especially, the lyric odes of the chorus, which are among the most lofty and the richest in love of nature in all the ancient drama. Eugene O'Neill, Jr., expressed the critical consensus in calling *The Bacchantes* "one of Euripides' greatest artistic creations." Macaulay declared it "a most glorious play . . . as a piece of language, it is hardly equalled in the world." The choral odes, original in their power and beauty, are embellished versions of the traditional chants of the Bacchic mysteries; the magnificent chorus, lines 64 to 169, follows not only the tenor but the terms of the ritual paean. *The Bacchantes* is indeed, as Cedric H. Whitman called it in *Sophocles* (1951), "a shattering paean of unreason, a hymn to the god of the beautiful but meaningless world."

The description of the wild sweep of the reveling Bacchantes through the wild woods mingles poetry and strangeness in ecstatic surge before the wakening horror. Nowhere else in the Greek, if indeed in any drama, is there such a mingling of beauty and terror, of wild exultation and bitter woe, as in *The Bacchantes.*

Among the many revivals of *The Bacchae:* London Mermaid, 1964, with Barrie Ingham as Dionysus; Josephine Wilson, Agave; Tom Courtenay; Lynn Redgrave; Diane Wynyard; Peter Cellier. Pentheus became a "transvestite Peeping Tom."

OffBway, 1968, adapted by Richard Schechner, with the ecstatic chorus amid the audience whispering seductive allure, and a slanging hippie Dionysus: "Feel pain; it's a gas!" At Yale, 1969, with Mildred Dunnock and Alvin Epstein. Clive Barnes called the 1969 Antioch Co. "strangely contemporary." London, 1972, adapted by Rob Walker, with a gymnastic Dionysus and erotic chorus.

In July 1972 the NT (Old Vic) opened a version by the Nigerian Wole

Soyinka, to general disapproval. John Walker (*Herald Tribune,* August 11, 1973) spoke of "the waywardness of the adaptation, with an irrelevant chorus of chain-rattling slaves" in ivy with great phalluses, and most of the choral speeches left out. Harold Hobson (*Times,* August 5, 1973) commented: "No amount of rushing about, clothed or naked, in a Greek city or an African village, will produce an authentic fever in the blood. An unidentifiable Maenad, with kissing bells on her exciting wrists, comes nearest to it; Constance Cummings is a brief, fine Agave, and Martin Shaw a serene Dionysus. The rest is sweating thighs, wobbling bottoms, and the propaganda of barbarism." On the other hand, the 1975 William Arrowsmith version at Wimbledon, London, Hobson found "outstanding," stressing a problem of today: discipline versus permissiveness. There was a London 1974 adaptation by W. H. Auden and Chester Kallman, with both psychoanalytic and political aspects.

The 1980 New York Circle in the Square, with Irene Pappas, directed by Michael Cacoyannis (who had directed it for the Comédie Française in Paris, 1977) set Dionysus in blue jeans and the Chorus in gypsy scarves. Ours today is largely a "director's theatre"; but directorial eccentricities cannot cover the searching and searing power of Euripides.

THE RECRUITING OFFICER   *George Farquhar*

George Farquhar (1678-1707) has been called the last of the Restoration dramatists, but the wit of this Irish playwright rises above the ethical indifference of his predecessors. To them, a gentleman was a natural rake; Farquhar's beaux may start out as gay deceivers, but love works to the good in them.

Farquhar's first connection with the theatre was as an actor. After badly wounding his opponent in a duel scene in Dryden's *The Indian Emperor,* he abandoned the stage and began to write. His first comedy, *Love and a Bottle,* 1699, was a success. He followed it with *The Constant Couple,* 1700, in which Robert Wilks made a hit. Its sequel, *Sir Harry Wildair,* 1701, was not so popular. Succeeding plays increased neither Farquhar's reputation nor his fortune; indeed, they left him in dire straits.

This state was slightly improved by *The Recruiting Officer,* the result of his experiences as a recruiting lieutenant in Lichfield and Shrewsbury. The play was produced by John Rich at the Drury Lane, April 1, 1706. (Rich also produced Gay's *The Beggar's Opera.**) In the autumn of that year, some of Rich's company went over to his rival Swiney at the new Haymarket, and the play was shown at both houses. Rich advertised that "the true Serjeant Kite"—Richard Escourt, whose performance Steele praised highly in *The Spectator*—was to be seen only at Drury Lane. In the first cast were also Robert Wilks as Captain Plume; Colley Cibber, Captain Brazen; Anne Oldfield, Silvia (she and Wilks went to the Haymarket).

From 1706 to 1800, the play missed only five seasons in London; in 1949 London saw it also in French. *The Recruiting Officer* was the first play shown in New York, opening December 6, 1732, in a windy barn at Pearl Street and Maiden Lane. The first regular theatre in New York, the Dock Street, opened in 1736 with Lewis Hallam's company from England in the play, which was shown also that year in Williamsburg, Va., and Charleston, S.C. During the American Revolution it was performed by British officers in garrison.

The great Garrick made his debut at the age of eleven in an amateur performance, as Serjeant Kite. Wilkes as Captain Plume, recruiting in Shrewsbury, was succeeded by Ryan; by Garrick (1742 and for many years); Barry (1756); Palmer (1758); Smith (1763); Charles Kemble (1797); and other leading actors. Peg Woffington first appeared as Silvia at Covent Garden in 1740. *The Recruiting Officer* was the first play produced in Australia, in a converted hut in Sydney, by a group of transported convicts, admission being paid in tobacco, wine, poultry, and corn. In New York, February 7, 1885, John Drew played Captain Plume; Otis Skinner, Brazen; Ada Rehan as Silvia and Virginia Dreker as Melinda had "cat-like exchanges." The next New York production was at the New School in 1931.

In the play Silvia, daughter of Justice Balance, is in love with Captain Plume; when her father, concerned for her virginity, sends her out of town, she returns disguised as a man and learns that the Captain, for all his bawdy remarks and insinuations, has remained true to her. Recruiting officers were commonly supposed to leave as many bastards behind as they took recruits to the battlefield; but, however free Plume's earlier conduct may have been, and despite the air of a gallant he wears, he resists Melinda and the other current temptations, so that he and Silvia are honestly united at the close.

The chief source of fun in the play is Serjeant Kite, Plume's assistant in persuading men to accept "the Queen's shilling," wherewith the rustics and the unwary citizens of Shrewsbury find themselves in the army. Kite disguised as a fortune-teller states that the word "demonstration comes from Demon, the father of lies"; but he manages to keep close enough to the truth to legalize his recruiting. When the Justice points out that a collier has a trade, and the law says that they are "to impress no man that has any visible means of a livelihood," Kite responds: "May it please your Worship, this man has no visible means of livelihood, for he works underground."

In the last score of years, *The Recruiting Officer* came again to popularity. Among productions have been: in England, December 10, 1964, in the first season of the NT, with Maggie Smith as Silvia; Lynn Redgrave, Melinda; Max Adrian, Justice Balance; Laurence Olivier, Captain Brazen; Robert Stephen, Captain Plume. In 1970, Cambridge; 1972, first play at the new Mercury Theatre, Colchester; 1978, Oxford; 1979, the Bristol Old Vic, also at the Edinburgh Festival. In the United States: 1967 at the Catholic University, Washington, D.C.; 1969, Goodman Theatre, Chicago, with Ronny Graham and Jerome Kilty; 1972, New Haven with John Horton; 1977, OffBway at the Cubiculo, with country dances and tumbling; 1981, BAM with a black recruiter. In 1976 Asolo played a modernized version by Eberle Thomas, *The Quibbletown Recruits.* In 1975 Stratford, Ontario, presented a version by Bertolt Brecht, first shown by the Berliner Ensemble in 1956. Called *Trumpet and Drums,* this was set during the American Revolution, and turned the play to propaganda purposes, with anti-imperialist sentiments and songs.

Alexander Pope early exclaimed: "What pert, low dialogue has Farquhar writ!" but the *Sunday Australian,* September 19, 1971, commenting on a Melbourne production, pointed out that Farquhar was not, like most of his Restoration fellow-playwrights, "peddling bed and bawd." Most comedies of the period introduced songs; one that runs through Act I, Scene 3, of *The Recruiting Officer* is still remembered: "Over the hills and far away." By those that have seen it, the whole play is well remembered.

THE BEAUX' STRATAGEM   *George Farquhar*

In 1707, during his last six weeks, while he was living on funds provided by Robert Wilks, Farquhar wrote his masterpiece, *The Beaux' Stratagem,* a lively social comedy which shows no trace of the fatal illness he was undergoing. He lived scarcely beyond the third night of its performance (the night the receipts went to the author), but he knew that the play was a success and that his two daughters would be provided for.

The play pictures two gentlemen, Archer and Aimwell, without resources but quite resourceful, who decide to work together toward a wealthy marriage. Archer passes as the servant of Aimwell. While the latter woos Dorinda, daughter of the wealthy Lady Bountiful, Archer and Mrs. Sullen, the mismated daughter-in-law of Lady Bountiful, fall in love. Aimwell comes to love Dorinda and confesses that he is penniless. Then honesty is rewarded; Aimwell's elder brother dies, leaving him title and estate. Mrs. Sullen wins a divorce, enabling the two couples to be both virtuous and happy.

The Beaux' Stratagem was for some time one of the most frequently played English comedies, enjoying constant revivals for a century. Opinions as to the morals of the play, however, have differed. In her preface to an 1808 edition, the pious playwright Elizabeth Inchbald observed: "It is an honor to the morality of the present age, that this most entertaining comedy is but seldom performed . . . Plays of this kind are far more mischievous than those which preserve less appearance of delicacy." But the 1829 preface says that the play "is absolutely a *sermon* compared with the productions of Wycherley and Vanbrugh; and, though this 1829 edition is assigning it but moderate praise on the score of decency, it may serve to show that Farquhar, at least, improved on the morals, if not on the wit, of his predecessors."

In *The Beaux' Stratagem,* Farquhar achieved a great success that broke with more than the ethics of Restoration drama. The scene of the comedy is a provincial town, Lichfield, and although two of the characters sigh to be in London, they no longer believe that city the sole habitat of endurable gentlefolk, nor that there are tolerable talk and admirable action only within earshot of Westminster chimes.

Several of the minor characters in the play have won lasting attention. Scrub, the servant of Squire Sullen, is a gem of his kind, one of the liveliest English descendants of the slave in the classical drama who holds the secrets and forwards the designs of the lovers. Boniface, the beaming innkeeper, was so popular that his name became proverbial for a genial host, and similarly "Lady Bountiful" became the general term (even to the heroine of an early "comic strip") for a wealthy and generous though somewhat gullible woman.

In the United States, *The Beaux' Stratagem* has also fared well. In New York, it was played in the first season of the New Theatre, 1732; at the Nassau Street Theatre, in 1750; and it was the opening piece for Hallam's American Company at the John Street Theatre, December 7, 1767. In Massachusetts, the House of Representatives in 1790 denied the petition of Hallam and Henry to open a theatre, but in 1792 an English company played *The Beaux' Stratagem* in Salem and Boston. It was presented again in Boston in 1807, a hundred years after its premiere.

More recent revivals include the Players' Club presentation in New York and on tour, 1928; one at the Mohawk Drama Festival, 1937; one with Aline

MacMahon in Charleston, 1939; and another, with Brian Aherne, at Woodstock, New York, summer of 1948. The Players' Club cast included Lyn Harding, Raymond Hitchcock, James T. Powers, Helen Menken, and Fay Bainter. A London production opened May 5, 1949, for 532 performances.

Brooks Atkinson (June 5, 1928) called the play "delightfully entertaining—a bundle of humors and rhymeless merriment." Allison Smith, in the *New York World*, declared that Farquhar's "intimations of a forthright and genuine consideration of life beneath the cynical persiflage of his stage bring a fresh breath into the studies of coffee house and boudoir." *The Beaux' Stratagem* matches the wit and the lively movement of the best of the Restoration comedies, while replacing their irresponsible licentiousness with a deeper understanding and a kindlier portraiture of the basic good qualities in human nature.

Archer states succinctly: "We have heads to get money and hearts to spend it." They have won it merrily in recent years: The Phoenix February 24, 1959; with June Havoc, 1966, OffBway; 1967, Chichester Festival. NT (Old Vic), 1970, with Maggie Smith; also on tour, across the ocean and continent to Los Angeles. In 1972, Baltimore; 1978, Melbourne. 1980, Hartford, Conn., Clive Barnes calling it "warm, witty, but with a steel-blade of realism running through."

Two of Farquhar's plays have won recent successful revival. *The Constant Couple* in London, 1945, 1952 (with Alec Clunes), and 1967, led Harold Hobson to call *Sir Harry Wildair* "one of the great creations of the English comic stage." He mistakes a debutante for a tart, and her titled mother for a procuress. Accused of cowardice, he draws himself up with a patrician smile: "A coward, sir? I have £8,000 sterling a year."

When *The Twin Rivals* (Drury Lane, 1702) came to London again in 1982, the *Times* declared: "The RSC has rarely done anything finer." The *Observer* announced "the most riotous duel I have ever seen." Mike Gwilym played crookback Benjamin Wouldbe, who sought (vainly) to win their late father's land and wealth from his elder twin brother, Hermes (played by Miles Anderson); their quarrel was "managed" by Mrs. Mandrake (Miriam Karlin), midwife to aristocratic mothers, and procuress to aristocratic gentlemen.

Farquhar maintained the earlier laughter, but discarded the earlier leer. The last lines of *Sir Harry Wildair* show Farquhar's awareness of the new note:

> *So, spite of satire 'gainst a married life,*
> *A man is truly blest with such a wife.*

LOOK AFTER LULU   *Georges Feydeau*

Leaving school in 1879, Georges Léon Julie Marie Feydeau (1862-1921) formed an acting company, but grew more successful as a mimic and a writer of monologues (for stars who used them at charity concerts and wealthy salons). For four years from 1882 he wrote one-act curtain raisers. Between 1894 and 1908 he wrote thirty-nine successful full-length comedies. Stricken by venereal disease in 1919, imagining himself Napoleon III, from the hospital he sent out invitations to his coronation—forestalled by his death in 1921.

Feydeau's comedies and bedroom farces were intricate but logical. He never allowed his characters to say or do anything "not demanded by their nature and the plot." He told a collaborator to cut out a witty line because it was not required by the play and therefore would interrupt the action. He often directed his own plays, watching every detail, through rehearsals that might take up to three months.

Feydeau's neatest farce, *Occupe-toi d'Amélie,* has had over three-thousand performances in France since it opened in 1908. It was taken to London in 1948 by the Renaud-Barrault Company; in French again, on December 6, 1956, when Queen Elizabeth II laughed heartily at the man and the pretty girl in bed—and the even prettier half-clad lass under it. (The play had been unsuccessfully adapted by Willard Mack in 1920, as *Breakfast in Bed.*) It was filmed in English in 1949 as *Oh, Amelia,* played as *Keep an Eye on Amelia*; then, adapted by Noel Coward as *Look After Lulu,* directed by Tony Richardson, it opened in London at the Royal Court Theatre, July 29, 1959, with Vivien Leigh, Anthony Quayle, and Max Adrian. Vivien Leigh was especially fetching under the bed, though the *Observer* observed: "There has been no prettier sight on the London stage for a long time than her moment in the last scene, wearing a mauve *déshabille* against the light, watching the Prince's trousers being flung from the window." Harold Hobson less joyously remarked that she "frisked about in her underclothes." Coming to the New York Henry Miller with Tammy Grimes and Cyril Ritchard, March 3, 1959, the play had thirty-nine performances.

The story has Feydeau's usual complex but clear events. Philippe, called for a month's duty in the Reserves, asks his friend Marcel to take care of Amélie for him. Marcel must explain the situation to his own mistress, the Countess. And he sends a picture of Amélie to his uncle, who has promised to settle a large sum on him when he marries. Uncle arrives, sees pretty Amélie, and decides to stay for the wedding. Desperately, Marcel plans a pretended wedding, with an actor dressed as the Mayor. Meanwhile, a Russian general tickles Amélie's fancy by informing her that his prince has fallen in love with her, and wants a meeting. There are lively doings, in and out and under beds. To cap the climax, Philippe, returning unexpectedly, finds that Marcel and Amélie have anticipated the mock wedding—we behold them, after a night on the town, awakening in bed together. Philippe cancels the actor, and the real Mayor ties them in a genuine wedding knot.

The play was again a hit at the New York Ziegfeld, in the repertoire of the Renaud-Barrault Company, which skittered through the plot, but gave New York a good sample of the superb style of French farce.

Of the production in English, Robert Coleman in the *New York Mirror* (March 4, 1959) said that Tammy Grimes, a luscious Lulu, "shoots off sparks like a Fourth of July pinwheel." John Chapman in the *News* selected another aspect: "New York hasn't seen anything like Polly Rowles' first-act hat since the opening of Brooklyn Bridge." (It should have been duplicated at the 1983 centennial of the Bridge's opening. But Chapman wrote before "my fair lady"* went to Ascot.) Walter Kerr was less amused: "I suppose there is a law of diminishing returns for eye-filling color, dizzying double-takes and lightning-quick changes of partners as there is for everything else . . . in persistently starting so high, Cyril Ritchard simply may not have reckoned with the distance down."

At the London Haymarket, London saw *Lulu* with Geraldine McEwen, Fenella Fielding, and Kenneth Haig. But French light comedies make demands not all English, and especially not all American, performers are equipped to meet, although the Noel Coward touch gives us a taste of the deft work of the man whom many French critics consider their greatest comic dramatist since Molière.

LE DINDON   *Georges Feydeau*

Le Dindon (1896; literally "the turkey"; figuratively "the dupe") is a riotous bedroom farce, with situations tumbling upon one another, a mad merry mixup of concupiscent and errant couples. Pontagnac follows Lucienne Vatelin home, with amorous intent. Vatelin, reconizing an old friend, invites him and his wife for dinner. He replies that his wife is in a wheelchair, with rheumatism, in Brussels. But the wife herself, Clotilde Pontagnac, cannot resist dropping in to see the friends her husband "visits" almost every day; she is young and healthy. Another friend, Redillon, on the prowl for Lucienne, drops in. Then there's a call from Maggie, with whom Vatelin had an affair in England; he explains that she's a client come to consult him as a lawyer and, seeing her alone, consents to see her that night, as she threatens to kill herself if he does not. Both wives are naturally suspicious; separately they promise Redillon that if their husbands prove unfaithful, they'll come to him: "What's sauce for the goose . . ."

At the hotel that evening, things, if possible, grow more complicated. Redillon is there with his cocotte Armandine; an army doctor is seeking rest with his deaf wife; Maggie's husband arrives; and they all fly around in an hilarious tangle of half-completed rendezvous, with a police inspector confounding the confusion. "Sauce for the goose," says Pontagnac, "but not with another gander." Somehow out of the tangle, the two couples rejoin. The audience is out of breath with laughter.

Among the many French revivals of the play was one by the Comédie Française in 1951, with Robert Hirsch as Redillon, Jacques Charon as Pontagnac. The French were again in London in 1959; at the New York City Center in 1961. London saw it in 1972, translated by Peter Meyer as *Sauce for the Goose*. New York saw it in 1971, as *There's One* [fool] *in Every Marriage*. A 1971 Stratford, Ontario, production also came to New York in 1972. The same year saw another version, *Ruling the Roost,* translated and directed by Richard Cottrell, at the Edinburgh Festival. In an English BBC broadcast of Peter Meyer's translation (August 28, 1972), Maggie from England was changed (who knows why?) to Heidi from Berlin, with the closing moments lightened: Lucienne overhears her husband unhappily tell Redillon that he loves her, and they share a joyful reunion.

Few farces have as many twists and intriguing counterturns, continuously unexpected and continuously amusing, as Feydeau devised for *Le Dindon*.

PASQUIN   *Henry Fielding*

Pasquin: a dramatic Satire on the Times, Being a rehearsal Of Two Plays, viz: A comedy called "The Election"; and a Tragedy called "The Life and Death of Common-Sense" is a further dramatic broadside by Henry Fielding against the shoddy in the theatre and life of his day. *Pasquin* was produced March 6, 1736; in 1737 Robert Walpole's Licensing Act closed the stage to political satire. (In 1749 Fielding became London's first police magistrate, and through the organization of the Bow Street Runners a pioneer in crime detection.)

Pasquin opens with a gathering at theatre of authors and players. Trapwit, author of the comedy, is late, and the tragic dramatist Fustian belittles the play, but when Trapwit arrives sings its praises. Trapwit modestly allows it one merit: "This I will say for it, that except about a dozen, or a score or so, there is not one impure joke in it." Throughout the two rehearsals, the watchers interrupt as they see fit.

The comedy "The Election" sets town against country. Squire Tankard and Sir Harry Foxchase are balanced against the city folk, who by influence and bribery try to sway the vote. Squire Tankard cries: "A man that won't get drunk for his country is a rascal!" Interest and Conscience, we learn, "are words of the same meaning." The Mayor of London, after the votes are counted, announces the reverse of the actual count, putting Lord Place in office instead of Sir Harry Foxchase. Since Colonel Promise marries the Mayor's daughter, all are reconciled. The comedy satirizes not only the constant opposition of city and country, and corruption in politics, but also petticoat rule. Thus, when the Mayor's daughter exclaims: "Would that the man I love best were here, that I might use him like a dog!" Fustian inquires: "Isn't that an odd wish?" and author Trapwit replies: "No, Sir; don't all the young ladies in plays use all the lovers so?"

By the fifth act of "The Election"—the third act of *Pasquin*—the critic Sneerwell has arrived. Fustian, asked to cut the Ghost, replies that he cannot; the Ghost is the main character. Interest in witches has been revived by the recent law against them; he's expecting a similar law against ghosts, and has set several in the play. First to appear is the Ghost of Tragedy, which "has walked all the stages of London several years."

Many satirical slashes occur during the rehearsal. A dancer objects to her secondary role, protesting: "I am sure I show more to the audience than any lady on the stage." Harlequin comes in with oddities to exchange for actors, among them two dogs that walk on their hind legs and impersonate human creatures so well, they might be mistaken for them . . . a human that impersonates a dog so well he might almost be taken for one. The oddities are for the afterpieces, which in those days were eagerly awaited; indeed, many came to the theatre only for the afterpiece. Of the early comers Fielding ironically remarked: "After the audience have been tired with the dull works of Shakespeare, Jonson, Vanbrugh and others, they are to be entertained with these pantomimes."

Although amid fantastic portents Ignorance comes to lord it over slumbering Common-Sense, Sneerwell is pleased to find that Common-Sense gets the better of it at the end. Whereupon Trapwit observes: "Sir, this is almost the only play where she has got the better lately."

Many of the sharp and popular barbs of satire are still pertinent. Fielding has ripened a genre that was continued from *The Rehearsal* to *The Critic*,* and was renewed in *Fanny's First Play** and the current *Accidental Death of an Anarchist*.* Tapering toward the theatre of the absurd, it still persists with laughter against formality and folly.

FILUMENA   *Eduardo de Filippo*

Eduardo de Filippo is the most significant Italian playwright since Pirandello.* His first play performed in English, *Saturday, Sunday, Monday*, opened at the London NT in 1973, directed by Laurence Olivier, with Joan

Plowright (Olivier's second wife, after the death of Vivien Leigh), and won the *Evening Standard* award as the year's best. His greatest play, *Filumena* (Marturano), was written in 1966 for his actress sister Titina; he himself played the husband in Italy. It came to the London Lyric, November 2, 1977, in adaptation by Keith Waterhouse and Willis Hall, directed by Olivier, with Joan Plowright and Colin Blakeley (followed by Frank Finlay in 1979), for 711 performances. It was filmed in 1966, and again, as *Marriage Italian Style,* in 1974.

The play opens with Domenico Soriano in a rage. After having taken Filumena from a brothel and lived with her for twenty-five years, he had been persuaded to marry her "on her death-bed"—whereupon she pops up, perfectly healthy, drives out the young Diana he had taken to replace her, and sits down to enjoy the dinner he had prepared for the girl. In his wrath, Domenico arranges to have the marriage annulled. Then Filumena springs another surprise: she has three grown sons from her early days, and one of them is Domenico's. Intrigued, he demands to know which; she refuses to tell him, for "either they are all equal or they are enemies."

The three young men are presented to him. They are neatly portrayed, with different class loyalties because they were brought up in families of different backgrounds. Domenico warms to them, and when the three of them address him as "father," his growth (as Bernard Levin put it in the *London Sunday Times*) "into the light of real humanity is complete."

In his final words, Domenico acknowledges the full legitimacy by giving her and them his name: "A mother's a mother, and sons are sons, Filumena Soriano." And with the "family reunion," Filumena for the first time sheds some tender tears. "If I had to pick a single moment from any performance presently visible in London to preserve for posterity as an example of what acting is about," said Sheridan Morley in *Punch* (November 16, 1977), "I think it would be that one." Joan Plowright gave a superb performance in a role de Filippo made robustious, tough, tender, tricky, and true.

The play had had an earlier unfortunate production in England: adapted by F. Hugh Herbert as *The Best House in Naples,* it closed after three performances. *Filumena* was less welcome in New York, too. Opening December 5, 1979, with Blanche Yurka, it attained only thirty-three performances. (In Cleveland, opening October 31, 1981, it reached twenty-six.) Howard Kissel in *Women's Wear Daily* said that "on the surface *Filumena* seems to be the Italian equivalent of a boulevard comedy, moving as it does between domestic comedy and farce. What makes it more special is the strong human feeling beneath the often predictable turns of plot."

Filumena was, however, popular all over Europe; in Russia, there were at one time thirty-six companies playing it. It was hailed in London (*The Guardian*) as rich with "the faultless rhythm and serene assurance of a comic classic"—"crying Yes" (Levin) "in a world largely afraid to do anything but mutter No." The *Financial Times* admitted that the story "is far from subtle, but its modulations keep it tense and entertaining, and there is hardly a part that doesn't give an opportunity for display."

The play is set in Naples, which is near Vesuvius; the *Observer* headed its review "Explosions in Naples" and went on: "What we first see is the volcanically quarreling couple, flanked by their respective servants. De Filippo, with the craft of either great cunning or great simplicity, has had it all ways. We are given the measure of Filumena's determination; and the play acquires the flavor of classic comedy while remaining a realistic drama." John Beaufort in the *Christian Science Monitor* remarked that

Domenico's "verbal explosions are no match for Filumena's implacable logic and maternal resolve."

Directed by Franco Zeffirelli, the play moved with Italian fire as what seems a merely local confrontation broadens to universal humanity. At the end (said Levin), "*Urbi et orbi* de Filippo gives his characters, and us, his blessing. The audience burst into cheers at curtain-fall, and I am only surprised that they did not burst into song." *Filumena* is a song to indomitable woman.

CAPTAIN JINKS OF THE HORSE MARINES   *Clyde Fitch*

Though shallow in its characterization and now familiar in its design, the lively and gay *Captain Jinks of the Horse Marines* was in its time one of the most talked of plays in New York. When it opened on February 4, 1901, it gave Ethel Barrymore her first stellar role and Broadway 168 performances of romantic dash and gay delight.

Clyde Fitch, said Alan Dale, "is certainly a wonder . . . The hero and heroine are so unconventional that you never know what they are going to do next . . . *Captain Jinks* is brimming over with fizzing novelties. No men and women who appreciate real genuine human humor—every line funnier than a whole book of 'jokes'—could fail to laugh." The *New York Evening World* called the play "one of the most delightful comedies New York has ever known." With five plays on Broadway at the same time—*Sapho, Lovers' Lane, The Climbers, Barbara Frietchie,* and *Captain Jinks*—Clyde Fitch became the king-pin playwright.

There was more laughter when Edgar Smith's revue *Fiddle-Dee-Dee,* a burlesque of *Captain Jinks,* bounced along, with David Warfield a hilarious Jinks, with Fay Templeton making ludicrous the graceful "Grecian bend" of Ethel Barrymore, with De Wolfe Hopper as the ballet master, and with a bevy of ballet girls played by males.

Ethel Barrymore proved a success in *Captain Jinks* again in 1907, and on the radio in 1936. A musical comedy made from the play, *Captain High Jinks,* opened September 8, 1925, with book by Frank Mandel and Laurence Schwab, lyrics by B. G. De Sylva, and music by Lewis E. Gensler and Stephen Jones. It ran for 167 performances, but moved slowly, lacking both the pace and the punch of the play. Ethel's niece, Diana Barrymore, was in a revival of the play, in 1941, at White Plains, New York, along with Gregory Peck, José Ruben, Philip Bourneuf, and Winston O'Keefe. *Captain Jinks* was seen again in New York in 1946 (OffBway) and 1948 (Fordham University). It is a bit dated, but amusingly quaint, and romantically charming.

The title came from a song (words by William H. Lingard, music by T. Maclagan) which Lingard brought from London to the Theatre Comique in New York, in 1868: "I'm Captain Jinks of the Horse Marines, I feed my horse on pork and beans, And often live beyond my means: I'm a Captain in the Army." The nonsense song made a sensational success, was used as the title of Fitch's play, and was sung in the 1931-1941 revivals of *The Streets of New York.** Lingard, incidentally, was the first of the long line of popular female impersonators.

The play begins on a New York dock, where newspapermen and others wait to greet the great singer Madame Trentoni, an American girl named after her native city, Trenton, who has won fame abroad. Among those waiting are the Purity Ladies, who have come to beg her not to sing in the "immodest" opera *La Traviata,* and Captain Jinks. The latter has wagered with his comrades that he can win the actress; if he succeeds, they all will live on what she earns for him. The inevitable happens: the officer and the lady fall in love; she learns of the wager and is brokenhearted. Not even her manager and ballet master, "Papa" Belliari, can persuade her to sing—until out of her wretchedness she cries "I'll sing to every woman's heart in that house." Then the genuineness of Captain Jinks' love reawakens her to joy.

Variations of this theme have scuffed its novelty, but there is undeniable deftness and lightness in Fitch's handling. The plea of the Purity Ladies is a slantwise attack upon the reception of his own play *Sapho* (from the story and play of Alphonse Daudet), the star of which, Olga Nethersole, went to jail. Belliari is a richly comic creation. The intertwining of the fuss and fret of theatrical preparations, the confused rehearsal of the ballet, with the officers' interest in their wager and Jinks' predicament in regard to Madame Trentoni, help make *Captain Jinks of the Horse Marines* a capitally amusing play.

The play was set to music by Jack Beeson, libretto by Sheldon Harnick, 1975, in Kansas City. A version with music by twenty composers from Stephen Foster to Verdi was presented OffBway (Cheryl Crawford Theatre) in 1981.

THE TWO NOBLE KINSMEN   *John Fletcher*

Best known for his dozen or more collaborations with Francis Beaumont,* John Fletcher (English, 1579-1625) also wrote some sixteen plays alone. He may have worked with Shakespeare on *Henry VIII* and Shakespeare may have had a finger in the making of *The Two Noble Kinsmen* (printed in 1634), Fletcher's best play.

The story of *The Two Noble Kinsmen* was told by Boccaccio in his *Teseide* and is *The Knight's Tale* of Chaucer's *Canterbury Tales.* The noble kinsmen are Palamon and Arcite, prisoners of Theseus, king of Athens. Theseus is married to Hippolyta, queen of the Amazons—their nuptials are celebrated in the opening scene of *The Two Noble Kinsmen,* and also in Shakespeare's *A Midsummer Night's Dream* *—and Palamon and Arcite love Hippolyta's sister Emilia. They compete for her in a tournament; Arcite wins, but shortly after is thrown from his horse and, dying, bids Palamon and Emilia wed.

To this tale, Fletcher added some episodes that enrich it with pathos. The imprisoned Palamon is freed by the gaoler's daughter who loves him and, when he spurns her, goes mad. The lover she has disregarded follows her faithfully, and his description of her is as touching as that of the mad Ophelia in *Hamlet.* * Indeed, said Kenneth Tynan in *He That Plays the King* (1950), "her mad scenes are exquisite, and better written, I think, than Ophelia's."

The authorship of *The Two Noble Kinsmen* has stirred more controversy than that of any other Elizabethan play. A drama about Palamon and Arcite mentioned in accounts of Queen Elizabeth's entertainment at Oxford in 1566 is ascribed to "Master Edwards of the Queen's Chapel." In the diary of theatre manager Philip Henslowe mention is made of a new play on the subject as of 1594. Critics are now generally agreed that the play was written by two writers of quite different style and temperament. The weaker portions, assigned to Fletcher, are marked by a large proportion of double (feminine) endings and a small proportion of run-on lines. The parts not by Fletcher are probably Act I, Scene 1 (except lines 1-40); most of Scenes, 2, 3, and 4; Act II, Scene 1; III, 1 and 2; most of IV, 3; V, 1 (except lines 1-19), part of 3, and 4 (except lines 99-113). These portions are very close in style to *The Winter's Tale,* * *The Tempest,* * and *Henry VIII,* * and give basis to the suggestion that Shakespeare lent a hand. However, the characterization—especially of the rather coarse heroine, Emilia—is less Shakespearean than the style.

Whosever the hand that penned them, the non-Fletcher parts of *The Two Noble Kinsmen,* as C. F. Tucker Brooke pointed out in *The Shakespearean Aprocrypha* (1908), contain "some of the most brilliant of Jacobean poetry." The play is easily the best of the few in the shaping of which Shakespeare may have had a minor share.

The Two Noble Kinsmen has had recent revivals on both sides of the Atlantic: 1955 at the Edinburgh Festival; 1956 at the Antioch, Ohio, Shakespeare Festival; 1959, Stratford-upon-Avon; 1973, York; 1974, in the open air at London Regents Park; 1982, by the Jean Cocteau Rep. Co., OffBway.

ACCIDENTAL DEATH OF AN ANARCHIST   *Dario Fo*

The Italian Communist Dario Fo (b. 1926) had three plays running in London in 1981. At the Criterion, for over a year, was *Can't Pay? Won't Pay!* a farce about women ravishing a shopping center—sidetracked by the tediously repeated maneuvers of a woman hiding a pack of groceries under her coat and pretending to be pregnant. (This was also shown at the New York Chelsea BAM in 1981.) *One-Woman Plays* (written with his wife, Franca Rame), at the NT (Lyttleton), has four one-act absurdist sketches of feminine subjugation, all the women played by Yvonne Bryceland. This was shown again at the NT (Cottesloe) in 1983. And, at the Wyndham, opening March 5, 1980, for 622 performances, *Accidental Death of an Anarchist.*

Based partly on a book, *The State Massacre,* 1970, *Accidental Death* focuses on the actual falling of Giuseppi Pinelli, pacifist though anarchist railway worker, from a third-story interrogation room while being questioned by the police in 1969, after a bank bombing in Milan. The police declared that Pinelli jumped, the window being "open" on a bleak December day. The bruise on his neck, court "experts" stated, was caused while the corpse was lying in the morgue. The coroner's verdict was not suicide, but "accidental death."

The play has been more successful than most radical dramas, such as the American Group Theatre's *Waiting For Lefty,* because Dario Fo recognized that the serious presentation of a particular point of view soon becomes boring to all but those already committed; he therefore wrote a farce, full of amusing situations, sparked with jokes by characters in obviously artificial facial makeup, with the point of the play slyly insinuated amidst the lively and amusing slapstick.

The play begins with a man in the Milan interrogation room, charged with impersonation. He admits six such disguises, and blandly presents documents showing he's been in various insane asylums. Dismissed, he sneaks back into the inspector's now empty room, puts on another disguise, and when the police return announces himself as an official from Rome, sent to investigate the case of Pinelli and Calabresi, the officer in charge of the investigation when Pinelli "fell." The remainder of the play, in absurd fashion, reveals the equal absurdity of the conflicting police explanations of Pinelli's death. In the Italian production, Fo played the "maniac."

The zany action, with frequent words directly to the audience, varied as the play ran and ranged. In the deft London version by actor-director Gavin Richards, we heard the story of three boastful men from three lands:

> American: We had an arm transplant, and in two weeks the person was looking for a job.

> Russian: That's nothing! We had a leg transplant, and in *one* week the person was looking for a job.

> Englishman: That's nothing! We had a whole person transplant— from Fleet Street to 10 Downing Street [journalist to Prime Minister]. And in no time at all, a million persons were looking for a job.

Toward the end of the play, a woman journalist comes on, asking questions that press home the play's basic point. Militant leaders are mentioned including "Rugged Ronnie Reagan"; she turns to the audience and exclaims: "Reagan! When this play was written, Reagan wasn't even heard of!"

As Irving Wardle noted in the *London Times,* March 6, 1980, "The masquerade is pushed to the point of lunacy to make the point that no false nose or fright wig can ever rival the limitless mendacity of the police."

The play was first produced by Dario Fo and his wife, with their newly formed Collectivo Teatrale La Commune. Its success may be partly explained by a program note for the London production: "Italy is the home of the Mafia, the Pope, the largest Communist Party in the capitalist world, of widespread corruption and never-ending scandal and of over 30 governments since the War. It has an impoverished peasantry, the world's largest backstreet abortion industry, and an almost unsurpassed record of political murders and assassinations ... an era of social, political and economic crisis that is still unresolved." Recent political kidnappings show that such conditions are reaching international scope.

At the close of the play, two policemen are handcuffed to the fatal window, to await the imminent explosion of a bomb. The "maniac" questioner leaves, tossing the handcuff key to the radical journalist. Shall she release them? If so, will they not leave her handcuffed there instead, the witness and soon reporter of their lies? She takes the chance—and they chain her there. The curtain falls before the bomb explodes. Her fate, said Catherine Itzin in the *Herald Tribune,* is "a consummate summing-up of present-day political dilemmas." Is violence to be forever countered with violence?

On its Italian tour, the play was refused the use of the Bologna Duse Theatre, seating 1,500; instead, it opened at the Palazetto dello Sport, to a sell-out audience of 6,000. It has been played widely in northern Europe; in Belgium the International New Scene collective has for five years shown only plays by Fo. Invited in 1980 to perform in New York at its first Festival of Italian Theatre, Fo and his wife were denied visas.

Accidental Death of an Anarchist is a lively illustration of the thought that laughter is a more potent weapon than anger. As the shrewd Voltaire used to pray: "Lord, make my enemies ridiculous."

When the play was filmed on British TV, September 15, 1983, there were more obvious comic effects, more disguisings; thus, when the journalist came, the "inspector" had turned into a one-legged veteran, with medals and crutch. There was also an audience, with whom the actors mingled, sharing drinks. Two endings were supplied. First, the bomb exploded, killing the four officials, destroying the office. Then the film ran backward through the catastrophe, until we again saw the four men manacled, waiting. And the journalist ran over and freed them. This satisfied the spectators, who cheered; but sacrificed the irony of the journalist's doom. On TV, Fo was no longer a potent foe.

'TIS PITY SHE'S A WHORE   *John Ford*

The greatest tragedy of the prolific John Ford (English, 1586-1640?), *'Tis Pity She's a Whore,* is a sombre story of incest, of the deep love between Giovanni and his sister Annabella. The latter, with child, marries Soranzo, but her husband learns their secret. Anticipating punishment, Giovanni kills Annabella, then slays Soranzo, and is slain.

On the picture of this doomed love, Ford lavished all his skills. As Havelock Ellis has said, "he concentrates the revelation of a soul's agony into a sob or a sigh."

The women of Ford's plays, especially Annabella, are probed more tenderly yet more deeply than those of his contemporaries. He writes of women, observes Havelock Ellis, "not as a dramatist nor as a lover but as one who had searched intimately and felt with instinctive sympathy the fibres of their hearts." Ford was not content with the gay or the majestic surface; he sought the soul.

'Tis Pity She's a Whore still finds occasional presentation. Maeterlinck's French translation, *Annabella,* was acted in Paris in 1894. New York saw the play in 1925-1926 and 1935; London had a revival in 1934; Hartford, Connecticut, viewed it in 1943. The 1926 production was advertised as *'Tis Pity.* The full title, the *New York Times* (January 24, 1926) explained, was "too stout by far for our delicate ears." The *Times* added: "Yielding all the connotations of this abnormality to the sweep of inevitable tragedy instinct in the theme, Ford composed a great work, shrouded in black like the paid murderers who cross the stage three times." W. A. Darlington, in the *London Daily Telegraph* (December 31, 1934) called *'Tis Pity She's a Whore* "work of a supremely dramatic imagination and a mind typically of the Renaissance. John Ford's ability to pile horror on horror's head was something better than the luridness of the author of a 'penny blood.'" The passion and the penetration, the temerity of the theme, and the tenderness of the treatment, make *'Tis Pity She's a Whore* a truly majestic achievement, a sombre searching of entangled and blasted souls.

The play has won more frequent attention. Among productions in Britain: Leeds, 1956. London (Mermaid), adapted by Bernard Miles, opening May 29, 1961, for fifty-four performances; Kenneth Tynan observed: "Shakespeare's people, to misquote *Measure For Measure,* are 'absolute for life' and when they die, we grieve; Ford's, on the other hand, are ripe only for death."

Edinburgh, March 1974, to Wimbledon, London, with Ian McKellen an "intensely adolescent Giovanni." In 1977, Stratford-upon-Avon; the poetry and the basic dignity of the characters mellowed the excess.

In America: Opening at the OffBway Orpheum, December 6, 1958, moving to the Macdougal Street for a run of nine months, came what Brooks Atkinson called "a progressively absorbing piece of theatre"; "brought vividly to life," added the *Post,* "by director Eugene Van Grona." Van Grona also wrote a modern version. *The Whore of Parma,* using pistols instead of stilettos, which alternated with the Ford.

Also 1960, Toronto. Yale, 1967, the Renaissance lust and fury in modern guise, with striptease dancing at the wedding party. OffOffBway, 1971, also 1978 (Walden Theatre).

To Paris, 1961, came *Dommage qu'elle soit une putaine.* And in 1975 (Théatre d'Ivry) the American director Stuart Seide tried to sustain the atmosphere with extracts from Shakespeare, Donne, and Webster in a simplified version of Ford. The *London Times* (June 28, 1975) reported that it gave the play "a Racinian austerity and clarity, and yet retains the rhythm and the earthy, vivid feel of the original." Center stage stood a banqueting table, with a bed and a throne at either end—the three regions of earthly pleasure—which turn into cemeteries, symbolizing not only Ford's tragedy but the coursing of our lives as well.

BIEDERMANN AND THE INCENDIARIES   *Max Frisch*

Also translated (with or without *Biedermann*) as *The Fireraisers, The Arsonists, The Firebugs,* this play by the Swiss Max Frisch (b. 1911) was first presented in German in Zurich, 1958.The author called it, borrowing the epic theatre term *Lehrstück,* "a learn-piece without learners."

A 1948 prose sketch, a 1953 radio play, became the six scenes and epilogue through which we watch the innocence of liberal-minded Gottlieb Biedermann. The set shows simultaneously his living room and his attic. In the dark, Biedermann strikes a match, saying, "You can't even light a cigar these days without thinking of fire." But fire is the last thing that comes to his mind when he shelters in his attic the "harmless peddler" Josef Schmitz, and then Josef's friend Willie Eisenring, a waiter from a burned-down hotel. Police come to report the suicide of an employee of Biedermann's hair-tonic firm, whom Biedermann had dismissed when he asked for a share of the profits from his invention. When the police wonder what the two guests are hauling upstairs, Biedermann tells them it must be his hair tonic; we know it's kegs of gasoline. Then, as Charles Marowitz reported from London in New York's *Village Voice* (February 1, 1962): "On the evening designated for the razing of Biedermann's home, the host invites his attic-boarders to a dinner party—carefully removing all his middle-class accoutrements so as not to offend their lower-class sensibilities. In a taut, menacing coda the firebugs consume their food, terrorize the family and, before they leave to ignite the inevitable blaze, request matches of their host. 'But surely if they had been fireraisers, they'd have had their own matches!' is Biedermann's final, paralyzed rationalization before the explosion that guts his house." The city is destroyed. One of the firebugs had remarked: "The third best camouflage is joking, the second best is sentimentality. But the best of all, and the most certain to prevail, is the plain and unadorned truth. Funnily enough, nobody believes it."

The Epilogue tosses out a feather of hope. It is set in Hell, with Eisenring as Satan; Schmitz, Beelzebub. Gottlieb and Babette Biedermann defend themselves and ask for reparations. Organ music sounds as the city is being rebuilt. Babette asks: "Do you think we are saved?" Biedermann answers: "It looks like it." But they are still in Hell as the curtain falls.

It is interesting to note the various ways in which the "lesson" has been interpreted. The *London Plays and Players,* February 1962, said the play "satirizes the growth of Nazism in pre-war Germany," the middle class, especially the misled liberals, forming the flock that blindly followed the hero-ram Hitler. Marowitz spread the application, calling the play "an indictment against the preposterous pseudo-morality of both East and West. The play sears us by declaring that we all live cosily with the knowledge of that grandiose sin which is the Bomb. In passing, it singes a dozen other hypocrisies which have become as familiar to us as any household item . . . that whole complex of known malevolence which exists as subject matter for liberal editorials and intellectual self-righteousness and little else."

Harold Hobson in the *Sunday Times,* December 24, 1961, looked beyond: Frisch "finishes believing that propaganda is what he has given us. In reality, apparently without knowing it, he has written something much finer, deeper, richer and more disturbing, whose values are rendered with an intensity and an assurance which pass with absolute ease from the amusing to the poetic macabre and the terrifying." Then he assigns the lesson geographically: "Who are the fireraisers? "If this piece is played in Moscow, the answer is Kennedy: if in New York, Khrushchev."

Jacques Cartier directed a Mordecai Gorelik adaptation with the Hartford Stage Company, which came to the OffBway Martinique July 1, 1968, with acrobatic clowns as firemen. He called the host George Upright and the two arsonists Sepp Smith and Willy Lee Irons, and converted the conflict into a color-conflagration, for the two were played by Richard Ward and Billy Dee Williams, Blacks, and Cartier explained: "Upright is an unscrupulous businessman who has been exploiting Blacks. Thus, the play is about the chickens coming home to roost." (Gorelik had in 1959 directed several scenes of the play, sponsored by Elia Kazan and Cheryl Crawford, at the Actors Studio, with Zero Mostel as Biedermann.)

There is a chorus of firemen, usually with clown makeup under their fire hats, symbolizing the people who always come too late, when the damage is done. In some productions, they began amidst the audience, offering surrealistic "tips" on fire prevention.

The play has had many productions. By 1962 there were seventy-five in German; the play had been shown in Poland, Hungary, Czechoslovakia, Israel (the Habima, 1959), Finland, Sweden, Spain. Paris saw *Les Incendriaires* at the Lutèce, October 29, 1960, and again, by the Théâtre National Populaire, February 24, 1976.

In England, as *The Fire-Raisers,* it opened at the London Royal Court, December 21, 1961, and again in 1962, in translation by Michael Bullock: "frightening to us as human beings, and sometimes extremely amusing," said *Punch,* January 3, 1962. At the Bristol Old Vic, December 4, 1962; at the Victoria, Stoke-on-Trent, April 18, 1972. In the United States, among others: at St. Marks OffBway, April 1962; at the OffBway Maidman, February 4, 1963, directed by Gene Frankel, with Boris Tumarin as Biedermann. In Seattle, November 20, 1965; Louisville, Kentucky, December 7, 1967; Washington, D.C., fall 1968; by policemen at the John Jay College of Criminal Justice (New York), as *The Firebugs,* May 9, 1969; at the OffOffBway Yankee Repertory, May 22, 1981.

In its apparently foolish fashion, the play points a warning still needed, and probably still unheeded, in the world today, of people inviting their own destruction.

THE LADY'S NOT FOR BURNING   *Christopher Fry*

The best writer of English dramatic verse today, Christopher Fry (b. 1907), blossomed suddenly, with five of his plays produced in London in two seasons. *The Lady's Not for Burning* is a story of witchery and love in the year 1400. Jennet Jourdemayne, hunted as a witch, seeks refuge in the home of Hebble Tyson, Mayor of the English market town of Cool Clary. A discharged soldier, a sardonic misanthrope, Thomas Mendip, tries to divert the charge from her by claiming to have murdered the man she is accused of having turned into a dog. All refuse to believe him, while taking her guilt for granted—until the tipsy return of the supposed victim clears the girl. Then she and Thomas go off together. Moral: love at least helps us to tolerate the unendurable.

Upon this slight story, Fry has woven a pattern of observation and reflection, spangled with bright imagery. His figures form an exciting blend of familiar objects and new attitudes; he reawakens the eye to the fresh strangeness of the world.

Fry wrote *The Lady's Not for Burning* as resident playwright of the London Art Theatre, which produced it on March 11, 1948. On May 11, 1949, it opened at the London Globe, with John Gielgud and Pamela Brown, for 294 performances. The same players brought it to New York, opening November 8, 1950, for 151 performances and the Critics' Circle Award.

Praise for the play was almost unanimous. Harold Hobson, writing in the *Christian Science Monitor* of June 4, 1949, found it too continuously brilliant: "It dazzles too consistently. It is like the long, hot sun of the tropics, which makes one throb for a little shade . . . With his belts of Orion, his astrolabes, and his metaphors from Archimedes, his familiarity with the obscurest saints, his knowledge of all learning, and his restless penetrating wit he astounds and a little wearies. If only now and again he were somewhat dull, how much more entertaining he would be! . . . Yet entertaining he certainly is."

As in all of Fry's plays, there is a sense that the riches of language are being renewed. New figures are minted from nature's ore: "When the landscape goes to seed, the wind is obsessed by tomorrow." Beyond the felicity of phrasing and penetrant wit and incisive widsom of *The Lady's Not for Burning,* there is the high lilt of romance, of the joyous spirit that accepts life as a challenge worth the taking. In this play, man walks with smiling, slightly self-mocking hopefulness toward the dawn.

Four of Fry's plays are linked with the seasons: *The Lady's Not for Burning,* spring; *A Yard of Sun,* summer; *Venus Observed,** autumn; *The Dark Is Light Enough,* winter.

The author was born as Harris; Fry is the name of his maternal grandmother.

Recent productions of *The Lady's Not for Burning* include: 1954, Ontario: 1955, New Zealand; 1957, New York Carnegie Hall Playhouse; 1962, Toronto; Boston, forty performances in 1962, there again 1964; 1964, Asolo; 1967, the first year of CSC; 1972, Chichester Festival, stressing an underlying vein of bitterness; 1974, Montclair, N.J.

On Fry's seventieth birthday, Eileen Atkins and Derek Jacobi opened in the main roles at the London Old Vic. Robert Cushman in the *Observer* (July 9, 1978) was a dissenting voice: "Poetry concentrates, but Fry's voice merely decorates . . . 'I love you,' says Thomas the soldier, 'but the world's not changed.' A finely balanced conclusion which fails to resonate because 'the world' has been kept firmly offstage." Francis King in the *Telegraph* (July 9) makes us still aware that Fry is "plainly someone who views existence as a constant source of mystery and wonder." That should gleam also, for "the world."

VENUS OBSERVED   *Christopher Fry*

The success of *The Lady's Not for Burning** led Laurence Olivier to commission Fry to write a play for the NT; he gave them *Venus Observed,* three acts of blank verse and lively wordplay, set in an English castle in the 1940s. Venus, of course, is both the goddess of love and the planet. The play was produced in London in 1949, with Olivier directing and playing the Duke, John Merivale as his son Edgar, Heather Stannard as Perpetua. It came to the New York Century with Rex Harrison and Lilli Palmer, opening February 13, 1952, for eight-six performances and the Critics' Circle Award. Of a 1957 production in Boston, Eliot Norton praised its "wit and wisdom and . . . rare kind of penetration."

The initial impulse in the play, though in wholly different social ambience and with wholly different treatment, may be seen in *The Farmer's Wife.** The Duke of Altair, as the years keep coming on, decides to marry one of his former mistresses, all of whom he invites. He gives his grown son, Edgar, an apple to bestow upon the chosen woman. But in the castle observatory, watching an eclipse of the sun by the planet Venus, the Duke offers the apple to his estate agent's daughter Perpetua, upon whom the reappearing sun shines. She shoots the apple from his hand; but she's ready to marry him to shield her father, who has been robbing the Duke for years. When the Duke tells her he has known this all along, Perpetua reveals her love for Edgar.

But the castle is on fire. They are rescued. One of the invited women, Rosabel, confesses that she has set the fire, out of jealousy. Perpetua goes off with Edgar. The Duke says he'll marry Rosabel in six months, when she is "disengaged from custody." He and his dishonest agent sit outside the castle, silent in "a unison of ageing."

The play glistens with Fry's love of language, as Rosabel's arson wins her the parson. Tempting Perpetua to a night of sin, the Duke invites her: "Let's be as mute as we are mutable." Rhyming slang slips in, Cockney style, with the rhyming word omitted: "Here's your tit-fer" (tat-hat); "Take a butcher's" (hook-look). When the Duke tells Perpetua that she "must try to use longer sentences," she responds with the longest sentence about a sentence in the English language; 295 words of continuous blank verse. The Duke's agent, wanting to curse, gives a figurative twist to a rare term: "God give me a few lithontriphical words!" (The nearest the many-volumed *Oxford English Dictionary* comes to this is *lithontriptic:* able to break up stones—in the bladder.)

Richard Watts, Jr., in the *New York Post* (February 14, 1952) said that the comedy displays "the witty, graceful, perverse, and enigmatic muse of Christopher Fry in its most uninhibited form." Brooks Atkinson in the *Times* sensed a serious note under the frivolity; he called *Venus Observed* "a poetic play about lonely people reaching out for love, understanding, or solace." Walter Kerr, in the *Herald Tribune,* was less captivated; he said the play is "fragile as glass and, like glass, shatters in the handling." It remains teasing theatrical fare, and a delight to all word fanciers.

THE BLOOD KNOT   *Athol Fugard*

The first of the searing plays of the white South African activist Athol Fugard (b. 1932) to reach London and New York was *The Blood Knot.* When it was shown in Johannesburg, the actors were briefly arrested. The play came to the London New Arts, February 21, 1963, with Ian Brennan as Morris Pieterson, Zakes Mokae as his half brother Zachariah. It played again in London, September 8, 1964, with Allan Miller as Morris, Douglas Turner as Zachariah. John Berry, who had directed the London premiere, also directed the OffBway production, opening March 2, 1964, and running for 240 performances. Fugard stepped in to play Morrie at the hundredth performance, May 30. He had acted Morrie in South Africa, with Zakes Mokae as Zachariah.

The play presents the two illegitimate sons of an ignorant black mother: Morrie, son of a white father; Zachariah, of a black. Morrie, who has passed as white, with a job as guard, part of whose duty it was to bar non-whites from the premises, has returned from the industrial town of Port Elizabeth to the hovel of his brother. Troubled by guilt feelings, he tries to teach the illiterate Zachariah, who grows restless, but brightens when Morrie arranges a pen pal for him. When she writes that she is coming to meet him, Zachariah in a panic buys "white" clothes for his brother. Then she gets engaged and cancels the visit. Morrie dons the "white" clothes and they begin to play racial roles, developing fantasies until (as Norman Nadel reported in the *World-Telegram*, February 3, 1964) "there is a terrifying and bleak beauty to the way they imagine themselves in the loathsome and violent passions of white and Negro at their worst."

There is a suggestion of an antagonism that began with Cain and Abel, as the one is anguished at his inability to better himself and jealous of the more successful brother, while the other is ashamed of the deception to which he lent himself to improve his lot, and therefore tangled in self-hatred and hatred of those to whom he had catered. Richard Watts, Jr., in the *Post* called the play "at once violent and subtle, bitter and impassionate, humorous and tormented, with a compelling power not easily forgotten."

In New York, J. D. Cannon played Morrie, James Earl Jones, Zachariah. The play has had numerous productions, including: Washington, D.C. (with Jones), and Hollywood, 1965; Arena Stage, Washington, and Queens College, New York, 1968; New Haven, 1971; Hartford, 1976; Atlanta and Pittsburgh, 1978; the Roundabout, New York, 1980, with Zakes Mokae. A 1977 London revival stressed the humor; but the play survives as a fierce yet compassionate picture of racial strains and the strong emotions that pour through them.

A LESSON FROM ALOES   *Athol Fugard*

Fugard continued active in the theatre, with premieres in Johannesburg, followed by productions in Britain and New York. *People Are Living There* was shown in Glasgow in 1968, in London in 1971. *Hello and Goodbye* opened OffBway, September 18, 1969, with Martin Sheen and Colleen Dewhurst, for 45 performances; London saw it in 1972. *Boesman and Lena* opened OffBway, June 22, 1970, ran for 205 performances, and was printed in Guernsey's *Ten Best Plays of 1970-71*. In the latter year, it played in London.

The most autobiographical of Fugard's plays, with characters drawn from his experience, is *A Lesson from Aloes*, which troubled him so that it took nineteen years to find shape; there were two earlier aborted efforts, *The Informer* and *A Man Without Scenery*. The play is set in a sun-baked yard in Port Elizabeth, where the author had his home. And there—historically—in 1958, when eight activists were meeting to discuss protests against apartheid, police broke in and arrested the black man who'd been banned from meetings. Obviously, there had been an informer, and naturally Fugard, being white, was suspected. On the other hand, he was under government surveillance. He was expelled from North Rhodesia for being at a bar with two black women—actresses in a play he was directing. His passport was withheld for three years. Recently, he has been in the United States, working with the Yale Repertory Company, with Lloyd Richards, Artistic Director.

In *A Lesson from Aloes,* set in Port Elizabeth in 1961, white Piet Beguidenhout and his wife, Gladys, are fussing about, preparing the table for the coming of Steve Daniels and perhaps his family. (They do not know how many to prepare for, but unfortunately their suspense is not shared by the audience, as the program shows only one more name, that of Steve.) But we learn that Piet and Gladys were white activists, broken by government harassment. Gladys has had hospital treatment with electric shock, and is on the brink of another breakdown. Piet, who had been a bus driver, is now devoting himself to the growth and study of a plant species, the aloe. Aloes, from which a bitter drug is extracted, have "an inordinate capacity for survival in the harshest of possible environments." They are, of course, a symbol here; Gladys asks: "Is this the cost of survival in this country— thorns and bitterness?"

In the second act, black Steve arrives, released after two years in prison. They share friendly memories; but Steve asks Piet whether he had been the informer. Piet is so astounded, and hurt, by the question that he gives no forthright denial. Gladys, approaching another breakdown—the police had taken her diaries; she bought a new diary, but it is blank—says to Steve: "They burnt my brain as black as yours."

Steve is preparing to leave for a new life in London. He tears up his beloved father's photograph, to destroy his past; but he repeats his father's words: "Only ourselves to blame." He accepts the ideal of individual responsibility—but they have all abandoned hope for any change at home.

In the London NT (Cottesloe) production, July 1980, Shelagh Holliday played Gladys; Bill Curry, Steve. In the United States the play was put on by the Yale Repertory in New Haven, March 28, 1980, directed by the author; this came to the New York Playhouse, November 17, 1980, with James Earl Jones—replaced January 17, 1981, by Zakes Mokae—as Steve; Maria Tucci, Gladys; Harris Yulin, Piet. The play ran for ninety-six performances, and won the New York Drama Critics' Circle award.

From New Haven Mel Gussow reported in the *New York Times* (April 1, 1980): "Just as the wife had been subjected to a kind of emotional rape by Government agents, in prison Steve had been unmanned by an insidious mockery . . . In common with his central character, the author has achieved a kind of heroic status—in his work and in his life. With his own aloelike stubbornness and his profound sense of morality, he offers a lesson to his audience."

The play was shown at the Mark Taper Forum, Los Angeles, from August 9 to September 4, 1981, with Peter Donat and Roberta Maxwell as Piet and Gladys, Louis Gosset, Jr., as Steve. It played in Atlanta, Georgia, opening October 29, 1981; at the Washington Arena stage, November 6 to December 20, 1981, with Stanley Anderson and Halo Wines as Piet and Gladys, Zakes Mokae as Steve. Called by Mel Gussow "a masterwork of soaring magnitude," *A Lesson from Aloes* is a searching study of persons beaten and broken by the forces of intolerance in the world.

"MASTER HAROLD" ... AND THE BOYS   *Athol Fugard*

Fugard's most piercing picture of black and white racial antagonism is *"Master Harold" ... and the boys.* Set in the St. Georges Park Tea Room on a wet and windy afternoon in 1950, at Port Elizabeth, South Africa, it moves without intermission from a merry opening to its blasting climax.

When the curtain rises young Willie and the older Sam, black employees, are preparing to close the tearoom for the day. Willie interrupts his scrubbing the floor to take some rather stiff dance steps, as Sam coaches him to greater ease, in preparation for the coming dance contest. Hally, the son of the white owners, comes in. A student in his late teens, he has grown under Sam's watchful and helpful guidance; they are at ease together. And Hally tries to help Sam, who still has difficulty reading the longer words. Together they try to name some of the world's great men. Willie and Sam try a fox-trot; Hally asks: "What happens at the contest if two couples collide?" They say that's impossible; then they drift into the dream of a world without collisions; if only class and class did not bump into one another; if only rich and poor, black and white, country and country, did not bump into one another! They sigh for the hopeless dream.

Then, as Willie listens, their talk drifts to happy memories—best of them, the time when Sam was making a kite for Hally; and Hally recalls his fears that it will not work and he'll be laughed at—and his triumph and joy when it soars.

But Hally is not happy. He is resentful of his parents, his mother's kowtowing to her husband's will, and his crippled father's ignorant, intolerant proud ways, darkened by his frequent spells of drunken bullying. His father is now in the hospital, recovering from such a bout. Hally's bitterest memory is of the time when he was called to a hotel bar where his father was lying dead drunk, and he had to walk home with his father on Sam's shoulders, Hally's head bowed in bitter shame as the whole town watched him walking behind a black man and a helpless father.

And now, over phone, Hally hears that his father is again blustering against his mother. He has decided to go home from the hospital, home, where he is boss. Frantically Hally bids his mother not to let him leave the hospital. When she says she can't stop him, Hally cries: "I'm warning you, when the two of you start fighting again, I'm leaving home!"

His shame and bitterness flare in anger, which, as he cannot turn it against his father, he spills upon the nearest person, Sam. And there bursts out the racial prejudice in which Hally, living in the white world of the town, has been steeped. The confused and angry boy, no longer a pal, but to these Blacks now the white "Master Harold," flings at the dumbfounded Blacks his father's favorite joke, a vicious and ugly wordplay, twisting two meanings of the word *fair*: just, and light-colored:

> *'Taint fair!*
> *What aint fair?*
> *A nigger's ass.*

And Sam is jolted into an equally ugly response. He pulls down his clothes, exposes himself, and cries: "See! It aint fair."

He stands over the still confused Harold, who looks up—and spits in Sam's face.

A moment's silence. Willie steps forward, enraged. Both men are bigger than the slim white Harold. But Sam checks Willie, taking control of the situation and of himself. In quiet though troubled dignity he reminds Harold of his devotion; it was after he had carried the drunken father home that he had made the kite, for he wanted the boy to look up to brighter thoughts and more rewarding days, to the open sky of friendship, clear of the clouds of prejudice, forerunners of the storms of oppression and mutual hate. And in his quiet talk Sam regathers his self-respect. Hally, in silence, but slowly and shaken, miserable but perhaps tangled in remorse, goes out the door. Willie and Sam silently finish readying the room for the morrow. Then Willie exclaims, "I'll walk home!" and puts his last coin into the jukebox. They try a few dance steps for the coming contest, then close the room.

The insulting racial joke and its violent consequence may seem bald and ugly in the telling, but as enacted (especially in the raging complex of emotions in Ronnie Price as Harold and the tremendous fight for self-control of James Earl Jones as Sam, with Danny Glover horrified and roused in counter-hate as Willie), it is a searing scene that scorches the beholders. Frank Rich (*New York Times,* March 17, 1982) wrote of its reception: "While some theatergoers struggle to stand and cheer, others cringe in their seats, their heads in their hands, so devastated that they can't even look at the stage . . . The author has journeyed so deep into the psychosis of racism that all national boundaries quickly fall away, and no one is left unimplicated by his vision."

This was at the world premiere of the play, directed by the author, at the Yale Repertory Theatre, March 16, 1982, the first of Fugard to have its premiere outside of South Africa. The Yale production came to the New York Lyceum, May 2, 1982, for 345 performances, after which it left for a national tour, starting in Boston, March 5, 1983.

Jack Kroll in *Newsweek* compared Fugard to O'Neill, "whom he has always resembled in the savage tenderness of his emotional honesty." John Simon in *New York* analyzed: "He avoids the spectacular horrors and concentrates instead on the subtle corrosion and corruption, on the crumbling of the spirit for which the cure would be heroic action that may not be forthcoming, and which the blacks try to assuage with the salve of dreams, the whites with the cautery of oppression." I know of no more powerful picture, in personal terms, of the foul degradation and conflagration of racial hatred than *"Master Harold"* . . . *and the boys.* Athol Fugard was given an honorary degree at Yale University in 1983. President Giamatti stated that his plays illuminate "our common capacity for inhumanity."

JUSTICE   *John Galsworthy*

The greatest play of John Galsworthy (1867-1933), *Justice,* came upon the British in 1910 with such a severe indictment of the penal system, and effected such an arousal of public indignation, that the nation's prison administration was reformed. *Justice* is indeed a powerful play. Its scene of solitary confinement, without a spoken word, is one of the most harrowing in the modern drama. After beholding this scene, Winston Churchill, then Home Secretary, reduced the allowable period of solitary confinement in English prisons from nine months to four weeks.

The play tells the story of William Falder, a law clerk who, to help the woman he loves break from her cruel husband, commits forgery, is found guilty, and is sentenced to three years in jail. Upon parole, his past haunts him, driving him from job to job. His former employers offer him a place, but the parole officer comes to arrest him for failing to report; the harassed Falder leaps from a stairway to his death.

First performed in the United States by the Hull House Players in Chicago, 1911, *Justice* came to New York, April 3, 1916, during a period of prison reform. With a cast including Cathleen Nesbitt, O. P. Heggie, Henry Stephenson, and John Barrymore (Falder), it took the city by storm. Thomas Mott Osborne, late warden of Sing Sing, said after opening night: "*Justice* does not come under the head of an amusement, for it is too pitifully somber, but there never has been a time when a play of such character would have so much chance of success as at present, when the local world is so stirred over prison reform." The *New York Review,* next day, added: "Mr. Galsworthy's play throws the big light on 'causes.' It helps you to understand how and why people go wrong. It paves the way to divine love and forgiveness . . . We can thank Mr. Galsworthy for giving us a drama of real uplift and one which has punch enough in the last act to satisfy the most determined low-brow." Channing Pollock saw the production as a crusade: "At the club there was but one topic, and in the street. Overnight the theatre has ceased to be a toy, a plaything—and had become a vital part of every day . . . *Justice* is not a play; it is an emotional experience, a tragedy in which you participate . . . the tremendous force of the treatment is in its simplicity and reticence." Other critics were less willing to enlist in the crusade; in the May, 1916, issue of *Theatre,* for instance, the success of the play was attributed mainly to the performance of John Barrymore: "He was one of the accidents, so to speak, that make for this unexpected success of a play not adapted to entertainment or even edification."

The power of *Justice* is indisputable; less can be said for its objectivity. The forgery is committed, not out of the mere prosaic desire to make money, but in order to free a sweet and harmless young mother from the brutality of a cruel husband. Also, though Falder is arrested while about to depart for South America with Ruth Honeywell, and returns to her as soon as he is released, Galsworthy takes pains to assure us there has been no sexual intimacy between them. So honest, so innocent, are these two victims of society that we almost expect a smile of heavenly approval for Falder's breach of man-made law. Indeed, the play closes with the words: "He's safe with gentle Jesus!"

Justice was revived in various parts of the United States in 1922, 1927, 1937 (Federal Theatre), and in London in 1922, 1928, 1932, and at a Galsworthy Festival in 1935.

It is interesting to note how critical opinion has shifted over the years. Leon M. Lion observed in the *London Era* of July 11, 1928: "The play stands now, as it did all those years ago, more as an indictment of the physical and mental horrors comprised in prison routine. Mr. Galsworthy, as always, has stated his case with the utmost fairness and clarity . . . Never, surely, was a play so subtly wrought, so carefully built up, as this one; how, with the firmest of blows, the hammer is wielded so that each point is driven in immovably!" In the *London Times,* after the April 1935 production, the same Mr. Lion observed: "It always was and still remains a mighty fine piece for sentimentalists priding themselves on their austerity, and for loose thinkers taking delight in their clearsightedness . . . What can it have been which in 1910 bluffed us into mistaking this piece of special pleading for a master-stroke of high unescapable tragedy?"

The fervor of a cause leads its adherents to give enthusiastic welcome to works that advance it—the more so when that cause seems at humanity's core. *Justice* today seems as obvious and as partisan as the novels of Dickens, though stodgier and less exuberant. It remains, however, a milestone in the drama of social fairdealing, which in every generation will wring new indignation and new pathos from abiding problems.

Galsworthy was awarded the Nobel Prize in 1932. *Justice* was revived in London in 1967, the hundredth anniversary of Galsworthy's birth, with Eric Portman, for forty-five performances. The problems the play pictures have been rather exacerbated than solved.

BLOOD WEDDING   *Federico García Lorca*

Although the fame of Federico García Lorca (Spanish, 1899-1936) had temporary glow from the fact that he was shot in Granada by Franco adherents, it rests solidly upon his work as the leading poet and poetic dramatist of his generation in Spain. Although university trained, Lorca chose his themes from the simple people of his native Andalusia, and for three years (1931-1934) he guided a traveling theatre, La Barraca, which brought classics of the Spanish stage to the people. In addition to a considerable body of distinguished poetry, and several light farces, Lorca wrote a group of three serious plays that set him high among Spain's playwrights. All three—*Blood Wedding,* 1933, *Yerma,* * 1934, and *The House of Bernarda Alba,* * 1936—present the same theme: the tragedy rising from frustrated women yearning to be fulfilled.

Blood Wedding deliberately moves within a non-realistic realm. Unlike those of the two other serious plays by Lorca, its characters, save for Leonardo, have not names but labels—the Mother, the Bride, Leonardo's Wife. Among the figures in the drama are Death and the Moon. With prose that breaks into poetry at intense and climactic moments, the play presses home the concept of human fatality. Without any conscious will, the characters are drawn to their destiny. The one person named, Leonardo, seeks his own destiny, but no more than the others does he shape its end. He and the Bride run off on her wedding day; the Bridegroom hunts him, and in fierce knife-combat both are killed. The three women—Leonardo's wife, the ravished bride, and the bridegroom's mother—mourn together.

It is the Mother who holds the play together. A knife thrust has already taken her husband away, and her other son—killed by Leonardo's kin. A brooding sense of doom hangs over her thoughts, hardly to be dispelled by the haunting beauty of the procession and dance before the wedding, for it is from that dancing that Leonardo disappears with the Bride.

Played in Madrid and Buenos Aires in 1933, *Blood Wedding* was enthusiastically received. It played successfully in Brazil, Italy, France, Portugal, Sweden, Norway, Denmark, Finland, Russia, Czechoslovakia, England, Canada, South Africa, Israel, and Ireland. In the United States, it has been well received in university theatres, but twice failed in New York. A Neighborhood Playhouse production on Broadway, February 11, 1935, under the title *Bitter Oleander,* with Nance O'Neil, Effie Shannon, and Eugenie Leontovich, ran for twenty-four performances. This version conveyed neither the taut violence nor the folk-quality of the original. Richard Lockridge (February 12, 1935) liked it more than most reviewers; he called it "a classic tragedy of love" and said that "at its best the play has poignant beauty . . . For all the stylization, the emotions are simple, unforced and untortured, real." As *Blood Wedding,* the play was presented by New Stages, OffBway, February 6, 1949, in a formalized production that, for all its sombre speech, had more of the quality of a brooding dance. The pathos, and much of the beauty, were felt, but the drive of drama was not carried across.

Although *Blood Wedding* sprang from a newspaper account of an incident in Almeria, Lorca deliberately generalized his treatment of the story. His brother, in the Introduction to *Three Tragedies of Lorca* (1947) relates that the play matured in Lorca's mind for years, then took but a week in the writing. In poetic beauty and intensity of feeling, with heavy sense of the implacable hand of fate, *Blood Wedding* and its two companion plays are the most poignant presentation of the love-starved and barren woman in the modern poetic drama.

Recent revivals of *Blood Wedding* include: 1955, Chapel Hill, N.C.; 1963, Royal Ballet, London; 1971, Boston; in New York in Spanish, 1973, also (Soho) 1979; 1975, OffBway (Cubiculo); 1978, University of Michigan; 1980, OffOffBway, adapted by Maria Irene Fornés.

Four composers have turned the play into an opera: American Hale Smith; German Wolfgang Fortner (*Die Bluthochzeit*); Yugoslav Kresimir Fribec; and Hungarian Sandor Szokolay, in the expressionist mode.

YERMA   *Federico García Lorca*

The title, *Yerma,* is the Spanish word for barren, and the play is a tragic poem of infertility and futility. Yerma is the childless wife of the hard-working farmer Juan, who loves her body and deems children unimportant; to her, they are all in all. Yerma's sense of honor prevents her from taking a lover, but also from enjoying sex—which, a lusty old neighbor woman tells her, is the cause of her barrenness. She consults a sorceress; she attends fertility rites, refusing another man; and when Juan comes and embraces her, she chokes him to death.

The play was produced in Madrid in 1934, with Margarita Virgu, who later (1967) directed a production in Spanish at Smith College, Mass. It was played by the Circle in the Square, OffBway, in 1952. In the 1952 production at the Arts Theatre, London, Madalina Nicol played Yerma. In 1966 at the Lincoln Center Beaumont, in an adaptation by W. S. Merwin, it ran for sixty performances; Gloria Foster played Yerma; Aline MacMahon, the sorceress.

In 1966 there was a Spanish production at the Greenwich Mews, OffBway; in the same year Antonia Ray as Yerma toured Central and South America. In 1968, it played in English at Cooper Union, New York.

In 1972, in the London World Theatre Season the Nuria Espert Company presented *Yerma* in Spanish. Harold Hobson in the *Times* commented on the setting: "a giant, diamond-like drum (trampoline), skin sometimes slack, sometimes tight, sometimes drawn up in the shape of a tent. In the center of this drum Nuria Espert's neurotic high-charged Yerma frantically rolls, locked in the arms of her husband, vainly striving to create the child for whom her whole being, and the teachings of her church, cause her to yearn . . . The entire play is a frenzied hymn of frustrated fertility." Along the edges of the drum, a chorus of village women danced and sang. The Espert company played in Washington, D.C., in the fall of 1972. *Yerma* was presented at Hunter College, New York, November 3, 1977; at Stratford, Ontario, in 1979. A musical *Yerma,* book by Paul Bowles, lyrics and direction by the dancer Agnes Enters, was played at the University of Denver in July 1958, with Libby Holman as Yerma; then at Ithaca College, New York.

It was a grim and foreboding dance. Lorca's drama is a frantic yet engrossing picture of a woman's anguished yearning for a child.

THE HOUSE OF BERNARDA ALBA   *Federico Garcia Lorca*

"Not a drop of poetry! Reality! A photographic document!" cried García Lorca, writing *The House of Bernarda Alba* for Margarita Virgu, who was starring in *Yerma.** In this play the feminine frustration is multiplied, for at her husband's death Bernarda orders her daughters to stay in the house, to see no man, for eight years of mourning. A hunchback daughter peeps out at passing men, and spies on the twenty-year-old Adela, who tries to rebel. A thirty-nine-year-old daughter of Bernarda's first husband is betrothed (for her money); Adela and the hunchback both love the man. (No man appears in the play.) But Adela goes to a tryst with him; the spying girl tells the mother, who takes a gun and shoots the man. Adela hangs herself; Bernarda dresses her for burial as though she had died a virgin.

Anticipating the "women's lib" movement, Lorca's plays of feminine yearning seemed to attract young women. Its first American production seems to have been in Hollywood in 1947; but in 1950 it was played at the Johns Hopkins University, Baltimore; in 1956 at Barnard College, New York (all women); in 1958 at Brandeis University, Conn; in 1963 at Smith College, Mass. (all women); in 1966 at Mercy College, N.Y. (all women).

It was presented at the ANTA, New York, with Katina Paxinou (the Greek star) as Bernarda, with Catherine Willard, Ruth Ford, and Helen Craig. In 1971 Diana Cartier danced "the venomous Bernarda" in the Joffrey Ballet presentation of *Feast of Ashes* by Alvin Ailey; there had also been ballets, by Kenneth MacMillan, *Las Hermanas*, and (92d Street Y) *Les Desanamoradas* by Eleo Pomare.

In 1973 at Greenwich, England, an overly jocular adaptation by Tom Stoppard* was shown. Bernarda's first word, and last word, is "Silence!" Stoppard has her say "Shut up!" Mia Farrow played Adela, "too ethereal for the basic eroticism"; June Jago made Bernarda "a suburban English matron." When the Stoppard version was presented in December 1973 by ACT, Leo Stutzin in the California *Modesto Bee* said that "Stoppard's wit deserted him in composing this obscenity-spiced bad joke on *The House of Bernarda Alba*."

García Lorca's play was presented in 1977 OffBway; in 1978 (March) at the Cincinnati Playhouse in the Park and (October) at the North Carolina School of the Arts. It remains a gripping picture of a frustrated feminine family, completing the playwright's trilogy of yearning.

THE BEGGAR'S OPERA   *John Gay*

John Gay (English, 1685-1732), apprenticed to a mercer, became known through several poems and plays before he wrote, following a suggestion by Swift, the one work that has given him enduring fame, *The Beggar's Opera*. This musical play was a satire on Italian opera (which for a time it drove out of style) and on the conniving of unscrupulous politicians with the London underworld.

In the midst of the play's underworld figures, the audience recognized the portrait of a judge who had recently been fined the enormous sum of £30,000 for taking bribes; they saw in the character of Peachum the living presentation of an actual informer (later hanged); and they had the delight of watching the Prime Minister and Chancellor of the Exchequer, Sir Robert Walpole, cry "Encore!" to the satire on himself. (Walpole had his revenge; *Polly,* the sequel to *The Beggar's Opera,* was forbidden the stage.)

The Beggar's Opera, produced in 1728 by John Rich at Lincoln's Inn Fields, was an instantaneous success, setting a record for its day of 62 performances. It "made Gay rich and Rich gay." Until 1773, it was regularly presented every season at both Drury Lane and Covent Garden. In 1773, the play was suppressed as "encouraging theft and other enormities." After its license was renewed, the play continued on the boards almost every season for 170 years. In 1728, its first year, it was played in Dublin by a cast of children under ten years of age.

Buxom Lavinia Fenton, the first Polly Peachum, within the year was married to the Duke of Bolton. *The Beggar's Opera,* in fact, lifted more actresses to the peerage than any other play. It was involved in other matters, too. When Covent Garden instituted its higher scale of prices with a revival of *The Beggar's Opera,* September 15, 1809, there were nightly riots for over a fortnight before arbiters decided that the increase was justified. In America (where the first performance was given in New York in 1750) the play was a favorite of George Washington's; the charms of the current Polly Peachum are said to have precipitated the duel between Alexander Hamilton and Aaron Burr.

With clever songs neatly interwoven with the dialogue, *The Beggar's Opera* gives an amusingly satiric picture of the disreputable London world of the eighteenth century, with a story that might well have happened, and still rings true. Captain Macheath, highwayman, is secretly married to Polly Peachum; when her father, who is both a fence and an informer, learns of this, he betrays Macheath to the authorities. Macheath, always gay and gallant, wins the heart of Lucy Locket, daughter of the Newgate Prison warder, who helps him escape. "By treating this material," Allardyce Nicoll observed, "almost in a spirit of romance, by artificializing, by jesting, by exaggerating, Gay has been able to create a new world of his own."

The Beggar's Opera has been one of the most frequently revived plays in the English theatre. In New York, however, it was not seen from 1870 until the Arthur Hopkins revival of 1920. A London revival, which opened June 5, 1920, ran for 1,463 performances. The British company that came to New York in 1920 had but a short run at the Greenwich Village Theatre, but toured successfully for eight years and then returned to New York. The *New York Times* then (March 28, 1928) called it "that incomparable blend of racy satire and song." The play has since been frequently performed. In 1940 it was shown at the University of California, at Yale University and in London (directed by John Gielgud).

In 1928, Bertolt Brecht wrote a German version, *Die Dreigroschenoper,* with music by Kurt Weill, which, retranslated into English as *The Three-Penny Opera,* has had some success; it was made into a motion picture in 1933. London was cool to Brecht's version, an experiment in "epic theatre" which, though set in 1837, seemed of the twentieth century. The scenic artist Mordecai Gorelik explained that Brecht sought to create "the social web of circumstances which can alone precipitate and qualify the story. The primary task of the *Opera* was not to parade the peculiar behavior of eighteenth century or twentieth century criminals, but to depict the connivance of criminals with supposed guardians of law and order." The more manifest social concern of Brecht did not improve his version.

More recently, December 26, 1946, there was presented in New York still another adaptation of *The Beggar's Opera,* with book and lyrics by John

LaTouche and music by Duke Ellington. Called *Beggar's Holiday,* it was set in twentieth-century Harlem, the Negro section of New York. John Chapman called the play "the most interesting musical since *Porgy and Bess*"; and Brooks Atkinson, who hailed it as "a gutter gavotte danced to the beat of an original, fresh, and animated score," seemed to prefer it to the original; Gay's version, he claimed, "always had more prestige than entertainment." (History proves, however, that the entertainment is what won the prestige.) The LaTouche version, Richard Watts declared, "doesn't come off"—and the public agreed. For LaTouche, in his effort to make his characters sympathetic, smiled also upon the vices in which they indulge—an error of which Gay is happily free. The liveliness of *The Beggar's Opera* came freshly through a production off Broadway in 1950, with thirty-five of the songs that at various times have brightened the play, at Columbia University in 1954.

Long without rival, *The Beggar's Opera,* the first of the great satirical musical comedies, is a play that is both excellent fun and a sharply pointed travesty of the abuses of its time. Both the abuses and the fun abide.

For much of the twentieth century, Gay's fortunes intertwined with Brecht's. The 1728 Gay opera was translated into German for Brecht in 1928; Brecht's *Three-Penny Opera* (Berlin, August 31, 1928; Leipzig, 1929) with music by Kurt Weill, came briefly to New York in 1933, then retranslated by Marc Blitzstein came again, with Weill's wife, Lotte Lenya, in 1952 and moving to the New York Greenwich Village Thèâtre de Lys, went on for 2,611 performances, directed by Carmen Capalbo. Some have credited much of Brecht's success to Weill's music; but a review of its first London production (1935) called this "cinema music . . . to treat this hotch-potch of jazz seriously would be a waste of time."

Brecht's version changed the locale to late nineteenth-century London Soho, making Peachum a genuine businessman, obviously therefore a scoundrel and a cheat. When this version was given at the New York City Center in 1952, there were protests at the use of city funds for un-American propaganda.

Productions of both plays have been too numerous to list. In 1978, the 250th anniversary of *The Beggar's Opera,* there were some fifteen productions of the play in the United States and England.

The Three-Penny Opera production at the London Prince of Wales, February 10, 1972, transferred to the Piccadilly April 10, in translation by Hugh MacDiarmid, directed by Tony Richardson, had Hermione Baddeley as Mrs. Peachum; when Macheath was led to the gallows, Peachum turned to the audience and (borrowing Barrie's idea for the fairy in *Peter Pan*) cried out: "Hands up who want Macheath to be saved!" The NYSF production in Central Park, 1977, restored the aggressiveness and anger of Brecht (which had been softened in Blitzstein's version) with "all the four-letter words" and the harshness of attack on the social system that was Brecht's intention.

The drive of the Brecht version swung back upon the Gay. Thus, the Scottish Opera Co. at the 1981 Edinburgh Festival, which went to London September 19, 1981, was commented on in the *Observer:* "David Williams' production aims constantly for the lowest common denominator, for the rawest belly-laugh and the tritest sentimentality. [The music] brings a touch of Tin Pan Alley to what can be a fresh and honest celebration of traditional tunes." And the NT (Cottesloe) *Beggar's Opera,* directed by Richard Eyre, 1983, emphasized the realistic squalor. Paul Jones was not the debonair, romantic highwayman of the eighteenth century, but a common trickster. The seven whores who consorted with him and appeared with his brats for his execution, said the *Observer,* were "so gaunt and bespotted that they were clearly in the last stages of syphilis." In contrast, in the London production ten years before, when the noose was slipped on Macheath, a Messenger on a magnificent horse brought the Queen's pardon, a peerage, a country house, and a pension of £10,000 a year. And on the other hand, a 1968 Seattle production introduced slides of race riots and police brutality.

Thus, one may still choose, between the freshness of the gay English songs and the cheerful fun of *The Beggar's Opera,* and *The Three-Penny Opera*'s savage satire, lacking compassion, driving hard at what it sees basically wrong in society today. Like drugs, violence requires ever stronger doses, and in our violent days Brecht has a continuing wide appeal.

Note the name Peachum; he sends his employees out on thieving errands, then "peaches" on them to gain the reward. Business is business, Brecht would repeat.

Polly was not produced until June 19, 1777, at the Haymarket. Its most recent revival was at the Oxford Playhouse, June 1983, then on English tour. Polly has followed Macheath to the West Indies, where he has become a pirate. The current adaptation, by David Pownall, directed by Bill Pryde, was turned to a satire on modern colonialism, with, said Francis King in the *London Telegraph* (July 10, 1983), "the settlers transformed into corrupt, randy men, and hideous, tennis-playing women (played by actors in drag), the pirates into vicious mercenaries, and the 'noble savages,' originally natives of the country, into imports from Africa." Unfortunately, the wit and frequent gaiety of *Polly* did not come through.

In December 1982 the English Royal Academy held an exhibition celebrating the 250th anniversary of the Theatre Royal, Covent Garden, which opened December 7, 1732, built by John Rich with money he'd won from *The Beggar's Opera.* Perhaps the final word on Gay's comedy was spoken by William Hazlitt, back in 1818: "It is a vulgar error to call this a vulgar play . . . The elegance of the composition is in exact proportion to the coarseness of the materials. By a 'happy alchemy of the mind' the author has extracted an essence of refinement from the dregs of human life, and turned its very dross into gold."

At York, England, June 1984, then Nottingham, July, Philip Prowse presented the Brecht play in translation by Robert David MacDonald, "funny, brutal, and rude, mixing slang with much of the original German— and the audience loved it" (*The Observer*). It opens with a wealthy woman playing Weill's overture on her grand piano. Then she goes to dinner. Beggars creep in and begin the play. The butler becomes Macheath, who at the end stabs the woman, and she dies atop the piano.

The *Three-Penny Opera* fits the current mood but does not preserve the deft and delightful satire, the gaiety of Gay.

THE BALCONY   *Jean Genêt*

Jean Genêt (b. 1910) from orphanage to criminal court had learned to hate society. He wrote two autobiographical books, *Notre Dame des Fleurs* (*Our Lady of the Flowers,* 1944) and *Miracle de la Rose* (1946), flaunting his homosexuality and his contempt for normal civilized life. In 1947, Louis Jouvet produced Genêt's one-act *Les Bonnes,* showing two maids, sisters in a love-hate relationship, enacting various situations, including how to do away with their mistress. The next year Genêt attained his tenth criminal

conviction, and was saved from a life sentence by the appeal of Sartre,*
Claudel,* Cocteau,* Gide, and other intellectuals. I had been offered the
translating of Sartre's *L'Être et le Néant* (*Being and Non-Being*), which I
passed on to my colleague Bernard Frechtman, who thereupon went over to
Paris, met Sartre and his group, and became the translator of all Genêt's
plays. These combine the theatre of cruelty with the theatre of the absurd;
they depict what Genêt sees as the rottenness of society; but there is no
denying their sheer theatricality. Most vivid are *The Balcony* and *The
Blacks.**

The Balcony, published 1956, presented in Paris, 1957, consists of nine
scenes in a brothel, in a country ripe for revolution; various characters enact
their sexual aberrations. A dwarfish gas-company workman, dressed as a
bishop, exacts confessions, then takes a whore, whom he reviles. Another
whore, Carmen, recalls her having acted in a fantasy of the Immaculate
Conception. Still another whore is being whipped by the "Executioner"; she
orders the "Judge" to lick her foot. "Tell me you're a thief." "Lick first." As
he obeys we hear the fire of machine guns. A "General" rides a girl as a
horse (in New York, 1960, Salome Jens); he "dies" as a war hero.

We glimpse the rebels plotting in "the real world." The Executioner, lover
of the brothel-keeper Irma, comes in for his share of the day's take; he is
shot, and cries out that the rebels have won. The Chief of Police, a former
lover of Irma, is the power behind the revolution; and the brothel men are
persuaded to make their roles real in the world outside. Irma, as Queen,
demands a statue in the shape of a giant phallus, and a mausoleum into
which she can retire to await posterity. Turning out the brothel lights, she
bids the audience go home, where "everything will seem even more false
than here."

The obscene dialogue of the play led to its being produced in London
(April 22, 1957) at the Arts "Club," to avoid the censor; Genêt, who objected
to the presentation, was not admitted. It was played the same year at
Oxford. In a modified version by Barbara Wright and Terry Hands, the RSC
brought it to the Aldwich in November 1971. Harold Hobson in the *Times*
called Genêt "priest not of the Resurrection but the erection, or rather, high
priest of impotence as the characters require fantasy to attain tumescence."
Modern life, Genêt suggests, survives, precariously, because it is built on
fantasy.

Lucille Lortel held an option for a New York production of *The Balcony* at
her Théâtre de Lys, but dropped it because of the extended run of Brecht's
*Three-Penny Opera.** *The Balcony* was staged by José Quintero for the
Circle in the Square, March 3, 1960, and ran for 672 performances. The
same year it opened in Berlin; in 1966 in Boston. A New York commentator
said: "It would require a committee of alienists to define all the abnor-
malities, and a committee of logicians to clarify all the meanings." Sartre's
Introduction to Genêt's collected works expanded to a separate volume,
which he entitled *Saint Genêt.* Genêt is the saint of the anti-world. Peter
Brook, who directed *The Balcony* in Paris, 1960, explained, "We were
continually moving into burlesque and farce as perhaps the only way one
can deal with extreme horror."

THE BLACKS   *Jean Genêt*

The Blacks, published 1958, produced in Paris 1959, revised 1960, calls
for an all-black cast, some of them made up as whites in grotesque caricature masks. In the play the Queen, Judge, Bishop and General (as in *The*

Balcony*) sit as civilized whites watching the weird rituals of African Blacks. The rites include the enacted seduction, through black "superior" sexual power, of a white woman—played by a black male in a blonde wig and with grinning red lips on the white female mask—then her rape and strangulation by the black priest. The watching "whites" are then assisted on their journey to Hell.

A directive states that if there is an all-black audience, some are to be in whiteface, to be overwhelmed by the play's final excoriation of the white world.

The Blacks was first presented in Paris, October 1958, directed by Roger B!in, who also directed the English production, briefly at Cambridge and Cardiff, then May 30, 1961, at the London Royal Court. It received harsh treatment from the London critics. Alan Pryce-Jones reported in the *London Times* on the Paris production: "From the middle on, the audience tends to behave like the musicians in Haydn's Farewell Symphony. One by one they creep out . . . Somehow, lodged like a grape-pip in the appendix, a festering significance works into the subconscious of those who cling on to the end. Does it amount to much more than the simple statement that black and white are much alike? I doubt it." He then adds, as though sensing the American reception: "But the bizarre embroideries hung round this conclusion evidently charm at least the younger generation, which has adopted Genêt, and his play, as a cause to be defended in the name of progress."

Of the London production, Kenneth Tynan reported (in the *New York Herald Tribune*, June 1, 1961) on "the recurrent Genêtic idea that all human relationships are power relationships, a timeless struggle between the ins and the outs . . . Thus described, the play sounds like a masterpiece *maudit*; and so it might have turned out in the hands of another writer . . . instead, it drowns in a flood of prose poetry . . . Genêt's mind moves from image to image, never from idea to idea." Tynan notes, however, that "the Lord Chamberlain has removed all the blatantly shocking words in what was expressly intended to be a blatantly shocking play." Bernard Levin was more forthright: white versus black is "a simple enough thesis; but it would be difficult to imagine anything quite as pointlessly, wearily, emptily obscure as what M Genêt has made of it . . . dialogue of a flatness matched only by its pointlessness . . . cock-a-doodle-dooing, reeling, writhing, and fainting in coils."

Then *The Blacks* came to the St. Marks Playhouse, OffBway, May 4, 1961, and ran for 1,408 performances—attended mainly by young whites. James Earl Jones headed the first cast; he and several others returned to perform for the play's last week. Director Gene Frankel admitted: "There are parts of the play even I don't understand." Ritual—even Black Mass—has its mysteries. In 1963 the company flew to Montreal for two performances at Her Majesty's Theatre. Norman Nadel in the *World-Telegram-Sun* called the play "a strong, dark preachment. It serves not only a theatrical but a sociological and moral purpose, in opening eyes, in irritating the raw areas, in making whites and Negroes more sensitive to the worst aspects of an intolerable situation." Actually, such a play is more likely to inflame passions than to stimulate calm consideration of remedy. Bernard Levin concluded: "Only at the Royal Court could the play have been put on in this country without provoking a riot. The whole sorry episode is a commentary on a culture which has decided that because the truth is incomprehensible, the incomprehensible must be true." Harold Clurman said that Genêt is "a man who no longer permits himself the luxury of forgiveness."

The play was produced at the Mark Taper Forum in Los Angeles in 1962, and there again in 1970 as a benefit for black and Mexican-American youth. Among other productions: 1964, Washington, D.C.; and at both the West Berlin Festival and the Venice Biennial. Also in 1964 in Darmstadt, West Germany, with white players in blackface, Genêt at first consenting, then ordering it stopped; but the producer claimed there were not enough black actors that knew German. In 1970, Oxford, England. In 1973, Kennedy Center, Washington; 1978, OffOffBway. No more violent attack on white supremacy and "superiority" has been staged than this savage clownerie, to use the author's term, by the lifelong rebel Jean Genêt.

PANTAGLEIZE   *Michel de Ghelderode*

The Belgian playwright Adolphe Adhémar Louis Michel de Ghelderode (1898-1962) wrote more than twenty plays, mainly in the absurdist mood, including a 1926 drama about a production of *Faust,** a 1929 parody of Pirandello's *Six Characters in Search of an Author,** and in the same year *Barabbas,* commissioned by the Belgian Popular Theatre for the Holy Week. In this, Barabbas, in prison with a silent Jesus, is spared at the Cross. Seeking to avenge the Christ, he is stabbed in the back and, dying, cries: "Hey, Jesus, I too am bleeding. But you died for something. I am dying for nothing; but I died because of you—for you. Jesus, my brother."

Ghelderode's one play to win wide repute outside of Belgium is *Pantagleize,* 1927, in which accidents determine the characters' fate.

Pantagleize greets his fortieth birthday with the thought that he is a living anachronism, with little distinctive save his odd name. He decides that his day's greeting will be "What a lovely day!"—little knowing that this has been set as the signal for an uprising. He enters a café where the revolutionists, watched by a plainclothes officer, await the word. When Pantagleize speaks, the uprising roars to a start; a pretty Jewess knocks out the officer and embraces the bewildered Pantagleize, whose word has awakened the world. Led by her, the triumphant Pantagleize bids the militia, "Go to the Devil!"—and they step aside; for this is their password. He carries off the State treasure. He is hailed at a banquet of the revolutionaries; and such is his euphoria that he fails to notice that the waiters are one by one overcoming the diners—until he himself is taken prisoner. The revolution thus failing, Pantagleize is condemned to death. Facing the firing squad, he thinks of the Jewess, and exclaims, "What a lovely day!" as he falls dead. There was a total eclipse of the sun that day, its "death" and "rebirth" symbolizing the immortality of beauty, however interrupted by the multiform murders of mankind.

In translation by George Hauger, APA-Phoenix offered the play for fourteen performances at its Ann Arbor season, with Ellis Rabb and Patricia Connolly, then brought it to New York, November 30, 1967, for fifty performances. Clive Barnes in the *Times* enthusiastically called it "a marvelous play: the production is excellent, the whole thing is funny, thoughtful, stimulating and entertaining." John Chapman in the *News* called it "a solemn, pretentious and badly written—or at least badly translated—morality play about good old Everyman." And Martin Gottfried in *Women's Wear Daily* deemed that it "fulfills the expectation of that N.Y. theatre audience hungry for the artistic, the original, and the rare." It remains an effective absurdist picture of motiveless life.

TRIAL BY JURY   *William Schwenck Gilbert*

The wit, satire, and sprightly humor of William S. Gilbert (English, 1836-1911), accompanied by lively songs set to the superbly accordant music of Arthur S. Sullivan (1842-1900), continue to delight theatregoers everywhere. The D'Oyly Carte Company, a permanent London troupe exclusively devoted to his operettas, is eagerly welcomed on its periodic trips to the United States, where the plays are even more frequently performed than in England. At one time, forty Gilbert and Sullivan companies were simultaneously touring the States. Almost five thousand performances of the plays are given by amateur and professional companies every year—a record not approached by any other playwright, even Shakespeare.

Trial by Jury, the first Gilbert and Sullivan success, was presented in London on March 3, 1875, as an afterpiece to Offenbach's *La Pericholo.* It opened in Boston on December 2, 1876, and in Chicago on January 7, 1877. Described as a "dramatic cantata," it is the only one of the operettas without any spoken dialogue. For the first time in comedy since Aristophanes, it uses the chorus as an integral part of the story—a satire on breach of promise suits. When the fair plaintiff declares that her betrothed is fickle, he responds that he is doing what comes naturally. After considerable frolicsome foolery and mocking of court procedure, the play ends with the judge's decision to wed the plaintiff himself.

It has been suggested that, in writing the play, Gilbert had in mind the trial of Bardell vs. Pickwick as depicted in Dickens' *Pickwick Papers.* He evidently also had in mind, and made the scene resemble, the Clerkenwell Sessions House, where he himself had practiced law.

It would be impossible to list all the times and places *Trial by Jury* has been played. In New York, it was presented in a full-length marionette version in 1940; in modern dress in 1942; in its regular costume presentation, many times before and after.

The London premiere was at the Royalty Theatre, of which the manager was Richard D'Oyly Carte (1844-1901). Recognizing their possibilities, he commissioned Gilbert and Sullivan to write a two-act opera for the company he organized. He leased the Opera-Comique, then built the Savoy Theatre, and all the later Gilbert and Sullivan operettas are associated with the D'Oyly Carte company, "the Savoyards."

The D'Oyly Carte Company was finally dissolved in 1982, because of rising production costs, not falling popularity. It is estimated that over two thousand companies in the English-speaking world still enact Gilbert and Sullivan. (Not to speak of other tongues, including Japanese; and I have heard a Yiddish *Gondoliers* that was hilarious.) In New York the goodly tradition is gallantly sustained by Light Opera of Manhattan (LOOM), with its imaginative and devoted director, William Mount-Burke. It has recently added a few other operettas to its repertory, but at first was and still is mainly noted for its ingenious G & S productions. In 1979 LOOM presented all the G & S plays. London's Sadler's Wells ran a series in 1984.

A word should be said of Gilbert before Sullivan. Mr. and Mrs. German Reed produced a number of Gilbert "entertainments." He made a most lively adaptation, *The Wedding March,* of *The Italian Straw Hat* * of Labiche. Perhaps freshest of his early plays is *A Sensation Novel,* which contains Lady Rockald's candid confession:

> *For innocents' affliction*
> *Guilty deeds I must prepare;*

I'm the lovely fiend of fiction
With the yellow, yellow hair.

A heroine's hair, of course, is golden. "Gentlemen prefer blondes."

In the illuminating introduction to her *Gilbert Before Sullivan,* 1957, Jane W. Stedman points out how the operas borrow from Gilbert's earlier works, and discusses pervasive motifs. There is what Sullivan, disapproving, called the Lozenge Plot, in which some supernatural or psychological force impels persons to behave contrary to their desires. "While Shaw prefers to attack human institutions, Gilbert more often exposes human nature." Then there is the Invasion Plot, wherein opposing groups penetrate each other's territory. In *Iolanthe,* for example, the Peers enter a fairy glade, and the fairies take over Parliament (the Queen of the Fairies falling in love with the Sentry). And we are given Gilbert's thought that "all humour, properly so called, is based upon a grave and quasi-respectful treatment of the ridiculous and absurd"—directly opposed to the mid-nineteenth-century burlesque, which was "a ridiculous treatment of the grave and respectful."

Among many discussions of the inimitable pair was an article in the March 1983 issue of the widely read *Reader's Digest,* emphasizing the supposedly opposed natures of "sour" Gilbert and "sweet" Sullivan. It declared that Gilbert, who watched over every detail of the productions, was "hated" by the casts, but failed to give him credit for the consequent excellence of the staging. (We owe to his insistence the fact that all the words of the songs may be fully understood, to the vast delight of countless audiences. Gilbert was also decorous in writing and in costuming; he spurned what *Punch* referred to as "leg-itimate" spectacles, which the respectable Victorians eschewed, though athirst for "innocent merriment.") The spirit of the Savoyards persists.

In 1975 (?) *Tarantara! Tarantara!* by Ian Taylor, came from Bristol Old Vic to London. It was set backstage at the Savoy, October 3, 1888, with producer D'Oyly Carte, star George Grossmith, and the cooperating but inwardly hostile two, at their peak, on the verge of their quarrel.

THE SORCERER   *William Schwenck Gilbert*

"Oh! My name is John Wellington Wells, I'm a dealer in magic and spells," sings the head of the old established firm of sorcerers with offices at Seventy Simmery Axe (St. Mary Acts), in *The Sorcerer,* the first of the Gilbert and Sullivan operettas to be presented, November 17, 1877, under the management of D'Oyly Carte at the Opera-Comique.

Founded on a story in a Christmas issue of an 1876 magazine, with borrowings from *The Elixir of Love* and the *Bab Ballads (The Cunning Woman),* this operetta builds its fun on a slight plot and the love philtres of John Wellington Wells. It pictures two lovers so happy that they hire the sorcerer to spread love around; such incongruous pairing develops that the happy ending is achieved by his removing the spell.

In *The Sorcerer* first appeared the patter song, a riotous racing rhyme that challenges the speed of the singer, and the one type of song in which Gilbert grew increasingly expert.

The patter song had an ancient forerunner in the strangler song (so called because the singer might choke on it) of the comedies of Aristophanes. Indeed, across the ages Aristophanes and Gilbert and Sullivan are fellow spirits, unmatched.

John Wellington Wells was first played by George Grossmith, who until he took the role was a police-court reporter by day, an entertainer by night. His son, and more recently Martyn Green, have succeeded him in the magician's role, which carries the bulk of the humor of the play.

The Sorcerer first takes full stride in comic operetta. It contains not only typical Gilbertian bubbling fun, and fund of wit and satire, but some of Sullivan's most catchy tunes. It began the series that, as William Archer says, "restored the literary and musical self-respect of the English stage."

H. M. S. PINAFORE   *William Schwenck Gilbert*

Gilbert and Sullivan first won their wide public with *H. M. S. Pinafore; or, The Lass That Loved a Sailor,* which D'Oyly Carte produced on May 25, 1878, for a run of 700 performances. The initial criticisms, however, were not all favorable. One now unknown prophet declared: "In the story itself there is not much of humor to balance its studied absurdity . . . a frothy production, destined soon to subside into nothingness." It has become the most popular of all the Gilbert and Sullivan operettas. *Pinafore* (with *The Mikado**) has most successfully undergone translation into German, and there is a Spanish version, *Pinafor,* 1885.

International copyright not yet existing, *Pinafore* was at once pirated in the United States. It opened in Boston in 1878 and in New York early in 1879. *The Spirit of the Times* (February 15, 1879) disparagingly commented: "we fear very much that those managers who have pinned their faith to *H. M. S. Pinafore* will find that they have trusted too strongly to public favor . . . it has scarcely those elements that will command the long lease of popularity which entrepreneurs would seem to anticipate." The more astute William Winter, in the *New York Tribune,* called the play "one of the neatest, brightest, funniest operatic burlesques in any language . . . The bright, fresh, sparkling music will take the popular fancy at once . . . There are lines that are destined to be famous."

Winter was right; the vogue of *H. M. S. Pinafore* grew into a craze. By the spring of 1879, eight rival companies were playing the operetta in New York. At Haverly's Theatre, in May, a children's company opened in morning and afternoon performances, with an adult company in the evening. (A London production by children opened January 17, 1880, and was highly praised; *The Illustrated London News* declared that the adult companies could take hints from the youngsters.)

In London, the popularity of the play grew slowly, in large measure as a result of the American furor.

As early as February 21, 1879, the San Francisco Minstrels presented in New York a burlesque of Gilbert's play, *His Mud Scow Pinafore,* using Sullivan's music and featuring Admiral Porter "bottled for use," Captain Corkonian, and a motley crew. At the peak of the play's popularity, over ninety professional companies were playing *H. M. S. Pinafore* in the United States.

In July 1879, at Providence, Rhode Island, sixty-three performances of *H. M. S. Pinafore* were given on a full-rigged ship anchored in a lake; Buttercup, the Admiral and the cousins and the aunts were rowed from shore to ship. In the following month the play was again presented on a real ship in real water at New York's Madison Square Garden (then on 25th Street). In 1935 a ship production was played off Jones Beach, New York. A Negro company, headed by Bill Robinson and Avon Long, produced in 1945 a musical comedy called *Memphis Bound,* in which a stranded show-boat company puts on a performance of *H. M. S. Pinafore.*

Plot ideas for *H. M. S. Pinafore* were drawn from six of the *Bab Ballads.* The play is a travesty of the once popular "shiver-my-timbers" nautical melodrama, with incidental satiric thrusts at politics and jingoistic patriotism. Just before the play opened in 1878, Disraeli had appointed W. H. Smith, a publisher, as First Lord of the Admiralty; hence the punch in the song ending:

> *Stick close to your desk, and never go to sea,*
> *And you all may be rulers of the Queen's Navee!*

On this satire Queen Victoria delivered her characteristic dictum: "We are not amused" (for details, see *The Pirates of Penzance**).

The plot of *H. M. S. Pinafore* revolves about the ambitious Captain Corcoran, who wishes his daughter Josephine to marry the Rt. Hon. Sir Joseph Porter, First Lord of the Admiralty, although she loves the plain tar Ralph Rackstraw. Villainous Dick Deadeye tries to help the Captain foil the lovers until the bumboat woman, Little Buttercup, reveals that Ralph and the Captain had been exchanged in the cradle—whereupon Ralph becomes Captain and marries Josephine, while the Captain becomes a common sailor and marries Little Buttercup. (The plot trick of a revealed substitution to solve the play's dilemma is a satire on theatrical fare of the 1870's; Gilbert used it again in *The Gondoliers**). The songs hold their place among Gilbert and Sullivan's best.

Amusing plot, swift wit, and lively varied songs combined to make this work the first sweeping success of Gilbert and Sullivan. It has remained a lasting favorite; only *The Mikado* comes near, in frequency of professional and amateur performance, to *H. M. S. Pinafore.*

In his next play, in the song of the Major-General, Gilbert takes a sly dig at the still-running *Pinafore.* The General is emphasizing his omniscience—except for military matters; he is pretending to hunt for rhymes: *strategy* (pause, then triumphantly) *sat a gee;* then he goes on:

> *I know our mythic history, King Arthur's and Sir Caradoc's,*
> *I answer hard acrostics, I've a pretty taste for paradox;*
> *I can hum a tune of which I've heard the music's din afore—*
> *And whistle all the tunes from that infernal nonsense Pinafore.*

THE PIRATES OF PENZANCE   *William Schwenck Gilbert*

Queen Victoria was quite displeased at the political satire in *H. M. S. Pinafore.** In *The Pirates of Penzance; or, The Slave of Duty,* Gilbert proferred a mock apology, but the play continued his satire.

The Pirate King declares that many a crowned monarch has to do more dirty work than he. The "very model of a modern major general" knows no more of military tactics and gunnery than a novice in a nunnery. The timidity of the police force is laughably brought home. Then, at the close of the play, comes a sudden change. The pirates, having overpowered the police, stand with drawn swords over their prostrate prisoners, until the captured police sergeant cries, "We charge you yield, in Queen Victoria's name!" At once the conquering pirates throw down their swords and kneel, crying:

> "We yield at once, with humbled mien,
> "Because, with all our faults, we love our Queen."

Queen Victoria, who had little sense of humor, never forgave Gilbert. She early knighted Arthur Sullivan, composer of oratorios, cantatas, of "Onward, Christian Soldiers," and of the Queen's favorite song, "The Lost Chord." When, in March 1891, a special performance of *The Gondoliers* was given before Queen Victoria "the piece was described," Gilbert has recorded, "as 'by Arthur Sullivan,' the librettist being too insignificant an insect to be worth mentioning on a programme which contained the name of the wig-maker in bold type!" Gilbert was knighted by King Edward VII in 1907; he accepted the belated honor because, he explained, "I am the only dramatic author upon whom, *qua* dramatic author, it has ever been conferred." The *London Times* inquired: "Is the knighthood compensation for the temporary ban that was placed on *The Mikado,* or a reward for the sublime mockery of the Peers in *Iolanthe?*"

The Pirates of Penzance is built on wordplay. Frederic, an orphan apprenticed to the pirates (his nurse misunderstood the word "pilot"), is in love with Mabel, one of the daughters of "the very model of a modern Major-General." Freed from his apprenticeship at the age of twenty-one, Frederic helps the unhappy and timid police, who have been sent against the pirates. Then comes "the most ingenious paradox": Frederic has been apprenticed until his twenty-first *birthday*; since he was born on February 29, leap year, he still has some sixty-two years to serve the pirates! A "slave of duty," Frederic warns his pirate masters of the police trap, and the police themselves are caught in it. Honesty and love triumph only through the power of "Queen Victoria's name."

Other "pirates" led Gilbert and Sullivan to journey to the United States to oppose the unauthorized productions of their works with an "official" production of *H. M. S. Pinafore.* The authors stayed to direct *The Pirates of Penzance,* which opened at the Fifth Avenue Theatre, with an English cast, on December 31, 1879; thus they secured United States copyright. The British rights were meanwhile obtained by an unannounced performance in a private theatre in the remote sea-side village of Paignton, South Devon. In the cast was a Mr. R. Mansfield, who later toured in the Gilbert and Sullivan operettas and grew to be the famous star, Richard Mansfield.

The Pirates of Penzance opened in London on April 3, 1880, for a run of 363 performances. The play was very popular in the United States. The Bostonians produced it in September 1880, with the first all-American cast; soon after, three companies were on the road. Tony Pastor (February 7, 1881) presented at his Broadway Theatre *The Pie-rats of Penn-Yan,* with Sullivan's music; this travesty gave Lillian Russell her first playing role. Alice Brady appeared in *The Pirates of Penzance* (1912); and among the men who have made names in its roles are George Grossmith, Frank Moulan, and De Wolf Hopper.

Among the countless productions of *The Pirates of Penzance,* that of Winthrop Ames is outstanding. Brooks Atkinson (December 7, 1926) averred: "On the word of Gilbert-and-Sullivan maniacs, whose mad eyes lit up the audience everywhere last evening and whose gestures endangered the safety of the common spectators, this is the best revival of *The Pirates* yet seen in the Milky Way." Alexander Woollcott nominated Winthrop Ames for the presidency of the United States.

"Gilbert's pirate king," William Archer stated, "seems to us an almost inconceivable caricature, but he does not exaggerate the poses and gestures that had been accepted as serious art until well on in the nineteenth century." The sense of travesty has gone, but the rippling wit, the amusing songs, the arrant nonsense of it all remain.

The Pirates, which had been shown in a WPA tent in a Greenwich Village empty lot during the Depression, and by the Federal Theatre in 1938 at a quarter for adults and 15 cents for children, took a new turn in Central Park, July 15, 1980, going to the OffBway Public, then to the Broadway Minskoff, January 8, 1981, for 807 performances. It opened at the London Drury Lane May 26, 1982, and as I write moves merrily toward 1984. The production is a sort of comic-strip, Keystone-cops version of the play, with constant acrobatics and horseplay. The Pirate King gets into a fight with the orchestra leader, his sword against the leader's baton—and loses. He thrusts—and the blade slips back into the hilt. He struts, blusters, domineers; the agile pirates cringe at his frown. The public raves. The sober New York Drama Critics' Circle issued a special citation. The *London Mail* found it "an explosion of laughter which for a couple of wild and wonderful hours obliterates all else." Even G & S fans were amused. And somehow the *New York Times'* full-page ad for the movie (February 6, 1983) found no room to name either Gilbert or Sullivan.

The large New York cast included Rex Smith (Frederic), Linda Ronstadt (Mabel), Estelle Parsons (Ruth), Kevin Klein (the Pirate King), George Rose (the Major-General). Much the same cast (save that Angela Lansbury played Ruth) was in the movie. Slipped into the play were the songs "My Eyes Are Fully Open" from *Ruddigore* and "Sorry the Lot" from *Pinafore.* The lively tunes and knock-down slam-bang action grew into the longest G & S single run.

PATIENCE   *William Schwenck Gilbert*

Patience; or, Bunthorne's Bride is many folks' favorite among the Gilbert and Sullivan operettas. It is a light and light-hearted spoofing of the "aesthetic craze" of the period in which it was written.

Based on the *Bab Ballad* "The Rival Curates," this operetta is a delightful satire on the poets that used "to walk down Piccadilly, With a poppy or a lily In their medieval hand" to fascinate the ladies. Bunthorne, the fleshly poet, loves the milkmaid, Patience; his rival Grosvenor, the idyllic poet, wins all the other maidens. But a revolt from the affectedly poetic ways duly arrives. When Grosvenor swears to be always a commonplace young man, Patience accepts him; the dragoons pair off with the other ladies; and the discomfited Bunthorne is left with his buncombe.

Gilbert was afraid that in *Patience* he had written merely a topical satire, which would soon lapse into oblivion. The *Illustrated London News* (June 18, 1881) saw that it was more: "This is at once the most subtle and most incisive of all the contributions to the exhaustive satire of aestheticism . . . To say ridiculous things with a grave face is but half Mr. Gilbert's method . . . He respects no one; and he shows ourselves not 'as others see us', but as we see ourselves. *Patience* . . . is terribly true. It is a satire of a human weakness, more than of a society craze. It will live in literature when the other plays and poems are long ago forgotten."

Allardyce Nicoll found in *Patience* "an enduring literary charm and a wit which is itself symptomatic of the change coming over English theatrical literature ... This opera is one long good-natured but severely critical attack upon that atmosphere which Oscar Wilde, the author of the *Poems,* strove to establish in London. It is the answer of wit to that outworn romanticism which called itself the aesthetic movement."

After opening at the Opera-Comique on April 23, 1881, *Patience* was transferred on October 10 to the new Savoy Theatre, built by D'Oyly Carte especially for the Gilbert and Sullivan operas—the first public building in England lighted by electricity. *Patience* ran in the two houses for 578 performances. Gilbert directed it, as he did all the operas, with an iron hand, sure and firm. (He had a model stage at home, with little figures representing the players, on which he worked out all the situations and movements in advance.) With specific reference to *Patience* he recorded that "the actors and actresses were good enough to believe in me and to lend themselves heartily to all I required of them," but George Grossmith, a star of the play, thought differently: "Mr. Gilbert is a perfect autocrat, insisting that his words shall be delivered, even to an inflection of the voice, as he dictates. He will stand on the stage beside the actor or actress, and repeat the words, with appropriate action, over and over again until they are delivered as he desires."

The rippling wit of Gilbert in *Patience* has been graced with an exceedingly bright score. John Mason Brown, who has called *Patience* his favorite of the operettas, says, "I know of no other score that tingles so incessantly with melodies which refuse to be forgotten, or that boasts lyrics which are more ingenious in their rhyming or amusing in their subject matter."

In sustained tomfoolery and in mockery of pretense, with merriment and tender music, none of the operettas is superior to *Patience.*

IOLANTHE   *William Schwenck Gilbert*

Having approached the pinnacle of popular approval with three plays whose titles begin with a P, Gilbert and Sullivan were hesitant about making a change. To play safe, they chose a subtitle that doubled the P and on November 25, 1882, presented the fantastic opera *Iolanthe; or, The Peer and the Peri,* which ran for 398 performances.

Iolanthe, based on "George and the Fairies" in the *Bab Ballads,* is a fusion of topsyturvydom and fairyland. After a period of exile at the bottom of a well for having married a mortal, the fairy Iolanthe is pardoned. She visits her son, Strephon, who is "a fairy down to the waist, but his legs are mortal." Strephon, who has grown up as an Arcadian shepherd, loves Phyllis, a ward of the Lord Chancellor. Various Lords in love with Phyllis lead her to surprise Strephon kissing the ever-young Iolanthe. Subsequently, the Lord Chancellor decides to give Phyllis to the most eligible suitor—namely, himself. But the Queen of the Fairies intervenes: Strephon will go into Parliament and throw the House of Lords open to competitive examination. Iolanthe then reveals that Strephon's father is the Lord Chancellor; the Peers marry the Fairies; the Queen of the Fairies marries Private Willis, the Parliament sentry; and Strephon and Phyllis are reunited.

This moonshine story is accompanied by some of Gilbert's choicest satire on the law and the House of Lords. The "highly susceptible Chancellor" has two songs in this satiric mood: "The Law is the true embodiment of everything that's excellent," and "When I went to the bar as a very young man."

Best known and best of all is the Sentry's Song, outside of Parliament: "When in that House M. P.'s divide, If they've a brain and cerebellum too, They've got to leave that brain outside, and vote just as their leaders tell 'em to."

In addition to its satirical songs, *Iolanthe* is bright with lilting lyrics of love: "I'm to be married today, today"; "None shall part us from each other"; "Faint heart never won fair lady," and more. The finale of Act I is one of the most lively in the operettas, with the Peers and the peris challenging one another in various rhythms and languages. And the nightmare patter song of the Lord Chancellor is far and away the most surprising, ingenious, and brilliant such piece in all literature.

As the Gilbert and Sullivan operettas appeared, the British press grew so fond of each one in turn that the next seemed inferior. Thus *Punch* insisted that "as a musical or a dramatic work *Iolanthe* is not within a mile of *Pinafore* or a patch on *Patience*." However, its gay tunes, sharp shafts of satire, and good-humored romping fun have endeared *Iolanthe* to generations of playgoers. It is comparatively difficult for amateur groups to produce because of the well from which Iolanthe rises, the wings that the Sentry sprouts, and other fairyland embellishments. But it is a joy to hear and see well done. The Winthrop Ames 1926 production in New York was one of the best.

THE MIKADO   *William Schwenck Gilbert*

The most popular of all the Gilbert and Sullivan operettas, *The Mikado; or, The Town of Titipu,* opened in London on March 14, 1885, for a run of 672 performances. It has been more frequently played by professionals and amateur groups throughout the world than any of the other operettas. Its wide appeal is attested by the fact that there have been three versions of it in German alone.

Although the atmosphere is that of an absurd Japan—the Japan we see "on many a vase and jar, on many a screen and fan"; Gilbert had Japanese teach the original cast the drape of their costumes and the play of their fans—the satire in *The Mikado* is directed against the English. Gilbert was both surprised and indignant when, during the delicate international situation of 1906-1907, performance of *The Mikado* was forbidden for fear of offending Japan. G. K. Chesterton was moved to remark: "Gilbert pursued and persecuted the evils of modern England till they had literally not a leg to stand on; exactly as Swift did under the allegory of *Gulliver's Travels* . . . I doubt if there is a single joke in the whole play that fits the Japanese. But all the jokes in the play fit the English . . ."

In *The Mikado,* Ko-Ko is Lord High Executioner; Pooh-Bah, Lord High Everything Else. Ko-Ko, in love with Yum-Yum, yields her to the wandering minstrel Nanki-Poo on the latter's promise to die at the end of the month so that Ko-Ko may have an execution to report to the Mikado. Meanwhile, the Mikado arrives, seeking his son, who has run away from marriage with the Mikado's daughter-in-law elect, the more-than-middle-aged Katisha. The kindly Ko-Ko and the timorous Pooh-Bah falsely report the execution—only to learn that the "wandering minstrel" is the Mikado's son. Ko-Ko placates Katisha by suing for her hand, and Nanki-Poo is enabled to stay alive, married to Yum-Yum.

All the songs are delightful. Some are delicate and charming: "A wand'ring minstrel I," "Three little maids from school," "Brightly dawns our wedding day." Some—like "The flowers that bloom in the spring," the titwillow song, and "There is beauty in the bellow of the blast"—combine lightness and laughter. Some are lively tumbling of good spirits and gay fun, with more than a hint of wisdom. The "little list" of folk that won't be missed is usually brought up to date for fresh performances of *The Mikado*. Gilbert himself set the precedent for this in a children's version of *The Mikado*—his last literary work.

Performances of *The Mikado* have been too numerous to detail. The first American amateur production was in Yonkers, New York, in 1891. There was a performance at the New York Metropolitan Opera House, December 5, 1900. Among those that have delighted audiences in the play are George Grossmith, William Danforth, De Wolf Hopper, Frank Moulan, Martyn Green. Fritzi Scheff played Yum-Yum in 1910, with Alice Brady making her debut as the third little maid, Peep-Bo.

In New York, 1885-1886, three companies played *The Mikado* while lawsuits tangled. One company, during the curtain speeches celebrating its 500th performance, was dumbfounded to see the Ko-Ko from the company across the street dash in costume onto the rival stage, and cry—pointing to the other Ko-Ko: "He's not upon my list, he sadly would be missed," and dash off again. He had effectively stolen his rival's thunder.

In 1939 two Negro companies appeared in versions of the play: the Chicago Federal Theatre produced *The Swing Mikado*, which visited New York, opening March 1; and in New York, March 23, *The Hot Mikado* introduced the famous "Bojangles" Bill Robinson as the Mikado. Both were well received. To Brooks Atkinson (March 2, 1939) it seemed "an original notion to slide *The Mikado* into the groove of black and hot rhythm"; Robinson's company, he observed, substituted "Harlem frenzy for an amateur swing serenade." However, the two companies were not first to hit upon the idea of "Sepia Savoyards." In 1886, Thatcher, Primrose, and West's Minstrels celebrated the 200th performance of "the most successful afterpiece ever produced on the minstrel stage"—Ed Marble's *The Black Mikado*. The program announced "Mick-ah-Do the Great, J. P. O'Keefe; Ko-Ko, Billy Rice; Pooh-Bah, his Cabinet, Ed Marble; Yanki-Poh and the three little maidens all unwary, plus Ah-There, Stay-There, The Yeddo Coconut Dancers and other curios too numerous to mention."

The popularity of *The Mikado* gives no signs of abating. The work is fresh and lively throughout, with the best-knit plot of the operettas, songs that spring naturally from the situations, and a constant spurting of humor and amusing topsyturvy. "In my humble opinion," George Ade once declared, "*The Mikado* is the best light opera ever written in English." Hosts of enthusiasts will concur.

RUDDIGORE   *William Schwenck Gilbert*

Though tempted to a new preference by every fresh production, the author of these lines, who has seen every professional Gilbert and Sullivan company in New York since 1908, concurs in fine with Gilbert himself, whose favorite of the operettas was *The Yeoman of the Guard*,* and whose second in favor was *Ruddigore*. (The original title, *Ruddygore*, so shocked Victorian London that Gilbert, ever considerate of the ladies, changed the spelling to *Ruddigore*).

Ruddigore; or, The Witch's Curse was not one of the most popular of the operettas, although, opening in London, January 22, 1887, it ran for eight months (288 performances) and netted Gilbert some £7,000. Based upon an early sketch of Gilbert's, *Ages Ago,* with ideas from the *Bab Ballads* ("The Modest Couple"), *Ruddigore* satirizes the "naughtycal" melodrama of the day, which brought the hero sailor home from the bounding main to foil the bold bad baronet who covets the innocent maid.

The "bold bad baronet" in *Ruddigore,* Sir Ruthven Murgatroyd, is a really good fellow at heart. He has inherited the family curse and (like a perverted Boy Scout) must commit a crime a day or die. To avoid this fate, Ruthven disguises himself as a farmer, Robin Oakapple; but his foster-brother Richard (home from the sea), his rival for the hand of sweet Rose Maybud, reveals Robin's true identity. The ancient Murgatroyds step down from their family portraits and force the present Murgatroyd to continue the family career of crime. Finally he finds a way out: since he will die if he does not commit a crime, to refuse to commit a crime is tantamount to suicide—and suicide *is* a crime; hence by refusing to commit a crime, he commits one. This paradox—in Gilbert's land of topsyturvy—frees Robin to marry Rose, and the fishing village of Rederring rejoices with Castle Ruddigore.

This "supernatural" opera contains Sullivan's liveliest and most varied score, Gilbert's most varied and deftest lyrics, and many shafts of humor in the dialogue. Two aspects of the play perhaps weight it against popular favor. The theme—with the ancestral curse, and Mad Margaret, who with her reformed Murgatroyd becomes a district religious visitor—lacks the airy grace and light-hearted charm of *The Mikado** or *The Gondoliers.** Moreover, the end comes rather abruptly. Although sudden turns end others of the operettas, the final turn in *Ruddigore* is a play on words, on the technical fact that suicide is a crime. This lessons the satisfaction at the play's close.

A more deft thrust, at a more universal impulse, is the device hit upon to keep the reformed Mad Margaret from lapsing into a passion. She and her husband agree upon a word, and whenever she seems ready to fly off the handle, he calls out, to warn and calm her:—"Basingstoke!" "Basingstoke it is!" and she is calm.

There are numerous humorous songs in varied mood in the play. The lightsome love song and the tender plaint are also sung in rich variety.

When *Ruddigore* was first produced, the press objected even to this title; but Sullivan had the good sense not to allow Gilbert to change it, as he suggested doing, to *Kensington Gore.* Gradually, however, the bad baronets grew into favor.

In the United States, *Ruddigore* has won a chorus of praise. Gilbert W. Gabriel (August 11, 1931) declared: "Sullivan never wrote handsomer music than the famous ghost scene, nor wittier music than the duet of Sir Despard's and Mad Margaret's conversion. Nor was his collaborator ever more intrinsically droll." The *New York Herald Tribune* (October 18, 1936) agreed that *Ruddigore* is "one of the most tuneful and humorous of their entire series." In this and in their next work, *The Yeoman of the Guard,* the talents of the pair are at their peak.

THE YEOMEN OF THE GUARD   *William Schwenck Gilbert*

Gilbert felt that *The Yeomen of the Guard* was the best of the Gilbert and Sullivan operettas; "and he was right," agreed his biographers, Sidney Dark and Rowland Grey, "the best thing they had done or were ever to do—a perfect work of art." *The Yeomen of the Guard; or, The Merryman and His Maid* opened October 31, 1888, for 423 performances.

In this operetta, Gilbert came nearest to making his quips and cranks and wanton wiles convey genuine portraits. His Phoebe Meryll, biographers Dark and Grey maintain, is "the most fascinating and human character he ever created"; and the melancholy Jaques, whom Shakespeare presents in *As You Like It,** has an active brother in Jack Point, the strolling jester of *The Yeomen.* Many see in this sad merryman Gilbert himself, who, at the public command—"Come, fool, follify!"—was brave enough to declare, "I ply my craft and know no fear, I aim my shaft at prince or peer," yet shrewd enough to know that "he who'd make his fellow-creatures wise should always gild the philosophic pill."

Rising to the challenge of Gilbert's more serious character study and more rousing and natural plot, Sullivan composed some of his most developed and effective music for *The Yeoman of the Guard.* The duet of the Merryman and his Maid, "I have a song to sing, O," is the finest music in the operettas, a masterpiece of cumulative sound and sense. Music critics have compared the opening song, "When maiden loves, She sits and sighs," sung by Phoebe as she spins, with the spinning chorus in Wagner's *The Flying Dutchman.*

The *Pall Mall Budget* (October 11, 1888) hailed the new operetta as undoubtedly in for a long run: "The delightful melodies, the plaintive ballads, the catching choruses, the lovely trios and quartets which are scattered so profusely through this new work, will give pleasure to millions . . . Sir Arthur surpassed his former efforts." The *London Times* (July 17, 1939) said: "There is more substance to *The Yeomen* than to the purely comic operas. Sullivan responded to its humanity and romance with music such as he could hardly write for Gilbert's merely cynical constructions." And in 1941, *The Yeomen of the Guard* was presented in London as "a dramatic play with music," emphasizing the romantic and pathetic interplay of characters.

The plot of *The Yeomen of the Guard* is serious, and intricately knit. Jack Point, a strolling jester, loves his singer, Elsie. He consents, however, for a hundred pounds, to have Elsie marry Colonel Fairfax, a prisoner within London Tower. Fairfax is to die within the hour; he wishes, by leaving a widow, to divert the inheritance from the relative responsible for his imprisonment and death-sentence. But Phoebe, daughter of the Sergeant of the yeomen of the guard, loves Fairfax. While singing a wooing song to the head jailor, "Were I thy bride," she steals his keys and releases Fairfax. The jailor discovers the secret; to silence him, Phoebe must grant him her hand. Reprieve comes for Fairfax, who stays married to Elsie, and Point falls fainting as the curtain falls.

Brooks Atkinson (January 24, 1939) remarked: "Criticism of the D'Oyly Carte productions should, and generally does, consist of rhapsodic encomium." His words most aptly apply to *The Yeomen of the Guard.*

George Grossmith, who had starred in most of the operettas, acted Jack Point in *The Yeoman of the Guard,* then left the company. The great collaboration was nearing its end. It had one more great satiric frolic to come, *The Gondoliers,** but it had reached its richest combination of earnestness and topsyturvy in *The Yeomen of the Guard.*

The story has an outpouring of wordplay such as Gilbert had not permitted himself since the *Bab Ballads,* the jester Point being the justification for the riot of verbal wit. There is a gala store of songs. "Is Life a Boon?" is a ballad of genuine beauty and neatly turned thought. Lighter songs, in various moods of love, include "Free from his fetters grim," "When a wooer goes awooing," and Fairfax' advice to Point on how to woo—while he practices what he preaches, and wins Elsie: "every Jack He must study the knack, If he wants to make sure of his Jill." There is further excellent humor in the descriptive song "Like a ghost his vigil keeping" as Point and the jailer tell how they killed Fairfax—who in disguise is listening. Advertising gets a glance as "I

> *vow my complexion*
> *Derives its perfection*
> *From somebody's soap—which it doesn't."*

Finally, there is the note of ringing patriotism in the Tower song:

> *On London town and all its hoard*
> *I keep my solemn watch and ward.*

Bubbling around these humorous or satiric songs are the freshest of love lyrics: "Roses white and roses red"; "Take a pair of sparkling eyes"; "When a merry maiden marries"—and the gay quintette that contains Gilbert's deftest pun:

> *Life's perhaps the only riddle*
> *That we shrink from giving up.*

Sullivan, whose friends were constantly telling him that he should write more of the serious music by which he would be remembered, frequently urged Gilbert to such more serious tasks. In 1880 Gilbert wrote the libretto for Sullivan's oratorio *The Martyr of Antioch*. But usually Gilbert shied away from such ventures. On February 22, 1889, he wrote a long letter, ending: "We have a name jointly for humorous work tempered with occasional glimpses of earnest drama. I think we should do unwisely if we left . . . The best serious librettist of the day is Julian Sturgis, Why not write a grand opera with him?" In 1891, while Gilbert and Sullivan were estranged, D'Oyly Carte opened his new Palace Theatre with Sullivan's grand opera *Ivanhoe*, libretto by Sturgis. It was a failure.

Gilbert then wrote a number of skits and sketches without music, including *Rosencrantz and Guildenstern*, 1891 (he acted in a benefit performance in 1902), which rings the changes on critics' notions of Hamlet's madness, summing up:

> *The favorite theory's somewhat like this:*
> *Hamlet is idiotically sane*
> *With lucid intervals of lunacy.*

On January 4, 1892, Gilbert's *The Mountebanks* was presented, with music by Alfred Cellier (this also laughs at Hamlet and Ophelia); *His Excellency,* music by Osmond Carr, opened October 27, 1894, with a doleful song of the king who must forever listen to the national anthem, and of the gloomy humorist who fears that "the mine of jocularity is utterly worked out."

Gilbert and Sullivan, reconciled, produced two more works together. *Utopia Limited* opened October 7, 1893, for 245 performances, with the most lavish production the Savoy had seen. But the outward glitter could not compensate for the loss of the inner spark; a satire on contemporary English life, *Utopia Limited* is limited indeed. Even less successful was *The Grand Duke,* March 7, 1896. Sullivan died November 22, 1900. Gilbert wrote two more fantasies, *The Fairy's Dilemma,* 1904, and in 1909 the blank-verse *Fallen Fairies,* music by Edward German. Then, oddly, a serious sketch of the last hour of a Cockney murderer, *The Hooligan,* 1911. On May 22, 1911, swimming and saving a drowning woman, the seventy-five-year-old Gilbert was drowned.

THE GONDOLIERS   *William Schwenck Gilbert*

Annoyed at the temperaments and inflated egos of their stars—George Grossmith left the Savoyards, August 17, 1889; Jessie Bond refused to renew her contract for less than £30 a week—Gilbert swore: "We'll have an opera in which there'll be no principal parts." And in *The Gondoliers* three men are equally entangled with three women. The men's identities are mixed; the two gondoliers (one of whom—but no one knows which—is supposed to be the king of Barataria) sing duets in which they divide the words, sharing even the silly syllabification. Gilbert was a thorough man.

The Gondoliers; or, The King of Barataria opened at the Savoy Theatre on December 7, 1889, for a run of 554 performances. It earned the most money of all the operettas. Over 70,000 copies of the songs were sold in a few days. In March 1891, Queen Victoria saw a command performance at Windsor Castle; the Queen had been sharply displeased by Gilbert's satire, and *The Gondoliers* was listed on the program as "by Sir Arthur Sullivan" (for details, see *The Pirates of Penzance**). *The Pall Mall Budget* (December 12, 1889) called the new play "an admirable specimen of melodious topsy-turvydom, in which neither author nor composer can be said to have fallen short of the Savoy standard. The humor of the libretto is unflagging, and the music is written in Sir Arthur Sullivan's brightest and most fascinating vein, and the whole surroundings of the piece are as picturesque and full of colour as possible."

Barataria, readers may recollect, is the island of which Don Quixote made his man Sancho Panza the governor, with queer results. In *The Gondoliers,* it is the island which the two gondoliers (ruling as twins until they learn which is king) set out to democratize. Whichever is king was betrothed in infancy to the daughter of the haughty Duke of Plaza-Toro. This fact embarrasses the gondoliers, because they have just been married to two charming Venetian girls. The Grand Inquisitor is distressed at their marriages, and also at the workings of democracy in Barataria, until it is revealed that the real king is Luiz, the drummer boy of the Duke of Plaza-Toro, whom the Duke's daughter loves.

Sullivan had more trouble with the music for *The Gondoliers* than for any other of the operas. His accomplishment was worth the trouble. The songs are his most varied; they are delightful in rippling merriment; they swing mock-martially, with rolling drum, for the "celebrated, cultivated, under-rated Nobleman, The Duke of Plaza-Toro," who leads his regiment from behind; and they prick home their barbs of satire. But they demand the most skillful of choruses; they call for tricky ensemble singing by the principals. Winthrop Ames, whose Gilbert and Sullivan productions have been among our best, said he wouldn't risk *The Gondoliers* with his troupe. "What *The Gondoliers* may lack," said the *Boston Transcript* (April 14, 1937) "in the matter of the usual gimlet-like wit, it makes up for in richness of color, grace, and lovely musical compositions." Its love songs are especially sparkling.

It is rich, too, in gay satire of snobbery, whether of aristocrat or of democrat. The gondoliers intend to improve Barataria by leveling up, not leveling *down,* hence:

> *The Lord High Bishop orthodox—*
> *The Lord High Coachman on the box—*
> *The Lord High Vagabond in the stocks—*
> *They all shall equal be!*

But the Grand Inquisitor, in a clever and lilting song, reminds the newborn democrats, "When everyone is somebodee, Then no one's anybody!" Originally, in this song, at the line "Up goes the price of shoddy," Sullivan introduced a few bars from *Yankee Doodle Dandy.* An American, present at a rehearsal, objected, and Sullivan removed the musical satire.

In *The Gondoliers,* we watch the twin kings, in a joint patter song, "embark without delay On the duties of the day." We see excitement boil and subside, and boil again in song, while between their passionate moments the excited ones peacefully sing "Quiet, calm deliberation Disentangles every knot." We hear the Grand Inquisitor's reassurance: "Of that there is no manner of doubt," when the mystery is greatest as to which is the king. We see and hear the gavotte of the Venetians who are being taught court manners, and the gayer romp, "We will dance a cachucha, fandango, bolero." We observe the pomp of the Duke of Plaza-Toro and the majesty of his wife, who, giving her daughter counsel, sings of how "I tamed your insignificant progenitor—at last!" And we note how the nobles (like moving picture stars and champions in sport today) lend themselves to causes for a fee.

It is folly to ask which of the Gilbert and Sullivan operettas is "best." Yet the *London Times* (January 26, 1938) said that *The Gondoliers* "has good claims to that distinction, especially today. For one thing, nothing in the libretto has dated."

When *The Gondoliers* first came to New York, it was savagely attacked in the *New York Herald,* and *The World* (January 8, 1889) said that "The general verdict is that it is not up to the standard of the former works ... The general effect is cheerful and inspiriting, but that the individual numbers are to be compared with those of *Patience,** *Iolanthe,** *Ruddigore,** or *The Mikado,** is absurd." Opinions changed, especially after the American debut of the new D'Oyly Carte company, September 3, 1934, and by March 4, 1942, Richard Watts, Jr., expressed the "general verdict" when he said that *The Gondoliers* is "a musical pleasure." The last line of *The Gondoliers,* indeed, is "We leave you with feelings of pleasure." There could be no more fit farewell to Gilbert and Sullivan.

The rest of the story of the two collaborators takes a darker tone. During the run of *The Gondoliers,* D'Oyly Carte spent £140 for a carpet for the theatre. Gilbert protested that this was an excessive sum. Sullivan sided with D'Oyly Carte. Buried resentments over prestige, over light versus serious music, swelled up, and the long and genial association came to an end. Later, Gilbert and Sullivan were reconciled, and produced two more works together. Both failed.

Isaac Goldberg, in a tribute to Gilbert, stated that "there is no figure of the past or present to whom Gilbert can be likened." He most resembles Greek Aristophanes,* that other staunch shaver of sham, who two thousand years earlier brought poetry and music together with mirth and social criticism, in a merry melange of satire and beauty. Between them, and since, they have no parallel.

SECRET SERVICE   *William Gillette*

For a stirring melodrama of war, in the days when war still carried the cloak of courtesy and gentlemanly dealing with a gallant foe, there is fire in the episode of the War Between the States presented in *Secret Service,* 1895, by William Gillette (American, 1855-1937). *Secret Service* remains, as William Archer has called it, "the best play of its type."

William Gillette, author and actor, tried out *Secret Service* in Philadelphia, May 13, 1895. He withdrew the work for improvement, however, and played all the next season in his farce *Too Much Johnson.* With himself as Captain Thorne, Gillette reopened *Secret Service* in New York, October 5, 1896. It ran for over 300 performances, followed by 150 in Boston, by a two-year run in England, and another successful season in New York. Gillette (turning from his adaptation of *Sherlock Holmes,* in which he played intermittently from 1899 to 1932) starred again in *Secret Service* in 1915. The play has had frequent community theatre production, and was seen in 1948 at the Putnam County Playhouse, New York.

The play is set in Richmond at the close of the War. Lewis Dumont, disguised as a Captain Thorne, a secret agent of the Northern forces, and Edith Varney, daughter of a Southern general, are in love. Arrelsford, a Southern agent, also in love with Edith, watches Thorne closely—while Thorne's brother, a prisoner surrounded while escaping, shoots himself to avoid betraying Thorne. But Arrelsford sets a trap and, while Thorne is telegraphing a misleading message, shoots him in the hand. Thorne is led away to be shot.

Edith has had her faithful Negro slave unload the guns; she tells Thorne to fall when they fire. He will not, unless she admits that she loves him. Modesty and Southern loyalty combine to keep her still. "Sergeant, look to your guns," says Thorne. "Thank you." "You're welcome." And the men reload. But the Southern surrender is announced; this saves Captain Thorne, and permits Edith to admit that she loves him. Arthur Hobson Quinn, in *A History of the American Drama* (1936) regretted that the saving of Thorne turned "a tragedy of uncommon power" into no more than a vivid melodrama.

Secret Service seemed, to its day, not merely a rousing spy melodrama of the late war, but "a remarkable contribution to the stage of any land." Such was the judgment of no less a critic than James Huneker, writing in the *New York Sunday Advertiser* (October 11, 1896), who said . . . "I can instance no other play by an American writer where the main current takes on such delightful, swirling eddies, and remember, the rush of the action never halts. The unities of time and place are rigorously adhered to. Even the diversion and sweet foolery of the young lovers melts into the story, and from being at first blush subsidiary, determines in reality the denouement. This is supreme art. The strands of this stirring tale are woven closely, yet is the fabric ever elastic, human, and not merely a triumph of the dramatic weaver's art."

There is a deftness of structure in *Secret Service* that utilizes all the resources of the stage, including silence. A most effective bit of wordless action comes as the curtain rises, with, as the *New York Journal* (September 27, 1898) described it, "the Richmond girl sewing for the hospitals, who enters the quiet room, crosses to a table to gather up some forgotten bit of work, her hesitating glance toward a window, where we see the flash of the siege guns, her weary glance through the parted curtains, and her silent exit. There is no reason why a thing so simple should be so tremendously impressive save that it is absolutely genuine. In the play's humor, its pathos, its heart-stirring climaxes, the same directness of treatment is maintained." "Above all else," said Arthur Hobson Quinn, "it is the absolute reality of the characters that is effective. Without a bit of heroics, they all move under the shadow of danger, playing the game."

The power of the play's hold, and the change in the public estimate of chivalrous conduct, are alike shown in an episode during the play's revival in 1915, a revival that the *New York Dramatic Mirror* (November 13) called "as effective as its first presentation nineteen years ago." When, on Edith's refusal to declare her love, Thorne tells the sergeant to look to his guns, a voice from the gallery cried "You damned fool!" A ripple of laughter bespoke the relaxing nervous tension, and in a moment the house was caught again in the drama's flow. Of the scores of melodramas drawn from the conflict of the Blue and the Gray, with love that crosses the lines, although closely followed by Bronson Howard's *Shenandoah*** and David Belasco's *The Heart of Maryland,** the most gallant, gripping, and vital is *Secret Service.*

Gillette played Captain Thorne some 1,800 times, spread through twenty years. There was a revival by Phoenix at the New York Playhouse, opening April 12, 1976.

SHERLOCK HOLMES   *William Gillette*

William Gillette starred in *Diplomacy (Dora***), The Admirable Crichton,** *Dear Brutus,** but especially in his own dramas. Most successful of these was *Sherlock Holmes* (1899), adapted from one of Arthur Conan Doyle's tales of the world's best-known detective and his companion Dr. Watson. It has been the most popular of the thirty-odd plays about Holmes.

Doyle had written a Sherlock play for Herbert Beerbohm Tree, which was acquired by Charles Frohman, who passed it on to William Gillette, who with the author's approval rewrote the drama. To introduce a love element, Gillette asked: "May I marry Holmes?" Doyle replied: "Marry him or murder him or what you will." Doyle himself killed Holmes at the chasm of the Reichenbach Falls, but public demand led him to bring the detective back to life.

Gillette's play, opening November 6, 1899, at the New York Garrick Theatre, ran for 336 performances, and, opening September 9, 1901, at the London Lyceum, for 216. Gillette played it constantly, coming out of retirement in 1919, aged sixty-four, to act Sherlock again; his last production was November 25, 1929, for 45 performances. In the 1905 London revival, Billy—first of the Baker Street Irregulars, originally lads nearby who occasionally lent a hand to the master—was played by a young actor named

Charles Chaplin. E. Hamilton Steward toured England as Sherlock, giving over two thousand performances between 1908 and 1918.

The Holmes story chosen for the play begins with Jim and Madge Larrabee holding Alice Faulkner captive in her own home, to obtain letters written by a foreign noble who had loved and left her sister and his child by her, in order to blackmail the noble family, by threat of scandal to prevent his imminent royal marriage. Sherlock Holmes is summoned to help her. A fire alarm (arranged by Holmes) is raised; as the others dash out, Holmes notes Alice's eyes turned toward a chair. From its depths he extracts the pack of letters—then returns them to the weeping Alice, saying she must give them to the noble's family of her own free will.

The blackmailers call Professor Moriarty, "Emperor" of English crime; he seizes the chance to foil his archenemy, Holmes. Trap and countertrap follow, until the crooks have Alice and Sherlock caught in the Stepney underground gas chamber. Holmes smashes the lamp, and with the glow of his cigar in the dark lures the men to the window, while he sweeps out of the door with Alice, dropping the outer bar to hold the criminals. To Holmes' office the next morning Moriarty comes disguised as a cabman; Holmes hands him a suitcase—and handcuffs him. Moriarty, led away, swears he will return.

The nobles come for the letters. Holmes proffers them—and is blasted as a fraud; these are counterfeits. Alice, from the anteroom where Holmes has placed her, comes in and gives them the originals. They go. She tells Holmes she loves him. To fend her off, he confesses all his little pretenses. She replies that she too can see beyond actions to real emotions; he protests that he's unworthy, but takes her in his arms as the curtain falls.

In 1922 London saw a dramatization of the story of "The Speckled Band." At the New York Century, October 30, 1953, a dramatization of *Sherlock Holmes* by Anita Rathbone with Basil Rathbone as Sherlock, could not compete; it lasted for three nights. Basil Rathbone, however, played Sherlock in fourteen movies based on the Holmes stories, and for seven years on radio and TV; he came to hate the role. Gillette's version was filmed in 1922 with John Barrymore. Gillette himself was on radio, 1930-1931. In 1955 on radio John Gielgud played Holmes; Ralph Richardson was his Watson.

In Berlin, opening July 2, 1906, Ferdinand Bonn's translation of the Gillette play ran for 239 performances. In Paris, December 20, 1907, Pierre Decourelle's, with Firmin Gemier as Sherlock and Harry Bauer as Watson, attained 335. To the New York Broadway Theatre, February 16, 1965, came the musical *Baker Street,* book by Jerome Coopersmith, music and lyrics by Marian Grudeff and Raymond Jessel, directed by Harold Prince, with Fritz Weaver as Holmes, Peter Sells as Watson, and Martin Gabel as Moriarty, for 313 performances. Among its songs were "It's So Simple," "Finding Words for Spring," "I Shall Miss You," "What a Night This Is Going to Be." The musical included a Queen Victoria Jubilee Parade by Bill Baird marionettes, and a ballet of mugging and murder in an alley of London's gaslit Soho, the victim danced by Joy Norman. It interlinked three of the Doyle stories: "The Adventure of the Empty House," "A Scandal in Bohemia," and "The Final Problem." The love interest was provided by Inga Swenson as Irene Adler.

The Gillette play was performed frequently in England between the two World Wars. And a January 1, 1974, revival at the Aldwych, which ran over 180 performances in the RSC repertory, was described by J. C. Trewin in the *Illustrated London News:* "A group of people had come to the theatre ready to laugh [as at old melodramas like *The Drunkard* and *East Lynne*]. Yet, less than twenty minutes after curtain-time the house was entirely still, held by the atmospherics of Frank Dunlop's production, by John Wood's assurance as the hawk of Baker Street, and by the night's sheer narrative power." It ran for 106 performances; then came to the New York Broadhurst, November 12, 1974, for 471. The play toured the United States again in 1977.

So well known is the detective, in story and play, that a private detective is often referred to as a Sherlock. The Baker Street Irregulars continue his reputation, and his most stirring dramatic presentation is still linked with the name of William Gillette.

SIEGFRIED   *Jean Giraudoux*

Jean Giraudoux (French, 1882-1944) was well known as a novelist, original in thought and in the structure of his works, before he turned to the theatre. He first won wide attention with the novel *Simon le Pathetique* (1918). His novel *Siegfried et le Limousin*, 1921, was awarded the Goncourt Prize; his first play was a dramatization of this novel, as *Siegfried*.

Giraudoux' years in German universities gave him background for the story, which sets a forgotten and forgetting Frenchman in Germany, after the first World War. A German nurse, Eva, finds a man wounded on a battlefield, without memory or identification. She nurses him, then becomes his secretary, as under the name Siegfried he becomes counselor of state and the liberal leader of the German people. The reactionary von Zelten, Siegfried's political rival, suspects that Siegfried is a minor French writer, Jacques Forrestier, reported "lost in action"; he imports Forrestier's fiancée, Genevieve Prat, to identify him. Genevieve comes, supposedly to teach French to Siegfried, who feels drawn to her. His identification is made. The two women urge their opposite claims: Eva tells him 60,000,000 people want him as leader; Genevieve says there's a little French poodle mourning its master. Siegfried returns to France. The close of the play bears the mellow hope that the good on both sides will prevail.

Such a fusion of Frenchman and German gives opportunity for showing the best of both countries. There are several emotional scenes in the play, and the conflict between the two women for Siegfried is a touching one, with audience sympathy finely balanced. Personal relationships, however, are on the whole subordinated to a searching and disillusioned picture of the ironies of political fame and fate, and the distortions of professional or jingoistic patriotism.

Produced in 1928, *Siegfried* ran for a year in Paris. Courtney Bruerton reported in the *Christian Science Monitor* (May 26, 1928) that the author showed "rich imagination and a great talent for poetic fantasy in realistic settings. . . . Most original figure in French letters for many a day." *L'Illustration* (May 19, 1928) said: "To hear Giraudoux is one of the rare pleasures of the spirit . . . The lack of likelihood in the story matters not; it is but a pretext for a development often profound and always sparkling on the German and French soul."

Siegfried was performed in New York in French, opening February 20, 1929; and in May of the next year in an English translation by Philip Carr at the Civic Repertory Theatre. Jacob Ben Ami was Siegfried; Eva Le Gallienne, Genevieve; Margaret Mower, Eva; Egon Brecher, von Zelten; also in the cast were Donald Cameron, J. Edward Bromberg, and Burgess Meredith (doubling in two minor roles).

The play, despite the flourishes of Giraudoux' imagination, holds its characters and situations in sharp relief. It was very well received in New York. Marc Connelly in the *Nation* (November 5, 1930) said *Siegfried* was "the first play I have seen in which the device of the amnesia victim has been used with artistic dignity." Howard Barnes (October 21, 1930) said Giraudoux "clothed this skeleton of a plot with rare artistry, and the climaxes of his dramatic movement are poignantly moving." Brooks Atkinson felt that the author "engenders beauties of thought and feeling quite unfamiliar to the stage. . . . occasionally drops into interludes of brisk Gallic irony, and turns one incidental scene in a frontier railway station into a vastly amusing caricature of French petty officialdom."

The scene at the railway station marks Siegfried's return to France, and brings home the irony of the change from a leading political figure before whom all bow to an ordinary citizen who must bow to border regulations and be tangled in red tape. With rich imagination, deft pressure of irony, and a subtle but sophisticated spirit, *Siegfried* manages to be both a neatly developed document for peace between nations, and a stirring play.

ONDINE   *Jean Giraudoux*

Since Baron Friedrich Heinrich Karl La Motte-Fouqué wrote *Undine* (1811), his story of the water spirit that loved and caused the death of a mortal has had wide popularity and many retellings. The opera *Undine* (1816, libretto by La Motte-Fouqué) with music by the composer and novelist Ernst Theodor Amadeus Hoffmann, became in turn the inspiration for Jacques Offenbach's *Tales of Hoffmann* (1880). The opera *Undine* was performed in England in 1843; in Berlin in 1932; in Vienna in 1936 and 1938. A play *Undine* by J. Benedict was presented in London in 1839; and *Undine* was a Christmas pantomime in London, 1858; a play by R. Reece was performed in London in 1870. (The legend was first set down by the sixteenth-century Paracelsus in his *Treatise on Elemental Spirits*.)

A version of *Undine* was first played in America at the Chestnut Street Theatre in Philadelphia on New Year's Day, 1822. Joseph Jefferson (grandfather of the Joseph that created the role of Rip Van Winkle) played the fisherman; Henry Wallach played Sir Huldbrand, the knight doomed by the love of Undine. The production was most spectacular, with underwater grottos, falling trees, and tumbling cascades.

In New York, in 1839, the noted Taglionis presented a ballet, *Undine*, which the *Spirit of the Times* (August 3, 1839) reviewed favorably. In New York also there was a play *Undine* by Grant Stewart in 1901. In Germany, the play *Undine* by Albert Lortzing, based on the original story, was presented in 1931.

The most recent, and the best, of the dramatic versions of the tale is *Ondine* by Jean Giraudoux. Directed by Louis Jouvet, *Ondine* opened in Paris with Jouvet as Hans and Madeleine Ozeray as Ondine on April 27, 1939. It was given once in English in New York, May 19, 1949; then, opening there February 18, 1954, with Audrey Hepburn, won the Critics' Circle Award as the best foreign play of the year.

In the La Motte-Fouqué version, the nymph Undine is reared by fisherfolk whose daughter has been kidnapped. The knight, Sir Huldbrand, encounters Undine; they fall in love. Undine is snatched back by the waterfolk, and the knight marries Bertalda, who is really the fisher-folk's daughter. The bride calls for a drink from the old well, and Undine is forced by the water-spirits to rise with the waters and bring about the death of the knight. Out of this tale, Jean Giraudoux created a supernatural fantasy that is also a human allegory, a poetic play with satiric overtones and shadings of wisdom and sadness.

In the Giraudoux play, Ondine, transparent as water, loves Hans von Wittenstein zu Wittenstein, opaque as earth. She is told by her uncle that Hans will die if he proves untrue. At court, Ondine mocks the courtesies and hypocrisies of the nobles. Her uncle, posing as a court magician, speeds the years along; Ondine disappears, and Hans is to marry Berthe. Now Ondine comes to save Hans; she tries to pretend that she was unfaithful first; but her love is too wholehearted for deception; it fools no one. Hans does not understand Ondine's attempt at self-sacrifice, but his love for her reawakens, and he dies. In the space of three sounds from the waters, Ondine has forgotten her mortal interlude, and is again one with the water-nymphs.

After the Paris production of *Ondine,* American opinions varied. The *New Yorker* correspondent (July 8, 1939) stated "It's a poor play, and nowhere does it touch on the fears and hopes now moving Frenchmen's minds, but Frenchmen flock to see the piece, which, for a relief, deals with the unreal." The reviewer for the *Christian Science Monitor* (June 3, 1939) was more sympathetic: *Ondine,* he said, "has indeed the fluidity of water, its freshness, its carefree babbling, and also here and there its pools hidden in the green shade, its still serenity, its depth, most of all its transparency."

The French newspapers were unanimous in enthusiastic praise of *Ondine.* All found the production superbly spectacular, yet delicate: "One of the most exquisite creations of Louis Jouvet," said Robert de Beauplan in *La Petite Illustration* (August 26, 1939). Several critics emphasized that Giraudoux had in *Ondine* most successfully combined reality and fantasy. "Never," said Pierre Audiat in *Paris-Soir,* "has Giraudoux been more accessible in his flashes of irony and philosophy; never has he gone farther in the exploration of the emotions." Most penetratingly, James de Coquet in *Annales* observed: "He seizes with uncommon clearness of vision the nature of things, the essence of forms, the course of events. Once in possession of these truths, so that they could be set down in figures and formulas, he gives them back to us in the colors of a dream . . . First he reduces things to their simplest expression, then he raises them to their highest power . . . He does not rest content with telling a story or demonstrating a truth; he must also lead the beholder into an imaginary world, far from our own in all appearances, yet very close in the character of its inhabitants." London saw *Ondine* in 1953.

The fairy-tale world of *Ondine* indeed comes close to our own, as the nymph Ondine loves Hans so much, and suffers so much for him, that she almost becomes human. As there is pathos—and all loving womanhood—in her attempt to sacrifice herself for Hans, so is there irony, and all natural indifference, in the forgetfulness of Hans that comes upon her as she, a force of nature, remains immortal while human generations die.

In addition to its poetry and its wisdom, *Ondine* is not without satire. The simple, superstitious fisher-folk are not spared, yet there is a kindliness in their exposure that becomes less gentle in the presentation of the absurdities and the hypocrisies of the court; and there is a searching comment in the manner in which Hans' doom is to be announced: when the peasant speaks poetry, the noble will die.

Ondine is a truly colorful and fanciful fairy-tale, delightful to behold, charming to the ear and the eye; it is also a moving and thoughtful picture of man's brief hold upon life and love in the endless indifferent flow of nature. In short, it is a play rewarding to the heart and to the mind.

Adapted by Maurice Valency, *Ondine* was performed in London in 1955 with Moira Shearer and Eric Porter, and in 1961 with Porter and Leslie Caron. It was shown at the Edinburgh Festival, 1968.

THE MADWOMAN OF CHAILLOT   *Jean Giraudoux*

Most rewarding of Giraudoux' slantwise satires of the life of our time is *The Madwoman of Chaillot (La Folle de Chaillot)*, 1943, which was produced in Paris, directed by Louis Jouvet, on December 19, 1945.

Vogue (March 1, 1946) considered the first production especially "notable for the inspired acting of Marguerite Moreno as the Madwoman, and Louis Jouvet as the Ragpicker; for the imaginative fantasy of Christian Berard's settings." After this production ran for over a year, Jouvet tired of a single role and returned to repertory. He has not revived the play since Mme. Moreno (aged 82) died.

A translation by Maurice Valency opened at the New York Belasco, December 27, 1948, with Martita Hunt (the Madwoman), John Carradine (the Ragpicker), Estelle Winwood, Clarence Derwent, and Vladimir Sokoloff. The costumes and the settings—a café terrace, and the vast cellar of the Countess—were brought over from France. In spite of unimaginative direction, the brilliance of the play shone through. It ran for 368 performances and, after a tour, returned to New York, June 13, 1950, for two weeks at the City Center. Martita Hunt was also in the cast of the London production which opened February 15, 1951, for 68 performances.

The Madwoman of Chaillot pictures a half-demented but quite competent and confident old crone who discovers that there is evil in the world and proceeds to dispose of it. A syndicate of astute exploiters plans to extract oil from the ground beneath Paris; the mad Countess, Aurelia, to save Paris from being destroyed by their greed, invites them, followed by journalists and sundry greedy groups, to her cellar, whence an endless staircase leads forever down. Thinking to find oil, they step down. "The pimps who little by little have taken over the world" thus removed, the clean world is left to the common people, the men of good will, the pure in heart.

The lucky Frenchman is born not with a silver spoon in his mouth, but with a golden pen in his hand. The French theatre-public believes, says Giraudoux, that "the soul can be made to open naturally, like a safe, with a word, and dislikes the German oxyhydrogen blow-torch method." Hence the flashes of improvisation in *The Madwoman of Chaillot*; sometimes they gambol for the sheer delight of verbal and mental play; sometimes they flicker with an eerie light over dark places within the human soul; sometimes they turn like a great revolving searchlight across contemporary life. "The logic of the scene," as Brooks Atkinson said (January 9, 1949), "seems to be impeccable, but the effect is crack-brained, original, and delightful . . . This vagrant style naturally suited Giraudoux, who was too sophisticated to believe in easy solutions but never lost faith in people and never renounced a young man's dreams of a happy world." When seen through Giraudoux' eyes, said John Mason Brown (January 15, 1949), "the mundane regains its wonder, the expected becomes unpredictable." Several critics compared the mood of the play with that of Lewis Carroll's *Alice* books. In Brown's opinion the Madwoman's was "the most hilarious and maddest tea-party given since the Dormouse, the March Hare, and a certain Hatter entertained Alice."

Those that complain that Giraudoux' cure for the evils of the world is too simple, overlook the fact that the cure is devised by the mad woman. Giraudoux not only looks with glint of irony at the evils of society; he also satirizes those that would adopt panaceas for social ills. In the seemingly mad cascading of the playwright's fancy, there is a subtle method as *The Madwoman of Chaillot* lights Roman candles over the gauds and the greeds, the shoddies and the needs, of human kind. Where realism must reckon with despair, Giraudoux focuses fantasy to light the intelligence with good theatre and brighten the vision with hope.

The Valency version of *The Madwoman of Chaillot* was given twenty-three performances in repertory at Asolo, opening July 6, 1967; and at Oxford, November 28, 1967, with Elisabeth Bergner. It was revived in New York in French, March 22, 1970.

A musical called *Dear World,* based on *The Madwoman,* book by Jerome Lawrence and Robert E. Lee, music and lyrics by Jerry Herman, came to the New York Mark Hellinger, February 6, 1969, with Angela Lansbury, for 132 performances. Among its songs are "The Spring of Next Year," "Kiss Her Now," "Each Tomorrow Morning." The title song is a plea to the "dear world" to somehow attain the ideal state of Aurelia's dream.

FAUST   *Johann Wolfgang Goethe*

The legend of Faust, a popular German folk tale supposedly based on the life of a real man who died about 1545, was first printed in the German *Volksbuch* of 1587. There was an English ballad on the subject in 1588; the great play by Christopher Marlowe* was written during the next year. During the Reformation, the legend was utilized for anti-Catholic propaganda, Faust being represented as a student of the Jesuits. Early versions of the story picture Faust as seeking material prizes: wealth, power, beautiful women; later, he is shown seeking more spiritual goals, until in Goethe his desire is equated with the highest, selfless quest of man.

Christopher Marlowe, in the opinion of the *London Times* (September 23, 1949), gave Faust "his true greatness when he divined the secret vitality of the story and made Faustus symbolize the human spirit's hunger for experience and power in the phase of the English Renaissance when that hunger was at its keenest. The symbol was too powerful to be confined even within the limits of a masterpiece. He found his way to the showman's booth and was immensely popular as a puppet. Swift saw him come off second-best to Punch. A gentleman walking in Smithfield in 1701 reports a performance at Bartholomew Fair of *The Devil and Dr. Faustus* [which is also the title of a motion picture shown in 1950]. It was as a wooden doll on wires that Goethe first saw the masterpiece upon which he was to labor intermittently throughout his creative life. Germany in the days of *Sturm und Drang* was as fascinated by the figure of Faust as Renaissance writers and showmen, and many *Fausts* were written while Goethe was at work. The creative spirit of the second coming of humanism found expression in the infinitely significant figure of the man who sought the same end."

The Faust legend captured the yearnings of the late Middle Ages, during which it arose. The goals of humanism, Faust achieves by the Devil's power: he hears blind Homer sing; he brings Alexander back to life; he weds immortal Helen. "That for which Faustus sold his soul," observed John

Addington Symonds in *The Italian Renaissance,* "was yielded to the world without price at the time of the Renaissance."

In 1775 Goethe (1749-1832) wrote his first, simple draft of the story, now known as the *Urfaust (Original Faust).*

In a play without firm dramatic structure—in quick, shifting scenes such as Goethe found in Elizabethan drama—but with some of the world's greatest poetry, Goethe gives his version of the Faust story. The First Part, completed in 1808, opens (like *The Book of Job**) with Mephistopheles in Heaven winning permission to tempt man. On earth, Faust agrees that the Devil may have his soul if the Devil gives him one hour so perfect that he would not have it pass. Chief of the seductions which Mephistopheles presents is the charming and innocent Margaret (Gretchen), whom Faust seduces; then, killing her brother who interferes, he leaves her to drown their child and to die.

The Second Part of *Faust* (completed in 1831, and so formless and complex that it is rarely acted) pictures Faust turning from the pleasures of the senses to the joys of the spirit, to a quest of aesthetic beauty and human worth. Helen of Troy is given to Faust. Their son, Euphorion, symbolizes at first the union of the classical and the romantic; then, more generally, the urge of mankind toward beauty. Both Euphorion and Helen, however, soar off into flaming air: beauty cannot be kept; ambition must hold its roots in earth. Faust then devotes himself to helping his fellow-men; he wears through years of service until finally, old and blind, he declares himself content. He has lost his wager, but he has found his way; and his soul is transported to Heaven.

Though the First Part is still frequently performed in Germany, *Faust* has undergone many transformations. The Hungarian Nicholas Lenau (N. N. von Strehlenau) rewrote *Faust* as an epic drama in 1835. Michel Carré made a French version, *Faust and Marguerite,* in 1850, which follows Goethe's Part One rather closely, but stresses the lighter moments of the play. The opera of Charles François Gounod (his first success), 1859, is based on Carré's version. London had earlier seen two forms of Part One. A version by George Soame, 1825 and 1827, was written in the style of the early nineteenth-century romantic drama, a mixture of song and dialogue, of Marlowe and Goethe and *Don Giovanni,* with Faust stung by a serpent in the final scene. Then came "the comic *Faust,*" a version by Lema Rede, 1849, set in contemporary London, with the Devil played as a buffoon. In 1863, and for some years after, London saw an English adaptation of Carré's French version of the German play. Of this adaptation, *The Spirit of the Times* (January 3, 1863), reviewing a Niblo's Garden production in New York, said: "The text bears no resemblance to that of Goethe's *Faust.* And it is well that it does not, for any attempt to put the original on the stage would be almost as absurd as an attempt to play *Paradise Lost* . . . Mephistopheles is . . . a limping, vulgar, noisy fellow, grinning like a monkey at every word or movement, and outraging all the proprieties of time and place with his loud ejaculations and perpetual boisterousness."

In Gounod's version, Faust is transported to hell; but in the opera of the Italian Arrigo Boito, *Mefistofele,* 1868, he is saved. Faust goes to hell again in *The Damnation of Faust* by the Frenchman Louis Hector Berlioz, which was presented as a dramatic cantata in 1846 and first played as an opera in 1880.

Notable among later *Faust* productions was, first, that of Henry Irving in a version by W. G. Wills played continually in London and New York from 1886 to 1896. Irving's performance as Mephistopheles was generally condemned, but Ellen Terry as Margaret won high praise. The production was highly praised by the *New York Dramatic Mirror* (November 12, 1887) and Clement Scott in the *Illustrated London News* (May 5, 1894).

Perhaps the best English acting version of Part One is that of Stephen Phillips, based on Bayard Taylor's translation of *Faust,* which Beerbohm Tree presented in 1908. Clayton Hamilton felt that "it compresses into comparatively few scenes the unrestrained sweep of Goethe's epical inventiveness . . . and reduces his main ideas to the simplicity demanded by a theatre-going public that yawns while it asks to be amused." Walter Pritchard Eaton, however, thought it a rather tawdry device to have the witch (drawing from Goethe's Part Two and Phillip's imagination) show Faust visions of Helen, of Cleopatra, and of Messalina. But Eaton conceded that there is a masterly touch in the witch's showing Faust the image of Margaret in prison, her dead baby at her feet. The sight wakes all the decency in Faust and Mephistopheles is foiled. "This is an idea," said Eaton, "quite in accord with Goethe's poem, and perhaps the best contribution of the new drama."

Of the original German work, James Huneker stated that "Goethe is not bound by the Faust legend; it is merely a springboard for his fantasy and wisdom." In weighing a performance of the play at Frankfurt, the *London Times* (August 15, 1939) declared: "Of the main themes, the lesser is the problem of the co-existence of good and evil; the greater, that of the insufficiency of man, who can aspire, god-like, to all understanding and all riches of existence and yet remain, when all is had, empty and unsatisfied."

Goethe's main idea was to picture human helpfulness as redeeming the soul; whereas Marlowe's was to picture a man who has gained the whole world at the cost of his soul. The frequent performance of Goethe's Part One without Part Two, however, has led many to consider the Gretchen episode as the main story. Thus Charles Lamb, in a letter to Harrison Ainsworth in 1823, before Part Two was written, declared: "'Tis a disagreeable, canting tale of seduction, which has nothing to do with the spirit of Faust." In Part One, Goethe probes depths of human pathos; in Part Two, he soars to heights of human majesty.

When the Henry Irving version of *Faust* was revived (January 3, 1927) with Gene Lockhart as Mephisto, the *New York Times* reported that it "turns a poem into a melodramatic costume tragedy, but there is something living in the play that histrionics cannot thwart." The next year (October 8, 1928), the Theatre Guild in New York presented a version by Graham and Tristan Rawson, with Dudley Digges (Mephisto), George Gaul (Faust), Helen Chandler (Margaret), Gale Sondergaard (the Witch), and Helen Westley (Martha). Later productions include one at Chapel Hill in 1932; one at Los Angeles, 1938, directed by Max Reinhardt, who in the same year produced a motion picture version with Walter Huston as Mephistopheles, Conrad Nagle as Faust, Margo as Margaret, and Lenore Ulric as Martha; and one by Equity Library in New York in 1946. Altogether, there have been over forty English versions of Goethe's play.

London saw *Faust* in German in 1852, 1853, 1901, and 1930; a performance by the Münchener marionettes in 1931, and the *Urfaust* in the centennial year of 1932. New York has also seen quite a number of German productions of Part One; recently, at the Barbizon Plaza, one opening November 28, 1947, with the eighty-year-old Albert Bassermann as Mephistopheles and Uta Hagen as Margaret. The year 1949, bicentennial of Goethe's birth, saw further revivals of *Faust*.

The symbolism of Helen, in Part Two of *Faust,* has been deeply explored.

In *The Classical Tradition* (1949), Gilbert Highet discusses various ways in which her impact on Faust may be interpreted.

In his recent book *The Fortunes of Faust* (1952), E. M. Butler refers to more than fifty translations of Goethe's play into English and almost as many retellings of the legend after him. Among the latter are fragments by Shelley, a serious play (*Gretchen*) by W. S. Gilbert,* Valery's *Mon Faust,** Thomas Mann's novel, *Doktor Faust* (1947), and Dorothy Sayers' *The Devil to Pay* (1945).

Faust, Eugene O'Neill has said, is "the one classic drama which is closest to the American mind of today." Though its turbulence and its tumultuous organization keep it from frequent full revival, *Faust* is certainly one of the world's greatest poetic dramas. Its story, being a legend, is timeless in that it can be interpreted anew to fit the fashions and the urges of every time; its theme is timeless and universal, being not merely man's questioning and heartbreak over good and evil in the world, but the quenchless thirst of humanity for meaning, for value, for direction on this dark journey we call life.

Gretchen's little game as she falls in love with Faust was called by the great critic Georg Brandes "the height of lyric eloquence . . . It was quite out of the question to portray anything more simple or familiar than the young girl who plucks the petals from the daisy and says 'He loves me, he loves me not!' But no one had availed himself of that theme before Goethe. It was the egg of Columbus; and its effect was incalculable. By this addition the field of art was extended."

Let us consider only productions in the 150th anniversary of Goethe's death, 1982. In West Berlin director Klaus Michael Grüber, at the Freie Volksbühne, reduced the cast to four actors. He omitted most of Mephistopheles' lines, and turned the Walpurgis Night into a play of lights on the curtains. In contrast with the young and naïve Margaret, the most distinguished West German actor Bernhard Minetti showed an old Faust, embittered by failure.

The CSC, fitly opening on Halloween, gave the first complete *Faust* One and Two, in the United States. The dialogue, somewhat colloquialized, showed Faust in three ages: first, in the Prologue, as an old man (played by Christopher Martin, who also directed); then as the young ardent poet (Gary Sloan); finally, the mature seeker (Tom Spackman). Gretchen (Margaret) was played by Ginger Grace, betrayed by Faust but returning to save him at the end. Amy Warner played Helen of Troy with a chorus of white-masked dancing nymphs. Noble Shropshire was the suave Mephistopheles. The Walpurgis Night became a "grand masque of witchery"; in the beer hall geysers of wine spurted from holes in the wooden tables. On the open stage sound, light, and costumes took the place of sets. In New York's Central Park, as Mel Gussow reported in the *Times* (November 4, 1982), "When Faust issues a sigh 'Thank God!' Mephistopheles momentarily shrivels, as if struck by a bolt of lightning." Goethe's *Faust* came as lightning in the nineteenth-century aesthetic sky.

THE INSPECTOR-GENERAL   *Nikolai Gogol*

Revizor (*The Inspector-General*), by Nikolai Vassilievitch Gogol (1809-1852) is the greatest Russian comedy. Its idea was suggested to Gogol by the poet Pushkin, perhaps from an actual happening. Gogol had already abandoned an unfinished play about an intriguing government official because he knew it could not pass the censor. But *The Inspector-General* was taken by the playwright Vassili Zhukovski to the Czar, who was so amused by it that he ordered it performed. Its devastating satire of corrupt petty officialdom has been played ever since throughout Russia, throughout the world.

The Inspector-General displays a small town whose officials hear that the Inspector-General is on a tour of inspection. The town hospital is filthy; the judge raises geese in the courtroom; the school superintendent draws his staff from the asylum; local accounts are in an incredible state. Dressed in the latest fashion, a nobody with haughty airs arrives from St. Petersburg. He is wined and dined, offered the Superintendent's best suits, the mayor's daughter, everybody's purse. When he leaves, by intercepting a letter they guess to be the secret report of the inspector, the town officials learn that they have been imposed upon. As they are gathering fury, hurling blame upon one another, a soldier announces that the Inspector-General has arrived.

The Inspector-General was played in Moscow and in St. Petersburg in 1836. New York saw it in Yiddish, with Maurice Schwartz, for sixteen weeks in 1923; then Schwartz played it in English, opening April 30, 1923. It was revived December 23, 1930, with Romney Brent, Dorothy Gish, Eugene Powers, and J. Edward Bromberg. The Moscow Art Theatre presented the play in New York, in Russian, February 17, 1935. It was played there again in Russian in 1949. In English there was a New York production by Equity Library in 1947. A film based on the comedy, with Danny Kaye in a setting moved to Middle Europe, was released in 1949.

In some Russian provincial theatres, the producers were afraid to stage *The Inspector-General* in the 1830's and 1840's. In Rostov-on-Don, when at the end of the play the "real" Inspector-General Skvosnik-Dmykhanovsky shouts "I'll send you all to Siberia!" Governor Zaguro-Zolorovsky jumped onto the stage and shouted, "You are insulting the authorities! I'll send you all to Siberia!!" He ordered the cast arrested; when shown the *exprimatur* of the St. Petersburg censor, he stomped out of the theatre.

When *The Inspector-General* was first shown in New York, only a few reviewers recognized its value. *The Call* (October 10, 1922) called it "a vivid human document, one of the famous comedies of all literature . . . Historically and socially, *The Inspector-General* has a value quite apart from its dramatic significance." Later performances were more widely hailed. In 1935, the *American* (February 18) said: "It is a living, universal farce, a great farce forever funny." Robert Garland called it "a political prank, a hilariously funny slapstick satire." More solemnly, of the centenary Leningrad production, B. M. Shushkevich, the director, declared in the *Moscow Daily News* (June 24, 1936): "I wanted to transmit the social force of laughter."

In 1929 a highly stylized production was given by Vsevolod Emilievich Meyerhold in Paris—the production for which the great Russian director Meyerhold is best known. This production romped about so freely that at length Balieff (the famous director of the Chauvre-Souris) rose in the audience and cried "Give us Gogol!"

In hilarious satire, with a clean integrity of malice, Gogol has pilloried for all time the petty, ignorant, grafting, rascally official, caught in one of the world's greatest comedies.

The CSC revived *The Inspector-General* in 1971. In a new, somewhat scatological translation by Gerard McLernon, the company obviously played for the laughs, not heeding Gogol's own warning: "The less an actor works for laughs, the funnier his part will be." A good comedian usually seems a little surprised that he is laughed at.

THE SERVANT OF TWO MASTERS   _Carlo Goldoni_

Although without the dramatic vitality of his later work _The Mistress of the Inn,* The Servant of Two Masters_ by Carlo Goldoni (Italian, 1707-1793) retains a considerable measure of liveliness and power. Written in 1740, it is still played in Italy. It was revived in German by Reinhardt in Vienna (1923), in Berlin (1924), and in New York, with Lili Darvas, Hermann and Hans Thimig, and Vladimir Sokoloff, January 9, 1928. Cambridge saw the play in English on June 8, 1935—the first time that a Cambridge Dramatic Club production used women—and it was revived there again in 1936, when Yale University also produced the play. The Barter Theatre played it in 1941; the New York Dramatic Workshop in 1954.

The Servant of Two Masters is built upon an intrigue involving two pairs of frustrated lovers. It is a comedy, somewhat after the Roman style, of confusions and mistakes, further complicated by the fact that Florindo, who loves Beatrice, meets Beatrice disguised as a man and deems her a rival. Most of the play's fun revolves upon the always hungry Truffaldino, who acts as servant both to Florindo and to the disguised Beatrice. He persuades both masters to order him a dinner, but his double-stuffing ends (with the play) when Beatrice's identity is revealed, and she weds Florindo.

The high point of the play is Truffaldino's final enjoyment of his meal, "an orgy among the edibles," said the _New York Post_ (January 10, 1928), "giving the stage the general appearance of a delicatessen store wrecked by a tornado."

In _The Servant of Two Masters,_ Goldoni had not yet broken away from the established patterns of comedy; especially, the use of stock figures. The triteness of such figures was especially noted by the _London Times,_ June 10, 1935, but a later review (October 23, 1936) conceded "they are nevertheless a lively lot . . . the intricate pattern they weave with their borrowed intrigues makes a charming effect." Considerable slapstick enlivens current productions, but _The Servant of Two Masters_ is sustained by Goldoni's good nature, gay spirits, and amused capture of the foibles of folk familiar to us all.

Its many recent productions include: 1968, London (Queens), with Tommy Steele as Truffaldino, one of the richest parts in all comedy, playing a corset like an accordion. In 1959-1960 Piccolo Teatro de Milano made a tour of ninety-two cities in twenty-two countries, from Tokyo and Buenos Aires to Moscow and Edinburgh, from Sadler's Wells, London, to the City Center, New York. In 1967, Chichester, England; Melbourne, Australia; Berlin; and Paris in French and in the Italian original. In 1971, Ottawa; Yale, and East Hampton, N.Y. In 1972, Vienna. In 1979, OffBway (La Mama) by the Pan-Asian Repertory, in English interspersed with dialects of China, Japan, Burma, Hawaii, and the Philippines. In 1982, Cambridge, with (_London Observer,_ July 25, 1982) "a dash and style that keep you gobstruck with admiration"; at the London (Richmond) with music by Martin Duncan and David Ultz, with fantastic wigs and makeup. Mingling with the audience at the London Ark, September 1983, Truffaldino shook hands; Pantalone urged "Don't be shy!" with the applause.

THE MISTRESS OF THE INN   *Carlo Goldoni*

In French and in Italian, Goldoni wrote well over 200 plays; by far the most famous of these is *La Locandiera* (*The Mistress of the Inn,* also known as *Mine Hostess* and *Mirandolina*).

La Locandiera was first presented in Venice, December 26, 1751. It is still very popular in Italy. Duse played in it in Paris, London, and, in 1893, New York. Stanislavski presented it in Moscow, December 2, 1898, and in New York, 1923. In English, *The Mistress of the Inn* was shown in Los Angeles in 1935, in New York by Eva Le Gallienne, 1926 on. As *Mine Hostess,* in adaptation by Clifford Bax, London saw it August 17, 1944. Equity Library, New York, produced it in 1947; the Hedgerow Theatre in 1948. In 1936, presented by the "First Collective Farm Arts Theatre" in a Moscow competition, it won first prize.

Robert Browning has said that "Goldoni, good, gay, sunniest of souls," reflects in his plays "the shade and shine of common life." These qualities, together with the pleasures and profits of innkeeping, are delightfully presented in *The Mistress of the Inn,* the story of the merry and independent Mirandolina, who is wooed, mainly for her wealth, by the niggardly old Marquis of Forlipopoli, and the eccentric Count of Albaforita. Mirandola, however, sets her cap for the woman-hating Cavalier, the Black Knight of Ripafratta. By flattery and good food she wins the Cavalier, then tumbles him aside for her head-waiter, Fabrizio. For she knows that the best way to secure her freedom is within the walls of matrimony.

A good deal of the play's fun is supplied by two actresses, Ortensia and Djaneira (omitted in the Duse version), who come to the inn; they pretend to be ladies of quality but on the slightest provocation behave like ladies of the evening. Mirandolina sees through their pretensions, and provides scope for their whole-hearted, lusty vulgarity. While all this fun, combined with kindly satire, keeps the action lively, the provident Mirandolina takes care to stuff not only her guests but the money-box of the inn.

"Papa Goldoni," as the Italians call him—father of the friendly comedy of manners, original in its mood though in its manner based on Moliere*— continues to be popular.

Of Eva Le Gallienne's production of the play, *Variety* (December 1, 1926) observed that it was "an amusing satire, in style quaint now and fan-like; but the essence of its characterizations is still of a piece with the quirks of human nature." In London, Harold Hobson said in the *Observer* (August 20, 1944): "This is a classic alternative to some modern methods of making antic hay."

Goldoni's conception of character was dynamic; he saw men as the instruments with which their own will could fashion a personality. The conception gives vigor to his figures and vitality to their movements. As Francesco de Sanctis points out in his *History of Italian Literature* (1931), "Goldoni has a marvelous gift for finding situations in which the character can be developed to the full . . . The author proceeds on his way swiftly and directly, without stopping to meditate or look into his soul, or to plumb the depths; but stays on the surface, content and joyous." This surface joy, rising from characters tinged with gentle satire and seen with sharp but amused eye, radiates from *The Mistress of the Inn.*

There were revivals in 1961 at Texas Christian University and San José State College, Calif.; by Asolo in 1963 and 1975; adapted by Clifford Bax, Bournemouth, England, 1966; also as a musical by Don Walker and Ira Wallace, Bucks County, Pa., 1957.

SHE STOOPS TO CONQUER   *Oliver Goldsmith*

Oliver Goldsmith (Irish, 1730-1774) seems to have been a blunderer as a man. After rejection for ordination and failure to earn a living as a physician, he took to literature. *She Stoops to Conquer* is based on an awkward situation from his own life.

At first the play had trouble in reaching the stage. Samuel Johnson, Goldsmith's friend, pressed it through to production at Covent Garden, where it opened, May 15, 1773. Although a claque almost spoiled the play's effect by over-applause, it was a hit. King George III enjoyed it; and it ran for thirteen performances to the end of the season. Revivals were produced almost every year until the end of the nineteenth century. Four editions of the play were printed in its first year. The title was suggested by Dryden; Goldsmith's original name of the play, *The Mistakes of a Night,* was kept as subtitle. At first, since the play did not employ the high-flown, over-colored speech then in vogue, actresses disdained the parts; but soon they were quarreling for roles, and Goldsmith wrote several Epilogues to satisfy the temperamental ladies. Garrick, sorry he had not taken the play for Drury Lane, wrote a Prologue.

Controversy over the play reached beyond the theatre. Johnson declared that no comedy in years had "answered so much the great end of comedy— making an audience merry"; but Horace Walpole demurred: "It is not the subject I condemn, though very vulgar; but the execution. The drift tends to no moral, to no edification of any kind ... It is set up in opposition to sentimental comedy, and is as bad as the worst of them." In the *London Packet,* "Tom Tickle" attacked the play; considering the attack a personal one, Goldsmith thrashed the publisher and was fined £50 for his pleasure.

The story of *She Stoops to Conquer* springs from a misunderstanding. Young Marlow, "one of the most bashful and reserved young fellows in all the world," with his friend Hastings goes to visit the Hardcastles, a match having been proposed between him and Kate Hardcastle. At night, Tony Lumpkin, Hardcastle's step-son, directs the two young men to an "inn," which is really the Hardcastle home; and Marlow treats Hardcastle bluffly, as the landlord, while he makes bold advances to Kate Hardcastle. Recognizing his misunderstanding, Kate "stoops" to the role of servant, so that Marlow may not be shy. The comedy rises mainly from the misunderstanding, but several of the characters are in themselves truly comic creations.

She Stoops to Conquer has been almost as popular in America as in England, being revived in Boston, for example, in 1870, 1871, 1874, 1875, 1876, and 1877. In New York a musical version by Stanislaus Stange, *The Two Roses,* was presented, opening November 21, 1904, with Roland Cunningham and Fritzi Scheff.

Many stars have performed in *She Stoops to Conquer.* Among them are Charles Kemble, Mrs. Langtry, Fanny Davenport, Rose Coghlan, Annie Russell, Julia Marlowe, Mary Shaw, Sidney Drew, Robert Mantell, and Cyril Maude. In New York, there was an all-star revival in 1905; another, the Players' Annual, in 1924, with Basil Sydney (Marlow), Dudley Digges (Squire Hardcastle), Ernest Glendenning (Tony Lumpkin), Elsie Ferguson, (Kate Hardcastle), Helen Hayes, Pauline Lord, and Selena Royle; and still another in 1928, with Wilfrid Seagram (Marlow), Lyn Harding (Squire Hardcastle), Glenn Hunter (Tony), Fay Bainter (Kate), and Patricia Collinge, with Pauline Lord delivering the Prologue. The first performance of the play in the United States was at the New York John Street Theatre on

August 2, 1773. More recent ones have come in 1933, 1934, 1936, 1937, 1938, 1940, and 1942. In 1949 it was played at the Old Vic in London with Michael Redgrave.

Of the 1924 revival, the *New York World* (June 10) declared: "This piece, which has made snobs of high school sophomores the land over and supplied safe fuel for languishing stocks, seemed in its glory." In 1928, Alexander Woollcott called the play "a singularly durable comedy"; Brooks Atkinson said it is "shot through with the homely simplicities of a pastoral jollification"; Allardyce Nicoll has pointed out that the play does not, like its predecessors, deal in pointed wit, but warms with an all-pervading humor. There is a basic love of mankind throughout; even the satiric strokes are friendly.

Revived as the first of the City Center series in New York, December 28, 1949, with Maurice Evans presenting a new prologue, and Celeste Holm, Ezra Stone, Carmen Matthews, and Burl Ives in the cast, *She Stoops to Conquer* again found the critics delighted. Atkinson singled out Tony Lumpkin as "one of the most objectionable brats in dramatic literature"; but noted that the play as a whole is stamped by "the good-hearted simplicity of Goldsmith's lovable genius."

Horace Walpole complained that *She Stoops to Conquer* "tends to no moral"; and, indeed, it presses no ethical point. But the play is so abounding in good humor, in gay and gentle and good spirits, that not only its fun but its fresh wholesomeness is infectious: it does not preach morals, it makes one better for the beholding. *She Stoops to Conquer* is the roast-beef-and-pudding, the ale-and-fare-well spirit of England, at its laughing heartiest.

Macaulay declared: "There have been many greater authors, but perhaps no other writer was ever more uniformly agreeable." And no other writer has written a masterpiece in every one of the four major literary forms—a minor masterpiece, one may protest, but a true one: poem, "The Deserted Village"; novel, *The Vicar of Wakefield*; essay, "The Chinese Letters"; drama . . . "How exquisite of its kind!" exclaimed Bulwer-Lytton in 1848; "the humour that draws tears, the pathos that provokes smiles, will be popular to the end of the world."

Among many recent productions: Pitlochry Festival, 1956. Phoenix, 1960, forty-seven performances in New York, directed by Stuart Vaughan, John Heffernan playing Tony. London, 1969, with Tommy Steele as Tony and Judi Dench as Kate. Roundabout, 1970-1971. Asolo, 1961 and 1978, the latter year also University of Michigan.

(Covent Garden, 1773; New York, 1973, "a massive satisfaction": Walter Kerr.)

Two musicals: *O Marry Me!,* book and lyrics by Lola Pergament, music by Robert Kessler, October 27, 1967, OffBway (Gate) for twenty-one performances, then 1963 to Windsor, England. *Liberty Ranch,* 1972 in Greenwich, England, setting the play in the American West, with Tony Lumpkin a halfbreed Indian, and Kate not in any sense the maid but "Ruby McLeod," a notorious femme fatale of the dance halls. And more—back to the old play at the London Lyric Hammersmith, 1982, with Betty Marsden a ludicrously bewigged and bedizened Mrs. Hardcastle, Tony Lumpkin an oaf you warm to while you laugh. "The first scene is a model of exposition," said Robert Cushman (August 15, 1982). "Like a good inn, it is clean, warm, funny, and hospitable . . . The production never stoops, the play conquers." The play continues its amusing hold.

THE LOWER DEPTHS   *Maxim Gorki*

Alexei Maximovich Pyeshkov (Russian, 1866-1936), left to fend for himself at the age of nine, drifted through Russia, grubbing at many jobs, was
imprisoned as a revolutionary, and wrote some short stories under the name
of Maxim Gorki (Maxim the Bitter). In 1900, several years after he organized a peasants' theatre in the Ukraine, he was invited to Chekhov's villa at
Yalta, where the Moscow Art Theatre under Stanislavski was rehearsing.
Shortly thereafter he wrote two plays, with Stanislavski's encouragement.

The first of the two, *The Petty Bourgeois* (also called *The Middle Class*
and *The Smug Citizen*) was weakened by censorship, but still aroused a
storm when it opened the new Moscow Art Theatre on October 25, 1902. On
December 31 of the same year, *The Lower Depths* was presented. It had
been censored in advance (over fifty passages were deleted), but the play
achieved the greatest triumph in the history of the Moscow Art Theatre. It
was revived, on Gorki's return to Moscow in 1928, after the Revolution, with
the full text and almost the whole original cast. On its thirtieth anniversary, the author's birthplace, Nizhni-Novgorod, was renamed Gorki, and
the theatre was rechristened "The Moscow Art Theatre in the name of
Gorki." In the meantime, the play was produced in London in 1903 and
1911; in Berlin (as *Nachtasyl*) for 500 performances in 1908. In New York it
was presented by Arthur Hopkins as *Night Lodging* in 1919; the Moscow
Art offered it in Russian in 1923; it was revived as *At the Bottom* in 1930, as
The Lower Depths in 1943 and at the City College in 1947; an all-Negro
version, *A Long Way From Home,* was produced by the Experimental Theatre of ANTA, opening February 9, 1948. Other American performances
include one in Cleveland, 1933; Dallas, 1934; Hollywood, 1935.

Following the Stanislavski method, of living oneself into the character,
the Moscow Art players prepared for the premiere of *The Lower Depths* by
visiting the slums and meeting such detritus of the human race as slumps
through Gorki's drama. Derelict thief, convict, run-down gentleman, one-
time actor ruined by alcohol, receiver of stolen goods, philosophic ragged
greybeard, whiner, aging prostitute, and profiteer seek anodynes or wait for
death in this dreary drama. Into the midst of the wastrels comes the
optimist Luka, who tells them that "no one is so low as to deserve the
degradation of another human's pity." He converts them to hope, but during
a murderous brawl, Luka simply goes off, and the derelicts drift back into
hopelessness. The drunken ex-actor Satin, after telling them that weaklings need Luka's lies but the strong man can face the truth—breaking into
a hopeful paean: "Man is higher than a full belly! Man is born to conceive a
better man."—proceeds to hang himself. In the brawl, the proprietor of the
cheap lodging-house, Kostylov, is killed; his sister-in-law in jealousy cries
murder against his wife and the thief her lover, and they are taken to jail.

The events in *The Lower Depths* are of less importance than the portraits.
These are devastatingly drawn, and have been superbly acted. In Russia,
Ivan Moskvin played the wanderer, Luka; Mrs. Chekhov played Nastya, the
prostitute. A superb cast—Gilda Varesi, Alan Dinehart, Pauline Lord,
Edward G. Robinson, and E. J. Ballantine—starred in the New York production of 1919, but the critics had mixed reactions. The *New York World*
(December 23) was impressed: "No pen has ever traced on paper a more
stark, shocking, loathsome, and yet strangely fascinating story of the flot-
sam and jetsam, the scum and dregs of miserable, abandoned, and hopeless
humanity. It is, perhaps, not a play at all, but a slow-moving graphic

panorama of unrelieved woe. Nevertheless, truth is stamped indelibly upon it; it is the work of a master of dramatic realism." But the *New York Times* remarked that "the average playgoer would be bored to extinction." The *Herald* deemed it "remarkable in being one of the most idly and feebly constructed plays ever written by an important author . . . a triumph of the dismal and the dirty may be of literary value, but for drama he has neither impressiveness nor coquetry. . . . As the play goes on you begin to look eagerly, even impatiently, for the doing in of a lot of the characters, but in spite of many spats—the word being employed in its most literal salivatory sense—there were comparatively few fatal atrocities . . . This is the mire out of which Bolshevism grew, and Gorki was one of the workers who spattered the mud into parlors."

When the Moscow Art brought its Russian production to New York, January 15, 1923, the critics, judging by the acting only, thought the play a sardonic comedy. Arthur Pollock said the production resembled the earlier ones "as a clown an undertaker." Only the *Times* (January 16, 1923) was bold enough to admit that, despite having read and seen the play several times, "two acts had passed before we could tell which was Mr. Katchaloff as the degenerated Baron, and which Mr. Alexandroff as the drunken actor." In this play of character revelation, the language barrier proved insurmountable.

In 1930, however, Leo Bulgakov (who had made his debut in *The Lower Depths,* in Moscow, 1911, and stayed in the United States after the Moscow Art visit in 1923) directed the play in English, with a cast that included John Wexley, E. J. Ballantine, Walter Abel, and Edgar Stehli. The translation into modern slang was ludicrously inept, but the production was vibrant and deep-toned.

The Negro version, *A Long Way From Home,* with Mildred Smith, Josh White, Fredi Washington, and Edna Mae Harris, was an almost line by line transportation of *The Lower Depths* into a slum flop-house in Durham, North Carolina. Celine, losing her lover Joebuck to her younger sister Marcy, goads her landlord husband into torturing the girl—with the same murderous consequences as in the Russian original. The setting, with the consumptive dying in the filthy room below, the cluttered yard outside, the mounting steps to the poolroom above, effectively evoked the drab atmosphere of the drama.

Gorki called the Russian Revolution "the sunniest and greatest of all Revolutions." Certainly there is no sun in the wretched world he pictures in *The Lower Depths,* the forerunner of that Revolution, which embodies what Gorki himself called "the terrific force of the theater."

There is too much that is gross and grim in the play to encourage frequent revivals. APA-Phoenix showed the play, directed by Ellis Rabb, opening March 30, 1964, for fifty-two performances. The hopeful Luka may remind us of Hickey in O'Neill's *The Iceman Cometh.**

THE MADRAS HOUSE   *Harley Granville-Barker*

Harley Granville-Barker (English, 1877-1946) was a force in the theatre that extended far beyond the influence of his plays. As an actor, he played Jack Tanner in the first production of Shaw's *Man and Superman.** As a director and producer, he managed the London Court Theatre, where he introduced simpler productions, with considerable attention to effects of lighting.

The Madras House develops its story in what has been called the symphony style—its four acts being four movements around the lives of the Huxtable and Madras families, and the great women's emporium that they own. First we see the six frustrated, unmarried Huxtable girls, who vainly strive, through local charity or watercolor painting, to give some meaning to their empty lives. Then we behold the several hundred spinster employees of the Madras House, who, coralled by the "living-in system," are doomed to dried-up years—from which one of them has burst to unmarried motherhood. We see the mannequins, parading in seductive finery copied from Parisian cocottes. Finally, in Philip's wife, Jessica, we see the attractive modern woman, whose beautiful flowering springs from the dead leaves of the workers in the store.

The author's fullest examination of the position of women is in the third act, when the partners meet to discuss an American millionaire's offer to buy the store. Among them is the head of the house, Charles Madras, called back from the Mohammedan land where he has been seeking refuge from woman's interference in politics, business and other parts of "man's domain."

Produced in London in 1910, *The Madras House* met but moderate welcome. It was played in 1921 at the New York Neighborhood Playhouse with Whitford Kane, Montague Rutherford, Albert Carroll, Eugene Powers, and Aline MacMahon. A program note by the author admitted that the external story of the play was somewhat dated, by the disappearance of the "living-in system"—which had never gained foothold in the United States—"by which the several hundred employees of a large department store are herded, men and women, in a mixture of barracks and boarding-school." Alexander Woollcott (October 31, 1921) found the play "alive and entertaining, a dramatization not of a human being but of a human problem. Its characters drift on and off its scene most casually, but the protagonist that marches through its four abundant acts is not a person. It is a question. How are the brains of the world to be cleared and the work of the world to be done, when that world is necessarily peopled with mutually exciting creatures and its energy so largely devoted to fomenting that excitability? . . . Variants of the woman question in a man-made world are provoked by every scene of *The Madras House*." The *London Times* (May 9, 1938), after a performance of Act I of *The Madras House,* called it "a pretty and malicious period piece . . . a recognizable but vanished past."

While the particular circumstances of women workers have changed, the basic attitudes and expectations remain. *The Madras House* continues to be a brilliant satire of the man that is a Turk at heart and the woman that is a siren at bottom.

What the "new woman" would think of her earlier kind, I have not seen recorded. There was a New York revival of the play in 1976 with Cathleen Nesbitt and Claude Rains; and one by the NT (Olivier) in 1977, the centenary of Granville-Barker's birth, with Paul Scofield. It has been suggested that the brilliant and paradox-prone Constantine Madras was based on the author's friend Bernard Shaw.

Mention may be made of Granville-Barker's *Waste,* which with wisdom and compassion pictures the ruin of a rising and sincere politician through fear of a scandal. Banned by the Lord Chamberlain because it includes an abortion that kills both the unborn child and its mother, *Waste* was given a public reading in 1908 by a cast that comprised Galsworthy, William Archer, St. John Hankin, Laurence Housman, Gilbert Murry, Mr. and Mrs.

H. G. Wells, Mr. and Mrs. Bernard Shaw. The play was performed in London in 1936 and (Leatherhead Theatre Club) 1966.

THE COMPLAISANT LOVER   *Graham Greene*

In the eighteenth century, this play by Graham Greene would have been called *The Complaisant Cuckold,* or, more succinctly, *The Wittol.* Twentieth-century attitudes toward sex alter the expectation. Clive Root, anti-quarian—a term he prefers to "secondhand bookseller"—also prefers women secondhand—that is, married—as less demanding, and safer. Except that his present choice, Mary Rhodes, sixteen years married to dentist Victor, with an alert ten-year-old son, has caught Clive hard. He wants to marry her. When the two manage a weekend abroad, Clive dictates a letter for the hotel valet to send to Victor, relating his wife's faithlessness. But Mary, though she clings to Clive, does not want to give up her family life and her son. Victor, it turns out, is equally unwilling to relinquish Mary and his equable married life; he suggests that they continue, and that Clive continue to "drop around." Reluctantly—the stage directions say "sadly"—Clive accepts his fate: "I expect I'll come."

"Readers of the play," says a Postscript on Censorship in the printed copies, "may have a little fun determining which adjective and which passage of three lines the Lord Chamberlain and his officers have found too indecent for the theatre." Asked, Graham Greene replied that he "simply cannot remember." Since censorship in England was abolished (in 1969) the lines presumably have been restored.

The Complaisant Lover opened at the London Globe on June 18, 1959, directed by John Gielgud, with Ralph Richardson as Victor, Phyllis Calvert as Mary, Paul Scofield as Clive, and ran for 402 performances. "With less wit but more depth than Noel Coward, Graham Greene probes intelligent persons involved in a situation far from uncommon in our time."

At the New York Ethel Barrymore the play opened November 1, 1961, with Michael Redgrave as Victor, Georgie Withers as Mary, Richard Johnson as Clive, for 101 performances. Walter Kerr made a neat distinction: "Other playwrights see trouble—and humor—roaring in from outside. Mr. Greene proposes that both bubble up from the inside." Kerr added that there is scarcely a line "without a deliberately provocative after-taste." Richard Watts, Jr., in the *Post* pictured Victor: "a futile, big baby of a man, who can't prevent himself from talking boringly of dentistry, indulges in feeble little jests that he knows too well aren't very good, plays infantile practical jokes; he grows in stature through the test of his feelings for his wife until he becomes almost heroic in his modest way." Walter Pidgeon and Martha Scott played the married pair in Philadelphia, 1962. The play is a comedy that grows to be touching in its probing of the natures and responses of a woman and two men in today's world.

THE TROUBADOUR   *Antonio Garcia Gutierrez*

A vivid and immediately successful melodrama, with all the turbulence and fire of gypsy Spain, was *El Trovador (The Troubadour)* by Antonio Garcia Gutierrez (1812-1884). Set in fifteenth-century Aragon and Biscay, this story is the source of *Il Trovatore,* by Giuseppe Verdi (Italian, 1813-1901), the music of which is probably more widely known than that of any other opera.

Manrico the troubadour, raised by Azucena, whose gypsy mother was executed for kidnapping Manrico, is now leader of the gypsies. He catches the heart of Countess Leonora. Count di Luna, who loves the Countess, seeks to kill Manrico. Leonora has taken shelter in a convent, from which, as the Count's forces near, she joins Manrico. But Azucena is taken prisoner by the Count; Manrico goes to her rescue and is also captured. The Count promises to free Manrico if Leonora will marry him; she promises, then takes poison. The perfidious Count has meanwhile ordered Manrico executed; the dying Azucena cries to the Count: "He was your brother! Mother, you are avenged!"

The violence of the story is tempered by the music. With book by Salvatore Cammarano, Verdi's opera was presented in Rome, January 19, 1853; at Covent Garden, London, in Italian in 1855; in English, at the Drury Lane, as *The Gypsy's Vengeance*, in 1856. Philadelphia also heard the opera in 1956; New York first on February 25, 1957. Especially memorable are the Anvil Chorus of the joys of gypsy life, which opens Act II; Manrico's "Tremble, ye Tyrants!" in Act III; and the Miserere—"Ah, che la morte!"—of Act IV. The tender story and the turbulent circumstances make a story of melodramatic power.

DEBURAU   *Sacha Guitry*

Among the various biographical plays of Sacha Guitry (French, 1885-1957)—in some of which his father, Lucien, acted; in some, Sacha himself—none is more deft and more tenderly touching than the story of the prince of pantomimists, *Deburau*, 1918.

Jean Baptiste Gaspard Deburau (1796-1847) was trained as an acrobat, and failed. The fool and butt of his family, he turned to pantomime and became, as David Belasco has said, "probably the greatest performer of Pierrot that ever lived." He played at a rather obscure theatre devoted to acrobats, jugglers and the like, until in 1839 Jules Janin proclaimed in the *Journal des débats*: "Gaspard Deburau, the greatest actor of our time, has revolutionized the actor's art . . . If you have nothing else to do, go to the Theatre des Funambules; whatever else you have to do, go to the Funambules—*and see Deburau!*" It was at a performance of Deburau's that Dumas met Marie Duplessis, whom Dumas set down in his drama *La Dame aux camélias.** She figures in Deburau's life as well.

As presented in the play, Deburau, peerless among the moon-face harlequins, is a lonely man. Admired and sought by many women, he shows them a portrait of his wife to ward them off. And his wife elopes. In single devotion Deburau follows his art; then he meets Marie Duplessis, and has two loves: his art, and his mistress, Marie. Subtly the drama traces the change in him. Deburau's serenity disappears; he is, in the words of W. L. Courtney in the *London Telegraph* (January 6, 1921), "no longer master of his emotions; he deserts his home; he is constantly in the house of Marie Duplessis. And the tragedy of it is that she has already become tired of him; while on the threshold of her flat appears the young man, Armand Duval, whose association with her is the theme of *La Dame aux camélias*. In a touching scene Deburau comes to her rooms, bringing with him his son, Charles, 10 years of age, and a bird in a cage, believing in his naïveté that such domesticity as he required would be found in the home of his beloved. He finds Armand Duval there and humbly takes his leave. He is not one to tear a passion to tatters; he accepts defeat with gentle stoicism more affecting than torrents of rhetorical passion."

His heart slowly breaking, Deburau gives up acting. But, jealously, he will not let his son, save under another name, carry on his career. Finally, yielding to persuasion, Deburau appears again at the Funambules. He is an utter failure. Then he turns and helps his son prepare for his debut, while outside the barker cries "A new Deburau! A young Deburau! A handsome Deburau! A better Deburau!"

Opening on February 9, 1918, for matinees only (Paris was under German fire), Sacha Guitry as author and actor made a sensation in *Deburau*. In an adaptation by Granville-Barker* the play had its English premiere in Baltimore, July 12, 1920, with Lionel Atwill and Elsie Mackay. Coming to New York, December 23, 1920, it ran for 189 performances. It opened in London, with Robert Loraine and Madge Titheradge, January 5, 1921, and was revived in 1935 with Morgan Farley. *Theatre* magazine (February 1921) called *Deburau* "a really fine play, a play of genuine human feeling, one that quickens the pulse, and stirs the emotions."

There is strong appeal in the worthy man who bears with fortitude the misfortunes of life. On a tragic scale, we see such a figure in *Oedipus.** Nearer our own human level, lonely but not forlorn, buffeted but not beaten, betrayed but not bitter, sad but not despairing, and out of the lees of life straining the wine of courage, wanly smiles Deburau.

It should be noted that the most gifted pantomimist of the 1970's and 1980's, Marcel Marceau, has never presented a full-length mime play, such as *Sumurun* (1910), which Friedrich Freska fashioned after an Arabian Nights tale. Marceau has created a chalk-faced figure, Bip, but shows him only in a series of anecdotes and moods. Deft and delicate as Marceau's art is, it lacks the fullness of a finished story. One might picture it as a range of exercises, preparatory to a complete work of art.

URIEL ACOSTA   *Karl Gutzkow*

A stirring drama of the conflict between sectarian prejudice and liberal thought is *Uriel Acosta,* 1847, by Karl Ferdinand Gutzkow (German, 1811-1878). The play was heatedly discussed during the surge of liberal feeling across Europe in the mid-nineteenth century.

Uriel Acosta, a seventeenth-century Portuguese Marrano (Jew "converted" by the Inquisition), fired by zeal for his faith, joins the community of Jews in Amsterdam. But through the literal ritualism of his co-religionists, his books are burned. Loyalty leads Uriel to recant, but he resumes his studies; the rabbinical authorities again accuse him of heresy and bring about his excommunication. Despite his desire for freedom of thought, Uriel feels the value of group unity; but when, after seven years, he once more seeks to return, the terms of penance set for him are so humiliating that he commits suicide.

Uriel Acosta was widely played in German; in English in London in 1905; there in Hebrew by the Habima in 1937; in Yiddish by Artev in New York in 1939. Theological dispute is dramatized as a personal problem of integrity; and there is a vivid ball scene of the early Amsterdam days, with, said the *London Times* (November 23, 1927), "some extremely telling songs, in a mood that enables the genuine gaiety of its opening to modulate with unbroken rhythm into the serious drama of Acosta's excommunication." An evocative picture of a Jewish community in seventeenth-century Europe, *Uriel Acosta* is also a moving drama of the struggle for freedom of thought.

FLORADORA   *Owen Hall*

This refreshing play by Owen Hall (pseudonym of James Davis, English, 1853-1907) has given lovers of light music a legended song—the unforgettable double sextet "Tell me, pretty maiden, are there any more at home like you?" Other tunes and a sufficient story make it one of the liveliest of comic operas.

The play opens in the Philippines. Dolores, daughter of the concocter of the perfume "Floradora," is in love with Frank, Lord Abercoed, manager of the firm that owns the perfume. The head of the firm, Gilfain, who has acquired the business illegitimately, hires Tweedlepunch, a detective disguised as a traveling phrenologist, to clear Dolores out of the way. Lady Holyrood, wanting Frank for herself, joins the conspirators. Frank, suspecting, is discharged; Dolores sets off after him to Britain. In Wales, Gilfain holds Abercoed Castle, but Frank breaks in. Tweedlepunch tells so fearful a ghost story that Gilfain confesses and restores the castle to Frank and the perfume to Dolores. The two join hearts and hands; Gilfain takes over Lady Holyrood; and his daughter Angela pairs off with Captain Donegal of the Life Guards.

This typical musical comedy plot, written in 1899, is furbished with gay music by Leslie Stuart (T. A. Barrett, 1864-1928).

Opening in London on November 11, 1899, *Floradora* ran for 455 performances; it had bright revivals in 1915 and 1931. In the United States, after a New Haven premiere, the show ran in New York (from November 10, 1900) for 552 performances, then toured for eight years. It played in New York again in 1905, and—with Gilfain changed to an American millionaire, and a sextet of six pretty stenographers and six English dudes—gave another 126 performances there beginning April 5, 1920.

The Floradora girls set the fashion in America for chorus girls' marrying wealth. Nightly they were besieged by stage-door Johnnies; orchids bore hidden gifts of jewels; champagne was drunk from slippers. Five of the six girls, snatched by tycoons, soon had to be replaced. Marjorie Relyea early married a nephew of Andrew Carnegie who dropped dead the night of the New Haven opening. Vaughn Texsmith (of Texas) married a New Jersey silk manufacturer. Marie Wilson got a Wall Street man, Frank Gebhard. Agnes (Mrs.) Wayburn divorced Ned to marry a Johannesburg diamond king. Daisy Green had to be content with a stock broker from Denver. Margaret Walker, apparently, just had to be content.

So famous is *Floradora*'s sextet song that "Tell me pretty maiden" has been heard all over the world. At a Navy benefit show in 1942 it was sung by Leonora Corbett, Eve Arden, Sophie Tucker, Tallulah Bankhead, Peggy Wood, Gertrude Lawrence, and, kneeling before them, Ed Wynn, Vincent Price, Clifton Webb, Danny Kaye, Boris Karloff, Eddie Cantor.

When *Floradora* returned to New York in 1905, the *American* (March 28) hailed it as "the most generally popular musical comedy ever sung hereabouts." The play itself is not badly tarnished by time. Only a song or two from *Show Boat** and possibly from *Oklahoma** seem likely to rival the popularity of the *Floradora* sextet. Its most recent revival was OffBway, 1981.

THE GEISHA   *Owen Hall*

The popularity of the Gilbert and Sullivan operettas led to many pirated productions and to imitations. Of the plays sprung on the trail of *The Mikado,** the most popular was *The Geisha,* by Owen Hall, with lyrics by Harry Greenbank and music by Sidney Jones. It opened in London, April 25, 1896, with Marie Tempest, for 760 performances; in New York, September 17, 1896, for 161. In New York, December 27, 1897, James T. Powers shared honors with Isadora Duncan. There was a colorful New York revival, March 4, 1931, with Powers and Lina Abarbanell.

The Geisha deals with the efforts of Imari, governor of a province of Japan, to take for himself the fascinating O Mimosa San, hostess of the Teahouse of Ten Thousand Joys. Lieutenant Fairfax, of H. M. S. *The Turtle,* though engaged to Molly Seamore, flirts with Mimosa. His actions bring Molly to the teahouse, disguised as a geisha; thinking she is Mimosa, Governor Imari buys her. In the ensuing complications the governor, discovering that he has the wrong woman—and a fearsome one—reconciles himself to marriage with Molly's friend, Juliette Diamant, who loves him. Molly wins back her sailor Fairfax, and O Mimosa San is happy with her soldier, Captain Katana.

There is a good deal of fun in the story, most of it flowing from the antics of Wun Hi, owner of the teahouse, one of Powers' happiest roles. Among the pleasantly tuneful songs are "The Amorous Goldfish," "Kissing," and the long-echoing "Chin, Chin, Chinaman, Chop, Chop, Chop"—which used to be shouted along the city streets. There are, said J. T. Grein in *The Sketch* (London, June 10, 1931), "at least half a dozen songs that set all London humming, strumming, singing, and whistling." It is mainly the music that kept *The Geisha* alive.

GASLIGHT   *Patrick Hamilton*

Among recent "shockers," few have had more success than *Gaslight,* 1938, by Patrick Hamilton (English, b. 1904), presented in New York as *Angel Street,* and on the screen twice (once under each title). A hit in London, the play opened in New York on December 5, 1941, and ran for three years. It was revived in 1945, 1946, and 1948. In the first New York production Vincent Price and Judith Evelyn enacted the married pair and Leo G. Carroll the detective. The City Center revival of January 22, 1948, starred José Ferrer and Uta Hagen.

The play is set in a private house on Angel Street in London during the 1880's. Pretending to be considerate, Mr. Manningham tortures his wife, seeking to drive her into insanity (in which state her mother died). Old Police Inspector Rough, when Manningham is out, convinces Mrs. Manningham that her husband committed murder in the same house fifteen years before, that he has now returned, and is seeking to get rid of his wife so that he may continue his hunt for jewels he did not find at the time of the murder. The horrified Mrs. Manningham is left to wait for her husband to return and betray himself. He almost does away with her—then, realizing he is caught, seems almost to persuade her to his aid—before in gloating triumph she delivers him to justice.

The devices of melodrama are deftly used, with constant breathholding suspense. The author, said Brooks Atkinson (December 6, 1941) "never raises his voice much higher than a shudder . . . never strays outside the bailiwick of dark, soft-footed nervousness."

Some of the play's devices are, if seriously intended, not well coordinated. The Inspector, for example, hides in the clothes-press, yet Manningham, who goes in and changes his suit, unaccountably does not find him. Such flaws led Louis Kronenberger (December 6, 1941) to declare: "The second act is thin and has to be padded out with a great many little tricks and pieces of hokum. But the last act regains some of the power of the first, and this ending, a kind of psychological denouement which comes after the plot has run its course, is a smash." Robert Coleman (January 23, 1948), on the revival of *Angel Street*, offered another explanation; he saw the play as at once a thriller and a satire on vintage thrillers: "There are those who put *Angel Street* on a pedestal, who conceive it as a deep psychological study. Let them. We've always thought it was a hokey chiller-diller that burlesques its breed with tongue in cheek. So apparently does the City Center Company's director."

Angel Street may be contrasted with *Kind Lady,** as a model of suspense built and maintained by successive turns of action and tricks of dramaturgy. At the end of the first act, when Rough has convinced Mrs. Manningham that her husband is a murderer, the basic suspense of the play appears to be over. Yet the author holds the audience in poised expectancy through two more acts, and at the very end, while we do not know whether or not Mrs. Manningham is yielding to her husband's hypnotic blandishments and desperate persuasion, a high peak of intensity is attained. In its quiet crescendo of psychological pressure, *Angel Street* stands out among melodramas of suspense.

The play takes the name *Gaslight* from a slight, but significant and sinister incident: the two know that the husband is searching in the attic because when he turns on the light, their gas flame, in the room beneath, lowers.

Revivals include: Chicago, 1972, 1975, 1980; Asolo, 1973; New York, 1976. At the London Criterion, 1976, the cast consisted of Nicola Pagett, Anton Rogers, and Peter Vaughan as Police Inspector Rough. Ingrid Bergman was in the 1944 film.

SHOW BOAT   *Oscar Hammerstein II*

Like Ol' Man River, *Show Boat* just keeps rolling along. Come of age for a fortnight at the New York City Center in 1948, it proved just as winsome and winning as when, twenty-one years before, it started its career on December 27, 1927, and had a run of 572 performances. It has been successfully revived a number of times since, notably in 1932 and in 1948, when it ran for 417 performances. Stars in it have included Norma Terris, Charles Winninger, Paul Robeson, Dennis King, and Helen Morgan.

The music of this perennially popular musical comedy is by Jerome Kern (1885-1945); he and the author, Oscar Hammerstein II (American, 1895-1960), together created what John Mason Brown has called "by all odds the most engaging musical romance known to our stage." Brooks Atkinson called it "the most beautifully blended musical show we have had in this country." The thrill that comes once in a lifetime swept over critics as well as less hardened playgoers when they heard, in immediate succession, the three songs, "Only Make Believe," "Ol' Man River," and "Can't Help Lovin' Dat Man"—which later in the evening were followed by the almost equally engaging "Why Do I Love You?" and "Just My Bill" (the words of the latter were contributed by the English humorist P. G.

Wodehouse). *Show Boat* was also most favorably received in England in 1928, and was remembered there a score of years later, when Harold Hobson called the music of *Oklahoma** "the freshest and most melodious we have heard in a musical comedy since *Show Boat.*"

The story of *Show Boat* at once exhibits and burlesques the life of the Mississippi River traveling troupe. Captain Andy of the "Cotton Blossom" takes his company upstream and down; we see them in the 1880's, at small town landings, with a barker urging in the curious; we watch part of an old-time melodrama interrupted by two hill-billies who take the villain in earnest. Andy's daughter Magnolia falls in love with gambler Gaylord Ravenal; married, he takes her to Chicago, where we watch the sideshows and stir of the 1893 World's Fair. Loving her still, but penniless, Gaylord deserts Magnolia and their daughter. Magnolia becomes a music hall singer, then a radio star. Twenty years later the two are reunited on the old "Cotton Blossom."

Interwoven with the plot are other episodes involving the comedy team and the star of the company, Julie, whom Magnolia loves. Julie turns out to be a Negress passing as white; her white husband, when the southern sheriff comes to arrest him for miscegenation, quickly pricks her with a knife and sucks the blood so he can swear he has Negro blood in him. Years later, Julie (after singing "Just my Bill"), at the Trocadero Music Hall, gets herself put out of the night club show to give the deserted Magnolia her chance to get started as a singer. The range of emotions played upon is wide, as the play's movement bears us from the picturesque to the pathetic, from the humorous to the sentimental, from burlesque melodrama to romantic love. Incidentally it affords a survey of the growth of the American dance, with the early two-step, the swishing skirt dance, the clog, eccentric dances, tap, waltz, a touch of the cancan, and variegated group work.

The play follows Edna Ferber's 1926 fiction best seller closely— "positively slavish," said the *New York Times* in 1927, adding that it has "about every ingredient that the perfect song-and-dance concoction should have." The *New York World* declared that "the amazing result has been the preservation of most of the old-time pathos and sympathy that made the story what it was."

Playgoers today would call the plot of *Show Boat* "corny"; but the corn is sweet, and there are flowers amid the stalks. The dialogue, as well as the story, has the lift of humor. In its color and story, its ability to laugh at itself, its muted sadness and irrepressible gaiety, its superb songs, its deft and agile dances, *Show Boat* is the most American of American musicals.

It opened in London in 1973 for over 800 performances. At the New York Uris, April 24, 1983, it ran for 73.

84 CHARING CROSS ROAD *Helene Hanff*

It is surprising what a tenderly touching drama can come out of Uncle Sam's and Her Majesty's mail. In 1949 the young American Helene Hanff mailed an inquiry to Marks & Co., antiquarian booksellers of 84 Charing Cross Road, London. Frank Doel responded, and for twenty years a correspondence developed between them, as she expressed her literary desires, which he strove to satisfy. They grew naturally more friendly, and increasingly chatty and informative. In time their letters became a book, which James Roose-Evans had the idea of turning into a play, and at the English Salisbury Playhouse, July 31, 1981, it became an overnight success.

The adapter directed it at the London Ambassadors, November 26, 1981, for 567 performances, and also in New York, December 15, 1982, where it ran for three months.

We watch Helene in her New York apartment, reading and writing; we watch Frank Doel and his fellow-bookfolk reading her letters, discussing how best to secure what she is seeking; and we share their genuine enthusiasm for the good life of good books. One touch is added: when Helene finally finds the funds for a trip to London, and visits Charing Cross Road, the store is closed. It is the end of an era.

Foyle's in London is transformed; it occupies more than one building. In New York, Brentano's has shut down. Dauber and Pine are struggling on lower Fifth Avenue. A lone survivor, amid jewelry booths and diamond-cutting workshops, is the Drama Bookshop on West Forty-seventh Street. The individual old-book shop, with a dealer who is sorry to see a choice volume leave his hands, has been replaced by a vast store, or chain of stores, with a large section of current and ephemeral paperbacks, where, except for a few standard reference works, such as dictionaries and *Roget's Thesaurus,* it would be hard to find any book more than two years old, and last year's best-sellers grow dusty. Here purchasers are served by faceless clerks, who need not even read—numbered buttons, punched, show what to give in change—and who may never have loved a book.

Book lovers, those who have read, not necessarily "great" books, but their personal favorites, more than once—every four years or so I reread Kipling's *Kim*; recently my grandson gave me a copy of it in French—those who find pleasure in reading, and browsing among good books, will enjoy the gleam of charm and the glow of warmth, as I trust succeeding generations will again fall under its spell, of *84 Charing Cross Road.*

John Beaufort in the *Christian Science Monitor* called the play, at the New York Nederlander, of "gentle serenity, reciprocal warmth of feeling, bookish humors and delights, and tender humanity." Clive Barnes in the *Post* expressed his surprise: "For a book list, what a helluva gamut! . . . full of pleasant little asides, insights, and quiddities." They gather into a portable package.

A RAISIN IN THE SUN   *Lorraine Hansberry*

Lorraine Hansberry (American, 1931-1964) had her first submitted manuscript accepted: *A Raisin in the Sun,* which opened at the Ethel Barrymore Theatre, New York, March 11, 1959, the first play by a black woman on Broadway. The title is from a poem by Langston Hughes:

> *What happens to a dream deferred?*
> *Does it dry up*
> *Like a raisin in the sun?*
> *Or fester like a sore —*
> *And then run? . . .*
> *Maybe it just sags*
> *Like a heavy load*
> *Or does it explode?*

In the play, in Chicago's South Side after World War II, Walter Lee Younger longs to escape his dull routine as a chauffeur; but his mother, Lena, from the $10,000 life insurance of her late husband, makes a down payment on a house—in a white neighborhood. Daughter Beneatha's dream was to become a doctor. Ruth stands with her mother to maintain the family dignity. Lena gives the rest of the money to Walter for safekeeping; he invests it in a liquor store, and is cheated out of it by one of the partners. The white neighbors offer to buy back the house at a big profit for the Youngers; but Walter now stiffens in refusal. Lena says to Ruth: "He finally came to manhood today, didn't he?" and the curtain falls as the Youngers prepare to move to their new home.

Winning the Critics' Circle Award, *Raisin in the Sun* ran for 530 performances, with Ruby Dee as Ruth; Sidney Poitier, Walter; Diana Sands, Beneatha; Claudia McNeil, Lena. It opened in London, July 1959, at the Adelphi, with Juanita Moon as Lena; Earl Hyman, Walter. In 1960 it was shown in Paris; in 1964 in Tokyo. In 1965 a production in Prospect Park, Brooklyn, was about to be stopped because of rain; the audience shouted, "No!" and sat it through. In 1972 Lyndon B. Johnson invited the drama club of his alma mater, Southwest Texas State University, to perform the play at the state park being named after him. It was revived in 1979 by the New Federal Theatre; on October 23, 1983, at the Chicago Goodman, and in November at the Yale Repertory.

Robert Nemiroff, Lorraine's widower (though they were divorced the year before she died), dramatized her letters and other writings, including a long excerpt from *A Raisin in the Sun,* as *To Be Young, Gifted, and Black,* which, opening January 21, 1969, ran OffBway for 380 performances, with the cast sitting around a table. It had a national tour, also a wide college tour, despite mixed notices. Of the February 19, 1974, opening in Chicago, the *Chicago Sunday Times* said: "arch, pretentious, outdated, awkward, and mostly drab," whereas the *Chicago Daily News* declared it "loving, warm, sensitive."

In 1973, with Charlotte Zaltzberg, Nemiroff turned the Hansberry play into a musical, *Raisin,* with music by Judd Woldin and lyrics by Robert Brittan. It opened in Washington, March 29, 1973, then at the New York 46th Street Theatre, where it ran for 847 performances. It went on a very successful national tour: two weeks in Boston, three in St. Louis, five in San Francisco, six in Los Angeles. It was an elaborate production, with scantily clad African maidens dancing to warriors' drums; and it won the Grammy and the Tony awards as best musical. It was played at the University of Michigan in 1977; in Switzerland, then Paris, in 1979.

Raisin in the Sun, with many poignant and some bitter lines, is a finely drawn portrait of a black family trying to maintain its dignity in white America.

FINIAN'S RAINBOW   *E. Y. Harburg*

Opening January 10, 1947, for a run of 723 performances, *Finian's Rainbow,* by E. Y. Harburg (American, 1896-1981) and Fred Saidy, with music by Burton Lane, is a musical show of the highest quality, with a social conscience. Pleasantly imaginative in conception, with deft lyrics, delightfully melodic tunes, and concordant dances, the play laughs gaily at the prime stupidity of racial prejudice.

The story springs out of a leprechaun, Og, who follows his stolen pot of gold. Finian McLonergan brings it and his grand-daughter Sharon from

Glocca Morra to Missitucky, to plant the gold and grow wealthy. (Have not the Americans buried their gold, and created great industries based upon it?) Much merriment and mischief develop before the folks learn that the greatest treasure buried in a land is what human labor develops from nature's resources. A southern Senator, a prejudiced fellow with designs on the land, is, through the magic of the pot of gold, turned black. He must therefore consort with Negroes; he joins a traveling quartet and becomes pure white inside. Even when his external whiteness is restored, the Senator remains a wiser and a more tolerant man.

Truly ingratiating were the three who came from Ireland: Albert Sharpe as Finian; Ella Logan as Sharon; David Wayne as Og, the leprechaun. The most beguiling song of the play is Sharon's wondering "How are things in Glocca Morra?"

On some of the play's details the critics disagreed. Louis Kronenberger enjoyed the fact that there is "message in its madness," but Brooks Atkinson found that "its stubborn shotgun marriage of fairy story and social significance is not altogether happy." Similarly, in London, Harold Hobson in the *Sunday Times* (October 21, 1947) insisted that "one seeks in vain for unity"; the American aspect of the play, he felt, "could hardly be bettered," but he too spoke of its "unhappy marriage" with the fanciful Irish legend.

In a lavishly colored first-act finale, "Come-and-Get-It-Day," all the poor folk in Rainbow Valley, Missitucky, prance about, bedecked in the gorgeous costumes that poor folks conceive in their dreams of sudden wealth. John Chapman delighted in this: "Seeing is believing . . . the costume designer rates a prize for this alone"; Atkinson rejoiced in the leprechaun; of Og's song "Something Sort of Grandish," he declared: "It and he should be inscribed in the Hall of Fame." John Mason Brown considered the same song "coy to the point of inducing emesis." All agreed with George Jean Nathan, however, that "the show is so superior to the common run of light entertainment that finding fault with it is much like finding fault with a charming supper simply because there is a little hole in the napkin."

Many Broadway dramas have attacked prejudice with indignation and in the fire of their own zeal have been consumed. *Finian's Rainbow* lets its social conscience peep through its fantasy and join in the laughter. We absorb the lesson; we remember the fun. At the end of *Finian's Rainbow,* there was the pot of gold.

Among the revivals: 1957, London, also 1961, directed by Robert Helpmann; 1965, Melbourne; 1967, New York City Center; also England, Blackpool, and six other cities, then London in June, with Donald Donnelly as the leprechaun. OffBway in 1973 and 1980 (St. Bart's).

LADY IN THE DARK   *Moss Hart*

An intricate interweaving of realism and fantasy gives pattern to the delightful movement of *Lady in the Dark,* a musical comedy in which Moss Hart (American, 1904-1961), having been psychoanalyzed, put his experience to profit in terms of the theatre. Aided by the music of Kurt Weill and the lyrics of Ira Gershwin, his story of a woman undergoing psychoanalysis provides tender scenes and uproarious moments. The shift from her real life to the display of her dreams is swiftly and colorfully managed, by the use of four revolving stages with fifty-one stagehands, for a cast of fifty-eight players.

Liza Elliott, editor of a charm magazine and mistress of the publisher, feels the need of psychoanalysis. Her life and the coursing of her dreams, enacted as she relates them to the analyst, run side by side until they merge. Her present problems—the publisher's wife won't divorce him; Liza feels drawn toward Randy Curtis, a movie star; and she can't abide the tough-minded advertising manager who wants her job—seem hinged upon the fact that, as a child, she had deemed herself ugly in comparison with her widely admired mother. In one of Liza's dreams, everybody adores her; in another, a whirling circus scene, she watches and at the same time is defendant at a trial for her indecision: "In 27 languages she couldn't say No." Gradually, as the incidents of her days and the indications of her dreams draw together, it becomes clear that Liza the clever and successful editor had always been yearning for feminine beauty, for submission to masculine power. Liza blossoms into beauty; the tough-minded advertising manager takes her place as editor, and she takes him to her heart.

The play opened at the New York Alvin, January 23, 1941, for 162 performances. Louis Kronenberger, in *P.M.*, declared: "The play will not make history but it will undoubtedly make conversation." George Freedley found it "a more than usually worthwhile libretto for the season's best musical score and the town's best dancing." Sidney Whipple reported in the *World-Telegram,* March 22, 1941, that he consulted a psychiatrist who was full of praise "for the technical skill with which Mr. Hart conducts us through mazes of psychoanalysis and arrives at a correct solution of the lady's problems of life and love."

Lady in the Dark is a rare combination of the theatre's opportunities. The complexity of its staging, and the demands on its star, have made productions infrequent; but, in the playing, the disparate elements are fused in a glow of gentleness alternating with jollity, in a single surge of delight. The play was performed in the summer of 1949 at Lake George, N.Y.; in 1950 in St. Louis; in 1951 at Milford, Conn., and in Detroit by the Civic Opera; by ELT in New York in 1952 and 1959, and in the summer of 1965 at Westbury, Long Island, with Jane Morgan as Liza. Celeste Holm in a Nottingham, England, production of 1981 won mixed notices. Robert Cushman in the *Observer* called her "sometimes charming, frequently elephantine . . . She sings beautifully about the ship. She also finds wit and warmth in the dialogue, but she often looks marooned."

The play works into one pattern a rollicking musical extravaganza of lively girls, songs, dances, and comic modes, with a tender and poignant story that grows through psychiatric treatment into a flowering of beauty and of love.

THE WEAVERS   *Gerhart Hauptmann*

The work of Gerhart Hauptmann (German, 1862-1946) coincided with the growth of the "new theatre movement" and the rise of social consciousness at the end of the nineteenth century. His most powerful social drama grew out of his father's stories of the 1844 revolt of the weavers in the Silesian Mountains. (Heine has a poem on the theme.) *The Weavers,* 1892, was stopped by the Prussian authorities after the first performance because of its socialist tendencies, but it was continued in the subscription performances of the Free Theatre. The play was also forbidden in provincial Germany and in many sections of Austria-Hungary.

New York saw the play in German at the Irving Place Theatre, opening October 14, 1894. The *New York World* said that "Its power comes simply from a curious, an almost repellent, accent of truth . . . The talk is positively ghastly, in its brutal, its ferocious, commonplace character." The *New York Sun* contrasted Hauptmann with Dumas, noting that the Frenchman, intending a sermon, gives us a play; the German never gets beyond the sermon: "*Die Weber* is sincere, it states terrible facts with terrible energy . . . but it does all this directly not incidentally; and therefore it is not a great or a good play, and there may be some doubt if it is a play at all."

By the time of the 1915 New York revival (December 14) in English, opinion had changed. *Theatre Magazine* (January 1916) called the play "one of the most stirring of realistic dramas dealing with modern social conditions. . . . the undercurrent of ferocity which breaks through at the climax is gripping and intense." Emanuel Reicher, who had been one of the first in Germany to hail Hauptmann, supervised this production. The *New York Dramatic Mirror* (December 25, 1915) contended that the play was probably the most graphic picture of human misery ever written: "The conventionalities of theatrical construction are disregarded . . . If it were a mere sop to sensationalism, or a case of special pleading, it would have its little day, and pass with the falling leaves; but it is not. It is the work of a poet with a deep insight into the philosophy of life and society, but it is supplemented in this instance by the work of an artist who has instilled life and verity into its scenes."

The Weavers was the first play with a composite hero. Despite the gallery of sharply etched individuals, the protagonist is the group of desperate weavers who rebel against wretchedness and starvation. Their bullying manager and their vain, vulgar capitalist employer are little more than caricatures, but there is a fierce power as the weavers go from the cheery tavern to destroy the house of their employer, a grim loom of future revolt in the suppression of the tumult by the soldiers, and a sharp stab of irony when a stray shot kills, at his work, the old weaver who has held aloof from the conflict.

Productions include a revival in 1937 at Yale University, another in 1937 by the Federal Theatre in Los Angeles. The play is generally recognized as not merely one of the earliest, but one of the best dramas of social conflict.

There was a revival of *The Weavers* in 1960, in Tavistock, with cuts to quicken the movement, and the locale changed to West Riding, Yorkshire. The original setting was retained in the Brooklyn College revival, in 1973.

HANNELE   *Gerhart Hauptmann*

The first play in the world theatre to have a child as its heroine was Hauptmann's sensitive study of the last days of an abused and wretched girl, *Hanneles Himmelfahrt* (*Hannele's Journey to Heaven*), 1893, known in English as *Hannele* (*The Assumption of Hannele*). Hannele is an illegitimate child who, brought up in a pauper's home, was taken by Mattern the mason, a drunken ruffian whose cruelty killed Hannele's mother. To escape this brute, Hannele tries to drown herself. She lingers in a spell of delirium as life obtrudes upon her vision of heaven, then she dies.

There is touching pathos as well as tender truth in Hannele's picture of the world to come. For heaven offers the things Hannele missed on earth— meat every day instead of hardened crusts, a white robe and Cinderella slippers replacing her rags, and a mother's undying love. A picture compounded of fairy-tales and a child's naïve notions of religion, spun in a fevered spirit, the play is, as the *Boston Transcript* said (December 26,

1909), "a strange, moving medley, grotesque and pitiful; yet, as all who have studied childhood know, well-nigh inevitable."

The visions of Hannele, though faithfully reported, mark a step of the author away from the naturalism of his earlier plays. The emphasis, however, is still upon things humanly caused, the correction of which is in the power of humans—the brutality and drunkenness of the mason are the results of poverty and ignorance. Not until *The Sunken Bell*, 1896, did Hauptmann move to the thought that tragedy is inherent in man's nature, that our very being, not merely our social circumstances, may lead us to our doom.

The pathos and implicit protest in the picture of Hannele perhaps contributed to the difficulties the play encountered. Hailed on the Continent, *Hannele* was banned in England (save for a private performance, February 29, 1904) until 1908, and it was not played again until 1924. In New York, after one performance, May 1, 1894, the play was banned as blasphemous. It was played again in 1908, in both English and German, without hindrance. Minnie Maddern Fiske and Holbrook Blinn starred in it in 1910. In 1946 it was presented in the Berkshires (summer theatre) and at Piscator's Dramatic Workshop in New York.

Set in Silesia, the play is written partly in Silesian dialect, in prose, and partly in simple, moving verse. Hauptmann, said the *New York Times* (May 2, 1894), "has avoided purely literary forms, his language is appropriately simple, and he rarely misses just the right word." Nevertheless, the *Times* moved to protest that "in the presence of such an assemblage of 'first nighters' and 'rounders', the performance seemed horribly sacrilegious." By 1908, the *London Leader* (December 9) questioned how anyone could object to such a "singularly restrained and beautiful treatment of the teachings of Christianity." And in America the *Boston Transcript* (date above) said that "Femininity and piety were surely seldom so wholly and so truly mingled . . . We find it all delightful, partly because in its very crudity it is precisely natural; partly because of the very human tenderness with which the author has treated it, and partly because it is, all in all, an exquisitely poetical piece of work." In essence, *Hannele* gives us the first picture, tender, searching, poignant, of a child protagonist building wretchedness into beauty. Surprisingly, I note no recent production of the play save in Vienna, 1974.

THE YELLOW JACKET   *George C. Hazleton*

Although J. Harry Benrimo admitted that he and George C. Hazleton (American, 1868-1921) barely "knew enough Chinese to swear at a laundryman," their drama *The Yellow Jacket*, 1912, is the most charming and enduring of the plays in the Chinese manner. The novelty of its presentation, the delicacy and poignant tenderness of its movement, softly conquer the seat of judgment, and win response from the heart. Clayton Hamilton declared it the most successful play of American authorship produced within his memory; the *Christian Science Monitor* (November 11, 1916) averred that "by many, *The Yellow Jacket* is considered the finest play written in America"; and Heywood Broun (November 10, 1916) declared: "You like the play, not because it is curious, but because it is beautiful."

When *The Yellow Jacket* opened, however, its fragile, exotic beauty won but a *succès d'estime*. Although the critics praised it, "Auditors couldn't agree whether it was comedy, tragedy, farce, or burlesque," reported the

New York Sun (November 5, 1912), "but they did agree it was both a novelty and a success." Connoisseurs saw the play again and again. Enrico Caruso during the first run attended thirty-five performances; Sir Herbert Beerbohm Tree crossed the Atlantic to have a look at it; and Charles Frohman prophesied, "This play will be seen all over the world."

The Yellow Jacket opened in London in 1913; by 1916 it had been seen also in Berlin (Reinhardt), Moscow, Shanghai, Hungary, Poland, Czechoslovakia, Norway, Spain, Japan, Sweden, Denmark and Holland. The Coburns took the play all over the English-speaking world and gave it successful revivals in New York in 1916, 1921 and 1928. A summer production in 1941 at Marblehead, Massachusetts, used Harpo Marx as the Property Man (the inimitable original was Arthur Shaw); *Life* (September 1, 1941) called it "the most interesting of the 150 shows produced so far this summer." The play still finds frequent performances.

Hazleton and Benrimo insisted that neither the plot nor the method of production was Chinese save in the most general fashion. The stage arrangements were, however, drawn from the old Jackson Street Chinese Theatre in San Francisco. The story itself has all the intricacy, all the naïvete, of a Chinese legend. When Che Moo, first wife of the provincial governor Wu Sin Yin, bears a sickly son, the governor wants to get rid of her so that a second wife can give him a healthy heir. The farmer hired to destroy Chee Moo kills instead her treacherous maid and takes the wife and child to hiding. Years later, the second son, Wu Fah Din, the Daffodil, has succeeded his father and has his mind set on marrying the beautiful maiden Plum Blossom. The sickly babe Wu Hoo Git has grown into an accomplished youth. With the help of a philosopher and his own talents, Wu deposes the unrighteous ruler, and takes the throne and the beauteous Plum Blossom.

The presentation of this story invests the tale with an exotic charm that adds novelty and frequent amusing moments to its beauty and emotional appeal. Most important is the supposedly invisible Property Man, a blasé individual who sits at the side of the stage drinking tea when he is not arranging or sustaining scenery in full sight of the supposedly unseeing audience. He holds a bamboo pole beside the two lovers: it's a willow tree; he drapes a scarf along two teakwood stands: it's a boat wherein the lovers share their dreams.

"For our part," said Heywood Broun (November 10, 1916), "neither Griffith nor Ince ever made us see a drifting boat and moonlit river as do Chow Wan and Wu Hoo Git as they sit on a few chairs and point across a bare stage . . . Only the hard of heart and the dull of eye can see anything except the picture which the mind conjures up. And if you laugh when Chee Moo ascends to the spirit land on a ladder, you are among the utterly damned who shall never know the true felicity of the theatre."

With gorgeous costumes, kindly face or villainous mask, each character on its first entrance explains its role in the play. The baby in Act One is, without disguise, a block of wood. When the treacherous maid is beheaded the Property Man hides her face with a red cloth and throws a red pillow (her head!) on the ground, while she walks off. And yet by the magic of make-believe, while we smile at the devices their artificiality quickly becomes a convention; we note them, we are amused for a moment, and we are caught again into the emotions of the play. We are touched by its tenderness, moved by its beauty.

During its early stages, the authors called the play *The Peacock Feather*, then *The Child of Chee Moo*; finally, they took the yellow jacket, symbol of royal power, as the title. The play starts with a pleasant address by the "Chorus," who asks the audience not to encourage the actors by too great signs of favor. The original "Chorus," the noted tenor Perugini, was stone deaf; he took his cues from the actions of the other characters. There is plenty of action in the play; indeed, the Property Man keeps it moving at a smart pace. If a warrior brandishes his sword too long, the Property Man calmly takes it from him and puts it in the closet. Or if the Property Man grows bored with the dialogue, he may begin to dust the dragon's head. Such interruptions, of course, are timed for a relaxing smile before the unbroken sweep to a climax, when the emotional flow rises undisturbed. There is at once a savoring of remote beauty and a nearly touching tenderness in the legend plucked out of the reign of time and set for continuing delight in *The Yellow Jacket.*

Among the lesser operettas of Franz Lehar (1870-1948), whose best-known work is *The Merry Widow,** is *Land of Smiles,* 1923, a musical version of *The Yellow Jacket.*

HEROD AND MARIAMNE   *Christian Friedrich Hebbel*

The best of Hebbel's dramas picture a person in conflict with environment. Out of the different impulsions of personal integrity and social convention, tragedy rises. The immediate driving force within the drama may be a specific emotion, as jealousy in *Herodes und Mariamne,* 1850, but beneath is the more basic contrast of the individual and his world.

The story of Herod the Great (73?-4 B.C.) and his second wife Mariamne has been told by many playwrights: in French, in *Mariamne* by Alexandre Hardy, 1610; by François Tristan l'Ermite, 1636, whose version made Richelieu weep; and by Voltaire,* 1724. Voltaire's play failed at its premiere because a remark in the pit started the audience laughing just as Adrienne Lecouvreur, as Mariamne, took her poison; shortly after, revised, it was a success. In English, Stephen Phillips* wrote *Herod* in 1900; and in Hebrew there is one by Falek Halpern, produced in Palestine in 1937.

An English version of Hebbel's play, written by Clemence Dane, opened in Pittsburgh, October 26, 1938, with Katharine Cornell and Florence Reed, and Fritz Kortner in his American debut. Besides cutting Hebbel's soliloquies and asides, Dane's adaptation neglected the play's psychological perceptions to emphasize the fierce jealousy of Herod; the production died on the road.

All the Herod plays present the same basic story. In continuing suspicion of his beautiful wife, Herod when departing on his campaigns leaves secret orders that if he falls Mariamne is to be slain; on returning, he kills her guards. She learns of and protests against these orders; this quickens his jealousy, for he assumes that she has employed her feminine charms to seduce the guard. Mariamne disdains to deny this and is condemned to die, leaving Herod sunken in a morbid spell. In Hebbel's psychological approach to this story, however, the jealousy of Herod is subordinated to the self-respect of Mariamne. A woman of dignity and moral force, she cannot consent to continue living in a world where a woman is no more than a man's possession. By such clear and dramatic presentation of the problem of individual integrity, and the tragic consequence of upholding ideals for which the time is not yet ripe, Hebbel made his mark as a dramatist.

A version of *Herod and Mariamne* by Paul Curtis was played OffBway in 1954.

THE FRONT PAGE   *Ben Hecht*

Starting as journalists, Ben Hecht (1894-1964) and Charles MacArthur (1895-1956) teamed on several plays, then went to Hollywood, where they wrote hit films and earned wide reputation as pranksters, the "Katzenjammer Kids" of the theatre. They were caricatured in *Boy Meets Girl* (1935) by Sam and Bella Spewack. They themselves in 1933 wrote a satire on Hollywood, *Twentieth Century*. Their best and most popular play is *The Front Page*, 1928.

In the play, Hildy Johnson, crack crime reporter of the *Chicago Herald-Examiner,* waits impatiently in the pressroom of the Criminal Court for the final word on the anarchist and murderer Earl Williams, held in the jail there, scheduled to die in the morning. Johnson's fiancée, Peggy Grant, presses him to leave for the honeymoon train; but the situation changes abruptly when, through the sheriff's stupidity, Williams escapes, and crashes through the pressroom skylight; Hildy, there alone, hides him in the rolltop desk. What a scoop! Walter Burns, the paper's managing editor, comes to help Hildy stave off his persistent fiancée; the other reporters come in; Burns in his excitement innocently bangs three times on the desk—which is Hildy's "All's well" signal for Williams, who pops out and is recaptured. The psychiatrist, seeking to reconstruct Williams' crime, asks the dumb sheriff for his pistol and hands it to Williams—who at once shoots him.

Tangled in the tale are Mollie Malone, "tart with a heart," who has tried to help Williams; and the fiancée's domineering mother, at whom the sheriff casts sheep eyes. A messenger from the Governor arrives with a last-minute reprieve for Williams; the sheriff and the dishonest mayor try to brush him away, in the hope of winning the imminent election, for the people want the murderer executed. There are assorted scrubwomen and comic cops. When finally reporter Hildy insists on leaving for his wedding trip, editor Burns (not so innocently) gives him his gold watch as a farewell present—then phones his assistant to have the train stopped and Johnson brought back: "The sonofabitch stole my watch!" Curtain.

The Front Page, opening at the New York Times Square Theatre, August 14, 1928, ran for 276 performances. Lee Tracy played Hildy Johnson; Osgood Perkins, his editor, Burns; Dorothy Stickney, Mollie Malone; Frances Fuller, fiancée Peggy Grant. Soon six road companies went out. Three movies have been made of the play: 1930, with Pat O'Brien and Adolph Menjou; 1939, *His Girl Friday,* Hildy's role made feminine, with Rosalind Russell and Cary Grant; 1974, with Jack Lemmon and Walter Matthau.

Editor Burns was drawn from an actual Chicago editor, Walter Howie; the play was accepted as a true picture of newspapermen. The language was colorful, though far from as bawdy as in plays since; but the dialogue was fresh. Thus, a reporter overphone: "Duncan, as in coffee and doughnuts." Reporter McCue, making full use of the free courthouse phone: "Is it true, Madam, that you were the victim of a Peeping Tom?" Allardyce Nicoll, noted theatre historian, declared that "vituperative rudeness of phrase is substituted for wit"; even if true, this is unfortunately no bar to public favor.

There was a revival of *The Front Page* at Mineola, Long Island, October 9, 1968; the first Hildy, Lee Tracy, died the day before. Anthony George played

Hildy; Robert Ryan, editor Burns; Anne Jackson, Mollie; Estelle Parsons, Peggy; Henry Fonda, reporter McCue. There was a benefit run for the Playwrights Company at the New York Barrymore in 1969, with all the cast accepting the Equity minimum, then $150.65 a week. In Chicago, July 6, 1974, the *Herald-Examiner* devoted an entire eight-page tabloid to the play.

On July 7, 1972, the play opened at the London NT (Old Vic) for 112 performances, with Dennis Quilley as Hildy, Alan MacNaughton, Burns; Maureen Lipman, Mollie; directed by Michael Blackmore. It was hailed, in Shakespearean words, as "a palpable hit." Harold Hobson in the *London Times,* July 9, 1972, declared: "It pretends to show with adult cynicism the corrupt world of Chicago in the 1920s, but really it is suffused with a shy, romantic adoration of tough, unscrupulous journalists, and golden-hearted tarts, and timid little men who turn honest when they find that graft holds no profit for them. It will delight every infant in the audience, especially those over forty."

The play's tricks are often absurd and unlikely, but amusing; its reporters are both amusing and convincing. In Los Angeles, 1974, Hugh O'Brien followed José Ferrer as Burns. The play was revived again at Los Angeles (California State University) and at Houston, Texas, in 1975. In 1978, State Theatre of Kentucky; in 1981, Goodman Theatre, Chicago; Manhattan Punch Line OffOffBway, and in July opening the new Festival Theatre, Santa Fe, New Mexico.

In London, July 20, 1982, with music by Tony Macaulay, book and lyrics by Dick Vosburgh, *Windy City* came to the Victoria Palace, directed by Peter Wood. It dropped the fiancée's mother and changed fiancée Peggy Grant to the frivolous and frustrated Esther Stone, of a top Hollywood family. Dennis Waterman played Hildy; Anton Rodgers, Burns; Diane Langton, Mollie; Amanda Redman, Esther.

The musical's set was superb, with two storeys of the Chicago police court, interest shifting from press room to prison cell to sheriff's office, with elevated trains going back and forth in the distance; but the music seemed to prize noise more than melody. Among the lyrics are "The Day I Quit This Rag," "No One Walks Over Me," "Long Night Again tonight." Esther sings "Perfect Casting" to show her pique that Hildy and Burns brush her aside: "Svengali and Trilby you'll still be, I know." *Punch* praised the "smashing big brass, sentimental, singalong succession of fifteen numbers," but the general opinion was that the songs checked the lively flow of the story. There is much, said James Fenton in the *London Times,* July 25, 1982, "in Anton Rodgers' portrayal of the editor which any journalist will recognize."

Robert Cushman in the *Observer* of the same date called *The Front Page* "greatest of American comedies." It is the most vivid stage picture of newsmen's ways; indeed, crime writers have tended to fashion themselves—at least for the public eye, and in fiction as well—on the Hecht-MacArthur model. Certainly the tabloids, with television often beating them to the public eye, continue the frenzied quest for the sensational scoop.

THE LITTLE FOXES   *Lillian Hellman*

The plays of Lillian Hellman (American, 1904-1984) present humans pressed in the throes of perverse passions—jealousy, hatred, greed. That the public favors such figures may be judged from the fact that out of six plays by Miss Hellman five have been hits. Two of the Hellman plays, colored by bitterness, deal with one family. These are *The Little Foxes,* which opened February 15, 1939, with Tallulah Bankhead and Patricia Collinge, for 410 performances, and *Another Part of the Forest,* which opened November 20, 1946, for 191 performances. The latter was a hit in Moscow in 1949 under the title *Ladies and Gentlemen.* The two plays present an unrelieved picture of greed and hate.

The Little Foxes (its title is taken from the *Song of Solomon*: "the little foxes, that spoil the vines") is a picture of rapaciousness working its own ruin. In Snowden, Alabama, about 1900, we see the end of the ruthless drive for power and wealth of the profiteers and carpet-baggers who have all but swallowed the milder-willed folk of the South. Petty, mean, grasping Oscar Hubbard has married timid and shrinking Birdie Bagtry, who dips her fear and aversion in wine. The older Ben Hubbard is shrewder and more controlled, but no less grasping. Their sister Regina, married to gentle Horace Giddens, is the most eager-clawed of them all. When Horace, sick of the Hubbards' vulpine dealings, refuses to join their latest project, Regina by not reaching over for his heart medicine lets him die. Although her daughter Alexandra breaks free, Regina in proud isolation holds the family power.

The characters of the play, etched in vitriol, are obnoxious, but not too unreal. "Between the crude short-changer Oscar," said *Time* (February 27, 1939) "and his greatly aspiring sister is the difference between a rat and an eagle: Not instinctive, but icily calculating, is their family sense: the same greed that divides them among themselves unites them against others . . . With such implacable people Playwright Hellman has dealt implacably, exerting against them a moral pressure to match their own immoral strength. Both the Hubbards and their playwright-inquisitor are a pitch too relentless for real life. But it is the special nature of the theatre to raise emotions to higher power, somewhat simplifying, somewhat exaggerating, but tremendously intensifying. Playwright Hellman makes her plot crouch, coil, dart like a snake; lets her big scenes turn boldly on melodrama. Melodrama has become a word to frighten nice-belly playwrights with; but, beyond its own power to excite, it can stir up genuine drama of character and will. Like the dramatists of a hardier day, Lillian Hellman knows this, capitalizes on it, brilliantly succeeds at it." Howard Barnes (November 1, 1949) called the play "a grim and numbing tragedy . . . One of the memorable events of the modern theatre"; and Atkinson hailed it as "one of the theatre's keenest dramas."

The author declared in the *New York Herald Tribune* (March 12, 1939): "I wanted especially to write about people's beginnings, to deal with the material that in most play construction is antecedent to the action, to show how characters more frequently shown in the maturity of their careers get that way . . . It seemed to me, in *The Little Foxes,* an essay in dramatic technique as well as an interesting business to depict a family just as it was on the way to the achievements that were to bring it wealth or failure, fame or obloquy. At the final curtain, the Hubbards are just starting to get on in the world in a big way, but their various futures I like to think I leave to the imagination of the audience. I meant to be neither misanthropic nor cynical, merely truthful and realistic." Miss Hellmen remains too external to the characters—presenting them as seen from the outside, by an onlooker who condemns, instead of with their own inner self-justifications—to achieve a sense of full truth; but she is certainly scorching.

Almost as much intensity surges through *Regina,* which opened in New

York, October 31, 1949, a musical version of *The Little Foxes,* written and composed by Marc Blitzstein, a powerful melodrama with many moments in which the music heightens the emotional quality of the play. Among such moments are the opening, which admirably illustrates Regina's character as she hushes the innocent merriment beneath her window; Birdie's tipsy singing of her cowed and frustrate life; and the closing contrast, after Regina lets Horace die, of the mourning Negroes outside the house and the quarreling family within.

The few persons in the play not wholly driven by powerful passions are weaklings. Alexandra, the exception, is the least rounded character in the play. Her father, Horace, is not well developed; he makes one feeble stand but his will cannot match his wife Regina's ruthlessness. Birdie, the *New York World-Telegram* (March 4, 1939) noted, "is beaten, crushed, and whipped into a state of fearful timidity and docility." However, she picks a swift moment's courage out of her own despair to help Alexandra escape the Hubbard will.

The play's blackguards, greedy, unscrupulous, hot-tempered folk, are shown with an incisive intelligence, a blunt, straightforward speech, and a sense of strong situation, that make *The Little Foxes* memorable.

Revivals of the play have been too numerous to list; here is a measured selection: October 26, 1967, directed by Mike Nichols at the New York Lincoln Center (Beaumont), with Anne Bancroft, for 100 performances, then on tour. On May 7, 1981, at the Martin Beck, the movie star Elizabeth Taylor made her stage debut, for 17 performances. The general opinion set her as a tyro among professionals, but the general question was not How does she act? but How does she look? Frank Rich in the *Times* spoke of her special gift "for making nastiness stinging and funny at the same time." Miss Taylor then made her first appearance on the English stage, March 11, 1982, at the London Victoria Palace, for a seventeen-week run, with mixed notices. Milton Shulman in the *Standard* gallantly rose to her defense: "If her performance is not good enough for unalloyed adulation, it is certainly not bad enough for crucifixion."

The musical *Regina* also had revivals. Among them: a single performance, June 1, 1952, at the 92d Street YM-YWHA, with author Lillian Hellman as narrator. New York City Center, April 2, 1953, and there again April 17, 1958, directed by Herman Shumlin, who had directed the original *Little Foxes.* The musical was later revamped, and toured: Santa Fé, New Mexico, 1959; Detroit, 1977; OffBway (Encompass), 1978, with a new jazz number in the second act.

John Mason Brown (*Saturday Review,* March 31, 1951) stated that Lillian Hellman "excelled at contrivances, at big scenes, and sulphurous melodramatics." Harold Clurman (*New Republic,* March 26, 1951) found that "love is present only through the ache of its absence." Joseph Wood Krutch (*Nation,* December 26, 1936) went further: She "is a specialist in hate and frustration, a student of helpless rage, an articulator of inarticulate loathing . . . She is fascinated by her own hatred." Audiences hearken in divided delight and dismay.

PORGY   *Du Bose Heyward*

Porgy, the crippled Negro of Catfish Row, Charleston, South Carolina, whose diminutive body housed an indomitable spirit, has had his story told in several forms. From his novel *Porgy,* 1925, Du Bose Heyward (American,

1885-1940) and his wife Dorothy fashioned a play, 1927. In 1935, with book by Du Bose Heyward and lyrics by Ira Gershwin, George Gershwin fashioned what he called the "grand opera" *Porgy and Bess*. In 1942, by reducing the recitatives to dialogue, and other simplification, Alexander Smallens gave the musical the more appropriate status of a "folk opera."

The story itself is one of violence. The play opens with a crap game at which bully Crown kills Robbins; when Crown flees, his girl Bess takes shelter with Porgy, who has always worshipped her from afar. His tenderness wins her affection, but when, at a picnic, Crown appears and summons her, Bess cannot resist. She comes back to Porgy, however; and when Crown seeks her in Catfish Row, Porgy kills Crown. While Porgy is being questioned by the police, the inconstant Bess goes off to New York with the carefree and pleasure-promising Sporting Life. On Porgy's release, he sets out in his rickety goat-cart to find New York and Bess.

Around these violent deeds pulses the warm life of crowded Catfish Row. The opening scene, of morning in the square, is rich in color and sound. The very noises grow in a rhythm of dawning: we hear snoring, then the taps of an early hammer, the swish of the morning broom, the sharpening of knives in the fish shop; then closer together or in concert the opening of windows, the banging of shutters, the flapping of towels, the beating of eggs, until the diapason is rounded with the human voice breaking into the cheery song "Good morning, brother!"

Two mass scenes in the play rise to great power: that in which all Catfish Row is gathered in Serena Robbins' room before her husband's burial, as the singing of spirituals rouses the Negroes, and that other dark scene in which the folk are huddled against the raging hurricane and a flash of lightning shows Crown at the threshold, Crown the bully and murderer, but now the only one that dares to brave the storm, dashing forth to rescue the frenzied woman whose husband is out on the waters. Alexander Woollcott (October 11, 1927) called the first scene "one of the most exciting climaxes I have ever seen in the theatre."

Many homely touches highlight the play. Vendors of food call their wares through Catfish Row. The gossip of the women, the gambling of the men, the stir of the fishermen preparing their nets, add considerable color. As a consequence of this fullness, Porgy becomes only the most prominent figure in a crowded panorama. "His simplicity, his frank rascality," said *Commonweal* (November 2, 1927), "his moments of grandeur, his confused vision of his limited universe—these all become the summing-up of forces eddying about him, a reflection, too, of the whole passion of a race . . . flashing with the ardor and the sultry magnificence of folk melodrama."

Porgy opened in New York on October 10, 1927, and ran for 217 performances, with 137 more on its revival the next year. It was seen in London in 1929. The play continues to be popular around the country, though in the larger centers it has, in the main, been replaced by *Porgy and Bess*. The opera, first produced October 10, 1935, ran for 124 performances, and did not cover its cost; the 1942 New York revival (January 22) ran for 286 performances with a return, after its tour, to the New York City Center in 1944. It was played in Zurich in 1945. It was revived again in 1952, with a brilliant cast, for export to Western Europe as a sample of American musical-theatrical culture.

The operatic score is fortified by frequent and delightful songs, including "Summer Time," "I Got Plenty O' Nuttin'," and "It Ain't Necessarily So!" There is a constant surge of emotion in the opera. It rests, said Brooks

Atkinson (February 1, 1942) "on a barbaric foundation of whirling terror, superstition and excitement . . . Even the gaiety is passionate." However, there is a loss of the cheery, everyday atmosphere that the play *Porgy* somehow maintains against the violent action; the opera lacks "the limpid give and take of community life." The songs and music of the opera are amusing or feelingful, but the pathos of the human story, of a staunch soul denying defeat, blends more successfully with the essential cheeriness within the tumult and trouble of a poor Negro community in the play.

Among revivals of *Porgy and Bess*: the Houston Grand Opera, 1976, produced by Sherwin M. Goldman, president of the American Ballet Theatre, directed by Jack O'Brien, came to the New York Uris and won the 1977 Tony award as "the most innovative production of a revival." The 1952 European tour, with Leontyne Price as Bess, played at La Scala, Milan, which brought it—the first American opera La Scala mounted—to the New York Radio City Music Hall, May 1, 1983, with a cast of over a hundred and the largest sets ever made for a stage musical; from the Music Hall it went on a seven-week tour.

Of *Porgy* and its author, Du Bose Heyward (not a black), Lenore G. Marshall said in the *Nation,* December 16, 1925: "Because he writes with poetry and penetration his story is a moving one; because he writes with detachment and tenderness, from keen-eyed acquaintance with these people, a fusion of comedy and tragedy is delicately achieved." The 1927 *Porgy,* directed by Rouben Mamoulian, with Frank Wilson as Porgy and Evelyn Ellis as Bess, had its Charleston tour forbidden by the producers because Charleston then had segregated audience seats.

A WOMAN KILLED WITH KINDNESS   *Thomas Heywood*

Thomas Heywood (English, d. 1650?) seems to have devoted his active years wholly to the theatre. Beginning as an actor with the Lord Admiral's Company in 1598, later with the Queen's Players, he became a prolific playwright. He admitted authorship of some 220 plays.

The simplest and most effective of Elizabethan domestic dramas, according to Allardyce Nicoll, is *A Woman Killed With Kindness,* 1603. Here, with unaffected, sincere sympathy, with language direct and of the English soil, in a play that moves without artifice, Heywood tells a story that touches the heart and manifests a Christian spirit unusual in his, or any, time.

The story is simple. Frankford, discovering his wife in the arms of his friend Wendoll, banishes her—to live in comfort, but without ever seeing him or their children again. In remorse, she pines away and dies. At her death-bed, Frankford grants her the forgiveness that is her last request.

What gives the drama its distinction is the noble spirit of the author. "In all those qualities that gained for Shakespeare the attribute of gentle," Charles Lamb declared, Heywood "was not inferior to him—generosity, courtesy, temperance in the depths of passion; sweetness, in a word, and gentleness." Lamb saw Heywood as "a sort of prose Shakespeare. His scenes are to the full as natural and affecting. But we miss the poet." It is Nicoll's opinion that the play displays "a universality of atmosphere; and contains, both in language and in portraiture, a strength which comes close to that of Shakespeare himself."

The two opening scenes show contrasted levels of charm and merriment as we watch the gentlefolk and the servants at the Frankford wedding celebration. The third scene presents another of the vigorous brawls

Heywood knew how to handle—this one over a wager between Sir Charles Mountford and Sir Francis Acton as to the skill of their hawks. Later there is an excellent scene, with play of words while Frankford, Mrs. Frankford, and Wendoll play at cards. Touching in its simplicity, yet dramatically most effective, is Frankford's hesitation before he enters his wife's chamber, where he expects to find—and does find—her lying with her paramour. Frankford withholds his sword—quite the opposite of Hamlet at Claudius' prayers—so as *not* to send them to death "with all their scarlet sins upon their backs."

The subsequent talk between the husband and wife is deeply scored with pathos. Mrs. Frankford, broken and contrite, speaks, as John Addington Symonds noted, in "monosyllables more eloquent than protestation."

Most of Heywood's plays have an almost independent sub-plot; this one, brought into homely English terms from an Italian novella by Illicini, pictures the plight of Sir Charles Mountford after the hunting brawl.

Mistress Frankford's gown in a 1662 performance cost six pounds and thirteen shillings—exactly thirteen shillings more than Heywood was originally paid for the play.

The play has not been recently presented in New York, though two scenes of it were enacted at the MacDowell Club in 1922. It was produced at the Malvern Festival in England in 1931, with Ralph Richardson as the faithful servant Nicholas. The *London Times* (August 5, 1931) found in it "many a happy touch . . . the unfolding drama challenges the judgment at every turn." *A Woman Killed With Kindness* is a simple and dramatic picture of domestic tragedy, with natural yet tender play of passions in a gentle soul. It was presented in England by the Marlowe Society in 1961, and the NT (Old Vic) in 1971.

THE RAPE OF LUCRECE   *Thomas Heywood*

Of the various plays Thomas Heywood wrote on classical themes or legends, the best known is *The Rape of Lucrece*. The story of the play was originally told in Livy's history of Rome and in Shakespeare's poem of the same name as the play. It is a stark tale of the beginning of the Roman Republic in 509 B.C. While Collatine, a Roman general, is at camp, Sextus, son of Tarquin the Proud, slips off to Rome and rapes Collatine's wife—the proud and chaste Roman matron Lucrece. She summons her husband, tells him what has occurred, and stabs herself. The patriot Brutus, drawing the sword from her breast, swears to sheath it in the tyrants' hearts, and leads the revolution that replaces Rome's kings by chosen consuls.

In Shakespeare's poem, only the last fifty of its 1,855 lines mention Brutus' hopes, and only the very last couplet tells that public consent led to "Tarquin's everlasting banishment." Heywood, on the contrary, gives almost the whole fifth act to the bloody consequences of Tarquin's rape and Lucrece's suicide. Porsena, King of the Tuscans, seizes the opportunity to march against Rome, and Heywood sweeps through episodes of this conflict. We see the heroic stand of single-handed Horatio at the bridge; we watch Scevola, caught trying to kill Porsena and threatened with torture, calmly hold his own hand in the torch-flame; we see Brutus the first Consul fight Sextus Tarquinius till they both fall dead—and promise of peace and freedom shines over Rome. Heywood's phrases and allusions in his play show his familiarity not merely with Shakespeare's poem, but also with his dramas, especially *Hamlet** and *Macbeth*.*

The play is one of striking and poignant contrasts. First we see the simple and refreshing homelike quality of Heywood's domestic dramas in the early scenes of Lucrece and her maids. Later, in Act IV, after watching the ravished and despairing Lucrece wake in the hateful arms of Sextus, we hear Valerius at camp sing a charming song to the dawn. In another moment, however, Valerius is singing a bawdy song about the general's wife, Lucrece; and when the clown comes from Rome with the message from Lucrece, the clown and Valerius sing a still more suggestive catch.

The songs, incidentally, contributed a great deal to the play's popularity and made outstanding the minor part of Valerius. The play, according to Alan Holaday's study (1950), was written in 1594, the year of Shakespeare's poem, and revised in 1607. Its first printed version, 1608, contains thirteen songs, inserted in the drama, says Holaday—all save "Pack, clouds, away"— "with blithe disregard of artistic propriety"; the fifth edition, 1638, contains twenty-two songs, many of which were quite popular.

Several other playwrights have told Lucrece's story. The Italian Alfieri covers it in his *Brutus,* published in 1783; in England Nathaniel Lee wrote *Lucius Junius Brutus,* about 1680; John H. Payne, *Brutus, or The Fall of Tarquin,* 1820. In France, François Ponsard wrote *Lucrèce* in 1843.

Five years later, at the Théâtre de la Republique (its name just changed from Théâtre Français) the entire Provisional Government and an excited populace watched Rachel in *Lucrèce,* cheering wildly at every reference to the earlier, Roman revolution, especially at Brutus' remark, "It is easier to destroy than to restore." The brother and the nephew of Napoleon were in the audience. At the end of the evening, Rachel, kneeling with the tricolor pressed to her heart, sang the *Marseillaise.*

In the twentieth century, André Obey wrote a French version of the story, which Thornton Wilder translated, and Katharine Cornell brought to the American stage: *The Rape of Lucrece,* in Cleveland, November 29, in New York, December 20, 1932.

The music drama *The Rape of Lucretia,* which opened in New York, December 29, 1948, with book by Ronald Duncan and music by Benjamin Britten, is an operatic form of the Obey version.

The varied moods of Heywood's play, without the almost ascetic quality of the twentieth-century version, but with a lusty vigor of life and a love of mankind and of justice, remain the best dramatic capture of the old Roman story.

The worldwide hold of the story shows in the October 14, 1955, production in Chile of *La Violación de Lucrecia.*

THE DEPUTY   *Rolf Hochhuth*

Considerable controversy was aroused by *The Deputy* (*Der Stellvertreter; The Representative; The Vicar*), 1963, of Rolf Hochhuth (b. 1931), a presentation of Pacelli, Pope Pius XII, putting expediency before principle, failing to use the power of his position against Hitler's campaign of Jewish genocide. The play was published February 23, 1963, dedicated "To the Memory of Father Maximilian Kolbe, Auschwitz inmate #16670," who, when a prisoner had escaped and the Nazis in retaliation picked ten men at random to sit naked in a cell until they starved to death, volunteered to replace an older Father (who survived). The book has sixty-five pages of "Sidelights on History." On the same day in Berlin, Erwin Piscator produced a shortened version of the play, which in full would run for six hours.

The Deputy pictures the Pope as timorous, justifying his silence by saying the Nazis were the chief bulwark against atheistic Communism. When he brushes aside the protest of the young Jesuit priest, Father Riccardo Fontana, the Father pins the yellow Star of David on his cassock, and goes to Auschwitz.

The German Kurt Gerstein, who has been secretly helping the Jews, comes with false orders for Riccardo's release. Riccardo wants a Jew to go instead; but a fiendish Nazi doctor foils them and has Gerstein arrested. The doctor says that Auschwitz "refutes Creator and Creation"; Riccardo retorts that the existence of the Devil proves the existence of God. When the sadistic doctor turns upon a Jewish woman, Riccardo intervenes, and is killed by the guards.

Hitler's legate at the Vatican approves publication of the Pope's innocuous proclamation—and a Voice reports that the gas chambers took their daily quota until the end of the war. Included in the production were harrowing film sequences of columns of condemned Jews, the gas chambers, high piles of human bones.

Reaction throughout Europe was vehement and almost immediate. There were productions in Stockholm (September 7, 1963), Helsinki (November 1, 1963), Paris (December 9, 1963); in 1964, Vienna, Frankfurt, Rotterdam, Hamburg, Munich, Athens. In London the RSC, in translation by Robert D. MacDonald as *The Representative,* opened the play on September 25, 1963, with Alec McCowen as Riccardo; Ian Richardson, the doctor, Alan Webb, Pope Pius XII.

The play was banned in Rome; in Brazil; in Chile, where in Santiago (May 10, 1965) a reading was given in a crowded theatre with police protection. In Brussels it was banned in French but in 1966 played in Flemish. In Madrid the Hochhuth play was forbidden, but *God's Deputy,* by Juan Antonio di Laiglessa, defending the Pope, had a brief run. The New York February 26, 1964, production, with Emlyn Williams, was picketed by neo-Nazis and Catholics, but ran for 318 performances at the Brooks Atkinson.

Albert Schweitzer spoke out in praise before the London production: "His drama is not only an indictment of history but also a clarion call to our own time." Max Lerner termed it "a shattering play." The *London Mail*; "Nothing has been produced since the War to set beside its profundity, its compassion, its understanding." The *New York Times* emphasized its "irresistible immediacy." Pope Paul VI was moved to state that a papal protest would have unleashed even greater calamities, and queried: "What is the gain to art and culture when the theatre lends itself to injustice of this sort?" The play presses an incisive indictment of "God's Deputy," and is the most vigorous expression of the cry of anguish after the horrendous attempt of Hitler to terminate the "Jewish problem" by exterminating the Jews.

Having attempted to destroy the reputation of Pope Pius XII, Hochhuth in *Soldaten* (1967) turned his fire on Winston Churchill. General Wladyslaw Sikorski, head of the Polish government in exile, demanded that the Red Cross check out the Katin murder of four thousand Polish officers, blamed on the Nazis, but actually committed by the Russians. And Hochhuth's play suggests that Churchill arranged the plane crash near Gibraltar in which Sikorski died, and provoked the "blitzkrieg" so that he could retaliate with terror bombings. The play's Epilogue puts it bluntly— "Did Churchill order Sikorski killed?" "If he thought it necessary, Yes; if not, No."—and ends with a supposed telegram: "The play has been banned in England." The NT refused even to consider the play.

RASMUS MONTANUS   *Ludwig Holberg*

Born in Bergen, Norway, Ludwig Holberg (Danish, 1684-1754) turned from the Latin of his day to found the Danish national literature. Professor, author in every literary form, he raised Scandinavian literature to a level of international worth. Between 1722 and 1727 he wrote twenty-eight plays.

In *Rasmus Montanus,* 1731, the leading character is the butt of a satire on the snobbery of learning that apes foreign ways and sneers at what is local and homey and of the native soil. The student son of the well-to-do peasant Jeppe Berg, Rasmus comes back from Copenhagen crammed full of Latin and disputatiousness. He shocks his parents by his air of superiority and the neighbors by his outlandish ideas. He actually tries to convince the bailiff that the world turns round. When the wealthy freeholder Jeronimus finds that Rasmus is not jesting, he wants to break the engagement between his daughter Lisbed and Rasmus. Toward his brother Jacob, the son whom Jeppe had kept at home to give a hand with the work, Rasmus is condescending; he expects Jacob to wait upon him. Gradually, however, the situation changes. The Deacon, who wept when Rasmus by chop-logic proved he was a rooster, outshouts Rasmus in almost-remembered Latin until the neighbors think he has out-argued the student. But Jacob's common sense refutes Rasmus' long-winded disputation. At length an army lieutenant comes, tricks Rasmus into accepting "press money," and orders him off to military service. Rasmus then sees the folly of his superior ways; he is let off and happily rejoined with Lisbed.

The satire is merrily and clearly pressed home. The play may lack the fire of passion, but it has the twinkle of intelligence. "There is no complexity of plot-making," said Brander Matthews in his *Chief European Dramatists* (1916), "the characters are drawn in the primary colors, and the story moves forward with the swift simplicity of a fable." Technically, *Rasmus Montanus* makes one useful innovation often credited to Lessing: the locale of the scenes changes only at the ends of the acts; there is but one set called for throughout an act. *Rasmus Montanus* is still performed in Scandinavia; it has survived two centuries as a lively and amusing satire on presumptuous pretension.

PRUNELLA   *Lawrence Housman*

Prunella; or, Love in a Garden, by Lawrence Housman (English, 1865-1959) is a charming blend of play, pantomime, and opera. It opens in a garden "where it is always afternoon." Although lessoned by Aunt Prim, Aunt Prude, and Aunt Privacy, Prunella listens to the mummer's lure of Pierrot, chief of the strolling players, who serenades her as she climbs down a ladder. While Prunella hesitates the statue of Love in the garden wakes and plays its viol. As Pierrette, Prunella goes away with her Pierrot. Two years later the sole surviving aunt, Privacy, sells the garden to a rich stranger. He is Pierrot, now despairingly seeking Prunella. He explains to Privacy: "She left me . . . I had been gone a whole year; but I came back again. You see now—it is not I who left her; she didn't wait for me long enough."

Pierrot wants to hear of the old troupe, to help him forget Pierrette; and Scaramel gives him word: "Coquette. Hmm. Her modesty's down at ankle now, like a slipt garter. Romp's a little heavier on the bounce than she used to be. Tawdry's much as usual, but dressed worse than ever, and costing more. The old faces, master, as you desired?" Then one disconsolate face slips in, of one to whom Pierrot had earlier sung "Little bird in your nest, are you there, are you there?" At first she does not recognize the rich stranger, but Pierrot is brought home to her by love: the statue floods with light and plays its viol, and the garden grows loud with song.

Prunella opened in London, December 23, 1904, with Harley Granville-Barker, who collaborated in its writing, as Pierrot. The music by Joseph Moorat was in constant flow beneath the dialogue, surging for the songs. The movements, almost as in pantomime, gave a fragile, delicate artificiality to the fantasy. The play was revived in London in 1906, 1907, 1910, 1930, 1933 (in the Priory Garden at Orpington, a perfect setting), and in 1937. In New York it opened October 27, 1913, with Ernest Glendinning as Pierrot and it ran for 105 performances. Sylvia Sidney played Prunella in 1926, when the *New York Telegram* (June 16) called it "an exquisite little fantasy . . . in just the proper key of visionary romance."

"There is a curious mounting something in Mr. Housman's rhythms," said the *New York Tribune* (October 28, 1913), "in the music which serves as an undercurrent to most of the lines, in the exquisite beauty and harmony of the colors and movement, which captures the doubtful spectator and is altogether perfect of its kind"; and the *Mail* called *Prunella* "as tender in sentiment as the love of a child, and worldly wise as the philosophy of a graybeard."

Prunella is a favorite, and a challenge to perform, in little theatres. The stock figure Pierrot is here a poetic symbol of the casual fancy that turns away, then recognizes the true worth of what it has left behind. In a delicate, dream-like blend of poetry, pantomime, music and drama, *Prunella* shows us such a fancy ripening into love.

SHENANDOAH   *Bronson Howard*

Bronson Howard (1842-1908), whose most popular play was *Shenandoah,* a vivid melodrama of the War Between the States, was significant in several ways in the growth of the American theatre. Upon the success of his light comedy *Saratoga,* 1870 (produced in England as *Brighton,* 1874), he became the first American to make a living solely from his plays. With *Young Mrs. Winthrop,* 1882, he presented the first serious study of American life on the stage. After *Shenandoah* (rewritten from his *Drum Taps,* produced in Louisville, Kentucky, about 1868) made a poor start (as a five-act play) in Boston in 1888, a four-act production by Charles Frohman opened in New York, September 9, 1889, with Wilton Lackaye, Henry Miller, and Effie Shannon, running for 250 performances. In Chicago the next year *Shenandoah* reached over 100 performances; for more than a decade it was exceeded in popularity in the North only by *Uncle Tom's Cabin,** on which the stars forever shone.

Shenandoah opens in Charleston, South Carolina, with Colonel Kerchival West, officer of the United States Army, declaring his love to Gertrude Ellingham. An explosion takes her to the window; it was a shell over Fort Sumter. She says to her beloved: "We are enemies now!" Gertrude must also part with her school friend Madeline West, beloved of her brother, Colonel

Robert Ellingham of the Confederate States Army. The plot intertwines the usual Civil War episodes of parted lovers and spies, but reaches its climax when the defeated and withdrawing Yankee forces hear the approaching hoof-beats of Sheridan's great ride, and the General calls out his famous command, "Turn the other way!" to shift the fortunes of the battle and the war. The last act of the play, with the war ended, presents a rousing review of the Union troops and unites the happy lovers.

Excellently intertwined in the war plot is the jealousy of old General Haverill as his young wife's letter, taken from their gallant son's body by the spy Thornton, is found by the General on the wounded Colonel West. Superb, too, is the manner in which Gertrude is torn between her southern patriotism and her northern love, until in a sudden heartwrung cry she urges on her own horse that is bearing Sheridan to save the day for the North.

Superlatives crowded the reviews of Shenandoah, especially for "the greatest battle scene ever shown upon the stage." A New York Academy of Music production included 250 men, many "late members of the U.S. Artillery, most of them from Manila where they have seen active service," and ended with a charge of over fifty horses across the resounding stage. Jack, the horse assigned to Sheridan throughout the run of the play, grew so attuned to the part that a dozen trainers could not hold him when his cue came; once when Sheridan was not in the saddle on time he galloped across the stage without him. "The government should open a recruiting station at the Academy," declared the New York Dramatic Mirror (May 17, 1898), "there would be a rush of volunteers after the performance of Shenandoah." It is impossible, the New York World stated (October 7, 1894) "to conceive that stagecraft can go any further than this scene takes it."

More than the fervor of Sheridan's ride gave Shenandoah its popularity. "Its clever character drawing and dialogue," said the Boston Post (October 7, 1890) "are in Howard's best and most polished vein . . . Love, war, and the varied emotions of the most stormy period in all our latter history are blended in one effective and consistent impression." "Its pathos is always deep and true," commented the New York Tribune (August 31, 1894); "Its humor is natural and appropriate, and its interest is that of human lives and human hearts."

Little more need be said. A 1917 production of Shenandoah, with Tyrone Power, was presented in Los Angeles. Along with David Belasco's The Heart of Maryland* and William Gillette's Secret Service* Shenandoah remains, as the New York Herald called it in 1894 (August 31): "the most interesting, the most exciting, the most dignified of modern military dramas."

After a film by James Lee Barrett, a new musical called Shenandoah, with book by Barrett, Peter Udell, and Philip Rose, lyrics by Udell, music by Gary Geld, was tried out in the summer of 1974 at East Haddam, Conn., then came to the New York Alvin, January 7, 1975, for 1,050 performances. James Stewart in the film, John Cullum in the musical, played Charlie Anderson, a Virginia farmer, widower with six sons and a daughter, who refuses to take sides in the Civil War, but becomes naturally entangled in its drive. The youngest son, who has found a Confederate hat and put it on, is taken prisoner by Northern troops; Charlie and four sons go in search of him. The eldest son, left to tend the farm, is slain. The daughter marries, and her husband at once goes off to fight. On their quest, the men stop trains and free the prisoners. They find the boy, and peace.

Among the songs are "Why am I me?" "We make a beautiful pair," "Violets and Silverbells."

The NBC reviewer called the musical "an attractive show, almost edging over to being corny, but maintaining its dignity . . . an anti-war musical with heart and humor. It is not afraid to believe in the goodness of man." Each of the two Civil War stories of *Shenandoah* presses validly home not the inevitable horror but the basic futility of war.

THEY KNEW WHAT THEY WANTED   *Sidney Howard*

After several adaptations from the French and an original melodrama of the Italian Renaissance, Sidney Howard (American, 1891-1939) came into his own with *They Knew What They Wanted*. With superb plot construction and a colorful capture of the fervor and vitality of life in the United States, the drama displays that gift of character portrayal which remains Howard's major achievement.

The story is set in a grape vineyard in California. Old Tony, whom Prohibition has made rich, writes to Amy, a waitress he had seen in San Francisco, proposing marriage. The proposition catches the lonely girl, and she comes to Tony, eager and hopeful. When she arrives, Tony's young helper, Joe, doesn't know what to make of her cordial though nervous greeting, until Tony—whose reckless driving to meet Amy's train ended in a ditch—is brought in on a stretcher. Then Amy discovers that Tony, timid because of his age, had sent her Joe's picture instead of his own.

What with Tony's broken legs and Amy's broken heart, the inevitable happens between Amy and Joe. But as she nurses her husband, Amy comes to recognize his sterling qualities. His ever cheery optimism, his understanding, his generous affection, awaken her love. But she is pregnant. It tears her heart to tell Tony this and to tell him she is leaving him; but Tony's need and Tony's love reach out to her. The casual Joe, an I.W.W., and a wanderer at heart, goes off; Amy and Tony in regathered love prepare a home for their child.

Howard has stated that the plot was "shamelessly, consciously, and even proudly derived from the legend of Tristan and Iseult."

They Knew What They Wanted, with Pauline Lord, Richard Bennett and Glenn Anders, opened November 24, 1924. Charges of immorality were made, and on April 26, 1925, the play was examined by a Broadway play-jury and cleared. The same day it was announced as the winner—the Theatre Guild's first—of the Pulitzer Prize, for "raising the standard of good morals, good taste, and good manners." The play has remained continuously popular. Tallulah Bankhead appeared in the London production in 1926; various companies in the United States have included June Havoc and Sally Rand as Amy. There was a New York revival, October 2, 1939, with June Walker; another, February 14, 1949, with Paul Muni. The film (1940) directed by Garson Kanin, starred Carole Lombard, Charles Laughton, William Gargan, and Frank Fay.

There was some objection, when the play was first produced, to its picture of unfaithfulness on the very night of a wedding and also to the husband's forgiveness of his wife's action. *Theatre* magazine (February 1925) called the drama "an unusually well-constructed play, smudged up with repellent situations." There is, however, a searching truth, almost an inevitability, in Amy's first reaction to the deception; her chagrin and her touched pride, and the picture of Joe she has come with, all drive her to Joe's arms. There is equal, but more winning, truth in Tony's forgiveness. Indeed, with his amusing Italian accent and curious ways, Tony is one of the most engaging figures of the modern American theatre.

The play as a whole, in Gilbert Gabriel's words (November 25, 1924), is "a winning little idyl of the California vineyards, nonetheless fond and sunny for the thumbprint of reality that is on it . . . a happy, lovable play. Yet it is a shrewd one, too, and sharp." Time has not altered this judgment of *They Knew What They Wanted,* which remains a colorful and a dramatic story, revealing finely responsive traits of human character.

The liveliest of several revivals of the play was by the Phoenix at the New York Playhouse, January 27, 1976, directed by Stephen Porter. Clive Barnes in the *Times* praised Louis Zorich as Tony, Barry Bostwick as Joe, but especially Lois Nettleton as Amy; "a bruised if not broken blossom, plucky, spunky, and with a sudden and delightful warmth, she is delightful, and plays her emotional scenes with a genuine passion."

In the meantime, Frank Loesser had sympathetically made the play into a musical, *The Most Happy Fella,* which opened in New York, May 3, 1956, with Robert Weede and Jo Sullivan, for 676 performances. Among the songs are "Somebody, Somewhere," "Standing on a Corner," "Warm All Over," "How Beautiful the Days!"

Howard retains the power of making his persons seem real.

ALIEN CORN   *Sidney Howard*

Brought to the stage February 20, 1933, by Katharine Cornell, Sidney Howard's *Alien Corn* combines its character studies with sheer theatrical excitement. It presents the difficulty of an artist trapped in an unsympathetic environment.

The title of the play comes from Keats' "Ode to a Nightingale":

> . . . *the sad heart of Ruth when, sick for home,*
> *She stood in tears amid the alien corn.*

The Ruth of Keats' poem is the biblical Ruth, who, on her husband's death, went to the land of her mother-in-law, Naomi. The "Ruth" of Howard's play is Elsa Brandt, a concert pianist who, when freedom died in Vienna, came as a refugee to the New World; she becomes instructor of music at Conway College, but feels stifled in the small midwestern town. Conway, with whom Elsa has an affair, plans a concert series for her; his wife, understandably, blocks this. When romantic young Julian, deeply in love with Elsa, discovers her with Conway, he kills himself. Encouragement for Elsa comes from a disillusioned newspaperman, Phipps, who had once dreamed of being a writer; and after the suicide and scandal Elsa packs off to try her artistic career.

The acting of Katharine Cornell, with the shrewd writing of Sidney Howard, won considerable sympathy for Elsa Brandt; American reviewers made no question of the importance of her career and the rightness of her struggle. In London the play opened at the Westminster in 1934; but at the Wyndham revival, July 8, 1939, James Agate, in the *Times,* declared that "the play invites us to consider to what extent the premonition of genius justifies its victim in immolating herself and other people." Howard seems to question neither Elsa's genius nor her deeds, and persuades most of the audience to similar approval.

Alien Corn came naturally out of the author's life. Howard was raised in a small college town; his mother was a professional pianist. Howard wrote, in the *Herald Tribune,* February 26, 1933: "When I was at Harvard, we used to say: 'May Heaven preserve us from ever being like Professor —, who has nothing to teach and is afraid to get out in the world.' That, I think, is the origin of *Alien Corn.*" He added: "The people who interest me most are those who are troubled to make both ends meet. I have never begun a play on the 'boy-and-girl' theme . . . Conway gets a glimpse of what life might be with Elsa, and then loses it; Julian, in his attempts to fit himself into the real world, comes to his end because of his inevitable futility; Phipps, clear-sighted, experienced, already is side-tracked, but bends his efforts to seeing that Elsa does not become a misfit, and, finally, Elsa gets 'booted' into the world where she belongs."

Brooks Atkinson (*New York Times*, February 21, 1933) said that Howard presents his story "with so much driving conviction and Miss Cornell plays it with so much spiritual torture that the effect is extraordinarily stirring . . . every incident gives the impression of being a crisis, and every person in the play lives in a whirl of excitement . . . *Alien Corn* is completely alive."

The *London Times,* however (July 6, 1939), queried: "Ought there to be quite so much excitement, so many moments of exaltation and hysteria, so much shrieking, and brandy, and suicide, before she can count the world well lost?" Even the English, however, admitted that the play achieves "a ranting, roaring *succés de théâtre.*"

Alien Corn has many shrewd and human touches. Elsa, of course, is our chief concern. But Conway, the successful businessman, philanthropist, and potential patron of the arts, is also excellently drawn. His attitude, on first hearing of Elsa's ambition, is naturally and neatly expressed: "Watkins says you're a genius. I wouldn't know. It puts you pretty far off my street. I mean I wouldn't buy stock in a company I didn't know from the ground up. And you're asking me to invest my money in something I can't even make a guess about." Conway's wife, a pretentious musical amateur, is a well-drawn figure, with no more exaggeration than satire demands. The characters are thus human enough to engage our interest, and the drive of the story captures and sweeps along our tense concern.

YELLOW JACK   *Sidney Howard*

The year that Paul De Kruif's *Microbe Hunters* was published (1926), Sidney Howard suggested to the author a dramatization of the eleventh chapter, which tells the story of the confirmation of the mosquito as the carrier of yellow fever ("yellow jack"), a finding that made possible the completion of the Panama Canal. With the help of De Kruif, Sidney Howard somewhat later found the time to write such a play, and on March 6, 1934, Broadway was pleasantly surprised with *Yellow Jack*. The play was hailed by Brooks Atkinson as "of tremendous importance to the stage . . . enlarges the scope of the modern theatre," and by the *New York Herald Tribune* as "a kind of minor miracle . . . it is almost as if, through the adroit use of lights, visible characters, spoken words, pause and spacing, and nothing else, life were given to an article in the encyclopedia."

The isolation by Army doctors in the Canal Zone of the mosquito as the carrier of yellow fever involved some opposition from conservatives and old fogies at Washington and elsewhere. Mainly it was a question of securing and observing two sets of four volunteers. One group was to live in a tent, filthy and foul with blankets and clothing of men who had died of the fever, but free of mosquitoes; the other group in a tent as clean as scientific prophylaxis could maintain it, but to which the mosquito was given full access. Out of the persistence of the "theorizing old fool" who entertained the mosquito theory, out of the enthusiasm and self-experiments of the doctors—one of whom died in the quest—and out of the seemingly dull waiting of the volunteers, Howard built a play of quiet but gathering intensity. "Without question," said producer Gilbert Miller, speaking of producer Guthrie McClintic's offering, "*Yellow Jack* is one of the greatest productions I have ever witnessed in the American theatre." Stephen Vincent Benét called the play "the finest thing ever done in the theatre by an American."

The story is advanced with complete realism of detail. The characters are natural, and the volunteers are effectively differentiated: the eloquent, almost grandiloquent Irishman; the radical Jew; the lazy southern lad; the man who wants to be a sergeant. The language and the attitudes of the speakers, moreover, are not only natural; they are historical. Only the staging departed from the realistic treatment. The various scenes were presented on a single setting, a simple stage architecturally disposed in various levels, with steps and curving bars marking off the doctors' office or the encampment site. Sufficiently suggestive and admirably apt, the staging permitted a rapid flow of the story.

Howard was perhaps justifiably afraid of the seeming barrenness of his theme, with an impersonal nurse as the only female in the cast and the villain literally an insect. For emotion he at times turned to theatrical standbys. As John Mason Brown (March 10, 1934) pointed out, he is "not above running up the American flag when he thinks he needs it, playing taps to guarantee a flood of tears, and closing many of his scenes with good old tag lines." Howard need not have resorted to such devices. The play holds its audience and is indeed a constant favorite with community groups. It was seen again on Broadway in 1947.

The theatre has often made reference to or incidental use of scientific discoveries. Rarely has it, as in *Yellow Jack,* made discovery itself the dramatic theme. The play was hailed by *Stage* magazine (April 1934) for depicting the heroism of science, which enlists not to kill men, but to save them: "The antagonist is so small as to be nearly invisible, even to the fine eye of the microscope, but deadly enough to call forth a strange and glorious kind of dramatic conflict . . . If there is one thing that differentiates our age from the age of antiquity, it is the faith in experimental science. If modern drama is to have a similar grandeur, it must not exclude such science from its theme. *Yellow Jack* has accepted that theme, and projected it with splendor . . . a notable contribution to the American theatre."

Unfortunately, the theatrical promise foreseen in the first quoted comment, and the last, has not been fulfilled. Stories of great scientific achievement have been frequent in motion pictures, which more smoothly than the drama can course through a laborious and hopeful life. *Yellow Jack,* therefore, remains distinctive as the dramatic presentation of a gallant fight of men against a long defiant foe of man.

There was a revival of the play by ELT on December 11, 1964.

A TRIP TO CHINATOWN   *Charles Hale Hoyt*

In the last decade of the nineteenth century, the increasing popularity of the ten-twen'-thirt' melodrama was matched by that of the lively farce with interpolated songs and dances that was one of the forerunners of the present-day musical comedy. Chief among the writers of such farces in the United States was Charles Hale Hoyt (1859-1900). Anna Held made her American debut and Maude Adams her first New York appearance in plays by Hoyt. His most popular play was *A Trip to Chinatown; or, An Idyll of San Francisco.* With its premiere in Philadelphia, January 26, 1891, and opening in New York on November 9, 1891, it ran for 657 performances, a record not broken until *Lightnin'* crackled in 1918. The dancer Loie Fuller made her serpentine "skirt dance" famous in *A Trip to Chinatown.* The play opened in London on September 29, 1894, for a run of 125 performances.

The characters in the play never get to Chinatown but the audience gets considerable fun by the way. Indeed, the destination is only a trick by which Ben Gay, a wealthy and strict widower, is persuaded to let his daughter Tony and his nephew Rashleigh Gay go out with Norman Blood, Isabelle Dame, and some other friends, (im)properly chaperoned by the widow Mrs. Daisy Guyer. Their intention is to go to the masquerade ball at the Cliff House. Mrs. Guyer's letter to Rashleigh making the arrangements is delivered to old Ben by mistake; he interprets it as a billet-doux making rendezvous, and he goes to meet the widow, first at the Riche Restaurant, then at the masquerade ball. After countless misadventures and tipsy venturing the younger folk surprise Ben in the midst of his pleasures and out of his discomfiture win greater freedom.

One manuscript of the play sets the last act not at the ball but in Ben Gay's home gymnasium (which permits the ladies to appear in shorts); here, Ben is exposed by his "I.O.U." on the Riche Restaurant menu.

Much of the fun of the play rises from Ben's old friend Welland Strong, who constantly checks his temperature and announces how much each gay spurt is taking off his life, but insists on joining the youngsters in all their reveling. There is a deal of dancing at the ball, and all the men, young and old, chase a high-kicking masquerader who turns out to be Mrs. Guyer's maid. The *Boston Transcript* (February 10, 1891) could well say that the play presents "a world in which conversation consists of diffusive slang and warmed-over waggishness, a world where high kicking is a high virtue, where a lady is reckoned as well and becomingly dressed in inverse ratio to the extent of her raiment, and where any and every member of society is prone, as well as expected, to break out at any moment, and with or without provocation, into song, dance, or other irrelevancy."

The songs in the play were epoch-making. Three by Percy Gaunt are "The Bowery," "Push Dem Clouds Away," and "Reuben and Cynthia." A song interpolated at a Milwaukee performance stopped the show; this was "After the Ball" (1892) by Charles K. Harris, which has sold well over five million copies. "Reuben, Reuben, I've been thinking" and "The Bowery, the Bowery, I'll never go there any more" are classics of popular song.

A Trip to Chinatown was constantly played for a decade. The *Philadelphia Record* in 1893 summed up its appeal: "The curtain goes up on silly merriment and almost three hours later the curtain comes down on silly merriment." Several years later (January 28, 1896) the *Boston Transcript* reported that the play captured "all that is most original and best in Mr. Hoyt's peculiar talent; in its way, it is a gem." Outside of sophisticate circles, *A Trip to Chinatown* still has much to please, and a little refurbishing would make it still shine on Broadway.

The play was revived by ELT in 1961, and OffOffBway (St. Bart's) in 1967. A program note declares: "The author begs to say that whatever this play may be, it is all that is claimed for it"—a statement those that have seen it and heard its songs are not likely to dispute.

HERNANI   *Victor Hugo*

The French Romantic drama, surging free from two centuries of classical rule, reached flood tide with the work of Victor Hugo (1802-1885). Already hailed as a leader by the young Romantics, Hugo in his preface to the play *Cromwell*, 1827, issued the direct challenge: "Let us take the hammer to poetic systems. Let us tear down the old plastering that conceals the façade of art. There are neither rules nor models; rather, there are no other rules than the general laws of nature."

In accordance with his own precept, Hugo wrote *Hernani* (1830), and at the prospect of its presentation at the Théâtre Français, blood began to boil. Seven members of the Academy petitioned Charles X to keep the theatre closed "against all productions of the new school, and reserved exclusively for writers who really apprehend the beautiful and the true." With kingly modesty Charles replied, "In literary matters my place, gentlemen, is only, like yours, amongst the audience."

As January 1830 moved along, classicists eavesdropped at rehearsals, caught snatches of the play and parodied them before the production. A burlesque of *Hernani, Hounded by the Horn*, even beat it to the stage. The Théâtre Français company itself was cold to the drama. Hugo received threatening letters. The painter Charlet offered him a bodyguard of four janissaries; boldly Hugo declared that on opening night he would dispense with the usual claque. Instead, the young artists of Paris rallied to him, led by Gautier in a new rose-colored waistcoat. Their passes to the theatre were red slips marked Hierro! (Spanish for "iron"—their mood for the evening). And on February 25, 1830, *Hernani* opened. The hisses of the classicists and the cheers of the romantics so drowned the play that hardly a word was heard from the stage all evening. For almost a hundred nights the tumult continued. Duels were fought over the drama's merits. Finally, *Hernani*, Romanticism and freedom won. The play stands as a milestone in the history of the French drama. On its centenary, February 25, 1930, Edmond Rostand, at a great celebration, read a poem "A Night at *Hernani*."

The story has all the turbulence and violence of the Spanish "cape and sword" drama, in which the *pundonor* (point of honor) drives young love to rapturous death. In the year 1519 the outlaw Hernani is in love with Doña Sol, who is betrothed to her old guardian Don Ruy Gomez. Don Carlos (King Charles V of Spain) covets her. Knightly obligations and the laws of hospitality out-balance jealousy. Don Carlos saves Hernani from Ruy Gomez; then Hernani spares the King, and Ruy Gomez hides Hernani from the King's pursuit. In thanks, Hernani gives Ruy Gomez a horn and his word that he will end his life when Ruy Gomez sounds it. Together they now pursue the King, who has carried off Doña Sol, and Don Carlos is saved only by the bells that announce his election as Holy Roman Emperor. Don Carlos grants amnesty to all below the rank of Count. Doña Sol exclaims that this spares Hernani, but the outlaw proudly proclaims his noble birth. The Emperor pardons him and sanctions his marriage with Doña Sol. But on the bridal day, Ruy Gomez sounds the fateful horn. Doña Sol snatches and shares Hernani's poison and Ruy Gomez also kills himself.

This surge of romantic heroism, of pride that dooms its owner, of love where "all is true, and all is good, and all is beautiful, and naught is wanting," Hugo has couched in majestical lyrical verse, with striking images, stark contrasts, and bold dramatic conceptions. Even without the excitement of the classical ire and romantic verve that led to "the battle of *Hernani,*" the play is striking enough to have been a great success. Its tumult, however, was part of the aesthetic and political turmoil of the day; those that cheered the play also helped put Louis Philippe on the throne in the revolution of July 1830.

The English felt the disorder as well as the power of the play. The *Foreign Quarterly Review* (October 1830) declared: "We cannot better compare M. Hugo's drama than to one of those Gothic castles, amidst which he has placed its scenes; it is vast and striking from the magnitude of its outline, varied from the accumulation of materials it contains, powerful from the wild strength which has been employed, or, rather, wasted in its construction; but, like it, incoherent in its plan, and mixed in its architecture; with pillars where it is impossible to trace any connection between the capital and the base, shapeless chambers, where meanness sits side by side with magnificence, and dark and winding passages, which terminate after all in a prospect of a dead wall, or an empty courtyard."

In 1844 Verdi based his opera *Ernani* on the Hugo play. Sarah Bernhardt acted in *Hernani* in London in 1879 and in the United States in 1887. Mounet-Sully brought it to America again in 1894, when the *New York Times* (March 27) said that in it, "passion never became effusive, nor heroism absurd" and the *Boston Transcript* (May 12, 1894) found it crowded with "people who have much of the stuff of humanity in them, whom we can imagine real, and whose emotions and actions we can reckon with . . . their humanity pierces the artificial, whimsical fantasticism of their surroundings, and to a great extent condones it. Surely there are few more emotionally powerful scenes on the stage than that terrible struggle between Hernani, Doña Sol, and Ruy Gomez in the fifth act."

The *Boston Transcript,* however, observed (April 12, 1930): "It is very evident that *Hernani* has become hopelessly old-fashioned for the modern stage." It is seldom acted; but it is often read. For, as the *Transcript* added, "it is sustained by the glory of the poet, by the brilliancy of the verse, and by a celebrity rare in the history of literature." Historic as *Hernani* stands, the drama of Hugo found few followers; only Rostand* has richly explored the Romantic vein. The characters are hollow as trumpets—but they make a trumpet sound. Dynamic in movement, superb in the vivid rhetoric of its verse, *Hernani* opened the French theatre to the romantic drama; it remains an outstanding example of the type.

BRAND   *Henrik Ibsen*

After the first fierce rebellion that followers of the established order rouse against exciting innovations, Henrik Ibsen (Norwegian, 1828-1906) was accepted as a classic, his plays familiar and frequent on every serious stage. After his first two great symbolic dramas, *Brand,* who followed his indomitable will to his doom, and *Peer Gynt,* who obeyed every impulse to the verge of destruction, came his series of more realistic studies of human striving and social ills. Great actresses have looked forward to awakening Nora's decisive bang of the closing door, or the otherwise awakening Hedda Gabler's decisive bang of the pistol shot.

A discussion of separate plays follows; at the end, after *John Gabriel Borkman,* there is a glance at some of the countless recent revivals.

The question of recognition of one's mission in life and of devoting oneself to it at any cost, was very much on Ibsen's mind when he wrote *Brand* in Rome in 1866. Brand is a stern pastor, whose motto is "All or Nothing." Through him, Ibsen shows the dangerous power of will without love. While the play pictures the destruction an iron will can bring upon its possessor and upon those around, who must be left free to make their own choice, it surges to an exaltation of faith in the spirit of man, "the one eternal thing."

Returning to the fjord valley of his youth, Pastor Brand challenges his country-folk to renew their faith. Young Agnes, about to run off with an artist, weds Brand and follows him. Brand fights the petty avarice of his mother, the self-seeking of the Mayor, the feeble humanitarianism of the doctor, the shrewd cynicism of the schoolmaster. As he denounces a church built on hypocrisy and compromise, his wife and child die of the cold of the countryside and the cold absolutism of his spirit. There is a conflict, implicit in his family's fate, between God as a force for order and God as a force for love. When Brand exhorts his congregation to follow him to the true church, he starts up the mountainside; and though the cold drives his congregation back, Brand continues the climb. An invisible choir warns him: "Earth-born creature, live for Earth!" The phantom of his wife appears, and pleads with him; he spurns, through her, the "spirit of compromise," the "falcon" that lures forever. And the rifle shot of Brand's last follower, the gypsy girl Gerd, fired to drop the falcon, loosens an avalanche that sweeps down and overwhelms Brand. Over the covering snow a great voice calls: "He is the God of Love."

Although *Brand* presents an eternal challenge in the idea that faith is essential though suffering is inevitable, the play's exhortation to Ibsen's countrymen had a more immediate application. When in 1864, as part of Bismarck's plan for the unification of Germany, Prussia and Austria invaded Denmark, Norway stood by, neutral. The result was that the defeated Danes abandoned all claim to the duchies of Schleswig, Holstein and Lauenberg. Ibsen—whose love for his country was deepened by his prolonged stay abroad—felt that Norway's action was a betrayal. The fierceness of his patriotic fervor gave particular point to the exhortations of Brand. Ibsen later declared, "Brand is myself in my best moments."

Brand was warmly received by a public that largely shared Ibsen's indignation. Its printed form ran through four editions within its first year. Although the play was not intended primarily for production, Act IV was enacted at the Christiania Theatre in 1866; the whole play was presented there in 1876, in 1885 in Stockholm, in 1895 in Paris, and in 1898 in Copenhagen and Berlin. The full production requires six and a half hours. Act Four, separately, has been much more frequently and more widely performed; it was given in London in 1893 and in New York in 1910. In its entirety, Brand was produced at Yale University in 1928 (Ibsen's centenary), at Litchfield, Connecticut, in the summer of 1938, and at Cambridge, England, in 1946.

Brand is written in four-foot rhyming verse; iambic for the more familiar and colloquial scenes, trochaic for the peaks of vision and passion and sober thought. The poetry is vivid, at times direct, at times mystic, always bearing an undertone of earnest emotion and a cloak of beauty. In 1906, C. H. Herford observed in the introduction to his translation of the play, that only those English readers "who can imagine the prophetic fire of Carlyle fused with the genial verve and the intellectual athleticism of Browning, and expressed by aid of a dramatic faculty to parallel which we must go two centuries backward" can understand the fascination of the play. Writing in *Black and White* on December 19, 1891, William Archer called *Brand* "one of the simplest, noblest, and most absorbing dramas in literature . . . among the two or three supreme poetic achievements of this century . . . the poet's farewell to popular theology—his passionate declaration that ideal Christianity is impossible, while possible and actual Christianity is a base compromise . . ."

This noble drama of a God of love whose "caress is chastisement," and of a faithful one who will not compromise but who summons mankind to the stern and stark alternatives of all or nothing, takes an imperious hold upon every reader. It poses the paradox of the human spirit: the absolute is destruction, yet compromise is a living death. *Peer Gynt,** the companion drama, is the wan comedy of eternal compromise; *Brand* is the bright tragedy of steadfast holding to one's high ideals.

PEER GYNT   *Henrik Ibsen*

In his dramatic poem *Peer Gynt*, 1867, Ibsen wrote a counter-movment to *Brand.** In Peer, all is compromise; instead of holding firmly to faith, though it lead to death, he abandons everything that may interfere with living. His life becomes inevitably a life of the senses. In *Brand* love means chastisement and death; contrariwise, in *Peer Gynt* love means forgiveness and life.

A happy-go-lucky lad, who drains each moment of its opportunity, Peer Gynt, boastful at a wedding, makes off with the bride, Ingrid, and after a night, abandons her; he dallies with the girls of the hillside farms; he accepts the virgin Solveig, who gives her life to him. He then returns to his dying mother, Aase, and in a tender make-believe drives her through St. Peter's gate to her eternal home. Away again, he comes upon the mountain trolls, and instead of man's motto, Be thyself, he accepts that of the trolls, Exist for thyself. Obeying this motto, Peer wanders lengthily. In a wild fourth act (not in the original plan of the play) he goes to Morocco with millions made in America. When the millions are stolen, he wanders in the desert and comes upon the Emperor's horse and jewels which were abandoned by frightened thieves. He meets Anitra, daughter of a Bedouin chief, who dances for him; he bears her off with the jewels. From behind the Sphinx at Gizeh comes a German, who takes Peer to the madhouse at Cairo, where a language reformer and other lunatics—among them a minister who thinks he's a pen, while everyone insists on using him as a blotter— hail Peer as their king, the Kaiser of Self-hood. Come home, he finds himself a legend. Peer then meets the Button-Moulder (Death); men, like buttons, are designed to have a definite shape in order to hold things together in the world, but Peer has "set at defiance his life's design." By never being firm, he has never been himself. He is destined for the melting-pot, unless in truth he can find himself—which he does, in Solveig's heart. It is Peer's recognition of his error that wins the grace of his salvation through Solveig.

The phantasmagoria of *Peer Gynt* confused many of the critics when it first appeared, even as others hailed it. Clemens Petersen, the most influential critic in Copenhagen, maintained it was "full of riddles that are insoluble because there is nothing in them at all." He called some of the playwright's devices "thought-swindling . . . not poetry, because in the transmutation of reality into art it falls halfway short of the demands both of art and of reality." As Ibsen had said earlier he'd be interested to hear what Petersen thought of the play, he now protested vigorously: "My book *is* poetry; and if it is not, then it will be. The conception of poetry in our country, in Norway, shall be made to conform to the book." This prophecy has been more than fulfilled: *Peer Gynt* was hailed by Alrik Gustafson, in *A History of Modern Drama* (1947), as "the great national poem of Norway."

Even Georg Brandes, though he later changed his mind, found the poetry and thought of the drama all wasted. The fourth act, he said, "is witless in its satire, crude in its irony, and in its latter part scarcely comprehensible . . . Contempt for humanity and self-hatred make a bad foundation on which to build a poetic work. What an unlovely and distorting view of life this is! What acrid pleasure can a poet find in thus sullying human nature?" Today the play is recognized as not merely a satire, but also a song to love.

In its entirety, *Peer Gynt* has seldom been performed. Ibsen recognized that the play required cutting and suggested that in place of Act IV there could be a great musical tone picture, suggesting Peer Gynt's wanderings all over the world, in which "American, English, and French arias occur as alternating and disappearing motives." At Ibsen's request, Edvard Grieg wrote the *Peer Gynt* suite, which is probably more widely familiar than the play. With Grieg's music, *Peer Gynt* was produced in Christiania in 1876, in Copenhagen in 1886 and 1892. In 1895 it was played in Stockholm, then it went on tour through Scandinavia. Paris saw it in 1896, at the Théâtre de l'Oeuvre; Vienna saw it in 1902. Richard Mansfield acted the role of Peer in the first performance in English, omitting Act IV, at the Chicago Grand Opera House, October 29, 1906, and later in New York. In 1923 the Theatre Guild produced the play with Joseph Schildkraut (Peer), Dudley Digges (the Troll King), Edward G. Robinson (the Button-Moulder), and Lillebil Ibsen (Anitra). The production was directed by Komisarjevsky. In 1924 Basil Sydney took on the role of Peer. Since 1930, *Peer Gynt* has been performed virtually every year by college theatres. New York saw it again, OffBway, in 1949, and with John Garfield in 1951. The first American presentation of the complete play was at Amherst, Massachusetts, in 1940.

Peer Gynt was produced in Edinburgh in 1908. In London, the Old Vic Company presented it in 1922 and 1935 and, with Ralph Richardson as Peer, in September 1944.

Despite the frequency of its performance and the variety of its acting versions, theatre critics in England and the United States have not given wholehearted praise to *Peer Gynt*. The first American production, for example, was dismissed by Albert Pulvermacher in the *New York Staats-Zeitung*: "What we saw on the stage was a hodge-podge of mere madness."

The Theatre Guild production of 1923 made clear enough the surge and sweep of the drama, but it left the critics divided. Heywood Broun (February 7, 1923) stated: "To the eye it is the most beautiful thing the Guild has ever done . . . Instead of being clearer when put upon the stage, more fog drifted into *Peer Gynt* than when we read it . . . The last two scenes are eternal drama. It has always seemed to us that the death of Aase is one of the most moving scenes ever written for the theatre." Alexander Woollcott declared: "To one who found the Jessner production in Berlin a singularly narcotic influence, the Guild revival seems an unexpectedly tonic and spiritual thing. *Peer Gynt* is an undisciplined, unedited play, a tremendous unfiltered stream fed from the springs of Norwegian folk lore and carrying with it no end of rubbish that fell in by chance as it was being written. The very process of cutting it down to the limits of a tolerable three hour and a half performance betters it some, and we could bear it if the entire gimcrack fourth act were dropped entirely. This . . . would leave intact all of the beauty which has kept the play alive for fifty years."

The English were even less hospitable to the Norwegian gallimaufry. On September 3, 1944, James Agate observed in the *London Times* (of a production that used Dame Sybil Thorndike as Aase, Ralph Richardson as Peer, Nicholas Hannen as the Troll King, Laurence Olivier as the Button-Moulder, and Joyce Redman as Solveig): "Last week, in an unguarded moment, I let slip my private opinion that Ibsen's *Peer Gynt,* like some other world-masterpieces, is all very jolly and boring! I withdraw and apologize abjectly. I now declare that there is neither iota nor scintilla of jollity in this cavernous and gloomy masterpiece . . ."

Despite the reservations of some critics, *Peer Gynt* holds firm place, not only as a national, but as a world masterpiece. The Norwegians naturally found in it many allusions to themselves. Björnson,* whose idyllic stories of peasant life Ibsen may have been satirizing, generously declared: "*Peer Gynt* is a satire on Norwegian egoism, narrowness, and self-sufficiency, so executed as to have made me not only laugh and laugh again till I was sore, but again and again give thanks to the author in my heart—as I here do publicly."

Although Peer Gynt comes partly out of Norwegian folk-tale, as do the trolls, the main story is Ibsen's invention; and as the adventures carry Peer around the world, so are the implications universal. *Brand* said that each man must hold to his faith and his ideals; *Peer Gynt* shows that each man must find, and be, his self. Bacchanalian and pagan in its imagery and rout, Christian and concerned in its thought and deeper feeling, Ibsen produced a unique and ebullient masterpiece in *Peer Gynt.*

PILLARS OF SOCIETY   *Henrik Ibsen*

Since events in Europe did not justify Ibsen's hopes of a gathering spiritual force, he turned to a succession of plays about everyday life with the second of his all-prose contemporary dramas, *Pillars of Society.* In the deliberate turn to commonplace themes, his English friend and translator, William Archer, thinks that Ibsen went too far, that this is "of all Ibsen's works the least characteristic, because, acting on a transitory phase of theory, he has been almost successful in divesting it of poetic charm."

This play is chiefly an exposure of sanctimonious hypocrisy, of the shaky pedestals that support the "pillars of society." The career of Consul Bernick, the leading citizen of a small but thriving Norwegian seaport, is founded on a lie: fifteen years earlier, he managed to shift onto his brother-in-law, Johan, gone to America, his own amorous indiscretion and a rumor of embezzlement. Bernick has, however, for the fifteen years, been a stalwart citizen, making the town a better place to live in and a richer field for his own double-dealing.

Faced with a threat of exposure, as the play opens, he plans to have the returned Johan sail on an unseaworthy ship—only to hear that his son has run away on the same vessel. Shocked to his senses, Bernick makes a decision and—though he learns in time that the ship has not sailed—before an assemblage of citizens confesses his earlier and present sins.

Two years in the writing, *Pillars of Society* opened at Copenhagen on November 18, 1877, with immediate and striking success. It was enthusiastically received throughout Scandinavia and German-speaking Europe.

In 1878, there were productions at five Berlin theatres within a fortnight; by the turn of the century, it had been played over 1,200 times in German. In France and England, the play was more tardily welcomed. Lugné-Poe produced it in Paris in 1896. A single London performance on December 15, 1880, was Ibsen's first appearance in the English theatre; there was another performance in 1889 and two more were given in 1901.

Pillars of Society came more lengthily to New York; it was played in German, opening December 26, 1888, and frequently thereafter; in English, it opened on March 6, 1891, to the usual Anglo-Saxon reception of Ibsen. The production, said the *New York Dramatic Mirror,* "served to show the dreariness of the one play of Ibsen's that seemed to give some promise ... The work is verbose and tiresome ... His 'realism' is evidently the commonplace unavoidable in a writer who has not the dramatic instinct nor the technical knowledge that permits a playwright of ordinary capacity to make a drama interesting and theatrically effective. In our humble opinion Ibsen is the veriest tyro in the art of playwriting. His pieces are sermons written in dramatic form ... Even the wildest of Ibsen faddists cannot fail to vote him an intolerable bore when he is acted."

In spite of this reception, the play has had numerous revivals in New York; notably in 1904 with Wilton Lackaye and William O. Hazeltine; in 1910 with Holbrook Blinn, Henry Stephenson, Fuller Mellish, and Minnie Maddern Fiske; in 1913 with young Edward G. Robinson; in 1931 with Moffat Johnston, Rollo Peters, Romney Brent, Frank Conlon, Edgar Stehli, Fania Marinoff, and Dorothy Gish.

By 1904 the *New York Dramatic Mirror* had changed its mind about the play: "... as fresh and as real today as when it was penned ... To an average audience perhaps more appealing than are the majority of Ibsen's plays ... Whether the drama is presented in Christiania or Cincinnati, its shafts of truth are pretty sure to strike as near home as one's next door neighbor."

Interwoven with the main theme of social pharisaism, Ibsen also stressed the drive of women toward moral and economic independence, which motivates his next play, *A Doll's House.* * In *Pillars of Society,* this emphasis is clearly shown in the contrast of three women. Martha, Bernick's sister, is all of the old generation: she fits into the pattern sketched in the first draft of *The Pretenders*: "to love all, to sacrifice all, and be forgotten: that is woman's saga." Dina, who marries Johan, is all of the new generation; she makes her own decisions; she does not yield to conventional claims. Standing between the two is the Bernicks' old friend, Lona Hessel; firm in her strength to turn Bernick toward the truth, when catastrophe comes she is equally firm in her devotion: "Old friendship does not rust." This may be, as Archer says, the only play of Ibsen's "in which plot can be said to preponderate over character"; the plot is ingenious, naturally developed, skilfully drawn together, with several powerfully theatrical scenes; yet the character of Bernick is probed with shrewd insight, and the women are neatly balanced in searching and sympathetic portraits.

In this play, Ibsen emerges as a searching analyst of the social scene, pondering universal human impulses in contemporary terms.

A DOLL'S HOUSE   *Henrik Ibsen*

With *A Doll's House* Ibsen broke the chains of the nineteenth-century well-made play with its happy ending. He also emerged as a world dramatist, for, although *A Doll's House* was not his first great play, it was the first to be widely performed and vehemently discussed in many tongues.

Before the play opens Nora Helmer, brought up in sheltered happiness, forges a check in order to help her sick husband. Krogstad, a clerk in Helmer's bank, after holding the forgery over her, returns the check; but in the meantime the attitude of her husband, Torvald, opens Nora's eyes. She has boasted that Torvald "wouldn't hesitate a moment to give his very life for my sake"; instead, he turns upon her and scolds her roundly for forging the check though she has done it to save him. And Nora recognizes that she has been, not a true companion, but a toy; she leaves her husband to find herself. The last sound in the play is the slamming of the downstairs door.

The closing of that door was heard around the world, in the surging battle for women's rights. Published and produced in Copenhagen (where it was Fru Hennings' greatest success), *A Doll's House,* 1879, within the year was played all over Scandinavia and Germany. Argument over the play—over the right or wrong of Nora's declaration of independence—so monopolized conversation and engendered such heated controversy that discussion of the play was by prior agreement barred at social gatherings.

Copyright laws did not then protect the text of plays, and Ibsen, confronted with perversions of the play's end, himself wrote a happy ending, in which the thought of her children works in Nora until she stays at home. Ibsen preferred, he said, "to commit the outrage myself, rather than leave my work to the tender mercies of adaptors." It is quite possible, indeed, that Ibsen originally planned a happy ending—which comes when Krogstad returns the forged check—but that the characters grew too real for such an outcome. Assuming a happy ending as Ibsen's original intention, however, explains certain inconsistencies in Nora, who seems at first too shallow for the great change that comes.

A rather remote adaptation of the play, called *Breaking a Butterfly,* by Henry Arthur Jones* and Henry Herman, was presented in London in 1884, but *A Doll's House* was not shown there until Janet Achurch enacted Nora with great success in June 1889. In America, Helena Modjeska had performed *A Doll's House* in Louisville, Kentucky, as early as 1883, but it was not until 1889 that it came to, and stirred, New York, in a version called *A Doll's Home.* "The Ibsen cult is not likely to achieve popularity in this metropolis," said the *New York Dramatic Mirror* (December 28, 1889) "if we may judge by the impression created by *A Doll's Home.* However profitable the study of the piece is to the sociologist, it is by no manner of means pleasurable from the playgoer's standpoint. Nora, the heroine, is a mixture of Frou-Frou and Featherbrain. She is of little dramatic value, because she is a freak rather than a type, and freaks are not welcome in the dramatic world ... [Ibsen] develops both character and plot in a tedious, halting fashion, using no lights and no genuine dramatic contrasts... The dialogue is wearisome—an arid desert without oases ... It is a dose that will make even the Ibsen cranks quail."

Ibsenites, however, rallied to the play, and it has been frequently revived. Actresses are attracted by the variety and increasing depth of the chief role, as the heedless and happy Nora, who dances the tarantella and skips to the masquerade ball, wakens to a responsible life.

In his introduction to *A Doll's House* (1906), William Archer remarked, "When Nora and Helmer faced each other, and set to work to ravel out the skein of their illusions, then one felt oneself face to face with a new thing in drama—an order of experience, at once intellectual and emotional, not hitherto attained in the theatre." Among the actresses who have partaken of, and transmitted, that experience, are the Germans Lucy Mannheim, Hedwig Niemann-Raabe, and Agnes Sorma; the French Réjane; the Italian Duse; the Russian Vera Komisarjevsky; and in English, Alla Nazimova, Minnie Maddern Fiske, Ethel Barrymore, Eva Le Gallienne, and Ruth Gordon.

A Doll's House has been popular in college theatres since 1920. The best recent Broadway production opened December 26, 1937, with Jed Harris directing a version by Thornton Wilder in which Ruth Gordon played Nora; Dennis King, Helmer; Sam Jaffe, Krogstad; and the screen star Paul Lukas made his Broadway debut as Dr. Rank. Atkinson called this production "one of the finest Ibsen revivals in years . . . Nora trying to hold the world back with a desperate tarantella; Nora driven nearly out of her mind with apprehension; Nora quietly coming into her own inheritance of personal pride and taking command of the situation—these are the portions of the play that Miss Gordon has completely mastered . . . the moral and spiritual triumphs of Nora are still full of the fire of life." And while John Mason Brown felt that "both specialists and general playgoers are forced to admit that their interest in A Doll's House nowadays is more academic than human," Robert Coleman declared that "the Norse giant's play still retains the ability to enlist and to hold the interest of modern audiences." The revival achieved a record run of 144 performances.

In A Doll's House there lingers a romantic juxtaposition of contrasted effects, not found in the later Ibsen social dramas. The tarantella, the Christmas tree, the toy-shop mood of the early scenes, are almost blinding in their brightness, held before Nora's dark self-questioning, and the cynical bitterness of her friend Dr. Rank. Despite these intrusions of an earlier dramaturgic method and mood, A Doll's House is a pioneer play in structure as well as in theme. It abandons most if not all of the tricks of the "well-made play" (though the confidant remains), and builds what has been called "the drama of retrospective analysis." The play starts, like the classical epic, in medias res, in the midst of things, when the events that will produce the crisis have already occurred, and the gradual revelation of the past as part of the present gives a double forcefulness to the happenings. This technique has been widely used by playwrights after Ibsen.

In idea, A Doll's House is a pioneer in the dramatic presentation of women struggling for independence, for equality of consideration and of treatment with men. Beyond the conflict of the sexes, however, the play continues Ibsen's dramatic portrayal of the basic conflict, of the individual against the mass, of personal integrity against the crust of convention and the rust of social mores and concerns. It is a world growing up, not merely a Nora, that is called upon to slam the door of its "doll's house."

GHOSTS   *Henrik Ibsen*

Opposition to Ibsen rose to a furious howl with his *Ghosts,* 1881. Intended as a sort of sequel to *The Doll's House,** in which Nora had refused to submit to social conventions, *Ghosts* pictures the life of Mrs. Alving, who does submit. Many critics of the time, however, mistook the son, Oswald, as the central figure of the play. Nor has this error lapsed; Freedley and Reeves in their *History of the Theatre* (1941), thinking they are praising *Ghosts,* declare "This play holds its own . . . the problems of inherited disease, insanity, and euthanasia are still as great as they were sixty years ago."

The same emphasis marks the summary of the play in Sobel's *Theatre Handbook* (1940; 1948).

Her love for the pastor Manders checked by his concern for convention, Mrs. Alving has devoted her life to a conventional hiding from the world of the dissolute, diseased nature of her husband, a retired ship captain. She has sent her son abroad, to shield him from the knowledge. As the play opens, Mrs. Alving, who is erecting an orphanage in her late husband's name, welcomes home her son Oswald, only to learn that he has come home to die—of inherited syphilis. He makes his mother promise to give him a deadly drug when insanity comes. The captain's illegitimate daughter, Regina, goes off to a life of pleasure, as the orphanage burns down and Mrs. Alving kneels beside Oswald, who is insanely calling, "The sun! Mother, give me the sun." His mother's concern for keeping up appearances has brought disaster down upon them all.

Oswald is often taken as the "ghost" of his father, but Ibsen's concern was larger, as Mrs. Alving reveals in the play: "I am half inclined to think we are all ghosts, Mr. Manders. It is not only what we have inherited from our fathers and mothers that exists in us, but all sorts of old dead ideas, and all kinds of old dead beliefs and the like."

Nazimova—who played Regina in St. Petersburg and Mrs. Alving throughout the United States—emphasized the same point: "It is only a very imperceptive person that sees in *Ghosts* the presentation of a single social problem. The true ghosts of the play are a whole legion of outmoded beliefs and ideals. They are dead ideas of conduct with which we have been brought up, notions of duty and obligation, conceptions of law and order which, in the lines of the play, I characterize as 'the cause of all the unhappiness in the world.'"

Ghosts is the first play fully utilizing the new technique of Ibsen. It is as "modern" as his ideas, which leap from his own time's conventional reticences to a forthrightness scarce seen since ancient Greece. Spare, stripped of all romantic trimmings and unnecessary adornment, it is austere in its direct and undeviating drive. While Pastor Manders may be somewhat of a type, the other characters are deeply revealed; we see them clear to the soul.

Ibsen's chief technical advance comes in the exposition of earlier essential facts as a part of the present drama. Each item—the late Captain Alving's dissolute nature, his being Regina's father, Pastor Manders' early rejection of Mrs. Alving's love—is revealed to the audience just when its impact is most forceful. This method, which had not been used in the drama since Sophocles' *Oedipus,* * became both a model and a challenge.

Another stark quality of *Ghosts* is its objectivity. Some have said that it is a sermon; but if so, it is one only in the sense that there are sermons in stones, books in the running brooks. There is validity in Ibsen's protest: "They try to make me responsible for the opinions certain of the characters express. And yet there is not in the whole work a single opinion, a single utterance, which can be laid to the account of the author. I took good care to avoid this. The very method, the order of technique that imposes its form on the play, forbids the author to appear in the speeches of his characters. My object was to make the reader feel that he was going through a piece of real experience; and nothing could more effectually prevent such an impression than the intrusion of the author's private opinions into the dialogue. Do they imagine at home that I am so inexpert in the theory of drama as not to know this?"

The charge of sermonizing, however, was the least of the accusations hurled against the author of *Ghosts*. Amid what Ibsen called a "terrible uproar in the Scandinavian press," only two staunch voices rang in his praise—that of Björnson,* whose early realistic plays had already appeared, and that of the greatest of Scandinavian critics, Georg Brandes.

The play was not produced until August 1883, with August Lindberg playing Oswald, first at Helsingborg, Sweden; then on tour through Scandinavia. Later that year *Ghosts* was played in the Royal Theatre at Stockholm. In 1899, when the National Theatre opened in Christiania, *Ghosts* was accepted in the repertory. Its first production in Germany was a private performance at the Stadttheater in Augsburg, April 1886. On September 29, 1889, it opened at the Freie Bühne (Free Theatre) of Berlin, which presented *Ghosts* as its initial offering. Berlin's Free Theatre, like that of Paris (Théâtre Libre) avoided censorship by a subscription scheme that made performances legally "private." The first production of Ibsen in France was given at the Paris Free Theatre on May 29, 1890. By the same subscription device, the Independent Theatre in London presented *Ghosts* on March 13, 1891. In the meantime, *Ghosts* had been forbidden in St. Petersburg, on religious grounds.

Ibsen expected that *Ghosts* would be attacked. "It may well be," he wrote in January 1882, "that the play is in several respects rather daring. But it seemed to me that the time had come for moving some boundary-posts. And this was an undertaking for which a man of the older generation, like myself, was better fitted than the many younger authors who might desire to do something of the kind. I was prepared for a storm; but such storms one must not shrink from encountering."

The play encountered considerable opposition in England; a storm of abuse followed the Independent Theatre production. The *Hawk* called the play "merely dull dirt long drawn out." *Truth* agreed that it was "not only consistently dirty, but deplorably dull." W. St. Leger, in *Black and White,* declared: "No one . . . could have been converted by the representation of that lugubrious diagnosis of sordid impropriety . . . The Ibsen craze is merely a cave of Adullam, to which resort all who would fain do some displeasure to Mrs. Grundy . . . There is not one theory, not one phrase, which bears the stamp of new thought, or of the vivid representation of the old. Some of his apologists see in *Ghosts* a great moral lesson—a moral lesson so great that, apparently, it is to excuse the writer for presenting to us a play which is dramatically as dull as it is generally unsavoury. And this new lesson is that the sins of the fathers are visited on the children! . . . His characters are prigs, and pedants, and profligates. Their lives are, no doubt, of interest to themselves, as the lives of the least estimable of creeping and crawling creatures are esteemed in creeping and crawling circles; but how any critical, let alone any wholesome mind can find pleasure in contemplating these morbid creatures it is hard indeed to comprehend." Clement Scott, in the *London Times,* called the play "an open drain; a loathsome sore, unbandaged; a dirty act done publicly; a lazarhouse with all its doors and windows open."

Among Ibsen's defenders were his English translator William Archer, George Bernard Shaw, and Justin McCarthy. The latter declared: "I think . . . that *Ghosts* is, for the days that pass, a great play; that it is in no sane sense unclean; that whether we like it or do not like it, it is obviously the work of a man of genius, and that above all things it is intensely interesting and intensely vital . . . I do not think that a more moral play than *Ghosts* was ever written . . . Sin was never more sternly unmasked, its shamelessness, its degradation never more mercilessly arraigned than in this tragic work of art, which is worth a wilderness of sermons."

Ghosts gradually worked its way to other theatrical centers. It was played in Italy in 1892. Its American premiere, on January 5, 1894, at the Berkeley Lyceum, New York, was hailed by William Dean Howells as "a great theatrical event—the very greatest I have ever known." In the same year, the play encountered censorship in Boston. Though long forbidden by the English censor, it was again seen in "private" productions in London in 1893 and 1894, and by 1900 was an accepted repertory play throughout the world. After an early New York production, opening May 29, 1899, directed by Emmanuel Reicher, the *New York Dramatic Mirror* (June 10) observed: "Some there were whose hearts and minds could not endure the hammer blows of the Norwegian dramatist's pessimism, and they moved noiselessly from the playhouse before the curtain fell . . . No less than as a philosopher and thinker is the Norwegian great as a dramatic craftsman. *Ghosts* is constructed with the scientific accuracy that a master engineer employs in building a suspension bridge. Every strand in the network of dialogue has its duty to perform in supporting the main theme. Every character, too, is as truly a part of the whole, and as necessary a part, as is each pier in the engineer's structure . . . to the analytical mind it presents itself as a monument of absolute truth."

In 1929 Alexander Moissi acted in New York in the Reinhardt German production of *Ghosts*. Nazimova played it in English at the New York Empire Theatre, with Romney Brent, in the season of 1935-1936. There have been productions of *Ghosts* every year since. A recent New York production was that of Eva Le Gallienne in 1948.

The timelessness of *Ghosts* is, of course, relative. In 1926, after a production with Lucile Watson, José Ruben, Hortense Alden, and J. M. Kerrigan, Gilbert W. Gabriel reported that he found it "the most completely dated and withered of Ibsen's plays." In 1935, Brooks Atkinson, praising Nazimova's performance, called *Ghosts* "now . . . only a temperate statement of an ugly thought with a milk-and-gruel attack upon authority and pious idealism." Atkinson partially retracted in 1948 (February 18): "Since *Ghosts* is planned and written by a master craftsman of the old school, it can still be made exciting by great acting or by a novel point of view . . ."

Unfortunately, the 1948 Broadway production was not effective. As Robert Garland said: "The fresh 'translation' credited to Eva Le Gallienne and the stale direction discredited to Margaret Webster help not at all." It was better received in England, with Beatrix Lehman, at the Festival of Britain in 1951.

There is the crux: every generation must continue the struggle against the chains of "convention," the clinging and clanking of outmoded ideas. Because of its stark presentation of this fact, the power of *Ghosts* remains in the reading, and in proper presentation. The play has admirably served its author's purpose, for *Ghosts* has set more "minds in motion" than any other drama of the last hundred years. It was, in many lands, the clarion call to realism and sharpness of technique, to freedom of thought and expression, in the modern drama.

AN ENEMY OF THE PEOPLE   *Henrik Ibsen*

The reactions of the public to Ibsen's previous plays strengthened his feeling that the majority, the conformers, had to be jolted from their smug sense of righteousness. His next play, *An Enemy of the People,* which his indignation hurried, was published in Copenhagen in November 1882.

This play takes a literal pollution as symbolic of the "swamp" in which the people's conscience had sunk. The noted health baths of a south Norway town, Doctor Stockmann discovers, are polluted; when he wishes to proclaim this fact, the "responsible" folk of the town denounce Stockmann as an enemy of the people for desiring to destroy their profits. Against the politicians and the press, Stockmann is powerless; he can console himself only with thoughts of the future, and with the closing reflection—an individual consolation out of a social defeat—that "the strongest man in the world is he that stands most alone."

Ibsen himself found consolation in the lonely rebel. Speaking of Dr. Stockmann in a letter to Georg Brandes, he declared: "The majority, the mass, the multitude, can never overtake him; he can never have the majority with him . . . At the point where I stood when I wrote each of my books, there now stands a fairly compact multitude; but I myself am there no longer; I am elsewhere and, I hope, farther ahead."

Going down to defeat, Stockmann nevertheless refuses to be "beaten off the field by public opinion, by the compact majority, and all that sort of devilry . . . I want to drive it into the heads of these curs that the Liberals are the craftiest foes free men have to face; that party-programs wring the necks of all young and living truths; that considerations of expediency turn justice and morality upside down, until life becomes simply unlivable." The battle of the baths has been lost, but the battle against hypocrisy goes on.

In spite of the personal indignation that spurred the drama, Ibsen is by no means one-sided in his presentation. He stirs in Dr. Stockmann a surge of energy and a genial humor; the aristocratic idealism of the man is beyond the grasp of the townsfolk. At the same time, he rouses in the good doctor a zealot's insistence, an uncompromising failure to grasp the other issues involved. Where a more moderate person might have won the town to take effective steps against the pollution of the baths, Dr. Stockmann by his insistence on instant public action, which would wipe out the town's income from the baths, succeeds only in turning every leading citizen against him.

An Enemy of the People, though William Archer called it Ibsen's "least poetical, least imaginative" work, is nevertheless a satirical comedy of technical excellence, buoyant good spirits, and surging vitality. In March 1882, Ibsen wrote his publisher: "It will be a peaceable production, which can be read by Ministers of State and wholesale merchants and their ladies, and from which theatres will not feel obliged to recoil." It was, indeed, quite popular. Within three months of its publication, it was played in Christiania, Bergen, Stockholm, and Copenhagen. Holland saw the play in 1884; Berlin, not until March 5, 1887, but frequently thereafter. In Paris, it was presented in 1895; on March 29, 1898, and in 1899; in 1895 and 1899 anarchist demonstrations accompanied the productions. In England, Beerbohm Tree, playing Dr. Stockmann first on June 14, 1893, appeared frequently in the part up to 1905. Its New York premiere was in 1895. Walter Hampden acted Dr. Stockmann first in 1927, then revived the play frequently until 1937. In that year (February 16) Richard Watts remarked that the play "continues to strike out with sardonic power, while its implications remain inescapably modern." Calling it a "mighty provocative play," Brooks Atkinson satirically observed: "Now that we have arrived at the golden age when governments and society welcome the truth in all things and never put convenience ahead of scientific enlightenment, *An Enemy of the People* is less pertinent." An adaptation by Arthur Miller* was produced in New York in 1950 with Frederic March, Morris Carnovsky, and Florence Eldridge. Miller "pepped up" the dialogue with many a "Damn!" and with current slang, but turned Dr. Stockmann, as Howard Barnes saw him, into a figure "part Galileo, part a man who refuses to testify whether he is or is not a Communist. The form and context of the original drama were far better than they are in the present reworking of the plot."

In any democracy, Ibsen's points call for pondering, lest the most well-meaning man find himself "an enemy of the people."

THE WILD DUCK
Henrik Ibsen

In two respects, *The Wild Duck,* 1884, marks a shift in Ibsen's thought. His earlier social dramas were concerned with themes; *The Wild Duck* is concerned with individuals. His earlier poetic plays raised the question of compromise—whether or not to hold absolutely to ideals. In *The Wild Duck* Ibsen begins to question ideals. Ibsen was going through a period of self-questioning; *The Wild Duck* is in a sense a spiritual autobiography. Little Hedvig in the play is modeled upon his own sister Hedvig, dearest to him of all his relatives. Gregers Werle, who insists upon telling the truth, to "enoble" those whose lives have been lived in the shadow of a lie, is an ironic self-portrait of the Ibsen that wrote *Brand;** Dr. Relling, the cynically despondent philosopher who sees through the shams and pretenses of people, is the Ibsen that now questions. One actor, in the role of the doctor, made himself up to look like Ibsen.

Freedley and Reeves in *A History of the Theatre* (1941) esteem *The Wild Duck* as Ibsen's "most appealing play"; many deem it his best one. After a 1936 production, W. A. Darlington, in the *London Daily Telegraph* (November 4) observed: "It may be a matter for argument whether *The Wild Duck* is the best of Ibsen's plays, but there is hardly room for doubt that it is the most durable."

In technique, *The Wild Duck* marks Ibsen's richest use of the "retrospective method." Only in *Ghosts* does as much of the essential action take place before the play begins, and in *Ghosts* the events are simple, almost bare. In *The Wild Duck* the whole play grows through our learning the tangled course of life that has already been run. And, as William Archer said in his introduction to the play (1908), "as every event is also a trait of character, it follows that never before has his dialogue been so saturated, as it were, with character-revelation." In no other Ibsen play do we feel that the characters and events are so real.

Through its story, *The Wild Duck* suggests that there are cases in which falsehood is essential to happiness, that there are persons who cannot carry on without a "life lie." Gina Ekdal is a practical soul; her shrewd common-sense keeps on a steady keel the household and the photography business of her dreamer husband Hjalmar. Their daughter Hedvig is a happy little creature; she loves the wild duck that old Ekdal, Hjalmar's father, has tamed and keeps in the attic. Like the Ekdals, the wild duck grows accustomed to its tame existence. But Gregers Werle, "suffering," as Dr. Relling puts it, "from an acute attack of integrity," insists upon telling Hjalmar that old Werle is contributing to the support of the Ekdal household, and may indeed be Hedvig's father. Hjalmar, contrary to Greger's expectation, is not ennobled by the revelation; he thrusts little Hedvig from him, and the girl goes into the attic and shoots herself.

Gregers speaks of maintaining one's ideals; Dr. Relling tells him he should speak, rather, the native word—lies. "Rob the average man of his life lie," says the doctor, "and you rob him of his happiness at the same stroke." "If you are right and I am wrong," says Gregers at the end of the play, "then life is not worth living." Dr. Relling responds: "Oh, life would be quite tolerable, after all, if only we could be rid of the confounded duns that keep on pestering us, in our poverty, with the claims of the ideal."

Presenting this idea in terms of character-development, Ibsen has created several of his most interesting figures. Little Hedvig is his most heart-warming, tender child. Her nature is interwoven with that of the wild duck in the attic, which grows tame and fat, but which is really at home only in the forest. Hjalmar once says that he would like to kill the wild duck; it is to show her love for Hjalmar that Hedvig goes to the attic and kills the little human bird Hjalmar has thrust aside—herself. Here, more moderately than in the later plays, Ibsen seeks to strengthen his psychological presentation by the use of symbols.

The figure of Gina is another triumph of character creation. Blanche Yurka enacted her role vividly in the New York Actors Equity production, which opened February 24, 1925.

Perhaps Ibsen's major creation in the play is Hjalmar Ekdal, at once a deeply pathetic and a broadly comic man; egoist, sentimentalist, poseur, dreamer, and failure, he lives on Gina's practical management and his life-lie. The fact that Ibsen has set this richly comic Hjalmar in circumstances that lead to tragedy—has even made him the fulcrum on which the crisis lifts—has misled the more solemn commentators. Thus Thomas Mann, looking for an image in which to cast his own dislike of the contemporary public, pontificates, in "Mankind Take Care," in the *Atlantic Monthly* (August 1938): "Put before an audience of today . . . a play like Ibsen's *The Wild Duck,* and you will see that in the course of thirty years it has become quite incomprehensible. People think it is a farce and laugh in the wrong places. In the nineteenth century there was a society capable of grasping the European irony and innuendo, the idealistic bitterness and moral subtlety of such a work. All that is gone . . ." Contrast with this the observation in the *London Times* (November 6, 1936), made of a revival of *The Wild Duck* in modern dress: "Of all Ibsen's plays it is most likely to disturb the moral and intellectual complacency of a modern audience"; or the remark of the *London Observer* (November 8, 1936) that "Dr. Relling diagnosing 'rectitudinal fever' is a national necessity in any country"; or Bernard Shaw's "Where can I find an epithet magnificent enough for *The Wild Duck!*"

Published November 11, 1884, *The Wild Duck* was, within four months, played throughout Scandinavia. Berlin saw it in March 1888; Paris, at the Théâtre Libre, in 1891 (when the dramatic dictator-critic Francisque Sarcey called it "obscure, incoherent, unbearable"). It came to London through the Independent Theatre Society, on May 4, 1894, when Clement Scott said: "To make a fuss about so feeble a production is to insult dramatic literature and to outrage common sense." London gave it a public performance in 1897; in 1905, Granville Barker played Hjalmar there. It was performed in Chicago in 1907, but New York did not see it in English until Nazimova played Hedvig in 1918. The thoughts of several critics were expressed by one who wrote that Nazimova's "bobbed sparkling black hair, that breathed a strangely missisvernon-castle spirit of rollick" broke the spell of the play; but Louis Sherwin in the *New York Globe* (March 12) said: "Last night I saw an Ibsen play acted as it should be acted . . . It was the most hilarious performance of an Ibsen play I ever saw, and the most commonsensible."

There being no single starring role in *The Wild Duck*, it has been less often performed than poorer plays that provide good acting vehicles. It is, however, frequently revived by repertory groups. There was a notable New York production in 1925 with Blanche Yurka as Gina, Helen Chandler as Hedvig, and Tom Powers as Gregers; Blanche Yurka played Gina in revivals up to 1937. There were other New York productions in 1938 and (Equity Library Theatre) in April 1944 and May 1945 with Albert and Else Bassermann.

The Wild Duck suggests that truth, like other valuable commodities, should be used sparingly. But it presents this thought in an observation of life at once so genial and so searching that *The Wild Duck* may well claim highest place in the field of domestic drama. In *The Wild Duck*, realism and symbolism, comedy and tragedy, integrate and fuse.

ROSMERSHOLM   *Henrik Ibsen*

Written in 1886, this play is the last of Ibsen's dramas based on social themes, and the first of his profound psychological studies. It is Ibsen's starkest tragedy.

When the play opens, the cultured and distinguished Johannes Rosmer, roused by the imperious Rebecca West, is ready to turn from his conservative post and take active part in the liberal and progressive movements of his day. Gradually, however, Rosmer becomes aware that the driving will of Rebecca, perhaps innocently and unconsciously at work, had pushed his wife Beata to suicide; his faith in his mission is broken. Rebecca sees but one way to restore it, namely, to kill herself; but Rosmer joins her and together they leap from the foot-bridge into the millrace that had earlier borne away his wife.

There is a parallel in the careers of Ibsen himself and Rosmer. Both were at first conservative; both turned liberal and were scorned therefor; and both found the change hollow. Ibsen visited Norway in 1885, just after the Liberal party triumph over the King and his Ministers destroyed the King's right to veto the decisions of Storthing (Congress). Ibsen found his countrymen turned into "cats and dogs," with snarling personal antagonisms that precluded urbane discussion of principles. "This impression," Henrik Jaeger has pointed out, "has recorded itself in the picture of party divisions in *Rosmersholm*. The bitterness of the vanquished is admirably embodied in Rector Kroll; while the victors' craven reluctance to speak out their whole hearts is excellently characterized in the freethinker and opportunist, Mortengard."

Ibsen himself, in an address to Norwegian workingmen (June 14, 1885), declared: "There remains much to be done before we can be said to have attained real liberty. I fear that our present democracy will not be equal to the task. An element of nobility must be introduced into our national life . . . Nobility of character, of will, of soul."

Although the actual incidents of *Rosmersholm* were suggested by a similar tragedy in the life of a Swedish Count, the theme of the play is the attempt of persons of nobility to square their life with their ideals or, as Ibsen himself said, "the struggle with himself that every serious-minded man must face in order to bring his life into harmony with his convictions." Rosmer is caught in the fateful dilemma of a constructive and progressive social purpose and a personal progress that has been reared on destruction. Rebecca West is pressed by an iron will that equally redeems and dooms.

Rosmersholm is knit with intricate skill. It employs the retrospective method as superbly as *The Wild Duck,** but the characters are more deeply sounded. The drama of the richly eventful past unfolds within the drama of the present in a complex yet clear and stately harmony.

Rosmersholm was published on November 23, 1886, and within four months played throughout Scandinavia. Ibsen saw the first German production at Augsburg in 1887. The play was produced in Vienna and in Paris by Lugné-Poe (who took his French Company on tour into Scandinavia), in 1893. In Italy, Duse enacted Rebecca West.

In Germany *Rosmersholm* is one of Ibsen's most popular plays, but in English it has never had a whole-hearted reception, though it was performed in London in 1891 and 1893 and in New York in 1904 and frequently thereafter. Minnie Maddern Fiske played Rebecca in 1907, and at intervals for eleven years. The Stagers' production opened on May 5, 1925, with Margaret Wycherly, Warren William, J. M. Kerrigan, Josephine Hull, and Arthur Hughes. Eva Le Gallienne played Rebecca in 1935; Equity Library Theatre put on the play in 1946 and 1947. London saw it again in August 1950.

Of the comments on the first English production, that of the *London Illustrated Sporting and Dramatic News* (March 7, 1891) is representative: "The filling-up of the play was the merest commonplace of domestic platitude. But the composition of the piece was no stronger than the comedy. I do not speak only of the straggling nature of the incidents and the want of action, but of the dramatic thinness of the work . . . With regard to the story of *Rosmersholm,* those who profess to know tell us it is a politico-social revelation . . . All that I gathered from the very dismal performance is that when a weak man loves a bad woman, the only thing open to both of them is to commit suicide . . . But where is the justice of awarding the same fate to a woman who deserved hanging and the man who should simply have been locked up for a fool? . . . The only emotion from beginning to end was the uncontrollable laughter produced by the naïve comicality of some of the serious lines." In America, although the *New York Dramatic Mirror* (April 9, 1904) allowed that "*Rosmersholm* is at once one of the deepest and—in the printed pages—one of the clearest of Ibsen's plays," it found that "the joy of anticipation was the only joy experienced by the auditors. The presentation was in almost every respect a disappointment."

Looking at the Stagers' production, the *New York World* (May 6, 1925) said that *Rosmersholm* was "like a fine granite chapel . . . all the cunning in design of its creator was preserved in the material provided by the builders. Yet somehow it was a chapel from which the worshippers had fled. There was a classic chill about it unrelieved by the warm humanity of hymns and whispers of life among the columns." By 1935, Brooks Atkinson (December 6) called the play "the mirror of a dead society," and John Mason Brown agreed that it was "tedious and talky and dated." Yet in 1947 George Freedley (November 25), speaking of the Equity Library production, said "*Rosmersholm* has got the season off to an auspicious start."

The unrelieved seriousness and unremitting introspection of *Rosmersholm* make it a heavy burden for the Anglo-Saxon spirit, accustomed to the comic interlude within the tragic drive; yet the play remains a masterpiece of psychological drama. Beneath the intellectual conflict of tradition and liberalism surge the ingrown forces and subconscious drives to which many persons awaken too late to dam before they themselves are damned.

THE LADY FROM THE SEA   *Henrik Ibsen*

In 1888, Ibsen published *The Lady from the Sea,* another psychological study of a woman caught in the quest of integrity. Nora, in *A Doll's House,* * breaks free at the play's close, going forth to find herself. Ellida, in *The Lady from the Sea,* discovers that with freedom comes power to accept responsibility, comes decision. When her husband leaves to her the choice whether or not to go off with her sailor wooer, Ellida chooses to remain at home.

The play is touched with a pleasant dry humor and tinged with tenderness, especially in the invalid Lyngstrand and in Ellida's younger stepdaughter, Hilda.

The Lady from the Sea was played in Scandinavia and in Germany early in 1889, and has always been popular there. At a Weimar production, on March 14, 1889, Ibsen, then sixty, was given a laurel wreath. London saw the play in 1891 and 1902; Paris, in 1892. New York saw it first on November 6, 1911, with Hedwig Reicher. Duse included it in her American tour, in New York in 1923, across the country in 1924. Revivals came in New York, with Blanche Yurka in 1929; in 1934; in 1948, an Equity Library production; and with Luise Rainer opening August 7, 1950, in a production that emphasized the personal story and slurred the general problem of integrity and freedom of choice, which remains most significant in our time.

HEDDA GABLER   *Henrik Ibsen*

Without wholly putting aside social satire, Ibsen places greater emphasis on individual psychology in this play than in any of his previous works.

Freedley and Reeves in their *History of the Theatre* (1941) call *Hedda Gabler,* 1890, "a character study pure and simple." Its namesake is neither simple nor pure—though quite attractive. Alrik Gustafson in *A History of Modern Drama* (1947) suggests that Hedda is "so repulsive in her cold, clammy spiritual sterility that we are attracted to the phenomenon as we are to a poisonous snake." Grant Allen, on the other hand, says Hedda is "the girl we take down to dinner in London nineteen times out of twenty." Hedda's is indeed a hypersensitive soul; she shrinks from all that is gross and prosaic. She desires power, but seeks it only along decorous avenues. Fastidious to excess, she avoids not evil but ugliness; rather than become tangled in a sordid, underhand liaison, she shoots herself.

Married to a dull pedant, George Tesman, Hedda finds his devotion to his aunts and his drudgery ways unbearable. In envy of an old schoolmate who has helped another writer, Eilert Lövborg, with his manuscript and has won him from drinking, Hedda lures Eilert back to his liquor and burns his supposedly lost manuscript. She then sends her pistols to Eilert, who shoots himself. When Hedda's cynical but observant friend, Judge Brack, indicates that he knows about the pistols, and expects Hedda's favors in return for his silence, Hedda finds one more use for the pistols, pointed at her beautiful but oh-so-bored self.

Freedley and Reeves call *Hedda Gabler* "perhaps Ibsen's best play." Written in colloquial prose, it has but seven characters, covers but two days, and its well-knit plot observes strict unity of place and action.

Published December 16, 1890, the play was performed in Munich, with Ibsen in the audience, January 31, 1891, with Frau Conrad-Ramlo as Hedda. In Copenhagen, Fru Hennings opened as Hedda, on February 25; Constance Brunn starred in Christiania the following night. The production with Elizabeth Robins, in London, April 20, 1891, made quite a stir, as did the Paris production, December 17, 1891. Mrs. Fiske brought the play to New York in 1903. Others who have played the proud Hedda include Eleanora Duse, Katina Paxinou, Mrs. Pat Campbell, Nance O'Neil, Alla Nazimova, Clare Eames, Emily Stevens, Blanche Bates, Blanche Yurka, and Eva Le Gallienne. Productions have come almost yearly in the United States; from Nazimova, whose first English role was Hedda in 1906 and who revived the part constantly, with excellent productions in 1918 and in 1936-1937, to Eva Le Gallienne, who enacted Hedda with the Civic Repertory Theatre in 1928, 1929, and 1930, and played the part again in 1939, 1941, and 1948. Such actresses are drawn to the part by qualities that led Justin Huntly McCarthy to say in the London *Black and White* (April 25, 1891): "*Hedda Gabler* is the name, to my mind, of Ibsen's greatest play, and of the most interesting woman that he has created . . . She is compact with all the vices, she is instinct with all the virtues, of womanhood." But the great Danish critic Georg Brandes said: "What deep impression can it make upon us, that such a creature throws her life away? It is with but cold regret that we see her lying dead on the sofa in the inner room."

Hedda Gabler presents no social theme; its action, with a few changes in details of setting, could occur almost any place in our time. Ibsen stated, in a letter of December 4, 1890, to his French translator, Count Prozor: "It was not my desire to deal in this play with so-called problems. What I principally wanted to do was to depict human beings, human emotions, and human destinies, upon a groundwork of certain of the social conditions and principles of the present day." This detachment of the playwright led to mixed judgments. Brandes declared: "In no earlier work of Ibsen has it been so difficult to discover what the poet wishes us to learn, or rather what is his underlying sentiment . . . it seems as though Ibsen this time has not had anything at heart which he particularly wishes to say—although surely his artistic conscientiousness has never been greater than in this play, and his technical mastership has never been more brilliant . . . In *Hedda Gabler,* it seems to me that Ibsen is at his best only as a calculating artist, not as the sympathetic poet." Yet William Archer called the play "surely one of the most poignant character-tragedies in literature."

When Blanche Bates (with Minnie Dupree, J. H. Benrimo, and Albert Bruning) opened in *Hedda Gabler* in Philadelphia, the *Ledger* (February 13, 1904) exclaimed: "What a hopeless specimen of degeneracy is Hedda Gabler! A vicious, heartless, cowardly, unmoral, mischief-making vixen." The *New York Sun* of April 18, 1918, cried out: "What a marvel of stupidity and nonsense the author did produce in this play! It is incredible to think that only a score of years ago the audience sat seriously before its precious dullness and tried to read something into its lines." Thirty years later (February 25, 1948) the *New York World-Telegram* had other words: *Hedda Gabler* "completely escapes the perennial blight of an Ibsen play—datedness—in its timeless theme of a woman revenging herself on the lover she rejected to her regret. In the title role, Eva Le Gallienne turns in an all-stops-out performance that ranks with Judith Anderson's *Medea.**"

The sentimentalist may be repelled by the photographic indifference of Ibsen's portrait; Ibsen presents, he neither condones nor condemns, the ways of the hapless Hedda. But few women have been more clearly and more completely revealed in moving drama.

THE MASTER BUILDER   *Henrik Ibsen*

Master Builder Solness (to translate the original title literally) was written after Ibsen had returned to his native land "to arrange his affairs." It is the first of the four plays he wrote in Christiania, and bears a symbolism that, while it has universal application, is also autobiographical.

Much of the drama is spun through conversation between Halvard Solness, architect, and the young Hilda Wangel, for whom he had once hung a wreath on a church steeple. He is no longer building churches, he tells her, only "homes for human beings." With the eager zest of youth, Hilda encourages Solness to build houses with high towers, perhaps even castles in the air. Spurred on by her, despite his fear of dizzying peaks, Solness climbs with a wreath to the pinnacle of his new house—and falls to his death.

In the play's vague, mysterious atmosphere, says William Archer, "though the dialogue is sternly restrained within the limits of prose, the art of drama seems forever on the point of floating away to blend with the art of music." Others have been less sympathetic, finding the mixture of symbolic and realistic elements confusing and Solness comprehensible only as a pathological study. Thus the *London Times* (February 24, 1893) declared: "The most ardent votaries of Ibsenism must be in some doubt as to whether a further prosecution of the cult is advisable. They must have left the theatre with an uneasy feeling that the master was laughing at them up his sleeve. It is only on some such hypothesis that the strange composition of the latest of Mr. Ibsen's plays can be accepted as the work of a wholly sane writer." With pretended sympathy, the *Theatre* (All Fools' Day, 1893) inquired as to the possible meanings of the play: "There is room for a score of interpretations . . . Presumably there is more in the play than meets the eye. Otherwise it is a very uneven, exasperating, and inconclusive jumble of brilliance and dullness, lucidity and obscurity . . . the characters of Solness and Hilda are vague, elusive, utterly lacking in sustained reality. At every turn, moreover, they bring one into a blind alley, and turn one back with the sense of having been rudely made a fool of."

Fifty-four years later, Harold Hobson declared in the *Sunday Times,* with reference to a production of *The Master Builder* that opened January 1, 1947: "I find this play, like the universe and the way of an eagle in the air, incomprehensible. But, incomprehensible or not, there blows through this play a loud and gusty wind of genius, which . . . sets everybody tingling with an invigorated and refreshed excitement . . . This is an evening to remember."

Published in December 1892, *The Master Builder* was first presented in Berlin with Emanuel Reicher on January 19, 1893; then in London the following February 20 with Elizabeth Robins. Christiania and Copenhagen saw the play on March 8, 1893. Lugné-Poe enacted Solness in Paris, opening April 3, 1894. The New York premiere was January 16, 1900. Other New York productions came in 1905; in 1907 with Alla Nazimova and Walter Hampden, in 1926 with Eva Le Gallienne and Egon Brecher, who revived it for a number of years. The work was brushed aside by the *New York Dramatic Mirror* (November 18, 1905) with the exclamation: "Enough for this week's recrudescence of Ibsenity." In London, the *Times* (March 15,

1936) called a revival of the play "enchanting." It was performed again in 1948 with Donald Wolfit and Rosalind Iden.

The later reactions show that the critics discerned order beneath the first semblance of confusion. Some saw it as the drama of a sickly conscience prodded by a conscience more robust, as the conservatism of age is pressed by the insistent seeming radicalism of youth. Solness' inability to climb as high as he builds thus symbolizes man's inability to act as freely as he thinks. Others, finding the symbolism and the psychology both true, examined the play on its realistic level. Thus the *London Observer* (March 15, 1936), calling it "an enthralling play," observed: "Here is no plain tale from the Norwegian hills, but a complex parable whose narrative surprises flower . . . with astonishing richness and fecundity from outset to denouement. Here, if anywhere, Ibsen begins where lesser dramatists leave off."

There is an autobiographical symbolism throughout the drama. The churches Solness builds represent Ibsen's historical and romantic plays. The homes for human beings are his plays of domestic realism, his social dramas. The towered buildings, "castles in the air," point toward the spiritual dramas, with psychological problems and symbolical overtones. Like Solness, Ibsen was insistently pressed by the younger generation.

The intertwining and overlapping of subject and symbol—surface story and suggested thought—make *The Master Builder* unique among the plays of Ibsen, the least derivative and most original of all his works.

JOHN GABRIEL BORKMAN   *Henrik Ibsen*

This play, written in 1896, was Ibsen's last intense drama of individual psychology. It is of interest especially as it shows Ibsen looking back upon, and weighing, his career.

John Gabriel Borkman opens with an intensity of feeling as Ella confronts her twin sister, Mrs. Gunhild Borkman, after a silence of eight years. Above them paces John Gabriel Borkman, self-imprisoned by hatred, after having been released from jail. Avid for power, Borkman had renounced Ella, whom he loved, to marry Gunhild, who could further his career. He feels no compunction for the embezzlement for which he'd been sentenced; if he'd been let alone, he bitterly reflects, he'd have doubled the money for everyone. And as Borkman paces his room, waiting for society to call upon his talents, the two sisters below struggle for power over Borkman's son, Erhart, who in the heedless passion of youth scorns both his mother and his aunt and goes away with the knowing widow next door. The unwanted Borkman walks out into the storm to die; over his body the sisters at last join hands.

This bitter study of individuals gathers meaning from its portraits. In it we find what Dumas sought in a drama: a painting, a judgment, and an ideal. For through the vivid portraits of the two sisters and the man they loved we discern the bitter end of ruthless self-seeking, the lees of the wine of self-concern and quest of power; and we behold how the killing of love slays what is best in man. Yet in Borkman's final vision, where the poet complements the dramatist as the doomed man tells his dream—weaving "a network of fellowship all round the world"—though his unscrupulous means dragged him to failure, Borkman in his dying moments holds high the ideal.

Published December 15, 1896, *John Gabriel Borkman* opened at Helsingfors in two theatres (one in Swedish, one in Finnish) on January 10,

1897; within the month, it was played all over Scandinavia. Germany took it up quickly, as did London, May 3, 1897, with Elizabeth Robins, and New York, in November of the same year. On March 19, 1897, the *New York Times* reported from Berlin that "the drama exhales an atmosphere of respectability mildewed and eaten away by vice." The play was revived in New York in 1915; by the Civic Repertory with Eva Le Gallienne in 1926, 1927, and 1928; by Eva Le Gallienne again, November 12, 1946, with Margaret Webster, Victor Jory, and Ernest Truex.

Every New York production has won mixed reviews. The *New York Dramatic Mirror* of April 21, 1915, noted the differences of opinion. Chapman, Garland, and Barnes were negative. Chapman: "Theatrical claptrap of an astonishingly cheap quality." Garland: "These woe-is-me-ers woe-is-me-ing on the frosty outskirts of Norway's Christiania are out of this world. And they certainly should be!" Barnes: "The rescue of the Ibsen drama from comparative neglect has been effected with more pains than flourish." Other critics were deeply impressed. Morehouse: "a play of gnawing and sustained bitterness ... steadily engrossing theatre." Watts: "this low-pitched but oddly arresting drama of anticlimax took on an absorbing sense of power and truth." Atkinson: "Put *John Gabriel Borkman* down as a tone-poem written out of Ibsen's angry passion, and dub the current performance as a masterpiece ... with the rhythm of a dance of death and the tone of a song of doom."

The swift movement of *John Gabriel Borkman* strictly observes the "unity of time." The time of the events is no more than the time of the performance. Yet at the end the intensity slackens somewhat as the dramatic drive gives way to a lyric exaltation before doom. Comparison with *Pillars of Society** shows the greater poetic power of the later play. In both dramas a business man of great ability has committed a crime, in both the man is torn between two sisters; in both he has turned from a woman he loves to a woman who can help his career. But *Pillars of Society* seems cluttered, and its end, if not tawdry, tame, beside the stark and inevitable movement of *John Gabriel Borkman*. Imagination and beauty combine with truth, to give the play grim yet magnificent power.

Among revivals:

Brand: translated by Michael Meyer, London, April 8, 1959. Edinburgh Festival, August 20, 1962. On April 28, 1978, the NT (Olivier) produced a felicitous translation by Geoffrey Hill, who replaced Ibsen's rhymed verse with pararhyme and consonance. Bernard Levin (*London Times*, April 30, 1978) says that the play's weakness is that Brand does not grow; on the contrary, it is his strength that he does not change. His name in Norwegian means fire, and he is himself the brand that is consumed.

Peer Gynt: Phoenix, thirty-two performances in repertory, opening January 12, 1960. Also at Oxford, November 27, 1961; at the Bristol Old Vic, March 30, 1966, with Fritz Weaver and Joanna Roos. In 1982 the RSC at the Other Place, Stratford-upon-Avon, then the London Barbican, with Derek Jacobi, used a version by David Rudkin that set the play in Ireland, with Irish sprites and spirits.

Pillars of Society: London, 1954, and 1970-1971, sixty-four performances in repertory.

A Doll's House: OffBway (Theatre 4), February 2, 1963, for sixty-six performances. A "slap-up-to-date" version by Christopher Hampton, New York, January 13, 1971, with Claire Bloom, reached eighty-nine performances; a revival was a London 1972-1973 hit, while Claire Bloom was running in the film. Cheryl Campbell, in the RSC revival (Stratford, 1981; Barbican, 1982), was a lively, sexy Nora, giving Dr. Rank a luring glimpse of a silk stocking. "It is no denigration of this fine performance," said the *London Telegraph* (June 20, 1982), "to wager that her Nora would take advantage of Ibsen's alternative ending and return home after sampling the difficulties of a single life."

Ghosts: London Old Vic, 1958, translated by Norman Ginsbury. OffBway (4th Street), September 21, 1961, with Leueen MacGrath, 216 performances, a *Ghosts* record. New York, August 29, 1982, adapted by Arthur Kopit, with Liv Ullman, for six weeks. Of a London 1973 revival, Harold Hobson (*Times,* August 5, 1973) commented on Oswald's last plea, "Mother, give me the sun": "Nothing in itself, in its context it is overwhelming. This capacity so to marshal the emotional strength that it can be concentrated into one shattering blow is what makes the encounter with a work of art a thrilling experience."

An Enemy of the People: February 14, 1958, London, with George Coulouris, the first adaptation by Arthur Miller in London; there again June 28, 1963. The Miller version was used in New York, February 25, 1958; February 2, 1959; and for fifty-four performances, March 11, 1971.

The Wild Duck: December 1955, London, Emlyn Williams as Hjalmar; Dorothy Tutin, Hedvig. APA-Phoenix, January 11, 1967, adapted by Eva Le Gallienne, forty-five performances with Will Geer (old Ekdal), Rosemary Harris (Gina), Donald Moffat (Hjalmar), Patricia Connolly (Hedvig). December 13, 1979, NT (Olivier), Eva Griffith (Hedvig), Michael Bryant, (Gregers).

Rosmersholm: London, November 18, 1959, with Eric Porter and Peggy Ashcroft. New York, April 11, 1962, fifty-eight performances with Nancy Wickwire and Donald Woods. Roundabout, 1974-1975.

The Lady from the Sea: New York, March 15, 1961, with Vanessa Redgrave, Andrew Cruikshank, Margaret Leighton. London, 1970-1971, twenty-five performances in repertory.

Hedda Gabler: New York, November 9, 1960, with Anne Meachem in a record 340 performances. On the Paris stage and British TV, 1962, Ingrid Bergman. London, 1963-1964, 101 performances with Joan Greenwood. OffBway, January 16, 1970, with Eli Siegel as "aesthetic advisor," 81 performances. Claire Bloom in New York, February 17, 1971, 46 performances. Susannah York in a pleasantly restrained natural performance at the London Cambridge, May 17, 1982, for two months.

The Master Builder: A Max Faber version, New York, 1955. Adapted by Emlyn Williams, London, June 9, 1964, with Michael Redgrave and Maggie Smith. London Old Vic, November 17, 1964, with Laurence Olivier and Maggie Smith. Roundabout, 1971-1972, 1983.

John Gabriel Borkman: Norman Ginsbury translation, London, 1961. Carmel Eban translation, London, 1963, with Donald Wolfit and Flora Robson. NT, 1975, with Ralph Richardson, Peggy Ashcroft, and Wendy Hiller.

PICNIC   *William Inge*

Encouraged by Tennessee Williams, Margo Jones at Dallas, Texas, put on the first play of William Inge (1911-1973), *Farther Off from Heaven,* 1947, which ten years later he rewrote as *The Dark at the Top of the Stairs.* Meanwhile, in 1953, his *Picnic* won the Pulitzer Prize. In 1956 it was filmed; then, in 1962, Inge rewrote this play as *Summer Brave,* which he called "more humorously true."

Picnic, itself expanded from a one-act sketch of five frustrated women on a porch in a Kansas town, adds the stir created by the arrival of the itinerant Hal Carter, a rough and ready knockabout (whose mother had had him sent to a reform school), who is paying for his breakfast by cleaning the yard. Flo Owens, a neighbor, sniffs at him, but he sweeps her daughter Madge into a swift affair. He goes off, and despite her mother's warnings, Madge packs a bag to follow him. A common enough story, illuminated by neat characterizations, which include a picture of a lonely schoolteacher who yields to a middle-aged merchant—who the next morning returns to marry her. *Picnic* seems an ironic title for this rouse of love in an eager maiden and a lonely spinster.

The play opened at the New York Music Box on February 19, 1953, for 485 performances. Brooks Atkinson said: "Taking a group of commonplace people in a small Kansas town, on a hot Labor Day, Mr. Inge has made a rich and fundamental play out of them that is tremendously moving in the last act . . . Peggy Conklin as the anxious mother, Eileen Heckart as a school teacher with a hunger for life and a knack for getting it, Paul Newman as a college lad infatuated with a pretty face, Ruth McDevitt as a wistful neighbor, Arthur O'Connell as a comically reluctant bridegroom, help to bring to life all the cross-currents of Mr. Inge's sensitive writing . . . Most of the characters in *Picnic* do not know what is happening to them. But Mr. Inge does, for he is an artist."

The Dark at the Top of the Stairs is a psychological study of a confused family. The father resents being dominated by his wife, for whom the son suffers an "Oedipus complex." Sister and brother-in-law have problems with their shy and oversensitive daughter, who is deeply disturbed when her escort, a Jewish cadet (whom she had left when at the dance he was insulted), commits suicide. And the son is unable to conceal his jealousy when he sees his mother going barefoot to join his father in the warm light at the top of the stairs.

Richard Watts, Jr., said of the play (*New York Post,* December 5, 1957): "It is a moving, perceptive and effective drama, demonstrating again Mr. Inge's notable ability to probe sympathetically into tortured souls under a facade of frequently humorous brightness." Atkinson added: "Teresa Wright as the wife, Pat Hingle as the husband, Eileen Heckart as his sister-in-law . . . preserve the homespun quality of the play but also disclose the darkness at the top of the stairs of their lives. Call *The Dark at the Top of the Stairs* Mr. Inge's finest play. Although the style is unassuming, as usual, the sympathies are wider, the compassion deeper, and the knowledge of adults and children more profound." It is the deft probing of the characters that lifts these not uncommon stories above the commonplace.

The revised *Picnic,* as *Summer Brave,* took its title from Shakespeare's "The Passionate Pilgrim":

> *Crabbed age and youth cannot live together:*
> *Youth is full of pleasance, age is full of care;*
> *Youth like summer morn, age like winter weather;*
> *Youth like summer brave, age like winter bare.*

To an Elizabethan, as Inge apparently knew, *brave* meant fresh, brightly adorned.

The new play was shown by ELT, April 5, 1973; by ANTA, October 26, 1975; OffOffBway (78th Street), June 5, 1980, and (St. Barts) January 29, 1981. Mel Gussow in the *New York Times* said that in *Picnic* Hal was a tornado; in *Summer Brave* he became a summer breeze, which left without altering the landscape. In the revision, indeed, instead of following the brawny Hal, Madge lapses at home in dreams. It is the general opinion, in which I concur, that *Picnic* is the stronger play.

RHINOCEROS   *Eugene Ionesco*

A leader in the school of the absurd, Eugene Ionesco (b. 1912) in a number of one-act plays tried by absurdist devices—characters in garbage pails, or sunk to the neck in dirt; accumulating chairs for a lecture, with no audience, and finally a speaker who merely grunts—to convey the idea that existence is meaningless, life a prolonged futility. In his full-length plays (*The Killer, Tueur sans gages,* 1958; *Exit the King,* 1962; *The Pedestrian in the Air,* 1963, etc.) he sets a character, Berenger, to represent the commonplace, routine-ridden citizen of the senseless world. His most comprehensible and most commercially successful of these plays is *Rhinoceros,* 1959. *Rhinoceros* was presented in London, in translation by Derek Prowse, April 28, 1960, with Laurence Olivier, Joan Plowright, Miles Malleson, and Alan Webb. In New York, opening January 9, 1961, with Zero Mostel, Eli Wallach, and Morris Carnovsky, it reached 260 performances, with 16 more in October.

In a small town in France, a rhinoceros suddenly appears. The wife of a missing worker, chased by the beast, cries, "It's my husband! He's calling me! I'm coming, my darling!" Gradually, most of the townsfolk have been transformed into a herd. Berenger watches his friend John, saying, "We must get back to primeval integrity," as John turns into a rhinoceros. (Zero Mostel, in the New York production, made this a triumphant theatrical transformation.) Only Daisy and Berenger remain human; then she succumbs. Berenger is unable to make the change; he cries: "People who try to hang on to their individuality always come to a bad end." Then he tries to take comfort in the thought that he is the last man left. His final words are "I'm not giving up!"

This ending is confusing. A program note to the Fayetteville, Arkansas, production states, "He was condemned to stay human." Howard Taubman in the *New York Times* protested: "Before his final speech Berenger has been one of the sweet, characterless sort. It is impossible to believe that he suddenly acquired the moral fiber to stand against mass psychosis." He didn't; his remark was sour grapes: if he can't join them, he *won't* join them.

It was perhaps a misfortune that Ionesco, his obscurity hailed as profundity, chose to become clear. For comprehension reveals his shallowness. When the logician in the play offers a syllogism, "All cats die. Socrates is dead. Therefore Socrates is a cat"—this is not even what the cartoon comics call a sillygism; it is a feeble, false banality, and falls flat. His choice of the particular beast to make the herd is surely absurd: *Encyclopaedia Britannica* states: "Most rhinoceroses are solitary . . . Interactions between individuals usually are avoided . . . normally ill-tempered and unpredictable." A poor symbol for the crowding unanimity of the mass! Intellectually,

Ionesco's talents are cloudy; he would probably declare that all thought is equally foggy, false, and fundamentally futile.

Time magazine (May 23, 1960) spoke of Olivier as Berenger "triumphing over the din-and-delirium direction of Orson Welles." The Barrault Company played *Rhinoceros* in Paris in 1960 where it was shown again (in Rumanian) in 1965. It was originally a short story, and Harold Clurman deemed the three-act play "overlong." The *Sun* spoke of a New York revival (October 1967) as a "dated message play." It was revived OffOffBway in 1974 and 1975; in Pittsburgh January 15, 1981. At its Dusseldorf world premiere (1959) it was taken as a picture of the subservient Nazis; Martin Esslin in *The Theatre of the Absurd* more widely called it "the pull of conformity."

Ionesco remains the champion of the absurd. Those that see no meaning in life may take comfort in his theatrical expression of mass meaninglessness. Considering this widespread prospect, his presence in this volume is as inevitable as it is absurd.

GREASE *Jim Jacobs*

Called by one critic "a happy and tuneful tribute to the 50's," while another declared: "It cocks an ironic, slightly appalled eye at the folkways it pretends to be celebrating," *Grease,* by Jim Jacobs and Warren Casey, opened in a basement theatre in Chicago in the spring of 1971 and ran for thirty weeks, returning in 1974 for another thirty-three. Meanwhile, on February 7, 1972, it came to the Eden OffBway, then moved uptown to the Broadhurst, the Royale, then the larger Majestic, and ran for a record-breaking 3,388 performances. (Second on Broadway was *Fiddler on the Roof,* with 3,242; third, the non-musical *Life with Father,* with 3,224. Opening May 21, 1975, *A Chorus Line** in October 1983 broke the record with 3,400 performances, and is still dancing on as I write, February 1984.) It played in London in 1973. It broke records in Manitoba, where it opened in 1981. It has been shown at over 1,100 theatres in the United States and Canada. In Paris, 1977, it was called *Brillantine*; in Mexico City it ran for two and a half years as *Vaselina*. Its title is explained as "in homage to the kid-stuff boys used in abundance to keep their ducktails in full bloom, with the aid of aphrodisiac pocketcombs." The play awoke nostalgic memories among the 1950 rock n' rollers, and envious hopefulness in the thronging adolescents of its days.

A huge blowup of James Dean formed the backdrop of most of the play, which deals mainly with the "blackboard jungle" denizens of Rydell High School, Anywhere, U.S.A. The boys' gang, in leather jackets, talk dirty; their favorite salute is an upthrust finger, sure to win an adolescent laugh. The girls' gang call themselves the Pink Ladies. A beauty-school dropout of impenetrable stupidity dreams of a rock star. The leader of the boys dares not show he's in love, for fear of the gang's laughter and loss of his dominance. There's a teenage love song, "It's Raining on Prom Night," and tears and rain together "are wilting the quilting in my Maidenform." There are wild dances, especially at the prom, where an incredibly high kick nearly decapitates the English teacher "chaperon." When a boy's arm slips down and the girl starts to leave the car, he protests: "Sandy, you just don't walk out of a drive-in!" The pluperfect mindlessness of the characters has infected the authors; but the picture is only slightly overdrawn, and the songs suit the surging singers. "Greased Lightnin'" has a resounding brutishness: "There Are Worse Things I Could Do" belts out a defense of unwed motherhood. As the *Philadelphia Inquirer* of January 14, 1973, put it, the play shows "a time when hubcaps are for stealing, girls are rated according to whether they put out . . . the detritus of the 50s has been gathered up with a fine, careless rapture and has been tossed at us, pell-mell, to the accompaniment of wittily banal music that succeeds in making rock 'n' roll more absurd than it really was."

And the teenage desire for freedom from social and moral restraint, for excitement and emotional arousal, found a vicarious outlet in *Grease* that led the play to the peak of pre-adult popularity. This is a sobering thought.

UBU ROI   *Alfred Jarry*

For so silly a play, performed so few times, *Ubu Roi* has made a great splash in the pond of avant-garde drama, especially the school of the absurd. When Alfred Jarry (1873-1907) was a student in Rennes, his classmate Henri Marin showed him a skit Henri's elder brother had written about Felix Hebert (Père Ebé), his disliked physics teacher. It was called *Les Polonais.* Jarry built a farce around this, which was enacted at the Marin home in 1889 and at his own home in 1890, "as played in 1888 by the marionettes of the Théâtre des Phynances." (Phynances—the theatre imaginary—is the farcical pomposity for finances.)

In 1891 in Paris, Jarry reshaped the piece changing Père Ebé (nickname of Hebert) into Père Ubu. He also wrote *Ubu Cocu: Cuckold Ubu.* On 10 December 1896, Lugné Poë, director of the Théâtre de l'Oeuvre, rebelling against the current "well-made" drama, persuaded the star, Fermin Gémier, to take the role of Père Ubu. Louise France played Mère Ubu.

Toulouse-Lautrec helped with the decor, which in one spread covered the couple's travels with palm trees, apple trees in blossom, and snowy hills. At the opening, Jarry spoke of the producers and friends, whose "well-meaning has seen Ubu's belly big with more satiric symbols than its swelling can hold. . . . You are free to see in M Ubu all the allusions you wish, or a simple marionette, a pupil's deformation of a professor who represents to him all that's grotesque in the world. . . . As to the action, now about to begin, it takes place in Poland, that is to say, Nowhere."

The play's first word is *Merdre!* (Not *merde,* but merdre.—Gershon Legman's translation of the play is called *King Turd.*) At once a riot broke out. In the audience the poet Mallarmé cheered; the playwright Yeats drew back in a wan smile. The play lasted for two performances. It was enacted with puppets in 1898, then lay forgotten for twenty-nine years.

In 1927 Roger Vitrac with Antonin Artaud, creator of the "theatre of cruelty," opened the Théâtre Alfred Jarry, hailing *Ubu.* And Jarry became the oriflamme of the radicals. The da-da-ist Hans Arp gave readings of the play; André Breton, who wrote the manifesto of surrealism, called it "the great prophetic, avenging play of modern times." The great French dictionary Larousse states that "the crude and inconsequential farce became the symbol of an egoistic and stupid bourgeoisie."

Ubu's ignorant conceit was exalted by Jarry into the creation of pataphysics, defined as "the science of imaginary solutions, which symbolically attributes the properties of objects, defined by their virtuality, to their lineaments." And in 1949 the College of Pataphysics was founded by Eugene Ionesco, René Clair, Raymond Queneau, Jacques Prévert, and the leader of the theatre of the absurd, Boris Vian. They held an "Expojarrysition," and several pataphysical works were published. *Ubu Roi* was produced again, by Jean Vilar at the Théâtre National Populaire in 1958. It had a brief run at the London Royal Court theatre in 1966. In 1967 it was played in Swedish at the Edinburgh Festival; in 1968 in Serbo-Croat, in London and New York. In New York in English, it had a few OffOffBway performances, the most recent in 1974. Nevertheless, it has been called (by Myron Matlaw in *Modern World Drama*) "a landmark in avant-garde drama"; and Cyril Connolly denominated Ubu "the Santa Claus of the Atomic Age."

In the play Ubu, ex-king of Aragon, officer of the Polish Dragoons, is urged by his wife (hence reminding some far-searching critics of Lady Macbeth) to kill the king. The cowardly Ubu gets Bordure to carry out the murder; then he snubs Bordure, "disembrains" the nobles, has the magistrates and the phynanciers killed, but flees when the king's son Bougrelas and Bordure bring Russian troops. Mère Ubu, escaping, meets him in a cave; they take ship across the Baltic to France, where Ubu hopes to become Minister of Phynance. "We must be making at least a million knots an hour," cries Ubu, "and these knots have been tied so well that nobody can untie them." The play ends as they utter the following gems:

> Père U: Wild and inhospitable sea, which bathes the land called Germany—so-called because the inhabitants are all cousins german.
> Mère U: That's what I call erudition! They say it's a beautiful land.
> Père U: Beautiful it may be, but it's not up to Poland. If there were no Poland, there'd not be any poles!

Ubu has been called vicious, cowardly, coarse, pompously cruel, and unashamedly amoral; a monster, says Martin Esslin in *The Theatre of the Absurd*, "that appeared ludicrously exaggerated in 1896, but was far surpassed by reality in 1945." Ubu, however, is also fatuous and stupid, which vitiates the comparison. In *Ubu in Chains* (1900), set in France, in order to be different in that "land of the free," Ubu turns himself into a slave.

King Ubu's favorite exclamation is "By my green candle"; and in the New York 1974 production he carried a foot-high green candle, which burned with a green flame and was in the shape of a phallus. Himself fat and pear-shaped, Ubu was surrounded by figures dressed as clowns, with painted chests, some with faces marked as with hideous disease. Note the name of the assassin, B/ordure and of the Prince Bougre/las ("worn-out sodomite"). The play, unfortunately, is feeble in its humor and in its satire unable to rise above Ubu. Although Henri Ghéon states that "it has been interepreted as an epic satire of the greedy and cruel bourgeois who makes himself a leader of men," there is more pertinence in Wallace Fowlie's remark that *Ubu Roi* "has reached the status of a myth." Fortunately for its reputation, more have hailed it than have seen it played. Its value is purely mythical.

THE LIARS   *Henry Arthur Jones*

With shafts of comedy, Henry Arthur Jones (1851-1929) in *The Liars* aims at the heart of society, its conventions and its petty evasions. Skillfully constructed, deftly told, *The Liars*, 1897, was Jones' most popular play. Written for Charles Wyndham and the Criterion Company (with Mary Moore), *The Liars* came to New York in 1898, with John Drew. It was a hit on both sides of the Atlantic, and was revived often in the United States, notably in 1915 with Grace Moore and Conway Tearle.

The play is set in English society. Lady Jessica, feeling herself neglected by her husband, Gilbert Nepean, meets the diplomat Edward Falkner at the "Star and Garter," where they are seen by her brother-in-law George. To clear Jessica, her sister Rosamond and her cousin Dolly join in an invented story, to which they make their men folk testify—until the unwitting Edward tells a conflicting story. The counsel of Jessica's old friend Sir Christopher keeps her from going off with Edward, who departs alone; while Gilbert, become aware of his error, begs Jessica to give him another chance.

When the play opened in London, its quality was quickly recognized. Observed A. B. Walkley in the *Speaker* (October 9, 1897): "The reality of the tragedy is not disguised by the somewhat cheap and facile conclusion . . . the comedy of the surface must be worked for all it is worth, and the tragedy of the undercurrent must be discreetly veiled." Walkley, however, put his finger on the high spot of the play; "There is one moment when we can all laugh without stint. It is in the capital scene of the play wherein Lady Jessica's friends engage in the concoction of a story which shall blind the husband . . . The facile fluent lying of the women, the helpless floundering of the men, the irritation of the one sex at the other's want of skill at the game and the blank amazement of the unskilled sex at the rich and ready resource of the skilled—all this, as I have said, is excellent comedy." Even Bernard Shaw, who usually pricks at his forerunners on the English stage, declared that Jones had extracted from this situation "all the drama that can be got from it without sacrificing verisimilitude, or spoiling the reassuring common sense of the conclusion."

Allardyce Nicoll has called *The Liars* a landmark in the history of modern drama: "The true comedy of manners is realistic in aim, but from the very fact that its main objective is the displaying of the manners of society it is artificial; it aims at the realistic depiction of artificial life, and frequently the success of the picture depends upon the subtle contrast instituted by the dramatist between the external veneer of society manners and the evidences of natural man (and woman) peeping through the veil. This quality often appears in the present play, and contributes much to its permanent interest." In its realistic capture of this artificiality, *The Liars* marks, said Nicoll, the beginning of a new period in the drama.

In New York, *The Liars* was favorably received. *The Dramatic Mirror* (October 1, 1898), however, regretted that "the three wives, Lady Jessica, Lady Rosamund, and Dolly, are silly, frivolous, and heartless. Their respective spouses are dolts of incredible density." The *Mirror* refused to have its "ideals of the stability of the English character . . . shattered by even so careful an observer of manners and morals as Mr. Jones." *Harpers Weekly* (October 8), preferred the play to the production; it called *The Liars* "a far better play than one is permitted to appreciate . . ."

Revivals found *The Liars* still effective. The *London Outlook* (April 20, 1907) declared it "one of the few plays that never stale." Of the New York 1915 production, Charles Darnton (November 19) said there is "still a great deal of interest and entertainment"; and the *Dramatic Mirror* (November 20) stated: "In the neatness of his characterization, in the effect of his spontaneity of wit, Henry Arthur Jones proves as magnificent a calculator, as expert a dovetailor, as the playwrighting world has produced." Neatly woven, with broad but savory strokes of characterization, beneath its amusing surface *The Liars* carries sobering thoughts of a widespread weakness of mankind.

MRS. DANE'S DEFENSE   *Henry Arthur Jones*

Mrs. Dane's Defense, set in nineteenth-century English middle-class society, contains Henry Arthur Jones' most vivid portraits, especially that of the quick-eyed scandalmonger, and it reaches its climax with a grilling inquisition the intensity of which is unmatched even in *The Thief** and *The Winslow Boy.**

Mrs. Dane and Judge Lionel Carteret are in love. The jealous busybody, Mrs. Bulsom-Porter, begins to sniff scandal, and Judge Carteret, to protect Mrs. Dane, begins to question her. From flat denial, she grows tangled in contradiction, recovers, makes inadvertent admission, then slumps through hysterical protest to sobbing confession of an irregular past: at fifteen, she had been seduced by the man of whose children she had been governess. The judge's mood, in counter-progression, moves through earnest faith, puzzled bewilderment, vague suspicion, outraged discovery, to a final pity that persuades him to conceal the story. He even extracts an apology from Mrs. Bulsom-Porter, but he sends Mrs. Dane away forever.

Opening in London October 2, 1900, *Mrs. Dane's Defense* ran for 209 performances. In New York, with Margaret Anglin, it opened December 31, 1900, for a run of 100. It played there again in 1928, with Violet Heming and Alison Skipworth; London saw it in 1902, 1912, and with Mary Ellis in 1946. The play has been continuingly popular in repertory companies.

The *New York Sun* (January 3, 1901) said that the play decorated and ennobled the stage. "There is in this drama the most scathing, bitterly truthful portrait of a scandal-monger that the stage has shown. This Mrs. Bulsom-Porter, who starts the dogs of scandal after Mrs. Dane—a woman who does more harm with her tongue in a day than a woman of Mrs. Dane's type does in a lifetime—can be met with any day right here in any circle of New York, and there is not a town in the country but boasts of at least half a dozen old 'ladies' of a similar species. The only trouble is that women of this type always declare it is an admirable picture of one of their best friends."

The *New York Tribune* dissented: "The drift of the piece is—in a mood of sentimental flummery—to assail an alleged injustice of social law, and to perplex and befog the perception of right and wrong. It is the old humbug business of trying to arouse mawkish sympathy with a hussy; the old folly of assuming that human law or custom—or anything else—can avert from anybody, man or woman, the inevitable consequences of sin. The way to attack 'the double standard' is not to lower women to man's adulterous level. The practice, under the Jones and Pinero dispensation, would, obviously, lead to the complete disruption of society."

That society has nearly sunk to such a level is indicated not only by our divorce statistics, but also by the comment on *Mrs. Dane's Defense* less than half a century later, in the *London Observer,* December 8, 1946: "Who cares in Sunningwater whether the smart young widow once slipped on the banks of the Danube? The Woman Who Did can hardly excite in an age when everybody does." At her earlier time, Mrs. Dane declared that the first rule of propriety is that one must not be found out.

Despite the changing attitude toward an early "slip," the play grips the audience. The leechlike hold of Mrs. Bulsom-Porter on a sip of suspicion leads implacably to the inquisition. "No description of this scene," said the *Sun,* "can do it justice. When Mrs. Dane finally shrieks out her guilt the whole effect seems so true that one feels almost guilty of eavesdropping." *Mrs. Dane's Defense* remains an excellent acting play, with several vivid character studies, and a climactic scene of unparalleled power.

EVERY MAN IN HIS HUMOUR *Ben Jonson*

Although Ben Jonson (English, 1573-1637) collaborated in the writing of a few earlier dramas, *Every Man in His Humour*, 1598, is the first play from his pen alone. At once it marked a new type in the English theatre. Jonson was aware of the novelty he had provided; in the prologue he scorns the drama that ranges widely through lands and years, like many plays of Shakespeare.

For the history play and the romantic comedy of Shakespeare, Jonson substituted the satiric comedy of humours. The word "humours" refers to the four moistures that, in medieval physiology, were held to determine a man's temperament, making him sanguine, choleric, melancholy, or phlegmatic. By the time of Jonson, the term had come to be applied to a man's dominant foible or passion; *Every Man in His Humour* turns its shafts upon the eccentricities and affectations of London types. There are Edward Kno'well, the town gull, whose father is over-solicitous of his son's behavior; Well-Bred, from the country; the lively Cob, the water-bearer; and especially Captain Bobadill, a boastful and cowardly soldier, condescending, affecting a niceness in his habits and associations, without humor in our sense of the term, but thoroughly phlegmatic in Jonson's. Gentlemen, merchants, and a genial magistrate, Justice Clement, are variously displayed in the drama.

The plot of the play, amusingly carried along with varied disguisings of Kno'well's man Brain-worm, revolves about the jealous merchant Kitely, whose wife proves credulous and jealous too, once her suspicions are aroused. The two meet at Cob's house, each thinking the other to adultery inclined. Kno'well, on the watch for his son, is mistakenly assumed by Kitely to be his wife's paramour, but young Kno'well has meanwhile been tied in lawful matrimony to Kitely's sister Bridget, and at Justice Clement's chambers the misunderstandings are cleared away. In the course of the story Bobadill, the haughty soldier, submits to a thrashing.

While the persons pictured in the play are as authentic English types— London types—as any in the theatre, they had their prototypes in the Greek drama, and indeed are embodiments of universal failings. When the play was first presented in 1598, it had Italian localities and names; these were changed to English in the version of 1606, when the play was revived at the time of the visit of the King of Denmark to his daughter Queen Anne. The characters are drawn from every level of life, as might well come within the compass of Jonson, a gentleman by birth, a citizen by training, a craftsman and a soldier by necessity, a scholar and a poet by nature, an actor by choice. The Prologue, announcing Jonson's satiric intention, was first printed in the 1616 folio edition of the play. Since Jonson holds up to ridicule all excess, and with the sharpness of his intellect almost mocks all enthusiasm, it is understandable that in this edition he omitted young Kno'well's praise of poetry, in which a genuine fervor richly rings. It might be noted that a great bulk of the play is written in vigorous—indeed, at times too full of oaths for the censor!—plain English prose.

In the first production of *Every Man in His Humour* by the Lord Chamberlain's servants at the Globe Theatre, the actor Shakespeare was listed as having a part. The play was revived after the Restoration, in 1675; in 1751 Garrick first played Kitely, who became one of his favorite roles. In the preface to his acting version, Garrick said of Jonson: "The basis of his dramas is one master-passion; to illustrate which, he brings forward a variety of strongly contrasted characters, drawn with the profoundest skill: the incidents maintain a perfect consistency; he never throws his personages into ridiculous situations to make the unskilful laugh . . . His too lofty contempt for the millions forbade him the use of pantomimic aid; nor would he sacrifice his own severe judgment to escape or insure the catcalls of their censure or applause . . . When the passion he set out with is illustrated, his play is done . . . The scene is laid in domestic life; the characters are striking and original; and the incidents are kept within the pale of probability. In depicting jealousy working in the bosom of a plain citizen, Jonson may stand in comparison with Shakespeare: indeed, Kitely is altogether a more masterly-drawn portrait than Ford [in *The Merry Wives of Windsor**]."

Through the eighteenth and first half of the nineteenth century, the play continued popular. Cooke and Kemble alternated in the part of Kitely; Macready also acted the part. Charles Dickens played Bobadill, making *Every Man in His Humour* the first production of his noted amateur company in 1845. In New York, the *Spirit of the Times* (April 4, 1846) commented of a revival that the comedy "has a peculiar adaptability to the stage where, when in proper hands, it cannot fail to convey a good moral, as well as to amuse."

The first American production was at New York's John Street Theatre in 1769. Of a 1905 performance at Stanford University, California, with even the audience in Elizabethan guise, *Stage* magazine observed that "its principal interest to a modern audience lies in the historical view it gives of the development in our social and economic conditions and in the realization that while our manners, our costumes, our pet hobbies and our chosen extravagances may change in three centuries, the fundamental 'humours' which make every man, remain unaffected by the swing of time." It seemed even more contemporary when revived in England in 1937 with Donald Wolfit and Rosalind Iden, marking the 300th anniversary of Jonson's death. Ivor Brown stated that "Iden Payne's production fully justifies the choice of play . . . a light and nimble masquerade of cozeners, gulls, and pretenders." And the *London Times* declared: "At no other time can one imagine such a conjunction of scholarship with quick and close observation of everyday affairs . . . not only in the slang and catchwords of their time but in language of wonderful richness and variety . . . It is surprising how real many of these types of a vanished age become."

Though the age has vanished the persons persist, and Jonson's picture of the "humours" of men has lost none of its validity and force.

The London 1960 Joan Littlewood production of *Every Man in His Humour* went also to Paris.

EVERY MAN OUT OF HIS HUMOUR   *Ben Jonson*

In his second play, *Every Man Out of His Humour,* 1599, also enacted by the Lord Chamberlain's company, Jonson followed the pattern of his previous hit, but the experiences between brought certain modifications. There is a greater measure of self-confidence, even of self-applause. There is a sharpness of satire, increasing to sarcasm, in the attack upon the follies of the time. Writers that have attacked Jonson are represented in the play: Carlo Buffone the jester may be Marston; Fastidious Brisk has been identified as Daniel; more directly, in two figures irrelevantly introduced, Orange and Clove—the character Cordatus calls them "mere strangers to the whole scope of our play"—the dramatists Dekker and Marston are satirized. On the other hand, the attack on human weaknesses, while more fully elaborated, is also more generalized; it is not so much individuals as representatives of common failings the audience watches on the stage. It opens, like Shakespeare's *The Taming of the Shrew,* * with an Induction, in which Asper and two friends, Cordatus and Mitis, argue about the purpose of comedy. Turned 'out of his humour,' Asper becomes a character in the play, called Macilente. Between episodes, the two friends continue the argument.

Various persons move about, exposing their natures, finally reveal them to themselves, and thus achieve improvement. In the printed copy of the play, Jonson gives a sketch of each character, from which we may cull examples: Puntarvolo, "A vainglorious knight, over-Englishing his travels, and wholly consecrated to singularity"; Carlo Buffone, "A public, scurrilous, and profane jester . . . His religion is railing and his discourse ribaldry"; Deliro, "A good doting citizen . . . a fellow sincerely besotted on his own wife."

Jonson's theories are presented mainly by Cordatus, described as "the author's friend; a man only acquainted with the scope and drift of his plot: of a discreet and understanding judgment; and has the place of a Moderator." In the Induction, Asper, who represents the author, rejects the dramatic unities, demanding for himself the freedom the ancients took, to alter and add to the drama's form and range. He recognizes the necessity of pleasing the audience, but insists that the audience seek more than pleasure, "and come to feed their understanding parts." At one point in the play, Mitis (who presents the views of Jonson's opponents) declares it would be more fun if in the story there were "a duke to be in love with a countess, and that countess to be in love with the duke's son, and the son to love the lady's waiting-maid"; whereupon Cordatus rests upon Cicero's definition of comedy: "the imitation of life, the mirror of manners, the image of truth."—Not a bad, nor a petty, goal; and in this play attained by Jonson.

The fustian and highfalutin phrases of Marston are neatly burlesqued in the speeches of Clove, but Jonson's own prose and occasional blank verse are vigorous and apt, with many effective figures and blunt but trenchant phrases.

For the performance of the play before Queen Elizabeth, Jonson wrote a special epilogue, altering the end so that Macilente loses his envy through beholding the Queen and feeling the force of her virtue; the London public objected to this panegyric, being then resentful of Elizabeth's treatment of their favorite the Earl of Essex, on his return from Ireland. (Essex was executed for treason in 1601.)

In *Every Man Out of His Humour,* Shakespeare comes in, if not for attack, at least for a few mocking allusions. When Clove and Orange are displaying their learning, they casually toss off the remark "Reason long since is fled to animals, you know"—a thrust at Antony's "O judgment! thou art fled to brutish beasts And men have lost their reason." Later, when Puntarvolo seals Carlo Buffone's lips with wax, Buffone's last words are "Et tu, Brute!" It has been suggested that this, besides its comic intent, sends a wink to the audience at Shakespeare's ignorance, as Caesar's dying words were different, and in Greek: *Kai ou, teknon* (You too, my son?)

Its episodic nature makes *Every Man Out of His Humour* less interesting to ages not so vividly caught in its figures; there is no record of its professional performance after 1682. There is too much learning in it, also— quotations from Erasmus and from the classics, frequently in Latin—to make for effective presentation before a modern audience, but reading reveals much that remains pungent and pertinent. *Every Man Out of His Humour* remains a brilliant example of satiric drama.

THE POETASTER   *Ben Jonson*

In this play, written in 1601, Jonson put aside most of his concern with current vices and devoted himself to the dramatists that had been having a fling at him. Though it is set at the court of Augustus Caesar, there is no doubt that Horace is Jonson; Crispinus is the playwright John Marston* and Demetrius the playwright Thomas Dekker.*

Jonson rushed the writing of *The Poetaster* to reach the stage before his rivals. It was completed in fifteen weeks, instead of the full year usual with Jonson. Better than most of his other plays, it holds closer to a single dramatic drive.

Captain Tucca, a foul-mouthed braggart and bully, overflowing with boisterous spirits and rich vocabulary (perhaps a portrait of an actual person of Jonson's time, one Captain Hannam), incites Crispinus and Demetrius to defame Horace, who pleads before Caesar for justice and accepts the great Vergil as judge. Lines from Marston's plays *Antonio and Mellida* * and *Antonio's Revenge* * are read; Crispinus and Demetrius are convicted of envy and put under oath to refrain from further attacks on the poet: "Neither shall you, at any time, ambitiously affecting the title of the Untrussers or Whippers of the age, suffer the itch of writing to over-run your performance in libel, upon pain of being taken up for lepers in wit and be irrevocably forfeited to the hospital for fools." (Here is obvious allusion to Dekker's *Satiromastix; or, The Untrussing of the Humorous Poet*). In addition, Horace is permitted to administer an emetic to Crispinus, who vomits up some thirty bombastic or unusual words—*gibbery, lubrical, magnificate; spurious snotteries, oblatrant, furibund*—twenty of which are drawn from Marston's plays, down to the last *obstupefact*.

In his concentration upon the literary quarrel, Jonson did not neglect the more general satire. In the background of Horace's successful defense are the loving citizen Albius and his ambitious wife, who dotes upon the Court; and Ovid, who's in love with Caesar's daughter and who lashes out at lawyers and boastful soldiers. For these attacks, Jonson was brought before the Lord Chief Justice, but protesting that, as claimed in his *Apologetical Dialogue,* "my book has still been taught To spare the persons and to speak the vices," he was exonerated.

Even though Jonson hurried the writing of the play, the persons he chose for characters made allusions to classical literature inevitable. His handling of the great personages is superb. Of his portrait of Augustus, Lamb has said: "Nothing can be imagined more elegant, refined, or court-like than the scenes between this Louis the Fourteenth of antiquity (Augustus) and his literati. The whole essence and secret of that kind of intercourse is contained therein: the economical liberality by which greatness, seeming to waive some part of its prerogative, takes care to lose none of the essentials; the prudential liberties of an inferior which flatter by commanded boldness and soothe with complimental sincerity." In his use of the ancient works, however, Jonson was spendthrift beyond dramaturgical prudence. As Herford has stated: "Few richer minds than his ever created drama; few so critical in temper so easily mistook their intellectual abundance for artistic wealth, or pursued the track of the ancient poets with so complete a disregard of the reserve, the austerity of classic art." Jonson gives us in this play an emendation of Marlowe's translation of one of Ovid's love poems (15th Elegy, Book I); a song from Martial; in the last act, twenty-eight lines from the *Aeneid* (Book IV, 160-188); and—added in the 1616 edition; Act III, Scene 2, on Horace's first appearance—an almost bodily borrowing of one of Horace's satires (I, Book II). Original to Jonson, however, and noble in spirit, are the several tributes to Vergil. Some critics like to think that Jonson here compared Vergil with his contemporary Shakespeare, but his other comments—as that Shakespeare had never blotted out a line; would he had changed a thousand!—seem to void such likelihood. Vergil more probably represented, if any contemporary, Jonson's close and admired friend, Chapman.

The Poetaster is the best example in the English drama of a particular quarrel turned to the ends of general satire. Through it the caustic vehemence and the noble integrity of Jonson shine.

VOLPONE   *Ben Jonson*

Into a gorgeous flowering of Renaissance tapestry, Ben Jonson wove his most savage attack upon the evil of his time. Instead of a motley crew of "humours," he shows in *Volpone; or, The Fox,* 1605, various faces of the same vice—cupidity. His vehemence as a moralist, moreover, is here coupled with his indignation at those that looked upon the theatre as antechamber to the brothel, "my special aim being to put a snaffle in their mouths that cry out "We never punish vice in our interludes"!"

"No such revolting figures as Volpone and his instrument Mosca," said C. H. Herford, "had yet been drawn with such sustained and merciless vigor, for the English stage. The hideous occupations of the parasite and the 'captator,' stock subjects of every Roman satirist, are reproduced with incomparable vividness before the relatively innocent English public . . . Of all professedly comic scenes, surely the most ghastly is that where Volpone's human playthings, the dwarf, the eunuch, and the hermaphrodite, entertain their master with 'songs' in which the intentional 'false pace of the verse' parodies their own imperfect humanity."

The same greed that leads Volpone (fox) to sham mortal sickness bends the various gulls, itched on by Mosca (gadfly), to give Volpone their wealth, hoping to be his heir: Voltore (vulture) the advocate, who would make out the will in his own favor; Corbaccio (raven), who would betray his own son; Corvino (crow), who would yield his own wife to Volpone's lust; Lady Would-Be, who would be all things to him, though Volpone cannot bear her constant chatter, her fussing over appearances, and her long-worded and long-winded pretense to learning. When Corbaccio's son, present by chance, rescues Corvino's wife from the attempted ravishing, Volpone is taken to court. Supremely impudent, he summons his gulls to lie for him, and in the flush of victory pretends to be dead, leaving as his heir—Mosca. And now the gadfly, who has been urging Volpone on, turns upon his master and tries to hold everything; as a consequence, their deceptions are exposed, and both lose all.

Played at the Globe Theatre in 1605, *Volpone* was an instant success; it was revived at once when the theatres were reopened with the Restoration (1660); and it was played frequently during the next century. In 1921 and in 1923, the Phoenix Society gave a few performances of *Volpone,* and it was played at the Malvern Festival in 1935 and at Birmingham in 1937. Donald Wolfit, producing it in London on January 1, 1938, called his the first production there for a century and a half. The London *Times* in 1935 (erroneously) declared: "In his own day, Jonson was an author for the few, and the English public continues to be estranged by the formalism of *Volpone* . . . At Malvern we learn among other things how to endure our own satirical masterpieces, and there was no abatement of satire in tonight's production. Briskly as the crow, the raven, and the vulture were drawn by the clever fly into Volpone's traps, Mr. Wilfrid Lawson saw to it that the farce was dominated by the sulphurous horror of an intelligence immensely alert in the pursuit of evil, and there was terror as well as laughter in the play. There was nothing of the cackling dotard about this Volpone. A fox in his flaming make-up, he was in essence a man whose cruelty and cunning and intellect had grown with age and were ripe for mischief on the grand scale."

Stefan Zweig adapted the play in German for a Berlin production of 1927. A hit, this version was also played throughout Germany. It was translated into French by Jules Romains (filmed with Harry Baur) and into English by Ruth Langner for an elaborate 1928 (1929, 1930, 1933, 1934) production by the Theatre Guild in New York and a 1929 production in London. The New York production in 1928, virtually an all-star one, included Alfred Lunt (Mosca) and Dudley Digges (Volpone).

Never having seen any version of *Volpone,* the New York critics gave glad greeting to Zweig's adaptation. They were fortified by the statement of R. G. Noyes of Harvard University that Zweig's version possessed a "compression, unity, heightened irony, conformation to the demands of the modern stage" that the original lacked. Alexander Woollcott acclaimed it "a gay and gaunty and slightly rakish feather in the Theatre Guild's cap." Brooks Atkinson called it "heavy in the central scenes, played straight without the poisonous edge of satire. But it begins with a flourish of buffoonery, and it concludes with a spectacular hailstorm of flashing gold coins. In between, the ingenuity of a complex plot and the rowdiness of Jonson's greedy characters make *Volpone* a welcome diversion." When the English saw the American translation of the German version, they were less enthusiastic. Sir Nigel Playfair quoted a friend: "If you want to make money, produce the version of *Volpone* they are doing here." To which Sir Nigel added: "I do want to make money, and so, most meritoriously, do most of my brothers in the craft. But I hope there exists in London an undertaker with a sufficiently macabre imagination to invent a suitable form of memorial service for anyone of us who follows her advice."

When the critics saw Jonson's own *Volpone* done by Donald Wolfit at the Century Theatre (February 24, 1947) for the first time in New York, they recognized the superiority of the original. Robert Garland declared: "It took the comedy almost three and one half centuries to get from London to New York. It was worth waiting for." Of the Guild version, he added: "Even with Digges, Lunt, Westley, Gillmore and the Guilded likes of them, it was neither Jonsonian nor joyful. At the Century, it is both of these."

Wolfit's London production of Jonson's *Volpone* opened April 9, 1947. Harold Hobson of the *Sunday Times* called it "a piece which, if it resembles a catalogue of diseases, a doctor's dictionary, is nevertheless a considerable work. *Volpone* has the teeming life of worms in a rotting corpse, and Mr. Wolfit plays it with all the fifty-seven kinds of relish."

In January 1948, Jose Ferrer and Richard Whorf, with John Carradine as a stalking, stooped, and black skeleton of a Voltore, brought *Volpone* to another success at the City Center.

It is clear that after a century and a half of neglect, *Volpone* has come back into its own. Swinburne earlier recognized its worth from the reading; he felt a coursing in the play of that "life-blood which can only be infused by the sympathetic faith of the creator in his creature—the breath which animates every word . . . with the vital impulse of infallible imagination." Desmond McCarthy has astutely pointed out that the chief quality of Volpone is not his evil, but his delight in the artistry of his devices.

Jonson's figures may seem abstract in the reading, but the virtue of the stage is that it gives living body to an author's figments. In the acting, Jonson's people are caught in the acid ink of a master pen. They continue to live in the continuing fire of human passion.

The ever-timeliness of *Volpone* brought many revivals. Among them: Joan Littlewood directed and played Lady Would-Be, Stratford-upon-Avon and Cambridge, 1955. Yale, 1959, directed by Clifford Williams of the RSC, a modern-dress version set in present-day Italy. In 1967, free performances by the NYSF in the city parks; also an "animalistic revival" by Tyrone Guthrie. In 1971, Stratford, Ontario, with Sir Politic and his Lady (the *Louisville Courier-Journal* pointed out) as "Texas-style Americans with mannerisms unmistakably akin to a recent U.S. President and his Lady (Bird)." In 1972, Los Angeles (Mark Taper Forum), adapted by Edward Perone, set in the 1872 California gold rush, with a song, "What is money to the poor?" October 9, 1975, free adaptation by Morris Carnovsky, OffOffB-way, his fourth involvement with *Volpone* since 1928.

NT (Olivier), April 6, 1966, directed by Peter Hall, Prologue by John Gielgud; Paul Scofield entered saying:

> *Good morning to the day; and next, my gold;*
> *Open the shrine, that I may see my saint.*

This production was in informal modern dress; it suggested that man's main drive is not for wealth but for the consequent power. Numerous changes sought to update the language; thus, *costive* becomes *constipation; kithings, kittens; The talk of the ordinaries, the gossip of the journals.* In 1979, at Asolo; by RSC at the Barbican, 1984.

It was converted into an opera by Francis Burt, shown at the London Sadler's Wells, April 24, 1961. Also, from the Zweig version, Larry Gelbart made the musical *Sly Fox*, shown at the New York Broadhurst, 1976; Foxwell J. Sly's love of God is fifty-fold increased when with the added L (Roman numeral for 50) God is revealed as GOLD.

The French Jules Romains version was presented at the New York Winter Garden, February 4, 1957, by the Renaud-Barrault company, and in Montreal in 1958. The play has been translated into a dozen languages, including Finnish, Hungarian, Hebrew, and Japanese.

Swinburne declared: "No other of even his very greatest works is at once so admirable and so enjoyable . . . The chief agents are indeed what Mr. Carlyle would have called 'unspeakably unexemplary mortals,' but the serious fervour and passionate intensity of their resolute and resourceful wickedness give somewhat of a lurid and distorted dignity to the display of their doings and sufferings." If there is no joy in the display of virtue rewarded, there is satisfaction in the spectacle of evil that outsmarts itself.

EPICOENE   *Ben Jonson*

The most popular of all Ben Jonson's plays for 250 years, *Epicoene; or, The Silent Woman,* 1609, still is an effective stage piece, but its emphasis has shifted from satiric comedy to farce. To many critics today, cruelty rather than humor glints in the tricking of a man who hates noise into a mock marriage with a "dumb" woman who turns out to be a noisy scold.

In the play, young Dauphine offers to free his uncle Morose of this nagging wife, if Morose will deed Dauphine his estate. When the transfer is signed and sealed, Dauphine reveals that the "wife" is a boy, disguised and imposed on Morose to win the property. This trick may have seemed a good joke three hundred years ago, but the sympathy of the modern audience veers toward the duped old man. Thus W. A. Darlington, after a 1936 performance, went so far as to say that "Dryden's verdict seems little better than nonsense nowadays."

In his *Essay on Dramatic Poesy* (1688), Dryden praised *Epicoene* for the manner in which it observes the dramatic unities, then added: "The intrigue of it is the greatest and most noble of any pure unmixed comedy in any language: the conversation of gentlemen, in the persons of Truewit and his friends, is described with more gaiety, air, and freedom, than in the rest of Jonson's comedies: and the contrivance of the whole is still more to be admired because it is comedy where the persons are only of common rank, and their business private, not elevated by passions or high concernments, as in serious plays." The characters in the play, however, do not advance beyond the stage of "humours"; nor is there growth, through the course of the play, in the persons' natures. Only at the end of the play, when bang! the head hits the hard wall of experience, is there awakening and consequent hint of change.

The *London Times* (August 3, 1938), after an Oxford production for which John Masefield wrote an Epilogue, made a measured judgment: "That the plot is brilliantly contrived is undeniable, but much of it serves the end of a rather cruel and insensitive humor . . . It is difficult to understand how this astonishing eloquence of dialogue, this miraculous fertility of illustration and metaphor, should accompany the unkind cozening of a poor old gentleman with a very natural distaste for noise . . . the characters, though they are wonderful caricatures, are much rougher in their outline than in their speech, and they must submit, in spite of their powers of discourse, to many rude indignities of farce."

The early success of the play is marked not only by frequent performances, but by printed editions in 1609, 1612, 1616, 1620, etc. It has been translated into the major European tongues, plus the Portuguese. Samuel Pepys mentioned *Epicoene* in his *Diary* five times. On April 15, 1667, he took his wife to the play and on the next day noted that "Knipp tells me the King was so angry at the liberty taken by Lacy's part to abuse him to his face, that he commanded they should act no more, till Moone (Mohun) went and got leave for them to act again, but not this play. The King mighty angry; and it was bitter indeed, but very fine and witty. I never was more taken with a play than I am with this *Silent Woman*, as old as it is, and as often as I have seen it. There is more wit in it than goes to ten new plays."

A 1735 production of *The Silent Woman* had as the afterpiece Moliere's* *The Mock Doctor; or, The Dumb Lady Cured;* Anatole France's *The Man Who Married a Dumb Wife* * is another version of the same theme. An adaptation of Jonson's play in 1776 by Colman made the mistake of having a woman (Mrs. Siddons) play Epicoene, and when the character was revealed as a "boy" at the end, the audience felt, not surprised, but cheated.

Inevitably, Jonson reaches out to ranges of satire beyond the play's main drive and shows us types of the day, sharply satirized. Yet the satire remains general; no particular person is travestied although common follies are ludicrously displayed. "The utmost effect," said C. H. Herford, "is got out of the few but felicitously chosen characters."

The two hundredth anniversary of Jonson's death led to revivals of *Epicoene*—as in London in 1936 and 1938, and at Fordham University, New York, in 1939. Though the novelty of its plot, with the final curtain surprise, has lost its freshness, the play still has a humor and a sting that reward imaginative revival. Richard Strauss in 1935 wrote an opera called *The Silent Woman*.

With *Epicoene*, the usually enthusiastic Jonsonian Swinburne makes a reservation: "—this most imperial and elaborate of all farces . . . His wit is wonderful—admirable, laughable, laudable—but it is not in the deepest sense delightful . . . The sneer of the superior person is always ready to pass into a snarl: there is something in this great classic writer of the bull-baiting and bear-baiting brutality of his age." That 'superior' persons are not limited to Elizabeth's days is manifest in the success of such later plays as *The Man Who Came to Dinner.**

THE ALCHEMIST   *Ben Jonson*

Many critics deem *The Alchemist*, 1610, the best of Ben Jonson's comedies. Coleridge went so far as to declare the swift-moving plot one of the best three in literature. It owes much to Giordano Bruno's *The Candle-Maker* (1580), a surprisingly vivid mixture of effective realism, lively indecency, and keen observation. In *The Alchemist*, as C. H. Herford points out, "Jonson, for the first and also for the last time, found a subject in which all his varied faculty could run riot without injury to the art quality of his work. The profession of alchemy, at once notorious and obscure, with its mountebank reputations and its mystic pretensions, its impenetrable Kabbala of subtleties, and its Rembrandtesque profusion of sordid and squalid detail—the most impudent, venerable, and picturesque of social plagues—was the fittest subject then to be found in Europe for such comedy as his."

From its first presentation to the end of the eighteenth century, *The Alchemist* was frequently played. Comparatively neglected during the nineteenth century, it has recently been restored to popular favor. A presentation in London in 1899, appropriately enough at Apothecaries' Hall, brought playgoers the robust humors of its satire, the imposing range and richness of its language—its blank verse is superbly adapted to natural dialogue and ranges from luxurious poetry to brisk and bawdy repartee—and the plain, downright fun of its coursing plot. There was a revival in 1904 at Cambridge, Massachusetts. More important were the productions at Malvern Festival in 1932 and in London in 1935, with Ralph Richardson as Face and Sir Cedric Hardwicke as Drugger. In New York, the depression of 1931 was lightened by a production, and London saw the play again (Old Vic) in 1947. New York enjoyed a revival in 1948 with José Ferrer as Face.

The story opens in the London plague of 1610. Lovewit leaves the city to avoid the plague. His servant, Face, lets into the house an alchemist, Subtle, and his punk, Doll Common. The three join forces to cheat the folk around. Among their victims is Sir Epicure Mammon, who hopes that Subtle will find him the philosopher's stone, which turns what you will to gold. Tangled in their devices are also Dapper, a lawyer's clerk; Drugger, a tobacco-man; a pastor of Amsterdam, Tribulation Wholesome, with his deacon Ananias—satiric portraits of Puritans, extended in *Bartholomew Fair**—the willing widow Dame Pliant and her brawling brother, Kastril. (The names, as you notice, catch at the characters. Kestrel, a hawk, was a term then applied in contempt to a boisterous ruffian.) A gambler, Pertinax Surly, suspects the impostures; he comes disguised as a Spanish grandee to expose the rascals, but the unexpected return of the owner of the house, Lovewit, makes Subtle and Doll Common flee. Face faces it out, and wins his master's pardon by marrying him to the quite content Dame Pliant.

Recent productions have won *The Alchemist* almost unanimous praise from the critics. The *New York Post* called the 1931 revival "a brawling, full-blooded, wholesomely bawdy thing, volleying its broad humors of a fresher time across three hundred years, to burst in laughter on a twentieth century target. Soothsayers and charm-vendors still flourish, taking pretty pennies from the wallets of the children of this scientific age. But aside from that, *The Alchemist* is a joy because of its perfection as a piece of dramatic craftsmanship." The *London Times* (April 2, 1935) remarked on the present timeliness of the characters: "The petty tradesman and the ambitious clerk, the young gentleman who is determined to be a dog, and the old one who creates a fool's paradise of infinite self-indulgence, in fact the whole company of the dupes and the self-deceived can still be seen flocking to the doors of any occultist charlatan or vendor of tickets in the Irish Sweep." Ivor Brown said in the *London Observer* (January 19, 1947): "Ben trovato, indeed! . . . Jonson went crashing into the theatre with a matchless torrent of polysyllables, Latinities, and lickerish rhetoric as gross as grand . . . Richardson's look of moon-calf innocence as he gulls and pills lackwit and greedyguts alike, and the superb incantations of alchemical bosh, are a simple, eternal, irresistible type of fun." The New York 1948 revival, which opened May 6 at the City Center, was likewise hailed.

The wealth of Jonson's language in *The Alchemist* makes a lavish display, apart from its contribution to the plot's movement. The delighted imaginings of Sir Epicure as he translates his fancied wealth into dreams of bedding and banqueting, lift just over the sunset brink of genuine splendor to the ludicrous, and woo us, as we laugh, to share his fancies.

Allardyce Nicoll discerned Jonson's deepening horror at the corruption of his time: "This note is continued in *The Alchemist* and in *Bartholomew's Fair,* two of his finest comedies. In the former all the men are either rascally or rapacious, the women vain and libertine; in the latter Jonson's lash falls with no sparing hand upon the Puritans and on current hypocrisy. These are among the best comedies in the English language, but the coarseness and even the brutality of Jonson's later style detract considerably from their beauty." Of these words, James Agate declared: "Read 'add' in place of 'detract,' and I agree." The vigor, the blunt and even brutal presentation, are part of the beauty.

In writing *The Alchemist,* Jonson was, as usual, conscious of his orderly method and insistent upon his pride of place as a dramatist. Throughout the sixteenth century playwriting was deemed either a schoolmaster's exercise or the shift of a poet for his purse's sake. The profession owes much of its later prestige to Jonson's integrity and sense of the theatre's high office. In his Preface to this play, Jonson wrote with vehemence of the art of the theatre, against those that "think to get off wittily with their ignorance . . . For it is only the disease of the unskilful to think rude things greater than polished: or scattered more numerous than composed." And in his Prologue to the "judging" audience, Jonson scorned the usual bending to plead for plaudits, and spoke with the same honesty as in the play itself he attacked not evildoers but the evils of the time.

Dryden sought to deny the originality of the story. Before Jonson's own edition of the play (1616), there had been presented before King James, at Cambridge in 1614, Thomas Tomkis' comedy *Albumazar,* twisting the ninth century astronomer Albumazar into a tricky astrologer and wizard, who transforms the boorish Trincalo into the shape of his absent master, with humor sought in the consequent absurdities. When this play was revived in 1668, Dryden wrote a Prologue in which he claimed that Jonson based his play on Tomkis'. As the two plays have very little in common—the *Albumazar,* though revived again by Garrick, is not only different in story, but lacking the gifts of language and satire—and as, furthermore, Jonson's play was enacted in 1610 and first printed in 1612, the relationship Dryden claims is nonexistent.

The reaction of Garrick to *The Alchemist* shows that it indeed has "fat" parts, and that genius needs not the star's place in order to shine. Garrick always took the little role of Abel Drugger, the tobacconist who is planning to open his own shop, and who comes to Subtle to be told how the planets fall, for favorable disposition of his wares in his store. What an actor long dead has made of a part, it is hard for later generations to recover, but we may glimpse something of Garrick's capture in his widow's memory. When Kean first appeared as Richard III, Garrick's widow drove to his lodging and presented him with the sword her husband had used in the part; some months later, she paid him a second call, and said: "Sir, you can play Richard; you cannot play Abel Drugger." Abel is but one of a dozen comic parts, rich in their opportunities, true and fresh in their satire today as when first set down, that bustle through the gay rioting of *The Alchemist.*

In the original cast of *The Alchemist* was Burbage; also, Hemmings and Condell, who prepared the first collection (1623) of Shakespeare's works. Charles II saw the play several times. (Coleridge's "best three" plots are *The Alchemist, Oedipus Tyrannus,* and *Tom Jones.)* Among many recent revivals: 1962, Princeton to OffBway; also, London Old Vic, November 28, 1962, directed by Tyrone Guthrie; it's the "flu," not the plague, that drives Lovewit out of London; the details are modernized with such items as flick knives and travelers' checks; yet one of the conycatchers threatens to splash others with a chamber pot of urine.

In 1968, Asolo. From Nottingham to the Old Vic, February 9, 1970. The *London Telegraph* lauded "the wonderful pseudoscientific gibberish mined for a maximum of sense"; but Harold Hobson made strong protest: "There has been only one Ben Jonson in literary history, and Stuart Burga's production for the Nottingham Playhouse contains nothing to shake my conviction that there is one too many." (Does the old hail "O rare Ben Jonson," then, really say "*Orare*"—Pray for Ben Jonson?)

The Young Vic, June 8, 1972, opening showed the play updated, with modern references from Cheapside to King's Road (where the then current hippies roamed); Tribulation Wholesome and his deacon were turned into two formidable women from the Salvation Army.

The RSC from Stratford-upon-Avon to the London Aldwych, May 19, 1977, had crisp minor figures, Susan Drury as Doll Common, a very tart tart; it opened with street cries: "Who wants fresh lavender?" and the awesome call of the plague year: "Bring out your dead."

Here Swinburne's enthusiasm is unreserved: "All the distinctive qualities which the alchemic cunning of the poet has fused together in the crucible of dramatic satire for the production of a flawless work of art, have given us the most perfect model of imaginative realism and satirical comedy that the world has ever seen."

BARTHOLOMEW FAIR   *Ben Jonson*

Despite his classical learning, Jonson was one of the most typical Englishmen of all time; he could not avoid writing about his home and his true love—London. After the failure of his second tragedy, *Cataline,* in 1611, he returned to comedy with *Bartholomew Fair,* 1614. In this play there is less savagery than is Jonson's wont; a more genial tone pervades it; so that the Londoners could recognize themselves and still be amused at the vivid and colorful pictures of their gross enjoyments.

From about 1150 until 1855, the churchyard of the priory of St. Bartholomew, Smithfield, London, was the scene of a fair on Bartholomew's day, August 24. In Jonson's time, the occasion was one of gay frolicking; and, of course, every type of gull was matched by a scheming knave. The whole of Jonson's play, after the opening scene, is at the Fair. On the broad canvas he set many characters: the ginger-bread woman and the roast-pig woman; the puppeteer; the ballad-singer who is a receiver for the pickpocket; the Captain who is a pimp for the blowsy bawds. Chief of those gulled is the young simpleton Bartholomew Cokes, come from the country to be married; overjoyed at the fair, he buys all that he sees, until he is robbed of his purse, his cloak and sword, and his bride-to-be. Amid all the crowding folk walk Littlewit, his submissive and pregnant wife whom he has persuaded that she has an insistent longing for roast pig, and the gluttony Rabbi Zeal-of-the-land Busy. The manners of these outwardly pious Puritans, and the tricks played upon them, were not the least reason why the Elizabethans made a favorite of the play.

Bartholomew Fair was revived immediately upon the Restoration; several command performances were given before King Charles II, who especially enjoyed the character of Cokes. The Puritan leader Collins, taken to the play, thought for a while (so deft is Jonson's satire) that he was watching a sympathetic portrait of Puritan life; he shouted in fury when he saw Rabbi Busy thrust into the stocks. Although he partakes gluttonously of the feast, the Rabbi protests that he is going to the Fair against his will and only to guard the pregnant Win-the-Fight Littlewit and her mother, the wealthy widow Dame Purecraft.

There is another group of Puritans at the Fair. The zealous Justice Adam Overdo has served on the Fair's pie-powder court (*Pie-powder,* from French *pied poudreux,* dusty foot: a special medieval court called to deal summary justice to the vagabond beggars, cutpurses, and brawlers that sought the opportunity afforded by the crowding, happy, heedless throngs at the fairs). And Justice Overdo, wishing to see things at first hand, mixes with the crowd disguised as a fool: "They may have seen many a fool in the habit of a justice; but never till now, a justice in the habit of a fool." Yet the naïve Overdo is himself beguiled by the sharpers; he mistakes the cutpurse Ezekiel Edgworth for an innocent boy, deems the madman wise, is put in the stocks for a pickpocket, and at the end discovers that the person he is about to sentence as a drunken bawd is his own wife.

Meanwhile, two gentlemen about town, Winwife and his friend Tom Quarlous, have been pursuing Dame Purecraft, on whom Rabbi Busy also has matrimonial designs. Justice Overdo has arranged a match between his well-to-do ward Grace Welborn and his country-bred brother-in-law, young Cokes. At the fair, Winwife and Quarlous meet and covet Grace; she dislikes Cokes so much that anyone else looks lovable: Winwife wins her in a game of words, but Quarlous steals the license.

The Elizabethans are so well caught in the comedy that they might indeed have continued the action at home after the play. The characters are rude and crude, using broad language, painted with broad strokes; but those were broad, bustling, brawly times. They are superbly sketched, with neat markings subtly held to the brink of caricature. Littlewit prides himself on his cleverness; never a quirk or a quiblin but he apprehends it and brings it before the constable of conceit. Justice Overdo is, like many of us, an honest but simple fellow. Only Zeal-of-the-Land Busy steps over the brink of caricature. The Elizabethans were well acquainted with such long-winded sanctimonious argument as that by which he justifies the Puritans' going to the fair.

Some little known features of the Elizabethan theatre survive in the Induction to the play. The booke-holder (whom we call prompter) ridicules the stage-keeper for presuming to deem himself a critic. There were two stage-keepers, usually in hideous false-face masks, on the Elizabethan stage. They furnished pipes and tobacco to the gallants seated there; they drew the curtain of the inner stage; and, if necessary, they helped curb the unruly in the audience. In an 1881 production of *Hamlet*,* William Poel used a pair of such curtain-drawers.

Recent performances of *Bartholomew Fair* have been mainly by community or college groups. These include one in Boston in 1908; another in London (at the Merchants Taylors' School: the fair was originally held for drapers) in 1936; one at Bryn Mawr in 1939. In 1950 the play was presented at the Edinburgh Festival and at the Old Vic in London. It is still a lively and homely play.

There have been many recent professional performances of *Bartholomew Fair.* Among them: Stratford-upon-Avon, 1959. In 1966, Bristol; 1968, Asolo. With RSC, October 1969, Alan Howard played Bartholomew Cokes, the chief "innocent abroad"; the pig-woman presided over a crowd of cripples, lepers, madmen—beggars all—drunks, and decaying whores. In 1975, outdoors at South Hill Park, London, with a pig roasted over a wood fire; 1978, London and an English tour, with a large cast of pigs.

At the Shaw Theatre, August 18, 1981, the National Youth Theatre celebrated its silver anniversary with *Bartholomew Fair,* with a busy gallery of grotesques "massively presided over by Sally Dexter as the greasy pig-woman." There is no livelier picture of early London lowlife.

EXILES   *James Joyce*

The one drama of novelist James Joyce (Irish, 1882-1941) *Exiles,* 1916, manifests the interest in intellectual analysis that pervaded his writings. Joyce's material is sex, even "the eternal triangle"; but of it he has worked a picture of tortured lives, too intellectualized for wide popularity, yet drawn from the inner core of tragedy. The most exalting type of tragic disaster is that which comes, not from villains without, nor from the pressures of society, but from good qualities within—a doom foreseen, and that may be avoided, but instead is freely chosen, elected as the noble, or, better, as the natural way of life. Such a choice, on one level, is that of Dick Dudgeon in

The Devil's Disciple;* on another level, it is that of the martyrs of all time. In *Exiles,* Joyce pictures a modern liberal doomed to torture by the inconsistencies of his ideals.

Richard Rowan, a writer, and Bertha have lived together, in love, but unwed, for a decade. Their best friend, the journalist Robert Hand, visits them. Sensing an attraction between Robert and Bertha, Richard tells Bertha she is free and leaves the two alone. Bertha needs a commanding spirit; she lacks the self-sufficiency of Richard. Loving him, she begs Richard to forbid her going to Robert. But Richard, having achieved his own freedom, insists on freedom for her as well. She goes. When she returns, Richard refuses to allow her to tell what happened. The audience is permitted to feel that Bertha has been faithful to him, but Richard, himself tangled in the contrary tugs of freedom and love, is condemned to continuing doubts and torture.

On an intellectual level, the tension in *Exiles* is that of high-powered electric wires. "The whole is lifted," said the *London Times* (February 16, 1926), "and throbs, like *King Lear,* with a capacity for suffering more startling even than the situation in which it is manifested."

Exiles was published in 1918 and first produced in German. New York saw it at the Neighborhood Playhouse on February 19, 1925; London, a year later. In the New York *Playbill,* Ernest Boyd wrote: "Technically, *Exiles* is an Ibsenite play, but for Ibsen's symbols and solutions Joyce substitutes doubts and irresolutions that are typically modern ... All its action is psychological and cerebral, and its strength lies in the superb delineation of character, notably that of Bertha, an instinctive woman, in the hands of a man who feels through emotional analysis rather than through emotion itself ... The people of this play are exiled from happiness, from the tranquility of doubts that can be stilled, into suffering."

It is possible to interpret Richard's nobility in quite another way. The free man, the anarch, by imposing his own freedom on others becomes a tyrant. Of the moment when Richard tells Bertha that she is free, the *London Times* commented: "At this point you begin to wish that someone would kick Richard, who is possibly a psycho-realist but certainly a cad ... We see in Richard a self-tormentor, a man with a perpetual grievance against life as it is lived, and yet with an absorbing interest in that life and a curiosity to see it actually lived under his eyes—a curiosity which leads him to actions that can only be qualified as odious." This judgment of the *Times* is based on Richard's application of the Golden Rule: Do unto others as you would have them do unto you. If made specific, the rule fails because natures differ; it might better read: Do unto others what they would want you to do unto them. There may be flaws in this, too, as a general principle of action, but Richard's conduct serves soberly to remind us that different natures demand different attitudes. Bertha is not, shall we say, "ready" for the freedom Richard insists is man's only good. Perhaps, indeed, freedom is not everyone's path to righteousness: in our Father's house are many mansions. By presenting—with sharp analysis, gripping dialogue, and ruthless penetration—the opposition of these two natures, and the tortures set upon both by their very nobility, James Joyce has given us in *Exiles* a drama of intellectual power and high distinction.

The play was revived at the London Mermaid in 1970, directed by Harold Pinter; in 1971 by the RSC at the Aldwych. In both productions, John Wood enacted Richard. In 1972 it was presented at Dortmund in German, as also in Vienna, 1974.

New York productions include: ELT, 1947 and 1957. OffBway, 1957; (Cubiculo) 1971; (Circle Rep.) 1977; (York Players) opening on St. Patrick's Day, 1978, directed by Vincent Dowling of the Dublin Abbey Theatre.

Dramatizations of other Joyce works have been staged. Perhaps best is Margery Barkentine's *Ulysses in Nighttown,* 1958, which Zero Mostel's performance helped make memorable.

FROM MORN TO MIDNIGHT   *Georg Kaiser*

In the great decade of dramatic expressionism which began in 1914, Georg Kaiser (German, 1878-1945) was the outstanding playwright. Germany hailed him, presenting in those ten years twenty-six of his dramas, which were promptly produced throughout Europe. The most popular of his works, and the most enduring, is the tragedy in seven scenes, *From Morn to Midnight,* written in 1916.

The play is expressionistic in its devices—that is, it seeks to externalize states of mind. It is a monodrama; all the characters and events are seen through the eyes of a single person. In its development, the drama is what Kaiser called a "think-play." Sweeping along with intense emotional power, it is the illustration of an idea.

The person through whose eyes we watch the multiplex happenings of the day and trace the author's thought is a bank cashier. Rebellion long pent in him flares with a whiff of perfume, as a lady awaits identification for a letter of credit. Off he goes to her with 60,000 marks—to discover that this glowing, seductive stranger is a perfectly respectable mother. He leaves her, then, for a carousing day of freedom, of frenzied spending at the races, at an all-night cabaret, with a sobering pause at the Salvation Army. But everywhere he remains imprisoned by his stodgy past and by his sense of guilt and of the imminence of retribution. As the police draw near, the bank clerk anticipates his capture and shoots himself.

The theme of this "think-play" is the persistence of illusion. In each scene, the cashier sloughs one illusion, only to have another cloud his mind. First is the simple sex illusion; the swirl of a silken skirt foreshadows a conquest. Then, on his flight, there is the illusion that he can laugh at death, at disillusion. Fear looms over him and shrouds him, to prove such laughter hollow. The next illusion is that he has proper place in some more glamorous sphere than his conventional home. Like most persons that dream exotic, golden dreams, he is a habit-ridden home-body; the rouse makes him restless, not full of zest. At the race track, he breaks the illusion that free spending frees the spirit, and at the night-club, that money can buy more than mechanical favors. The last illusion of the man in the play is that men have learned the futility of living for money. He learns that lesson—learns, indeed, the futility of living at all. Freed of illusions, he takes his life, leaving the illusion that life might be worth living to those watching the play.

From Morn to Midnight was produced in Berlin by Max Reinhardt. In New York, The Theatre Guild offered it for two special performances, in May 1922, in translation by Ashley Dukes. Encouraged by the play's reception, The Guild opened it in June for a regular run. The critics were respectful, but deemed the treatment a bit difficult for American audiences. Maida Castellun, in the New York *Call,* called it "an amazing emotional drama . . . crashing to its doom while terror and sardonic humor seize the spectator, as well as the clerk, who tastes life only while he is gambling with death . . . There can be no question about the arresting quality of its spiritual telegraphy, its swift staccato dialogue, its explosive soliloquies, its soul-shattering revaluation of the pleasures and duties of life." Audiences have since become more fully acquainted with the expressionist technique, but *From Morn to Midnight* remains a challenge to the imaginative producer. It has been widely revived in community theatres, for beyond its technical challenge is a searing picture of the wish-dreams of an ordinary man come horribly true.

From Morn to Midnight was banned by the Nazis in 1933. It had American revivals by ELT, 1948; New York Actors Playhouse, 1959; University of Vermont, 1978.

BORN YESTERDAY   *Garson Kanin*

Out of Hollywood Garson Kanin (b. 1912) came to direct his first play on Broadway. *Born Yesterday* opened in Boston, December 25, 1945, with Jean Arthur; it came to New York, February 4, 1946, with Judy Holliday (Jean Arthur having a strep infection), and stayed for 1,643 performances. Laurence Olivier directed it in London, January 20, 1947. It has been shown in Argentina, Poland, France (in Paris, directed by René Clair), Sweden, Denmark, Finland, Holland, and Australia. Revivals persist. In 1948 army chaplains forbade its showing in Tokyo, but it was allowed in Yokohama. In 1950 it was presented by the Communist Theatre in Vilna, with the "representative American businessman charging through the play like something caught in the jungle." In 1953 Edna Mae Robinson, wife of middleweight champion Sugar Ray Robinson, headed an all-black cast. In 1973 Lynn Redgrave played Billie Dawn in London. Other productions include one at Asolo, 1971; Palm Beach, 1974; and Seattle, 1981, thirty-five years after its New York premiere, to the day. Phoenix played it in 1982.

Born Yesterday is a comedy of sex and social conscience. The social significance is superficial enough not to interfere with its entertainment, as a dumb blonde turns the table on her rich but uncouth racketeer lover and goes off with a poor but more learned and socially conscious guy.

The play carries on in a hotel suite in Washington, D.C., "a setting as repulsive," said the *Christian Science Monitor,* "as the character who is paying $235 a day for it . . . a veritable Hollywood nightmare." The character is Harry Brock, who by means more foul than fair has built a hundredweight of scrap iron into millions of dollars. With him is chorus girl Billie Dawn. Brock loves her, in his fashion, but won't make it legitimate: "This way, I give her something, and I'm a hell of a guy; we get married, she thinks it's coming to her." In Washington, as Brock must meet senators, his woman must have "class"; therefore he hires a *New Republic* reporter, Paul Verral, to teach Billie. Paul teaches her enough for her to discover there is poverty and evil and justice in the world; she goes off with Paul and 125 profitable junkyards that Brock, to protect himself, had carried in her name.

Pretty Billie, at the play's start, is both dumb and hard. Under Paul's teaching, she grows not more learned, but more wistful, and more soft. She has not learned to think for herself; she has merely transferred her devotion from Brock with his wealth and power to Paul with the pressure of his social ideals. When Brock yells at her, she quietly points out that he's been guilty of using a double negative. Instead of being authentically tough, she has become synthetically sentimental.

The play also grows sentimental at the close, as the tricky triumvirate—Brock, his lawyer, and the senator Brock owns—remain after Billie and Paul have gone away. The lawyer, tipsy, proposes a toast, "To all the dumb chumps and all the crazy broads, past, present, and future, who search for knowledge and search for truth and civilize each other—and who make it tough for sons of bitches like you [the bribe-taking senator] and you [Harry Brock] and me." The *Christian Science Monitor* declared this ending incredible: Harry puts up "only a feeble defense, and is left at the final curtain reading a book to find out what all this intellectual stuff is about ... In such an event, I am sure, he would find forceful ways of taking revenge, and these would include Billie's sudden and permanent disappearance." The *Boston Post* pointed out that there is not a decent person in the play. "Everyone behaves like the heel he, or she, is, and that goes for the tutor too, who is represented as a white knight in armor, but does not hesitate to work on salary for the junk man while engaged in stealing his girl."

It is only when we disregard white knights and concentrate on bright lights that *Born Yesterday* can be praised. Burton Rascoe said it "rings the bell on all counts as sheer entertainment." More exhaustively, George Jean Nathan explained: "The chief industry of Hollywood, topping even divorce, million dollar lawsuits, social fisticuffs, fortune tellers, and hamburgers with lichee nuts, is widely rumored to be sex. It is therefore only natural that Mr. Kanin, who is no stranger to the place, should, like most other members of that cultural parish who have their eyes on the theatre, export a considerable cargo of it in his play ... a somewhat labored but ribaldly amusing comedy."

The author turns the machine-gun fire of gags upon a major enemy of society; but we rather imagine that the racketeer, and his tribe, will survive; and the audience loses its indignation in the laughter. Crowded with wisecracks, deftly attuned to its time, shrewdly melodramatic, with swift pace, keen suspense, and forceful physical action, *Born Yesterday* stands out among plays fashioned expertly to swell the eager box-office line.

LUTE SONG   *Kao-Tong-Kia*

It is possible to classify the plays of the Ming Dynasty in China, roughly, as northern or southern. The North China drama was in the main concerned with historical and legendary (supernatural) events, while the South China drama was in the main concerned with romance. Both expected the audience to stay lengthily in the theatre; the dramas were as much danced as acted, with stately movements and elaborate costumes; and the dramatic episodes were interspersed with lyric poetry, often of considerable power and beauty. Outstanding among the plays of South China was *P'i P'a Chi (The Story of the Lute)*, written by an obscure provincial schoolmaster, Kao-Tong-Kia, in the mid-fourteenth century, and adapted for court presentation (in twenty-four acts) by Mao-Taou in 1404. Played before the Ming Emperor Yuan Lo, and by strolling companies throughout China, the drama became a classic. It has been played often ever since, and was recently produced in the New York Chinese Theatre. In fact, it was Will Irwin's hearing *P'i P'a Chi* in San Francisco's Chinatown theatre about 1910 that led to its production in English. (The Chinese audience cried like children, Irwin tells us.) Developed from an 1841 French version of *P'i P'a Chi, The Lute Song* was adapted by Sidney Howard and Will Irwin, with lyrics by Bernard Hanighen and music by Raymond Scott. It was presented in 1930 at the Berkshire Playhouse; in 1944, by the adventurous Catholic University of Washington, D. C. On February 6, 1946, a superb company—including Mary Martin and Clarence Derwent—opened at the Plymouth Theatre, in New York, "with $185,000 worth of scenery, lights, and costumes" by Robert Edmond Jones.

Lute Song is a sad story of family fortunes, in the true Chinese manner. A young student, successful in the examinations, leaves his wife and doting parents. Become a magistrate, he is forced by the prince's edict to marry a princess; nor can he send word to his family. His parents starve. His first wife, as a mendicant nun, begs her way across China, seeking her husband. When they meet, the Princess wife, being of noble heart, helps to bring about the reunion.

This tale, despite the attempt to retain the Oriental coloring—which led Robert Coleman and others to declare that "Jones, in our opinion, is the real star of the evening"—was sadly transmogrified into an overdressed musical. It had a few good lyrics but on the whole it was wrecked by Broadway pretentiousness, sumptuousness, and expensive shoddy. John Chapman said: "arty as all hell"; Burton Rascoe headed his review: "Authentic, No Doubt, and a Bore." George Freedley was as strangely altered as the play; in his *History of the Theatre* (with John A. Reeves, 1941) he says of *P'i P'a Chi* that "its lugubrious story of filial piety is rather sickening to the western mind"; in his review of *Lute Song* (February 6, 1946), he called it "one of the most touching plays, in incredibly beautiful production." George Jean Nathan was probably thinking of the Chinese original when he wrote: "What is slight about it is the characteristic Chinese butterfly-wing approach to it, and what is simple about it is the customary and relishable Chinese practice of avoiding complexity where simplicity will better serve . . . charming, delicate, and leisurely story . . ."

For the original Chinese has merits that the adapters have caught as those that seek to snare the secret of genius, and copy only its cough. All entrances, the Chinese convention dicates, are made from the right; all exits are made to the left. The bridal veil is red, the color of blood; mourning color is white, the pallid hue. These external conventions are carried over into *Lute Song*. But *P'i P'a Chi* is rich in Chinese culture, and in satire of Chinese ways. It satirizes the Imperial examinations, wherein tests in classical literature and verse writing are given prospective canal builders and road-menders. It satirizes the ubiquitous grafter (long a disastrous element in Chinese life), and the arbitrary user of power (still dangerous in any land).

P'i P'a Chi is the only play that presents, sympathetically, the three great Chinese religions: Confucianism, Buddhism, Taoism. The genii, the supernatural elements that the simpler Chinese accept, the talking animals, are aspects of the ancient Taoism. The student Tsai-Yong and his family are Buddhists.

The Prince in the play exemplifies the reaction from the liberal Buddhist attitude, to the deep-rooted, noble but conservative family piety of Confucius. Indeed, many of Prince Nicou's remarks in the play are direct quotations from Confucius. Thus *The Story of the Lute* deservedly became a Chinese classic, combining as it does a tender and realistic story with poetry of beauty and ideas of grace and truth, together with a satire of general abuses and a wide picture of the richly colored Chinese life.

With Mary Martin and Clarence Derwent were McKay Morris, Rex O'Malley, Yul Brynner, Mildred Dunnock, Helen Craig, and Augustin Duncan. Among the enchanting songs are "Mountain High, Valley Low" and "Monkey See, Monkey Do."

Dolly Haas and Yul Brynner played *Lute Song* in Chicago, 1947; and in London, 1949. Joanne Roos played it at Stockbridge, Mass., in 1954. A 1959 New York City Center production used Dolly Haas as the wife; Leueen MacGrath, the Princess; Estelle Winwood, Philip Bourneuf, and Clarence Derwent. In 1974 it was shown at New York University.

BEGGAR ON HORSEBACK   *George S. Kaufman*

The finest fruit of the collaboration of two experienced journalists and men of the theatre, George S(imon) Kaufman (American, 1889-1961) and Marc Connelly,* is the fantastic comedy *Beggar on Horseback.* The story and much of the technique of the play are taken from the German satire *Hans Sonnenstresser Goes Through Hell,* 1912, by Paul Apel. Transplanting the characters to an American scene, with many comic inventions of their own, the American authors concocted a hilarious satire of the money-centered life. The title of the play was taken from the proverb "Set a beggar on horseback and he will ride a gallop," which implies that sudden riches are soon spent, that the proper use of any value demands preparation and understanding.

The play opened in New York with Roland Young and Osgood Perkins to music by Deems Taylor and a delightful pantomime danced by Grethe Ruzt-Nissen on February 12, 1924. The story is a simple one. The young and struggling composer, Neil McRae, in love with Cynthia Mason, the girl across the hall, contemplates—urged on by Cynthia—marriage with the wealthy Gladys Cady, so as to gain freedom for his creative work. In a dream, he marries Gladys, and envisions his enslaved life; he kills his in-laws, and is sentenced to work in an "art production factory." When he awakens from this nightmare, Cynthia gives him her hand. The basic situation is sentimental; the dream device with the awakening turn is a familiar one. What gives *Beggar on Horseback* its distinctiveness is its rich satire, its good-humored but unsparing wit, and the freshness of its individual comic devices by which machine-age efficiency and money values are lampooned. The banal mother-in-law with an appalling nasal voice, who knits and nods and gossips, is bound to her rockingchair; the father-in-law, Cady, has a telephone strapped to his vast, self-satisfied middle and on his golf bag is a stock-market ticker.

The dream shows the overpowering effect of great wealth by a multiplication of butlers: almost a score of them stand, formidable, forbidding, in the composer's way, helping to bind him to convention. When the dream-murder has been committed, newsboys rush down the theatre aisles with copies of *The Morning Evening,* which has big headlines, full details of the crime, a picture of the accused, and a special article headed, "No Crime Wave, Says Commissioner." A ragtime burlesque of courtroom and trial follows; the verdict is announced through a loud-speaker. In the "Cady Consolidated Art Factory," to which the composer is condemned, novelist, song-writer, poet, painter, sit in cages at work on art as anodyne. When the composer determines to make a break for freedom, he discovers that the cage is unlocked; all he needs is the will to walk away. Then he awakens and chooses poverty, love, and freedom.

The critics gave the play a most hearty reception. "All the good qualities of the heart and of the head," said Alexander Woollcott (February 13, 1924), "went into the making of this wise, witty, and leaping comedy"; and John Corbin declared: "It bristles with sly and caustic satire, brims with novel and richly colored theatric inventions, and overflows with inconsequent humor and the motley spirit of youth . . . It is all quite mad, utterly delightful, and inerrant in touching off our mundane fads and follies."

Beggar on Horseback opened in London on May 7, 1925. It has been popular everywhere and is a favorite with community theatres. Swift in its flow, and topsy-turvily satiric in its ridicule, *Beggar on Horseback* is a tilting of laughter against the idea that money makes the man.

The words of Ludwig Lewisohn in the *Nation,* February 27, 1924, are still pertinent: "I wish to congratulate the authors of *Beggars on Horseback* most heartily for this, that they laugh at fatuousness and gross materialism, at triviality of mind and soul, at stubborn stupidity—and dishonor no longer conscious of itself, not as these qualities are contrasted with some specious moralistic idealism, but as they are contrasted with art, with the eternal creative spirit, with the quest of him who is drawn despite himself to pursue that beauty which is truth."

The farcical aspects of the play were somewhat overstressed in the New York Lincoln Center (Beaumont) revival, May 14, 1970.

ONCE IN A LIFETIME   *George S. Kaufman*

The feeling that the motion picture industry was a threat to the theatre was decupled when, in 1929, the first talking pictures were heard. The theatre, "the fabulous invalid," has, of course, never been the same since cinemanufacture, but it is far from moribund. More than once, it has smiled indulgently at grandiloquent and resplendent Hollywood. The most genial yet devastating of these theatrical glances at the movies is *Once In A Lifetime* by George Kaufman and Moss Hart (1904-1961). It still deserves Gilbert Gabriel's comment (September 25, 1930) that it is, "in its own, loose, loping, sly-eyed way, the funniest satire the movies have yet had."

When "sound" reverberated in Hollywood, it startled the actors of the silent films. What had they to do with English! *Once In A Lifetime* pictures a rescue team, around whom many aspects of the Hollywood spectacle are pricked in the full of their foibles. A refugee from vaudeville, Jerry, seeing a talking picture in New York, decides to entrain for Hollywood. His friend May suggests opening a voice-culture school and, with the simple-minded and semi-literate George Lewis, they launch forth. The impression they make on film magnate Herman Glogauer approximates that of a snowflake on the mid-Pacific—until George angrily gives Glogauer a piece of his mind. Since no one else has ever dared let Glogauer even glimpse a mind, the magnate at once makes George boss of the studio.

Meanwhile, there is shown the making of a film on a Hollywood set, a wedding scene of super-supreme splendor, though the "Bishop" sends for a racing-sheet just before the camera clicks. The famous playwright, with a sumptuous workroom at the studio, has been six months without an assignment. The Boss has dodged a script-writer scene after scene, then comes out crying "Masterpiece!" after the writer shrewdly left his manuscript in the Boss's bathroom. The presently-successful scorn the not-yet-arrived, while quick oblivion envelops the has-beens. There is broad and deft capture of the sham and the shame, the flimflam and the flame, of Hollywood. George Lewis, the dumb-bell, reading *Variety* and cracking nuts with his teeth, finds Hollywood an easy nut to crack.

Once In A Lifetime opened in New York on September 24, 1930, with Jean Dixon and Spring Byington; it had an enthusiastic press and a run of 401 performances. "I laughed so steadily," George Jean Nathan reported, "that everyone thought it must be a couple of other fellows from Fort Wayne." Brooks Atkinson called it "a hard, swift satire, fantastic and deadly, and full of highly charged comedy lines . . . The skinning of Hollywood is neat and complete."

Kaufman staged the play in New York, making his stage debut as Lawrence Vail, the transplanted and lonely playwright. Hart staged it on the West Coast, playing the same part. *Once In A Lifetime* went to Birmingham, England, on January 28, 1933; to London, February 23. The *London Daily Mail* called it "the funniest play in recent years."

Once In A Lifetime has been popular with amateur groups; 1932 saw a production even in Hollywood High School. Now that the lush days of the movies are (at least temporarily) over, what with wars and recessions and radio and television, *Once In A Lifetime* remains a unique capture of the fabulous phantasmagoria that once was Hollywood.

Once In A Lifetime was the first play in the fruitful collaboration of Kaufman and Hart. Revivals include: ELT, April 25, 1956; Washington Arena Stage, November 23, 1962 and November 23, 1975; Circle in the Square, July 6, 1978. The RSC revival came from Stratford-upon-Avon to the London Aldwych, August 30, 1979, to the Piccadilly on February 20, 1980, with Zoe Wanamaker as May; Peter McEnery, Jerry; Richard Griffiths, George. *Variety* (September 19, 1979) reported: "The jokes still crackle, the vulgarities and lunacies still boggle, but the characters remain involving and sympathetic." It was revived at Asolo in 1981. And always, throughout the play, George keeps cracking Indian nuts.

OF THEE I SING   *George S. Kaufman*

A rousing musical comedy and an uproarious political satire, *Of Thee I Sing* by George S. Kaufman and Morrie Ryskind, with music by George Gershwin and lyrics by his brother Ira, is the only musical comedy to win a Pulitzer prize. Opening in New York on December 26, 1931, with William Gaxton, Victor Moore, and Lois Moran, *Of Thee I Sing* ran for 441 performances, then toured for 24 weeks. It has been revived often; in New York, at Jones Beach and at Randall's Island in 1937; and by Erwin Piscator in 1949.

The story is an amusing one. The political party that has nominated John P. Wintergreen for President resolves to carry the country on a platform of love. A beauty contest is held; Wintergreen is to marry the winner. In the meantime, however, he falls in love with Mary Turner, a campaign worker who can cook wonderful corn muffins. In a whirlwind campaign, John publicly proposes to Mary in forty-eight states. The campaign speeches at the climactic Madison Square Garden rally are accompanied by a comic wrestling match and emphasized by placards with such slogans as "Wintergreen—The Flavor Lasts," "Vote for Prosperity and See What You Get." John is elected; inaugural and marriage are one ceremony.

However, Diana Devereaux, pride of the Southland and winner of the beauty contest brings suit. Since "She's the illegitimate daughter of an illegitimate son of an illegitimate nephew of Napoleon," the French Ambassador interests himself in the case. Public sympathy swings to the deserted Diana; all that saves the President is Mary's timely announcement that he is about to become a father. What will the child be? The Supreme Court's decision is twins, one of each sex. As a consolation prize, Diana Devereaux is delivered to the moon-faced, roving-eyed Alexander Throttlebottom, the lost and forgotten fellow who was made Vice-President. All ends with a hey-nonny-nonny and a ha-cha-cha.

Many other touches of satire enliven the play; some press particular issues and personalities, some prick general foibles of our time. In addition, there is much good humor with lively or genuinely comic songs (the lyrics were written first, reversing the Gershwins' usual procedure). The title song illustrates one secret of the musical's success. It is drawn from the familiar anthem: "My Country 'tis of Thee," but with a comic twist. In the musical the song goes: "Of Thee I sing, *Baby!*" That is to say, the seriousness and the satire, the earnest intent and the comic spirit, are fused. There is one integrated movement, one drive of laughter throughout.

Of Thee I Sing brought wide ripples of laughter to the land. Brooks Atkinson called its authors "as neat a pair of satirists as ever scuttled a national tradition . . . transposed the charlatanry of national politics into a hurly-burly of riotous campaign slogans, political knavery, comic national dilemmas and general burlesque." Several reviewers, indeed, felt that, in such moments as the entrance of the six blue-bearded secretaries of the French Ambassador or the deliberations of the nine old men of the Supreme Court, we approached an American equivalent of Gilbert and Sullivan. This peak of high humor, however, is not maintained in the writing, but the Broadway production helped sustain the mood. As Atkinson said: "Satire in the sharp, chill, biting vein of today needs the warmth of Victor Moore's fooling and the virtuosity of Mr. Gershwin's music. Without them, *Of Thee I Sing* would be the best topical travesty our musical stage has created. With them, it has the depth of artistry and the glow and pathos of comedy that are needed in the book."

The 1949 revival showed that *Of Thee I Sing* remains timely. The strokes of satire are broad enough to smack firm upon general follies, while sparing individuals that fall. There were scattered votes, in the Wintergreen election, for Mickey Mouse, for light wines and beer, and for Mae West. Democracy votes for what it likes best. The public gave a hearty, and a deserved, vote to that leveling of laughter at democracy's failings, that self-mockery spun out of love, *Of Thee I Sing*.

The play was heard again at the New York Ziegfeld, 1952; by ELT, 1968; at the New York City Center, 1969; around the straw-hat circut, 1976; OffBway (4th Street), 1978.

YOU CAN'T TAKE IT WITH YOU   *George S. Kaufman*

The most madcap of all the George S. Kaufman-Moss Hart products is the picture of the completely irresponsible, completely captivating Sycamore family, *You Can't Take It With You*. With Josephine Hull, Henry Travers, and Paula Trueman, the play opened in New York on December 14, 1936, for a run of 837 performances and the 1937 Pulitzer Prize. It has been widely played since. England saw it in 1937 (Manchester, December 13; London, December 22) and New York enjoyed it again in 1945.

Root of the Sycamores is Grandpa Vanderhof. A quarter of a century before the play begins, he went up in the office elevator, reflected while rising that drudgery is a silly game, and came right down again. Ever since, he's been luxuriating at home; for variety, he attends commencements, throws darts, hunts snakes, and manufactures fireworks. Having sheltered a milkman who died without mentioning his last name, Grandpa has the milkman buried as Vanderhof. Since then he has opened no mail; thus he hasn't paid twenty-two years of income taxes.

The Sycamore family is made in Grandpa's image. His daughter Penelope is an aimless but eager muddlehead. Since the day a typewriter was delivered by mistake, she has been writing a play. It's about monks; she inquires: "If a girl you loved entered a monastery, what would you do?" Penelope is also a sculptor; Mr. De Pinna—an iceman, who has been their guest for eight years—poses for her, as a discus thrower. Easie practices ballet dancing; her husband, the xylophone. The fireworks explosives cook in the cellar. A tipsy actress comes in to give her opinion of Penelope's play. It is the wrong night for the supercilious, society Kirbys—but they arrive.

Tony Kirby wants to marry his typist, Alice Sycamore; he brings his family to meet hers. The Kirby brows wrinkle higher; their noses tip more loftily back—when F.B.I. men, suspecting the cellar gunpowder, carry them all to jail. The Kirbys' experiences in jail—while Mrs. Kirby is being searched, a tipsy strip-teaser sings an undressing song—knock them thump off their pedestal. They consent to the marriage. The curtain falls with Kirbys and Sycamores around the festive table as Grandpa says grace before the meal: "Well, Sir, here we are again. About all we need is our health. The rest we leave up to You."

Each of the figures in *You Can't Take It With You* is an individual study in oddity. The Kirbys, who represent orderly society in contrast to the irresponsible brood of Sycamores, are mildly satiric types. The two lovers, most nearly normal, seem almost an intrusion upon the genially madcap scene. Kolenkhov, the xylophonic husband of the ballet dancer, declares: "A Russian feels life chasing around inside him like a squirrel." The doings of the Sycamores, undirected by mundane motives, denying the monetary standards of humdrum life, responsive to the moment's whim and the apt suggestion, whirl around like the colored chips of a kaleidoscope.

The reviewers whirled into superlatives. John Anderson (December 15, 1936) said that *You Can't Take It With You* "puts the 'tops' in topsyturvy." *Time* magazine (December 28, 1936) said that the play "mounts into the stratosphere of literary lunacy." The *Brooklyn Eagle* (August 27, 1938) called the Sycamores "the goofiest but at the same time the most likable family the legitimate stage has ever presented." John Mason Brown (September 14, 1938) thought the entire piece "one of the most lovable and uproarious products of our contemporary stage."

No doubt some of the contemporary references—to Father Divine and to Franklin D. Roosevelt's attempt to hog-swallow the Supreme Court—will date revivals unless deleted. But the substance of the play survives as a charade against grubbing and grinding and hoarding in a world that can, instead, be enjoyed.

Among revivals of *You Can't Take It With You*: APA-Phoenix, November 23, 1965, at the New York Lyceum and on tour for 255 performances. In 1979, Chichester Festival; *Stage and TV Today* (August 16, 1979) said: "It is still a play of comic distinction, its framework, development and details freshly intact, every part diverting." In 1980, Washington Arena Stage, then to the Hong Kong Arts Festival. Paper Mill Playhouse, N.J., January 12, 1983, to New York March 30, 1983, directed by Ellis Rabb; Jason Robards, Grandpa; Colleen Dewhurst, Russian countess; George Rose, Kolenkhov; Paul Dobson and Elizabeth Wilson, Mr. and Mrs. Sycamore; Lawrence Weber, Mr. Kirby. and NT (Lyttleton), August 4, 1983; Geraldine

McEwen, Penelope; Jimmy Jewel, Grandpa; Brewster Mason, Kolenkhov; the English cast, said the *Herald Tribune,* "plumbs new depths of local inadequacy." In 1973, at the New York West Side Gay Theatre, there were homosexual variations, with the female roles in drag.

From the Paper Mill Playhouse director Ellis Rabb brought *You Can't Take It With You* to the New York Royale, where it closed December 3, 1983, after 312 performances. Jason Robards played Grandpa Vanderhof; Colleen Dewhurst (for two months, Eva Gabor) played the Russian Grand Duchess who is a waitress at Child's. The play retains its casual but amusing unconcern with our even more cockeyed world.

THE MAN WHO CAME TO DINNER   *George S. Kaufman*

To that element of the public which succumbs to snob appeal, there are few more admirable—or at least amusing—men than the supercilious, arrogant, and self-satisfied snob Sheridan Whiteside, the title character of George Kaufman and Moss Hart's *The Man Who Came to Dinner.*

Radio Town Crier and raconteur Whiteside, on a lecture tour in the Midwest, slips on the ice of his host's porch and is confined to a wheelchair. Housed there for several weeks, Whiteside pours insults on all and sundry. The eccentric characters who visit him are also victims of his tarantula tongue, further envenomed by his injury and enforced stay. When his secretary, Maggie Cutler, tells him she is leaving to marry a newspaperman, he pours his bile on her as well; but, since such sharp tongues as Whiteside's are traditionally accompanied by a tender heart (and what else can he do?), he relents at last, and with the aid of a mummy case in which an actress has been imprisoned lets Maggie go her matrimonial way. To the infinite relief of the household, Whiteside himself is about to take off—when, flourishing his cane in triumphant farewell, he crashes to the floor again. He is being carried back into the house as the merciful curtain falls.

At the time of Beau Brummell, persons with few qualifications other than insolence made themselves socially prominent in a milieu where insults were *de rigueur* and indignities accepted as wit. "I have the right to be impudent," says a character in Farquhar's *Sir Harry Wildair* (1701), "I am an Oxonian." The Three-Hours-For-Lunch Club at the New York Algonquin Hotel reveled in the same "right" of which Jonathan Swift, in his anticipatory (1731) verses on his own death, gave downright opinion:

> *For he abhorr'd that senseless tribe*
> *Who call it humour when they gibe.*

The Man Who Came to Dinner rests on the assumption that such affronts are still admired. And the more Whiteside insults the unoffending, the more the audience laughs. To a friendly overture he rejoins: "Listen, Repulsive." He calls his efficient and helpful nurse "Miss Bedpan." (To an actress: "Good morning, Miscast.") The situations in the play, however, are always lively, often absurd, and frequently touched with irony; and the characters are deftly drawn and neatly barbed.

Whiteside was recognizable as Alexander Woollcott, chief proponent of Algonquinese. When offered the role, Woollcott said that to act in it would be bad taste. It opened in New York, October 16, 1939, with bearded Monty Woolley, and ran for 739 performances. In London, opening December 4,

1941, it attained 709, with Robert Morley. In Dublin, although a film version preceded the play, it was also a hit. Among those who have played Whiteside on tour are Clifton Webb, author Kaufman, and—Alexander Woollcott, who could not resist the temptation to reveal himself onstage.

At a June 1, 1965, performance at Paramus, N.Y., there was a sudden electrical blackout. Playing Whiteside was Kenneth Banghart, a well-known CBS broadcaster, who ad-libbed: "NBC probably had something to do with this." For fifty minutes, with choir boys (in the play onstage), the audience joined in song, until the lights were restored and the play went on.

The army laughed at the play at Fort Eustace in 1976. In 1979 it was played in Minnesota; also in an updated version at the English Chichester Festival. There, for Whiteside's Christmas broadcast from his wheelchair, Muhammed Ali and Henry Kissinger spoke over the phone, and Dr. Christiaan Barnard from Capetown by satellite. (English critics wondered how such a "literary monster" could be considered funny.) The play was revived by the Circle in the Square, June 28, 1980; and in 1981 in Covington, Kentucky, and Melbourne, Australia.

On March 28, 1967, *Sherry,* music by Lawrence Rosenthal, book and lyrics by James Lipton, came for seventy-two performances. The very name showed misconception: who would dare call venomous Sheridan Whiteside "Sherry"? (French: *cheri*-darling!) The songs—including "Why Does the Whole Damn World Adore Me?" and "How Can You Kiss Those Good Old Times Goodbye?"—and the dances, despite Dolores Gray's best efforts, were irrelevant interruptions to the offbeat incidents of the story; and the presentation overlooked the fact that, for all his verbal ferocity, somehow Woollcott was liked!

The play is a portrait etched in carbolic acid. John Mason Brown called it "Broadway's top-notch best comedy, as gay, giddy, and delectable a comedy as our stage has seen in years." Brooks Atkinson agreed that it was the funniest comedy of the season. "If it is not cricket, it is at least croquet . . . bowls 'em over." It is really more like ten-pins, as Whiteside "bowls 'em over" with strike after strike. The trouble with the play is that the authors seem to feel, or want the audience to feel, that their bullying bellower is really an admirable chap with whom we should all sympathize—stuck there in the dreary Midwest with those dreary middle-class bores!—whose sharp tongue we should at least envy, if we cannot emulate. Imaginative as some of its effects may be, *The Man Who Came to Dinner* survives as a "candid camera" portrait of one of the nastiest-tongued poseurs in the comic theatre.

THE SHOW-OFF   *George Kelly*

Two of the most reliable figures in the theatre are the braggart that is humbled and the genial incompetent that makes good. George Kelly (American, 1897-1974), fused the two figures in *The Show-Off,* and achieved what has been called "one of the three or four best comedies the modern American theatre has had."

The play is an expanded version of a vaudeville skit. It depicts Aubrey Piper, a $32-a-week clerk in a railroad freight yard in West Philadelphia, who talks as though he were an executive involved in tremendous deals. Amy Fisher adores Aubrey and his grand ways; her family are less pleasantly impressed. They suffer still more after Aubrey and Amy are married, for Aubrey's inefficiency runs into debts the family must pay and when Amy's baby is due, Ma Fisher reluctantly gives them shelter in her house.

Despite his sister-in-law Clara's plain speaking, Aubrey persists in his magniloquent ways—until his high assumption of authority and his important airs double the amount offered for an invention of Amy's brother, bringing $100,000 and peace to the Fisher household. The show-off's bluff, at the last, comes through.

Opening on February 5, 1924, *The Show-Off* attained 571 performances and has since been very popular. It "combines a keen commentary on human nature with a steady flow of scintillating dialogue," said Kelcey Allen. When the play reached its first anniversary, Stark Young pointed out the qualities in Aubrey Piper that take hold upon the audience: "For all his garish bluff, he makes a woman happier than her mother has ever been, and happier than the childless sister whose well-off husband is more than indifferent to her. The mother with her household, her stewing and fretting, and her blunt goodness, becomes a wistful rhythm through the play. Aubrey has wild wings and a thick skin. He is always second-rate, commonplace, and soaring. He is a liar with an overwhelming truth of his own, a parrot among hens, the irony of art over utility. He is an intolerable, inconsiderate breeze blowing through, but from this on the room will be stuffy without him." "Of course," said Heywood Broun, "it may truthfully be said that Aubrey lives in a fantastic dream world of his own creation; but once he has built his world he stands by it. God himself has done no more."

Aubrey is a combination of comic butt and hero. He is a figure in the tradition of Rip Van Winkle* and 'Lightnin','* with a touch of the grandiose braggart warrior, laughed at down the ages. *The Show-Off* sets the eternal pretender against a characteristic background of our time and, with touches of tenderness and pathos, builds his bluff into a successful deal and a perennially amusing comedy. See *Craig's Wife.* *

The Show-Off opened in London, October 26, 1924, to a rave review by James Agate. A New York 1932 revival reached 119 performances. It had 50 performances at the New York Negro Theatre in 1937. In 1967, APA-Phoenix, at the New York Lyceum with Helen Hayes for four weeks, went on tour with Nancy Walker, for 114 performances. In 1978, Roundabout, with Paul Rudd as Aubrey.

A musical by Leonard Drum, *The Kid From Philly,* based on *The Show-Off,* was announced in 1962, but did not reach Broadway. The most recent revival OffOffBway (St. Bart's) was in 1980, when the critics agreed that the play "will never be out of date."

Eleanor Flexner, in *American Playwrights,* 1938, discussed the two plays: "In *The Show-Off* the action is desultory. Instead, the talk is so real, so untheatrical, that one seems to be actually listening to the conversation of a typical American family at supper . . . It is no part of Kelly's technique to condense or imply; his characters indulge in no mental or verbal shortcuts. The result is a degree of realism overwhelming in its intensity.

"With *Craig's Wife,* Kelly took off his gloves and wrote one of the most devastating and effective plays of the decade. In it he shows how tragedy inevitably overtakes a woman whose sense of values has become so corrupted that she sacrifices everything to material security." She is, in excess, the epitome of countless women who deem themselves excellent housewives.

CRAIG'S WIFE   *George Kelly*

Craig's Wife, the first full-length play by George Kelly not expanded from a vaudeville skit, won the 1925 Pulitzer Prize. It opened on Broadway

October 12, 1924. London was hospitable to only ten performances in 1929, but Broadway liked it again in 1941, with Pauline Lord, and again in 1947, when *Variety* said that it "remains Grade A theatre." Although it lacks the genial spirit of Kelly's best play, *The Show-Off,** and occasionally presses its point too heavily, *Craig's Wife* is one of the most keenly etched, most devastating portraits of a woman in the modern theatre. The apparently devoted wife and loving home-maker, whose living-room reflects her excellent taste and her insistence on order, is gradually revealed as a woman who will sacrifice everything, including her husband's happiness, for the sense of security that springs from her hold on her home.

Under the guise of love, Mrs. Craig weans her husband from his friends, even from his business associates. The time comes when relatives, servants, and her finally awakened husband turn from her, leaving her with her home and her security—alone. With head high, she accepts the roses a friend brings for the departed aunt, then—first sign of misgiving—as though in a daze, she plucks the rose petals, and on the floor where up to now a flicker of ash would have aroused her fury, she lets fall the petals one by one.

The entire action of the play grows out of and turns ever back to Harriet Craig, whose early fears have built her into an unscrupulously selfish woman. Every word of the play, said the *New York World* (October 13, 1924), "is dedicated to the steady, cruel illumination of Harriet Craig . . . To this one purpose of hers, she is faithful within the limits of her purely feline intelligence. That purpose expresses itself in a thousand ways, from her entirely cold calculation with regard to her husband to the watchful prowl she maintains behind her servants, running her sceptic finger over every lintel they have dusted, crouched for a vengeful pounce if one match-end or a rose petal is found on the rug." The portrait achieved is not only absorbing, but disturbingly true; it is the portrait, as Alexander Woollcott said, of "a woman who would rather have her husband smoke in hell than in her living room. At every matinee of this play there will be some uncomfortable squirming in the audience."

The action of the play extends only from 5:30 one evening until 9 o'clock the next morning. It shows, declared *Theatre* magazine (April 1926), "genius in conception and craftsmanship." Without doubt, *Craig's Wife* is a penetrating portrait, especially revealing because it sinks below appearances to basic motives and bone-bred drives. In milder form, many a Mrs. Craig is taken as a model wife. As her character is brought to life before us, the development is as horrid as it is true.

MARY, MARY   *Jean Kerr*

Everyone knows the old formula for a love comedy: boy meets girl; boy loses girl; boy gets girl. Jean Kerr (b. 1923), deft at all things, enlivened the standard plot by reversing the first two actions. *Mary, Mary* (1961) is quite contrary.

The interlocutory divorce decree of Bob and Mary McKillaway has still two weeks before it becomes final; but Bob has already picked Mrs. Number Two; nor is Mary without her ardent admirers. When they all come together, Bob is at first taken aback. "Bob thinks that when he brings a book back to the library it will never go out again." But soon interest and love reawaken, and by mutual consent Mary too is taken back.

Jean Kerr's wit had earlier been noted in the prose of *Please Don't Eat the Daisies* and in another book, the title of which she attributed to her young son. He had the part of Adam in Eden in a Christmas play; Jean asked him if he had much to memorize, and he responded: "No. The snake has all the lines." As her husband is the distinguished drama critic Walter Kerr, theatre is frequent fare in the family.

Mary, Mary opened at the New York Helen Hayes Theatre, March 8, 1961, to a run of 1,572 performances. John Chapman said next day in the *News*: "*Mary, Mary* was much more springlike than last evening's weather, containing no slush." Barbara Bel Geddes played Mary; Barry Nelson, her not quite ex-husband Bob. Oscar Nelson, shrewd attorney, was played by John Cromwell; Dick Winsten of Hollywood, who hoped to be Mary's next, by Michael Rennie; Tiffany Fields, Bob's perhaps too self-assured fiancée, by Betsy von Furstenberg. During the long Broadway run, Mary was also played by Nancy Olson, Julia Meade, Inger Stevens, Diana Lynn, and Mindy Carson; while Barry Nelson as Bob was followed by Scott McKay, George Grizzard, Tom Preston, Biff McGuire, Wayne Carson, and William Prince. Nelson and Cromwell were in the 1963 film, along with Debbie Reynolds, Diane McBain, and Hiram Sherman.

Meanwhile, from 1961 through 1965, there were productions and touring companies all over the United States. Orson Bean opened in the play at Paramus, May 5, 1965. Betsy Palmer played Mary at the Paper Mill, N.J., at Christmastime the same year. Paris hailed the play at the Théâtre Antoine, September 26, 1953. (There was a cartoon pun on Mari?-Mari?— the not finally divorced husband.) The play came from England's Brighton to the London Queen's Theatre, opening February 27, 1963, then September 2 to the Globe, for 395 performances. Milton Shulman said: "What saves *Mary, Mary* from sinking in a lather of soap suds is Mrs. Kerr's wit and a joyous comic performance by Maggie Smith." More recent productions include Lake Tahoe, April 4, 1972; Tuckahoe, N.Y., April 23, 1975; New Orleans, with Janet Shea and John Wilmot, June 6, 1979, with some of the topical references brought up to date. The play has proved especially popular in Germany and Greece.

The New York critics found a fresh and scintillating spirit in Jean Kerr's work. John McClain in the *Journal-American* (March 9, 1961) praised her "delightfully ludicrous approach to life's more sombre moments . . . triumph of lines and situations over a threadbare theme. There are countless jokes, but most of the hilarity is founded in true wit, emerging from character." Howard Taubman in the *Times*: "Her mind is agile, her observation of the small frailties of people is sharp, and her skill at coining a lively phrase is sure." Judith Crist, in the *Herald Tribune,* added: "Mrs. Kerr has a remarkable talent for taking even a cliché and, with humor and worldly widsom, giving it novelty and sophistication." And I might add that, although her Mary is gifted with a tart tongue, unlike many that take the stage today, Jean Kerr does not seek a laugh by making any individual the butt of her humor. She has succeeded in telling a simple story with subtle skill and smiling wit.

ARSENIC AND OLD LACE   *Joseph Kesselring*

"The funniest play about murder ever written," as the *Baltimore Sun* (March 26, 1941) called it, *Arsenic and Old Lace* has audiences on both sides of the ocean half-seas over with applause at poisoning. Opening in New York, January 10, 1941, the play ran for 1,437 performances. London saw it first December 23, 1942; it ran for 1,337 performances and reopened in April 1946. It was played in Spanish in Buenos Aires in 1942, and has had corpses in window seats and audiences in stitches on every continent. It was the first play ever presented in sign language (at Gallaudet College for the Deaf, Washington, D.C.). The author, Joseph Kesselring (American, 1902-1967), we are told, intended the play as a serious melodrama; during rehearsals, its mood was changed to farce.

The play revolves about the sweetly homicidal mania of the mild old maid Brewster girls of Brooklyn, Martha and Abbie. The local police drop in for cozy comfort on cold nights; the women are charitable; everybody loves them. They have three nephews. Teddy Roosevelt Brewster, who lives with them, is amusingly cracked; he digs the Panama Canal in the cellar and he constantly charges up the stairs blowing a bugle for the taking of San Juan Hill. Nephew Mortimer, who loves the minister's daughter next door, is a drama critic. Mortimer discovers a corpse and then finds out that his aunts, with humanitarian motives, welcome lonely, friendless, homeless old men, ply them with elderberry wine spiked with arsenic, and bury them in Teddy's Panama Canal. This corpse makes their twelfth victim.

While Mortimer ponders what to do about his tender aunts, nephew Jonathan arrives. Abbie learns of him when she discovers a strange corpse in the window seat; "Now who can that be?" she wonders. Jonathan, a more direct homicidal maniac, is disguised as Boris Karloff (Boris Karloff created the role); he travels accompanied by his personal face-lifter and plastic surgeon. Jonathan, as Abbie observes, always was a mean boy; he couldn't bear to see anyone get ahead of him: he too has accumulated his twelfth corpse. The police account for Jonathan, but Mortimer manages to arrange to have his aunts taken to a private "home." When the custodian arrives, the gentle ladies suggest that he have a drink before they leave. They serve him the arsenic and elderberry as the curtain falls.

We will not render lip-service to the two benign old ladies, but they almost capture our hearts. We are less concerned than amused when a playwriting cop, finding Mortimer tied in a chair (one of Jonathan's pranks), seizes the opportunity to read the critic his play. (The falling curtain spares the audience.) It is not less than inevitable that Mortimer, being a drama critic, is a bastard—and thus, spared the Brewster heritage of insanity, is free to marry the minister's daughter. Richard Watts, Jr., claims (or confesses) that the drama critic is partly patterned after him.

Insanity not only runs in the Brewster family; it gallops. The dramatic effects—in the New York production of Howard Lindsay and Russel Crouse, directed by Bretaigne Windust—were equally cavorting. The climax was top-hatted when, during bows after the final curtain, up from the cellar streamed the thirteen murdered old men. The total impression, said *Time* (January 2, 1941) is "as if Strindberg had written *Hellzapoppin*." Certainly no such genial pair of lethal spinsters has elsewhere made murder so hilarious as in this corpse-ridden play.

The original lethal pair, in the New York *Arsenic and Old Lace,* were Josephine Hull and Jean Adair. In the first London cast were Lilian Braithwaite and Mary Jerrold. Among the many revivals: the 1956 tour, with Gertrude Berg as Abbie, was the play's fifth Boston showing. London, February 7, 1966, with Sybil Thorndike and Athene Sayler, for 300 performances. In 1969, Pitlochry Festival. In 1975, record broken for the Cincinnati Playhouse; the same year played by two actual sisters, Eva and Zsa Zsa Gabor. OffOffBway, 1972 and 1976. In 1977, twenty-six performances in Vancouver. Paris saw it again in 1981. Hamlet speaks to the King of "murder in jest"; Kesselring made this actual for the public.

MEN IN WHITE   *Sidney Kingsley*

The doctor has been caricatured or satirized in the modern drama, from the ailing Molière* to the vegetarian Shaw.* Sidney Kingsley (American, b. 1906), in *Men in White,* favorably presents his physicians in the atmosphere of a modern hospital. The old chief of staff, Dr. Hochberg, is an ideal surgeon, a scientist with a whole-hearted devotion to his profession. Dr. Levine, a once most promising intern, shows the social and intellectual poverty that may be pressed upon a physician whom an early marriage drives into the humdrum and wearing routine of ill-paid general practice. Between them stands young Dr. Ferguson, who wants a good career, while his fiancée, Laura, wants only a good time.

The problems implicit in these contrasted figures, however, are given scant attention in the play's rather trite story. Dr. Ferguson, happy at the success of a risky operation, kisses nurse Barbara Dennin. He thinks nothing of it, but Barbara goes to his room and waits for him. "The inevitable" grows between them until Barbara needs an emergency operation— which intern Ferguson is called to perform. Barbara dies. Laura, discovering the situation, is quickened to a sense of deeper reality. Dr. Ferguson leaves, to study abroad; a more understanding Laura accompanies him.

The play has, according to John Mason Brown (October 7, 1933) "a piffling script, mildewed in its hokum, childishly sketchy in its characterization and so commonplace in its every written word that it in no way justifies its own unpleasantness." But, as the *New York Herald Tribune* (February 4, 1934) declared, "all this is the surface of *Men in White.* Beneath its innocently phony exterior there are problems, solved and unsolved. What, it seems to ask, are the Hippocratic pledges, and how obediently can they be observed? Must a young student of medicine consecrate himself absolutely to the duties of science, or should he be humanly selfish now and then and compromise with the ideals and the ethics?" Even beyond this, the power of the play lies in the atmosphere, in the general stir of life within hospital walls, in the medical aspects of the play, more significant than its love story.

We see the big, modern, city hospital from the inside, with its many facets: the loudspeaker calling the interns; the anxious inquiries of relatives and the professional calm sympathy of the nurses; the almost military precision of operation procedure; and also (as Arthur Ruhl pointed out in the *New York Herald Tribune,* October 22, 1933) "the politics of the hospital board room; sharply revealing incisions into the lives of various kinds of patients . . . grouped round the central story in a swift sequence of scenes, vividly set, told with moving sincerity, without a trace of flub-dub or waste of words."

The "expert" was pleased with the picture: An editorial in the *Journal of the American Medical Association* praised the atmosphere of the play; doctors thronged to see it. They did object, however, to the earlier scene of the over-insulinated child; to the doctors, this is comparable to a sergeant's snatching papers from a general and issuing orders.

The second operating-room scene is indeed a major one. It was rehearsed over a hundred times. Nine-tenths of it is in pantomime; there are no speaking cues; each one is busy and cannot watch the others. Sand-glasses were used to time washing and other actions, as the regular routine of an operation speeds upon the stage, with the doctor driving on, quick step by step, and the nurses in instant time with the required instruments. It is rich, said Brooks Atkinson, with "impact in the theatre, and it is warm with life and high in aspiration"; and, said Arthur Pollock, "it is a really remarkable drama. It will make you feel once more that there is nothing quite like the theatre, and never will be."

Men in White was presented by the Group Theatre in New York, September 26, 1933, with Morris Carnovsky, Alexander Kirkland, Luther Adler, and J. Edward Bromberg. It ran for 367 performances and was awarded the 1934 Pulitzer Prize. (The play jury unanimously recommended Anderson's *Mary of Scotland,** but was overruled by the Board of Trustees.) In London, *Men in White,* adapted by Merton Hodge to English medical practices, opened June 28, 1934, for a run of 131 performances. It played at the same time in London, Baltimore, Cleveland, Los Angeles, and Budapest; also in 1934, Myrna Loy and Clark Gable acted in a screen version. While it presents the problems of the medical profession through the medium of an obvious and sentimental story, the play is a shining example of how the theatre can create a living atmosphere and a moving mood. The swift surge of hospital events largely replaces the story; the characters gather a sense of human worth; the play speeds a vital emotional drive upon the stage.

Walter Pritchard Eaton in the *New York Herald Tribune,* April 1, 1934, declared that *Men in White* "captures reality with almost a passion of sincerity and breathes a spirit of idealism." Dissatisfaction with the action of the Pulitzer Prize board helped the creation of the New York Drama Critics' Circle in 1935. *Men in White* was revived by ELT in 1955; OffOffB-way in 1979.

DEAD END   *Sidney Kingsley*

This play by Sidney Kingsley vividly captures the opposed extremes of city life. A gripping melodrama, it is, in the opinion of Arthur Pollock, "very close to being the last word in realistic playwriting and presentation." The street scenes, said the *New York Herald Tribune* (November 10, 1935) are "so literal, so apparently genuine, that you are fascinated in the belief that you are a spectator at real events." Opening in New York, October 28, 1935, the play ran for 687 performances, and it has become a little theatre favorite.

"We see the whole drama of our social order," said the *New York Times* (November 3, 1935) "concentrated in a foul and ugly tenement street that lies at the rear of an aristocratic apartment house and debouches into the East River . . . The jeering, bullying, slippery restlessness of the hoodlums, the pool of quiet around the artist who is sitting on the stringpiece, the tired anxiety of the older sister for one of the boys, the condescension of an apartment-house adventuress, the pompousness and assurance of the uniformed doorman, the nervous distaste of the rich for the mean street they have to follow—all this pother of a thousand and one Manhattan days, Mr. Kingsley has reproduced so literally that at first it appears to lack significance . . . Presently, however, you perceive that this casual pier scene represents in Mr. Kingsley's mind something of current social importance."

Some of Kingsley's shrewdest writing is in the interplay of the youngsters, for in them is the heart of this drama. Its story concerns Babyface Martin, come back to his boyhood haunts hunted by the police. He has taught little Tommy some of the gangsters' tricks; with them Tommy trips up the supercilious Philip Griswold, 2d, scion of wealth, and swipes his wrist-watch. The lame architect, whose emotional life is thwarted but whose ethical direction holds straight, promises Tommy's sister that the reward money for Martin's capture will be used to help Tommy. And perhaps not all of these lives will move like Martin's, through violence to a dead end.

Rich in vivid moments and swiftly coursing emotions, *Dead End* keeps melodrama within the range of reality. Especially gripping, in their psychological truth, are Babyface Martin's moments with his mother and with his early sweetheart. As the *New York World-Telegram* (January 15, 1937) declared: "Many will remember Mrs. Martin's fierce denunciation of her son as a wonderful scene, but there is an equally dramatic sequel of even more significance—the recoil of Babyface. For even to his killer, Mr. Kingsley gives a human touch. Dismayed by her anger, Martin offers her money as a last gesture. She spurns it and turns away, leaving him with her awful curse. 'Well, whatdaya tink o' that,' says Hunk, Martin's trigger man. 'Whyn't ya slap her down?' 'Shut up!' says Martin. Although smarting, a shade of sadness crosses his face, which is relieved only when he thinks of his coming meeting with Francey, his one-time sweetheart. And then along comes Francey—now a diseased prostitute. Again, Mr. Kingsley caps the drama of this meeting. Unlike the mother, Francey accepts Babyface's money—and asks him for an extra $20. One of these scenes would be outstanding in any play, but to introduce two in such a way that the second is in no way an anticlimax, is playwriting of a high order."

The appeal of wealth, of luxury, is one of the strongest along the dead end streets of the city, the breeding ground of go-get-it girls and of gangster elements. But we hear Evolution's warning, lest civilization be approaching its dead end: "Now, men, I made you walk straight, I gave you feeling, I gave you reason, I gave you dignity, I gave you a sense of beauty, I planted a God in your heart. Now let's see what you're going to do with them. And if you can't do anything with them, then I'll take them all away. Yes, I'll take away your reason as sure as I took away the head of the oyster; and your sense of beauty as I took away the flight of the ostrich, and men will crawl on their bellies on the ground like snakes or die off altogether like the dinosaur."

With a vivid setting by Norman Bel Geddes and a blending of blue and white lights that simulated out-of-door daylight so well the players needed no make-up, *Dead End* proved a strikingly realistic presentation, beyond the strong melodrama of its story, of a problem basically dramatic and crucial in all city life. Children at both extremes are problems, spoiled Philip as much as neglected Tommy; and as they grow the city will grow, to fruitful future or to dead end.

Dead End was shown again at the New York 41st Street, with Sylvia Sidney (then Ruth Hussey) and Humphrey Bogart; in the same year by ELT; and OffBway in 1978.

THE BROKEN JUG   *Heinrich Kleist*

Within the vehemence of the German *Sturm und Drang*, Bernd Heinrich von Kleist (1777-1811) lived turbulent days, sensitive and brooding to the brink of madness, until in jealous passion he shot his sweetheart, Henriette Vogel, and himself. His tormented life found echo in his intense dramas, which swing from despair to jubilation, which delight in sharp contrast of emotion. Even in his comedies there is a turbulence, as is shown in the thirteen scenes of his comic masterpiece, *The Broken Jug*, 1808.

In this play Frau Marthe Rull comes before the village judge, Adam, to claim damages for her broken jug from Ruprecht, the sweetheart of her daughter Eve. The district judge, Walter, present on a tour of inspection, watches the case. The jug has been broken by a midnight visitor to Eve's bedroom. This turns out to be not Ruprecht but Judge Adam himself, who, inventing a summons to Ruprecht for military service in the East Indies, has come to promise Eve to let the lad off in exchange for her favors. The trial ends with the ignominious flight of the exposed judge.

The play—translated into English in *Poet Lore,* 1939—gives an excellent picture of the life of ordinary folk, much in the style, as several critics have observed, of the Flemish masters of painting. "What an atmosphere of everyday reality is spread over it!" exclaimed Kuno Francke in *A History of German Literature* (1901). "How squarely they stand before us, this slovenly and slothful justice of the peace with his club foot, his blackened eye, and his big bald head; this sleek, thin, officious clerk, constantly on the alert for an opportunity to thrust himself into the position of his chief; this quarrelsome and loquacious Frau Marthe, not hesitating to drag the good name of her daughter into the courtroom if there is a chance of recovering damages for her broken jar; and, in pleasant contrast with all these, this sturdy peasant lad and his sweetheart, whose love, though sorely tried, is proven to be genuine and true!"

Natural as the development of the story seems, there is deft art in its construction. *The Broken Jug* has been called the comic counterpart of *Oedipus,** which it resembles in the skill with which the gradual revelation is achieved through constant action, the present progressing as it unveils the past. Presented by the Federal Theatre in New York in 1936, *The Broken Jug* proved still rich in its satire of hyprocrisy and in its capture of the comic drama within ordinary happenings to simple folk.

An adaptation by Donald Harron was presented at the 1958 Stratford Canada Festival; the first non-Shakespearean play the Festival sent on tour, it came to New York with the Phoenix, April 1, 1959. This set the story in a small settlement in western Canada during the War of 1812. Also in 1958, in a rhymed adaptation by Ashley Dukes, it was played at the Edinburgh Festival with Donald Wolfit, George Curzon as the inspector and Nan Munro the daughter.

There was an operatic version, called *The Jug,* by Fritz Geissler, in East Berlin's Linder Oper in 1972; and in 1975 a dramatic version by Henry Livings was shown in Nottingham, England. In the 1978-1979 season, 170 years after it was written, *The Broken Jug* was on more West German stages than any other play, totaling 421 performances. As *The Broken Pitcher,* adapted by Jon Swan, it opened OffBway (Martinique), October 2, 1981. The irony of a judge's presiding over a case in which he himself is the real criminal still has dramatic power.

PRINCE FRIEDRICH VON HOMBURG   *Heinrich Kleist*

The uncompromising spirit of Bernd Heinrich von Kleist, his refusal to accept the limitations life imposes, is marked in his serious dramas, by which he hoped, with a blending of Greek and Shakespearean elements, to lift the laurels from Goethe's brow.

Kleist's greatest drama, *Prince Friedrich von Homburg,* 1810, opens with the Elector of Brandenburg making plans for the battle of Fehrbellin (June 28, 1675) against the Swedes; Homburg, in charge of the cavalry, is to await the order for the finishing blow. Word sweeps across the field that the

Elector is dead; Homburg charges, and gains the victory. He then declares his love to Nathalie, Princess of Orange. The Elector, however, is alive; and Homburg is condemned to death for disobedience. In the presence of Nathalie, Homburg abjectly begs the Electress to plead for his life. Nathalie, though scorning Homburg for his cowardice, intercedes, and bears him a letter from the Elector: "If you believe I have been unjust, say so, and I shall return your sword." Homburg refuses to make that claim, and publicly asserts the code of honor and patriotic service: a commander must first of all learn to obey. Expecting to die, he is now restored to freedom, honor, and happiness.

The drama, with its costumed spread through palace and dungeon, begins and ends in a garden; but beneath the melodrama and the flowered romance one may discern—as in Homburg's revulsion from the thought of death—a more realistic understanding of human nature. Christian Hebbel,* praising the play, pointed out that not death but no more than "death's darkening shadow" was needed to produce the "moral purification and apotheosis of the hero."

The play had its American premiere at Brown University, April 29, 1935, and manifested a freshness and power that have kept its issues vital.

It was banned in its day as seditious, but acclaimed by the Nazis for its emphasis on obedience. In translation by Jonathan Griffin it was produced in 1976 at Manchester and London; the English saw in von Homburg's charge a resemblance to Horatio Nelson's action at the Battle of the Baltic. There were two OffBway productions in 1976: Theatre Four; and the BAM translation of James Kirkup adapted and directed by Robert Kalfin. *Prince Friedrich von Homburg* came into the NT (Cottesloe) repertory in 1982. In its basic situation, opposing individual initiative to expected obedience, there is dramatically developed substance for thought.

THE SPANISH TRAGEDY   *Thomas Kyd*

Written by Thomas Kyd (English, 1558-1595?) in the early Shakespearean years, *The Spanish Tragedy; or, Hieronimo Is Mad Again,* 1589? was the greatest Elizabethan stage success and the most popular English drama for a century. Licensed October 6, 1592, the play had numerous printings between 1594 and 1633. Familiarly known as *Hieronimo,* it was frequently alluded to in other works. "Its thrilling theme," Allardyce Nicoll noted, "with murders galore, ghosts, madness, and love, easily captured the attention of contemporaries, and even when, in later years, it was ridiculed by literary men with pretensions to taste, it kept its hold on the popular imagination."

Although Kyd's blank verse is rough, his construction and use of dramatic irony is effective and many of his melodramatic devices reappear in unnumbered blood-and-thunder plays thereafter. Even *Hamlet* * following *The Spanish Tragedy* uses an opening ghost, the dumb-show, the play within the play as an instrument of vengeance, the innocent woman whom the horrors drive to madness and self-slaughter. Any criticism, said John McGovern and Jesse Edson Hall in the June 1908 issue of *National Magazine,* "that dwells on the horrors of Kyd's drama falls with nearly equal harshness on *Hamlet,* and we think the general construction is the better in *Hieronimo.*"

The Spanish Tragedy is set against the background of Spain's victory over Portugal in 1580. Andrea, the beloved of the Spanish lady Bel-imperia, has been slain by the Portuguese Prince Balthazar, who has in turn been captured by Horatio, son of the Spanish marshal Hieronimo. The play opens with the ghost of Andrea and the spirit of Revenge, but for much of the time Revenge sleeps. Balthazar is delivered to Lorenzo, the brother of Bel-imperia, who sees his own political advantage in marriage between his sister and Balthazar. He and Balthazar spy upon Bel-imperia and Horatio whom she has come to love; murderers then stab and hang Horatio, and Bel-imperia is carried off. The murderers themselves are slain so that they cannot betray their masters, but Bel-imperia sends Hieronimo word writ in blood, of their villainy. Hieronimo, who himself has cut down his son's body, has spells of madness, but he is shrewd enough to awaken Revenge. He arranges a play, in which he and Bel-imperia, and Lorenzo and Balthazar, are to act. As part of the play's action, Hieronimo and Bel-imperia stab Lorenzo and Balthazar; Bel-imperia then kills herself. The audience onstage think this but part of the performance—then discover it is fatally real. Hieronimo bites off his tongue, so that he cannot be forced to speak. Given a quill pen, he motions for a knife to sharpen it; with the knife he stabs Lorenzo's father and himself.

Many of the lines of the play have a surging power; some, even the lift of beauty. However, the style is unsustained—so much so that Charles Lamb was led to stretch a resemblance into a collaboration, suggesting that the passages added in the 1602 edition are not by Kyd but by Webster, displaying "that wild solemn preternatural cast of grief which bewilders us in *The Duchess of Malfi.**" Certainly the mad speeches of Hieronimo point toward the aberrations, the method in the madness, of Shakespeare's Hamlet.

Turbulent, melodramatic, for our taste long-winded, Kyd's play borrowed many elements, of ghostly avenger, of harrowing horror, from the Roman Seneca;* but the deeds of violence reported by messenger in the Roman drama were in *The Spanish Tragedy* enacted before the eyes of the audience on the English stage. It was the first and long the most popular of the blood-and-thunder dramas.

In a 1978 Glasgow revival, Revenge is made both a commentator and a participant; the set is a tumbledown bombed-out ruin of the Civil War in Spain; and over a menacing gallows that dominates the shambles hovers the ghost of Andrea. At the NT (Cottesloe), September 22, 1982, ghosts and the spirit of Revenge (smoking a cigarillo) remain onstage throughout the play, "hell being a city much like Seville." On June 14, 1984, it reopened at the Lyttleton, ending (not as with *Hamlet,* with peace) with revenge still preparing.

THE ITALIAN STRAW HAT   *Eugene M. Labiche*

Among the plays of Eugene M. Labiche (French, 1815-1888) written with sheer intent to amuse, is *Le Chapeau de paille d'Italie (The Italian Straw Hat),* 1851, which has enjoyed a great success and many years of revivals. "F. L. Tomline" (W. S. Gilbert*) rendered it into English as *The Wedding March,* which opened in London on November 15, 1873, and ran for 119 performances. Gilbert later rewrote it as an operetta, *Haste to the Wedding,* with music by George Grossmith, first enacted July 27, 1892. As *Horse Eats Hat,* September 22, 1936, adapted by Edwin Denby and Orson Welles, it was one of the high spots of the Federal Theatre in the United States. The antics of the farce are well fitted to the films and were set delightfully on the screen by René Clair.

On his wedding morning, a young man goes horseback riding; when he stops, his horse eats a hat of Italian straw instead of grass. The hat belongs to a woman with a jealous husband; she is now with an irascible army man, who demands that the bridegroom at once replace the hat. The wedding party turns into a mad chase for the hat. It stops at a milliner's. The owner of the shop happens to be an old sweetheart of the bridegroom and wants to renew their amours. However, he manages to learn that the hat's only twin has been bought by a Countess. Off they go to the Countess only to find she is having a party. The bridegroom is mistaken for an entertainer; the wedding party makes itself at home at the Countess' feast. The Countess has given her hat to her niece. At the niece's home a suspicious husband awaits and the groom finds he's been chasing the very hat his horse has eaten. Everywhere the bride's father, Nonancourt, carries a pot of myrtle for the bride; each time he encounters the groom he announces "Tout est rompu!"—"It's all off!"—whereupon the bride is at once embraced by a drooling cousin who had hoped to marry her. The right two are finally married at the City Hall in the course of the hunt for the hat. Everywhere, too, the bride's deaf uncle carries a gift box he refuses to set down; it turns out to contain an exact copy of the eaten hat! But before the groom can get it to the lady, her jealous husband appears, the wedding party is arrested, and the audience has worn itself with laughter.

Although the motion pictures quickly borrowed the stir and excitement of the chase, it still carries interest on the stage. The doings at the Federal Theatre production were characterized in the *New York Times* (February 28, 1936): "It was as though Gertrude Stein had dreamed a dream after a late supper of pickles and ice cream, the ensuing relevations being crisply acted by giants and midgets, caricatures, lunatics, and a prop nag. They pulled down the scenery and jumped into the aisles, were mummers of a Hallowe'en parade and the victims of slapstick from the age of innocence."

The ludicrous names of the French original are recaptured in the Gilbert version. The bridegroom is Woodpecker Tapping; the Uncle, Bopaddy; the Cousin, Foodle. The irate military man is Captain Bapp; his lady of the eaten hat is married to Major-General Bunthunder. Much of the Gilbertian humor is in the songs, but the music is not Sullivan's, and the absurdities of the story all stem from Labiche.

In 1955 Joan Littlewood directed a London production of *The Italian Straw Hat,* adapted by Theodore Hoffman. Peter Coe directed the play at the Chichester Festival, 1967.

OffBway, 1957, in a translation by Richard G. Mason and Regina Wojak, Richard's father, Gabriel Mason, then principal of Abraham Lincoln High School, properly pompously played the jealous Tardiveau. In 1963 the play was directed by Norris Houghton at Cambridge, Mass.; 1968, New York Hunter College; 1977, Saratoga Springs. A 1981 production OffBway (Manhattan Punch Line) showed that fanciful foolery can still fill a house with laughter.

THE VOYAGE OF MONSIEUR PERRICHON   *Eugene M. Labiche*

Hailed by many as the chief comic dramatist of nineteenth century France, Eugene M. Labiche moved from light vaudevilles and lively farces to plays that, while no less amusing, were centered on a core of character or a nugget of thought. The best of these is *The Voyage of Monsieur Perrichon (Perrichon's Trip),* 1860, which entertainingly presses home the psychological point that we are grateful to and like not those that have helped us but, rather, those that we have helped.

The play starts with the confusion of a railway station, and the Perrichons—a bourgeois husband who is proud, petty, and vain; a hopeful but muddled wife; their charming daughter Henriette; and six pieces of luggage—on their way to the Alps. Henriette has two suitors, Armand and Daniel. In the Alps, at the edge of a glacier, Armand saves M. Perrichon's life. The women shower Armand with attentions, but the shrewd Daniel pretends to slip and offers M. Perrichon the opportunity to save him. Thereafter Daniel sings M. Perrichon's praises and Perrichon centers his affections—and his daughter—upon the man that he believes he has saved. It is only when the cocksure Daniel boasts and Perrichon learns how he has been tricked that Henriette and Armand are united.

The psychological factor that motivates *The Voyage of M. Perrichon* is subtly traced and neatly developed. It may seem obvious now, but as the *London Times* (March 8, 1933) declared, it is "a platitude only because this once brilliant discovery has now been known for a long time. And it is worked into an excellent and amusing plot." Its structure is direct and clear; the dialogue is straightforward and without subtleties, but amusing and keen. When the play was written, according to the *New York Times* (November 2, 1937), "it was the fashion of the drama to caricature the bourgeoisie. It was the vogue among dramatists to imitate the simple diction and idiom of Voltaire.—For this last reason *The Voyage of M. Perrichon* has been academically perpetuated, so that few French classes, few French dramatic societies, have escaped it." But surely mere imitation could not ensure the continuously friendly greeting the play receives. Its situations are amusing, its basic point is both ironic and true.

When *The Voyage of M. Perrichon* was produced in New York in 1937 (in French, November 1), *Theatre Arts* of January 1938 observed "Le Théâtre des Quatre Saisons dusted off the gay comedy of Labiche and redecorated it with some of the glitter and wit it had a half century ago." In Paris *Le Monde* (February 6, 1946) remarked that "the humor remains alive." The play remains an excellent light-hearted, laughing dramatic picture of man's natural tendency to find virtue where it makes him shine.

In 1977 to OffBway came *Bon Voyage,* book by Edward Malby from Labiche's play, and lyrics set to music by Offenbach. (That year Jay Gorney wrote a song, "Steal a Tune from Offenbach.")

SUMMER OF THE SEVENTEENTH DOLL   *Ray Lawler*

Written in 1953, a hit in Melbourne in 1955, *Summer of the Seventeenth Doll* is the best play to come out of Australia. Bernie and his pal Roo are cane-cutters in the outback of Queensland, who in the slack season spend five months dallying in Victoria, Bernie with Nancy and Roo with Olive, to whom he brings a doll every year. But this year, their seventeenth, things are different. Bernie's girl has married; in her place smiles hopeful Pearl, a widow, barmaid in the pub with Olive. (The girls, who had been millinery workers, became barmaids for the greater freedom and the company of the men.) But Roo also has changed. Bernie explains that Roo has strained a muscle; but actually a younger man has surpassed him. Roo is only too aware that he can no longer boast of being the best cane-cutter, that he is growing old, that he is broke.

Instead of enjoying the holiday, Roo wants to settle down; he gets a job, and asks Olive to marry him. She responds hysterically, beating his breast, crying, "I want what I had!" The bewildered Roo smashes the doll. Bernie vainly tries to comfort him, then leads him away, to the aging pattern of their days.

The Australian company, with the author playing Bernie, came to the London New Theatre, April 30, 1957, for 254 performances; in the same year it played at the Bristol Old Vic. At the New York Coronet, opening January 22, 1958, it attained only 29 performances—"the fun goes out of the vacation and of the play," said George Oppenheimer in *Newsday*—but at the Washington Arena Stage, opening April 30, 1958, directed by Alan Schneider, it broke the theatre's record. It was revived OffBway in 1959, 1968; 1975 at New York University, and 1976. The 1968 production, at St. Marks OffBway, was by the Negro Ensemble Company, with the locale changed to a black neighborhood in New Orleans, with the cane-cutters speaking accordant dialogue, the men "blokes," the women "cats." Clive Barnes in the *New York Times* said (February 21, 1968): "Mr. Lawler describes this time of crisis, the end of easy youth, with skill and compassionate insight." The play was filmed, as *Season of Passion,* in 1966.

In Melbourne, opening in December 1975, John Sumner directed a Lawler trilogy: at 10:30 a. m. *Kid Stakes,* showing the first summer; at 2:45 *Other Times,* with the cane-cutters released from the army at the end of the war; and at 8:30 *The Summer of the Seventeenth Doll.*

Instead of the philosophical optimism of Browning's "Rabbi Ben Ezra":

> Grow old along with me,
> The best is yet to be

(for which see *The Chinese Prime Minister**), the play shows us the reality to which, if we survive that long, most of us are implacably drawn.

INHERIT THE WIND   *Jerome Lawrence*

At the notorious "monkey trial" in Tennessee, John T. Scopes, defended by Clarence Darrow and prosecuted by William Jennings Bryan, was found guilty (June 10, 1925) of teaching the theory of man's evolution. On June 20 the verdict was overturned on a technicality, and Scopes never paid the $100 fine.

Thirty years later Jerome Lawrence (b. 1915) and Robert E. Lee (b. 1918) fashioned the story into the gripping *Inherit the Wind.* Refused by several Broadway producers, the play was opened right in the Bible Belt by courageous Margo Jones, January 10, 1955. Favorable reports took it, produced and directed by Herman Shumlin, to Philadelphia, then to the New York National, April 21, 1955, with Paul Muni as Henry Drummond (Darrow) and Ed Begley as Matthew Hanson Brady (Bryan). On August 29, 1955, Muni withdrew for an eye operation; Shumlin reopened the play September 19 with Melvyn Douglas, again to excellent reviews. Muni was able to return to the cast in time for Bella Muni to wish author Lawrence "Merry Christmas!"—and the play went on for 806 performances. Douglas played it on the road.

The title is from the Bible, Proverbs 11:29: "He that troubleth his own house shall inherit the wind."

The play, showing a courtroom and the town square beyond, opens with the crowd awaiting the famous Brady, three times almost President of the United States, while the Reverend Brown whips them up with a dramatic story of the Creation, to the climax of the sixth day, when God made man, with the directive: Be fruitful, and multiply, and replenish the earth, and subdue it. Brown's daughter Bertha, torn between family devotion and her interest in the young accused teacher, Cates, is perplexed at the intensity of feeling the case has roused. Drummond, counsel for Cates, tells her: "Murder a wife, and it isn't nearly as bad as murdering an old wives' tale."

Brady says to Drummond when they meet: "There used to be a mutuality of understanding and admiration. Why is it, my old friend, that you have moved so far away from me?" Drummond says slowly: "Perhaps it is you who have moved away—by standing still."

The trial scene is one of the most blistering the stage has shown, with Brady taking every opportunity to denounce the "Bible-haters, the Evilutionists"; but Drummond, despite the judge's continual objections, riddles his opponent's biblical assumptions. Notwithstanding the "Guilty" verdict, Brady knows he has been made ridiculous; he collapses, and as he is borne out to die, he utters an inaugural address, as though elected President. Bertha and Cates go off together. Drummond puts the Bible and Darwin into his briefcase, and crosses the empty stage as the curtain falls.

Walter Winchell, always punctual with a pun, proclaimed: "The star is Paul Munificent." *Cue* called Brady "an invincible innocent Fundamentalist . . . a phrase-making charlatan"—unjust to both Brady and Bryan, for we watch not a charlatan but an earnest and sincere believer, whose biblical faith is battered by the merciless logic that leaves him baffled as much as beaten down, largely by quotations from his own book, the Bible. But Drummond, the defense attorney, is compassionate; he was seeking not triumph but truth; and he puts in his place the pseudo-clever reporter who tries to cheapen the victory for truth by the journalistic assumption that it has only one side.

Other productions of *Inherit the Wind* were widespread. From Croydon (theatre in the round) it went to the London St. Martin's, March 16, 1960, with Andrew Cruickshank as Drummond, Henry McCarthy as Brady. The 1961 Habimah production in Hebrew marked the twenty-eighth language in which the play was produced; Mandarin Chinese in 1983 was the thirty-second. In 1963 at Rockford High School, Ill., the principal forbade the play under school auspices; as did, after five Baptist ministers had protested, Vestal High School in Binghampton, N.Y. It was played in Brooklyn's Prospect Park in 1967. In 1973 the Washington Arena Stage took it to Moscow. In 1974, Asolo and Honolulu; 1975, London, with Henry Fonda as Drummond; 1979, New York's Little Church Around the Corner; 1981, Baltimore, Md. Spencer Tracy and Fredric March were in the 1960 film.

In 1965, Tennessee revoked its 1925 statute against teaching evolution; but, as Lawrence and Lee stated: "It might have happened yesterday. It could happen tomorrow." The theory is still being challenged by those who demand equal time for teaching the Bible story, which they now call "Creation science." Both sides may claim that, in Darrow's words: "The right to think is on trial." As Felix Barker put it in the *London Evening News:* "The drama belongs to the arena of the world. This sort of thing is the true stuff of the theatre . . . The fight becomes the eternal one of enlightenment versus reaction."

It is a good token, not only for the authors, that somewhere in the world, every night for a quarter of a century, there has been a performance of

Inherit the Wind. The freedom to fight for one's belief, in the challenge of science and faith, has no more vivid dramatic presentation.

THE NIGHT THOREAU SPENT IN JAIL   *Jerome Lawrence*

While *The Night Thoreau Spent in Jail* is perhaps too much of a thesis play for the commercial theatre, it is a prime example of a drama that speaks widely to the people. Jerome Lawrence and Robert E. Lee gave it to the American Playwrights Theatre, which they created to stimulate college and community groups to seek original work instead of relying upon the backwash of Broadway. Opening at Ohio State University and the University of California at Los Angeles in 1970, it has had, not a tour, but 154 separate productions around the country. It was directed by Lawrence in Dublin, March 17, 1972.

The play builds upon Henry David Thoreau's statement: "If a man does not keep pace with his companions, perhaps it is because he hears a different drummer." And it takes body from Thoreau's imprisonment for refusing to pay a federal poll tax in 1845, levied for what he deemed an evil purpose: support of the Mexican War. The play quotes a Congressman opposing the war—one Abraham Lincoln. Meanwhile, the soldiers train to the tune of "Hate-2-3-4; Hate-2-3-4 . . ."

Center stage is the cell, which expands into a schoolroom, where Henry Thoreau is ordered by Deacon Nehemiah Bell of the school board—a stereotype of rigid conformity—to flog the questioning students (theirs not to question why). Ralph Waldo Emerson (with whom Thoreau lived from 1841 into 1843) bids "Cast conformity behind you." Henry resigns as teacher in the public schools of Concord; Waldo resigns as pastor of the Boston church. But Emerson is inclined to weigh issues lengthily, holding back from action. The play's first act ends with the retorted question:

Emerson: Henry! What are you doing in jail?
Thoreau: Waldo. What are you doing out of jail?

The stage spreads, also, into a flowery meadow, into Walden Pond, where the strongbox becomes a boat. The women seem conservative. Mrs. Emerson remarks: "In order to get along, you must go along." And Henry's mother helplessly echoes Emerson: "He keeps casting conformity behind him."

John [Henry's brother]: What the hell, he's been to Harvard.
Mother: Never say—
John: Harvard. I'm sorry, Mother, I'll never say it again. (to Henry): What do you plan to do?
Henry: Well I think I'll think for a while. That'll be a change from college.

When Henry is released, as his aunt without his knowledge pays his tax, he "strides up the aisle of the theatre to the sound of his own different drummer."

Among the still timely remarks in the play is that there is "a whole country of us who only want to be liked." The playwright-novelist J. B. Priestley said to me at dinner once: "There's one thing I cannot understand about you people. It has been the fortune—or misfortune—of various countries to have a predominant position in the world. The ancient Romans.

They rode roughshod over all opposition. In the last century, England. We thought so much of ourselves that what others thought didn't matter. Now, the United States. But you want to be liked—the two don't go together!" Always *to be liked* (which implies conformity) must be weighed with *to be right,* which implies individual judgment. The one—oneself—is what mattered to Thoreau. As he wrote in *Civil Disobedience* (1849, but still a challenge): "There will never be a really free and enlightened State until the State comes to recognize the individual as a higher and independent power, from which all its own power and authority are derived." One and God make a majority. *The Night Thoreau Spent in Jail* is a vivid presentation of the continuing problem of finding a balance for the apparently irreconcilable values of society and the individual.

AUNTIE MAME   *Jerome Lawrence*

Patrick Dennis (actually Edward Everett Tanner III) wrote a story about his aunt Marian Tanner, *Auntie Mame,* which sold a million and a half copies. It told of an eccentric, wealthy, but bohemian woman who in 1928 inherited the ten-year-old Patrick and took him off to see the world. She was a warmhearted woman who matured as her relations with her growing ward progressed.

Auntie Mame was dramatized by Lawrence and Lee, presented at the New York Broadhurst, October 31, 1956, attaining 663 performances. Rosalind Russell, the first Mame, took nineteen costume changes for the play's twenty-five locales. She was succeeded by Greer Garson, Eve Arden, Sylvia Sidney, and more, including Beatrice Lillie, who played the role at the London Adelphi, September 9, 1958. Five road companies were out at the same time. Sylvia Sidney played Auntie Mame at the New York City Center, then on tour. Among numerous productions, it appeared as *Min Fantastike Tante* in Norway, 1959, with Lillebil Ibsen, Henrik Ibsen's granddaughter; at the Dublin Gate, July 3, 1963; OffOffBway (St. Bart's) in 1977. A Greenwich Village performance in 1982 was attended by eighty-one-year-old Marian Tanner, the real Auntie Mame.

With music and lyrics by Jerry Herman, choreography by Onna White, book by Lawrence and Lee, *Mame* opened in Philadelphia, April 4, 1966, then at the New York Winter Garden, May 24, with Angela Lansbury. Janis Paige, Jane Morgan, and Ann Miller followed; *Mame* moved to the Broadway for a total of 1,508 performances. The *Globe* called it "the brightest book for a musical in many a dull musical moon." The London Drury Lane production, running from February 20, 1969, to March 14, 1970, starred Ginger Rogers. *Mame* was played in many countries, twice in Mexico, twice in Japan. Among revivals: Bowdoin, Me., 1978; St. Bart's, 1979; New York, 1982, again with Angela Lansbury.

In addition to the title song, the musical was brightened with "It's Today," "Open a New Window," "My Best Girl," "The Man in the Moon Is a Lady," "If He Walked Into My Life." It was filmed with Lucille Ball in 1974.

Brooks Atkinson called Rosalind Russell "tall, slender, willowy, inexhaustible, incredibly fast with a joke, incredibly versatile in her changes of pace; she is consistently uproarious." Mame's adventures carry her from a brief spell as a Macy's salesgirl to social days at Beekman Place; to an encounter with a correctly Wasp Connecticut family, to a Georgia plantation, to the Matterhorn, to the Pyramids—always fresh and always smiling. "You're odd, but loving," says the nephew's nurse to Auntie Mame. The audience seconds the judgment.

Both the play and the musical combine character growth with highly amusing vicissitudes that strike home as warm and real.

THE GOLEM   *H. Leivik*

The Golem takes on significance as a dramatized legend symbolizing the eternal struggle of a people against oppression. According to Jewish legend, Rabbi Judah Low fashioned in Prague, about 1575, a "golem," a giant man made of clay, to help the Jews. After killing the tyrant who persecuted them, the golem (like Frankenstein's monster of a later day and the robots in *R. U. R.* *) turned upon its own people and had to be destroyed. This story is presented against a background of rich local color depicting the Jews of the East-European ghetto.

In its picture of the messianic hopes of the Jews, the play poses the problem of physical force as opposed to spiritual power. There is symbolic coincidence in the fact that a production by the Habimah Players of Tel-Aviv opened in New York on May 15, 1948, the day the Jewish state of Israel came into being.

The life of the author is also linked with the problem of the play. Studying for the rabbinate, he was expelled for reading modern Hebrew works. He then became part of the revolutionary movement of his native Russia. Sentenced in 1906 to four years in prison and to exile in Siberia for life in 1912, he escaped the next year and made his way to New York.

Written by H. Leivik (Leivik Halpern, 1888-1962), the play was published in Yiddish in 1921. Its first professional production was in Hebrew in 1925 by the Habima Players, who brought it to New York in 1927. The play was translated into English in 1928 (published in *Poet Lore*) by J. P. Augenlicht, and performed the next year. Motion pictures of the legend were made in 1921 and 1936; an opera with music by Eugen d'Albert was heard in Danzig in 1927; an oratorio with music by Vladimir Heifetz played at New York's Carnegie Hall in 1931.

American reactions have not been especially favorable to *The Golem.* The Yiddish Ensemble Art Theatre production in 1931, according to *Variety,* transformed "a theme and a plot that should have been treated with subdued reverence into a hybrid music-tragedy-comedy-farce" with the "story sequence submerged in a mass of extraneous horseplay." The *New York Herald Tribune* called it "a grim artistic triumph," but the *New York Times* declared it "slow-moving, undramatic."

To the 1948 Hebrew presentation the *Times* was more generous: "Things happen plainly enough to engage an onlooker's interest and emotions . . . The final conflict is vivid enough to render translation unnecessary."

The Golem is a dramatic monument to a period that has gone and to a question that remains unanswered: Must force be used, or can one rely on spirit, against the oppression of tyrants?

The Golem was produced OffBway (Center Stage) in 1958 and (Jean Cocteau Rep.) 1982. Marc Chagall designed sets for a "new approach" by Lionel Abel, which did not find a stage.

THE MERRY WIDOW   *Victor Leon*

When *Die Lustige Witwe (The Merry Widow)* opened in Vienna on December 30, 1905, its gay and lively airs took the city by storm. It became a great success all over Europe. Based on *La Petite Ville,* 1801, by Louis

Baptiste Picard (French, 1769-1828), the best playwright of the Napoleonic era, *The Merry Widow,* with book by Victor Leon (Austrian, 1858-1940) and Leo Stein (1872-1947) and music by Franz Lehar (Austrian, 1870-1948) opened in London, June 8, 1907, and ran for 778 performances. By the time of its New York premiere, October 21, 1907, with Donald Brian and Ethel Jackson, there were a hundred "merry widow" variations romping on a hundred stages. The operetta ran for 419 performances in New York and started a vogue of "Merry Widow" hats, dresses, drinks, and conversation. London saw revivals in May 1923, in May 1924, in 1932, in March 1943, in September 1944, and in April 1952. The operetta was burlesqued in New York, January 2, 1908, for 156 performances. *The Merry Widow* itself was revived in New York in 1921, 1929, 1931, and 1932. On August 4, 1943, it opened for 318 performances with Jan Kiepura, Martha Eggerth, and conductor Robert Stolz, who had conducted the Vienna premiere. It was seen again in New York in 1944—this time at the City Center. It has had some 250,000 performances in twenty-four languages and is still in live repertory. There were film versions in 1911, with Wallace Reid and Alma Rubens; in 1925 with Mae Murray; in 1934 with Jeanette MacDonald and Maurice Chevalier, and in 1952 with Lana Turner.

The story is a simple one. Sonia of Marsovia, widowed young, takes her good looks and some twenty million francs to have a good time in Paris. Many men naturally seek her hand, but the Marsovian Ambassador, Baron Popoff, has instructions to see that she marries a Marsovian. The Baron picks as husband-to-be Prince Danilo. He and Sonia had loved before she married money; piqued, he is having a good time with Fifi, Jou-Jou, Clo-Clo, Lo-Lo, and other French girls at Maxim's. Sonia, too, is piqued at the thought that she should marry to order, but after considerable gaiety and roundabout dalliance, the old love wins through.

The Merry Widow has continued to be popular because its comedy is gay, wholesome, and fresh, but mainly because its music is tuneful, lively, and easily remembered. At the New York premiere the waltz "I Love You So" spurred a spontaneous demonstration of cheering and wild applause such as is seldom heard. *The Merry Widow* remains one of the most engaging and delightful of operettas.

Among innumerable performances: Kiepura and Eggerth sang it again in London in 1955, and at the New York City Center in 1957, its fiftieth anniversary. (Kiepura sang the martial song in Polish. There was new choreography by George Balanchine, but the two did not dance—in the original they quarrel while waltzing.)

In 1962 the original German was sung at New York Carnegie Hall, with a running humorous narrative delivered by Hiram Sherman. In 1964 Mischa Auer played Popoff in New York and on a seventeen-week tour. In 1967 the play opened for the seventh time at the Paper Mill Playhouse, N.J. In 1974 it was presented in Spanish at the New York City Center; at one time in Buenos Aires it played in five theatres in five languages. London saw it again in 1980; in summer 1981 it traveled the U.S. straw-hat circuit. Among those who have played the young and merry widow are Maria Jeritza, Fritzi Massary, Patrice Munsel, Kirsten Flagstad, Evelyn Laye, Kitty Carlisle, and Margot Fonteyn.

BRIGADOON   *Alan Jay Lerner*

Seldom in a single season does Broadway rejoice in two musical shows that prove lengthily haunting; but, scarcely two months apart, *Finian's*

Rainbow* was followed by *Brigadoon*. Opening on March 13, 1947, the latter won the Critics' Circle award as the best musical of the year. After 560 performances and a successful tour it returned, May 2, 1950, for three more weeks in New York. Some 886 performances were at His Majesty's, London, opening April 14, 1949.

What chiefly lifted *Brigadoon* above similar plays was the complete integration of the theatrical arts it achieved. The music by Frederick Loewe, the dances by Agnes de Mille, and the book and lyrics by Alan Jay Lerner fused in a rich union.

Brigadoon takes us to Scotland and to whimsyland, where two American hunters come upon the village of Brigadoon on the one day in every hundred years on which it rises from the mists of magic to become a living, pulsing village once again. When the town comes to life the two hunters are entranced with its ways, and with two Brigadoonian maids. So deeply is one of the men smitten that, after his return to the United States, he journeys back to the forest glen in Scotland, where love works its magic and bears him again to Brigadoon.

The heart of Brigadoon is MacConnachy Square. The name is a cue to its Scottish fantasy, for James M. Barrie called his "unruly half—the writing half" by the name of M'Connachie. George Jean Nathan noted that the plot is "a pleasant, if strangely unacknowledged, paraphrase of Friedrich Wilhelm Gerstächer's little German classic, *Germelhausen*." The German story, written in 1862, does not have the final episode of the modern man returning to the old-time girl in the vanished village. In truth the American play might well have omitted this, too; for here, as Kronenberger said, the piece "flops down to a banal Broadway level."

Especially attractive is the manner in which the dances, beautiful in themselves, lead on the action. "A kind of idyllic rhythm flows through the whole pattern of the production," declared Brooks Atkinson. "The funeral dance, to the dour tune of bagpipes, brings the forestep of doom into the forest."

The village of Brigadoon has more charm and reality than most existing communities, and displays it in a feat musical.

The choreography by Agnes De Mille included a lively Sword Dance. Among the songs were "I'll Go Home with Bonnie Jean," "Come to Me, Bend to Me," "It's Almost Like Being in Love."

The New York City Center played it in 1957 with Helen Gallagher and Scott McKay; played it again in 1962, 1963, 1964, 1967, 1968. In 1980 it came to the National Theatre, Washington; to New Orleans; and to the New York Majestic with ice skates.

MINNA VON BARNHELM   *Gotthold Ephraim Lessing*

Educated for the priesthood, Gotthold Ephraim Lessing (German, 1729-1781) preferred social criticism and the theatre. In 1766 the newly organized Hamburg National Theatre invited him to be its official poet. Not wishing to grind out plays to meet popular need, he refused the post, but he accepted appointment as critic and began the penetrating body of criticism known as the *Hamburg Dramaturgy*, deemed by many to rank next to Aristotle's *Poetics* among the world's considerations of the drama.

In 1767, Lessing's *Minna von Barnhelm* was produced at the Hamburg National Theatre. This first German comedy to present contemporary life was an immediate success; it has proved a lasting favorite. It was produced in New York in 1904 and in 1920, in German, at the Irving Place Theatre.

Germany saw productions in 1928, 1931, 1934; on the radio from Munich in 1937; and in Berlin in 1940. Of a 1937 London production, W. A. Darlington observed in the *Telegraph* (July 14): "To me, the play was a very pleasant surprise . . . By modern standards it is stiff and conventional, but there is no mistaking the life in it."

Modern standards have indeed made the central theme of the play seem less a basic social problem than a stickler's scruple. In the drama, a Prussian army officer, Major von Tellheim, is discharged on an accusation of embezzlement. Despite her faith in him, he releases the wealthy Minna von Barnhelm from their engagement. When he clears his honor, Minna for a time gives Tellheim a dose of his own medicine, pretending to have lost her fortune and to refuse him because of their unequal status.

The story is thin, but the characters are delineated with keen observation, with natural and sympathetic colors, and with a deep sense of integrity. The lofty concept of womanhood in it, and of the nobility of the army officer, helped keep the play a favorite on the German stage. "Since Sara Sampson and her lover perished by violence on the Frankfort stage," said Magnus, "the weeping heroine of everyday life has dominated the social problem drama." And since Minna taught her lover a lesson on the Hamburg stage, Sara's smiling sisters have shown the theatre that, given love and faith and a firm spirit, many social problems can be solved. In both types of social drama, Lessing was a vigorous pioneer.

In translation by Anthony Dent, London saw the play beginning December 10, 1964. In New York in German, it was played at Barnard College, 1957, and at the Barbizon Plaza, 1968.

NATHAN THE WISE   *Gotthold Ephraim Lessing*

After Lessing became involved in religious controversy, the authorities forbade his further critical writing on the ground that he "antagonized the principal doctrines of the sacred writings of Christianity." He therefore determined to try the theatre again. In the meantime, he had lost his wife and child; out of his grief and loneliness grew a spirit of tolerance and peace. The fierce attack his opponents expected in his new work proved, instead, a compassionate picture of understanding and love—Lessing's best play, *Nathan the Wise,* 1779. The plot was to some extent suggested by *Edward and Eleonora,* a play by James Thomson, published in 1739. Lessing called his play "the son of my old age, whom polemics helped to bring into the world." It was the rich product of his maturity.

Set in Jerusalem, the play presents a tangled tale through which to reach its moral of tolerance. A Christian knight is given permission by the Jew Nathan to wed his daughter Recha. The Patriarch of Jerusalem, learning that Recha is really a Christian child brought up by the Jew, wants to have Nathan killed. The case is brought before the Sultan Saladin, whose clear-sighted justice and objective tolerance set an example for Christian and Jew alike.

The most famous part of the play is the story of the three rings (also told in Boccaccio's *Decameron),* which Nathan tells in his defense before Saladin. For generations, Nathan says, a royal line had left the favorite son a most precious ring, a talisman of love and peace. At length came a king who had three sons, equally beloved. He called in a jeweler and had two duplicates of the ring made, and when he died each son claimed to be the heir. The judge ruled that each should hold a third of the kingdom; after years had gone by, the prevalence of justice and peace would prove which was authentic. Similarly, by the spread of love and justice and peace, humanity may know which is the true religion.

"If God held all truth in his right hand," said Lessing, "and in his left nothing but the ever-restless impulse toward truth, though with the condition of ever erring, and said to me 'Choose!', I should humbly fall at his feet and say 'Father, give me the left; pure truth is for Thee alone'." This recognition that to err is human was at the core of Lessing's spirit; it brought calm in the midst of passion, love in the midst of hate.

Produced posthumously, 1783, the play passed almost unnoted, but after Goethe and Schiller revived it at Weimar in 1801 it became tremendously popular and has never gone out of favor in the German theatre. It was the first play Max Reinhardt presented in Berlin after World War I. Burned by the Nazis in 1933, it was acted in London by a German company during World War II. In New York, the play has had numerous productions in German. In English, Erwin Piscator's 1942 Dramatic Workshop production was so well received that it moved to the Belasco Theatre on Broadway; the play was revived again at the Dramatic Workshop in 1944.

The Dramatic Workshop used an English translation of Ferdinand Bruckner's adaptation of Lessing's play. Bruckner,* said John Mason Brown (March 12, 1942), "denies the plot its multiplicity and suspense, exiles the Sultan to the wings and eliminates entirely such helpful characters as Hofi and the Sultan's chess-playing sister," but helps by omitting the "lost-baby combinations" at the end. Brown found the play powerful: "The blaze of Lessing's intellect and heart is such that no Nazi could hope to survive it." Robert Coleman stressed the play's "eloquent, timely, and timeless words . . . a literary landmark." Richard Watts was a dissenter; he called the play "a garrulous and undramatic work, with the nobility of its spirit atoning for its essential tediousness." Brooks Atkinson considered it "an admirable and profoundly moving play."

It is the simplicity and the calm of its plea for the brotherhood of man that give the play its permanent power. Robert Garland well said (February 22, 1944): "It is this quality of quietude, of composure and control, that gives the work its undeniable effectiveness . . . Something to think about, something to take home with you and treasure."

One may cavil at the end of the play (omitted by Bruckner) in its revelation that the Jewish Recha is a Christian after all (a twist also seen in *Gentleman's Agreement,* a 1948 novel), for this removes rather than solves the problems of interrelationship; but this is a detail in an otherwise superbly integrated dramatic study of understanding and love.

Productions in England include London Sadler's Wells in German, 1958; English at Croydon, 1968. London saw the Bruckner version, adapted by Jack Lindsay, in 1967 at the Mermaid.

Clarence Derwent gave a dramatic reading of an adaptation by Melchior Lengyel at the Library of Congress, January 24, 1953. New York heard it in German (Düsseldorfer Schauspielhaus) in 1962; in the same year (March 22, 1962) in English OffOffBway (Finch College) for two weeks; and OffOff Bway (Soho), February 1982.

DEATHTRAP   *Ira Levin*

Deathtrap, part guessing game, part parody of the old-time mysteries, was the first play of Ira Levin (b. 1929), whose best-selling novels of suspense, *Rosemary's Baby* and *The Boys from Brazil,* were also hit films.

The plot concerns Sidney Bruhl, playwright, who has not had a hit in ten years; his last four ventures were flops. Then a pupil of his, Clifford Anderson, sent him what seems a surefire "smash" drama. Sidney is tempted; he invites Cliff to his Westport, Conn., home, telling him to bring along the other copy of his play. At the home is lawyer Porter Milgrim, also bitten by the writing bug. Another guest is Helga ten Dorp, a misty medium reminiscent of the weird Madame Arcati in Noel Coward's *Blithe Spirit.** Will Clifford get away safely with his play? Will Sidney get away with it, and recapture his reputation? The plot twists and turns, with unexpected discombobulations, deftly and amusingly swerving just before each crisis.

A program note, as in the good old mysteries, requests that the outcome remain unrevealed. Obediently, every Broadway reviewer kept it untold. Ruthlessly, I continue. Sidney's wife, at first horrified at his intention, then accepts and welcomes Cliff. But when she dies, of a "heart attack," there is a suggestion that Sidney's plot against Clifford was really a device to get rid of her. Clifford becomes aware of Sidney's purpose, and suggests that *there* is a surefire plot; they cooperate, to make the playing team "Bruhl and Anderson" as famous as "Rodgers and Heartless." But they constantly bicker, with pistol shots, handcuffs, and other stabs at mayhem; until Sidney shoots Clifford with a crossbow, arranges the scene, calls the police, announces that his secretary Clifford has attacked him with an ax, and he has killed him in self-defense. As he talks, the bloody Clifford rises, stabs Sidney viciously with the crossbow bolt, and collapses. Stage direction: "Sidney gasps and twitches and dies."

Since this is their last appearance, we must assume that these deaths are final. In the next scene, the medium—who claims she has forecast the deaths—and the lawyer decide to take over and complete the "surefire hit." But they quarrel about splitting the profits; the lawyer calls her foul names; she goes for him with a dagger; they circle the stage for combat as the final curtain falls. When the police arrive (we now may prophesy) the entire cast will be corpses.

The play opened at the New York Music Box, February 26, 1978, with John Wood as the desperate playwright, and ran for 1,793 performances, with Patrick Horgan twice (August 28 to September 3; November 27 to December 11) and then Stacy Keach (January 15, 1979) replacing Wood. At the London Garrick, October 26, 1978, Denis Quilly played Sidney; Rosemary McHale, his wife; Philip Sayer, Clifford; Joyce Grant, the medium Helga. Robert Moore, who'd played Sidney twelve times in New York, on tour stepped into the role at the last minute in Fort Lauderdale, Fla., instead of Patrick Macnee. The play reached Toronto on December 3, 1979. In London, then Chicago, and thereafter, with Brian Bedford as Sidney, the ending (coda) was restaged. The play was given twenty performances in Anchorage, Alaska, opening February 26, 1978. It held for twenty-five performances in Richmond, Va., beginning December 26, 1980.

Jack Kroll in *Newsweek* said that watching *Deathtrap* was "like a ride on a good roller-coaster when screams and laughs mingle." T. E. Kalem in *Time* (with a double *ass* to avoid a cliché) exclaimed: "If you care to assassinate yourself with laughter, try *Deathtrap*." The play is an ingenious mixture of parody and stress, a delightful deviation from the usual drama mystery.

SPRINGTIME FOR HENRY   *Benn Levy*

One of the most popular farces among stock companies and summer theatres is *Springtime For Henry,* written by Benn Wolf Levy (English,

1900-1973) in 1931. It is a crackbrained farce that turns the moral code topsyturvy and elevates the reckless spirit of man against the curbs of commonplace convention.

The story is absurdly simple and simply absurd. Henry Dewlip, a wealthy London automobile manufacturer, is a gay old roué; under the influence of his new secretary, Angela Smith, who likes "the Decent Thing," he reforms; then he relapses. But this story has many other twists. It turns out that the secretary, Angela Smith, is a self-made widow; she shot her husband in the Touraine. He was a Frenchman who brought two mistresses home to tea, an act which Angela thought a bit excessive and a bad example for their little boy. The jury acquitted her. It turns out, too, that when Henry reforms he gives up his flirtation with the wife of his best friend Jelliwell; this throws her back on her husband's company—to the desperate boredom of both. Jelliwell complains to Dewlip; his happiness depends upon his wife's having an extramural interest. The reformed Henry has also been boring his friends at the Club. So, out of regard for his fellow-men, Henry goes back to his rakish ways. As he proceeds toward the consummation of his intrigue with his friend's not unwilling wife, Jelliwell and Miss Smith disclose that they have discovered love in the mirror of one another's eyes.

This story came to New York on December 9, 1931, for a run of 199 performances. Its hilarious situations and slily twinkling dialogue were an instant joy. Leslie Banks (later, Henry Hull), Nigel Bruce, Helen Chandler and Frieda Inescourt excellently conveyed its "intelligently slapstick mood," said Robert Garland; "it had the audience in hysterics." When the play opened in London on November 8, 1932, it won equally favorable comment; the *Evening News* called it "that rarest of productions, a farce that does not insult the intellect."

Springtime For Henry is indeed, as Brooks Atkinson has said, "a marvelously demented bit of impish fancy. . . . the most skillful farce written in English in many years." The dialogue is as unexpected as it is hilarious. There are few funnier narrations in any drama than the story of Perseus and Andromache that Jelliwell tells to Angela. Situations and details of stage business continuously freshen the fun.

Especially effective in the play were the devices of Edward Everett Horton, who began playing Henry in 1933, and, after eighteen years of touring the United States, brought the play to New York on March 14, 1951. The date of the story was wisely set back to 1911, giving it a delightful period flavor.

In 1931, the play provided a lift of laughter against the depression. A decade later, the Texan *Dallas News* (April 6, 1940) called it "as complete an escape from the war, taxes, politics, the census, and canker worms as can be had outside a flagon of spirits." But a basic value of art, even comedy, even farce, is that it provides not an *escape from* but a *springboard to* a world where irresistible social and natural forces are irrelevant in the face of the soaring independence of man. *Springtime For Henry* continues to be a delightfully irreverent thrust of sheer absurdity against the solemn forces that would burden and bind the spirit of man.

The New York Golden showed the play in 1951, and again in 1957. After a revival at the Oxford summer festival, August 6, 1974, *Stage and TV Today* found "the dialogue invariably funny and often witty, with crisply turned phrases . . . the action bubbles briskly along."

Edward Everett Horton played Henry over 1,100 times. Not especially as a result of his play, Benn Levy was elected to Parliament in 1948.

LIFE WITH FATHER   *Howard Lindsay*

Begun as a series of sketches in the *New Yorker* by Clarence Day (American, 1874-1935), *Life With Father* was issued as a book in 1935, then transformed by Howard Lindsay (American, 1889-1968) and Russel Crouse (American, 1893-1966) into a play that achieved the world's longest unbroken run. Opening at the Empire Theatre on November 8, 1939, it closed on July 12, 1947, with a record of 3,224 performances, forty-two more than its closest rival, *Tobacco Road*. Actor, manager, play doctor, and author Lindsay and Broadway journalist Crouse drew out of virtually no story, merely a series of lively episodes from Clarence Day's memories, a delightfully real picture of family life in a fairly well-to-do New York home of the 1880's.

Such plot as there is revolves around Mother Day's determination to have Father Day—whose parents had neglected the ritual in his childhood—consent to be baptized. But it is the wholesome vitality of the bewildering Days and their four red-headed sons that maintains the constant comedy.

Foremost, of course, is Father Day, by turns irascible and complacent, king-pin, cock of the walk, roaring "My Gawd!" in frequent anger, constantly concerned over the family expenditures and Mother's inability to keep accounts; yet tender and even sentimental on occasion. Mother Day, who bows to her proper master, is humorless and naïve, yet knows how to turn a situation to her advantage. Through sheer misunderstanding she wins her way in money matters, as her love and warmth and bending persistence guard her brood. These are buoyant, living people. "Merely as a play it may be unimportant," said John Mason Brown, "but as a biography of everyone's family, except Caspar Milquetoast's, it is as shrewdly drawn as it is ingratiating." Brooks Atkinson called it "a perfect comedy."

It is such an amusing piece of Americana, such an "authentic part of our American folklore," as Atkinson said, that we might expect the play to be attacked by those that profess to despise the American way of life. The one dissenting critical voice did come from the Communist *Daily Worker*: "There is not a moment of honest joy or passion in its daguerreotype tableaux. Father is a stuffed shirt who never condescends to a lovable moment of human uncertainty. . . . When it becomes a matter of chivalry, understanding, and simple human compassion, we'll take one of Saroyan's drunks—in a pinch . . . *Life With Father* may be good propaganda, but it's bad art."

It's hard to see what these dramatized character sketches are propaganda for—other than the basic goodness of human nature—but, as deftly presented in *Life With Father*, they rise to excellent theatrical art. Howard Lindsay himself played Father Day in the original cast; his wife Dorothy Stickney played Mother. In the eight years of the play's run, those that played Mother Day included Lily Cahill, Nydia Westman, Margalo Gillmore, Dorothy Gish, and Lillian Gish. Several "generations" of young actors outgrew the roles of the Day boys.

In England the play opened June 5, 1947, and was received with polite enthusiasm. Critic Harold Hobson called it "simple, rollicking fun."

This epic of the brownstone front with its lively and genial picture of old New York went so gently into the hearts of its beholders as to win the play a preeminent place among long-loved productions in the American theatre.

Life With Mother, by the same authors, also with Lindsay and his wife in the cast, opened in 1949 for 265 performances. In the *Father* play, the problem was his baptism; in the *Mother* play, her problem was that, although married for twenty-five years, she had never been given an engagement ring. Life is a chain of trivial links.

STATE OF THE UNION   *Howard Lindsay*

Out of the current headlines and the national situation, "obviously inspired by Wendell Willkie," said the *New Yorker,* November 24, 1945, the team of Lindsay and Crouse, abetted by the deft director Bretaigne Windust, produced a swift and sharp comedy of American life, *State of the Union.* A personal situation of natural figures is blent with a national problem of basic issues.

In the play, Grant Matthews, a straightforward and successful airplane manufacturer with a breezy personality and eloquent, engaging ways, is picked by the power politicians as a presidential candidate. On his campaign tour he must of course be accompanied, not by Kay Thorndike, the ambitious newspaper publisher who is his mistress, but by the sedate and sensitive wife from whom he has been alienated. Mary Matthews, understanding the situation, consents to go with Grant because she loves him. And on the trip, helped by her unobtrusive understanding, he comes to see that he is an implement of Kay Thorndike's compromising ambition and a cat's-paw for the politicians. At a dinner party at which the birds of prey are gathered, Mary helps Grant set the eagle free: over the radio he repudiates his scheming backers, and promises to give the public his own ideas and his unbossed service. In Mary's words, Grant sears his discarded sponsors: "You're all thinking about the next election instead of the next generation."

The play opened in Philadelphia, October 10, 1945; it came to New York, November 14, 1945, with Ralph Bellamy, Ruth Hussey, and Kay Johnson, for 765 performances and the Pulitzer Prize, followed by a national tour and a 1948 film with Spencer Tracy and Katharine Hepburn. In 1960, somewhat updated, it was shown at the Bucks County Playhouse. Lewis Nichols in the *Times* stated that "with wonderfully funny lines and situations, this new comedy about politics also has enough sentiment to keep it from being farce and enough idea to show that its heart is in the right place . . . about the serious side of their play, they are not joking at all." Lewis Kronenberger found virtue even in the play's failings: "By not trying to say too much, it says what it does with simple vigor; by not trying to cut too deep, it has its own kind of quick, sharp sting; by not becoming too involved about problems, it remains interesting about people . . . a plea that never becomes a preachment, and a lot of fun to boot."

The marital story of Grant and Mary is neatly knitted with the political drive of the play. Grant's manager, his mistress, his wife, and Grant himself are drawn to human measure; in and through them we see, on an individual scale, the conflict between opportunism and integrity that, on the national scale, is the country's major conflict. The representatives of the power groups are more typical figures. The southern judge and his bibbling wife, the bullying millionaire, the female leader of a national pressure group, are at once near enough truth to be broad satire and near enough caricature to be gay fun. The husband-and-wife relationship, incidentally, was prophetic of an actual situation in a recent presidential campaign. As long as such plays as this can be prizewinners and can tour the land to crowded theatres, there is still a bright aspect to the state of the union.

HADRIAN VII   *Peter Luke*

Frederick William Serafino Austin Lewis Mary Rolfe (also known as Baron Corvo, 1860-1913) was a man disappointed in his desire, in what he deemed his vocation, to become a Catholic priest. He led a life of austere poverty, supporting himself by writing *Hadrian VII* (1904) and other books. Out of his life and works Peter Luke (b. 1919) fashioned the drama *Hadrian VII*.

When the play opens, we see the impoverished Rolfe, in his forties, visited by two bailiffs threatening to take his belongings, as he refuses the help of his concupiscent landlady. The bailiffs come again, but in the guise of Rolfe's friendly old Bishop of Caerleon and the Cardinal of Pimlico. The Cardinal is on the Vatican committee to seek a new Pope, the Conclave in Rome having been unable to achieve the required two-thirds majority. In their questioning of Rolfe, both his bitterness and his basic righteousness come through. When they leave, Jeremiah Sant, a fanatic Protestant demagogue, comes in; he taunts Rolfe with his poverty, and threatens doom to all papists.

In Rome, although, like the real Rolfe, he had been twice expelled from seminaries, Rolfe, confessed and absolved, is elected Pope. He chooses the name of the only English Pope before him, Nicholas Breakspear, Hadrian IV, Pope 1154-1159. The new Pope at once dismays the Cardinals by attempting to clear the Church of secular activities and concerns. More personally significant, in George Arthur Rose, whom he makes his secretary, Rolfe recognizes a young, questioning, troubled nature, as once was his, and in the Pope there awakens a fellow-feeling; his bitterness is dispelled by a new humanity, the birth of a spiritual love that ennobles him.

Meanwhile, his old landlady, who has become intimate with the Protestant Sant, like Potiphar's wife turns the facts about, claiming that Rolfe had sought to seduce her; the gloating Sant spreads the scandal, and comes to Rome to seek revenge. Rolfe calls Sant his own enemy, and in a rage Sant shoots him.

As Brother Rose makes tearful encomium and the funeral cortege moves off, Rolfe as we saw him at the beginning comes on, and Rose and Rolfe together say: "Let us pray for the repose of his soul. He was so tired."

In a final scene, Rolfe is back in his shabby London boardinghouse; we recognize that Rome and the papacy have been a wishful dream. The landlady announces two men: "Oh yes, of course, Their Lordships. Show them up, please." The two bailiffs enter and proceed to take the furniture. One picks up a manuscript. Rolfe explains:

> "It's about a man who makes the fatuous and frantic mistake of living before his time."
> "Any value?"
> "It's a masterpiece and therefore probably not worth tuppence. At the same time, it is probably beyond price."

They take out the last of the furniture. One bailiff returns and takes the manuscript from Rolfe . . . and the curtain falls.

Hadrian VII was produced in Birmingham, May 9, 1967; at the London Mermaid, April 18, 1968; moving to the Haymarket, March 18, 1969, it attained 988 performances, with Alec McCowen and Sydney Sturges as the landlady. It was recognized as a vivid portrait of a man who feels unjustly denied his proper place in the scheme of things, a widespread malaise in the modern world. Harold Hobson in the *Sunday Times* observed that the play "appeals to extremely powerful elements in human nature. Everyone who feels in himself the presence of extraordinary abilities which an envious world has failed to recognize, will find this splendid, colorful, recklessly melodramatic and vituperatively brilliant drama speaks to him in irresistible tones." The New York critics, on its opening at the Helen Hayes, January 8, 1969, also with Alec McCowen, were equally impressed; it had 166 performances. Whitney Bolton in the *Telegraph* called it "a moving, at moments shattering play of pageantry and dimension, a play of violent colors and wrenching frustrations." McCowen and his first two replacements (Barry Morse and Douglas Rain) played Rolfe as a "wiry, crabby would-be martyr whose humanity remained obstinately obscured behind a vitriolic wit"; Paul Daneman, who succeeded these, emphasized his awakening from church concerns to human values.

Also in 1969, Hume Cronyn as Rolfe went from Los Angeles to Stratford, Ontario; then (March 2, 1970) to Washington, D.C., as part of a national tour. The play has been produced in Greece, Italy, Mexico, Spain, France, Japan, Denmark, Norway, Finland, and Iceland. In 1980 Hadrian found shelter in the Church of the Heavenly Rest, OffBway. Rousing in its humor, deep in its compassion, *Hadrian VII* presents in its fantasy world emotions pertinent and penetrant in our own.

BABES IN TOYLAND   *Glen MacDonough*

The charming musical extravaganza *Babes in Toyland* is an American offshoot of the typical English pantomime such as *Babes in the Wood.* *With book by Glen MacDonough (1866-1924) and music by Victor Herbert (1859-1924), the play opened in Chicago, then came to New York, October 13, 1903, for 192 performances. Although it calls for a large cast, and invites spectacular settings, it has been frequently played about the country. In 1937 it set a record for attendance in St. Louis, with 71,365 persons at seven performances.

A "small" version on tour came to New York's Town Hall in 1972. The full show was on tour in 1973; at Westbury, L.I., Music Fair in 1977. In 1979 a tour of twenty-two cities ending at the New York Felt Forum brought a "contemporary version," with three "babes" of a rock group stumbling into an old amusement park called Toyland; it made use of giant puppets for many of the toys. The original was played in Toronto in 1980. With a somewhat "more cheerful story" the book was adapted by the ingenious director of LOOM, William Mount-Burke, and Alice Hammerstein Mathias, and entered the LOOM repertory, its biggest hit in 1978. In this version, the brother and sister run away from Toyland, and eventually humanize their rigid parents, with love unselfish and abiding.

Babes in Toyland opens in Mother Goose Land, in the garden of Contrary Mary. Bo Peep, Red Riding Hood, Tom Tom, Bobby Shaftoe, and many more of the nursery rhyme folk are there. The rich miser Barnaby, uncle of Alan and Jane, has seized Mother Hubbard's cottage for debt. The gay country dances, the carefree songs, are chilled by the miser's scowl. Act II shifts the scene to Toyland, particularly to the shop of the Master Toymaker, whose toys in human shape become possessed of the spirit of evil and kill their maker. In Act III Alan is brought to the scaffold for the murder; then old

Barnaby drinks the poison he had prepared for Alan; and his death solves the problems.

The sentimental appearances of the Mother Goose figures in their rhyme adventures, the jollity of the dialogue and of the familiar folk in episodes irrelevant but endeared by childhood associations: all these, as the *New York World* remarked, are "linked together with some of the most enchanting melodies Victor Herbert ever wrote, surviving far beyond the magic of childhood.

Best remembered of the songs is the delightful

> *Put down six and carry two;*
> *My, but this is hard to do . . .*
> *I don't care what teacher says,*
> *I can't do that sum.*

"Rock-a-bye Baby" and the Mignonette serenade also linger, as does the delightful March of the Wooden Soldiers to the rescue, down the stairs of alphabet blocks. *Babes in Toyland* retains all the charm of the hours in which one watches one's grandchildren at happy play.

MANDRAGOLA   *Niccolò Machiavelli*

The brilliance and the cynicism of the Italy of the Medici shine in this lively and bawdy drama. When the Medici family re-entered Florence in 1512, Niccolò Machiavelli (1469-1527), suspected of having plotted against them, was given "four twists of the rack" and sent into exile. He subsequently wrote *Mandragola*. Printed in 1524, it was supposedly based on an actual occurrence in 1504. When Machiavelli was restored to favor, *Mandragola* was presented before Pope Leo X at Rome; the Pope ordered a theatre built so that the people could see the play. Catherine de Medici and Henri II of France saw it at Lyons in 1548. *Mandragola* is, said J. A. Symonds in *Renaissance in Italy* (1876) "the ripest and most powerful play in the Italian language." Macaulay esteemed the play below only the best of Molière. Voltaire said he would surrender all of Aristophanes to have *Mandragola*.

The story is simple, in the Renaissance taste. Old Nicia wants a cure for his wife Lucrezia's sterility. Her would-be lover, Callimaco, disguised as a doctor, administers the fecundating mandrake (mandragola) root. But there is a hitch. The first one thereafter to lie with her, so they assure Nicia, will absorb the poison of the mandrake and be in peril of death. Nicia and the doctor seek a victim to purify Lucrezia; they pick—Callimaco.

This is, as the *Los Angeles Times* (April 22, 1935) averred after a performance in its city, "a lusty tale, which the brilliant wit of Machiavelli wove into a complicated intrigue, sinister yet ripe with the hearty swing of a swift medieval pungency." Around the intrigue move typical figures of the Italian Renaissance, shrewdly pricked with darts of satire or illuminated with beams of wit. Prominent among these is the cynical confessor, Frate Timoteo, a prime representative of mocking monks.

A German version by Paul Eger, acted in Berlin in 1912 to music by Ignatz Waghalter, was presented in New York with book by Alfred Kreymborg, March 4, 1925. It contained some charming songs, especially one in praise of love, sung by Bianca, niece of old Pandolfo (the names were changed), but in general the pungency and wit of Machiavelli were not recaptured. There was more vigor and bustle in the Ashley Dukes adaptation shown in London in 1939, which, according to the *New Statesman and Nation* (December 23), was "not Machiavelli, but excellent entertainment."

Harold Hobson, in the *Christian Science Monitor* (March 9, 1940), noted a present significance in *Mandragola* in that "it windows a mentality that has deeply deflected the course of human events, and is said to influence the policy today of some leading figures of Central Europe."

The incidents of *Mandragola* were used as though they had happened to Machiavelli himself in W. Somerset Maugham's story *Then and Now* (1946). The gullible old husband, horned on his dilemma, might be offered a different remedy today, but the characters of *Mandragola* are still as full of life as the bawdy play is full of the joy of living.

The nature of the story made the play a prime target for college humorists, with puns and all sorts of suggestive jokes. Among these: translation by I. A. Portner, Harvard University, 1963; English by Frederick May and Eric Bentley, Amherst, 1968; Columbia, 1979. Yale sent a company on tour as far as Los Angeles.

Inevitably came the musical, February 15, 1967, book and lyrics by Michael Alfreds; music, mixing jazz and old-style musical comedy, by Anthony Bowles, reaching the London Criterion, April 16, 1970. *Mandrake,* as they called it, unfortunately tried too hard; "flounders funnily, but sinks," said the *Observer* (April 19, 1970). The dialogue ranged from cute to crude; one sugary love song includes a four-letter word that rhymes with *luck.* On the whole, more bored than bawd.

In April 1970, the Cinoherni Klub of Prague used *Mandragola* to open the World Theatre season at the Aldwych. In modernized translation by Wallace Shawn (who played Prologue and the wily servant), it opened December 6, 1977, at the New York Public, "a 450-year-old story about today." The NT (Olivier), opened June 14, 1984, is a modernized, bawdy dance of deceit.

THE BLUE BIRD   *Maurice Maeterlinck*

In *The Blue Bird,* 1908, the gloom and pessimism of Maurice Maeterlinck (1862-1949) are wholly dissipated by the sun of happiness and love. Here symbolism and fantasy combine with complete clarity in a charming play that has remained popular with theatregoers of all ages. Soon after it was written, the play was produced in Russia and in England. New York saw it in 1910, 1911, 1913, 1915, and 1923; Pasadena in 1929 and 1937; Seattle in 1934; Chapel Hill, North Carolina, in 1938. After its world premiere in Russia (September 30, 1908), the play enjoyed popularity in that country right up to 1930, in Stanislavsky's and other companies. It was revived there in 1936. At one time it was being shown by fifty-nine different companies in almost as many countries.

The story concerns a poor woodcutter's children, Tyltyl and his sister Mytil, who set forth on Christmas Eve to seek the blue bird of happiness, accompanied by Milk, Fire, Water, Bread, and Light, as well as by the Cat and the Dog. They first hunt for happiness in the past. In the land of memory, they find their grandparents, kept alive by the children's thoughts. Next they visit the Kingdom of the Future. Many adventures entangle them, including an escape from the forest in which the Cat would destroy them. In the end, they come back to find the blue bird of happiness awaiting them at home. They give the bird to a sick neighbor child. After the neighbor has tasted joy and the children have found happiness in the giving, the bird flies away.

The theme of the play charmingly grows through the quest of the children. Even through their joyous journey, we constantly glimpse the dark forces of the universe, lurking and watching for a relaxed moment in man's vigilance, ready to thrust humanity back into the seething depths of evil.

Maeterlinck visualizes the story of man as a lonely adventure in a hostile world. In a discussion of the play, he declared: "We are alone, absolutely alone on this chance planet, and, amid all the forms of life that surround us not one, excepting the dog, has made an alliance with us . . . In the world of plants we have dumb and motionless slaves, but they serve us in spite of themselves, and, as soon as we lose sight of them, they hasten to betray us and return to their former wild and mischievous liberty."

Maeterlinck's idea was further developed in a review of the play in the *New York Dramatic Mirror* (October 5, 1910): "every object, animate or inanimate, has its own soul or essence of being . . . All this symbolism is lost, however, in the panoramic splendor of the production . . . *The Blue Bird* may nest as long as it wishes to at the New Theatre, secure in the support of a wide popular interest in ornithology."

This play has indeed been popular all over the world. The reasons for its success were well put by the French statesman Leon Blum: "The originality of Maurice Maeterlinck, as a thinker, lies in his having united in a single system the Alexandrian or German mysticism and the Anglo-Saxon ethics, the mysticism of knowledge and the morality of practical life . . . But . . . it must not be assumed that *The Blue Bird* is pedantic and boring. It is the most pleasant, the most charming, often the most delightful, of spectacles . . . One feels constantly present that sort of imagination, special and rare, which consists in seeing and seizing, in the slightest concrete detail, or in the merest word, the way of giving expression to the abstract thought . . . a work both very lofty and very beautiful."

The play wears well. Upon seeing it in 1923 John Corbin observed that it had "grown" considerably: "Or perhaps it is we who have grown. In either case, the play is, or seems to be, of far greater stature both as the holiday entertainment which it is on the surface and as the wisely thoughtful and amiably humorous fantasy which it is fundamentally . . . By some magic of his own Maeterlinck has woven into this seemingly naïve fantasy far more of wisdom and of humor, of penetrating observation and of deeply quiet thought, than are to be found in many a ponderous tome." In London's *Saturday Review* (December 18, 1909) Max Beerbohm traced the progress of Maeterlinck from his early plays, when the problem of existence moved to the enigma of death, to the deathless joy of *The Blue Bird*: "For proper appreciation of Maeterlinck, you must have, besides a sense of beauty, a taste for wisdom . . . In his youth, the mystery of life obsessed him. He beheld our planet reeling in infinity, having on its surface certain infinitesimal creatures, all astray, at the mercy of unknown laws. And he shuddered . . . Little by little, the shudders in him abated . . . If we are but the puppets of destiny, and if destiny is, on the whole, rather unkind, still there seems to be quite enough of joy and beauty for us to go on with. Such is the point to which Maeterlinck, in the course of years, has won; and such is the meaning he has put into *The Blue Bird*."

Maeterlinck was constantly preoccupied with the basic problems of the human soul, which he approached at times more realistically, at times more fantastically, but always delicately, with a luminous aura of suggestion and symbol around the dramatic figures. Nowhere, however, has he achieved a happier and richer combination of his best qualities than in *The Blue Bird*. The play lends itself to revival at sentimental times, such as Christmas. Thus, London, December 26, 1962.

PEG O' MY HEART   *J(ohn) Hartley Manners*

As dewy sweet as an April morning in Killarney, *Peg O' My Heart*, by John Hartley Manners (English, 1870-1928), has touched the hearts of theatregoers everywhere. Opening in New York, December 20, 1912, with Laurette Taylor, who in that year married the author, the play attained 692 performances. Within the year there were five touring companies. It opened in London, October 10, 1914, for 710 performances, was revived June 19, 1916, for 289 more, and again in 1920 and 1931. It was revived again in 1948 by On-Stage, New York, and in the summer with Julie Haydon, who had heard many stories of the play during her run with Laurette Taylor in *The Glass Menagerie*.

A popular song, "Peg O' My Heart," not in the play, by Fred Fisher, was widely sung in 1914. The play has been seen in India, Holland, France, Spain, Italy, and all the English-speaking world. In 1918-1919 there were still eight *Peg* companies touring the United States and Canada. Laurette Taylor was Peg on the silent screen in 1923; as a 1933 talkie it gave Marion Davies her best role. Laurette Taylor's faithful companion Michael appeared in 1,250 performances, a stage record for a dog.

In 1967 a musical version by Robert Emmett, based on an adaptation by Michael Sawyer, with music and lyrics by Johnny Brandon, had a pre-Bway tryout at Valley Forge. In 1974 an all-black version appeared OffBway, changing the events to the "swing era" of 1924. In 1977, with Sophia Landon as Peg, the original play was shown in two houses OffOffBway; and opening January 3, 1980, with Beth Austin, it was revived at Springfield, Mass. The troupe presented it OffOffBway, July 8, 1982.

The play begins when Peg, a plain Irish-American lass, arrives with her mongrel dog Michael at the cold household of her supercilious English relatives, the Chichesters of Regal Villa, Scarboro. She is received with hostility, and only because her uncle's will has left her the bulk of the family fortune. By her simple honesty and good spirits Peg breaks down the coldness of the family, saves Ethel Chichester from elopement with a married man, and wins the heart and title of an honest Briton. "Laughter is not dead in this house," says Peg, and proves it.

Her words proved true also of the theatres where she played. Charles Darnton in the *Telegram,* December 21, 1912, said that the author, "who called it a comedy of youth, might have described the play more accurately by calling it a comedy of truth. By the simple expedient of telling the truth and confounding her hypocritical English relatives the little Irish girl from America keeps the house in roars of laughter." Peg's dog Michael was replaced at the last minute by a female, who kept the name.

Robert Garland in the *Journal-American,* July 22, 1948, declared that the play "never ceased to be an old corn-fritter, even when it was new." But corn-fritters are delicious with syrup, which Peg generously supplies. *Peg O' My Heart* is the best of the Pollyanna comedies, wherein innocence and freshness bring warmth, joy, and virtue to the stodgy, the calculating, and the cold. The musical was played at the London Phoenix, 1984.

FALSE SECRETS   *Pierre Marivaux*

The plays of Pierre Carlet de Chamblain de Marivaux (French, 1688-1763) were greatly influenced by the Italian commedia dell' arte. His first success, *Harlequin Polished by Love,* was presented by the Italian Comedians in Paris in 1720; his most successful play, *False Secrets* (in which Harlequin is the heroine's servant) had its premiere with the same company on March 16, 1737. Of Marivaux's thirty-two plays this one and three others are still in the French repertory.

Although some of Marivaux's characters are drawn from Italian comedy, they are not stock figures, but endowed with a graceful life of their own, among the solid bourgeois and the lesser nobles. In the generation before the French Revolution, Marivaux dealt not with social problems but with social dalliance. Gallantry and intrigue occupied society and the stage, but Marivaux was concerned less with the erotics than with the metaphysics of love-making. His elegance and ease of thought and expression (which gave birth to the word *Marivaudage*) and his exquisite though trifling dialogue are in delightful harmony with his delicate sentiment and refined analysis. The actions and reactions are less in the deeds than in the emotions of his characters. They tell not merely what they feel but what they feel the others feel they should feel. His is indeed the theatre of the salon.

False Secrets (Les Fausses Confidences) shows the scheming servant Dubois working by indirections to arrange a marriage between his former master, Dorante, and the beauteous, wealthy Araminte. Dubois whispers to Araminte that Dorante is madly in love with her. Like the disguised Rosalind in *As You Like It,** Araminte laughingly suggests that seeing her often may cure Dorante of his love; she employs him as her steward. From this point, as Arthur Tilley declares in *Three French Dramatists* (1933), "the gradual awakening of a reciprocal love in her heart is portrayed with a marvelous skill and delicacy." Araminte's ambitious mother, an impecunious Count, and a maid, Marton, who thinks Dorante is in love with her, add complications to the story. More important are the sparkle and interplay of sentiment, the gathered grace of "the kingdom of the tender."

Later periods grew in appreciation of Marivaux. Araminte was a favorite role of the famed Mlle. Mars, in the 1830's; and when Mme. Arnould-Plessy played the part in 1855, Théophile Gautier called it "one of the pleasantest in the theatre." The United States premiere of *False Secrets,* by the Madeleine Renaud–Jean-Louis Barrault Company, November 12, 1952, was the play's thousandth professional performance. The Renaud-Barrault production was a great success in New York, as it has been in Paris. After the French premiere Gabriel Marcel, in *Les Nouvelles Littéraires* of July 11, 1946, said that "the exquisite spirit of Marivaux is at its best . . . His good will is a grace as much as a virtue . . . The tenderness does not exceed the span of a sigh, an exclamation withheld; but the emotion the actor suppresses the audience feels." Out of artificial comedy Marivaux has fashioned real delight.

False Secrets was presented at the Malvern Festival, 1966; the deft ELT production, January 6, 1971, was the first New York showing of the play in English. It was in modern dress, with Araminte wearing trousers. Marivaux' other plays still in the French repertoire are *The Game of Love and Chance,* 1730; *The Legacy,* 1736; *The Test,* 1740.

TAMBURLAINE THE GREAT   *Christopher Marlowe*

The advent of the plays of Christopher Marlowe (1564-1593) brought the English drama to its full freshet power in one great springtide surge. In the naked freshness of exuberant youth Marlowe opened the door to the modern theatre.

It may be that Marlowe is more poet than playwright. Certainly in his first play, *Tamburlaine the Great,* 1587, he presents less a well-knit story than a succession of dramatic episodes. Yet these episodes move with such vigor that they took Marlowe's unaccustomed age by storm.

The story of Tamburlaine (Timur the Lame, 1336?-1405) is drawn from the Spanish *Timur* (1543) of Pedro Mexia, translated in 1571 as *Foreste* by Fortescue. The First Part of Marlowe's play shows the Scythian shepherd, Tamburlaine, rising in power until he marries the daughter of the Sultan of Egypt, Zenocrate, and crowns her Empress of Turkey and Persia. The Second Part carries Tamburlaine further upon his career of conquest— kings draw his chariot, champions tremble at his name—until he is confronted by death.

The pomp and majesty of this play must have been especially rousing to the many who knew the court of Henry VIII. "The lures of Tamburlaine," said Lamb, "are perfect midsummer madness. Nebuchadnezzar's are mere modest pretensions compared with the thundering vaunts of the Scythian shepherd."

Marlowe lacked the creative imagination of Shakespeare, who boldly refashioned whatever he took; but he, too, made old material new. The wonder of Tamburlaine, said Havelock Ellis in his Preface to the Mermaid edition of the work, "lies in the wild and passionate blood, in the intensely imaginative form, with which he has clothed the dry bones of his story." The successive scenes are held together by the surging personality of Tamburlaine (whose sweep toward power and beauty was akin to the Elizabethan) and by the impact of Marlowe's words. He was the first to reveal the power of blank verse in the English drama.

Despite lapses into bombast and rant, the play is rich and forceful.

Swinburne has said of this play: "In the most glorious verses ever fashioned by a poet to express with subtle and final truth the supreme aim and the supreme limit of his art, Marlowe has summed up all that can be said or thought on the office and the object, the means and the end, of this highest form of spiritual ambition." The poet in Marlowe makes the playwright soar. In his *History of Elizabethan Literature* (1887), Saintsbury avers that "Shakespeare himself has not surpassed . . . no other writer has equalled the famous and wonderful passages in *Tamberlaine* and *Faustus.*"

For many years *Tamburlaine the Great* (especially the First Part with its magniloquent lines) held the stage. In 1702 Nicholas Rowe condensed the two parts into one play: *Tamerlane.* Instead of a conqueror blood-thirsty and afire for power, Rowe paid tribute to King William by converting his hero into a calm, philosophic ruler.

Tamburlaine the Great had its American premiere January 26, 1758. It was played again in 1762, 1784, and 1799. In the nineteenth century, its popularity waned because of its long speeches and episodic structure. In England, it was revived at Oxford in 1933, when the Second Part was played for the first time since the seventeenth century.

Although long stretches of *Tamburlaine the Great* would stall on the stage today, many passages still flash with the fire that was Tamburlaine's—and Marlowe's.

The lasting power of the drama was demonstrated recently when Donald Wolfit acted Tamburlaine in an Old Vic company production which opened in London, September 24, 1951. Harold Hobson reported in the *Christian Science Monitor* of September 29 that "the play is packed with horrors which were preserved from becoming ridiculous only by becoming revolting," but he recognized it as "the most tempestuous, wildest, most frantic play in the English language."

Tamburlaine the Great remains tremendously important as the first flag Marlowe raised in that new realm he helped create—the modern English drama.

The classical Ben Jonson demurred: "The true artificer will not run away from nature . . . And though his language differs from the vulgar somewhat it will not fly from all humanity, with the Tamer-lanes and Tamer-chams of the late age, which had nothing in them but the scenical strutting, and furious vociferation, to warrant them to the ignorant gapers."

The 1951 production, adapted by Tyrone Guthrie, was repeated at the New York Broadway, January 19, 1956. In 1964, four hundred years after Marlowe's birth, London saw the two parts, abridged by Robert Pennant Jones. In 1972 at Edinburgh, there was a different actor for each phase: Rupert Frazer as Tamburlaine the erotic adventurer, Jeffery Kissoon as the brutal bombastic killer; Mike Gwilym for the dignity and world-weariness of age. Death was the only comer the conqueror could not defeat. The stage showed the prow of a huge galleon, on its sides chariot wheels with the skeletons of victims, while from every part of the theatre Tamburlaine's foes sent shuddering cries.

On October 4, 1976, *Tamburlaine,* directed by Peter Hall, was the first play at the new NT (Olivier), with Albert Finney "all iron and gut" and Susan Fleetwood as Zenocrate, served by bare-breasted concubines. "As for me," said Harold Hobson, "I was overwhelmed by it. Its swelling, bursting words sweep in floods across the hall. They are a revelation in their imaginative grandeur, and in their sense, which I do not find in Shakespeare, of unknown worlds of thought and being on the very verge of birth."

DOCTOR FAUSTUS   *Christopher Marlowe*

Probably first produced in 1588, *The Tragical History of Doctor Faustus* by Christopher Marlowe was not officially registered until 1601. The first edition was not printed until 1604; other editions followed in 1609 and 1616, the latter with many comic additions. The story (for its sources, see Goethe's *Faust**) is based on an old German legend, but the spirit is all of Marlowe's England and Elizabeth's.

Magic and hell are to Marlowe no symbol, no subject for irony, as with Goethe; they are hot, passionate reality. Doctor Faustus is a vivid figure of the times, a master of the alchemical knowledge of the Middle Ages, yet afire with the lust for power that marked the Renaissance. Against the earlier conception of duty to one's superiors, against the divinity of kings, against God himself, Marlowe for the first time in modern drama set the assertion of individual responsibility and individual worth. Yet, because of his position in time, his Dr. Faustus is torn between the two conceptions; Faustus seeks power, raising himself against the world, yet he acknowledges his sinfulness. He knowingly rebels against the rule of God, and he admits the justice of the doom for which the devils hale him off to hell. Legend has it that at one performance the actors noticed one devil too many amongst them; they spent the evening not at the tavern but in prayer. "Why, this is hell, nor am I out of it!"

While Marlowe thus raises the legend to a symbol of that rebellion of the individual against authority which characterized the Renaissance, he also spiritualized his drama, freeing it from the physical signs of hell-fire and the other material horrors that delighted the medieval audience (some of which were reinstated by the author of the 1616 comic additions). Marlowe's conception of hell itself, as existing wherever the damned may go, is more modern than that of either Dante or Milton.

In the article "Faust on the Stage" in *All the Year Round* (June 28, 1879), edited by Charles Dickens, the differences between Marlowe's and Goethe's Faust are pointed up: "Marlowe's work is the outcome of an undoubting mind, not the statement of a great problem yet unsolved. After the old simple fashion, Marlowe points his moral before he begins to adorn his tale . . . Goethe's earth and air spirits are abstractions; Marlowe's are concrete actualities; and throughout the Englishman's wonderful play there is no hint, any more than there is in a medieval mystery, that the events in it are either impossible or even improbable . . . This Mephistophilis is not the mocking fiend of Goethe, but rather the awful Lucifer of Milton . . . Not only is Faustus duly handed over to the foul fiend at the conclusion of the tragedy, but a perpetual conflict is maintained between his good and bad angels. He is shown, within the compass of eight days, the face of heaven, of earth, and of hell. The seven deadly sins appear before him, and describe their attributes; he is given every chance of repentance—in vain. His power to decide is assumed by the frequency of the appeals made to him. He is vanquished by one weakness—sensuality."

The lust for power that led to the excesses of the Renaissance—the slaughter of Montezuma and countless American Indians, the launching of the Armada, the very creation of the English Church out of Henry's spleen—is epitomized in Dr. Faustus, whom it scorches to hell. The visit of Dr. Faustus to Rome, in the play, with the Pope and the Cardinals burlesqued, pays tribute to the passions of the times. In the very year of the play's production, the 132 Spanish ships of the Invincible Armada set sail to bring the rebellious English back to the fold of the Church. On every side Puritan and Catholic stood, sword, dagger, pistol, and poison in hand. In the religious and political intrigues of the time, the government agent Christopher Marlowe lost his own life. Vigorously, but through the force of will rather than through physical force, Dr. Faustus chose his own path toward power though it end in damnation.

Out of this earnest presentation in *Dr. Faustus* of a theme that shaped his own life, Marlowe rolled his "mighty line." Amid the prose passages of the play, his blank verse takes more powerful and more beautiful surge than in the earlier *Tamburlaine,* * which marked its first effective use in the drama. As Swinburne said in the Prologue to an 1896 production: "Then first our speech was thunder."

The dramatic power of *Dr. Faustus* has been manifest in a number of productions. The *London Telegraph* (July 25, 1934) observed: "Faustus is the one figure in English drama whose mind is shown at war with itself, and whose inner struggle is expressed by direct means." "*Faustus* at its best," declared Arthur Symons, "seems to me much finer than *Faust.*" There can be no question that Marlowe's is a more effective stage play than Goethe's. American productions included one almost every year of the decade 1931-1941, somewhere in the United States; Orson Welles played

Faustus and directed the Federal Theatre production in New York in 1937. Brooks Atkinson called his "a brilliantly original production . . . grim and terrible on the stage." To John Mason Brown this production suggested the spirit of the Elizabethan stage "in exciting modern terms." Richard Watts, Jr., noted that the play "contains some of the most haunting poetry in the English language." Those that find the writing uneven should note that only Act I, Scenes 1 and 2 of Act II, and eighty-seven lines more of the twelve scenes up to the last of Act V, have come to us in Marlowe's own words.

There was a Federal Theatre production of *Dr. Faustus* in New Orleans in 1937; another in Boston in 1938; Rex Ingram played Mephistophilis in 1940. The play ran in London in 1940 during a defense blackout; the *New Statesman and Nation* (March 9, 1940) observed: "It is astonishing how well it acts, and how overwhelming is the effect of the sustained tragedy of damnation." In 1941, the play was presented in Los Angeles by six masked readers while dancers enacted the parts.

Marlowe was denounced as an atheist; his plays give ample evidence at least of his questioning nature. Three of his four chief figures are infidels. All are vibrant with hot desire for beauty, power, wisdom; they reach out beyond the limits of human grasp. The illimitable desire in Marlowe's plays turns them to tragedy. Lamb has looked into this relationship: "The growing horrors of Faustus are awfully marked by the hours and half-hours as they expire and bring him nearer and nearer to the exactment of his dire compact. It is indeed an agony and bloody sweat."

The spirit of Tamburlaine and of Faustus is Marlowe's own spirit, on the fervent quest that led him toward beauty, toward power—therefore toward danger and toward evil: a quest that resulted in four masterpieces and ended on a dagger's point.

Christopher Marlowe, who died in his thirtieth year, is the author of some of the greatest English dramas. Of these, *Dr. Faustus* probes most deeply into the soul of man.

Among revivals, in Britain: RSC, 1961; again 1968, with smoke bombs, gold-faced angels, writhing devils, "brazen theatrical splendour," and Maggie Wright "tastefully nude" as Helen of Troy:

> *Was this the face that launched a thousand ships*
> *And wrecked the topless towers of Ilium?*

In 1970 RSC used the full range of comedy (often much omitted), including a custard-pie routine in the Vatican. In 1974, Edinburgh Festival. In 1980, Hammersmith, London, an all-male cast (as originally), Helen in a diaphanous jumpsuit over a jockstrap; it began with gowned students around a library table, on which at the end Faustus died. The Pope was played by a three-and-a-half-foot dwarf with a Cockney accent, who gobbled a sausage while being hauled off crying, "Oh, I am slain!" In a 1981 Manchester production by Adrian Noble the magic pranks of Faustus fell flat; Helen flew (said Francis King in the *Telegraph*, September 20, 1981) "like a Folies Bergère beauty from the flies." Devils Baliol and Belcher rode round on whirring bicycles. At the end Mephistophilis resembled Christ on the cross; Faustus was blown "like a sere leaf into the pit of hell."

In America: Phoenix, October 5, 1964, to sixty-four performances. RSC, Los Angeles, with Eric Porter, 1967 and 1969. Milwaukee Rep, 1974 (fifty performances); again 1976. CSC OffBway, 1979. Oak Park, Chicago, 1981.

The 1966 film with Richard Burton and Elizabeth Taylor had adviser Neville Coghill, who gave Lechery a line from *Edward II**; Avarice, from *The Jew of Malta**; Envy, Pride, and Wrath, from *Tamburlaine,** in the play's Masque of the Seven Deadly Sins.

THE JEW OF MALTA   *Christopher Marlowe*

Shakespeare is supposed to have drawn his Shylock in *The Merchant of Venice** after Barabas in *The Jew of Malta,* 1588?. But the compound of villain and buffoon the Elizabethans saw in Shylock bulked concentrate, horrendous in Barabas.

The first impression the play makes is majestic; only Milton has surpassed Barabas' opening soliloquy, Swinburne has said. But as the incidents gather and break, the first grandiose conception of Barabas shifts to the caricature of a crafty villain. Resisting the tax demand, when Malta must pay tribute to the Turks, Barabas has his properties confiscated. His house is turned into a nunnery. He poisons his daughter Abigail and all the nuns. He betrays Malta to the besieging Turks, who make him governor. Then, seeking to ensnare the Turks, he is caught in his own trap and spilled into his own boiling cauldron.

Charles Lamb gave these reasons why *The Jew of Malta* was not often played: "Barabas is a mere monster brought in with a large painted nose to please the rabble. He kills in sport, poisons whole nunneries, invents infernal machines. He is just such an exhibition as a century or two earlier might have been played before the Londoners, *by the Royal Command,* when a general pillage and massacre of the Hebrews had been previously resolved on." It was, in short, popular in its own day with much the same appeal as bear baiting. It was usually performed at Shrovetide, when the rowdy audience demanded low comedy and violent action. Today, occasions for reviving this play seem less frequent. It was performed at Yale University in 1940. London saw it in 1922 for the first time since 1818.

The *London Times* of November 12, 1922, declared that some "may, with some justice, ridicule the element of buffoonery in his comedy, the preposterous intrigue of his tragedy; but no one can deny the wild poetry, the raging sublimity of his words, the force, the passion, of his rhetoric and verse . . . The soul of the sea is in almost every line of Marlowe. His music surges up against our ears with tidal beauty. His power of rhythm is oceanic alike in its serenity and its tumultuousness. While we cannot bring ourselves to think seriously of the incidents in such a play as *The Jew of Malta,* whilst the skeleton of its plot is grotesque and absurd, there is always a magniloquent grandeur in its verbiage, a turgid beauty in its thoughts . . . It is a stage creation of undeniable vitality . . . there is throughout directness of characterization, swiftness of action, and felicity of dialogue."

At first, in vivid lines, Barabas prizes the beauty of precious stones, as well as the power of riches.

"The vigorous design and rich free verse of *The Jew of Malta,*" Havelock Ellis points out, "show a technical advance on *Dr. Faustus.**" While the beauty of the verse gathers turbulent power, the beauty Barabas desires is lost in his uncontrolled lust after power over men. Like all Marlowe's protagonists, Barabas reaches too far and topples.

In the development of the Malta Jew we find all the traits woven by Shakespeare into the Jew of Venice. "There is not a single note in Shylock," the *London Times* of November 12, 1922, declared, "that primarily Barabas does not indicate or suggest."

Despite the grim course of Barabas' plotting, *The Jew of Malta* surges not only like the sea, but like the spring, and morning. "Now Phoebus ope the eyelids of the day!" cries Barabas; and morning wakes with Marlowe on the English stage.

The most vivid recent performance came in Marlowe's four hundredth anniversary year, 1964, by the RSC at Stratford-upon-Avon, then London, with Eric Porter (followed by Clive Revill) alternating in Shakespeare's *Merchant of Venice*. The *Sunday Times* declared: "Porter has all the verve necessary. In addition he has a fundamental dignity and gravity that make Barabas a worthy and potentially tragic representative of a stricken and persecuted race." (Despite this, a scheduled 1977 performance at Basle was cancelled because of the protest of the Jewish community.) By contrast, said the *Times,* Porter's Shylock had "argument instead of passion. The hints of grandeur he has given to Barabas he here totally abandons. This is Fagin. This is the villainous Jew used to frighten Christian children."

The most prominent, if not the only, Jew known to Londoners of the time was Roderigo Lopez, physician to Queen Elizabeth, hanged for attempting to poison her, in a Spanish plot. Lopez died protesting his innocence, reportedly crying (in what must have seemed a curtain line of ironic genius) that he loved the Queen as much as he loved Jesus. He was hanged June 7, 1594—twenty days after *The Jew of Malta* was registered. *Lupus* is Latin for *wolf*; and Lopez may have been in mind when in *The Merchant of Venice* Gratiano calls Shylock

> *a currish spirit*
> *Governed by a wolf hanged for human slaughter.*

EDWARD II   *Christopher Marlowe*

The last of Christopher Marlowe's great dramas, *Edward II,* 1590?, is by many deemed his masterpiece. While it lacks some of the fire of his earlier verse, it is more fully integrated as a work of art, not so much a mere succession of stirring scenes as a coordinated and swiftly progressing drama. The characters, too, are more individually drawn. There are sensitive portrayals, especially of Isabella, Edward's queen, and of young Edward III, the best drawn child in the Elizabethan drama. In *Edward II,* as Havelock Ellis said, Marlowe's "passionate poetry is subdued with severe self-restraint in a supreme tragic creation."

Edward II is a "history play" of the turmoil in England from 1307, when Edward, newly crowned, recalled his Gascon favorite Gaveston, to 1327, when Edward was forced by his wife Isabella and her lover Mortimer to abdicate, and was brutally slain. There is broad sweep of passions across the stage as the nobles resent the king's infatuation for Gaveston, whom they force Edward to banish. The domestic and the international intrigues are interwoven with a skillful hand. Isabella, at once a political pawn and a passionate woman, turns from Edward to Mortimer and from love to murder. "The reluctant pangs of abdicating royalty in Edward," said Charles Lamb, "furnished hints which Shakespeare scarce improved in *Richard II*; and the death scene of Marlowe's king moves pity and terror beyond any other scene in ancient or modern drama with which I am acquainted." Havelock Ellis expressed the opinion that "the whole of Shakespeare's play, with its exuberant eloquence, its facile and diffuse poetry, is distinctly inferior to Marlowe's, both in organic structure and in dramatic characterization."

First acted in 1592, *Edward II* was printed in 1594, 1598, 1612, and 1622. It has been broadcast both in England and in the United States in the "great plays" series. It was presented at Oxford in 1933; the *London Times* of February 10 of that year stated: "Although Marlowe's drama pursues its way without the relief of any lighter interludes in the Shakespearean manner, yet the play as it was performed tonight never appeared heavy or tedious." Of a production at New York's City College in May 1948, George Freedley wrote: "One of the noblest and best of English tragedies . . ."

The words of Edward (opening Act V) after he has been imprisoned, have the nobility and fire of true majesty. We can readily understand how the boatmen on the Thames used to sing Marlowe's *Hero and Leander*; how Marlowe's young contemporary Petowe could declare that "men would shun their sleep in still dark night to meditate upon his golden lines." Truly, as Drayton declared, Marlowe "had in him those brave translunary things that our first poets had." He was England's first great dramatic poet—cut down in his thirtieth year. Tradition has it that he was slain over a wench in a tavern brawl, but research has shown that Marlowe was in the government secret service, and his death may well have been the outcome of such intrigues as still sunder the world today, and as he pictures, with power and sympathy, in his great historical drama, *Edward II*.

The play opens with Edward's beloved minion, the low-born Gaveston, planning the games he will play with the newly crowned king, who has summoned him from exile:

> *Sometime a lovely boy in Diane's shape,*
> *With hair that gilds the water as it glides,*
> *Crownets of pearl about his naked arms*
> *And in his sportful hands an olive tree*
> *To hide those parts which men delight to see,*
> *Shall bathe him in a spring . . .*
> *Such things as these best please His Majesty.*

It is Edward's obsessive love of Gaveston, his refusal to send him away, that provokes the nobles to revolt. One time, he cries that they may divide his kingdom among them,

> *So I may have some nook or corner left*
> *To frolic with my dearest Gaveston.*

Queen Isabella had truly loved Edward, and lamented:

> *For now my lord and king regards me not,*
> *But dotes upon the love of Gaveston.*

In despair she had turned to Mortimer, and acquiesced in his order for the killing of the king. At the end, however, when Mortimer shows that as

Regent he intends to rule young Edward III and England, she orders Mortimer put to death.

A version of Marlowe's play by Bertolt Brecht, first shown at the Munich Kammerspiel, March 19, 1924, omits Gaveston's opening speech and the homosexual emphasis of the play (as when Mortimer Senior, I, 4, lists great men, such as Alexander and Socrates, who have had their Ganymedes), to stress the violence and the rebellion against royal rule. The Brecht version was shown by the NT (Old Vic) in 1968.

Edward II was shown in the New York ANTA matinee series, 1958, with Clarence Derwent as Narrator. From Leicester it came to London (New Arts), July 1, 1964. OffOffBwy, 1970; again (Riverside Church), 1973 and (CSC) 1974. By the Marlowe Society, Cambridge, then London, 1976. Marlowe was the first, and remains one of the greatest, to command the majestic march of blank verse in the drama.

ANTONIA AND MELLIDA AND ANTONIO'S REVENGE   *John Marston*

In sharp contrast to most of his contemporaries, John Marston (English, 1575?-1634) dedicated his works "to everlasting oblivion." Yet some of them still send clear echoes along the corridors of time. For a while, Marston was engaged in the "War of the Theatres" against Ben Jonson, who in *The Poetaster** attacked *Antonio and Mellida,* 1599? and *Antonio's Revenge,* 1600? William Gifford, who in the early nineteenth century edited Jonson, declared that these two plays of Marston's "are distinguished by nothing so much as a perpetual bluster, an overstrained reaching after sublimity of expression, which ends in abrupt and unintelligible starts, and bombast anomalies of language." A century later, however, the more objective Allardyce Nicoll observed that "of the sixteenth century revenge plays with thrilling and bloody plots . . . none is more entertaining than *Antonio and Mellida.*"

The two parts of the story were published in 1602 as "sundry times acted by the Children of Paules." In the First Part, Andrugio, Duke of Genoa, defeated by Piero Sforza, Duke of Venice, has been hiding in the Venetian marshes, with a price on his head. The son, Antonio, likewise outlawed, goes disguised to the court of Piero, whose daughter Mellida he loves. They run away, but Mellida is brought back. Then, in stately funeral procession, Andrugio bears the body of Antonio to Piero's court and claims the offered reward. Piero, now assuming neighborly forbearance and grief, says he'd give half his fortune, or his daughter's hand, to have the young prince alive again. Thereupon Antonio rises from his bier, and the two lovers are united.

The Prologue to the Second Part, *Antonio's Revenge,* is fraught with the dark presage of overhanging doom as are few passages in our literature. "This Prologue," said Charles Lamb, "for its passionate earnestness, and for the tragic note of preparation which it sounds, might have preceded one of those old tales of Thebes or Pelops' line which Milton has so highly recommended . . . It is as solemn a preparative as 'the warning voice which he who saw th' Apocalypse heard cry'." Piero had once courted Andrugio's wife, Maria; he now poisons Andrugio, and presses himself upon the widow. He also has a friend of Antonio's slain and the body placed in Mellida's room to make it seem that she has been unfaithful. Antonio is told the truth in Elizabethan fashion by his father's ghost, but meanwhile Mellida has died.

Maria has feigned acceptance of Piero's suit; at a banquet on the eve of their wedding, Piero is offered his own son to eat, then is hacked to death. Instead of taking control of the two dukedoms, Antonio seeks such peace as he can find in the seclusion of a religious house.

Through the glooms and horrors of this bloody story, Marston moves like a majestic storm—now with great lightning flashes and reverberant thunder roll, now with heavy drench of rain in the irksome dark. His tones are clear and massive, but occasionally he strains, especially in diction, on the quest of sublimity or awesomeness of passion, laying himself open to Jonson's satiric shafts.

In 1607 Marston entered the church and closed the door upon his brief writing career. *Antonio and Mellida* and *Antonio's Revenge* are his best plays, and in underlying nobility and dignity of spirit the most rewarding of the blood-and-thunder dramas.

The two *Antonio* plays were shown at Nottingham, 1979. Of other plays of Marston's few have won recent revival. *The Dutch Courtesan,* 1603, opened at the London Royal, April 24, 1959, directed by Joan Littlewood. The *Observer* said: "Seeing it is not a scholarly duty but a theatrical pleasure." It came from the 1964 Chichester Festival to the London NT, October 13, 1964, called by *Stage* "a fertile, bawdy comedy with a crowd of rich parts, witty, varied and verbally luxuriant," contrasting the vying charms of a prosperous courtesan and the virtuous love of a sheltered young woman with the subplot of a pretended murder that almost backfired.

The Malcontent, played in 1604 by Burbage of the Shakespeare company and also the rival boys of Blackfriars, with a tangle of deposed dukes, and deaths continually plotted, though nobody dies, came from Nottingham to London with Derek Godfrey, June 11, 1973. It also played OffBway (Classic Theatre), November 1977.

Finally, *The Fawn,* 1606, at the NT (Cottesloe), July 1983, for perhaps the first time since its opening days. While it carries the courtship of Tiberio, Prince of Ferrara, and the daughter of Gonzago, Duke of Urbino, it is a lively picture of the follies of court life. These we see through the eyes of the Prince's father, who had first desired the girl for himself, but when he comes incognito helps his son. The old man acts as a flatterer, hence the play's title; Robert Cushman in the *Observer* (July 17, 1983) could not resist heading his review with "Fawnication." Actually, Marston called the play *Parasitaster; The Fawn* is the subtitle. Through the old man the widespread follies of the self-satisfied and self-deceived, mainly directed against women, are laid bare.

Most of the follies Marston pricks are still familiar, not of course in ourselves, but clearly in our neighbors. Chief of the self-satisfied is Gonzago, supposedly modeled on King James I, whom history has recognized as "the wisest fool in Christendom." Look around.

A NEW WAY TO PAY OLD DEBTS — *Philip Massinger*

There is a proud spirit, a dignity, a sense of human values, in the dramas of Philip Massinger (English, 1583-1640) who came, said Arthur Symons, as "the twilight of the long and splendid day of which Marlowe* was the dawn." Massinger collaborated on a score of dramas with Fletcher,* with Dekker,* and with Beaumont.* He is sole author of some thirty plays, the seven earliest of which are lost, having been used leaf by leaf for baking piecrust by William Warburton's cook.

Razor sharp in its satire of contemporary manners, and the most popular Elizabethan play after Shakespeare's and Jonson's, is *A New Way to Pay Old Debts,* written about 1625. In this play, according to Allardyce Nicoll, Massinger "has shown his power of depicting boldly limned characters, and his fine knowledge of stage effect. Sir Giles Overreach is a perfect masterpiece, drawn with lines which seem to come between those of the 'humorous' style of Jonson and the individual style of Shakespeare. He is a man, and yet he is a monstrous type . . . *A New Way to Pay Old Debts* is essentially a theatre play; it acts much better than it reads, although its dialogue has a certain straight and rhetorical beauty of its own."

The central situation of this play was drawn from Middleton's *A Trick to Catch the Old One,* * but the plot was based upon an actual political scandal of the time (1620), when the Jacobean monopolist and extortioner Sir Giles Mompesson was degraded from knighthood and banished. In the play, the wealthy but avaricious Sir Giles Overreach seeks to marry his daughter, Margaret, to the rich Lord Lovell, and to ruin, and secure the property of, his nephew Wellborn. Lord Lovell and Lady Allworth connive to fool Overreach, who unwittingly consents to his daughter's marriage with young Tom Allworth. When he finds out how he has been deceived, Overreach goes mad and is sent to Bedlam. (In some acting versions, Overreach has a stroke, and dies.) Wellborn gets his property back, and Lord Lovell weds Lady Allworth.

Few roles have been more desired by stars than that of Sir Giles. It was the greatest role of Edmund Kean (1787-1883). A study *The Amazing Career of Sir Giles Overreach,* by Robert H. Ball (1939), is devoted to the history of the part. For a decade, beginning 1816, Edmund Kean, Charles Kemble, and Junius Brutus Booth all essayed Sir Giles, and the reviewers took vehement sides. Looking back at Kean's debut, to the moment of Sir Giles' going mad, the *Theatre* (August 1, 1895) recalled: "Not a few women, like Lord Byron, went into hysterics; the pit rose as one man and cheered; even the other players, hardened as they must have been in their art, were beside themselves with emotion. Mrs. Glover fainted; Mrs. Horn sobbed over a chair; Munden was so far spellbound that he had to be taken off by the armpits." A decade later, when Kean revived *A New Way to Pay Old Debts* at Drury Lane, his admirers and his detractors created a riot.

A New Way to Pay Old Debts actually won favor slowly; even when revived by Garrick it found no great success. Throughout the nineteenth century, however, it was performed in England almost every year. Edwin Booth brought it to New York in 1849, and kept Sir Giles in his repertoire until 1886, when the *New York Times* (February 17, 1886) reported that he showed Overreach "a man confident of his own power, stooping to use the meanest craft to gain his ends, of course, but never losing the sense of his own dignity and vast importance . . . the death of the usurer was powerful and realistic; the effect of the stroke of paralysis falling suddenly in a moment of violent passion was vividly manifested."

E. L. Davenport essayed the role of Sir Giles in 1871 in Boston, where Booth was also playing it; he took it to New York, and by 1874 had played the part more than 500 times. In 1922, Walter Hampden played Sir Giles.

A New Way to Pay Old Debts was presented in New York, by Equity Library, in 1945, in an arena theatre; George Freedley found it "curiously effective." Of a 1932 production the *London Times* observed that "it tells vigorously an interesting story that appeals to any age."

The money-seeking devices of Sir Giles Overreach seem too obvious to our more circumspect age, but *A New Way to Pay Old Debts* remains dramatically vivid and historically important. Coleridge declared it "the nearest approach to the language of real life at all compatible with a fixed meter."

There was an OffOffBway (Jean Cocteau Rep.) revival in 1977, also by the RSC at Stratford-upon-Avon, June 1983. OffBway (Classic), 1983; Owen S. Rackloff's playing of Overreach reminded Mel Gussow in the *Times* (October 2, 1983) of William Hazlitt's warning to Edmund Kean "to contrive not to frighten the ladies into hysterics."

THE CIRCLE   *W. Somerset Maugham*

The most ironic of the dramas of English society by Somerset Maugham (1874-1965) is *The Circle,* 1921, which presents a recurrent pattern of marital infidelity. Elizabeth Champion-Cheney persuades her husband, Arnold, M.P., to be reconciled with his mother, Lady Kitty, returned from a long stay abroad after she'd eloped with Lord Hughie Porteus, both then married, with Hughie's career ruined by the scandal. To ease the tension, Elizabeth invites a few guests.

Porteus is ill-tempered, constantly troubled by his false teeth. Lady Kitty is overdressed, shallow, vain. "She's a silly, worthless woman because she's led a silly, worthless life." Such were the realistic consequences of their heedless romantic impulse.

Now, however, Elizabeth falls in love with one of her guests, Edward Luton, owner of a Malay plantation. She tells her husband, Arnold, who refuses to divorce her and orders Luton to leave. Kitty begs Elizabeth not to make the mistake she did. "The tragedy of love isn't death or separation. One gets over these. The tragedy of love is indifference."

Old Clive Champion-Cheney tells his son Arnold to offer Elizabeth her freedom, and she'll come to her senses. He does, but while the three old folks congratulate one another, and laugh at the foolish girl's abandoned notion, Elizabeth and Luton slip away to enjoy their spell of love.

The Circle opened at the London Haymarket in March 1921, and at the New York Selwyn September 12, 1921, for 175 performances, with Mrs. Leslie Carter (Kitty), John Drew (Porteus), Estelle Winwood (Elizabeth), Ernest Lawford (Arnold), and John Halliday (Edward). Among its many revivals: Cambridge, England, 1929; the New York Playhouse, 1938, produced by William A. Brady with Grace George (Mrs. Brady), Tallulah Bankhead, John Emery (then Tallulah's husband), and Dennis Hoey, directed by Bretaigne Windust, for seventy-two performances. The *New Yorker* (April 30, 1938) called it "still an intelligent man's guide to irony and adultery." In 1942 Fritzi Scheff played it in Cape Cod. In 1944 the London Haymarket showed John Gielgud as Arnold, with Yvonne Arnaud as Elizabeth and Rosalie Crutchley as Lady Kitty. In 1960, Ipswich, with Alan Judd and Julia McCarthy; 1965 at the London Savoy, with Evelyn Laye and Frank Lawton. In 1966 Helen Hayes took the play on a U.S. tour. The *New York World* assessed it as, except for Shaw,* "the deftest, wisest, most searching and true study that has come out of London since Pinero.*"

New York saw the play at the Roundabout in 1974; in England, a Chichester production with Googy Withers and John McCallum went to the London Haymarket October 13, 1976, for a two-year run, then on to Ontario, Canada. The ACT showed it in San Francisco in November 1977, again a year later, and in 1979 took it to Westport, Conn.

The American version of *The Circle* was bowdlerized; in London Lady

Kitty, emphasizing the boredom and the shabby edges of her faded romance, confessed to some amiable missteps with ardent Italians. The play remains a sharp reminder of how few profit by the mistakes of others; how often we assume that our situation is a thing precious and apart; while life tips the irony and in its tangle of hasty hearts prepares to renew the sorry circle.

THE CONSTANT WIFE   *William Somerset Maugham*

This play is a challenge to the double standard of morality. It depicts the charming Constance Middleton, fifteen years wedded to an eminent London surgeon. Providing Constance with an excellent home, John Middleton freely goes his own emotional way. Constance blandly wards off all attempts of relatives and friends to tell her of John's affair with her best friend, Marie Louise Durham; and when Durham himself comes with what he thinks is proof of the liaison, Constance convinces him that he must be mistaken. After he leaves, Constance lets Marie Louise and John know that she has known of their affair all along, but is behaving as a proper, "constant" wife. She then proceeds to make herself self-supporting, and announces to John that she is going to take six-week holiday with her old friend Bernard. Chagrined though he is, John sees that he is being given a dose of his own medicine, and he reconciles himself to being a constant husband on Constance's return.

Opening in New York, November 29, 1926, with Ethel Barrymore, *The Constant Wife* was an instant success. The London opening, April 14, 1927, was marred by a ticket error that sent half the pit into the stalls, creating a confusion that blurred the play. Not until ten years later did the London reviewers have proper view of it. Then the *Times* (May 20, 1937) said Maugham "has a story to tell; he has something to say which is both entertaining and, so far as it goes, true." The *Telegraph* of the same date called Maugham "one of the greatest craftsmen of our theatre . . . with brilliant and incisive dialogue."

As a craftsman, Maugham recognized the value of effective curtain incidents. He had ended *The Circle* with ironic laughter; in *The Constant Wife,* the final moments turn upon the husband the full irony of the "enginer hoist with his own petar."

The *Boston Transcript* (November 10, 1928) pointed out that the play appeals to those "preferring the smile of intelligent amusement to the guffaw of knowing derision" and admired the play's "exercises in pure reason . . . neatly decorated with verbal if usually sardonic, minor ironies, vignettes of manners, contrast of characters." Yet it noted that, when Constance's old sweetheart returns, opportunity fed by jealousy breeds inclination, till, "catching these pebbles of sentiment in her shoe, pure reason goes alimping." This fallibility makes more engaging the portrait of the understanding woman.

The Constant Wife was revived in New York on December 8, 1951, with Katharine Cornell as Constance, Grace George as her mother, and Brian Aherne. In spite of unimaginative direction, the irony and sparkle of the comedy retained their hold.

It was revived in Cambridge, England, January 30, 1967; also at the London Albery, September 19, 1973, directed by John Gielgud, with Ingrid Bergman brilliant in her second comedy role (her first was Lady Cicely in Shaw's *Captain Brassbound's Conversion**). It broke records all over the United States when Ingrid Bergman, with Jack Gwyllim as John, took it on a 1974-1975 tour. (She broke her ankle, and played in a wheelchair for a week. Act III was too intimate for the butler wheeling her to hear, and she twice wheeled herself into the wall. She limped until Washington, D.C.) The play reached the New York Shubert in April 1975, for thirty-two performances. The Bergman accent was still foreign; Harold Hobson in London did not like her work. The play was revived at the New York Lincoln Center in 1978.

THE MIDNIGHT REVEL (THE BAT)   *Henri Meilhac*

Henri Meilhac (French, 1831-1897) and Ludovic Halévy (French, 1834-1908) were masters of structure.

They built neat comedy dramas and swift farces, with little concern for character probing, but with every regard for lively situations. As a consequence many of their plays, with or without credit, have provided the basis, the plot and groundwork, of other works. In their original form, as they kept breaking upon a delighted public, Meilhac's comedies made half a century laugh. His collaborations with Ludovic Halévy were produced from 1861 to 1881.

Le Reveillon (The Midnight Revel), 1872, was a frisky farce, which Haffner and Genée, with music by Johann Strauss (Austrian, 1825-1899), converted into the operetta *Die Fledermaus (The Bat).* Opening in July 1874, *The Bat* achieved only 16 performances, but the next season it became a hit. It has grown to be the most popular of all light operas and, as *Life* observed (December 14, 1942), "It remains just about the prettiest operetta ever written." The boulevardier spirit of Meilhac, his brilliant and fertile fancy, and the agile turns of his wit, sparkle with the Strauss music throughout the play.

The story of the play is trickily complicated, with many opportunities for slily patterned, laughing amours. Baron von Eisenstein, out on his own recognizance, instead of going to jail decides to go first to Prince Orlofsky's ball. When Eisenstein doesn't reach the jail, the Warden goes to Eisenstein's, where the Baron's wife, Rosalinda, is dining familiarly with Alfredo Allevante, who has serenaded his way into her home. A true gentleman, Alfredo goes to jail as though he were the husband. But Rosalinda, masked, goes to the ball, where her own husband madly flirts with her. Also at the ball is her maid, Adele; dressed in her mistress' finery, she is a pert and pretty lass, and the Prince does more than flirt with her. After the ball, Eisenstein goes to the jail to begin his sentence. When the Warden, who has also been at the ball, finds two men who both say they are Eisenstein, he thinks himself more tipsy than is his wont. The wife is sent for, and after confusion, discovery, recrimination, and forgiveness, the curtain descends before a happy audience.

The title, *The Bat,* is drawn from the costume the Baron's friend, the Notary Falke, had worn a while before, when the Baron tricked him into having to go home in broad daylight in that disguise. It is the Notary that persuades the Baron to go to the ball before going to jail, and in the resultant confusion finds his revenge. In the Reinhardt production, the roof of the Warden's office in the jail had the shape of a hovering bat.

After its false start, *The Bat* flew to success. By 1880, it had been played in 171 German theatres. The French (Wilder and Delacourt) wrote their own libretto, as *La Tzigane (The Gypsy).* Its American premiere was in Brooklyn, 1879. Translations of it have taken many names. In London, beginning December 30, 1911, titled *Nightbirds,* it had 133 performances. In New York, it started on August 10, 1912, as *The Merry Countess,* with the Dolly Sisters, and had 129 performances. Opening on October 31, 1929, as *A Wonderful Night* (with one Archie Leach, later somewhat more familiar as Cary Grant), it had 125 performances. On October 14, 1933, it reappeared as *Champagne Sec,* with Peggy Wood, and ran for 113 performances. There have also been *The Masked Ball; Fly-By-Night*; and more. In the meantime, in 1929, with the production freshened and beautified by Reinhardt, *Die Fledermaus* ran for 300 performances in both Berlin and Paris. That production came to New York, October 28, 1942, as *Rosalinda,* with Oscar Karlweis as the Prince, for 521 performances; to London, March 8, 1945, as *Gay Rosalinda,* for 413 performances.

As *Die Fledermaus,* it remains in light opera repertory everywhere. The New York Metropolitan Opera Company gave it a lively production in 1951, with book by Garson Kanin but strained and hard-to-sing lyrics by Howard Dietz. The most successful English rendering of *Die Fledermaus* is that of Ruth and Thomas Martin, first heard in San Francisco in 1942, the biggest hit of the 1949 summer season at Central City, Colorado, and of the 1950, in Cincinnati, Ohio, and on tour throughout the United States, as also the Kanin version, in the fall of 1951.

The delightful music of Oscar Strauss permeates *The Bat,* and gives further touches of charm and beauty to its piquancy, its fun, its colorful frolicking. Among the songs it is hard to choose. "Dove that has escaped" is the romantic serenade that opens Rosalinda's window, if not quite her heart. Other gay tunes are "Come with me to the ball"; a lively drinking song; and the Prince's popular "Each to his own taste, sir! Chacun à son gout!" *The Bat,* fledged from *The Midnight Revel* of Meilhac and Halévy, is deservedly the favorite among light operas.

In 1967 came the New York remark: "It wouldn't be New Year's Eve at the Met without old bubbly *Fledermaus*"; and for a long time there was the same tradition in Vienna. Public television caught it up in 1981.

The Paris Opéra, under the New York OffBway director Richard Foreman, sought a "bacchanal atmosphere" with twelve nude women dancing the waltz of the final ballroom scene. Forty ballet dancers onstage at intermission proclaimed they had refused the roles; the disapproval of public and critics was so pronounced that on the second night seemly gowns—and general enjoyment—were restored.

CARMEN   *Henri Meilhac*

Out of Prosper Merimée's novel *Carmen* (1847) Henri Meilhac and Ludovic Halévy fashioned a play with music by Georges Bizet (1838-1875), that was called a light opera but has since established itself firmly in all opera repertoires. It was not especially well received on its world premiere in Paris, March 3, 1875; Bizet died thinking it a failure. It had 15 performances in Paris up to February, 1876; then was not heard there for six years. In the meantime, however, it won plaudits around the world. It was played in New York first at the Academy of Music, October 23, 1879. In its first performance at the Metropolitan Opera House, December 20, 1893, Emma Calvé made her tumultuously welcomed debut. She sang the thousandth performance at the Metropolitan on December 23, 1904. Others that have sung the role of Carmen are Olive Fremstad, Risë Stevens, Adelina Patti,

Rosa Ponselle, Mary Garden, Geraldine Farrar, and Gladys Swarthout. Carmen is a superbly challenging part, in a fiery play.

The story of *Carmen* is set in Spain, about 1820. Don José, commanding a troop of dragoons in Seville, flirts with Carmen, a gypsy girl working in a cigarette factory. After a fight among the girls, Don José arrests Carmen, but, fallen under her spell, lets her escape. Also under her spell, he insults a superior officer and joins Carmen's mountain friends, a gang of smugglers. José spurns the faithful Michaela, who has led him to his dying mother's bedside. He then watches Carmen, now bored with his jealous attentions, flirting with the famous bullfighter, Escamillo. As Escamillo is returning successful from the arena, Don José in jealous fury stabs Carmen to the heart.

Carmen moves with a speed and a passion unusual in opera. It has, at least it had in the original version, moments of dialogue instead of recitative, as well as many memorable airs: especially Carmen's songs "Love is a rebellious bird"; the coquettish "Near the walls of Seville"; "When the gay guitars ring out," a lively gypsy tune; and her more defiant "In vain I sort the cards." There is a vivid opening march of the soldiers; later a stirring smugglers' march. José has a vigorous song when he cries to Carmen: "You must hear me! This flower you once gave me is dishonored!" Best known of all is the Toreador song of Escamillo, a bravado cock-crowing that shivers along female spines.

The success of *Carmen* has given rise to other tellings of the story. It was presented as straight drama in 1869 both in London (version by Henry Hamilton) and in Boston (version by Marie Doran and Mollie Revel) without success; but Olga Nethersole made a hit in a play version on tour in the United States. A burlesque of the play, *Carmen-Up-to-Date,* by Henry Pettit and George R. Sims, music by Meyer Lutz, ran in London, opening October 4, 1890, for 248 performances. In New York, a Negro version, *Carmen Jones,* which opened December 2, 1943, followed the Bizet score, with book adapted to American Negro life by Oscar Hammerstein II, and restored dialogue instead of recitative. This "sizzling sexy saga of a rapacious Dixie wench," as *The Journal of Commerce* aptly called the Billy Rose production, ran in New York for 500 performances with Muriel Smith as Carmen, then toured the country and returned, May 2, 1946, for four weeks at the New York City Center. The cigarette factory was converted into a war-time parachute plant in a Southern town; the tavern became a hot-spot night club, with fantastically swank décor. Don José became Corporal Joe; Michaela became Cindy Lou; the toreador Escamillo became the prizefighter Husky Miller But Carmen remained her carefree, flirtatious, fiery self, and all the passion of the story was sustained.

Another recent transformation of *Carmen,* even more fiery, was into pantomime and dance, choreography by Roland Petit, who also danced Don José, in Les Ballets de Paris company, to the torrid Carmen of Renée Jeanmaire. This dance drama, seen in New York in 1949, turned Carmen into a savage French apache, with one dance of desire that scorched the accustomed stage.

In its various forms accompanied by music, *Carmen* proves irresistible. As *Le Temps* (March 3, 1925) remarked on its fiftieth anniversary, "It charms a philistine and the cultured alike. It exercises a strange attraction in its mixture of primitive passion, frivolity, and fear. The red flower which the cigarette-maker holds between her teeth has not yet faded. It blooms anew every season." Its appeal strikes basic chords of lust and stormy passions, as well as higher tones of beauty and final atoning calm.

Carmen continues in constant repertory. It was presented by an all-black cast in 1959; also heard by a great crowd in New York's Central Park, as part of the 350th anniversary (1609) of the Hudson celebration. A Peter Brook production in Paris, 1981, used three alternating international casts.

Carmen Jones, having been kept offstage abroad by injunction of the Meilhac and Halévy heirs, had its European premiere and first tour August 14, 1973.

The play *Lulu Belle,* by Edward Sheldon and Charles MacArthur, has been called "almost pure *Carmen,* down to Leonore Ulrich's last shiver."

A significant change came with *La Tragédie de Carmen,* adapted from Bizet by Marius Constant, Jean-Claude Carrière, and Peter Brook, who directed the 83-minute condensation. After 150 performances in Paris, this reopened the restored Beaumont at New York's Lincoln Center November 17, 1983, still running as I write. Despite a more resigned Carmen at the end, the play won rave reviews from the theatre critics, but faint praise, with head-shakes over the singing, from the critics of opera. Harold C. Schoenberg, in the *New York Times* (November 27, 1983), summed up the opinions: "To many musical and most theater people the point is that a stage director has taken music and singers to create a new kind of theatrical environment."

Without intermission, on a dirt stage, the gypsy Carmen flirts with and teases various men who fight over her. Three little bonfires onstage die to embers and are stamped out with the dawn break. The temptress reappears, but now in sober, churchly black. The toreador mimes the approach of a bull; he goes out, and is borne back dead, killed in the bull ring. Carmen, refusing to go off with Don José, is stabbed by him, where the tarot cards had appointed her death.

THE ARBITRATION   *Menander*

By the time Alexander the Great of Macedon had gained ascendency over all Greece (335 B.C.), the Old Comedy had given way to the New Comedy— that is to say, the gods and heroes, as characters, had been replaced by the upper middle-class citizens of Athens, with their entourage of slaves, parasites, procurers, courtesans, pompous physicians and boastful soldiers. The stories of the plays, however, were not localized, but remained general tales of intrigue, romance with all its difficulties and happy ending—often with a surprise recognition at the close. The setting, too, was generalized: the stage became a city street or public square, with two houses in the background; the action was all outdoors.

In the opinion of the ancients, the greatest writer of the New Comedy was Menander (Greek, c. 342-292 B.C.). Of his hundred-odd plays, sections of three survive: *Samia, The Shearing of Glycera,* and *The Arbitration.* These fragments, said Goethe, "gave me so high an idea of him that I look upon this great Greek as the only man that can be compared with Molière."

Menander's *The Arbitration,* written about 300 B.C., is not a farce, but a social problem play, with individualized characters excellently drawn, and with an approach to the interrelationships of the sexes that even today seems enlightened and advanced. The play, moreover, is admirably constructed and rich in thought of the highest moral tone. It is swiftly paced and effectively mounts in interest to an absorbing close.

The story, while intricate in detail, moves clearly along the usual pathway of misunderstanding to surprise recognition. The surprise is not that of the audience; a prologue informs us of the situation in advance. We know that the man who assaulted Pamphila during a festive night, the father of the babe she exposed, is the very man she later marries. With this knowledge, we can watch with amusement the complications that develop, sure that the happy ending will ensue.

The marriage, as usual in those days, was an arranged one, but the charming Pamphila and the upright, if somewhat stern, Charisius come to love each other. Thus, when Charisius learns of his wife's lapse, he is heartbroken. He moves away and embarks on a life of reckless extravagance; but he leaves untouched the courtesan he hires; he cannot get drunk; he cannot forget; and he cannot shake off his love of his wife. Then he hears his wife's father urge her to divorce the dissolute husband who has abandoned her. This she refuses to do. Her simple trust and integrity work upon her husband's spirit; ashamed of his excesses and transgressions, he determines to seek his wife's pardon. In the meantime, we have seen, step by step interwoven with this action, how the exposed babe is saved, then freed, then (presented by the courtesan) accepted as Charisius' bastard son, and finally recognized as a legitimate son and citizen, cementing the family ties of respect and love.

The Arbitration presents a moving and dramatic story. In the period of Athens' decline, it nobly maintained her best ideals of faith and self-respect and human dignity.

In 1945 at Haverford College—its first production in the United States—the play proved as lively as in 300 B.C. Most of the original is extant; Gilbert Murray courageously and apparently competently filled the gaps. His version was presented in London July 2, 1965.

In Sydney, Australia, April 20, 1981, the Amphitheatre Co. from Athens presented its modern Greek version by Tassos Rousos, each of the five acts in a different style, showing "Menander down the ages."

OLD HEIDELBERG (THE STUDENT PRINCE)   *Wilhelm Meyer-Förster*

Wilhelm Meyer-Förster (German, 1862-1934), used his own story *Karl Heinrich* (1899) in writing this romantic play.

Old Heidelberg opened in Berlin on November 22, 1902, took the city by storm and within two months was playing all over Germany and Austria and in Russia. Soon after, it was translated and produced in Poland, Denmark, Sweden, Greece, and Italy. It opened in London, at St. James's, in English, March 19, 1903, for 189 performances, and had revivals there in 1909 and 1925. In New York it was for some years the most popular play at the German Irving Place Theatre. Richard Mansfield played it in English, opening October 2, 1903. It was revived in 1910.

The story is a charmingly nostalgic one. Karl Heinrich, grandson of the King and heir to the throne of Sachsen-Karlsburg, comes from the stiff formality of his early training to spend a year at Heidelberg. There, by the banks of the Neckar, he joins in the student life, and he and Käthie, the pretty maid at the inn, fall in love. After four months of idyllic happiness, Karl is summoned to assume the responsibilities of the throne. Two years later, Kellerman, a tippler from the Heidelberg tavern, arrives at court to claim a promised job. Memories awakened, Karl revisits the college town. The students hail him with formal and solemn respect. Käthie tells him: "I shall marry my cousin; you, your princess. But we shall remember how we loved each other."

Old Heidelberg touched a tender chord. "In its own style the play is a gem," said the *Boston Herald* of December 22, 1903, "a dim, sad-colored gem, finely cut, perfectly proportioned. . . . The author's hand is firm, exact, and cultured in expression, and his constructive skill is considerable. He produces exactly the effects he desires."

The songs can be discussed more fitly in connection with *The Student Prince,* a musical comedy that Dorothy Donnelly (American, 1880-1928) fashioned from *Old Heidelberg,* with music by Sigmund Romberg (1887-1951). The musical follows the story closely, with emphasis on the male chorus of students; it has been even more successful in English than the play. Opening in New York, December 2, 1924, it ran for 608 perform-ances and had revivals in 1931, 1936, and in 1943 for 149 performances. The year 1945 marked its twelfth return to Philadelphia, and the musical has had equal popularity in other cities. London saw it in 1926, 1929, and 1944. On its New York premiere, the *New York Times* stated: "It is many a year since so glorious an opera has graced the stage of this city. From beginning to end it was a triumph." The *Sun* reviewer said he had "never heard an opera that was more alive," and the *World* called it, "the finest, the most robust, and most stirring of all American light operas."

Traditional student songs are in both *Old Heidelberg* and *The Student Prince.* Many a member of the audience, beneath his breath, joins in as the chorus swells with "Gaudeamus igitur"; with the drinking song "Ergo bibamus"; with the traditional "Old Heidelberg"; with the universal "Hoch soll er leben!" To these the musical added a student's march; a "rough house" song; and love ditties such as the Serenade and the tender "Deep in my Heart."

There are moments of comedy in the play, drawn in good part from the contrast between Karl's formal valet, Lutz, and the rollicking students. Karl's old tutor, Dr. Juttner, dies while at his alma mater, giving a prior touch of pathos to the final scene between Käthie and Karl. But essentially the power of both *The Student Prince* and *Old Heidelberg* rests in the effective evocation of the spirit of youthful hours, of students ways in college days, in the nostalgia of memories of a happy, wholesome, and love-warmed time.

Among many recent revivals: March 2, 1959, Brighton, England. In 1961, American Savoyards, Greenwich Mews, its first production OffBway. In 1968, London, eliciting the comment: "If you don't come out humming 'Deep in my heart I have a dream of you'—you're tone deaf!" In 1973, New York, Philadelphia, Washington (Kennedy Center), Chicago, State Fair of Texas, and tour. In 1966 and 1978, Paper Mill, N.J., again 1979, with Harry Danner as the Prince; Danner again in 1980 at Lake George, N.Y., August 1980, New York City Opera with Leigh Munro.

A TRICK TO CATCH THE OLD ONE   *Thomas Middleton*

Thomas Middleton (English, 1570?-1627) was a prolific playwright, in tragedy, romantic comedy, and political satire. His social satire of greed and intrigue, *A Trick to Catch the Old One,* 1607, the popularity of which led Massinger* to borrow its plot, is Middleton's most enduring drama.

Lucre, an old usurer, maintaining it is better to be fleeced by one's kin than by strangers, secures to himself the property of his spendthrift nephew, Witgood. The latter persuades a courtesan to impersonate a rich widow; Lucre and a rival usurer, Hoard, at once compete for the new prize. Playing one against the other, Witgood recovers his property from his uncle, marries the courtesan to Hoard, and mends his profligate ways.

The picture of London life in *A Trick to Catch the Old One* is colorful and drawn with a swift, unerring hand. The play moves rapidly through a well-knit story. Swinburne praised "the vivid variety of incident and intrigue, the freshness and ease and vigour of the style, the clear straightforward energy and vivacity of the action."

The play was quite popular in its time, and had numerous revivals through the seventeenth century. Unlike most of Middleton's plays, much of it is in prose, which retains the vitality of its tumultuous period.

In the *annus mirabilis* 1611—the year of the King James Bible and the Chapman translation of Homer—Middleton and Dekker wrote *The Roaring Girl,* based on the notorious Mary Frith, known as Moll Cut-Purse (1584-1659). In the play, Sebastian Wentgrave loves Mary Fitzgerald. With the friendly aid of Moll, Sebastian pretends to be madly in love with her; his horrified father urges that he wed the one he really loves. Moll, thief and forger, is pictured as a sort of female Robin Hood. The play was in RSC repertory in 1982.

Middleton's *The Changeling,* 1623 (BBC Play of the Month, January 1974), which many deem the best tragedy of the period, after Shakespeare, is especially modern in its picture of the sexual obsession of Beatrice with the hideously ugly yet domineering De Flores.

A Trick to Catch the Old One is one of the best of the early comedies of manners. It toured Scotland and Wales in 1978.

DEATH OF A SALESMAN   *Arthur Miller*

With *Death of a Salesman,* Arthur Miller (American, b. 1915) at one stroke won the Critics' Circle Award, the Pulitzer Prize, the Antoinette Perry Award, and the distinction of having written the only play ever selected for circulation by the Book-of-the-Month Club. The demand for tickets before and long after the Broadway opening on February 10, 1949, exceeded capacity and helped precipitate an official investigation of the fees charged by ticket brokers. The commonly careful John Mason Brown went so far as to say that the play "provides one of the modern theatre's most overpowering evenings."

In *Death of a Salesman,* many reviewers saw a searing indictment of the American way of life. It opens with Willy Loman's return to his Brooklyn home after an abortive start on a selling trip. Willy is sixty-three, and just cannot summon the concentration and the will to go on selling, even to go on driving his car. Flashbacks give glimpses of happier days, when Willy's two boys were growing up: Biff, the high school football star, and Happy, the worshipful younger brother. Their mother, Linda, was also happy; the household was thriving. Then Biff, rushing to his father in a crisis, discovers him with another woman, calls him a "phony," turns into a petty thief, and leaves home. Biff might have found himself as a farmer, but some family bond always brings him back, to quarrel with his father and leave again. Happy has grown into a complacent, self-centered lecher. Linda, loving and understanding her husband, defends him against the contempt of his sons, but can bring nothing to sustain Willy, as he wonders vaguely and glumly about the downward turn of life. Finally, his salesmanship slumps so low that he cannot even persuade himself to go on living. His insurance, he comes to think, makes Willy "worth more dead than alive."

The story is presented through a succession of scenes that flow freely through time. Some are in "the present"; some are in the past as it was (as the author sees it); some, apparently, are in the past as Willy sees it; and some scenes are entirely in Willy's imagination. Just which are which, it is sometimes hard to tell; but this physical confusion is important as a symptom of deeper confusions in the play.

The very theme of *Death of a Salesman* is a matter of sharp difference of opinion. John Mason Brown declared the play "the most poignant statement of man as he must face himself to have come out of our theatre." Miller himself, in commenting on the play, said: "Willy is Everyman who finds he must create another personality in order to make his way in the world, and therefore has sold himself." On the other hand, Miller has told the present writer that he had discussed his play with Harold Clurman, and that subsequently Clurman, in *Tomorrow* (May 1949), had expressed Miller's intention "better than I could myself." Clurman was emphatically with those that saw a wide social significance in *Death of a Salesman*. The play, he declared, "is a challenge to the American dream . . . of business success. . . . Salesmanship implies a certain element of fraud: the ability to put over or sell a commodity regardless of its intrinsic usefulness. . . . The death of Arthur Miller's salesman is symbolic of the breakdown of the whole concept of salesmanship inherent in our society."

The critics did not agree. Willy's story is one of an individual's incompetence, not of society's insufficiency. Willy does not fail because his standards are false; he just fails to meet his own standards. Other men, he declares, can sit and get orders by phone; but he has to have his mistress pass him through to her boss. This is no criticism of salesmanship. In fact, Willy's family life with his growing sons is very happy. The seeds of corruption in it are by no means inherent in Willy's occupation or ideals; they are, simply, flaws in Willy.

More than confusion and the failure to establish its theme mars *Death of a Salesman*. Willy's killing himself, telling himself it's to help Linda financially, is a dumb, pathetic step, that gives none of the exaltation of tragedy. Most of the minor figures in the play are left uncomfortably undeveloped; Willy's boss, his mistress, his brother, who's made a fortune in Alaska and in the jungle, are cartoon characters.

Most, of the reviewers, nevertheless, praised the play. Brooks Atkinson called it "one of the finest dramas in the whole range of the American theatre"; John Chapman, "One of those unforgettable times in which all is right and nothing is wrong"; Robert Garland, "One of the lasting rewards that I, as a professional theatre-goer, have received in a long full life of professional theatregoing." The supersalesman W. Howard Fuller, president of The Fuller Brush Company, in *Fortune* (May 1949), sought to explain why salesman Willy Loman's story had such wide appeal: "Nearly everyone who sees it can discover some quality displayed by Willy and his sons that exists in himself and his friends and relatives. It is this close identity between the audience and the characters that lends such poignancy to the tragedy."

A few reviewers seemed disturbed by the play's success. Atkinson later remarked (May 29, 1949) that seeking the basis for its favorable reception would be "a job in mass *psychiatry* terrible to contemplate." Yet Dr. Frederic Wertham inquired before interviewing Arthur Miller for the *New York Times Book Review* (May 15, 1949): "What is the basis of its universal success? The people have spoken. But have they listened?" They attended, at any rate, 742 performances in New York. Lee J. Cobb, Gene Lockhart, Albert Dekker, and Thomas Mitchell in succession played the role of Willy Loman.

Partisan Review (June 1949) saw in the play "an intellectual muddle and lack of candor that regardless of Mr. Miller's conscious intent are the main earmark of contemporary fellow-traveling. . . . This is a very dull business which departs in no way that is to its credit from the general mediocrity of our commercial theatre . . ." George Ross in *Commentary* (February 1951), discussing the Yiddish production of *Death of a Salesman,* had this to say: "What one feels most strikingly is that this Yiddish play is really the original, and the Broadway production was merely Arthur Miller's translation into English." He suggested that Miller "make another try at a more imaginative translation of his material into English; the attempt might result in a more authentic and, by that same token, a more moving play." *Death of a Salesman,* in truth, is even closer than the early works of Clifford Odets to the sob-stuff of the Yiddish drama.

Harold Hobson struck at this mixture of James Barrie and *Esquire* when he said that the play's "fusion, or confusion, of them is its greatest artistic defect, yet it may prove again its financial salvation. For the world is full of people who like to eat their cake and have it."

British reviewers were cool toward a London production which opened July 28, 1949, for 204 performances. Ivor Brown reported in the *New York Times* (August 28, 1949): "There were cheers for Paul Muni, but no tears for Willy Loman . . . its pathos is more easily recognized in Brooklyn than in Balham. . . . The play has an immediate, and specious, appeal because it makes the little man the hero. . . . It is Lowman, not Highman, who throws Broadway into compassionate lamentation."

Viewed from overseas, *Death of a Salesman* lacked universality as well as sharpness of outline. Arthur Miller has exemplified, rather than caught into conscious art, the muddled strivings, the distorted rather than false ideals, and the consequent confused sense of guilt, of our time.

Among revivals of *Death of a Salesman*: New York Circle in the Square, 1975, with George C. Scott; 1979, Providence, R.I.; 1980, Pittsburgh; 1981, Boston and Brooklyn College; May 1, 1983, Peking, directed by the author. To the Chinese cast, Miller explained that it is a play about the love between a father and a son; and at the New York Broadhurst, March 29, 1984, the final scene between Dustin Hoffman as Willy and John Malkowitz as Biff, Frank Rich in the *Times* called "the transcendent sum of two of the American theatre's most lowly, yet enduring, parts."

In the September 20, 1979, NT (Lyttleton) production, repeated in 1980, Warren Mitchell pictured Willy as weary, spiritually dead, from the start.

Miller's Introduction to his *Collected Plays,* 1958, explains: "The first image that occurred to me, which was to result in *Death of a Salesman,* was of an enormous face the height of the proscenium arch which would appear and then open up; we would see the inside of a man's head. In fact, *The Inside of His Head* was the first title. It was conceived half in laughter, for the inside of his head was a mess of contradictions." This may explain the mess of reactions to the play. It is indeed gripping, yet lacks the lift of tragedy.

THE PRICE   *Arthur Miller*

The outstanding American playwright of his period was Arthur Miller (b. 1915). Although his first Broadway play, *The Man Who Had All the Luck*

(1944), ran for but four performances, his next two plays, *All My Sons* (1947) and *Death of a Salesman** (1949) won the Critics' Circle Award—the second, also the Pulitzer Prize. Less distinguished was *The Crucible* (1953), originally called *Those Familiar Spirits,* a vivid presentation of the McCarthy anti-Communist activity as a witch hunt—although there were no witches, and there were Communists. Of a 1976 revival at Stratford, Conn., Alan Rich wrote in the *New York Times*: "Its relevance to the times has dissipated, leaving only its shrill didacticism and its ludicrous attempt to create atmosphere by its hokey pseudoarchaic language (consisting largely of bad grammar)." The NT January 19, 1965, showed *The Crucible* at the Old Vic, directed by Laurence Olivier, but its October 30, 1980, revival was relegated to the tiny Cottesloe.

Miller's *After the Fall* (1964) was equally attacked (by John Simon in the summer 1964 *Hudson Review*): "The most painful flaw of *After the Fall* is its megalomania combined with hypocrisy. A forthright, smiling self-love can be harmless and even likeable. But here we have Miller telling us that he is relentlessly baring his, or his blatantly autobiographical hero's, chest—only to emerge as someone whose faults are as nothing compared to those of almost anybody else." Miller's *Creation of the World and Other Matters** lasted only forty-one performances.

His reputation was restored by *The Price,* which opened at the Morosco, New York, February 7, 1968, for 429 performances, with Pat Hingle as Victor Franz; Kate Reid, his wife, Esther; Arthur Kennedy, his brother, Walter; Harold Gray, Gregory Solomon (replacing David Burns, who fell ill on the pre-Broadway tour).

Victor, a uniformed New York policeman, talks with his wife in the attic of his late father's house, where all the furniture is piled, awaiting disposal. Esther points out that Victor's brother Walter owes them "a moral debt; he could never have finished medical school if you hadn't taken care of Pop"—who died sixteen years ago; now the building is to be torn down; now the brothers will meet for the first time since the funeral.

The real creation in the play is Solomon, the ninety-year-old second-hand-furniture dealer, who instead of being businesslike, making an assessment and offering a price, talks about his four wives, his daughter's inexplicable suicide; a genuine though comical old man. (Miller suggests an intermission with the arrival of Walter, but prefers "an unbroken performance, as in the original Broadway production.")

Business: Esther argues that $1,100 is not enough. Walter, now a successful surgeon, refuses to take any of the money; Vic has earned it; "It's yours." Solomon and Walter go into the next room; Walter comes back with a proposal: they can get an estimate of $25,000 for the furniture; he'll donate it to the Salvation Army and get a saving of some $12,000 in taxes, which they can split. Victor turns this down. Walter tells them he's had a nervous breakdown; he's changed. Instead of owning three lucrative nursing homes, he now spends half his time in city hospitals. Victor is still hostile; Walter tries to break through; their talk is dramatic, convincing, emotion-wrung. Solomon comes in; Walter goes, Victor cries out and starts after him; Solomon stops him: "Let him go." Esther accepts the situation; she and Victor go out to a movie. Solomon plucks at the old harp, turns on the phonograph. The Laughing Record plays; with the comedians, Solomon laughs, tears in his eyes, as the curtain falls.

At the Duke of York's, London, opening in March 1969, directed by the author, the play ran for over 100 performances, with Albert Salmi as Victor, Shepperd Strudwick, Walter; Harold Gary, old Solomon; Kate Reid, Victor's wife. The apostle of the avant-garde, Charles Marowitz, in *Plays and Players,* April 1969, analyzed "Miller's assumption that some concrete and knowable truth *can* be known, that if enough layers are stripped away, one eventually reaches a bedrock which one can celebrate as the truth. It is this unshakeable belief in demonstrable revelation which is what makes him seem old-fashioned. That, and his irresistible weakness for sociological melodrama.... As with *All My Sons* and *Death of a Salesman,* the real villain is self-delusion.... If there can be such a thing as a beautiful expression of a dying artform, *The Price* is it."

Strudwick, with Michael Strong as his policeman brother, was in the 1970 Chicago production. Leningrad acclaimed the play in 1969; Paris, at the Vieux Carré, in 1971. In New York, 1979, Joseph Buloff played Solomon; Mitchell Ryan, Victor; Fritz Weaver, Walter; this Playhouse production was also at the Spoleto Festival (Charleston, S.C.). There were productions January 27, 1981, in Allentown, Pa., and February 19, 1982, in Lowell, Mass. In Communist China it was the first translated play, in 1980, when Arthur Miller and his wife, the photographer Inge Morath, were there preparing a book on their journey.

Miller, in his production notes to the script of *The Price,* wrote: "As the world now operates, the qualities of both brothers are necessary to it; surely their respective psychologies and moral values conflict at the heart of the social dilemma." He has revealed them more fully than those in any other of his plays. *The Price* is considered by many to be Arthur Miller's best play.

THE TRUTH ABOUT BLAYDS   *A. A. Milne*

A. A. Milne (1882-1956) set a serious situation into a comic frame in *The Truth About Blayds,* 1921. The *London Times* of December 21, 1921, called the play "comic, both in the vulgar and in the strict sense: [Mr. Milne] provokes hearty laughter, and also calls up the serious emotions that are not too serious to be within the province of comedy." In two ways—these only, for their moods are wholly unlike—*The Truth About Blayds* resembles Ibsen's *The Wild Duck**: both plays picture the havoc wrought by a sudden revelation, in a household dwelling comfortably upon a lie: and both seem to point the moral that not all truths are always to be told.

The play concerns ninety-year old Oliver Blayds, who is venerated as the last of the great Victorian poets, their equal and their friend. His daughter Isobel, who has relinquished the man she loves, the critic Royce, to devote her life to her father, comes from the latter's deathbed to announce to the family his confession: all his poetry, save the one book the critics damned, has been stolen from manuscripts left him by a long-dead friend.

The reactions of the family give rich irony to the play. Son-in-law Blayds-Conway, who is planning a biography of the genius, brushes the confession aside, and there is a condescending reference to "another Shakespeare-Bacon controversy." Isobel, indignant at having wasted her life on a fraud, wants to give the truth to the world at once, and rehabilitate the dead genius, Jenkins. Blayd's works have brought them all a tidy sum; the news that Jenkins had made his best friend, Blayds, his heir eases their financial worry, but does not ease their consciences. With the thought that the poetry, not the name of the author, is what matters, they decide not to waken scandal. Isobel finally accepts her Royce, and Blayds-Conway settles down to his biography, in which he promises to make reference to the Jenkins shadow in Blayds' background: "It is our duty to tell the whole truth about that great man." The satire is particularly effective in the way each relative completely loses all human feeling, all sense of personal relationship, in regard to old Blayds. He is just an antique; the question is, whether or not he is genuine.

The Truth About Blayds was a hit on both sides of the ocean. London saw it, December 20, 1921, with Irene Vanbrugh, Dion Boucicault, and Norman McKinnel. The *Telegraph* said it had "less sparkle than usual because there is more depth." In New York, the play opened on March 14, 1922, with O. P. Heggie, Alexandra Carlisle, Leslie Howard, Frieda Inescort, Gilbert Emery and Ferdinand Gottschalk. Alexander Woollcott called it "an engrossing play . . . wise, finely wrought." Percy Hammond remarked: "Any plagiarist who could steal, as Blayds did, his friend Jenkins' *Ode To Truth* and other works, and live to be ninety in the spurious glamour of their fame, is himself a poet of distinction. It was a beautiful achievement in mendacity, and we were all glad when it was decided last night to let it stand."

The play was revived in New York, April 11, 1932, with O. P. Heggie, Effie Shannon, Pauline Lord, and Ernest Lawford.

Pauline Lord also acted, the next autumn, in a sort of obverse story to *The Truth About Blayds,* the very successful *Prenez garde à la peinture* (1932), by René Fauchois (b. 1882) which within the year Emlyn Williams* adapted for England, and Sidney Howard* for the United States. In New York, as *The Late Christopher Bean,* it opened October 31, 1932, with Pauline Lord, Walter Connolly, Beulah Bondi, Clarence Derwent, and Ernest Lawford. The English version (with Sir Cedric Hardwicke) was set in Wales; the American, in New England. It pictures Abby, the faithful drudge in a country doctor's family, the only one who had befriended the poor and neglected painter, Christopher Bean, until he died. Then a critic hails him as a genius; art dealers rush upon the doctor's family, whose greed is awakened. They rescue Bean's paintings from plugging leaks in the roof, from serving as backs to the chromos the doctor's daughter made. Abby resists their pressure to give up Bean's portrait of her; it turns out that she has eighteen further authentic Beans. It turns out, further, that the paintings the doctor has been setting the dealers at odds to buy are also Abby's; for she is the widow of the late Christopher Bean.

Pauline Lord played Abby again in 1938. June Walker assumed the part in 1934, with Geoffrey Kerr and Montagu Love; again in 1939. Others who have appeared in this popular play are Helen Mencken, Charlotte Greenwood, and Catherine Alexander. It has been a favorite of colleges and community theatres.

The Truth About Blayds remains Milne's most serious drama, an ironic comedy that lays bare the personal interest behind pretense.

The Late Christopher Bean was revived in Toronto, 1970; Broadway saw it again in 1982, with Jean Stapleton as Abby.

SAMSON AGONISTES   *John Milton*

The final great poem of blind John Milton, *Samson Agonistes* (Samson Wrestling), 1672, though in dramatic form, was not, like his *Comus,* intended to be played. It was, however, produced in London on April 7, 1900, and in 1908, 1935, and 1938. The story is the familiar one of the Bible (*Judges* XVI). In prison at Gaza, blind Samson is visited by his Jewish friends, who form the Chorus, then by his old father, Manoa, who still hopes for his release, and by Delilah, his wife, who asks forgiveness, but reveals herself still his evil spirit. Taunted by Harapha, a strong man of Gath, Samson is taken to the temple of Dagon, for the sport of the Philistines celebrating there. A messenger bears word of Samson's destruction of the temple, which took the Philistines down with him in death.

Following the pattern of a Greek tragedy (with chorus, and with action not presented but reported) *Samson Agonistes* also follows the spiritual course of Milton's life. Like Samson, Milton felt that he was guilty of that noblest of tragic faults—hybris, rebellious pride. Like Samson, Milton had to walk in darkness, stumble in the Valley of Humiliation, learn that God doth not need either man's work or His own gifts: through full submission he might come again to serve. In Samson's travail we find "the inner agony of Greek tragedy in its darker moments" until the Greek catharsis is achieved.

On the title page of the play's text Milton quotes Aristotle's definition: "Tragedy is the imitation of a serious action . . . through pity and fear effecting a purgation [catharsis] of such emotions."

It is the need of submission to the Lord that makes Samson seem to some a passive, undramatic figure. Writing in the *Saturday Review* of Dec. 19, 1908, Max Beerbohm denied the play any dramatic quality: "even Dalila, the one dramatically imagined person in the play, has a taste for copybook headings." However, James H. Hanford, in his *John Milton, Englishman* (1949), had this to say: "The resolution of conflict is on a different level from anything we have met elsewhere in Milton's work. There is no God from a machine. Samson accomplishes his restoration to favor by his own effort. He is dynamic even in bewailing his hard lot or confronting the image of his guilt. His final act, though felt to be divinely instigated, is yet an act of passion. . . . It is not right reason which triumphs, but the will of man."

Milton, as Cromwell's Latin Secretary, was opposed both to the Catholic Church and to monarchy. His feeling against the latter rings through the drama.

Samson Agonistes is a great poem cast in dramatic form. Its chief classical model is the *Prometheus Bound**** of Aeschylus, which it follows in majesty of conception and character, as well as in general form, even in such matters as having one character lengthily alone onstage. Like Aeschylus, Milton achieves poetry of the highest order in *Samson Agonistes*. The play's ending rises to theatrical power. "The climax was made exciting," declared the *London Times* of April 11, 1938, "by a breathless but brilliant recitative effort on the part of the Messenger." The best appreciation of *Samson Agonistes* as a stage piece is probably that of the *Times* a few years earlier (July 24, 1935): "There is the grandeur of the poetry . . . a grandeur which Milton himself never surpassed, and there is also the intrinsic interest of feeling everywhere in the play the poet's final reflections on his own experience, his blindness, his unhappy marriage, and the defeat of his spiritual and secular ideals. . . . While Samson laments in exquisitely subtle monologues over what has passed, slowly forms the resolve to do some great deed and steadily establishes the theme that man is regenerated by the use of his will to resist temptation, the stage is more or less static . . . except in the closing scene, which is magnificent in its swift drama."

The redemption of man through the exercise of his will, however static the stage, is a dynamic conception and a powerful motivating force. In *Samson Agonistes,* expressed in majestic poetry, the integrity, the thought, and the feeling of Milton reach their dramatic height.

The play has had recent vivid productions. A July 1956 presentation at

Birmingham, England, went on to the Ludlow Festival. Sir Michael Redgrave played Samson at Guilford in 1965, with Max Adrian and Fay Compton; Faith Brook as Dalila. Dartmouth College, N.H., saw it January 1959. Of a London production before the altar of St. Martin's in the Fields (Trafalgar Square), the *Times* observed: "Behind its classical severity and its simple directness lie a profundity of thought and a mastery of construction, rivalling that of Racine, which make it one of the supreme achievements of tragic drama . . . Abraham Sofaer, who surely has one of the richest and most beautifully modulated voices of today, gives Samson a dignity worthy of the tragic, passionate, resigned rhythm of his words."

THE NEW YORK IDEA   *Langdon Mitchell*

Although the cast of *The New York Idea,* when it opened in New York on November 19, 1906, included Emily Stevens, George Arliss, and Dudley Digges, the play is usually associated with Minnie Maddern Fiske as the fetching divorcee, Cynthia Karslake. Even before the Broadway run, her work was hailed. The *Chicago Record Herald* of October 16, 1906, declared: "Pathos springs from laughter, and reverts to it, in the twinkling of Mrs. Fiske's eyes . . . Mrs. Fiske played with her audience—tossed laughter to it as she might in mischievous frolic have tossed thistles to stick on the garments of self-satisfaction." The play is a mixture of merry comedy and satire on divorce.

Langdon Mitchell (American, 1862-1935), son of the physician and novelist S. Weir Mitchell, was basically serious in his intent. "The humor is only incidental," he stated in the *Boston Transcript* of January 19, 1907. "It is only such humor as happened to come to me, spontaneously evolved from the situation. . . . I do not consider it a funny play but, on the contrary, a very serious one. . . . The essence of this comedy sermon of mine is contained in Karslake's line: 'Ours was a premature divorce, and you are in love with me still.'" Despite Mitchell, and despite the appalling increase in the divorce rate since it was written, the play holds to this day because of the humor of its situations.

Cynthia, the divorced wife of Jack Karslake, comes to stay with the family of her fiancé, Judge Philip Phillimore, for a few days before the wedding. She is liked by none of the Judge's conservative Washington Square family. When Cynthia's ex-husband and the judge's ex-wife call on business—Jack wants to sell his horse, named Cynthia K—the relationships have to be explained to the English visitor, Sir Wilfred Cates-Darby. Wilfred, who has come to America to marry wealth, is ready to take either of the ladies, but when Vida, the judge's ex-wife, sets her flirtatious cap for Cynthia's ex-husband, Cynthia decides she has to save the susceptible Jack from Vida's lures. In the process, the Karslakes discover that they are still in love. The venerable judge and his reverend brother are left waiting at the altar, and the discovery that the Karslake divorce was not valid, after all, speeds the closing reunion.

When first shown, *The New York Idea* seemed a daring, breath-taking play. The *Chicago News* of October 16, 1906, called it "decidedly astonishing in its courage and ribald satire. . . . The *New York Post,* however, reacted unfavorably to the out-of-town praises: "Instead of the hoped-for comedy . . . there was a sort of farce, or extravaganza . . . pert, audacious, nonsensical, utterly insignificant, and occasionally, unmindful of good taste." The sole aim of this play, the *Post* added, is to extract laughter out of the least respectable possibilities of a notoriously scandalous institution."

The *New York Dramatic Mirror* of December 1, 1906, deemed *The New York Idea* "a satire of social circumstances, whose ridicule bites as deep and hurts as long as the tragic realism of one of Ibsen's dramas, though it is clothed in the pleasing robe of comedy . . . a marvelously vivid, coherent, and effective work." Later performances—Grace George played it around the land, and it has had frequent amateur and little theatre production—have emphasized the comedy. The satire comes a bit obvious and the characters are not deeply probed, but it remains good fun. As George Freedley said in 1948, *The New York Idea* is still "an amusing and frequently hilarious comedy."

Much of the liveliness and lightness of the play springs from the deft and sparkling dialogue. Striking out, lightly but neatly, at hasty divorce when the adage "Marry in haste and divorce in Reno" was beginning to shape the American mores. *The New York Idea,* compared in 1906 to the dramas of Ibsen and Shaw, remains an entertaining study of the eccentricities of smart society.

Among recent revivals of the play: 1952, New York Ziegfeld; 1962, ELT; 1963, Harvard University; 1976, Berkshire Theatre Festival and the straw-hat circuit; 1976, Asolo, "the light touch, and the right touch"; 1977, BAM. Sir Wilfred in the play sums up the United States: "You know, Mrs. Karslake, I like your country. No fear and no respect. No cant and lots of can." The play continues to "amuse, baffle, surprise and stimulate its audience."

THE AFFECTED YOUNG LADIES   *Molière (Jean B. Poquelin)*

Jean Baptiste Poquelin (1622-1673)—he took the name Molière when he became an actor—is the greatest French comic dramatist. Indeed, as Saintsbury says in his *History of French Literature,* "If we leave purely poetic merit out of the question, and restrict the definition of comedy to the dramatic presentment of the characters and incidents of actual life, in such a manner as at once to hold the mirror up to nature and to convey lessons of morality and conduct, we must allow Molière the rank of the greatest comic writer of all the world."

An active man of the theatre, Molière was actor, manager, and play-wright for his company. For some twelve years, he toured France with the Béjart family in "The Illustrious Theatre Company." On November 14, 1659, the one-act farce *Les Précieuses Ridicules (The Affected Young Ladies)* had its première. When it was played, early in 1660, before Cardinal Mazarin, King Louis XIV leaned incognito on the Cardinal's chair; he gave the company 3,000 livres; and "Monsieur," the King's brother, took the company under his protection. Molière was launched.

Les Précieuses Ridicules was the first modern social satire. It ridiculed the feminine coterie then in high repute throughout France. Women such as Madame de Sévigné, Madame de Lafayette, Mademoiselle de Scudéry, gathered all the great figures of the day in their salons, seeking to improve the taste of the time, to avoid extremes of pedantry and vulgarity, to lend elegance to language and to manners.

Deriding the excesses of such gentlewomen, *Les Précieuses Ridicules* por-trays two affected ladies come to Paris, where they spurn their lovers, seeking more delicate gallants. The lovers have their valets masquerade as gentle-men. They are greeted by the ladies in this fashion: "I beg you, Monsieur, do not be inexorable to this easy chair, which has been opening its arms to you for a quarter of an hour; satisfy its desire to embrace you." The valets match the affected talk of the ladies with grandiose absurdities, until the lovers, returning, force the valets to unmask—and properly lesson the ladies.

Mascarille, the comic valet, was acted by Molière; by Jodelet; most effectively in recent years by Coquelin (Benoit Constant Coquelin, 1841-1909). When he is unmasked, Mascarille takes off waistcoat after waistcoat (as does the gravedigger in *Hamlet**) in perennial comedy.

The satire struck home. All fashionable Paris attended the opening, but the coterie was cold; the play was banned for a fortnight. Molière protested that he was attacking only excess. After the King showed his favor, the play reopened and played to crowded houses, twice daily, at double prices, for four months. Amused audiences have rejoiced in its fresh fun and pungent satire ever since. But the hostility of the nobles, against the "presumptuous player," Molière, pursued the playwright to his grave.

Everywhere *Les Précieuses Ridicules* has proved a delight. Of an American production, the *New York Dramatic Mirror* of October 13, 1888, reported: "An admirable skit . . . a bit of grotesque exaggeration of amazing proportions."

When *Les Précieuses Ridicules* was played in 1938, the *Post* called it "hilarious mockery"; in the same year, a copy of the first edition brought £880 in London. "Les Compagnons," of Montreal, played the farce in Boston and in New York in 1946.

A somewhat different attitude toward the satire is urged by Ashley Dukes. Writing for *Theatre Arts* (August, 1937) he said: "In the apparent realism of Molière the most important thing is its poetic fabric. . . . I should say that the comedies of Molière never moralize, in the usual sense, and we must see in them quite simply the most perfect expression of the French spirit, a new form of what Rabelais called *pantagruelisme*—a certain gaiety preserved in defiance of fortuitous events—an attitude of mind, which is distinctly superior to a moral."

There may be exaggeration rather than photography in *Les Précieuses Ridicules,* but there is essential truth in its capture of pretentiousness and continuing delight in its good-natured mockery.

For more general discussion of Molière, see the end of *The Imaginary Invalid.**

THE SCHOOL FOR WIVES   *Molière*

Produced in Paris in December 1662, this highly amusing play has a story artfully woven for expectancy, suspense, and surprise.

Three characters in the play are excellently developed. Arnolphe (originally played by Molière) is a man of forty, who has raised the girl Agnes in sweet and simple innocence to be his wife. In a dozen amusing soliloquies, Arnolphe reveals himself to us; jealous but not a dupe, to awaken our laughter and sympathy. Arnolphe is, as noted by Paul Benichon in *Morals of the Grand Century* (1948), "the most thoroughly revealed figure Molière has given us of the bourgeois in love."

Agnes' very innocence, however, defeats Arnolphe. For when young Horace makes love to her, she knows no reason why she should not respond. She is completely frank when Arnolphe questions her. Horace, too, tells the old man of all his meetings with the ward of "M. de la Souche," unaware that he is talking to that very man. The situations are superbly handled— so deftly, in fact, that Voltaire insisted the play seems to be all action when it's really all narrative, and Sainte-Beuve marvelled how interest is maintained in a five-act love story when the audience doesn't see the lovers meet until the middle of the last act!

Through sycophant writers and rival theatrical companies, nobles hostile toward Molière denounced the play on three grounds. Listing a few remarks of double meaning, they called it indecent; in that it seemed to approve revolt against one's lawful guardian, they called it immoral; and, as Arnolphe's list of commandments for a wife might be construed as a parody of a sermon, they called it impious. In the eyes of Louis XIV, however, such satire served to strengthen his power, now firmly held against the nobles. On the list of annual pensions in 1663 were Corneille (2,000 livres as "the foremost dramatic poet of the world"), young Racine (800 livres, as "French poet"), and—the only actor included—Molière (1,000 livres, as "excellent comic poet"). When the King asked which writer under his reign had most honored France, the poet and law-giver of the drama, Boileau, answered: "Molière." Yet Molière saw himself not merely as a dramatist, but fully as a man of the theatre. When he was offered membership in the French Academy if he would stop acting, he refused. The seat was given to Racine.

The School for Wives was first performed in America at New York's John Street Theatre on May 8, 1788. London saw it in the same year with English setting and names. More recently, it was presented in New York, in French, in 1933, by the Abbey Theatre in Dublin in 1934, and in Montreal, then in New York, with Louis Jouvet, in 1951.

To the many contemporary objections to this play, Molière answered with a one-act prose comedy, *Critique of The School for Wives,* which opened in Paris on June 1, 1663. A series of conversations, with characters neatly contrasted, of marvelous variety and vivacity, this "dialogued essay in criticism," remarked Brander Matthews, "is one of the most adroit and characteristic of Molière's comedies." The *Critique* evoked a number of responses, published, or performed by a rival company at the Hotel de Bourgogne; and Louis XIV, in his first direct command, ordered Molière to retort. He had a week's notice before presenting what he called (October 14, 1663) the *Impromptu de Versailles.* This ingenious handling of the problem begins with Molière's telling members of the company they are to perform. They suggest postponement; he says they must defer to the King's command. Then we watch Molière, the stage manager, conducting a rehearsal, telling the company what and how to act; Molière, the author, presenting his writing creed; and Molière, the man, in dignity defending himself against personal abuse. One character remarks that the best answer to criticism is another good play. (And, indeed, thereafter Molière never again responded to attacks). Amid these displays of virtuosity, Molière freshened his satire with some lively sallies between man and wife (his own wife rejoined the company for the *Critique,* after bearing a son, to whom the King condescended to act as god-father). As in the *Critique* and the *Impromptu* Molière showed understanding and dignity in defending his art; so in *The School For Wives* and other plays he sets his own passions and pains in their proper perspective. He was often a victim, but never a dupe. Through his genius, his lapses and sufferings in life become sources of laughter and of a finer perception of truth.

TARTUFFE   *Molière*

On the sixth day of the Versailles Spring Festival of 1664, three acts of *Tartuffe* were presented.

There was at once a howl of protest from the pious; the Queen-Mother exacted a promise that it would never be shown again. After she died, the King authorized its production; it was shown in August, 1667, but with the King off at the wars, the Mayor of Paris closed the play. Not until February, 1669, when the Jesuits and Jansenists had quieted their feud and their fervor in "the Peace of the Church," did *Tartuffe* achieve a run. It was an instant and lasting success. "The best title of Louis XIV to the recollection of posterity," Lord Morley has said, "is the protection he extended to Molière."

What was this play, which roused such pious wrath? Into the home of the substantial citizen Orgon (originally played by Molière) comes cunning, hypocritical Tartuffe, who, palming himself off on an honest and refined family, tries to drive the son away, marry the daughter, corrupt the wife, ruin and imprison the father, and almost succeeds, not by clever plots but, as Taine described it, "by the coarse audacity of his caddish disposition." When Orgon's wife pretends to yield to Tartuffe, in order to let her husband hear, and the hypocrite is exposed, he brazens out the situation. Presenting Orgon's deed of gift, Tartuffe claims the house as his, and only a message from King Louis saves Orgon and sends Tartuffe to prison.

When an Italian company performed *Scaramouche and the Hermit,* Louis XIV said to Condé: "I'd like to know why those that are so scandalized by Molière's play do not object to this *Scaramouche*." Condé replied: "That's because this *Scaramouche* shows up religion and Heaven, about which these gentlemen care nothing; but Molière's comedy shows them up—and this, they will not allow."

The excellent workmanship of *Tartuffe* has won highest praise. The play is simple without being bare, direct without being obvious; it is powerful in conception, unswerving in movement, and, given the characters, inevitable in its situations and turns. Of its opening, Goethe exclaimed: "Only think what an introduction is the first scene! . . . It is the greatest and best thing of the kind that exists." Of the climactic drive, when the exposed Tartuffe turns with renewed demands upon his baffled victims, Brander Matthews wrote: "It is one of the most effective scenes ever shown in a theatre, startling when it comes, and yet perfectly prepared for and immediately plausible." When Molière's company took the play to London in 1879, the French critic Sarcey noted that *Tartuffe* was the easiest, if not the only, play for those unfamiliar with the language to watch with unflagging interest.

Only one great critic has objected to a structural aspect of *Tartuffe*. Taine considered the ending careless, for bringing the King casually in as a *deus ex machina*. Even the dramatic hack, Taine remarked, could tell that "the catastrophe of half of Molière's plays is ridiculous." But Scribe*—the "hack" *par excellence* of Taine's own time, the master of the well-made play—found the ending "has one great merit: without it, we should not have had the play, for Molière would probably not have been allowed to produce it, had he not given the King a role in it. . . . Here is an honest man who has bravely served his country, and who, when deceived by the most open and odious of machinations, does not find anywhere, in society or in law, a single weapon wherewith to defend himself. To save him, the sovereign himself must needs intervene. Where can a more terrible condemnation of the reign be found than in this immense eulogy of the King!"

After its first vicissitudes, *Tartuffe* continued to have a varied history. Voltaire commented in 1739: "Scarcely anyone now goes to the *Tartuffe* that once drew all Paris." Napoleon said he'd never have permitted even the first performance of the play, yet he saw it several times, preferring a production of elegance and almost affected nicety to the direct, robustious presentation.

The Romantic movement paid fullest tribute to Molière. In 1800, Madame de Staël remarked: "We feel a vague sentiment of sadness in the most comic scenes of *Tartuffe,* because they bring to mind the natural wickedness of man"; in 1801, Chateaubriand said: "It is remarkable how the comedy of *Tartuffe,* by its extreme profundity and, if I may say so, by its sadness, closely approaches the tragic gravity." A one-act play, written by Merle and Désessarts in 1809, *Down With Molière,* could not stem the tide. From 1815 on, *Tartuffe* was welcomed by packed houses. Stendhal, in 1825, said of Molière that he "has seen clearly into the depths of the human heart" and hailed him as the greatest genius in French literature. The *Paris Globe* of March 18, 1826, declared: "In general, if the English tragedies hold more truth than our own, their comedies hold less; and we prefer Molière to Shakespeare, just as we prefer Shakespeare to Racine." Many outside the English-speaking countries feel the same. The popularity of Molière was summed up by Gustave Lanson in his *History of French Literature* (1894): "Hardly was he dead when all attacks, all jealousies, all reservations ceased; he was ranked as a genius, inimitable and without equal, and never perhaps has a reputation been sustained as consistently as his."

The traditional single set for *Tartuffe* was not varied until 1907, when *L'Illustration* pictured the five sets Antoine introduced for the different acts. Lucien Guitry ventured a new interpretation of the title role, which, however, even the English rejected. The *London Stage* (March 29, 1923), remarked that Tartuffe "untidy in appearance, with the boorish manners of a peasant, and an accent that smells of garlic, would never have been intimately received in Orgon's household . . ." Another change came with the very successful 1950 production in Paris, with Louis Jouvet; for this, the costume of Tartuffe, and the sets by Georges Braque, were a somber black. The end was arranged as a surprise tableau, the rear wall parting to reveal the King.

American performances include one in English, March 13, 1913, at the American Academy of Dramatic Arts with Edward G. Robinson as a sheriff's officer, one by Albert Lambert and Cecile Sorel in New York in 1922, one at New York University in 1938, and one in Boston in 1924. Of the last production, in the traditional vein, the *Boston Transcript* (March 13, 1924) said: "Molière so acted is exceeding good for an American audience to see and hear . . ."

Closest to the hearts of French playgoers, quickening the spirit with laughter even as it sobers and stirs the mind, *Tartuffe* remains the most vivid presentation of a hypocrite, preying upon the weaknesses of ordinary folk, etched in enduring drama.

THE DOCTOR IN SPITE OF HIMSELF   *Molière*

One of Molière's most amusing comedies is *Le Médecin malgré lui (The Doctor in Spite of Himself),* first played August 6, 1666, in three acts in prose. Suggested by a medieval painting, *The Rascally Apothecary,* the play was developed from an earlier farce of Molière's, *The Shuttlecock Doctor.*

The Doctor in Spite of Himself begins with Sganarelle, originally played by Molière, as a cunning but improvident woodcutter, once the servant of a doctor, now married to a shrew. Their neighbor Géronte has a daughter Lucinde, who loves Léandre; to avoid her father's choice, she pretends to be dumb. Various doctors fail to effect a cure.

In the meantime, Sganarelle has thrashed his wife, and she, in revenge, has told the neighbors that Sganarelle is a great doctor, who will not admit it unless he is beaten. Soundly beaten, Sganarelle diagnoses Lucinde's ailment, with a rigmarole jargon of mixed French and pseudo Latin, Hebrew, and Greek. However, when he takes Léandre as his assistant, Lucinde is forthwith cured. Sganarelle thereupon decides to remain a doctor.

The frolicsome, farcical satire of the play has made it highly popular. Fielding based a farce on it, *The Mock Doctor,* which opened in London in 1733 and reached New York in 1750. Gounod made an opera from Molière's play (the Prologue shows the court assembling to watch the comedy); it was heard first in Paris in 1857; recently in New York, 1936, and New Haven, 1941.

The Molière comedy has been translated numerous times, often with a changed title, such as *The Frantic Physician* and *The Doctor by Compulsion.* It is frequently played in community and college theatres. It was acted in Wilmington, Delaware, in 1943, with modern slang and colloquial dialogue. In New York, it was presented in adaptation by Anne Gerlette and the Czech comedian George Voskovec in what claimed to be the first professional production of the play in English. George Freedley (May 30, 1946) called this "certainly one of the best of the Equity-Library productions."

The Doctor in Spite of Himself was produced in Moscow in 1936. In the original French, New York saw the play in 1937, produced by Le Théâtre des quatre-saisons, which had toured the French provinces playing it in the open air. Of the play, as they performed it in a *commedia dell' arte* spirit, *Les Beaux Arts* (May 28, 1937) declared: "The humor of the situations still produces full-throated laughter." A French Canadian group, Les Compagnons, acted the play in Boston and New York in 1946.

As a human being, Molière walked in the valley of tears; as an artist, he knew both that life is too serious to be taken solemnly and—more important—that by laughter man reasserts his values in the face of defeat. Out of the buffeting of comedy, as out of the battering of tragedy, the dignity of the individual indefeasibly rearises.

THE MISANTHROPE   *Molière*

Since the Queen-mother had just died, *The Misanthrope,* June, 1666, was not shown at court. The depth and earnestness of the play's portrayals took the public slowly, but with increasing favor. George Brandes observed that "by most French critics this play is held to be the loftiest achievement of French comedy, the unapproachable masterpiece of the foremost of comic dramatists;" and George Eliot called it "the foremost and most complete production of its kind in the world."

Lord Morley noted its wide social range: "Without plot, fable, or intrigue, we see a section of the polished life of the time, men and women . . . flitting backwards and forwards with a thousand petty worries—and among them one strange, rough, hoarse, half-sombre figure, moving solitarily with a chilling reality in the midst of a world of shadows."

In her salon, the gay and charming Célimène receives the polite world of courtiers and women of fashion, whose varnish of politeness cannot quite conceal vulgarity of taste, polished without being decent, well-bred without being sincere.

Amid this group looms Alceste, insistently sincere. He tells the blunt truth, whether it be a question of his salvation or of a poetaster's love sonnet. He cannot endure the pretense, the affectation, that abound; yet his extravagance is as ridiculous as the others' foibles are bad. His rigid righteousness carries him to extremes. In love with Célimène, he alternates between jealousy of the courtiers whose company feeds her social sense, and impatience with her for enduring them. When she finally consents to marry him, he sets the condition that she abandon the world of fashion and its dazzling insincerities. She refuses; Alceste rushes off to the desert alone; the play ends as his friend Philente goes off to persuade him to return.

Alceste has no pettiness of soul; there are in his make-up true manliness, fervor, and force, but the acid of Célimène's etchings of the folk around has eaten into his soul; in contrast, he grows perhaps overproud of his virtue. He is essentially humorless.

"Célimène," said George Meredith in his essay on *The Idea of Comedy* (1877), "is worldliness; Alceste is unworldliness." Nowhere are two lovers more deftly set in contrast.

The Misanthrope lacks the close-knit structure of *Tartuffe** and the variety of incident of *Don Juan*, but its superb character portrayal wins every audience. Of Richard Mansfield's performance, the *New York Daily Mirror* of April 22, 1905, said: "The character of Alceste has little sympathy, for he appeals more to the reason, but Mr. Mansfield played him so sincerely, with such nobleness . . . he quite won our warm regard."

The performance of Jacques Copeau, in French, 1919, was greatly admired; that of Lucien Guitry, 1922, was not. The work of Cecile Sorel as Célimène won praise (in New York, in French, with Albert Lambert, 1922; with Louis Ravet, in 1926). The play was performed, in a verse translation, in London in 1935. The best recent production in English was in 1937, with Lydia Lopokova as Célimène.

Some critics discern an autobiographic tone in *The Misanthrope*. Molière and his wife were, at the time, estranged; he had reason to believe she was unfaithful. Yet onstage Madame Molière was playing Célimène to her husband's Alceste: what wonder if his jealous tirades lashed with genuine green fire! This suggestion, however, is weakened by the fact that some of Alceste's despairing jealousy is cast in words borrowed from Molière's *Don Garcie*, written long before his marriage.

THE WOULD-BE GENTLEMAN   *Molière*

In 1670 Molière presented before Louis XIV the five-act prose comedy that is today his most frequently performed work, *Le Bourgeois Gentilhomme* (*The Would-Be Gentlemen*).

This picture of the *nouveau riche,* the wealthy citizen who would like to be accepted as a gentleman of fashion, is superb and perennial in its capture. The central figure, Monsieur Jourdain, like most of Molière's best figures, displays in excess a quality within us all. As in *Tartuffe** and *L'Avare*, we watch the disintegrating effects, within a single family, of the folly of its head. The quick-witted and outspoken Nicole, who rebukes Jourdain for his pretensions, ranks, with Dorine of *Tartuffe*, among the best of the maids in comedy—a stock figure lifted to a genuine character presentation.

The play comprises three acts of Molière's best character comedy, followed by two of fantastic farce. The first two acts show Monsieur Jourdain with his various instructors, learning to be a gentleman. In the third act, love enters the scene; for of course widower Jourdain and his daughter Julie must marry as befits Jourdain's hoped-for station. Jourdain aims at Dorimène, Marquise de Montignac, who loves an adventurer and swindler, Dorante, Comte de Chateau-Gaillard (Count of Jolly-Castle). For Julie, these schemers provide the Son of the Grand Turk, who naturally, cannot marry the daughter of a commoner; Jourdain is raised to the rank of "Mamamouchi." But the Grand Turk's son, who marries Julie, is just plain Cléonte, her lover, in disguise. Jourdain is left with his hopes of distinction dashed, but really the better off, as Dorimène and Dorante also decide to marry. The Turks come in for caricature at the end of the play, probably because the new Turkish envoy to the French court had displeased Louis XIV.

Monsieur Jourdain is, as Brander Matthews said, "a constant source of unquenchable laughter, as we behold him delighted to discover that he has spoken prose all his life without knowing it, and as we see him, pricked by the foil in the hands of Nicole, protesting that she is not fencing according to the rules." But there is more than laughter within this portrait. As the critic of the *New York World* (October 3, 1928) noted after the Civic Repertory opening of *The Would-Be Gentleman*: "Jourdain is a fool, a buffoon, a monster of ignorance, crudity, and complacency. But his befuddled destiny is played against a background of snobbish, contemptuous exploitation on the part of the gentlemen he envies; and some of this he dimly feels—and swaggers the more, to combat it. Before the genuine pathos in this picture your own contempt crumbles."

There have geen innumerable productions, in various lands, of *Le Bourgeois Gentilhomme*. It was a favorite role of Coquelin. Firmin Gemier brought his French company to New York in 1924, with romping onstage and amidst the audience. The *New York World* (November 20) reported that "anything funnier or more finished than the Odéon's presentation of the delicious old comedy has not been seen in New York. It was comedy run wild, but never out of hand; absurdity carried to the last degree, but always adroit."

In English, The Civic Repertory presented the play in New York in 1928, in an adaptation by F. Anstey (acted in London in 1928, with Nigel Playfair) with Egon Brecher (Jourdain), Walter Abel, Donald Cameron, Alma Kruger, and J. Edward Bromberg. Pierre de Rohan, in the *New York American* (October 3, 1928), commented: "Molière's immortal comedy has been preserved to us without the loss of a single flash of wit and without the necessity of modernizing a single allusion." Productions at college, community, and summer theatres have been numerous; *The Would-Be Gentlemen* was presented at Cornell University in adaptation by Lady Gregory in 1929; with Jimmy Savo at Westport, Connecticut, in 1936; at the Mohawk Drama Festival in 1937, with Charles Coburn; at Yale in 1937 also; in 1939 at the University of California and at Pennsylvania State College; in Philadelphia, in 1941; at the University of Texas, with Walter Slezak, in 1942; and by ELT in 1945.

With elaborate changes by and with Bobby Clark, *The Would-Be Gentleman* was turned into a masterly display of Clark's comic mannerisms, in a production that opened in New York January 9, 1946. Clark (like Molière) took many liberties. Though it ran for only 77 performances, the production was well received. Robert Coleman called it "a glittering rough-house of fun;" Howard Barnes, "a wonderfully funny show." If there were lapses, some felt, with Louis Kronenberger, that "the fault is mostly Molière's." However, Arthur Pollock insisted that the character comedy of the play, with all its deeper implications, had been sacrificed to the farce: "Clark has taken out all the flavor and, surrounded by a cast of pretty bad actors, simply grinds out the comedy all evening like a cement-mixer."

The original play is, of course, a fast and funny frolic; but it is also a searching exposure of human weakness, and in consequence a reassertion of human dignity. These qualities combine to make Molière's *The Would-Be Gentleman* both a provocation and a delight, one of the world's richest comedies.

THE LEARNED LADIES *Molière*

Molière's *Les Femmes Savantes* (*The Learned Ladies*) was first produced in March 1672.

This five-act play in verse, which Brander Matthews called "the ultimate model of high comedy," follows the fair sex in its fashionable progression from the frills of preciosity (pricked in *Les Précieuses Ridicules**) to the blue stockings of philosophical and scholarly conversation. It was favorably received, but not by Molière's aristocratic foes.

Again, as in *Tartuffe,* L'Avare,* and *Le Bourgeois Gentilhomme,** Molière drives home his theme through a single family; beyond them, too, the social milieu is neatly caught and deftly laid bare. Two generations are shown. Of the old: Chrysale (played originally by Molière), well-intentioned but weak-willed, led by his dominating wife Philaminte, who has been educated beyond her intelligence; and Chrysale's resourceful and sensible brother Ariste, whose flighty old maid sister, Bélise, thinks all the young men are courting her. Of the younger generation, we see Chrysale's two daughters: the pretentious and self-important Armande, her mother's girl, and the simpler and more readily satisfied Henriette (played originally by Madame Molière, then reconciled with her husband).

The play opens with a superb scene in which Armande mocks Henriette for taking her discarded suitor Clitandre; in Molière's deftest dialogue the nature of the two girls is revealed: the prurient prude who shrinks, beneath a mask of would-be learning, from the normal responsibilities of a woman's life; and the charming, straightforward girl of solid affections and simple ways. Philaminte, however, wants Henriette to marry the man she thinks is a paragon of wit and learning, Trissotin. When Uncle Ariste announces that the family money is lost, Trissotin withdraws, and the steadfast Clitandre gets Henriette, as old Ariste reveals that his story of the lost money was just a device to expose Trissotin.

The play is rich in contrasting characters. Trissotin is a sharp portrait of an actual person, the Abbé Cotin, who had translated Lucretius, but had attacked Molière and his friend Boileau; two of Trissotin's epigrams are drawn from the writings of Cotin, who in the play is pilloried for literary pretentiousness. "The comedy as a whole has a unity of intent and a harmony of tone which Molière was rarely able to attain," wrote Brander Matthews.

Les Femmes Savantes pokes fun at pretentious women with Molière's neatly barbed shafts of wit. Tucked into the dialogue are many apt phrases, some of which have become proverbial: "seasoned with Attic salt"; "grammar, which controls even kings."

It was a pleasant bow to the old master when the young women of Hunter College, New York, produced *Les Femmes Savantes,* opening November 5, 1938, the tercentenary of the birth of Louis XIV.

THE IMAGINARY INVALID   *Molière*

Though the title figure in the comedy *La Malade Imaginaire (The Imaginary Invalid)* is a hypochondriac, Molière, while playing the role, himself was seriously ill. He had a convulsion while taking the burlesque oath at the end of the play, during the fourth performance, February 17, 1673, and died before his wife could reach his side.

The Imaginary Invalid carries along Molière's frequent attack upon the quacks and pretending physicians of his day. A sentence of the play—"Most men die, not of their diseases, but of their remedies"—was too nearly true in Molière's time for any but rueful laughter.

Argan, the hypochondriac, wants his daughter to marry a physician, so that there'll always be a doctor in the house. He is attended by a doctor, Purgon; an apothecary, Fleurant; and two other medicos, Purgon's brother-in-law Diafoirius, and young Thomas Diafoirius, whom Argan wants to marry his daughter Angélique. The girl, however, prefers another man. With the help of Argan's solid, clear-headed brother, Béralde, and the shrewd maid Toinette, who at one point puts on the disguise of a doctor, Angélique gets her Cléante. When Béralde suggests that Argan has learned enough to be a doctor himself, Argan agrees, and the play ends with the lifting farce of his induction into doctorhood, with the "right to purge and bleed and kill throughout the world."

The Imaginary Invalid (sometimes translated as *The Robust Invalid*) has been frequently and widely played. It is in the repertory of the Moscow Art Theatre and of the Habimah (Hebrew) Players. When the Coburns played it in New York, Arthur Hornblow in *Theatre* magazine (April, 1917) considered it "the funniest play of the season." The Coburns played it again in 1922, the tercentenary of the birth of Molière. The Old Vic, in London, showed it in English in 1929 in F. Anstey's sprightly version, with Martita Hunt as Madame Argan and Margaret Webster as the maid Toinette. It was presented again at the Old Vic, in French, in 1933, when the *London Times* observed that it had "plenty of wit, and kept fully alive its knockabout fun." Radio versions were broadcast from Munich in 1933 and from London in 1937.

American productions were given at the Mohawk Drama Festival in 1936; at Tuscaloosa, Alabama, in 1939; at Great Neck, Long Island, in 1945; at Piscator's Dramatic Workshop, New York, in 1947; and in Delaware, Ohio, in 1948. Elisabeth Bergner starred in a revival entitled *The Gay Invalid* which opened in London, January 24, 1951. The play shows that the great comic spirit of Molière was vigorous and rich and vital to the end.

In 1680 King Louis XIV founded *La Maison de Molière,* which became the Comédie Française, the oldest theatre company in the world, which still has all Molière's comedies in its repertoire. In 1973, the tercentenary of the playwright's death, most of them were presented. Here can be mentioned just a few of the many productions and adapatations in English.

The School for Wives in 1966 reached its 1,500th performance. In addition to almost annual productions in Britain and the United States—1957, Stratford-upon-Avon; 1959 and 1967, London Old Vic; 1964, Oxford, England; 1967, tour of twenty-three cities in Virginia; 1968, APA-Phoenix and again for 120 New York performances in 1971; 1975 tour of the Midwest in the excellent rhyming couplets of Richard Wilbur—there were two musicals and a Scottish adaptation: *The Amorous Flea,* by Jerry Devine with music and lyrics by Bruce Montgomery, OffBway (78th Street), 1963 for ninety-three performances; *Gold Diggers of 1664,* book and lyrics by Lee Gold-smith, music by Lawrence Hurwit, Miami 1975, mingling seventeenth century France with modern absurdist modes; and *Let Wives Tak Tent,* by Robert Kemp, 1981 at Glasgow and Edinburgh, set in a fortresslike house where the young girl could be incarcerated.

Tartuffe was shown in London, 1961, in the felicitous Miles Malleson translation. In 1965 in Wilbur's verse for seventy-four performances at the New York Lincoln Center; again, directed by John Wood, at the Circle in the Square in 1977. The Wilbur version came to the London NT (Old Vic) November 21, 1967, with John Gielgud and Joan Plowright. The Malleson version returned to London in 1983, as did also a Christopher Hampton translation with the RSC; both of these made the hypocrite so obvious a scoundrel that Eric Shorver in the *Telegraph* (August 26, 1963) suggested that the actors of Orgon and Tartuffe exchange roles.

The Doctor in Spite of Himself was adapted as *The Reluctant Doctor* by George Graveley, at Farnham, England, February 24, 1958; translated by John English at Cardiff, June 3, 1958; adapted as *Doctor's Joy* by Charles Drew at the Bristol Old Vic, December 2, 1958. *The Love Doctor,* concocted by Robert Wright and George Forrest from Molière's medical plays, came to London in 1959. Molière's comedy was shown OffBway in 1955 (Lenox Hill) and again in 1977.

The Misanthrope was played at the Edinburgh Festival in 1961. It was adapted by P. D. Cummins as *All For Truth,* London, 1962. At the NT (Old Vic) a version by Tony Harrison came in 1973, directed by John Dexter, with Alec McCowen and Diana Rigg; this came to the Kennedy Center in Washington for a sold-out month, then to the New York St. James March 12, 1975, for ninety-four performances.

The Wilbur version—with Brian Bedford as Alceste; Mary Beth Hurt, Célimène; Carole Shelley, Arsinoë; Stephen D. Newman, Philinte—came to the Circle in the Square January 28, 1983, and moved Walter Kerr (*Times,* February 6, 1983) to elaborate on the play's problem. In full sincere frank-ness, Alceste proclaims:

> We should condemn with all our force
> Such false and artificial intercourse.

His more discreet friend Philinte demurs:

> In certain cases it would be uncouth
> And most absurd to speak the naked truth.

"The issue is still generalized," says Kerr, "still abstract. Nothing, for instance, has been said about honesty where intimacy has been concerned. Nothing has been said about love. At which point—perhaps some fifteen minutes after the larger issue has been joined—Philinte politely but point-edly asks if he may enquire whether

> ... these hard virtues you're enamoured of
> Are qualities of the lady whom you love?"

Thump! For his beloved Célimène, though charming and indeed adorable, is a coquette. Her chief pleasure lies in the wordplay and half-truths of dalliant discourse. "The scale of the playwright's preparation for this moment," continues Kerr, "the deliciousness with which he's delayed its arrival, the rifle-crack with which the news now detonates in our faces—all of this is literally stunning." It is indeed theatrical exposition at its comic best.

The Miser was played by the Phoenix, 1957-1958; by the Roundabout, 1966-1967; at the New York Lincoln Theater, May 8, 1969, for fifty-two performances. A London adaptation by Max Loding came April 20, 1966. See *The Pot of Gold,* by Plautus*.

The Would-Be Gentleman was played at Stratford, Ontario, and at the Chichester Festival, England, in 1964, translated by H. Baker and J. Miller. To Oxford October 17, 1968, came *The Bootleg Gentleman,* lyrics and music by Michael Bogdanov; set in Chicago in the mid-1930's, it pictures Jordani, a speakeasy hoodlum grown rich among the molls and mobsters, seeking social acceptance. In 1972 a translation by Michael Feingold, directed by Alvin Epstein, came to Yale. In 1977, ACT, translated by Charles Hallahan and Dennis Towers; also in 1977 a lively London show, adapted by Sally Pinder, called *All the Best People.* OffBway (Lehman College) translated by Albert Bernal, with emphasis on song and dance. There was a German version in Vienna, 1973, called *Bürger als Edelman* (*Citizen as Nobleman*).

The Learned Ladies came to London, 1959, as a challenge to "fem lib." The long-suffering husband says to Philaminte: "I live on good soup, not beautiful language." OffBway (Barbizon) saw a modern setting in 1967, "Molière in miniskirts." It went on a Canadian tour in 1979, also to Australia, New Zealand, Tahiti.

The Imaginary Invalid in 1966 reached its 1650th performance at the Comédie Française. In English: April 20, 1966, adapted by Max Loding, combined with *The Miser* at the London Mermaid; 1968, straw-hat circuit; 1974, Stratford, Canada, which led Walter Kerr to exclaim: "How extremely funny an embalmed man can be!" The musical *Toinette,* book by J. I. Rodale, music and lyrics by Deed Meyer, ran OffBway October 20, 1961, for thirty-one performances. In 1977, translated by Morris Bishop, at Topeka, Kansas, there were three interludes: a mimed Pierrot sequence with Toinette; a ballet of trees and flowers; and a doctors' ballet. At the New York Edison, March 5, 1970, a musical adaptation called *Show Me Where the Good Times Are,* book by Lee Thuna, music by Kenneth Jacobson; lyrics by Rhoda Roberts, converted the locale to a Jewish section of New York's lower East Side; Argan became Aaron, played with a Jewish accent and much clowning by Arnold Soboloff, although he was in bed most of the time. Among the songs were "I'm Not Getting Any Younger" and "Staying Alive." There was a conniving wife waiting for the invalid to die. The musical has not been revived; but *The Imaginary Invalid*—and Molière—seem destined to survive for many years more.

A play called *Molière,* by the Russian Mikhail Bulgakov, translated by Helen Rappaport and adapted by Dusty Hughes, was produced by the RSC in 1982. The two authors had similar life stories: Molière was protected by Louis XIV, but his *Tartuffe* was banned for five years from 1664, and many nobles continued to resent his work; Bulgakov was "protected" by Stalin, but from March 1929 his plays were banned in Russia, and his death was not mentioned in the Soviet press. His play pictures Molière's entangled ways with his actress wife, Armande Bejart, whose infidelities tormented him and are reflected in his own comedies. (He thought Armande was the younger sister of his former mistress, but rumor whispers that she was actually his own daughter by the mistress. This legend is accepted in the Bulgakov play, which was revived in London in 1983). Bulgakov's play, while helping to evoke the early period, with Derek Godfrey an imposing Louis XIV, took some sideswipes at the Soviet regime—there is an inquisition scene suggestive of the Russian Cheka—but the farcical treatment of Molière, with false nose and constant stammer, destroys any serious application.

Molière remains at the summit of the comic art.

LILIOM   *Ferenc Molnár*

The suave and subtle comedies of Molnár (Hungarian, 1878-1952) neatly constructed, deft in dialogue, are admirable examples of plays written to entertain. Rarely does their author offer more than lively, slightly ironic, superficial theatrical fare.

Liliom, 1908, gains especial interest because it reaches beyond sentimentality and cynicism to probe a simple, ineffectual heart. It tenderly unfolds a tragedy of the inarticulate. "Liliom" (the nickname "Lily" means Toughy), a swaggering barker in a cheap amusement park, is watched with jealousy by his boss, Mrs. Muskat, as he flirts and then goes away with naive little Julie. Despite Mrs. Muskat's attempts to lure Liliom back, something holds him and Julie together. His impatience at his joblessness, his inarticulate love, his wordless urges, come out in beatings for Julie. Equally incapable of giving words to her thoughts and feelings, Julie somehow understands. When she tells Liliom they are to have a child, he seeks money for it; he permits "The Sparrow" to guide him in a hold-up attempt—which fails; and Liliom stabs himself to escape arrest. Again, beside the dying man, Julie understands.

At the Police Magistrate's Court up yonder, the unregenerate Liliom is sentenced to sixteen years in the purgatorial fires, after which he is allowed a day to return to earth and try to atone. On that day, he brings to his daughter Louise (now sixteen) a star he has stolen from heaven. Julie has told Louise her father was a fine man; when this "stranger" says he knew Liliom, who had beaten her mother, Louise scolds him for lying, and he slaps the girl. Liliom turns away with a sense of defeat, but Louise turns in surprise to her mother: the blow has borne no sting. "It is possible, dear," says Julie, with memoried love, "that someone may beat you, and beat you, and beat you—and not hurt you at all."

When Eva Le Gallienne, Helen Westley, Joseph Schildkraut, and Dudley Digges opened in *Liliom,* on April 20, 1921, its tender pathos won instant favor. The *New York Times* called it "Barrie done in terms of realism instead of sentimentality." Heywood Broun allowed: "There is some sentimental tosh in the play, but it is almost the best tosh we have ever heard." Alexander Woollcott was comparative: "There are such scenes of human squalor in it as Gorki might have written, but now and again there are dancing lights that Barrie might envy, and at times a cathedral hush settles over the play for those out front who have a prayer in their heart." *Liliom* was revived in 1932, again with Eva Le Gallienne and Schildkraut; Burgess Meredith was also in the cast, as he was again (this time with Ingrid Bergman) in 1940.

With music by Richard Rodgers, lyrics by Oscar Hammerstein II, choreography by Agnes De Mille, and the setting transplanted to the New England shore, the play reappeared on April 19, 1945, as the musical *Carousel*. Save for the transposition to New England, with a chorus of factory girls and fisher men, the story of *Liliom* is followed closely in *Carousel*. Songs and dances delightfully carry along the gayer mood: "June is bustin' out all over," "If I loved you," and "This is a real nice clam bake." The musical was welcomed with cheers. Ward Morehouse spoke of its "charm and compassion in musical play form . . . something rare in the theatre." It attained 890 performances in New York and 650 on the road, then went back to New York for four more weeks at the City Center. It well achieved the author's aim, to be "not *Liliom* with some songs added, but truly a musical play based on *Liliom*." A London revival of 1950 enjoyed 567 performances.

For the revival in the year of George V's coronation, with Alexandre Carlisle and Robert Loraine, Bernard Shaw revised the translation of the latter's lines. Molnár, though he couldn't read them, said they must be the best in all his plays. *Carousel* opened in Manchester, England, July 4, 1984.

THE GUARDSMAN   *Ferenc Molnár*

A Testör, translated as *The Guardsman,* shows another aspect of Molnár's deft handiwork, with the added fillip of an ending with more than one possible interpretation, which kept audiences arguing long after the play was over.

Married just six months, the Actor is worried that his wife, Marie, also a star in the Vienna theatre, may be growing bored; her previous emotional attachments, he tells his friend the critic Bernhard, have all lasted no more than half a year. He confides to Bernhard that he has been testing her, sending her roses as from an imaginary guardsman, Prince Wassilly Samsonov, and she has finally consented to see him. We have heard her playing a Chopin nocturne, with the roses on the piano.

The Actor invents a three-day engagement to take him out of town. Dressed in full uniform as a Russian Guardsman, he visits Marie, who flirts with him, but insists that she loves her husband; then, in a theatre box, she permits him to kiss her: "At last, a man!" and bids him come to her home next day at five.

The Actor returns, unexpectedly. It's almost five; Marie bids him take a half-hour walk; he says he'll go as soon as he unpacks his costume for the evening. They talk as, behind his trunk, he changes dress; at the stroke of five, in full Russian regalia, he confronts her. She smiles: "Good afternoon, Prince." He accuses her of acting; she says No, he's acting; she's just joining in, as she did yesterday. She had recognized him at once: his way with a cigarette, his kiss, the ardor in his eye. A bill collector, coming in, knows him at once. Marie sits down and plays the Chopin nocturne—and the Actor will never be sure.

Does the audience know?

The play was first presented in Budapest in 1910, with Irene Varsunyi, and Gyula Csortos, who had earlier turned *Liliom** from a failure to a resounding success. Actors Hegedus and Csortos alternated in the title role, the first more subtle, the second dashingly romantic. The play had a brief run in London in 1911, as *Playing with Fire*. In New York in 1913, as *Where Ignorance Is Bliss,* adapted by Philip Littell, with William Courtenay and Rita Jolivet, it was a quick and quiet failure. Meanwhile, it was popular in Europe; in 1913 with Leopold Kramer in Vienna, Alfred Abel in Berlin, stressing the Actor's role; in 1920 in both Vienna and Berlin with Anton Edhofer and Traube Carlsen, the two main figures given equal prominence.

Then, in a translation by Grace I. Colbron and Hans Bartsch, adapted by Philip Moeller, it was presented by the Theatre Guild at the Booth on October 13, 1924, with Alfred Lunt and Lynn Fontanne, Dudley Digges as the critic, Helen Westley as Mama, and ran for 248 performances. This version came to London in 1925 with Seymour Hicks, who also directed, and Madge Titheredge. It was frequently revived around the United States: 1927, Newport; 1929, Seattle; 1930, Ann Arbor; 1940, with Miriam Hopkins, White Plains, N.Y.; 1950-1951, Jeanette MacDonald and Gene Raymond on tour; 1954 on the straw-hat circuit; 1957, Sacramento; 1968, Palm Beach. In London, March 1, 1978, in a version by Frank Marcus, *The Guardsman* was directed by Peter Wood at the NT with Richard Johnson and Diana Rigg.

Alexander Woollcott noted the underlying seriousness of the lightly handled situation: "The tormented wooer relishes every hint of conquest as evidence of his skill as an actor—and writhes at every such sign as evidence of his failure as a husband."

The question as to just when the actress saw through the Guardsman disguise divided even the critics. Woollcott said that many playgoers would at once buy tickets again, to weigh every nuance of voice and movement, to discern at what moment Marie recognized the trick that was being played on her. Percy Hammond stood firm: "Fooled? Of course she wasn't. It is an authentic theory of acting and the drama that no actor can deceive his wife." Pressed on the matter at an interview, Lynne Fontanne smilingly dodged every question. The author, in a cynical 1950 *Note for an Autobiography*—set down in exile in New York, with his third wife, the actress Lili Darvas, and his secretary, Wanda Bartha in a patently pleasant *ménage à trois*—wrote: "Audiences everywhere in the world laughed at a perfectly agonizing play of mine in which a lovelorn suffering actor in disguise seduces his own loose-loving wife."

Frequently a merely good play receives added illumination (French *illustration*: lustre) from the brilliance of the performance. This quality arose from the teamwork of Alfred Lunt and his wife, Lynn Fontanne. *The Guardsman* is the first play in which they acted together; from it was made in 1931 the only motion picture in which they consented to play. They were in a great husband-and-wife tradition: in the generation before them Charles and Iva Coburn; John and Louisa Drew; Maurice (né Herbert Blythe) and Georgina Drew Barrymore, whose children were Lionel, Ethel, and John; in the generation after, Hume Cronyn and Jessica Tandy; and in France, Madeleine Rénaud and Jean-Louis Barrault—husband and wife offstage; onstage, consummate acting team.

Despite the author's later cynical observation, *The Guardsman* treats with light hand a grievous theme (that would have appealed to the often enanguished cuckold Molière*): how a suspicious husband, seeking surety, by his own device hangs himself more securely on the hook of doubt.

THE PLAY'S THE THING   *Ferenc Molnár*

Its title from *Hamlet, The Play's the Thing* "wherein I'll catch the conscience of the king," was adapted by P. G. Wodehouse from the Hungarian of Ferenc Molnár. It sparkles its way through a bantering, amoral land where virtue does not triumph, but where ingenuity comes to the aid of beauty to preserve the young lover's faith in his beloved.

The plot is simple. A young composer, Albert Adam, accidentally over-hears his beloved, Ilona Szabo, who is to star in his first operetta, amo-rously yielding to a former lover. Disillusioned, Albert contemplates suicide; but his friend, the playwright Sandor Turai, quickly drafts a com-edy skit employing the very words Albert has overheard. Ilona and (reluc-tantly) the "other man" put on this playlet; Albert thinks he has eavesdropped on a rehearsal, and all is well.

Holbrook Blinn's makeup bore "facial and sartorial" resemblance to Mol-nár, pointing up the autobiographical nature of the comedy. For Molnár had once actually overheard his third wife, the fascinating actress Lili Darvas, uttering words that left him with little doubt of her unfaithfulness—then was overjoyed to discover they were part of a play she was rehearsing.

Adapter Wodehouse not only added a few comic absurdities of his own concoction, but summarized the story in seventeen quatrains, ending:

> Girls, there's a moral to this tale,
> And one that worth its weight in candy:
> Be good—and if you can't, don't fail
> To have a clever playwright handy.

The play had its world premiere in Great Neck October 21, 1926, and came to New York November 3, with Catherine Owen and Holbrook Blinn, for 313 performances, the longest run of any Molnár play. On April 28, 1948, Mrs. Elliott Roosevelt (Faye Emerson) made her Broadway debut in the play, with Louis Calhern, Ernest Cossat, and Arthur Margetson. It was on the straw-hat circuit in 1953 with Ezio Pinza, Philip Loeb, Vilma Kurer—and Francis Compton as the butler, who is the butt of one of Wodehouse's additions:

> Why are you so late?
> I fell downstairs, Sir.
> Well, that oughtn't to have taken you so long.

The Hungarian original (Play in the Castle) opened in Budapest November 27, 1926. It was played in New York in German in 1954. The English version was produced by ELT in 1952 and 1957. In 1973 it was shown in New York at both the Booth and Roundabout; also in Milwaukee, and in Melbourne, Australia. The next summer Lake Forest, Ill., saw it with Tammy Grimes and Edward Mulhare—the latter again with Patrice Munsel (of the Metropolitan Opera) in 1978 at Ogunquit, Maine, and on tour. In the same year Carole Shelley played Ilona at BAM. England saw it again in 1979, with Julia McKenzie and John Moffat. Princeton, N.J., in 1981.

The play pictures a world concerned not with the worth but with the gusto of living. Gilbert W. Gabriel in the Sun, November 4, 1926, called it "a wittily garnished dish of sex soufflé. . . . You are earnestly exhorted to take all this with much more than a single grain of perfumed bath salts." Brooks Atkinson saw in it "no more substance than a sprinkling of star dust . . . with sparkles of extraneous conversation, sudden twists of action and informalities amazing in the successful effect . . . the gay holiday mood of a dramatist bored with the conventionalities of his craft."

Theatrical tricks are deftly turned. "Suppose you were writing this situation," Sandor inquires; "How would you end your second act?" Several proposals are enacted; each time the curtain starts to fall and Sandor waves it back; then he summons everyone for an important announcement; we fear that the moment of Ilona's exposure has come, and he says, "Now let's have the curtain."

At the April 1948 New York revival of *The Play's the Thing* Molnár, then in his seventieth year, must have glowed. For at the same time Memo Benassi, Duse's onetime partner, starred in Molnár's *The Devil* in Italy; *Liliom,* * revived in Paris, moved on in French to London, Geneva, Brussels, and Berlin, and in its original language to its original theatre in Budapest; and Austria, Switzerland, Germany, and Italy were also seeing *The Play's the Thing.* "Molnár at his best," said Brooks Atkinson, "theatre-wise and saturnine, writing of nothing with an impishly inspired pen." The play remains a freshly amusing picture of the resourceful maneuvering of sex. "Happiness is a state of being well deceived."

THE PRIVATE SECRETARY   *Gustav von Moser*

Out of the very successful German farce of Gustav von Moser (1825-1903), *Der Bibliothekar,* Charles Hawtrey (1858-1923), the English actor-manager, wove one of the most popular English farces, *The Private Secretary.* The play opened in Cambridge in 1883 and was brought to London, March 29, 1884, for the then phenomenal run of 785 performances. It has been frequently revived. By 1900, the *Hull* (England) *Mail* estimated that the play had already "shaken the sides of the great British public 468,000 times." New York saw it September 29, 1884, with William Gillette, opening a run of 200 performances; Gillette revived it in New York, December 12, 1910, for a fourteen weeks' run. He played the title role more than 2,000 times, and the part was considered his best comic characterization.

The play presents a galaxy of varied characters, including, as the *Boston Herald,* November 15, 1910, listed them, "the shrinking country clergyman who, as a new tutor for a couple of lively girls, is hurled into the company of two gay young London blades, a dunning tailor, a sporty rich uncle from India, a languishing chaperon seeking spiritualistic manifestations, and a doting wife with unnumbered small children, all stirred into a rattling mixture of cross purposes, misunderstandings, and mistaken identities." The private secretary, the Reverend Robert Spaulding, is a meek fellow who wears galoshes, plays the piano, and always carries an umbrella. Douglas Cattermole, a wild young man who has accumulated a host of debts, persuades the timid Spaulding to change places and names with him. Meanwhile old Cattermole from India, Douglas's rich uncle, comes back to help his nephew sow a few wild oats; he won't leave his money to any prissy pallid boy. The "nephew" he meets, the timid Spaulding in the gay blade's stead, disgusts him. Finally he and the tailor with his bill descend upon the innocent impostor and the complications are cleared away. Uncle Cattermole is pleased to discover that his nephew is a lively, high-spirited fellow after all, and the two girls are no less pleased with their swains, as the Reverend Robert Spaulding rejoins his sedate better half.

Much of the fun rises from the misunderstandings. The dialogue abounds in malapropisms, mispronunciations—Cattermole is called Cattleshow, Shattlemow, Mattercole—and other verbal play. The buffeted private secretary was born to be the butt of practical jokes, a fellow you like while you laugh at him. "His sufferings," said the *Boston Herald,* "excited such genuine sympathy that one felt half ashamed to laugh at the poor fellow."

"Farcical comedy that is worthy," the *New York Telegraph* commented (December 13, 1910), "has a quality in common with good wine—age adds to its flavor. As the droll Reverend Robert Spaulding ... Mr. Gillette was delightful." The play provides perennial entertainment. Certain of its outer devices are now dated, but the basic situations and comic characters of *The Private Secretary* continue to justify its wide repute as one of the funniest of modern farcical comedies.

Among recent revivals: London (The Arts), 1954; Pitlochry Festival, 1960, "a glorious romp," said the *London Times*; 1975, the U.S. straw-hat circuit.

The umbrella is a fashion attributed to his fellows ever since: "The German with his pipe, the Frenchman with his mistress, the Englishman with his umbrella."

FASHION   *Anna Cora Mowatt*

The first American social comedy, and still the best of the early pictures of budding American society, is *Fashion; or, Life in New York,* by Anna Cora Mowatt (1819-1870). Beginning her theatrical experience with an amateur group in Flatbush, New York, then turning to the professional stage, Mrs. Mowatt designed the play wholly as an acting comedy. "A dramatic, not a literary, success was what I wanted." She had her wish. *Fashion* opened, March 24, 1845, and attained the then phenomenal run of 28 nights. Mrs. Mowatt had the pleasure of starring in her own play in London.

Fashion has lasted well; a 1924 revival in New York ran over seven months, and London in 1929 saw the "famous old comedy." Various groups have constantly performed the play all over the country; it played in New York again in 1941 and (Equity Library) 1948.

Fashion shows the conflict between homely American ways and the supposed high society manners of old Europe. The action takes place in the home of the Tiffanys. The *Albion* (March 25, 1845), described the Tiffanys as follows: "(He) is a New York merchant doing an extensive business, has risen from a peddler to his present importance, and conducting his affairs upon the high steam pressure of the day, becomes involved in and resorts to false indorsements for the support of his declining credit. Mrs. Tiffany, also of obscure origin, uneducated, vulgar, and full of pretension, aspires to lead in so-called fashionable society by extravagant display and aping of foreign manners." She wants her daughter Seraphina to marry Count Jolimaitre, a valet posing as a noble, who, while wooing the wealthy Seraphina, also flirts with the beautiful governess, Gertrude. Also, more honestly, attracted to Gertrude is Colonel Howard, U.S.A. Adding varied color to the play are such figures as the sycophantic and villainous bookkeeper, Snobson, and the poet, T. Tennyson Twinkle, who makes no less than seven unsuccessful attempts to read his poems in Mrs. Tiffany's drawing-room. The complications of the plot are disentangled by Adam Trueman, well-to-do farmer from Catteraugus, upstate. In Adam, the first diamond-in-the-rough American, there is moving power, as well as rustic earnestness. He reveals that Gertrude is his daughter and bestows her on Colonel Howard. Graciously, the play ends with a restoration of honest manners.

Fashion is not without standby characters and situations, and it is indeed, as the *Chicago Journal* (December 7, 1926) remarked, "one of the earliest American manufacturers of hokum." Edgar Allan Poe, writing in the *Broadway Journal* (March 24, 1845), blasted the original direction for its "total deficiency in verisimilitude . . . the coming forward to the footlights when anything of interest is to be told; the reading of private papers in a loud, rhetorical tone; the preposterous asides." Nonetheless Poe went to each of the first five performances of the play, and his final judgment of it was that "Compared with the generality of modern drama, it is a good play; compared with most American drama, it is a very good play; estimated by the natural principles of dramatic art, it is altogether unworthy of notice." As literature, *Fashion* is of little consequence; as theatre (which, after all, was the author's aim) the play achieved and has held a prominent place on the American stage.

There have been frequent revivals of the play, especially at college theatres. In 1941 at Hunter College, New York, with its president, George N. Shuster, playing T. Tennyson Twinkle. ELT presented it in 1948, and gave a dramatic reading in 1957. Smith College, 1955. In Boston, 1959, then OffBway, Will Geer played Adam Trueman; Enid Markey, Mrs. Tiffany. In 1963, Yale. Songs were added: "Not for Joseph," "A Boy's Best Friend Is His Mother." There were OffOffBway productions in 1968 and 1973.

WHITE HORSE INN   *Hans Müller*

White Horse Inn is one of the most successful of spectacular musical comedies. It is based upon a farce by Oskar Blumenthal (German, 1852-1917) and Gustav Kadelburg, the comic actor (Austrian, 1851-1894), which was itself successful both on the Continent and (in adaptation by Sydney Rosenfeld) in New York in 1899 with Amelia Bingham and Leo Dietrichstein. *Im Weissen Rössl (White Horse Inn)* has book by Hans Müller (Austrian, b. 1882), and music by Ralph Benatzky and Robert Stolz. The musical version played over 1,000 performances in Vienna; it ran for two years (from September 1932) in Paris; had 416 performances (from November 1930) in Berlin, and has been seen throughout Europe as well as in Palestine, Africa, and Australia. London saw it, opening April 8, 1931, for 651 performances, and for 268 more beginning March 20, 1940. In New York, it ran for 228 performances beginning October 1, 1936, with Kitty Carlisle and William Gaxton, with lyrics by Irving Caesar. It is said to be the longest-run show in European history. "Never before," said *Play Pictorial* (May 1931), "has the London stage seen such an elaborate production." In New York, the Center Theatre spread the Inn and its Tyrolean surroundings across its wide stage and out along the sides. Everywhere the spectacle has been colorfully and lavishly adorned. Robert Coleman fitly warned his readers: "Bring along your St. Bernard and your skis."

The White Horse Inn is situated in the village of St. Wolfgang, on an Alpine lake. The proprietress, Josepha Voglhuber, has been loved by each of her head waiters; she turns from the present one, Leopold, to Valentine Sutton, an English solicitor and a guest at the Inn. Also present is Mr. Ginkle (McGonigle in the English version), the bathing suit king, now presenting his latest "Lady Godiva" model, and his daughter, Ottoline, whom Sutton admires. Leopold deliberately confuses the suits of Ginkle and Sutton, who are on opposite sides of a law suit. The Emperor Franz Josef, on hand for the Tyrolean festival, gives the proprietress some good advice. She settles back with her Leopold, and Ottoline bridges the Ginkle-Sutton abyss.

The play is lively, gay, and amusing. There are also a few good songs: "Star Dust," "The White Horse Calling To Me," and the rousing march "Good-Bye." Most appealing are the spectacles, swirling with dancers in variegated costumes. "The real heroine of the evening," said John Mason Brown, "is the wardrobe mistress." In New York, there was a cow-milking scene and song, with real cows in a village cowshed; the visitors for the Tyrolean festival arrived in a real, full-size motor omnibus, greeted with ballets and folk dances; a great revolving stage took them around the fair grounds, and to the public baths; the Emperor arrived by steamer, and the Tyroleans passed before him in review. As the *London Era* (April 15, 1931) declared: "All the resources of modern stage-craft have been used. Colour, light, music, and movement are perfectly blended in an entertainment that is almost breathless in interest. . . . I rarely remember a more thrilling scene than the procession that preceded the arrival of the Emperor." The lavish display, the gay movement of light-hearted comedy, the tuneful and cheery songs, combine to make *White Horse Inn* one of the greatest world favorites of musical comedy.

The elaborate production makes the play prohibitively expensive; but there was a showing in Peterborough, Mass., in 1950, with welcome memories.

TANGO   *Slawomir Mrozek*

Tango, by the outstanding Polish dramatist Slawomir Mrozek (b. 1930), reverses the usual generation gap, but presses home the point that power rules the world. Arthur is ashamed of the permissiveness of his parents, which in a world wherein they see no basic values has led his father, Stomil, to complacency and his mother, Eleanor, to promiscuity. She is currently sleeping with Eddie, an opportunistic hanger-on watching for his chance. Stomil and Eleanor had once, in a youthful gesture of rebellion, made love in the front row at a performance of *Tannhauser.*

Arthur surprises his cousin Ala by wanting to marry her; she was ready to sleep with him freely. With his father's gun, he seeks to make the family tidy up, dress up for the wedding; then he recognizes that the old conventions cannot be brought back by force. The only one who had seemed sympathetic was Arthur's uncle, a glib sentimentalist with gentlemanly manners and an addled head. The watching, philosophical grandmother goes quietly to her coffin and dies.

When Arthur turns threateningly on his uncle, Ala, to divert him, cries out that on the wedding morning she slept with Eddie. Eddie smashes down the bemused Arthur, and with the old uncle dances a tango over the idealist's corpse. The history of a nation is recapitulated in the story of a family: the intellectual is not ruthless enough to exercise naked power; the stupid and insensitive Eddies will rule the world.

"Who is Eddie?" Walter Kerr asked; and answered: "Good question. Eddie has been hanging around the house, having an affair with the mother; Eddie has been the butler; Eddie has been Nobody. . . . He is the nameless face that steps into power whenever a vacuum exists, the pure opportunist, the common man become uncommonly arrogant."

Presented in Warsaw in 1965, though the author claimed it was a straightforward story, *Tango* proved sufficiently allegorical to escape prosecution; but the triumphant dance of the totalitarian at the close confused the London audience when on May 28, 1966, the RSC put on the play, adapted by Tom Stoppard from Nicholas Bethell's translation, directed by Trevor Nunn, who stepped into the role of Arthur when Dudley Sutton fell ill. Patience Collier played the grandmother; Pauline Jameson, the wife; Ursula Mohan, daughter Ala. Eddie was played by Mike Pratt.

The play has been shown in most of Western Europe. it was produced in St. Paul in 1962, and opened OffBway January 18, 1969, for sixty-seven performances. Richard Watts, Jr., praised its "savagely sardonic black humor that is almost always bitingly alive, and it succeeds in presenting a sense of doomed hopelessness in provocative terms of defiant and blistering scorn." *Tango* is an indirect but nonetheless powerful picture of reasonableness and moderation beaten down by brute force.

THE CAPRICES OF MARIANNE   *Alfred de Musset*

Alfred de Musset (1810-1857) is widely known as the "enfant terrible" of the French Romantics, the poet of passion and regret, one of the fated lovers of George Sand. Among his published works is *Comedies and Proverbs,* a volume of charming, cultivated dialogue and keen psychology. Years after the publication of this book it was discovered that it contained plays that made delightful theatre pieces.

"The theatre of Musset," said Jacques Porel in 1936, "is a marvelous accident, unique in our dramatic literature. . . . Poetry, in all its forms, irony, melancholy, mystery—in one sweep invaded the stage. A grave lightness, a sort of sweet madness, animates all these ambiguous personages. Each of them, even the most ordinary, seems to bestride a little cloud all his own. Their voices have the sonority of an echo. Beholding them, we feel freed from our chain of reason; we come out of ourselves to journey in unknown regions of the spirit."

Best of Musset's comedies is *The Caprices of Marianne,* published in 1833 and first produced at the Théâtre Français (at that time called the Théâtre de la République), June 29, 1851, introducing the new star Madeleine Brohan. Théophile Gautier, in his comment, regretted the changes and cuts in a "text that everyone knows by heart. . . . Nonetheless, *Les Caprices de Marianne* won the most brilliant success, and will further popularize the author's name." It was frequently performed by Louis Delauncey from 1851 to 1887; in 1906 it became a permanent part of the repertoire of the Comédie Française.

The play is in two acts and nine scenes. It portrays young Marianne, married to ugly old Claudio and adored by handsome young Coelio. The timid Coelio sends his friend Octave to plead his cause; he does so well that Marianne is drawn to him. She sets a rendezvous with Octave, who sends Coelio; but Claudio has been watching, and Coelio is killed. Marianne would be consoled by Octave, but he says, "I do not love you; it was Coelio who loved you." Marianne, said *Le Théâtre* (February 11, 1906), "has 'caprices' in vain; she is not a coquette, *la grand coquette,* as they say in the theatre; she is *l'amoureuse,* the loving woman." Following a revival on October 16, 1922, *Le Théâtre* (November) called *Les Caprices de Marianne* "a work that does not age."

Once Scribe and Musset were discussing their work. "My secret," said Scribe, "is to amuse the public."

"My secret," said Musset, "is to amuse myself."

When *Les Caprices de Marianne* was published, Musset (aged twenty-two, not yet entangled with George Sand) was asked where he had met this Marianne: "Nowhere," he replied, "and everywhere. She is not a woman, she is woman." The rest of the secret is the capture of character in sparkling dialogue, and the discerning vision that beholds and sets forth that irony which robs us of our pretenses and leaves us reduced to the simpler dimensions of human dignity and beauty. Alfred de Musset is amused at love's little subterfuges and more damnable ways, but he—and his audiences— remain in love with humans, and with love.

Musset's one-act comedy, *A Door Must Be Either Open or Closed,* has had over 1,000 performances in the Comédie Française repertoire. *Les Caprices de Marianne* was shown at the Ohio State University in February 1960.

HE WILL HAVE HIS FLING   *Johann Nestroy*

Of the scores of farces and melodramas written by Johann Nestroy (Austrian, 1802-1862), mainly in Viennese dialect, that delighted the Austrian public in the mid-nineteenth century, one achieved international success. This is an amusing comedy of an aging small-town merchant who goes to the big city to have a good time and get a second wife. Nestroy took the idea from the farce *A Well Spent Day* by John Oxenford (English, 1812-1877) and called it *Einen Jux will er sich machen* (*He Will Have His Fling*). Thornton Wilder adapted it as *The Merchant of Yonkers,* 1938, and revised it as *The Matchmaker,* a smash hit in 1955.

The Wilder version opens in the 1880's in the gilded drawing-room of the elderly Yonkers merchant Horace Vandergelder. After berating his niece Ermengarde for fancying a "scalawag artist," Horace goes off with the pert minx Mrs. Molloy, a milliner, to have a gay time in the wicked city of New York. Two of his clerks, also on a spree, engage Mrs. Molloy in their champagne festivity, and Horace's old friend, Mrs. Dolly Levi, née Gallagher, takes over as his guide and adviser. Her advice is that Horace marry her; accepting it, he can no longer object to the union of his niece Ermengarde and her artist.

The play opened in Boston, December 12, 1938, with Jane Cowl and June Walker, and in New York, where it ran for five weeks, December 28. An over-elaborate production by Max Reinhardt slowed the rippling pace of the comedy, which makes merry use of the well-tried tricks of farce. Indeed, as the *Boston Transcript* (December 13, 1938) remarked, the author "has penned a tongue-in-cheek satire on the conventions of farce, decorating his gentle fable with all or anyhow a good parcel of the traditions thereof . . . The jokes, if mild, are neat, and even they are less important than the philosophical pleasantries that adorn the play." "Sheer funny business," said the *New York Sun*; "Laughter-compelling," declared the *World-Telegram*. Nestroy was a master of the popular theatre, and Wilder has converted his Viennese comedy into a lively American frolic, spiced with a little wisdom.

Revivals of *The Matchmaker* include: the Edinburgh Festival, then London, November 4, 1954, directed by Tyrone Guthrie, with Sam Levene as the merchant, Ruth Gordon as Mrs. Levi, Eileen Herlie in the hat shop, for 274 performnces. Dolly Levi was Wilder's happy addition to the plot. New York, 1955-1956, for 488 performances; again 1962 by Phoenix, directed by Harold Prince, with Sylvia Sidney as Dolly. July 1978, Cambridge

Theatre Co. in London. In 1979, Williamstown Festival, Mass. In 1980, OffOffBway (YM-YWHA).

The popularity of the play was augmented by the musical *Hello, Dolly!*, book by Michael Stuart, music and lyrics by Jerry Herman, choreography by Gower Champion, which opened at the New York St. James January 16, 1964, with Carol Channing, and shone for 2,844 performances. Among the songs were "Before the Parade Passes By," "It Only Takes a Moment," and the humorous antics of the restaurant staff before Mrs. Levi, down the grand stairway, makes her magnificent "Hello, Dolly!" entrance, which always stops the show.

Mary Martin was the first London Dolly, December 2, 1965, for 794 performances. She also took the musical to Tokyo and on an Asian tour, sponsored by the U.S. State Department. In London again in 1967, Dora Bryan was "an unquestionable smasheroo." After eight weeks at the Sahara, Reno, Nev. (where the longest run for any prior play had been three weeks), Carol Channing went in 1980 to London's Drury Lane for 141 performances, then to the Shaftesbury for six months more.

Among other actresses who have played Dolly are Ginger Rogers, Martha Raye, Betty Grable, Bibi Osterwald, Phyllis Diller, Eve Arden, and Dorothy Lamour. When Ethel Merman took the role, Lewis Funk in the *Times* (March 30, 1970) gave her a rave review. Two songs were added for her: "World, Take Me Back" and "Love, Look in My Window." Pearl Bailey, with Cab Calloway, headed an all-black production; on October 10, 1967, in its pre-Broadway showing in Washington, President and Mrs. Lyndon B. Johnson took curtain calls with the cast. When it came to New York, Walter Kerr (*Times,* November 26, 1967) declared: "Eventually, people are going to stop going back to see *Hello, Dolly!* They'll just settle down and live there." The film had Barbra Streisand as Dolly, "all glitter," and Walter Matthau as the merchant, "all grouch"—until Dolly took him on.

Onstage or onscreen, *Hello, Dolly!* is superspectacular.

On the trail of these successful variations, Tom Stoppard—helped by the literal translation of Neville and Stephen Plaice—went back to Nestroy for his *On the Razzle,* which opened at the Edinburgh Festival, then came to the NT (Lyttleton), August 22, 1981, directed by Peter Wood, with Alfred Lynch, and Felicity Kendal in a breeches role as the younger clerk, Christopher (a role played in Berlin in 1926 by Elisabeth Bergner). It keeps the story in Vienna, but (like the American versions) abandons the satire for a dazzle of verbal wit. As John Walker put it in the *Telegraph*: it offers "an unremitting fireworks display of puns, crossword puzzle tricks and sly sexual innuendos . . . so thick on the ground that they are in danger of tripping the actors." Robert Cushman in the *Observer* went so far as to say: "It is very rare indeed for anyone to say anything that cannot be misinterpreted or that isn't. . . . His jokes, unlike, say, Neil Simon's, are not there to lighten or to accentuate the situation; they *are* the situation." Thus, the pompous grocer feels "like the cake of the week—no, cock of the walk." (Alliteration in itself is not funny.)

> *Unhand my foot, sir!*
> *I love your niece.*
> *My knees, sir?*

A projection of musical designs is used to cover scene changes; Nestroy used songs.

The basic situation remains that of the two apprentices seeking a more exciting life, if only for a few hours, so that their daily drudgery routine may gleam with memories. But the action onstage suggests footlight toil, as the verbal play suggests midnight oil. The public laughed—but the crowds went to *Hello, Dolly!* The plot went through half a dozen changes, but has sustained its value for theatrical use.

'NIGHT, MOTHER   *Marsha Norman*

Marsha Norman was born (1948) in Louisville, Ky., where several of her plays were produced. The first, *Getting Out,* 1977, presents the struggle of a juvenile prostitute, a psychopathic murderer, to reconstruct her life after prison, as her defiant spirit seeks to adjust to the new conditions. The play came to the New York Phoenix with excellent reviews, transferred (1979) to the Théâtre de Lys, now the Lucille Lortell, OffBway, for eight months; it has been translated into eight languages, and shown in Yugoslavia, Israel, Ireland, Norway, and Poland.

Marsha Norman's grimmest play to date is *'night, Mother,* which came March 31, 1983, to the New York Golden and won the Pulitzer Prize. It pictures Jessie Cates informing her mother, Thelma, that she intends to commit suicide. Without intermission (no break in the tension would be tolerable), the mother struggles against her daughter's resolve while Jessie both explains why she must die and tries to prepare her anguished mother for continuing life without her. We gather that she misses her dead father; she resents her husband, who had walked out on her (her mother reveals that he had first been cheating on her); and she laments her son, who had stolen her rings and run away. "There's no reason to stay, except to keep you company; and that's not reason enough, because I'm not very good company, am I?"

Jessie tries to comfort her mother with little chores; she makes her some cocoa, and tells her to clean the pan while waiting for the police. Thelma protests that she won't. She pounds on the locked bedroom door through which Jessie has gone with her father's pistol. But when Thelma turns the telephone dial, she is clutching the cocoa pan.

The two women in *'night, Mother* are played by Kathy Bates as plain Jessie and sixty-one-year-old Anne Pitoniak in her Broadway debut as mother Thelma (although she had played the mother in the author's *Getting Out* in Louisville). And it should be mentioned that the two were voted "best actresses of the year" by the Critics' Outer Circle.

'night, Mother, directed by Tom Moore, who also directed *Grease,* * Broadway's longest-running play, exercises unusual power over the audience, provoking sober thought, compassionate understanding, and perhaps a stronger resolve. The writer Wilfred Sheed once said that "suicide is the sincerest form of criticism of life." Conversely, the impulse may be a challenge to proper survival. One comes from the play to face that challenge.

JUNO AND THE PAYCOCK   *Sean O'Casey*

"Everyone was getting tired of the Abbey plays, so I decided to write one for them." These were the words of a 37-year-old Dublin bricklayer, Sean O'Casey (Irish, 1884-1964). His first play was rejected, but his fourth attempt, *The Shadow of a Gunman,* was accepted and well received. The promise of the fourth play was richly fulfilled in *Juno and the Paycock,*

1924, which James Agate (*New York Times,* August 29, 1937) called "the greatest play written in English since the days of Queen Elizabeth." Juno— so named because she was born in June—is the suffering and eternally hopeful wife and mother; her husband Jack Boyle is the self-satisfied strutter, the "peacock." Juno's son Johnny was hurt, as a boy, in the Easter Rebellion (1916) and lost an arm in a later uprising. When a neighbor is killed, Johnny, whom his mother is called to identify, is accused of betraying the man and executed. To ingratiate himself with the family, the school-teacher Charlie Bentham, who seeks the hand of Juno's daughter Mary, brings word that Boyle's uncle has left them a fortune; the family buys new furniture and holds a celebration. But Charlie's news is a lie; he goes off, leaving Mary pregnant, whereupon Jerry Devine, another suitor, turns from her. Creditors carry off the new furniture while the Paycock and his tipsy crony Joxer Daly philosophize, and Juno gathers the debris to start to build anew.

Dublin greeted the play with cheers and resentment. London saw it, opening November 16, 1925, for 202 performances, and awarded it the Hawthornden Prize. The play was revived in 1927, in 1934, and with Sara Allgood and Arthur Sinclair in 1937. New York saw the play first on March 15, 1926; again in 1927, 1932, 1934, 1937, in 1940 with Barry Fitzgerald for 106 performances, and in 1947 at Piscator's Dramatic Workshop.

The play's tragic aspects have an impact that is increased by verbal understatement and a broad vein of comedy. "Mr. O'Casey does not drive his comedy home with a hammer, as he does his tragedy," said the *London Sphere* (November 28, 1925). "It seems to come almost before he is aware of it himself." But in all the tragic aspects, as James Agate said, "the play is keen and alive." The comedy, drawn mainly from the "Paycock" and Joxer Daly, is none the less amusing because these men are, at bottom, poignantly pathetic figures of a spent generation.

The Dublin city speech of O'Casey's characters matches the rural Irish dialogue of Synge.* "The beauty of words is a thing all but forgotten by the London theatre, and our great indebtedness to Mr. O'Casey is for his rediscovery of words," said the *London Times* (June 27, 1934). "But beauty of language can disguise many forms of poverty, and there is no denying that Mr. O'Casey's rhetoric helps him over a number of serious lapses.... We have the rich humour and the variously shaded pathos of his conversational passages, and the violent, unprepared-for assaults on the emotions of his 'drama.' The two main notes of the play are isolated; they alternate, but never harmonize. The only unity comes from Juno herself in her indomitable bravery, tenderness, and humour, who subdues the breaking waves within her heart. The contemporary theatre, nevertheless, has few things as rich to offer us." A later writer in the same paper (September 21, 1951) felt a greater unity in the play: "The language flows freely and at the same time acknowledges by instinct the restraint of dramatic economy. Through scenes of high humour and rich, racy fooling the tragic story moves on with that inevitability which is the mark of organic design." There are, nevertheless, in *Juno and the Paycock,* successive drives of feeling, rather than a sustained and gathering power. Though the disasters fall upon the members of a single family, we feel their severance rather than their union. The play thus presents a gallery of portraits—sardonic, bitter, hopeful, gentle— all touched with the shadow of doom, poetically and powerfully drawn and deeply moving.

Among many revivals of *Juno and the Paycock*: August 1, 1961, Dublin, with Siobhan McKenna; Peter O'Toole's accent was flailed by the Dublin critics. From the Dublin Abbey to London, September 20, 1964. NT (Old Vic), August 1, 1966, with Joyce Redman and Colin Blakeley. Alan Dent declared: "It manages at one and the same time, and against practically all the rules of playwriting, to be glorious farce as well as tragedy serene and eternal." In 1972, Washington. March 1973, Long Wharf, New Haven, with Geraldine Fitzgerald, who also played it with Roundabout in 1982. London Mermaid, July 2, 1973; Siobhan McKenna directed, and played Juno. December 1980, RSC, Aldwych.

Boyle: The world's in a terrible state of chassis.
Joxer: It's better to be a coward than a corpse.

The musical *Juno,* book by Joseph Stein, music and lyrics by Mark Blitzstein, came to the New York Winter Garden March 9, 1959, with Melvyn Douglas and Shirley Booth, but managed only sixteen performances. The Paycock was called "Darlin' Man." The musical, revised and now called *Darlin' Juno,* tried again May 20, 1976, at the New Haven Long Wharf, with Geraldine Fitzgerald and Milo O'Shea, with no better results. The play has all the glory.

WITHIN THE GATES   *Sean O'Casey*

The leap into imaginative writing that marked one act of *The Silver Tassie* animates the whole of O'Casey's *Within the Gates,* 1933. The play is a symbolic drama of life, set in a sort of Hyde Park in London. Each act is a season, and has its own song and dance by the people in the Park.

The Park gates open. The characters within have not names but labels: the Young Whore; the Young Dreamer, her lover; the Atheist, her stepfather; the Bishop, her real father; and the Down and Outs. The Bishop comes to the Park daily, "to mingle with the people," and we observe his spiritual dearth beneath his sprightliness. When the Young Whore seeks his help, the Bishop demurs: "But you can't discuss such things with a man and a perfect stranger, Girl." To which she retorts: "You're neither a man nor a stranger; you are a priest of the most high God." But despite the poverty, the cruelty, and the shabby unconcern for others we see in the play, there is a thrusting up of the human spirit, courage, hope, and exaltation. The Young Whore, her last days made happy by the dreamer poet, dies bravely in the arms of the Bishop, ready to face whatever may be in store.

The Down and Outs, who come to our attention first in an offstage chanting, then a gathering macabre shadow, at the end sweep in and engulf the scene—the Young Whore escaping them by dying. The Evangelists in the Park have the last word: "Offer not to God the dust of your sighing, but dance to His glory, and come before His presence with a song." The Dreamer, crying: "Make way for the strong and the swift and the fearless!" breaks through, to live.

Published before it was produced, the play won critical acclaim. The *London Times,* November 28, 1933, said: "It emerges as a work of art more significant in its promise of dramatic liberation than any other play written since Strindberg moved away from naturalism . . . new in contemporary theatre, the consummation of a long struggle to build, on the foundations of naturalism, an alternative to it, and to discover a flexible instrument of dramatic poetry, not blunted by antique uses as the instrument of blank verse has been."

Later reflection found the *Times* (*Literary Supplement,* September 21, 1951) less enthusiastic, feeling that O'Casey's quest for abstraction had led him to use "the stock types of melodrama. With his masterly transitions from naturalistic to poetic speech and his richness of utterance, he achieved some magnificent effects, but the total impression is that of a dyed-in-the-wool romantic pretending to be a scourge of society."

Most of the book's reviewers believed that *Within the Gates* was to be read rather than acted. Performance proved them wrong. The play opened to acclaim in London February 7, 1934. In New York, opening October 22, 1934, with Lillian Gish, Mary Morris, Bramwell Fletcher, and Moffat Johnson, it ran for 101 performances. Banned in Boston, it returned to New York. Brooks Atkinson in the *Times,* October 26, said that it "has given the drama greater compass and a more exalted spirit than any new drama I have seen . . . theatre incarnate, not to be savored apart from the stage . . . the most glorious drama in the contemporary English-speaking theatre." The play was revived by ELT in 1953.

The play shows that, despite the world's disorder, distress, and self-concern, simple folk can attain both courage and wisdom. When the Young Whore dies in the arms of the Bishop, she stirs in his arid spirit the waters of compassion. *Within the Gates* shows us the park of life—where beauty can flower along dusty walks, where fallen leaves prepare the ground for future growth. "Our mother the earth," sings the chorus: "Our mother the earth is a maiden again, young, fair, and a maiden again." Hope walks beside beauty to lay on the drooped shoulders of despair the gentle hand of reassurance.

The *London Times* (February 8, 1934) called *Within the Gates* "that very rare thing—a modern morality that is not a pamphlet but a work of art . . . his art purges the dross from his controversy."

Lillian Gish, in the April 7, 1974, *New York Times,* forty years after she acted in *Within the Gates,* declared: "It would have a better chance for success today than when it was written in 1934, and it might be time for a spiritual drama." Indeed, the play's potency is not only timely, but of all time.

AWAKE AND SING   *Clifford Odets*

The first produced play by Clifford Odets (1906-1963) was the fiery one-act *Waiting for Lefty,* of taxi drivers waiting for their leader, to decide whether to strike; he is brought in—dead, struck down by company goons. Encouraged by its success, Odets reworked a full-length play he had called *I've Got the Blues,* which the Group Theatre (founded in 1931 by Harold Clurman, Cheryl Crawford, and Lee Strasberg; disbanded in 1940) had rejected. The Group now took the play, with a new title, *Awake and Sing,* from the Bible, Isaiah 26:19: "Awake and sing, ye that dwell in the dust . . . for thy dew is a dew of light." It opened February 19, 1935, for 209 performances.

Percy Hammond (*Herald-Tribune,* February 20) expected "a rebellious war-whoop summoning the under-dog to revolt" but found "a sober study of unhappiness in the Bronx." A supercilious Gothamite once remarked that art is the quickest way out of the Bronx, but Clifford Odets, in *Awake and Sing,* brought the Bronx into art.

The Bergers are struggling in the Depression, with Mother Bessie firmly ruling the roost. She drives her pregnant daughter, Hennie, into marriage with a man not the father, the slaving but respectable Sam. She breaks up her son Ralph's social life to keep his salary home; she browbeats her ineffectual husband, Myron. When Hennie tells her husband the child is not his, and runs off with one-legged veteran Moe Axelrod, whose financial status as a bookie is somewhat more sound, Bessie pours out her wrath on her old father, Jacob, the sad philosopher of the family, who finally jumps from the roof so that his $3,000 insurance may help to liberate Ralph. Ralph, however, decides to remain at home and use the money for the family, though he vows to fight for a better (Marxist) world.

While resenting the economic conditions of the time, the characters are caught in personal relationships that are natural and vivid. As one critic noted, most of the play takes place during, just before, or just after, meals. There are touching true moments, as when Pa Berger sadly remarks: "Don't think life's easy with Mama." Old Jacob, on his final trip to the roof, takes along his friend, the dog. Brooks Atkinson (*Times,* March 10, 1935) declared: "If Mr. Odets has this much appetite for life and this much comprehension of the theatre, nothing else really matters. I have rarely read a script so bursting with the pressure of longing, frustration and conflict in terms of character."

In the original cast were Stella Adler as Ma Berger, twenty-eight-year-old Morris Carnovsky as seventy-five-year-old Jacob, Phoebe Brand, J. Edward Bromberg, Jules (later John) Garfield, Luther Adler, and Sanford Meisner. The play has had many revivals, among them: ELT, 1947; Iowa State University, 1959; OffBway, 1970, with Sylvia Sidney as Ma Berger, directed by Harold Clurman; 1971, Arena Stage, Washington; and London with Patience Collier as Ma Berger. And in 1975, after forty years, Morris Carnovsky again, and, said Clive Barnes (*Times,* March 14, 1975): "When he takes the long walk up to the roof with the little dog, there is still a very proper shiver running through the audience." In 1977 San Francisco and OffOffBway; 1979, the Roundabout, and "the play seems surprisingly new"; 1981, the Jewish Rep OffOffBway; 1982, Seattle, Wash. Essentially, *Awake and Sing* remains a revealing and moving portrait of a middle-class family trying to hold up its head while making ends meet.

BEYOND THE HORIZON   *Eugene O'Neill*

When Eugene G. O'Neill (American, 1888-1954) registered in the fall of 1914 for George Pierce Baker's famous playwrighting course at Harvard, he showed Baker an already finished one-act play, *Bound East for Cardiff.* Baker pointedly said it was not a play at all, but it was the first of O'Neill's works to be produced.

"There was a fog on the night in 1916," said the *London Times* (April 10, 1948), "when Mr. O'Neill's first play to be publicly performed, a short sea-piece entitled *Bound East for Cardiff,* was produced in a fish-shed on a wharf in Provincetown, on the coast of Massachusetts. The fish-shed had been transfigured, and was now the Wharf Theatre, with a 'capacity' of ninety persons: a little smaller than the Bandbox in Bergen in which Bjornson and Ibsen learnt their craft. The cast included the author who, however, failed to convince his audience that his father [who had played *The Count of Monte Cristo* some 6,000 times] lived again on the stage. . . . The fog entered Mr. O'Neill's soul that night and has remained there ever since." Three years later, O'Neill had completed three other short plays of the forecastle. The four are usually presented together under the collective title *S.S. Glencairn.*

Eugene O'Neill's first full length play to be produced, and his first play to reach Broadway, *Beyond the Horizon,* opened in New York on February 2, 1920. It ran for 160 performances and won a Pulitzer Prize.

The play depicts Robert Mayo, a restless plowman whose dreams of the open road end in the squalor of neglected fields. About to ship for a voyage with his uncle, Robert tells Ruth Atkins, his brother Andrew's girl, that he loves her. She responds, and Andrew, who would have been a fine farmer, ships away instead. When he returns, a wealthy man with Ruth wholly out of his mind, he finds the farm in ruin and the marriage sodden. Robert and Ruth have slumped from mutual hate to dreary indifference. Robert, dying of tuberculosis, fevered, babbling, still looks beyond the horizon, dreaming the vain hope that when he dies Ruth and Andrew will find happiness together.

Through the 1930's, the play was produced by some ten college and community groups every year. In 1937, the year after O'Neill was awarded the Nobel Prize, it had its Scandinavian premiere in Oslo. In the same year Helen Hayes played Ruth on the radio, after a long dispute with the Federal Communications Commission over the use of what it labeled "profane and indecent lines," and Margalo Gillmore acted Ruth (without the lines Helen Hayes had retained) in a 1938 broadcast. In 1947 Equity Library staged the play in New York.

"O'Neill begins crudely but honestly and frankly with a scene in which two of his chief characters sit down and tell the audience the things they ought to know," said Heywood Broun (February 4, 1920), "but after this preliminary scene the play gathers pace and power, and until the final act it is a magnificent piece of work, a play in which the happenings are of compelling interest and, more than that, a play in which the point of view of everyone concerned is concisely and clearly set forth in terms of drama. . . . The power of the play is tremendous . . . it is as honest and sincere as it is artistic." The *Boston Transcript* (February 5, 1920) observed that "since the days of *The Great Divide* no such significant piece has passed to our stage."

In England, the play was less favorably received. Charles Morgan, reporting in the *New York Times* (March 30, 1938) spoke of the "rigidity" with which O'Neill identified the two aspects of his thought with the two brothers, Robert and Andrew Mayo: "Andrew, keen, eager, practical, is a first-rate portrait. . . . And the setting of the play—the father, the seafaring uncle, the life of the farm—all these are Andrew's natural background. His brother Robert is an invader of the play, not because he is a youth born out of his element, for that is natural and true enough, but because O'Neill has poeticized him and has written of him in a tone and idiom different from that employed in the writing of the rest of the play. For this reason, *Beyond the Horizon* gives an impression of being a studio piece. Its poetry is not fused with its observation."

Even sharper was the double-edged attack in the *London Times* (April 10, 1948): "Mr. O'Neill's technique has been extolled for its experimental character, but it is clumsy and sometimes surprisingly ingenuous. He was not a novice when he wrote *Beyond the Horizon,* yet that play, which has six scenes when three would suffice, is singularly incontinent and full of loose ends. . . . This play is intellectually, as well as physically, tuberculous. Its lungs are full of holes. Mr. O'Neill does not let his audience off a single hacking cough. . . . It is in this play that the theme of all Mr. O'Neill's plays is set out: frustration and disillusionment."

Beyond the Horizon is on the whole overdrawn, perfervid, not carefully wrought, as though the playwright's memories were too turbulent to be set in polished order. Partly for this reason, the play has a disturbing power. Its ultimate effect is not so much the exultation and the exaltation of purging tragedy as it is a sense of pity, almost of self-pity, at thought of what life can do to the ineffectual beings most of us mortals are.

THE EMPEROR JONES   *Eugene O'Neill*

Eugene O'Neill's power of presenting the breaking down of a human mind is nowhere more vividly displayed than in this short play of eight episodes.

The first scene sets the background for the story. From the sycophancy and cowardly hatred of Smithers, a trader and the only white man on a small West Indian island, and from the boastfulness of Brutus Jones, an ex-Pullman porter and ex-convict who has imposed himself as Emperor upon the superstitious natives of the island, we learn that Jones has amassed a fortune; also that he has cached a boat on the farther shore of the island against the day when the natives will revolt. We learn, then, that the day of revolt has come. Lightheartedly Jones sets forth for the forest and safety.

The rest of the play depicts the fantasied flight of Jones. Reaching the forest by dark, he grows less confident. Nameless fears take shape in his mind. His fancy gives body to his crime; he envisions the slave auction block, the slave ship, and the voodoo god of his ancestors. He dispels each vision with a revolver shot; to drive off the last, he uses the silver bullet he had been saving for himself. All this time he hears the throb of the tom-tom which had summoned the natives to revolt and which ebbs and floods with his emotions. Dawn finds Jones, half dead with fatigue and fright, not at the haven of the farther shore, but returned in a circle to the forest's edge, where a silver bullet moulded by the natives brings him down.

If racking the nerves be a function of the drama, *The Emperor Jones* fulfills it. In this it was highly successful, according to the *New York American* of October 13, 1926. The *London Times* (September 11, 1925) called the whole thing "one brutal attack on your nerves." "The tom-tom stunned us as it stunned the Emperor Jones," said St. John Ervine, "and if it had not stopped when it did, I should not have been surprised to see some of my less controlled colleagues climbing onto the stage and doing a war dance."

Brutus Jones, who after the first scene plays virtually a monologue, was acted in the New York premiere (November 1, 1920, for 204 performances) by Charles S. Gilpin. Paris saw the play in 1924; London, with Paul Robeson, beginning September 10, 1925. In German, the tom-tom apparently had less effect; the critics dismissed the production by Reinhardt in Vienna, 1926, as "melodramatic rot." The play has, however, continued to be widely popular. Dublin saw it in 1927 with a white actor playing Brutus Jones. 1932 saw it performed by puppets in Los Angeles. It was also made into an opera in 1932 with music by Louis Gruenberg; Lawrence Tibbett sang it at the Metropolitan in 1933. In 1933 it was also memorably filmed with Dudley Digges and Paul Robeson. Colleges and communities have frequently revived the play. Canada Lee acted in a radio version in 1945.

The Emperor Jones unquestionably is stirring. It brought a new thrill to the theatre with its impact of fear that sends a man back toward the brute, and its hypnotic and cumulatively bloodcurdling sound. It evoked, said Richard Dana Skinner, "a mood in the theatre never before felt."

Although he spells us into a state of emotional intensity, O'Neill does not find a way to lift us with its movement. The breaking down is completely effective, but the building up—as often in O'Neill—does not follow through. Though Heywood Broun (November 4, 1920) deemed *The Emperor Jones* "the most interesting play that has yet come from the most promising dramatist in America," he was constrained to add: "He has almost completely missed the opportunities of his last scene, which should blaze with a tinder spark of irony. Instead, he rounds it off with a snap of the fingers, a little O. Henry dido." The *London Times* (September 11, 1925) more bluntly observed: "Your Ah! of admiration ends in the Ugh! of repulsion." The sum total is negation, the conclusion is defeat. Since this powerful and compelling play is the drama of a man without faith, it can only rouse emotions, it cannot direct them. Bernard Shaw called O'Neill "a Fantee Shakespeare who peoples his isles with Calibans." *The Emperor Jones* remains on the level below thought.

Among recent revivals: Boston, 1964, James Earl Jones, with a ballet element; Jones took it to the Edinburgh Festival in 1967; 1967, also, the Venice Festival. OffOffBway (7 Ages), 1977, and tour. In 1979, New York, Fordham University with African demon dance.

ANNA CHRISTIE   *Eugene O'Neill*

Out of Eugene O'Neill's drinking and seafaring days came one of the most vivid of his dramas. The saloon in which, according to George Jean Nathan, O'Neill used to sleep under the bunghole of a whiskey barrel is Jimmy-the-Priest's, where *Anna Christie* opens. Chris Christopherson, captain of a coal barge, hates "dat ole devil sea"; he has had his daughter Anna brought up, safe from its terrors, on a relative's Minnesota farm. Now, in the saloon, as he tells his mistress, Marthy, that she can sail with him no more, for Anna is coming to stay with him, and "She is goot girl, my Anna," Anna bristles in through the family entrance, orders a drink: "Gimme a whiskey—ginger ale on the side. And don't be stingy, baby!" And only Anna's father, onstage or off, is unaware that the girl is a member of her sex's oldest profession.

The sea that Chris hates cleanses Anna. Out of that sea through the fog comes Mat Burke, a shipwrecked sailor, to make honest love to her. In the peace and salve and release of her soul, Anna tells of her horrible days of ill-treatment on the farm, where her cousin had seduced her, and of her bitter life before joining her father. The fury of Mat flames against the fury and remorse of Chris; the men quarrel, then get drunk together, then return to be reconciled with Anna. The two men—still on the edge of mutual slaughter—have signed on the same ship; Anna will wait for Mat.

Originally entitled *Chris Christopherson*, the play was tried out with Lynn Fontanne as Anna; it was withdrawn in Philadelphia for revision. On November 2, 1921, it opened in New York as *Anna Christie,* with Pauline Lord, for 177 performances. The London production, opening April 10, 1923, ran for 103 performances. The play has been frequently revived: in 1941, Ingrid Bergman played Anna in Santa Barbara; in 1942 both play and film (the latter with Greta Garbo and Marie Dressler) were seen in Baltimore; June Havoc essayed the title role in 1948. In 1922 the play was awarded the Pulitzer Prize.

The authenticity of atmosphere, both saloon and sea, won considerable praise. A captain of the British merchant marine, author and twenty-two years a sailor, David W. Bone, commented in the *New York Times* (January 15, 1922) that the play "has brought our true environment to the boards." Praise went also to the characterization of Anna. In the *London Observer* (April 11, 1937) Ivor Brown likened her to "every broken blossom that ever drifted through a brothel and emerged to allure the lusty youth of the waterfront." After the New York premiere, Kenneth Macgowan stated: "Miss Lord's Anna Christie is the most perfect piece of naturalism I have ever seen on the American stage." One other naturalistic aspect of the play, its salty use of language, was noted by the *London Times* (April 8, 1937): "This is a comparatively early example of the many American experiments in inarticulacy. . . . For here is not only the confused utterance and worn imagery of the illiterate, but Anna herself, in the crisis of her life, turns naturally to the 'language and gestures of the heroics in the novels and movies' with which she is familiar."

Despite the chorus of praise, the play aroused considerable controversy. The two main points of dissatisfaction were mentioned in the London *Punch* (December 6, 1944), which insisted that Captain Chris's "confusion between devil and deep sea is the play's most trying repetition," then bracketed the other objection with its praise: "For about five-sixths of its length—until, indeed, the author yields to the melting mood in the flat calm of a happy ending—the play is a tough, passionate drama, talking at the top of its voice and holding us with the gaze of the Ancient Mariner." "What is really the matter with this play," said the *London Times* (April 11, 1937), stressing the first point, "is that big red herring, the ocean. What is the strength of old Christopherson's 'Dat ole devil sea!' which he reiterates so often? Even in 1923 it didn't seem to have much point."

Although O'Neill provides little justification for Chris's deep distrust of the sea, *Anna Christie* is well motivated and constructed. However, the very critics who had previously lamented the unending dreariness and depression of O'Neill's plays, now objected to his happy ending, calling it unnatural and conventional. When O'Neill went so far as to boast, in the *New York Times* (May 11, 1924), that the last act "was the most courageous and original act of the play," the *London Times* (April 11, 1937) retorted: "Nonsense."

Anna Christie speaks vividly and powerfully of the sea and the sea's influence upon three quite different persons. Like the sea, from which it springs, it is turbulent; it is sunny, with sudden storms; and within the "very ordinary little drab," Anna, we can feel what is within most ordinary folk, the urge of a dream toward a finer self. This upward urging, mystic within the summons of the sea beyond the conventional drop of a happy curtain, gives the play considerable distinction.

O'Neill had tried three tragic versions of *Anna Christie* before he released it in 1920, with "ominous comments on the happy ending." Among numerous revivals: 1952, New York City Center with Celeste Holm, moving to the Lyceum with Ralph Meeker as Chris. In 1952, all-black cast, set in Panama, with Sylvia Earle as a New Orleans prostitute. Oxford, England, with Jill Bennett. In 1962, Philadelphia, with Salome Jens, Meeker, and Luther Adler. New York Imperial, April 14, 1977, with Liv Ullmann for 124 performances. September 18, 1979, RSC, Stratford-upon-Avon. London NT, June 1980.

A musical, *New Girl in Town*, book by George Abbott, music and lyrics by Robert Merrill, came briefly to New Haven, Boston, and New York, May 14,

1957; it played the Massachusetts straw-hat circuit in 1958, with Evelyn Ward and George Wallace (Matt), and was revived by ELT, January 9, 1975.

DESIRE UNDER THE ELMS   *Eugene O'Neill*

This farmhouse tragedy is another O'Neill play that builds cumulatively to an effect of great power. It opened in New York, November 11, 1924, for 208 performances. With its frank language, its "distresses," as the *New York Herald-Tribune* called them, that range "from unholy lust to infanticide, and include drinking, cursing, vengeance and something approaching incest," the play was at once attacked. It was exonerated by a citizens' play jury in New York, February 25, 1925. In London it was banned by the censor until 1938; though it had a private production there, opening February 24, 1931, it was not publicly enacted until January 20, 1940. In Los Angeles the cast was arrested (February 18, 1926). Nevertheless, the play has been widely performed: Prague, 1925; Moscow, 1932; Stockholm, 1933; and it has been given by community groups in the United States, for its manner of production is a challenge to little theatre ingenuity. The play was revived off-Broadway by The Craftsmen, November 21, 1951, so effectively that they wished to transfer their production to Broadway, but were prevented by ANTA, which opened its own Broadway revival January 16, 1952.

To a New England farmhouse of 1850, old Ephraim Cabot has taken as his third wife young Abbie Putnam, who welcomes the security he offers. Two of his sons decide to go west, but Eben, who hopes to inherit the farm, remains behind, hating the new wife. Not having a son by Ephraim, Abbie seduces young Eben, and their child is born. Eben feels that he has avenged his mother upon his father. At the celebration of the baby's birth, Ephraim dances while the neighbors snicker behind the back of the seventy-six-year-old farmer. But the combined urge for security and lust in Abbie have melted into a love for Eben; to prove that she did not merely want an heir to claim the farm, she kills the child. Eben leaves to report the murder to the Sheriff, while Abbie tells the enraged Ephraim that it was not his child. When the Sheriff comes, Eben deepens in his love of Abbie enough to share the blame and go off to prison with her. In a surge of personality rare at the end of an O'Neill play, the main figures rise to face their bitter lot.

The power of the play is impressive. On its New York opening, the *New York Herald-Tribune* declared that "O'Neill again eats his heart out in the bitter torments of despair"—overlooking the fact that the play ends not in a slump of despondency but with a lift of resolution in the midst of disaster. The *Times* found it "essentially a story of solitude, physical solitude, the solitude of the land, of men's dreams, of love, of life." Gilbert W. Gabriel commented: "Some moments were vivid and great ones. Some sloughed off into maudlin dreariness. Some wrenched the clothes from gnarled, grimy farm folk. Others reclothed them in poetic masquerade and togas of deliberate oratory. It is a story so grim it will sour the spittle in most persons' mouths." Alexander Woollcott remarked: "A strong tide swept through it, it was hewn from the stuff of life itself; and it was marked from first to last with boldness and with imagination." Burns Mantle called it "stark, morbid, forbidding tragedy; a cheerless, fascinating, hopeless, thrilling human document."

As the title indicates, the drama develops variations on the theme of desire. Old Ephraim desires to maintain the farm and keep warm o' nights; sons Simeon and Peter desire freedom from the hard New England farm life; son Eben desires to hold on to what his mother had; and Abbie desires a home, security, then love. Rooted in insecurity and insufficiency, their desires are doomed to be frustrate.

The stage set of *Desire Under the Elms* is most effective. It shows the ground before the Cabot farmhouse, and the front of the building, with the windows of four rooms, two on each story. The walls of these rooms are removed at will, so that we watch the action outdoors, or in any of the rooms, or in several at once, with not only a continuity but an intimacy of action.

O'Neill's efforts to give symbolism and universal import to the play are frustrated by the very complexity of the detailed incidents themselves; such a series of happenings and actions can bear no general application; it is possible only as a unique train of events involving particular individuals. Hence, again—as most often in O'Neill's plays—the accumulated power is lost as in a fizzling fuse. Hence the reversal of Woollcott's first enthusiasm, and his conclusion that the play "falters feebly at its climax and remained, when seen in retrospect after the final curtain, essentially unimportant."

Despite O'Neill's usual failure to give an individual story universal overtones, *Desire Under the Elms* has all his depth of human analysis, his emotional power, and, in addition, a lift of courage and constancy at the end that does not let the human spirit die.

The play was revived in London in 1955. Opening at the New York Circle in the Square January 8, 1963, with Rip Torn and Colleen Dewhurst, directed by José Quintero, it ran for 380 performances. Asolo, 1977. Off-OffBwy (American Stanislavsky Theatre), 1982. Pennsylvania Stage Co., 1983.

STRANGE INTERLUDE   *Eugene O'Neill*

The nine acts of this Pulitzer Prize play required that performances begin at 5:30 p.m. when it opened in New York on January 30, 1928, running for 426 nights with Lynn Fontanne; Pauline Lord and Judith Anderson have also played its leading role. When Boston banned the play, it opened at nearby Quincy on September 30, 1929. London saw it February 3, 1931, with Mary Ellis and Basil Sydney. It was cut to three hours' playing time for Europe (Vienna, 1936). Lynn Fontanne acted in a radio version in 1946.

George Jean Nathan hailed O'Neill's play as "the finest, the profoundest drama of his entire career, a drama, I believe, that has not been surpassed by any that Europe has given us in recent years and certainly by none that has been produced in America." The *Boston Transcript,* (October 25, 1929) concurred: "It has affirmed his originality and power as a dramatist, his insight into the dark places of human living, his intrinsically tragic imagination, his ambition to widen and deepen the scope of the stage. His tendency to excess, his occasional obtuseness, his unconscious lapses, are less faults in themselves than the price his temperament pays for virtues."

Beyond its length, *Strange Interlude* marked the continuing of O'Neill's experimentation, in its use of "asides"—though "forethoughts" might be a better term. Time and again the characters utter their thoughts aloud before speaking to those around. The audience is thus carried along on two planes of reality: the outer, audible level on which the characters address and show themselves to one another; and the inner, self-conscious level of thoughts and recognized feelings.

The story revolves around Nina Leeds who, at her father's insistence, has waited to marry until her beloved Gordon comes back from the war; he does not return. In agony at not having given herself to him, Nina becomes a promiscuous war-bride, until, we are assured, she can clear away her neurosis by rearing her own children. Loving her hero still, she marries his male idolator, the ineffectual but wholesome Sam Evans, and by him becomes pregnant. Told by Sam's mother that there is insanity in the family, Nina aborts the burden; then, at old Mrs. Evans' suggesion, she picks a healthy man and has his child. Sam thinks the boy is his and although Nina and the real father, Dr. Edmund Darrell, fall in love, Nina refuses to leave or to disillusion Sam. Nina's friend, Charlie Marsden, watching all this, suspects and is jealous. The boy, named Gordon after Nina's ideal, resents Darrell's intrustion into the family life and thus comes to hate his actual father while he loves Sam. Finally Nina, piqued by her son Gordon's growing away from her, closer to his fiancée, Madeline Arnold, and closer to his "father" Sam, decides to tell Sam that Gordon is not his child. Sam's heart-failure prevents this. The love between Nina and Darrell has grown cold and empty, and Nina settles down "with drowsy gratitude" to warm the rest of her nights with "dear old Charlie" Marsden.

The examination of Nina Leeds is thorough and complete. She might seem, indeed, a more natural person were the analysis less thorough, for we note that (as in *Mourning Becomes Electra** with incest) O'Neill has taken pains to include every possible relationship of heterosexual love. We observe introspective Nina and her dream-ideal lover; her father; casual "lovers"; husband; father of her child, who becomes a true lover; understanding friend; and son. The study, granting all these relationships, and the quirks of the story (with its intruding insanity and the son growing in the dream-lover's image) is psychologically profound, but the strain of granting all these fortuities, which in a novel might (through the 25 years the play covers) be clothed in explanatory and solidifying atmosphere, reduces the drama to a tour de force that is true in the details of its character observation, yet essentially false. O'Neill explores the caverns of love as one bearing light through a labyrinth; he reaches the Minotaur, but he holds no Ariadne's thread to lead him out to the sky once more.

The chief merit of the play, according to Gilbert W. Gabriel (*New York Sun,* February 6, 1928), is its use of spoken thought: "The whole worth—not only the novelty, the passing originality, but the whole big worth—of *Strange Interlude* is hung upon these soliloquies and asides. It is these that make dualism out of Sardoualism. It is these that plunge the play's violences back into deep vistas of each character's past, illuminate each of those memories and motives which play even greater parts than do the living bodies before your eyes." Brooks Atkinson, on the other hand (January 31, 1928) remarked: "One irreverently suspects that there may be an even deeper thought unexpressed than the nickel-weekly jargon that Mr. O'Neill offers as thinking." And St. John Ervine, in the *London Observer* (March 13, 1932) maintained that if *Strange Interlude* "were shorn of its last two acts and its valueless asides, it would make a moderately interesting play."

Analysis of the asides shows that they do not forward the action of the drama. In many cases, the character "thinks aloud" a thought or feeling, then speaks it. Dudley Nichols put his finger on the fault when he said in the *New York World* (January 31, 1928): "This is a psychological novel of tremendous power and depth put into the theatre instead of between the covers of a book." O'Neill—son of an actor whose work he despised—blunts the actor's part by his various devices: in *The Great God Brown* masks blank the mobility of expression; in *Strange Interlude* the double wording of thought or feeling dams the actor from creative expression. "The characters are automata," said Brooks Atkinson (May 13, 1928). Such intensity as develops springs from the emotional baring of the story, and the personal power of the performer, breaking through the artificiality and loquaciousness of the device.

"Whatever one may think personally of the story and the significance of Mr. O'Neill's long drama," said Atkinson (May 13, 1928, shortly after it was awarded the Pulitzer Prize) "it is a heavily-freighted piece of work, uncompromising, forceful, and sustained." The complex intertangled relationships of Nina Leeds and her men make the fullest study of a woman in the American theatre. It loses in intensity through the very logic of its completeness, but its analysis is as implacable as complete, making *Strange Interlude,* though unsuccessful in its experimental features, richly revealing. Elmer Rice in *Harper's Magazine* (Spring 1932) called it a "bitterly anti-feministic play," but O'Neill has merely laid bare a woman's soul.

Directed by José Quintero, first play of the Actors Studio, at the New York Martin Beck March 11, 1963, *Strange Interlude* ran for 107 performances, with Geraldine Page as Nina, Ben Gazzara (replaced by Rip Torn), Pat Hingle, Betty Field, Jane Fonda, and Franchot Tone. There was a brilliant performance by Glenda Jackson at the London Duke of York's, opening April 6, 1984.

MOURNING BECOMES ELECTRA   *Eugene O'Neill*

Following the plot pattern of the *Oresteia** trilogy of Aeschylus, *Mourning Becomes Electra* is O'Neill's most neatly constructed play. With names suggestive of the ancient Greeks (Ezra Mannon for Agamemnon, Orin for Orestes), O'Neill set his trilogy at the time of the American Civil War. "Homecoming" shows Christine Mannon, while her husband is at war, having an affair with an outcast cousin, Adam Brant. Christine's jealous daughter, Lavinia, discovering the affair, notifies her father whom she idolizes; on Ezra's return, Christine poisons him. "The Hunted" shows Christine using her power over her son Orin to induce him to marry Hazel Niles. Her plan might have succeeded, but Lavinia and Orin overhear Brant and Christine planning to go away together. Orin shoots Brant and virtually forces Christine to kill herself. In "The Haunted," Orin and Lavinia, returned from a long voyage, have failed to rid themselves of "the curse of the house of Mannon." Lavinia seeks a way out in marriage with Peter Niles. Orin, after making more than brotherly overtures to Lavinia, in disgust of soul shoots himself. When Peter Niles is repelled by the morbid intensity of Lavinia's desire, she makes the Mannon home her living tomb.

The play takes five and a half hours to perform; in New York the curtain rose at 5 p.m. The play opened there October 26, 1931, for a run of 150 performances with Alla Nazimova, Alice Brady, and Earle Larimore. On tour, then in New York, were Judith Anderson, Florence Reed, and Walter Abel. London saw the play opening November 19, 1937, for 106 performances. Erwin Piscator produced it at his Dramatic Workshop, New York, in 1947.

There is a surging power in *Mourning Becomes Electra*. It is, thought the *London Times* (April 10, 1948), "O'Neill's masterpiece, and is superbly constructed." It moves, said John Mason Brown in *Seeing More Things*

(1948), "with the white heat of tragedy," at least for the first two parts, "before the play became mired in Freud." The three parts, said Burns Mantle (October 27, 1931) are "artistically important and physically wearying." More enthusiastically Gilbert W. Gabriel declared: "They capture a firmness of wording, a litheness of incident, a burning beauty, which insure them rightful place among dramatic masterpieces of the world today."

The length of the trilogy was scored vehemently by St. John Ervine in the *London Observer* (March 13, 1932): "Mr. O'Neill is a verbose author who declines to be economical in his writing. He will not use one word where he can use six, nor say in a sentence what he can say in a page. . . . This spendthrift habit has grown upon him to such an extent that he cannot now write a play in less than thirteen acts. . . . Only a born dramatist could have written the first nine acts of *Mourning Becomes Electra*; only a Greenwich Villager could have written the last four. . . . Mr. O'Neill *knows* when to stop, but willfully goes on." The *London Times* (March 10, 1932) pressed a further point: "O'Neill has asked of his chosen medium more than it has power to give. As though aware of this, he has tentatively introduced here and there groups of townsfolk—'a chorus,' he says, 'come to look and listen and spy on the rich and exclusive Mannons.' This was his way out; by using a chorus he might so have enriched his medium that his stage-directions and the play's spiritual intent were fully expressed in their comments. But having introduced his chorus, he makes surprisingly little use of them, preferring to hustle them off the stage and revert to the methods of direct naturalism. No play ever stood in greater need of a chorus than this trilogy. They might have been the tongue of its tragic spirit which, in their absence, cannot speak plain."

By the form and substance of his trilogy, O'Neill challenged comparison with Aeschylus. Their most obvious difference, said the *London Times* (April 10, 1948) is that Aeschylus loved mankind, while O'Neill "feels only contemptuous pity for it. The strongest passion animating his characters is hate." Clytemnestra had several substantial reasons for murdering Agamemnon—among them, his sacrifice of their daughter Iphigenia, an innocent child, to win back the wanton Helen. Clytemnestra herself, though a dutiful wife, had never loved Agamemnon; she was one of his spoils of war. The motives of Christine are vaguer and less substantial; she behaves, said the *Times*, like "a mawkish schoolgirl with a crude, novelettish mind." In Aeschylus' plays the crimes are open, even flaunted; in O'Neill's they are concealed, and sordid.

In two other ways, O'Neill loses power by deviating from the Greek spirit. In the classical trilogy, there are not only three plays but three stages of spirit: the curse, the doom, and the deliverance. These may also be envisioned as the Christian pattern of sin, penitence, and redemption; both approaches imply a religious understructure. Without such religious ground, O'Neill cannot show the reclamation; his trilogy but lengthens out the doom. Hence *Mourning Becomes Electra* does not achieve the catharsis that would purge audiences of fear and pity and send them asoar with exaltation; instead, it leaves them in a dismal slough of despond. Secondly, having added the element of incest, O'Neill is not content to leave it humanly individual, but, as in *Strange Interlude*,* like a conscientious syntagmatist he must ring all the changes on his theme, compile a complete catalogue: Mrs. Mannon is drawn only toward her son, but Lavinia is stung with desire of her father and her brother; Orin, of his mother and his sister. Such a thorough surging of incestuous desire, while it may enlighten Freudian neophytes, and while it may pile horror upon horror in melodramatic pitch, will hardly seem to add to the play's credibility or to its art.

With all its shortcomings and long-windedness, *Mourning Becomes Electra* probes deeply into the tortured souls of Orin and Lavinia Mannon, and renders poignantly vivid the trail of their pitiful lives.

The 1947 film starred Rosalind Russell, Michael Redgrave, Raymond Massey, Katina Paxinou, Kirk Douglas, Nancy Coleman, and Henry Hull. Recent revivals of the play include one in 1969 at Berkeley, Calif., 1971 at Stratford, Conn., and 1972 by the Circle in the Square.

AH, WILDERNESS!   *Eugene O'Neill*

This is a strange, pleasant interlude among O'Neill's threnodies of disaster. Presented in New York on October 2, 1933, it ran for 289 performances and was revived there in 1941. London saw it in 1936, Oxford in 1946. It has been popular in community theatres.

Ah, Wilderness! is O'Neill's only play that follows the conventional pattern of contemporary comedy. Picturing the problems of a smalltown family, it is an affirmation of the tolerance and goodness of the American way of life. Nat Miller, Connecticut newspaper publisher, has a problem, among his four children, in the shape of his rebellious son Richard. The boy's mother, Essie, is worried. Her own brother, Sid Davis, a good-natured fellow, has never amounted to anything because of his drinking; and Nat's sister Lily is an old maid from refusing to marry Sid. When rigid neighbor David Mc-Comber thinks Richard too wild for his daughter Muriel, the boy goes off on a binge and pretends to be as knowing as Belle, "the swift babe from New Haven," whose vulgarity and amorous readiness really scare him. On Richard's drunken homecoming, Sid takes charge. Then his father helps straighten Richard out and his sweetheart Muriel washes away the bitter taste of his wild oats with a pure kiss.

This sentimental vein, most unexpected in O'Neill, brought, as the *London Times* (April 10, 1948) remarked, "mingled pleasure and surprise" and showed "how skillfully he can construct a play, how charmingly he can create presentable people."

Deftly and sympathetically produced, and with David's father understandingly played by George M. Cohan in New York and Will Rogers on the road, *Ah, Wilderness!* was received like an engagement present. The mood is, of course, more of a dream delight, a creation of wishful memory, than a living span of days, but, as Richard Dana Skinner said in *Eugene O'Neill: A Poet's Quest* (1935): "This appealing and innocent and tender little comedy of adolescence is really much more important than it seems in the poet's unconscious scheme of things. It marked an end to that terrible fear which had made every symbol of youth appear like some hideous monster. It was unquestionably the beginning of a third and entirely new period in O'Neill's creative life, the period of full manhood of the soul."

Skinner's prophecy proved less accurate than his description; O'Neill returned to his restless seeking, moving downward to despair. Robert Garland (October 3, 1933) said of the play that it was "strong with the strength that is tenderness, warm with the ineffable sweetness of everyday life. . . . It came with laughter, tears, and good old-fashioned sentiment. And with acting, settings, and direction that must have been made in heaven." George Jean Nathan maintained it is "a folk comedy of such truth in humor, such gentle and sympathetic raillery and such imaginatively photographic character that it must be given sound rank in the list of O'Neill's accomplishments."

O'Neill drew his title from FitzGerald's translation of the *Rubáiyát of Omar Khayyám:*

> *A book of verses underneath the bough,*
> *A jug of wine, a loaf of bread—and thou*
> *Beside me singing in the wilderness—*
> *Oh, wilderness were paradise enow.*

In addition to professional revivals, as at Ann Arbor, 1949, with Ernest Truex, the Bristol Old Vic in 1956, Chicago and Toronto, 1957, there is hardly a year without a college or high school or other amateur production of the happy play (Wesleyan, 1952; Swarthmore, 1961; Boston University, 1963). The Community Theatre Company of East Hampton, N.Y., opened it May 4, 1984.

In contrast with O'Neill's more experimental but more straining and perfervid plays, *Ah Wilderness!* provides a mellow evening and shows that sentiment and hopefulness, and the bounding bounty of youth, were at least once within the grasp of our grimmest dramatist.

THE ICEMAN COMETH   *Eugene O'Neill*

After a twelve-year lapse in the production of his new plays, O'Neill's drama of illusion, *The Iceman Cometh,* written in 1939, had its premiere on Broadway, October 9, 1946. In this work, he went back to "the best friends I ever had," the derelicts in a New York saloon of 1912, and to his old depressive mood, his characteristic preoccupation with despair. "The Mr. O'Neill who wrote *Beyond The Horizon* in 1920," said the *London Times* (April 10, 1948), "is the Mr. O'Neill who wrote *The Iceman Cometh* in 1946," and John Mason Brown (October 19, 1946), in discussing the latter play, quoted references to "Jimmy-the-Priest's, a waterfront dive," in an O'Neill interview of 1924. They could have gone farther and fared better; in the magazine *Seven Arts* of June 1917 is a short story, "Tomorrow," by Eugene G. O'Neill, which is a detailed summary of *The Iceman Cometh.* O'Neill has, in the play, dramatized his earlier story.

The play opens in the saloon of Harry Hope, with a spread of back room tables on most of which lie the heads of sleeping bums. Among them we find Larry Slade, one-time anarchist; Pat McGloin, an ex-policeman; Willie Oban, a Harvard Law School alumnus; Piet Wetjoen, a General; and James Cameron (Jimmy Tomorrow), a correspondent, Harry Hope, once a ward heeler, hasn't gone out of doors in twenty years. The persons most alive are three streetwalkers—Margie, Pearl, and Cora—and the bartender pimp. A young frightened fellow, Don Parritt, comes from the West Coast; Slade, who at first refuses to be the kid's confessor, gathers that the boy has betrayed his I.W.W. pals—including his mother; then Slade talks the boy into suicide.

None of these half-alive dreamers in Hope's haven considers himself down and out. They all "hit the pipe of the future." On that fateful tomorrow, each will venture forth and again do a man's job in the world. Their present interest centers upon the imminent coming of Theodore Hickman, "Hickey," a salesman who periodically leaves his wife "with an iceman" to enjoy a spree at Harry Hope's. His coming is a feast for all. But this time when Hickey comes, he brings a new faith which he insists upon imparting to Harry's soaks, has-beens, and tarts. Face yourself, he tells them; see yourself as you are, and you will change, you will act, you will be happy. Tomorrow is here. Against their will, as though hypnotized by his fervor, one by one they set forth; even house-held Harry Hope steps beyond his door. Then one by one they slink back, unable to face themselves or the life beyond the saloon. They discover that Hickey's faith itself is built on death; he has killed his wife, he tells them, to end her suffering over his infidelities and drunkenness. Hickey has himself summoned the police, and his departure is welcomed by the besotted cowards in Hope's saloon, who shrink back again behind their drinks and their illusions. "They will relapse with relief," said the *London Times*; "the swine return to their swill. They are, Slade asserts, converts to death." At the end of the play, in its printed form, Larry Slade slumps over a table; in the performance, he walks slowly toward the door through which the boy Don Parritt went to jump to death.

This shrunken universe of dregs and depression, of persons seeking consolation for life in drink and dreams, takes four hours to enact upon the stage. One speech of Hickey, telling why he killed his wife and urging the sodden souls to live their dreams, takes nineteen minutes. To all rehearsal suggestions that the play be cut, O'Neill was adamant: "Cut out a minute, and I'll add a half hour." Yet the one point on which all the critics agreed is that the play is much too long. John Mason Brown "kept wondering for an hour and a half when the play was going to begin." Ward Morehouse found it "too verbose, too slow in starting, too digressive once it was started." Kelcey Allen remarked that Act I began with most of the characters asleep and ended with most of the audience asleep.

Beyond this there was sharp division of opinion. Richard Watts (October 19, 1946) called the play "a drama of great emotional and creative power." Brooks Atkinson declared that it "ranks toward the top of his collected works . . . the drama that seems tediously wordy in the reading glows with promethean flame." Despite its verbosity, Morehouse felt that it is "one of the few plays of genuine stature brought to the theatre of the century's fourth decade." George Jean Nathan broke into cheers for his friend's return to the theatre: "Hallelujah, hosanna, hail, heil, hurrah, huzza, banzai and gesundheit!" He called Hickey's peroration one of the most impressive pieces of writing in contemporary dramatic literature. On the other hand, Howard Barnes maintained that the play "has not increased O'Neill's artistic stature . . . more promise than substance." "One trembles to imagine," said John Mason Brown, "what people would think of *The Iceman Cometh* if it did not bear Mr. O'Neill's mesmerizing name." Sterling North headed his review of the printed play "Iceman Cometh Stinketh."

The play suggests a symbolic meaning which according to Atkinson becomes in the glow of the performance "no more than an unimportant afterthought." It has, however, troubled other reviewers. John Mason Brown suggested several possibilities: "What the drummer in Mr. O'Neill's drama symbolizes—whether he means death by robbing men of their life-sustaining dreams, or whether he (and the whole play) represent Mr. O'Neill's subconscious protest against those who have chaperoned and tidied up his own recent living—is a matter for individual conjecture. One thing is certain. Mr. O'Neill has turned on the meddlesome idealists as fiercely as ever Ibsen did."

The *London Times* (April 10, 1948) summed up the dramatist through his work by saying that "Mr. O'Neill . . . has no hope of anything better, here or hereafter. The world is futile and so are its inhabitants. There is no other world, and this one had better be ended. . . . There is nothing here of courage and endurance, nothing of unflinching faith, nothing of self-sacrifice deliberately made. The O'Neill world is a dirty pub, frequented by drunks and disorderlies and shiftless loafers; and periodically raided by corrupt cops."

The lack of courage in the play, its "nothing of unflinching faith," suggests examination of Nathan's statement that the play yields "the profound essences of authentic tragedy." Each may frame for himself his own definition of tragedy; for many—for O'Neill himself—tragedy rings with the affirmation of human worth or dignity. Out of the depths of physical disaster, one is borne to the heights of spiritual triumph. The simple reassumption of a staunch stand against overwhelming forces—human or superhuman—brings a companioning exaltation that makes tragedy a rich and a purging experience. O'Neill's world comes to its end in no such stalwart wise, not laconically brighteyed against the terrors, but lengthily drooling evasions in its beer. It is as a picture of this piteous world of the coward, not as a tragic stand but as a pathetic fall—a picture the more heart-rending because the playwright is within the frame—that *The Iceman Cometh* makes its dark appeal.

The 1946 production marked O'Neill's last Broadway presentation before his death, after a lingering illness, in 1954.

The Iceman Cometh was revived by the New York Circle in the Square May 8, 1956, with Jason Robards, Jr. It opened again in London January 29, 1958, and in Liverpool October 21, 1958.

O'Neill's Posthumous Plays

Word seems appropriate as to how O'Neill's posthumous plays came to be produced. Shortly after O'Neill's death, Dag Hammarskjöld, Secretary General of the United Nations, asked me at lunch one day: "What's the matter with you people of the American theatre?"

"We've been accused of many things. What in particular is on your mind?"

"Why aren't you allowing the Swedish Royal Theatre to produce O'Neill's posthumous plays?"

"I understand that he doesn't want them shown in the States for twenty-five years. I don't know whether he felt the same way about productions abroad. I'll check."

O'Neill's press agent had also died; but at my request the office manager consulted Carlotta, O'Neill's widow, then explained the situation to me. In her first anguish, Carlotta had said no to everything. More calmly, she remembered that Stockholm had given world premieres of some of Gene's plays. She didn't want to contact them for fear of a rebuff; but if they were to approach her again, there might be a more favorable response.

This information I conveyed to Dag Hammarskjöld, and in the fall Ahmed Bokhari, Dag's assistant secretary, asked what theatre folk I'd suggest to meet Karl Ragnar Gierow (b. 1904), director of the Swedish Royal Dramatic Theatre, who was coming to the United States to arrange details for the production of the posthumous plays. A dozen of us, including Elmer Rice and Tennessee Williams, gathered for luncheon in Dag's quarters atop the U.N. building.

When we were introduced, Karl Gierow said to me: "I understand you're the midwife of this project."

I responded: "I'm glad it's being turned over to a competent pediatrician."

Without adding a word to O'Neill's, but cutting and tightening, fitting many pages of dialogue into the frame of taut drama, Gierow presented the world premieres of whatever could be salvaged from O'Neill's papers. O'Neill had planned a series of one-act plays, *By Way of Orbit*. Only one of these proved usable: *Hughie*, a virtual monologue in which an habitué of a shoddy New York hotel becomes a friend of the new bartender while telling him about the old one, Hughie. This had been written about 1941; it was produced in Stockholm in 1957, in New York in 1958.

O'Neill had also planned a series of eleven full-length plays, *A Tale of Possessors Self-Dispossessed*, tracing one family from Revolutionary days to our own. Two of these were well enough developed to be made presentable. *A Touch of the Poet*, fifth in the series, written about 1936, was shown in Stockholm in 1958 and reached Broadway later the same year. *More Stately Mansions*, which followed it in the series, was cut from more than ten hours of manuscript to five hours for production, in Stockholm and New York in 1962.

Let me end this note with the last sentence of my chapbook, *The Art of Eugene O'Neill* (University of Washington Press, 1928), the first survey of the playwright's work: "Whatever untried dramatist comes most richly to reveal the many-sided genius of the American theatre, will owe no small debt to the prior experiments and achievements of Eugene O'Neill."

LIST
of planned plays, conceived beginning 1933,
to form the cycle

A Tale of Possessors Self-Dispossessed

Title	Setting
1. *The Greed of the Meek, Part I*	Rhode Island, 1755-1775
2. *The Greed of the Meek, Part II*	(Same as above)
3. *And Give Me Death, Part I*	Rhode Island and Paris, 1783-1805
4. *And Give Me Death, Part II*	(Same as above)
5. *A Touch of the Poet*	Outside Boston, 1828
6. *More Stately Mansions*	In and near Boston, 1837-1846
7. *The Calms of Capricorn*	New England, and aboard a clipper, 1857
8. *The Earth's the Limit*	San Francisco and the Sierras, 1858-1860
9. *Nothing Is Lost Save Honor*	San Francisco, New York, and Washington, 1862-1870
10. *The Man on Iron Horseback*	New York, Paris, Shanghai, and Midwest, 1876-1893
11. *A Hair of the Dog* (earlier, *The Life of Bessie Bowen*, then *The Career of Bessie Bolan*)	A Midwest mansion, 1904-1932

While the unfinished cycle was in process, O'Neill completed *The Iceman*

Cometh, 1939; *A Long Day's Journey into Night,* 1940-1941, and *A Moon for the Misbegotten,* 1943.

Most of the cycle dramas were either destroyed by Eugene O'Neill or left in unusable fragments. The fifth and the sixth, as noted hereafter, were reshaped by Karl Gierow and produced.

LONG DAY'S JOURNEY INTO NIGHT   *Eugene O'Neill*

Written in anguish, harrowing its writer, *Long Day's Journey into Night* was dedicated in 1941 to Eugene's wife, Carlotta, who "gave me the faith in love that enabled me to face my dead at last and write this play." It is avowedly autobiographical, "Tyrone" a pseudonym for O'Neill. Mother Mary is addicted to morphine, which she'd been given at the difficult birth of her third child, which had soon died. James Tyrone, Sr., is a bitter man, his career ruined by his continuing success in a single role in a potboiler play. (Eugene's father had for years toured successfully in *The Count of Monte Cristo.*) Elder brother Jamie is a dissipated soul, who at times tries to draw Edmund (Eugene) into the same sort of wasted life, at times more soberly tries to help him. Edmund (like Eugene) has consumption; his miserly father—who excuses himself by saying that his early poverty had made him parsimonious—wants to send him to a state sanitorium.

The family love-hate relationship is implacably developed in its tawdry details, through a day in 1912 in their summer home in New London, Conn., until Mary comes in, flaunting her old wedding gown—greeted by Jamie with "The mad scene, Enter Ophelia"—as the men drink and the curtain comes slowly down.

Long Day's Journey into Night opened at the New York Helen Hayes on November 7, 1956, directed by José Quintero. It ran for 388 performances, and won the 1957 Pulitzer Prize. Fredric March and Florence Eldridge played the parents; Jason Robards, Jr., the alternately sadistic and loving elder brother; Bradford Dillman, Edmund, the author's picture of himself. The Swedish National Company played it at the New York Cort May 15, 1962, with Inga Tidblad the mother; Georg Rydeberg (in Stockholm Lars Hanson) as the father; Ulf Palme, James junior; Jarl Kullo, Edmund. It was revived May 13, 1971, and at Asolo in 1979. There was an all-black cast OffOffBway, with Earle Hyman, in 1981.

O'Neill's play won instant acclaim. Walter Kerr (November 9, 1956) called it "the searing and sorry record of the wreck of his family." Brooks Atkinson: "Scene by scene the tragedy moves along with a remorseless beat that becomes hypnotic as though this were life lived on the brink of oblivion . . . a stricken family in which the members are at once fascinated and repelled by one another. Always in control of the material, he has also picked out and set forth the meaning that underlies it." Brooks does not tell what that meaning is.

Of the London 1958 production, Harold Hobson called the last act one "of incomparable pathos and beauty." There were eighty-seven performances at the New York Public Theatre, opening March 18, 1981. It came to the London Westminster, spring 1984. *Long Day's Journey into Night* makes clear the anguish out of which Eugene O'Neill's genius flamed bright.

A MOON FOR THE MISBEGOTTEN   *Eugene O'Neill*

Written in 1943, tried out on the road in February and March 1947, *A Moon for the Misbegotten* came to Broadway after O'Neill's death, opening at the Bijou May 2, 1957, directed by Carmen Capalbo, and running for sixty-eight performances.

The play centers upon the plight of James Tyrone, Jr. (representing Eugene O'Neill's brother), a cynical alcoholic, haunted by the memory of his drinking and whoring binge while bringing his mother's body back East for burial. He is a braggart on the surface, but a lonely child at heart. We watch him dallying, in a superior, cynical way, with Josie, an oversized Irish woman of twenty-eight, daughter of Phil Hogan, a stingy, persnickety tenant on Tyrone's Connecticut farm. Josie has built a reputation as a promiscuous gadabout, but is actually a virgin; and the play culminates under the moon when the drunken Tyrone lies on her breast while she tenderly comforts him as a mother.

Brooks Atkinson in the *Times* called the play flawed; it is too long, but O'Neill forbade any cutting. John McClain in the *Journal-American* called it "long but fiercely great, with fierce qualities of introspection, the ruthless examination of forces and frustrations that pursued his tragic family to their separate graves." The play elaborates an episode mentioned in *Long Day's Journey into Night,* * which is a fuller autobiographical dirge.

Wendy Hiller and Franchot Tone, with Cyril Cusack and Glen Cannon, starred in the New York production, and Atkinson observed: "Thank Mr. Capalbo for realizing that even a minor O'Neill play deserves a beautiful production and admirable performance." London saw the play briefly in 1960. It was revived in New York by the Circle in the Square, June 12, 1968, and at the Morosco December 29, 1973 with Jason Robards, Jr., and Colleen Dewhurst, for 313 performances. Despite its unnecessary length, it is endowed with O'Neill's anguished longing for better days beyond the grasping. As Browning puts it in "Andrea del Sarto":

> *Ah, but a man's reach should exceed his grasp,*
> *Or what's a heaven for?*

The London Riverside Studio (June 1983), production of *A Moon for the Misbegotten* emphasized the role of Frances de la Tour as Josie, unable to conquer her own self-loathing, but winning deep audience sympathy with her understanding love of a man without capacity for return. She renews her quarreling with her father as soon as James Tyrone leaves. There was a revival at the London Mermaid, September 6, 1983, with Ian Bannen and Alan Devlin, and one at the New York Cort, April 19, 1984.

The Tyrone-O'Neills were a family marked for a tormented living, out of which Eugene wrought his tremendous but flawed art.

A TOUCH OF THE POET   *Eugene O'Neill*

Written about 1936, *A Touch of the Poet,* fifth of the projected series of eleven plays following one family from Revolutionary days to our own time, was presented by Gierow in Stockholm in early 1958; in New York at the Helen Hayes October 2, 1958, directed by Harold Clurman, for 284 performances.

The action takes place in 1825, in a gloomy tavern near Boston run by Cornelius Melody, an Irish braggart tyrant, a drunken, meddlesome, lazy fraud, who rides a horse, puts on aristocratic airs, despises the shanty Irish "scum," and scorns the Yankees—who consider him trash. His proudest memory, which he celebrates every year, is of the battle of Talavera, at which, he boasts, he distinguished himself under Wellington. He behaves as an overacting Byronic lord with, says his wife, Nora, "a touch uv a poet."

Nora Melody, whom he also despises, having picked her out of the Irish bogs, is shrunken and shabby, but deeply loves her husband. While Cornelius piles on debts, Nora keeps the tavern going. Their daughter Sara, who hates her surroundings, has determined to marry the well-to-do young American tradesman Simon Harford, who is sick upstairs in the inn. We do not see him, but his mother, Deborah, is a gentle and charming contrast to the forcefulness if not violence around.

Simon's father sends an offer of money to Cornelius, to keep Sara from marrying his son. Cornelius, considering himself insulted, gallops off to Boston to challenge old Harford to a duel. Meanwhile, there is a magnificent scene in which Sara confronts her mother, who cries out: "There is no slavery in it when you love!" And, while Sara is trying to tell her mother that she'd allowed herself to be seduced in order to win the young man upstairs, Nora is pleasantly contemplating how Cornelius will carry things off in Boston. Melody comes back, beaten not in a duel but in a brawl with the police—and bailed out by Simon's father.

Disillusioned and vowing to change, Cornelius shoots not himself but his favorite mare, and goes out to join his new "pals" among the Irish. Nora understands: "He had to live all his life alone in the hell of pride." Sara weeps for her father's loss of his pride and his illusions. "Shame on you," Nora chides her, "when you have love." And Sara's mind turns to her future with the young Yankee upstairs.

In the New York production Eric Portman played Cornelius; Helen Hayes, Nora; Kim Stanley, Sara; Betty Field, the quiet aristocratic Deborah Harford. The *World-Telegram* emphasized the author's penetration of his characters, especially Nora, who "can work up a big hatred, but would rather forgive, for inside her heart stars are singing." The audience is proffered a mixed potion of illusion, sham, and shame.

MORE STATELY MANSIONS   *Eugene O'Neill*

More Stately Mansions follows *A Touch of the Poet* in the family series O'Neill had projected. Its title is taken from Oliver Wendell Holmes' "The Chambered Nautilus":

> *Build thee more stately mansions, O my soul,*
> *As the swift seasons roll.*

The action is set in the Massachusetts home of Sara and Simon Harford, from 1832 to 1841. Simon has lost his early idealism and becomes a ruthless and weathly businessman, with the single-minded drive of a Yankee on the make. Between his weakened mother, Deborah, with illusions of an aristocratic society life, and his wife, Sara, with the illusion of her husband's love of her rather than of money, there is a struggle for possession of the man. Simon seems to pay more heed to his mother, until she goes mad. This leaves Sara—who shares Simon's robust and rapacious nature but still expects the ideal—to hope for the day when Simon will withdraw from the money-maze and write the masterful "book that will save the world and free men from the curse of greed." But Simon burns his book in self-disgust. The soul has gone out of the mansion.

O'Neill destroyed what he thought was the final copy of this play, but enough dialogue was found among his papers to call for ten hours of playing time. The Gierow production in Stockholm, November 1, 1962, compressed this to five hours; for New York, director José Quintero cut it to more nearly normal time; but the play is still flawed. This is not to be blamed, said Walter Kerr, on "the familiar demons that dogged O'Neill throughout his creative life: the inexplicably flat prose [I should prefer to say, his inability to achieve poetic power], the obvious overambition." The play *is* unfinished; its seeming conflict between idealism and materialism is a cobweb in a corner of an empty house.

More Stately Mansions opened at the New York Broadhurst October 31, 1967, and attained 142 performances. Ingrid Bergman played Deborah (who'd had one big scene in *A Touch of the Poet*), still living in the early American dream.

In Colleen Dewhurst as Sara the changing emphases were rife. Arthur Hill as Simon showed the conflict between dream and desire. Helen Craig played the continuing Nora Melody, Sara's mother, still in love with dead Cornelius.

Walter Kerr, in the *Times* November 12, 1970, recalling an apartment building left half finished in the Depression, and ultimately not finished but torn down, applied this image to *More Stately Mansions*: "The play is born a ruin: a great architectural emptiness derived from slaved-over blueprints, an eyeless, topless tower that cannot escape the earth in which it is deeply embedded. The draughtsmanship is finished. The earth has been dug. No one will ever live there." The play remains as the final, though maimed, expression of the greatest American playwright thus far to reach our stage.

LOOK BACK IN ANGER   *John Osborne*

The "angry young men" who were so vehement for a score of years took impetus from the play *Look Back in Anger,* by John Osborne (b. 1929), which had its premiere May 5, 1956, at the London Royal Court Theatre, a house hospitable to avant-garde drama. The cast included Kenneth Haigh as Jimmy Porter; Alan Bates as Cliff Lowes, his partner in a sweetshop; Mary Ure (Osborne's second wife) as Alison Porter; Helena Hughes as the girlfriend, Helena Charles. Richard Burton starred in the film.

Anger at all life kindles the play, flaring beyond the puny plot, which the *London Times* summarized: "A scruffy but eloquent hater of class distinctions is sadly deserted by his adoring wife." He calls her upper-class friend Helena an evil-minded little virgin; she slaps his face; he weeps in despair; she kisses him passionately, draws him down upon her, and the curtain also draws down. "When his wife comes groveling back, the mistress magnanimously concludes that she has been wrong to break up the marriage." (Jimmy had tried to break his wife out of her "beauty sleep. If only you could have a child and it would die." Before returning to him Alison has had a child, stillborn.) "The play consists largely of angry tirades. The hero regards himself, and clearly is regarded by the author, as the spokesman for the younger post-war generation, which looks round at the world and finds nothing right with it."

That the author shared his hero's bitterness is clearly shown in a letter he wrote from Paris in 1961: "This is a letter of hate. It is for you, my countrymen. I mean those men of my country who have defiled it. . . . You are its murderers, and there is little left in my own brain but thoughts of murder of you." The anger of Jimmy Porter, however, seemed to most critics too widely diffused; "we discover," said Gareth Lloyd Evans in *World Drama*, "that he really needs protection; the bombastic and belligerent attitude which he assumes is that of a frightened child." John Gassner said that the play "is limited by the nihilism of its author and the crackle and sputter of fireworks in a mist." Kenneth Tynan, expectedly, praised the play's "evident and blazing vitality. . . . He certainly goes off the deep end, but I cannot regard this as a vice in a theatre that seldom ventures more than a toe into the water."

In Paris, of the 1958 production, Guy Dumur observed: "After the films of James Dean and the novels of Françoise Sagan, we are now at the third stage of journalistic speculation on youth. The film, the novel, and now the theatre, have taken some real anxieties of youth, some questions which confront youth, and have returned a pale, undisturbing image of them."

What is fundamentally wrong lies in the emotion that produced the play; anger is both too superficial and too physically immediate to be a proper response to social life, or an effective avenue to art. Anger may be exorcised in art, but not if it spews itself indiscriminately around. A Turkish friend of mine, a high cultural official, describing a case of political malfeasance, ended: "I was so mortified that I went home and wrote a poem." It is as a signal, then as a symbol, that *Look Back in Anger* retains significance.

The play was shown at the Bristol Old Vic, April 22, 1957; in London again, May 11, 1957, with Alan Bates, directed by Tony Richardson; and again, opening October 29, 1968, for 127 performances. The New York production, opening October 1, 1957, ran for 407 performances. It played at the Asolo in 1962 and 1968; at the Roundabout in 1980.

Frank Rich, in the *New York Times* of March 1, 1982, declared that the angry playwrights are here again, "a dominant force in the post-World-War II theatre." Their anger now, he continues, is born of despair, "of a deeply felt, at times tragic, sense of futility." Neither sense of futility nor fisted anger is likely to spawn art. Allardyce Nicoll, theatre critic and historian, looking in the other direction, declared: "All the elements, or ingredients, of this theme are exactly similar to those which were largely cultivated between 1900 and 1930." Thus, it seems that Osborne was merely giving vociferous contemporary expression to the ever-rising resentment of rebellious youth, the noisy, sometimes violent, but usually frustrate gabbling at the generation gap.

LUTHER   *John Osborne*

Anger is prominent again in Osborne's *Luther*, 1961, with good reason, as the religious reformer's chronic constipation made him bitter and intolerant. Many of Luther's actual words are used in the numerous brief scenes of the play. "I'm like a ripe stool in the world's straining anus," he exclaims, "and at any moment we're about to let each other go."

On October 31, 1517, we watch Luther nailing his ninety-five theses to the Wittenberg church door; urged to be prudent, he declares: "If I break wind in Wittenberg, they are likely to smell it in Rome." On word of his excommunication, Luther burns the papal decree, excoriating Pope Leo X as "an over-indulged jakes-attendant to Satan, a glittering worm in excrement." At the 1521 Diet of Worms, Luther refuses to retract. Blamed in 1525 for inciting the slaughter of peasants, he retorts: "They rebelled against God's word."

Toward his wife, a former nun, and toward his young son, Luther reveals a more tender aspect, which invites more sympathy. For he is not only in physical pain; he is in spiritual anguish. As he puts his boy to bed, torn between hope and doubt, he cries: "I believe. I do believe. Only help my unbelief."

Osborne has put much of his own power and passion—and unbelief in man's future—into the play.

A PATRIOT FOR ME   *John Osborne*

In the days when men were beginning to identify themselves as German, or English, instead of the vassals of some noble or king, a man was recommended to Franz II of the Austro-Hungarian Empire as a staunch patriot. Franz asked: "But is he a patriot for me?" Ironically, this title is applied to Alfred Redl, a highly respected officer in Vienna at the turn of the century. Osborne's play is based on a biography by Robert A. Asprey.

Redl, ambitious, finds that his rise is helped by the officers' code of homosexuality. He moves from a tender innocence, beaten up by the accomplices of the first boy he sleeps with, to a depraved cruelty. This was caused partly by the anguish of distaste and fascination within him—as at the annual Vienna ball, with half of the Austro-Hungarian officers in drag, led by Baron von Epp as Queen Alexandra, her "court" including Marie-Antoinette, Messalina, the Czarina, and Lady Godiva.

Countess Sophie Delyanoff, who has tried to seduce Redl, is a Russian spy; through her the Russian spymaster, Colonel Oblensky, blackmails Redl to treachery. For the officers' code includes not having the homosexuality "found out." Redl's impulses lead him to more blatant and sadistic acts, and to his exposure as a spy. Maintaining the officers' code, he shoots himself. This is in 1913.

Historically, Redl served the Russians so well that the Austrians in 1914 were unaware of the seventy-five Russian army divisions, "more than the whole Austro-Hungarian army," said Austrian Count Adalbert Sternberg; "hence our eagerness to go to war, and hence our defeat."

A Patriot for Me, in twenty-four swift scenes, including brothel, gymnasium, homosexual bedrooms, and the lavish ball, gives a vivid picture of the disintegrating glory of Middle Europe on the brink of the First World War, which reshuffled the rulers and the lands.

The play, with public performance forbidden by the Lord Chamberlain in 1965, was presented as in a club, at the London Royal Court. Then, from the Chichester Festival in 1983, the production came to the London Haymarket, August 8, 1983, and is still playing to crowded houses as I write, with Alan Bates as Alfred Redl. Critical opinion was on the whole favorable. Eric Shorter in the *Telegraph* (August 9, 1983) called the play "extraordinarily compelling," but added that when Redl "'comes out,' as we say today, the dramatic pulse of the piece gives way to melodrama and yawns." Harold Hobson in the *Sunday Times* called it "full of sadness, beauty, and distress."

Osborne has now, in half a dozen plays, apparently outgrown his widespread anger, and in *A Patriot For Me* he takes proper place among the outstanding British playwrights of the day.

(The old Osborne reasserted himself in a *London Sunday Times* review

(September 28, 1983) of the diaries of Sir Peter Hall, director of the National Theatre from the time of its occupancy of the new buildings: "this numbing record of banal ambition, official evasiveness, and individual cupidity . . . this chronicle of our dull and overweening times.")

VENICE PRESERVED   *Thomas Otway*

This play has long been hailed as the greatest English tragedy since Shakespeare. As late as December 18, 1910, the *New York Sun* drama critic maintained that "outside of Shakespeare there is no English tragedy that can compare in power, pathos, and passion with *Venice Preserved*." Today the play's plot and treatment seem rather melodramatic, but there is no mistaking, even now, the strong emotional impact in its tense opposition of the claims of loyalty and love. It is the masterpiece of Thomas Otway (1652-1685).

Based on *The Conspiracy of the Spaniards against Venice in 1618,* a work by César Vichard de Saint-Réal (Paris, 1674), *Venice Preserved; or, A Plot Discovered* presents the disastrous dilemma of Jaffier, a noble young Venetian who, against the will of her father, Senator Priuli, has married Belvidera. When Priuli seeks to oppress the impoverished pair, Jaffier joins the Spaniard Pierre in a conspiracy against the Senate. Belvidera begs Jaffier, for love of her, to save her father and the State. Yielding to his love, he reveals the plot to the Senate on its promise to spare the conspirators—a promise that it promptly breaks. On the scaffold, Jaffier stabs his friend Pierre, then himself; Belvidera, her mind and her heart broken, joins them in death.

With Thomas Betterton and Otway's beloved Elizabeth Barry, the play opened in London on February 7, 1682. It was a fiery success, and it was revived constantly for two hundred years: by Mrs. (Susannah Maria) Cibber, 1738; David Garrick, 1743; Spranger Barry, 1747 (for a decade Barry and Garrick alternated as Jaffier and Pierre, with Mrs. Cibber as Belvidera); Mrs. (Sarah Kemble) Siddons and J. P. Kemble, from 1774 to 1811; William Charles Macready and Eliza O'Neill, 1819; Charles Kean, 1820 and the next decade; Charles and Fanny Kemble, 1829; Macready with Helen Faucit up to 1837. New York first saw the play at the Nassau Street Theatre February 20, 1752. More recent performances include one in London, 1920; Oxford, 1932; and an elaborate production at Yale, 1933. Hugo von Hofmannsthal translated it into German in 1905. The London production opening May 15, 1953, with John Gielgud and Pamela Brown, was called by Harold Hobson, in the *Christian Science Monitor* (June 6), "about the most contemporary play now to be seen in London . . . as much an example of *le théâtre engagé* as any work of Sartre or Camus." New York saw it in 1955.

The fiery speeches, the swift variations of passion, the conflict of motives, make *Venice Preserved* a superb acting play. Its prime value, as Allardyce Nicoll has said, "rests in its masterly construction and in its fine characterization, but its final impression is added to by the nervous blank verse, essentially theatrical, which Otway, after many experiments in various styles, had taught himself to write." The character of Belvidera is warm and richly revealed, as she moves upon her own path too ardently to recognize where it may lead the man she loves.

There are some allusions to contemporary affairs in *Venice Preserved,* which added to its appeal. The Venetian Senator Antonio was recognized as a caricature of the Earl of Shaftesbury. England in 1682, with its "Popist plots," with one revolution not far behind it and a second just ahead, could find much pertinent in conspiracies and divided loyalties. Without such timely tugs of interest, *Venice Preserved* remains nonetheless a richly colored, invigorating drama. The tragedy results, not from villainy, but from the flaws in decent men, from Pierre's too inflexible resolve and firm-set faith, from Jaffier's love-swayed vacillation, which is redeemed by his manly action at the end. "Now, now," gasps the dying Pierre, "thou hast indeed been faithful. This was done nobly." Jaffier's is an old-fashioned nobility (if indeed, nobility itself seems not to many old-fashioned!) as *Venice Preserved* is an old-fashioned play, that still trails clouds of glory.

Richard Watts, Jr., said in the *Post*: "It takes on such life and vividness and emotional intensity that it deserves all the pains that have been lavished on it. . . . There is an amazing episode of sheer and unashamed bawdry in the highly explicit session [omitted in the nineteenth century] between a courtesan and her senile protector."

The NT (Lyttleton) in repertory April 12, 1984, with Jane Lapataire, and Michael Pennington as Jaffier, restored this "Nicky-Nacky" scene of the decadent senator playing "doggie"; the courtesan takes his purses but kicks him as he backs under the table, then whips him out—adding to the play's picture of current corruption. Charles II died in 1685; three years later came the Bloodless Revolution.

TOPAZE   *Marcel Pagnol*

A hit in Paris, where it opened on October 9, 1928, *Topaze,* by Marcel Pagnol (French, 1895), with its warm humor and gentle irony, also scored in London and New York. Frank Morgan and Clarence Derwent headed the New York cast in 1930, which played 141 performances. A French company played it in New York in 1931, and the comedy has been revived frequently by little theatres and college playhouses. The play has been performed all over Europe, and remains an excellent ironic study of human nature.

Watching Topaze conduct a class of mischievous boys, we find him scrupulously honest and quite naive. He refuses to raise a student's marks to please an important patron of the Pension Muche, and is fired. To his great surprise he is offered a much better job. And gradually Topaze grows aware that he is being used as an honest front for dealings in community graft and that the lady who has befriended him and given him the work is the chief grafter's mistress. Thus wakened to the ways of the world, Topaze tosses aside his old adages, turns rogue, and deftly proceeds to supplant the grafter both in the spoils of the city and in the smiles of his mistress. As the curtain falls, his old pedagogue colleague is deciding to leave school to become Topaze's secretary, hoping also to reach the rainbow's end.

The play delights with the deftness of its portraits, the neatness and the fineness of its satire. Its theme—the decision of an upright person to match the manners of the world and play its "practical" game, with its implication that the honest man makes the best thief—while it may amuse a laissez-faire society, is hardly acceptable as a jest in these more bureaucratic days, when graft would be too large-scale for persiflagic trifling. But it is always a comfort to see the innocent tool turn on its cynical users, and in *Topaze* the characters are excellently drawn, the episodes humorously manoeuvred, and the dialogue crisply pertinent.

Benn W. Levy* made the English adaptation, which Gilbert W. Gabriel (1930) said lacked a little in raciness, vigor, edge: "It manages, though, to do Anglo-Saxon justice to the delicacies, whimsicality, little bendings of hu-

manity that are most Gallic and most charming about M. Pagnol's play . . .
a play that should tickle the humor of all students of what rogues these
mortals be."

From its schoolroom scenes, which touch teachers with intimate humor
and understanding satire, to those in which the emancipated manipulator
of men masters the woman also, *Topaze* is a delightful capture of human
nature devoted to truth, turning aside to acquire riches.

Topaze was deemed novel at a time when most French comedies had
actual or attempted infidelity as the central theme. A version called *I Like
Money*, with Peter Sellers, came to New York May 18, 1962.

THE SOCIETY WHERE ONE IS BORED   *Edouard Pailleron*

Among the deft comedies of the French Academician Edouard Pailleron
(1834-1899), *Le Monde où l'on s'ennuie* (*The Society Where One Is Bored*),
1881, has become a classic both of the French stage and of the classroom. It
is a shrewd but light-handed satire of the pretentious and pompous society
in which literary and political reputations are sometimes made and often
marred. The play was produced in London in 1893, and has often been
presented by student groups.

On the surface the play depicts a complicated set of amours. Roger de
Céran loves Suzanne de Villiers, the pretty adopted daughter and heir of
the Duchesse de Réville. Suzanne, however, has a "crush" on Professor
Bellac, who is also admired by the bluestocking English girl Lucy Watson.
The main business of the drama, however, is not in matching these couples,
but in making clear the character of the Professor and of the Raymonds. The
Professor (drawn from life after Professor of Philosophy Caro of the Sorbonne) has made a name as "the ladies' philosopher," the savant à la mode;
he is a neatly caught prototype of the latter-day popular lecturer and author
of guides to "mature behavior." Paul Raymond, a young sub-prefect of a
small town controlled by Roger's mother, the Comtesse de Céran, has
taught his bride Jeanne how to bow and say the right word, with apt
quotation, to win the Comtesse's favor and Paul's promotion. The play ends
with Paul successful and Jeanne relieved of this duty.

Mildly pleasing in its romance, the play is superbly deft in its satiric
delineation of literary and political pretenders of a sort that still seek
prominence in our age.

DISRAELI   *Louis Napoleon Parker*

According to its author, Louis Napoleon Parker (English, 1852-1944), this
"is not an historical play, but only an attempt to show a picture of the days—
not so very long ago—in which Disraeli lived, and some of the racial, social,
and political prejudices he fought against and conquered." Parker's portrait,
richly and roundly drawn, is not only an effective dramatic seizure of
Disraeli, but in performance the most famous of George Arliss's characterizations. *The New York Mail* (September 19, 1911), noted that "The play
itself, with its story of international intrigue, is but the frame or background for the portrait, an artistic and harmonious setting with its lords
and ladies in their picturesque Victorian costumes, its every detail blending
to create the atmosphere of that golden age."

The play centers on the intrigues that preceded English control of the
Suez Canal project, and ends with a reception to Queen Victoria, new

Empress of India. Charles, Viscount Delford, who seems an idler but is an astute statesman, and the charming Clarissa Pevensey form a background to the intrigue. Disraeli's clerk, Foljambe, is a Russian spy, as is the vivacious Mrs. Travers. The shrewd Disraeli, aware of their interest, keeps them properly misinformed. But Russian manoeuvring manages to bank-rupt Meyers, on whom Disraeli depends for funds for the Canal deal; whereupon Disraeli threatens to smash the Bank of England unless its head, Sir Michael Probert, grants him credit. This credit carries through the deal, which is celebrated in the reception to the Queen. At this point, personal concerns enter the story. Disraeli has been greatly worried over his wife's health. He receives a telegram, but does not dare open it; he is still holding it as his wife arrives at the reception.

The four-act play opened in Montreal January 23, 1911, and failed. It displeased audiences in Detroit, Toledo, Columbus and Chicago. The trouble seemed to come at the end of the third act, at which point, pressed by Disraeli, Sir Michael grants credit to cover the purchase of the Canal, and the curtain falls. In the new version, Sir Michael, forced to give Disraeli credit, goes. Then Disraeli, smiling, bows Mrs. Travers, who he knows is a spy, out of the room. Clarissa exclaims: "Oh, Mr. Disraeli, thank God you have such power!" Disraeli confides: "I haven't, dear child; but he doesn't know that."

After this change, business jumped from $3,000 to $15,000 a week. Opening in New York on September 18, 1911, the play ran for 282 perform-ances; in 1913 it attained over 150 performances in Boston; in London, where it opened April 4, 1916, it reached 128. George Arliss played Disraeli also in a talking film, with Joan Bennett, in 1929.

It is more than the fact that Arliss played both roles that now brings thought of the Rajah of Rukh in *The Green Goddess.** There is in the man Disraeli a similar stroking with the velvet glove, the polished courtier concealing the shrewd and ruthless politician. Disraeli, fighting for the creation of the empire, used weapons fitter to disrupt it. An excellent picture of the times, the means, and the man is built in the political melodrama *Disraeli,* still a powerful piece in the theatre.

THE TEAHOUSE OF THE AUGUST MOON   *John Patrick*

The Teahouse of the August Moon opened at the New York Martin Beck October 15, 1953, to win the Drama Critics' Circle award, the Pulitzer Prize, and several other citations as the best play of the year. It ran in New York for 1,129 performances. The play is a delightful combination of genial satire, deft staging, and warm sense of human fellowship. At once mellow and mocking, it was neatly fashioned by John Patrick (American, b. 1907) from the novel by Vern Sneider. Outwardly, it shows the natives of Tobiki Village, Okinawa, getting what they want by shrewd handling of the U.S. occupying authorities, but beneath the amusing patterns of the play we discern that democracy—decency in dealing with others—may, with the modicum of luck (or God's favor) all things human require, point the way to living together. East and West, the presumably impossible twain, do meet.

A genial interpreter, Sakini—played first in New York by David Wayne; Eli Wallach in London, 1954, then New York; Burgess Meredith and Larry Parks on the road—sets the Oriental point of view before the audience, with touches of Oriental philosophy: "Pain makes man think; thought makes man wise; wisdom makes life endurable." Sakini is also interpreter, within the play, to Captain Fisby, whose task it is to democratize Tobiki according to Army Plan B. Fisby is not liked by his superiors, having one major fault: he does not know how to refuse what someone deeply wants. Thus, somehow the jeep that is to take Fisby to the village carries also a heaped-up cargo of natives, with baggage and goat. On his arrival, among the natives' gifts to the Captain is a geisha girl, so naturally, instead of the Plan B schoolhouse, it is a teahouse that gets built. Under Fisby's democracy, the village thrives, especially as its sweet-potato brandy is a boon to the army posts—until the literal-minded colonel arrives and in horror orders the teahouse torn down. The United States, however, now heir to the process of muddling through, gives orders that restore the teahouse and one's faith in democracy, that make the natives happy, and the audience too.

Several companies took the play on tour, including one in Spanish for South America in 1956; and it has had over eighty productions abroad. Among revivals have been Bergen County, N.J.; Farmingdale, N.Y., and Long Beach, Calif., in 1967 and 1968.

In August 1970 a musical, *Lovely Ladies, Kind Gentleman,* with music and lyrics by Stan Freeman and Franklin Underwood, came to Philadelphia, and on December 28, 1970, in New York it was picketed by the Oriental Actors Association for having too few Orientals in the cast. The musical version sharpened the satire—Davy Burns as the rule-ridden colonel gives the order: "Teach these people democracy, if you have to shoot every one of them!"—but it lost the sense of fellowship. It closed after sixteen performances. The songs, including "One Side of the World" and "This Time," interrupted rather than enhanced the flow of the story. Clive Barnes was cruel, beginning his review with a memory of Antony's words of dead Caesar: "I come to bury *Lovely Ladies, Kind Gentleman,* not to praise it." Next day, the cast paraded Lady Astor, the play's goat, in front of the *Times* building, with a placard: "Clive gets my goat." They should have stayed with Patrick.

Over and beyond the play's "rich and deliciously humorous and touching qualities as sheer entertainment," said Richard Watts, Jr., in the *Post,* "the most enchanting quality of *The Teahouse of the August Moon* is its gay, smiling tribute to the human spirit and the capacity of mankind for mutual understanding." The reviews were studded with such phrases as "the delicacy of a porcelain bowl . . . the ease and airiness of a magic carpet." At the Majestic, London, opening April 22, 1954, the play had a run of 964 performances; English critics described it as "America laughing at itself." The moon of August is the most mellow; more than any other play in a lustrum of August moons, *The Teahouse* blends satire, comedy, charm, and warmth of man toward fellow-man.

When I saw the film version, with Marlon Brando at his best as the shrewd interpreter, there was an added spell of beauty in the geisha dance at the opening of the teahouse, along with a touch of genuine pathos toward the end, besides the constant laughter.

THE OLD WIVES' TALE   *George Peele*

As engaging a romp as has come to us from the Elizabethan theatre is *The Old Wives' Tale,* written about 1590 by George Peele (c. 1557-1596). Like Cervantes' novel *Don Quixote,* this play was intended as a satire on the romantic writings of the time. Its prose, and occasional rhyme, and deliberately inflated blank verse, with here and there a touch of mock Latin, present a merry mixture of reality and make-believe, a potpourri that might well be called "The Follies of Fairyland." Peele's first plays were written for the court; then, as in *The Old Wives' Tale,* he carried qualities of the courtly style to the public theatres.

The play begins with a combination of romance and reality as three starving knights-errant, Antic, Frolic, and Fantastic, break in and find hospitality with the plain smithy Crunch and his old goodwife Madge. Madge begins her tale, and the fairies come romping—and out of the fireplace bursts one of the characters of the story. Madge the narrator joins the delighted spectators as the story she was about to tell unfolds before our eyes.

The story is an amusing tangle of tales. Two brothers, Calypha and Thelea, in quest of their sister Delia, who is held by the magician Sacrapant, are also made his prisoners. In the magician's power are Erestus and his lady love; indeed, the sorcerer has changed bodies with Erestus, who hobbles about as a bent old man, while the magician takes youthful, vigorous strides.

A number of other legendary figures enter the story, such as Lampriscus, a villager unblessed with two unmarried daughters who find their fortunes at a magic well. The sorcerer is finally bested by the knight Eumenides, with the help of the ghost of Jack the Giant Killer, who helps because the knight has paid for Jack's burial. Sacrapant's victims are rescued, and Delia, beloved of Eumenides, turns out to be the Sleeping Beauty. Madge prepares a cup of ale and some breakfast, as the drama ends.

Pleasantly contrasted, amidst this merry travesty of romantic and fairy plays—the first dramatic travesty in English—are the village dances and songs of the harvest men and maids and the tripping rounds and lilting roundelays of the fairies. In an American production of *The Old Wives' Tale* (at Middlebury College, June 20, 1911, supervised by Frank W. Cady) the music arranged by Mrs. Maude S. Howard found old English tunes for Peele's delightful songs: "All ye that lovers be" and the impatiently charming "Whenas the rye–."

The Old Wives' Tale is crowded with literary allusions, most of them intended to spice the satire. The mood of the play and certain of the relationships made Thomas Warton remark, in *Milton's Poems* (1791), that *The Old Wives' Tale,* "which might have been a favorite of his early youth," suggested to Milton the general movement of his *Comus.*

There is considerable amusement still to be drawn from Peele's extravaganza, which presents, as Allardyce Nicoll has said, "a peculiarly original handling of the romantic material. Stories of chivalrous adventure, of sorcerers, of spirits who rise amid thunder and lightning, had been popular on the stage for well over a decade, but such themes had been treated in a serious manner. . . . By the use of a typical romantic colouring, this serious treatment of adventurous themes has been blended with burlesque, and real persons meet on the same plane with fictional characters who step out of the story and enact their own parts. It is not too much to say that we have here a kind of strange anticipation of Pirandellesque methods." Fresh after 395 years, *The Old Wives' Tale,* first of dramatic travesties, can hold its own against many more recent burlesques. With little change, it might make a merry Yuletide frolic in the theatre.

PAOLO AND FRANCESCA   *Stephen Phillips*

Dante Alighieri, a fellow-soldier of Francesca's brother Bernardino, first told Francesca's story in the fifth Canto of his *Inferno.* Her father, the

Guelph lord of Ravenna, losing in battle to the Ghibelline Traversari, sought aid from his former rival, Malatesta di Verucchio, the notorious "mastiff" of Rimini. As seal to the pact of friendship, Francesca was sent in 1275 to marry Malatesta's son Giovanni. How she and Giovanni's younger brother Paolo fell flamingly in love, how they loyally sought to beat down the fire, how they were consumed—and by Giovanni killed—has since been a tender theme for poets.

In 1814, Silvio Pellico wrote an Italian play on the subject, seen in Milan in 1815, which gave the fourteen-year-old Adelaide Ristori her first great role; the play became a classic. In 1820, it was used as the basis of an Italian opera; in 1882 it was fashioned into a French opera by Ambroise Thomas. D'Annunzio's tragedy on the theme, much more emotional, was written for Eleonora Duse in 1901. George Henry Boker (American, 1823-1890) wrote a blank verse tragedy, *Francesca da Rimini*, 1855, which was revived in 1882 as rewritten by William Winter. In another play on the same story, 1902, by Marion Crawford (American, 1854-1909), Sarah Bernhardt starred. In England, when Stephen Phillips' poems (1897) induced the actor-manager Sir George Alexander to commission a poetic drama, Phillips (English, 1868-1915) wrote *Francesca da Rimini* in 1899. The play was produced in 1902, by Herbert Beerbohm Tree. Phillips wrote several lesser poetic dramas.

When the play was first produced in New York as *Paolo and Francesca* the hand of fate was felt to be too heavy on the lovers. The *New York Dramatic Mirror* (October 13, 1916) quoted blind Agatha's prophetic words in the play—"His kiss was on her lips ere she was born"—and added: "Thus is the drama from the start shadowed, like a Greek tragedy, with an impending doom . . . There is nothing commanding in Paolo, and but little that is appealing in Francesca."

On its revivals, the play was better received. It won praise, too, for the character Phillips added to the story, a widowed and childless cousin of Giovanni's, Lucrezia, who out of her own bitter emptiness envies and spies on the lovers. She it is that betrays them to Giovanni. In a touching scene, the troubled Francesca turns to Lucrezia for help, and the aching need of love in Lucrezia responds, too late.

Paolo and Francesca was revived in New York on December 2, 1924. The *Times* said that it "held the interest beyond expectation. . . . A certain high quality emerged and an atmosphere more beautiful than in any other play in town . . . the best role, that of Lucrezia, the most original and most powerful motive in the play, that of the barren woman with her jealousy and thwarted nature." On April 1, 1929 the play again opened in New York, with Philip Merivale and Jane Cowl. Brooks Atkinson said that "if this luscious sort of drama—'not pretty, but beautiful, and passing sad'—has fallen out of favor, it is because the proper actors are lacking to make it alluring." The present company, he added, "have brought off this verse tragedy with deep-shadowed beauty."

The poetry of Phillips is rhetorical, with some lush coloring. But the play is neatly built and the emotions are both natural and profound. The recurrent conflict between loyalty and love has no tenderer telling than in Phillips' dramatic capture of the story of these two star-crossed children.

THE FARMER'S WIFE   *Eden Phillpotts*

An engaging drama of rural life is the story of the marital aspirations of Samuel Sweetland, a prosperous Devonshire farmer in *The Farmer's Wife,* by Eden Phillpotts (1862-1948). Samuel, a widower and the owner of Applegarth Farm, tells his housekeeper, Araminta Dench, that he will pick as his next wife one of the eligible neighbors. Araminta helps him list them and he pops the question. With his daughters, Petronell and Sibley, also finding mates, there are half a dozen proposals in the play, all variously amusing. To Samuel's increasing surprise and chagrin, none of the women will have him. They know him, as *Theatre Magazine* (December 1924) described him, as "blustering, selfish, convinced that women were invented only for his pleasure." Soon, however, the thought of Samuel's substance and doubtless many worthy though unperceived qualities begins to tip the balance, and the country ladies one by one let him know that they have changed their mind. By now, it happens, Samuel has found the woman he really wants right at home, in the person of his quietly observant and briskly competent housekeeper. The hired man approves, because "the next best thing to no wife be a good one."

With apt dialogue, there is shrewd capture of human nature in the play. Especially amusing is Thirza Tapper's tea party in Act II, which T. C. Kemp in his book *The Birmingham Repertory Theatre* (1948) hailed as "the classic example of fun among the teacups." The *New York World* (October 10, 1924) called the play "a large and glowing two hours of love among the simple folk."

Many of the lines press a shrewd thought in homely utterance, as when Samuel says of the wistfully young old gal who has refused him that she is "too fond of dressing her mutton lamb-fashion." There is a pleasant song in the play, which begins:

O Daisy dear, wi' eyes so blue—

and after telling of Daisy's deception, ends:

And the Devil, though black as a parson's shoe,
Has doubtless got eyes of a beautiful blue!

The play had its premiere in Birmingham, England, November 11, 1916. The March 11, 1924, London production, with Melville Cooper and Cedric Hardwicke, ran for 1,324 performances. It was revived in London in 1928 and 1932. Charles and Mrs. Coburn produced it in New York, opening October 9, 1924, for 120 performances. The Federal Theatre in San Francisco revived it in 1936. In 1941, Basil Sydney played Samuel in a motion-picture version. The play was shown again at the English Chichester Festival, May 30, 1967.

On June 13, 1951, a musical based on *The Farmer's Wife* came to New York: *Courtin' Time,* book by William Roos and lyrics and music by Jack Lawrence and Don Walker, with Joe E. Brown, directed by Alfred Drake, for thirty-seven performances. It set the farm in Maine, but followed the story faithfully, with much of the original dialogue. The opening words of both play and musical are "Love is in the air." The chief changes were the strange omission of the sharp-tongued hired man, Churdles Ash, and some variations at Thirza Tapper's party, when in her delight at Samuel's proposal she summons all the guests and asks them to share her joy, before she turns Samuel down. In this scene, at the New York premiere, Carmen Matthews as Thirza stole the show. Among the musical's lyrics are "Today at Your House, Tomorrow at Mine," "Fixin' for a Long, Cold Winter," "I Do, He Doesn't," "Smile a While."

Despite the county-fair clowning of Joe E. Brown in *Courtin' Time, The Farmer's Wife* is richer in comedy, particularly in that mellow humor which rises out of simple folk viewed with a congenial twinkle. With kindly satire and neatly caught characters, *The Farmer's Wife* sets the folk of a friendly countryside into a heartwarming drama.

(Note: There was a comedy called *The Farmer's Wife* by Charles Dibdin, with a dozen country songs, that opened at Covent Garden May 5, 1814, and was quite popular in repertory there for a score of years. Both titles probably sprang from the old counting-out jingle "The farmer takes a wife." Note also that Christopher Fry's *Venus Observed** utilizes the same wife-seeking idea, but with the farmer replaced by a lord.)

SWEET LAVENDER   *Arthur Wing Pinero*

One of the most tender of the plays of Arthur Wing Pinero (English, 1855-1934), *Sweet Lavender*, 1888, marks the transition from the spectacular and passion-torn melodrama of the mid-nineteenth century to the psychological social drama of the century's end. It shows, as Allardyce Nicoll has said, "the new style at an early period in its career. With a sure sense of the theatre the author has told a story . . . which did much to accustom audiences to a better dramatic technique. The crude world of melodrama disappears in face of the spirit of this play."

Sweet Lavender is well named in the drama; she is the freshly gentle daughter of Ruth Holt, housekeeper and laundress in the London Temple. Among the lawyers chambered there is Dick Phenyl, a rough old barrister who drinks. With him rooms the student Clement Hale, ward of the banker Geoffrey Wedderburn and in love with Lavender. Geoffrey, disapproving this love, is about to cut Clement out of his will when he discovers that Ruth is his own early sweetheart, Lavender his natural daughter. Ruth comes to nurse Geoffrey through an illness; his love is reawakened, and three marriages shine at the end of the play.

Sweet Lavender opened in London March 21, 1888, and ran for 684 performances. In New York it opened November 13, 1888, for a run of 128 performances. In both cities it has had a half dozen revivals, and it is a popular play in college theatres. The London *Piccadilly* (October 2, 1890) called it "as fresh as the sweet bloom after which it was named." The *New York Herald* (January 7, 1923) said "Sir Arthur's humor and pathos and sentiment are so firmly based on changeless complexes of human nature that the play is moving throughout. Sweet Lavender herself is believable even to a generation accustomed to flappers."

The play's chief distinction rises from the care and the color with which the characters are drawn. Several critics have placed them—especially old Dick Phenyl—in the gallery with Dickens' and Thackeray's. The *Boston Transcript* (November 15, 1888) said that Phenyl "serves to introduce an element for which Anglo-Saxon and Celtic audiences have always evinced a profound and touching sympathy, no matter how administered, and this is *Rum.*" The colorful characters and tender conflicts of *Sweet Lavender* make it good material for the current vogue of turning plays into musicals. In quite different mood, and with the sexes reversed, it tells much the same story as Oscar Wilde's *A Woman of No Importance.** It lifted the author from his Pinerotic trifling to solid worth.

As the *London Graphic* (December 30, 1922) remarked, *Sweet Lavender* "is old-fashioned but not out of date." Some may feel that Lavender herself is a bit too sweet and that her lover was picked from the top layer of a chocolate box, but sentiment is no outworn commodity in the theatre. The story of the play is well-constructed and moving, the Temple background is excellently caught, and the characters are not only limned with sympathy but limbed with truth. *Sweet Lavender,* combining the emotion and sentiment of melodrama with the character drawing of latter-day realistic plays, is not merely an interesting transitional drama, but in itself a pleasant and still moving play.

THE SECOND MRS. TANQUERAY   *Arthur Wing Pinero*

Beginning his long career with farces in the liveliest Victorian curtain-raiser mood, Arthur Wing Pinero later turned the course of English drama toward a serious examination of social problems, then lived to be surpassed by richer talents along the path he pointed. At the height of his career Pinero wrote a drama that broke through the politeness and Victorian reticences of the day to expose a burning social situation, the problem of a woman with a past—*The Second Mrs. Tanqueray.*

The story is stark. The widower Aubrey Tanqueray marries Paula, thinking that this respectable action will cloak her past. She is, however, not accepted by society. Aubrey's daughter Ellean goes off to Paris; when she returns, engaged to Captain Ardale, Paula feels it her duty to the girl to inform Aubrey that the Captain is one of her former lovers. Ellean, thus prevented from marrying the Captain, bursts out against Paula; and, despite Aubrey's offer to start life over with her away from England, Paula kills herself. Too late, Ellean wishes she had been more understanding.

When the play was offered, the leading actresses of the time refused to assume the part of Paula. It was finally given to an unripe girl from the provinces, who later wrote in her memoirs, "During the first act, I was simply paralyzed with fear, and I am afraid did but scant justice to my work." Pinero, walking in the Embankment Gardens—he had not dared enter the theatre nearby—was told after that first act, that the performance was a fiasco. He rushed to the actress' dressing room, clasped her damp and trembling hands, and exclaimed: "Magnificent, dear Lady! Magnificent! Only play the next three acts as you have played the first, and we are made!" The actress went back, and made history for Pinero and for herself. She was Mrs. Pat Campbell.

The play took London by storm. Said the *Star* (May 29, 1893): "The dialogue is wonderfully telling; the situation nakedly true. . . . This is a really fine play. . . . We are filled with an abiding compassion for the poor woman: we feel as we should feel in tragedy, not the horror, but 'the pity of it.'" The *Times* called it "decidedly a play à thèse. . . . The purpose of Mr. Pinero's latest play is to exhibit the hopelessness of the attempt to raise the profligate woman to the position of the honoured and happy wife." The *Standard,* however, although it called the drama "one of the most powerful and absorbing plays the modern stage has produced," rejected the *Times'* point of view: "An idea has prevailed that *The Second Mrs. Tanqueray* is an example of that most unpleasant thing, a play with a purpose, that it was written to enforce a moral, that Mr. Pinero was bent on departing from the true purpose of the stage by expounding a social problem. He is far too able a dramatist to do anything of the sort. . . . He furnishes themes which suggest, and, indeed, enforce reflection; but his main purpose . . . was . . . to write a drama which should awaken and sustain interest and not to preach a sermon in the guise of a play. . . . Primarily the drama is a study of character and of a character so complex that the lucidity with which the author has carried out his design is especially notable."

Accepted by most that saw it as a searching study of a sore problem—Mrs. Pat Campbell's superb performance helped give the illusion of universality—the play really presents a very special situation, as was recognized by the *London Illustrated Sporting and Dramatic News* (June 10, 1893): "If we must have productions which some of us would not wish our womankind to see, let them at least help the world forward. There is no such justification for *The Second Mrs. Tanqueray.* Mr. Pinero raises an unpleasant question, and then lays it down; he tells us of the life, and brings about the death, of an exceedingly improper young person, and there we are left. . . It is no use saying that this is life; it is not life; it is, bad as we are, one of life's rare exceptions . . . the tragedy of the finale appears to me more a matter of momentary impulse than the natural outcome of the play . . ."

Bernard Shaw put his finger on another major flaw in the play when he observed that Pinero was no profound student of human nature, but "an adroit describer of people as the ordinary man sees and judges them." The "ordinary man" of today has tasted so much of Freud, even though in diluted pourings, that the surface attitudes of the turn of the century seem outmoded and thin. Pinero, lacking profundity and universality, does not survive as a living playwright. But his dramatic structure is excellent, building naturally and powerfully from simple opening to gripping climax; and his theme burst upon the contemporary public like a social atom-bomb. James Agate, in *At Half-Past Eight* (1923) said it "began like a bombshell and endures as a landmark. With it English drama emerged from the . . . nursery, and took for the first time since the eighteenth century a man's look at the world."

Bernard Shaw, regardless of the fact that Pinero blazed the path he himself followed, mercilessly averred that Pinero never wrote a line that might reveal him as a contemporary of Ibsen, and that even his acclaimed stagecraft is feeble. In *The Second Mrs. Tanqueray,* for instance, Shaw declared, two whole actors are wasted on "sham parts" in the exposition, while the hero has to rise from his own dinner party and go out "to write some letters," so that something can be said behind his back. "What most of our critics mean by mastery of stagecraft is recklessness in the substitution of dead machinery and lay figures for vital action and real characters." Still, Shaw grants that Pinero is "a writer of effective stage plays for the modern commercial theatre." In truth, he was an innovator as well as a success.

In both England and America, the play has had a long, successful career, serving as a vehicle for such famous thespians as Mr. and Mrs. Kendal, Olga Nethersole, Mrs. Pat Campbell, Mrs. Leslie Carter, Gladys Cooper, and Ethel Barrymore. There have been many productions around the United States; Tallulah Bankhead essayed Paula in the summer theatres of 1940. London was still deeply moved by a revival which opened August 29, 1950, for 206 performances.

In 1893, the New York critics were cold to the play. The *New York Dramatic Mirror* declared that "Mr. Pinero's play makes a false start and leads to a false conclusion. It is unreal from first to last, and such skill as it exhibits is purely theatrical and technical." The same paper, on May 22,

1905, said of the play: "Emotions are by no means wanting, but rather etched in with steel-point cunning by that master of technique, A. W. Pinero." And on February 3, 1913, the same paper reflected: "How times do change! . . . Today our women with pasts become the wives of our presidents . . . the neat cleverness of the dialogue and the firm vigor of construction still win our admiration."

The play was still admired in the Arthur Hopkins revival with Ethel Barrymore. Percy Hammond (October 28, 1925) said: "The old tragedy has stamina and stubbornness; it tells the story of the unfortunate Paula as skillfully as any playwright of today could do it." And Alexander Woollcott called it "still engrossing . . . a play that you all must see."

Paula affords an acting part that will lure a star, in a play so well constructed that its climax remains intense. *The Second Mrs. Tanqueray,* though it no longer seems deeply searching, is a powerful presentation of a story that, in its day, woke the theatre to a concern with social themes, and paved the English stage for Ibsen and for Shaw.

The play was soon translated into German, Italian, and French; it became a triumphant vehicle for Eleonora Duse. It was revived at Croydon, England, October 30, 1961, and entered the NT (Lyttleton) repertory in December 1982, with Felicity Kendal, still "heartstopping," said the *Mail*.

THE BENEFIT OF THE DOUBT   *Arthur Wing Pinero*

In 1895 theatrical England was in the midst of a revolution. The realistic plays of Ibsen had staunch advocates and vehement opponents. Would the native drama follow in the foreign steps? Champions were waiting to hail the venturer; stalwarts, to deride him, when Arthur Wing Pinero wrote *The Benefit of the Doubt*.

The play opens with the Frasers, the Allinghams, and their friends awaiting a court verdict: Mrs. Allingham had sued her husband, Jack, for divorce, naming Mrs. Theo Fraser. The court gives Mrs. Fraser "the benefit of the doubt." Her husband, proud Fraser of Lochbeen, naturally disapproves of the conduct of his wife, of a background that makes her free and easy, though capable, she feels, of "drawing the line." Fraser insists they go abroad to live down the scandal; hurt at what she deems his lack of trust, Theo seeks an appointment with Allingham. Theo arrives hungry, is given champagne, and grows tipsy. While her apprised relatives and Mrs. Allingham, who had demanded of Jack that she listen too, lie concealed, Theo Fraser begs Jack to run off to Paris with her. The others break in, and the discomfited Theo retires in social quarantine to an episcopal retreat with the bishop, her uncle.

The play opened in London October 16, 1895, with Winifred Emery and Cyril Maude as Mr. and Mrs. Fraser, Lily Hanbury as Mrs. Allingham. In New York January 6, 1896, were William Faversham, Viola Allen, and May Robson. The second act, with the concealment and exposure, lasted an hour and eighteen minutes, probably the greatest length until the first act of O'Neill's *The Iceman Cometh*.* Naturally, attention centered upon it. Clement Scott, in the *Illustrated London News,* praised "the masterly construction and climax, which I hold to be the finest thing the author has done in dramatic literature."

The crucial point, however, was the validity of the play's approach to life. Bernard Shaw declared "*The Benefit of the Doubt* worth *The Profligate, The Second Mrs. Tanqueray,** and *The Notorious Mrs. Ebbsmith* rolled into one and multiplied by ten." For the play, Shaw said, "keeps within the territory he has actually explored; and the result is at once apparent in the higher dramatic pressure, the closer-knit action, the substitution of a homogeneous slice of life for the old theatrical sandwich of sentiment and comic relief, and the comparative originality, naturalness, and free development of the characters." Israel Zangwill hailed it as "the great realistic play I have asked for ... the fusion of tragedy and humor, pathos and farce as the great Master, Life, fuses them." On the other hand, Austin Fryers, in *St. Paul's* (November 2, 1895), declared: "There is no art in painstaking detail. The artist is never true, because the mere truth is commonplace, and its faithful depiction lies in the province of the auctioneer, not that of the poet. Mr. Pinero's play is so true that he might have collected it with the camera and the phonograph." The *London Times* countered: "There may be two opinions as to its propriety, but Mr. Pinero has unquestionably the truth of human nature on its side."

The battle against the foreign "moderns" was drawn. Clement Scott challenged: "There are things in this play far finer than anything yet done by the accepted masters of the modern school. The theme is sad, but never morbid. The lives painted for us are inexpressibly sorrowful, but the pictures are delicately drawn and always in good taste ..." Across the sea the contest continued. The *Boston Post* struck hard for Pinero: "The offense of it all—and that there is offense has been shown by the lavish abuse heaped upon Mr. Pinero—lies in the uncovering of social evils, and in stating things as they are, not as we wish they were. . . . There is nothing in modern dramatic literature comparable to this play. . . . Of the Ibsen or the Suderman influence, *The Benefit of the Doubt* shows not a trace. Ibsen preaches all the time; every character is a living sermon, a walking specimen of some social ill to be reformed, or some social good to be propagated. Pinero asserts, and leaves the rest to the intellectual processes of his audiences."

To our time, when divorces are as plentiful as spring peas, the to-do over Mrs. Fraser may seem overstrained. The *London Telegraph* (June 17, 1935) said of a revival, "a magnificently successful piece of stagecraft. But how utterly incredible the whole affair seems today!"

The Benefit of the Doubt retains considerable power as a period piece. In its day, in the English theatre, it set a firm paving of native materials and craftsmanship on the road toward a sound realistic drama that was still to come.

The play was more happily received in later revivals: January 3, 1978, Cincinnati; Washington (Folger Theatre), April 4, 1979. The *London Times* looked beyond: "As to the lives of the characters after the final curtain is drawn, there is a greater degree of uncertainty than the average playgoer cares to contemplate." In the best plays, life leaves unfinished edges.

THE GAY LORD QUEX   *Arthur Wing Pinero*

After the great success of *The Second Mrs. Tanqueray,** Pinero continued to explore situations involving a man with a woman of different social milieu. *The Notorious Mrs. Ebbsmith,* 1895, in which Mrs. Pat Campbell and Johnston Forbes-Robertson joined forces, showed the unsuccessful attempt of an advanced woman to live out of wedlock with an unhappily married man. *The Thunderbolt,* 1908, another excellent example of vigorous stagecraft, shifted the problem to provincial family life. The lightest and most deft Pinero handling of this constant theme is in *The Gay Lord Quex,*

1898. This shows Sophie Fullgarney, a manicurist, seeking to save her sister from marriage to the roué Lord Quex by luring him to lavish attention upon her. She overhears him in a last farewell to an old flame, the Duchess of Strood, and seeks to expose him. Discovering, however, that Lord Quex has undergone a genuine reformation, Sophie flirts away with her sister's other admirer, Captain Bastling, and leaves the field clear for her sister's marriage to the still gay but honest Lord Quex.

This comedy, written for Irene Vanbrugh as Sophie, opened in London in 1899, in New York in 1900. It was revived in Pittsburgh October 8, 1917, then in New York November 12, 1917, with John Drew and Violet Kemble Cooper. In the audience were alumnae of John Drew companies: Laura Hope Crews, Billie Burke, and Ethel Barrymore. Augustus Thomas declared the revival better than the original production. The play was again revived at the Mohawk Drama Festival in 1935. John Gielgud, who had long urged a revival of *The Gay Lord Quex*, directed it in London, opening at the Albery June 16, 1975, with Judi Dench and Daniel Massie, and Sian Phillips as the Duchess of Strood.

Lewis Sherwin in the *Globe* declared: "There is no more famous example of his best than the smashing scene between Lord Quex and the manicurist at midnight in the Duchess' bedroom. The sheer dramatic force of this clash of wills is something nobody can resist." Max Beerbohm stated: "There is no better play for stagecraft." *Vogue* (January 1, 1918) had called this "the cleverest and most effective act that has ever yet been written in the English language. . . . All that the theatre has to show, in suspense and in surprise, seems summed up and incorporated at the climax of this quite incomparable episode."

The remark that Pinero is full of platitudes reminds one of the remark that Shakespeare is full of quotations. It is true that our social studies in the theatre have passed beyond Pinero. Before and after him, characters have been more profoundly probed, emotions more truly and more deeply captured and conveyed. But it is only since Pinero that the English stage has given wide welcome to serious searching of the social scene and the problems of everyday domestic relations. Shaw may have scoffed at the Pinerotic, saying that "in his fertile, live moments . . . Mr. Pinero has no views at all." But Pinero—perhaps himself blinded by the light—held up the torch by which the public noticed Shaw. *The Gay Lord Quex* remains live theatre, and is one of the best and most forceful plays by which Pinero prodded the theatre onward.

TRELAWNEY OF THE WELLS   *Arthur Wing Pinero*

Trelawney of the Wells, opening at the London Royal Court January 20, 1898, for 135 performances, is the best of Pinero's comedies.

Rose Trelawney, lively ingenue at the Wells Theatre in London, is engaged to Arthur Gower, whose grandfather, Vice-Chancellor Sir William Gower, insists that she come for a while, before marriage, out of the theatre environment to live with him and his sister. Her fellow-actors give her a farewell party at Mrs. Mossop's lodging house. Among them is Tom Wrench, a minor actor writing unproduced realistic plays, not the fashionable Wells trashy society comedies. (Tom Wrench is intended as a tribute to Thomas W. Robertson,* Pinero's predecessor, who turned the fashion from romantic society comedies to more serious realistic "cup-and-saucer" drama, *Caste* * and *Society*, which paved the pathway to our time. His real doorknobs on real doors were the first step toward Elmer Rice's real garbage pails on paved sidewalks in *Street Scene.**)

Rose cannot stand the sober, almost somber, life of the Gower household. She invites over her friends from the Wells. Avonia and Gadd have married, it's cheaper; Gadd is tipsy and quarrelsome. Tom is there too. The noise brings in the three Gowers; Sir William orders the players out of the house. Rose goes with them, telling Arthur she's a gypsy; he's not.

In Mrs. Mossop's lodging house we learn that Rose's return has been a failure; she can no longer act the empty roles of the Wells plays. Imogen Parrott, who has left the Wells for the better Olympic, brings word she's found a backer to rent the Pantheon for Tom's play. Sir William comes, demanding that Rose tell him where Arthur is. She had no idea that Arthur had left home to become an actor in Bristol, to match his ways with those of Rose. Sir William becomes aware of the change in Rose; he learns that her mother had played opposite Edmund Kean. He beams, tries on Kean's sword, and agrees to put up the rest of the money needed for Tom's play.

At the rehearsal, Sir William watches. Tom is directing. He calls for an actor, Gordon, for a role based on Arthur. Gordon *is* Arthur—neither he nor Rose knew the other was in the cast. They are reunited. Rehearsal call: "Miss Trelawney, late of the Wells," and the curtain falls.

The original London cast included Irene Vanbrugh as Rose, Edmund Gwenn, Whitford Kane, Dion Boucicault (son of the playwright*), May Whitty, Lewis Casson (husband of Sybil Thorndike), Mary Jerrold, and O. P. Heggie, who long continued in the play. Sadler's Wells had a theatre from 1753; Bagnigge Wells nearby (supposedly the company in the play) never had one.

Coming to the New York Lyceum November 22, 1898, the play ran for 131 performances. Among its numerous revivals, London New Theatre September 7, 1917, for 113 performances during the war. There stands out the all-star American tour of 1927, with Helen Cahagan as Rose, Peggy Wood, Estelle Winwood, Henrietta Crosman, Effie Shannon, F. M. Kerrigan, O. P. Heggie, Otto Kruger, John Drew, Rollo Peters, Wilton Lackaye, John E. Kellerd, Lawrance D'Orsay, Eric Dressler, Frieda Inescort, and the eighty-two-year-old Mrs. Thomas Wiffen playing the boardinghouse landlady, Mrs. Mossop.

More recent productions include ELT, November 25, 1961; Chichester Festival, summer 1965, coming to the NT (Old Vic) November 18, 1965, with Louise Purnell as Rose. The *London Times* praised the satire of the old-style theatrical mannerisms: "The absurdities of the Wells company were painted with Dickensian brio, the posturing, the enormous gestures, the transformation of the simplest remarks into baroque grandiloquence." It was from such artificialities that Rose had been transformed into a modern spirit.

Joseph Papp put the play on OffBway (Public Theatre) February 26, 1970—closed by the transportation strike after forty-six performances; again at the Lincoln Center Beaumont, September 3, 1976, for sixty-three performances, changing the locale from London to New York, with Mary-beth Hurt as Rose, but (said William Glover) "with a spirit of crass vulgarity and clownish excess." The play was shown in Manitoba, Canada, 1970; in London, 1971, with Audrey Woods, Julian Slade, and George Lowell; at Asolo, 1974; at the London Old Vic, December 19, 1980, with Lynne Muller; and at Williamstown, Mass., July 24, 1982.

A musical, *Trelawney,* by Guy Bolton and John Mitchell, music by Eric

Coates, opened at the Bristol Old Vic, January 12, 1972, with Gemma Craven as Rose, Ian Richardson (in his first musical), as Tom Wrench, Max Adrian, Joyce Carey, and Elizabeth Powers; it went on to the London Sadler's Wells, then to the Prince of Wales. *London Stage and TV Today* said that it turned Pinero's play "with sympathy, tact, and taste, into a rousing, touching, colourful show."

The *London Times* (November 18, 1965) called *Trelawney of the Wells* "an irresistibly affectionate play, of warm humanity and great theatrical cunning." It is the Pinero play for which Bernard Shaw—who in general mocked the Pinerotic flavor—expressed a few favorable words. Its appeal remains.

THE TREASURE   *David Pinski*

One of the masterpieces of the Yiddish drama, *The Treasure* first brought David Pinski (1872-1959) international attention. In its ironic portrait of human greed, the play depicts the family of Chone the gravedigger, who lives in contented poverty until Judke, his feeble-minded son, goes out to bury a dog and returns with a few gold coins. The family blossoms. Judke's sister Tille, a sharp-witted, sharp-tongued girl, mean, worldly, and ambitious, decks herself in finery, condescends to the neighbors, and sets about securing a fit husband. A host of assorted parasites crowd around: marriage brokers, charity collectors, rabbis, "schnorrers" of every sort, as the village fumes with envy, fawning, vanity, and greed. Chone is most evasive as to the treasure; the truth is the half-wit Judke has forgotten where he found the coins. At night, the villagers swarm upon the cemetery, regardless of whose grave they are defiling—until Judke remembers; and they find four more pieces of gold.

There are many swift serio-comic sketches of the greed-struck villagers in the play. It works with vivid realism to the close, when, as the *Boston Transcript* (June 6, 1928) observed, "the night wind blows across the graves; upon it, some hear the plaint of the dead at the cupidity of the living." Following a pattern used later for other ends in *Our Town,** *The Treasure* closes with a conversation of the dead, pressing home the point of the play—that it is not money, but the love of money, that is the root of all evil. Some good, however, has come of the village flurry. Chone returns content to his job; and Tille is happier since even her new mite of a dowry may bring a worthy husband.

The play was produced by Reinhardt in Berlin in 1910, by the Theatre Guild in New York, October 4, 1920.

What chiefly distinguishes *The Treasure,* apart from the universality of the drive of human greed and the humor that softens the sharpness of the satire, is the deft etching of the various portraits, the many aspects of avariciousness in the realized characters that give the play the essence of vivid truth.

THE BIRTHDAY PARTY   *Harold Pinter*

"More rubbish has been written about Harold Pinter than all his contemporaries put together," says Simon Trussler in his book about the plays, 1973. Which is the rubbish depends upon your point of view. Thus, Martin Esslin in *The Theatre of the Absurd* calls Pinter "one of the most promising exponents of the theatre of the absurd." (Pinter prefers the label "comedy of menace.") "We have been entertained, we have admired the author's ability," said London's Bernard Levin, "we have not been bored. But we have advanced our understanding and our humanity not a whit, and every experience we have had has been of an entirely superficial nature." Clive Barnes has remarked: "Silence falls upon silence like rose petals pretending to be a slender snowstorm." Of the same play, Ted Kalem (in *Time*) averred: "His familiar pauses seem to be toothless gaps in the text." The immediate theatrical effect of his plays is clear, even when what he is driving at remains deliberately obscure. How long that effect will hold audiences, the future will tell. Somehow, Barnes felt: "The nonsense in his dialogue makes a terrible lot of sense." *Terrible* is a two-edged word. John Chapman (in the *News*) wondered: "Even though they don't seem to be going anywhere, Pinter's characters are sharply drawn. But why?"

Pinter has already been used as a point of comparison. *Supplement III* of the great *Oxford English Dictionary* lists the word *Pinteresque,* with fifteen lines of quotations. It adds *Pinterian, Pinterish,* "hence *Pinterishness, Pinterism,*" with nineteen more lines of quotations, including 1960: "Miss Quayle as a Pinterish woman on top of a bus"; 1975: "A precisely structured script, only very occasionally dropping into those meaningless meanings now known as Pinterisms"; 1975: " . . . Pinterism—relaxed circumambient dialogue with lots of significant spaces between the words." Not many persons find their ways defined by their name.

The first full-length play of Harold Pinter (b. 1930) was *The Birthday Party,* 1953, using characters and situations from *The Room* and *The Dumbwaiter,* two of his one-act plays of the year before. Opening at the Hammersmith Lyric, May 19, it lasted five days. More successful abroad, it returned to London November 24, 1962, with Lynn Redgrave as Meg, and again at the RSC Aldwych, June 18, 1964, directed by the author. In New York it opened October 3, 1967, at the Booth for 126 performances. It is one of his most popular plays for radio and TV. Among productions: Phoenix, 1974; San Francisco's Actors Workshop, July 15, 1980; given its U.S. eastern premiere February 10, 1966, at Baltimore's Center Stage; played the same year in Washington, D.C., and Ann Arbor, Mich.; May 11, 1967, at Cincinnati Playhouse in the Park; 1971 at New York's Lincoln Center; at the ACSTA, May 1976; on Bank Street OffOffBway, May 28, 1980; and January 31, 1981, at the New York 92d Street YM-YWHA.

In the play, Stanley Webber, an unsuccessful concert pianist, is a lodger at a run-down seaside-resort boardinghouse, run by a former deck-chair attendant, Patsy, and his senescent wife, Meg, who mothers the lodger. Stanley asks neighbor Lulu to go out with him, but "there's nowhere to go." Two sinister strangers, Nat Goldberg and Seamus McCann, arrive and take over; they arrange a birthday party for Stanley. During this they alternately play tricks on him—blindfolded, he stumbles into a toy drum—and threaten him. McCabb: "You betray our land." Goldberg: "You betray our breed." They gradually break him down, then announce that he's had a breakdown. Incidentally, Nat seduces the willing Lulu. The next morning, Stanley appears in bowler hat and neat suit, and despite Patsy's feeble protests they carry Stanley off, as he utters nothing more than a few inarticulate gurgles. Meanwhile, housewife Meg thinks happily of the last night's party: "I was the belle of the ball."

Pinter's effects, said the *London Times,* "are neither comic nor terrifying; they are never more than puzzling, and after a time we tend to give up the puzzle in despair." Various explanations have of course been given: a play *must* have a meaning. Thus, "two exploited and spat-upon races (Irish and Jewish) turn the tables upon their persecutor"—if so, they picked an odd man. (Pinter is the son of a Jewish tailor.) Trussler in his book calls the play "simultaneously an allegory about the rise of Fascism, a seaside social comedy, and a sexual farce." His later plays follow the same enigmatic pattern. Asked what they are about, Pinter answered: "the weasel under the cocktail cabinet." Pop goes the weasel.

THE CARETAKER   *Harold Pinter*

The Caretaker, 1960, takes place in the winter, in a dilapidated room in west London occupied by two unloving brothers, the clever and decisive Mick and the elder but weaker Aston, who has undergone shock treatment in a mental hospital. Aston brings in a tramp, who calls himself Davies, but wants to go—though always finding reasons for not going—to Sidcup, where he says there are his "identity" papers. Whitney Bolton describes this tatterdemalion tramp "the militant bum with torn clothes and defiant mind, the little man who leads with his chin in his encounters with life, who hates with cold scorn, is suspicious, wary and—neatest touch of all—an unswervable snob." Asked to help as caretaker, he tries to play one brother against the other. There is a scene of his terror in the dark attic; he drops his matchbox, which is retrieved and rattled by a crawling taunter; he then hears the whine of a sucking vacuum cleaner; finally a dim light goes on, to reveal a mocking Mick.

Recognizing Mick as the stronger, Davies plays up to him, telling Aston that Micky's his friend: "So don't you start mucking me about. *I* never been inside a nuthouse." But Mick calls Davies "a stinking liar and a troublemaker," and they cast him out.

The Caretaker opened in London April 27, 1960, and was voted the best play of the year. Pinter enacted Mick for four weeks before the company left for New York, opening at the Lyceum October 4, 1961, for 165 performances, Donald Pleasance playing Davies; Robert Shaw, Aston; Alan Bates, Mick. Among its many stagings are: Asolo, 1968; the Roundabout, opening July 2, 1973, and again February 24, 1982; Random Theatre OffOffBway, November 3, 1977; Westport, Conn., January 29, 1980; Soho OffOffBway, May 16, 1980. In London, the Mermaid March 2, 1972, with Leonard Rossiter as Davies; Jeremy Kemp, Aston; John Hurt, Mick. The Young Vic, November 8, 1973; and the NT (Lyttleton), November 1980, with Warren Mitchell as Davies; Kenneth Cranham, Aston; Jonathan Price. Mick. Young Vic again, September 1983.

Again opinions were sharply divided. Howard Taubman in the *New York Times* said: "Pinter finds comedy, tenderness, and heartbreak in all three" of the characters. Walter Kerr contrariwise: "Even when the three characters are talking in broad daylight—and they talk incessantly—the hearts of all concerned echo a hollowness as insistent and resounding as the drip of water into an empty bucket from a crack in the ceiling." Taubman continues: "Mr. Pinter has been vehement in his assertion that his play is no more than the story it tells. But he cannot prevent his audiences from finding in it a modern parable of derisive scorn and bitter sorrow. Who will take care of the caretaker?" Robert Coleman did not find it so: "Pinter writes like an old-fashioned vaudeville comedy scripter. He gains laughs by repetitious nonsense and pantomimic tricks. For instance, a scene in which the trio do football passes with a handbag had the first-nighters howling.

The actors' histrionic dexterity fascinated us to the extent that we almost forgot that much of the evening we were being bored stiff." The play found faint praise in the remark that it avoided the three common themes of current drama: violence, psychiatric probing, and sex. (We are told that Pinter's first intention was to end with the violent death of the tramp.)

Norman Nadel sensed a deeper feeling: "It is the sorrowing undercurrent of three-sided loneliness that has the most lasting effect." Martin Esslin in his *Theatre of the Absurd* builds the play into universal significance, declaring that the final heaving out of Davies "assumes almost the cosmic proportions of Adam's expulsion from Paradise." Pinter had hardly shown him in a Garden of Eden. . . . The play will probably be shown again soon, so you can choose your side.

THE HOMECOMING   *Harold Pinter*

The Homecoming was shown by the RSC at the London Aldwych, opening June 3, 1965, directed by Peter Hall, for ninety-one performances. Pinter called it "the only play which gets remotely near to a structural entity which satisfies me." Trussler in his book on the Pinter plays calls it "his most explicit and least satisfying work. Each thing melts in mere, unmotivated oppugnancy. . . . I felt myself actually soiled and diminished." John Lahr compiled the contrasting comments in his 1971 *Case Book of Pinter's Homecoming*. The playwright, as I say, has acquired dictionary status, with the terms *Pinterian, Pinterism, Pinteresque*.

It is Teddy, an American Ph.D. and professor, who with his wife, Ruth, after six years comes home to the north London house of his father, Max, a retired butcher; his bachelor uncle Sam, a taxi driver; and his two younger brothers, Joey and Lenny, a pugilist and a pimp, both seedy. Almost at once Ruth and Lenny pump up and down on a couch; then go upstairs to complete the connection. The family decides, and Ruth agrees, that she shall stay with them, at their sexual service, and also sell the service to help support the family. Teddy without protest returns to his professorship and their three children. Papa Max, who has been alternately eulogizing and vilifying his dead wife, Jessie (who had made love with his friend MacGregor in a car uncle Sam was driving), protests that he's not too old for Ruth, and on his knees cries, "Kiss me!" as the curtain falls.

In the RSC Aldwych production Paul Rogers played Max; Ian Holm, Lenny; Vivien Merchant (then Pinter's wife), Ruth. The play was revived at the London Garrick, May 1, 1978, with Timothy West as Max; Michael Kitchen, Lenny; Gemma Jones, Ruth. In 1966 it was shown in Paris. In New York the RSC production directed by Peter Hall opened at the Music Box May 1, 1967, for 324 performances, winning the Tony and the Critics' Circle awards. It was revived at the Bijou OffBway May 18, 1971; in Boston it opened in March of that year, with emphasis on the comedy. Beginning October 26, 1974, it toured thirty Italian cities, playing for a month in Rome. It was shown again OffBway, at the Wonderhorn, November 6, 1975; and in Montclair, N.J., in January 1979. It reached a run of 200 at the London Garrick by October 21, 1978.

Several critics have spoken, in phrases hard to justify, of Pinter's "infallible ear for the rhythms of language, menacing and compassionate"; his "acute ear for conventional platitude"; but he insistently uses *which* when *that* is preferable. And he has, said John Chapman, "a fine gift for creating stage characters. . . . But he seems to lack one gift that might make him a really important dramatist: good taste."

Pinter has, no doubt, as *Variety* put it, "a flair for enigmatic drama with an air of profundity." The characters act without any suggestion of a motive; there they are—or are they? John Simon gives illustrations to show that "every character, sooner or later, becomes the opposite of himself." And director Peter Hall seems to agree: "Any proposition we draw from one side of the play we can contradict or modify by a proposition from some other side." But Pinter himself rejects all meaning-hunters. "*The Homecoming* means what it says; exactly what it does, exactly what happens on the stage. . . . Any search for meaning behind everything is a little wasteful of the energies of the people who participate in it." This leaves those desirous of meaning as frustrated in Pinter's theatre as they are in life offstage. Director Peter Hall deemed it necessary to rush to the defense, protesting that Pinter's people "are not all profoundly repulsive, or utter nullities."

In *The Homecoming,* less menacing than his other plays, Richard Cooke said: "the ennui is only occasionally interspersed with interest." Saturated with sex as is none of Pinter's other plays, *The Homecoming* demands current consideration, though the permanence of its appeal may be suspect. Ray Bradbury, asked to read Pinter by Paul Newman, did, then wrote: "I refuse to praise Pinter to please Paul."

BETRAYAL   *Harold Pinter*

Pinter's least eccentric, most sensitive play so far, with neither menace nor mystery, is *Betrayal,* which was a hit at the London NT in 1978, directed by Peter Hall, as also at the New York Trafalgar, January 5, 1980, where it ran for 170 performances. It was shown in French, as *Les Infidèles,* in Ottawa from April 24, 1981, to May 2. It presents a simple story in nine scenes, told backward.

We first see Jerry and Emma, who meet as "friendly strangers," two years after their affair is over. He is a literary agent. Emma, who has opened an art gallery, but can get away afternoons, is the wife of Robert, a publisher and Jerry's best friend. She has told her husband of the affair (of which he had long known; he had remained quiet, unwilling to raise the issue with either wife or friend) and she is now contemplating a new affair with Casey, the best-selling author of the two other men.

The rest of the play moves back through the years of the love life of Emma and Jerry, from 1977 to 1968. There is a luncheon of Jerry and Robert, with the husband expressing his emotions only by intimation, trying to taunt, to bait the lover while outwardly engaging in friendly chatter. Thus, the sequence in Venice, as Walter Kerr said in the *New York Times,* "is a small masterpiece of hidden challenge." The movement of the couple's love is "a hothouse flower opening wide as we watch." But now Emma hangs hesitant. (She was played by Blythe Danner; Jerry, by Raul Julia; Robert, by Roy Scheider.)

Douglas Watt in the *News:* "Pinter's craftsmanship has never been so delicate and sure . . . with the deceptive strength of a spider's web. . . . For a change in Pinter, the only enigma is the heart's great and insoluble one." Note, as incidental to the main story, that both men have children, never seen; that Robert the cuckold has himself been cheating on his wife; that Jerry's wife does not appear in the play, but, as he thinks her ignorant of his infidelity, he has no qualms, no sense of guilt. This attitude is no doubt not uncommon in "intellectual" society today, but makes it seem, as John Beaufort remarked in the *Christian Science Monitor,* that "the trio inhabits a world in which it is more important to articulate than to feel." We watch rather a game of words than a life of passions. "With Pinter's usual flair for the theatrical, however, *Betrayal,* despite its basic triviality, commands the audience's interest. Perhaps that will survive.

SIX CHARACTERS IN SEARCH OF AN   *Luigi Pirandello*
AUTHOR

Although the Frenchman Benjamin Crémieux and the Irishman James Joyce had earlier called attention to Luigi Pirandello (Italian, 1867-1936), it was with the production of his *Six Characters in Search of an Author,* 1916, that an awareness of his genius flashed through the theatrical capitals of the world. Fame came late to this brilliant Italian, who began his career as a writer of short stories (writing over 300, many of which he later turned into plays) and who taught literature in Rome from 1897 to 1922, while supporting his insane wife. In 1925 he organized a theatrical troupe which presented his plays in Europe and America. His fame, however, preceded his trip to the United States; his *Six Characters in Search of an Author* had opened in New York on October 30, 1922, with Moffatt Johnston, Margaret Wycherly, Florence Eldridge, and Ernest Cossart. The germ of the play was a short story, *The Tragedy of a Character,* in which a "character" complains about the role given him in a book Pirandello has read.

The play passes so adroitly from the unreal world to the real that the two are fused—indeed, the created characters seem to have more reality than the actual persons beside them. The audience is watching a director rehearsing a play by Pirandello, for which there is not much enthusiasm, when it is interrupted by six lugubrious figures who announce themselves as characters of a play abandoned by their author. They pulse with the life started in them and plead with the director to let them play it through. Unwilling at first, the director grudgingly consents; they go off to arrange a scenario. (The curtain remains up; but this is the end of Act I.)

The characters return with their story ready. When the actors take over their roles, the characters watch, at first with amusement, then with astonishment and disgust, as the actors transmogrify their passions. Finally, they protest: "Of my nausea," cries the stepdaughter, "of all the reasons, one crueler and viler than the other, that have made this of me, you want to make a sentimental, romantic concoction." The daughter turns to the mother: "Shout, mother! shout as you shouted then!" and the mother cries out in genuine anguish. "Good!" says the director. "The curtain can fall right there." A listening stagehand by mistake lets down the curtain, and we have the second intermission. In the last act, the characters work through their dreary doom. The director will have none of them and their story, shrugs over his wasted day and turns back to his own rehearsal as the final curtain falls.

The pattern of the play permits a close examination of the relationship of art and life. A playwright's usual quest of verisimilitude is derided as a covering for the lack of true creative power. The artist foolishly seeks the verisimilar, when "life is full of infinite absurdities." Is not Hamlet more real, better and more fully known, more rounded and actual a person, than most of your neighbors? "When a character is born," says Pirandello, "he acquires immediately such an independence of his author that we can all imagine him in situations in which the author never thought of placing him, and he assumes of his own initiative a significance that his author never dreamt of lending him." This independence is symbolized by the plight of the six characters who have been abandoned midway of their story.

A sordid and a gloomy story comes through Pirandello's theorizing with undiminished power and poignancy. The father, an intellectual, after sending his son to a farm to be reared like a healthy peasant, turns over his simple, domestic wife to his secretary, by whom she has three more children. Years later, in a fashionable establishment that sells expensive garments and expansive girls, the Father is being embraced by a sly young wanton when the Mother, now a seamstress and a pander, cries out "She is my child!" (This scene reaches almost unendurable poignancy as the stepdaughter insists on the truth: "I went there, you see, and with fingers that faltered with shame and repugnance, I undid my dress, my corset." It is here, on the Mother's shouting, that the curtain falls.)

The Father takes back the family, but their tangled relationships breed only torment. They live in a seething stew of hatred, rebellion, and remorse, until the four-year-old girl is drowned in the garden pool, and the adolescent son, gazing after her, shoots himself.

The *Christian Science Monitor* (March 21, 1922) called the play "one of the freshest and most original productions seen for a long time past," a verdict it was accorded everywhere. The play was revived in New York in 1931, with Walter Connolly and Flora Robson; and again in 1933, 1939, 1947, and (Phoenix) 1955. London saw a private performance in February, 1922, but the play was not licensed there until 1928. It was revived in London in 1932, when the *London Times* (February 19, 1932) said: "Repetition cannot dull the brilliance of the play's attack on theatrical shams; it cannot stale the tragedy which we receive in fragments and yet perceive as a whole; but it does persuade us that the Pirandellian parlour-game for metaphysicians is a rather tiresome contrivance . . ." A brilliant production of the play was given in London opening November 21, 1950, with Karel Stepanek as the father, *Theatre World* (January, 1951) reported, "striving with every fibre of his being to explain and justify his equivocal life." Analysis of Pirandello's intention came from the *Boston Transcript* (January 23, 1922): "It is as if the stage has become the teeming brain of Professor Pirandello, and the audience, by some strange psychic license, has been permitted to look right into the throbbing mechanism of a dramatist's mind at work." Some critics discerned Pirandello's frequent method of covering with ludicrous externals a tragic soul. Gilbert W. Gabriel (April 16, 1931) called it "Pirandello's most amazing play. Certainly his most amusing one." And the *London Telegraph* (February 28, 1922) considered it "a comedy in which the humorous element springs from, and is wholly dependent on, a theme of the utmost gravity."

The subtitle of *Six Characters in Search of an Author* is "A Play Yet to be Written," but in it Pirandello presented not only a gripping and a piteous tale, but one of the most searching questionings of the drama. The stage manager says: "Let's see how cleverly we can turn an illusion into a reality." But the father protests that they are turning a reality into an illusion: living ("real") characters die; characters in the drama are immortal.

The Phoenix, production, December 11, 1955, adapted by Tyrone Guthrie and Michael Wager, had 65 performances. In translation by Paul A. Mayer, it ran OffBway, March 8, 1963, for 529 performances. London (Mayfair) saw it with Ralph Richardson, June 7, 1963; it ran there again in 1965.

For other Pirandello revivals, see page 505.

RIGHT YOU ARE (IF YOU THINK YOU ARE)   *Luigi Pirandello*

The problem of illusion and truth, in the spell of Pirandello's dramatic weaving, grows tense with the anguish of truly realized persons in this play, written in 1917.

Its action is motivated by the curiosity of gossips in a provincial town, who thrust themselves into what seems a mystery and insist upon learning the truth. To that town has come Signor Ponza as secretary to the Prefect. He and his wife live on the top floor of a building in which his mother-in-law, Signora Frola, occupies the ground floor. Although Ponza is most considerate of, even tender toward, his mother-in-law, he never permits her to visit his wife. The two women shout greetings to one another or exchange messages in a hoisted basket. The gossips break in upon the family to find out what this is all about. Ponza tells them that his first wife, Lina, died four years ago, and that her mother's affliction was so great that when he took Giulia to wife, the mother found comfort in the delusion that the wife was still her daughter Lina. Then Signora Frola tells her side of the story—*i.e.,* that Ponza was so stricken when Lina went to a sanitarium that on her return he thought she was another woman, whom he called Giulia. To appease him, they had even held a second marriage ceremony. A genuine sad vein of humanity runs through the concern of each to keep the other happy. So thoughtful of each other are Ponza and his mother-in-law that the neighbors do not know which to believe. One kindly but amused observer, Lamberto Landisi, bids them accept both stories. Instead they turn to the wife herself. Veiled, vague, almost blurred, she comes to them. She tells them she is Ponza's second wife, and Signora Frola's daughter, and, to herself, no one. In her compassion she has drowned her personality in the truth of their desires.

The play is, of course, a purely symbolic fable. Yet, "with no more substance than this fable to go upon," said Brooks Atkinson (February 24, 1927), "Pirandello manages to work up a passionate, comical rigamarole with a thousand penetrating intimations. . . . Approaching philosophy in a light fantastic mood, Pirandello has written a thoroughly delightful metaphysical melodrama."

The American premiere of the play was at Cornell University, with Franchot Tone among the student players. Atkinson's remarks were made after the first of a series of New York matinees opening February 23, 1927, with Edward G. Robinson and Morris Carnovsky. On July 22, 1942, in Cleveland, Marta Abba (Italian star in most of his plays) made her first American appearance in a Pirandello play as Signora Frola. After the New York opening, John Anderson called the play "fresh and provocative drama . . . deft and engaging foolery, cloaking with silken delights of comedy some suavely savage stuff of human illusion and absolute truth." *Commonweal* (May 11, 1927) added: "There are certain scenes of rare dramatic poignancy and others of highly strung suspense."

Those that consider Pirandello as caught in abstruse intellectual concerns should weigh the title of this drama. He is psychological in his symbols and methods, but he sees danger in the cold intellect; he is almost anti-intellectual in his idea. He declares that, instead of abandoning himself to the warm flow of instinct, man thinks; man sets up theories about himself and about life. Other creatures simply live, but man watches himself live, with the aid of an infernal machine called logic. Hence we begin to classify persons: he is unjust; she is immoral; he is serious; she is a prude. Reality rebels at these clear-cut classifications. Reality is manysided; reality is fluid, warm. Hence there is a clash between intellect and instinct. Reality cannot always be revealed, hence the dilemma within *Right You Are (If You Think You Are)*. The play leaves the townsfolk, and the audience, in doubt as to the "absolute" identity of the wife of Signor Ponza. The usually cautious Mr. Atkinson wagered "one pistareen on the husband's insanity." What, asked jesting Pilate, is truth? The point is that there is no single answer. Pirandello shapes and sharpens that point into a vivid play.

HENRY IV   *Luigi Pirandello*

One of the most popular plays by Pirandello, *Henry IV*, 1922, was performed all over Europe, notably by Georges Pitoeff in Paris in 1925. In England it was shown at Cambridge in 1924 with sets and costumes by Cecil Beaton; in London in 1938 and 1940. New York saw it as *The Living Mask* (Pirandello attended the opening) on January 22, 1924, and again (Equity Library) in 1947. Paris saw another production in 1950.

The play opens in the majestic throne room of the Holy Roman Emperor Henry IV (1050-1106), with courtiers talking of intrigue and Pope Gregory. When one of the courtiers wants to light a pipe, and when another arrives in the costume of the court of Henry IV of France, which dates some five hundred years later, we know that we are beholding a masquerade. We learn that twenty years before, when his beloved Matilda, in a masque and pageant, dressed as Countess Matilda, her suitor Henry matched the costume by dressing as Henry IV. But a rival, Baron Belcredi, pricked Henry's horse, so that he was thrown; when he regained consciousness, he believed himself the actual Emperor. His wealthy sister provided a castle and other means for him to live in that delusion. Now, twenty years later, Matilda, widow, and mistress of the dominating, cynical Belcredi, comes with her daughter Frida and her lover to the castle. A psychiatrist has suggested that if mother and daughter both appear, with the daughter in the costume of the Countess, the shock may restore Henry's mind. It happens, however, that for eight years Henry has been sane, but has preferred the splendor of the eleventh century to the cold shock of return to the modern world. The sight of beautiful Frida dressed as the Countess rouses him; her warm vitality sweeps through the coldness of his "lucid insanity"; he embraces her madly: "She's mine!" Belcredi steps forward; Henry kills him—and recognizes that now he must wear his mask of madness forever.

This "satirical comedy," as Pirandello has called it, works upon the interplay of rationality and irrationality in our lives. Thus Alexander Woollcott could call the work (January 23, 1924) "a psychopathic play of the retreat from reality—a mad flight along a road which a good many of your neighbors travel for a little distance every day of their lives." George Freedley (December 12, 1947) declared it "one of the most brilliant plays of the modern theatre."

This absorbing drama probes the troubled depth of human consciousness. For all the masquerade that is built around Henry, his problem is a poignant and modern one. "When the Emperor Henry IV disappears," as Domenico Vittorino has noted, "and the man looms in all the agony that tortures him, his humanity is as complex and deep as the figure of the Emperor was stately." Is his enforced madness any less a "lucid insanity" than that which impels this atomic age toward a third World War? *Henry IV* is a profound philosophical fantasy on the plight of the human personality in a complicated and unchosen world.

NAKED   *Luigi Pirandello*

A deft probing into the human soul—with its tangled skein of motives, intentions, designs, and desires beyond our powers of judgment—gives significance to Pirandello's *Vestire gli ignudi,* 1924 (*Clothe the naked*), which has been translated as *Naked.* Centered upon the suicide of young Ersilia Drei, the play also reveals the minds of the three men that helped to shape her days.

Ersilia had longed for only a modest sort of beauty, such as even a commonplace person might hope to achieve. A nursemaid in the home of the Italian Consul in Smyrna, she was engaged to an Italian naval officer, Franco. When he left her, the baby in her care fell from a terrace and was killed. Returning to Italy, Ersilia found Franco engaged to another girl, and took poison. The play begins when that first attempt at suicide fails, and a novelist, Ludovico Nota, attracted by her story, invites her to his home.

But the story was hers to die with; living, she feels only revulsion against the men who have given her ugly days. When Franco, contrite, wishes to marry her, she will have none of him; when he had left her, she had given herself to the first passerby. In a grueling scene, the Consul and Ersilia accuse one another: he had wanted only to be as a father to her; it was the light in her eyes (kindled for Franco!) that had inflamed him. And we learn that it was while they were making love that the Consul's baby fell to its death.

Thus all the passion that in Ersilia's death-tale seemed tenderly and sorrowfully romantic becomes sordid, and wormy with disgust. Nor are the motives any cleaner than the acts. Ersilia wished to die, not for love, but because life was too grim a burden. The novelist takes her in, not out of compassion, but as good material for a romance. Franco returns because, on reading Ersilia's story, his new fiancée casts him aside. Nevertheless, these men, and the Consul, all turn in anger and scorn upon the wretched girl, as they learn her story. Why—they cannot understand—why did she lie?

Naked has stirred audiences deeply wherever it has been played. It was a sensation throughout Europe. It opened in London, March 18, 1927, with Charles Laughton. New York saw it in French, with Mme. Simone, in 1924; in English with Augustin Duncan, opening November 8, 1926 for 32 performances. Its poignance was again revealed in a Studio production off-Broadway, opening September 6, 1950. The *New York Sun* (October 29, 1924) spoke of "the same old metaphysical shell game," but Gilbert W. Gabriel considered it better than *Six Characters in Search of an Author.* *

London emphasized Pirandello's usual concern, *Stage* (March 24, 1927) insisting that he "harped again on his one and only theme, that the unreal is more real than the real, that what is imagined is more actual than the actual." Life put a vivid illustration of this thesis before Pirandello one evening while he was watching a performance of Maurice Rostand's *General Boulanger.* After the suicide onstage, a man in the audience rose and cried: "You don't die only for love; you can also die from eternal persecution." There was a slight crack, as of clapping hands. "See!" said Pirandello to Saul Colin, "the fiction is in the audience; the reality is on the stage." And the unperturbed audience watched the rest of the show—to learn next morning that there had been a suicide in their midst.

Naked, however, presses the problem of reality and irreality to the realm of motives and intentions. Ersilia's impulses, not her deeds, were imagined; the lie was about not her action, but its cause. And her lie, as the *New York Post* (November 9, 1926) points out, "attains glorious heights in the literary imagination of her benefactor, acquires essential vitality in her relations with a former lover, dwindles to pathetic cheapness in the reality which leaves her naked, becomes mystically significant in her own neurotic imagination." Yet that lie, around which the others fang and tear at her spirit, gives pathos, gives dignity, to the wretched nursemaid. It is her pitiful grasp at beauty, the one step she can take to give semblance of decent human meaning to the life she is too miserable to hold. Caught unawares by life, she seeks to assume a better pose for dying. When this fails, she goes indeed naked from the world—but, as Vittorino remarked, "Pirandello has clothed her with his sympathy, and with the beauty of his art." Ersilia, however, is not the only one stripped naked, left quivering and raw, by Pirandello's play. The three men in the drama—and uncounted audiences— can hardly cast the first stone.

MAN, BEAST, AND VIRTUE   *Luigi Pirandello*

In this play, written in 1925, Pirandello indulges in an ironic gambol over the relationship of reason, instinct, and morality. Far from having to be taught virtue, he seems to say, we travel toward it by instinct. The same instincts may, it is true, lead us along other paths; then reason has to harness the "beast" in us, so that it may haul us back to virtue.

The thought is presented as a tragedy drowned in a farce. If the play is accepted purely for its surface value, it is a bawdy, risqué skit, with titillating situations. It was offered in New York at "milkman's matinees"— midnight performances for "the tired business man too tired to go home"— opening December 3, 1926, with Osgood Perkins, who, said Gilbert W. Gabriel, performed like a "Yankee at King Boccaccio's Court." The situations of this "boulevard farce," said Brooks Atkinson (December 6, 1926), "are conventionally ribald, and easy to understand once you have caught the salty meaning . . ." Long-stemmed flowers were given to the opening night audience with a tip to the English title, *Say it With Flowers.*

The story is simple. Captain Perrella, on his journeys home, always stops to see his mistress in the next port; his wife receives none of his attentions. She notifies Professor Paolino that he has consoled her so successfully that her good name depends upon her husband's immediate and intimate interest. Paolino takes charge. The Captain laughs boisterously when his wife comes to dinner powdered and painted, and in a low-cut gown. Hopes fall, but rise again when the Captain eats a large portion of the cake that has been liberally dosed with an aphrodisiac. Signora Perrella is to signal Paolino next morning by placing a flower pot on her balcony. Watching early, he rejoices at length to see her—but what is this?—it is with strangely mixed feelings that he watches her setting out not one flower pot but five.

Man, Beast and Virtue, said the *New York Telegraph* (December 6, 1926), is "a highly amusing combination of banter and burlesque . . . a frisky and risqué story now and then is relished by the most philosophical of playwrights . . . The moral, if any, is that you *can* eat your cake and have it too." Dancing on the surface of a triangle of sex, Pirandello shows how Man may summon the Beast to attain Virtue.

Exposed passions seem ridiculous, the play declares. Instinct is honest; reason, hypocritical. Virtue is the name given to the successful mask.

TONIGHT WE IMPROVISE   *Luigi Pirandello*

The oppositions that tear upon art and life, as each strives to be the other, are pressed in *Tonight We Improvise,* 1929. In *Six Characters in Search of an Author,** Pirandello abandoned his persons midway of their tale; in the present drama, he turns them over to Dr. Hinkfuss (Lamefoot), the director, who boasts that he will bring the author's work to life on the stage. After two acts of Hinkfuss's theatrical calculations, the persons of the story throw the director out, and move with all their living blood and anguish to their destined doom.

The story presents a dominating woman, Signora Ignazia Palmiro, who comes with her four daughters and her meek husband from gay Naples to sober Sicily. Her daughters have a lively time entertaining officers of the Flying Corps. They are all "very beautiful, plump, sentimental, vivacious, and passionate." Mommina, the eldest, sings excellently. One aviator does not join the gaiety. He watches jealously, quarrels, and asks Mommina's hand. Married, he imprisons her, fiercely jealous of her past, the pleasure of which he imagines and fancies her always remembering. Mommina grows old before her time, secluded from all society; but when her sister Totina comes to town on a singing tour, Mommina's thoughts are so strong that they summon her mother and sister. Totina sings the *Trovatore* aria; Mommina joins her in a great burst of song, and with it her heart bursts, too.

Until the last scene, the movement of the story is variously interrupted on three levels of concern. There are the fussy endeavors of the director to extract dramatic values; when the Father is brought home from the cabaret dying, the director protests there is no drama in the entrance, only blank, soggy death. Then there are the efforts of the actors to fit into their parts; they resent the director's using their offstage names and are already beginning to live the persons assigned them, even in actions not set down in the script. Finally, there is the Palmiro family, with its entourage of lively aviators. The latter are seated in the orchestra with the audience. They watch a motion picture, along with us, and make loud comments while we are politely dumb. The quarrel they start in their seats is continued onstage and takes fire again in the lobby during intermission.

"The play runs smoothly for a time," said the *London Times* (January 29, 1935), "and then, with no warning, a confusion of human temperaments overwhelms it. . . . Nonsense and tragedy, ugliness and beauty, vulgarity and fastidiousness, all here are mixed." Complicated in the telling, *Tonight We Improvise* gains power in the performance. Much of its meaning and most of the poignancy of the story come through.

Pirandello was at the opening of his play not only in Italy, but also at the Pitoeff Paris production on January 17, 1935. An Italian company presented the play at the Vienna Drama Festival of 1936 and toured Switzerland and Italy in 1939. The Berlin reception of the play in 1930 was tempestuous; opponents of Pirandello's ideas and methods thronged the theatre; some say that a Reinhardt clique arranged the attack. When the characters in the audience began to quarrel, others in the audience proceeded to throw vegetables. A riot ensued; the play did not reopen.

The American premiere of *Tonight We Improvise* was at Vassar College, December 20, 1936. In New York, Erwin Piscator presented the play at his Dramatic Workshop in 1943 and again in 1946 and 1948. The drama offers no easy anodyne, but probingly examines the bases of human action and sets a provocative pattern along that lightning-lit, that dark but intriguing and intricate region where life blends with art.

AS YOU DESIRE ME   *Luigi Pirandello*

The basic plot of *As You Desire Me,* 1930, was taken from an actual situation in Italy: Brunelli, a professor of Greek at Verona, was reported missing at the front; some years later, Signora Brunelli, in Turin, saw a man who called himself Canella; she insisted that he was her husband, that his denial must be the result of amnesia. The force of her faith convinced the man that he was Brunelli. Pirandello switched the sexes of the chief characters and the result, as Robert Garland (January 29, 1931) said, was "shot with the Italian's metallic and entirely mental sense of comedy . . . a sort of metaphysical mystery melodrama combining most that is worthwhile in Signor Pirandello with most that is worthwhile in Mr. Samuel Shipman . . ." The woman, he added, "plays with fact and fancy as a cat plays with a mouse; saves her soul and loses her body. On paper, it sounds complicated and dull; onstage it is uncomplicated and exciting. From curtain rise to curtain fall, Signor Pirandello's story grips you."

In Pirandello's story, the Unknown One, as the woman is called, is found by the artist Boffi, who had once painted Lucia Pieri's portrait. He is sure that she is Lucia. The woman, a singer in a Berlin cabaret, is the coarse and debauched mistress of the novelist Carl Salter; the latter is a Kraft-Ebbing super-sensualist whose life is a tumult of depravity and violence. Salter shoots himself, and the Unknown One goes off with Boffi. At Bruno Pieri's home she is welcomed as Lucia returned from the dead. Kindness and faith restore her nobility, ravaged as it has been by the horrors of the war. But there are doubts: Bruno does not find on her body a mark that Lucia bore, and the woman wonders whether Bruno welcomes her spirit, or her body, or indeed the estate that her uncle now deeds back to her from her sister. Then Salter, recovered from his wound, brings from a Vienna sanitarium the Demented One, whose mangled body bears a likeness to Bruno's Lucia. Which is the real wife?

The Unknown One scorns the need of proof. If she has the loveliness and bloom of Lucia, if she has all the husband desires of his long-missing wife, is she not more truly his wife than the walking cadaver dragged from the asylum? But seeing that in Bruno and his relatives faith hangs upon the weight of physical proof, the Unknown One goes off with Carl Salter. Pirandello does not disclose which body is the wife's. Plagued with the question, Pirandello once responded: "That is not the point. Even if she was Cia, she is now another person." Life keeps us always changing. It is not in the cold constructions of reason, but in the surety of faith, that human integrity and unity abide.

Onstage, said Robert Garland, *As You Desire Me* is "a straightforward and arresting tale . . . a play among plays," but Brooks Atkinson, after seeing the same performance, on January 28, 1931, with Judith Anderson, was at first more reserved: "The trouble seems to be that the design of the play does not arouse your loyalty for the heroine—which is essential." By the last act, however, all was well: "You instinctively take sides yourself, and you want to believe, which is the essence of Pirandello's doctrine." More detached than the reviewer, Pirandello asks you, not to believe, but to observe the effects of belief and disbelief. According to the expectations and the belief in her, the Unknown One—"a drunken, baleful slattern," as Atkinson described her, "living in sin with a German brute"—becomes gracious, kindly, noble, dignified, until, when doubt smudges the woman she has become, once again there rises the scornful slut, contemptuous of mean-spirited folk; and from their meanness with a satanic nobility she walks away.

"The Strange Lady of Pirandello's metaphysical drama remains a fascinating person." There is rich truth in these words of the London *Stage* (January 22, 1948) on a revival of the play with Mary Morris. "The play itself seems melodramatic in the first act, when the vices of post-Great-War Berlin are the feature; but as soon as we are at the villa, the conflicts and doubts concerning the Lady clearly appear, gathering in strangeness and intensity. Then the play becomes real, and absorbing. Pirandello's stage craft is magnificent. Few modern dramatists have known as well as he how to write effective dialogue and work out a situation so brilliantly. Even for those that do not care for the speculations on human life and understanding, there is an evening of first rate 'theatre', full of excitement, surprise, and character interest." *As You Desire Me,* in addition to being a superb dramatic statement of the problem of reality and the power of faith, is one of Pirandello's best plays.

WHEN SOMEONE IS SOMEBODY   *Luigi Pirandello*

Although it was after he had met Bernard Shaw in 1933 that Pirandello wrote this tragicomedy or cosmic farce of what life does to its leading figures, and although some of the chief figure's characteristics bring Mark Twain to mind, the author could easily have plucked the story from his own days. For every noted man is condemned to be the image the public have formed of him. "They make a statue of you," protests the poet in the play, a figure always dressed in white, his long flowing hair swept back from the majestic brow, a "public property, like the face on a coin." So completely has fame stripped away the poet's personal identity that he is indicated in the drama by no name: three asterisks show that he is a fixed figure, but of stellar luminance.

The play presents ***, just turning fifty. His wife, Giovanna, has the grim, devoted face of a custodian of glory. Their daughter, Valentina, lives in a withdrawn atmosphere, as though she lacked true existence. Their young son, Tito, sums up his world in the constant word "Pappa! Pappa!" Then, at his nephew Pietro's villa, *** finds—in Pietro's sister-in-law Veroccia, who has come to Italy from Russia by way of the United States—a renewed intensity, a fresh vitality, truly the breath of new youth, of a new world. Veroccia cuts ***'s hair short, has him put on sports clothes, and, under the name Delago, his volume of love poems in a new style wins acclaim. Giovanna the wife arrives—the world for too long has missed the light of ***'s glory—and as she strokes the poet's head his hair grows again into its familiar lines. The public figure reassumes its public guise. A second volume reveals that Delago is ***; the public laughs and dismisses the name as an amusing hoax. In the heart of *** this is a bitter tragedy; his own life,

his reasserting youth, have been denied him. The image of the great one
has been restored; the idol crushes the man. At the fiftieth birthday of ***,
he is created a count; the State gives him a palace for his remaining days,
after which it will in his name become an orphanage. The speech on this
occasion might well be his funeral oration. Indeed, Veroccia, who had given
hope to his renewal of youth, exclaims "He is dead." A group of children
come to *** as he sits on a bench beside the garden wall. He speaks to them,
and after they are gone, as he muses alone, his last words to them light up,
like a golden inscription, on the wall behind. And as *** sits in the twilight,
the bench moves up and back, the wall with its inscription makes a pedestal: the great man has become his own statue.

Saul Colin, who was with Pirandello when he met Bernard Shaw, has told
me that Shaw remarked: "If only you had written in English, you'd have
been even more famous than I." In 1934 Pirandello received the Nobel Prize.
Throughout Europe he was constantly pestered by gaping admirers. Like
Shaw's, his image was taking its mold. In the play *When Someone Is
Somebody,* the great writers on the wall of the poet's study, Dante, Aristo,
and the rest, come down and gesticulate, silently arguing the problems of
art and of the world, each in the too-familiar way, the frozen attitude fame
has assigned him. The drama builds into an ironic and deeply moving story
of a great and famous man, a vision of the lonely pedestal upon which every
public figure is doomed to become his own statue.

Among recent Pirandello revivals:

Right You Are (If You Think You Are) March 16, 1965, London Mermaid,
translated by Frederick May; described as "buried treasure." OffBway
1954; George Freedley pointed out that it tends to be overlooked that the
play's "fantastic approach and satirical treatment are nicely balanced by its
great compassion." APA-Phoenix, March 4, 1964, for fifty-three performances; again November 22, 1966, with Helen Hayes and Donald Moffat, for
forty-two. In 1967, Expo-Montreal. Roundabout, October 11, 1972.

Henry IV often kept the Italian title *Enrico IV* to distinguish it from
Shakespeare's. New York, August 21, 1950, with Herbert Berghof and Gale
Sondergaard. Pitlochry Festival, 1962. Phoenix, 1966 (University of Michigan). OffBway (Sheridan Square), translated by William Murray, April 27,
1967, for thirty performances. Toronto, January 8, 1972, and sixteen-week
tour, with contemporary dialogue by Stephen Rich. The English premiere
was at Cambridge, June 7, 1924, with an all-male cast.

Naked: Oxford, November 1, 1960, with Diane Cilento, who played it
again at the London Royal Court, April 4, 1963. In America: ELT, 1954; Los
Angeles (University of California), 1965. OffBway 1967, thirty performances as *To Clothe the Naked*. In 1977, Roundabout.

Man, Beast and Virtue: The *London Times* January 12, 1956, called it "an
evening of delightful impropriety" and added: "The best bawdiest jokes are
made by men of genius, Aristophanes, Shakespeare, Pirandello."

Tonight We Improvise: First English showing, Leeds, 1955. The Living
Theatre, November 6, 1959, directed by Julian Beck, with Judith Malina,
seventy-seven performances. I was then American representative of the
Théâtre des Nations, and for its 1960 season in Paris I recommended the
Living Theatre, which there took first prize. *Tonight We Improvise* was
shown again at Toronto, 1968; in 1974, at the Chichester Festival, directed
by Peter Coe.

As You Desire Me: ELT, 1945. London Lyric, January 8, 1958; the same
year at Toronto.

SWEENEY TODD   *George Dibdin Pitt*

The story of Sweeney Todd, the demon barber of Fleet Street, has long been popular. Mr. Todd's shop has a chair that can suddenly be dropped through a trap-door into the cellar; the occupant disappears and the next day there is a fresh supply of veal pies. The sailor Mark Ingestrie tempts the fate of the chair by showing the barber his string of fine pearls; down he thumps. "Every trick in the whole calendar of melodrama," as the *New York World* (July 19, 1924) put it, is played before the barber can be trapped and taken to his doom.

The story of Sweeney Todd is not in the Newgate Calendar of London crimes, but his shop on Fleet Street is still pointed out. There is reference in *The Life of the Late Earl of Barrymore* by Anthony Pasquin (John Williams, 1761-1818) to a pastrycook play in 1793, in which the joint of a child's finger is found in a Senator's pie. The story originated in Venice, with sliding trap-door and underground vault; the barber was added in Paris; and it came to England, via the periodical *The Tell Tale*, in 1824. For twenty-five years the story circulated in "penny dreadfuls," and on March 8, 1847, there was produced the play *The String of Pearls; or The Fiend of Fleet Street,* by George Dibdin Pitt (English, 1799-1855). Charles Dickens in the London *Morning Chronicle* exclaimed, "No one should miss seeing Sweeney Todd!" The play remained popular until Frederick Hazelton's version, *Sweeney Todd, The Demon Barber of Fleet Street,* appeared in 1862. Pitt's version ends in the court room at the trial of Sweeney Todd, when the escaped sailor Mark appears; Todd thinks he's a ghost, and confesses. In the Hazelton version, the still free Todd is shown drawing a razor across the baker-woman's throat to kill off betrayal, when the trap gives way and he plunges into the blazing bake-house.

Later versions include one by Matt Wilkinson, shown from 1870 to 1928; one by Andrew Melville, 1927 and 1932. Most recent productions return to the Pitt version and exhibit the crude melodrama for the superior amusement of our sophisticate age.

When Queen Victoria saw the play—her first command performance—she found it thrilling. Even today, laugh as we may at its exaggerated and obvious horror, there is a measure of uneasiness beneath our amusement. In 1924 the *New York Tribune* (July 18) called it "full of thrills," and the *World* (same date) declared that "it lacks some of the modern gloss of the trade, but the core of it is identical with the hair-raising hokum of all crook plays, detective dramas, and murder trials seen in these parts for eighty years." Less rousingly active and less pathetic than such plays as *The Streets of London,**** but with more horror in its theme and as much suspense in its unfolding, *Sweeney Todd* is the epitome of the grisly melodrama.

The play has had several fresh versions. With book and lyrics by Donald Cotton and music by Brian J. Burton, it came to London in 1958 as *The Demon Barber* and again in 1962. With music and lyrics by Terence Hawes it came to Southgate, England, January 20, 1966. More elaborately, with book by Hugh Wheeler, music and lyrics by Stephen Sondheim, it opened in New York, March 1, 1979, with Angela Lansbury and Len Cariou, for 526 performances. Effective songs included "The Ballad of Sweeney Todd," "Green Finch and Linnet Bird," "The Worst Pies in London," "By the Sea," "Not While I'm Around"—but the story took little emotional hold. The stars took it to Los Angeles in 1981. June Havoc took the play on tour in 1982.

THE MENAECHMI   *Titus Maccius Plautus*

The most vigorous and robust of the Roman comic writers, Titus Maccius Plautus (c. 254-c. 184 B. C.) probably began his career as an actor. His name Maccius is derived from Maccus, the clown of ancient farce. His plays are all based on Greek originals now lost. He wrote exclusively the *fabula palliata,* or comedy in Greek dress (from *pallium,* the mantle worn by Greek male citizens). The exact dates of most of his surviving plays (twenty out of a hundred) are not known; certain references make it seem likely that *The Menaechmi* (also translated as *The Twin Menaechmi*) was written about 215 B.C.; if so, it is Plautus' earliest extant comedy.

Plautus' best comedy of mistaken identity, the play is, in the words of J. W. Duff, "a triumph of fun without challenge." Menaechmus of Syracuse, seeking his long-lost twin brother, comes to Epidamnus, where he is mistaken for his brother by a cook, a parasite (Peniculus, "Sponge"), and by the mistress, the wife, and the father-in-law of his brother, until his slave Messenio recognizes the error and the twins come together. The comedy, of course, rises from the misunderstandings onstage; Plautus is very careful to have the audience well aware which brother they are beholding. He is also very skillful in building up reasons why the visiting Menaechmus does not understand the mistake all these folk are making.

The two Menaechmi, being the figures through whom the situations unroll, are less fully developed than some of the other characters. The money-seeking courtesan Eratium ("Lovely"); the shrewish wife; the self-important doctor—apparently a stock figure, but here first surviving—with his countless irrelevant questions, his technical jargon, his absurd diagnosis and, of course, the most expensive prescription: these are all richly comic figures, swept along by the story at a pace that never flags. The play is one of the most popular of the comedies of Plautus, most frequently revived in schools.

The Menaechmi was the first ancient comedy to be acted in a modern translation. An Italian version by Niccolo da Correggio was performed for the Duke of Ferrara in 1486; an adaptation of this, in Italian prose, called *Calandria,* ("calandro" means "booby"), by Bernardo Dovici, Cardinal Bibbiena, was presented at Lyons in 1548 for Henry II of France and Catherine de' Medici. Others that have adapted the play, or used its theme, are Trissino, 1547; Sachs, 1548; Firenzuola, 1549; Cecchi, 1585; Rotrou, 1636; Regnard, 1705, and Shakespeare, in *The Comedy of Errors.* *

Shakespeare's play perhaps added some fun to the plot, but lessened its plausibility, by matching the twin masters with twin slaves. Shakespeare also gave the story a romantic note, ending with the reunion, not only of the twins, but of their parents. Shakespeare, according to Hardin Craig, "loved to play with edged tools. Somebody's life or somebody's happiness is at stake even in his comedies." In *The Comedy of Errors,* the visiting twin will lose his life if identified, whereas in *The Menaechmi* he is in danger of losing only his fortune. Plautus, Craig has also pointed out, "in his realistic world begins with truth and then involves his characters in error; Shakespeare in the mad world of Ephesus begins his episodes with error and enlightens them with flashes of truth." Plautus maintains the cooler, cynical spirit of his comedy to the very end, where the Epidamnian Menaechmus, planning to return to Syracuse with his brother, offers all his property, including his wife, at auction. Shakespeare's play, says George E. Duckworth in the

Complete Roman Drama (1942), is "usually considered inferior to its Latin original." In eighteenth century London *The Theatrical Inquisitor* declared that Shakespeare's "ignorant modernization of its senile manners is peculiarly unpalatable," but Craig found the Shakespearean version, though "in dramatic manipulation not superior" to the Roman's, "of far greater general significance." Plautus' characters, however, are perennial types.

Plautus apparently introduced into the Roman drama songs and dances that break up the dialogue. These, in *The Menaechmi,* with the pacing of the farcical situations, make Plautus rather than Shakespeare the spirit behind Broadway's hit musical *The Boys From Syracuse* (1938). In its basic value as entertainment, Plautus' comedy retains more than merely historical interest.

The April 30, 1938, showing of *The Boys from Syracuse* at the New York Alvin, with Jimmy Savo and Teddy Hart as the twins, and Burl Ives, ran for 235 performances. It was directed by George Abbott, with music by Richard Rodgers, lyrics by Lorenz Hart, choreography by George Balanchine. Among the songs were "Falling in Love with Love," "This Can't Be Love," "Ladies of the Evening," "Sing for your Supper," "Oh, Diogenes." Other revivals of the musical were 1954 (straw-hat), Skowhegan, Maine; 1957, Cleveland; 1963, OffBway (Theatre 4). The play *The Twin Menaechmi* alternated with *The Comedy of Errors* at the University of Minnesota in 1957.

THE BRAGGART WARRIOR   *Titus Maccius Plautus*

This play, written about 205 B.C., is the best ancient representation of that frequent butt of humor, the soldier who deems himself a champion in battle and in love. Nothing but the title is known of the Greek drama, *The Braggart,* on which Plautus' play is based, but the type it inaugurated has been a favorite in the drama from ancient Greek days to our own.

For Plautus the story is rather complicated. The soldier Pyrgopolynices has carried off to his home in Ephesus both the slave and the sweetheart of the young Athenian Pleusicles. Notified by the slave, Palaestrio, the young Athenian comes to live next door and meets his beloved by means of a connecting passageway. Finally, through a courtesan disguised as a neighbor's wife, Palaestrio seduces the soldier and tricks him into sending himself and the kidnapped girl away. The girl is restored to her lover and the soldier is flogged as an adulterer. While intrigues are kept clear in the minds of the audience, suspense is not sacrificed. At one moment, suspicion begins to breed in the soldier's breast; but quickly Palaestrio recovers control, switches his tactics, and proceeds deftly to regain the confidence of the conceited soldier, whose vainglory leads him to the disastrous end.

In this lively but rude farce, the characters are vividly portrayed, and the braggart soldier is a full-blown caricature. Amusing, too, is the old bachelor—an unusual figure in Roman comedy—who has little part in the main action but who comments keenly on the affectations of society and the blessings of a bachelor's life. There is also effective contrast between the two courtesans, the faithful sweetheart of Pleusicles and the hussy hired to deceive the braggart soldier, the *miles gloriosus.*

The very names of the characters are comic; Pyrgopolynices means "conqueror of many towered cities"; Artotrogus (the parasite), "bread-chewer"; Acroteleutium, "tip-top"; Philocomasium, "lover of drinking bouts"; Palaestrio, "trickster."

Of all Plautus' plays, this has been the most popular. The Roman games of 205 B.C. were held for seven extra days, probably to lengthen the run of the play's performance there. While there are boastful soldiers in other ancient plays, it is from *The Braggart* that later variations stem. Among these may be mentioned Captain Matamore in Corneille's *The Comic Illusion,* 1636; in England, *Ralph Roister Doister**; Falstaff and Pistol in Shakespeare; Captain Bobadill in Jonson's *Every Man In His Humour.** More recent variants include Rostand's *Cyrano**; and the type is recognizable in such comedies as George Kelly's *The Show-Off,** as well as in figures of any war play (*Mr. Roberts,* 1948; *At War With The Army,* 1949; the musical *South Pacific,* 1949) or motion picture. Pyrgopolynices, in Plautus' play, declares that his progeny will live "for a thousand years, from one age to the next"; they have more than doubled the span of the soldier's boast.

Note that the Romans laughed especially at the *Miles Gloriosus, The Braggart Warrior,* because he was enacted in Greek uniform. The play was presented in 1958 at the Hebron Academy, Maine, with the Prologue in Latin, most of the rest in English. Translated by E. F. Watling as *The Swaggering Soldier,* it was played at Farnham, England, in 1968. In English by Eric Segal, OffOffBway (Amateur Comedy Club), October 1971.

THE POT OF GOLD *Titus Maccius Plautus*

One of the best known of Plautus' comedies is *Aulularia (The Pot of Gold),* 194? B.C. While there is much incidental comedy in the play, the interest is centered on the character of the miser Euclio, who worries over his pot of gold. Euclio's concern is tangled with his family's story. A wealthy old neighbor, Megadorus, urged by his sister to take a wife, speculates upon the extravagances of a wife who comes with a dowry, and therefore asks Euclio for the hand of his daughter Phaedria. To prepare for the wedding feast, Megadorus provides food and sends cooks to the "poor" Euclio; their presence so worries the miser that he takes out his pot of gold for safer hiding. He is noticed, then spied upon, by the slave of Lyconides, a young man who has seduced and who loves Phaedria. The slave steals the pot of gold and gives it to his master. Although the end of the play has been lost, we know from the Prologue, and from the acrostic "argument" prefixed to Roman comedies, that Lyconides returns the gold to Euclio and in exchange marries the miser's daughter.

Among the neat turns of movement in the play, two are especially clever. Just after Euclio misses his gold, Lyconides comes to confess his seduction of Euclio's daughter; and for some time, while the young man is talking of the girl, the miser thinks he is referring to the gold. Even trickier is the effort of Lyconides' slave, once he perceives that his young master will, honestly, return the gold to Euclio, to retract his story that he has stolen it. Throughout the play, the suspicions of Euclio, his apprehension that everybody knows about his treasure, his constant scurrying to make sure that it is safe—until his very fear of losing it leads to its loss—maintain a high pitch of comic interest.

Among plays that have used the theme of *The Pot of Gold* are Gelli's *The Basket,* 1543 and Jonson's *The Case Is Altered,* 1597. Two plays called *The Miser,* by Shadwell, 1672, and Fielding, 1732, are more directly taken from the most famous descendant of Plautus' play, Molière's *L'Avare (The Miser),* which was produced in Paris September 9, 1668.

Among other sharp contrasts, the miser of Molière's play is the very incarnation of avarice; Plautus' Euclio is a human being, once poor, to whom the coming of wealth brought also the tormenting fear of its loss. At the end of *The Pot of Gold* (a fragment of the conclusion is extant to tell), when Euclio has given away his daughter and with her his gold, there is pathos as well as comedy in his final words, "Now I shall sleep." Molière's savage satire more thoroughly castigates the avaricious type; Plautus brings us laughter, but also a tinge of sympathy for one who has, gigantic, a fault we all feel nursling in ourselves.

THE ROPE   *Titus Maccius Plautus*

Many critics hail *Rudens (The Rope)*, 194? B.C., as the masterpiece of Roman comedy. It is not comedy in the sense of broadly humorous farce, but rather like the romantic comedies of Shakespeare. Its mood and opening movement remind one of *The Tempest*,* and its heroine comes into the action by being cast ashore after shipwreck, as in *Twelfth Night.** Her lyric of lament and the song of the fishermen that follows are among the most beautiful in Plautus. And the swift movement of its romantic tale, a tender story pricked through with sardonic humor, with emotional depths plumbed, villainy exposed, and virtue rewarded, justifies the comparison.

Based on a Greek comedy by Diphilus, the play begins with a characteristically long prologue. (We are told that when Diphilus complimented the hetaera Gnathaena on the coldness of her well water, she replied that she kept it cold by throwing his prologues into it.) Plautus' Prologue, spoken by the god Arcturus, explains that the basic coincidence in the action is produced by the will of the god to mete out justice.

The unique setting instead of a city street represents a stretch of the African coast backed by a temple of Venus, with hard by the cottage of Daemones, an old man from Athens. To that temple the procurer Labrax has bid young Plesidippus go, and Labrax has sailed away with Palaestra, a slave girl he was supposed to deliver to the young man. Wrecked by Arcturus on that selfsame shore, Palaestra and another girl held by Labrax take shelter in the temple. Labrax seeks to drag them forth and Daemones, acting as judge in the dispute, discovers—the proof is in a casket which the fisherman Gripus has roped in the sea, salvage of the wreck—that Palaestra is his own long-lost daughter. Palaestra and Plesidippus thus are free to wed.

While the play moves on its course with a well-knit and tender plot, many of the successive scenes are gems of satire or humor. The second young woman rescued from the waves is a lively vixen; when she comes from the temple to Daemones' house for water, there is a sprightly and pointed conversation between her and Sceparnio, the slave. When Labrax and Charmides, the man who had advised him to ship to Sicily, haul their bedraggled bodies to shore, their shivering and wailing (Labrax even has a vomiting spell) and their growly wordplay make a vivid scene. Labrax, for all his villainy, is a courageous fellow; he stands up boldly for his claims until Daemones' overseers bear him down; then, losing the girls, he tries to trick Gripus out of the treasure Gripus has fished from the sea. Trachalio, the slave of Plesidippus, has several amusing scenes: one gives the play its name, when he discovers Gripus with his "hamper-fish" and they begin a verbal and physical tug-of-war for its possession. Throughout, the quick dialogue is enlivened by puns and other word-play, not all translatable.

Between scenes of low comedy the romantic movement of the plot drives to its happy close.

Plautus' drama, according to W. Y. Sellar, "entirely enlists both the moral and the humane sympathies." It is one of the most original and most effective of Plautus' plays; in quality of the lyric passages, in surge of spirited dialogue, in variety and interest of character-portrayal, it is the most modern in tone of the ancient Roman comedies.

CURCULIO   *Titus Maccius Plautus*

The amusing *Curculio,* 193? B.C., one of the shortest of Plautus' plays, is packed with interest. Its plot combines the two most frequent devices of ancient comedy: guileful deception and mistaken identity. The characters that move through it, however, though they are the usual comedy figures, are individualized and made human. Curculio ("Weevil"), the parasite, is also a messenger; he, instead of the usual shrewd slave, slowly relates the news and cleverly carries through the deceits played on the pimp and the captain; he pours abuse, neatly satiric of conditions in Rome, equally upon pimp and banker; and he adds considerably to the lightness and speed of the comedy.

The action is set in Epidaurus, where the pimp Cappadox is spending the night at the temple of the god of healing, Aesculapius. The young Phaedromus sends Curculio to raise money to buy, from Cappadox, the girl Planesium. Curculio, however, steals the ring of Captain Therapontigonus, who also loves the girl and who has deposited money for her purchase with a banker. Using the ring as a seal, Curculio brings the banker a letter, supposedly from the Captain, so that the money is paid and the girl delivered to her lover, Phaedromus. When the Captain discovers the fraud, his seal identifies the girl as his own sister, who was separated from her nurse when the seats at a festival collapsed during a storm; he joins Phaedromus at the wedding feast; and the pimp, having no claim upon a free-born girl, has to return the money.

The play is rich in all sorts of word-play, and perhaps has more obscenity than is usual with Plautus; but the obscenity is counterbalanced by the fact that Planesium has preserved her chastity, a fact that was essential to the Roman audience since she turns out to be free born. Phaedromus is so enamored of the girl that he sings a *paraclausithyron,* i.e., a serenade to his sweetheart's door—the first in Latin literature of what was to become a frequent form of love poetry. The meetings of the lovers have a tenderness underlaid with respect.

The Captain, also deftly drawn by Plautus, is a "braggart warrior" in his speeches, but by his actions is brought down to human size. At the end, though still truculent with the pimp, he is a friendly companion to the man that is to marry his sister. There is a neat passage in the play, when the banker, receiving the letter with the Captain's seal, asks suspiciously why the Captain himself hasn't come. The disguised Curculio answers that a gold statue is being erected to him in Caria, "because the Persians, Paphlagonians, Sinopians, Arabs, Carians, Cretans, Syrians, Rhodes and Lycia, Eatonia and Tipplearia, Centaurfightiglia and Onenipplehostania, all the coast of Libyia, all Winepressbacchanalia, half the nations on earth, were all conquered by him single-handed in less than twenty days." "Damned if you don't come from him," the banker declares, "you jabber such nonsense!" and he proceeds to pay the pimp to release the girl.

A unique feature of *Curculio* is an address to the audience by the property man. Immediately after the scene in which Curculio hoodwinks the banker, the property man comes forth and wonders whether, with such a sharper around, he'll get back the costumes at the end of the play. He then gives a miniature guide to Rome, telling in which quarters what sorts of person can be found. He then departs and the play goes on. His speech is the only vocal appearance of the property man in Roman drama.

In these several respects, *Curculio* is of unusual interest. Despite its brevity, it carries through a typical Roman plot with realistically conceived and humorously developed characters, and it presents an unusually vivid picture of Roman ways. It was played in English in Manchester, England, December 9, 1965.

PSEUDOLUS   *Titus Maccius Plautus*

One of the liveliest of Plautus' comedies, *Pseudolus*, 191 B.C., evidently was a favorite in ancient times. In his essay *On Old Age* Cicero tells us that Plautus rejoiced in the play in his last years. In the first century B.C. the famous actor Roscius played the part of Ballio.

The opening situation is not unusual: a young man needs money to buy his sweetheart from a pimp who has already taken a deposit on the girl from a rival. But the rest of the play is more novel. The Prologue, for instance, instead of containing the usual exposition, consists of but one warning sentence: "You'd better stand up and stretch your legs; a long play by Plautus is about to be staged." The exposition, which follows in the first scene, is given in a highly amusing letter from the girl to her sweetheart Calidorus, in which she laments her imminent departure when the balance of the rival's payment is made.

After the exposition, Calidorus' slave Pseudolus sets his ingenuity a test. He admits the situation to Calidorus' angry father, Simo, and wagers that he'll not only secure the girl, but get the money for her from Simo himself. Later, the pimp, Ballio, is warned that he will be tricked and, though on his guard, he is amusingly cozened; he delivers the girl to the false messenger; when the real messenger comes for her, he thinks him a pretender and pokes fun at him for a time before he learns the truth. Thus the girl is turned over to her sweetheart, and Pseudolus collects his wager and a round bellyful of wine.

Ballio and Pseudolus are both well developed figures. The pimp is the most rapacious and scoundrelly in Roman comedy. He summons forth his covey of courtesans, upbraids them each by name, demanding that they extort from their lovers great gifts for his birthday, or off they'll go to the common brothel. Pseudolus, however, is one of the jolliest of slaves, enjoying every one of his sly devices, faithful to the interests of his young master, but not afraid to match wits and bandy words with the citizens. His final drunken moments are not the conventional carousal, but continue the comic characterization, until his old master goes off with him to drink away the wager.

It is worth noting that, except when the courtesans appear, to take Ballio's abuse, and when Calidorus' sweetheart steals from Ballio's house (none of them saying a word), there are no women in the comedy. With the informal, free and easy tone of the play and the sprightly dialogue, full of quips and contemporary references and verbal play, Plautus enjoys himself as he entertains the audience. When Calidorus wants to know something, his slave nonchalantly but directly answers: "We're acting this play for the benefit of the spectators here. They know; I'll tell you later." The audience is amused, and the action goes on. With the fun enjoyed both on the stage and off, with light and lively action, *Pseudolus* is a gem of Roman comedy.

The play *Pseudolus,* translated by Patric Dickinson, was played in Stoke-on-Trent in 1969.

Pseudolus is also the name of the slave in *A Funny Thing Happened on the Way to the Forum,* which came by a skip, hop, and a jump from Plautus to the New York Alvin, May 8, 1962, for 964 performances. Book by Burt Shevelove and Larry Gilbert, music and lyrics by Stephen Sondheim, it was directed by George Abbott there, and in London October 3, 1963; it was played in Paris in 1964. Among its songs are "Comedy Tonight," "Everybody Ought to Have a Maid," "Impossible."

Zero Mostel was Prologus, also the tricky slave (*Pseudolus* means *Little Faker*) to Hero, helping him win a beautiful virgin (by misfortune trained as a courtesan) from Miles Gloriosus, who had bought her from a rascally procurer. David Burns played Senex, an old rake seeking his last wild oats despite a termagant wife. Jack Gilford played Hysterium, a timid slave who hides in woman's clothes. Pseudolus, the critics agreed, though "not the noblest Roman of them all, was one of the most entertaining."

THE CAPTIVES   *Titus Maccius Plautus*

One of the finest comedies of ancient times, *The Captives,* 188? B.C., deserves the name comedy only because it has a happy ending. While there is considerable quiet humor in the play, fundamentally it has a lofty theme and an inspiring tone, far removed from the usual bawdy Roman farce. Plautus, indeed, in his Prologue deemed it necessary to warn the audience that "there are here no filthy verses that one can't repeat; no perjured pimp appears today, no infamous abandoned courtesan, no braggart warrior"; and in the Epilogue he added that "few comedies of this sort will you find, where those already good may learn to be better. . . . Who vote for modesty, applaud our play."

Set in Aetolia, the play pictures the sorrow of old Hegio, who has lost two sons, one kidnapped long ago, the other recently taken captive in battle and held at Elea. Hegio hopes to regain the second son by an exchange of prisoners. The Elean citizen Philocrates, a prisoner of war in Aetolia, seeks to protect himself by changing places with his slave Tyndarus. Hence Philocrates (who the Aetolians think is the slave) is sent to negotiate the exchange of prisoners, while the slave Tyndarus (supposedly the citizen) is held as hostage. But, despite Tyndarus' fears, Philocrates makes the exchange, and comes back with Hegio's son. Then Tyndarus himself turns out to be the long-lost other son of Hegio.

The exchange of places by Tyndarus and Philocrates is made clear to the audience by the device, which occurs only this once in Roman comedy, of having both characters appear in the Prologue, to be pointed out while the situation that is to come in the play is explained. The audience also knows (as the characters within the play do not) that Tyndarus is Hegio's lost son; this gives frequent dramatic irony to the situations, and lightens with an overtone of humor the old man's grieving at his loss.

The one stock figure, Ergasilus the parasite, is well employed as a foil to Hegio. When the father is hopeful at the prospect of recovering his son, the parasite appears in the deepest dumps; when the father is depressed, when even the lyric measures of the play shift to a tragic pathos, the parasite enters in a state of the highest elation. In addition, through the parasite the play maintains some measure of the low comedy the Romans enjoyed.

The characters possess a dignity and an integrity that give a noble tone to the drama. Master and slave evince mutual loyalty, if not always mutual trust; Hegio (whose name means "leading citizen") is the most self-respecting and venerable old man in Plautus. There is comic irony in the names of the three youths—Philocrates, "lover of conquest"; Aristophontes, "best slayer"; Philopolemus, "lover of conflict"—when all three have been taken prisoner in battle; but they are sober and decent young men. The quality of its persons, and the exalted tone of its theme, led Lessing to call this of all comedies "the finest piece ever put on the stage."

It is interesting to note, during present days of high costs in the theatre, that finances bothered the Romans too. The two sons of Hegio are never onstage at the same time; in all probability, to save expense, one actor doubled in the roles. It may also be noted—though not as a matter of economy, since men played all parts—that there are no female characters in the play.

Among plays that are based on *The Captives* are Ariosto's *I Suppositi*, 1502?, which Gascoigne adapted as *The Supposes*;* Jonson's *The Case is Altered*, 1597; Massinger's *A New Way To Pay Old Debts*;* and Rotrou's *The Captives*, 1638. With individualized characters, natural though noble, decent without sentimentality, and with a serious theme borne along through swift-flowing incidents in lively lyric patterns, *The Captives* is one of the richest comedies of ancient times. It was played at the New York Park Theatre, June 22, 1795; in London, 1980, and at St. Francis Xavier's, New York.

THREE-PENNY DAY   *Titus Maccius Plautus*

With its action drawn from the usual basic comedy situation, *Trinummus (Three-Penny Day)*, 187? B.C., has a moral tone almost on a level with *The Captives*;* Lessing ranked it second among Plautus' comedies. A serious study of a Roman social problem, it contains many reflections upon the life of the day.

When the play opens, we find Luxury, speaking the Prologue, sending her child, Poverty, into Lesbonicus' house. For the young Lesbonicus, during his father's absence, having squandered the family fortune in riotous living, is planning to sell the family home. Here, however, the resemblance to the usual Roman farce ceases. Lesbonicus' sister (there are no women actually in the play) should have a dowry, or the family's social position will drop; it is to secure money for this dowry that Lesbonicus and his slave bend their wits. The old neighbor, meanwhile, has been watchful; asked to keep an eye on Lesbonicus, he it is that buys the house. He also provides a dowry, for three pennies hiring a swindler to pretend to bring it from the absent father. The returning father comes upon the swindler, with amusing misunderstandings which resolve themselves as Lesbonicus promises to reform and both the children prepare to wed.

The direct and comparatively simple movement permits concentration on the characters. While modern taste would provide young women in a story of this sort, only respectable women are called for in the action, and Roman custom would keep these off the stage. The men, however, are diversified and natural. Contrasted with frivolous and spendthrift young Lesbonicus is his serious-minded friend, whose father suggests the Polonius of Shakespeare's *Hamlet*,* not merely in the general aspect of his prosy moralizing but also in the details of his observations; his warning to his son against lending is directly echoed in Polonius' admonition to his son. The son in Plautus differs from Laertes in that he takes his father's moral sermons so literally that he takes his father aback: he wants to marry Lesbonicus' sister even without a dowry. His early song against loose loving, incidentally, has considerable lyrical beauty and great charm.

While the dialogue of the drama is not enlivened with spicy or suggestive wit, it is fresh and figurative, as when the slave characterizes the sharpers: "Any one of them could steal the sole of a shoe right off a runner at top speed."

Three-Penny Day has been consistently considered one of Plautus' best works. Its theme recurs in Cecchi's *The Dowry*, 1550; Destouches' *The Hidden Treasure*, c. 1730, in whose sentimental comedy the two young women take a considerable part; Lessing's *The Treasure*, 1750; Colman's *The Man of Business*, 1774. With its simple situation and its shadowing forth of typical problems of Roman life, natural characters are soundly built into an effective play.

TRUCULENTUS *Titus Maccius Plautus*

The tight hold that a loose love may exercise upon a man has been no more sardonically portrayed than in *Truculentus*, 186 B.C. There are few complications in the plot of this play, which is, rather, a picture of how a courtesan, most fair and most unfair, can squeeze the last coins out of her eager victims.

Four men whose lives are ruined by the courtesan Phonesium are balanced one against the other; the courtesan teases them to vie in extravagance for her favors. The soldier gives her all the trophies of his wars; the countryman lavishes upon her the produce and the profits of his farm; the young citizen, Diniarchus, having already ruined himself for her, continues to scrape up sums for the scraps of her favors; and the "truculent" slave is tantalized by the lust of the others into sloughing his rudeness and bringing forth his savings, to taste of the courtesan's joys.

The intrigue of the play rises from the courtesan's insatiable greed. To gain more gifts from the soldier, she pretends to have had a child by him and hires a child born out of wedlock. Diniarchus turns out to be the child's real father; but even when he goes off to marry its mother, he promises to drop in on the courtesan every now and again. He is so entangled in her snares, indeed, that he lets her keep his child a few days, as bait for the soldier. The yokel and the soldier recognize that they will have to share the courtesan; each wants more frequent hours of her bounty, and the play ends, as her maid sums it up, with "a fool and a madman competing for their own ruin."

Truculentus is a portrait of a courtesan etched in vitriol. Diniarchus starts the play by remarking that "An entire lifetime isn't really long enough for a lover to learn how many roads there are to destruction. If only," he continues, "we could pass on to our descendants the wisdom of the past, then, I'd guarantee, there'd be no more pimps and harlots, and there'd be a lot fewer spendthrifts."

The characters in *Truculentus*, while they are the usual ones, are turned from their usual development to fit the purpose of the author. The soldier on his first appearance notifies the audience that he is no braggart warrior. The slave Truculentus begins as a moral blusterer, worried about his country master cozened by the city courtesan, but instead of devising tricks to extricate his master or to further his master's desires, Truculentus himself turns lecherous. Phronesium is, throughout, more barefaced in her iniquity than Plautus' other courtesans.

Along with *Pseudolus,* Truculentus* was the author's favorite play. Some moralists among critics have objected to the tone of the drama. Others, like Paul Lejay, deem it Plautus' most satiric comedy, one that evokes not heedless laughter but pertinent thought, as do the more serious dramas of Molière.* This realistic study, in dramatic terms, of a frequent evil in Roman society is a powerful play, not without pertinence to our own times.

AMPHITRYON   *Titus Maccius Plautus*

The most popular of Plautus' plays, *Amphitruo (Amphitryon),* 186? B.C., is also the only extant Roman comedy that presents a travesty of gods and heroes. With exuberance and gay horseplay matched only in the work of Aristophanes, it romps with delightful abandon over the ancient legend of the birth of Hercules.

In a night made extra long by the god, Jupiter comes to Alcmena disguised as her husband Amphitryon, who is away at war. Mercury, disguised as Amphitryon's servant Sosia, is on guard outside when the real Sosia returns just ahead of his master. The fun of the play is made up of the bewilderment and discomfiture of the mortals, the increasing anger of Amphitryon, and the mischievous amusement of the gods. Finally, we are told of the birth of twins to Alcmena, and the exploit of one of them in killing two snakes that attack the cradle. In a crack of thunder, Jupiter reveals himself as father of the strong babe, Hercules, and Amphitryon decides, for his love's sake, that yielding to a god is being faithful. In a long jesting Prologue, Mercury states that since gods are in the play it cannot be a comedy; since a slave is in the play it cannot be a tragedy; hence he will make it a tragicomedy. The rest is farce. Sosia enters, delivers another Prologue; then Mercury, the false Sosia, beats away the real one, and completes his Prologue.

The only character not developed solely for the fun is Alcmena, whom J. W. Duff calls Plautus' sweetest and purest woman. "She is a devoted and faithful wife to Amphitryon; his reproaches, when he thinks her unfaithful, bewilder and grieve her." Her character, indeed, gives a dignity and loftiness to the play, for all its boisterous fooling. Arthur Palmer called it "the most simple, dignified, and tender of all the plays of Plautus." It was a great favorite in ancient times, always performed in Rome by public authority when the state was threatened with pestilence, famine, or other calamity, on the theory that showing the god enjoying amorous exploits would please the god and win his favors.

Many later plays have told Amphitryon's story: *The Sosias,* by Rotrou, 1638; *Amphitryon* by Molière, 1668; by Dryden, 1690; by von Kleist, 1807. Roughly estimating the number before him, Jean Giraudoux called his 1936 version *Amphitryon 38.*

There are several differences in detail, in the later versions. Molière introduces Sosia's wife, an ill-favored, ill-natured scold, completely without a sense of humor, as a feminine foil to her witty husband. Dryden, in addition, has a maid for Alcmena, a selfish creature who garners gifts from the gods. In Plautus, there is a pilot who refuses to arbitrate between the two Amphitryons. In Dryden there is a Judge Gripus, through whom the playwright lashes at his time (thinking of Judge Jeffries when the judge in the play is abused): "Thou seller of other people, thou weathercock of government: that, when the wind blows for the subject pointest to privilege, and when it changes to sovereignty, veerest to prerogative."

More basic are the differences in tone. Plautus maintains the high ideals of Roman life; the home is sacred and the woman honored therein; all the abounding humor, even to the pail of slops dumped on Amphitryon, sets no strain upon the social structure. Molière trifles more along the feminine lines, as one might expect at the court of Louis XIV, but he, too, is basically earnest. Dryden, for all his polished wit, reflects the lower tone of the cynical court of Charles II and seems today to exceed the limits of good taste. Sir Walter Scott sums up the French and the English attitude: "Dryden is coarse and vulgar where Molière is witty, and where the Frenchman ventures upon a double meaning, the Englishman always contrives to make it a single one." The coarseness broadened into a leer in the musical comedy *Out of This World* which, with book by Deems Taylor and Reginald Lawrence and music by Cole Porter, opened in New York November 30, 1950, and clumsily set the god's descent in our own times.

Giraudoux is subtler in his humor, turning it also on the gods. His play opens with a delightful scene of Jupiter and Mercury perched on a cloud, looking at earth below, and revealing that, in some respects, the gods are only human. Later, this impression increases; where Plautus has the disguised Jupiter telling Alcmena of his exploits in battle, Giraudoux has him complacently speak of his exploits that long night in bed, and Alcmena innocently reminds him of other, livelier, more enjoyable nights, thus exalting human love above even divine imitation.

Giraudoux' *Amphitryon 38,* adapted by S. N. Behrman, with Alfred Lunt, Lynn Fontanne, and Richard Whorf, was a great success in both America and England. It is interesting to compare the reactions to the play in New York and in London. To New York reviewers, the play was no more than a bedroom farce. John Mason Brown said (November 1, 1937) that it "attempts to approach Bulfinch with a bedside manner"; and Brooks Atkinson elaborated the point: The play "may wear the robes of the time of Greek fables and talk of the gods of Olympus, but it is bedroom farce and only human. It is also the most distinguished piece of theatre the Guild has had the pleasure of presenting to the subscribers in some time. . . . Although the bedroom joke is more durable than most, it is still only one joke for the space of three acts, and it stumbles through a monotonous stretch in the middle of the evening. In several of the scenes, particularly in the sententious prologue, the authors have scribbled some coruscatingly witty dialogues between Jupiter and Mercury, contemplating from on high the strange love customs of the mortals. There is also one colloquy of vibrant irony when Alcmena belittles Jupiter's genius and politely cries down the story of creation. But *Amphitryon 38* does not dazzle the bedroom joke with inexhaustible brilliance, playing all the changes that might be gayly rung on a god's night out among the gullible mortals." Only Richard Lockridge, and he without analysis, felt a richer quality, when Jupiter, facing Alcmena as a god, "grants forgetfulness with a kiss and climbs back to his cloud in radiance. But a little of that radiance is left over for the human couple, lighting their little island of fidelity."

In contrast with these comments, and with George Jean Nathan's dismissal—"The play itself is slight stuff, but it provides a sufficient share of agreeable and witty boulevard entertainment"—were the discerning observations in the *London Times* (May 18, 1938), of the same production and play: Here, the dramatist Giraudoux "is, in the theatre, that increasingly rare specimen, a civilized man who speaks but does not shout and who, having something to say, dares to say it not with bludgeons but with wit, entertainingly, remembering the stage, eschewing the solemn and abominable tub. . . . Here, if you please, is an essay on the disadvantages of being a god and so, by implication, on the delights of mortality. Alcmena is offered immortality and refuses it. It would bore her to be a star and shine endlessly. She possesses, what the gods have not and our own Elizabethans had supremely as a quickener of all their poetry, the joy of transience, the delight of instants, the blissful necessity, of which Olympians can know nothing, to taste the cup, to be a connoisseur of time, before both are snatched away. This is the nature of M. Giraudoux' 'civilization': he preaches not greed but selectiveness and that connoisseurship of life by which the Anglo-Saxons are still a little shocked but which forms a link between Paris and Athens. 'Preaches!' It is the wrong word. As there is no tub, so there is no pulpit, and whoever will may lean back in his stall and enjoy the legend only, the delicious absurdity of Jupiter and his messenger chatting on a cloud, their feet (and more) in the air, or the dashing gaiety of Alcmena, who, with the help of Miss Lynn Fontanne, gives to all truth the aspect of high comedy." Enduring in its wit, timely in its thought, and comic in its staged misunderstandings—knowledge of which sets the audience on a par with the gods—Plautus' *Amphitryon* is a joyous play in its own right, as well as a fruitful stimulus to playwrights.

There have been many revivals of the later versions. A cynic remarked that Molière's *Amphitryon* (1668) "was written by a pimp to gratify a rake": to persuade Madame de Montespan that the greatest honor that can befall a virtuous wife is to commit adultery in a royal bed; she and Louis XIV watched the premiere side by side. In 1968, the play's tercentenary, it reached its 1,000th performance at the Comédie Française, with Robert Hirsch as Sosie. The Molière version was played May 1970 at the London Aldwych, in January 1970 at Washington, D.C. and February 3, 1970, at the New York City Center, with Hirsch. The translation by Peter Hacko from the German of Ralph Manheim, opening May 28, 1970, at the New York Lincoln Center, ran for twenty-eight performances in repertory.

Amphitryon 38, with Lunt and Fontanne, opened in 1937 in San Francisco and Los Angeles, at the New York Shubert November 1, 1937, and at the London Lyric May 17, 1938. The NT translation of Giraudoux, opening June 23, 1971, directed by Laurence Olivier, starred Christopher Plummer, Geraldine McEwan, and Constance Cummings, for forty-six performances in repertory. Praised by *Stage and TV Today* (July 1, 1971): "It gives the work all its sinewy strength, shafts of poetry and delicately shaded brilliance," it was condemned by the French critics, as having "betrayed Giraudoux" with "leering and provocative" lines.

Phoenix revived it for the summer 1974 at East Hampton, Long Island. Plautus rings clear, neatly in the defense of human marriage: Alcmena prefers her husband's lovemaking to the god's.

CASINA   *Titus Maccius Plautus*

Originally known as *Sortientes (The Men Who Drew Lots),* 185 B.C., and based on a Greek comedy of that name by Diphilus, this popular play of

Plautus' was revived in antiquity as *Casina,* the name of the heroine who never appears in it. It is a lively farce, much of which is sung; the basic indecency, to our standards, of its final situation makes it no less amusing.

Old Lysidamus and his son both covet the fair young slave girl, Casina. Each tries to arrange to have a slave marry the girl, as a cloak for his own gratificatigon. Lysidamus sends his son out of town, but his mother, suspecting her husband's intentions, continues arguing for her son's slave. The two slaves, in an amusing, quarrelsome scene, draw lots; the old man's proxy wins. The wedding is held, but Lysidamus' wife substitutes a disguised male slave for Casina, and out of the bridal chamber tumble first the male "bride" and then the old master, completely duped and shamed.

The comedy flows along with quick repartee and gay lyric movement, and was probably set to sparkling tunes. Its usual theme of the old man tricked was given a new variation that must have tickled the Roman fancy. As in many of the more exuberant farces, there is occasional breaking of the dramatic illusion by talk or reference to the audience, as when the wife, after enjoying her husband's exposure and discomfiture, says that she'll forgive him, "less reluctantly, so as not to make a long play still longer." Neither Casina nor the son appears in the play; the Prologue tells us not to expect the young man: "Plautus did not wish him to come, and broke down the bridge that was on his route."

It is noticeable that the later plays of Plautus have a greater lyrical element, as though the playwright grew fonder, or found his audience fonder, of music. The taste of the audience probably accounts for the increase of exuberant vulgarity in the later plays, though among these are also Plautus' chief satires on vice. Some influence of the early (pre-Roman) Atellan farces, with their frank sex play, may leer in these later comedies. *Casina,* the last of Plautus' surviving plays, is the most care-free and the bawdiest in its plot, as well as one of the liveliest in its movement.

DANGEROUS CORNER   *J. B. Priestley*

John Boynton Priestley (1894–1984) first became known for his novel *The Good Companions,* a story of a troupe of performers, which he dramatized in 1931 with Edward Knobloch. Then the author was strongly influenced by *An Experiment with Time,* by J. W. Dunne, and wrote a succession of "time" plays.

Time and the Conways, 1937, shows Mrs. Conway and her six children at Kay's twenty-first birthday, picturing their rosy future. Twenty years later we behold them; one who had dreamed of becoming a stage star is dead; Kay, instead of being a noted novelist, is a grubby journalist; all are variously unhappy. The last act shows them back at the twenty-first birthday party. Unambitious brother Alan quotes Blake:

> Man was made for joy, and woe;
> And when this we rightly know
> Safely through the world we go.

—and they go blithely on into the future.

An Inspector Calls, 1947, presents another ironic time sequence. A police inspector questioning Arthur Birling, a factory owner, about a girl's suicide, causes a tumult in the family. Birling's son and daughter and the others have had moral lapses; they are apprehensive about a possible scandal—

until they discover that the call is false. The inspector goes; and the family lapses into smug self-satisfaction; then there's a phone call: the factory girl has just committed suicide, and an inspector will call. When the play was revived at the London Mermaid, August 29, 1973, Priestley called it "more topical than when I wrote it."

First and most popular of Priestley's "time" plays was *Dangerous Corner,* 1932, wherein we watch two publishers and their wives, a novelist and his secretary, at dinner. "Telling the truth's about as dangerous as skidding around a corner at sixty—and life is full of dangerous corners." Noticing his dead brother Martin's cigarette box, Robert Caplan wonders why Martin had shot himself: was it because he felt guilty of stealing the firm's check for £500,000? Robert's insistence on pressing the inquiry unearths the actual thief, a partner who smilingly comes through undismayed, while "dangerous corners" in the lives of the three women are exposed; the tranquility of Olwen is torn away, revealing double depths of suffering; and a quite different version of Martin's death comes to light.

In the final act, we are back at that early dinner; as they rise from the table, no one pays attention to the cigarette box; the radio is turned on, and the couples dance happily as the curtain falls.

Dangerous Corner opened at the London Lyric in spring 1932, with Flora Robson as Olwen and Frank Allenby as Robert, and was at once successful. Ivor Brown called it "really original in its method and really exciting in its result." It opened in Paris in December 1932, with Marie Ney and Richard Bird. On October 26, 1932, Cecil Holm and Barbara Robbins played it at the New York Empire, for 206 performances. George Jean Nathan said that "each turn of character, each motivating thought, and each deduction from thought and act is logical, shrewdly understanding, and convincing."

Of the October 19, 1938, Westminster revival, the *London Times* declared, we "marvel afresh at its ingenuity."

The play has been very popular in local stock companies and student drama groups. Among revivals are: in the United States, the Theatre Guild, March 1938; ELT, January 22, 1946; Faye Emerson and John Forsyth on tour (Olney, Md.), 1952; in London, the Ambassador's, December 17, 1980.

The play's events are not tied to any specific period; its various levels of appeal and the novelty of its turning thus remain fresh, and ensure its lasting hold upon theatregoers, as each of us embarks, all unwitting, toward our own dangerous corner.

BRITANNICUS   *Jean Baptiste Racine*

When *Britannicus* was produced in 1669, Pierre Corneille, aged 63, reproached the 30-year-old Jean Baptiste Racine (French, 1639-1699), with having made Britannicus live two more years than history accorded him. Racine retorted that Corneille had allowed the Emperor Heraclius to reign twenty years when history accorded him eight.

When Floridor produced *Britannicus* in December 1669, Corneille sat almost alone at the premiere; the crowd was off watching the beheading of the Huguenot Marquis de Courboyer. The few who saw the play did not at once grant it their favor. Boileau, however, expressed the view that *Britannicus* has "the most finished and the most sententious" poetry of Racine's plays. King Louis XIV joined in its praises and its success was assured—

though Racine later declared that *Britannicus* won both more applause and more censure than any other of his dramas.

Britannicus presents the climactic moments in the rivalry between Nero and his stepbrother, Britannicus, whose beloved Junie Nero covets. Britannicus is killed, but Junie saves herself by becoming one of the Vestal Virgins. There is little dramatic movement in the play, but intense analysis of the emotions of the characters. Saint-Evremond (striking a blow for Corneille) declared: "There once was a time when one had to choose good subjects, and to handle them well; now all one needs is characters." Racine's interest lay in character rather than theme; but the counterbalance and the analysis of his characters itself grows intense and exciting.

Boileau wrote of the premiere: *Britannicus* "touched me so deeply that the happiness he was apparently soon to enjoy having made me laugh, the story they came to tell of his death made me weep; and I know nothing more pleasant than to have at any given moment a fund of joy or of sadness at the very humble service of M. Racine. . . . Others who, for the thirty sols they'd given at the door, thought they had the right to say what they thought, found the novelty of the catastrophe so astonishing, and were so touched to see Junie, after the poisoning of Britannicus, go to become a religious of the order of Vesta, that they would have called the work a Christian tragedy, if they had not been assured that Vesta was not Christian."

Though not so frequently revived in France as Racine's *Phèdre* and *Andromaque*, *Britannicus* has remained popular. It is worth noting that Nero is reproached in the play for having performed before his courtiers; after the premiere of *Britannicus,* Louis XIV never again danced in public. In England, the play proved fairly popular. Thomas Gray, we are told in Norton Nicholls' *Memoirs,* "admired Racine, particularly the *Britannicus.*" The play was warmly received by English romantics in general—though Sir Brooks Boothby, who translated it in 1803, wondered whether there was a place for "so simple and chaste a tragedy on a stage where even Shakespeare must make way for ballets of action. . . . The characteristic of Racine is purity of taste. He seldom attempts to create, but is content to imitate, and this he always does with great force and infinite propriety of art. His versification is generally agreed to have reached the summit of perfection, in a language the least of all formed either for melody or for figurative expression; and when it is remembered that he has restrained himself to the difficult unities of time and place, suited to the regular and simple construction of his plays, the best performances of Racine will always be considered as masterpieces of dramatic art."

Racine is primarily a musician. His exactness, of both psychology and versification, has led the French to prefer his plays to those with Corneille's "noble fire." His verse, as Laurie Magnus observed in the *Dictionary of European Literature* (1926), is, "at its height, incomparable for its passion, restraint, majesty, and music." These very qualities—passion *and* restraint—however, suggest the reason for the lack of full appreciation of Racine outside of France. Thus F. Y. Eccles in *Racine in England* (1922), states: "His rarest virtue of expression is not exactness, nor propriety, but an ardor robed in discretion, which most foreigners perhaps—and some of his own countrymen—do not distinguish from frigidity and rhetoric." Both a poet and an analyst of characters torn by the opposite claims of devotion and duty, Racine in his chosen range is without a peer.

Britannicus was shown in London in French, by the Comédie Française, in 1953, 1960, and 1961. In English, at London Hammersmith, 1981. New

York, Phoenix, November 28, 1958; New York City Center, February 21, 1961, and on tour (Washington, Princeton, Philadelphia, Boston).

For Racine's *Phèdre,* see Euripides,* *Hippolytus.*

HAIR, ETC. (NUDITY IN THE THEATRE)   *Gerome Ragni, etc.*

Any survey of the theatre that covers the 1960s and 1970s must discuss the outbreak of nudity and not only the mention but the display of (simulated) sexual activities. To indicate this properly, mention will be made of plays that have no other place in this volume; but more than one of them have proved a great financial success, a *coup de théâtre,* if not a work of art.

The first exposure of a nude form on the legitimate stage probably came in *Marat/Sade** (1964), when a male inmate of the insane asylum comes silently but nakedly up through a trapdoor to merge into the onstage crowd. The first precise sexual act perhaps came in 1967, in *The Beard,* by Michael McClure. This pictures Billy the Kid and Jean Harlow in the hereafter, engaged in a verbal duel, mainly of four-letter words, which ends with her removing her panties, which he tosses back over her head; she opens her legs, he kneels and nuddles. She shouts "Stars! Stars!" Kenneth Tynan, after the London production at the Royal Court, November 4, 1968, called the play "a milestone in the history of heterosexual art." The *Saturday Review* of November 11, 1967, after the New York opening, declared that at the end "there is a sense of ecstatic flight toward the stars that reminds one of Dante's emergence from the Inferno." (The critic should, at least once, read Dante.)

I say this is "perhaps" the first, because *Time* (November 3, 1967) calls this "a continuation of the second-act curtain of Albee's *Tiny Alice* (1964) in which Irene Worth, shielded from the audience by her robe, seemingly displayed her nude body to John Gielgud, who dropped to his knees before her while she uttered orgiastic cries." *The Beard* was revived OffOffBway in 1973, in a new version with four characters; also in 1977. A June 24, 1974, performance at Cambridge, Mass., was stopped by the police. The title does not refer to the fringe of white paper that adorned the chins of the two characters in their haven in the hereafter, reminiscent of ancient gods or monarchs.

After *The Beard* came *Hair,* which, opening OffBway on November 3, 1967, moved to Broadway in April 1968 and attained 1,750 performances. By Gerome Ragni and James Rado, directed by Tom O'Horgan, it was, said the *New York Times,* "a wild, indiscriminate explosion of exuberant, impertinent, youthful talents." It opens in "the age of Aquarius" and it listed the staff astrologer on the program. It has been played in over twenty-two countries and fourteen languages. King Moshoeshoe II attended the 1974 premiere in Lesotho. It began its London run in 1970; four years later the roof of the Shaftesbury Theatre collapsed, and the play was transferred to the Queen's. It had over 1,000 performances in Australia. A tape recording of the work, by the original cast, went with Apollo 12 to the moon. In New York's Central Park on June 5, 1972, its songs were sung in English, Japanese, Hebrew, and as much as the cast could manage of the other languages in which the play has been performed. The music remains the best part of the play, especially the song "Let the Sun Shine In."

Called "the American tribal love-rock musical," *Hair* came in a period of rebellion, and was a protest against many things the young deemed wrong in contemporary life, especially war; it is, said the London press, "not about love but about hate," and in 1974 Benedict Nightingale declared: "Time has removed its alibis, and *Hair* stands revealed for what, I fear, it always was: maudlin, aggressive and mindless . . . nasty, brutish and long." Its notorious "nude scene" at the end of Act I lifts a long scarf to reveal a file of unclad male and female bodies. This lasts, a San Francisco commentator pointed out, "for a few seconds in such dim light that an unsuspecting playgoer who wasn't watching closely might miss it entirely." None the less, director O'Horgan boasted that for the next few years every play, on whatever theme, would have its obligatory nude scene.

There seemed some measure of truth in O'Horgan's prophecy. In 1972 a Lady Macbeth rose from her bed unclad and went nude throughout her sleepwalking scene. In the opera in New Orleans in 1973 Thais opened her robe for the temptation of Paphnutius, then dropped it for the contemplation of the audience. In 1974 *Equus** showed a nude—tender and touching— attempt at lovemaking, as the young maiden tries to woo the boy from his horses.

Meanwhile, *Che,* by Lennox Raphael, opening OffOffBway in April 1969, used varieties of sexual activity as symbols of political action. Its chief characters are Che (Guevara) and "President"—the nationality marked by a red, white, and blue waistband that, with a top hat, is his only garb. They perform varied simulated sex acts on each other and the two female characters, until the President shoots Che and a woman, and lies embracing their bodies, leaving the stage to a man dressed as a gorilla, strumming a guitar.

CHE is also the acronym of the Campaign for Homosexual Equality. In 1974 at the London Royal Court a play called merely *X* used the story of a seventeen-year-old girl who seldom achieved orgasm to press the notion that children should be introduced in their earliest years to the delights of cunnilingus and fellatio, so that they might grow into a richly varied sex life, escaping the furtiveness and the frustrations of adolescence and the tensions that strain in many a neurotic adult. Following the play there surfaced a group, Paedophile Information Exchange, PIE, advocating sex between an understanding, tender adult and a child who would thus accept sex without guilt. And PIE was approved by CHE. On August 24, 1983, after the imprisoned spy Geoffrey Prince had been linked with PIE, three of its members were arrested on various sex charges.

One play, *Grin and Bare It,* by Tom Cushing (written about 1928, brought up to date by Ken McGuire and produced at the New York Belasco March 16, 1970) attempted an appropriate use of nudity. It pictures a proper Bostonian young man visiting the family of his fiancée in California, to discover that they are practicing nudists. The play had been presented, in the summer of 1969, at the New Jersey Circle H Ranch, with the audience invited to join the cast in the swimming pool after the performance. Unfortunately, it was a bad play.

Also in 1970 in New York, in 1971 in London, was *The Dirtiest Show in Town,* ending with the simulated copulation of five naked couples, but announcing that it was intended to depict "the destructive effects of air, water, and mind pollution." The general verdict was that while it was perhaps the dirtiest show, it was certainly the worst show in town. Clive Barnes paid it a second visit, then found it "a good-natured spoof of dirty shows."

The year 1969 took nudity, *in* and *per se,* clearly and plainly for its own sake, out of brothel and stag show, onto the "legitimate" stage. Erstwhile critic Kenneth Tynan (1927-1980), who had hailed *The Beard,* who in *Who's*

Who listed his recreations as "sex and eating," then gathered a few kindred spirits, including Samuel Beckett, Jules Feiffer, John Lennon of the Beatles, and Sam Shepard, and made a successful bid for a fortune with *Oh! Calcutta!* The title seems to be an English intellectual's idea of an interlingual pun, from *Oh! quel cul t'as!*, the play's programs and posters showing a prone woman, with a rose lying across the intended area, presenting the posterior for posterity. The play opened at the OffBway Eden June 17, 1969, for 704 performances.

Walter Kerr, the most seasoned newspaper critic of the time, said that from *Oh! Calcutta!* "taste, an ear for wit, an eye for form, a heart that usually insists on being pleased only in the highlands, had all vanished. The clumsiest, most labored of jokes were permitted to succeed one another in obsessive monotony. . . . Language no longer mattered. Anything would do so long as it met two requirements: that the actors undress and that they engage in simulated sex play. . . . The people were not engaged in being amusing or pertinent or impertinent or imaginative. They were engaged in being naked. It was an exclusive occupation." In 1984, Walter Kerr remarked that there were 24 plays running on Broadway, "unless you count *Oh! Calcutta!*, which I do not."

Not all of the show's fourteen sketches are performed in the nude. The masturbating women wear riding costume. The masturbating men have their backs to the spectators, and are looking up at slanted mirrors that show us their fantasies as they pump. Most of the men, of course, visualize women, but one of them fancies the galloping Lone Ranger. There is one nude pas de deux, a tender adagio, that has genuine charm, and makes one wonder whether young men and maidens dancing in unclad innocence on a moonlit lawn might not indeed present a graceful and aesthetic delight. Perhaps in the ballet. . . . The rest of *Oh! Calcutta!* not only lacks both wit and beauty, but palls into what one reviewer called "more corn than porn."

The first Broadway run of *Oh! Calcutta!* attained 1,314 performances. The 1976 New York revival at the Edison was still drawing crowds in 1983. The American road company of 1977-1978 played over 500 performances in 119 cities in the United States and Canada, with only occasional police interference; the cast was arrested three times. The show has been played in most of the countries of Europe. In London, it has been running continuously since 1969; January 28, 1970, at the Royalty; January 28, 1974, at the Duchess, with over 4,000 performances, exceeding the New York run of *Grease*.* It was on tour in England in 1981-1982, and proclaims its "fifteenth international year."

The success of *Oh! Calcutta!* was followed on January 8, 1974, by another nude frolic. With a tasteless reversal of Moses' cry to the Pharaoh, Earl Wilson Jr.'s *Let My People Come* came to the Village Gate in New York City's Greenwich Village, where the spectators might sit at tables and sip while the show went on. The State Liquor Authority revoked the Gate's license, but the show went on, moving uptown to the Morosco on July 27, to attain 1,327 performances. I have read, but find it hard to believe, that it had over 1,000 performances in Philadelphia. The show has been popular elsewhere, too. It ran for six months in Boston. In Paris, in 1975, it was adapted by Jacques Lanzmann as *Lève-toi et Viens (Rise Up and Come)*. At the London Regent Theatre it ran for two years.

At the first showing in downtown New York, the cast, needing no costume changes, mingled with the spectators during intermission and at the end waited for comments near the exit, nude. As Dr. William Hitzig said after being invited onstage to dance with the topless chorines of the Paris Folies Bergère: "They're pretty, but how they sweat!"

An opening song insists "There are no dirty words," to prove which it repeats and repeats them. Apparently believing also that there are no "dirty acts," the show spends the rest of the evening simulating sexual performances. A group of females, with one male, take lessons in sucking a banana; in his eagerness, the young man bites off the top. There are two homosexual songs: "I'm Gay" and "Take Me Home with You."

Critics were not invited—a practice other producers (as Joseph Papp with his *Macbeth*; "swinishly bad," said John Simon) have followed with plays they think likely to be damned by the critics. Of course, nudity in itself has a strong appeal to the emotionally adolescent, especially, as Harold Hobson says, those over forty. So the critics paid, and saw, and spoke. The *London Times*: "After the feeble *Oh! Calcutta!*, the repellent *Dirtiest Show in Town*, the idiotic *Let My People Come*." The *London Guardian* was more analytic: "Rather like *Godspell*,* it belongs to the hortatory school of OffBway revues in which missionary fervor replaces sophisticated persuasiveness; and just as the former show offered a kindergarten view of religion, so this one is full of adolescent excitability at the discovery that sex isn't half fun. . . . As in all sex shows I've ever seen, the law of diminishing returns inevitably sets in: once the motion's been carried that sex is here to stay, the cast are all undressed with, intellectually, no place to go." The critic confessed to a perverse, rebellious impulse to go home and be chaste. As with Mae West, though less entertainingly, sex had become its own anaphrodisiac. In December 1982 *Let My People Come* came to the New York Carter, OffBway.

By the 1980's, nudity was routine. Although the plays that exploit it romp ever along for ever new adolescents, sex may now be taken for granted if it fits the story. Thus, *Steaming*, by Nell Dunn, showing a group of women at a municipal Turkish bath, came to the London Theatre Royal, Stratford East, July 6, 1981, and moved to the Comedy, August 20 for 840 performances. It came to Stamford, Conn., November 10, 1982, then to the New York Brooks Atkinson, opening December 3, 1982.

The New York critics were divided. Several complained that the women were too professionally shapely for a casual municipal gathering—which may be why they more frequently discarded towels or robes than the London ladies. Clive Barnes in the *Post* called the play "for the most part sharp, pointed, and witty." *Variety* said it was "women's lib for beginners." The only male, incidentally, is the handyman, unseen but heard through the opaque glass door. The play was directed by Roger Smith in London and New York.

In a grand but decaying bathhouse the attendant, Violet, and five women bathers talk about families, digestion, and of course sex, with lively and ribald humor, viewing men "from scathing disgust to affectionate slanderous exasperation." There are an abrasive censorious Cockney mother, Mrs. Meadow, and her repressed, retarded daughter; a good-hearted exhibitionist hooker, who needs a man to keep her in fine clothing and fine fettle ("Each morning I wake I pray for courage and a good sex life"); an educated ex-hippie; and an inhibited middle-class housewife whose husband left her after twenty-two years (seventeen, in the New York version). They bare their bodies, souls, and fantasies; they are sketched with firm and compassionate hand. The author, said Benedict Nightingale in the *New Statesman*, shows "lonely women finding a fresh sense of identity, confidence and purpose as they launch into battle with bureaucratic churlishness; and she shows it good-naturedly and well." The bureaucrats are the local council, which is planning to close the municipal bath (and erect a library); and the women work themselves—and the play—into a most unusual climax as they stage a symbolic "sit-in," in a gaggle of protest jumping together into the pool, as the final curtain falls.

It seems relevant to mention the report, in the New York *Village Voice* (December 21, 1982)—for which the Reverend William Archibald Spooner may vouch—that on the London theatre scene "there's an English feminist theatre called the Cunning Stunts."

(There was an earlier play by Charlton Andrews and Avery Hopwood, *Ladies Night in a Turkish Bath,* sometimes called by just the first two words, and in a version by Cyrus Wood called *Good Night Ladies,* which opened August 10, 1920, at the New York Eltinge for 450 performances and had extensive tours and many revivals. It was filmed in 1928. The Wood version, 1942, played over two years in Chicago before coming to the New York Royale in January 1945. The play came to the New York Selwyn February 17, 1956; it opened at the Eleanor Gould OffBway March 14, 1961; also, in a version by Donald Kvarse, June 1974. At the London Aldwych December 14, 1933, adapted by Austin Melford and Douglas Furber, it was seen by the King and Queen of Denmark. In those days, the women onstage were not nude, but their varied shapes were clearly revealed in one-piece swimsuits. The play had more of a plot than *Steaming:* a gambling den next door was raided, and to escape the police, men put on women's garb and mingled with the ladies. Charles Ruggles was in the Eltinge cast. The producer, Al H. Woods, was hailed as "a genius for picking a sure-fire winner.").

To all this discussed and displayed sex, there is amusing counterplay in *No Sex Please, We're British!* by Anthony Marriott and Alastair Foot, which opened in London in 1971 and has been playing there ever since, to towns-folk and tourists, with now over 5,000 performances, the world's longest-running comedy. (It has been exceeded only by the Agatha Christie mystery *The Mousetrap,* * with over 12,000 performances in London and continuing; Rostand's mock-romance *Les Romanesques,* * translated as *The Fantasticks,* almost 10,000 OffBway and going strong; and the old-time melodrama *The Drunkard,* which opened at the Theatre Mart in Los Angeles July 6, 1933, and was laughed at for 7,510 performances.)

No Sex Please, We're British! opened in 1971 in Johannesberg. Washington saw it in 1972, on the way to New York, where in 1973 it ran for only thirty-eight performances, but went on: 1974, Chicago; 1977, Omaha; 1979, Palm Beach and the Papermill Playhouse, N.J.; with productions in over thirty countries. Alastair Foot died while the play was rehearsing for a 1971 opening in Edinburgh. It was put on by Volcano Productions, and though it sends forth more smoke than fire, the volcano is certainly still live.

It pictures the embarrassment of the Hunters, who live over the bank in which Peter Hunter is a clerk, when by error cartons of pornographic books are shipped to them from Scandinavia. As he strives to keep the family, including his uncle Brian Runnicles, the bank manager, unaware of the contents of the cartons, the audience chuckles at thoughts both of his plight and of the books—which are not proffered with the programs but may be sampled at any bookstore in London's Soho.

The display of sex, concurrent, will probably continue as long as permissive laws allow and human nature endures.

THE WINSLOW BOY   *Terence Rattigan*

It is through the implications behind its story that *The Winslow Boy,* by
Sir Terence Rattigan (1912-1977) takes on significance. The audience is told
in advance that the play is based on an actual case, the fight of a middle-
class family against the British Empire; although the author warned us, in
Theatre Arts (April, 1947), that "the facts, as stated in the play, are wildly
inaccurate and the characters bear no relationship whatever (unless by
accident) to the Archer-Shee family and Lord Carson." The play itself (aided
by deft direction and sensitive acting) gathers a sense of universality
through the quiet persistence of Mr. Winslow until, as Richard Watts
emphasized, "in the end you feel that the Winslow victory has really been a
triumph for human rights." In days of totalitarian pressure and the subor-
dination of the individual to the state, it is heartening to watch (in life and
in the theatre) the plucky and successful fight of a plain citizen to maintain
the family integrity—to find an empire on the brink of war pause in its
widespread, epochal concerns, to lean down over a personal problem and
repeat the traditional but tremendous formula with which Parliament
grants review of a government action: "Let right be done."

Terence Rattigan's history did not prepare us for the American success of
The Winslow Boy. In England, his earlier plays had been popular, two of
them having run for over 1000 performances, but all of these plays found
Broadway unreceptive. The American theatre was setting Terence Rattigan
down as a journeyman whose products had a merit limited to his own land.
Then *The Winslow Boy,* which won the Ellen Terry award in England, with
a London run from May 23, 1946, to September 6, 1947, came on October
29, 1947, to the Empire Theatre. It ran for 215 performances, and the New
York Drama Critics' Circle voted it the best foreign play of the year. On tour
through the United States, the play achieved a total of 899 performances,
terminating with a condensed television performance by the stage cast,
back in New York.

The play is a dramatized version of the story of George Archer-Shee,
dismissed for petty theft from the Royal Naval Academy, and of his father's
long fight for the right to reopen the case and establish the boy's innocence.
"A small boy and the Magna Carta", said John Mason Brown, "suddenly and
somehow found themselves fused." Alexander Woollcott wrote lengthily
about the case; and Brown's review of the play gave details of a fight against
discrimination in the United States.

This "challenging and memorable piece of theatre," as Barnes called it,
succeeds through the earnestness and honesty of its cause, and through the
very natural, recognizable reactions of the various members of the family to
the situation thrust upon them when the expelled boy shrinks home,
ashamed of his position yet proudly staunch in his innocence. These early
scenes, said Atkinson, "are heart-breaking in their simplicity and
directness."

If the wider implications fail to reach across the footlights, the play may
seem, as it did to John Chapman, "frightfully genteel and more than faintly
tedious." For if you strip the story bare, as George Jean Nathan pointed out,
it is the familiar tale of a person wrongly accused who, "after more
vicissitudes than an audience can shake a stick at," is declared innocent and
reunited with his family. Usually the climax of such a play is a courtroom
scene; here, the noted barrister grills the boy with grueling questions

before accepting the case, and the actual trial occurs offstage—told in a neatly humorous variation of the messenger's report, as old as the drama of ancient Greece. To strengthen these familiar situations, Louis Kronenberger felt, the play "falls back more and more on hokum and muted heroics."

For most persons, however, the play successfully carried over the broader implications and the surge of human justice. There is something pitiful as well as heroic in Arthur Winslow's perseverance, while his ordinary wife completely fails to see the significance of his fight and wishes he would drop the matter, for the neighbors are beginning to think them queer. Young Ronnie Winslow himself loses interest; while the trial is coming to its end, Ronnie is out enjoying a motion picture. Equally natural are the reactions of Ronnie's older brother Dick and sister Kate, the boy pluckily urging his father on, even though the mounting expenses of the case mean that he must drop out of college; the girl taking the cause as her own, though therefor she must break with her over-conventional fiancé. And the play neatly avoids the sentimental in merely allowing us to surmise that the barrister—whom Kronenberger called "the icy lawyer with the heart of an oven"—may choose, after the trial is over, to ripen his acquaintance with Catherine Winslow.

The Winslow Boy is an intense and roundly developed drama. With the bright fire of a fine fight for justice illuminating the play, Terence Rattigan made of it a drama of rich significance, a stirring presentation in theatrical terms of the eternal vigilance and the dogged tenacity of purpose that are the price of individual integrity and freedom.

The 1983 revival of *The Winslow Boy* at the London Lyric Hammersmith, with Ian Hogg as the barrister, laid a strong stress on Barbara Jefford as the mother, who complains that her husband has become a fanatic, ruined his health, depleted their income, blasted the daughter's hopes of a marriage and the elder son's university career—stressing that the pursuit of justice has counterbalancing costs.

A BEQUEST TO THE NATION   *Terence Rattigan*

A Bequest to the Nation had its premiere at the London Haymarket September 23, 1970, directed by Peter Glenville, with Ian Holm as Nelson, Leueen MacGrath as Frances, Lady Nelson, and Zoe Caldwell as Emma Hamilton. It was made into a film, *The Nelson Affair,* in 1973, with Peter Finch as Nelson and Glenda Jackson as Emma Hamilton.

The play covers the last month of the life of Admiral Horatio Nelson. Emma Hamilton is already the widow of Lord William Hamilton, late his Majesty's Ambassador to the Court of Naples, complaisant cuckold of Emma, who has borne the Admiral a daughter, Horatia (who does not appear in the play).

The devoted Frances, Lady Nelson, is pictured as a loving, forgiving wife, still hoping that when the flames of passion have died, her errant husband will return to rekindle the hearth fire. The family has gone with the Admiral, thriving socially and financially in the light of his glory—save for his young nephew George, who is troubled by Nelson's attitude toward his wife. George cannot understand why her forgiveness makes Nelson the more bitter. Nelson's character is complex. He himself, referring to his wife's forgiveness, exclaims: "Jesus told us how to answer a blow on the cheek. He never told us how to answer a kiss." After the London Haymarket opening

September 23, 1970, Harold Hobson (*Times,* September 27, 1970) analyzed: "It was only because he was ashamed of the sin he could not help committing that this Nelson committed a sin graver still. He could not forgive forgiveness. He could not forgive himself, either." Death, he seemed to recognize, was his life's solution.

The besotted Admiral is aware of his folly. In a moment of self-scorn he pictures the public laughter at his devotion to one who, as he describes her, "displayed herself naked for show at fourteen in Vauxhall Gardens, who was sold by Greville to Hamilton in payment for a bad debt, and had been bedded by half the nobility and gentry of England before becoming Sir William's wife." (She had in fact been a "love goddess" in a fashionable Garden of Love, where gentlemen copulated with sinuous sirens to strains of sentimental song.) But to Nelson the ecstasy of the nights not only justified but somehow spiritualized the sordidness of the days; sustaining within him a wondrous renewal of his earliest hours with Emma. "I found—why should I be ashamed to say it?—that carnal love concerns the soul quite as much as it concerns the body. For the body is still the soul, and the soul is still the body."

We see Emma, alas, not as the beauty whom Romney painted, but as a vulgar woman, boastful of her vulgarity, of frequently scatological speech, too often tipsy, obescent, proud of her power over the Admiral, in reference to whom she sings a parody of the National Anthem, ending "God bless *my* King." Her one act of generosity is to release Nelson from his vow to stay with her for a year, thus enabling him to head the English fleet against the French and Spanish armada, to meet the enemy at Trafalgar, October 21, 1805, gaining victory—and death.

In his cabin, on the morning of the battle, Nelson made his will, ending: "I leave Emma, Lady Hamilton, a legacy to my King and Country, that they will give her an ample provision to maintain her rank in life." How little his will was followed is foreshadowed in the play's last scene, a confrontation between Nelson's widow and his mistress as his home is already being stripped of its valuables by cormorant creditors. As the city bells still toll for Nelson, "Emma's head, whether through drink or despair, crashes on the keyboard, emitting a jangled discord, and the bottle of brandy held in her hand spills slowly on the floor." Frances Nelson says, with genuine pity: "Poor Lady Hamilton," and leaves as the stage grows dark.

THE FORTY THIEVES   *Robert Reece*

The Forty Thieves, by Robert Reece (1839-1891), with versions by many others, along with *Babes in the Wood* * is one of the best and most lengthily popular of the British pantomimes. This theatrical form, starting in the early nineteenth century mainly as a Christmas spectacle, added songs to its elaborate scenic devices and grandiose dances. It drew in elements from many sources; fairies and folklore figures intermix with characters of olden stories; frequently there is conjoined burlesque on topical themes. Subsequent authors added freely to these spectacles, which, except for Christmas revival, developed into the modern musical comedy. Thus, *The Forty Thieves,* although still revived, gave its theme to the musical comedy that for its time had the longest run of a musical on the London stage, *Chu Chin Chow.* *

The Forty Thieves first appeared on the London stage on April 8, 1806, as a romance by George Colman the Younger (1762-1836), with music by

Kelley. The story is the well-known tale from *The Thousand Nights and One Night (The Arabian Nights)*: the poor woodcutter Ali Baba discovers the cave of Abdallah, captain of the forty thieves, and by overhearing their password "Open, Sesame" carries off much of their treasure. His rich brother, Cassim, worming the secret out of Ali Baba, goes to the cave, but once inside forgets the password, and is caught by Abdallah. The thieves, seeking to kill Ali Baba, are smuggled to his new home in forty great oil jars—and in these are destroyed by Ali's faithful slave Morgiana, "the pearl of Bagdad." Some versions of the tale have Ali's son Ganem in love with Cassim's daughter, Amber; others picture him enamored of Morgiana.

A version opening March 12, 1810, attributed to Richard Brinsley Sheridan,* was a great success, enabling the theatre to recoup its losses of the last year: "What forty honest souls had lost, the Forty Thieves return." For a time, the play was shown as an afterpiece; on April 14, 1828, at Covent Garden, Edmund Kean as Othello was "followed by *The Forty Thieves*." The "Sheridan" version included Ali Baba's protectress, Ardenelle, fairy of the lake, drawn over the water by swans. It flourished; it came to Boston in 1876, "performed originally at the Theatre Royal, Drury Lane, London, upwards of 200 nights to crowded houses."

By that year, the spectacle had accumulated a galloping charge of the robbers on real horses against a caravan, seizing the beautiful daughter of a Bashaw; a forest scene at the abode of Orcobrand, the spirit of the forest and protector of the thieves, with his four Infernals, Fraud, Famine, War, and Rapine; with a subterranean scene in the grotto of the fairy of the lake— and a dozen sentimental or humorous songs. The *Boston Register,* January 29, 1876, said that the spectacle "was produced in a style of magnificence that has never been equalled."

In the meantime a travesty by Harry B. Farnie (d. 1889) played at the New York Niblo's Garden on February 6, 1869: "The Lydia Thompson Burlesque Troupe in the Gorgeous Oriental Spectacular Burlesque Extravaganza *The Forty Thieves; or, Striking Oil in Family Jars!*" Lydia Thompson played the boy Ganem, and, said Richard Grant White in the *Galaxy* (August 1869): "It was as if Venus, in her quality as the goddess of laughter, had come upon the stage. And if there is a likeness to Venus in costume, as well as in manner, I must confess that I saw in it no chance of harm to myself or to any of my fellow spectators, old or young, male or female. Indeed, it seems rather to be desired that the points of a fine woman should be somewhat better known and more thought of amongst us than they have been. They seem to me quite as important, and I think they are quite as interesting, as those of a fine horse; and I should be sorry to think that they are more harmful, either to taste or to morals." This production (apart from the famous critic's early thrust at decorum) also had a real train crossing the stage, and such other treats as "the can-can as only Niblo's could-could" and "Grand Resurrection of the thieves; they have not been potted but preserved!"

In 1878 an amateur production was given in London. The *Advertiser* (February 16, 1878) told of "the pantomime written by a grand confederation of comic powers, composed of Messrs W. S. Gilbert,* H. J. Byron, Farnie, and Burnand ... W. S. Gilbert wielded Harlequin's magic wand, and danced, pirouetted, and took flying leaps through doors and windows as if to the manner born."

Not only throughout Britain, but widely in the United States, *The Forty Thieves* toured. Also in 1878, during a performance in Nevada, the real mule turned recalcitrant; it kicked down Ali's bags, and was demolishing the scenic cave, while miners in the audience shouted bets on its perform- ance, until the combined cast managed to control it.

In Queen Victoria's Jubilee Year, a special version of *The Forty Thieves* outdid its predecessor in splendor. The play, said the *Illustrated London News* (January 1, 1887) had "never been adorned hitherto with such a wealth of pageantry." The first scene was "a peep at Paradise, gay with pretty faces and graceful forms, bedight in charming silks and satins." The climax was historical: "Commencing with an allegory of the conquest of India, this splendid crowning effect comprises a processional and choreo- graphic gathering of the clans which go to make up the British Empire, and ends with a gorgeous ballet before a large statue of Her Majesty, with the singing of Mr. Clement Scott's Jubilee Ode to the Queen."

Productions and adaptations continued. Most successful was that by Robert Reece, with music by Meyer Lutz. Opening December 24, 1880, it ran for 232 performances. This was revived a dozen times, always with over 100 performances; opening December 26, 1935, for 186. Thus, the *London Times*: "It is evident that the old bright songs, dances, and puns of this most successful burlesque have lost none of their freshness and charm."

A 1900 version written by Fred Bowyer made Mrs. Ali Baba "the terror of Bagdad; she has many vices, but one virtue: she makes a lovely steak puddin'." Sophie, Ali Baba's donkey, was played by a man; the four lieuten- ants of the Forty Thieves Ltd. were played by women. A 1925 production boasted comedy acrobats, a children's harlequinade, and "the Masa- Madatsu troupe of Japanese marvels." The *Times* on December 27, 1935, reported: "It holds hardened playgoers as well as children for four hours on end. . . . Here are all the vital elements of entertainment in their simplest forms. From the Lyceum pantomime a painstaking scientist might deduce the whole nature of theatrical man."

Begun as a spectacle, the British pantomime had become a sort of the- atrical grab-bag full of choice and surprising treasures of the theatre. A motley of song and dance and legend and fairy lore, of pun and slapstick fun and travesty and satire, of beautiful spectacle and theatrical legerdemain, the pantomime is a holiday festival for the child in all of us. Among these productions, one of the most enduringly delightful is *The Forty Thieves*.

ON TRIAL   *Elmer Rice*

When *On Trial*, by Elmer Rice (Elmer Reizenstein; American, 1892-1967), opened in New York August 19, 1914, Broadway "experienced one of those thrills for which it lives," according to the *New York World*. Shrouded in secrecy until the opening, the play captured audiences not only with the power of its melodramatic story but with the novelty of its technique.

On Trial was the first play to convey its story through a movement akin to what is called "the flash-back" in motion pictures. The idea was sug- gested to him, Rice told me, by an article of Clayton Hamilton's in the *Bookman*, which suggested a play with scenes in inverse sequence; Rice hit upon the more dramatic movement of going back in order to go forward. The scene of his play is a courtroom during a trial; as the trial advances, new witnesses are called. As the witness begins his story, the stage darkens, then changes—and we watch the story in action. Thus, as we behold the past scenes, our interest is always in the present; we are balancing this episode among the others for its effect upon the jury and as it shapes our own attitude toward the defendant.

The story itself is really less important than the method of presentation. Originally the play was all about a Kentucky feud. By the time it was sold— through Arthur Hopkins, to Cohan and Harris—it told the story of a murder in New York. Mr. Strickland, catching his wife in a lie, and on its trail discovering that she has been visiting his best friend, Mr. Trask, himself pays a visit to this gentleman and shoots him. The play opens with Strickland on trial for murder. The evidence discloses, however, that Mrs. Strickland was not unfaithful: that Trask had compromised her years ago, when she was an unwitting girl of seventeen, and that now he's been ruthlessly blackmailing her. If Strickland knew this, his crime was clearly not immediate impulsive killing but coldly deliberated murder. Strickland claims that he had no knowledge of these facts; indeed, in good faith he had just paid his friend Trask $10,000; but there is no trace of the money. We watch the jury in its vigorous debating of the case. One point is not clear; they wish to recall a witness. And in a last moment surprise, the trap is sprung: Trask's secretary, tangled in his own words, confesses he has stolen the $10,000—and Strickland is freed.

The play's reception was enthusiastic. The audience rose in its seats and cheered. The play, said Acton Davies in the *Tribune*, "made an instant appeal not alone by the compelling power of its story and the big human note which throbbed through all its acts, but by the unique manner in which its scenes were presented. . . . Elmer Reizenstein has not only dared to take his dramatic bull by the horns but has, to carry the animal simile further, actually put his cart before the horse with immense success." The play, said the *World,* "grips with the tenacity of a well spun detective yarn."

Outstanding in memory is the craftsmanship of the play itself. Technique, said Rice, is "not merely the framework of art, but almost its very essence. . . . For it is craftsmanship that channels the tumultuous flow of fantasy and gives body and form to the nebulous stuff that dreams are made of." That craftsmanship is one of Rice's firmest gifts. It is manifest in his first play, *On Trial,* not only in the new stage device of stepping back to leap forward, but in the tenseness of the witness scenes themselves, in the neatly incidental way in which the husband learns of his wife's past—an excellent playing upon his emotions, and those of the audience—and in the climactic surprise when the case seems over, upon the jury's request that the secretary be recalled.

The young lawyer author was freed by the play's success to devote himself to the theatre. In many ways—as one of the organizers of the Federal Theatre, as a president of the Dramatists' Guild, as an astute director as well as a warm-hearted, social-minded playwright—he has worked for the good of the theatre. In his plays, along with an uncanny capture of natural dialogue, he manifests a superb plot sense, an unerring sense of construction—which gave power, and significance in the history of the American theatre, to *On Trial.*

Among recent revivals: OffBway (Hotel Diplomat), February 20, 1979; Houston (Alley), Texas, November 25, 1982—still holding emotion and suspense.

THE ADDING MACHINE   *Elmer Rice*

This is the best American play in the expressionist mode. The Theatre Guild produced it in New York, March 19, 1923, with Dudley Digges and

Edward G. Robinson. It was almost immediately produced in London by the Independent Labor Party, and in 1928 by Barry Jackson, and it has had countless revivals in England and throughout the English-speaking world. Foreign language productions have been given in Argentina, Austria, France (by Gaston Baty), Germany, Holland, Hungary, Japan, Mexico, Norway. The play continues to be a challenge to community and college theatre directors.

With tenderness and tragic irony the play pictures the regimentation of middle-class life in a money-bound world. The characters are identified by labels, not names—Mr. Zero; Mrs. Zero; their friends, Mr. and Mrs. One to Seven; the Boss—except for the delightful heaven-sent dream-companion Daisy Diana Dorothea Devore. Mr. Zero, the patient bookkeeper, expecting praise and a raise after twenty-five years of devoted service, is told by his boss that an adding machine will supplant him—he is fired. Fired by these words, Mr. Zero snatches up a filing spike and stabs the boss. Condemned to death, he reawakens in the next world. There he wanders in a flowery field with Daisy Diana, who had been his office assistant, the secret object of his unsatisfied love; but when nobody seems to care that they are together, Mr. Zero's shocked conventionality sends him away. He then finds himself more at home (which is heaven, which hell?) as he stalks about on a gigantic adding machine, stepping from key to key until he is reassigned to the old routine on earth, sentenced once more to be alive. The drudgery round, being the creation of a commonplace mind, is dreadfully and endlessly renewed.

The structure of the play roused considerable controversy. The New York *Freeman* (May 2, 1923) attacked it violently, as "a concoction of strident modernity that would be difficult to explain on any more charitable basis than that it is a clever exploitation of expressionism . . . there is no direct plagiarism—only a complete and audacious surrender to modern forms that is disagreeable in proportion to its calculated hope of succeeding." Contrariwise, the London *Spectator* (March 22, 1924) said: "It is in Mr. Rice's bold and novel presentation that the play's force resides"; and the *Boston Transcript* (December 14, 1926) called the play's production America's "emergence into theatrical day."

The *New York Times* (March 20, 1923) upheld expressionism as "the form of dramatic expression best conveying the illusion of reality in the presence of the obviously unreal." It came to Rice, despite the *Freeman,* as the natural form for his subject; for, as Rice told me: "I had never seen or read any expressionistic plays when I wrote *The Adding Machine.* In fact, the writing of that play was about the most extraordinary experience I have ever had. I was working on another play and suddenly *The Adding Machine* came to me, practically complete—characters, story, situations, and even some of the dialogue. I began writing it eight hours after the idea hit me and finished it in eighteen days."

The superb structural sense of Elmer Rice and his subtle handling of dialogue are in evidence throughout the play. The opening scene shows Mr. Zero in bed; his wife, combing her hair, delivers herself of a monologue of inconsequential gossip interspersed with spurts of nagging at her recumbent husband, which admirably sets the tone of the play. At the office, Daisy reads the figures with dullest monotony as Mr. Zero books them. But between the numbers their thoughts, dreams of their unavowed romance, drift into audibility. "The thought sequences," the *Spectator* noted, "wander like arabesques, sometimes converging till they almost touch, sometimes interrupted by irritable outbursts between the two thinkers. The dialogue, apparently desultory, fills out the intimate characters of the speakers, and gives their present and past relations to one another in a masterly fashion. It is a skilful and beautiful piece of writing." At the Zeros' party, the friends appear in mechanical reduplication. "They make," the *Spectator* continued, "one after another like a peal of bells, remarks of an inconceivable and desolating banality. The effect is not only comical but terrible; and it is entirely appropriate, for by illustrating symbolically the mechanical monotony of Zero's life and his everlasting concern with sums and figures, it lights up and intensifies the *motif* of the play."

There is similarly effective use of robot responses in the courtroom, with the puppet-like jury automatic in its attention, its whispered deliberations, its unanimous raising of the right arm to point the "Guilty!" But here is the play's most pathetic moment, when Mr. Zero, perhaps dimly discerning the truth that to understand all is to pardon all, tries to make the jury understand his action, and in his inarticulate groping can achieve only a continued mechanical repetition of incoherent phrases. This is at once a true stroke of psychological insight and a pressing of the play's point: so far has mechanization proceeded that it has infected the very soul. This insight continues in the next world, where Mr. Zero dallies with Daisy, and, as the *Freeman* observed, "his prosaic conventional soul asserts itself against the passionate glow of life, which he could endure only by labeling it immoral."

Of the specifically expressionistic devices of the play, that marking the moment when Mr. Zero loses his job is typical. Galsworthy,* in a satirical comment that struck home, characterized expressionism as revealing the inside of a situation without showing the outside. When one receives sudden and shocking news, one grows dizzy, the world seems to spin. Mr. Zero is told that he is fired. And at once the part of the stage on which he stands begins rapidly turning, spinning him around and around. Out of this dizzying whirl, he grasps the fatal spike and kills the Boss.

"Examine this play scene by scene, symbol by symbol," said Ludwig Lewisohn in the *Nation* (April 14, 1923). "The structure stands. There are no holes in its roof. It gives you the pleasure of both poetry and science, the warm beauty of life and love, the icy delight of mathematics . . . Here is an American drama with no loose ends or ragged edges or silly last-act compromises, retractions, reconciliations. The work, on its own ground, in its own mood, is honest, finished, sound."

Striking in its production methods, vivid in its moving scenes, strong in its indictment of the deadening effects of routine working and routine thinking, *The Adding Machine* is a symbolic expressionistic drama that strikes home.

The 1923 Guild production omitted one of the eight scenes of the play, brought back by the Phoenix revival of February 9, 1956: with Mr. Zero caged on display as "The North American Murderer." Sam Jaffe played Zero; Margaret Hamilton, his wife; Ann Thomas, Daisy Diana. London (RADA) saw the play October 27, 1956, again at the Gate August 10, 1980, when the *Times* expressed "admiration" for the way Rice's vision has endured.

COCK ROBIN   *Elmer Rice*

Cock Robin, 1927, is as deft, and as unexcited, a mystery thriller as one might find in a blue moon of theatrical murders. Opening in New York January 12, 1928, for a hundred performances, it was a critics' joy and ever since has been the amateurs' delight. Hard-boiled *Variety,* commenting on its "absence of thrills," added "it will go nicely for small stock." The more urbane *Boston Transcript* (December 27, 1927) called it "a smooth play, a mystery play for gentlefolk, possibly the first of the kind."

Elmer Rice is modest about the melodrama. He wrote me: *"Cock Robin* was cooked up by P. L. Barry* and myself, in the course of a voyage to Europe. We were both hard up and thought it would be a good idea to write a play that contained all the sure-fire ingredients of success. (Maybe that is why it did not do well.) Anyhow, we worked out the plot on the boat, separated at Le Havre and never saw each other again until six months later when the play went into rehearsal. The collaborating was done entirely by correspondence, with Phil sitting in Cannes and me moving around through Italy, Austria, Germany, Belgium, France, and God knows where."

The structure of *Cock Robin,* as with most Rice plays, is superb. The play opens in an eighteenth century English grog-shop where, while an anguished wench is held in check, two gentlemen fight a pistol duel. One drops. There are shouts "The Guard!" They start to dash away—and the Landlord stops the proceedings. At this point, we discover that these are amateur theatricals: The Cape Valley Dramatic Society is in dress rehearsal. The "Landlord" is the professional director the group has engaged. During the discussion of the rehearsal, we learn that most of the Cape Valley folk dislike Hancock Robinson ("Cock Robin"), and with reason. Indeed, he has, though married, persuaded young Carlotta Maxwell to sail to Paris with him the day after the performance.

Act Two we watch from behind the scenes. The duel goes on again—and Robinson remains lying on the floor, dead. The remainder of the play carries through the investigation until the revelation of the killer, with a number of neat and novel turns. After twisting and twining to discover how the loaded shell got into the revolver, the cast move the body—and find that Robinson was killed by a knife thrust in the back. The cast itself carries on the inquiry, without the usual smart-aleck or brow-beating detective or buffoon officer of the police. Maria, the assistant director, despite her thick glasses has a "kodak eye"; it is through her observation of seemingly insignificant details that the criminal is finally pinned. But all the company recognize that this has been, if ever, justifiable homicide. No one knows anything. The summoned police knock. Maria says, "I didn't see a thing! How could I, with *my* eyes?" She polishes her glasses, as the door is opened, and the curtain falls.

Audience emotions, while watching *Cock Robin,* are divided between amusement and excitement. The high point of amusement is the speech of welcome by Chairlady Mrs. Montgomery to those that have come to see the Cape Valley players performing for the benefit of the General Hospital. That speech is a comic gem, an uproarious burlesque of the amateur theatricals chairlady. Said Leonard Hall: "Seldom have I heard anything funnier, and seldom have these old ears listened to such howling and bellowing in a playhouse." Percy Hammond recorded that Robert Benchley laughed so heartily those around thought he must be a claque, and added: "Nothing more quietly cheerful in the way of minor satire is on sale in the Times Square canteens."

Smiles soon give way to shivers as death strikes and suspicion stalks from the wings. The development, however is a deftly woven argument, progressing through the pressing of logical points, not gun points, with frequent surprise. A program note requested that no one reveal the actual criminal;

recent re-reading, however showed that the play is tense even when the ending is known. As the *London Times* observed (February 25, 1933), "The game is played fairly and with a quite brilliant sense of the theatrical possibilities that lie in the reconstruction of a crime."

Neither Rice nor Barry has often written with a collaborator. This collaboration, born of the accident of an ocean voyage together, produced one of our suavest and most amusing mystery plays.

STREET SCENE   *Elmer Rice*

Broadway producers were initially quite indifferent to the lure of this play. "It was peddled around for over a year," Rice wrote me, "and was turned down by practically every New York producer. . . . Nobody had any confidence in the play. A number of actors turned down parts because they thought it had no chance of success. George Cukor, the only first-class director who could be interested in the play, walked out on it in the middle of casting, so I had to take over the direction myself, though I had never directed a play before. Even after an enthusiastic opening and rave notices, the ticket agencies refused for some time to buy, believing the play had no popular appeal. Brady himself thought the play's appeal was confined to New York, and it took me a whole year to persuade him to send a company to Chicago. He was so skeptical about England that he let the English rights lapse, enabling me to do the play there myself."

The play opened in New York on January 10, 1929; it ran for 601 performances and won the 1929 Pulitzer Prize. It has been played wherever English is spoken; also in Argentina, Denmark, France, Germany, Greece, Holland, Hungary, Japan, Mexico, Norway, Palestine, Poland, Spain, and Sweden. While it is a difficult play for a small theatre to present, it is widely popular as the fullest dramatic capture of the teeming life of the tenement folk of a great city. As the *Montreal Herald* declared (October 28, 1930): "Last night we saw the soul of a city, and its body too; felt its mad, despairing lusts, its ruthlessness, its dumb good-heartedness; its gentle hypocrisies and, withal, its inherent dignity . . . life raw and unlovely, without illusion, pretense, or convention. Realism and force there are to this work of Elmer Rice, and a muscularity of Gargantuan proportions."

The scene of the play is the front of a cheap apartment house, its windows wide open, for the action occurs on a hot night and day in June. The plot is simple and melodramatic: Frank Maurrant discovers his wife in the arms of the milkman; he kills them both, runs away, and is caught by the police. Interest, however, lies less in this than in the swarming folk around, whose diverse characters and interests jostle and intertwine up the stairs and on the flagstones of the city. Again and again in reviews recur the words "a slice of life"; "the sidewalks of New York." The *New York Post* (January 19, 1929) admiringly exclaimed: "Along comes a man who merely sits on a New York front stoop for a few hours and tells us about it." The *World* (January 14) declared: "With your first shadowy glimpse he gives you the sights and noises of a shabby New York thoroughfare in mid-summer, dominated by a chipped and dusty brownstone dwelling, still bearing the remnants of a sturdy dignity through the pathos of the better days it has known." Suggested by an actual house on New York's 65th Street, wherein dwell Swedes, English, Italians, Negroes, and Germans, all is authentic, even to the garbage can on the stone sidewalk outside the basement rail.

There is more than the street, however, to the play. Brooks Atkinson probed: "What distinguishes *Street Scene* from a host of synthetic forerunners is Mr. Rice's remarkable sense of character. Here are not merely the automatons of the giddy city streets but the people—the intellectual Jew who runs on endlessly about the capitalistic classes, the Italian musician who dreams of the flowery land from which he came, the office girl who wants to move out to Queens, the pleasant woman who is quietly sacrificing her life to a sick mother, the ruffian taxi driver, the flirt, the school-teacher, all brought into focus with telling stories of character portrayal. . . . Mr. Rice's flowing, somewhat sprawling drama catches the primitive facts of child-birth on the third story, the chicken for soup, the petting after dark, the common hatred of the Jew—race prejudices, class morality, jolly, broad humor, sympathies, jealousies. Again, he expresses no point of view about the matters. For those who are interested it is sufficient that he has done his portrait with remarkable artistic integrity." Maurrant tells Kaplan to go back where he came from. "Listen," said the *Boston Transcript* (May 6, 1929), "to Maurrant and Jones pummeling everything outside their experience of life and their own courses of conduct as so much Bolshevism, while Maurrant's implement of rectitude is a smoking pistol and the Jones children go cheerfully to the devil in their own way." Out of these many vignettes of city life, the wistful love of young Sam Kaplan and Rose Maurrant as well as the more desperate clutch after happiness of Rose's mother, the play gathers its power.

In 1929 Deems Taylor wanted Rice to write the book for an opera based on *Street Scene*; Rice refused, thinking the play might make a musical almost without change. It did, coming to the stage January 9, 1947, with music by Kurt Weill and lyrics by Langston Hughes. For the musical, the composer felt that *Street Scene* was admirably constructed, "very much like Greek tragedy, with tight unity of time and space, and the inescapability of fate." *Time* (January 20, 1947) called the new version "more folk opera than musical"; *PM* called it "Broadway's first real opera." There are spoken dialogue, recitative at tense moments, and song—solo, duet, quartet, wide chorus. The songs are not just dragged in by the chorus, as in many musicals; they are integrated with the story. The musical nevertheless throws more emphasis upon the melodrama, less fully captures the spirit of the street or reveals the characters of those that walk it through their destiny. The original remains the better play and the finest dramatic capture of the dust and dreams, the degradation and the dignity, the sham and shame and striving honesty and urging simple nobility of the many folk whose ways make up the street scene of the city.

The play was revived at the London Globe, 1971; by ACT February 4, 1975; also OffOffBway (Quaigh) July 8, 1975. The Rice-Weill musical has entered into light opera repertory, as by the New York City Opera in 1960, also 1978; the New York Lincoln Center (State), 1966; ELT, January 7, 1982. It was acclaimed at its London premiere at the Royal Academy of Music, June 7, 1983, echoing Alexander Woollcott's earlier words: "The curtain falls—slowly, reluctantly—on a living and beautiful play."

SEE NAPLES AND DIE   *Elmer Rice*

Elmer Rice's *See Naples and Die,* 1929, is a comedy of vapid society folk on a crowded terrace overlooking a street in Naples, a bubbling delight of craftsmanship and lively caricature. The *New York Telegram,* September 27, 1929, called it "a satirical high farce." Several critics contrasted the new play with Rice's *Street Scene,* * then playing to crowded houses across Forty-eighth Street. Others were led to feel, as Barrett H. Clark put it, that the author "intended to prove that he was not merely a social reformer." More probably Elmer Rice, recovering from an illness, felt in the mood for a frolic. He called the play "the story of the incredible happenings that befall extraordinary people." The story may be incredible, but it is also most enjoyable.

An American heiress, Nanette Dodge, has married a Russian prince, Ivan Kosoff, to save her sister from his blackmail. Immediately after the wedding, she ran away to Naples, whither the Prince and her American admirer, Charlie Carroll, follow her.

On the hotel terrace where the action occurs, several innocents abroad add humor, as several Europeans add color, in the play's movement. "Mrs. Evans from Ohio" is a delightful caricature of the fussy and self-important leader of the small town social group, quite unaware what a ridiculous figure she is cutting. The various servants might make material for a Neapolitan "street scene." The Russian prince is a genuinely comic portrait, too aimlessly mellow to be held seriously as a villain, "one of Mr. Rice's vague and irreverent memories," said the *London Times* March 23, 1932) "of the melancholy, shiftless, childish characters of Russian literature."

Throughout the play, two chess players sit silently at a corner table. So long do they sit motionless that it becomes a moment of high dramatic tension when, finally, one of them moves a piece. Toward the end of the play, loud shot-like sounds are heard from the street, but we are reassured: it is not a vendetta; it is just one of those cross-country automobile races that shoot through the cities of Europe. As one automobile roars by, the Rumanian General Skulany, totalitarian dictator, appears on a balcony near the terrace. The two chess players rise and fire at the General. He falls dead. Prince Ivan, Nan's husband, in the line of fire, falls dead too. And as soon as Charlie and Nan can picture their future together (and the Neapolitan guardsman slips into the bedroom after the pretty maid), the curtain falls.

This engaging comedy opened in New York September 26, 1929, with Claudette Colbert as Nan, Pedro de Cordoba as Ivan, in London March 22, 1932, with Olive Blakeney and Antony Holles. It was a great hit in England; London saw it again in 1936, 1937, and 1938. The *London Times* declared that Rice "writes extravaganza with a very supple wrist, never failing to give a fresh turn to his mockery just when it threatens to degenerate into buffoonery . . . a persistent crackle of wisecracks, nearly all of which have a fine cutting edge."

The extravagant aspect of the play was stressed in a University of California performance, which had a prompter seated in the audience, the actors entering down the aisles, and other devices to increase the delightful artificiality of Americans on tour in a prewar Europe. And within the characters, as behind the incidents, we sense the spiritual hollowness, the constant quest of gaiety hiding from heartbreak, that let the world drift toward another war.

THE LEFT BANK   *Elmer Rice*

In comic guise a serious study of Americans abroad, *The Left Bank*, 1931, with Elmer Rice's continuing craftsmanship to sustain audience interest, examines the attitudes and the problems of the American expatriate in Paris.

Between the exodus of the White Russians and the first blarings of Hitler, hosts of American "intelligentsia," oppressed by the Philistinism they thought too rampant in their land, fled to the Parnassian hills of Paris, and the "freedom" of the artist. Rice lets us observe the life there as two American couples find it. John and Claire Shelby (played by Horace Braham and Katherine Alexander) live on the Left Bank with their child in a boarding shcool. Waldo and Susie Lynde (Donald MacDonald and Millicent Green) are on their first visit to Europe. Neatly and dramatically, through these crossing lives, the problems of intellectual freedom, modern education, adult responsibility, and the amenities of monogamy are examined, until opposed interests tear the couples asunder. Claire and Waldo return to the United States, leaving the two seekers for freedom imprisoned in their own vacuity.

Opening in New York October 5, 1931, the play ran for 244 performances. George Jean Nathan called it "real in its characters, real in its dialogue, and consistently intelligent." Brooks Atkinson called it Rice's "maturest play . . . the shrewdest contribution to the literature of the American Emigré in Paris . . . Rice has an uncanny ear for dialogue, and he enjoys discussing literate topics . . . argues the case for intellectual sincerity with tolerance, with humor, and with generous understanding." Arthur Ruhl, in the *Herald Tribune,* called *The Left Bank* a better play than *Street Scene.* *

London, in 1933, was not receptive to the play. The *Times* September 27, 1933) gravely shook its head, remarking that the play contains "a Fourteenth of July [Bastille Day] celebration to enable Mr Rice to show how sadly gay his countrymen may become in mass, in exile, and in drink." Wilella Waldorf, in the *New York Post,* December 7, 1933, explained this cool reception: "The British don't care a whit how Americans carry on in Paris so long as they stay across the Channel." W. A. Darlington in the *London Telegraph* confirmed her point: "To decent Americans, it must be a matter of great concern that Americans of no account flock to Paris and there make a craving for culture an excuse for the practice of promiscuity. But the problem seems to me to concern Americans, and Americans only." The basic drive of the characters, however, is more universal.

The play is civilized theatre, free from such melodramatic fireworks as give plot to *Street Scene.* * It is often richly amusing, but it is also provocative of thought, thought about individuals and their problems of interrelationship, but also thought about the individual's relationship to his native land. Rice recognizes that it is hard to be fruitful, save where one has roots; just as there are unlikely to be spiritual riches, save where there is love. These thoughts find clear and vigorous expression through the wonder and resolution that give dramatic drive to *The Left Bank.*

DREAM GIRL   *Elmer Rice*

Brief mention should be made of the play Elmer Rice wrote for Betty Field, then his wife, a tongue-in-cheek parody of the usual "success" star play. It opened at the New York Coronet December 14, 1945, for 348 performances. It was played at Youngstown, Ohio, April 7, 1961, and in Cleveland December 6, 1962.

Most of *Dream Girl* displays the daydreams of Georgina Allerton, a beautiful lady who runs a bookshop at a loss. She dreams that she goes to Mexico with a publisher who "knows the ropes," but—is that a lady's sometime thought?—ends as a streetwalker. In a more attractive reverie, she is at the theatre when the actress playing Portia is stricken; rising from her seat, Georgina steps forward and consummately completes the performance. She ends by marrying a book reviewer who attains the post of sports reporter.

Lewis Nichols in the *Times* December 15, 1945, stated: "Part fantasy, part farce, *Dream Girl* is always human and always pleasant."

From Detroit to New York November 13, 1965, came Julie Harris in her first musical, *Skyscraper,* a version of *Dream Girl,* for 227 performances; book by Peter Stone, music by Jimmy Van Heusen, lyrics by Sammy Cahn. The girl now lives and sells antiques in a brownstone house she tries not to sell to a skyscraper builder. The play is a mixture of her dreams and her social-mindedness, with dynamic choreography by Michael Kidd around the scaffolding rising next door. On the play's pre-Broadway tour the *Detroit News,* September 15, 1965, said the book had "both chic and cheek."

When I spoke to Elmer Rice about his parodic intention, he lamented that most took it seriously. Critics praised *Dream Girl,* but the device of travesty found less public favor than Rice's direct comedies and dramas. Even played straight, it remains good fun.

NOT FOR CHILDREN   *Elmer Rice*

The cool reception of three of Rice's plays turned his attention upon the problems of the theatre; and in *Not for Children* we have an extravaganza of dramatic criticism in the form of a play. At times skylarking, at times dealing body blows with the power of Joe Louis, at times looking innocently from an orchestra chair to ask what the shooting's for, Elmer Rice managed to put a deft finger upon almost every weakness in the body dramatic—and to make the audience smile as it gulps the dose.

It seems that a producer has bought a play he doesn't understand. He hires Prudence, a lecturer on the drama, and Ambrose Atwater, professor of applied psychology, to explain. Their discussion precedes, then interrupts, the play; at times, they become part of it. In the play, a character is writing a play; this second drama also gets into the action. The players exchange roles; they clamber over the footlights and tangle the audience in the movement. In one of the plays a husband and wife, breakfasting beside a large bed, are contemplating divorce. With the suggestion of the commentators that they, too, go to bed, the play seems to end. Then Rice, in a slanting attack on the conventional curtain, wonders what would happen if the love climaxes were continued beyond the point at which the curtain discreetly drops. Like as not we'd see the couple in a violent quarrel—but the British censor apparently had other thoughts, for he forbade public performance of *Not for Children.*

The world premiere was therefore given by the Stage Society, London, November 24, 1935, with Jack Minster and Martita Hunt as the two commentators. After the play, the Society held a discussion, led by John Drinkwater and Clemence Dane. They felt the play not only a satire on the theatre, but through the lens of the theatre a satire on contemporary life.

GREEN GROW THE LILACS   *Lynn Riggs*

One of the liveliest of American folk plays is *Green Grow the Lilacs,* 1930, by Lynn Riggs (American, 1899-1954), a tale of Indian Territory in 1900, seven years before it became the State of Oklahoma. The play is, said the

New York Times (March 1, 1931), "a gusty gambol of the great open spaces . . . with a contingent of hell-for-leather cowboys, who would just as soon shoot you as look at you."

In the midst of all the gaiety and lusty youthfulness coils a picture of repressed perversion. Curley McClain, a care-free bronco-buster and sweet-singing cowboy, loves Aunt Ella Murphey's lovely niece Laurey Williams. To tease Curley, Laura encourages the farm-hand Jeeter Fry, who hides his lust in his room in the Williams' smoke house. Laura lets Jeeter take her to the dance at Old Man Peck's, but Curley takes her away and marries her. At the shivaree (serenading and roughhouse of the wedding party), Curley and Laurey are gaily taken by the revelers and pitched on top of a haystack. The brooding and jealous Fry sets fire to the haystack. When this attempt is foiled, he rushes upon Curley; in the ensuing fight, Fry falls upon his own knife and is killed. Cowboy Curley decides to become a farmer and do his share in the growth of the land.

Riggs called his play "a ballad in dramatic form," and song has a part in it—the strumming of a guitar with folk songs and border ballads. The title itself is from a frontier folk song. The play opened in Boston December 8, 1930, and in New York, January 26, 1931, with Helen Westley, June Walker, and Franchot Tone in his first outstanding part. England saw the play in 1935. It has been popular throughout the United States; Burgess Meredith played in it in the summer of 1939.

The press accepted the drama's authentic folk capture. Brooks Atkinson found it "full of sunshine and the tingle of the open air . . . life drips from every fibre of its narrative." John Mason Brown said that it "gives, as few of our plays have succeeded in doing, a refreshing and authentic sense of having sprung from the earth and belonging to it." It is at once real and quaint, the revivification of a vanished epoch of American growth. Thus the *Cleveland Press* (December 4, 1941) called the play "a series of old-fashioned stereopticon views, animated." Animated is a good word for the colorful exuberance of the play.

In large theatrical centers, *Green Grow The Lilacs* is best known in its musical transformation into *Oklahoma!*, book and lyrics by Oscar Hammerstein II, music by Richard Rodgers, and dances by Agnes De Mille. *Oklahoma!* delays the story seven years so that it can end with Indian Territory's becoming the state.

The chief attraction of *Oklahoma!*, however, is its use of song and dance, by which it simply and beautifully captures the surge and youthfulness and joy of growing America. Instead of the conventional opening chorus, the play begins with Aunt Ella alone on the stage, while Curley, approaching from the distance, sings "Oh what a beautiful morning!" The choral dances, instead of swinging and swaying hips in the conventional musical comedy style, surge and romp in gay folk rhythms—the modern dance fused with the folk dance in vivid theatrical patterns—and a new era in musical comedy was born.

The story behind the production of *Oklahoma!* shows that, in the theatre, Anguish Avenue abuts on Ecstasy Street. The Theatre Guild, after a series of failures, had found itself forced to lease its fine Guild Theatre for radio. Oscar Hammerstein II had had no success in a dozen years; Richard Rodgers had just separated from his successful lyricist Lorenz Hart. Because of such conditions, the musical version of *Green Grow The Lilacs* had trouble finding backers. It opened (as *Away We Go*) in New Haven, then moved to Boston; on March 31, 1945, it came to New York as *Oklahoma!* and stayed for 2,248 performances.

Oklahoma! was a hit in London, too, opening at Drury Lane on April 30, 1947, for a run of 1,548 performances. It "has shaken London up," said Harold Hobson, "more than anything that has hit it since the first flying bomb. . . . It is almost impossible to imagine anything better in its own particular way than *Oklahoma!*" The success of the play was repeated in many parts of the world; in Johannesburg, South Africa, the annual opera season was canceled, to keep the theatre for *Oklahoma!*

Oklahoma! is a gayer and a livelier play than *Green Grow The Lilacs,* managing to convert even the suggestions of perversity into good-humored fun. As a musical, especially in the fresh form of its opening and the ingenious blend of its dancing forms, *Oklahoma!* has been a challenge to later musical comedies. For college and community theatres, however, *Green Grow The Lilacs* remains a sparkling and stimulating folk drama of western frontier days.

CASTE   *Thomas William Robertson*

Eldest of the 22 children of an English actor (whose youngest daughter became the actress Dame Madge Kendal), Thomas William Robertson (1829-1871) was a pioneer in the growth of the modern realistic drama. In a succession of plays produced by the actor-manager Squire Bancroft at the Prince of Wales Theatre in London, Robertson established the cup-and-saucer drama: plays of a conventional social code, with natural dialogue and ordinary folk in domestic settings. Within the comedy, these folk are faced with a serious situation, as in the later, more radical, social problem play. In particular, as the *Baltimore Sun* (July 7, 1932) expressed the widely recognized fact, "the original ancestors of a good many present-day characters and culminations" are contained in *Caste.*

In the play, despite the objection of his haughty mother, the Marquise de Saint-Maur, the Honorable George D'Alroy marries the ballet-girl Esther Eccles. George, a Dragoon, is sent to India to help quell the Mutiny; rumor of his death widens the chasm between his wife and his mother; but he returns to Esther and their child, and Esther's pluck and firm dignity and persisting love at length win her mother-in-law's affections.

There is considerable humor in the play, rising especially from the contrast between George's haughty friends and family and Esther's frowzy relatives. Her sister Polly, engaged to a journeyman gas-fitter, is, as Charles Darnton (April 27, 1910) called her "a vulgar, good-hearted, lively little creature," while the shabby old fraud their father, a loud, tipsy fellow, searching deep in his pockets in the hope that some one will offer him tobacco, "fills his pipe with comedy." The *New York Dramatic Mirror* (April 29, 1910) indeed, went so far as to say that, "next to Falstaff, old Eccles is probably the most humorous character in English comedy." The *New York Times* earlier (January 24, 1897) remarked that *Caste* is a model of construction: "It could be acted intelligently from beginning to end without a spoken word."

Produced in London in April 1867, the play was announced in New York, by Lester Wallack, for September 2 of the same year. To his surprise, the play opened at the Broadway Theatre on August 5, with Mr. and Mrs. William J. Florence as George and Polly. Wallack opened in Brooklyn and went to court, to discover that Florence had memorized the whole play from the London production, without making a single note, and could not be restrained by law.

The play has had many revivals. Often produced in London before the end of the nineteenth century, in 1867, 1871, 1879, 1889, it attained a hundred or more performances. It was revived at the Old Vic in 1929. The New York revival of 1910 starred Marie Tempest and Elsie Ferguson. Bit by bit, however, the reviews grew less enthusiastic, until in London in 1925 the *New Statesman* (August 8) declared: "*Caste* has no body to it. It has neither psychology nor wit, the humor is crude, the sentiment obvious, the language stilted and platitudinous. . . . Yet Robertson was the best English playwright of his age." *Caste* had suffered the fate of all pioneers: later comers had traveled farther along the trail it blazed. It remains as a landmark, and the earliest of the realistic dramas that still can hold the stage.

At its first production, *Caste* established a new theatrical practice, being the first evening devoted to a single drama, without the thitherto usual comic interlude or afterpiece.

A London revival December 3, 1970, ended with the reunion embrace, doing away with the usual and often boring denouement, the old "Victorian family tidy-up"—another welcome innovation. A September 9, 1972, revival was still "combining satire with simple human affection." Eccles, reminding some of Falstaff, may have been in Shaw's background when he created Doolittle of the "undeserving poor" in *Pygmalion*.*

DANTON   *Romain Rolland*

Less episodic, less tumultuous, than Büchner's *Danton's Death** on the same theme, *Danton,* by Romain Rolland (French, 1866-1949, drives with direct and concentrated force through the days of the French Revolution in March and April 1794.

The play has been a great success whenever played; as directed by Max Reinhardt in Berlin, March 1920, with a cast of a thousand, a *succès fou.* Paris saw the play December 29, 1900; England (first at Leeds, November 14), 1927. Reinhardt, said the *Boston Transcript* (April 1, 1920) "has made the public take part in the Revolution, lose its natural equilibrium, and cheer."

There are minor illuminating episodes and figures in the drama: Lucille, the frantic wife of Camille Desmoulins; Eleonore, the platonic admirer of Robespierre; the Widow Duplay, Robespierre's matter-of-fact landlady, who complains of matters again recently pertinent, the lack of coal and butter, the standing long in line to receive—two eggs. But the tremendous movement of the play comes in the last act, the trial of the men whom Robespierre has doomed. On the one hand, said the *Transcript,* "is Robespierre, the man of duty and of virtue, who speaks of revolutionary discipline just as Kerensky spoke of it and as the moderate leaders in Germany have spoken of it, who demands the personal sacrifice of every one for the good of all, of personal liberty for the freedom of the people; and on the other, Danton, the passionate partisan, the all-too-human, live-and-let-live friend of the people, the untamed lion, hard to rouse but terrible in his wrath. The conflict between these two makes the drama. Then there are Desmoulins the literary agitator, weak, spoiled, and effeminate, but of a poisonous tongue and pen; St.-Just, the fanatical avenging angel of the Revolution; the blustering General Westermann, and the cynical Hérault de Séchelles, a charming remnant of the *ancien regime,* who sees more clearly than all."

At the trial, after Desmoulins' outburst, Danton, rising to the charge that he has conspired against liberty, cries "Liberty is here!" and strikes his heart. He demands that his accusers face him; and the President of the Tribunal grows alarmed as the people side with Danton and shout in his favor. "The thunder of the populace outside," said the *New York Post* (July 15, 1920), "the hurly-burly, threats, and breaking of furniture within, the whole popular hysteria, with the stentorian voice of Danton above it, shake one's very marrow." The presiding judge sends Danton's demand to the Convention.

The mob has quieted. The Convention refuses the demand; the judge orders the noisy prisoners removed before the trial proceeds. The resurgent mob is checked by the guards, the timely arrival of the formidable St.-Just, and the welcome announcement that a distribution of wood and flour is being made at the docks. The howling Desmoulins is dragged out; Danton walks calmly to his doom. Rolland makes explicit his thoughts at the play's close through the words of Robespierre's friends, left in the courtroom, triumphant—till their turn shall come.

The psychology not only of the French Revolution but of revolution—the various motives that animate the leaders, the fickle surge and baying of the mob—quickens with surging power the dramatic drive of *Danton,* to the inevitable doom of death out of which new and—we can hope—better living will rise.

As a German critic remembered the Reinhardt production, which used 1,000 actors before a crowd of 5,000: "We didn't know where the audience commenced. . . . It was not acted, it was a real revolt, a cry for humanity and freedom . . . I was a dramatic critic in Paris for seven years; I was often in London; nowhere have I seen anything to equal it."

DR. KNOCK   *Jules Romains*

Jules Romains (Louis Farigoule, French, 1885-1972) has written in two distinct veins. As a serious artist, he inaugurated the school of unanimism, which states that the unifying elements in men, in social groups, and in nature, are more basic than the individual diversities.

Quite distinct from the unanimist works are the several satiric farces, beginning with *Knock, or The Triumph of Medicine,* 1923 (translated by Granville Barker,* 1925, as *Dr. Knock*) that made Romains the outstanding comic playwright of the period. This most penetrating of his studies of human frailty and human folly, is the liveliest and most widely known of Romains' plays.

The first scene shows the dilapidated automobile of old Dr. Paraplaid, who is leaving the small town of St. Maurice because it is too healthy. His successor, Dr. Knock, proceeds like a sort of inverted Coué to build up disease. Setting up ominous charts and maps of the human system, he offers the bait of free consultation; and those that crowd in, hale and hearty, drop out with every type of symptom and complaint. The local hotel is converted into a hospital; sanatoriums crop up on every corner; and the once tiny village grows into a vast health resort.

The figure of Dr. Knock is an imposing one. He marches through the play, said the *Boston Transcript* (May 3, 1928) "in wider and wider swath. He is the anxious and advising friend; the discovering and urgent physician; the prince and prophet of medicine's new triumph up and down St. Maurice. He pervades the play and yet crowds not one of the others into the corner. There they are—crier, school-master, chemist, townsfolk and countryfolk, none too far from human semblance and the workings of human nature, yet each in place in the scheme of satirical extravaganza. . . . Finally, observe in the little world a microcosm of the larger world beyond—ready to believe what it is told to believe; taking every missioner, political, social, artistic, scientific, commercial, at his own value, so long as he is urgent enough; catching at everything proffered to its ignorance, dread, credulity, or faith. The pity of it—as it is easy to say—but also the humor of it!"

Several reviewers, as the *London Era* (May 19, 1926), called Dr. Knock "a magnificent charlatan . . ." Yet Dr. Knock is more than a charlatan. He is a man with a mission: to convince men of their ailments. His motto is: The healthy are those that do not know they are ill.

At the close of the play, providing an amusing finish, Dr. Paraplaid, returning for his first quarterly check, himself falls victim to Dr. Knock's calm suggestion, and with a bottle of tablets quakes over an imaginary complaint. To his predecessor, Dr. Knock points out the advantages—not to himself, but to the community—of his devices and methods. Not only does it do folk no harm to stay in bed for a time, but they actually relish it. Amid the paraphernalia, the thrice-a-day thermometers, night lights, cautionary lectures, the townsfolk are for the first time really enjoying themselves, and living intensely. Not only is the doctor the most popular man (and one of the richest) around, but the whole countryside is thriving as never before. He is their benefactor, their prophet, their saviour. They kiss the hand that coddles them.

Produced in France by Louis Jouvet, the play ran for four years. It was presented in London April 27, 1926; again December 6, 1928. New York saw it opening February 23, 1928. It was tried again, at Westport, Connecticut, in 1936, in a romanticized version by Laurence Langner and Armina Marshall. In this, the nurse becomes enamoured of the doctor, is repelled when she comes to the conclusion that he is a quack, and returns to his embraces when she recognizes how much well-being (and how much wealth) he has produced. "These are bold and spinning scenes of delicious satire," said the *New York Times* (July 14, 1936), "mixed neatly with a sauce of running humor that keeps the play in a lilting vein." The whole is, said Robert Garland, "a neatly nasty nose-thumbing at the ultramodern medico, his diets, his lamps, his paying inability to let well enough alone." The 1936 version also Americanized the locale and the townsfolk, with, as Garland listed them, "a motley and amusing parade of New York caricatures: an undertaker, a druggist, a miser, a manufacturer, a spinster, a widow, and a couple of local roughnecks."

Dr. Knock is an amusing lesson in the fine art of creating something out of nothing but human faiths and human fears. Psychology and satire romp through this superb dramatic picture of a master salesman, and the credulous folk who succumb to his double-edged sales talk.

Dr. Knock has been frequently revived, especially in France. In 1950 it was performed by the doctors at Kings Park State Hospital, Long Island. Of a London October 21, 1973, production (Meadow Players), directed by Minos Volanakis, the *Observer* said that "Alfred Burke enacted a competent sharper where the text demanded a great manic rogue." The audience laughs at the sharper and feels for the public and the rogue.

PINS AND NEEDLES, ETC.   *Harold Rome, etc.*

The garment industry is so closely identified with New York that it was inevitable that its activities would find their way into the theatre. Its first lively expression came in dramatizations of the Potash and Perlmutter stories of Montague Glass, a feature of the *Saturday Evening Post*. When the play *Potash and Perlmutter* opened at the George M. Cohan Theatre, August 16, 1913, no author's name was on the program; the expert hand of Cohan was suspected, as well as that of Charles Klein. Hugh Ford was also suggested.

The play was at once popular, destined, said the *Mirror,* August 16, 1913, "to take its place with the stage classics of the day . . . it travesties in an enjoyable manner a phase of contemporary life." The *Dramatic News* called it "the most laughable play on record . . . three hours of solid fun . . . with spontaneous warmth and extraordinary dexterity."

The activities take place in the workrooms of a shop in the garment district, with women at the sewing machines, and a notable parade of models. While there is a plot—of a refugee wanted in Russia for murder, whose forfeited bail bond of $20,000 totters the firm toward bankruptcy until the Russian is cleared, to marry Potash's daughter, while Perlmutter marries the designer from Paris—the play centers on the humor rising from the bickerings, reconciliations, and petty intrigues involved in the dealing on small margins with small capital. "$17.85 expense account for one meal?" (This is 1913.) "He must have dined on gold fish." "$22 for a sleeping car, and he was recommended as a wide-awake salesman!"

Abe Potash was played by Barney Bernard; Mawruss Perlmutter by Alexander Carr. Mrs. Potash, with a mania for pinochle, was in the deft hands of Elita Proctor Otis; beautiful Louise Dresser came over from vaudeville to the role of Ruth Snyder, the designer from Paris. The play was soon shown in all the large cities of the United States, on and on, with Robert Leonard touring in it from 1914 to 1923. Beginning March 1914, London laughed through 1915.

In spring 1916 to the New York Lyric came *Potash and Perlmutter in Society,* by Montague Glass and Roy Cooper Megrue; it came to London in September of that year, and was revived at the New York Park April 5, 1935. On August 31, 1926, *Potash and Perlmutter Detectives; or, Poisoned by Pictures* by Montague Glass and Jules Eckert (Goodman) came to the New York Ritz. The laughter was so continuous that the audience missed some of the lines. The names Potash and Perlmutter are still remembered in the (once mainly Jewish) garment district of New York.

For the weaving of one hit the workers themselves, members of the ILGWU, the International Ladies Garment Workers Union, went on stage. The actors' regular jobs were listed on the program: buttons and novelty, underwear, cutters, pressers, knitters, and more. The play was *Pins and Needles,* with music and lyrics mainly by Harold J. Rome, sketches by Arthur Arent, Marc Blitzstein, Emanual Eisenberg, Rome, Charles Friedman, and David Gregor. It opened November 27, 1937, at Labor Stage (Princess Theatre) and ran to high acclaim for 1,108 performances. Although the tone was liberal—"Sing Us a Song of Social Significance"—its first aim was entertainment, with propaganda occasionally slipped in. "It can laugh as merrily at itself as at its foes," wrote Richard Watts, Jr., in the *Herald-Tribune* on December 13, 1937, expressing the general critical opinion, "and that is a quality both disarming and persuasive."

Included were a perceptive and hilarious burlesque of Brecht's *Mother Courage**; "The Little Red School House," which "makes sharp and merciless fun of those serious and professionally radical dramas the Theatre Union used to put on" (Watts); and "Four Little Angels of Peace," a slapstick caricature of Mussolini, Hitler, Anthony Eden, and a gentleman of Japan. Rube Goldberg and Karl Marx were conjoined in a sexy lyric. Other songs included "Doin' the Reactionary" and "One Big Union for Two," a "hit" number with the women brandishing rolling pins.

A "second edition" in April 1939—the play had moved to the Windsor Theatre—added what the *Times* (April 23, 1939) called "a masterpiece of burlesque" (after *The Hot Mikado* and *The Swing Mikado* had been popular on Broadway): *The Red Mikado,* with Gilbert and Sullivan picketing with "Unfair" signs; followed by a "Lesson in Etiquette" with a society lady protesting, "It isn't cricket to picket."

Songs from *Pins and Needles* were sung at the Manhattan Theatre Club February 26, 1976. The play was revived, updated by Joe Schrank, June 1967 in the first Roundabout season, and by Roundabout again in the play's fortieth anniversary year, May 30, 1978. [Note that there was an earlier *Pins and Needles,* "a revue with points" mainly by Albert de Courville, with Wal Pink and Edgar Wallace, presented briefly at the London Gaiety in 1921, at the New York Shubert in 1922, with a detective skit, a "Tropical Fantasy," and a large "Vanity Bag." Songs included "Love Spans the World," "The Piccadilly Walk," "Off We Go," "All Pull Together." On a program at the Lincoln Center, New York Theatre Collection someone wrote: "Very ordinary and vulgar."] The ILGWU *Pins and Needles* was called by the *Washington News:* "unequivocally one of the brightest developments of the modern theatre." Eleanor Roosevelt mildly wrote: "No one could be disappointed by this entertainment."

Less bouncy but more substantial in its picture of garment district ways is *The Fifth Season* of Sylvia Regan (b. 1908), which presents the "ups and downs, gags and gimmicks" in the fitting room and office of Goodwin, Pincus, a struggling firm on lower Seventh Avenue, New York. They are suffering the effects of the garment trade's "fifth season": spring, summer, fall, winter—and slack.

Again we have a picture, less farcical than *Potash and Perlmutter* but richly comical, of a firm's financial concerns, complicated by the weekend that married Benny Goodwin spends with a model. As John McClain (in the *Journal-American,* January 24, 1953) puts it: "With the creditors closing in, one of the models who has her eye on Benny, the attractive 'front' for the firm, steers a rich buyer into the premises. This saves the life of the business, but leads to no end of other difficulties, mostly domestic, and eventuates in a romance for Pincus. This is a perfectly practical structure, and Miss Regan has provided many resoundingly funny situations and lines which have lost none of their lustre through the direction of Gregory Ratoff." "It moves with its own gay and touching rhythms" said William Hawkins in the *World-Telegram.* "Some of the sexiest models in the dress business not only parade about, flaunting their Marilyn Monroes, but make their changes in full view of the audience, a most instructive and unusual view of this aspect of the dress business." Robert Coleman in the *Mirror* called it "a hit filled with laughs. . . . It boosts heart and hilarity."

Critical opinion of the play was divided. The white-collar *Herald-Tribune* and the *Times* sniffed at the play, although Brooks Atkinson declared that "some of *The Fifth Season* is uplifting in an off-hand way." It opened at the New York Cort January 23, 1953, and ran for 657 performances, the longest run at the Cort since Laurette Taylor in *Peg o' My Heart,* opening the new theatre in 1912, attained 692 performances. *The Fifth Season* was shown around the country for the next dozen years (New Haven December 25, 1952, then Philadelphia, before New York), including 1954, Los Angeles; 1956, Milwaukee; 1960, New Orleans; 1967, New Milford, Conn. After six weeks in Houston in 1981, it went for a 1982 tour in Canada.

The slowest time in the theatre was for many years the week before Christmas; actors' contracts used to make concessions for that week; and during the week before Christmas at the Chicago Erlanger, 1956, stage manager Carl Benson posted some verses:

> *The time has come upon us all*
> *When BO grosses start to fall,*
> *When SRO is much too rare*
> *And should-be yocks receive a stare . . .*   *(4 more verses, then:)*
> *So don't lose heart—you know the reason:*
> *We're going through our own fifth season!*

Joseph Buloff played Maxie Pincus in the three-week tour beginning in Glasgow February 8, 1953 on its way to London. In the New York run, Benny Goodwin was played by Richard Whorf; Maxie Pincus by the Yiddish star Menasha Skulnik, acclaimed by every critic as an outstanding comic actor, here in his first English-speaking role. Brooks Atkinson exclaimed: "There are not many things in life more enjoyable than a melancholy Jewish comedian."

At the New York Second Avenue Eden on October 12, 1975, there opened a musical version of *The Fifth Season,* book by Luba Kadison, music and lyrics by Dick Manning—in English and Yiddish. Joseph Buloff played Pincus; Stan Porter, Goodwin, for the musical's 122 performances. Among the songs, besides the title song, were "Believe in Yourself," "How Did This Happen to Me?," "From Seventh Avenue to Seventh Heaven." The garment trade, with its perennial fifth season, is funny enough without music.

(Sylvia Regan was not new to Yiddish theatre, for which her husband, Abraham Ellstein [1907-1963], along with Jacob Rumshinsky and Sholem Secunda, provided music for the annual productions at the height of the Yiddish theatre, which for several decades at the beginning of the twentieth century had twelve playhouses in New York. Among its stars, besides Skulnik, were Boris Tomashevsky, David Kessler, and the patriarch Jacob P. Adler, whose children Luther and Stella moved over to the English-speaking stage. World classics were played by Maurice Schwartz at the Yiddish Art Theatre, and by German-speaking Rudolph Schildkraut at the Irving Place on East Fifteenth Street. The Yiddish theatre was a lively aspect of the New York scene in the early decades of the century.) The garment district is still a vital part of the city's industry, still a rich source of satire and comedy, although it is no more than a muted background in Arthur Miller's *Death of a Salesman**.

ME AND MY GIRL   *L. Arthur Rose*

There is something perennially amusing in the good-natured misfit, in the worthy but unpolished person shown amidst formal surroundings. Humor and satire may flow side by side from such a situation. The audience is left with the comforting if sentimental reflection that kind hearts are more than coronets. An American comedy on this theme is *Peg O' My Heart**; an English musical comedy, *Me and My Girl,* by L. Arthur Rose (English, b. 1887) and Douglas Furber (b. 1885), with music by Noel Gray. Opening in London on December 16, 1937, with Lupino Lane as the Cockney interloper from Lambeth and George Graves as a somewhat downsliding aristocrat, it ran for 1,646 performances. The June 25, 1941, revival ran for 208 performances; the August 6, 1945, for 304; the December 12, 1949, for 75 performances.

The play presents Snibson, a Cockney bookmaker's tout, arriving to claim an aristocratic seat as Lord Hareford's heir. He brings his girl along; there are contrasted choruses of Cockneys and aristocrats, and in spite of one persnickety "old baronial bean," as the *London Observer* (December 19, 1937) sedately observed, "the clash of class is satisfactorily solved."

Me and My Girl won universal praise. The *Tatler* (August 17, 1938) called it "one of the best musical low comedies ever invented. . . . The book is naive but comic and full-bodied; the gags are vulgar but funny; and the tunes are as catching as the common cold." "Only a very superior person indeed," said the *London Times* (December 19, 1937), "could survey this bold spectacle without quickly thawing into a smile. It is the theatrical equivalent of those picture postcards which, when in the holiday mood, we send from the seaside to disturb our sedate acquaintances. The story is the perennially entertaining one of the urchin who suddenly finds himself among hoity-toity relations, and it is zestfully unfolded amid scenes loaded with the insignia of aristocracy."

The two main roles receive equal acclaim. "Mr. Graves," declared the *Sketch* (January 29, 1937) "endears us to the blood that runs blue, though the nose is red. He may be said in this piece to represent the aristocracy on its mellower side. There are severer faces. There are those who would tame Mr. Snibson and improve his manners. They gloriously fail." As the Cockney Snibson, Lupino Lane tumbles and somersaults downstairs in velvet and ermine. He sucks a Countess's cocktail through a straw. Asked "Will you help the Old Ladies Home?" Snibson inquires: "Have they got far to go?" He is continually putting his foot in his mouth. "Fortunately, bless the human heart" said James Agate in the *Times* (August 19, 1945) "there are some 'incongruities and fantastications' which are, so to speak, born funny."

The music made some of the critics praise Sullivan. Among the sprightly numbers is a Sextette for Servants. The songs include "You'll Find Us All," and the very popular "Doin' the Lambeth Walk," which gave birth to a new dance. The basic idea of *Me and My Girl* is old but sure-fire; it has been woven into a merry madcap musical, especially appealing to the English love of fun poked at the upper class.

LES ROMANESQUES   *Edmond Rostand*

In the heart of the naturalistic movement in France, Edmond Rostand (1865-1918) shrewdly returned to the romantic verse drama. His first produced play, *Les Romanesques,* 1894, entered the repertoire of the Théâtre Français. Its period was "any you like, provided the costumes are pretty enough." The story is a fine flower of romance, tinged with satire. Sir Percinet and Sylvette are in love; they meet across a wall (like Pyramus and Thisbe) because their fathers are enemies (as with Romeo and Juliet). The fathers hire a bravo to stage a bogus abduction—which fails—and the lovers learn that the fathers are friends, pretending to part them as the surest way of drawing them together. Disillusioned, Percinet demolishes the wall; and they part to seek genuine love elsewhere. After various adventures, they learn that their fathers' pretense did not make their own lives less real:

> Poetry, love: but we were crazy, dear,
> To seek it elsewhere. It was always here.

The wall is being rebuilt as the curtain happily falls. Good fences make good neighbors. The play is thus at once romantic and a charming satire of romance, as the lovers (and the audience) eat their cake and have it too.

Among productions (called in English *The Romantic(k)s* or *The Fantasticks*) have been: October 22, 1901, New York Empire; George Fleming converted Rostand's hexameters into rhyming pentameters. University of Birmingham, England, February 16, 1923. London, June 22, 1931; the *Times* praised its "pretty pantomimic trippings and miniature ballet." New York Hotel Sutton, 1932. In 1933, London Hammersmith Lyric, with Sir Nigel Playfair. June 1937, Worcester, England, open-air in French. London Leatherhead Rep., January 21, 1957, directed by Hazel Wallace. London Regents Park, June 25, 1956, with Angela Baddeley and Sir Nigel Playfair.

Then two young men from theatre-conscious University of Texas pondered the play; Tom Jones wrote book and lyrics, Harvey Schmidt composed music, and on June 3, 1960, *The Fantasticks* opened at the New York Greenwich Village Sullivan Street Playhouse. It went for a summer week (August 1960) to catch its breath after a slow start, then back to the Village for a run that, twenty-four years later, shows no sign of a stop. (As a gesture, it returned July 17, 1981, for another summer spell at East Hampton, Long Island.) On October 3, 1980, its millionth ticket was sold in a theatre of 153 seats.

In the meantime, the play counts over six-thousand performances elsewhere in the United States, and over 300 productions in fifty-four other countries, in fourteen languages. The London production, September 7, 1962, ran for forty-four performances. (By contrast, *The Mousetrap*,* now in its thirty-second year in London, ran for three months OffBway, New York.) The London *Stage* commented that its lively action, in the mode of a court masque, "often hovers on the edge of elegantly contrived farce." The January 1979 revival in San Francisco was that city's fifth.

The musical's best songs, "Soon It's Gonna Rain" and "Try to Remember," are not easy to forget. They have been recorded by Barbra Streisand—who had failed to win an audition before the play opened.

Jones and Schmidt had originally planned a Broadway spectacular musical, which they called *Joy Comes to Deadhorse*, combining ideas from *Romeo and Juliet* and *Les Romanesques*, when *West Side Story* opened, based on the Shakespeare play. They modified the story and modestly reduced its scope, and *The Fantasticks* emerged. It has had some five-thousand productions around the world, is especially popular in Japan, and is a favorite in high school drama groups.

CYRANO DE BERGERAC   *Edmond Rostand*

In 1897, after Sarah Bernhardt had starred in several of his plays, Rostand reached his peak when Coquelin the elder (Benoit Constant Coquelin; with his son Jean playing Rageneau) took the title part in the poetic drama that won the most enthusiastic popular reception in dramatic history: *Cyrano de Bergerac.*

The story of the play is based very loosely on the life of an actual French poet and soldier (1619-1655), a free-thinker, author of a few plays and of the satires *The States and Empires of the Moon* and—*of the Sun.* In the play, Cyrano is a long-nosed daredevil who, thinking himself too ugly for Roxane whom he loves, aids the inarticulate Christian to woo her. Cyrano writes Christian's love letters, and, in a superb balcony scene, whispers from the dark the poetic phrases that gain Christian entrance to Roxane's heart and to her chamber—while Cyrano below keeps off a noble rival. Christian dies in the wars. Many years later Roxane in her convent discovers, as Cyrano is dying, that he was the author of the letters, that his was the spirit she had always loved. Roxane sighs: "I loved but once, yet twice I lose my love." Cyrano's sense of inferiority he bends to his glory; his love leads to his sacrifice. Yet the final moment of ecstasy atones for a barren lifetime. This is the acme of romance.

The story is presented in a style that recaptures both the swagger and the preciosity of the seventeenth century. Its verse mingles bombast and grandiloquence, the flourish and gallantry of D'Artagnan with the sadness and devotion of Don Quixote. The lightness of the period is caught in pastry-cook Rageneau, patron of poets. Its recklessness gleams on the clashing swords, as Cyrano composes a ballade while fighting a duel. The play is a colorful and consummate tapestry of Romance, beneath its care-free bravado playing a quiet undertone of sacrifice and sadness. (This undertone is to be noted also in Rostand's later plays, *L'Aiglon* and *Chantecler.**)

Opening in Paris on December 28, 1897, the play ran for 200 nights to great public and critical acclaim. The usually severe Francisque Sarcey called it "an admirable work, a work of marvelous poetry, but especially and before all a masterpiece of the theatre." *Le Théâtre* (January 1898) said that Rostand "has the triple merit of being remarkably witty, thoroughly dramatic, and entirely clear."

Within the year, there were many production of *Cyrano* in Europe and the United States. One in Philadelphia and one in New York opened on the same night, September 28, 1898: the former in an Augustin Daly version, with Ada Rehan and Tyrone Power; the latter in a version by Howard Thayer Kingsbury, with Richard Mansfield and Margaret Anglin. The *New York Dramatic Mirror* called the Kingsbury adaptation "nothing more than a romantic melodrama abounding in all sorts of theatrical tricks."

The play was a great success everywhere. Sarah Bernhardt and Coquelin played it in French in New York, opening December 10, 1900. Almost a dozen English versions have been produced; the most popular of these is that of Brian Hooker, in sometimes pedestrian but often swashbuckling, witty, or tender verse. This version was used by Walter Hampden, who opened as Cyrano on November 1, 1923, and gave his thousandth performance of the part on May 18, 1936. The *New York Times,* after the opening, called Hampden's "a production thoroughly worthy of his ambition, which is the highest. . . . It would be difficult to exaggerate its charm for all who love humor and fancy, the thrill of valiant deeds and the glamour of romantic love, enveloped in an atmosphere of poetic eloquence and shot through by the lightning flash of wit." The *Telegram* declared: "Here are romance and heroism, beauty and poetry. Mr. Hampden has made a production of such beauty that it easily surpasses Mansfield's and Coquelin's alike." Whatever the merits of the playing, there is no question of the perennial power of the play.

Cyrano de Bergerac was made into an opera by Walter Damrosch and William J. Henderson, performed in Chicago and at the New York Metropolitan in 1913 and revived at Carnegie Hall, with Pasquale Amato and Frances Alda, in 1938. It was twice reshaped as a musical comedy, the better version with music by Victor Herbert, book by Stuart Reed, lyrics by Harry B. Smith, and Lew Fields as the comic Cyrano.

Of the many later productions of the play, most notable in English is that with José Ferrer, in the Brian Hooker version, which opened in New York October 8, 1946. The revival was heartily welcomed. Robert Garland said: "When a great play meets a great performance, that's good news on Broadway"; Robert Coleman, "For our money, *Cyrano de Bergerac* is the greatest theatre piece ever penned"; and Louis Kronenberger, "Rostand's play offers all those dashing, pathetic, impossibly romantic things for which the human heart secretly hungers; offers them in abundance, moreover, and offers them with authority."

After a London production (October 25, 1946) by the Old Vic with Ralph Richardson, Harold Hobson of the *Sunday Times* contrasted Brian Hooker's "pedestrian translation" with the original: "Those verses are swift and delightful, their rhymes are marvels of cleverness, they are both clever and musical, they entrance with their beauty, and they make one laugh." Hobson also reminds us that, as the French critic Lemaitre pointed out, *Cyrano* is full of reminiscences: the tumultuous opening recalls Gautier; the cake-shop, with Cyrano displaying a heart as tender as his sword is sharp, is redolent of Hugo; the scene with Roxane at the war-camp might have been drawn by Dumas; the attempted self-sacrifice of Christian—matching Cyrano's great-heartedness—has parallels in Alfred de Musset. "To a French audience, then, *Cyrano* is not only a pleasure in itself, but a means of recalling other pleasures. It is a recollection as well as an experience, and combines a crowded and agreeable past with a most acceptable present." Even to those without these prior associations, *Cyrano* is a continuing delight.

Before World War II, *Le Miroir du Monde,* in Paris, asked its men readers which literary hero they would like most to be; the women, which hero they liked most. The first three choices coincided: the men chose Cyrano by a hundred votes over Jean Valjean, with D'Artagnan a close third; the women chose Cyrano by a clear 1500. Cyrano would probably be the choice in other lands as well. Rhetoric and rue combine in the madcap part the gallant, grand-manner picture of the grand century, in what Brooks Atkinson has called "the cloak-and-doggerel vein"—in what, next to Hamlet, is the theatre's most popular part: the romantic hero that gives his name to *Cyrano de Bergerac.*

Cyrano is a difficult role, yet even in our unromantic time still tempting. Among revivals: with music and lyrics by Richard Maltby, August 28, 1928, Williamstown, Massachusetts. In the Brian Hooker version, Bristol Old Vic, May 19, 1959, with Peter Wyngate and Ingrid Hofner. London, translated by James Forsyth, July 12, 1967, for fifty-two performances. The Forsyth again at New York Lincoln Center, April 25, 1968, forty-two performances, with Robert Symons as Cyrano. New York with Christopher Plummer, 1973. Phoenix (University of Michigan), 1974. RSC, 1983, in repertory.

CHANTECLER   *Edmond Rostand*

When ill health sent Edmond Rostand to the Basque countryside, in 1899, there came to him the idea of using the birds of the farm to capture something of mankind, "to express my own dreams and to make live, before my eyes, a little of myself." Illness intervened again and again. He told the idea to Coquelin in 1905; the play was ready for rehearsal in 1909, when Coquelin suddenly died. *Chantecler* finally opened in Paris, with Lucien Guitry in the title part, on February 7, 1910, to one of the most brilliant—and most expectant—audiences in the history of the theatre. In New York, despite the eagerness of Sarah Bernhardt and Olga Nethersole, both friends of Rostand, Charles Frohman gave the role of Chantecler to Maude Adams.

In both countries the production was a disappointment. The reason was well put in the *New York Tribune* (January 25, 1911): "The piece loses immensely in the playing. The actors, masked and hampered by their feathers and beaks and claws—only the principals show their faces, and gesturing is of course impossible—are neither one thing nor the other. Comparatively few of their lines get across as they should, and much of the play's poetry and dramatic quality is untranslatable into the visual terms required by the stage." To dwarf the humans to bird size, they are shown against gigantic properties and sets; but something of the play's seriousness and profundity seems also dwarfed thereby.

When read, the play reveals a brilliance that no production has yet captured; a witty satire of mankind, and a proud tribute to humanity withal. A special *Chantecler* number of *Le Théâtre* (No. 268, February 12, 1910) looked beneath the feathers for the heart of the story. The cock, who knows that his crowing wakes the sun, who recaptures his faith even after the hen-pheasant has made him over-sleep the dawn: he is "the Gallic cock," the embodiment of the French love of order. Said Nozière: "He wants to protect the brains of his countrymen from obscurity, and from bad taste. He wants to get society beyond reach of disorder. Never has a more nationalistic piece been written. Yet M. Rostand belongs to no party. There is in his work no bitterness nor hate. His allegorical hero is as resigned to the ingratitude of the many as is Jesus. . . . The play is a hymn to enthusiasm, nature, tradition, work. . . . *Chantecler* defends the French tradition against the foreign and the foreigner. . . . Never has he found accents more human than in this play devoted to the beasts."

Coquelin had seen Chantecler as a creature of gaiety; vain, but buoyant; inventive, a resourceful observer. Guitry interpreted Chantecler as a believer in work, as a thinker, a creature of gravity, a lover of beauty. Maude Adams tried to combine these interpretations, but essentially to show that one must "do one's work, though it cost one's love and one's life." Max Beerbohm felt that Guitry was too steadily grave: "For Chantecler is a dual part. The cock is at once a great figure and a figure of fun." When the sun rises without his summons, "Chantecler, though troubled, is undismayed. The sun, he reassures himself, has risen in answer to the still resounding echoes of some previous day's song. There is grandeur in the thought, as in all the thoughts of Chantecler; but the grandeur of Chantecler is the measure of his grotesqueness."

That grotesqueness, but also that grandeur, gleam in the spirit of man. There is the rivalry of the sexes in the play: the quiet victory of the female; and the complacent self-assurance of the male that turns defeat into a greater triumph. There is a satiric picture of the French people. But beyond these—through the Gallic sense of order that shadows man's attempt to cope with the mysteries of the universe; through the vanity that cloaks man's erection of his powers against nature's driving force—*Chantecler* is a wise and witty, a smiling and searching, a tender and revealing drama of the human spirit in search of beauty and truth.

A version with book and lyrics by Anthony A. Piano and music by Michael R. Colicchio opened OffBway, 1981.

JANE SHORE   *Nicholas Rowe*

The beautiful and witty Jane Shore (died 1527)—wife of a London goldsmith, mistress of Edward IV, accused of witchcraft and forced to public penance in 1483—has been the subject of several literary works. Chief among these is the tragedy of Nicholas Rowe (1674-1718), which opened in London on February 2, 1714, and remained a favorite for almost two hundred years. New York saw it first at the new Nassau Street Theatre, March 4, 1754. W. G. Wills made a version of the drama that ran in London, opening September 30, 1876, for 116 performances and, in revival November 24, 1877, for 162 more. The play was popular enough in 1894 to evoke the burlesque *Jaunty Jane Shore,* by Richard Henry (Richard Butler and H. Chance Newton). Among those that have acted in the play are David Garrick and Mrs. Cibber, 1758; Mrs. Siddons, 1789; William Macready and Helen Faucit, 1837; Junius Brutus Booth, and Charles Kemble. Mrs. Siddons declared that the most effective line she ever uttered was Jane's exclamation: "'Twas he! 'Twas Hastings!"

The play complicates the action through the passing love of Hastings for the Lady Alicia who, when his desires turn from her to Jane Shore, denounces both to the suspicious ears of Gloster (to be Richard III, brother of King Edward IV). Jane has repulsed Hastings, but jealousy plagues Alicia on. Hastings is ordered killed, and Alicia goes mad. Jane is condemned to walk the streets clad only in a sheet, with death the penalty for giving her shelter or food. Her husband—who, disguised as Dumont, has been serving Jane throughout her prosperity—comes in his own guise to succor her; he is arrested, and Jane dies in his forgiving arms. Hastings and Alicia, said the *London Chronicle* (November 7-9, 1758) "are pillars which while they add to the beauty, are absolutely necessary to the support of the fable, and not like those little abominable Gothick nothings which we, nowadays, see foisted into the structure of every dramatic poem, without being either ornamental or useful."

The chief interest in the play is the character of Jane Shore, in the picture of whom the poet improves on the historian. She is a sympathetic figure. As Samuel Johnson says, "the wife is forgiven because she repents, and the husband is honored because he forgives." "There was a plaintive sweetness in her early scenes," the *London Theatrical Observer* (January 3, 1837) said of Helen Faucit as Jane, "exactly in accordance with the poet's portraiture of the repentant fair one; her vindication of her rights of the children of her royal paramour was finely impassioned, and her death scene was uncommonly effective: it affected the imagination without shocking the senses." Jane is made still more appealing in an adaptation of Rowe's play by Mrs. Vance Thompson and Lena R. Smith, which came to New York March 27, 1905; for this pictured her not as King Edward's willing mistress, but forced into submission of his lust. Thus the *Sun* saw her as a "tender woman who has repented of a compulsory sin, and who afterward, because of her steadfast fidelity to duty, is persecuted, starved, exposed to the rigors of wintry weather, and slowly and cruelly driven to the final agony of heartbreak and death. The component attitudes of the character are simplicity, gentleness, innate goodness, and the capability of heroic endurance."

In simple blank verse that, while rarely exalted, is seldom bombastic,

Jane Shore combines the surging qualities of a chronicle play with searching and sympathetic character portrayal.

The German critic A. W. Schlegel pointed out that the part of Gloster is directly borrowed from Shakespeare's *Richard III.* He added: "This play, consisting chiefly of domestic scenes and private distress, lays hold upon the heart." There was a revival by the London Hovender Theatre Club, November 18, 1962.

PASSENGER TO BALI   *Ellis St. Joseph*

Using his successful novella as a springboard, Ellis St. Joseph with *Passenger to Bali,* "a modern allegory," challenged the catchwords of the time. The play, with Walter Huston hopelessly miscast, opened in New York on March 14, 1940, with the play praised and the performance damned. Within the year, three publishers printed the play, which was soon shown in England, Holland, and Sweden. Among those who have appeared in it are Charles Laughton, Boris Karloff, Robert Morley, and Gene Lockhart. When Orson Welles acted the Passenger on WABC, John Crosby in the *Herald-Tribune* (July 8, 1946) called it "possibly the greatest radio performance of all time."

The meaning of *Passenger to Bali* has widely struck home. In 1946, it was broadcast on the U.S. radio to Europe, as a force for democracy. In 1949, it was one of the first plays shown on television. Our time is catching up with the play's symbols.

The action of the play takes place on the tramp steamer *Roundabout,* out of Shanghai. Captain English has taken the Reverend Walkes as a passenger to Bali; but when the ship arrives the Netherlands officer declares Walkes is a troublemaker, and will not let him land. When they discover that no port will receive him, the mates, Mr. Wrangle and Mr. Slaughter, would dump Walkes overboard; but Captain English lives by law. Meanwhile, Walkes debauches the crew, and threatens to wrest command of the ship from the captain. A great storm sweeps upon them. Captain English orders the men to man the boats. Walkes provokes a rebellion—and this gives English a law. He holds a gun on Walkes, says, "God forgive me!" and leaves him on board as they abandon ship. Walkes cries, "We'll meet again soon enough!" as the curtain falls.

Despite some inability to leap the story to the allegory, which the characters' names help to point, the reviewers were stirred by the play. Richard Lockridge in the *Sun* (March 15, 1940) said: "There are rousing scenes of human and natural violence in *A Passenger to Bali.* The stage roars with a storm at sea, lightning flashes on reeling men, and the deck of the doomed ship Roundabout rocks in a fashion to scare a landlubber out of his boots. But even in these circumstances Ellis St. Joseph finds time and room enough to turn a phrase. Now and again the author's eloquence outroars the wind." And Arthur Pollack in the *Brooklyn Eagle* (March 17) declared the typhoon "the most exciting storm at sea you ever saw, a storm that sent a ship to the bottom, and ended the tyranny of a Nietzschean gentleman who had caused the deaths of thousands in the South Seas and made that ship a ship without a country. A curiously interesting, often fascinating play, it tells a story into which can be read all sorts of things, though the author has been careful to keep his meanings free of the obvious . . . a shrewd, wise play about good and evil, centering in an unusual character, a man of intelligence and rare intuitions and no conscience of any kind."

Others at the time thought *Passenger to Bali* not so much "free of the obvious" as obscure; but, as with many other works—think of Browning!—time has weakened that charge. *Passenger to Bali* is an allegory of Fascism and democracy; not merely of these, for the "Reverend" walks the earth forever, but of tyranny and the forces of freedom through law and order. Walkes is a seeker after power, a dictator in search of a country. The ship of state, under English, is governed by law, but a tyrannous spirit sows evil; too often the enemies of evil take on the semblance of what they would destroy. Thus, in this dream, while the force of tyranny is held at bay, it still threatens its world.

Rampant individualism is inevitably at odds with the social order of democracy. The adjustment between individual and society is the crux of the world's problem. *Passenger to Bali* suggests that violence applied to either may destroy both—though perhaps the "English" lifeboats will weather the storm. And they will find that water has not drowned the destructive forces that also, seemingly forever, "walk" the pathways of the world.

The uncontrolled natural human forces (the emotions) must be, not beaten down, but properly directed. Since these forces are usually presented either as champion and hero or as enemy and villain, a play that looks at them objectively is likely to fall between two stools. It may be uncomprehended, or damned from both sides. *Passenger to Bali* ran counter to current slogans. A play that fits its day's slogans—*Death of a Salesman*,* for instance—may win readier acceptance; *Death of a Salesman* marks its author's triumph as a salesman. There is more insight, fraught with warning to the world, within the grim story and gripping storm of *Passenger to Bali*.

DIVORÇONS   *Victorien Sardou*

The peak of Sardou's comedies of conflicts between the sexes, in saucy triangulation, is *Divorçons*, which ran for 400 performances in Paris, 1880, with Eleonora Duse. The stellar role of Cyprienne des Prunelles has attracted the greatest actresses: Bernhardt, who grew famous in her Sardou roles, Réjane in 1895 in Paris and the United States; and Minnie Maddern Fiske in 1897—each of whom, we are told, lifted the farcical idea to the realm of high comedy. New York saw the play in French in 1882 with Paola Marie; in English with Grace George in 1916; with Alexandra Carlisle in 1917. Marta Abba played it in Italy, and in English in Cleveland, 1941. *Divorçons*, said the *Chicago Herald* October 21, 1901, "is one of the smartest comedies that ever came out of France."

Written by Victorien Sardou (1831-1908) and Émile de Najac, the play shows a trivial but amusing idea turning a family topsy-turvy, as a charming lady decides that the way to keep a husband is to make him a lover instead. For Cyprienne decides that what makes a husband a bore, and a lover an excitement, is not the person but the position that he holds. Come, she says to her husband, let's divorce (*Divorçons!*); let me marry my present lover and you take over his role. The result of this amusing though muddleheaded proposal is that des Prunelles and Cyprienne have their rendezvous like a pair of clandestine lovers, and find that love can be adventurous—without the divorce. In their movement to this conclusion, there is considerable deft dalliance with sex.

For a time, *Divorçons* seemed too risqué for the English stage. In a toned-down version called *The Queen's Proctor* (the Proctor, at that time, had to be

petitioned in cases of divorce), it came to London June 2, 1896. The scene
was transferred from Rheims to the English shires. The married couple
were Sir Victor and Lady Crofton; an attaché of the Italian Embassy, Cesar
Borgia, was the lover. Crofton was a baronet and master of foxhounds; the
French restaurant with mirror-lined *cabinets particuliers* became the
White Hart Hotel, "like all English hostelries, a home of unblemished
reputation." Arriving there in the rain while the married couple are celebrating the divorce, Borgia looks the fool, and drives the others together
again. The *London Graphic* lamented the change: "yet a few more years and
Divorçons will be recognized as what it is—a masterpiece. Unedifying in
parts, indelicate and almost coarse in its outspokenness, it nonetheless
shows the high-water mark in farcical comedy of its author, and is the
happiest conceivable instance of that sauciness of speech which wins acceptance in French, and in other languages tends to incur reprobation. Its
second act is the most humorous in modern French comedy." Bernard Shaw
saw the same English production, with Violet Vanbrugh. He lost his temper
at the opening, with Sardou's "inevitable two servants gossiping," those
servants whose pretended function, said Shaw, is to present the exposition,
but whose real purpose is to bore the audience so much that it will welcome
the main characters. "Sardoodledum!" he exclaimed. As the play progressed, however, Shaw praised, "its witty liveliness" and ended by congratulating producer-player Bourchier on "his first genuine success."

The American version of *Divorçons* was also expurgated, but the idea that
illegitimacy lends spice, and the character of the woman who conceived the
notion, made an amusing counterpoise that lilted the play with laughter.
The *New York Evening World,* May 8, 1897, caught this balance in Mrs.
Fiske's performance: "It was the centre of an event that did more in its brief
two hours for the elevation of the stage art and the refinement of the stage
atmosphere than all the purification theorists will do in a century with
their fads of expurgation and of morality in the play . . . a dear, delightful,
piquant little wife she was, positively and charmingly sure that she had
read out and thought out the great marriage and divorce problem to an
unanswerably right conclusion. And yet we saw all the time that not the
faintest conception of the real gravity and obscured immorality of the case
had ever entered her small, busy, self-satisfied brain. She had been a pretty
pet and had petted herself into an absurd idea; and the only way to get her
out of it was to keep on petting her, as her fond, middle-aged husband did."
Almost a half century after the play's premiere, *Variety* (March 10, 1926)
called it "as fresh and unhackneyed, as apt and as appropriate today as
when written . . . constantly amusing, with a first act that gets down to
business and discards preamble and talkiness. The laughs come thick and
fast, and most of the fun is inherent in the play itself."

The play, translated by Angela and Robert Goldsby, was shown in Manchester, England, in 1959, announced as the English premiere. An adaptation by Diane Hart and Louis Manson, called *Divorce à la Carte,* was
presented at Oxford in 1962. On June 2, 1966, the Goldsby version, called
Let's Get a Divorce, came to the London Mermaid: the *Times* called it "the
most polished and well cast play I have as yet seen at the Mermaid." The
same version came to St. George's Chapel, OffOffBway, in 1978. Toronto saw
it in March 1977. In translation by Brian Kelly, *Divorçons* entered the Asolo
repertory March 30, 1979. Alvin Klein exclaimed: "How utterly right this
too long lost piece of sensible frivolity seems and sounds today! And what a
lovely, funny testament it is to real romance!"

Divorçons starts with an amusing twist of the triangle, setting the apex at the base; and it ends with the thought that nothing may be quite so upsetting as getting just what you thought you were longing for. *The Devil's Dictionary* (the amusing "cynic's handbook" of Ambrose Bierce) defines opportunity as "a favorable occasion for grasping a disappointment"; Cyprienne can draw back just in time, giving another amusing fillip to a play full of suggestion, spice, and charm.

MADAME SANS-GENE   *Victorien Sardou*

A vivid historical play, and one of Sardou's most immediate and most lasting successes, is *Madame Sans-Gêne* (Madame Free-and-Easy), 1893. Written with Emile Moreau, the play gave Gabrielle Réjane her first great popularity. She brought it to the United States in 1895 and it has been popular in stock ever since. Henry Irving and Ellen Terry opened in the play in London on April 10, 1897, then toured England and the United States. Mme. Simone played it, in French, in New York, in 1924; Gloria Swanson made a film of it the next year. Cornelia Otis Skinner played it in the summer of 1938. Nina Marshall was in a Spanish film version in 1945. A version, *Madame Devil-May-Care,* with Sarah Churchill, was on television in 1951 and 1974. This story of Napoleon put in his place by a laundress is a continuously popular blend of historical rouse and amorous entanglement, with brilliant dialogue.

Madame Sans-Gêne is Catherine, who in August of 1792 is laundress to a company of soldiers, which includes Lefebvre, who marries her, Fouché, a shrewd, unfeeling fellow, and a certain Napoleon Bonaparte, a jolly corporal who cannot always pay for his laundry. This much is in the Prologue; the play opens in the year 1811, when Lefebvre is Marshal of France. His wife, who is taking lessons in deportment, is scorned by Napoleon's sisters, who suppress their mutual jealousy to crush the light-hearted and naive Catherine, and have her discarded. Through a succession of palace plots and political intrigues, Catherine, innocent but sharp-witted, works her way. She softens the angry Emperor, then presents a long overdue laundry bill; as they laugh together, she reconciles Napoleon with the out-of-favor Fouché; and the Emperor is happy to have her remain with her husband, Lefebvre.

The major points of Sardou's drama are historical. François Joseph Lefebvre (1755-1820) married Catherine Hubscher, his company's laundress, who retained throughout her husband's rise, under Napoleon and Louis XVIII, the outspoken frankness and quick tongue of a woman of the people. She was, as Sardou pictures her, a vivandière during the early fighting of the Revolution. In the play, the constant simplicity of Catherine's ways, contrasting with the increasing finery and formality of the Emperor's entourage, gives effective character portrayal behind the political intrigue of Sardou's story.

Madame Sans-Gêne retains its power. As the *New York Times* declared (November 4, 1924), the play "remains one of the delightful and blooming pieces of the theatre. It has verve and a hearty spirit; it has wits about it, and a breeze of inexhaustible life. The jolly craft abounding throughout has plenty of style upon it, and its story rattles along with a good French vivacity and tang." The deft construction of Sardou's well-made play drives home the neatly turned situations; the characters have more breath of life than is usual with Sardou, as the historical canvas reveals traits that are common to Catherine, the Emperor's Lady, and the woman next door. These are caught into delightful action in *Madame Sans-Gêne*.

MY HEART'S IN THE HIGHLANDS   *William Saroyan*

After having attracted considerable attention with some short stories, William Saroyan (American, 1908-1981) turned to the theatre. *My Heart's in the Highlands* was first printed in *The One-Act Play Magazine*; it was lengthened and produced in New York on April 13, 1939, first by the Group Theatre, then taken over by the Theatre Guild, and achieving 43 performances. It brought a fresh, or a long disused, note into the American theatre: a simple love of man, an acceptance of the worth of humble people and the joy of simple living.

There is hardly any story to the play. An unpublished poet, with his adoring son and a few friendly mice, lives in a shack near Fresno, California. A kindly, frustrated storekeeper, himself on the brink of bankruptcy, gives them credit. They shelter an old Shakespearean actor, out of a home for the aged, who plays the trumpet—evoking nostalgic moods in the neighbors, who come to listen, bearing little gifts. The actor dies. The poet and the boy are evicted. The shopkeeper sees his store failing. The curtain falls.

Pervading all this straitened sequence is a quiet dignity, a self-respecting, non-complaining acceptance of one's lot, a love of living that makes defeat an endurable episode in a journey toward a bright horizon. The nearest the play offers to complaint, to propaganda, is the final remark of the poet's son, a chip off the old happy-go-lucky block: "I'm not mentioning any names, Pa, but something's wrong somewhere."

Like most works of fresh quality, *My Heart's in the Highlands* divided the reviewers. Those that disliked the play, Saroyan answered. Thus the *New York World-Telegram* (April 14, 1939) said: "You will search in vain for any trace of truth, beauty, or moral in it." And in that paper, the next day, Saroyan declared of his play: "It's wonderful, in the very truest sense of that dead word. It is full of wonder from the rise of the curtain to the fall of it. . . . The message of the play is the simplest and earliest message of man to man: For the love of God, be alive; be grateful for the miracle of possessing substance, of being able to draw energy from the great source of energy, and for the instinct to approach danger and death with pride, humor, and humbleness. . . . As for the moral of the play, it is the very simplest: It is better to be poor and alive than to be rich and dead. In short, it is better to be a good human being than a bad one. P.S. The idea is not original with me. It is simply that it got misplaced two or three years ago." The *New Yorker* (April 22) observed: "The singular hodge-podge of geometrical scenery, trump playing, crepe hair and tangled prose on exhibition in 52d Street conveys no rational message to anybody. . . . I think we'd better forget all about it as soon as possible." Saroyan had anticipated this, in the *New York Journal American* (April 19): "I'm sure it is going to live because it is alive. . . . Of its kind it is a classic." In the Preface to the printed play, Saroyan elaborated: "A classic is simply a first work, the beginning of a tradition, and an entry into a fresh realm of human experience, understanding, and expression. I believe *My Heart's in the Highlands* is a classic."

Although no "tradition" along the play's lines is yet manifest, its lyric quality, and its love of and faith in people, give it continuing values. These were not unrecognized by the reviewers. Arthur Pollock (April 30) remarked that the play is "written with the grace of a hummingbird. . . . It is very important. . . . His heart is in the right place. His heart is in the high lands." And more fully Richard Watts (April 23) declared that the play "is evocative rather than explicit, and its quality perhaps resembles that of music in its intangibility and its appeal to suggestion. . . . He is attempting to create in the manner of a dreamy recollection of childhood a picture of the artistic life of those that have the gift to feel the meaning of beauty but not to put it in words." In a "rag bag of bright scraps—Mr. Saroyan never bothers his head much about continuity, logic, or transition"—said Brooks Atkinson (May 7), "he has created a group of lovable characters who live with each other in amusing or pathetic harmony and give a sunny impression of natural kindness in the midst of a hard, grim, fatally wrong-headed world."

It is not to the head but to the heart that Saroyan's characters look for guidance. The song the old actor trumpets, that gives its name to the play, is a symbol of the high-hearted buoyancy that gives these little figures—and the play—a high significance.

THE TIME OF YOUR LIFE   *William Saroyan*

Saroyan's easy affability, his unreflecting joy in life, his casual use of the drama as a meeting place for important nobodies—important because they are human beings engaged in occupying a soul—swept the New York reviewers and public into an enthusiasm for *The Time of Your Life* that made it the first play to win both the Critics' Circle Award and the Pulitzer Prize. It was initially performed by the Theatre Guild on the road and brought to New York by Eddie Dowling on October 25, 1939, with Dowling and Julie Haydon, for 185 performances. London saw the play February 14, 1946.

The action of the play occurs in "Nick's Saloon and Entertainment Palace" on the San Francisco waterfront. The chief figure is a guy named Joe, who drinks champagne because it gives him interesting thoughts, and who makes a dancing doll to help Kitty, a sort of ethereal prostitute, keep her thoughts from her profession. Kitty is quitting her profession, for the fellow she loves has finally taken a job, so that they can marry. Also in the saloon are the usual hangers about. There's Willy, the pin-ball maniac, forever at the machine. Harry is a lively tap dancer; there's an Arab with a harmonica; and a Negro comes in and plays the piano so well that he's given a job. Old Kit Carson tells tall tales of the west, none of which the habitués believe; some of his stories start and never finish, like his hopeful beginning: "I don't suppose you ever fell in love with a midget weighing 39 pounds."

Into this company comes a group of society slummers. They are paid scant attention by the rest; but a sudden irruption breaks: Blick, the head of the Vice Squad, enters on an angry prowl. His abusive language sets the slummers fleeing; he intends to arrest Kitty, but first—in savage scorn and sadistic pleasure—he orders her to dance a strip tease. As the bewildered Kitty stands hesitant, the braggart Kit Carson pulls out his gun and shoots Blick. The pin-ball machine hits the jackpot; to the shower of coins the machine lights up the words *American Destiny*.

This comedy, which Saroyan says he wrote in six days, shows no signs of careful construction. It is casual; it does not make efficient use of the theatre; some of its movements seem merely injected vaudeville turns. It does not bother with questions of verisimilitude; there is no indication, for instance, of the source of Joe's freely spent money. The play has, instead of these dramatic qualities, a buoyant love of life and of the living.

Saroyan has, said Walter Prichard Eaton, reviewing the printed play in the *New York Herald Tribune* (January 14, 1940) "a genuine love for all underdogs, and a deep understanding of the essential dignity of each individual spirit, however lowly; and this understanding is not clouded with any materialistic political propaganda." While *The Time of Your Life* is refreshingly free from propaganda, it does at times attempt philosophy, and then, commented Brooks Atkinson—but what can we expect of saloon drifters?—"when Saroyan permits himself to discuss ideas he can write some of the worst nonsense that ever clattered out of a typewriter." When, however, Saroyan contents himself with displaying, in tender understanding and respect, persons that do not let life's barrenness parch their soul, then, Atkinson declared, "some of the warmest and heartiest comedy in the modern drama comes bubbling up through Mr. Saroyan's pungent dialogue, and although it is not realism it is real." "Its compassion is as irresistible," said John Mason Brown, "as its humor is gay. . . . The characters have blood in their veins, real air in their lungs, and joy in their hearts."

Sometimes a novelist like Dickens may be sentimental, almost saccharine, except for his ink-black villains—may ignore the formal elements of construction in seeming haphazard spread of life, yet by the very exuberance of that life and his love of living infuse into his characters a pulsing vitality that makes them moving, makes us consider them, not as book folk, but as neighbors, as persons on our block. Similarly Saroyan, in *The Time of Your Life,* in seemingly casual construction gives warmth and dignity and human stature to the persons that have found harbor in Nick's waterfront saloon.

Among revivals of *The Time of Your Life*: New York City Center, January 19, 1955. New York Lincoln Center, November 6, 1969, for fifty-two performances. Asolo, 1972; also a tour covering Los Angeles, Chicago, Philadelphia, and Washington, with Henry Fonda as Joe. August 18, 1975, Boston; also 1975 OffOffBway (Harkness). ACT, July 15, 1976.

John Gassner, in *Theatre at the Crossroads,* 1960, declared of Saroyan: "A sharp gamin's intelligence played behind the mask of his naïveté and behind the sentimentality of his protestations of brotherly love. . . . There was a measure of provocative impudence in his gospel of brotherly love which pulled down the mighty. His sentimentality, the element of his work most frequently deplored, sometimes concealed and sometimes flaunted a cutting edge that both his admirers and his detractors tended to overlook." The *Times* said his plays were for a time "when people still believed in people." Zoe Wanamaker and Daniel Massey were in the Barbican Pit revival July 1, 1984.

THE FLIES   *Jean-Paul Sartre*

Most vivid of the modern retellings of the Orestes story is *The Flies,* 1944, by Jean-Paul Sartre (French, 1905-1980). The account of Orestes' slaying of his mother Clytemnestra and her paramour and consort Aegisthus, after they had killed his father and usurped the throne of Argos, was a favorite among the ancient Greek dramatists. It is presented with emotional intensity in the *Choephori** of Aeschylus. Sartre endows the story with a modern psychological complexity. Although *The Flies* was presented unmolested in Paris during the Nazi occupation, 1943, it is a bold defense of freedom against the dictator. It is also the fullest dramatic development of Sartre's philosophy of existentialism.

The new play introduced some variations into the olden story. It pictures Argos as a pestilence-ridden city, plagued by the flies, symbols of the guilt and the remorse of the citizens who, in accepting Aegisthus as their king, share in his crime. The king himself, out of his sense of guilt, has established an annual Day of the Dead, when the citizens wallow in remorse, the graves are opened, and the spirits of their dead torment the living.

On such a day Electra, courageous with Orestes' homecoming, defies her mother and the king. Zeus, watching Orestes with a mixture of cynicism and amusement, expects to plant in the young man the seeds of fear, guilt, and pious reverence. But Orestes calmly dispenses justice in dealing death to his mother and King Aegisthus. He knows neither fear nor remorse.

The flies now cluster like Furies around Orestes and Electra. The citizens of Argos assail the temple where they rest. Orestes tells the crowd: "Aegisthus you did not fear; you read in his eyes that he was of your kind, he had not the courage of his crimes. . . . My crime is wholly mine." Orestes by his deed has taken the guilt from the citizens; they no longer have their old king's murderer as their king. And Orestes, having dealt justice, feels no guilt. The flies, therefore, are powerless over him; and Zeus, baffled by a human who feels no guilt nor remorse, fears for his own reign.

The weaker Electra sinks in remorse before the flies; but Orestes freely goes on his way. The citizens of Argos, without the burden of guilt, must now, he declares, work out the pattern of their days.

The doctrine of existentialism may be traced through the actions of Orestes. He comes to his native city, with no intention of seeking revenge, merely as a curious passerby. Then he learns that to live is to be engaged in life; one may choose one's action, but one must act. One must act, despite the seeming hopelessness of every course of action: "human living begins on the far side of despair." Hence there is anguish involved in any action; also, the burden of responsibility, because whatever one does helps shape the world around. Thus Orestes' killing of Aegisthus frees the citizens of remorse. They wish Orestes, son of their rightful king, to stay and rule them. But he will not. For (as it was put by Simone de Beauvoir, Sartre's associate): "You can help people to be in the position to be free, but you can't be free for them: they must find freedom in their own hearts." Each for himself must freely choose, then create, his own life pattern.

This philosophy underlies the moving drama of *The Flies*. As Simone de Beauvoir said to me, "Zeus is the philosophic exponent, Aegisthus the unthinking expression, of authority, conventional morality, established religion, political power—Petain!—trying to oppress and mystificate the people." *The Flies* is also a stirring drama of strong emotions and stark action, thoroughly effective on the story level. Given vivid presentation by Erwin Piscator in New York, 1947, and revived at his Dramatic Workshop in 1948 and 1949, *The Flies* commanded close attention and deep feeling. Richard Watts (April 18, 1947) spoke of its "several levels of provocative interest" and called it (May 3) "one of the few genuinely distinguished dramas of the post-war world theatre." *Esquire* (November, 1947) pointed out (Piscator's being a non-professional group) that "the most exciting play on Broadway this season is not, as it happens, on Broadway at all."

Several of the scenes in the play are truly gripping. Most impressive, perhaps, is that of the hilltop temple and cave of the dead: the rock rolled from the entrance stops before Electra, who is defiant, exhorting the abased citizens to rouse from their submissive and piteous remorse—"a mass scene of terror," said Thomas R. Dash (October 20, 1947) "that is orchestrated superbly into a ballet of lament and misery," as the swaying throng falls back into its subjection and fear.

The Flies was enacted in London (University College) and in the United States at Vassar and Western Reserve. In February 1948, a production by the German director Jürgen Fehling, in the United States sector of Berlin, was widely hailed—except by the Communist press. Since the play advocates the freedom of the individual, since Orestes refuses to guide, direct, or rule the citizens: let them work out their own way of living, and since the Communists for such reasons were already opposed to existentialism, the press of the Soviet sector sneered at *The Flies* as "Heidigger with a shot of effervescing inanities from the Café de Flore." All other comments paid tribute to its philosophy and its power.

The Greeks, though they did not discover all the answers, knew the basic questions of man's life and the course of human action. Religion; individual freedom; individual responsibility; fear as enslavement; the necessity of choice for wholesome living: these problems are all imbedded in Orestes' ancient story, and illuminated for modern pondering in the tense dramatic action of *The Files*.

Oxford saw the play, in translation by Vernon Dobtcheff, November 20, 1956. Not to be outdone, Cambridge put on a version by Margaret Drabble, February 18, 1958. It entered the APA-Phoenix repertory 1966-1967.

THE LION-TAMER   *Alfred Savoir*

The Lion-Tamer; or, English As It Is Eaten (*Le Dompteur,* 1925) is the best example of a type of drama in which Alfred Savoir (French, 1883-1934) excelled: the farce of ideas. With a sprightly plot, much in the mood of the nineteenth century French vaudeville, Savoir interwines a play of fancy and a play of thought, by comic devices and situations presenting, as in a distorting mirror, his serious theme. He might be called the satirist of *Savoir faire.*

The playwright reached this form by a roundabout path. Coming from his native Poland (where his name was Posymanski), Savoir first wrote serious, bitter dramas, such as *Baptism,* 1908. From this mood, he turned to sparkling comedies of sex, of which the best-known is a hilarious picture of husband-taming, *Bluebeard's Eighth Wife,* 1921. This delighted New York audiences—the New Haven try-out was stopped by the authorities—in 1921, with Ina Claire and Edmund Breese, in adaptation by Charlton Andrews.

Delightful farce, but considerably more, is *The Lion-Tamer,* which was an instant hit both in French and in English: (1925 in Paris, with Spinelli; October 8, 1926 in New York, with Dorothy Sands, Ian Maclaren and Albert Carroll). The play presents Lord Lonsdale carrying on the family tradition. For many generations, the Lonsdales have fought and died for the oppressed; the last frail remnant of the great family can do no less. But he can do no more than travel with a country circus, hating the cruel lion-tamer, hoping, with the incorrigible hopefulness of the idealist, that some day the lions will eat the trainer. The trainer rules his beasts and his wife through fear; Lonsdale tries to soften the trainer by making love to his wife—but at last it is Lonsdale that the lions eat.

The Lion-Tamer has meat beyond the surface story. Beneath its lightly-handled plot runs the opposition of mastery over idea and mastery over man, a symbolic conflict of idealism and absolutism. It is the idealist that is swallowed up. But not so simply. For, as Savoir pointed out, justice and beauty bear with them the inevitable counterpart of beautiful things: revolt, heresy, anarchy. And if the lion-tamer represents power, brutal reality, cruelty, vulgarity, he also stands for order, civilization, law, and the harmony of the universe. "Evil brings forth good, and good, evil. . . . They are at once two aspects of the same phenomenon."

Some of the reviewers of the American version did not reach out to the play's symbolism. The *New York World* asserted: "The scene in which arrangements are duly made for encompassing the wife's infidelity is one of the naughtiest and at times one of the most amusing episodes now on view in this much indulged city," but added (October 28) that the play "is full of bell-boys' wisdom, pseudo-philosophy, cheap boudoir wit, fiddlings with sex as disgusting and deathly as the dreams of an impotent old flaneur." On the other hand, the *Telegraph* averred: "Mr. Savoir recognizes one cosmic truth that most men never discover: that the intimate relations between man and woman, over which murders are done, high and low crimes committed and many heart-breaks and tears wasted, are, in essence, comic." Alexander Woollcott called *The Lion-Tamer* "a highly meaningful, excessively roguish, and distinctly entertaining fable." Barrett H. Clark in the *New York Sun* (November 13, 1926) spoke of the play's superb structure: "It has not a superfluous comma" and said that "it stems from Racine* . . . the analyst of love, the delicate commentator on the erotic ailments of unfortunate women and the sexual tempests of heroic men." The *Telegram* remarked: "Savoir is mocking the public as well as the mad design of the universe, but it would be a dour public that did not enjoy being mocked in such a manner." In *The Lion-Tamer,* sex becomes a vehicle for satire, farce the conveyor of fertile thought.

THE ROBBERS   *Johann Christoph Schiller*

The challenge to the existing order in *The Robbers* came red-hot from the author's life. The frail Johann Christoph Friedrich von Schiller (German, 1759-1805) hated the strict discipline at his regimental school. He later declared: "Of men, the actual men in the world below, I knew absolutely nothing at the time I composed my *Robbers.* Four hundred human beings, it is true, were my fellow-prisoners in this abode: but they were mere taut-ologies and repetitions of the self-same mechanical creature, like so many plaster casts of one statue. Thus situated, of necessity I failed. In making the attempt, my chisel brought forth a monster, of which (fortunately!) the world had no type or resemblance to show." Thomas DeQuincey called this work of the nineteen-year-old Schiller "beyond doubt the most tempestuous, the most volcanic, of all juvenile creations anywhere recorded . . . has never failed to convulse the heart of young readers." *The Robbers* bears as motto the passage from Hippocrates: "What herbs cannot cure, iron cures; what iron cannot cure, fire cures." Here is, bluntly, the appeal to fire and sword!

Further events of Schiller's life sprang from *The Robbers,* which was published at his own expense in 1781. In January, 1782, Schiller, by then Regimental Surgeon for the Duke of Württenburg, left without leave, to see the production of the play at Mannheim. All the youth of Germany boiled with unparalleled enthusiasm; the conservatives were proportionately shocked. When the Grisons complained to the Duke because the play called

their city "the thief's Athens," the Duke ordered Schiller to confine his
future writings to medical treatises. The next year, Schiller fled the Duchy,
and travelled about Germany for a decade.

The Robbers, in romantic spirit, breathing defiance of law in the name of
a noble freedom, pictures Karl von Moor abandoning the evils of his father's
court for the free forests of Bohemia, where he lives like a German Robin
Hood. Karl's brother, Franz, at the conventional court, is a coarse, scheming
villain, holding in his power Karl's beloved Amelia, until— "Only by Moor's
hand shall Moor's beloved die"—Karl himself puts an end to Amelia's
sufferings. Through the play extravagant incidents sweep with wild passion; strong patriotism—the famous *Lebt Wohl* song; virile and intense love
of action; as horror heaps on violent death and enthusiasms outleap order.
We are told that, after seeing the play, one German noble abandoned his
estate and took to the woods like Karl von Moor. Another German prince-
ling, however, stated: "If I had been God at the moment of Creation and had
foreseen that *The Robbers* would be written, I would have left the world
unmade."

The Germans of the Storm and Stress period, who soared with the
"untamed hope of wild and noble self-expression" of *The Robbers,* were
outmatched by the young English romantics. Coleridge, in a letter to
Southey, in 1794, exclaimed: "I had read, chill and trembling, when I came
to the part where the Moor fixes a pistol over the robbers who are asleep. I
could read no more. My god, Southey, who is this Schiller, this convulser of
the heart? Did he write his tragedy amid the yelling of fiends?" Later,
Coleridge added: "Schiller introduces no supernatural beings; yet his
human beings agitate and astonish more than all the goblin rout—even of
Shakespeare." Wordsworth borrowed freely from *The Robbers* for his *The
Borderers.*

Later in the century, the Schiller cult rose in Bulwer Lytton almost to
worship. Thackeray, in the German town of Erfurt, saw Devrient, "the Kean
of Germany," as Franz von Moor, and cried: "I think I never saw anything so
terrible. There is a prayer which Franz makes while his castle is being
attacked, which has the most awful effect which can well be fancied: 'I am
no common murderer, mein Herr Gott.'" Most fully, in his *Life of Schiller,*
Carlyle discussed *The Robbers*: "A rude simplicity, combined with a gloomy
and overpowering force, are its chief characteristics; they remind us of the
defective cultivation, as well as of the fervid and harassed feelings of its
author.... The tragic interest of *The Robbers* is deep throughout, so deep
that frequently it borders upon horror. A grim inexpiable Fate is made the
ruling principle; it envelops and overshadows the whole; and under its
louring influence, the fiercest efforts of human will appear but like flashes
that illuminate the wild scene with a brief and terrible splendor, and are
lost forever in the darkness. The unsearchable abysses of man's destiny are
laid open before us, black and profound, and appalling."

Carlyle recognized the personal impetus behind the play, which gives
such impassioned strength, for instance, to the fiery soliloquy on life and
death, yet makes its chief personages more figments of the poet's wild fancy
than mortal men. Karl von Moor, said Carlyle, "had expected heroes, and he
finds mean men; friends, and he finds smiling traitors to tempt him aside,
to profit by his aberrations, and lead him onward to destruction: he had
dreamed of magnanimity and every generous principle, he finds that prudence is the only virtue sure of its reward ... Amelia, the only female in the
piece, is a beautiful creation; but as imaginary as her persecutor Franz.

Still and exalted in her warm enthusiasm, devoted in her love to Moor, she moves before us as the inhabitant of a higher and simpler world than ours. . . . She is a fair vision, the *beau idéal* of a poet's first mistress; but has few mortal lineaments."

In England, even more than in Germany, those hostile to this exuberant rush of unrestrained emotion also spoke forth. In the *Anti-Jacobin* of June, 1798, for example, there appeared a satiric play, *The Rovers,* the joint work of Canning, Frère, and Ellis. Its barbs were directed partly against Goethe's *Stella,* but mainly against Schiller's *The Robbers* and *Ingrigue and Love.* The Preface sardonically stated that *The Rovers* aims to instill "a wild desire of undefinable latitude and extravagance," and referred to the German play "in which robbery is put in so fascinating a light that the whole of a German University went upon the highway in consequence of it"—a statement that won wide credence in England.

The first English translation of *The Robbers* was banned by the censor; after being tamed it was produced in London in 1799 under the title *The Red Cross Knights,* with the robbers transformed into knights errant, and the good brother living happily at the end.

Of the early dramas of Schiller, all in prose, *The Robbers* is by far the most vigorous, fiery, and dramatically intense. The characters and the diction are flush with the extremes of passion, bold in the black-and-white vision of the world that often appears to idealistic youth. But it is the youth of a genius that created *The Robbers*; in it surge the power and the majesty that make Schiller the greatest of all German playwrights.

In its two hundredth anniversary year *The Robbers* was performed (March 10, 1982) OffBway (13th Street).

Schiller's *Mary Stuart, Queen of Scots,* another drama of the proud, doomed royal lady, should be mentioned. (See also Maxwell Anderson.*) Produced in Weimar, 1800, directed by Goethe, it was revived by Madame Modjeska in New York in 1898 and 1900. Later, ELT, December 20, 1944. Phoenix, directed by Tyrone Guthrie, December 1, 1957, with Eva Le Gallienne as Elizabeth and Irene Worth as Mary. With Miss Le Gallienne and Signe Hasso (as Mary) it went on a national tour beginning October 5, 1959, Schiller's two-hundredth anniversary year. At the NT (Old Vic), September 17, 1958, "the highly combustible meeting of the two imperious females," said Milton Shulman in the *Standard,* "turns out to be the play's highlight." Among others: 1959, Vancouver Festival, Agnes Moorehead as Elizabeth, and Viveca Lindfors. Translated by Stephen Spender, New York Lincoln Center, October 30, 1971. Alternating with *Hamlet,* OffBway (Circle), 1979. Los Angeles, 1981. The intense drive of Schiller's drama has made it more frequently performed than Maxwell Anderson's *Mary of Scotland.**

WILHELM TELL　　　　　　　　　　　　　*Johann Christoph Schiller*

Though named after a man, this play, written in 1804, is the drama of a great people. It pictures the citizens of a Swiss canton, in 1308, gathering in a crescendo of indignation at their mistreatment by the Governor, impelled by their sturdy self-reliance to strike for liberty, and to establish the oldest democracy in Europe. Somewhat as in the Shakespearean history-play, we behold all classes of society: the nobles, conservatively inclined, by their privileges bound to the Emperor, yet in the crisis taking stand for freedom; the solid citizens, burghers attentive to their rights; and the common people, hunters, farmers, shepherds, whose Swiss cantons instill deep breath of freedom with the mountain air. Binding these pictures together is the legendary story of the Swiss archer, Wilhelm Tell, ordered by the tyrant Gessler to shoot an apple from his own son's head, but with a second arrow beneath his cloak for Gessler's heart, if the first had missed its mark. Arrested for this, Tell escapes and kills Gessler, thus giving start to the struggle that ends Austria's domination, sets Switzerland free.

Schiller's *Wilhelm Tell,* said Carlyle, "exhibits some of the highest triumphs which his genius, combined with his art, ever realized. The first descent of Freedom to our modern world, the first unfurling of her standard on that rocky pinnacle of Europe, is here celebrated in the style which it deserves. There is no false tinsel decoration about *Tell,* no sickly refinement, no declamatory sentimentality. All is downright, simple, and agreeable to Nature; yet all is adorned and purified and rendered beautiful, without losing its resemblance. . . . The feelings it inculcates and appeals to are those of universal human nature, and presented in their purest, most unpretending form. . . . It is delightful and salutory to the heart to wander among the scenes of *Tell,* all is lovely, yet all is real. Physical and moral grandeur are united; yet both are the unadorned grandeur of Nature. There are the lakes and green valleys beside us, the Schreckhorn, the Jungfrau, and their sister peaks, with their avalanches and their palaces of ice, all glowing in the southern sun; and dwelling among them are a race of manly husbandmen, heroic without ceasing to be homely, poetical without ceasing to be genuine."

Wilhelm Tell was played in Philadelphia by Joseph Jefferson in 1812. It was frequently played in England in the nineteenth century. In Paris, the play was supplanted by the opera based upon it in 1829, with book by Hippolyte Bis and Etienne Jouy, and music by Gioacchino Antonio Rossini; this closes with the rousing hymn to liberty and to the woods and mountains where freedom was bred: "I boschi, I monti!" This popular opera was first played in New York in 1857 and later produced at the Metropolitan Opera House in the 1888-1889 season.

An American production of *Wilhelm Tell* opened in Hollywood on May 25, 1939; it was played by a group of refugees and directed by Leopold Jessner. The latter had produced the play successfully in Europe on a cubistic set with platforms, runways, and steps. His presentation did not please the American audience, though *Variety* (May 31, 1939) reported that "distinctly in its favor is the timeliness of its theme, the deadly parallel to despotic rule in European countries at this time."

In a Schiller centennial address in 1859, William Cullen Bryant declared: "Wherever there are generous hearts, wherever there are men who hold in reverence the rights of their fellow-men, wherever the love of country and the love of mankind coexist, Schiller's drama of *Wilhelm Tell* stirs the blood like the sound of a trumpet." Its stirring rouse for freedom makes *Wilhelm Tell* a valid and vigorous drama as long as the need to rouse for freedom makes a prison of some part of earth.

LUV   *Murray Schisgal*

The frequent one-act plays of Murray Schisgal (b. 1926) began with *The Typist* and *The Tiger,* OffBway 1963, with the husband-and-wife team Eli Wallach and Anne Jackson, who were with him still in *Twice Around the Park,* 1982. Walter Kerr commented: "In Schisgal's lunatic universe, nothing is merrier than misery." In the "West Side" playlet of this last group, a black policewoman comes down to protest the noise her neighbor is making, to discover that he plays a record of his dog barking to keep intruders away when he is out. Embittered by the injustice of life, the policewoman complains that the last time she haled a prostitute to court, the judge married her. Of course, she and her white neighbor, each away from an unhappy marriage, grow tempted to try it again, making (according to Kerr), "a kind of pop theatre, which comes perilously close to being like a daytime soap opera."

Schisgal's "merriest misery" comes in the full-length *Luv*, which opened at the New York Booth November 11, 1966, for 901 performances, to show a bench, a garbage pail, and a bridge. Naturally, Harry is preparing to jump into the river, when Milt arrives in time to stop him. They recognize each other as old school pals; then in a lugubrious scene they try to outdo each other in telling of the wretched days of their childhood. Harry's current failure is symbolized by the dog that wet his pants in the park. Milt boasts that he loves his wife—but she refuses to grant him a divorce. Wife Ellen comes in, and opens a graph she's kept of their love life; it ended on July 22. She also has a knife ready for her husband—who stumbles over the bridge. Ellen and Harry are drawn to each other; they kiss. He admits to having had six women once, and one woman twenty-two times; she says there's been only Milt. Harry throws her mink coat into the river; she bids him prove his love for her by jumping in. Milt, all wet, comes up in time to stop Harry. He has filled a bag with junk from the garbage pail, and borrows five dollars from Harry, to go home.

A few months later Ellen and Milt meet at the bridge again, happy with their new partners, "deliriously happy." Then Milt bursts out: "She left me—walked out," and Ellen confesses she's miserable, but will stick to take care of Harry: "I know where my duties are." Harry arrives; they try sneakily to push him over the bridge; Milt stumbles and falls off. By the time he gets back, Harry jumps over. Ellen and Milt go off together. Harry climbs back, and cries: "Where's my 5 bucks, you cheap bastard!" A dog comes in; Harry jumps, and hangs on to the crossbar of the lamppost with the dog gripping his pants leg as the curtain falls.

Luv was revived in Los Angeles and at Palm Beach with Barbara Bel Geddes, in 1966; in 1969 in Texas. John Simon, in the *Hudson Review*, spring 1965, analyzed Schisgal's achievement: "It is plain and simple burlesque and vaudeville . . . the old burlesque device of repetition by way of a slow comic build-up serves a dual purpose here: it stretches out a mere playlet into the more marketable commodity of a play, and it allows the playwright's essentially commonplace mind to revel in its natural habitat . . . Schisgal is not quite up to what he is trying to poke fun at." Henry Hewes in the *Saturday Review* (November 28, 1964) saw the paradoxical nature of Schisgal's drive: "We are in a comic world in which conventional responses and clichéd superficialities have their own logic and compelling force. . . . Devastating events are to be accepted lightly as a matter of course, but trivial annoyances can evoke furious passion."

Eli Wallach and Anne Jackson were again amusingly on hand, as Milt and Ellen with Alan Arkin, "a thing of rags and poses," as Harry, the final victim of a wire-haired terrier.

The *Wall Street Journal* discerned in *Luv* "the theatre of sense masquering as the theatre of the absurd." Howard Taubman in the *Times* found it "a delicious spoof on many matters . . . you name it, and the author probably has a guffaw at its expense." Walter Kerr in the *Herald-Tribune* went further: "*Luv* is probably the answer to existentialism, bad dreams, Sigmund Freud, fear and trembling . . . and the ever-present problem of underarm unpleasantness. It is certainly the answer to a theatergoer's prayer."

The complex nature of what is at once a parody and a sort of Picasso portrait gives both amusement and afterthought to *Luv*.

ANATOL   *Arthur Schnitzler*

In considering the plays of Arthur Schnitzler (Austrian, 1862-1931), it must be kept in mind that he was a physician, the author of papers on hypnotism and psychotherapy, and a contemporary of Freud. His plays are explorations of "the vast domain" of the soul. After 1895, when Schnitzler turned almost entirely to literary work (novels and short stories, as well as plays), he helped form the "Young Vienna" group, opposed to the naturalism then triumphant in Berlin. Beyond the individual soul-studies of his dramas spread the various levels of Viennese society, even in his comedies finding overtones of melancholy in the declining Austrian culture. Schnitzler, Sol Liptzin has said, "caught in his gentle hand the last golden flow of Vienna's setting glory, and converted it to art." He seems to saying, "Eat, drink and be wistfully merry, for tomorrow civilization will die."

By far the most popular of Schnitzler's plays is *Anatol*. Perhaps Anatol is in some measure Schnitzler himself; for under the pseudonym "Anatol" he issued his earliest works. In the play, Anatol talks of his experiences to his friend Max, with a wit and irony constantly turned upon himself, and with a wistfulness that sends him to his wedding, at the end, sophisticate and almost cynical, but fluttery, nervous and hopeful as any young bride. Of the seven short episodes in the play, most amusing is that in which Anatol prepares to tell Mimi all is over between them—then is caught in surprise and chagrin when Mimi beats him to the break with word of her own new love.

Beneath the frivolity of Anatol, however, one can sense the yearning for an association more firmly tied by understanding, wherein love is not a game one side must lose, but a way of life two folk may walk together. A way unfound, yet ever to be seeking. It is this underlying wistful sense of search—as well as the deft craftsmanship and the witty, charming dialogue—that has won such success for *Anatol*. A life-long flitting from love to love would be a bitter emptiness, as Schnitzler himself indicated in a later playlet, *Anatol's Megalomania,* produced in 1932, which shows Anatol as a shuffling old pantaloon.

Several scenes from *Anatol* were enacted at Ischl, Austria, in 1893; the whole group was not produced until 1910 in Vienna and Berlin. The translation of *Anatol* by Granville Barker, *The Affairs of Anatol,* was presented in London in 1911; in New York, in 1912 with John Barrymore. It was revived in New York in 1931 with Joseph Schildkraut, Walter Connolly, Patricia Collinge, and Miriam Hopkins. Barrymore presented five and Schildkraut six of the original seven episodes. Various episodes have been frequently presented by college and little theatre groups. Equity Library revived *Anatol* in New York in 1946, directed by Mady Christians (who had played in it under Reinhardt in 1924), with Tonio Selwart and Carmen Matthews.

When *Anatol* was first produced in America, the theme of the play disturbed some reviewers. The *New York Dramatic Mirror* (October 16, 1912) declared: "Anatol is the polygamous animal in which Herbert Spencer once summed up all mankind. But the lovely thing about him is his geniality and utter detestation of hypocrisy. He runs the whole gamut of possible 'affairs' without once besmirching his honor. . . . He sins as a perfect gentleman should, if he should sin at all." In Chicago, where the "gentleman" is apparently not so important, the *Record Herald* (December 18, 1912) complained: "The skit is about a gull and his girls. . . . As these triumphs are merely the carryings-on of a green youth who flops about like a belated Byronic derelict; no interest attaches to them as experiences in life. . . . The mawkishness of the composition occasionally is assuaged by its deft mockery. . . . The intention of the thing is deplorable, its effect is tedious and insipid."

The public taste seemed to mellow with revivals. Gilbert W. Gabriel (January 17, 1931) called *Anatol* "still a treasurable, immensely actable, delightful little roundelay of sentiment and cynicisms, of farce-lined wit and charming heart-break. . . . Here, in many ways and many smiles, is the most inviting revival New York has been granted in your day and mine." Vernon Rice (June 5, 1946) found in the play "variety, contrast, and consuming interest." Anatol is a lasting figure, for he moves in smiling earnest on an eternal quest.

Anatol is the most popular picture of the eternal playboy, dwelling in a wish-world. What gives depth to the character, and the play, is that beneath the frivolous desires that live in the moment, beneath the urges that spend themselves on the present joy, stirs a basic yearning—almost too urgent, too unrealizable, for utterance—for a more stable life of love and understanding that somehow will endure.

Each of the seven episodes in the play shows Anatol with another light o' love, as he seeks, and fails to find, a permanent attachment—from Cora, the seamstress, whom he hypnotizes to ask if she's been untrue, and then is afraid to ask, to Ilone, whom he takes home the night before his wedding. The audience is left to speculate on how long the marriage of such a man will endure. Will he be unfaithful—or become a cuckold?

PROFESSOR BERNHARDI   *Arthur Schnitzler*

The most complex of Schnitzler's studies of human nature is *Professor Bernhardi*. In this intense drama, the conflict of ethical and religious standards flares from a Vienna hospital and widely and deeply tries men's souls.

Acted in 1912 in Berlin, then all over Europe, by Fritz Kortner, *Professor Bernhardi* everywhere aroused a storm of discussion. The play was banned in Germany in the 1930's. New York saw it in German in 1914 and 1918. It was presented by the Jewish Drama League in London in 1927. It was acted again in London in 1931, translated by Hetty Landstone, directed by Heinrich Schnitzler, the author's son, and in 1936, translated by Louis Borell and Ronald Adam; both times, with Abraham Sofaer as Dr. Bernhardi.

Freedly and Reeves in *A History of the Theatre*, 1941, called *Professor Bernhardi* "a far from faultless play about anti-Semitism, which is robbed of much of its force because its author began it with a situation which was insufficient to explain the forces released, and because the conclusion of the play seems ineffectual." The play is more rewardingly captured, however, when the view is taken that anti-Semitism is not a basic drive but a hatred roused when desires are thwarted. In a situation where one cannot have one's way, what easier diversion than to snarl upon the Jew!

It is a simple humanitarian act, so it seems to Professor Bernhardi, that brings the storm upon him. A charity patient, in the hospital that he heads, is unaware that she is dying. The priest, Father Reder, wishes to see her, to save her immortal soul; the doctor forbids the priest's going to her, so that her last living hours may be happy. An officious Catholic nurse, Sister Ludmilla (the only woman we see in the play) informs the girl that the priest is waiting; the shock kills her. Personal enmities, then political and religious motives, gather force from this incident to bring about the Jewish Professor Bernhardi's resignation, then his imprisonment. Such animosities are aroused that Sister Ludmilla testifies falsely at the trial, making it seem that Professor Bernhardi has denied religious consolation to one seeking it. The priest, for testifying that in his opinion Bernhardi was honestly doing what he thought best for the patient, is transferred to a dreary Polish parish. When Bernhardi, released because prince Constantin needs the best medical attention, learns these facts, he is urged to apply for a reopening of his case—and he refuses. He has done what he considers right; let each examine his own conscience.

Professor Bernhardi shows Schnitzler's character-drawing at its best. Each of the dozen doctors at the hospital, Jewish and Christian, is deftly differentiated, his ideas and his prejudices humorously yet honestly caught. There is a superb scene at the end between Bernhardi and the priest, Father Reder, wherein the latter admits the potency of Bernhardi's attitude, but declares he could not say anything that might be so construed as to harm the Church. The fine balance maintained in this scene may be observed through two concurrent interpretations of it, after the London 1927 presentation. Said the *Era* (February 14): "One of the finest things in the play is the beautifully written scene at the end in which the Jewish doctor and the priest, both idealists serving their idea of right, come to an understanding and shake hands." The *Stage* (February 14), stating that the play strikes "the human note in the final colloquy with Reder, come ostensibly to confess that Bernhardi had been in the right, but really to safeguard his own position," ended its comments with the remark that the Jewish doctor and the Catholic priest "shake hands across the chasm, without looking down into it."

As a matter of fact, the two men do understand and respect one another. Their points of view are on opposite sides of a chasm, it may be, a chasm too deep to fill; but across it understanding and mutual respect may build a bridge. *Professor Bernhardi* is a genuine dramatic contribution to such understanding. "Its enduring power," said the *London Times* (June 16, 1936) "is as a discussion, first, of two opposed systems of thought, and, secondly, of two differing sets of moral values." In fuller detail, Charles Morgan observed this "genuine study of differing sets of values. Bernhardi himself is by no means exempt from criticism; his stubborn refusal to compromise in little things, his fanatical lack of proportion, his special variety of spiritual pride, are set side by side with the excessive desire of priest and politicians to excuse their immediate failures or weaknesses by saying that it is often necessary to subordinate the means to the end. Schnitzler is not impartial; he has his own prejudice and he does not conceal it; but his satire is by no means undistributed. The result is a play of rare balance and subtlety and one that rewards every perceptive delicacy of the players."

The anti-Semitism in *Professor Bernhardi,* thus, is no more than summoned ammunition in several intertangled wars. We see the opposition of the scientific and the religious spirit; more precisely, of the sceptical and the mystical temperament. And beyond this opposition of the scientific humanitarian concern for the immediate welfare and the Catholic concern for the eternal soul, there presses still another basic issue, that of integrity of spirit, of harmony between end and means, of honesty in the advancement of one's own cause. Both of these problems—what one believes, the immediate versus the ultimate values; and how to move toward one's objectives: does even the shiniest goal excuse a tarnished striving?—remain basic in our post-war world. And both of them, naturally fused in the drama of living, are searchingly and sharply revealed in *Professor Bernhardi.*

The Vienna Burgtheater brought *Professor Bernhardi* to New York for six performances in 1968.

Another tangled sex-play of Schnitzler's is *Reigen,* in French *La Ronde,* in English *Hands Around* and *Merry-Go-Round.* Privately printed in 1900, it was banned in 1903 as obscene, produced in 1912. The Reinhardt production of 1920 was "driven off the Berlin boards."

There is in it less depth of character, merely sketches, as a prostitute and a soldier meet, make love, and move on. Through ten such episodes, each with one person from the episode before, the same event takes its various ways—until a count awakens with the prostitute of the first episode, who tells him that he came in so drunk that he just fell asleep. A lesser play, yet the RSC referred to its 1982 production (the last at the Aldwych, before moving to the Barbican) as "Schnitzler's classic."

Anatol, played at Birmingham, England, in 1956, was paraphrased by Harley Granville Barker, London, June 9, 1964. With music and lyrics by Arthur Schwartz and Howard Dietz, book by Fay and Michael Kanin, *The Gay Life* opened in New York with Walter Chiari as Anatol, November 18, 1961, for 113 performances. The "classic" *Reigen* is Schnitzler at his most trifling. *Anatol* is provocative; *Professor Bernhardi,* profound.

THE LONELY WAY   *Arthur Schnitzler*

Schnitzler's quietest and most searching play, *The Lonely Way,* turns from his concern with the interrelations of men and women to probe depths of the individual soul. Those who do not give of themselves must tread the lonely way. Schnitzler's thought looks along the path of self-indulgence, which every journeyer without companioning footsteps will find a barren walk. Only as we live in and with others, sharing ourselves with others, do we abide in the hearts of others, and hold their love and comradeship to fortify our days.

How much one can truly give of oneself Schnitzler has pondered in several plays. *Living Hours* (1902) in four one-act plays explores this problem from the point of view of the artist, who draws upon those around him for his art. The strongest of these playlets, *Literature,* is a savage satire of the self-centered exhibitionist. Three one-act plays grouped as *Marionettes* (1906) question what choice we have in determining our own way; they suggest that all humans have only the illusion of freedom. And *Comedies of Words* (1915), another group of three, suggests that our words, our public behavior, set an appearance between the world and our real selves: far from seeking understanding, we hold up a mask that may seem to shield us, but eventually estranges us, bars us, from those around. Thus, we prepare for ourselves the lonely way.

These thoughts are, of course, embodied in dramatic stories, which Schnitzler moves with sure sense of theatrical construction, with characters involved in natural situations, and dialogue that flows with a poetic pulsing yet with the fervor and conviction of life. *The Lonely Way* shows the futility of self-centered lives through the stories of two men of great promise, the painter Julian Fichtner and the poet Von Sala. Julian had seduced, then "for the sake of his career" deserted Gabrielle, who was engaged to his friend, the art student Philip Wegrat. The play opens as Frau Wegrat is dying; she has two children, Felix and Johanna; Felix is the son of Julian. After a life spent in the pursuit of pleasure, Julian returns to claim the love of his son—to find that love bound to Wegrat, the hard-working, responsible man, now professor of art and head of the Academy. And Julian recognizes that "we have to tread the downward path alone—we, who have never belonged to anybody but ourselves. The process of aging must be a lonely one for our kind, and he is but a fool that doesn't prepare himself against having to rely on any human being.* Even the lesson Julian learns is distorted by his lonely self-concern.

The fate of the self-centered Von Sala presses its point more sharply home; for Johanna, loving him, drowns herself, and he brings his sterile life to its end.

The subdued movement of *The Lonely Way*, the melancholy rhythm of the dialogue, the atmosphere as of a golden day of dying autumn, have endeared the play to European audiences. In America it has been less heartily welcomed. The Theatre Guild presented an adaptation by Philip Moeller in Baltimore and Washington in 1931, with Violet Kemble-Cooper, Glenn Anders, Joanna Roos, and Ralph Roeder (replacing Tom Powers, who had fractured a leg bone). New York had to await an OffBway production (Drama Studio) in 1952.

Those that know Schnitzler only through his *Anatol** are unaware of the searching scalpel with which he can reveal more sombre depths of the human soul. These depths are dramatically sounded in *The Lonely Way*.

A GLASS OF WATER   *Augustin Eugène Scribe*

Augustin Eugène Scribe (French, 1791-1861) wrote all or part of some 400 plays, most of them very successfully appealing to the nineteenth-century French playgoer. He was the chief manufacturer of the "well-made play," in which the effects are wrought by the well-timed use of theatrical devices, with firmly-knit construction of an often complicated plot leading to a powerful climax. For the most part, the persons of Scribe's plays do not seem real inhabitants of earth, but dwell in what Brander Matthews labeled "the pleasant land of Scribia." Reading several of Scribe's plays in succession does indeed give one an uneasy sense of scribbledeedee; but taken one at a time, many of them are workmanlike models of dramaturgy, truly effective theatre pieces.

One of Scribe's best plays, still in the repertoire of the Comédie Française, is *A Glass of Water*, 1840. It was performed in New York in 1930, in Pasadena in 1936. London saw a fresh adaptation by Ashley Dukes in 1950. The play pictures how great events may spring from little causes; the history of England is altered because a favorite spills a glass of water on a Queen.

From 1702 to 1711 the Duke of Marlborough was virtually the Regent of England, through the influence of his wife, as Mistress of the Robes, Keeper of the Privy Purse, and trusted though imperious companion of Queen Anne. The play shows the Queen as an amiable, good-natured, but weak and over-romantic woman, more interested in the state of her affairs than in the affairs of her state. She and the Duchess of Marlborough are both in love with a gentleman of the court, who prefers the charming but baser born daughter of the Queen's jeweler. Spun along with this quadrangular romance are the swirl and intrigue of national politics, as the Tory Bolingbroke seeks to oust Marlborough and the Whigs. The destinies of the state hang upon the caprices of the court; and Scribe lifts the play to a strong climax when the Duchess' spilling of a glass of water on the Queen's dress floods out the Queen's long-dammed resentment, and sweeps the Duchess to disgrace and Marlborough to his ruin.

There is an effective battle of wits between Bolingbroke and the Duchess as Scribe deftly handles the intertangled themes of politics and sex. The dialogue is undistinguished, but apt and lively. The play, tightly woven and economically built, alternates amusing and dramatic moments, until the two drives, of men's concerns and women's, concenter their forces in the climax.

Plays of this sort, "well-made," mechanically deft but with characters undeveloped while situations are strongly played, may grow a bit dated, with sophisticated audiences. Outside of theatrical centers, A Glass of Water is still sure-fire material. It has been frequently played, and was a favorite in Russia until the Revolution.

When A Glass of Water had its first American production in English, Robert Garland (March 6, 1930) found it "lovely to look at, arty to listen to, and more than a wee bit tiresome." John Mason Brown insisted this Glass of Water was "hard to swallow," but the New York Herald Tribune deemed it "still good theatrical stuff." The French encyclopedia Larousse Universel, 1922, called it "one of Scribe's most delightful comedies."

In his plays, Scribe reduced great passions and historic events to the level of the plain citizen of the middle class. He was so deft at rousing curiosity and sustaining suspense, at resolving intricate entanglements, at combining the amusing and the moving, that during the performance his characters move with semblance of life, with that illusion of reality which is the secret of great drama. Scribe's works—among the best of which is A Glass of Water—carry to the peak of its potentialities the well-made play. It was revived OffOffBway, translated by Dewitt Bodein, in 1979.

ATSUMORI   *Seami Motokiyo*

This is one of the No plays, which constitute the classical drama of Japan. These plays, lasting about an hour apiece, but usually presented in groups of five with farcical interludes (kyogen), were the chief theatrical entertainment of the aristocratic Japanese for almost 600 years.

The No drama is an outgrowth of several earlier forms of entertainment. There were ballad-singers and wandering reciters of popular poetry. There was the masquerade (sarugaku) that enlivened the Shinto ceremonies. By the tenth century, the countryside juggling and acrobatics (dengaku) had been given shape in a sort of opera with recitative and dance. The Chinese pantomimic dance had been introduced at the Japanese court. This courtly dance (kagura), in delicate and formalized patterns of movement, was blended with elements of these other forms by Kwanami Kiyotsugu (1333-1384), thus creating the No. About 1375 Kwanami, priest of a temple near Nara, was taken under the protection of the shogun Yoshimitsu, a patron of the arts. Kwanami's son, Seami Motokiyo, 1363-1443, further fashioned the form and brought it to its highest peak.

The No drama, acted entirely by masked and elaborately costumed men, is architectonically constructed as a movement of music and dance. The walking about the stage, and the posing during the dialogue, are formalized; in addition, there are wordless dances, such as the many battle scenes and duels, the special dances of the various gods, and a characteristic slow dance (*mai*) mimicking the crane. In most of the plays, the characters are either gods, or ghosts reliving an earthly experience. This device of having an olden story re-enacted by the wraiths of those involved imparts a "distancing" to the events that softens the emotions. The ghosts are wistful wisps of a remembered past; thus the No dramas deal in reticences, in understatement, in delicacy of mood and of diction. Often something lies beneath the surface (*yugen*); this is symbolized by a white bird with a flower in its beak. The dialogue is reinforced with familiar passages from well-known poems (*tanka*) from the classical anthologies; and the pattern of growth of the drama is advanced by pivot-words: puns, words of two meanings that as they approach bear one significance and as they recede take on another. The chief moods of the No plays, beyond the dances of gods, flower spirits, and other supernatural beings, are praise of the gods; the rouse and especially the pathos of battle; revenge; and grief.

Seami has written plays in all these moods. Most representative of his No dramas is *Atsumori,* written about 1400. It is the story of Kumagai, who in 1184 killed Atsumori in battle, and gave to his own son a flute he found beside the fallen warrior. The play shows Kumagai, who regrets his action (for in an earlier incarnation Atsumori had done him a kindness) now become a priest under the name of Rensei. As he laments, reapers appear and sing the responses. One of the reapers, a flute player, lingers, and reveals that he is the ghost of Atsumori. They re-enact the fatal fight; save that, this time, Atsumori lifts his sword over Kumagai.

In recent years Japan has developed a drama fashioned after that of the western world, but the No plays proffer gentle patterns of quiet and beauty in a noisy world.

THYESTES   *Lucius Annaeus Seneca*

The complicated events of Roman history during the lifetime of Lucius Annaeus Seneca (Roman, 4? B.C.-A.D. 65) made literary references to current happenings inadvisable. As an official in Rome, Seneca incurred the dislike of Emperor Caligula, who aptly characterized Seneca's style as "all sand and no mortar." Caligula was murdered, A.D.41. In the same year Messalina, third wife of the new emperor, Claudius, had Seneca banished—on moral charges but political grounds. Messalina was killed by Claudius in 48. The next year, Claudius' fourth wife, his niece Agrippina, recalled Seneca, and made him tutor of Nero, her son by an earlier marriage. Agrippina poisoned Claudius in 54, establishing Nero on the throne. To ensure his own safety Nero poisoned his stepbrother, Britannicus (see Racine's *Britannicus**) in 55. When Agrippina tried to dominate her son Nero, he killed her, A.D. 59. Despite these murders, the early years of Nero's reign, guided largely by Seneca, were comparatively moderate. About the year 63, however, Seneca found himself thrust out of the Emperor's councils. A conspiracy of Piso, in A.D. 65, was held to involve Seneca, who by imperial order committed suicide.

Seneca, the most influential writer of Latin prose after Cicero, wrote many essays in philosophy. He was interested in science, geography, and natural history and wrote the influential *Natural Questions*. As a playwright, he wrote nine tragedies, all based on Greek dramas, all drawn from Greek mythology.

These olden legends, however, far away though they may seem, ring the changes on thoughts and actions in the Rome of Seneca's day. The long rhetorical speeches, as well as the pointed epigrammatic turns, reflect the oratory of the day. The emphasis, much more than in the original Greek, is on the violent emotions, the outrageous crimes. The sensational, the horrible—with the raising of ghosts, for deeds so abominable the very ghosts do blench—accord with the turbulence of Messalina's and Nero's Rome. From the stories, an alert audience might well draw the immediate allusion. The tyrant is a frequent figure in the plays. The stepmother recurs. And constantly the stories drive home the lesson that crime leads to further crime in endless repetition. The Roman citizen saw the truth of this all around him.

Although there are records of nine Greek plays and eight Roman plays named *Thyestes*, the only one extant is that by Seneca. *Thyestes* is the most gruesome of ancient tragedies. Throughout, it is marked by an atmosphere of gloom, and driven by the spirit of hatred and revenge. The play opens with one of the Furies calling forth the ghost of Tantalus, who shrinks from the dire deeds ahead. For Atreus has, on a pretense of peace, called back his brother Thyestes, who has seduced Atreus' wife. Thyestes returns, although mistrustfully, and asks for his sons. Atreus responds: "I'll restore them to you: and never more shall you be parted from them." There is a banquet of reconciliation. At the end of the feast, the heads of Thyestes' sons are brought in, and Atreus tells him he has fed upon their bodies.

Something of the Stoic fortitude with which Seneca himself ended his life is manifest in his characterization of Thyestes. There is dramatic tension, too, in the politeness and restraint—hatred boiling under the kettle's hood—of the brothers' meetings. But the power of the play lies, first, in the overhanging sense of dread, and then, in the burst of horror with the foul revenge. Sharply it observes the tyrant, so cruel a man that "death is a longed-for favor in my realm."

(The sons of Atreus are Agamemnon and Menelaus, so that in the generations ahead Thyestes is avenged, with the doom of the House of Atreus reaching through four generations.)

Thyestes, the most influential of Seneca's tragedies, gave birth to the Elizabethan blood-and-thunder play, the tragedy of revenge, as in Shakespeare,* Kyd,* Marston,* and Chapman.* A line of Seneca's *Agamemnon,* "The only path that's safe for crime is crime," which is the motif of *Thyestes,* is quoted in Latin in *The Spanish Tragedy,*^ and in *The Malcontent,* by Martston; it is paraphrased in six other Elizabethan dramas. Even Seneca's tricks of style, his neat epigrams, his stichomythia, his closing ethical tags, were copied by the eager Elizabethans.

Two lines of the play—"For whom the morning saw so great and high Thus low and little 'fore the eve doth die"—are quoted in Marlowe's *Edward II*^ and form the final couplet of Jonson's *Sejanus.*

Scholars for a long time, because of their many rhetorical passages, believed that the plays of Seneca were intended for recitation only; current opinion has it that they were performed. Although the tragedies have many sensational scenes and supernatural apparitions (not gods so much as ghosts), they bring their legendary characters nearer to human proportions than do their Greek originals. The demigods have been reduced to the human level, with human motivations. However extreme, Atreus still is human in his hatred and in his lust for vengeance. That human life, furthermore, as in *Thyestes* at the bitter end, retains its dignity. Man is viewed as acting of his own free will; descending, perhaps, into blackest villainy, but capable also of Stoic fortitude, of clean integrity despite the disintegrating forces of the world. Many may stand erect, proudly human, in the face of disaster.

At the same time, man moves in a world of brutality and crime, the excesses of which were all around Seneca, who put them full and stark into his dramas. His pattern has been the most influential on all tragedy since. See Sophocles' *Oedipus the King.* *

SLEUTH   *Anthony Shaffer*

Anthony Shaffer (b. May 15, 1926), after collaborating with his twin brother, Peter, on three mystery novels, wrote his first play, the two-act mystery thriller *Sleuth.* As a prank, he named it *Who's Afraid of Stephen Sondheim?* When his friend Sondheim protested, he changed it to *Anyone for Tennis?* (hence the two curtain lines); then *Anyone for Murder?* Finally, he settled on *Sleuth.*

The play was produced in London in 1970, and ran for 2,359 performances. On November 12, 1970, it opened at the New York Music Box, where it had 1,226 performances. In both cities, Anthony Quayle played Andrew; Keith Baxter, Milo. Although there are offstage noises, and other names on the program to keep the audience expectant, *Sleuth* is the only two-character mystery play.

It plays "the game of death." Milo Tindle, a travel agent, is the lover of the wife of Andrew Wyke, a writer of mysteries, who plans to divorce her, but not to give her up to a neighbor whom he hates. During their verbal duel, Andrew suggests that Milo disguise himself and "steal" the Wyke jewels; Milo can sell them, Andrew can collect the insurance, and each go his separate way. When the "burglar" Milo appears, Andrews shoots him, crying, in tennis terms, "Game and set!" as the curtain falls.

In the second act, a detective calls on Andrew; when his questions grow alarming, he reveals himself as Milo—Anthony had fired a blank. The "game" continues, until an approaching police-car light flashes through the window; a loud knocking shakes the door, and Milo cries, "Game, set, and match!" as he again drops dead.

Clive Barnes called *Sleuth* "an entertaining tale of detective-story mayhem with a touch of urbane intellectualism added for savor. . . . It has a ponderous frivolity that sparkles like golf-course sunshine on early-morning corpses." It is, said Ted Kalem in *Time,* "urbanely and unashamedly literate, clawingly tense, and playfully savage."

It is always hard to sustain interest in a two-character play, especially in a mystery, where the essential hold is not merely interest but suspense. *Sleuth* is unique in that its two figures are neatly contrasted; audience intelligence is quickened as the "game" progresses; and even at its ending one may speculate as to the end. The maneuverings of two doomed men keep the play alive.

It seems worth mention that Anthony Shaffer's next play, *The Murderer* (1975), begins with thirty minutes of speechless action, as we watch an artist, in a rear room, strangle a model and limb by limb dismember the hapless corpse. When the dialogue beings, "she" turns out to have been a dummy.

Sleuth, called in London "a brilliant thriller that parodies thrillers," has had numerous productions. Paris, and Sydney, Australia, 1970; Los Angeles, 1972; Pocono Playhouse, 1974; Barter Theatre of Abingdon, Va., 1975; Williamstown Festival, 1976; Long Island, 1977; Midland, Tex., 1978. At the London Savoy, opening March 7, 1978, Patrick Cargill played Wyke; Tony Anholt, Tindle. The Pennsylvania Stage Co., October 1983. Laurence Olivier was in the film. The game of death, deftly played, keeps the audience alive and guessing.

FIVE-FINGER EXERCISE   *Peter Shaffer*

Into the family of Stanley Harrington, in *Five-Finger Exercise,* by Peter Shaffer (b. 1926, twin brother of Anthony*), comes the tutor Walter Langer as a catalytic agent. Nineteen-year-old Clive is afraid of his father and dominated by his mother; his fourteen-year-old sister is eager for life. Between them and their parents, there is not only a generation gap, but an inability to bridge it. Walter quickens something in them all.

Stanley is a prosperous furniture manufacturer, who is certain that he is doing all right. His bored wife sees Walter as a possible lover; when he does not so deem her, she dismisses him as a bad influence on the children. But he has been a friend to Clive, a stimulus to the girl; and his departure brings on a crisis. Clive faces his family, and sees that they must "pray for courage" to grow together in trust and love. "For all of us, O God, give it!"

Running a year in London in 1958, directed by John Gielgud, and at the New York Music Box December 2, 1959, for 337 performances—with Roland Culver as Stanley; Jessica Tandy, his wife; Brian Bedford, Clive; Michael Bryant, Walter; Juliet Mills, the girl—the play is a well-constructed and searching study of a frequent family concern.

THE ROYAL HUNT OF THE SUN   *Peter Shaffer*

The Royal Hunt of the Sun, by Peter Shaffer, was first presented by the NT at the Chichester Festival June 7, 1964. This "play concerning the conquest of Peru" was so brilliantly designed by Michael Annals that the author described it: "A huge aluminum ring, 12 feet in diameter, hung in the center of a plain wooden back wall. Around its circumference were hinged twelve petals. When closed, these interlocked to form a great medallion on which was incised the emblem of the Conquistadors; when opened, they formed the rays of a giant golden sun, emblem of the Incas." Within this sun, from his first appearance in Scene 3 until Scene 8, the climbing of the Andes, stands Atahualpa, sovereign Inca of Peru, Sun-god, Son of the Sun. Robert Stephens played Atahualpa; Colin Blakely, Pizarro.

The play opens with old Martin Ruiz, who speaks to the audience of this story "about ruin and gold." Pizarro in Spain enlists volunteers for his third expedition to Peru; young Martin joins as his page. With his 187 men and 27 horses are two representatives of the Church, and the Overseer for King

Charles V of Spain. Pizarro is a rough and cynical commander, a bastard, "reared in a pigsty," suffering from an old, never-cured wound. Young Martin is an eager naïve youth; when he protests: "But, Sir, a noble reason can make a fight glorious," Pizarro retorts: "Give me a reason that stays noble once you start hacking limbs off in its name."

Atahualpa—himself a bastard who has defeated his legitimate half brother, rival for the throne—is a trusting soul in this socialist land, where every age has its appointed tasks, its duties and rewards; where, as the interpreter describes them to the Spaniards: "Not poor. Not rich. All same." Despite his counselor's advice, the king will see these newcomers.

We watch the Spaniards advancing, past a miming of Indians sowing and reaping; into a mime of the great ascent of the Andes, to the meeting with Atahualpa, who asserts his rule, examines and scorns the proffered Bible, and precipitates the massacre of his unarmed men. A mime of the great massacre of three thousand Indians, with the Inca's crown tossed to Pizarro, while from the middle of the sun howling Indians rush with a vast bloodstained cloth that bellies out over the stage, brings the act to its end.

In the second act, the cynical Pizarro is softened. He has said, of tenderness to women: "What is it but a lust to own their beauty, not them, which you never can: like trying to own the beauty of a goblet by paying for it. And even if you could, it would become you, and get soiled." But now he feels a tenderness for Atahualpa, whom he promises to free unharmed when the Indians have filled a room with gold. The Catholic priests and the King's Overseer clamor for the Inca's death, but Pizarro remains firm in his promise—even wondering why Christ is the only one to rise again after death: perhaps in this land "beyond all maps and scholars" . . . until Atahualpa declares that, once freed, he will spare Pizarro but must avenge on the Spaniards the massacre of his three thousand unarmed men. Pizarro then turns him over to the Church authorities, and we watch the garroting of Atahualpa. The Indians keep watch too, wearing the golden funeral masks of ancient Peru, until the sun rises; but as its rays touch his body Atahualpa does not move, and they shuffle away in dejection and defeat.

Martin comments that the Europeans have given Peru "greed, hunger, and the Cross: three gifts for the civilized life." To the audience, "God save you all," and Martin goes. Pizarro, left alone with the dead king, lies down beside him, singing the Inca's song:

> *See, see the fate, O little finch,*
> *Of robber birds, O little finch.*

"The sun glares at the audience" as the curtain falls.

From summer 1964 at Chichester the play came to London December 8, 1964, the first play by a contemporary presented by the NT. Bernard Levin in the *Mail* the next day declared: "No greater play has been written and produced in the language in my lifetime." Harold Hobson in the *Sunday Times* December 13, 1964, detailed his delight in "the great pictorial set pieces, like the opening of the golden rose to reveal the figure of the painted god, the irruption on the stage of the feathered Incas, the slow, painful climbing of the Andes by the rapacious and stunningly courageous Spaniards. . . . The finest scene in a very fine play is the chorus of masks around the dead body of Atahualpa waiting for the first rays of the rising sun to touch him, and fill him once again with radiant life . . . Atahualpa . . . incomprehensible to human thought, and unforgettable to human memory."

On November 6, 1965, the play came to the ANTA in New York, for 261 performances, then went on a national tour. Richmond and Cleveland saw it in 1969. In 1977 the London Coliseum briefly showed it as an opera, "the play with music tacked on." Manitoba saw the play in 1978; Cleveland, in 1982. Proper production is costly, but London's National Youth Theatre revived it in 1983.

The author pictures the play as "the encounter between European hope and Indian hopelessness, between Indian faith and European faithlessness"; but it has deeper undertones and challenging thoughts, as when the Franciscan De Nizza declares that Satan is in "this country which denies the right to hunger." Pizarro: "You call hunger a right?" "Of course; it gives life meaning. Look around you. . . . They have everything in common, so they have nothing to give each other. . . . All men are born unequal: this is a divine gift. And want is their birthright. Where you deny this and there is no hope of any new love; where tomorrow is abolished and no man ever thinks "I can change myself," there you have the rule of Anti-Christ." Perhaps he was mistaken who wanted man free fom fear; fear is one of the things over which man must maintain his power. . . . *The Royal Hunt of the Sun* maintains its power over the audience.

EQUUS   *Peter Shaffer*

With striking theatrical effect the horses in *Equus* dominate the stage and vivify the story. With heads outlined in wire, and stilted silver shoes, the men-as-steeds (*Equus* is Latin for horse) form an epic in motion, waking memories of myth; they fascinate the audience, which can sympathize with if not wholly share the obsession of young Alan in the play. A seventeen-year old stableboy, Alan used to go riding, naked, at night; the horses gave him exhilaration and even sexual release. Then one day, after a tender maid's unsuccessful attempt at lovemaking (played in the nude), Alan with a hoof pick blinded six horses. We learn these earlier events as the psychiatrist probes.

The psychiatrist who is treating the boy is himself seeking escape from the boring routine of his days with his provincial wife; in the process of helping Alan, with the sympathy of a woman magistrate who becomes in a sense his mother confessor, he finds his own maturer adjustment. As a blunt but honest critic pointed out, save for the horses, the story is pure soap opera. But the horses are there. ("Save for the poetry, Shakespeare . . .")

The July 26, 1973, NT (Old Vic) production with Alec McCowen as the psychiatrist Martin Dysart, and Peter Firth as the young Alan Strang, ran for ten months; the play returned at the Albery April 4, 1976, with Colin Blakeley and Gerry Sundquist. It opened in New York October 24, 1974, with Anthony Hopkins, followed by Richard Burton, Anthony Perkins, and Alec McCowen as the psychiatrist, with Helen Hayes entering the cast as the magistrate, for a total of 1,209 performances. Along the way it took the Tony and the Critics' Circle awards. Anthony Hopkins directed and acted in the nationwide 1976-1977 tour. The play has been performed widely around the world: Catholic Madrid, in 1976, permitted the nude scene, which was banned in Dallas and Atlanta. In 1979 the play was performed in Los Angeles by the West Coast Performing Arts Center for the Deaf, with voice and Ameslang (American sign language). The NT revived the play November 2, 1979; Broadway, December 17, 1980. Clive Barnes found in it "a quality of thoughtfulness that is rare in the contemporary popular theatre." John Beaufort analyzed this: "The artistic achievement lies not merely in what the conflict unfolds but in what it suggests about the human mystery. . . . Although the work is multi-layered, the expression is a model of clarity."

On March 19, 1980, Baltimore saw the world premiere of the ballet *Equus,* supervised by Peter Shaffer, music by Wilfrid Josephs, choreography by Dany Reiter-Soffer. The ballet was danced in 1980 in Brooklyn; in 1982 by the Dance Company of Harlem.

The play, with the double psychological problem of the boy and his doctor, achieves individuality and distinction through the superb theatricality of the dominating horses.

AMADEUS   *Peter Shaffer*

The notion that Antonio Salieri, court composer to Emperor Joseph II of Austria, in jealousy poisoned his younger rival Mozart is accepted as fact in the poetic play *Mozart and Salieri,* by Pushkin (1832), which Rimsky-Korsakov set to music. Peter Shaffer prefers to leave it in doubt.

Shaffer's play opens in 1823, thirty-two years after the death of Mozart. Seated in a wheelchair, the seventy-three-year-old Salieri looks back upon the years of Mozart's stay in Vienna. Flashbacks present the events of the rivalry, but of course it is the Kappelmeister's point of view that colors the picture. Mozart is shown as an unbridled libertine with a wide range of gutter talk, a contemptible figure—save that he echoes "the music of the spheres." Salieri is a well-meaning man, even a pious man, content to present his music to the court—until Mozart arrives with no virtues save his genius. Then, as Frank Rich puts it in the *New York Times* (December 18, 1980:) "When he discovers that there is no connection between virtue and the talent he covets, Salieri must confront the most profound emptiness—the one that comes when man ceases to believe that he lives in a rational universe governed by a divine plan. By obsessively plunging into that void Salieri escalates his plight until he arrives at a tragic rendezvous with madness. . . . To the extent that we identify with them [Salieri and Mozart], their helplessness before the irrationality of fate becomes our own." If Salieri did not actually poison Mozart, he poisoned many hours of his days. Mozart died in 1791, at the age of thirty-five.

The play has many neat touches. Thus, when the two first meet, Salieri plays a commonplace march he had composed. Mozart at once plays it straight through; then he replays it, plays with it, until—lo! it becomes the aria "Non piu andra" in the first act of Mozart's *Figaro,* which he was then composing.

Amadeus opened at the NT (Olivier) November 2, 1979, with Peter Scofield as Salieri, Simon Callow as Mozart, Felicity Kendall as Constanze Weber, Mozart's wife (who almost throws herself at Salieri once, to spare her husband). Despite reservations by several newspapers, including the *Telegraph* and the *Sunday Times,* the play is still running as I write. It came to the National Theatre in Washington in November 1980, opening at the New York Broadhurst December 17, 1980, to what Clive Barnes in the *Post* called "a total, iridescent triumph." The American cast was headed by Ian McKellan as Salieri; Tim Curry, Mozart; Jane Seymour, Constanze. Peter Hall directed both productions.

Shaffer made a number of changes and cuts for the New York production. He omitted the death of the Emperor, as irrelevant. More significantly, he took out the part of Greybig, Salieri's majordomo and assistant in the harrowing of Mozart; this made Salieri more active, more provocative, in the effort to keep down and humiliate his rival. And Shaffer added a scene at the premiere of *The Magic Flute,* which Salieri had tried to prevent.

The play was a continuing hit in New York also. Roman Polanski put on the London version in Warsaw, 1981, then in Paris; elsewhere—Vienna, Berlin, Sydney, and on U.S. tour in 1982-1983—the later changes were used.

Incidentally, Mozart's name at his baptism was Johannes Crysostomus Wolfgangus Theophilus Mozart. The Greek form, Latin Amadeus, German Gottlieb, all mean beloved of God; he usually signed himself in French, Amadé.

Amadeus, while it is sprung of music and the eerie haunting of death, takes hold upon the audience as the conflict within the soul of a man who sees unworthiness prospering through divine favor while his own honest striving wins only the bitter gains of mediocrity.

William Shakespeare
1564-1616

Merely to list the productions of Shakespeare's plays would crowd this volume. The Royal Shakespeare Company (RSC) has two theatres in London—long at the Aldwych, in spring 1982 moved to the new Barbican—and two in Stratford-upon-Avon. Stratford, Ontario; Stratford, Connecticut: there are some twenty major Shakespeare Festivals in America and Europe, including Russia. Mention should also be made of the free Shakespeare in New York's Central Park, initiated by Joseph Papp, and the mobile theatre around the city's five boroughs.

In 1964, Shakespeare's 400th anniversary year, Louis Marder, editor of the *Shakespeare Newsletter,* estimated there were in the United States 433 productions of thirty-one Shakespeare plays, the most being *Midsummer Night's Dream* (46), *Twelfth Night* (45), *The Taming of the Shrew* (36), *Othello* (30), *Romeo and Juliet* (27), *Hamlet* (24). In the same year (its 104th season) the Stratford-upon-Avon company presented the history plays in chronological order: *Richard II, Henry IV, Henry V, Henry VI* (Edward IV), *Richard III.*

Stars will continue to seek Shakespeare roles, each reinterpreting a well-known character through his or her dramatic personality. Recent emphasis has in quest of novelty turned upon external aspects of the plays. Costumes have varied, from those imagined to fit the time of the story to various periods from Elizabethan to contemporary, with occasional imaginative hybrids. Witches have ridden broomsticks; ghosts have been wisps of smoke; fairies have flown across the stage. A 1972 *Macbeth,* "in the spirit of the times" showed Lady Macbeth in her somnambulant scene walking nude. An Edinburgh Festival production of *As You Like It,* in 1981 made "frantic and even frenzied efforts to be funny, original, and spectacular. . . . The play's visual extravagances may appeal to those who know no English."

The thought of Shakespeare for the semi-literate turns us for a moment from stage to books. "Comic strip" Shakespeare has offered *Much Ado About Nothing, Julius Caesar,* and more, with guards and soldiers like Keystone Cops. And in 1976 the plays were "translated" into "modern" English. With little regard for Shakespeare's metaphors, and even less for his rhythm and style, with indifference to subtlety and even ignorance of idea, the "translation" justifies the Italian saying *traduttore, traditore:*

translator, traitor. For "Out, out, brief candle" we read "Burn out, burn out, brief candle of life." "To be or not to be, that is the question" becomes the misleading "To be or not to be, that is what really matters," when Hamlet is thinking not generally but of his own life: "To be or not to be, that is my problem." "Oh, what a rogue and peasant slave am I!" is transmogrified into "O what a bum and miserable flunky I am!", as though *bum* were the cue to Hamlet's mood, and *flunky* were more familiar to the half-literate than either *peasant* or *slave*. Lord Chesterfield advised his son: "Let blockheads read what blockheads write."

At the London Old Vic, 1914-1916, all of Shakespeare's plays were presented. In 1981-1983 British television put on all the plays of Shakespeare, in a series taken over to the United States; in New York, via Channel 13. The ones I have seen, on either side of the Atlantic, confirm the fact that Shakespeare's characters are three-dimensional.

Some of the plays have been turned into musicals, which may be mentioned with the particular play. Many have been played in the open air, on platform stages, or on spreading lawns near "another part of the forest." Within theatres, the actors may sit on chairs on an otherwise bare stage until it is their turn to rise and take part; or there may be the most elaborate realistic construction; or fancy may seek variety. Metal rods have created walks on several levels, so that, for instance, the Lords Capulet and Montague may meet for a confronting silent and sullen moment above their quarreling retainers. Center stage in Erwin Piscator's *King Lear*, circular steps led to an area that was the edge of the Dover cliffs, and the heath whereon Lear and the Fool outfaced the raging storm, and the platform whence Sam Jaffe as the dying Lear spoke words (from *Troilus and Cressida*) to press Piscator's point that a man himself presents Destiny with the instruments of his own doom.

As Allardyce Nicoll reminds us: "Particularly the texts of Shakespeare's tragedies and comedies have been mangled and mauled by actors and directors, many of them, like Caesar's murderers, most honorable men, yet dominated, like many honorable men, by overweening belief in their own superior skills and rectitude." (In the fourth century B.C. Lycurgus established official texts of the great Greek tragedies; any producer deviating would be fined.) Almost every current Shakespearean director makes cuts and other alterations.

There are many volumes discussing the plays onstage. Well known are the G. Odell 1920 *Shakespeare from Betterton to Irving* and the 1970 Ivor Brown *Shakespeare and the Actors*. Two series are in process: *Plays in Performance*, edited by Julie Hankey, beginning with *Richard III*; and *The Masks of Macbeth . . . Othello . . .* by Marvin Rosenberg. The annual *Shakespeare Survey* and the older German *Shakespeare Jahrbuch* give reports of worldwide events and trends in the field.

The discussions that follow seek to present insights and highlights in the story of each drama and in its history on the stage. For a play sprung of *Hamlet,* see the end of that discussion; several plays sprung of *Macbeth* follow discussion of it.

Since the Meiji Restoration of 1868, which opened Japan to the West, the Japanese Kabuki theatre has been drawn to the works of Shakespeare. The name Koshiro is perhaps the most famous of the players: Koshiro VII acted Shylock and Othello; the onnagata (Kabuki player who enacts women) Bando Tamasaburo was Desdemona. The present Koshiro IX has been more diversifed: Hamlet, Lear, Othello; but also musicals: *The King and I,*

Sweeney Todd,* twice *Man of La Mancha**; and in 1982 Salieri in *Amadeus.** Shakespeare remains the Western dramatist most frequently played in Japan.

In his tragedies, Shakespeare's puns pierce to the core of the character or the essence of the theme. Thus, Hamlet's puns—of which there are some ninety—spring from his battle with himself, revealing the conflict in his deepest feelings, while the wordplay of Polonius is mainly the rhetorical affectation of a court counselor. In comedy, while suited to the speaker, one aspect of them is caught in Viola's comment to the Fool Feste: "They that dally nicely with words may quickly make them wanton." Most of the witty wordplay in Shakespeare is either wanton or aggressive. (It may be noted that in those days even a clown could speak Latin. Feste says, "Cucullus non facit monachum." Today it is wise to translate.)

The individual plays follow in chronological order.

LOVE'S LABOR'S LOST   *William Shakespeare*

Played in 1598 before Queen Elizabeth, *Love's Labor's Lost,* 1590 ?, first of the Shakespearean plays, satirizes the dainty devices of the courtiers of the Virgin Queen. Their extravagant fashions and elaborate manners were matched by their highly adorned speech, especially after the success of Lyly's prose romance *Euphues,* 1579: the Italianate gloves and feathers; the smirk and bow of the Spanish grandee; the words fetched from the ink-horn, piled in pedantic periods, heaped in high hyperbole. In the play, hearing the curate and the schoolmaster, Moth observes: "They have been at a great feast of language, and have stolen the scraps." But William Shakespeare seems to enjoy, as well as satirize, extravagant language.

The play's substance concerns the trifling of four sets of lovers. The King of Navarre and his three courtiers have sworn to eschew feminine company and to devote themselves to study. They must, however, grant audience to the Princess of France, who comes with three of her ladies. The inevitable does not delay; and the movement of the play arises from the manner in which each of the men discovers that the others are also in love. With the spring cuckoo song— 'When daisies pied and violets blue'—hinting woman's infidelity, and the winter owl song—'When icicles hang by the wall'— suggesting domestic toil, the play lilts with laughter to its close. In the words of the German critic and translator of Shakespeare, Schlegel: "The sparks of wit fly about in such profusion that they form complete fireworks, and the dialogue for the most part resembles the bustling collision and banter of passing masks at a carnival." The many-colored light verbal banter remains delightful.

Less bantering times found the play less pleasing. When Queen Anne, the wife of James I, saw a performance, she could well have echoed the contemporary criticsm: "This play no play but plague was unto me." Jeremy Collier in 1699 said "the whole play is a very silly one." In 1740, a version of *As You Like It* borrowed the Spring Song; in 1762 an adaptation called *The Students* was published but apparently never performed. Until the Romantics, indeed, *Love's Labor's Lost* was quite neglected.

Coleridge saw the play as foreshadowing Shakespeare's greater comedies, "as in a portrait taken of him in his boyhood. I can never sufficiently admire the wonderful activity of thought throughout the whole of the first scene, rendered natural, as it is, by the choice of the characters, and the whimsical determination on which the drama is founded." Swinburne goes a step further: "During certain scenes we seem almost to stand again at the cradle of newborn comedy, and hear the first lisping and laughing accents run over from her baby lips in bubbling rhyme; but when the note changes we recognize the speech of gods. For the first time in our literature the higher key of poetic or romantic comedy is finely touched to a fine issue."

Beneath the romantic dalliance of love, however, Shakespeare presents a deeper thought. "What is the end of study?" Biron asks in the opening scene. The play gives answer. Benjamin Franklin caught the point in a *bon mot*: "A single man . . . is an incomplete animal. He resembles the odd half of a pair of scissors." From Biron's great speech on the education that shines within a woman's eyes, to the final songs with the bird of careless love and the bird of barren wisdom, the play presses home the thought that neither wisdom nor love, neither man nor woman, is whole without the other.

Much has been said of the artificial devices and dialogue of this play. They are attacked by Johnson: "A quibble is to Shakespeare what luminous vapours are to the traveller! He follows it at all adventures; it is sure to lead him out of his way. . . . A quibble was to him the fatal Cleopatra for which he lost the world, and was content to lose it." They are defended by Pater: "Below the many artifices of Biron's amorous speeches we may trace sometimes the 'unutterable longing,' and the lines in which Katharine describes the blighting through love of her younger sister are one of the most touching things in older literature." This early play sets the battle—ornate, sumptuous diction versus simple, direct statement—that Shakespeare fights until his writings end. From beginning to end, however, he is sparing in the use of the common copulative (*is*), giving us a great variety of vivid transitive verbs, that carry on the action.

The travesty of *The Nine Worthies,* enacted by the common folk in the play for the Princess, is one of the earliest burlesques in the English theatre.

The first New York performance of the play was on February 21, 1874, at the Fifth Avenue Theatre; it was produced again at Daly's in 1891. More recently in England, Stratford saw the play in 1934; London, at the Old Vic, in 1936. All Shakespeare's plays are performed in series by London's Old Vic: 1914-1923; 1953-1958. New York saw this play again in 1953.

After the 1874 New York production, the *Spirit of the Times* declared the play "undoubtedly one of Shakespeare's weakest in point of construction. . . . Whatever attraction the play possesses is not in its incidents or plot, but in the beauty and poetry of its lines."

An age in which the art of conversation, and even the sense of leisureliness that is prerequisite to that art, have been hurried away in the gallop of time, finds diminishing returns from this early frolic of Shakespeare's. However, those in whom a love of language persists, who joy in balanced syllables and fair matched phrases, as well as in the round-about indirections by which love romps at last home, will still enjoy their feat display in *Love's Labor's Lost.*

There was a lively revival of the play by RSC in 1979, with Michael Pennington as Berowne; Jane Lapotaire, Rosaline; Tony Church, Don Armado; directed by John Barton.

The play contains over two-hundred puns. As pointed out by M. M. Mahood in *Shakespeare's Wordplay,* 1957, these are divided in a pattern that continues through the comedies, between "the simpletons, who are at the mercy of words they do not fully understand, and the sophisticated wits, who show their mastery of words by ringing all possible changes on their meaning. In this way Shakespeare's comic puns, from being the wisecracks of an intrusive clown, are transformed into puns of character."

KING HENRY VI   *William Shakespeare*

The three parts of *King Henry VI* are separate plays. Scholars believe that Part Two was written first, about 1590. They follow chronologically the history of the king and the Wars of the Roses, with a fidelity to fact no other dramatist has maintained. In fact, arranged in historical sequence, *Richard II,* * *Henry IV,* * *Henry V,* * *Henry VI, Richard III,* * and *Henry VIII* * present a three-century panorama of English history, tracing its course to the birth of Henry VIII's daughter Elizabeth, patron of the playwright. The plays were presented in such sequence at Stratford-on-Avon in 1905 and at Antioch College, Ohio, in 1952. The German critic Schlegel declared that they constitute "a national epic." The plays, teeming with armies embattled against the French, against uprisings of the people or pretenders to the throne, offer vivid portraits of the English kings and emphasize the importance of a strong hereditary line to maintain due order in Britain. They helped contribute to the patriotic spirit of the time; it is said that after Shakespeare's speech of Henry V at Harfleur, the recruiting sergeant had no difficulty in filling his company. The story is drawn from Raphael Holinshed's *Chronicles* (1578). References by Nash, Greene, and others indicate the play's success. However, jealous Ben Jonson sneered at playwrights who used such material.

Part One opens with the dead march for the funeral of Henry V. The successor is an infant and intrigues begin. The adherents of York pluck white roses, the followers of Lancaster pluck red. In France, Joan La Pucelle (Joan of Arc; pictured as in league with the Devil) hurls back the English. The play shows the horrid consequences of rivalry among the nobles, common also while Shakespeare was writing.

Part Two begins with Suffolk; who as procurator for the King had married Margaret in France, delivering his charge to Henry in England. He does not relinquish her wholly, however; and Margaret (O tiger's heart wrapp'd in a woman's hide!) and Suffolk plot the overthrow of the Duke of Gloster, Protector during Henry's minority. The villainy rebounds upon Suffolk. A rebellion of the Kentish commoner Jack Cade is fomented by the Duke of York. This insurrection is travestied in the play, though several of the commoners' remarks are given pungency, referring to the humble origin of all men, the wretched lot of the people, and the lack of redress for wrongs. Jack Cade himself is killed by a Kentish gentleman. York now sweeps into open rebellion against the weakling Henry, and at St. Alban's field defeats the King's forces.

Part Three shows the Duke of York entering London in triumph, despite Henry's earlier boast: "Thrice is he armed that hath his quarrel just!" The forces of Henry then rally, led by the forceful Queen Margaret; York is captured, taunted, and slain. Spurred on by the Earl of Warwick, the sons of the murdered York—Edward; George, Duke of Clarence; and Richard, Duke of Gloster—scour the fields. Henry is imprisoned in the Tower; there, the bloodthirsty Gloster (later to be Richard III) kills him. Edward IV is established on the throne.

Although the March, 1592 performance of *Henry VI* took in the largest sum reported in Henslowe's *Diary* of receipts, the three parts of *Henry VI* are rarely performed. Some of the lines in Part Three were once well known through Colley Cibber's incorporation of them into his popular adaptation of *Richard III.** The three plays have sometimes been compressed into a single play, as by Edmund Kean in 1817, and in the earlier version of John Crowne, 1680, shaped to emphasize the antipapal feeling of his day. John Barrymore acted in a revival in 1920; Parts Two and Three were produced in Pasadena in 1935.

Some critics, deeming the *Henry VI* plays unworthy of Shakespeare, have declared that they are not his. Thus Tennyson ventured: "I am certain that *Henry VI* is in the main not Shakespeare's, though here and there he may have put in a touch." But Samuel Johnson insisted: "The diction, the versification, and the figures, are Shakespeare's." Most critics today agree with Johnson, surely for Parts Two and Three.

In Elizabethan days, the people had their attitudes shaped at least in part by the theatre. *Henry VI* was an instrument toward this end. "It is," said Hardin Craig, "as if Shakespeare had taken England for his hero." Certainly he was setting before the people a clear and searching examination of government, of a ruler's problems and ways. He pressed sharply home the still needed warning against civil dissension. Sharply, too, he stressed the chaos that follows the conqueror. Henry V is scarcely buried when a sentence comparing him to Julius Caesar is interrupted with word of the crumbling of his newly won empire in France.

Henry VI recognizes that the aggressive man is far from the best ruler; he makes the point about his hero-father. It is here to be noted that Henry VI is the only one of Shakespeare's English kings to possess all the "king-becoming graces" listed by Malcolm in *Macbeth.** Thus the play balances the odds of power and virtue.

At Stratford-upon-Avon on June 28, June 30, and July 2, 1977, RSC played the three parts of Henry VI, directed by Terry Hands. The large cast included Alan Howard as King Henry; Helen Mirren as his Queen; Charlotte Cornwell, Joan la Pucelle; James Laurenson, Jack Cade; Ron Cook, Edward Prince of Wales; Emrys James, Duke of York; his son, later Edward IV, Alfred Lynch; Richard, later Duke of Gloucester, to become Richard III, Anton Lesser. See *Richard III.**

THE COMEDY OF ERRORS   *William Shakespeare*

This play literally began with a riot. To the first recorded performance, at Gray's Inn on Holy Innocents' Day, December 28, 1594, the members of the Inner Temple were invited. Even standing room was lacking, but they pushed in, and the comedy was delayed by the disturbance. It has been played to crowded houses ever since.

The play, the shortest of Shakespeare's, is also his most artificial, with balanced speeches, occasionally in alternate rhyming, with puns, quibbles, and doggerel verse. Coleridge felt that "Shakespeare has in this piece presented us with a legitimate farce in exactest consonance with the philosophical principles and character of farce." Perhaps this is due to his close following of his source, the comedy *The Menaechmi,** by the Roman Plautus. Shakespeare, however, doubles the Roman twinship by providing the master twins with a pair of twin servants. Early separated, one Antipholus (with his Dromio) has grown to prominence in Ephesus; the other Antipholus (with his Dromio) comes there from Syracuse. The wife Adriana, the mistress, and sundry other citizens mix up the pairs, who confuse their own servants and are tangled in odd situations and threats of jail—until the meeting of the identical twins resolves the confusion. The deeper human sentiment rising from the presence and the reunion of the Antipholus' parents, Aegeon and Aemilia, is another contribution of Shakespeare's. The playwright's removal of the locale to Ephesus may have been influenced by the evil reputation of that city, its inhospitality to strangers, that helped produce Paul's *Epistle to the Ephesians,* in the *Bible.*

The Comedy of Errors has been highly popular; there have been frequent adaptations in German, France, Rumania, and other lands. One German version, by Hans Rothe—from Shakespeare from Plautus from a lost Greek original—was re-Englished by Ashley Dukes and performed in London in 1936; the *Times* said "the result of this geminiculture is a cheerful little charade," although this version omits Aegeon, and "with Aegeon goes the scene that touches the Shakespearean comedy with beauty."

Shakespeare deepened the play's mood, not only with the twins' parents, but with the serious notes of jealousy and shrewishness in Adriana, which some scholars deem a reflection of Shakespeare's own home life.

American performances include one by the Ethiopian Art Theatre in 1923. Heywood Broun called this "tiresome . . . but we cannot imagine its being very funny under the most favorable circumstances. It seemed the mustiest foolery possible." Others liked the performance, which was staged on a central platform. John Corbin felt that "the play is frank farce and can be run off successfully only at a heightened tempo and with the action at times running riot in the grotesque." The play was presented at the Century of Progress in Chicago in 1934 and at the World's Fair in New York in 1938. In 1938 and 1939, indeed, it was produced at Columbia, Yale, Northwestern, New York, and Louisiana Universities, at Cleveland, and at Stratford-on-Avon.

In 1938 Richard Watts, Jr. declared: "If you have been wondering all these years just what was wrong with *The Comedy of Errors,* it is now possible to tell you. It has been waiting for a score by Rodgers and Hart, and direction by George Abbott." The musical comedy *The Boys from Syracuse,* with pantomimist Jimmy Savo as Dromio of Syracuse, had come to town in time for Thanksgiving. The critics gave thanks. Brooks Atkinson called it "an exuberant musical comedy . . . giving Shakespeare a commendable assist in the modern vernacular. . . . Let us pass over their bawdries with decorous reserve, pausing only to remark that they are vastly enjoyable, and let us praise them extravagantly for such a romantic song as 'This Can't Be Love' and such gracious mischief as the 'Sing For Your Supper' trio." Sidney B. Whipple was even more emphatic: "I believe it will be regarded as the greatest comedy of its time." John Mason Brown, however, thought it not "really funny," dragging with long waits between the laughs, and too many twin confusions; but he was willing to put the blame for these on Shakespeare: "Mr. Abbott has made a valiant effort to get the great William out of academic hock. . . . With the exception of two or three lines, Mr. Abbott has tossed Shakespeare's dialogue out the window. Even when he follows its content, he does not hesitate to rephrase it in an idiom which is sometimes lusty and always contemporary. . . . One leaves *The Boys from Syracuse* congratulating Mr. Abbott for what he has done and almost—I say, almost— forgiving Shakespeare for his youthful indiscretion."

This 'youthful indiscretion,' *The Comedy of Errors,* has been a vehicle for the transfer of laughter from the ancient Greek theatre to stages of every land and recent time.

It was played with music devised and directed by Peter Wood, London,

1956. *The Boys from Syracuse* opened OffBway April 15, 1963, for five-hundred performances, and in London November 7, 1963. With music by Guy Woolfender and lyrics by Trevor Nunn, the play was voted the best British musical of 1976. In 1981, a modern version of the story, *Oh Brother!*, book and lyrics by Donald Driver, music by Michael Valentine, was attempted, with the twins separated in infancy by an airplane hijacking; the *New York Times* dismissed it as "a spectacularly silly Las Vegas floor show." While *The Comedy of Errors* is "the only Shakespearean play without a deep philosophical idea," said John Masefield, "it is also his first play that shows a fine, sustained power of dramatic construction."

THE TWO GENTLEMEN OF VERONA   *William Shakespeare*

It is the wandering heart that Shakespeare pictures in *The Two Gentlemen of Verona*, 1592 ?, though the mood is romantic comedy. Two of the most popular medieval and Renaissance themes are joined in the play—the pursuit of a wayward lover by a maiden disguised as a page and a man's wooing of the lady-love of his sworn bosom friend. Valentine, at the court of Milan, falls in love with the Duke's daughter, Silvia. Following Valentine from Vienna, his dear friend Proteus, forgetting his own sweetheart Julia, also becomes enamored of the irresistible Silvia. The lonely Julia disguises herself as a man, the first of a long line of similarly disguised women in Shakespeare; she follows Proteus and discovers his infidelity. The usual complications end with the usual readjustment and pairing of the two sets of lovers.

Ideas for the play were drawn from several earlier works, especially the Portuguese Jorge de Montemayor's *Diana Enamorada,* 1542. Hazlitt, indeed, called the play "little more than the first outline of a comedy loosely sketched in." Aspects of it are more fully bodied forth in Shakespeare's later comedies. Thus Julia's disguise as a servitor, bringing messages from the man she loves to his new inamorata, foreshadows the role of Viola in *Twelfth Night.** The philosophical words of Valentine, banished to the forest, look forward to the thoughts of the banished Duke and of Jaques, in the Forest of Arden in *As You Like It.** The matching of wits between the servants, Speed and Launce, however, is amusing in its own right. Indeed, in the version Garrick used in 1762, two extra scenes were added for the antics of Launce and Speed.

The Two Gentlemen of Verona was transformed into an opera in 1820. In 1938 the play was enacted at Stratford as though by boys and girls; this seemed to smooth over one difficulty. There had been considerable critical objection, when Proteus and Valentine are reconciled, to the latter's volunteering to give up his beloved to his friend: "All that was mine in Silvia I give thee." One critic declared that this shows "there is no longer even *one* gentleman of Verona!" Playing in the mood of youthful frolic, the *London Times* pointed out, takes the sting from this otherwise difficult line. To the Elizabethan gentleman, however, that declaration of Valentine was natural and proper, for the Renaissance held friendship more binding than love. A quite different interpretation of the play by Harold C. Goddard sees the ending as part of the irony underlying the story, in that the "gentlemen" of Verona are portrayed as far from gentlemanly or gentle. Launce accurately calls Proteus "a kind of knave" and Valentine "a most notable lubber"; and Launce's treatment of his dog is a Quixotic burlesque of gentlemanly behavior. This suggestion gathers worth from Shakespeare's satiric portrayal of gentlemen in other comedies.

American performances include one in 1916 at the University of Wisconsin; 1927, at Pasadena; 1935, at the University of Oklahoma; 1939, with Whitford Kane, at Ann Arbor, Michigan. Of the first American production, by the Keans, at the Part Theatre, New York, October 1846, the *Spirit of the Times* stated: "It was admirably put upon the stage, and . . . we can truly say it was entirely successful throughout." Noting that some believe parts of the play may not be Shakespeare's, the 1846 critic claimed the whole work for the bard. The Bristol Old Vic company produced the play in London in 1952.

In production, the comic elements are usually emphasized; thus Bernard Shaw (heading his review "Poor Shakespeare!") called Augustin Daly's 1895 adaptation "a pleasant vaudeville." But the shafts of laughter strike the bull's eye in human nature with an aim eternally true.

Shakespeare's earlier plays make us aware of his gift of language, said Logan Pearsall Smith, "but it is only in *The Two Gentlemen of Verona,* with the song 'Who is Sylvia?', with the line 'The uncertain glory of an April day,' and the passage about the brook that makes sweet music as it strays, that his power over words becomes a magic power, and his golden mastery of speech begins to almost blind us with its beauty." There is, said Swinburne, "an even sweetness, a simple quality of grace in thought and language, which keeps the whole poem in tune, written as it is in a subdued key of unambitious equality."

All of this quality is cast aside in the musical version, adapted by John Guave (who wrote the lyrics) and Mel Shapiro (who directed), music by Galt MacDermott, with the Black Passion Quartet. It was presented December 1, 1971, by Joseph Papp, absurdly bedecked with superlatives as "the best musical ever." There was an equally exaggerated limerick contest, with "the biggest prize ever"—for an ill-conceived melanized production, which nevertheless attained 613 performances.

KING RICHARD III   *William Shakespeare*

This play, evidently written in 1593, offers magnificent acting opportunities in the role of "Crouchback" Richard, fierce, ruthless, valiant, every inch a King—save that his mind, like his body, is crooked. So popular was the play in Shakespeare's time that between 1594 and 1620 a dozen other plays quoted or parodied the famous line: "A horse! a horse! my kingdom for a horse!" The image of the horse prominent in this play is closely related to its fierce drive of energy. (Harold C. Goddard called it "a sort of biography of force.") From Pegasus through medieval nightmares and proverbial spurring beggars to Freudian dreams, the horse has been the symbol of the unconscious energy that gallops beneath and often runs away with our conscious selves. *Richard III* is the most rapid in action, the most concentrated in energy, of Shakespeare's plays.

The role of Richard is especially luring in the adaptation made by Colley Cibber in 1699, which converted Shakespeare's drama into a one-man play. Although Sir Henry Irving, in 1896, attempted to restore the Shakespearean scope, later productions (even John Barrymore's in 1920) have preferred to cut nearer the Cibber concentration on the villainous Richard. The Cibber version added bits from others of Shakespeare's history plays; it put the last scene of *King Henry VI** at the beginning, and thus opened with

Duke Richard stabbing Henry. David Garrick made his London debut, October 19, 1741, as Richard in the Cibber adaptation, and established himself as the outstanding actor of the day. Garrick was a "natural" performer, in 1746 he challenged the rhetorical, violent James Quin, and they appeared as Richard on successive nights: the public preferred Garrick.

This was the first of Shakespeare's plays to be performed in America; Thomas Kean played the Cibber version at the New York Nassau Street Theatre, March 5, 1750.

The story is drawn from Holinshed's *Chronicles,* based on Sir Thomas More's (biased, and challenged by modern historians) life of Richard. "No poet in history," said John Masefield, "opens a play with more magnificent certainty." Richard, then but Duke of Gloster, brother of King Edward III and son of the Duke of York, is alone onstage, pondering his fortunes:

> *Now is the winter of our discontent*
> *Made glorious summer by this sun of York.*

Intrigues follow in quick succession. The body of the late king, Henry VI, whom Richard had slain, is borne in, accompanied by his daughter-in-law Anne, whose husband, Richard, has also killed. With cool effrontery challenging her hatred, Richard woos her. Woos, and wins. At Richard's order his elder brother, Clarence, is taken to the Tower, and there murdered. When King Edward IV dies (oddly, for the times, at peace in bed) Gloster has the two young sons of Clarence smothered to death, and with the aid of the Duke of Buckingham is declared King Richard III.

Margaret, widow of Henry VI, weeps with Elizabeth, widow of Edward IV, and with the old Duchess of York, mother of Edward, Clarence, and Richard, over the orgy of murder that steeps the land in blood. Then Richard cold-bloodedly orders his wife, Anne, killed, so that he may plead with his sister-in-law, Edward's widow, for her daughter Elizabeth's hand. Again—the crouchback villain must have exercised an eerie charm!—he succeeds in bending the woman to his will. But Buckingham, recoiling from the course of wholesale murder, joins with Henry, Earl of Richmond, against the ruthless Richard. At Richard's orders, Buckingham is taken and slain. Sleeping near Bosworth Field, Richmond and Richard are visited by the ghosts of those Richard has killed, who comfort Richmond and curse their murderer. The next day, in furious combat, Richmond kills Richard and takes the throne as Henry VII. By marrying King Edward's daughter Elizabeth, Henry joins the rival houses of Lancaster and York, ending the strife of the White Rose and the Red, and starting the Tudor line. The play ends with the prayer that England be spared another civil war.

That prospect faced the first spectators of Shakespeare's play, for Queen Elizabeth had no child; after the Virgin Queen, chaos might come again. Indeed, a prophecy lent force to this foreboding: "When hempe is spun, England's done." For HEMPE spelled the initials of Henry VIII and his children: Edward, Mary with Philip, and Elizabeth. And the prophecy came true—but happily; for Elizabeth's successor, James I, was king of not England but Great Britain.

Swinburne, after praising *Richard III*, sets it in the tradition of the mighty line of Marlowe: "It is as fiery in passion, as single in purpose, as rhetorical often though never so inflated in expression, as *Tamburlaine**** itself." The play makes excellent use of stichomythia with sharp thrust of repartee like the rapid play of sword on sword in fencing.

Bernard Shaw has called the drama the best version of *Punch and Judy*—even to the hump: "Shakespeare revels in it with just the sort of artistic unconscionableness that fits the theme. Richard is the prince of Punches; he delights Man by provoking God, and dies unrepentant and game to the last." There is typical hyperbole in his cry on the battlefield, "My kingdom for a horse!", when he wants the horse in order to preserve his kingdom. There is frank cynicism in his appeal to the nobles at Bosworth Field. The truculence of Richard, indeed, leaves few interpreters of the role mindful of the observation of Henry James, that this part can "best dispense with declamation." Indeed, James feels that the play should never be performed. "The attempt to make real," he argues, "or even plausible a loose, violent, straddling romance like *Richard III*—a chronicle for the market-place, a portrait for the house wall—only emphasizes what is coarse in such a hurly-burly and does nothing for what is fine. It gives no further lift to the poetry and adds a mortal heaviness to the prose."

The swashbuckling performer is nonetheless drawn to Richard. With his wit, adroitness, mordant humor, and unflinching courage, he wields a fascination within his villainy. The final fight of the furious monarch is always a fierce duel, as attested by those that saw David Garrick, Barry Sullivan, Edwin Booth, or Edmund Kean. Coleridge said that watching Kean play Richard was like "reading Shakespeare by flashes of lightning." *Blackwood's Edinburgh Magazine* (January, 1820) pictured Macready, who, "after the mortal wound, lifts himself to more than his natural height and comes pouring down upon his adversary till he reaches him, and then falls at his feet like a spent thunderbolt." The *London Times* (November 16, 1951) quotes a critic of the 1890's as declaring: "Absolutely Henry Irving's Richard is the most Satanic creature I have ever seen on the stage." Yet somehow in New York there was in the mid-nineteenth century a rash of performances by women and children (one Ellen Bateman, aged 4) as Richard, such as that of Charlotte Crampton with a troop of trained horses for the battle scene. The streamlined version of Richard Whorf (first played for the Army's Biarritz-American University in December, 1945, and brought to Broadway on February 8, 1949) oddly omits the final duel of Richard and Richmond, substituting a stylized ballet-battle of the armies—an ineffectual close to an ill-conceived production.

An opportunity for imaginative revelation of Richard's character comes while Richard awaits the result of Buckingham's plea to the Mayor and citizens of London that Richard be crowned. Richard accepts Buckingham's suggestion that he be seen by the Londoners "between two churchmen," with a prayerbook in his hand. Richard Mansfield, playing the part, when the others onstage were not looking righted the prayerbook, which he had been carrying upside down. And when Richard accedes with seeming reluctance to the Mayor's plea that he accept the burden of the Crown, and the Mayor leaves to prepare for the Coronation—Mansfield exultantly flung the prayerbook high in the air. Fit gesture for a spirit that feared not heaven or hell.

Although Shakespeare provides a wide historical canvas, with many figures of all ranks and stations, the play is one great thrust of energy, a single drive of the quest for power finding inevitable doom, as humanity recoils from the arbitrary actions, tyranny, cruelty, and crime. Set in England from 1471 to 1485, *King Richard III* is a horrid picture of emotions and ambitions such as are still loose in the shaken world.

There was a powerful *Richard III* at Asolo in 1978. John Barber in the *London Telegraph,* October 5, 1981, contrasts the Richard of John Wood at the NT with the "abysmal grandeur" in the malevolence of the Russian Ramaz Chkhikvadze, whose Richard was "a bug-eyed clownish bully who projected a crude Elizabethan dynamism rare in the modern theatre." John Wood, said Barber, "seemed anxious to explain Richard, psychologically, as a prodigious child. He played with toy soldiers, and when the Duchess of York cursed him, he curled up into a foetal ball and sucked his thumb."

Barber reviews the survey of Richards in Julie Hankey's first book in the series *Plays in Performance,* and mentions that Colley Cibber—whose own Richard was derided—added seven soliloquies and some effective lines: "Off with his head! So much for Buckingham" and "Perish the thought!"—both of which are retained in Laurence Olivier's film of the play. The Cibber version brought fame to David Garrick, who played it at Drury Lane in 1741 and after, closing his career with it in 1776. Later, Edmund Kean's violent and subtle Richard saved Drury Lane from bankruptcy.

There was an energetic OffOffBway (West Park Church) production December 2, 1982, the five-hundredth anniversary of Richard's brief triumph. At Stratford in 1984, black-clad Anthony Sher had also black crutches, which propelled him quickly, and were also weapons; he acted "like a giant malevolent tarantula."

TITUS ANDRONICUS   *William Shakespeare*

Shakespeare's earliest tragedy, *Titus Andronicus,* 1592 ?, is also his most gory. The Roman Titus Andronicus, returning victorious over the Goths with their Queen Tamora and her three sons captive, makes Saturninus Emperor. Thereupon Saturninus spurns Titus' daughter Lavinia, to marry Tamora. Meanwhile Titus' sons, to avenge their brothers slain in the war, have killed Tamora's eldest son. Tamora and her paramour, the Moor Aaron, begin her vengeance by killing Bassianus, the Emperor's brother, in such a way that suspicion falls on Titus' sons Quintus and Martius; the Queen's sons ravish Lavinia, then cut off her hands and her tongue. Aaron promises to send Titus his imprisoned sons if he will cut off his hand as ransom; his hand is returned to him, with their heads. The maimed Lavinia manages to communicate her despoilers' identity. Lucius, Titus' surviving son, seeks the aid of the Goths; they capture Aaron and his new-born son by Tamora. A parley is held at Titus' home. There Titus, after serving Tamora a pie made of the flesh of her sons, kills her and Lavinia. Saturninus kills Titus and is killed by Lucius, who, condemning Aaron to be buried breast-deep and left to die, takes over the Empire to set its days in order.

The spurt of blood across the stage of *Titus Andronicus* has shocked many scholars, some to the extent of protest that the play cannot be Shakespeare's, some—who face the evidence—to the suggestion, made among others by J. Dover Wilson and Richard Watts, Jr., that Shakespeare was burlesquing the tragedy-of-revenge tradition. Actually the play was seriously received and popular; its first recorded performance, January 23, 1594, filled the house, and it had frequent revivals for thirty years.

The play is in the tradition of Kyd's *The Spanish Tragedy* *; its horrors echo from Seneca's *Thyestes* * and the legend of Philomel in Ovid's *Metamorphoses.* Shakespeare, as Lucius' closing words make clear, uses the dismemberment of the human body to symbolize the disruption of the body politic.

A version of the play by Edward Ravenscroft, enacted at Drury Lane in 1678, ended with Aaron perishing in flames onstage; but as the public display of atrocities grew less appealing, *Titus Andronicus* lapsed from favor. The role of Aaron was a favorite of James Quin's in the 1740's, though the 1860 playbills of Ira Aldridge as Aaron bore the words "not acted for 200 years." There was an Old Vic production in 1923, one at Cambridge, England, in 1953, and a well-received one, the first at Stratford-upon-Avon, with Laurence Olivier as Titus, Vivien Leigh as Lavinia, and Anthony Quayle as Aaron, opening August 16, 1955. *Punch* (March 25, 1953) observed that, in the face of our tabloid sensations, gangster films, and horror comics, "to wrinkle our noses at the gruesomeness of Titus Andronicus only labels us as hypocrites." Harold Hobson, after the Stratford production, called *Titus* "in some important respects, a remarkably contemporary play." We still commit atrocities, we shrink only from displaying them onstage.

Aaron vies with Iago in *Othello** as Shakespeare's closest approach to an unmitigated, unmotivated villain; like Iago, he glories in his evil and goes defiant to his death. Note that in *Titus Andronicus* the source of corruption is in the aliens in power; in Shakespeare's later Roman plays, the corruption springs from the Romans themselves. G. B. Harrison calls the characters inconsistent, but their drive is more direct than Hamlet's. The play makes fierce emotional impact. Its horrors call for careful handling, lest today's finical audiences indeed treat them as burlesque. Properly presented, *Titus Andronicus* shows young Shakespeare testing his varied powers.

Laurence Olivier, with Vivien Leigh, played *Titus* in Paris, 1957. In 1981, the RSC abbreviated *Titus Andronicus* and *The Two Gentlemen of Verona* and played them as one bill—to critical consternation. The cuts sometimes were of half-lines, breaking both image and meter. Francis King, in the *Telegraph* June 9, 1981, commented: "Peter Brook's 1955 production of *Titus* with Laurence Olivier showed how, properly handled, it can exert a horrendous power; but here it appeared to be played largely for laughs . . . *Two Gentlemen,* on the other hand, appears to be played largely for speed." When not performing, the actors were herded at the back of the stage, with their costumes in baskets or on hooks. The august RSC, it was felt, proffered two half-baked halves of different loaves, instead of their usual good bread.

KING JOHN   *William Shakespeare*

In no history play does Shakespeare press the lesson to be drawn from earlier events more closely home than in *King John,* 1594 ?. After the death of his brother, Richard the Lion-Hearted, John has seized the throne; he must maintain himself by force. Against the French Dauphin, against young Arthur of Bretagne whom Richard has named as heir, against English lords enraged when the imprisoned Arthur is killed, and against the power of the Pope, John must defend his throne. When John dies, poisoned, the Dauphin withdraws, and peace comes to the land as John's son mounts the throne as Henry III. Troubled by the consequences of his own deeds, King John knows no peace; only with the approach of death can he say "now my soul have elbow-room."

There is a scene of tender pathos, unmatched elsewhere in the history plays, when Prince Arthur wins over the King's chamberlain Hubert, come to burn out the young Prince's eyes. The part of Constance, too, Arthur's mother, has attracted actresses because of the deep maternal affection and the heart-rending sorrow she displays. But the major movement of the play is an illustration of King John's words "There is no sure foundation set on blood, No certain life achieved by others' death."

Two elements of Shakespeare's style first became prominent in *King John*. Here first his images progress, a metaphor once uttered suggesting further development. This associative rise of the image develops in the plays until, as Charles Lamb observed, "Shakespeare mingles everything, he runs line into line, embarrasses sentences and metaphors; before one idea has burst its shell, another is hatched and clamorous for disclosure." The second element of Shakespeare's style, present in *Richard III* but richer here, is the driving home of an abstract idea with a concrete metaphor, as in *cloud of dignity* or *dust of old oblivion*. Metaphors have largely replaced similes, supplanting the looseness of comparison with the tight hold of identity; increasingly, in Shakespeare's plays hereafter, a metaphor grows to a leitmotif. The power of the images is thereby increased and sustained.

The earliest form of this play bears the title *The Troublesome Raigne of John, King of England*. Its events are related in Holinshed's *Chronicles*. Infrequently produced, the play is a succession of alarums, excursions, and tableaux, rather than a unified drive of dramatic action. From the time the theatres were closed in 1642, it was not seen until 1737, and then and lengthily therafter in a version by Colley Cibber, which minimized the role of the Bastard Faulconbridge and gave great prominence to Constance. Shakespeare's emphasis, reversed by Cibber, is definitely on Faulconbridge, the illegitimate son of King Richard I, whom Shakespeare depicts as an upright and proud Plantagenet, counterbalancing the tyrannical John. In the history plays, Shakespeare usually gives the final words to the person of highest rank; in *King John* not only the final words, but the last words in four of the five acts, are spoken by Faulconbridge.

With Faulconbridge's lines extensively cut, Samuel Johnson, in 1768, observed that the play lacked "the happy force of some other of his tragedies, nor can be said much to affect the passions, or enlarge the understanding." Tennyson, however, in 1883, highly esteemed its poetry: "As far as I am aware, no one has noticed what great Aeschylean lines there are in Shakespeare, particulary in *King John*." The *New York Dramatic Mirror* questioned, in 1915, "what curious turn of courage or whimsicality prompted Mr. Mantell to open his season of repertoire with *King John*? It is by far the least interesting of Shakespeare's historical tragedies. Most of its action depends on parades of pageants, and ensembles; and its central character is so uncertainly drawn that it commands neither respect nor admiration."

It is, indeed, less on the men in the drama than on Constance that actors' efforts and critical attention have centered. Garrick himself was astonished at Mrs. Cibber's performance in the part, and the audience was "electrified, when she threw herself upon the ground in agony." Of the same moment in another production, the moment when Constance learns of her son Arthur's death, Leigh Hunt declared: "All who remember Mrs. Siddons must remember its electrical effect, and how marvelously she reconciled the mad impulse of it with habitual dignity. Miss Kemble (Mrs. Siddons' niece) was almost stationary in her grief. Mrs. Siddons used to pace up and down, as the eddying gust of her impatience drove her." Julia Neilson is among the others that have essayed Constance's role.

King John was produced in 1935 in Pasadema; in 1938, in New York. What time permits to remain, of even the greatest men, is summed up in King John's self-estimate: "I am a scribbled form, drawn with a pen Upon a parchment." The play takes life and continuing significance because that pen was Shakespeare's.

King John was produced by the OffOffBway Cocteau Repertory January 13, 1984, director Eve Adamson interpreting the play as showing the futility of war.

A MIDSUMMER NIGHT'S DREAM   *William Shakespeare*

At the court of Athens, and in the woods nearby, moves *A Midsummer Night's Dream,* 1594 (?), a charming idyllic illustration of the remark made in the play: "The course of true love never did run smooth." Without scenery, the Elizabethan dramatist showers us with magic of description in verse. The desire for elaborate decoration overdressed the play and it fell from popularity. Samuel Pepys in 1662 could not endure it; it became an opera, *The Fairy Queen,* in 1692; Garrick also made an opera of it, *The Fairies,* in 1775. It was seen only in adaptations until 1840, when Charles James Mathews and his wife, Lucia Vestris, brought the original version to Covent Garden. All this substitution emphasizes Puck's comment: "Lord, what fools these mortals be!"

The framework of the play (told earlier in Chaucer's *Knight's Tale*) is provided by the wedding of Theseus, Duke of Athens, and Hippolyta, Queen of the Amazons. Probably written for a court wedding, the play seems to some scholars a hint that Queen Elizabeth herself ought to accept the golden chains of wedlock.

The royal nuptials within the play are watched over by the fairy King, Oberon, and his Queen, Titania, with whom Oberon has quarreled. Temporarily bemused by a love elixir Puck spreads at Oberon's command, Titania falls in love with weaver Bottom, temporarily topped as an ass. (E. A. Robinson begins his poem *Ben Jonson Entertains a Man from Stratford* with the comment that Shakespeare "alone of us Would put an ass's head in fairyland.") The lovers Demetrius and Helena, Lysander and Hermia, are intertangled, then properly paired by elfin Puck. Bottom, released from his transmogrification into an ass, is free, along with his fellows—Quince, Snug, Flute, Snout, and Starveling—to present, at the royal wedding feast, "the most lamentable comedy, and most cruel death of Pyramus and Thisbe." After their performance, all go off to bed. The Master of the Revels urged Theseus not to hear these horny-handed sons of toil, for it would be cruel to laugh at their earnest efforts, but Theseus is more tolerant and defends all players. Remarks of this sort, scattered through his plays, show that Shakespeare pondered deeply the problems of actors.

Even in the formal and "classical" eighteenth century, the romantic qualities of the play were appreciated, though Samuel Johnson seems almost grudging of his praise: "Wild and fantastical as this play is, all the parts in their various modes are well written, and give the kind of pleasure which the author designed. Fairies in his time were much in fashion; common tradition had made them familiar, and Spenser's poem had made them great. . . ." A century later, Swinburne was more unreserved: "Here each kind of excellence is equal throughout; there are here no purple patches on a gown of serge, but one seamless and imperial robe of a single dye."

The different characters in the play use as different speech. Royalty— including Oberon for official dicta—uses blank verse. The lovers talk mainly in rhymed couplets. The fairies lilt in a lyrical measure (trochaic tetrameter). *Pyramus and Thisbe* is presented in a parody of the ballad meter. The meaning of the *Pyramus* Prologue is reversed by pauses after the wrong phrases—a humorous device used earlier in *Ralph Roister*

Doister.* The "rude mechanics" speak prose. Thus the patterns of sound accord with their utterers.

The play itself, as well as Bottom, was "transmogrified" by the earlier Tyrone Power in 1836, as *O'Flannigan and the Fairies*; and 103 years later in a black version, *Swinging the Dream*; as a motion picture in 1909 and 1935. A colorful production of the play in its own shape was presented by the Old Vic company in London in December, 1951. American productions include Whitford Kane's in 1934; one at New York University in 1937; one outdoors in 1937 by the Caravan Theatre; one in 1940 at Schenectady; one in 1942 at the University of Washington in Seattle, and one in New York at the Dramatic Workshop in 1952.

The motion picture version of 1935, by Max Reinhardt and William Dieterle, was a pretentious, rococo, overdone filming, with fairies dancing through heavy mist in shimmering streamers of cellophane; but with one or two good movements, especially the rehearsal of Bottom (James Cagney) and Peter Quince (Joe E. Brown) as Pyramus and Thisbe, just before Bottom acquires the head of an ass; and the chasing through the forest night of the lovers misguided by Puck (little Mickey Rooney whisking to fame in an excellently acted but atrociously conceived role). The picture, furthermore, omits much fine material.

There has been a tendency in productions to emphasize mechanical devices. It is a neat touch, when Bottom awakes after his asinine lovemaking with Titania, to have him find hay in his pouch. But to have Puck pop out of an opening flower, or (as when Ellen Terry played Puck for Henry Irving in 1859) rise seated on a mushroom that sprouts miraculously from bare ground; or at the words "I'll put a girdle round about the earth in forty minutes" to let Puck slip behind a tree while a dummy flies far into the clouds—and once Ellen Terry had to return before a guffawing audience and carry off the dummy, which had plummeted thudding back onto the stage:—these more questionably follow the play's spirit of make-believe. Augustin Daly, bringing American science to England, in 1895 equipped his fairies with individual electric lights which, commented Bernard Shaw, "they switch on and off from time to time, like children with a new toy."

Not earthy Bottom and his mechanics, however, nor all the obtrusive mechanical devices, can dim the magic of the play itself, in the eternally springtide music of its verse and the spell of its poetry.

Director Peter Brook in London, 1970 (New York 1971) employed "dazzling acrobatics," the fairies flying through the air. The RSC in 1982 rashly tried a Victorian setting, with plush seats, ferns, and a decorated chaise longue for Titania; the fairies were blown in as wisps of silk, then became dolls worked by dark-hooded "invisible" manipulators—some grotesque, one cracked, one legless, one with big bare breasts: the straitlaced Victorian world uncomfortable in fairyland. Mike Gwilym and Juliet Stevenson doubled as Theseus and Oberon, Hippolyta and Titania. "Nevertheless," said Hartley Coleridge, "it is all poetry, and sweeter poetry was never written."

THE MERCHANT OF VENICE *William Shakespeare*

Two popular Renaissance themes—the nature of true love, and the relative power of love and friendship—are here dramatized. They are presented through four movements: the bond story; the ring story (these two are found together in the Italian tale *Il Pecorone*, about 1379, by G. Fiorentine, called Ser Giovanni); the choosing of a casket (in Boccaccio's *Decameron, 1353*);

and the opposition of Christian and Jew, culminating in the final order that Shylock become a Christian.

In friendship, Antonio lends Bassanio money wherewith to equip himself to woo Portia—though Antonio must himself first borrow the 3,000 ducats from the Jew Shylock, "in merry jest" assigning as forfeit a pound of flesh nearest his heart. Of three caskets, gold, silver, and lead, among which Portia's suitors must choose, Bassanio picks the leaden casket, finding therein Portia's picture, which means her hand. Shylock's daughter Jessica meanwhile deepens her father's sense of wrong by eloping with Lorenzo, a Christian, and when Antonio's ships are delayed, Shylock in dead earnest demands his forfeit. Then in her love Portia, disguised as a lawyer, with a verbal trick saves Antonio: Shylock may have his pound of flesh, but not one drop of blood. As her reward for saving Antonio, Portia (unrecognized) demands the ring she herself has given Bassanio, and which he has sworn never to relinquish while he loves her. Back home, Portia asks Bassanio where the ring is; his explanation seems feeble, until she shows him the ring in the recognition scene that ends the comedy.

It is in recognition of Portia's quality that Henry James, in 1880, condemned the work of Ellen Terry: "Miss Terry has too much nature, and we should like a little more art. . . . The mistress of Belmont was a great lady, as well as a tender and clever woman; but this side of the part quite eludes the actress, whose deportment is not such as we should expect in the splendid spinster who has princes for wooers."

In 1788 Horace Walpole declared: "With all my enthusiasm for Shakespeare, it is one of his plays that I like the least. The story of the caskets is silly." Hazlitt also disapproved: "Portia has a certain degree of affectation and pedantry about her, which is very unusual in Shakespeare's women. The speech about Mercy is all very well, but there are a thousand finer ones in Shakespeare. We should like Jessica better if she had not deceived and robbed her father, and Lorenzo, if he had not married a Jewess, though he thinks he has a right to wrong a Jew."

Hazlitt's reservations regarding Portia accord with the interpretation of Harold C. Goddard, who points out that the casket, the bond, and the ring episodes all involve a contrast between the outer seeming and the inner reality. Likewise there is a contrast between the flashy exterior of the "golden" world of wealth in the play and the plain exterior of the "leaden" world of worth these gentlefolk do not attain. Their society sparkles; but underneath, it is empty and dull. The first words of Antonio: "In sooth I know not why I am so sad", of Portia: "By my troth, Nerissa, my little body is aweary of this great world," of Bassanio, and of Jessica all indicate their boredom.

Portia herself, of radiant outward beauty, is at the most charitable estimate completely self-satisfied. She is wholly content to be adored. She plans to go to the trial with more attention to the fun of her disguise than to her serious purpose, the hope that her quick woman's wits may save Antonio. She is made somewhat more pleasant if the actress so plays the part as to make it seem that the trick by which she extricates him flashes into her mind at the last moment—if when she asks Shylock to have a surgeon at hand lest Antonio bleed to death and he replies "Is it so nominated in the bond? . . . I cannot find it; 'tis not in the bond," *then* Portia recognizes that the bond contains no mention at all of blood. Otherwise, Portia most cruelly tortures her husband whom she loves, and permits Antonio even to make his last farewells, while all the while she keeps her secret, just to tease on the Jew. Her speech on mercy does seem genuine; but Portia reveals herself, in a few minutes, completely devoid of that quality of mercy, and even interferes when the Duke seems ready to be merciful. Her coaxing of the ring from her grateful husband is lightly intended, but the jest jars. Of all Shakespeare's fair-seeming heroines, Portia of Belmont, "richly left," is poorest in character, complacent, vulgar, unfeeling. The play is indeed Shakespeare's subtlest contrast of reality and seeming. Even in Shylock, as we shall note, there is the outer villain or buffoon and the inner man by nature kindly but by neighbors wronged.

In like contrast, Launcelot Gobbo's play at being torn between his conscience and the fiend is an echo, if not a burlesque, of the conflict between the virtues and the vices that was a stock subject of the medieval debates and the morality plays.

A new use of images is developed in *The Merchant of Venice*. The metaphors at times are premonitory. Thus, even in the conversation on love (Act II, Scene 6), Gratiano employs the figure of ships tempest-tossed; in the next act, we learn that Antonio's ships have been lost in a tempest. This device of the premonitory image is subtly effective; Shakespeare employed it increasingly in the tragedies.

Emphasis on the comedy and the romance was manifest in Fritz Leiber's 1930 production of the play. Thus the *New York Times* called his Shylock "often moving, but never venomous. He is the butt of jest, but not of savagery, and what comes out of the play is rather the charm of a love story than the dread of a fierce forfeit." Of the same production the *Boston Transcript* said: "The play becomes what any lad can see is a 'tight little comedy.' If some of the poetry seems lost, none of the glamour is missing. What if the courtroom scene lends a sinister note? Through it runs the amusing grimace of Portia and her maid over the lost rings. Who cares about Shylock and his shekels, if the laugh comes last?. . . . For once the lads and their girls roaming the Venetian streets prove convincing. Real mandolins, real guitars, are strummed. . . . Plainly, Shylock notwithstanding, *The Merchant of Venice* may be taken lightly and enjoyed in this year of 1930."

What happened was a break in the tradition, and a change in the English heart. The play was not performed for much of the seventeenth century. An adaptation by Granville in 1701 was called *The Jew of Venice*; the famous clown Thomas Dogget played the title role. Forty years later the emphasis shifted; the comedy of tested and responding friendship and love, with a Shylock buffoon, became the tragedy of a wronged individual and a persecuted race. In 1741 Charles Macklin—walking through rehearsals, lest the manager prohibit the new interpretation—startled and conquered the audience with a serious and sympathetic, deeply wronged Shylock. Pope exclaimed, with more fervor than knowledge: "This is the Jew that Shakespeare knew!" Shylock, at first a buffoon, then a villain, became more and more a dignified individual, who thrusts back at last against unbearable infamies, intolerable wrongs. He became the symbol of his oppressed people. For fear of offending, the New York City Board of Education withdrew the play from the high school list of required reading. "When Shylock is played as a man of dignity and character," said Brooks Atkinson, "his experience is more than a tabloid sensation, it is a tragedy. In the twentieth century, perhaps we know better than Shakespeare did how painful a tragedy it is."

In this more serious mood, for the 150 years before Hitler, the Germans adopted *The Merchant of Venice*. One of their versions calls itself "vergrössert und verbessert"—enlarged and improved. The Jews, a bit later, took hold of the play as essentially theirs. David Warfield essayed the role in an elaborate Belasco production in 1923; unsuccessful, he retired from the stage. Stars of the Yiddish theatre have variously interpreted the part: Jacob Adler's Shylock was dignified and haughty as an Oriental potentate, Rudolph Schildkraut's was an almost ragged miser, Maurice Schwartz's was pious, proud of his Jewishness. (In 1948 Schwartz produced a play, *Shylock's Daughter* [based on the novel *Jessica, My Daughter*, by Ari Ibn-Zahav], to show, under the circumstances of Shakespeare's plot, the dignity and honor and restraint with which a pious Jew would really have behaved.)

It should thus be clear that there is a wide range for interpretation of Shylock and for feeling about him. Early critics speak of Cooke's "savage and determined method of whetting his knife on the floor, and the fiend-like look that accompanied it." The *London Morning Post and Daily Advertiser* of November 9, 1781, speaking of Charles Macklin's "coming down to the footlights and twisting up his face like the horribly tragic heads of Japanese sculpture," reports that, fronted by such a spectacle, "a young man in the pit fainted away." Charles Kean—whose production with Ellen Tree, on December 28, 1848, was Queen Victoria's first command performance—also sharpened his knife on the floor; Edwin Booth, as many after him, stropped the blade on the sole of his shoe. Of Edmund Kean's Shylock, earlier in the century, George Henry Lewes declared: "From the first moment that he appeared and leaned upon his stick to listen gravely while moneys are being requested of him, he impressed the audience like a chapter of Genesis." (Kean's Shylock stick brought five guineas at the posthumous sale of his effects.)

In the grim tradition was the performance of Henry Irving, to which the *New York Dramatic Mirror* (December 10, 1887) objected: "We take liberty to think that Mr. Irving chooses the absolutely lowest possible side from which to paint the Jew of Venice. . . . It is possible to give the Jew a fine dignity, an intellectual loftiness, and a tragic, fateful intensity of which Mr. Irving has apparently but faint concentration. The ideal Shylock is a gentleman—a wicked one, if you choose, but a man of mental training, clear ideas, and fixed purpose which make the good-natured, gullible Antonio and the selfish egotist Bassanio seem vulgar by comparison. Mr. Irving's Shylock is a wolf."

Henry Irving enacted the role as late as 1905 (with Edith Wynne Matthison); but the "ideal" Shylock prevailed. Later American productions include one in French, with Firmin Gemier, in 1924; one in 1925, with Walter Hampden and Ethel Barrymore; in 1928, George Arliss and Peggy Wood; 1930, Maurice Moscovitch; 1931, Otis Skinner and Maude Adams; 1931, Fritz Leiber, Tyrone Power, Helen Menken, Viola Roache, William Faversham, and Pedro de Cordoba; 1935, Ian Keith and Estelle Winwood; 1935 also in modern dress; 1937, Blanche Yurka; 1937 (at Ann Arbor), Peggy Wood, Rex Ingram, Gareth Hughes, and Albert Carroll; 1947, Donald Wolfit and Rosalind Iden. During March 1953 it was seen at the New York City Center.

There were two good OffBway productions in 1955, one excellently conceived, the other marked by the understanding performance of Clarence Derwent, with a superb moment as his look abashes the mocking Gratiano after the trial.

By creating a less sympathetic Shylock, two productions roused critical controversy. Of the 1924 Gemier production, J. Ranken Towse declared:

"The notable feature of his Shylock is its consistency. It is minutely and beautifully executed, but it shows no gleam of inspiration. It is a striking figure in a spectacular romance, but it is not Shakespeare." Gilbert W. Gabriel countered with the thought that "We are so used, here in America, to oversentimentalized, pro-Jewish Shylocks, that M. Gemier's must seen to many of us an inhuman fiend, a monument to Hate, a constrictor writhing in the net. Whereas, as a matter of fact, M. Gemier's Shylock is probably as close an approach as the modern mixture of audiences will permit to Shakespeare's writing." Similarly, Mr. Wolfit's 1947 performance provoked disagreement. Brooks Atkinson said that it "lacks stature." Louis Kronenberger said his Shylock was "both a hammy and a not too happily conceived one . . . more heartless than drained of heart, more bloodthirsty than bitter—a man, for example, who during the trial scene coldly whets his knife against his shoe." This time, George Freedley took up the cudgels. Admitting that Wolfit is "given perhaps too much to hurling himself physically on the floor with a thud that could be distinctly heard in Row M," Freedley continued: "He plays Shylock uncompromisingly enough to satisfy the most ardent anti-sentimentalist . . . closer to the part that Shakespeare wrote. Beginning with David Warfield, we have been invited to sob over the injustice dealt to Shylock, with little or no thought of honest and generous Antonio. For this service, at least, Mr. Wolfit cannot be praised too highly."

"Which is the Jew that Shakespeare Drew?", an article in the autumn 1981 issue of *The American Scholar,* shows that the interpretation of the role is still unsettled. In the 1701 adaptation *The Jew of Venice,* by George Granville, Thomas Betterton played Bassanio; Mrs. Anne Bracegirdle, Portia; Shylock was played by the low comedian Thomas Drugget. Later, he was played by the company's star: John Gielgud, with Peggy Ashcroft, in 1938. Laurence Olivier, in 1970, leaving at the end of the trial, murmured the Jewish mourner's *kaddish.* He acted the role of a sort of nineteenth-century Rothschild, against Joan Plowright as Portia. By contrast, in London, 1978, Patrick Stewart was a shabby and surly Shylock, given to hand-rolling cigarettes. Alec Guiness at Chichester, 1984, added little to the role.

When Shylock is played sympathetically, audience reaction is often intense. King George II reported that the night he saw the play, he could not sleep. The words of Heinrich Heine show the response of a sensitive poet, born a Jew but, like Shylock's daughter, turned Christian: "When I saw this play at Drury Lane, there stood behind me in the box a pale, fair Briton, who at the end of the Fourth Act fell a-weeping passionately, several times exclaiming 'The poor man is wronged!'. . . . Towards evening, when, according to Jewish belief, the gates of heaven are shut, and no prayer can then obtain admittance, I heard a voice, with a ripple of tears that were never wept by eyes. It was a sob that could come only from a breast that held in it all the martyrdom which, for eighteen centuries, had been borne by a whole tortured people. It was the death-rattle of a soul sinking down dead-tired at Heaven's gate. And I seemed to know the voice, and I felt that I had heard it long ago, when, in utter despair, it moaned out, then as now, 'Jessica, my child!'"

Put such feelings aside, and consider that Shylock appears in only five of the play's twenty scenes, not at all in the last act, where the major drive of the play should be pressed home. And the end—"On such a night as this"— is a delightful movement of romantic love. Leigh Hunt called the line "How sweet the moonlight sleeps upon this bank" "the happiest instance I remember of imaginative metaphor."

Shylock and Portia and poetry combine in a play the beholder will long remember. (See *The Jew of Malta.* *)

ROMEO AND JULIET   *William Shakespeare*

Shakespeare's tragedy of "the ardours and errors of impetuous youth," of the star-crossed lovers Romeo and Juliet, has fair claim to be called the world's best-loved play. Certainly this struggle of love for happiness despite family feuds has been one of the world's most frequently performed dramas.

The story of *Romeo and Juliet* (1594?), was first told in a novello (1554) by the Italian Matteo Bandello, dramatized in *Adriana,* 1578, by Luigi Groto (Italian, 1541-1595) and put into English poetry in 1562 by Arthur Broke, whose nine months for its events are compressed by Shakespeare into five days. In Verona Romeo, a Montagu, and Juliet, a Capulet, fall in love; the enmity between their families leads them to marry in secret. Romeo tries to stop a brawl in the families' feud, but his friend Mercutio is killed, whereupon Romeo kills the fiery Tybalt and flees to Mantua. The Capulets wish to marry Juliet to Paris; on the advice of Friar Laurence, she takes a sleeping potion and seems to die. Word of this device is delayed, and does not reach Romeo; at Juliet's tomb he kills first Paris then himself. The waking Juliet, seeing her beloved dead, takes her own life. In the shock of the tragedy the feuding houses are reconciled.

A summary gives scant idea of either the excitement of action or the rouse of beauty that the drama holds. The poetry of young love is ardent throughout, as in the balcony scene, where Juliet ponders and Romeo climbs to claim the first admissive kiss; and the lovers learn, when the lark succeeds the nightingale, that "parting is such sweet sorrow." Their ardor, however, drives them to swift doom, leaving others to sip "adversity's sweet milk, philosophy." In many situations since, of futile quarrels, men have echoed the words of the dying Mercutio: "A plague o' both your houses!"

The emotions, tossed on tempests of love and hate, cannot be continuously sustained. In his tragedies, Shakespeare has often set what is called "comic relief." This does shift the emotional response, relaxing the tension; but usually by its theme (as the porter's talk of eternal damnation in *Macbeth* *) it reenforces the major mood. Occasionally Shakespeare goes farther, introducing even burlesque. Thus, when the Capulets mourn Juliet, the audience knows she has but taken a sleeping potion. Shakespeare therefore gives voice to the family grief in exaggerated tones of wailing and follows by the irreverent tomfoolery of the hired musicians. Thus are the audience's emotions preserved for the play's drive to the abyss of doom.

Popular as it may be in its lure to actors, the play has not always been well received. Pepys, in 1662, seeing the first performance after the reopening of the theatres (closed for twenty years by the Puritans) declared: "It is a play of itself the worst that ever I heard in my life." Pepys saw a version by James Howard, in which a happy ending and the tragic ending were presented on alternate nights. Thomas Otway's version (*Caius Marius,* 1679), which supplanted the original until 1744, had Juliet awaken before Romeo died. This variation was used by Colley Cibber and by David Garrick, was retained until the mid-nineteenth century, and survives today in Gounod's opera.

Dryden, in 1672, noted that: "Shakespeare showed the best of his skill in his Mercutio, and he said himself that he was forced to kill him in the third act, to prevent being killed by him. But, for my part, I cannot find he was so dangerous a person: I see nothing in him but what was so exceeding harmless that he might have lived to the end of the play, and died in his bed, without offense to any man." In 1818 Coleridge paused in his praise of the play to express an opposite opinion: "All congenial qualities, melting into the common *copula* of them all, the man of rank and the gentleman, with all its excellences and all its weaknesses, constitute the character of Mercutio!"

A number of critics have felt that having the closing deaths come through the accident of Friar John's failure to reach Romeo with word that Juliet had drunk a potion—"the mere mischance of an undelivered letter"— lessens the stature of the play. Thus Hazleton Spencer called it "more pathetic than powerful," and George Pierce Baker labeled it a melodrama rather than a tragedy. The play is, however, by this device (which Shakespeare took from his source) rendered more lifelike; given Romeo's impetuous nature and the need for concealment, the tragic end is inevitable, but (as in *Hamlet**) the instant and the avenue of doom are seemingly haphazard. A different approach is taken by Bertrand Evans in *The Brevity of Friar Laurence,* in PMLA (September, 1950). Picturing the play as a tragedy of unawareness, Evans points out that it is less Friar John's failure to reach Romeo than Balthasar's bringing him the false news of Juliet's death that precipitates the fatal end. All five of the young folk—Tybalt, Mercutio, Paris, Romeo, and Juliet—die ignorant of the facts that would have saved them. And at the close, Friar Laurence has to explain to the two families what twisted fate has linked them.

A further analysis of the theme was ingeniously made by G. M. Matthews, in *Essays in Criticism* (April, 1952); he declared that the moving idea in *Romeo and Juliet* is its flouting of contemporary convention in that the marriage contract with Paris is broken by Romeo's intrusion. *The Merchant of Venice,** however ("In Belmont is a lady richly left"), and more emphatically *The Taming of the Shrew** ("I've come to wive it wealthily in Padua") start with the thought of a convenient marriage which more conventionally ripens into love.

This is the first of Shakespeare's plays to dwell upon the relation between the generations, which recurs in *Lear** and *The Tempest,** and which dominated the ancient drama. It also contains Shakespeare's frequent linkage of violence and lust, which are conjoined in Mercutio. Romeo moves toward bodily death when he falls spiritually by lunging from love and peace to bloody vengeance. Juliet moves toward bodily death but triumphs spiritually when she spurns the lust of her nurse's urging that she wed Paris, and consents to the agonizing simulacrum of death to hold steadfast in love to her husband. Romeo's violence companions him to the tomb; there, it mingles with Juliet's love as he exclaims "Thus with a kiss I die!"

A famous theatrical war was waged through the play. In 1750, Garrick's prestige as star and manager was being disputed. Actors Spranger Barry and Mrs. (Susannah) Cibber left Garrick and Drury Lane to work with John Rich at Covent Garden. When they were announced to open the season (September 28, 1750) in *Romeo and Juliet,* Garrick at once announced himself as Romeo, with Miss (George Anne) Bellamy as Juliet. After twelve nights of simultaneous performances, Mrs. Cibber withdrew, and Garrick triumphantly played one night more. For years the merits of the rival Romeos were disputed; but Margaret Barton, in *Garrick* (1949), stated that "either presentation of the play was almost certainly better than any other of which we have records."

Romeo and Juliet was filmed in 1908 and 1911, and in 1936 with Norma Shearer and Leslie Howard; also 1955. American productions of the drama include one with Rollo Peters and Jane Cowl, in 1923, for 157 performances; one in 1934 with Katharine Cornell and Basil Rathbone, Brian Aherne the Mercutio, Edith Evans the earthy Nurse, and Orson Welles the Tybalt; in 1935, Katharine Cornell and Maurice Evans, Florence Reed the Nurse, and Ralph Richardson the Mercutio; in 1940, Vivian Leigh and Laurence Olivier. The record run of 186 performances was achieved by the London production of 1935-6, with Peggy Ashcroft as Juliet and John Gielgud and Laurence Olivier alternating as Romeo and Mercutio. Olivia de Havilland opened as Juliet in New York, March 10, 1951, like a bobby-sox gushling. Earlier productions included one with Charlotte Cushman as Romeo; and Juliet has been played by many a star: Mrs. Patrick Campbell, Julia Marlowe, Olga Nethersole, Modjeska, Ellen Terry, and Ellen Tree. The Germans have tried to claim Shakespeare as their close kin; Goethe's adaptation of *Romeo and Juliet* was played at Weimar in 1812. The play (as also *Macbeth, Hamlet, Othello,* and *Julius Caesar*) had some thirty French versions in the nineteenth century; and in the mid-twentieth century five complete translations of Shakespeare into French were made.

Productions have not met with as favorable a critical reception as the play itself, though Bernard Shaw warned that "the parts are made almost impossible, except to actors of positive genius, skilled to the last degree in metrical declamation, by the way in which the poetry, magnificent as it is, is interlarded by the miserable rhetoric and silly logical conceits which were the foible of the Elizabethans." Katharine Cornell's production won the most praise in recent years—"realizing brilliantly," said Howard Barnes, "the pageantry, violence, poetry, and passion of the classic." John Mason Brown stated that "seldom has a production of such drama mellowed and matured as magnificently as Katharine Cornell's revival." Of the Laurence Olivier-Vivian Leigh production, however, Brown declared that the play, "so hot in its impulses, so youthful in its spirit, so tumultous in its fatuous action, becomes a dead march from the rise of the first curtain." Brooks Atkinson began his review: "Much scenery: no play." Earlier productions were no better received. Of the 1895 revival Bernard Shaw declared: "Mrs. Patrick Campbell's dresses, says the program, 'have been carried out by Mrs. Mason, of New Burlington Street.' I wish they had been carried out and buried." And Mr. Forbes-Robertson's Romeo, Shaw continued, "was a gentleman to the last. He laid out Paris after killing him as carefully as if he were folding up his best suit of clothes. One remembers Irving, a dim figure dragging a horrible burden down through the gloom 'into the rotten jaws of death.'" How well "one remembers" Irving may be judged from Henry James' comment on Irving's work: "It is the last word of stage-carpentering. . . . The play is not acted, it is costumed; the immortal lovers of Verona become subordinate and ineffectual figures. I had never thought of *Romeo and Juliet* as a dull drama; but Mr. Irving has succeeded in making it so."—Irving's opening scene, of the city square of Verona, had children romping, donkeys passing through laden with wares, and housewives craning from windows as the Montagu-Capulet retainers began their quarrel.

It may be suspected that the audience liked some of these productions more than the critics. For the play itself is as eternal as spring. It summons the youth within us all to the savoring of one of the world's best-known and best-beloved love stories—a savoring that loses none of its tear-pearled pleasure when renewed.

The basic idea of *Romeo and Juliet* was converted—Jerome Robbins' concept—into a musical of New York street-gang rivalry, *West Side Story,* with book by Arthur Laurents, lyrics by Stephen Sondheim, music by Leonard Bernstein. With songs including "Something's Coming," "Tonight," "Cool," "Jet Song," "Somewhere I Have a Love," with spirited dancing, opening September 26, 1957, Carol Lawrence, Larry Kert, and Chita Rivera carried it through 1,039 performances.

The London reception was less enthusiastic. Thus, Harold Hobson (*Sunday Times,* July 15, 1973): "This Ruritanian exhibition of feeble wit and out-of-date political commentary makes a sad evening . . . the scrapping is called choreography." When the musical was revived at the New York Minskoff February 14, 1980, Clive Barnes called it "better than ever."

In 1973 Peter Ustinov tried another rivalry linkage, *Romanoff and Juliet,* set in "Concordia," with Igor Romanoff loving the all-American Juliet; the *Observer* (July 15, 1973) called it "a reasonably winning mixture of lightly parodied romance, political satire, and bizarre local color." London saw it again (Her Majesty's) in 1984. Shakespeare survives.

In Shakespeare's play, critic Georg Brandes called the lines Romeo speaks on first climbing to Juliet, beginning "With love's light wings did I o'erperch these walls," "the most exquisite words of love that ever were penned."

In addition to its tenderness, its superb poetry, and its contrasted yet combining themes of old family feuds and youthful flame of love, *Romeo and Juliet* contains more than 175 puns. M. M. Mahood, in *Shakespeare's Word Play,* 1957, concludes: "It is the prerogative of poetry to give effect and value to incompatible meanings. In *Romeo and Juliet,* several poetic means contribute to this end: the paradox, the recurrent image, the juxtaposition of old and young in such a way that we are both absorbed by and aloof from the lovers' feelings, and the sparkling wordplay. By such means Shakespeare ensures that our final emotion is neither the satisfaction we should feel in the lovers' death if the play were a simple expression of the *Liebestod* theme, nor the dismay of seeing two lives thwarted and destroyed by vicious fates, but a tragic equilibrium which includes and transcends both these feelings.

THE TAMING OF THE SHREW   *William Shakespeare*

This rollicking farce sets a man's mastery against a woman's will and leaves the man comfortably assured that he is the victor—while the audience notes that the woman still has means to have her way. Its popularity led to an answer, *The Woman's Prize; or The Tamer Tamed,* by John Fletcher, about 1624, in which a shrewd Maria tames the widower Petruchio. *The Taming of the Shrew* was written about 1594.

Petruchio of Verona, come "to wive it wealthily in Padua," finds the lovers of "gentle" Bianca in dismay because she may not marry until her elder sister, the shrewish Katherina, has been wed. In a very whirlwind, Petruchio woos wild Kate. He and her father Baptista arrange the wedding; Petruchio comes late, dressed like a madman; he boxes the priest's ears and drags Kate off before the wedding feast. Countering her every wish, snatching fine food from her lips as burnt, tearing rich gowns as rags, he bends her to complete submission: if he say so, then is the sun the moon. Bianca is won by young Lucentio, whose tricks enliven the play and outwit his rivals. At the close, Katherina makes a speech that wins Petruchio the wager as to who has the most obedient wife. But when Kate (Julia Marlowe) at two o'clock agrees with Petruchio that it is seven, behind his back she holds two fingers to the audience to let us know her concurrence is but policy. And when Kate (Lynn Fontanne) lectures the other wives on the virtue of obedience, her twinkle tells us that she is but exploiting a pleasanter way to get what she desires. The "shrew" is tamed, but nowise daunted. In truth, Petruchio is no cruel wife-beater, as in the popular ballad that earlier told the story. In his excesses he is parodying Kate's faults; she—being truly less shrew than shrewd—ultimately recognizes this, helps play the joke, and is cured. Throughout he calls her his "sweet and lovely Kate," and she becomes so. Her "gentle" sister Bianca, outwardly sweetly obedient, is finally revealed as a spoiled and pettish girl.

The play has gained in popularity down the years. Samuel Pepys noted in his *Diary* (1667) that it "hath some very good pieces in it, but generally is a mean play; and the best part, 'Sawny,' done by Lacy, hath not half its life, by reason of the words, I suppose, not being understood, at least by me." What Pepys saw was John Lacy's adaptation, *Sauny the Scot,* 1667, which transported the characters to England, enlarged the role of Petruchio's clownish servant here called Sauny, and supplanted Shakespeare's play until the mid-eighteenth century. Garrick in 1736 made a shorter version, *Catherine and Petruchio,* which was very popular. Among those that have played in this version are Kitty Clive, 1736; J. P. Kemble and Mrs. Siddons, 1788; Helen Faucit and Ellen Tree, 1836; Barry Sullivan, 1855; and Henry Irving and Ellen Terry, 1867. The full play, including the *Induction,* was not seen after Tudor times until 1887, when Augustin Daly, in New York and in London, revived it for Ada Rehan. More recently, the play was performed in New York: in 1920 by E. H. Sothern and Julia Marlowe; in 1921 by both Walter Hampden and Fritz Leiber; in 1924 by the visiting French company of Firmin Gemier; in 1927 by Basil Sydney and Mary Ellis in modern dress (as also, the same year, at Harvard University and in Birmingham, England); in 1935 by Alfred Lunt and Lynn Fontanne in a slapdash performance with Richard Whorf as Christopher Sly; in 1936 with Rollo Peters and Peggy Wood; in 1939 at the Old Globe Theatre at the New York World's Fair; in 1940 again by the Lunts, to aid the Finns. In 1948 the play was revived in Chicago, and by Margo Jones in Dallas, Texas. A Margaret Webster production toured the United States in 1949-1950, and in New York Clare Luce opened in a City Center production April 25, 1951.

Many theatrical folk today have lost sight of the purpose of Shakespeare in the *Induction* to the play. This is a shrewd instance of the way in which the playwright appropriated to dramatic use the theatrical conventions of his day—as he employed the upper and the inner stage; as the enacting of female parts by men invited him often to disguise his heroine as a male. One feature of the Elizabethan theatre—humorously detailed in the chapter "How a Gallant Should Behave Himself in a Playhouse," in *The Gull's Horn Book,* 1609, by Thomas Dekker*—was the practice of the gay young blades to sit on the stage itself, and to make loud comments on the actors, their carriage, their clothes, their reading, and their lines. The playwrights of the time must have itched for a way to counter or control these gadflies; with his *Induction,* which leads to the play-within-the-play, Shakespeare neatly turned the trick. (See also *The Knight of the Burning Pestle.**)

The *Induction* shows a lord and his retainers, homing in gay mood from a hunt, come upon a drunken village tinker, Christopher Sly. As a lark, they carry him to the manor; when he awakes, he is addressed as Your Honor, and told that he is the Lord of the Manor, now recovered from a fifteen years' nightmare. In his hangover, the befuddled Sly is all confused—until a page enters, dressed as a Lady and announced as his loving wife. Sly is then ready to believe and to act accordingly. Then word comes that players have arrived: in honor of milord's recovery, they will put on a play.

The play they present is *The Taming of the Shrew.* After one more reference, Sly is not mentioned by Shakespeare. He with his "hangover," the tipsy page his "wife," and the others, sat on the stage amid the gallants who had paid an extra sixpence for the privilege. But there is no doubt that the company's most quick-tongued wits were cast as Sly and the Page, and that their *ad lib* comments on the play they watched, and their shafts of repartee exchanged with the gallants onstage, convulsed the delighted groundlings.

Soon after Shakespeare's time, the bloods were transferred from the stage to boxes; and the function of Christopher sly, protagonist of the *Induction,* became obscured. Ben Webster and Samuel Phelps had Sly fall asleep; Daly did not bring him back after the first act. Later, the *Induction* was often omitted altogether. Alexander Woollcott, indeed, said it was not played from Daly's time until the Basil Sydney production of 1927; he overlooked the Gemier *Shrew* of 1924. The *New York Times* called the Gemier production "loud and boisterous, merry and broad, even bawdy at times, with the dash and swing of a college burlesque. . . . Except for one brief scene some moments later, Shakespeare forgot the roistering Christopher and left him to fall into a broken slumber. Not so Mr. Gemier." M. Gemier was wiser than that critic. So were the Lunts, in whose production Sly stood and stared reproachfully while embarrassed latecomers hurried to their seats, and otherwise created diversion that made Gilbert W. Gabriel remark: "It puts a madcap on the old *commedia dell' arte.* It walks in beauty like a nightmare. . . . The yellow sun which seems to pour so much light down on these pranks and spanks must have the fat, shining face of an all-lovable clown."

Of the 1935 performance by Alfred Lunt and Lynn Fontanne, Brooks Atkinson exclaimed: "The Lunts have stuffed it with all the horseplay their barn loft holds." On their return in 1940, however, he added: "For this theatregoer's personal enjoyment they have painted the lily a trifle too gaudily . . . it begins to lack spontaneity." But they could hardly have been more obstreperous than Cécile Sorel in her 1920 performance at the Comédie Française, in Paris; one night, she tumbled from the stage into the orchestra pit!

The production of Basil Sydney and Mary Ellis went wildly modern, with Petruchio in plus fours tearing up Katherine's wedding gown of latest twentieth century style; with movie cameras to "shoot" the bride; radio sets; and a return to Padua in a tumbledown automobile. (This, incidentally, was equipped with three motors: one to turn the wheels, one to make the sound of a driving engine, and one to blow the actors' clothes as though they were whirling along in an open car.) Alexander Woollcott thought that this production "succeeded in making a pretty good show out of that usually somewhat trying relic"—the play, not the auto—but the *Times* observed that "these little sundries furnish momentary pictorial amusement, but are likely to arouse an expectation greater than they can fulfill. The joke is soon over, but must necessarily be prolonged for the duration of the scene."

A somewhat different, but delightful arousal came to New York on December 30, 1948, when the musical comedy *Kiss Me Kate* took the town with music and lyrics by Cole Porter, book by Bella and Samuel Spewack, choreography by Hanya Holm, sets and costumes by Lemuel Ayers, and a deft cast headed by Alfred Drake, Patricia Morison, Harold Lang, and Lisa

Kirk. *Kiss Me Kate* is the tempestuous story of two theatrical folk, akin to Petruchio and Katherine, in a company engaged in playing *The Taming of the Shrew*. The production is somewhat slowly paced and a few of the lyrics are quite irrelevant, but the *Shrew* scenes are delightfully colorful satire, and some of the lyrics are both appropriate and highly amusing. A travesty and a treat is whipped out of Shakespeare in *Kiss Me Kate*. The musical attained 1077 performances in New York, returning after a long tour, with a different but equally effective cast on January 8, 1952. It has played in Europe and Australia, and for 501 performances in London, where it opened March 8, 1951. Despite its hilarious and its graceful moments, however, the musical's two movements, of actors living and actors acting, are not wholly integrated; the experienced theatregoer will still prefer Shakespeare's *The Taming of the Shrew*.

Some scholars think that not all of the play is Shakespeare's; others contend he revised an earlier play. "I can think of no other Shakespearean play that has so little essential Shakespeare in it," said Harold Hobson in the *London Sunday Times* after a November 4, 1947, revival. Swinburne earlier put the matter in more complimentary form: "The refined instinct, artistic judgment, and consummate taste of Shakespeare were never perhaps so wonderfully shown. . . . All the force and humor alike of character and situation belong to Shakespeare's eclipsed and forlorn precursor; he has added nothing; he has tempered and enriched everything." The likelihood is that the "earlier play" is a pirated version of Shakespeare's own comedy, set down from a player's memory. In any event, Shakespeare in *The Taming of the Shrew* has spangled with sequins of delightful observation rich cloth of human nature.

Kiss Me Kate was played in Los Angeles in 1955 and 1964; revived at the New York City Center in 1956 and 1965. Among its engaging songs are "We Open in Venice," "I've Come to Wive It Wealthily in Padua," "So in Love," "Where Is the Life That Late I Led?" *The Taming of the Shrew* was performed commedia dell'arte style by ACT in 1974, with masks and merry slapstick.

KING RICHARD II   *William Shakespeare*

Among the portraits of English kings in Shakespeare's history plays, perhaps none searches more deeply into a monarch's soul than that of Richard II. To rule effectively, a king must have authority of will and power of both mind and hand. Not only are these lacking in Richard, but he knows their lack, and can but watch himself slump to his downfall. His "unstaid youth" rejects the wise admonitions of his uncle, John of Gaunt. He seeks to compensate for his lack of drive with wild expenditures. The handsome lad lends ear to every flatterer, but also breaks into sudden impetuous acts. One of these acts, his seizing the wealth of John of Gaunt and John's banished son Bolingbroke, as soon as Gaunt has died, costs him his throne. Henry Bolingbroke comes back from France; Richard is forced to abdicate; and, soon after Bolingbroke mounts the throne as Henry IV, in response to the new king's desire Richard is slain. Such a stark opposition of two chief figures—here, Richard and Bolingbroke—was new in the English drama.

The essential events of the play are drawn from Holinshed's *Chronicles* and Stowe's *Annals*. It was early involved in English politics. Although the play, written about 1594, was first published in 1597, the scene of Richard's abdication was not printed until 1608 for fear of offending Queen Elizabeth, who more than once compared herself to the gentle Richard. On the other hand, it was enacted on February 7, 1601, the day before Essex' rebellion, in order to encourage the plotters against Elizabeth. For general patriotic purposes, however, no more ringing words can be found than Gaunt's praise of England, before he dies. The entire speech was often heard on the British radio during World War II. More philosophical is Richard's soliloquy upon the death of kings, which, said William Bliss in *The Real Shakespeare* (1949), "is almost the most perfect thing Shakespeare ever wrote."

The play has not been frequently revived. Nahum Tate's version of 1680, *The Sicilian Usurper,* with references to the current Popish Plot, was suppressed after the second performance. Lewis Theobald's version of 1719, obeying the three dramatic unities, was little more successful. The play was produced but twice in the eighteenth century. In the nineteenth, Richard was played by Edmund Kean and his son Charles; by Edwin Booth; and by Sir Frank Benson at Stratford in 1896 and 1899. There were productions in London in 1905, with Herbert Beerbohm Tree and his daughter Viola; in 1916 at Fordham University, New York; in 1917 at the Old Vic in London; in London by Henry Boynton in 1925; again in 1934 at the Old Vic. In New York the play was not professionally produced from Edwin Booth's appearance at Daly's Fifth Avenue Theatre in 1875 until Maurice Evans played in it in 1937, when it achieved the record run of 171 performances. In the same year, John Gielgud enacted the doomed Richard in London. The play was performed in 1948 in Germany, Italy, and France. Evans revived it in New York in 1940 and for another fortnight opening January 24, 1951; and later in the year Michael Redgrave acted Richard at Stratford-on-Avon.

In 1937 the vitality of the play took the New York critics by storm. Brooks Atkinson called it "one of the most thorough, illuminating, and vivid productions of Shakespeare we have had in recent memory. Although Richard II was no hero, now we know that the anguish of his soul is heroic and has the power to make our hearts stand still. . . . It is the distinction of Richard that his mind grows keener with destruction before his enemies; although he lacks the power to rule, he has the courage to be his own confessor, and he is most kingly when the crown has been snatched from his head." Gilbert W. Gabriel was more emphatic still: "No other play of the bard's has so many lines in it of ringing steel and patriotic bronze." And John Anderson went so far as to declare that "our theatre has no scene to put beside this Richard's abdication." When Evans brought *Richard II* back in 1940, Atkinson said that it "seemed again one of the most absorbing of Shakespeare's plays."

The king gives a new sort of unity, of tone and feeling, to the play; Walter Pater compared it to a musical symphony. Yet Richard turns constantly from action to talk; such words as *tongue, mouth, speech, word* are frequent in the play. For full appreciation, *Richard II* should be viewed as the first play of a tetralogy, followed by the two parts of *Henry IV* and by *Henry V*. This view, taken by E. K. Chambers in *Shakespeare: A Survey* (1925), sees Henry V as "the ideal king, the divinely chosen representative and embodiment of the spirit of England. . . . He holds the tetralogy together, from the first mention of his frolic boyhood at the end of Richard II, through the riot and the budding valours of *Henry IV,* until he takes his kinghood on and blazes forth, 'his vanities forespent', in the glittering careers of Agincourt." Both Henry V and Richard II spent an "unstaid youth," but the great monarch of action stands as a counterweight to the feeble monarch of words. That kings are but actors on a larger scale is implied in these four plays, by repeated comparison of state and stage.

King Richard recognizes that his life is like a performance. Yet, reflecting on his betrayal and recalling the betrayal of Jesus—the King being God's deputy—the actor becomes a man, and while remaining a symbol of ineffectual divinity rises to human dignity.

Early in the nineteenth century, Hazlitt observed: "*Richard II* is a play little known, compared with *Richard III* . . . yet we confess that we prefer the nature and feeling of the one to the noise and bustle of the other." There was, nevertheless, but a single revival of the former—by the little known Jones Finch—in London, from 1858 to 1900; it required our age's interest in introspection to make the play popular again. Hazlitt found the appeal of *Richard II* in the fact that "the sufferings of the man make us forget that he ever was a king." In appraising a 1947 revival, Harold Hobson of the *London Sunday Times* found the secret of the play's popularity in Richard's self-pity: "He creates, out of the artistic fecundity of his mind, the image of a king who *has* been royal. . . . Self-pity: lamentation: hysteria. . . . The world today darts hither and thither directionless. It grieves over the hardness of its fate, as Richard did. Of all Shakespeare's kings, he is its prime spokesman. And, if not with spirit, if not with courage, he speaks beautifully, with words that twine about the heart." Too close to ourselves for comfort, *Richard II* is a sympathetic but a warning picture of a well-meaning king too weak to rule.

The frequently experimental CRC, March 18, 1982, set the play in the legendary world of the Celts about A.D. 100, with the nobles as Druids, stressing the love of language of Richard, and the mythical pattern of his finding his humanity in his yielding to death.

KING HENRY IV

William Shakespeare

The popularity of the two parts of *Henry IV*, 1597?, featuring history and Falstaff, has been continuous with good reason. As Samuel Johnson stated in 1768: "Perhaps no author has ever in two plays afforded so much delight. The great events are interesting, for the fate of kingdoms depends upon them; the slighter occurrences are diverting and, except for one or two, sufficiently probable; the incidents are multiplied with wonderful facility of invention, and the characters diversified with the utmost nicety of discernment, and the profoundest skill in the nature of man." The play is generally esteemed as the best of Shakespeare's histories.

Part One, drawing its history from Holinshed's *Chronicles,* presents Hotspur's rebellion, and his death at the hands of Prince Hal. In Part Two, the serious historical concern is less; the comic scenes are more varied and especially lively with Doll Tearsheet at Boar's Head Tavern. Yet there is a sound talk between Henry IV and his wild son; much indication of the evils of rebellion; and the significant incident in which Prince Hal tries on the crown while his ailing royal father is still alive. Originally Falstaff was called Oldcastle, and pictured as a Lollard hypocrite misleading the young Prince; presumably the Earl of Cobham, a descendant of Oldcastle, objected, for the name was changed and an apology was inserted in the Epilogue to Part Two, where it is promised that "Falstaff shall die of a sweat, unless already 'e be killed with your hard opinions; for Oldcastle died a martyr, and this is not the man."

Falstaff knew his own limitations, as he shows, sighing "There live not three good men unhanged in England, and one of them is fat and grows old." Maurice Morgann (in 1777), denying that Falstaff, like earlier clowns, was a "mere stage mechanism compounded of rogue and gull," described him as "a man at once young and old, enterprising and fat, a dupe and a wit, harmless and wicked, weak in principle and resolute by constitution, cowardly in appearance and brave in reality, a knave without malice, a liar without deceit, and a knight, a gentleman, and a soldier, without either dignity, decency, or honour." Hazlitt, about a century later, called him "perhaps the most substantial comic character that was ever invented . . ." From these, Bernard Shaw's is a dissenting opinion: "Falstaff, the most human person in the play, but none the less a besotted and disgusting old wretch." Audiences can enjoy Falstaff, though he is not only humorous but also objectionable; the Victorians ignored or resented this conjunction, wishing to laugh only where they felt morally sound. Harold C. Goddard, who also pointed out, in *The Meaning of Shakespeare*, 1951, that the immoral Falstaff and the immortal Falstaff exist in one body, called the robustious knight a "symbol of the supremacy of imagination over fact."

Many Freudian commentators have rushed in on Shakespeare. Perhaps most effective was Dr. Franz Alexander; in his study he shows the parallel between the development of Prince Hal and the typical Freudian picture of the ego's struggle for adjustment: (1) rebellion against the father; (2) conquest of the super-ego (Hotspur, glory rigidly conceived); (3) conquest of the id (Falstaff, anarchic self-indulgence); (4) identification with the father (putting on the crown while the king still lives); (5) assumption of mature responsibility. The last of these comes suddenly, but the sequence is natural.

In 1804 Stephen Kemble—the *big* not the *great* Kemble—played Falstaff without stuffing; in 1895, Julia Marlowe played Prince Hal. Notable, more recently in New York, are the all-star revival in 1926—Otis Skinner as Falstaff; Philip Merivale as Hotspur; Basil Sydney, Peggy Wood, and Blanche Ring, with the *Prologue* spoken by John Drew; the production of Part One by Margaret Webster, starring Maurice Evans, in 1939; and the coming of the Old Vic company in May 1946. Stratford-on-Avon saw the play in 1951 with Michael Redgrave as Hotspur and Anthony Quayle as Falstaff.

Of the Evans production, January 30, 1939, John Anderson declared: "It was the first time that I can remember a Shakespearean play at which the audience laughed at a clown as loudly as it would at Ed Wynn, without worrying about Divine William at all." Regarding the Old Vic production of Part One, Robert Garland recorded: "Slowly, but surely, a feeling of disappointment began to take possession of the audience. What might have been an integrated projection of a second-string historical play began to be a disintegrated vehicle for the showy actorial portraiture of Laurence Olivier as Hotspur and Ralph Richardson as Falstaff." Robert Coleman, who had found Evans' work "a gorgeous performance of a rousing and risible play," called Olivier's "definitely inferior to many Shakespearean revivals that have been given here with half the fanfare." As Hotspur Olivier seemed a minor Evans. With Part Two, however, opinions abruptly veered. George Freedley wondered why Part One had been played the more often. John Chapman also failed to understand "why this play has not been produced here in almost eighty years . . . a glowing, vigorous work whose drama is relieved by superbly lusty, delightfully lewd comedy."

There is drama as well as history in the vivid portraits of the king and his son, and in the sudden sweep of Falstaff to bewildered pathos at the close. Whether to play the fat knight with exaggerate swagger or more realistically roistering, has divided performers. Falstaff's carrying off of Hotspur, for instance, may be troublesome: a critic remarked that Quin "had little or no difficulty in perching Garrick upon his shoulders, who looked like a dwarf on the back of a giant.—But oh! how he tugged and toiled to raise Barry from the ground. . . . It was thought best for the future, that some of Falstaff's ragamuffins should bear off the dead body." Arthur Colby Sprague urged moderation: "If, too, a good deal of the business was stuffy and uninspired, it might at least serve as a check on such extravagances as we have to put up with, at times, today. Mr. Orson Welles, as Falstaff, in the Play Scene in *Henry IV*, chose to wear a saucepan on his head as a crown. Surely, the cushion which Falstaff names and tradition might once have dictated is quite as funny—and Shakespearean, as well." As a reminder of the more serious portions of the play, there is Leigh Hunt's comment on the 1830 production at Drury Lane: "Mr. Cooper's costume as Henry IV was a real historical picture. We saw the King himself before us, with his draperied head; and the performer, as he rose from his chair, and remained lecturing his son with his foot planted on the royal stool, displayed the monarch well—his ermined robe, stretched out by his elbow, making a background to the portrait."

The plays themselves are a portrait of a period, and of a richly comic life-loving man.

The Memorial Theatre of Stratford-upon-Avon opened in 1932 with *Henry IV*. The RSC opened its new Barbican Theatre in 1982 with *Henry IV*.

Naturally, Falstaff always draws attention. In 1700 *Falstaff's Wedding* briefly took the stage, as in 1829 *The Life and Humours of Falstaff*, by C. S. William Hazlitt discerned: "Falstaff's wit is an exuberance of good-humour and good-nature; an overflowing of his love of laughter and good-fellowship; a giving vent to his heart's-ease, and over-contentment with himself and others." J. I. M. Stewart sought farther: "All true drama penetrates through representative fiction to the condition of myth. . . For Falstaff, so Bacchic, so splendidly with the Maenads Doll and Mrs. Quickly, a creature of the wine-cart and the cymbal, so fit a sacrifice (as Hal early discerns) to lard the lean, the barren earth, is of that primitive and magical world upon which all art, even if with a profound unconsciousness, draws."

In August 1983 the Colletivo of Parma, at the London Riverside Studios, added Italian violence and horseplay, including pickpocketing, to the tavern scenes, with leather jackets pouring in for the Gad's Hill robbery, on blaring and glaring motorbikes.

KING HENRY V   *William Shakespeare*

Although frequently shown, this play, Shakespeare's most rousing patriotic pageant, always worries the producers for the reasons set down by Henry James after an 1875 performance: "The play could be presented only as a kind of animated panorama, for it offers but the slenderest opportunities for acting. . . . Illusion, as such an enterprise proposes to produce it, is absolutely beyond the compass of the stage. . . . To assent to this you have only to look at the grotesqueness of the hobby-horses on the field of Agincourt and at the uncovered rear of King Harry's troops, when they have occasion to retire under range of your opera-glass. We approve by all means of scenic splendors, but we would draw the line at invading armies." Shakespeare himself felt the limitations of the stage for such a play as this, as the *Prologue* shows. It was written about 1598.

Read the play and you have an entirely different impression, as recorded by Ruskin: "That battle of Agincourt strikes me as one of the most perfect things, in its sort, we have anywhere of Shakespeare's. The description of the two hosts: the worn-out, jaded, English; the dread hour, big with destiny, when the battle shall begin; and then the deathless valour: 'Ye good yeomen, whose limbs were made in England!' A true English heart breathes, calm and strong, through the whole business; not boisterous, protrusive; all the better for that. There is a sound in it like the ring of steel." So too, E. K. Chambers in *Shakespeare: A Survey* (1925) speaks of "The unfailing imagery, the abundant eloquence, the swelling phrase . . . the martial ring and hard brilliance of so much of the verse of the play, in which Shakespeare's style reaches its zenith of objectivity and rhetoric."

The story of the play is drawn mainly from Holinshed's *Chronicles*. Prince Hal, now Henry V and a truly royal monarch, after the French Dauphin has sent him a tun of tennis balls as a scornful inauguration gift, invades France. After a stirring appeal leading his men through the breached walls of Harfleur, watching with quiet prayer through the night before Agincourt, Henry triumphs over the more numerous French forces and wins peace with marriage to Katherine of France. With Falstaff dead, his erstwhile comrades Pistol, Nym, and Bardolph are, as William Hazlitt says, "satellites without a sun"; but England's new sense of national unity is suggested, and the humor sustained, through portraits of sturdy Britishers: English Gower, Irish Macmorris, Scots Jamy, Welsh Fluellen with his leek for St. Davy's Day—which the fierce coward Pistol must eat (though of course the stage "leek" has a slice of apple inside!).

Productions have varied in splendor, with Sir Henry Irving's in the 1870's perhaps most scenically elaborate. John Ranken Towne compared Richard Mansfield's, in New York 1899, to Irving's, but added: "the driving force to give animation and dramatic vitality to all the elaborate preparation was wanting." Charles Kean (1830) and after him Macready (1839) had King Henry, in France, pray before Agincourt in a fashion to which *John Bull* objected: "the actor literally kneels down with his soldiery, and the curtain falls to the solemn strains of an organ, brought from England we suppose for the purpose." Few today question music to match a play's mood. In his quest of realism Charles Calvert in Manchester in 1872 raised scaling ladders before Harfleur, with volleys of arrows. His wife's *Memoirs* record that "the supers rose each night to such a pitch of excitement that as he rushed up the eminence, followed by the shouting soldiery, the moment he was out of sight of the audience, he had to jump down and get underneath the platform, or he would, most assuredly, have been mowed down by his own men."

Produced in Pasadena in 1935, in London by Laurence Olivier in 1937 and Ivor Novello in 1938, at Stratford-on-Avon in 1943, and by the London Old Vic opening January 30, 1951, *Henry V* was seen in New York in 1924 with Irene Bordoni and Philip Merivale, in 1925 and 1928 with Walter Hampden, and again in 1931. Percy Hammond called the Hampden production "a substantial and earnest endeavor to bring one of the most cadaverous of Shakespeare's plays back to life," although again the battlefield settings seemed troublesome.

The difficulties of staging, revolving as they do around spectacle and charge, make the play a likely one for motion pictures; and the best film version of a Shakespearean play is the Laurence Olivier *Henry V*, widely shown in 1946. Pictorially superb, with rousing battle scenes, it does not overlook the other values of the play (though it gilds the lily by adding a line from Marlowe). For through the drama comes a feeling that kings are, after all, men; that they have responsibilities as well as—nay, rather than—rights. This most imaginative and stirring of Shakespeare's histories is a surface show of a high-spirited ruler riding to national glory.

Below the surface of the play are more somber depths. Richly, as Harold C. Goddard observed, there is a continuance of Shakespeare's subtle irony, hinting the difference between seeming or saying and being. Georg Brandes objected that the playwright "manifests no disapproval where the king sinks far below the ideal, as when he orders the frightful massacre of all the French prisoners taken at Agincourt. Shakespeare tries to pass the deed off as a measure of necessity." It is, of course, not Shakespeare but Henry that argues necessity as the excuse for slaughter. While the Chorus praises Henry as "the mirror of all Christian kings," the mirror of the play itself shows a conceited and unscrupulous conqueror. As abruptly as he has discarded Falstaff, Henry orders Bardolph executed for robbing a church, whenas his own French campaign is being financed by a church bribe. In disguise at camp, he gives a glove to soldier Williams, pledging his honor to match it man to man; then, as king, his first fobs the challenge off on Fluellen, then tries to pay Williams off; the soldier, more manly than his king, cries "I will none of your money!" As for fighting, King Henry takes as little part in the Battle of Agincourt as Prince Hal in the Gadshill robbery—and, as Goddard remarked, there is scarce any higher ethics in the royal plundering. Almost the first words of Shakespeare's *Henry VI* indicate the crumbling of the power Henry V had gained. Under the bright panoply and gilt costumes of power, Shakespeare lets peep the soiled undergarments of violence, greed, and pride.

The RSC production of *Henry V* in London, 1975, and New York, 1976, directed by Terry Hands, sets by Farrah, music by Guy Wolfenden, with Alan Howard as Henry, was called "definitive" by Clive Barnes. The actors walk about in modern dress, chatting—until the French enemy enters in fifteenth-century court dress; the stage blossoms with bright heraldry; and the actors assume their English costumes—save for Emrys James as the Chorus, who retains his modern clothes throughout the play. "Definitive?" Clive Barnes questions himself, and adds: "In the plundered world of Shakespearean production nothing is definitive."

Falstaff, brushed aside by the reformed Henry, is granted a death scene of which John Middleton Murry declares: "There is nothing remotely like it in all the literature of the world. How should there be? It is Shakespeare's requiem over the darling of his imagination." The death scene is realistically described by Mrs. Quickly, now married to Pistol, hostess of the Boar's Head, Eastcheap. King Henry knew he must cut clean.

John Masefield set the play in its wider perspective. It ought, he said, "to be seen and judged as a part of the magnificent tragic sequence. . . . It is about a popular hero who is as common as those who love him . . . Henry V is the one commonplace man in the eight plays. He alone enjoys success and worldly happiness. He enters Shakespeare's vision to reap what his brokenhearted father sowed. He passes out of Shakespeare's vision to beget the son who dies broken-hearted after bringing all to waste again.—'Hear him but reason in divinity!', cries the admiring archbishop. Yet this searcher of the spirit woos his wife like a butcher, and jokes among his men like a groom. He has the knack of life that fits human beings for whatever is animal in human affairs." He is the most attractive figure in the history plays.

THE MERRY WIVES OF WINDSOR   *William Shakespeare*

One of the most successful of Shakespeare's comedies, with a long history of revivals all over the world, is *The Merry Wives of Windsor,* (1598?), which, legend tells us, he wrote in a fortnight, on Queen Elizabeth's mention that she would like to see Falstaff in love. Hartley Coleridge commented on this idea in 1948 with Victorian emphasis: "That Queen Bess should have desired to see Falstaff making love proves her to have been, as she was, a gross-minded old baggage. Shakespeare has evaded the difficulty with great skill. He knew that Falstaff could not be in love; and has mixed but a little, a very little, *pruritus* with his fortune-hunting courtship. But the Falstaff of *The Merry Wives* is not the Falstaff of *Henry IV.* * It is a big-bellied impostor, assuming his name and style, or, at best, it is Falstaff in dotage." Saintsbury, fifty years later, counters this notion: "It is mistaken affection which thinks him degraded, or 'translated' Bottom-fashion. He is even as elsewhere, though under an unluckier star." The Falstaff of *Henry IV,* however, is always resourceful; the Falstaff here is always helpless, and an easy butt.

John Dennis, in 1702, altered the play into *The Comical Gallant*; but this time the original drove the vulgar perversion from the stage. Opinions of the comedy have varied little over the centuries. Thus Samuel Johnson said in 1768: "The conduct of this drama is deficient; the action ends often before the conclusion, and the different parts might change places without inconvenience; but its general power, that power by which all works of genius shall finally be tried, is such, that perhaps it never yet had reader or spectator, who did not think it too soon at end." And Hardin Craig called it, in 1948, "one of the liveliest comedies in dramatic literature. It has greatness in dramatic situations; and situations, rather than wit, are the basis of English comedy. There is a wealth of incidents, all presented in a breathless bustle."

Shakespeare has ingeniously mixed the ingredients of this English trifle. Some of the material came from the Italian tales of Ser Giovanni Fiorentino, but *The Merry Wives of Windsor* is Shakespeare's only comedy with a setting in contemporary England, and his only play almost all in prose. There are comically exaggerated pictures of ordinary English citizens, Mistress Ford and Mistress Page, their husbands, and the country-folk around, including Justice Shallow and his cousin Slender, a mere puff-ball of foolish froth made immortal. There is Pistol, who cries "The World's mine oyster, which I with sword will open"—and who informs the husbands of Falstaff's rendezvous with their wives. The wives, too, have mischief in their heads; so that first we see Falstaff, hidden in a laundry basket, dumped with the dirty wash into a ditch; then we watch him, disguised as a woman, belabored and beswitched as a polecat, a runyon, a witch; and finally we behold him in the forest at night, wearing horns he'd have loved to plant on the husbands, plagued and burned and pinched by the company disguised as a satyr and fairies, in a burlesque of the May Day stag-mummers' hunt, popular in England from pagan times. It is during this frolic in the forest darkness that the love-story steals off for its climax. For Shakespeare has intertwined with all this rioting and horseplay (indeed, Beerbohm Tree as Falstaff, in 1902, came in on a white horse) the threads of a tender romance. Sweet Ann Page—whom Hartley Coleridge called "a pretty little creature one would like to take on one's knee—is ripe for a lucky man's picking. Her father would marry her to Slender, with his wide lands and heavy beeves; her mother's eyes are turned to the fashionable and imposing Frenchman, Dr. Caius. Ann's heart belongs to Fenton, whose oats are mainly wild, but who has gentlemanly birth and is full of promise. Three disguised couples steal away during the forest frolic: Dr. Caius and Slender each finds himself with a boy; and the Pages reconcile themselves to Fenton's marriage with Ann.

Productions have tended to stress the foolery or the grotesque extravagances of Falstaff. Thus Oscar Asche in the role devoured an entire fowl at each performance, tearing it asunder with his fingers and pitching the drumsticks at Bardolph. Beerbohm Tree tangled in the dress he put on to try to escape the irate husband, tripped and crawled along the floor while Ford belabored him on the buttocks. Vegetables tumbled from the bag he carried, with which Mistress Page (Ellen Terry) pelted him as he made his way out.

Among American performances was one in 1927 with Mrs. Fiske and Otis Skinner, of which John Mason Brown observed that "Mrs. Fiske romped through the farce, adding to the gaiety of a script which, in spite of its riotous moments, is none too hilarious at best. They created happy memories." The play was also produced by Mr. and Mrs. Coburn, in 1935; by the Federal Theatre in Los Angeles, in 1938; and in a "swing version" at Hollywood in 1940. It was revived at the Old Vic in London, opening May 31, 1951, with Peggy Ashcroft as Mistress Page and Roger Livesey as Falstaff.

In New York an April 1938 production was damned by the critics and ran for but four performances. Brooks Atkinson declared: "Although Queen Elizabeth asked to see Falstaff in love she did not require him to woo in a straw hat nightmare. . . . Taking advantage of Shakespeare's death, Robert Henderson has dumped old tub o' guts into a frantic production like an experiment in practical joking . . . Queen Bess would have marched Shakespeare off to the hangman if *The Merry Wives* had looked like that in her decisive day." Despite such critical words—which in sober truth the production deserved—those that saw the play seemed to enjoy it; and the *Journal-American* said there is "good solid entertainment in Shakespeare neat at the Empire." Even a bad performance, however critics cavil, cannot destroy all the fun of the audiences watching *The Merry Wives*. The child in us all will laugh at Falstaff's discomfiture; the youth in us all will rejoice in love's winning with sweet Ann Page. More maturely, we shall smile at the all-too-human weaknesses of the earnest husbands and the merry wives.

The merry wives are a delightful pair, said Hartley Coleridge. "Methinks I see them, with their comely middle-aged visages, their dainty white ruffs and toys, their half-witch-like conic hats, their full farthingales, their neat though not over-slim waists, their housewifely keys, their girdles, their sly laughing looks, their apple-red cheeks, their brows the lines whereon look more like the work of mirth than years."

JULIUS CAESAR   *William Shakespeare*

Based upon North's translation (1579) of Plutarch's *Lives, Julius Caesar,* possibly written in 1598, tells the story of the assassination of the great Roman and the death of the conspirators against him. Partly history, partly tragedy, the drama shows how the idealist may be misled by the practical man, and the practical man doomed by the idealist. For the honest Brutus, once ensnared, overrides the crafty Cassius. During the conspiracy he insists that they take no oaths, that they do not draw Cicero in, and that only Caesar and not Antony be killed; and after the assassination he insists that Antony be allowed to speak and that the foe be met without delay at Philippi. In all these decisions Brutus was honest, pigheaded, and unwise. When craft and honesty seek to work together, both succumb.

Julius Caesar is studded with gems of rhetoric. Working upon his upright friend, Cassius remarks: "The fault, dear Brutus, is not in our stars, but in ourselves, that we are underlings." After the soothsayer bids him "Beware the Ides of March!", Caesar scoffs at fear: "Cowards die many times before their deaths; The valiant never taste of death but once." He goes to the Capitol, is stricken by the conspirators, and falls dead. There is superb contrast in the funeral orations of Brutus and Antony. Brutus is straightforward and reasonable, but utterly unconvincing. Antony, after a disarming start, with shrewd persuasiveness whips the populace to a destroying frenzy against the "honourable men" that have killed Caesar.

The quarrel between Brutus and Cassius before the battle of Philippi is also noteworthy. Brutus is intolerant of Cassius' "itching palm"; but Cassius' shrewdness and Brutus' weight of grief at news of his wife's death effect a reconciliation. Coleridge declared: " I know no part of Shakespeare that more impresses on me the belief of his genius' being superhuman, than this scene between Brutus and Cassius." Bernard Shaw loosed a blast at this bardolatry: "A conceited poet bursts into the tent of Brutus and Cassius and exhorts them not to quarrel with one another. If Shakespeare had been able to present his play to the ghost of the great Julius, he probably would have had much the same reception. He certainly would have deserved it."

Shakespeare's ability to develop characters under the strain of circumstance is shrewdly shown in the presentation of Brutus. Brutus, the only member of the conspiracy with disinterested motives, must convince himself that his honorable intentions justify questionable deeds. He therefore pictures the murder of Caesar as a ritual—"Let's carve him as a dish fit for the gods. . . . Let's be sacrificers, not butchers"—but the performance of this "ritual" demands deceit. Thus the initial two scenes of the play—with Shakespeare's frequent device of reiterative imagery—give stress to rituals and ceremonies first performed then desecrated or mocked. The symbolism of ceremony, and the irony, continue through the play as, in Brutus, dedication slumps to policy, then draggles in petty moods. We see the end evoked to give dignity to the means, which then proceed to debase and befoul the course of living. Brutus is an "honourable man" whose very honesty, on an ignoble course, forces self-deception and widens the doom. For Brutus, though honorable at the play's start, is coarsened by the dilemma life has set him. He scorns to secure money by such means as Cassius employs, yet rails at Cassius for not sending him any. His toploftiness in the quarrel— "For I am armed so strong in honesty . . ."—echoes Caesar's vainglory— "But I am constant as the northern star"—and shows that one grows to be the thing one hates.

Ben Jonson (see *Every Man Out of His Humour**) took a fling at a few passages in the play. However, a line he called ridiculous seems really the epitome of a tyrant's self-justification: "Caesar did never wrong but with just cause." Though changed in later editions, these words ensnare the spirit of any man with power. It has been charged that Shakespeare, in his treatment of the common people in this play and elsewhere, shows himself opposed to democracy. This is much like accusing a caveman of not reading newspapers. In Shakespeare's day, the problem was for England to achieve unity and maintain peace under a strong, wise head. Examination of many of Shakespeare's plays shows that although the mob is referred to as a foul many-headed beast, individuals are esteemed according to their worth, not their rank. The sturdy, solid, manly commoners in the plays, indeed, are outnumbered only by the stupid or villainous gentlemen. It may be this charge, nevertheless, that led Bernard Shaw to attack the spirit of *Julius Caesar.* Declaring that it is the craftiest stage job ever done and praising

Shakespeare's full organ tones, Shaw protested in 1898 that the portrait of Caesar is a travesty, that not a statement of his is worthy of even "an average Tammany boss. Brutus is nothing but a familiar type of English suburban preacher . . . Cassius is a vehemently assertive nonentity." Shaw's indignation, however, died at thought of Antony: with him "we find Shakespeare in his depth; and in his depth, of course, he is superlative."

Superlative, too, though briefly seen, are the wife and the servant boy of Brutus. Portia stands staunchly by her husand; she divines, and insists on sharing, his concerns. She, and the innocent boy Lucius, whom Brutus is always rousing from his slumbers, partake of the nobility and slumbering innocence of the misled leader. Lucius, who has fallen asleep over his musical instrument in Brutus' tent, catches in his half-waking words the way his master has been played upon: "The strings, my lord, are false." Once embarked, Brutus urged the conspirators to put on a false face, and the train of violence, falsehood, and greed was started on its repetitive journey.

Productions of this drama have usually been simple, though one in 1875 ended with a great tableau of Brutus' funeral pyre. Junius Brutus Booth found a fit gesture when as Cassius he strode unconcernedly over the fallen Caesar. There was less propriety when, in an Edwin Booth production, the First Citizen and the Second Citizen, each weighing well over 200 pounds, stepped conspicuously forward as Julius Caesar exclaimed, "Let me have men about me that are fat!"

Outstanding American productions have included Edwin Booth and Lawrence Barrett (1871), Robert Mantell (1906), William Faversham and Tyrone Power (1912). In 1940 the play was presented in Cleveland Heights, Dallas, and (in modern dress), Kalamazoo, Michigan. The most exciting recent version was the one, condensed to ninety minutes without intermission, of the Mercury Theatre in New York in 1936, with Orson Welles as Brutus, against the brick wall of the theatre, with modern uniforms. A company from Amherst College presented the play at the Folger Shakespeare Museum in Washington in 1949. An arena production, with Basil Rathbone as Cassius and Horace Braham as Caesar, opened in New York on June 20, 1950.

Of the Mercury production, Brooks Atkinson said: "It is revolution taken out of the hands of men and driven by immortal destiny . . . Caesar's resemblance to Mussolini in appearance and manner defines the play so exactly that the dialogue sounds curiously restrained, as though the author could not speak the words he needs for so ominous an occasion." John Anderson felt that the production succeeded "enough to blow the hinges off the dictionary." John Mason Brown concurred: "I come to praise *Caesar*, not to bury it . . . the heart of the drama beats more vigorously in this production than it has in years."

Few productions of the play, however bad, have been able to destroy its vigor. It continues its challenge as—in Bernard Shaw's relenting words— "the most splendidly written political melodrama we possess." Even more, it is a dramatic picture of calculation failing, and dragging down nobility in its ruins. In *Julius Caesar* Shakespeare, writing for the first time under the double influence of the Roman Seneca and the Greek Plutarch, reaches out toward new heights of tragic power.

MUCH ADO ABOUT NOTHING   *William Shakespeare*

Borrowing the serious story of *Much Ado About Nothing*, (1598?), mainly from Bandello's *Novelle*, 1554, Shakespeare added all that gives the play its sparkle and its life. The virtuous heroine made, by a villain's plot, to seem wanton, so that her lover denies her—as Claudio at the church casts off the innocent Hero—was a widespread medieval motif. Widespread too was the device of having her then play dead so as to effect a final happy restoration. But the absurd constable Dogberry and his Watch, who stumble upon and disclose the villainy, are a unique Shakespearean creation. And Shakespeare brought into the play the love-game played upon Beatrice, "the sauciest, most piquant, madcap girl that ever Shakespeare drew," and Benedick, who swore to remain a bachelor, but whose name is now the byword for a married man. The way in which the two are enticed into a courtship—their friends arranging to have Benedick overhear them say that Beatrice loves him; and Beatrice, that Benedick loves her—leads to some of Shakespeare's merriest trifling. As Coleridge in 1818 summed it up: "Take away all that is not indispensable to the plot . . . take away Benedick, Beatrice, Dogberry and the reaction of the former on the character of Hero—and what will remain?" Swinburne felt that the borrowed and the original parts were admirably fused by Shakespeare: "For absolute power of composition, for faultless balance and blameless rectitude of design, there is unquestionably no creation of his hand that will bear comparison with *Much Ado About Nothing.*"

One of the most popular of Shakespeare's comedies, the play was performed at court in 1613 as part of the wedding celebration of the daughter of James I. In 1649 Leonard Digges, in doggerel verse, attested to its unfailing popularity. In 1662 Davenant's *The Law Against Lovers,* a version combining the Beatrice-Benedick plot with that of *Measure for Measure,** supplanted Shakespeare's play; the original was not acted again until 1721. It was popular in Garrick's repertory around 1750; but gradually the play came to be chosen by women stars attracted to the role of Beatrice: Helen Faucit, Ellen Terry, Ada Rehan, and Modjeska. Peggy Ashcroft and John Gielgud acted the play at Stratford, opening June 6, 1950.

The first American performance of the play was in New York at the John Street Theatre, March 17, 1787. More recently, it was produced here by Sothern and Marlowe in 1904, and by the Stratford-on-Avon Festival Company in 1930. It is very popular in college and community theatre revivals. Gielgud played it again in London, opening January 11, 1952. Claire Luce was in a New York production opening May 1, 1952, that lasted for only four performances. The New York production with Ellen Terry and Henry Irving, in November 1884, was an elaborate one. Said the *Times:* "The wit, the tenderness, the playful satire, and the humanity . . . charmed an audience that filled every part of the Star Theatre. . . . There have been in our day more comely and less ungainly Benedicts than Mr. Irving. . . . But surely there has never been a better Beatrice than Ellen Terry. . . . Infused with the spirit of all that is pure and lovable in womanhood, sparkling with merriment that does not hide the tenderness of her heart . . . certainly one of the best dramatic achievements of its time." Viewing the play again in March, 1885, the *Times* reconsidered: "Mr. Irving's Benedict improves on acquaintance. . . . He still seems crusty and odd, but his surliness disappears, and we find him a good-humored, fair-minded, warm-hearted, brave gentleman, not so young as he was, but all the better for having seen the world and learned wisdom by experience. He is still a bit fantastic too, and overfond of dress and jewelry; but how well the hues of his raiment harmonize with the colors of the scenes through which he strolls! . . . a delightful glimpse of the sunny land of romance."

To the chorus of praise of the play, Bernard Shaw set a countering solo:

"The main pretension in *Much Ado* is that Benedick and Beatrice are exquisitely witty and amusing persons. They are, of course, nothing of the sort. Benedick's pleasantries might pass at a sing-song in a public house parlor; but a gentleman rash enough to venture on them in even the very mildest £52-a-year suburban imitation of polite society today would assuredly never be invited again. From his first joke . . . to his last, he is not a wit, but a blackguard. . . . Precisely the same thing, in the tenderer degree of her sex, is true of Beatrice. In her character of professed wit she has only one subject, and that is the subject which a really witty woman never jests about, because it is too serious a matter to be made light of without indelicacy. Beatrice jests about it for the sake of the indelicacy."—Surely this was the moment for someone to quote, against Shaw, from the play itself: "Speak, cousin, or, if you cannot, stop his mouth with a kiss!'

A more serious moment in the play is that in which Benedick first asks Beatrice what he can do to show his love for her. Beatrice, full of resentment against Claudio for his having spurned Hero at the altar's foot, cries out "Kill Claudio!" Harold Hobson of the *London Sunday Times* contrasted the weakness of the Robert Donat revival at the Aldwych Theatre (October 16, 1946) in this scene, with the varied strength of two other performances, of this "climax and crisis of the play. When Marie Ney played Beatrice on the radio, in the church scene she spoke her two tremendous words "Kill Claudio!" in a voice as sharp, as clear, as cold as an icicle. I froze in my chair as I listened. When Mr. D. A. Clarke-Smith was Benedick in another production, he sprang back three paces on his horrified reply, "Not for the wide world!" In the first performance, I have forgotten the Benedick; in the second, the Beatrice. In this scene at the Aldwych I shall forget both." With such keen observation are the details of Shakespearean performance watched! E. K. Chambers, in *Shakespeare: A Survey* (1925), also indicated the significance of this moment in the play. He called Beatrice: "High-spirited, witty, honest, shrewd of apprehension, capable of tenderness: all this we had seen or guessed her earlier in the play; but for the dialogue with Benedick in the church we should never have known her inmost soul is wrought of forged steel and gold." Chambers, however, felt that the genuine depth of Beatrice's emotion clashes with the predominant moods of the plot. Claudio and Hero are acceptable, he declared, only on the plane of melodrama, not on the more realistic plane of comedy to which the Beatrice and Benedick episodes in the main shift them. In answer to this, it should be noted that both couples are set in opposition to the romantic idea of love. There is a humdrum realism in the businesslike joining of hands in Claudio and Hero's marriage of convenience. And the other couple join in despising, not love, but the artificial jargon that often masks it; they slough the romantic make-believe and find true love.

The title of the play, as Harold C. Goddard has pointed out, calls for further pondering. There may be an immediate verbal play, for the Elizabethans pronounced "nothing" like "noting," and noting (eavesdropping) starts the action moving. But there are deeper divinings. For "nothing" is what the poet gives a local habitation and a name. "Nothing," said Timon of Athens, "brings me all things." And "nothing," what Cordelia had for Lear, is the choicest human giving. In a sense, the play grows out of nothing, out of things that do not exist. The two bases of the main plot—Don John's statement that Hero was untrue to Claudio; Friar Francis' statement that Hero is dead—have nothing of substance. Here imagination works toward disaster. Out of nothing also rises the underplot: Beatrice and Benedick each hears talk of the other's non-existent love. Here imagination works upon nothing to create something good, as faith in the love helps it into their hearts. A mighty deal may thus burgeon from nothing! One need not be surprised that a later poet, William Butler Yeats, declared: "Where there is nothing there is God." Out of nothing, here, beckons the god of love.

Some of Shakespeare's neatest verbal play adorns *Much Ado About Nothing,* as the lovers polish the language, and Dogberry polishes it off. There is neat implication when the Sexton says, of the conspirators against Hero, "Let these men be bound" and Constable Dogberry emphasizes: "Let them be opinioned." The constable's tongue tied the play's theme: "to be opinioned is to be bound"; on the free imagination, one may soar. Here Shakespeare's fancy soars, as he shoots "the paper bullets of the brain" with expert marksmanship. With Dogberry's malaprop phrases, and the blunderings of the Watch that save the situation, the playwright has built some of his best low comedy scenes. In Beatrice and Benedick, he has smilingly satirized human nature while weaving a romped romance. And the feast is further spiced with homely and sound reflections; in a superb play, bountiful in excitement, wit, and beauty.

There was a vivid production of *Much Ado* in 1981, at the NT (Olivier), directed by Peter Gill, with Tim Woodward as Claudio; Caroline Langrishe, Hero; Michael Gambon, Benedick; Penelope Wilton, Beatrice; with a colorful masked ball and effective music by George Fenton, but with the comic scenes run perhaps too swiftly. A 1981 production at the Great Lakes Shakespeare Festival (founded 1962) set the play in Cleveland's Little Italy after World War II.

ALL'S WELL THAT ENDS WELL   *William Shakespeare*

Among the six comedies by Shakespeare mentioned in *Wit's Treasury,* 1598, is *Love's Labour's Won;* this is in all likelihood the play now known as *All's Well That Ends Well.* Some scholars, indeed, trace two styles in the comedy, and aver that the rhymed couplets, the lyrical dialogue, the many puns and conceits, are relics of the early version, while the run-on lines of blank verse with feminine (unaccented syllable) endings, are signs of the revision. The play apparently called for revision, for it was not popular. We have no record of its performance before 1741. It was produced perhaps once a decade, usually in an expurgated version by Kemble, from 1763 to 1900. It was played in Birmingham, Alabama, in modern dress in 1927; in San Diego, 1935; Pasadena, 1937; and Richmond, Virginia, 1938.

The plot of the play—borrowed, via William Paynter's *Palace of Pleasure,* 1556, from Boccaccio—seems a bit far-fetched to have wide appeal to modern audiences. Bertram, Count of Rousillon, ordered by the King of France to marry Helena, decides that "a young man married is a man that's marred." Influenced by his boon companion, the rascally Parolles, he goes through the ceremony, then leaves for the wars, declaring that when Helena presents him with his own seal ring and his own begotten son, he will acknowledge her as his wife. Helena in disguise follows Bertram; substituting for the pretty Diana at an assignation, she secures Bertram's ring, and in due time fulfills the second condition.

The value of the play lies, then, less in the story than in the characters. The play stands out artistically, said Bernard Shaw, by the sovereign charm of the young Helena and the old Countess of Rousillon, and intellectually by the experiment, repeated nearly three hundred years later in *A Doll's*

House,* of making the hero "a perfectly ordinary young man, whose unimaginative prejudices and selfish conventionality make him cut a very mean figure in the atmosphere created by the nobler nature of his wife." Among the minor figures, the old Lafeu and the adventure-dreading, adventure-boasting coward Parolles are especially neatly drawn. And, as Hardin Craig well put it: "Helena is beautifully attended and vouched for, largely by elderly people. Nothing graces youth more than the friendship of the old. The wise, kindly, clear-eyed Countess of Rousillon loves her as a daughter and knows her heart." A quite different interpretation was advanced by E. K. Chambers, in *Shakespeare: A Survey* (1925). He saw the play as a picture of the way in which love blinds and betrays a noble woman into a poor choice and into demeaning herself to win and hold him, "not Helena's triumph but Helena's degradation. . . . It is a poor prize for which she has trailed her honour in the dust." This evaluation, however, smacks more of the doctrinaire twentieth century than of the sentimental sixteenth.

Although it has not been a stage favorite, the play rewards the reader. Hazlitt considers it "one of the most pleasing of our author's comedies. The interest is, however, more of a serious than of a comic nature. The character of Helena is one of great sweetness and delicacy. She is placed in circumstances of the most critical kind, and has to court her husband both as a virgin and as a wife, yet the most scruplous nicety of female modesty is not once violated. There is not one thought or action that ought to bring a blush into her cheeks, or that for a moment lessens her in our esteem." The men are of quite different nature. In some productions, the play was cut so as to make the scoundrel Parolles the central figure; King Charles I, in his copy of the Second Folio edition of Shakespeare's dramas, wrote as title for this play, *Monsieur Parolles.* Bertram is a cad, to whom Samuel Johnson could not reconcile his heart: "a man noble without generosity, and young without truth; who marries Helena as a coward, and leaves her as a profligate; when she is dead by his unkindness, sneaks home to a second marriage, is accused by a woman whom he has wronged, defends himself by falsehood, and is dismissed to happiness." These portraits are so tinged that Harold C. Goddard has suggested that there is an irony in this picture of two gentlemen of France similar to that in *Two Gentlemen of Verona,** with their polished exteriors and their putrid core. At the end, there is only a hope that Helena and awakened love will change Bertram, but the King closes the play with an optimistic couplet.

An important element in the drama is the dialogue itself, prose and poetry. The ear is the sure clue to Shakespeare. Whether it be pure tone of beauty or sly twinkle of fun, the words in sound and echo fit the mood. The more important events of the play may seem far-fetched, but the motives and emotions are natural, are in us all. Combined with the character studies are enough poetry and comedy to make the reader find enjoyment still in thinking "all's well that ends well."

The RSC, setting the play in a World War I Edwardian glass pavilion, staged *All's Well That Ends Well* at Stratford-upon-Avon in 1981, the London Barbican in 1982, and the New York Martin Beck in 1983. Peggy Ashcroft played the Countess in England; Margaret Tyzack, in New York. Michael Billington in the *Guardian* called the play "a masterly realist fairy-tale that sends you out of the theatre with a radiant, overpowering happiness." Frank Rich, in the *New York Times* (April 14, 1983) said that at the end "the ostensibly reconciled lovers pull apart from each other in mid-step and walk side by side but separately into the dark. It's not the happy finale of a comedy—just the perfect ending for this rare production that captures the elusive glow of a play as melancholy and peculiarly radiant as a lunar eclipse."

AS YOU LIKE IT   *William Shakespeare*

Based upon the prose romance of *Rosalynde,* written in 1590 by Thomas Lodge, William Shakespeare's smiling artificial comedy *As You Like It,* 1599 ?, is "the play most ideal of any of this author's plays" in the opinion of Hazlitt. It captures the mood of courtship in a forest filled with sunshine.

Rosalind, daughter of the banished Duke, watching Orlando wrestle at court, falls in love with Orlando, who with his old servant Adam flies from his brother Oliver's jealous treachery, to the Forest of Arden. Rosalind, herself banished, flees with Celia, the present Duke's daughter and her dearest friend, to the same forest. There, disguised as a boy, she promises to cure Orlando of his love; and a mock courtship carries the days lightsomely along, with the shepherd and court Fool and forest philosopher, until the bad brother and the bad Duke repent, and Rosalind's lifting of the disguise brings on four weddings.

For the Elizabethan gentlefolk, the play deftly balanced the advantages of the town and the country, the court and the forest. For those that fell out of royal favor (and frequent were the occasions and many the persons, with Elizabeth's short temper and shifting politics!), there is proffered consolation. The play burlesques three things: the pastoral vogue in literature; country life itself, though that is also lovingly drawn; and the courtiers that sigh for the country but hurry back to town. The audience is not expected to take the emotions in the play seriously; the very verse grows artificial to weaken the impact on the feelings, as, for instance, when starving Orlando breaks in upon the Duke's company, and the Duke echoes Orlando's words. This artificiality is, at one place, pointed out by Shakespeare himself: When Orlando greets his beloved, "Good day and happiness, Dear Rosalind!", Jaques takes his leave, exclaiming: "Nay, then God be wi' you, an you talk in blank verse." The melancholy Jaques is the first in the long series of observing commentators in the English drama, and Touchstone, a Fool at court, is a philosopher in the forest. (About 1598, the comic actor Will Kemp left the Lord Chamberlain's Company and was succeeded by Robert Armin, a quite different type of comic. This may help to account for the fact that such figures as Bottom and Falstaff were followed by such others as Touchstone and the Fool in *King Lear.**)

Charles Johnson's version, *Love in a Forest;* 1723, with rapiers instead of the wrestling, with Oliver committing suicide, with passages added from *A Midsummer Night's Dream,** was short-lived; by 1741 Shakespeare's own play again commanded the boards. Among the actresses whom Rosalind has lured are Fanny Davenport, Helena Modjeska, Julia Marlowe, Maude Adams, and Marjorie Rambeau (in 1923, the first production of the American National Theatre). The comic scenes and the wrestling match have frequently been stressed in productions. (Wrestling always provides entertaining stage action; *see The Apple Cart.**) In a production offered at the University of Washington, then brought to New York, in 1945, the French fop became a woman: Madame La Beau. In this "modern" production, as *Variety* put it, Rosalind and her companions were garbed "in the loveliest Basque shirts and pastel shorts this side the Abercrombie and Fitch windows."

Further comedy has always been sought in the scenes where Rosalind is disguised as a boy. *Blackwood's Magazine,* in the mid-Victorian year of 1890, protested: "What can Miss Ada Rehan mean by pulling down her doublet . . . as though she would accomplish the impossible feat of hiding her legs under it—an indelicacy of suggestion at which one can only shudder!" The magazine contrasted with this the decorum of Lily Langtry who gave no sign of embarrassment when in her disguise she encountered Orlando, and "carefully avoided all vulgar clowning in passages referring to her male attire, but when she spoke the line—'Here, on the skirts of the forest, like a fringe on a petticoat'—she put out her hand with a perfectly natural gesture to pick up her own petticoat, and finding none, paused awkwardly for half a second." Rosalind's charm is almost actor-proof. "Who ever failed, or could fail, as Rosalind?" asked Bernard Shaw. "Rosalind is not a complete human being: she is simply an extension into five acts of the most affectionate, fortunate, delightful five minutes in the life of a charming woman." Her pleasant fellowship contrasts sharply with the snobbish wit of Touchstone.

Bernard Shaw disapproved of much of the play after the 1896 London production. Yet he declared that "it has the overwhelming advantage of being written for the most part in prose instead of blank verse, which any fool can write. And such prose! The first scene alone, with its energy of exposition, each phrase driving its meaning and feeling in up to the head at one brief, sure stroke, is worth ten acts of the ordinary Elizabethan singsong." Part of that exposition, however, is presented without concealment, as though Shakespeare were indifferent to this minor problem of dramaturgy: "What's the new news at the new court?" "There's no news at the court, sir, but the old news"—whereupon we hear what both onstage know but the audience must be told. Sheridan poked fun at such direct recital, in Act II Scene ii of *The Critic.* *

The Park Theatre, in New York, opened on January 29, 1798, with *As You Like It.* More recently, the play was performed in New York in 1937; at the World's Fair in 1939; with Helen Craig in 1941; with Donald Wolfit as Touchstone in 1947; and with Katherine Hepburn opening January 26, 1950. There was a production in Rome in 1948, with surrealist scenery and costumes by Salvador Dali; it was presented at the Stratford Festival in 1952. Elizabeth Bergner was Rosalind in the screen version. Recent productions have won scant critical praise—George Freedely thinks the best was "an eighteenth century rendering" by Hilpert at the Deutsches Theater, in Berlin in 1934—but the play itself, even though it is required reading in schools, still has a strong hold on popular favor.

The song "Under the greenwood tree Who loves to lie with me" well illustrates Shakespeare's use of music. In addition to breaking the audience's tension (as does comic relief in the tragedies), this song states the theme of the play, helps establish the forest setting, fills time for the preparation of the Duke's banquet, and by contrast with gay Amiens builds the character of the "melancholy" Jaques.

Orlando's brother, Jaques de Boys, mentioned in the first scene of the play, does not appear until the last, when he speaks the sixteen lines that wind up the plot. This was called "the shilling speech" in the old Shakespearean companies: if the actor was word-perfect, he was given a shilling—which was rarely won. The speech makes Shakespeare's least effective denouement, of the "old religious man" that converts the usurping Duke Frederick, who returns the dukedom to his brother.

It is interesting to note that Shakespeare himself was not wholly bemused in the merry romp of the enchanted courtship. As foils to Rosalind and Orlando, he sets three other pairs. Touchstone takes up with Audrey about as one decides to wear old shoes to an outing. To this casual cohabitation is added another doomed match when the disguised Rosalind tricks young Phebe into marrying the doddering Silvius, whom she detests. Finally, Oliver repents, Celia is nearby and unattached: let's mate them! These cynical counter-currents in the stream of happy love add to the reflective mood that underlies the comedy, as we consider that indeed "all the world's a stage . . . and each man in his time plays many parts."

In its surface sunshine of romance, however, we echo the line in the play Shakespeare borrowed from Marlowe: "Who ever loved that loved not at first sight?" Samuel Johnson matter-of-factly wondered: "I do not know how the ladies will approve the facility with which both Rosalind and Celia give their hearts."

The NT gave forty-five performances in repertory, 1974, to an *As You Like It* with an all-male cast. The RSC gave a gracious production at Stratford-upon-Avon in 1980, at the Aldwych in 1981, with John Bowe as Orlando and Susan Fleetwood as Rosalind. The Birmingham Rep. at the 1981 Edinburgh Festival, overdid themselves, making, said John Barber in the *Telegraph* August 19, 1981, "frantic and even frenzied efforts to be funny, original and spectacular." The play is a comedy, said Georg Brandes, "in which all the notes the poet strikes, of seriousness and of raillery, of passion, of tenderness, and of laughter, blend in the richest and fullest concord."

TWELFTH NIGHT   *William Shakespeare*

"A silly play, and not at all related to the name or day," Samuel Pepys wrote in his *Diary* in 1663, after seeing a performance of Shakespeare's *Twelfth Night; or, What You Will,* 1559?. During the formal times of Pope and Johnson the play was seldom performed. A version by William Burnaby, called *Love Betrayed; or, The Agreeable Disappointment,* had mediocre success in 1703. The original comedy was revived in 1741; but it did not become popular until the nineteenth century. Its presentation at Daly's Theatre in London in 1894 saved that theatre after the disastrous failure, the season before, of Tennyson's *The Foresters.* More recent productions, in New York, include that of Sothern and Marlowe in 1919; Fritz Leiber in 1930; Jane Cowl and Leon Quartermaine in the same year; The Federal Theatre in 1939; Helen Hayes and Maurice Evans in 1940; the Dramatic Workshop, with Marlon Brando, in 1944. There were two effective productions of the play in the United States in 1949, one with Betty Field, one with Frances Reid. Several outstanding French directors have produced the play; Jacques Copeau (in 1914 and 1919), Gaston Baty, George Pitoeff, and Firmin Gemier. In London, the Granville-Barker production of 1912 broke the long tradition of elaborate sets and came, as the *Tatler* said, like "a breath of fresh air over a world super-stuffy with the theatrical conventions of centuries." This simple and charming production was the success of the season and unmatched until the Old Vic 1950 production opening November 4 with Peggy Ashcroft as Viola, which led W. A. Darlington to declare, in the *New York Times* (December 3, 1950) that "to many people, myself most emphatically included, *Twelfth Night* is the nearest thing to a perfect comedy yet composed in English." The deft New York production in 1955, by the Shakespearewrights, would not incline you to disagree.

Twelfth Night, the feat of Epiphany (the visit of the Magi to the infant Jesus), was traditionally a time of jollity and merry-making. The title thus indicates the mood of the play, as does Sir Toby Belch's query to the sour steward Malvolio: "Dost thou think, because thou art virtuous, there shall be no more cakes and ale?" Hazlitt, in the nineteenth century, showed how far opinion had shifted from Pepys' day: "This is justly considered as one of the most delightful of Shakespeare's comedies. It is full of sweetness and pleasantry." "Structurally it is a joy," Hardin Craig says of *Twelfth Night;* and the play neatly interweaves the stories and the levels of action. For the nobles, it combines two frequent Renaissance themes: identical twins and the consequent confusions; and the maid disguised as page to the man she loves. Thus Viola, as page to Orsino, duke of Illyria, bears his love-messages to Olivia—who falls in love with the page. Orsino also finds himself attracted to the page; so that the complications are agreeably smoothed when Viola's twin brother Sebastian marries Olivia, and Viola, revealed as a maiden, marries the Duke.

Linking this romantic realm with the more humorous everyday world is Olivia's turbulent toss-pot uncle, Sir Toby Belch, who with his timid bean-pole friend, Sir Andrew Aguecheek, and Olivia's maid Maria, wages war upon the steward Malvolio. Malvolio was a figure quickly recognized in Shakespeare's day, being frequent and well-hated: the upper servant that bullies those below him in station. Thus there is much amusing frolic in the tricks played on Malvolio, especially with the letter supposedly from his mistress Olivia—"Some are born great, some achieve greatness, and some have greatness thrust upon them"—that tempts him to come before her cross-gartered, in antic disposition, so that the others gleefully incarcerate him as insane. Malvolio's misadventures, however, must be handled with deft lightness. Thus Beerbohm Tree—who as Malvolio was attended by four tiny pages aping him in dress and deportment—majestically descending the great staircase, slipped to a "crash landing," but, as Bernard Shaw reported: "Tree, without betraying the smallest discomfiture, raised his eyeglass and surveyed the landscape as if he had sat down on purpose." Hardin Craig complains that great actors, playing Malvolio, have been inclined to make his final threat of vengeance too emphatic. The *New York Dramatic Mirror,* in 1920, made this charge specific: "We of the present day cannot laugh at madness, and when Malvolio is tormented with the belief that he is mad, we are tormented also. . . . Mr. Sothern elects to play it seriously. The result is that his audience pities him, weeps for him perhaps, and is deeply moved, but feels under its skin that some extraneous mood has crept into the theatre."

There are abundant opportunities for comic business in the play. The drunken bout of Sir Toby and Sir Andrew in Olivia's kitchen is the first such scene in English comedy; it has been almost invariably successful in countless plays since. The many opportunities for comic byplay, indeed, are so tempting as sometimes to lead to excess. Mme. Modjeska, in the duel between the disguised Viola and the cowardly Aguecheek, refrained from hitting her timorous adversary; Julia Arthur first beat him with her sword and then spanked him as he dodged about. In 1820 Aguecheek tried to get out of the way by climbing the proscenium of the stage; in 1825, he scurried up a handy rope-ladder; later, he clambered up a tree. In 1901, Julia Marlowe protested: "We cannot go far wrong if we let the lines have the center of the stage and allow them to show the poet's meaning. We cannot aid him by a multitude of gestures or by creating intricate business." But still, in 1940, Brooks Atkinson had to exclaim that "the beauty of the current *Twelfth Night* is overladen with a desire to be funny at any cost." Of the same production, Richard Watts, Jr. observed: "Although *Twelfth Night* contains some of the worst features of Elizabethan comedy, it has charm, grace, and loveliness, and these saving qualities are captured in abundance in this handsome and skillful new production."

In addition to the romance and the comedy, the play affords us the lilt of delightful poetry. From its opening words—"If music be the food of love, play on"—to the Clown's song that closes the play—"with hey, ho, the wind and the rain"—as Viola says of Olivia, "'tis beauty truly blent." *Twelfth Night* is perhaps Shakespeare's most effective commingling of love and lyrical beauty and rowdy laughter . . . and something more. For here, as often in his comedies, Shakespeare plants, for the discerning, guideposts to further thoughts. These were developed by Harold C. Goddard in *The Meaning of Shakespeare* (1951), who noted that the figures in Illyrian society are all marked by excess of various sorts. Sentimentality and sensuality blind their days. It is a seventeenth century version of *Heartbreak House*,* Goddard declared, "with the difference that whereas Bernard Shaw depicts his heartbreaking society with blasts of satire and on top of that writes a blistering preface that nobody may miss his point, Shakespeare just holds up what is essentially the same world and allows it to amuse us or break our hearts as we choose. *What You Will*." There is hope at the end that Viola and Sebastian, rescued from the sea (across which in legends the deliverers come) may bring those drowning in the ocean of sentimentality back to friendly earth and through love reawaken the spirit.

Three musicals based on *Twelfth Night* have been tried. *Love and Let Love,* adapted and with lyrics by John Lollos, music by Stanley J. Gelber, came OffBway January 3, 1968, for 14 performances. On January 13, 1968, also OffBway, came the rock musical *Your Own Thing,* book by Donald Driver, music and lyrics by Hal Hesher and Danny Apolinar. This had the twins shipwrecked on Manhattan Island, used slides and film, and attained 933 performances; reaching 59 the next year in London. And on December 20, 1976, *Music Is,* opened beginning with Duke Orsino's words: "If music be the food of love, play on"; book and direction by veteran George Abbott, music by Richard Adler, lyrics by Will Holt. Inevitably, one wished for Shakespeare.

HAMLET   *William Shakespeare*

The longest of Shakespeare's plays, *Hamlet,* 1600?, is the most widely discussed of all dramas. Despite the melodramatic vicissitudes of the Prince, many persons find much within themselves like "the melancholy Dane," hesitant before the deed. William Hazlitt went so far as to declare in 1817: "It is *we* who are Hamlet." One reason for the pervasive power of the play is that it closely follows the pattern of the nature-myth of the seasonal death and resurrection of the fruitful world, which lies deep within our human ways.

The story of Hamlet (Amleth) comes down from the twelfth century *History of the Danes* of Saxo Grammaticus. In the play, returning home for King Hamlet's funeral, Prince Hamlet finds his mother Gertrude remarried and her new husband, the late King's brother Claudius, on the throne.

Informed by his father's ghost that the death was not natural, but murder by Claudius, Hamlet plans retribution. To make sure the ghost is not a deceiving fiend, and to expose Claudius' guilt to the court of Denmark, Hamlet arranges for visiting players to enact a similar crime: "The play's the thing Wherein I'll catch the conscience of the King." The King's councillor Polonius thinks Hamlet mad for love of his daughter Ophelia, whom he and Claudius try to use as a decoy to discover Hamlet's thoughts. After the players' acting reveals Claudius' guilt, Hamlet wrings his mother's heart with his reproaches, until, hearing a noise behind the arras, he stabs through it and kills the listening Polonius. Ophelia, broken by the strain, goes mad and drowns herself. Polonius' son Laertes, returning to avenge these deaths, is turned by King Claudius against Hamlet, and persuaded to engage him in a "friendly" duel, with Laertes' foil unbuttoned and poison-tipped. For double assurance, Claudius prepares a poisoned drink for the Prince. As a consequence the Queen, Laertes, the King, and Hamlet, all die. The strong arms of Fortinbras, King of Norway, bring promise of peace to the land.

In addition to containing some of the greatest of all poetry, such as the well-known soliloquy beginning "To be or not to be," *Hamlet* is a superbly constructed drama. The very reticences of the playwright mark his genius. One of the most important moments of the play is a scene unseen, reported by Ophelia to her father. After wandering all night, broken with the dreadful story of his father's ghost, Hamlet comes for comfort to the woman he loves. Instead of springing to help him, Ophelia draws back, scared out of her wits; she runs to her father—"O, my lord, I have been so affrighted!"— and Hamlet recognizes he can put no trust in her.

The weakness of Ophelia, which leads to her later madness, gives the clue to Hamlet's emotional state, left with no one to share his awful burden. His first words in the play, two answers to the King, are twisted, bitter puns. His later distracted manner has led critics, up to our own generation, to argue as to whether Hamlet is mad or merely feigning. Charles Kemble acted Hamlet as mad: his brother John Philip Kemble cut the wilder parts and made him feigning. Samuel Johnson is emphatic: "Of the feigned madness there appears no adequate cause, for he does nothing which he might not have done with the reputation of sanity." Modern psychology enables us to understand his conduct. Pressed with an excessive emotional burden, Hamlet could not suppress, but could direct, his outbursts. Thus to Polonius he speaks of Ophelia; to Rosencrantz and Guildenstern, the King's spies, of his discontent with the narrow confines of his position in Denmark. In the original Amleth story, the madness is feigned, as indeed in other hero tales, such as those of Greek Odysseus and Jewish David. Hamlet's attitude toward Ophelia has troubled many critics. He came to her from the ghost, William Bliss remarked in *The Real Shakespeare* (1949), not only for consolation but also for renunciation. Dedicated to revenge, he could not ask the child Ophelia to share his lonely destiny. This notion was earlier put forward by Lamb to explain "the asperity which he puts on in his interview with Ophelia . . . a profound artifice of love to alienate Ophelia by affected discourtesies, so to prepare her mind for the breaking off of that loving intercourse which can no longer find a place amidst business so serious as that which he had to do." Productions usually, after Hamlet has come upon Ophelia at her prayers, supply some ground, most obviously the king's peeping from behind a curtain, for the sudden suspicion that turns Hamlet's tongue to bitter words. Many critics have complained of Hamlet's procrastination, of his habit of thinking too much on the event. Thus Coleridge called the drama a "tragedy of weakness of will." Other critics have gone so far as to say that the delays arose from Shakespeare's clumsy joining of two earlier versions of the story. Still others, trying to look upon Hamlet with Elizabethan eyes, consider that he has broken from the medieval Christian view of a world dependent upon God's grace, but is unable to decide between the two Renaissance attitudes—the one that finds an essential dignity in man, and the other (Calvin; Montaigne) that sees man as base. Hamlet's wavering actions are then the result of his wavering thoughts. Psychologically, however, the delay is the natural struggle of a sensitive, peace-loving soul against violence. The mind orders an action against which the spirit rebels. When we consider the Prince's task, furthermore, we recognize that the entire action flows in a smooth continuity. For first Hamlet (within the beliefs of Shakespeare's day) must make sure that the apparition of his father is not a fiend tempting him to his own damnation. Then he must fulfill the conditions of a fit revenge: the guilty one must know he is being dealt just punishment; the public (the court) must know this is not murder but revenge; and the punishment must fit the crime, i.e., Claudius, who killed King Hamlet with all his sins upon him, must not be dispatched to heaven while at prayers. Once the prior conditions are met, that is, after the play scene, the drama speeds to its tragic conclusion.

A neat reticence of the author is in regard to the Queen's share of guilt. Knowing that his mother was unfaithful to his father, Hamlet naturally wonders whether she was party to the murder. He flings his suspicion at her in contemptuous words, and the only idea the audience is given as to the Queen's share in the murder must come from the actress' answer: from whether she replies like one confounded in her guilt, or like an innocent one dumbfounded by the accusation. Most actresses seek sympathy by taking the latter tone; and indeed, after Hamlet's reproaches, Gertrude's love of him and her remorse lead her to shelter him against the King. John Barrymore followed Freud's comments and played the scene in Hamlet's mother's room with a suggestion of incestuous love. In the Quarto, Gertrude denies her guilt.

The drama is prominently mentioned by those that indicate in the Elizabethan plays the practice of "episodic intensification," building the immediate scene for its own effect and fullest power, without regard to its value in the scheme of the play as a whole. Sometimes, even, items drawn into the play are hard to account for logically. Critics are still arguing, for instance, as to whether the King sees the pantomime that precedes, and shows the same story as, the play that "catches" his conscience. And, if Ophelia drowns near enough for somebody to give the Queen a graphic description of her last moments, why didn't that somebody save the lorn princess?

The movement is speedy. There is, for all Hamlet's seeming irresolution, a constant bustle of action in the play. In addition to the traveling players, *Hamlet* stirs with the mad scene, with a restless ghost, a wrestling match in a new-dug grave, and a duel with swords flying. Thus the play is "much more a variety show than the later tragedies," avers S. L. Bethell in *Shakespeare and The Popular Dramatic Tradition* (1944). "Its greater popularity on the stage is due to sheer 'entertainment value'; and it is a favorite with the critics because its imperfections leave more room for discussion, and the peculiar character of its hero provides a fascinating subject for every variety of armchair quackery." Viewed within the story's scope, however, as we have seen, Hamlet is so far from peculiar as to be universal; and it is less the play's "imperfections" than its many-sidedness that continually rouses discussion. Note, for instance, the deft but apparently casual contrast of three sons that have lost their fathers by violent death. The sensitive yet impetuous Hamlet and the hotheaded Laertes both unwittingly bring on their own doom; the cool-headed Fortinbras comes in at the end and takes control.

Also notable is the artistry of what T. S. Eliot* in *Poetry and Drama* (1951) called "as well constructed an opening scene as that of any play ever written." Eliot praised the subtle variations in the verse which urge their emotional effects unnoticed, the economy and harmony of the diction—"The first twenty-two lines are built of the simplest words in the most homely idiom"—and the manner in which the poetry promotes the dramatic purpose of the scene.

The play is a masterpiece of irony. Double meanings abound. Hamlet is often acting a part, as the play's reiterative imagery reminds us. In addition to such outstanding instances as the advice to the players and the play to catch the king, images drawn from the theatre carry overtones of this idea. The last three speeches of the play contain puns on theatrical terms (*audience, performed, stage*). The frequent puns themselves, of course, add further force of irony, being understood one way by the listeners on stage, and another by the listeners off. This sense of double meaning is also fostered by the looking-glass image that runs through the play. Art, says Hamlet to the Players, holds a mirror up to nature, and the play within the play mirrors the king's murder. Hamlet tells his mother he will hold up a glass to her—yet the faults Hamlet attacks in others he exhibits in himself. He urges the Players to temperance, and their play rouses him to rage. He kills Polonius on the moment's impulse, than lectures his mother on self-control. The man that holds a mirror up to others sees not himself. Even more dominant in the play is the image of an ulcer, a "worm in the bud." The murder of Hamlet's father, his mother's incestuous marriage (as it was deemed by Shakespeare's England), the usurpation of the throne, all mark a corruption, "something rotten in the state," that the imagery presses home.

Various aspects of the drama are in the tradition that grew from Seneca,* whose complete works had been translated into English by 1571. Thus the gloomy, introspective, self-dramatizing hero, the ghosts urging revenge, the various treacherous horrors and rearing violence, are all in Seneca. Nashe, in the Preface to Greene's *Menaphon* (1589), sneered at writers who copied, from "Seneca read by candlelight . . . whole *Hamlets,* I should say handfuls, of tragical speeches." It need hardly be said that, though Shakespeare borrowed freely, he transmuted the old material into new gold.

The play has been performed continually, since Shakespeare's day. There were performances on the East India Company's ship *Dragon* in 1607 and 1608. The seventeenth century was varied in its reaction to the play, as notes of two diarists attest. John Evelyn set down, on November 26, 1661: "I saw *Hamlet, Prince of Denmark* played, but now the old plays do begin to disgust this refined age." Samuel Pepys, however, noted on August 31, seven years later, that he was "mightily pleased with it, but above all with Betterton: the best part, I believe, that man ever acted." Its first New York performance was at the Chapel Street Theatre, November 26, 1761.

To name the men that have acted Hamlet (women too, e. g., Charlotte Cushman; in a translation by Alexandre Dumas, Sarah Bernhardt) would be to list the most famous players of many lands. Children also have essayed the role; in the 1804-5 season, the English House of Commons, on motion of Pitt the Younger, adjourned to see the fourteen-year-old William Betty play Hamlet. Legend says that Shakespeare played the Ghost, at the Blackfriars' Theatre, in 1603. Most Hamlets have presented the Prince in an elocutionary, rhetorical, almost grandiloquent manner, even approaching the style that Hamlet, in his advice to the players, tells them to avoid. Thus David Garrick (1742) achieved a truly sepulchral melancholy; so violent was his starting at the entrance of the ghost as to rouse critical attack. Garrick's friend Boswell, defending him, asked Samuel Johnson: "Would you not start, as Garrick does, if you saw a ghost?"—to which Johnson relied: "I hope not. If I did, I should frighten the ghost!" The actor Edwin Forrest hissed William Macready's Hamlet in a rivalry that led to twenty-two deaths; for details, see *Richelieu.* * Edwin Booth, after his early exuberance in the role, adopted (1864) a more natural, but still intense and gloomy Hamlet that continued the tradition.

A more natural tone was sought in the Hamlet of Edmund Kean (1814), as in that of Sir Henry Irving, who in 1874 established the record run of 200 performances. This natural quality is also marked in the Hamlet of John Gielgud, who enacted the play in 1939 at Elsinore Castle, Denmark, and in New York in 1936 with Lillian Gish as Ophelia and Judith Anderson as Gertrude, and again for 132 performances in 1944-45, and—although some prefer the performance of Paul Scofield at Stratford-on-Avon in 1948—is perhaps the best Hamlet of our generation. Jean-Louis Barrault played Hamlet in Paris in 1947 in a translation by André Gide. Donald Wolfit enacted the prince on his American tour in 1947. In London, Michael Redgrave was hailed as Hamlet in an Old Vic production opening February 2, 1950. Alec Guinness starred there in 1951 as Hamlet with a beard but public opinion quickly shaved him. Charles Albert Fechter, in London in 1865, in New York in 1870, was much more successful as an active Nordic Hamlet, with flowing blond hair.

In 1925, at the Birmingham Repertory Theatre, Sir Barry Jackson's production in modern clothes touched off a round of similar productions, including those by Basil Sydney and Orson Welles. The American premiere of the motion picture version, with Sir Laurence Olivier as Hamlet, was completely sold out, in Boston (August 18, 1948), despite picketing by a "Boycott Britain" group, a century after the anti-British riots at the Astor Place Opera House in New York. Olivier, by the way, says that Sir Johnston Forbes-Robertson, who played Hamlet frequently from 1897 to 1913, was "by all accounts the finest Hamlet of the present century." An American company of actors, headed by Robert Breen, presented the drama in the summer of 1949 at Elsinore Castle, Denmark, the historical scene of the story.

Whatever the style of the production, the audience is rewarded with an intense dramatic character study, in richest poetry, relentless in its drive toward the inevitable doom, although, as in life, the immediately fatal circumstances seem almost accidental. *Hamlet* is one of the greatest plays, and unquestionably the most continuingly popular play, of all time.

Tennyson raised an interesting point when he declared: "The Queen did not think Ophelia committed suicide; neither do I."

"Hamlet dies on a note of certitude," said F. E. Halliday, "his assurance emphasized by the unexpected Latinisms so exquisitely set between lines of homely monosyllables:

> *If thou didst ever hold me in thy heart,*
> *Absent thee from felicity awhile,*
> *And in this harsh world draw thy breath in pain,*
> *To tell my story.*

"It is out of this poetry, this synthesis of lyric, epic, and elegy, subdued and made dramatic, that the best loved of Shakespeare's characters is fashioned; for by now it is axiomatic that poetry is character, and this poetry *is* Hamlet."

Hamlet opened in the New York Lunt-Fontanne April 9, 1964, for 137 performances, with Richard Burton as the Prince; Alfred Drake, Claudius; Linda Marsh, Ophelia; Eileen Herlie, Gertrude; and John Gielgud as the unseen ghost.

There were three productions of Hamlet in New York in 1969. The APA-Phoenix, opening March 3, had Ellis Rabb directing and playing Hamlet in a Nehru jacket. Other actors wore turtlenecks with long chain necklaces and medallions; at times they walked through the audience. A shapely, lusty Ophelia—instead of a frail, uncertain one—in her madness bared a breast to give suck to a rag doll. Oddly, Rabb used the First Quarto version, which lacks the passion and the power of the 1623 Folio. The curtain fell for intermission in the middle of Hamlet's speech to the players. Walter Kerr said that, as director, Rabb was "all thumbs and all banged thumbs at that. The poetry of the play seems to have been reduced to the Elizabethan equivalent of Choctaw."

More surprising was the bearded Hamlet of Nicol Williamson, opening May 1 at the Lunt-Fontanne, directed by Tony Richardson to stress a loving Prince. Hamlet woos Ophelia; his "Get thee to a nunnery" is a laughing jest to a sweetheart—repeated but savagely transformed when he spies Polonius peering around a corner. His bitter scene with his mother ends in a long embrace.

But even more surprising was the travesty presented free on July 3 by Joseph Papp in Central Park, then on tour in the boroughs. This had Cleavon Little as Hamlet, and his blackness is emphasized in the play, for when Polonius asks what he is reading, Hamlet replies: "*Ebony,* baby!" At one point Horatio treats Claudius to a custard pie (full in the face). To the gravedigger not Hamlet but Claudius speaks; dressed as a policeman, the King cries, "Don't give me any of that Shakespeare crap!" Vincent Canby in the *Times* described this as "Mr. Papp's desperate declaration that he can be *Hair*-hip and anti-intellectual. The audience laughed—rather guiltily and masochistically—like onlookers at a Black Panther meeting. . . . It has as much relation to the original Shakespeare as cole slaw has to cabbage." It was a bad year for the tormented Prince. More fittingly, the greatest play by the world's greatest playwright was the first production at the new home of his native land's National Theatre (Lyttleton), where on March 16, 1976, Albert Finney played the troubled Prince.

Joseph Papp grew reckless again December 2, 1982, when at his New York Public he presented the virtually untried Diane Venore as the latest in the line of women (recently Eva Le Gallienne, Siobhan McKenna, Judith Anderson) to play the Prince. A representative comment is that of Walter Kerr, who was struck by Hamlet's "readiness to slip back into the emotional bursts of his childhood" manifest in the "far, far too many times" when, instead of "Hamlet's familiar rage" at his own ineffectual hesitancy, "the actress most often falls to her knees, groans in anguish, doubles over in tears." *Hamlet* will survive.

Of plays by others woven from Shakespeare, there were thirteen by Eli Siegel, which he condensed into three, presented OffBway (Gramercy Arts): *Hamlet and His Father,* April 29, 1963; *Hamlet and Ophelia,* May 6; *Hamlet and the World,* May 13. In 1976 came a rock musical, *Rockabye Hamlet,* with a black Prince and somebody called Meat Loaf playing a priest; of which Alan Rich said in the *Times*: "For the most part the sound was as loud and coarse as the words were mindless."

Best of the plays out of *Hamlet* is Tom Stoppard's, here discussed.

ROSENCRANTZ AND GUILDENSTERN ARE DEAD   *Tom Stoppard*

In 1891 W. S. Gilbert wrote a burlesque, *Rosencrantz and Guildenstern* (see *The Yeomen of the Guard*).* In 1967 Tom Stoppard followed with *Rosencrantz and Guildenstern Are Dead.* Stoppard was born in 1937 as Straussler in Czechoslovakia. His doctor father was killed by the Nazis. In India his mother married a British officer; they went with him to England. He has brilliantly mirrored the story of Shakespeare's *Hamlet* through the eyes of the two wondering victims, so vague that they sometimes confuse their own identities, but whose questioning enlivens the tale and enlightens the beholders.

The play begins with Guildenstern tossing a coin that Rosencrantz catches, announcing a continuous run of ninety-two heads—during which they wonder about the laws of probability and the reason for their summons to the royal court of Denmark. On their way—they are on their way—the Players enter, and try to draw the two men into a performance (with a glimmer of sexual activity; Alfred, the small boy among the Players, is ready to assume a woman's role). The Players leave, the chief Player lifting his foot off the last tossed coin. Rosencrantz: "I say, that was lucky." "What?" "It was tails."

On the tail of this Ophelia rushes, frightened, onto the stage, followed by Hamlet (bedraggled, as in Shakespeare's play Ophelia describes him to her father), and the most significant unshown scene in all drama is here performed, as "he falls to such perusal of her face as he would draw it . . . he raises a sigh so piteous and profound that it does seem to shatter all his bulk and end his being." Hamlet breaks off; Ophelia runs away. Before Rosencrantz and Guildenstern move, King Claudius and Gertrude enter and with Shakespeare's words greet them and accept their instant promise:

> And here give up ourselves in the full bent
> To lay our service freely at your feet
> To be commanded.

They practice questioning each other as they will Hamlet, with slips of the tongue and puns sliding in. Hamlet beards Polonius with his "Buzz, buzz" as the Players are announced. Stage directions inform us: "The context is Shakespeare's Act III Scene 1," and they ask the Players:

Guild: What is the dumbshow for?
Player: Well, it's a device, really—It makes the action that follows
         more or less comprehensible; you understand, we are tied down
         to a language that makes up in obscurity what it lacks in style.

Another scene Shakespeare merely relates is now enacted: the ship trip to England. Rosencrantz and Guildenstern open and read the letter that calls for Hamlet's immediate death. In the dark night, we see Hamlet extracting the letter and slipping in another. In the morning, music comes from three barrels on the ship's deck, out of which emerge the Players. Pirates attack; Hamlet, the two pals, and the Players jump into the barrels. When the pirates are beaten off, all come out of the barrels—except Hamlet.

> Rosen.   He's dead, then. He's dead, as far as we are concerned.
> Guild.   Or we are, as far as he is.

They again read the letter, which now calls for their own sudden death. As the boat sails irrevocably on, Guildenstern threatens the chief Player, who had died onstage a hundred times, with real death—and stabs him. The players applaud, their fallen chief rises; Guildenstern presses the dagger at the Player's hand, and the blade slides back into the hilt. Rosencrantz and Guildenstern, still bewildered and mildly protesting, are lost in darkness.

When the stage lights come up, the actors are arranged as at the end of Shakespeare's play, with the King, Queen, and Laertes lying dead, and the dead Hamlet in the arms of Horatio. Standing are Horatio and ambassadors from England. In Shakespeare's words an Ambassador speaks:

> The sight is dismal,
> And our affairs from England come too late.
> The ears are senseless that should give us hearing,
> To tell him his commandment is fulfilled,
> That Rosencrantz and Guildenstern are dead.

> Horatio: Not from his mouth,
> Had it the ability of life to thank you.

And as Horatio continues with Shakespeare's words, the stage slowly darkens and the final curtain falls.

Beginning as a one-act burlesque, *Rosencrantz and Guildenstern,* in Berlin in 1964, the full play was shown at the Edinburgh Festival in 1966, by an Oxford group. In London, 1967, it was the first play by a new dramatist presented at the NT; it went on tour in Europe, India, and Pakistan: Opening on Broadway October 16, 1967, it ran for 421 performances and won the Critics' Circle Award, "shot through with eloquent observation." Brian Murray played Rosencrantz; John Wood, Guildenstern; both had played Guildenstern in Shakespeare's drama. In London, it was presented again, by the Young Vic, in spring 1973 and fall 1975. It was seen in Alberta in 1976 and Melbourne in 1980. American productions include CSC in repertory, 1970, 1972, 1973; Cleveland, 1974; the Williamstown Theatre Festival, 1977; Tulane, and the Madison, N. J., Shakespeare Festival, 1978; OffOffBway ("The Lone Wolf Co."), 1981. The play is a tour de force that is forceful, and takes us on a delightful and enlightening tour around Shakespeare's *Hamlet.* (For *Dogg's Hamlet,* see plays after *Macbeth.*)

TROILUS AND CRESSIDA   *William Shakespeare*

Many have declared that this is Shakespeare's wisest and least pleasing play. Its unheroic picture of Greek legend has long puzzled critics. Some have seen in the play a symbolic parallel to the battle of the theatres—of boys' companies and adult actors—of Shakespeare's time. Some have even suggested that Shakespeare is burlesquing the Greek heroes out of jealousy of Chapman's translation of Homer; this notion is taken for granted in a scholar's letter to the *London Times* of February 2, 1951. In all probability Shakespeare is simply telling the story, as was often done in the middle ages, from the Trojan point of view. In any event, the drama's origin is so complex that Gilbert Highet calls it "a dramatization of part of a translation into English of a French translation of a Latin imitation of an old French expansion of a Latin epitome of a Greek romance." It may have been written by 1598.

Pointing out that none of Shakespeare's plays is harder to characterize, Coleridge observed: "I am half inclined to believe that Shakespeare's main object, or shall I say his ruling impulse, was to translate the poetic heroes of paganism into the not less rude, but more intellectually vigorous, and more *featurely,* warriors of Christian chivalry—and to substantiate the distinct and graceful profiles or outlines of the Homeric epic into the flesh and blood of the romantic drama." Dryden sought to improve the play. In the Preface (1679) to his revision he explained: "The tongue in general is so much refined since Shakespeare's time, that many of his words, and more of his phrases, are scarce intelligible. And of those which we understand, some are ungrammatical, others coarse; and his whole style is so pestered with figurative expressions, that it is as affected as it is obscure. . . . The author seems to have begun it with some fire; the characters of Pandarus and Thersites are promising enough; but as if he grew weary of his task, after an entrance or two he lets them fall; and the latter part of the tragedy is nothing but a confusion of drums and trumpets, excursions and alarms. Yet, after all, because the play was Shakespeare's, and that there appeared in some places of it the admirable genius of the author, I undertook to remove that heap of rubbish under which many excellent thoughts lay wholly buried."

From the point of view of frequency of performance, the play may well be referred to as Shakespeare's only failure. Goethe, however, saw it as Shakespeare at his most original: "Would you see his mind unfettered," said Goethe in his *Conversations with Eckermann,* "read *Troilus and Cressida.*"

The two movements of this comedy of disillusion are not well knit together. On the Trojan side is the love story, with Pandarus (whose name gives us the word *pander*) furthering Troilus' desire for Cressida. Cressida swears eternal love to Troilus—then, sent in an exchange to the Greek camp, at once is free of her lips to the generals, and makes a rendezvous with Diomedes. Cressida is not mentioned nor seen throughout Act Two, which carries along the military aspect of the drama. Ajax, while Achilles sulks, is sent to fight Hector; their single combat ends with their shaking hands. Then Achilles, spurred by the death of his friend Patroclus, takes the field, and comes upon Hector unarmed. The play, like the *Iliad,* ends with the death of the Trojan hero Hector.

There have been several important productions in recent years: 1916, at Yale University; 1932, the Players' annual revival in New York (the first professional production of the play in America; it included Otis Skinner as Thersites, Eugene Powers as Pandarus, Charles Coburn as Ajax, Edith Barrett as Cressida, and Blanche Yurka as Helen of Troy); 1938 in modern dress in London; by the Marlowe Society in London in 1948. A 1948 production at Harvard University afforded a delightful instance of serendipity (happy accident, frequent in the theatre); wire shapes were used for makeshift helmets—leaving faces and expressions completely visible—when the ordered helmets failed to arrive.

This is the most explicitly philosophical of Shakespeare's dramas. Through its two courses of lechery and war—two scenes of the last act end with a railing upon "lechery: wars and lechery"—the play pictures the passions corrupting their human victims, until all is "fair without and foul within." The central theme of violence with its two faces of war and lust, both with resplendent surface and "putrified core," is embodied in Helen, in Cressida, in the war itself—in all war, with the pumped glory and the blood-soaked sod. The same thought runs through many of the works of Shakespeare. Here is pressed home the final thought that those engaged in war and lust end in their own destruction.

Also in this play is Shakespeare's most explicit political thinking. His belief in the value and social need of an hierarchical order, evident in several of his plays, finds fullest expression in Ulysses' famous speech on degree and the consequences of establishing a false equality. However, the conduct of Ulysses, in ironic contrast to his words, should warn us against assuming that he speaks the playwright's own opinions.

Beyond these basic considerations, the incidental wisdom of the play reveals itself in such lines as "To be wise, and love, exceeds man's might," "A plague of opinion! a man may wear it on both sides, like a leather jerkin," and "One touch of nature makes the whole world kin." Harold C. Goddard has expressed the view that the play includes "a hundred-odd of the most wonderful lines in Shakespeare." Though seldom seen, *Troilus and Cressida* continues to be read for its swift action and its often bitter but always searching reflections on human nature. There was an NT production in 1976.

MEASURE FOR MEASURE   *William Shakespeare*

The essential plot of this play originally appeared in Whetstone's unproduced tragedy *Promos and Cassandra* (1578), based on the Italian Giraldi Cinthio's *Hecatommithi* (1565). Like *All's Well That Ends Well*,* it resolves its complications by the Boccaccionian bed-trick of the substituted woman. Its theme, however, is more serious, and perennial, being (as the *New York World* said, at a 1929 production) a "startlingly familiar study of the hypocritical reformer . . . of the agonized conflict in those creatures that spend their days in enforcing laws and their nights in breaking them. Shakespeare makes him a sick and tormented soul who would delight the modern psychiatrist."

Vincentio of Vienna, leaving his Dukedom in charge of Angelo, watches in disguise. Angelo presses heavily upon evil-doers; he condemns Claudio to death for his pre-marital relations with Juliet. Then Angelo promises to spare Claudio if Claudio's sister Isabella will yield to his desire—but secretly he orders Claudio killed nonetheless. The disguised Duke arranges that the assignation with Angelo is kept, not by Isabella, but by Angelo's affianced, then discarded, sweetheart Mariana. The next day, revealing himself, the Duke weds Isabella, orders Claudio to marry Juliet, and spares Angelo when he accepts Mariana as his wife. The Duke does, however, mete punishment to Lucio, who has lied and has slandered the Duke's name—such civil sins being less tolerable.

The play was presented by the King's players, December 26, 1604.

In versions by William Davenant in 1662 and Charles Gildon about 1690, *Measure For Measure* did not win popularity. Revived in 1720, the play held interest throughout the eighteenth century. The Romantics neglected the work, although it contains some of Shakespeare's richest dramatic poetry, and Isabella is one of his noblest characters. Later in the nineteenth century it grew popular again, with Adelaide Neilson, Helena Modjeska, and Sarah Kemble Siddons in the role of Isabella. Swinburne, disliking the play, felt that it could not be all Shakespeare's; he insisted it was "very far from thoroughly worthy of the wisest and mightiest mind that was ever informed with the spirit of genius of creative poetry." On the other hand, Pater states that as "the poetry of this play is full of the peculiarities of Shakespeare's poetry, so in its ethics is it an epitome of Shakespeare's moral judgments . . ."

The actions of the Duke, as well as biblical references and other allusions, show him serving as a sort of pastor tending his people. Some of the play's underworld figures—the condemned murderer Barnardine, for instance—are uncommonly interesting. With tolerance and lack of pretension, Shakespeare reminds you to judge not, that ye be not judged.

The play is, in essence, a study of the effect of power on character; it demonstrates that those in authority are often caught in the foul dilemma of having to employ falsehood or force. This is most sharply shown in the scene between Isabella and Angelo, the sheer theatrical effectiveness of which, as Harold C. Goddard said in *The Meaning of Shakespeare* (1951) "can easily blind us to the tangle of moral ironies and boomerangs it involves."

To a post-Elizabethan there may seem certain confusions in the play. E.K.Chambers, indeed, in *Shakespeare: A Survey* (1925), asserts that "many honest readers of Shakespeare quite frankly resent the very existence of *Measure For Measure*. . . . Here are the forms of comedy, the byplay of jest and the ending of reconciliation. But the limits of comedy, which may be serious but must be suave, are sorely strained. There is a cruel hint in the laughter, and the engineer of the reconciliation is surely a cynic." It may seem as though tragic material has been forced into the mould of comedy. There are moral ambiguities in the Duke's intriguing and in Isabella's self-righteousness, not to mention inconsistent details in the story. Because of these confusions, some scholars maintain that much of the play is the work of an inferior hand. It may clarify the play's movement, however, to suggest that Shakespeare was writing a politico-moral thesis play; the title is from the *Bible: St. Luke VI 38*, and all Chapter Six of *St. Luke* comes to mind beneath this dramatic examination of the Elizabethan concept of justice and mercy. The difficulty E. K. Chambers feels may arise from the fact that the play combines elements of the sunny romantic comedy with elements of the caustic comedy of humours Jonson* had just made popular. With understanding of these contemporary concerns, the play gathers into an effective pattern.

In 1929 New York was offered a modern version, *The Novice and the Duke,* by Olga Katzin, with Leo G. Carroll. The Stratford Players presented the play on their American tour in the 1930's, and it was performed at Stratford-on-Avon, with John Gielgud as Angelo, opening March 19, 1950. In 1929, Wilella Waldorf called the play "alarmingly up to date. What Shakespeare has to say . . . is uncommonly interesting, too, or would be were it not so completely tangled up in a lot of decidedly uneven quality, interspersed with doubtful comedy which strikes a particularly sour note when played in modern surroundings." Without the modern clothing, in its own atmosphere, *Measure For Measure* may be accepted as an olden plot that continues to have present validity in its pointing of a permanent truth.

Herbert Read felt that the scene wherein Claudio, to save his own life begs his sister to accept Angelo as a lover reaches "the very perfection of poetic diction." Georg Brandes more widely stated that "one feels throughout, even in the comic episodes, that Shakespeare's burning wrath at the moral hypocrisy of self-righteousness underlies the whole structure like a volcano, which every moment shoots up its flames through the superficial form of comedy and the interludes of obligatory merriment." The play should be viewed, said Wilson Knight, "not as a picture of normal human affairs, but as a parable, like the Parables of Jesus."

RSC showed the play in 1962, with Judi Dench as Isabella, Ian Richardson as Lucio.

OTHELLO   *William Shakespeare*

Its story taken largely from the Italian Cinthio's *Hecatommithi* (1565). *Othello* (1604) is by many deemed Shakespeare's greatest play. It is often referred to as a tragedy of jealousy. Young Macaulay seems to have regarded it so: "*Othello* is perhaps the greatest work in the world. From what does it derive its power? From the clouds? From the ocean? From the mountains? Or from love as strong as death, and jealousy cruel as the grave?" Samuel Johnson saw the drama as driving home a lesson: "We learn from *Othello* this very useful moral, not to make an unequal match. . . . I think *Othello* has almost more moral than any other play." The Romantics analyzed the play more aptly. Lamb, in 1834, remarked: "Othello's fault was credulity." Coleridge, a dozen years earlier, plumbed to the heart of the matter: "Jealousy does not strike me as the point in his passion; I take it rather to be an agony that the creature whom he had believed angelic, with whom he had garnered up his heart, and whom he could not help still loving, should be proved impure and worthless. . . . It was a moral indignation and regret that virtue should so fall. . . . In addition to this, his honor was concerned." In truth, once Othello was persuaded of Desdemona's guilt, he took, regretfully, the sole course that his honor allowed. For Shakespeare's picture of jealousy, note Leontes in *The Winter's Tale*.

As Coleridge analyzed it: "*Lear* is the most tremendous effort of Shakespeare as a poet; *Hamlet,* as a philosopher or meditator; and *Othello* is the union of the two. There is something gigantic and unformed in the former two; but in the latter, everything assumes its due place and proportion, and the whole mature powers of his mind are displayed in admirable equilibrium." Even Bernard Shaw conceded the play's greatness: "When the worst has been said of *Othello* that can be provoked by its superficiality and stageyness, it remains magnificent by the volume of its passion and the splendor of its word-music, which sweep the scenes up to a plane on which sense is drowned in sound. . . . Tested by the brain, it is ridiculous; tested by the ear, it is sublime."

The story moves with simple directness. Desdemona, won by the Moor Othello's nature and his stories of his battles for Venice, defies her father to marry him, and goes to Cyprus where Othello is to govern. Iago, Othello's "ancient," invaluable in the battlefield, finding he is of less use in civil affairs, feels slighted; he seeks to turn Othello against his wife, and by stealing a handkerchief Othello has given Desdemona, convinces the Moor of her unfaithfulness. Still loving Desdemona, Othello finds no course open save to kill her. After smothering her, he discovers his error and stabs himself, while the still gloating Iago is led to punishment.

The drama is permeated with irony. In the first act, Othello is called to justify his love before the City Councillors. He does; and, as G. G. Sedgwick points out in *Of Irony* (1949): "At the very moment the speech ends an extraordinary irony, prepared for by a previous order, is enacted before our eyes, baldly suggested by a stage direction, 'Enter Desdemona, Iago, and attendants.' Just as Othello has scored his great and only triumph, his sworn enemy appears as the trusted guard of his wife. There can be no more effective entrance in the range of drama."

It is the honesty in Othello's heart that makes him easy victim: it is the deep love in Desdemona's heart that makes her vulnerable. She has taken out her handkerchief, when Othello says his head aches, to bind his forehead. Already tainted with the suspicion Iago has implanted, Othello brushes her away: "Let it alone." If Desdemona had loved Othello less— Harold C. Goddard pointed out, in *The Meaning of Shakespeare* (1951), the subtle psychology of this critical moment—"she would naturally have noticed the fall of the handkerchief and would, however unconsciously, have stooped and picked it up. But every fiber of her soul and body, conscious and unconscious, is so totally devoted to Othello that the handkerchief for the moment ceases to exist. The slightest deflection of her eye in its direction as it dropped would have been a subtraction from the infinity of her love—just as the movement of Othello's hand when he pushed her hand away measured his distrust of that love, gave the villain his unique opportunity, and sealed his own doom forever. Is there anything in all the drama of the world, I wonder, to equal this in its kind?" The full measure of Desdemona's love is in her dying words when, asked by Emilia "Who hath done this deed?" she responds, "Nobody; I myself. Farewell!" Again, in this play, Shakespeare pits violence against love; the bodies succumb to violence, but love is undismayed, and the spirit exalted.

Othello is one of Shakespeare's most popular dramas. Many stars, among them Booth and Irving, have alternately enacted Othello and Iago. Almost every noted actor has essayed the title part: Quin, Garrick (though Garrick's rival Spranger Barry was more favored in the role), Macready, Forrest (deemed over-violent), Fechter, Kemble. Hazlitt declared that Edmund Kean's Othello was not only the greatest of Kean's roles, but the highest effort of genius on the stage. The Negro Ira Aldridge made his debut, in London in 1826, as Othello; on tour (in Belfast) his Iago was Charles Kean—who played the same role to his father Edmund's Othello on March 25, 1833, when Edmund collapsed on the stage in his final illness. The Italian Ernesto Rossi played Othello in Rome (1873) and in Paris (1876); Henry James deemed him excelling in the moods of violent passion: when Iago seeks to rouse Othello against Desdemona, Rossi as Othello "seized Iago's head, whacked it half a dozen times on the floor, then flung him twenty yards away." Alexandre Dumas, in 1868, protested against such intensity; but to little avail. The performances of Tommaso Salvini were also noted for the ferocity of the playing, as he toured England and the United States in the 1870's and 1880's—he speaking in Italian, while the rest of the company (Edwin Booth was once his Iago) used the English lines. More than once, in various productions, when Othello has taken Iago by the throat, shouts have come from the audience: "Choke him!" The power of the drama leaps the footlights.

The popularity of the play led to much discussion, even to disputes over the rendering of lines. In Henry Fielding's *A Journey From This World to the Next* (1743) Shakespeare, asked how to deliver the line "Put out the light, and then put out the light," scolds his questioners for petty arguing. In Eliza Haywood's novel *The Husband* (1756) a quarrel over the same line leads to a duel and two deaths.

The smothering of Desdemona was a controversial point, protested by critics in 1717, 1766, 1770, and later. *Town and Country* magazine for April, 1773, declared that "We carry our enthusiasm so far, that we entirely suspend our senses toward his absurdities . . . devoutly view Desdemona stifled to death, then so perfectly restored to life as to speak two or three sentences, then die again, without another oppressive stroke from the pillow." The critic Rymer retorted: "A woman never loses her tongue, even after she is stifled"; but for over a century a dagger was also used; until Salvini put his knee on the actress' breast to speed Desdemona's end. Fanny Kemble, in 1848, objected: "The Desdemonas that I have seen, on the English stage, have always appeared to me to acquiesce with wonderful equanimity in their assassination. On the Italian stage they run for their lives." Something is to be said for Desdemona's acceptance of her fate; but Macready as her Othello eased Fanny Kemble's apprehension by letting down the bed curtains before the despatch. Ira Aldridge, as late as 1865, pulled Madge Kendal as Desdemona out of bed by her hair and dragged her around the stage before he smothered her. The audience hissed; but later performers (as Rossi in 1881) have strangled Desdemona with her own hair; or have struggled with her in the center of the stage and then carried her to the bed for the final disposal. Partly because of this treatment, Desdemona's part has not been sought by actresses, although the first performance ever given by a woman on the English professional stage was that of Margaret Hughes as Desdemona, on December 8, 1660. (There had been a French company with woman players in London in the 1630's, and women had long performed in private masques, especially noble ladies in their own homes.) The role of Desdemona demands a star, yet she is quite subordinate to Othello. Nor, indeed, is Desdemona always admired. James Agate in 1939 exclaimed: "Desdemona? I have never been able to see how any actress could make anything out of this extraordinary hybrid. Before the curtain rises she puts up a display of social daring which Ibsen's Hilda Wangel and Mr. Shaw's Ann Whitefield couldn't have come anything near. After which she shows herself to have fewer brains even than Cordelia, and stands next to that immortal gumph in Ruskin's list of Shakespeare's perfect women." Ruskin, however, comes closer to the general estimate of Desdemona, who loved perhaps not wisely, but certainly well.

In the French theatre, the struggle between the classicists and the Romantics, which burst out over the production of Hugo's *Hernani** in 1830, erupted in a riot the year before when in a production of *Othello* the word *handkerchief, mouchoir,* was spoken: the word was deemed by the classicists too vulgar for dignified drama. (In 1907, the Dublin riots over *The Playboy of the Western World** similarly broke out at the word *shift.*). Alfred de Vigny is among the half hundred that have translated the play into French. The Spanish playwright Manuel Tamayo y Baus in 1867 wrote *A New Drama,* which presents *Othello* as a play within a play, arguing the problem of jealousy. Similarly the motion picture *A Double Life* (1948, with Ronald Colman) shows a man so caught into the role of Othello that he goes forth and finds a "Desdemona" to kill.

There have been a number of recent performances of the drama in New

York and on tour: in 1926, 1933, and 1934, Walter Hampden; in 1935, Philip Merivale and Gladys Cooper; 1936-1937, Walter Huston and Brian Aherne; 1940, in modern dress; 1943, the black Paul Robeson and José Ferrer; 1944, the black Canada Lee at Erwin Piscator's Dramatic Workshpop; 1945, the Robeson company, back from its tour, at the New York City Center. London saw a gripping production in 1947, with Frederick Valk as Othello and Donald Wolfit as Iago. In October 1951 Orson Welles and Douglas Campbell opened in separate London productions. In an OffBway production of 1953, Earle Hyman was a striking Othello; William Marshall was effective in a Brattle Players production at the New York City Center opening September 7, 1955. The play was made into a silent motion picture in 1922, with Emil Jennings and Werner Krauss, less successfully into a sound film with Orson Welles in 1955.

Of the 1935 New York performance, general opinion was reflected by Arthur Pollock: "When the plot begins to thicken, and excite the interest of the audience, as it always does, when the actors grow more and more animated, you can hardly notice the playing, you are so wrapped up in the play." It was, declared John Mason Brown, "as perfect an example of scenes drained of their emotions, of fast-moving dialogue and exciting plotting as the whole history of the theatre boasts." The work of Robeson was another thing. There were ten curtain calls for the black Othello at the opening; director Margaret Webster and Howard Barnes were favorably impressed, but others were sharply critical. To Wilella Waldorf Robeson was "definitely disappointing" and John Chapman found himself "wishing now and then that he would stop intoning and do something else with speech." George Freedley, a year later, raised another issue: "I find it difficult to accept the idea of Othello's being played by a Negro when Shakespeare so clearly states that this noble general is a distinguished Moor, which is quite another thing. Granted the premises, however, Canada Lee makes a creditable showing in the part. . . . He seems to feel and act the part with more conviction than does Paul Robeson, whose very sonority is his most tragic weakness." George Jean Nathan said bluntly: "Black or white, the whole question rests on whether the actor can act the role. Robeson acts it poorly." The production with Robeson, nevertheless, achieved the play's record run of 280 performances, and showed that it retains its tremendous tragic power.

Some critics have called Iago Shakespeare's one real villain, acting from "motiveless malignity"; but he has at least as strong a motive for his treachery as Benedict Arnold had for his treason—a gnawing sense of merit unrewarded. Shakespeare balances Iago against Othello in many ways. Up to the handkerchief episode, ACT III Scene iii, Othello speaks 240 lines; Iago, 574. Othello's words, however, make the poetry of the play; Iago's the machinery and, through the foul figures that he uses, the foreboding.

The drama's conclusion is one of the rare instances of Shakespeare's use of surprise. When the Moor has learned the truth, that he has slain an innocent woman whom he most dearly loves, he tells his tale, and catches the others onstage unawares as he stabs himself, "one that loved not wisely but too well." Othello's lack was less in his love than in his judgment; being honest himself, he could not conceive that another could lie to such cruel ends. *Othello* is not a drama of jealousy, but—here intensified and fiercely lighted by contrasting stations, strong natures, and deep love—a tragedy, oft recurrent in the world, of wily deceit ensnaring simple honesty, and— less common but more exalting—of love holding steadfast against despair.

Robeson continued in the role, with Zoe Caldwell, in 1959 at Stratford-upon-Avon. More recently, the black James Earl Jones has enacted Othello; in six productions over a dozen years: Los Angeles, 1970; a nine-city tour beginning at Stratford, Conn., August 1981, reaching the New York Winter Garden February 3, 1982—still finding new facets of the Moor. Thus, there is a tender touch in Jones' moment in his next-to-the-last scene with the brief-bowed and fallen Desdemona: within himself the anguished struggle between love and sense of honor silences him as he leans and draws the voluminous folds of his cloak over her too; instead of the usual anger or horror, he whispers in aching hope-against-despair: "O Desdemona! away! away! away!" The appealing innocence of Diane Wiest, and the superbly shown cunning of Christopher Plummer as Iago, using honesty and virtue in others as the means of their destruction, make this—grown from its earlier presentation at Stratford—an outstanding production of the play.

MACBETH   *William Shakespeare*

This tragedy moves with a fiercer drive than any other of Shakespeare's dramas. It is, as Harold Hobson of the *London Sunday Times* remarked, after a December 18, 1947 revival, "the shortest, most energetic, concentrated, and vehement" of all his tragedies. And A. W. Schlegel said, in his *Lectures on Dramatic Art* (1809-1811), "Nothing can equal this picture in its power to excite terror . . . otherwise the tragic muse might exchange her mask for the head of Medusa."

From the moment that the three weird sisters meet the Scottish generals Macbeth and Banquo returning victorious from battle, and prophesy that Macbeth will be king (succeeded by Banquo's sons), we feel the ominous march of doom. When Lady Macbeth learns of the prophecy and hears that King Duncan is coming to spend the night in Macbeth's castle of Dunsinane, she resolves that he will never thereafter step forth. The death of the King and the piled horrors are inevitable train. After the murder, Macbeth feels fear, which leads him to more murders; Lady Macbeth feels remorse, which leads her to suicide. When Lady Macbeth, after her sleepwalking revelation of her guilt, succumbs and dies, Macbeth voices his sense of futility. Thereafter the witches' prophecies are wryly fulfilled. They have assured Macbeth that he is quite safe until Birnam Wood comes to Dunsinane. Now a guard breaks in upon Macbeth with news that the Wood is nearing: the troops carry branches before them, to camouflage their force. They have told Macbeth that no man born of woman can do him harm. And, facing Macbeth, his fiercest foe reveals: "Macduff was from his mother's womb untimely ript." False assurance swept away, Macbeth summons his manhood: "Lay on Macduff, and damn'd be him that first cries 'Hold, enough!'" Macduff lays Macbeth's head before Malcolm, hailing the new king.

Here Shakespeare faced his most difficult dramatic problem. For he took as his protagonist, not a wronged man (Hamlet), a man imposed upon (Othello), or a noble man weakened by age (Lear), but a vigorous champion at the peak of his power and the height of his honors, turning to fourfold sin. Macbeth is a friend that violates the trust of his friend and benefactor, a soldier that turns upon his commander, a subject that betrays his king, a host—and for this Dante holds the deepest circle of hell—that uses the cloak of hospitality to murder his guest. In Holinshed's *Chronicles* (1577), Shakespeare's source, Macbeth is an open enemy of Duncan; the dramatist sought fuller measure of evil by adding the treachery, which Holinshed has in the story of Macdonwald. While the audience understand Macbeth's temptation—in our lesser fields, which of us has not been assailed?—we watch his acts with gathering horror; yet Shakespeare must so enwrap us in the mood that we follow also with sympathy, that is, with emotional involvement in the flow of Macbeth's feelings. Hence the tragic exaltation of the close, when Macbeth accepting his doom reasserts his human stature, and in his dying struggle is defying the witches, the Fates, as much as Macduff.

Indeed (and this is a measure of Shakespeare's mastery), we feel from the first that the conflict is no mere battle for a crown (save as in this we see the Crown of Heaven) but a gathered onslaught of the forces of evil upon the goodness of the world. With many Biblical parallels, the play drives home thoughts of man's eternal striving; "the murder of Duncan and its consequences," said Roy Walker in *The Time Is Free* (1949), "are profoundly impregnated with the central tragedy of the Christian myth." The witches, as Schlegel said, "are ignoble and vulgar instruments of Hell." Hecate (who may have stood silent in Shakespeare's play; many scholars feel that her speeches are interpolations; her songs appear also in Middleton's play *The Witch*), Hecate is the spirit of evil presiding over the witches' brew at which Macbeth is the sole human figure—contrasted with the feast of the living, from which Macbeth is barred by Banquo's silent ghost, the sole supernatural figure and portent of the defeat of evil. The Porter, who comes when there is knocking at the door after the King is murdered, tipsily muses: "If a man were porter of hell-gate, he should have old turning the key." "Ay, my good fellow," A. C. Quiller-Couch commented in his *Cambridge Lectures* (1943), porter of hell-gate: *"that is precisely what you are!"* The "third murderer" at Banquo's death is in all likelihood the hovering spirit of Macbeth. The play is a specific manifestation of naked evil.

Adding to this general effect of supernatural forces engaged in grim conflict is the atmosphere in which Shakespeare enshrouds the play: darkness, and blood. The first creatures we behold are the witches, who cry: "Fair is foul and foul is fair." The first human we behold is a man bathed in blood. Macbeth's first words are "So foul and fair a day I have not seen." All continues in blood and darkness. "Stars, hide your fires!" Macbeth cries. Lady Macbeth makes black summons: "Come thick night, And pall thee in the dunnest smoke of hell . . ." Of the play's twenty-six scenes, twenty-two are in darkness or gloom; the four bright scenes are all in the last act, as the forest advances, bringing the forces of righteousness to their triumph. Throughout the play, as Caroline Spurgeon showed in *Leading Motives in the Imagery of Shakespeare's Tragedies* (1930), the figures of speech are clotted with images of blood. These blood-soaked stimuli strike at all the senses. Lady Macbeth in her sleep-walking smells blood on her hands. Macbeth sees a bloody dagger; he hears a voice crying "Sleep no more, Macbeth does murder sleep"; he feels his victims' clotted blood on his hands; and as he cries "I have supped full with horrors!" there is the taste of blood on shriveling palates. The three weird sisters stirred their pot about the time of the publication of King James' book on *Demonology*, which led to the passing of more stringent laws against witchcraft and had eerie echoes in the American colonies. The play thus had a fascination for its time we can but dimly recognize. If, as Henry N. Paul documented in *The Royal Play of Macbeth* (1950), its first performance was at Hampton Court on August 7, 1606, before King James I and his brother-in-law King Christian of Denmark, it came to a London still clouded with the effects of the Gunpowder Plot of Guy Fawkes (November 5, 1605) and the exceptionally severe equinoctial storms at the end of March 1606.

Later, and for almost two hundred years, *Macbeth* was played in an adaptation by Sir William Davenant (1663?). This omitted the Porter's scene and ended the play with a fight between Macduff and Macbeth. David Garrick in 1743 wrote a dying speech for Macbeth. Samuel Phelps in 1847 tried to restore the original ending, which has the duel offstage, with Macduff bringing back the head of Macbeth. The public's love of a good fight, however, made this unpopular, and productions vied with one another in the closing battle. From eighteenth century Charles Macklin, through Henry Irving in 1888 to Michael Redgrave in 1948, soldiers have dashed across the stage in wild conflict, with echoing clashes beyond; Macduff and Macbeth have fought with sword and dagger to the fatal end. Otis Skinner as Macduff with a downswing of his broadsword once narrowly missed cleaving the skull of Edwin Booth. Irving's Macbeth, losing his sword, fought on with dagger until his weakening fingers clawed the empty air. Redgrave's Macbeth, in a knockabout duel that might have roused the envy of Douglas Fairbanks, finally fell upon his own dagger, snatched by his enemy's hand. Shakespeare's ending was used in the 1951 Dramatic Workshop revival directed by Erwin Piscator, which excellently conveyed the brooding darkness of the drama.

Macbeth (1601?–1606) was perhaps first conceived not, as some have thought, to honor the new Stuart King, James I, who was one of the line of Banquo's sons, but by showing the violence on the northern reigns to help justify Queen Elizabeth's execution of Mary Queen of Scots. Today the play is sought, by both actresses and actors, as a vehicle to test their powers. One of its greatest performances was doubtless that at Drury Lane in 1785, with John Philip Kemble and his sister, Mrs. Sarah K. Siddons, who also enacted Lady Macbeth on her farewell appearance in 1812. Since Helena Modjeska's performance in 1888, the sexual tie between Macbeth and his Lady has been emphasized: Lily Langtry in 1889 snuggled amorously in Macbeth's arms while tempting him to the assassination; Lillah McCarthy in 1909 dominated him like an Elizabethan courtesan.

Also variously stimulating the imagination has been the appearance of the three weird sisters. From the Restoration until 1833 their roles were commonly enacted by company comedians playing primarily for the laughter of the gallery. The flying "machines" used by the witches in the Davenant version led to the earliest travesty of a Shakespearean play, *A New Fancy, After the Old and Most Surprising Way of "Macbeth,"* 1675, by Thomas Duffett. In this burlesque witches sing in mid-air and devise lightning before the eyes of the audience with "mustard-pot and salt-peter." Another travesty was written by Francis Talfourd in 1850. In some productions the witches have been invisible spirits, but most have shown them fully embodied. The German Schiller, in his adaptation of *Macbeth,* played at Weimar in 1800, practically denatured the witches by endowing them with philosophy. His countryman Schlegel knew better: "Shakespeare's picture of the witches is truly magical: in their short scenes, he has created for them a language of their own, which, although composed of the usual elements, still seems to be a faggoting of formulas of incantation."

In an 1860 production, during the murder of Duncan, the three witches exulted within a transparency, high in the castle wall. Their platform collapsed and one of the witches, proving mortal, was killed by the fall.

The manner in which the two murderers reveal their guilt is noteworthy. Macbeth is startled at the hallucination in the banquet scene, when he sees the dead Banquo take his place at the table. This is presented in elaborate, ornate verse. Lady Macbeth makes her guilt known through the troubled words of her sleep-walking. These are of the utmost simplicity: of 170 words, all but twelve are of one syllable. Throughout the play, Shakespeare shows full command and rich variety of poetic expression.

In many ways, *Macbeth* is a counterpiece to *Hamlet.* The one opens with the ghost, as the other with the witches, to set the mood of the drama. In each play—with superb craftsmanship—we have twice seen the supernatural figures before they meet their main objective; hence, when the man comes, we can concentrate not on them but on the human reaction. What matters is how their message is received. Against these structural similarities the two protagonists move from opposite sides in a spiritual pilgrimage: Hamlet must plunge into sin to achieve salvation; Macbeth must chastise (make chaste) the world through the fires of sin. As Roy Walker has observed, Hamlet is noble despite his world; the world is noble despite Macbeth. Macbeth, in his final rebellion, is man again, is mortal, and attuned to die: evil has died, and "the time is free." Goodness and peace once more may walk abroad.

It is also noteworthy how the witches make use of the three types of dramatic prophecy. Simplest is the prophecy that the prophet (the playwright) makes come true. Thus, in *Julius Caesar,** "Beware the Ides of March!"; in *Macbeth,* the witches' word that Banquo's sons will rule (made true in the vision). Subtler is the prophecy that comes wryly true; it has a literally true outcome but twists unexpectedly, as when "Birnam Wood" comes to Dunsinane, and a man "not born of woman" slays Macbeth. Most difficult is the prophecy that makes itself come true: once the kingship is in the minds of Lady Macbeth and Macbeth, granted their natures, nothing could stop them in their wild course towards its securing. The wryly true prophecies are but one form of the Delphic effects in the play, words or deeds capable of a dual interpretation, of which *Macbeth* contains more than any other of Shakespeare's dramas. These help to build the impression that behind the material world of lustful action there boils a deeper world of supernal forces, the well-springs of human energy and desire.

The play is so short that some have suggested we possess but an acting version of a longer drama. This might explain the swift rush of time. With specific chronology, Shakespeare is careless; but of the sense of time—in amble or gallop—he holds command. He is, however, careless also with anachronism, as in the jokes of the Porter, who in the year 1055 turns his humor upon Elizabethan London. The knocking at the gate, on which DeQuincey wrote a most discerning essay, has been the subject of considerable discussion. The Romantics tended to consider the Porter's role a blot on the play. Schiller, in his adaptation, substituted a Watchman with a charming song to the rising sun. Coleridge let loose a notorious heresy: "This low soliloquy of the Porter and his few speeches afterwards, I believe to have been written for the mob by some other hand." DeQuincey's essay thrusts aside these genteel scruples; today this moment is recognized as the turning-point of the play, the annunciation. "What hand is on the hammer? Whose step is on the threshold?" asked Quiller-Couch: "It is, if we will, God. It is, if we will, the Moral Order. It is, whatever our religion, that which holds humankind together by law of sanity and righteousness. It is all that this man and woman have outraged. . . . From this moment the moral order reasserts itself to roll back the crime to its last expiation." The Porter thus does not merely bring comic relief between two moments of high tension— the thrust of evil, and the returning thrust of good. He serves also, by the matter-of-fact contrast, to emphasize the blackness of the night and of the appalling deed. And also, as with the grave-digger in *Hamlet** and the farmer that brings the asp in *Antony and Cleopatra,** by the impact of his unwitting appearance—this simple man, unaware of the great events that overhang—he sets a moment of normality with which we may take bearings in the tragic dark.

There have been many revivals of *Macbeth.* One in 1927 with Fritz Leiber. In 1928, with Florence Reed (later, Margaret Anglin), and William Farnum, with sets by Gordon Craig. Richard Watts, Jr., found this "more than a little disappointing," and John Hutchens (in the *New York Post*) declared it "gleaming with pictorial excitement, and steadily done almost to death by its players." In 1934, with Walter Hampden. In 1935, with Gladys Cooper and Philip Merivale. In a Cleveland Heights modern version, Macbeth made his first entrance in an armored car. *Macbeth* was played at the Stratford Festival in 1952. In 1936 the black unit of the Federal Theatre presented a Haitian version arranged by Orson Welles. This was hailed by Brooks Atkinson, who called the witches' scene "a triumph of theatre art."

Macbeth has long appealed on both sides of the footlights. Thus Goethe, who knew the theatre from both sides, declared in his *Conversations with Eckermann:* "*Macbeth,* I consider Shakespeare's best acting play, the one in which he shows most understanding of the stage." Thomas Campbell in 1834 and Henry Hallam in 1854 are among the many that have said, with Abraham Lincoln, "I think nothing equals *Macbeth.*"

The 1948 revival by Michael Redgrave and Flora Robson dragged the murky melodrama from its Scottish lair and flung it into the teeth of the audience. Atkinson again gave praise: "A superb *Macbeth* has come to town. No one else in the contemporary theatre has drawn so much horror and ferocity out of it . . ." Whatever the success of the particular performance, the play continues its challenge to the greatest players, for in no other of Shakespeare's tragedies is such sustained power of poetry combined with such surging of emotion and such unremitting force of action.

The London Comedy Theatre production of October 10, 1914, ran for 710 performances. The London Old Vic, at the New York City Center, 1962, showed John Clements as a vigorous, villainous Macbeth, reveling in gore. Two of the witches were male, not shrouded in mist, but explicit, earthy. A Zulu production, *Umbatha,* was shown briefly in London in 1972. In New York, 1977, *Macbeth* played in two OffBway houses, La Mama and (all-black) Henry Street.

At the Stratford, Ontario, Festival, 1978, a grim and graphic Douglas Rain was matched by Maggie Smith with, said Richard Eder in the *Times,* June 9, 1978, "terrifying exaltation."

In London, also 1978, Peter Hall directed the NT with Albert Finney and Dorothy Tutin; while Trevor Nunn directed the RSC with Ian McKellan and Judi Dench, who went from Stratford to London and a national tour. In New York, Sara Caldwell directed the play in 1981 at the Beaumont, not well received. And in 1982 Nicol Williamson directed and starred at the Circle in the Square; Walter Kerr said he "loses just about every gamble he takes. . . . Certainly he makes no effort to avail himself of Shakespeare's cadences and Shakespeare's music." It is, however, hard to fail with Macbeth.

An RSC production, directed by Howard Davies, at Stratford-upon-Avon, then (August 1983) at the London Barbican, sought variety by having the players in modern dress, reciting most of the lines directly at the audience, interrupted by all sorts of devices. Doors opened suddenly; lights flared or died; and high on the steel-poled gym that was the setting, two percussionists were quick with rattle and other noisemakers. The witches were not old hags, but pretty lasses who turned cartwheels—and spouted blood. Bob Peck played Macbeth as "a power-mad gangster" in jeans or a military greatcoat.

The poet Lamartine asserted that "all the great crimes in Shakespeare are inspired by wicked women; men may execute, but cannot conceive them." While this may apply to Macbeth, Iago and Richard III would smile a caustic smile.

Several plays spider-spun out of *Macbeth* are here considered:

MACBETT   *Eugene Ionesco*

Ionesco said that he called his play *Macbett* so that it would not be confused with Shakespeare's. He was not only joking, but ironic, for he knew that in several languages, including German and French, the two names are pronounced alike, *th* given the *t* sound, as in Thomas. He also said: "Shakespeare was the father of the absurd. Macbeth defines it when he says that life is a tale told by an idiot, full of sound and fury, signifying nothing." Then Ionesco proceeds to transmogrify poetry into absurdity. With a false echo of *Ubu Roi,** when in Ionesco's travesty Birnam Wood comes to Dunsinane, Macbett cried "Shit!" (Then was the dunce inane.) Thomas Quinn Curtis, in the February 9, 1972, *New York Times,* reviewing the Paris production, called the play *"Macbeth* seen in a nightmare after too many Welsh rarebits."

Beyond its grotesque humor, the play has a serious purpose: to show how a devoted revolutionary, destroying and supplanting a vicious tyrant, becomes in his turn a sadistic, lecherous villain, ad infinitum. Glamis and Cawdor; Duncan; Macbett and Banco; Macol. To emphasize the repetitious pattern of perverting power, Ionesco in the successive situations repeats the phrases. The list of vices that the worthy Malcolm piles falsely on himself to test his allies, Ionesco, quoting from Shakespeare, makes real in his Macol. But absurdity rules, with its need to shock; the characters, rising rarely beyond the level of a macabre joke, fail to move us. The pervasive complacency and corruption Ionesco sees in the world today are not conveyed by the anachronisms that leap from old times to ours. Macbett's favorite exclamation is "Son of a gun!" The guillotine is assisted by machine guns.

Lady Banco—who, like her lady-in-waiting, is really a witch—seduces Macbett into killing her husband. (Banco's kilt is pulled off, revealing frilly feminine underthings.) Lady Banco sits sipping tea, counting heads as twenty thousand rebel soldiers are executed, while she plays footsies under the table with Macbett. She then marries the new king, becoming Lady Macbett, and murder piles on murder. No man born of woman, remember, can kill Macbett; Lo, Macol is the son of Banco and a gazelle. Leaving the world to the assassins, Lady Macbett flies ecstatically off on a broom.

Macbett played in Vienna in 1972. It came to Coventry, then to the London Globe, July 1973, adapted and directed by Charles Marowitz, known for his avant-garde work in the theatre. In the same year it was played in Ottawa in French, and in the Marowitz version at Yale. Harold Clurman, in the *Nation,* May 28, 1973, declared: "Though there is something tart and mischievous in Ionesco's humor, even at times a touch of the macabre and the frightening; the whole of his work breathes a pathos which is at the core of its subjective origin." After the Marowitz London production, Harold Hobson in the *Times* called the play "a vulgar, banal, transvestite lacy-knickered, bottom-kissing, belly-shaking, belching, bellowing, brutal bore." Then, having read the Donald Watson translation of the play, he recanted: it is "a powerful study of the corrupting effects of power, and it has much beauty and dignity. . . . Mr. Marowitz has ruined it." If life is a tale told by an idiot, Ionesco's *Macbett,* full of sound and fury, dances to the absurdly tattered tune.

MACBIRD   *Barbara Garson*

In an underground pamphlet Barbara Garson (b. 1941), a rebellious undergraduate at the University of California at Berkeley, first issued her play *Macbird,* compressing Ionesco's generalized cliché—first Baron Acton, 1904: "Power tends to corrupt and absolute power corrupts absolutely"—into specific instance. Her title springs partly from "Lady Bird" Johnson, wife of Lyndon Baines Johnson, Vice-President of the United States until the assassination of President John F. Kennedy, then succeeding him. The play extends the idea of corruption to all the Kennedy family, and to everyone around. Ms. Garson more than hints that Johnson arranged the assassination. She implies that the death of Adlai Stevenson—in the play Lord Stevenson the Egg of Head—was similarly inspired: "the rumor goes that near the body a poison dart was found." She suggests that Bobby Ken O'Dunc, who has won the power struggle, will be equally obnoxious; at the close of the play, Bobby points the recurrent story:

> *So, choked with grief, I pledge my solemn word*
> *To lift aloft the banner of Macbird.*

No one—Stevenson; the Earl of Warren (Chief Justice of the U. S. Supreme Court, Earl Warren); Wayne (Thane?) of Morse (U. S. Senator Wayne Morse)—escapes the lash of vilification. As Walter Kerr put it: "By scattering her fire unselectively across the landscape, leaving no motive or course of action or personal characteristic unassailed, the author wipes the slate clean (or muddies it irremediably)."

The three witches—a young beatnik demonstrator; a Black Muslim; and an old leftist—open the play. (In the Joan Littlewood production at the Theatre Royal, Stratford East, London, opening April 8, 1967—presented as at a membership club to avoid the censor, after the Lord Chamberlain had forbidden two prospective West End showings—the play started with Shakespeare's witch scene; then an actor addresses the audience: "Bet we had you worried. You probably thought you were at the other Stratford." The play lasted in London for 43 performances, although at the New York Village Gate, opening February 8, 1967, then at the Circle in the Square, then at the Garrick Theatre, it attained 386. It toured the United States, had earlier (1966) been shown on Canadian TV, and has been produced in fourteen countries, most of them shaking their delighted heads at American villainy. The *New Haven Register* approved, calling it "good unAmerican fun from beginning to end." Peter Brook, director at the RSC, pondered: declaring that no other country in the world would permit such a picture of its own rulers, he called *Macbird* "a positive and glowing refutation of all antiAmericanism . . . the most powerful piece of pro-American theatre in a long time."

The American left, and many self-styled liberals, hailed the play, leading the *London Times* (February 9, 1967) to question: "What kind of intellectual climate is it in which a trifling pantomime can be described by Robert Brustein (Dean of the Yale Drama School) as 'one of the brutally provocative works in the American theater, as well as one of the most grimly amusing' and by Eric Bentley (Columbia University Professor of Dramatic Literature) as a warning against the American way of life?"

As Macbeth cannot be killed by a normal man, Robert Ken O'Dunc is superhuman: his father had replaced the heart of his newborn son with a "precision apparatus of steel and plastic tubing." There are twisted lines from other Shakespeare plays; thus, a Hamlet soliloquy becomes the Egg of Head's pondering:

> To see or not to see, that is the question:
> Whether 'tis wiser as a statesman to ignore
> The gross deceptions of outrageous liars
> Or to speak out against a reign of evil
> And by so doing, end there for all time
> The chance and hope to work within for changes.

The *New Yorker* tried to deny the play's existence, not reviewing it, not including it on its theater listing; but it finally spoke, calling the play "not satire at all; it is a libel thinly disguised as a high-spirited undergraduate prank. The substance of *Macbird* is not truth carried to absurdity—another component of satire—but a lie. Lyndon Johnson did not kill John F. Kennedy. And all the rest is talk."

The playwright achieved a *succès de scandale*. Far from the Swan of Avon, Barbara Garson (as one critic put it) "took a swan-dive into an empty pool. . . . *Macbird* is for the birds." Despite its violence, *Macbeth* goes strikingly on.

DOGG'S HAMLET AND CAHOOT'S MACBETH   *Tom Stoppard*

This odd combination had its world premiere at the Washington Kennedy Center September 4, 1979, running until the end of the month. It was dedicated to "Dr. Dogg," whose troupe had put on *Dogg's Our Pet* at the London Almost Free Theatre in December 1971. It shows boys from an English public school, under tutelage of Dogg, helping a workman put up staging, and putting on a fifteen-minute capsule version of *Hamlet,* followed by a two-minute reprise. *Cahoot's Macbeth* shows a similar capsule and reprise of Shakespeare's *Macbeth,* but put on in the living room of Czechoslovakian theatre folk whom Stoppard knew, who were barred by the government from public performance.

(The proscribed playwright was Pavel Kohout; Stoppard dedicated *Cahoot's Macbeth* to him.) The Cockney carpenter in the first movement becomes in the second a police officer who harangues the players, and questions the propriety of their presentation.

Of the London Collegiate production, July 28, 1977, the *Observer* said:

"Hic, haec, hype, hokum"; some called it quite extraordinarily funny. It played in San Francisco, opening December 19, 1979, presented by the British American Repertory Company (BARC); Gerald Nachman in the *Chronicle* said it was "BARCing up the wrong tree.... Intellectual masochists may love the thrill of being flipped and bumped about by Stoppard and Ed Berman (the American he's in cahoots with) like a pinball in a philosophical phantasmagoria which ends, finally, in 'tilt.'" When it came to New York—four weeks at the 22 Steps Theatre, opening October 3, 1979—the program cover quoted *Hamlet:* "A hit! a very palpable hit!" But Stoppard's is a verbal duel, or duet.

The *Daily News,* calling Stoppard "a screwball," added: "He depends upon a dazzling technical command of language and flights of absurdist humor to carry off his theatrical impostures." For instance, when the platform stage is being built, to the cries "Plank! ... Block! ... Slab! ... Cube!" different shapes are handed out; but we are not to assume that's what the words mean. For if the actors know in advance which pieces to pass along, the words might mean "Ready ... O.K.... Next ... Thank you." Knowy no-he, Stoppard springs from the Humpty Dumpty remarks in *Alice through the Looking-Glass,* "When I use a word it means just what I want it to mean.... The question is, which is to be master—that's all." Stoppard asserts the mastery. The boy playing Ophelia wears an obviously ill-fitting blond wig. Shakespeare would not have called it ill-fitting to travesty his plays. They should, however, aspire toward his quality.

These trivialities aside, let me roundabout approach my final words on *Macbeth.* In his widely read and recorded monologue from the works, *The Ages of Man,* John Gielgud was led by his editor into one error, when he calls his author cynical, quoting Sonnet 130:

> *My mistress' eyes are nothing like the sun;*
> *Coral is far more red than her lips' red*
> *If snow be white, why then her breasts are dun....*

Shakespeare was being, not cynical, but sarcastic; he was quietly mocking the poetasters who pile hyperbole upon exaggeration for their fair lady's favor. For his sonnet ends:

> *And yet, by heaven, I think my love as rare*
> *As any she belied with false compare*

Similarly, the absurdists are in error who seek support by quoting "Life is a tale told by an idiot, full of sound and fury, signifying nothing." They are, of course, quoting not Shakespeare but Macbeth. And they are quoting Macbeth only in a moment's dash of despair. For when he is pressed, despite despair, despite the supernatural forces—the "moving" wood, the man "not born of woman"—he goes down not with a whimper but with a bang. He holds high the shield of his insuperable self, his still held manliness, the one thing death can destroy but may not humble. In the face of inevitable disaster he remains the captain of his soul. And this is why *Macbeth* is not merely a drama of bloody revenge, not merely the melodramatic story of a villain who gets his just deserts, but that ineffably higher form we call a tragedy.

There is perhaps one higher form of tragedy, hinted at in Shakespeare's picture of Coriolanus, but not at the core of any of his plays: the action of a free man, conscious of his choice, holding steadfast to what he believes is right although he knows it means his doom. Not, for instance, of the scientist Galileo, who publicly recants—and privately murmurs: "Still, it moves."—but rather, of the peasant girl Joan of Arc, who refuses to deny her voices and, frightened but firm, goes to the fire. Many a man is a martyr *jusqu'au feu:* up to the flames; the tragic figure walks steadfast to the end. Such a person justifies not merely tragic drama, but human life.

KING LEAR   *William Shakespeare*

Drawn from the *Chronicles* of Holinshed, *King Lear* (1605) tells a well-known story; Shakespeare was the first to give it an unhappy ending. His play is his richest study of the relation between the generations, the favorite theme of the ancient dramatists, here pointed in Lear's exclamation: "How sharper than a serpent's tooth it is to have a thankless child!" Henry V heeds his father's wish that he take up arms against France. Hamlet hesitates to obey his father and is lost. Desdemona rebels against her father's will. Cordelia alone maintains both full filial love and spiritual freedom. Like Desdemona's, her words before she dies breathe understanding love, save that Desdemona thinks of her husband Othello, while Cordelia cries to her father Lear that he has "no cause, no cause" for self-blame. In Shakespeare's plays of parent and child other than *King Lear,* however, the emphasis, as their titles show, is on the younger generation. We watch in Prince Hal's growth the way by which a man becomes a king. Cordelia is briefly, though brightly, shown; we watch in Lear the way in which a king becomes a man.

Through Lear's actions, more deeply, the play presses the problem of authority, the maintenance of one's personal standards and proper place. As through the man Hamlet we see into the inner life of all men, so through Lear we see a man's life in relation to all. And since Lear is a king, the whole range of order in the universe hangs on his right rule: with his relinquishment, the family is disrupted, then the kingdom, then civilization (decency), then the soul (sanity itself). Caught into this whirl is the problem of human responsibility, of a man's obligation to assume and maintain the order and the station to which he is called. Man's passage along his years is a growth to mature tasks, mature responsibilities, until, the new seeds scattered, the plant falls. And the safety of all hangs upon each man's assumption of his proper tasks.

Lines of the play contrast two basic attitudes toward responsibility: "As flies to wanton boys are we to the gods: They kill us for their sport"—and the sobering thought: "The gods are just, and of our pleasant vices make instruments to plague us." The second is hammered home in the mocking words: "An admirable evasion of whoremaster man, to lay his goatish disposition to the charge of a star!"

Lear moves, as S. L. Bethell emphasized in *Shakespeare and the Popular Dramatic Tradition* (1944), to a "gradual enlightenment of spiritual blindness." And "as Lear unbuttons and casts off his lendings, so Shakespeare strips him of the accidents of personality, so that only universal humanity remains." Sight is a symbol running through the drama. Goneril declares that she loves her father "dearer than eyesight." When Lear disinherits Cordelia and banishes Kent, that worthy noble cries "See better, Lear!" Gloster, who with his good son Edgar and his villainous bastard Edmund

piteously parallels Lear's own more tragic case, is physically blinded—
"Pluck out his eyes!" orders Goneril—even as Lear is spiritually blind. The
play is a study in spiritual darkness and light. Behind this growth to
enlightenment spreads an even more general opposition. Nature is strong in
the play: wild nature in the stress of the storm on the heath; animal nature
in the vivid imagery of the speech; and pagan nature fronting the Christian
attitude toward the world. Religion appears in many forms, from Kent's
superstition to Gloster's piety; its teachings grow manifest in Poor Tom,
whom the Elizabethans would have recognized as "o' Bedlam," as they
watched "the mystery of suffering laid bare to an ancient king by the
contemporary village lunatic." From this point of view, Cordelia takes her
place as the Christian good: she echoes Christ's words—"O dear father, it is
thy business that I go about" (Act IV, iv, 23; see St. Luke II, 49)—and she
stands as the goal of Lear's purgatorial struggle. Only through suffering
come true understanding, deep love, and lasting peace. The play, however,
eschews Christian terminology; it is set in a pagan environment, and
heaven is invoked as a pagan deity, or referred to as a part of nature. The
play is rooted in nature, its piety is natural. *King Lear* is a play of maturity,
moving toward death; no person in it is parent of a young child; no allusion
nor reference brings childhood to the mind. The weight and the woe of age
lie on the drama.

The title role has lured the greatest actors, containing a variety of moods
that serves as a high challenge. The fond pride of the aged king—succumbing to the flattery of his daughters Goneril and Regan, so that he divides
the kingdom between them, rejecting the true love of his youngest daughter
Cordelia when she scorns to play the sycophant—must journey through
humiliation as the daughters drive him forth, through the dignity yet
heart-rending pathos of his mad movements with the Fool on the wild
heath, to a final recapture of sanity that breaks, and breaks the heart, with
the simple tenderness and poignancy of the death of Cordelia and of Lear.
Through the play, said Swinburne, "we look upward and downward, and in
vain, into the deepest things of nature, into the highest things of Providence; to the roots of life, and to the stars; from the roots that no God waters
to the stars that give no man light; over a world full of death and life
without resting-place or guidance. . . . Here is no need of the Eumenides,
children of Night everlasting; for here is very Night herself." Hazlitt said
Lear is the best of all Shakespeare's plays;" Shelley called it "the most
perfect specimen of the dramatic art existing in the world." C. E. M. Joad in
Decadence (1949) suggested that "*King Lear* is superior as a play to
Hamlet, precisely because in *Lear* a cosmic theme, man in revolt against
the moral law of the universe and incurring the wrath of the angry gods, is
substituted for the rather squalid drama of purely human relations." Basic
moral law, and the conflict of the generations, are of course present in
Hamlet as well; the difference is that Hamlet has his problems thrust upon
him; Lear's own nature creates his problems for himself.

So tremendous is the burden that the play puts upon actor and audience
alike, that many have felt *King Lear* cannot be fitly acted. James Agate has
listed the qualities a Lear must convey: "First, majesty. Second, that quality which Blake would have recognized as moral grandeur. Third, mind.
Fourth, he must be a man and, what is more, a king, in ruins. There must
be enough voice to dominate the thunder, and yet it must be a spent voice."
Lamb, in 1810, was blunt: "To see Lear acted, to see an old man tottering
about the stage with a walking stick, turned out of doors by his daughters in

a raining night, has nothing in it but what is painful and disgusting." Henry James in 1883 reiterated this position: *"Lear"* is a great and terrible poem—the most sublime, possibly, of all dramatic poems; but it is not, to my conception, a play, in the sense in which a play is a production that gains from being presented to our senses. . . . I cannot speak of a representation of *King Lear* without protesting primarily against the play's being acted at all."

Nevertheless the play has been frequently performed. It was shown to James I, at court, on St. Stephen's day in 1606. In 1681 Nahum Tate wrote a version with love scenes between Edgar and Cordelia, with the Fool omitted, the language Tatified, and Lear restored to his throne. Most eighteenth century productions continued the happy ending, which was occasionally used by David Garrick. Edmund Kean, about 1815, restored the tragic close, but after three performances had to revert to the happy ending. It was not until 1838 that the original play was revived, by William Macready. The Macready production at Drury Lane achieved startling effects with the first use of limelight in the theatre. The title role has been essayed also by Phelps, Wallack, Kemble, Irving, Salvini, the Booths, the younger Keans, and Forrest. In 1892 Jacob Gordin wrote a *Jewish King Lear* in Yiddish, transposing the theme from a king's court to the home of a rabbi. In 1930 Fritz Leiber presented Shakespeare's play in New York. It was presented in London and at Stratford in 1936. In New York in 1940 Erwin Piscator made an "epic theatre" production, strengthening the play's lesson for our time with inserted words of World War II refugees, and a final speech borrowed from *Troilus and Cressida.** In 1947, Donald Wolfit opened his New York season with *King Lear,* and Louis Calhern played Lear in New York in 1950. London saw it again, at the Old Vic, in 1952.

More than with any other of Shakespeare's plays except *Hamlet,* details of performance in *King Lear* have drawn critical attention. Bernard Shaw objected to Irving's waste of time over "the trumpery business" of Kent's tripping the steward. In the midst of the wild storm on the heath, Wallack had Kent place his cloak upon Lear's shoulders; Salvini as Lear put his own cloak upon the shivering Fool. Oscar Wilde praised the sensitivity of Salvini's conceptions, especially when, to test the dying Cordelia's condition, he took from Kent's cap the feather he put to Cordelia's lips: "This feather stirs; she lives!"

Critical opinions as to performances have differed greatly. Brooks Atkinson objected to Leiber's 1930 arrangement because it "lops off the story recklessly. *King Lear* is as finely wrought as a piece of architecture in terms of emotions, and you cannot omit the flying buttresses without letting the structure sag." Howard Barnes, however, declared that Leiber "has succeeded brilliantly, in his arrangement, in loosening the sombre tragedy from the dry rot of textbooks and traditional productions." Of Donald Wolfit's work, in London and in New York, opinions differed even more widely. Atkinson called the evening "a carnival of bombast and attitudinizing." However, James Agate declared in the *London Times:* "I say deliberately that his performance was the greatest piece of Shakespearean acting I have seen." Harold Hobson, Agate's successor on the *Times,* after the Old Vic revival of September 24, 1946, recalled Irving's entrance—"Coming down a flight of stairs, he leaned on a huge scabbarded sword which he raised with a wild cry in answer to the shouted greeting of the guards"—then spoke with even greater praise of Laurence Olivier as Lear, referring to his performance as "among the greatest things ever accomplished upon the English stage." Even a poor performance cannot disguise the grandeur, the gloomy magnificence, that strikes to the heart of human nature, and to the hearts of the audience, with *King Lear*.

The American poet Eugene Field, during his journalistic years, forever marked the career of Creston Clarke, who had essayed the role of Lear, with the declaration that "he played the king as though under the apprehension that someone was about to play the ace." Yet he was loudly trumped at the playwright's hometown in 1982; there at Stratford-upon-Avon the RSC set Michael Gambon as Lear, Anton Sher as the Fool, against a dominating gray block of a building until Lear is cast out of his daughters' houses, to rove through a shadowy wasteland. For, on the next night, the audience is assailed with Edward Bond's play, *Lear,* with rifles and modern technology, such as the machine to remove Lear's—not Gloucester's—eyes. Lear has built a wall to protect his territories, but moves from tyrant to madman to pacifist; and he dies trying to destroy the wall. It is rebuilt by the revolutionaries, led by Cordelia (a sort of female Stalin; she has married the pig-boy who had earlier sheltered Lear). All government, we should see, is sadistic and oppressive; it should be replaced by a "rustic, anarchistic community, free of strife, cupidity, and ambition."

The 1984 Ingmar Bergman production of *King Lear* in Stockholm ended with Edgar and Albany with drawn swords, setting an endless struggle for power in place of Shakespeare's usual ending of peace and order.

Of Shakespeare's play, A. C. Bradley comments cogently on the words of the dying Lear before the dead Cordelia: "Lear's five-times repeated 'Never,' in which the simplest and most unutterable cry of anguish rises note by note till the heart breaks, is romantic in its naturalism; and to make a verse out of this one word required the boldness as well as the inspiration which came infallibly to Shakespeare at the greatest moments. But the familiarity, the boldness and inspiration are surpassed (if that can be) by the next line, which shows the bodily oppression asking for bodily relief. Where else are we to seek the imagination that could venture to follow that cry of 'Never' with such a phrase as 'Pray you, undo this button,' and yet could leave us on the topmost peaks of poetry?"

TIMON OF ATHENS   *William Shakespeare*

Based upon North's version of *Plutarch's Lives,* this play, possibly written in 1605, is the tragedy of the honest, trusting man who looks for equal honesty and generosity in his fair-weather friends. Having lavished his fortune on his friends, Timon turns bitter when they desert him. He then invites his former guests to a last banquet at which he scornfully serves them warm water—and goes to live in seclusion in the woods. Word that he has found gold draws visitors again, but the dying Timon curses all the Athenians—while young Alcibiades breathes hope of better days in the city.

In 1678 Thomas Shadwell added love interest to the story, declaring in his Preface, "I can truly say I have made it into a play." More interesting are the thoughts implicit in the story or given cogent expression in the verse. Samuel Johnson observed that "the catastrophe affords a very powerful warning against that ostentatious liberty which sanctions bounty, but confers no benefits, and buys flattery but not friendship." Johnson possibly had in mind his own experiences; his letter to the Earl of Chesterfield helped destroy the old system of literary patronage. *Timon of Athens* reached the height of its popularity in this age of patrons, with its theme of the patron betrayed.

In the nineteenth century, the play was used mainly as a vehicle for such stars as Kean, Phelps, and Macready, but the twentieth century finds present pertinence in the bitter attack on materialism in Timon's arraignment of Athens; in the program of the 1940 production (in modern dress) at Yale University, Allardyce Nicoll stated that "among Shakespeare's plays, *Timon* addresses our own age as directly as any." The play was performed at Stratford in 1928; in London in 1935; in Pasadena in 1936. The satire rather than the tragedy of the play was emphasized in a production, vividly directed by Tyrone Guthrie, that opened at London's Old Vic in May 1952.

Timon is one of the few plays, according to Hazlitt, in which Shakespeare "seems in earnest throughout, never to trifle nor go out of his way. He does not relax in his efforts nor lose sight of the unity of his design. It is the only play of our author in which spleen is the predominant feeling of the mind. It is as much a satire as a play: and contains some of the finest pieces of invective possible to be conceived, both in the snarling, captious answers of the cynic Apemantus, and in the impassioned and terrible imprecations of Timon." On the level of history instead of poetry, *Timon* is even more vehement against ingratitude than *King Lear*.* The two plays are alike in the condemnation of flattery, the frequent curses, and the animal imagery, as when Timon addresses his fair-weather friends. They both press the thought that misery leads to enlightenment and (like most of Shakespeare's and the Greek tragedies, but unlike those of Ibsen*) they end with the promise of peace. Throughout *Timon,* however, there is irony (as when Timon's bitter sincerity makes the thieves talk of reform) and there is deep intensity.

Indeed, the play is usually enacted with bursts of passion. Of Edmund Kean's performance, in 1816, at the words "Tear me, take all, and the gods fall upon you!", the *Theatrical Inquisitor* declared, "Mr. Kean gazed at the bloodhounds who were preying upon his existence, tore open his vest to enforce the offer he had urged, and at length broke from the clamours his distraction could not silence, with an imprecation of tremendous horror on the throng that assailed him." The *Examiner* stressed the brighter vision at the close: "While the squalid misanthrope still maintains his posture and keeps his back to the strangers, in steps the young and splendid Alcibiades in the flush of victorious expectation. It is the encounter of hope with despair." On "life's uncertain voyage," the journey of Timon is one whose vicissitudes we today well may ponder.

"Timon, in love or hate," said G. Wilson Knight, "bears truly a heart of gold. He is a thing apart, a choice soul crucified. . . . The profoundest problems of racial destiny are here symbolized and fought out. In no other play is there a more forceful, a more irresistible, mastery of technique—almost crude in its massive, architectural effects—employed. But then no play is so massive, so rough-hewn into Atlantean shapes from the mountain rock of the poet's mind or soul, as this of Timon."

Some critics, including Edmund Chambers and Ivor Brown, suggest that Shakespeare wrote *Timon* "under conditions of mental and perhaps bodily stress," on the brink of a breakdown.

ANTONY AND CLEOPATRA   *William Shakespeare*

Although "nothing much greater than *Antony and Cleopatra* has ever been written," as Louis Kronenberger has asserted, this play has not been generally popular. Dryden's version of the story, *All For Love; or, The World Well Lost,* 1678, is one valid play among all the attempts to improve Shakespeare, took its place for almost a century and a half. In 1818, Coleridge tried to restore the values: "Of all Shakespeare's historical plays, *Antony and Cleopatra* is by far the most wonderful. There is not one in which he has followed history more minutely, and yet there are few in which he impresses the notion of angelic strength so much. . . . This is greatly owing to the manner in which the fiery force is sustained throughout, and to the numerous momentary flashes of nature counteracting the historical abstraction . . . And if you would feel the judgment as well as the genius of Shakespeare in your heart's core, compare this astonishing drama with Dryden's *All For Love*." Even after this, the play had but occasional revivals. When it was produced in 1897, with Louis Calvert and Janet Achurch, Bernard Shaw said: Strip any passage "of that beauty of sound, by prosaic paraphrase, and you have nothing left but a platitude that even an American professor of ethics would blush to offer to his disciples."

Shaw wrote to me that in his battle against bardolatry he deliberately overstressed his case. There is, in truth, a tremendous conflict in this drama, pointed by imagery of a colossal scale. On the surface the opposition is Egypt and Rome, empire and love: Antony has to choose. But within Cleopatra shine the Egyptian traits; from Octavius Caesar the Roman values frown. They present opposed attitudes toward the universe: love versus duty; generosity versus prudence; indulgence versus restraint; emotion versus reason; impracticality versus worldly wisdom; spontaneous impulse versus common sense. In Cleopatra burn the hidden energies of life; her qualities affirm, those of Rome deny. The good life, even in some measure the Christian good life, is built upon her values. Antony chooses her path, returning to her "from the world's great snare uncaught." Theirs is the right choice—save that they sin through very excess of virtue. Excess, exclusiveness, of love becomes self-love. Hence comes their defeat on earth— but heavenly triumph; for through defeat they lose their weight of self. Shakespeare accepts suicide only in his Roman plays; in them, it is the fullest sacrifice of self. Through this final deed, Roman fortitude blends with Egyptian sensitivity and love. And Antony, who had made "his will Lord of his reason," becomes a full man in his decisive choice.

The facts of the play (1607?) are drawn from North's *Plutarch's Lives*. Several critics have deemed it loosely constructed; thus Samuel Johnson declared it "without any art of connection or care of disposition." Viewed in the light of its major conflict, however, the play, as S. L. Bethell stated in *Shakespeare and the Popular Dramatic Tradition* (1944), is "seen to be a careful pattern of interwoven and contrasting episodes, all duly subordinate to the main design." That design takes glowing shape in the amorous queen. There is naturally much appealing to an actress in this story of the Queen of the Nile whose love so held a Roman that he idled away the Empire in her arms. Wooed back to Rome and wed to Octavius Caesar's sister, Antony still found the silken chains of love too strong. He went again to Egypt and Cleopatra; there, defeated by the Romans, he killed himself. Rather than march a slave in Caesar's triumph, Cleopatra—here at last a resolute monarch—gave suck to an asp and died. The woman's role in the play is as important as the man's. This is true, among Shakespeare's tragedies, only of his love dramas, which mark the equality in their titles. Lady Macbeth, save for the sleep-walking scene that precedes her death, drops from *Macbeth** after the third act; Antony dies in the fourth act, leaving the final act wholly to the Queen.

Of the 42 scenes in the play, many are vividly dramatic. Among these is the meeting of Pompey and the triumvirate, Antony, Lepidus, and Octavius Caesar, on Pompey's galley off Misenum, a bitter mockery of temporal power, as we watch the three drunken men that rule the world. All three, in truth, are more deeply drunken—Lepidus with self-importance, Octavius with lust for power, Antony with infatuation—until sober resolution in extremity clears the mind and illuminates the spirit.

Antony's gentle dealing with his friend Enobarbus, who deserted him after the defeat at Actium, and Enobarbus' consequent remorse and suicide, give further touch of nobility to the decay. The drama is a rich tapestry of magnificence luxuriating to its ruin. There is wide opportunity for scenic splendor; but, most of all, for variety of mood and surging passion in Cleopatra's part. Emotional actresses have therefore been especially drawn to the role. When Lily Langtry essayed the part in 1890, the *Saturday Review* attacked her break with tradition, in that Cleopatra did not lie on a couch for her death scene, as Enobarbus pictures her on the barge when she first met Antony. The *Athenaeum,* however, deemed it a sound innovation to have her seated on the throne; "The aspect of the queen, motionless and erect in her robes, with her handmaids prostrate and dying before her, is superb." In a nineteenth century French production, elaborately staged, a mechanical asp was introduced, which before biting Cleopatra raised its head and hissed. The critic Francisque Sarcey commented: "I agree with the asp."

The final scenes of the play, whatever the vicissitudes of production, are a proud surge of beauty. The earliest meeting of Antony and Cleopatra, as described by Enobarbus, was a magnificent display, a triumph of the senses: "The barge she sat in, like a burnisht throne, Burnt on the water; the poop was beaten gold."

The final meeting of the two lovers, and the movement toward Cleopatra's death, show the triumph of the spirit. The Egyptian sensuality, the pride and passion, in the face of disaster have deepened to steadfast love. Cleopatra faints when Antony dies; her first words on recovering reveal that the vainglorious queen has become "no more but e'en a woman;" yet her resolution is manifest when the dying Antony admonishes her to seek of Caesar her honor with her safety. "They do not go together," she replies, and all her words and actions thereafter prove that Cleopatra has moved through humility to humanity, and to the nobler resources of the spirit. The whole movement, as Harold C. Goddard summed it up in *The Meaning of Shakespeare* (1951), is "one of the supreme things in Shakespeare. The atmosphere of sunset—which Charmian's single phrase, "O eastern star!" turns into sunrise—the universal character of every image and symbol, and above all perhaps the sublimity of the verse, conspire with the action itself to produce this alchemic effect. Here, if ever, is the harmony that mitigates tragedy, the harmony, better say, that creates it."

Little wonder that actresses have been eager to play the part! Or that the reviewers have disagreed, over almost every performance: Helen Modjeska in 1889; Sothern and Marlowe, 1909; Jane Cowl and Rollo Peters, 1924; Tallulah Bankhead and Conway Tearle, with music by Virgil Thompson, 1937; Katharine Cornell and Godfrey Tearle, 1947. Jane Cowl was most favored. John Corbin praised her capture of "the infinite variety of this marvel of courtesans, this mistress of all that is mentally intoxicating, all that is spiritually baleful in feminine allure." Heywood Broun declared that "nothing could be better for the tired business man." The performance was really better than the reviewers, and caught the deeper values of the play.

Tallulah Bankhead fared the worst. John Mason Brown led off with the caustic remark: "Tallulah Bankhead as Cleopatra barged down the Nile last night—and sank." Yet, the *Brooklyn Eagle* declared: "Tallulah took the old script and went to town with it. . . . She lifts a rather doll-like character out of a wallow of sentiment and makes her a vital, passionate woman." Katharine Cornell's less tumultuous Cleopatra was less violently received. Robert Coleman called it "superlative . . . the only satisfactory production we've seen in our time." Brooks Atkinson observed: "Apart from being a queen, Cleopatra is also the world's most celebrated coquette, sensual as well as capricious. As a poet Shakespeare admires her, but as a man he knows she is a royal slut. The qualities of character we esteem in Miss Cornell are not those of 'the Egyptian dish' that has drugged Marc Antony's will to action. That is the basic weakness of this beautifully caparisoned performance." Opening in London, May 11, 1951, Laurence Olivier and Vivien Leigh presented *Antony and Cleopatra* on alternate nights with Shaw's *Caesar and Cleopatra*;* they brought the two plays to New York on December 12, 1951, the Shakespeare play receiving its most distinguished production of our generation.

Cleopatra will continue to lure great actresses to this drama of the conflict between love and empire. The struggle the play presents on its kingly height is far from unfamiliar on the level of homely hearths. But in *Antony and Cleopatra* the conflict between duty and desire glows with the radiance of the setting sun, through the passionate spirits of a man that might have ruled the world, and of a queen that learned to be a steadfast woman.

London in 1973 saw two contrasted performances. At the Bankside Globe, Tony Richardson directed Julian Glover and Vanessa Redgrave in modern clothes and ridicule; John Walker (*Herald-Tribune* August 18, 1973) said: "Cleopatra is a puritan gone off the rails and pretending, not very successfully, to be a tart. With her carroty red hair, her cheap gypsy clothes like a fairground fortune-teller, her cigarette ever dangling from the corner of her mouth, she is a shrill, shrewish, silly woman who throws Coke bottles at messengers and collapses drunkenly in public. . . . They appear to ignore the poetry in the hope that it will go away."

With the RSC at Stratford in 1972, the London Aldwych in 1973, Trevor Nunn for the first time directed Shakespeare's Roman plays in juxtaposition: *Coriolanus; Julius Caesar; Antony and Cleopatra; Titus Andronicus.* His fateful pair were played by Janet Sugman and Richard Johnson, with respect. They give substance to the comment of John Masefield, on Cleopatra's words as she fondles the asp after Charmian's cry "Oh eastern star!"—

> Peace, peace:
> Dost thou not see my baby at my breast,
> That sucks the Nurse asleep?

—calling them "among the most beautiful things ever written by man."

Georg Brandes compared the swarthy Cleopatra with the "dark lady" of the Sonnets, concluding: "Now he was a maturer man, a gentleman, a landed proprietor and tithe-holder; but in him still lived the artist Bohemian fitted to mate with the gypsy Queen."

CORIOLANUS   *William Shakespeare*

The tragic satire of *Coriolanus,* 1607?, based on North's *Plutarch's Lives,* presents Shakespeare's most advanced political thinking. The Renaissance was marked by an increasing assertion of the importance of the individual; more and more the "common man" was thrusting himself into public affairs, demanding that his needs and his desires be taken into account. It was natural that such an urge be pictured in the drama; and there was apt parallel to the current trend in the power of the tribunes of the people, and the custom of the candidates for consul to submit themselves to the plebs, in ancient Rome. Thus the Roman general Caius Marius—for his victory at Corioli surnamed Coriolanus—when selected as consul by the Senate, has to come before the plebs. The people resent his pride and, incited by the tribunes, effect his banishment. In his rage Coriolanus cries "I banish you!" He allies himself with the Volscians, headed by Tullus Aufidius, and they march triumphantly against Rome. Outside that city, his family's pleas move Coriolanus to relinquish the war and, as he expects, he falls by the swords of Aufidius's followers.

The play moves at a swift pace; it was written with fierce rapidities of speech, especially as Coriolanus pours forth his scorn upon the people. Some critics have read from this play a similar scorn on the part of the author. Thus Hardin Craig, thinking that he was defending Shakespeare, said that he "did not hate the common people, but he did apparently think them unfit to rule the state." This puts Coriolanus' conception of the people into Shakespeare's heart—overlooking that the point of the play is that Coriolanus is at fault. Successful in the field as he may be, and well-meaning in the peaceful state, he has a stiff-necked pride that refuses even to try to understand the people among whom he must dwell, and for whom as consul he proposes to rule. The pride of the aristocrat must learn humility. At first, Coriolanus' mother, Volumnia, prods him on the warlike way; later, she, and especially his wife Virgilia, help him to a final acceptance of the spiritual path—an end approached in others of the later plays of Shakespeare, *Antony and Cleopatra* * and *King Lear,* * but not in *Hamlet.* * Coriolanus turns from vengeance, knowing that his choice leads to death.

The political attitude is analyzed by Hazlitt: "The arguments for and against aristocracy or democracy, on the privilege of the few and the claims of the many, on liberty and slavery, power and the abuse of it, peace and war, are here very ably handled, with the spirit of a poet and the acuteness of a philosopher." Where did Shakespeare stand? "The language of poetry naturally falls in with the language of power. . . . The principle of poetry is an anti-leveling principle. It aims at effect, it exists by contrast. It admits of no medium. It is everything by excess. . . . It puts the individual for the species, the one above the infinite many, might before right. . . . We feel some concern for the poor citizens of Rome when they meet together to compare their wants and grievances, till Coriolanus comes in and with blows and big words drives this set of 'poor rats,' this rascal scum, to their homes and beggary before him. . . . Our admiration of his prowess is immediately converted into contempt for their pusillanimity. The love of power in ourselves and the admiration of it in others are both natural to man: the one makes him a tyrant; the other, a slave . . . Coriolanus complains of the fickleness of the people; yet, the instant he cannot gratify his pride and obstinacy at their expense, he turns his arms against his country. . . . He scoffs at their tribunes for maintaining their rights and franchises: 'Mark

you his absolute *shall?*' not marking his own absolute *will* to take everything from them—his impatience at the slightest opposition to his own
pretensions being in proportion to their arrogance and absurdity." Thus,
though he may seem to attack the people, Shakespeare makes even stronger
case against their would-be master. While there is considerable railing
against the mob in Shakespeare's plays, they abound, as Harold C. Goddard
remarked in *The Meaning of Shakespeare* (1951), in "little touches that
reveal an almost Wordsworthian faith in the existence of nobility and
wisdom in obscurity." Shakespeare does not stress these, but leaves them
incidental, as in life itself. In his plays, the number of upright and independent commoners is exceeded only by the number of rascally or ridiculous
gentlemen. But value lies in the individual, not in the mass.

After the close of the theatres in 1642, London did not see the play for
forty years. Versions by Nahum Tate, 1681, and John Dennis, 1719, were not
popular. James Thomson in 1749 wrote a stately rhetorical version that was
fused with Shakespeare's until the nineteenth century, as by John Philip
Kemble in 1789, 1806, and 1811. Shakespeare's play was performed in
London, and in Philadelphia by Jefferson, in 1813; and from the time of
Macready (1819) it has been fairly popular. British performances include
two in 1901, one with F. R. Benson, and one "of grand spectacular display"
with Henry Irving and Ellen Terry, which Irving had been promising since
1879; one in 1916 at the Stratford tercentenary; in 1936 and 1939 again at
Stratford; in 1938, the Old Vic in London with Laurence Olivier and Sybil
Thorndike; and again at Stratford, opening March 13, 1952, with Anthony
Quayle and Mary Ellis. The *London Times* reviewer (April 20, 1938) did not
like the play, declaring: "There is only one thing to do: keep up the pace and
beat the drums."

The first New York performance of the drama was in 1799. Salvini acted
the title part in America in 1885. Coriolanus was the best remembered role
of Thomas Sowerby Hamblin, about 1850; one of the best roles of Edwin
Forrest, in the 1860's. A French production at the Comédie Française in
1934 played to especially crowded houses because, after the February sixth
riots, the French drew a parallel between the play and their own times. In
1937, a condensation by Arthur Hopkins was presented by the Federal
Theatre at Roslyn, Long Island, with the mob rushing up aisles from all
parts of the house. Favorable criticism brought this to New York in February 1938. Richard Watts commented: "The author expresses with considerable enthusiasm his (sic) distaste for the common people, assailing them
for their manners, their odors, their language, and their habiliments, until
there are moments when you are inclined to believe that he must have
called in Mr. Lucius Beebe as collaborator. . . . The poetry of the play seldom rises to the greatest Shakespearean heights, but the drama remains
a work of unquestioned force and power, and was most decidedly worth
reviving."

The power of great acting may be seen even in silent moments, as in the
performance of Mrs. Siddons as Volumnia. The actor Charles Mayne Young
has pictured it: "I remember her coming down the stage in the triumphal
entry of her son, Coriolanus, when her dumb-show drew plaudits that shook
the building. She came, alone, marching and beating time to the music;
rolling from side to side, swelling with the triumph of her son. Such was the
intoxication of joy which flashed from her eye and lit up her whole face, that
the effect was irresistible." There are, thus, varied production opportunities
in *Coriolanus:* mob scenes, individual moments of intensity; and closing

spectacle. Forrest, for instance, in 1863, ended with an imposing funeral pyre for the body of Coriolanus. In the 1838 Macready production, warriors raised the dead body of the conqueror on their shields, draped over it the colorful trophies of war and, trailing their steel pikes in mournful memory, marched slowly up the stage to doleful music. Such an ending, up an inclined road into the distance, was utilized at Fordham University, in a striking 1949 production. Supposedly taking place in the year 2048 (in the "costumes of the time," including atomic rapid-fire guns), this began with the death of Coriolanus. A lecturer explained the play's current pertinence; then we watched the movements of the conflict between the insistent people and the unbending leader, until the common soldiers bore away the corpse of the general. The play seemed equally timely when presented over television, June 11, 1951, with Richard Greene and Judith Evelyn.

"The beast with many heads butts me away," says Coriolanus on his banishment. Today, in many lands, the prowling of this beast gives sharp significance to *Coriolanus*.

PERICLES   *William Shakespeare*

The movement of *Pericles,* 1607?, differs so greatly from that of Shakespeare's other plays as to suggest that it is only in part his work. Some critics put a specific point to his hand's entry: the storm scene in the third act, which opens with Pericles' cry: "Thou god of this great vast, rebuke these surges!" The early portion of the play some scholars attribute to George Wilkins, who did write a prose paraphrase of the story. But in the very first scene of the play Pericles, beholding King Antiochus' daughter, exclaims: "See where she comes, apparell'd like the spring"—and Wilkins was no second Shakespeare, to have written such a line! A more probable suggestion is that, as preserved, the first two acts are from the hand of a poor reporter. There are, incidentally, some 3,500 obvious misprints in the First Folio edition (1623) of Shakespeare's works.

Throughout the play shine noble passages of rich beauty or sound sentiment attuned to the purpose. Instead of tense dramatic conflict there is unfolded on the stage the long course of an adventure tale, in the vein of the popular late Greek and medieval romances. The English poet John Gower told the story in his *Confessio Amantis* (1390); and in *Pericles* Gower speaks the Prologue to each act, and the Epilogue.

Our thoughts travel through many lands and years. First Pericles, Prince of Tyre, discovers that Antiochus' daughter, whom he would wed, is living incestuously with her father. Leaving them, he brings aid to Cleon and his wife Dionyza, rulers of famine-stricken Tarsus. Shipwrecked, Pericles comes to Pentapolis, where in a tourney he wins Thaisa, the lovely daughter of King Simonides. At sea, Thaisa gives birth to a girl they name Marina; but Thaisa remains unconscious, is thought dead, and in a wooden casket is buried at sea. The unhappy Pericles leaves Marina at his friend Cleon's palace. As Marina grows in loveliness, Dionyza in jealousy for her own daughter would have the girl slain; at the brink of death she is snatched by pirates, who sell her to a brothel-bawd in Mytilene. To Pericles, Cleon reports that Marina is dead. But the purity of the girl, as resistant as her beauty is alluring, beats off the attempts upon her chastity in the brothel; she leaves it and lives honestly but humbly until Pericles, passing by, hears her story and recognizes his daughter. Then, in a vision, the goddess Diana bids him visit her temple at Ephesus; in the priestess there he discovers his long-lost wife, Thaisa—who had been rescued from the chest and recovered from her coma—and the marriage of Marina is happily arranged. The movement of these episodes is enlivened by dumb-show and dancing. The situations vary from the gallant assemblies of aristocrats, and the households of honest citizens, to the seashore toil of humble fishermen, and the earthy grubbing of the brothel pander and the bawd. At the play's close, Gower points the moral of the enacted story.

To those troubled by the far-fetched story, it has been suggested that in his last plays Shakespeare subordinates the plot to the dramatic meaning as a whole. They are to be judged not by the credibility of the (often supernatural) events but by the genuineness of the emotions and the significance of the theme. Thus Derek Traversi in *Shakespeare: The Last Phase* (1953) states that in *Pericles* plot exists "as a function of imagery, and imagery, in turn, is directed to the elaboration of a kind of dream in the course of which normal human qualities, detached from their customary attributes and elevated above their usual status, undergo a process of poetic sublimation to become symbols of a moral rebirth." In *King Lear** this awakening comes too late; in the last four comedies. the family division is healed—in every case through a daughter, symbolically named: Marina, Fidele (Imogen), Perdita, Miranda. And the reconciliation companions restoration and moral regeneration. Pericles says of his daughter, "Thou that beget'st him that did thee beget," recognizing the rebirth. In *Cymbeline,** *The Winter's Tale,** and *The Tempest**—out of storm and tempest the new life is born—the moral redemption is likewise manifest, marking the concern of Shakespeare, in his last comedies as well as his great tragedies, with basic problems of harmony and human worth.

Printed in 1609, 1611, 1619, and 1630, the play was a popular stage piece during the Stuart reigns. Thereafter, it was not performed until Samuel Phelps revived it at Sadler's Wells in 1854, in a spectacular production using seven miles of canvas for rolling billows and moving panoramas as the ship glides along the coast toward the temple of Diana at Ephesus. The play was performed at Pasadena in 1936.

In the reading the play gathers power; seeming at first a sort of mythological adventure tale, it grows more intense because it grows more human. The unusual incidents are accompanied by universal emotions; the passions, more closely involved, make the dangers seem more real; and the motives touch closely to the core of human nature—until, without echoing, we can understand the rapturous tones of Swinburne: "What shall I say that may not be too pitifully unworthy of the glories and the beauties, the unsurpassable pathos and sublimity inwoven with the imperial texture of this play? . . . what, above all, shall be said of that storm above all storms ever raised in poetry? . . . Nothing but this, perhaps, that it stands—or rather let me say that it blows and sounds and shines and rings and thunders and lightens as far ahead of all others as the burlesque sea-storm of Rabelais beyond all possible storms of comedy." The roused passions and personal dangers of *Pericles* make perennially pathetic this medieval romance put into poetry and dramatic form.

In London Toby Robertson set the whole play in a brothel, "the complete whorehouse divertissement," said Robert Cushman in the *Observer* (August 26, 1973), "packaged with transvestism and a great deal of snappy music . . . what used to be known as swinging." Robertson also directed the play OffBway (Jean Cocteau Rep.) in 1981.

"Even in the scenes in the brothel at Mytilene," said J. W. Mackail, "the supple elastic prose shows the master hand. . . . The recognition scene in Act V is unsurpassed—one sometimes is inclined to say unequalled—for sheer perfection of beauty in the whole of Shakespeare's work. Speech has become music."

CYMBELINE   *William Shakespeare*

The mood of this play is like the air of an Indian summer, with a low morning haze that lifts over clear, crisp beauty. The play, 1609?, with its challenging incidents, its ringing lines, and its lovely songs was an instant and long-continuing favorite. We are told that, on New Year's day, 1634, it was "well liked by the King." Tom D'Urfey in 1682 rewrote the play as *The Injured Princess; or, The Fatal Wager,* a pathetic version that held the boards until 1720. Other versions were tried in 1755 and 1759. Garrick appeared as Posthumus in 1761 for the then unusual run of sixteen nights. J. P. Kemble in 1785, Charles Kean, Macready in 1818, and Irving in 1896 have also played that part. (When young, Irving appeared as Pisanio; and John Drew as Cloten.) Still more appealing to players has been the role of fair Imogen, acted by Mrs. Siddons in 1787; in New York by Adelaide Neilson in 1880; by Helena Modjeska in 1888 and again in 1892 with Otis Skinner; by Ellen Terry, with Irving in 1896, a "gorgeous production" with sets by Lawrence Alma-Tadema; by Margaret Mather also in the 1890's; Viola Allen in 1906; Julia Marlowe in 1923 with E. H. Sothern.

The story, drawn from Holinshed's *Chronicles* and from Boccaccio, complicated in the telling, is unfolded on the stage with neat simplicity. Cymbeline, King of Britain, wishes his daughter Imogen to marry his stepson Cloten. Posthumus Leonatus, who is already secretly married to Imogen, flees to Italy—where Iachimo ("little Iago") wagers he will succeed in seducing Imogen. Held off by her purity, by a trick he convinces Posthumus that Imogen has yielded, whereupon Posthumus arranges to have her killed. Imogen, warned by servant Pisanio, flees in disguise. After many adventures—meeting her two brothers, who had been stolen and supposedly killed in infancy; drugged in a cave to awaken beside the headless body of Cloten dressed in the clothes of Posthumus, so that she thinks her husband dead; serving as a page to the Roman commander come to collect tribute, who is routing the defiant British when "a narrow lane, an old man, and two boys" turn the tide of battle—Imogen is brought among the Roman prisoners to Cymbeline's court. In the play's final scene, twenty-three separate steps of revelation unravel the tangled threads, restore his children to Cymbeline, and reunite Posthumus and Imogen. Beneath the events of the play we can discern that the battle between lust and purity, and the battle between tyranny and freedom, are basically one conflict.

Thoughts on other phases of life may be found in the drama. When Posthumus, thinking he has killed Imogen, doffs his Italian finery for a British peasant's garb, we may see in symbol the best impulse of the Reformation sloughing the excesses of the Renaissance. And with the two young princes—repeated with Perdita in *The Winter's Tale** and with Miranda in *The Tempest**—we find a prime pattern for education: good blood, unaware of its heritage, brought close to nature but reared in love by a person of civilized wisdom.

Desite its poetry and its thought, *Cymbeline* has been attacked. Samuel Johnson prosaically declared: "To remark the folly of the fiction, the absurdity of the conduct . . . and the impossibility of the events in any system of life, were to waste criticism upon unresisting imbecility, upon faults too evident for detection;, and too gross for exaggeration."

Alan Dale stated: "There is no other heroine in the Shakespearean repertoire as charming and as rational as Imogen, and it is difficult to understand why we seem to prefer the lunacy of Juliet, the imbecility of Ophelia, the farcicality of Katherine, the heroics of Lady Macbeth, the flippancy of Beatrice, or the moonshine of Rosalind. Imogen is infinitely superior.

Even Bernard Shaw succumbed to Imogen. "Pray understand that I do not defend *Cymbeline*. It is for the most part stagey trash of the lowest melodramatic order. . . . But I am bound to add that I pity the man who cannot enjoy Shakespeare . . . the Imogen of his genius, an enchanting person of the most delicate sensitiveness . . ." Shaw, in correspondence with Ellen Terry, suggested the device of having blood on the flowers that are strewn over Cloten's body beside the waking Imogen; but he stressed Imogen's horror at finding this headless man, rather than her agony a moment later when she recognizes on the body the clothing of her own husband, which Cloten had donned in his scheme to ravish her. Shaw, in fact, declaring that "*Cymbeline*, though one of the finest of Shakespeare's later plays now on the stage, goes to pieces in the last act," himself joined the long line of would-be improvers of Shakespeare by writing a new fifth act for the play, which was presented in London in 1937. Shaw's post-Ibsenic conclusion makes the two sons of Cymbeline refuse the new royal life offered them, in favor of their country simplicity, and makes Imogen resent the supposedly "happy ending" that restores her to her husband who had wanted to kill her. In spite of Shaw's claim that he stands "in the same relation to Shakespeare as Mozart to Handel, or Wagner to Beethoven," his rearrangement—setting twentieth century attitudes on a sixteenth century mood—tumbles him awkwardly from Shakespeare's shoulders. In the fifth act of the original play, after the vision of his ancestors that Posthumus has in gaol (which Shaw omits), with Jupiter mounted on an eagle descending in thunder and lightning to foretell the happy end, Shakespeare at once provides contrast in the gaolers gloating over the condemned Posthumus; and by swiftly succeeding shifts of fortune he holds interest in the fate of the characters. Although the story may have lost flavor of reality since Boccaccio told it, the characters move truly and are truly moving. Those that think they have improved on Shakespeare are usually mistaken.

The sense of gentle sadness, of calm autumnal movement toward the Reaper's scythe, behind which is a harbor of grace abounding, rests as a peaceful cloud over the turbulent stir of *Cymbeline*.

The play was put on in 1978 by fringe director Mike Alfreds, with the cast in white judo suits, and much doubling. The BBC production, shown on U. S. TV just before Christmas 1982, was one of the most highly praised of the series, with Helen Mirren as Imogen. Swinburne earlier declared: "I have always loved this one beyond all the other children of Shakespeare."

THE WINTER'S TALE   *William Shakespeare*

Time has triumphed over Greene's novel *Pandosto; or, The Triumph of Time* (1588), but its story lives on in Shakespeare's *The Winter's Tale*, 1610(?). Despite the unreasoning and unjust jealousy of Leontes, King of Sicilia, and little Mamillius' remark "A sad tale's best for winter," the movement of the story, after its first severities, is kindly and mellow, with country gaiety and revel. King Leontes interprets his queen Hermione's courtesy to their guest, Polixenes, King of Bohemia, as sign of love, and—despite the oracle's declaration that she is pure—he drives her forth. The Queen is given up for dead; her son Mamillius dies of grief; but to the sea-coast of Bohemia ("where there is no sea by near a hundred miles," Ben Jonson chided; but the error is in *Pandosto*) her child the new-born Perdita is brought by old Antigonus. Antigonus is chased away by a bear; a shepherd rescues and rears Perdita. Sixteen years later the charming maid is loved by Florizel, son of King Polixenes, who naturally resents his son's fondness for a shepherd's daughter. Florizel and Perdita therefore flee to Sicilia, where the identity of Perdita is discovered. She is thus restored to her father, Leontes—who, come to view a new-made "statue" of his long-lost wife, finds that the statue breathes, and is indeed Hermione.

Tangled in the story is the light-fingered pedlar and thief Autolycus, a rogue without malice, "a snapper-up of unconsidered trifles," who with his easy ways and merry songs is one of Shakespeare's deftest creations. The plot itself would tax credulity if such things were intended to be believed; but the play's charm lies in its background, its verse, and its pictures of human nature. "For sheer joy in life and breath at the present moment," said Harold C. Goddard in *The Meaning of Shakespeare* (1951), "the fourth act of *The Winter's Tale* is one of Shakespeare's pinnacles . . . a very superfluity of comic and romantic riches." The close, the reappearance of Hermione stepping off the statue pedestal, is one of Shakespeare's few uses of dramatic surprise. (See *Othello.* *)

The wide range of *The Winter's Tale,* in mood, in manner, and in time, has drawn critical objection. Most flagrantly it violates the three dramatic unities (just before *The Tempest,* * which most closely observes them). But this gadding about builds into a unity, as the initial scenes in Sicilia, of friendship breaking through jealousy to violence, pass through the pastoral paradise of Bohemia to the final realization of exalting love on earth.

The play has been quite popular, being performed at court in 1611, 1612, 1624, and 1634. In 1751 Macnamara Morgan wrote a pastoral version, *Florizel and Perdita,* which five years later Garrick revised and in which "foolish, lovely Mary 'Perdita' Robinson was adored." For fifty years this version was frequently performed; then in 1802 John Philip Kemble played Leontes in the Shakespeare play, to his sister Mrs. Siddons' Hermione. Charles Kean in 1856 made a lavish and almost archaeological production of the play, opening with Leontes and his guests reclining on couches "after the manner of the ancient Greeks"; the boy Mamillius (played by the young Ellen Terry) had a toy cart modeled after a terra-cotta cart in the British Museum; and—said *Punch*—the bear that chased Antigonus "was an archaeological copy from the original bear of Noah's ark." In the almost equally lavish production of Herbert Beerbohm Tree in 1906, Ellen Terry played Hermione. Some actresses, for instance Mary Anderson, have doubled in the roles of Hermione and Perdita. The *New York Dramatic Mirror* (Nov. 13, 1888) disliked Mary Anderson's English company, calling the setting of the piece beautiful and the whole representation highly picturesque and interesting, but objecting that the performers "all talk in the thick, choky guttural distinctive of the Cockney second-rate actor. . . . They all murder their lines with a serene insensibility to taste and meaning. . . . Their manner of pronouncing *knowledge no ledge,* for instance, will always seem apocryphal to an orthoepist not trained in an English *co lege.*" Evidently London was sending New York as poor a supporting cast as New York for many years sent with its stars to the rest of the United States!

The English production by Granville-Barker in 1912 helped set a simpler fashion for Shakespearean plays. Though the *London Times* mocked a bit: "The costumes are after Beardsley, and still more after Bakst ... the bizarre smocks and fal-lals of the merry-makers at the sheep-shearing come from the Chelsea Arts Club Ball," it concluded its judgment: "It is very startling and provocative and audacious, and on the whole we like it." The public liked it even more; and the vogue of artful simplicity of production was launched. American revivals include a tour in 1910; a New York production in 1921; the Stratford Company tour in 1931; productions in Pasadena and Chicago in 1937; New York in 1938; Ann Arbor in 1940; and the Theatre Guild production of 1945 with Henry Daniell, Romney Brent, and Florence Reed. George Jean Nathan stated: "Just why the Theatre Guild, in its conceivably somewhat less spacious than infinite wisdom, elected to launch what it has announced as a Shakespearean program with *The Winter's Tale* jilts the critical faculties. . . . The exhibit itself has persisted in being a potential masterpiece hopefully starting on a doomed climb to a slippery mountain peak and ending as a crippled theatrical occasion." Lewis Nichols conversely declared that "on the whole, the trip is successful." Burton Rascoe went further: "In spite of three hundred years of criticism that it is a minor tour de force which doesn't quite come off, this Theatre Guild production of *The Winter's Tale* shows me that it is one of the Bard's great theatrical masterpieces, poignant, lively, entertaining, and beautiful." John Gielgud revived the play in London, opening June 27, 1951; a French production opened in the same month in Paris. The *Christian Science Monitor* of July 14 called the English production "a profound aesthetic experience; Gielgud as Leontes gave the best performance of his distinguished career."

The boy Mamillius, snatched from us while beginning to tell his mother a tale of sprites and goblins—"There was a man dwelt by a churchyard"— lingers in the mind. Swinburne cannot rid himself of thoughts of him: "Even in her daughter's embrace it seems hard if his mother should have utterly forgotten the little voice that had only time to tell her just eight words of that ghost story which neither she nor we were ever to hear ended." As vividly comes Autolycus, crying his "lawn as white as driven snow," traversing the countryside with cheerful song, leading us into a land where heartsease grows, and "daffodils that come before the swallow dares, and take the winds of March with beauty." There is a haunting, perduring beauty in *The Winter's Tale*.

The play was directed in 1948 by Anthony Quayle, with Diana Wynyard and Esmond Knight; its first with RSC was in 1960 with Eric Porter, Elizabeth Sellers, and Peggy Ashcroft; Judi Dench in 1969.

KING HENRY VIII   *William Shakespeare*

The most immediately political of William Shakespeare's plays, bringing the story of England up to the birth of Elizabeth, *King Henry VIII*, 1610?, may have been written in part by John Fletcher; probably, it was dashed off quickly, for a theatrical or political emergency. The Prologue states that this is "no merry bawdy play," but a tale of greatness tumbled from its high estate, as "mightiness meets misery." That Fletcher wrote part of the play (perhaps his was the later revision) is maintained by A. C. Partridge, in *The Problem of "Henry VIII" Reopened* (1949). By the frequency of typical words, grammatical constructions and abbreviations—Fletcher would use 'em and ye; Shakespeare, more often, *them* and *you*—Partridge attributes specific parts of the play to each writer, *e. g.,* Act III, ii, the first 203 lines to Shakespeare, the remaining 257 lines to Fletcher. In addition to these lines, there is general agreement that Shakespeare wrote Act I, i and ii; Act II, iii and iv; and Act V, i. Samuel Johnson remarked that Shakespeare's genius, if not his pen, comes in and goes out with Katharine.

Opening with a description of the Field of the Cloth of Gold (1520) *Henry VIII* progresses, faithfully following Holinshed's *Chronicles,* to the christening of Anne Bullen's daughter, the infant Elizabeth, in 1533. Within that period we watch the ruin of the Duke of Buckingham, the annulment of the marriage of Queen Katharine, and the downfall of Cardinal Wolsey. In Wolsey's place we watch the rise of the "good and great" Thomas Cranmer, Archbishop of Canterbury, author of the *Book of Common Prayer.* Elevated by Henry VIII, Cranmer was the forerunner of Bishop Parker and Lord Burghley; he paved the way for Elizabeth's greatness as in the play, at her baptism, he heralds it. The Tudor rose, planted in conflict and grown through bloody war, came to full blossom in Elizabeth.

The play thus had present pertinence to its first audiences, showing the rise of England's national independence and picturing the fight against the papacy, which was still claiming victims. Productions of the drama were marked by splendor then unusual—set forth, Sir Henry Wotton complained, "with many extraordinary circumstances of pomp and majesty . . . sufficient in truth to make greatness very familiar, if not ridiculous." Wotton's account is of a performance at the Globe Theatre on June 29, 1613, on which occasion the theatre, "filled with people to behold the play," took fire when ordnance ignited the thatched roof, and burned to the ground, though fortunately "nothing did perish but wood and straw." It was rebuilt in 1614 at a cost of £1400.

Henry VIII has had a fairly steady popularity. Samuel Pepys was of two minds about it. In his *Diary* for 1664, he set down: "Saw the so much cried-up play of *Henry VIII;* which, though I went with resolution to like it, is so simple a thing made up of a great many patches, that, besides the shows and procession in it, there is nothing in the world good, or well done." Four years later, however, an entry reads: "to the Duke's Playhouse, and there did see *King Henry VIII,* and was mightily pleased, better than I ever expected, with the history and the shows of it." The acting tradition of the play is continuous; we are told that when Betterton, in 1663, played the king, he was "instructed in it by Sir William (Davenant) who had it from old Mr. Lowen, that had his instructions from Mr. Shakespeare himself." There were over a dozen revivals of the play in the eighteenth century; a production at Drury Lane in 1727 spent the then enormous sum of £1,000 to decorate and costume the procession for the Coronation of Anne Bullen as Queen. In the nineteenth century the play continued popular; Kemble, Kean, Macready, Edwin Booth, Otis Skinner, all put it on; in 1892-1893, to Henry Irving's Wolsey, Ellen Terry was Katharine and Forbes-Robertson was Buckingham. More recently, Beerbohm Tree made an exciting and sumptuous production in New York in 1916, which he considered the greatest success of his career. There was one at Pasadena in 1932; Ann Arbor, 1937; Stratford, 1938; and one with Walter Hampden as Wolsey and Eva Le Gallienne as Katharine, the first production of the American Repertory Theatre, running thirty-nine performances in New York in 1946-1947. This production used two Narrators to speed the action and clarify the history to a modern audience.

Actresses are especially drawn to the part of Queen Katharine, whose demeanor throughout her trial is a noble combination of submissive gentleness and high pride and queenliness; she may be cast off, but cannot be cast down. In the play (though in history she did not die until 1536) she sends her dying blessing to the King. Mrs. Siddons told Samuel Johnson she deemed Katharine the most pleasing of Shakespeare's heroines; and he concurred. Charlotte Cushman, Helena Modjeska, and Fanny Kemble also played the part. The role of Wolsey, in turn, appeals to the actors: Wolsey who worked so faithfully for England, though he raised himself with royal pride to almost kingly state—and strove so zealously for Henry, though his intriguings failed with the Pope's refusal to divorce Katharine, and Wolsey fell. There is a dignity in the Cardinal's behavior as he faces ruin that recaptures the audience's sympathy, as it animates his farewell words. As a neat detail in the production, Charles Kean and Beerbohm Tree, as Wolsey, carried an orange. This marked the Cardinal's fastidious nature; for in Tudor times the segments of the fruit were removed and the skin "filled up again with the part of a sponge, wherein was vinegar and other confections against the pestilent airs," when the Cardinal walked abroad amid the crowd.

Of the two main figures, in the 1946 revival, George Freedley said: "As the ill-treated Queen Katharine, Eva Le Gallienne gives the finest performance of a distinguished career. She is beautiful as well as touchingly tender, majestic, and extremely forceful. . . . Walter Hampden's Wolsey is a revelation of simplicity, restraint and malevolence in a role that could be and frequently has been overplayed." The production, Freedley considered "the handsomest Shakespearean revival in the memory of the oldest inhabitant." "Out of an indifferent play," declared Brooks Atkinson, "the A R T has fashioned a memorable performance and a notable production." George Jean Nathan saw it as appealing only to "resolute students of classical curiosae" (sic); but surely there are many that still find the past pregnant with the future. To these, there is more than splendid pageantry in *King Henry VIII;* there is the spectacle of over-vaulting ambition tumbled to the dust, of perennial passions and plottings, of pride too arrogant and pride in self-respect—human dignity sustained against disaster's tide—caught into rich poetry and vivid drama.

The RSC played it in 1967 and 1983. Shakespeare, said G. Wilson Knight, "thinks poet-wise, drama-wise, through persons or, failing that, ritual and symbol, and has little truck with the abstractions normally current as powers of thought, so here he says nothing of England as a 'nation,' still less of a national 'destiny'; and yet, in working his story, with all its tragic, historic and theological overtones, all its humanity and humour, and all its ritual and crowds, to the culminating ceremonial from which the prophecy flowers—as prophecy should flower from poetry—he has not only defined the indwelling spirit of his nation, but also outlined that greater peace, those 'olives of endless age' whose cause that nation was, and is, to serve; has thus pushed his art up to a proclamation and a heralding, lifting his whole lifework to this point, with cumulative force and authority." With this bow to his late Queen, Shakespeare was preparing to set down his pen.

THE TEMPEST   *William Shakespeare*

Many critics consider Shakespeare's last play, *The Tempest,* 1611 ?, a symbolic autobiography. All sorts of allegories have been found in its lines.

"It shows us," says Richard Garnett, "more than anything else, what the discipline of life had made of Shakespeare at fifty—a fruit too fully matured to hang much longer on the tree." More than anything else, the drama presents a probing of human nature in loveliest poetry.

Samuel Johnson dismissed the play as a mere rippling of the author's fancy: "Of these trifles enough."

Prospero, Duke of Milan, whose "library was dukedom large enough," with his daughter Miranda takes refuge from his brother Antonio's treachery on an island where they live with the help of the air-sprite Ariel and the earthy slave Caliban. When Miranda is a young lady, Prospero uses his book-learned magic powers to summon a tempest (Shakespeare's favorite symbol of tragic conflict) to wreck upon the island Alonso, King of Naples, with his son Ferdinand, Antonio, and others who had connived in the deposing of Prospero. Ariel annoys and perplexes the shipwrecked gentlemen, while Caliban grows drunken with the jester and the butler, Trinculo and Stephano, and plots rebellion against Prospero. Ferdinand, falling in love with Miranda, makes himself her servant. After further exercise of Prospero's magic—in a banquet placed before the newcomers which, even as they reach for the viands, vanishes; and in a wedding pageant and dance of Iris, Juno, Ceres, and nymphs and reapers—Prospero has all the people on the island come together; he reveals his identity, forgives the contrite nobles, and lays his blessing upon his daughter and the prince. "How many goodly creatures are there here!" exclaims Miranda in glad wonder. "O brave new world, That has such people in it!"

The Tempest has been one of the more popular plays of Shakespeare. Dryden and Davenant wrote a version of it in 1667, with numerous new features. This made Prospero guardian of a youth, Hippolyto, who has never seen a maiden, thus balancing Miranda, who has never seen a youth. Miranda has a sweet sister, Dorinda; Caliban has a lecherous sister, Sycorax; and Ariel has a companion spirit, Milcha, for his love. This version was shaped into an opera in 1674 by Thomas Shadwell, and Hippolyto remained on the stage until William Macready brought back Shakespeare's play in 1838. The original play was performed in New York as early as 1773, at the John Street Theatre. It has had frequent revivals throughout the country.

The nineteenth century produced the comedy with magical tricks and spectacular devices. Frank R. Benson, as Caliban, hung head down from the trees with a fish in his mouth. Beerbohm Tree also used the fish. Macready had his Ariel fly about the stage; Charles Kean had Ariel borne on a large bat; at the end of the play, he had a spectacle of the ship's departure, with Ariel watching. Tree used a similar spectacle, but with Caliban looking on "in mute despair." In a Boston production of 1856, Prospero waved his wand: a tree trunk fell, and opened into an armchair for him and Miranda. At another wave of Prospero's wand—with Arnold Daly, in 1897—a sapling shot up, upon which the magician nonchalantly hung his robe. In 1897, Bernard Shaw attacked these stage effects: "The poetry of *The Tempest* is so magical that it would make the scenery of a modern theatre ridiculous." The extravagance, nevertheless, has persisted; George Jean Nathan quoted Shaw and reiterated the point after the New York production of 1945.

In 1928, the play was presented in New York with John Barrymore and Louis Wolheim; in 1941 at the University of Washington; in 1942 at the University of California; in 1944 at Vassar College. The 1945-1946 New

York production showed Arnold Moss as an imposing Prospero, the Czech comedians Jan Werich and George Voskovec overacting as Stephano and Trinculo, the dancer Vera Zorina miscast as Ariel, and the black Canada Lee overly uncouth as Caliban. The Stratford production, opening March 25, 1952, with Ralph Richardson and Margaret Leighton, was more accordant with the play's beauties. In its first season (1955) the playhouse at Stratford, Connecticut, ventured a production of the play.

The 1945 production, despite its inept casting and direction, was cleverly set, according to a plan of Eva Le Gallienne. A central elevation which we first behold as the deck of the storm-tossed vessel, for the rest of the play is used as the top of a high rock, on which, and around its base as it revolves, the remainder of the action occurs. Several of the critics liked even the acting; but Nathan said that it is "strongly recommended as a valuable education in what, at least partly, a production of *The Tempest* should not be." Louis Kronenberger condoned its faults, calling the play "perhaps the hardest to project corporeally" of all of Shakespeare's: "Its beguiling side, its air of poetry and enchantment, almost eludes human presentation; while its baser side, its plot twists and comedy scenes, almost exhausts human patience." Yet he must add that "Zorina is not an effective Ariel, nor Canada Lee an effective Caliban." Robert Garland declared that "Canada Lee, camouflaged as the hideous and unhappy Caliban, looks more like a bush walking than anything else I can think of." The 1916 New York production, with Fania Marinoff as Ariel and Walter Hampden as Caliban, was handled with much more delicacy and deftness of touch. With the text uncut, with an Elizabethan simplicity in the staging, this was a delight to all beholders, and won almost unanimous critical praise. The *Tribune* prophesied that it would undoubtedly be forty years "before theatregoers are again enabled to witness as competent a performance as is that now on view." These words still hold true; but even the over-elaborate production of 1945, with its too posturing Ariel and its too growling and groveling Caliban, found a receptive audience, establishing, indeed, a record run of 100 performances.

Ariel and Caliban have drawn considerable attention, as Shakespeare's fullest non-human figures. Ariel—compounded of the two finer elements, fire and air—fulfills his tasks and finds joy in their doing, but would nevertheless be free of them. Caliban—compounded of the two coarser elements, water and earth—must serve, but hates his labors. Men are made of the four elements and a soul; they can rise higher, and sink lower, than these spirits. The play pictures, in the humans, liberty, love, and wonder, but also their opposites, tyranny and license, hatred and lust, and banality and prodigies. As Ariel shows no human signs of affection or personal loyalty and leaves Prospero without regret or any sense of friendly ties, so Caliban lacks the depravity, the lechery or the greed of the degenerate drunken humans. Hazlitt, who calls Caliban one of Shakespeare's masterpieces, says that his character "grows out of the soil where it is rooted, uncontrolled, uncouth and wild, uncramped by any of the meannesses of custom."

Some of Shakespeare's most delightful songs are in this play—"Come unto these yellow sands"; "Full fathom five thy father lies"; "Where the bee sucks, there suck I"—nor is there any better phrased reflection on mortality than Prospero's words after the goddesses' pageant (which were held, in the 1945 production, until the end of the play): "We are such stuff As dreams are made on, and our little life Is rounded with a sleep."

The symbolism of the pageant scene is multiplex, as humans enact persons watching other humans enact spirits that vanish with their play. It seems, said S. L. Bethell in *Shakespeare and the Popular Dramatic Tradition* (1944), "as if Shakespeare had deliberately crowded into a few moments of his last play all that can suggest the manifold mystery of experience." Taking August Strindberg's characterization of the play as "a Buddhist dream," Paul Arnold (editor of *La Revue Théâtrale*) declared that it is a wish-fulfilment dream and the first forerunner of symbolism, Freud, and surrealism on the stage. The characters reveal "so completely and so directly their subconscious tendencies, that they seem to be more like X-rays of the soul than studies of human types." Consequently, M. Arnold continued, "*The Tempest* is like a new table of laws. . . . The poet has endowed all art and especially dramatic art with a means of expression of immeasurable power, and has given to the dramatist, by a representation quite like a dream, access to our subconscious life." It is unfortunate that only the post-Freudians can recognize the new "laws" Shakespeare is here said to have set down; and that, in the eerie land to which M. Arnold pointed, the dream is too often a nightmare. It seems, however, that more than man's fate is involved in the play's action; the primal elements are also ranged in battle. Shakespeare here is still the consummate playwright; he provides a varied and a moving action; within this, he snares us into thought of the various levels of reality and bids us contemplate the bases of human existence.

The play drives its creatures on a nameless island in Never-Never Land. No source has been traced for the plot. At Yale University in 1953 the play was produced as science-fiction: a space-ship was wrecked; Prospero watched by television the scenes away from his cell. As often in art, strangeness in one aspect is counterbalanced by tradition in another: Bernard Knox in *English Stage Comedy* (1955) has detailed the resemblances between the characters in *The Tempest* and the stock figures in the comedies of Plautus.* In particular, master and slave—the master helped in his intrigues by the shrewd slave who thus earns his freedom; and everyone save Prospero is in some way at some time enslaved. At the end, however, not only freedom and property are restored, but human worth.

Caliban's meeting with Stephano and Trinculo parallels on its level that of Miranda with Ferdinand, the traditional and continuing low take-off of the high folks' doings. Caliban uses, as Dryden pointed out, "language as hobgoblin as his person." The only touch of low sexual humor in *The Tempest,* Knox continues, "is Caliban's unrepentant laughter when reminded of his attempt on Miranda's virtue; but that one laugh is enough to remind us that he has an ancestry reaching back through scurrilous Plautine slaves and Aristophanic comic actors wearing a leather *phallos* to the ithyphallic satyrs of the Greek vase paintings."

In a sense, *The Tempest* is a memory play. The catastrophe occurs at the start. The images are not premonitory but reminiscent, the sea and the storm constantly recurring in figures. The images, furthermore, appeal to all our senses, sight and hearing fortified by touch, taste, smell. Thus the supernatural in the play is given solid ground of concrete reality, as the characters look back at their earlier days, and we look back upon nature budding into man. Misery, says Trinculo, as he stumbles upon Caliban in the thundery dark, "acquaints a man with strange bedfellows;" but there is lovely as well as odd companionship, and food for thought, throughout the play.

A French attempt at a sequel, *Caliban Set Free,* by Gonzague de Reynold, was produced in Geneva, Switzerland, in 1948. Picturing Caliban, recognizing the baseness of his drunken companions, reformed and made ruler of the island, the play offers an allegory of man's present state. The critic Georges Bonnard called it "a good instance of the profound influence exerted by Shakespeare on modern minds anxious for the future of the values to which he has given shape and form for all times." In addition to the values inherent in the characters and in the symbolism of Shakespeare's play, Prospero makes the closing statement: "The rarer action is In virtue than in vengeance. They being penitent, The sole drift of my purpose doth extend Not a frown further." Here is the judgment on all violent acts. These values, in *The Tempest,* are spun by richest poetry in our souls.

At the London Old Vic, in 1957, there was a pleasant, well-received revival of the Dryden-D'Avenant version, with score by Henry Purcell.

In the 1982 RSC production, with Derek Jacobi a commanding Prospero, Ariel leads a cluster of five sprites tormenting Trinculo and Stephano, with yapping skeletal phantom dogs. The London Actors Touring Co. in 1983 had Christine Bishop as "the Ariel of my life," said John Barber (*Telegraph,* June 20, 1983), who "could have flitted into a Jonson masque. . . . At his knee he wore a tabor, and briskly thrummed it to bring the clowns to heel." And there came, after these many years, a new interpretation of a Shakespearean episode, when Prospero keeps his promise to release the spirit:

> *Then to the elements*
> *Be free, and fare thou well.*

And then (Barber) "a wondrous thing happened. Ariel fell dead. The spirit had quit the body it was using, and Prospero watched while his darling flew invisibly, high overhead, to the blossom that hangs on the bough. Caliban carried out the abandoned corpse."

The importance of time in *The Tempest* (the word *tempest* springs from Latin *tempus,* meaning time, season) is explored in Frederick Turner's *Shakespeare and the Nature of Time,* 1971, and specifically by D. S. McGovern in the Autumn 1983 issue of *English.*

> *Time flies, you say? Ah, no.*
> *Alas, time stays. We go.*

"And still the sense is royal," said Sir Arthur Quiller-Couch: "we *feel* that we are greater than we know. So on the surge of our emotion, as on the surges ringing Prospero's island, is blown a spray, a mist. Actually it dwells in our eyes, bedimming them; and as involuntarily we would brush it away, there rides in it a rainbow; and its colors are wisdom and charity, with forgiveness, tender ruth for all men and women growing older, and perennial trust in young love." And thus we bid farewell to Shakespeare, with a misty smile.

(George) Bernard Shaw
Irish, 1856-1950

Bernard Shaw, whose revivals are too numerous to list, for a period was first a music critic, then a drama critic. In the latter capacity, he sent many shafts at Shakespeare (on whose shoulders he claimed to stand), belittling his intellect while admiring his poetry—deliberately, as he wrote me, over-stressing his attack to counteract the bardolatry of the time. Being passionately involved in the social problems of the day, he came to many of the next generation to seem out of date. Thus, John Osborne,* known for his *Look*

Back in Anger, wrote in 1977 to the *Manchester Guardian:* "Sir: Having recently seen *St. Joan* in London and *Caesar and Cleopatra* in Sydney, it is clearer to me than ever that Shaw is the most fraudulent, inept writer of Victorian melodrama ever to gull a timid critic or fool a dull public. He writes like a Pakistani who learned English when he was twelve years old in order to become a chartered accountant." To this came a rejoinder from Michael Crawford (later elected "actor of the year"): "Sir: I suggest that Shaw will be remembered with respect when no one looks back in anger—or any other emotion—at the rabid rantings and pompous twaddle of John Osborne."

In 1925 Shaw was awarded the Nobel Prize. The Malvern Festival in England began in 1929 as a tribute to Shaw. The *Shaw Review* gives an annual account of his plays around the world. These were multiplied in 1956, Shaw's centennial year.

One deeply interested in the playwright should consult the printed works, for Shaw has written lengthy prefaces developing his ideas, as well as books on social and religious themes. It is likely that his less determinedly social dramas will be more lengthily remembered.

Some major revivals of his plays will be mentioned—and *My Fair Lady,* the musical from *Pygmalion,* added—at the end of the discussion of *In Good King Charles's Golden Days.*

MRS. WARREN'S PROFESSION   *Bernard Shaw*

In his earliest plays, which Bernard Shaw called "unpleasant," the thesis drives with a vehemence that precludes the sparkle of wit. The same intensity, however, and perhaps the censorial necessity of conveying some of his meaning in hints, rendered the dialogue unusually pregnant and compressed. Critics who have disliked the subject matter of these plays, in perhaps unconscious self-exculpation, have attacked their artistic quality. As the plays' themes were rooted in current attitudes, they have lost some of their timely significance, but they remain vivid comments on social evils.

The first of the "unpleasant" plays was *Widowers' Houses,* 1892, which began as a collaboration between Shaw and William Archer; the collaboration ended because Archer was aghast at Shaw's battering of the "well-made play" formula. Subsequently Shaw developed the two acts of the attempted collaboration into what he called "a grotesque realistic exposure of slum landlordism." *The Philanderer,* 1893, the second "unpleasant" play, is a satire on sexual attitudes and relations—based perhaps on Shaw's own early experiences.

In the third "unpleasant" play, *Mrs. Warren's Profession,* 1894, Shaw returned to his stark presentation of social evils with a picture of prostitution as the result not of sinfulness but of poverty. The play shows Mrs. Warren as the prosperous proprietress of a chain of brothels across Europe. One of her half-sisters died of drudgery; and rather than "let other people trade in our good looks by employing us as shopgirls, or barmaids, or waitresses," Mrs. Warren systematically traded, first in her own advantages, then in those of an increasing number of impoverished or adventuresome young women. Her daughter Vivie has grown in respectable ignorance of her mother's means of livelihood, and when the play opens she is a very practical young person, of high attainment at Cambridge, looking forward to a professional career as mathematician and engaged to the rather inconsequential Frank Gardner, son of a clergyman. Mrs. Warren arrives with two of her gentleman friends. Vivie keenly questions her mother, breaks through the woman's surprised defenses, and discovers her mother's "profession." In anguish, the mother pictures her early days, and Vivie understands, sympathizes, accepts, and kisses her mother good night. One of Mrs. Warren's friends, Sir George Crofts, a partner in the business, falls in love with Vivie and proposes marriage—even though there's a chance that he is her father. When Crofts, who has invested in the brothels not out of need, but for the high rate of profit, is made the butt of Vivie's scorn, he retaliates by revealing that the Rev. Gardner may be her father— her fiancé Frank, her half-brother. Despite her mother's plea, Vivie rejects the ease and wealth she might enjoy, and turns from her mother, whom she despises as a "conventional woman at heart," living one life and believing another. Vivie has determined to make her own honest living, as a modern woman should. Vivie's rejected Frank dallies with the idea of following Mrs. Warren to Vienna.

Forbidden the stage by the Queen's reader of plays, the drama was published in 1898 with a preface vehemently attacking censorship. It was given "private performance" by the London Stage Society in 1902. In 1905, despite Shaw's warnings, Arnold Daly presented it in the United States. It was banned in New Haven, but opened October 30 in New York, with 2500 persons turned away, and Police Commissioner McAdoo offering $30 for a seat. In his curtain speech—after the uproar had somewhat subsided— Arnold Daly declared: "I do not think Mr. Shaw's play appeals to the lewd minded, but should be taken as it is—as a strong moral lesson on a phase of society that some might not care to see portrayed." The police disagreed and closed the play; when the courts acquitted the company, public interest had waned. The critics, in general, sided with the police. The *New York American* (October 31, 1905) quoted the Rev. Thomas B. Gregory: "From beginning to end the play—if play it may be called—is a veritable abyss of the vile and the infamous." The *Times* gave a column and a half to discussion of the excitement, half a column to the play: "Mr. Shaw takes a subject, decaying and reeking, and analyzes it for the edification of those whose unhealthy tastes find satisfaction in morbid suggestion . . . it is not only of vicious tendency in its exposition, but it is also depressingly stupid." Echoing the attacks on Ibsen came the *Herald:* "You cannot have a clean pig stye," and the *Sun:* "It is a dramatized stench." The *Post* shrewdly struck at Mrs. Warren's attempted justification of her means of livelihood: "There is nothing so offensive to the normal, clean, and healthy mind as the affectation of a lofty motive in the commission of a mean and dirty action." The practical *World,* on opening night, gave slips to those entering the theatre, asking them to mark their opinion of the play: *Fit* or *Unfit* for the American stage. It collected these after the performance; the next day on the first page, under the heading *"Mrs. Warren's Profession* Is An Offence," the *World* italicized its findings: "The verdict of the majority of those present at the first performance was that Mr. Shaw's play was unfit for presentation on any stage"—and on an inner page revealed the figures: *"Fit*—304; *Unfit*—272; *Not Voting*—424!"

Shaw's Preface suggests in part the cause of these reactions: "The play's dramatic power is used to force the spectator to face unpleasant facts. No doubt all plays which deal sincerely with humanity must wound the monstrous conceit which it is the business of romance to flatter." When the British ban ended in 1924 (with performances opening October 3, 1925 and again March 2, 1926), the attacks were renewed. After a 1935 performance in modern dress, W. A. Darlington, in the *London Telegraph* (July 23) dismissed the play: "Its value, as a tract for the time, has disappeared. Its value as a work of art never existed." The later American reception was more favorable. After a performance by Mary Shaw (who presented the play in 1917 and frequently through the decade thereafter) the *New York World* (April 12, 1918) called it "one of the strongest plays of the modern theatre." Although it has had wide production in Europe, the play was stopped after the first rehearsal in Budapest in 1936 as offensive to morality. The theme is not conducive to frequent amateur performance; but undeniably its presentation is powerful, as New York saw again in the off-Broadway production that opened October 25, 1950. The scene in which Vivie discovers her mother's profession, and her mother defends it, is pitiless and poignant; William Irvine, in *The Universe of G.B.S.* (1949), calls it "perhaps the most powerful situation in any of his plays." It is a crowning irony that the most conventional person in the play is Mrs. Warren; her standards, her indignation at the lack of filial sense of duty, of recognition of her maternal prerogatives, even her attitude toward the brothels whence her income flows: all these mark her as basically a commonplace Victorian. The character of her daughter is also unsparingly limned; her mother's sentimentality is countered by an equally reprehensible hardness in Vivie. As in *The Philanderer,* Shaw condones neither excess. The characters in *Mrs. Warren's Profession,* however, despite the somewhat exceptional source of Mrs. Warren's wealth, come close to such persons as we may still see about. Within the frame of its particular thesis, the play sets universal characteristics.

To some extent, in truth, the characters are not so much persons as living arguments, but the play has been acclaimed as "a masterpiece of realism." The facts are real; the points are potently pressed; the persons are given enough life to color the contention and infuse it with human warmth. Three interlocking ideas are pressed in the play. Shaw makes a moving defense of the woman that turns to prostitution. With equal fervor and sharper pen, he castigates the society that perpetuates and exploits that institution. And beyond this, in the conflict between Vivie Warren and her mother, he puts into human terms the basic struggle between decency and corruption. Shaw is aware that his play probes fundamental questions. It is no accident that, at the final meeting of the two women, he speaks in Biblical terms that recall, and reverse, the relationship of Ruth and Naomi. Bidding her mother farewell, Vivie says, "Your work is not my work, and your ways are not my ways."

In its treatment of Mrs. Warren's profession, the play flings the Marxian economic challenge into the theatre. The prostitute of French novels and plays (a French story had been suggested to Shaw by the actress Janet Achurch, as possible play material) has become the self-analyzing vehicle of a social argument, maintaining that all society shares in any guilt of Mrs. Warren. Indeed, said Shaw in his Preface, "Rich men without conviction are more dangerous in modern society than poor women without chastity." He added, on the 1926 program to *Mrs. Warren's Profession:* "I have only to point to the amount of the dole to remind you that we still are willing to do everything for the virtue of British womanhood except pay for it." Other countries, in the afteryears of another war, show that the play's point is continuously timely.

ARMS AND THE MAN   *Bernard Shaw*

First of what Shaw called his "pleasant" plays, *Arms and The Man,* after a cool reception on its London opening, April 21, 1894, grew to be one of the most popular of the playwright's comedies. It was an immediate hit in New York, opening September 17, 1894 with Richard Mansfield and Lillah McCarthy. London saw the play again in 1906 with Arnold Daly—"a success," said the *Telegraph* (April 17, 1906) "in spite of the Daly handicap"; in 1908; and on the return of the Old Vic Company after the War, October 1944, with Laurence Olivier and Ralph Richardson. Daly played it in New York in 1916; Lynn Fontanne and Alfred Lunt in 1925. Throughout the United States amateur and little theatre productions appear almost every year. New York saw it again, opening October 19, 1950, at the Arena Theatre. Both the amusing dalliance with the romantic attitude in the very act of satirizing it and the constant shafts of thought-provoking dialogue have kept the play entertaining and stimulating.

The play opens in Bulgaria in 1885, in the bedchamber of Raina Petkoff, whose fiancé, Sergius Saranoff, has just been hero of a victory over the Servians. Into that bedroom comes a fleeing Servian captain. Raina, after her first alarm, remembers that the Petkoffs are a family of wealth and refinement; she has seen *Ernani* and, like the host in that opera, will not betray her guest. The prosaic Captain Bluntschli, a Swiss mercenary, completely fagged out, is glad to be rescued but takes it as a matter of course. The chocolate he carries instead of cartridges is all gone; scornfully, Raina offers him a box of bonbons. He falls asleep on Raina's bed. Sometime later, the war over, Bluntschli returns. With swift and amusing tangle and double-barbed banter, he takes Raina for his own. The pompous "hero" Sergius is ensnared by the haughty maid-servant Louka. The servant Nicola, engaged to Louka, relinquishes her as a bride, preferring her as a wealthy patron of the shop he plans to open.

In spite of the rapid and constant action, the play has really little story. Even Shaw's good friend William Archer at first could see in the play no more than promise: "I begin positively to believe that he may one day write a serious and even an artistic play, if only he will repress his irrelevant whimsicality, try to clothe his character-conceptions in flesh and blood and realize the difference between knowingness and knowledge." But after some years had passed the English public grew more attuned to the Shavian method. Thus Max Beerbohm, in the *Saturday Review* (January 4, 1908) declared: "I have come to see that much of this seeming fantasy and flippancy was a mere striving after sober reality, and that the reason why it appeared fantastic was that it did not conform with certain conventions of the theatre which the majority of playgoers took as a necessary part of truth to life. . . . Fourteen years ago he was not so far ahead in form, as he was in matter, of the average playwright. In form, indeed, he was merely abreast of the time."

The matter of substance of the drama is its realistic, common-sense attitude toward militarism and war, which in the theatre before Shaw had worn the cloak of glory. The title of the play is drawn, sardonically, from the first lines of Vergil's *Aeneid:* "Arms and the man I sing." When the play was produced in Vienna on June 16, 1921, a protest of the Bulgarian Legation and threats of Bulgarian students there closed it after the first performance; but, as the *Boston Transcript* (April 21, 1897) had earlier remarked, "although its scenes were laid in Bulgaria for the sake of giving a fantastic and picturesque atmosphere, the play proved to be a keen and pungent satire on modern English life." Indeed it has been suggested that Shaw's soldiers had actual English models; for glamorous Saranoff, the aristocratic traveler Cunninghame Graham; for efficient Bluntschli, the economist (and a founder of Shaw's Fabian Society) Sidney Webb.

We are shown that war is humdrum, that it has become middle-class. Shaw seems in truth to object less to war than to the romantic allure spun around it. He knows that the most important man in the army is the supply-man. His final thrust of satire in the play comes through the servant Nicola, who has kept out of the army and who at the end willingly gives up a wife to get a customer. Here (as with the flowergirl in *Pygmalion* *) Shaw has written a success story of the working class: hotel-owner's son makes good. The playwright might wish the audience to believe that, in succumbing to matrimony, Bluntschli has suffered defeat; but Raina Petkoff will keep her husband secure in the sense of his triumph.

This play, says George Jean Nathan in the *Theatre Book of the Year 1946-1947,* "is after all essentially a libretto with dashes of malapropos satiric wit and, when these are reduced to a minimum, it is as naturally suited to the operatic form as almost anything of Gilbert's." The Germans recognized this quality of the work; Rudolph Bernauer and L. Jacobson fashioned a libretto, with music by Oscar Straus (1909) superbly done and—in English by Stanislaus Stange, as *The Chocolate Soldier*—one of the most successful of recent comic operas. Opening in New York on September 13, 1909, it ran for 296 performances, with New York revivals in 1921, 1930, 1934, 1937, 1942, 1947, and frequent production around the country. In London, the 1910 production ran for 500 performances; the musical has had several revivals. *The Chocolate Soldier,* said the *Musical Courier* (January 15, 1910), is "filled with melody of a distinctly superior quality." Several of the songs have both charm and vitality; "My Hero," "The Chocolate Soldier," and "Falling in Love" are widely remembered and sung. The libretto, too, is continuously effective; it leaves out the sting of Shaw's satire, and manages to make even the practical Bumerli (Captain Bluntschli has become Lieutenant Bumerli) a romantic figure.

The parent play combines with humor and charm a laugh-provoking satire on the stir and contagion and muddle-headedness of war. It quite decapitates the militarist in each of us while leaving us complacently and thoroughly amused. *Arms and the Man* deftly substitutes feminine for military arms.

CANDIDA   *Bernard Shaw*

Shaw's most frequently presented play, *Candida,* 1894, was written with Ellen Terry in mind, but was first performed by Janet Achurch, March 30, 1895. It has since attracted many stars. New York saw the play with Arnold Daly, December 8, 1903; it was also presented in 1905 and 1906; in 1915 again with Arnold Daly; in 1924, 1937, 1942, and 1946 with Katharine Cornell; in 1932 with Blanche Yurka; in 1933 with Peggy Wood. In 1937 in London the play presented Ann Harding, who had played Candida at the Hedgerow Theatre outside Philadelphia in 1924. New York saw it again in 1939 with Cornelia Otis Skinner; Jane Cowl was Candida in the summer of 1942; Elissa Landi in 1943; Congresswoman Clare Booth Luce essayed the role in the summer of 1945. The play has also been constantly performed by college and community theatres, including a "modern dress" revival in Detroit in May, 1948.

More than any other of Shaw's plays, *Candida* presents a personal problem. Candida, wife of the somewhat pompous and complacent Reverend James Morell, is drawn toward the young poet, Marchbanks, who falls flamingly in love with her. The sensitive and keen-witted poet scorns Morell, "moralist and windbag." Morell tells Candida she is free to choose between them; he offers her his strength; Marchbanks offers his weakness. Morell tells Candida he trusts her goodness and her purity; she tells him he'd be wiser to put his trust in her love. And Candida shrewdly knows which of the two is the weaker, needs her the more; she stays with her husband—knowing also that the poet's desolation will ripen and enrich his maturing spirit.

"Mr. Shaw has never written a better speech," said Harold Hobson of the *London Sunday Times,* after the revival opening March 27, 1947, "than that in which Candida talks of those little, nameless, unremembered acts by which a self-sufficient man's wife or mother enables him to burgeon and to glory before an admiring world." Something of the tenderness of the Barrie that wrote *What Every Woman Knows** is here compounded with the wit of the usually more caustic Shaw. In truth, there is no genuine conflict between Marchbanks and Morell. The poet is purposely given but 18 years. He merely precipitates the clarification of the relationship between the Reverend James and Candida Morell. Through his irruption into their lives, they achieve frankness and understanding. Their attitudes toward one another, as G. K. Chesterton pointed out in *George Bernard Shaw* (1909), are harmoniously parallel: "She regards him in some strange fashion at once as a warrior who must make his way and as an infant who is sure to lose his way. The man has emotions which exactly correspond; sometimes looking down at his wife, and sometimes up at her; for marriage is like a splendid game of see-saw."

The universal implications, thrusts at conventional morality, revealments of the relations between men and women, rich observation of life, are integrated with the story: here are no long Shavian lectures; this is a full-blooded and moving play. To its story the minor figures—the naive curate, "Lexy" Mill; Burgess, whom Shaw describes as "a vulgar, ignorant, guzzling man, offensive, and contemptuous to people whose labor is cheap, respectful to wealth and rank, and quite sincere and without rancor or envy in both attitudes;" Morell's typist, the abrupt but sensitive Proserpine ("Prossy") Garnett, who Marchbanks at once observes is in love with Morell (and the thought that a woman *can* love Morell terrifies the poet)—all make rich contribution, caught in the author's keen insight and amused outlook. The various minor figures therefore call for careful casting; Mildred Natwick has made a living person out of Prossy; and for Katharine Cornell's 1946 production Burton Rascoe (April 4) headed his review with words of businessman Burgess: "Hardwicke Steals the Show." Shaw emphasized in his Preface that he entered sympathetically into the point of view of every person in the play.

In the play are embodied, as Arthur H. Nethercot reminds us in *P M L A* (September, 1949), the three types of person listed in 1891 in Shaw's *The Quintessence of Ibsenism.* Of every thousand persons, classified according to their attitude toward marriage and the family, Shaw declared, there are 700 philistines, 299 idealists, and one realist. Candida, basically content with the current system of matrimony, is a philistine. Her husband, recognizing but unable to face the flaws in the system, hence building elaborate defense of it, is an idealist. The realist, with courage to face the truth, is the poet Marchbanks. Shaw instanced the poet Shelley as a realist, and in the early productions young Marchbanks was made up to bring to mind the young Shelley, "femininely hectic," Archibald Henderson described him, "and timid and fierce."

The commingling of salvation and sex is a frequent Victorian theme, travestied in the pale young curate of the Gilbert* operettas. But Shaw was enough of a socialist for his early plays to move as "dialectic," from thesis to antithesis, showing—as he put in his words on *Candida*—the ideal's "own revolt against itself as it develops into something higher."

Candida herself is one of the most appealing figures in the modern theatre. As the *New York Dramatic Mirror* said (May 26, 1915): "So wholesomely moral is Candida in her immorality and so captivatingly immoral in her morality that she is one of the most fascinating exhibits in the entire Shaw museum ..." Opinions of Candida and her "morality" have nevertheless varied widely. Shaw himself, in a 1904 letter to James G. Huneker, unmercifully dissected the sweet wife: "Don't ask me conundrums about that very immoral female, Candida ... Candida is as unscrupulous as Siegfried: Morell himself sees that 'no law will bind her.' She seduces Eugene just exactly as far as it is worth her while to seduce him. She is a woman without 'character' in the conventional sense. Without brains and strength of mind she would be a wretched slattern and voluptuary. She is straight for natural reasons, not for conventional ethical ones. Nothing could be more coldbloodedly reasonable than her farewell to Eugene: 'All very well, my lad, but I don't quite see myself at 50 with a husband of 35.' It is just this freedom from emotional slop that makes her so completely mistress of the situation." Again one must beware, as Shaw himself warns, of taking Shaw at his face value. Candida may be a Shavian philistine, in that she embraces an attitude that Shaw deems petty and petty bourgeois; but in her conduct within the framework of that system, she is both a realist and a woman of astuteness and command. Candida is, said Eric Bentley, "the sweeter for not being all sugar." She is Shaw's most provocative woman of modern times.

The play has found few detractors. John Mason Brown called it "the wisest, tenderest, and most perceptive of all the realistic plays that have come from Shaw's active pen." In April 1946, Kronenberger felt that "the play itself shows its age and ailments," but most agreed with Barnes: "The plain fact is that *Candida* has the power to withstand the seasons." This is still true.

YOU NEVER CAN TELL   *Bernard Shaw*

Shaw's first attempt at popular, commercial drama resulted in what Freedley and Reeves call "one of his least characteristic plays"— *You Never Can Tell*, 1896; but you can always tell that a surprise will come with Shaw. This play has the first dramatic use of the legal separation of man and wife and the first stage exhibition of a dentist making an extraction.

Shaw's attempt to write a "well-made play," to suit his drama to contemporary taste, was, John Mason Brown remarked in the *Saturday Review* (April 24, 1948), like putting on a hobble skirt: "Nowadays, it seems as absurd as a hobble skirt would. It is the confinements of its pattern that got in the way of Shaw. . . . By his own admission, *You Never Can Tell* found Shaw stooping to conquer. Fortunately Shaw was never meant to be a stooper. All of us are the better off because he has led rather than followed us. Leading is his life work." It is wise, however, not to take Shaw at "his own admission"; if he stooped, it was to put a firecracker beneath the audience's complacency. The play is indeed, as William Irvine says in *The Universe of G. B. S.* (1949), not a copy of but "a satirical compromise with fashionable comedy. . . . The total result suggests the Pickwick Club at the height of election excitement."

Shaw for a time seemed mistaken, however, in thinking he had struck the popular vein. Cyril Maude took the play for his company to produce at the Haymarket; but the actors themselves were so confused by the script that Shaw withdrew it. The New Stage Society made it the first of their private ventures, opening November 26, 1899. In 1900 it was shown for a fortnight of matinees in London. Chicago saw an amateur production in February 1903. But it was not until January 9, 1905, in New York, that the public welcomed it for a run of 150 performances with Arnold Daly and Mabel Taliaferro. It had been offered to Richard Mansfield, who refused it, saying that one couldn't popularize a dentist in America. In London, later the same year, H. Granville-Barker produced the play with Nigel Playfair. Since then there have been scores of revivals, one in New York opening on March 16, 1948, with Patricia Kirkland, Frieda Inescourt, and Leo G. Carroll.

The play tells us of Mrs. Clandon, a "modern" woman and authoress, who carried her son Philip and her two daughters, Dolly and Gloria, to Madeira to keep them from the middle-class influence of their father. After eighteen years—when the play opens—they are back at "a watering place" on the coast of England. Here a "five-shilling dentist," Dr. Valentine, falls in love with Gloria—though his joy is mixed with dismay when in twelve short hours she sweeps him into matrimony; and the family is reunited with the father. The idea that a man is reluctant to embrace matrimony, whereas a woman seeks always to snare him into that state, becomes less playful in Shaw's later treatment; here, as Irvine said, it is "an elaborate joke in the process of becoming an elaborate dogma." The suggestion has been put forward that the play is to some extent autobiographical, picturing as Gloria Miss Charlotte Payne-Townshend, whom Shaw—after many delays and hesitancies—eventually married.

The wit of the Shavian dialogue, the crisp, character-catching repartee, cannot be gathered into bouquets for brief savoring. When the play was first produced in New York, the *Dramatic Mirror* called it "the most enjoyable of all Shaw's plays, pleasant or unpleasant, to read to one's self or aloud. . . . It is so full of whimsical turns and odd half-lights on human nature that it is brainy champagne with all the sparkle left in. With this clever Irishman there is nothing holy in love; it is only a chemical reaction, or more, perhaps, like a game of chess, where the cleverer party advances her pawns boldly until she can cry 'checkmate' to her fleeing victim, man." However, few critics of 1905 were ready to look upon Shaw as a serious commentator on life.

The play grew to be tremendously popular throughout the world, but when it was revived in New York in 1948 it received mixed notices. Brooks Atkinson tried to defend it: "Let's say this much . . . no other comedy of that period (early 1900's) would be even tolerable. . . . It was directed in a key that would make an ordinary farce unbearable." Others spoke more praisefully. George Jean Nathan contended that the play "still retains a deal of its original amusement." George Freedley hailed it as "one of Shaw's most delightful and graceful comedies." Quotations from these mixed reviews were used by the producers, the Theatre Guild, in a *New York Times* (March 18, 1948) advertisement headed "Shavians Arise! Heresy! Sabotage! Treason!" The Shavians rallied enough to give the play a run of five weeks.

In retrospect, the English critic W. A. Darlington has declared: "I have always thought Shaw's chance of becoming a classic rests chiefly on two

plays, *St. Joan** and *You Never Can Tell*." With more of a plot and with less
lengthy speeches than many of Shaw's other plays, the latter remains a
delightful picture of the "new" woman succumbing to the old emotion—
then, like the eternal feminine, taking command. The Shavian woman, who
as the instrument of the Life Force subdues the male, first flutters and
flowers in *You Never Can Tell*.

THE DEVIL'S DISCIPLE   *Bernard Shaw*

The first of Bernard Shaw's "Three Plays for Puritans," *The Devil's
Disciple*, 1897, is also a play about Puritans. Mrs. Dudgeon, the mother of
Dick, "the devil's disciple," is a strict Puritan; she is also an old harridan;
she hated her late husband; she bears with "intensely recalcitrant resignation" the blows the Lord has let fall upon her head. It is in revolt against her
harsh piety and the sanctimonious hypocrisy he sees around that Dick
Dudgeon has declared himself a diabolonian, and has been content to be an
outcast from these over-righteous townsfolk. Dick hates the rigid religiosity
that makes children weep and old women nags or witches. When his father's
will makes Dick master of the house, old Mrs. Dudgeon is mortally stricken;
all the members of the family turn from him, except the "irregular child" of
Dick's Uncle Peter, Essie, whom Dick alone has treated with respect. More
urgent events sweep on; for this is Westerbridge, New Hampshire in 1777;
and the British, driving through the state, as an example and warning are
hanging a leading citizen in every town. Nearby, they have hanged Dick's
Uncle Peter; in Westerbridge they come for Parson Anderson. But the
Parson is out and, to his wife Judith's distaste, Dick Dudgeon is there. He
has taken off his coat because it is wet with rain; he does not disclose his
identity and the soldiers carry him off in mistake for the Parson, to be
condemned to hang next day at noon. Parson Anderson gallops off to safety.
The sentimental Judith—doubtless romantic at heart beneath her drab
Puritan garb—swings from hatred of Dick to deep concern and love. To the
severe English Major Swindon comes the suave General, "Gentlemanly
Johnny" Burgoyne, who chats amicably with the prisoner, especially when
Judith frantically cries out that he is not her husband. Identified, Dick is
still to be hanged; but in the nick of time, the American officer who the
night before drove back the British arrives with a safe-conduct to discuss
the terms of their evacuating Westerbridge. Dick is saved. The American
officer is Parson Anderson. Judith is ashamed at having thought her husband a coward, and relieved at Dick's promise of silence; the British march
off, with the village band playing Yankee Doodle behind them.

This tomfoolery and satire is peppered with wit and wisdom. The plot is
swift-moving; beneath it flows an inner action. Parson Anderson is superbly drawn; his tolerant calm in the face of Dick's insults wins Dick's
respect and our own. His wife Judith is a superbly satiric capture of the
moony, romantic dreamer within the seemingly sober and solid pious
woman. Most interesting is the contrast between Dick Dudgeon and his
mother. Shaw dwelt on this in his Preface (1900) to the play, comparing
Mrs. Dudgeon to Mrs. Clenman in Dickens' *Little Dorrit*. The critics, said
Shaw, "took Mrs. Dudgeon at her own valuation as a religious woman
because she was detestably disagreeable. And they took Dick as a blackguard, on her authority, because he was neither detestable nor disagreeable." Shaw neglects to observe that the other characters in the play also
accept that evaluation. Not quite for the reasons Shaw gives; but it takes a

revolution to upset the Puritan values. Opposed to Mrs. Dudgeon's almost vindictive self-sacrifice is Dick's unintended heroism. "On the stage, it appears, people do things for reasons," remarked Shaw. "Off the stage they don't: that is why your penny-in-the-slot heroes, who only work when you drop a motive into them, are so oppressively automatic and uninteresting."

This is not the remark of a cynic; rather, as the portrait of Dick Dudgeon shows, it is the reflection of one who has faith in the essential goodness and dignity of human nature. William Irvine, however, in *The Universe of G. B. S.* (1949), points out that such an assertion of human dignity usually springs in a stable moral climate, from a basic moral tradition and self-discipline—which Dudgeon rejects. "In glorifying the product while deprecating the cause, Shaw is close to moral melodrama." Rather, Shaw is placing in 1777 an early instance of his man-to-be, whose impulses are so ordered that he will do as he pleases, and do right. Shaw complained in his Preface that a critic and the actors rewrote the play, destroying its point by giving Dudgeon a secret love for Judith Anderson. "Dick Dudgeon every night confirmed the critic by stealing behind Judith, and mutely attesting his passion by surreptitiously imprinting a heart-broken kiss on a stray lock of her hair whilst he uttered the barren denial." Shaw took so firm a hand in the productions of his plays that this acting trick was probably never performed, but invented for the satiric effect of the telling—though a motiveless good deed may indeed be, to some persons, inexplicable.

Shaw wrote *The Devil's Disciple* after three years of reviewing bad plays—to show that there were better ones available. He made his point; the play was well received. It had its world premiere in Albany, October 1, 1897, and moved to New York on October 4, with Richard Mansfield. Some of the critics called the play "original"; Shaw laughed at them, pointing out that he used many of the hackneyed devices of the current theatre. What most critics praised was the play's paradoxical twists of thought, its barbed shafts of wit.

Much of the wit strikes sparks that fly between Dick Dudgeon and General Burgoyne. The latter has no essential part in the play; he seems onstage mainly because Shaw—who devoted a long prefatory note to him — was attracted to the man. (John Burgoyne was not only a general, but also a playwright. His *Blockade of Boston* was being performed in Boston in 1776 when an attack on the city interrupted it—as the hanging of Dick is interrupted in *The Devil's Disciple*.)

Perhaps because it shows a defeat of the English, the drama has been always one of the most popular of Shaw's plays in Dublin; the *Irish Times* commented (April 10, 1940): "Written as a melodrama, it became, and it remains, something that is a great deal more." Its English premiere was on September 26, 1899. It has been popular in England as in America. The American company of 1923 included Basil Sydney as Dick and Roland Young as Burgoyne. Percy Hammond said (April 23, 1923): "This humorous old nick-o-timer caused many of us to sit on the edge of our chairs last night and grow quite feverish over its beefsteak pudding incidents, as Mr. Shaw called them." The London *Stage* (August 1) in 1940 found the play still a "rollicking bit of realism and odd mixture of picturesque melodrama and ironic farce." The New York production opening January 25, 1950, at the City Center was so well received that it moved over to Broadway for 111 performances; it balanced Maurice Evans as Dudgeon and Dennis King as Burgoyne in a superb display of wit and fine acting. The play's clever use of the appeals of melodrama while it mocks the devices it is using, its sharp and witty attacks upon militarism, its topsy-turvy turns of accustomed attitudes, and its neat exposure of the difference between the religiose and the decent human being, keep *The Devil's Disciple* lively, timely, and fresh.

CAESAR AND CLEOPATRA   *Bernard Shaw*

Most challenging of "Three Plays for Puritans" is *Caesar and Cleopatra,* 1898, which was written by Shaw not, as some say, to show how Shakespeare should have composed a play, but to set straight the earlier playwright's values. After Shakespeare has pictured Antony as "the soldier broken down by debauchery" and Cleopatra as "the typical wanton in whose arms such men perish," Shaw averred, "Shakespeare finally strains all his huge command of rhetoric and stage pathos to give a theatrical sublimity to the wretched end of the business, and to persuade foolish spectators that the world was well lost by the twain." Shaw felt, moreover, that "sexual infatuation" is dramatically effective only in the comic vein. "To ask us to subject our souls to its ruinous glamor, to worship it, deify it, and imply that it alone makes our life worth living, is nothing but folly gone mad erotically." In Shaw's play the Roman conqueror merely dallies with the Egyptian queen in his moments of relaxation. When war comes he brushes her aside. When he sets out for home, only her calling to him reminds him of her existence. Love, which Shakespeare presents as felling potentates, Shaw sets as a byplay in the recess-time of a busy life.

In the character of Caesar, Shaw likewise differs from Shakespeare; here, Shaw specifically declared that he had improved upon the earlier picture. In the first place, "It cost Shakespeare no pang to write Caesar down for the merely technical purpose of writing Brutus up." In the second place, Shaw "saw the old facts in a new light." Shakespeare presented the Romans—and this is what many fail to see—not as ancient Romans really were, but as persons he might have known, "according to his own essentially knightly conception." The characters in *Julius Caesar** and in *Antony and Cleopatra** talk Shakespearean, and think Elizabethan ideas and values. The characters in *Caesar and Cleopatra* talk Shavian and think twentieth century "advanced" thoughts. Cleopatra, of course, is a mere child of sixteen; but Shaw is careful to explain that such childishness as hers—coquettish, malicious, and supremely selfish—"may be observed in our own climate at the present day in many women of fifty." All of Shaw's persons are essentially of the present day. "They had not the telephone", commented the London *Saturday Review* (November 30, 1907) critic, "and we don't torture our domestics, at least physically. Barring these trifles, I agree with Mr. Shaw that the difference between Julius Caesar and Cecil Rhodes, or Cicero and Mr. Balfour, is one of costume and slang." Take off the trappings, and Caesar—history's, or Shakespeare's, or Shaw's—is a human being even as you and I. Hailed as a novelty, Shaw's treating historical figures as contemporaries really continued the great tradition. He assumed that the Greek warriors of Plato's day had no less of native wit, not to speak of valor, than the soldiers of our own time. The Egyptians of Caesar's time enjoyed a comparatively high culture.

In Shaw's play we meet a Caesar somewhat like Shaw in a toga. Perhaps the character is mellow because, though romantic love is brushed aside, Shaw wrote the play on his honeymoon (he was married in 1898). The portrait is, however, a marked step in Shaw's efforts to find a cure for the ills of society: a definite turn from socialism to the superman. This prospect is given further treatment in *The Apple Cart* and fullest development in *Back to Methusaleh.* * "Caesar," said Sir Cedric Hardwicke in the *New York Times* (December 18, 1949), "is of course Shaw." Hardwicke then quoted Shaw's words of 1918 to his biographer, Hesketh Pearson: "It is what Shakespeare called a history; that is, a chronicle play; and I took the chronicle without alteration from Mommsen. I read a lot of other stuff, from Plutarch, who hated Caesar, to Warde-Fowler; but I found that Mommsen had conceived Caesar as I wished to present him, and that he told the story of the visit to Egypt like a man who believed in it, which many historians don't. . . . Although I was forty-four or thereabouts when I wrote the play, I now think I was a trifle too young for the job; but it was not bad for a juvenile effort."

In the play, we come upon Caesar amid his later triumphs, when he is already fifty-four. After the opening alarm of the Egyptians as the conquering Roman cohorts come near, we watch a situation in which ironic comedy deftly blends with tenderness. "Shaw's portrait of an elderly gentleman coaching a girlish queen in the etiquette of ruling," as the *New York Times* observed (August 22, 1935), "is full of admiration and sympathy." The frightened Cleopatra, huddling for shelter between the paws of a Sphinx, takes counsel of an elderly man apostrophizing there. He tells her she is safe from Caesar only if she faces him like a queen. As they walk back to the palace, we watch her drawing assurance and courage from his easy confidence, assuming authority and when it works, lashing out like a tyrant; fighting for self-control as her slaves drape the royal robes upon her trembling form; recognizing that it is "bitter to be a queen"; and, as she stands desperately proud while the Romans troop noisily in, discovering that the elderly man who has soothed her and strengthened her and brought her back to face the Roman terror—is the man to whom the soldiers lift their swords and shout, "Hail, Caesar!" Cleopatra's feline disposition prevents her emulating Caesar's politic clemency. She has her nurse Ftatateeta kill the ambitious eunuch Pothinus for carrying tales to Caesar; and for fear lest the nurse give suck to further treachery, Caesar's blunt bodyguard Rufio passes his sword through her throat. Meanwhile the roused Egyptians have fired the city; the great Alexandrian library is consumed in the flames; and Caesar takes precarious post at the Pharos lighthouse. Into the tumult of this surging history, Shaw sets both comedy and beauty. Apollodorus, patrician dealer in aphorisms and art, brings rugs for Cleopatra: "My calling is to choose beautiful things for beautiful queens. My motto is Art for Art's sake." The prosaic sentinel objects: "That is not the password." Cleopatra, who wants to join Caesar at the Pharos, has herself wrapped in a rug and, thus concealed, rowed to the lighthouse station. There she is hoisted on a crane to Caesar; and when the Egyptians advance and Caesar dives to swim to his nearing vessels, Rufio at his call pitches Cleopatra after him. When timely reinforcements cement Caesar's conquest, he sets out for Rome, leaving Cleopatra the consolation that he will send her the captain she once saw and coveted, a dashing young Roman named Mark Antony.

This mingling of ancient history and modern thoughts and perennial humans is a merry frolic garnished with provocative ideas. Its main flow of satire springs from the contrasted and neatly drawn characters, especially the "unadulterated Briton . . . ancestor of Mr. Podsnap," the dignified prude, the literal-minded, the humorless, honest, devoted and brave Britannus. All through the play, ideas and action interflow in a swift coursing.

Between Caesar and young Cleopatra the teacher-pupil relationship, frequent in Shaw's plays, may be observed: a realistic and somewhat cynical person awakening and quickening toward fulfilment a younger person not yet deeply aware.

The play was given an amateur production in Chicago, in May 1901. Its professional premiere came in New York October 30, 1906, with Sir Johnston Forbes-Robertson, and was coolly received. The *Tribune* said: "The purpose of it is the deliverance of satirical jibes from behind a stalking horse of farcical history. It seems to be the conviction of this author that everything existent, including human nature, is wrong, and that all things ought to be made over and newly fashioned, according to Shaw." There were similar comments after the London opening, as in the *Illustrated Sporting and Dramatic News* (December 7, 1907): "*Caesar and Cleopatra* made me sleepy at the Savoy. . . . The pleasantest moments to myself during the performance were—to put it Irishly, which Mr. Shaw should not mind—the waits while the performance was suspended. . . . It is not a history, it is not a tragedy, it is not a comedy, it is not a farce, it is not a burlesque—it is not anything that I can name; it is four acts of mixed negations, not one of which is strong enough to dwell upon." Comparison with Shakespeare was inevitable. The London *Saturday Review* (November 3, 1907) favored its contemporary: "Mr. Shaw has more learning, and a great deal more wit and humor, than Shakespeare, though he lacks the pathos of the latter." A quarter of a century later, Brooks Atkinson (August 30, 1935) similarly declared: "*Caesar and Cleopatra* is superior to *Julius Caesar* and *Antony and Cleopatra* in thinking and form, being inferior only in passion, which is perhaps the whole thing."

Forbes-Robertson played the role again in 1913, adding the rug-and-swimming act, which he had omitted in the earlier production. Helen Hayes and Lionel Atwill opened the new Guild Theatre in New York with the play on April 13, 1925; Helen Hayes acted in it again ten years later. In 1925, in London, Sir Cedric Hardwicke played Caesar; he returned to the role in New York in December 1949, with Lilli Palmer, for 151 performances. In the summer of 1950 Paulette Goddard acted in the play. London saw it again in 1951 with Laurence Olivier and Vivien Leigh, opening May 10, and alternating with Shakespeare's *Antony and Cleopatra.** This production came to New York on December 19, 1951, Olivier playing Caesar as a world-weary, wise old man. In 1944, in the most expensive film ever made in England, Vivien Leigh played Cleopatra to Claude Rains' Caesar. For this filming, Shaw wrote a brief bath scene intended to bring the Queen's childishness to the level at which Shaw pictured the movie audience. For his theatre audience he employed the usual tricks of the trade while keeping a vivid story swiftly flowing to bear his ideas along. Thus there are few that will not find harvest of entertainment and thought in this play.

CAPTAIN BRASSBOUND'S CONVERSION   *Bernard Shaw*

The central figure of this play, written in 1899, is Lady Cicely Waynflete; she produces the change noted in the play's title. Although Richard Watts, Jr. calls her "chiefly a sort of middle-aged Candida," Lady Cicely has youth and charm enough to wind around her little finger all the men she meets. With her to Morocco has come her brother-in-law, the English judge Sir Howard Hallam; among the others in the small town there, are a Scotch missionary, a Cockney hooligan, and a desperately serious brigand. The brigand, Black Paquito—less romantically, Captain Brassbound—has a score to settle with Judge Hallam, who happens to be his uncle, and the instrument of his mother's having been sent to prison. Brassbound arranges to have the judge taken into slavery by a Mohammedan sheik; but in a scene of superb comedy, Lady Cicely, with feminine matter-of-fact, explodes Brassbound's romantic notions of revenge. This, however, empties his life of its meaning. Meanwhile a United States gunboat, getting word of the brigands, has sent out an expedition; the captured Brassbound is held by the gunboat's Captain Kearney. Before him Lady Cicely, always in complete command of herself and any situation, tells the truth and nothing but the truth—when Judge Hallam reminds her that "the English law requires a witness to tell the *whole* truth," she retorts: "What nonsense! As if anybody ever knew the whole truth about anything!"—and she manipulates the hearing with such apparently innocent astuteness that Brassbound is exonerated. With Brassbound free and his life's purpose gone, there seems nothing left but for Lady Cicely to marry him. She is holding out her hand to him when a broadside from his pirate ship breaks the spell; Brassbound dashes off.

Explaining the play's publication as one of the "Three Plays for Puritans," Shaw said: "I have, I think, always been a Puritan in my attitude toward art. . . . The nineteenth century has crowned the idolatry of Art with the deification of Love . . . the pleasure of the senses I can sympathize with and share; but the substitution of sensuous ecstasy for intellectual activity and honesty is the very devil." It is the delight arising from intellectual activity that one feels here, for, as Desmond McCarthy said, since Swift "no such insistent preacher has so leavened his lesson with laughter."

Lady Cicely is a superb creation, at once imbued with romantic charm and equipped with such deftly managed store of woman's wiles as makes a mockery of romance. She balances with her common-sense the romantic notions the men hold of revenge as justice; and by her motherliness and her encouragement of the right course (and her artful assumption of candor) she smooths away the masculine villainy and ill-will.

The play was produced in London by the Stage Society in December, 1900. A revival opened on March 20, 1906, with Ellen Terry, for whom the part was conceived, as Lady Cicely. She played it again, opening January 28, 1907, with James Carew (whom she married) as Captain Brassbound. The *London Telegram* (January 29, 1907) conceded that Miss Terry "easily made Lady Cicely charming," but insisted that the play "is pretty tiresome." Subsequent opinion has been more favorable. Grace George appeared in the play in New York in 1916; Gladys Cooper, during the summer of 1939; Jane Cowl, in 1940. Then, Robert Coleman (July 13, 1940) declared it "gorgeous burlesque; an excellent example of what super-fun can be whacked from a slapstick in the hands of such artists as Shaw, Cowl, and company." In 1937 the play was produced in Warsaw under the title *The Pirate and a Lady*. Six years later Dame Sybil Thorndike enacted Lady Cicely in Dublin. In this role, Edna Best showed, at the New York City Center opening December 27, 1950, that the play is still amusing and provocative, with shrewd character study. London felt the same about the revival at the Old Vic, with Roger Livesey and Ursula Jeans, opening April 17, 1951.

The nature of things peeps out, in deft revelation and humorous concern, from beneath the romantic color and adventure and brilliant dialogue of *Captain Brassbound's Conversion*.

MAN AND SUPERMAN   *Bernard Shaw*

With *Man and Superman*, 1901-1903, Shaw moved for the first time in
the full grip of the "life force." For his panacea for the ills of the world he
turns from socialism to the superman who was to come into being through
"creative evolution."

A. B. Walkley, the critic, had asked Shaw for a Don Juan play. The usual
treatment, Shaw felt, had been fully exploited by Molière* and Mozart;
hence his use of the storied figures is concentrated into the seldom played
third act presenting a dream of hell with Don Juan and the Statue and the
Devil in long arguments that end with Don Juan going up to heaven to live
in contemplation, while the Statue decides there's more fun to be had by
staying in the other place. In Shaw's irony hell is a place where one may
have all one desires—save intensity of thought and feeling. The Devil
himself is suspiciously like a Congressman. One of Shaw's most biting
speeches is Don Juan's long description of the Devil's "friends," a piece of
rhetoric perhaps intended to outvie Shaw's hated-beloved master, Shakespeare, who uses such patterns of word play, as in the curate's characterizations in *Love's Labor's Lost*.

In the play proper, Don Juan is represented by the Englishman John
Tanner and Donna Ana by Ann Whitefield. "Instead of presenting a diabolonian scoffer who horrified respectable believers by his skepticism," as
William Irvine states in *The Universe of G. B. S.* (1949), "Shaw must
present a fanatical revolutionary who horrifies respectable skeptics by his
faith. Instead of depicting a libertine who pursues women, he must depict a
Puritan who is pursued by them." John Tanner, gentleman by birth,
wealthy by class, revolutionary by theory, bachelor by luck, is annoyed at
having been made guardian of the sweetly feminine Ann Whitefield. When
friends, including his practical chauffeur, open John's eyes to Ann's designs
upon him, he flees to Spain. There, in the hands of the bandit Mendoza
(formerly a London waiter, fled in despairing love of the chauffeur's sister),
in the Sierra Nevada Don John Tanner dreams his magnificent dream-
dialogue in hell. But even to the mountain fastness, Ann follows him. She
says that her mother insists on her marrying John; her mother denies it.
Tanner rejects her; she announces publicly that she has accepted him, and
"swoons" at his feet. Ann spins her feather boa around his neck; for she is
the serpent the Life Force has sent to wrap John in her toils, for the
movement of mankind toward the superman. Her feminine frailty is the
velvet over the steel of her undeviant purpose.

Tanner is somewhat like Sidney Trefusis in Shaw's novel *An Unsocial
Socialist* (1883). There is also Shaw's early sketch *Don Giovanni Explains*
(1887), in which the man is the pursued. H. M. Hyndman has been mentioned as model for Tanner, but in many ways the latter resembles Shaw
himself. He pours forth Shaw's ideas and, like Shaw's, his ideas are met
with rejection and ridicule; and he is swept willy-nilly into matrimony.
John Tanner wrote a *Revolutionist's Handbook,* which is printed as a
postscript to the play. It sears with the full bitterness of Shaw's disappointment in democracy and Fabian socialism; its dicta reflect the opinions of
the poet Blake and suggest those of Ambrose Bierce's *The Cynic's Word
Book* (1906). "Revolutions have never lightened the burden of tyranny," says
John Tanner-Shaw; "they have only shifted it to another shoulder. . . . We
must eliminate the Yahoo, or his vote will wreck the commonwealth. . . .

The art of government is the organization of idolatry. . . . Positive: mistaken at the top of one's voice. . . . Marriage is popular because it combines the maximum of temptation with the maximum of opportunity. . . . Learning: the kind of ignorance distinguishing the studious. . . . Applause: the echo of a platitude. . . . "He who can, does. He who cannot, teaches," declared the most didactic of modern playwrights. (*Positive, learning, applause* are from Bierce.) Tanner's handbook is in the cynical fashion of his time. Shaw was a Victorian, not as inverted as he liked to seem; his major characters are aristocratic.

The play, opening in London May 25, 1905, with the dialogue in hell left out, was better received by the public than by critics. Granville-Barker played Tanner in a red beard, to resemble Shaw. The play was revived in London in 1905 and 1906; opening September 28, 1911, for 191 performances; in 1912, 1927, twice in 1930, 1931, by the Old Vic in 1938 and 1951. The hell scene was first played in London on June 4, 1907, with Robert Loraine. London saw the full play in 1925, 1928, 1935, 1951. It was performed complete in Germany in 1906. The American premiere (without hell but with Robert Loraine) was on September 5, 1905; the play ran for 192 performances. Maurice Evans, opening in New York in the abridged version on October 8, 1947, ran for 295 performances.

In 1947, Shaw had three plays on Broadway: Evans in *Man and Superman; John Bull's Other Island** with the Dublin Gate Company; and Gielgud in *You Never Can Tell.* Don Juan in Hell,* as the dream episode is called, was presented by Charles Boyer, Charles Laughton, Cedric Hardwicke and Agnes Moorehead—without scenery, on a two-year tour, in New York at Carnegie Hall October 22, 1951, and for runs on Broadway in the winter and spring of 1951-1952.

After the London premiere of the dream of hell, Max Beerbohm declared in the *Saturday Review* (June 8, 1907): "Mr. Shaw has never contrived so good an expression of his genius as *Don Juan in Hell*. In no other work of his is one so struck by the force and agility of his brain, by the spontaneity of his humor, and by the certainty of his wit." Quite different were the reviews of the entire play. In the *London Times* (November 27, 1938), James Agate declared that "the characters are doubly dead for the good reason that they never were alive." To lend emphasis, Agate then quoted Max Beerbohm on the main figures of the play: "We can no more be charmed by them than we can believe in them. Ann Whitefield is a minx. John Tanner is a prig. Prig versus Minx, with the gloves off, and Prig floored in every round—there you have Mr. Shaw's customary formula for drama. The main difference between this play and the others is that the prig and the minx are conscious not merely of their intellects but of the 'life force.' Of this they regard themselves, with comparative modesty, as the automatic instruments. They are wrong. The life force could find no use for them. They are not human enough, not alive enough."

Across the ocean, the *New York Telegram* (September 6, 1905) took the playwright to task for stating in the Preface that his point of view is akin to that of Shelley, Ibsen, and Nietzsche: "Save the mark! Shelley, whose sense of beauty was his all, and Mr. Shaw has absolutely none; Ibsen, whose moral force moved the mountains of Norway, and Mr. Shaw confesses he is a wobbler; Nietzsche, whose gigantic sincerity is even painful, and Mr. Shaw doesn't even know what it means." In supplementing these comments George Jean Nathan remarked that though *Man and Superman* is "beautifully written," time has a way of turning saucy platters into platitudes. In truth, there seems in this drama a considerable pother of talk for the simple story. Shaw's inability or unwillingness to curb his character's conversation, and his refusal to let producers cut his lines, explain why Mrs. Pat Campbell (whom Shaw called "perilously bewitching") was moved to protest, in 1912: "It's too late to do anything but accept you and love you—but when you were quite a little boy somebody ought to have said 'Hush!' just once."

Despite these objections, the play is adroitly attuned to its purpose. The characters may not be humanly real, but they have gusto. Ann Whitefield may not be any particular woman, but she is Everywoman (Shaw conceived her, indeed, after seeing a performance of *Everyman* *). The development of the play is, if delayed, richly adorned, by the trenchant wit, and the dialogue is at the peak of Shavian coruscation. Shaw's most characteristic ideas are presented in sharpest focus. And if, as E. Strauss suggests, in *Bernard Shaw: Art and Socialism* (1942), the love story in Shaw's plays reflects their thought, then the acquisitive woman represents capitalism; and Tanner's succumbing to Ann well captures the modern man's predicament, snared inextricably in the capitalistic mesh and mess, condemned to enjoy its advantages while decrying its deficiencies—until man has been supplanted by superman. But, Shaw admonishes us, beware the Yahoo, whose scion will be Superman of the comics! This danger Shaw does not see how to avert, save by more desperate endeavors of the Life Force, intellect and will joining instinct in the course of creative evolution. Meanwhile the intellect finds wholesome, tasty food in *Man and Superman*.

MAJOR BARBARA   *Bernard Shaw*

In *Major Barbara,* 1905, which Shaw disarmingly labels not a drama but "a discussion," he created one of his most fully realized women, Barbara Undershaft—and gave his usual social satire an unusual turn. For the millionaire munitions manufacturer, Barbara's father, Andrew, preaches that poverty is the vilest sin of man and society: "It is our first duty not to be poor." And Barbara, whom social ills have so deeply wrung that she has joined the Salvation Army, learns that the capitalism she detests maintains the charities on which she pins her faith; she sees that the workers in her father's plant are well-off and contented; and, if she does not come wholly to agree with her father about the futility of helping the poor, at least she comes close to feeling that social evils rise out of the degradation that comes with poverty. These ideas Shaw bandies back and forth, mainly in the last act, with much physical action around the Salvation Army, in which Barbara is a major. The unregenerate Bill Walker "bashes the face" of the harmless little salvationist, Jenny Hill—which, said the London *Truth* (December 7, 1905), "is a disgusting spectacle, and sickens the soul of every decent man and woman in the theatre." Barbara, with not meek but militant Christianity, tumbles Bill from his defiance. Greek professor Adolphus Cusins has joined the Army in love of Barbara; Undershaft comes to her shelter—and plays the trombone in the Army band—on condition that Barbara visit his factory and his workers' homes. There, amid busy and happy surroundings, Cusins shifts jobs from Army to munitions plant; Barbara still will marry him. Social work can do less for the shiftless than hard workers can do for themselves.

At the London premiere on November 28, 1905, Prime Minister Balfour was highly amused, but the critics were divided. The *London Graphic* was enthusiastic, calling the play "bewildering, vastly amusing. . . . So witty is the dialogue, and so shrewd, that we do not care to miss a line of all the lengthy speeches. There is not an ounce of padding in the play and there is enough material to supply half a dozen dramatists with half a dozen plays." The *Times* most cogently advanced adverse charges—charges to which Shaw more than once pleaded "Guilty, and I don't care." Said the *Times:* "Mr. Shaw has no dramatic skill, has apparently no dramatic instinct, but he is a thinker who from first to last deals with things worth thinking about. And so we turn with relief, nay, with positive joy, from the intellectual eccentricity of Mr. Shaw. We do it against our better judgment. We feel that the dramatic medium is being wasted and misused. We sorrowfully recognize that Mr. Shaw will never recognize what Pater called the responsibility of the artist to his material. But then the other people, who do possess this sense of responsibility, are so mediocre! And Mr. Shaw is so amusing! A dramatist he is not, but he is a splendid pleasure monger. That is why he has become the fashion in a pleasure seeking world. But we venture to address to him one word of warning. He must not abuse his vogue. Amusing as he is, he is not amusing for quite so long as he supposes. The truth is, he doesn't know when to stop. He lapses into longueurs. Before the end of *Major Barbara* was reached, we caught ourselves yawning."

The play has nevertheless been very popular. New York saw it on December 9, 1915, with a scintillant cast including Grace George and Conway Tearle. On November 19, 1928, New York saw it again with Dudley Digges and Helen Westley. *Variety* (November 21) reported that "*Barbara* isn't dated like some of the other pieces." A London production the next year, the *Era* (March 13, 1929) called "spendidly alive . . . the second act is as good as anything in modern drama . . . the long last act touches, despite its extravagances and humors, profundities that make the subjects of most other pieces appear as soap bubbles . . ."

Barbara stands beside Candida as Shaw's most appealing woman. There is broad humor in his treatment of her; she leans over the big bass drum for a tender kiss. There is practical common-sense behind her social rebellion. There is a staunch and vigorous will behind her devout religion. And her various qualities blend to form a rounded and charming creature. "There is a vein of poetry in Mr. Shaw, amongst all else that he is or chooses to be," said the *Boston Transcript* (December 31, 1929); "in *Major Barbara,* it touches Barbara herself with beauty."

Despite its vivid portraits and its well-directed shafts of satire, the play has been called the most widely misunderstood of all Shaw's dramas— probably because Shaw in his prefatory "First Aid to Critics" explained his purpose and thus roused the critics' suspicions. This is clearly his most Marxian play; in it, as William Irvine stated in *The Universe of G. B. S.* (1949), he "impatiently sweeps away meditation and ideas as totally incapable of influencing the world of action, and finds in the violent clash of materialistic egotisms themselves the promise of a Marxist millennium." Looking upon the wretchedness of the world around him, Shaw was seeking a cure. In *Man and Superman* * he concluded that it is thought, in the long run, the intellect dictating to the will, that shapes history. In *Major Barbara,* dismissing ideas as impotent, he declared that the pressure of events will forge a Marxian utopia. Barbara compromises with capitalism; but Cusins, while going over to Undershaft's factory, works with the dream of a revolution. In *Androcles and the Lion,* * Shaw saw salvation in faith, in the individual sense of moral values. Barbara is saved by compromise; Lavinia (in *Androcles and the Lion)* does not compromise but is saved by a deus ex machina, the Emperor; Joan of Arc (in *Saint Joan**) refuses to compromise, and moves to martyrdom. Barbara and Cusins are dreamers; representing the Christian morality that most folks preach, they embrace the gunpowder morality that most folks practice—telling each other they will make gunpowder work for Christian ends. But Shaw gives little comfort to this optimism of force.

The drama's ideas have to squeeze through incidents and surface drives that keep the stage lively and the audience amused. Among recent productions was one in "modern dress," opening in London March 5, 1935, with Maurice Evans as Cusins. Community theatres constantly revive the play. It was turned into a film in 1941, with Wendy Hiller and Rex Harrison. *Variety* observed: "One more crack about this Shaw guy. He'd make a hot Hollywood gag man." The evidence: when the guard reminds old Undershaft he mustn't take anything combustible near the plant, his wife exclaims: "Sir, I hope you're not referring to me!" W. S. Gilbert before Shaw observed that for public consumption one must always gild the philosophic pill. Shaw—who always proclaimed that his chief concern was with the gilders—in *Major Barbara* makes delightful mixture of merriment and meaning. We laugh as our prejudices bark their shins against the stumbling blocks of common-sense alternately set in our path by practical Andrew Undershaft and romantic Major Barbara.

THE DOCTOR'S DILEMMA *Bernard Shaw*

Shaw calls *The Doctor's Dilemma,* 1906, a comedy about death, a tragedy because "its theme—that of a man of genius who is not also a man of honor—is the most tragic theme to people who can understand its importance." In the Preface to the play he states: "Even the comedy which runs concurrently with it: the comedy of the medical profession as at present organized in England, is a tragic comedy, with death conducting the orchestra. Yet the play is funnier than most farces. The tragedy of Dubedat is not his death but his life; nevertheless his death, a purely poetic one, would once have seemed wholly incompatible with laughter."

Behind the play are several actual incidents. Shaw had heard one of his medical friends, Sir Almroth Wright, once ask if a patient was worth saving. William Archer in the *London Tribune* (July 14, 1906), in praising the tragedies of Ibsen,* commented on the fact that Shaw's characters never die: "It is not the glory, but the limitation, of Mr. Shaw's theatre, that it is peopled by immortals." And that summer, Granville-Barker came to Shaw in search of a play. Out of such impulsions Shaw wrote *The Doctor's Dilemma,* which Granville-Barker, acting Dubedat, produced in London on November 20, 1906, with Lillah McCarthy as Jennifer. The play was successful from the very first.

Of several doctors in the play, one, old Sir Patrick, has no faith in physicians whatsoever. Each of the others has his pet nostrum or treatment. "Stimulate the phagocytes." Dr. Walpole diagnoses every case as blood poison; his prescription: remove the nuciform sac. Sir Ralph Bloomfield Bonington ("B. B.") cures all by vaccination, though Sir Colenso Ridgeon warns him: Inoculate in the positive phase and you cure; inoculate in the negative phase and you kill. But B. B. has cured little Prince Henry with Ridgeon's new discovery, opsonin; hence Ridgeon's knighthood and eminence. It is the scant supply of opsonin (which "butters the disease germs so the white corpuscles eat them") that creates the doctor's dilemma. Jennifer

Dubedat beseeches Ridgeon to save her husband, a brilliant but amoral artist. Dr. Blenkinsop, less successful than the other physicians, also needs the treatment. Ridgeon can take but one—which? He invites Dubedat to a dinner with his colleagues, after which he will decide. At the dinner, Dubedat borrows money from all the doctors he can separately "touch," including Blenkinsop. When he leaves, the maid discloses that she is Dubedat's wife—Jennifer is living with him without benefit of clergy. Partly for these reasons, partly because he himself is in love with Jennifer, Ridgeon takes as his patient Blenkinsop, leaving Dubedat to B.B. Dubedat dies; Blenkinsop lives to no good purpose. At the posthumous showing of Dubedat's paintings, Ridgeon meets Jennifer, who is writing "The Story of a King of Men. By His Wife." Jennifer is happy; and Ridgeon is aghast to discover that she dislikes him intensely, that she looks upon him as an old fogy, and that, in accord with Dubedat's wishes, she has already remarried. Then, murmurs Ridgeon, "I have committed a purely disinterested murder."

In the conversation of the doctors, Shaw satirizes the stupidity and the cupidity of the medical profession. Balanced against the doctors, who deem themselves men of science, is the man of art, Dubedat. He is not always granted the better argument. Thus—in a passage omitted from the 1921 Boston production—when Dubedat declares "I don't believe there's such a thing as sin," Sir Patrick retorts: "Well, sir, there are people who don't believe there's such a thing as disease, either. They call themselves Christian Scientists, I believe. They'll just suit your complaint. We can do nothing for you." At his death, however, Dubedat has, if not the last word, the most challenging. The "exquisite beauty of his deathbed statement of the artist's creed," as John Mason Brown called it (March 15, 1941), presses a genuine tenderness into the caustic satire of the drama. Hence Gilbert Gabriel (November 22, 1927) declared that the play "manages, for all its Molieresque maunderings against the medical men, its wordy clash of travesties on the inoculators, the vivisectionists, and the fashionable quacks, to lash itself into a loveliness of romantic foolery. Such a smile is on it as even the shadow of the tombstone cannot darken. . . . He has made high comedy of death. Pitifully, terribly, before your eyes a rascally young genius dies—and Shaw gives you grace to laugh at it." In truth, the scene is touched with irony, for Dubedat overhears the doctors say that he is putting on a performance and he agrees with them. His "performance" is impeccable, as a last performance should be. A rascal in his living, he proves himself an artist in his dying.

The play had its New York premiere March 26, 1915, with Granville-Barker and Lillah McCarthy. Among New York revivals are that of 1927 by the Theatre Guild with Alfred Lunt and Lynn Fontanne; and that of 1941 with Katharine Cornell and Raymond Massey, which ran for 254 performances. There were London revivals in 1923, 1926, 1939, and 1942. The play continues popular, partly because the layman's awe of doctors makes him ready to laugh at them, partly because of more intrinsic merits. After the 1942 opening, the London *Stage* (March 12) exclaimed: "After nearly forty years it has still the power continuously to compel attention by the sheer interest of its story, the coherence of its argument, the cut-and-thrust dialogue, the sharply defined characterization, and the stinging wit with which Shaw pricks the medical profession." The New York City Center production, opening January 11, 1955, was equally well received.

The conscienceless artist, we are told, is drawn from an actual person, Edward Aveling, with whom Karl Marx's youngest daughter lived much like Jennifer—even to the episode with the maid. The value to society of such a genius-scamp is moot. Indeed, in the play "we are never certain," *Stage* continued, "whether the doctor sacrifices Dubedat on strictly ethical grounds . . . or because he hopes to marry the widow. This obscurity or, it may be, this dual motive, is a flaw in the play." On the same grounds, Desmond MacCarthy objected that "Ridgeon does not do justice to his own motives; he did not decide against Dubedat entirely because he coveted his wife, or because he wished to save her from disillusionment; so this admission on his part confuses the audience's recollection of what has gone before." Rather, it may quicken an alert audience to note that there is no inevitable correspondence between word and deed; not only deliberate liars may say one thing and act another. Life is quite likely to leave a man not fully aware of the comparative weights of the mixed elements in his motives; and—especially when a fate we all must meet is involved—it is good theatre to let the audience exercise its own judgment. There is intellectual exercise aplenty in *The Doctor's Dilemma*.

FANNY'S FIRST PLAY   *Bernard Shaw*

One of the less earnest of Shaw's pieces, this play, written in 1911 as "a potboiler," combines satire of middle-class society with humorous prodding of the drama critics of the day. It remains a delightful trifle, and a trifle more. As the *London Times* (August 1, 1935) remarked after a revival, the play "has become a costume piece living on its wit. It has enough wit to live on very well."

The play contrasts Count O'Dowda and his daughter Fanny. The Count is a "Count of the Holy Roman Empire"; in the twentieth century, he shuts the nineteenth carefully beyond his doors, and dwells by choice in the costumes and the manners of the eighteenth. His daughter, a bright young lass out of Cambridge, has written a play and the pleased papa is producing it, anonymously, with four London critics as his guests. Fanny's first play turns out to be something quite other than the eighteenth century pastoral masque the Count her father expects. It is a modern picture of middle-class life, with Bobby Gilbey and Margaret Knox—children of two shopkeeper partners— both on separate frolicking parties landing in jail. Bobby, held in check at home by his respectable parents, has been seeking a checkered career with "Darling Dora" Delaney. Margaret, guarded by her pious folks, felt freed by an evening's prayer at a Salvation Festival, went to a dance hall and in a fracas knocked out two teeth of a policeman. The children, back from a fortnight in jail, break the engagement their parents had pressed them into; Bobby teams up with Darling Dora; and Margaret finds a mate in the footman, Juggins—who turns out to be the brother of a duke, led by his social conscience to take a job.

After this play, the four critics invited by the Count discuss, not its merits, but who the author might be. (The fact that *Fanny's First Play* itself was presented anonymously added further spice to this discussion. A program note read: "The epigram in the second act is by Bernard Shaw"). Suggested as authors of Fanny's piece are Granville-Barker and Shaw, who thus come in for analysis. The critic Flawner Bannal, a composite caricature, is asked by the Count whether it is a good play. He responds: "If it's by a good author, it's a good play, naturally. That stands to reason. Who *is* the author? Tell me that; and I'll place the play for you to a hair's breadth." The rather broad caricatures of the critics are thinly disguised exaggerations of actual writers; one of them, Shaw said, assisted in the make-up with which the actor simulated his appearance. The critics whom Shaw did not introduce, he impishly reported in the Preface, "were somewhat hurt." ("Trotter," in the play, is the critic Walkley, "Vaughan" is Baughan, and "Gunn" is Cannan.)

Subordinate to the critical spoofing, yet present and pressed, is the social satire. The eighteenth century Count protests that he would not have minded "what people call an immoral play. Love beautifies every romance and justifies every audacity." What the Count does object to is the lack of respect the children show to their parents, to the general frankness, to the way they "tear down the veils." One critic—in the play—detects, "beneath all the assumed levity of that poor waif and stray," Darling Dora, a note of genuine passion and compassion. Another critic protests: "What does it all come to? An attempt to expose the supposed hypocrisy of the Puritan middle class of England: people just as good as the author anyhow." Another critic, Charles Darnton—outside the play, after the New York opening— declared: "*Fanny's First Play* is really a three-ring circus, with a human menagerie containing the only collection of trained drama critics . . . Not only does complacent Respectability get an awful biff in the eye, but frilled Romance is knocked clean over the ropes." Shaw's Fabian friends thought he was treating his subjects too lightly. Beatrice Webb wrote to Lillah McCarthy: "I wish you could persuade G. B. S. to do a piece of serious work, and not pursue this somewhat barren tilting at the family."

The first London production was on April 19, 1911, by and with Lillah McCarthy. It ran for 622 performances. New York saw it on September 16, 1912. It has been widely and frequently played since, especially in colleges; for its social satire pricks gently for the freedom of youth, and satire of critical pretension—though really the play buffets men of straw—always pleases young folk interested in art. Shaw's neatly delivered blows feel to each person like a pat on the back; it's his neighbor gets the drubbing! The multiplex smile of the master gleams in *Fanny's First Play*.

ANDROCLES AND THE LION   *Bernard Shaw*

In this play Shaw retells the old tale of the Christian wanderer who plucks a thorn from the paw of an anguished lion and later, "flung to the lions" in a Roman arena, is recognized and fawned upon by the beast he has befriended. The story occurs in the *Attic Nights* of Aulus Gellius, about A.D. 150. Shaw extracts all the circus fun out of the situation, showing Caesar scared to death of the beast, then taking credit for taming it. At odd moments somehow he lifts the play from low comedy to simple yet high assumption of human dignity. Throughout, there is constant probing of basic religious problems.

Accompanying Androcles on the march to the arena are several other Christians. The fierce and brawny Ferrovius is capable of breaking the neck of their Roman guard. And there is the beauteous and aristocratic Lavinia, whom the Roman Captain is perplexed to find dooming herself to the arena. They are all Christians; yet, by a Shavian turn, each holds a separate, individual creed in time of crisis. Thus, as Shaw points out in the Preface, "Androcles is a humanitarian naturalist, whose views surprise everyone. Lavinia, a clever and fearless freethinker, shocks the Pauline Ferrovius, who is comparatively stupid and conscience-ridden." Ferrovius is an early Puritan, wrung with suppressed desires. Caesar, taken with the lion's meek behavior, lionlike spares the martyrs.

The world premiere of the play was in Berlin, November 25, 1912. London saw it on September 1, 1913, with O. P. Heggie and Lillah McCarthy; the same two enacted the play in New York on January 27, 1915; the *Commercial Advertiser* reported that the play was "irresistible even to the gentry who are irritated by the Shavian satire and dialectic." In December 1925, the New York Theatre Guild presented the play, with an eerie forest, painted by Miguel Covarrubias, in which Androcles in fear and the lion in agony crawl toward one another. A black Federal Theatre group had a run of over 50 performances in 1939. In the spring of 1946 Ernest Truex played Androcles; on December 19 in that year he came to New York in the play, sponsored by the American Repertory Theatre. While George Jean Nathan disliked the production, he declared that the play's "propulsive wisdom and wit have not materially dimmed." It is still a delightful romp, with a lift for the mind and the spirit. It opened the new playhouse in Cleveland, December 12, 1949. The deft dialogue between the Christian maid and the pagan Captain recalls that in Wilson Barrett's novel *The Sign of the Cross* (1895), in which the Roman prefect walks hand in hand with the maid into the arena.

In a note for the London premiere, Shaw stated: "There is nothing incredible in the story except the theatrical coincidence of the meeting of the two in the arena. Such coincidences are privileged on the stage, and are the special delight of this particular author." For the American production, he added: "None of the characters are monsters: they are just such people as may be found in the United States today, placed in the monstrous circumstances created by the Roman Empire." We can, in truth, recognize such figures in the world today. More searchingly, we find still insistent in our lives the questions moot in the play. Most happily, *Androcles and the Lion* not only provides excellent entertainment but also that exhilarant sense of human worth, that exaltation of the spirit, which is the noblest puissance of the drama.

PYGMALION   *Bernard Shaw*

Annoyed at the English reception of his earlier plays, Irishman Shaw arranged for a continental premiere of *Pygmalion*. It opened in Vienna on October 16, 1913, and was produced in Berlin a fortnight later. Mrs. Patrick Campbell and Herbert Beerbohm Tree appeared in the play in London on April 11, 1914. At curtain call on opening night, Beerbohm Tree apologized that "the author had been so upset by the loud and frequent applause that he could not stand it any longer and fled in disgust." Shaw sought the notoriety that sprang from insulting the public. Part of the excitement rose from the fact that Mrs. Pat Campbell as Eliza first used the exclamatory word *bloody* on the London stage.

It was a series of such antics, in his life and in his plays, that long kept Shaw's measure from being properly taken. In *Pygmalion* the story is artificial, pleasantly comic; the social implications reside in minor characters and behind the tale. The tale itself is a modern parallel of the story of Pygmalion, legendary sculptor and King of Cyprus, who fell in love with his own statue of Aphrodite. At his prayer, Aphrodite brought the statue to life as Galatea, and Pygmalion married her. Shaw's "Pygmalion" is Henry Higgins, Professor of phonetics, who, come upon a Cockney flower-girl in a rainstorm, wagers that in three months he can so transform her as to pass her off for a lady. To Higgins, this is but a task that he accomplishes, a wager that he wins; but in Eliza Doolittle, the flower girl, a new personality has been created. With the manners and speech of a lady, she cannot fall back into her old life, and with those ways has come an asserting will, which selects Henry Higgins, her "creator," as her mate. To Higgins' dismay, he finds that his "laboratory case" has surged into all his life, with emotional entanglements he had not anticipated. "Driven to extreme exasperation," as Brooks Atkinson put the play's ending, Higgins "proceeds to wring Eliza's infernally beautiful neck; and the light of victory instantly gleams in her eyes." Higgins has won his wager, but Eliza has won her man.

The play leaves the "victory" to be inferred. In a later Epilogue, not part of the play, Shaw says that Higgins would never marry, and he mates Eliza with Freddie—the friend with whom Higgins made the wager—and they set up a green-grocery shop.

Beneath the comedy lies a satire on the superficiality of class distinctions. This is made explicit in the character of Eliza's father, Doolittle, who calls himself one of "the undeserving poor" and is one of Shaw's richest comedy creations.

The story of Pygmalion and Galatea occurs in Ovid's *Metamorphoses,* about A.D. 15. It was dramatized in English by John Marston,* as the *Metamorphosis of Pygmalion's Image,* 1598. W. S. Gilbert* used the story for his comedy (without music) *Pygmalion and Galatea,* 1871, which makes the sculptor a married man; under the fire of the wife Cynisca's jealousy, Galatea decides that her original state was happier, and turns back into a statue. Shaw has combined a modern transformation of the Pygmalion story with that of a Cinderella girl, in one of his liveliest comedies.

Shaw said of the play: "I delight in throwing it at the heads of the wiseacres who repeat the parrot cry that art should never be didactic. It goes to prove my contention that great art can never be anything else." Aristotle earlier observed that all art is didactic—to the adolescent mind.

Mrs. Patrick Campbell brought the play to New York on October 12, 1914, with Philip Merivale replacing Beerbohm Tree, after a German production at the New York Irving Place Theatre. The play is one of Shaw's most popular, with revivals every season or two all around the country. New York saw it in 1926 in Spanish, with Catalina Barcena, and in a Theatre Guild production with Lynn Fontanne. In 1931 Frieda Inescourt and Tom Powers played the leading roles; in 1940, Ruth Chatterton enacted Eliza. The revival on December 26, 1945, with Gertrude Lawrence, Raymond Massey, and Melville Cooper was, as Robert Coleman remarked, "one of the nicest holiday gifts." Wendy Hiller and Leslie Howard acted in the filmed version made in 1938.

Of the play, in the Theatre Guild production, Brooks Atkinson (November 16, 1926) declared: "What remains most vividly is what Mr. Shaw understands more shrewdly than anyone else: the jumble of human relations." Gertrude Lawrence's performance in 1945 was charming but sentimentalized.

Pygmalion continues the Shavian thesis, first seen in *You Never Can Tell,** most fully developed in *Man and Superman,** that the woman is the pursuer in the struggle of the sexes, while the man too tardily wakens to his fate. The popularity of *Pygmalion*—in addition to the continuing sparks the steel of Shaw's wit strikes from the flint of the alert mind—rises from its amalgamation of the social satire and the story and (granting the initial artificiality of the wager) from the engaging conflict of contrasted personalities that not merely reveal themselves but grow through the development of the tale. Eliza grows more aware; Higgins grows more human. The audience grows in discernment and delight.

HEARTBREAK HOUSE   *Bernard Shaw*

The upheavals of the first World War shook Shaw's thinking into distinctly pessimistic channels. Influenced by Chekhov, especially *The Cherry Orchard,* he worked for several years upon "a fantasia in the Russian manner on English themes" which developed into *Heartbreak House* in 1919. However, he would not permit its public reading or presentation amid the escapist frivolities of the current theatre in a land where his attempted objectivity was being labeled pro-German. The play was printed in 1919, and given its world premiere—on Shaw's insistence being held until after the presidential election—by the Theatre Guild in New York on November 12, 1920.

In the long Preface to *Heartbreak House* Shaw envisaged but one generation before another war, with Germany and Russia, defeated in World War I, again great powers in the world. In his Preface, Shaw explains that "*Heartbreak House* is cultured, leisured Europe before the war," where futile culture and talk spread through an economic, political, and moral vacuum. In England, the alternative to Heartbreak House was Horseback Hall, where the same vacuum was filled with futile talk and hunting. In the play, we watch a group of futile humans, in the Sussex home of old Captain Shotover, endlessly talking of culture and politics and one another, flirting, maneuvering for power or security, laying their souls bare.

Among those gathered in the home of the 88-year-old sea captain are his daughter Mrs. Hesione Hushabye and her philandering husband, Hector; his other daughter, Lady Ariadne Utterwood, just back after years in the Colonies her husband governs; Ellie Dunn, a young thing who loves Hector, woos the Captain, and for a time wants to wed Boss Mangan for his money; Ellie's father, Mazzini Dunn, "a born soldier of freedom" who wrote pamphlets and watched the world and saw that nothing ever really changes; Mangan, who mistakes Hesione's effusion for invitation; and a burglar who deliberately gets himself caught, so that he can pour out a sob story and take a collection. These folk discuss all possible subjects, including the world and its movement toward self-destruction. The burglar and the business man scorn the others' talk, talk, talk, but do not hesitate to seek advantage from their impracticality. When enemy bombs begin to break nearby, the practical burglar and the business man Mangan run out to the cave in the gravel pit—which is where a bomb strikes, sparing the aimless talkers in the house. Yet these are held in the grim prophecy of the Captain, of the ship they voyage in, "the soul's prison we call England . . . She will strike and sink and split. Do you think the laws of God will be suspended in favor of England because you were born in it?" Staunchly against that prophecy England still battles today.

Both Chekhov's *The Cherry Orchard* and Shaw's play show the decomposition of society through a group gathered in a country house; but, as William Irvine pointed out in *The Universe of G. B. S.* (1949), the characters in Shaw's play are allegorical; in Chekhov's typical. Thus we find the Captain standing here as stalwart old England. "His house, built like a ship, somehow symbolizes the sea-trading out of which English wealth and commerce grew. The selling of his soul to the devil in youth and his marriage with a black witch in Zanzibar signify the ruthless colonial exploitation and the savage insistence on prestige inseparable from imperial power . . . When he looks into the past he is Sir Francis Drake—and Bernard Shaw when he looks into the future. He is noticeably Bernard Shaw, for he is fond of macaroni and generally regarded as mad." The other characters likewise symbolize aspects of English life. Lady Utterwood is the Empire; Hesione Hushabye, the British home. Mazzini Dunn is the Victorian liberal—still a lingering form: sentimental and therefore ineffectual. His daughter Ellie is the modern girl, who joins with the Captain as youth and "Old England" must unite. From these symbolic figures as contrasted with Chekhov's types, it follows that "*The Cherry Orchard* is prophetic as a slide beneath a microscope is prophetic; *Heartbreak House,* as the interpretation of a formula or the demonstration of a theorem." The warning stands, that, without our most careful bolstering, civilization will fall.

This brilliant though pessimistic satire was given a superb production by the Theatre Guild, with Helen Westley and Dudley Digges. When the Guild expressed a desire to cut the play, Shaw cabled "Abandon play. Cancel contract." By mail he explained: "I knew that the cutting of a single syllable would mean failure, as I had myself cut the play down to the bone, as I always do, before printing it. . . . Nothing would induce me to consent to the omission of one word of the text, or the curtailment of one minute of the time. . . ." The play was produced verbatim; and although it ran for 129 performances, the critics felt there was too much of it. The *New York Sun* called it "a conversational debauch"; Heywood Broun said "we like the needle, but we could dispense with the haystack." The *New York Times* considered the play "a rehash of all his often reiterated scoldings and complaints against everything in English domestic and political life with which he happens to disagree." The play opened in London October 18, 1921; Birmingham saw it in 1923 and 1930; London again in 1932 with Cedric Hardwicke and Edith Evans, and in 1936-1937. New York saw a revival by the Mercury Theatre in 1938 with Orson Welles. On-Stage presented the play in 1950, off Broadway.

The *London Times* (April 26, 1932) sought to analyze the play: "The first act of *Heartbreak House* is exceptional in Mr. Shaw's theatre, for the pleasure it gives is predominantly aesthetic. It has form as well as substance. . . . Somewhere about the middle of the second act one ceases to believe in the stable existence of any of the people on any one imaginative plane . . . feeling is dead, and form is broken." There is general agreement that this is one of Shaw's greatest plays, but that the exuberance of the drama detracts from its form and therefore from its power. Brooks Atkinson said (April 30, 1938): "It is the play of a clown and a prophet, full of caustic insight—but O Lord, how long!" Richard Watts felt that "most of it is so shrewd, so wise, so brilliant and so prophetic that the flaws seem of little importance." John Mason Brown was a bit more reserved: "Although genius sails proudly upon the windtossed oceans of its speech, it sails on a vessel which is covered with barnacles, burdened with a poorly packed cargo, steered in a haphazard manner, and manned by an unruly crew." Similarly divided was the English critic Ivor Brown, in the London *Observer* (March 14, 1937): "Captain Shotover is one of the greatest of Shavian creations: half fire and air, half rum and realism, he is archangel, inventor, master-mariner, and tough old critic of the social scene. His memory is a morass, yet his mind is sharp as a sword. But he trumpets his verities under handicap. His delivery of judgment on the world is not prolix in itself, but is spoiled by the prolixity of others. Mr. Shaw is rarely guilty of creating a bore, but Mr. and Mrs.

Hushabye come as near to it as any of his creatures, and Randall Utterwood is little better ... *Heartbreak House* has the quality of a masterpiece, though here and there the quantity be swollen and the matter over-ripe."

It is, nevertheless, the conversation in *Heartbreak House* that burgeons to searching and searing criticism of the well-meaning, esteemed, and apparently estimable people that help to ruin the world. Some works, like *Moby Dick*, like Rabelais', achieve virtue through their very excess. In refusing to allow his drama to be cut, Shaw showed that a dramatist may be wiser than his critics. They may have the last word on first nights; but his words continue their challenge beyond the footlights.

BACK TO METHUSALEH   *Bernard Shaw*

Shaw's ponderings about the sorry state of the world led him to the conclusion that only if men live long enough to grow really mature and wise (say 300 years), can civilization be saved. His theory of creative evolution, partly suggested by Samuel Butler's *Life and Habit* (1877), is developed in the Preface, and illustrated in the five parts of Shaw's longest play, the "metabiological pentateuch," *Back to Methuselah*, 1918-20. The preface has some 30,000 words; the play, 90,000.

Part I, "In the Beginning," opens in the Garden of Eden, where Lilith tears herself asunder to create Adam and Eve, and where the Serpent reveals to Eve the secret of continuance. Eve has been asking "Why? Why?"; the Serpent starts evolution on its way by asking "Why not?" A few centuries later, we see Adam, the digger, waiting for death; Cain, the killer, grasping power and thereby hastening death; and Eve, hoping for something that will make life worthwhile.

Part II, "The Gospel of the Brothers Barnabas," is a satire of society, especially of politics, at the time of the writing. Joyce Burge and Lubin are thinly disguised portraits of Lloyd George and Asquith. The idea of longevity is introduced by Professor Barnabas, and the politicians, thinking he has an elixir, want to decide which persons are to be allowed to use it. When they discover that Barnabas has only a biological theory based upon the human will, Burge plans to use it as a plank in his election campaign.

Part III, "The Thing Happens," set in the year 2150, presents Burge-Lubin, President of the British Isles, conferring with Barnabas about an American invention of a method of breathing under water, which may upset their tables of life-expectancy (according to which all persons work only between the ages of 13 and 43. The country is well-governed, because the public services are manned by Chinese: "Justice is impartiality. Only strangers are impartial.") Motion pictures, shown by the American inventor, of well-known persons that have drowned, reveal that the Archbishop has survived the generations. We knew him as the Reverend Bill Haslam of Part II; he is now 283 years old. The Domestic Minister, Mrs. Lutestring, has lived for 274 years. The two determine to perpetuate the race of long-livers, as the Chinese Chief Secretary points out (with double-edged satire) that the English are still children at sixty and seventy, hence "are potentially the most highly developed race on earth, and would actually be the greatest if you could live long enough to attain to maturity."

Part IV, "Tragedy of an Elderly Gentleman," is set in A.D. 3000, when the "normal" (long-lived) people have taken control, and the short-lived are attended by nurses. The capital of the British Empire is now Baghdad. A short-lived elderly gentleman has come with the Prime Minister to Ireland, center of the normal, to consult the Oracle. She bids the Minister "Go home, poor fool!"; but the elderly gentleman begs permission to stay, and by her compassionate glance the Oracle kills him.

Part V, "As Far As Thought Can Reach," shows children, in A.D. 31,920, hatched from eggs, born adolescent, living some four years in love and play, in artistic creation and procreation—then transmuted to "Ancients." The Ancients live endlessly, until an accident fells them; they spend their centuries without need of nourishment or sleep, in profound and almost wordless meditation. One of the youngsters, a sculptor (Pygmalion; Shaw again uses the name), creates two living dolls that call themselves Ozymandias, king of kings, and Cleopatra-Semiramis, whose human misdemeanors and petty emotions disgust the young ones, until an Ancient wills them to die. The youngsters are briefly bored until the Ancients leave; then briefly bewildered as one of their own group goes off: it is his time to become an Ancient. As night falls, the ghosts of the first living creatures appear from the distance of 4004 B.C., and weigh the centuries. The serpent says "I am justified. For I chose wisdom and the knowledge of good and evil; and now there is no evil; and wisdom and good are one." Lilith, who had given Eve "the greatest of gifts: curiosity," bids the ages dread, of all things, stagnation; she looks forward to, "the whirlpool in pure intelligence that, when the world began, was a whirlpool in pure force," and to the day when life shall fill and shall master the myriad starry mansions to their uttermost confines.

Shaw declared, in the *Candid Friend* (May 11, 1901): "I exhausted romanticism before I was ten years old." He has been creating his own brand ever since; *Back To Methusaleh* is its fullest flowering. However, the play lacks the mellowness that the theme deserves; it is embittered by Shaw's disillusionment and rage at the hideous folly of World War I. Thus, in what many think the most vigorous of the parts, "The Gospel of the Brothers Barnabas," he lashes savagely at his political butts, although for his buffetings he has fashioned hardly more than men of straw. In "The Thing Happens," his successful candidate for the House of Commons "was released from the County Lunatic Asylum a fortnight ago. Not mad enough for the lethal chamber: not sane enough for any place but the division lobby." A sharpness has taken the place of the often more even-toned wit; but Shaw is waging the most serious war of his dramatic struggles. *Back to Methusaleh*—more intense than *Man and Superman,** more wide-ranging than *Heartbreak House**—shows long conflict and the ultimate triumph of hope over despair. It is a wry and dry faith that conquers.

Back To Methusaleh undoubtedly represents Shaw's fullest and most deeply pondered study of the problems of mankind. It is, however, scintillant and searching, satiric and expository, rather than dramatic: a thesis in the theatre. The basic problem man faces, as Shaw presents it, is to grow strong enough to surmount the destructive forces that man's own development has loosed within the world. He can achieve this through the creative evolution of the self-conscious mind, achieving indefinite longevity. This leaves him free for the ecstatic contemplataion of the free intelligence, which Shaw, in a measure, equates with God.

The play, searching thus widely down the centuries, is far too long for an evening's presentation. In its world premiere (opening February 27, 1922), the New York Theatre Guild divided it into three parts, showing each for a week in turn, to a total of 25 complete performances; in England, under Sir Barry Jackson in Birmingham beginning October 9, 1923, and in London beginning February 18, 1924, the parts were played on successive evenings and matinees. The play was presented in Berlin in 1925; in public readings in New York in 1933; again in London in 1935; in Pasadena in 1938.

After a London revival that spread the various parts over several evenings of February and March 1947, Harold Hobson of the *Sunday Times* was condescending. When "The Tragedy of an Elderly Gentleman" was reached, he declared (February 25) that the play "seems to be approaching the anecdotal instead of the apocalyptic." His shrewdest remarks (March 18) came for the last and best of the Methuselah plays: "To argue the hind leg off a dog isn't quite the same thing as to convince him. The dog may lose his leg and retain his opinion. In fact, in *As Far As Thought Can Reach,* Mr. Shaw, the master of paradox, gives the impression of being paradox-trapped. What is he trying to prove? That the emotions are a discarded foolishness; that art, which appeals to them, is useless. How does he try to prove it? By the resources of his art . . . declaring in cadences of undying loveliness that nowhere in life is there any loveliness at all. Every argument Mr. Shaw brings forward is contradicted by the overtones of the phrases in which he expresses it." By this time, however, *Back To Methusaleh* had been widely accepted on the stage, and even more widely read.

The critics that saw the premieres were on the whole unimpressed. The *New York Sun* (March 14, 1922) called it "not merely undramatic; it is antidramatic." Heywood Broun declared Shaw "so passionately sincere in this play that it is embarrassing. And after embarrassment has begun to wear off, it is boring." Kenneth MacGowan was annoyed at Shaw's classifying artistic creation as adolescent play, "using art to foreswear art . . ." In England, J. T. Grein declared in the *Illustrated London News* (March 8, 1924) "The play is a magnificent jest—the greatest literary jest ever attempted by a great man, who, conscious that he could do with his public as he pleases, pulled it by the leg and—pulled both off, leg, as well as jest."

A condensed version of the play, arranged by Ellis St. Joseph, was effectively presented by Valerie Bettis, Bramwell Fletcher, Arnold Moss, and Blanche Yurka at New York University, December 11, 1952.

A shrewd criticism of Shaw's ultimate concept was advanced in the *London Times* of January 18, 1952: "Mr. Shaw's Utopia, in which everyone lives to the age of Methuselah and dies at last by accident, is a kind of composite photograph of all the more serious heresies, dominated by the supreme intellectual heresy that the Divine Life consists of contemplation . . . Once again we have a religion that is not good enough because it is the expression of a nausea for actual things, of a mere desire for release . . . This barren climax has come to religious thought again and again, so long as it has been thought about religion mistaking itself for religion."

Whatever its shortcomings, *Back To Methusaleh* gave timely expression to far-searching thoughts on an insistent problem. Its length may cause it to remain largely a reader's drama; but it remains a delightful experience for the mind in quest of maturity. The play both indicates and illustrates that quest.

SAINT JOAN   *Bernard Shaw*

Unquestionably the most dramatic treatment of the martyred Maid's story is Shaw's *Saint Joan*. Written out of no social or socialist urge, it is probably his greatest play. Archibald Henderson has expressed the view that it is "the greatest play in English since Shakespeare."

It was not to be expected that Shaw would present the mere story of the Maid. While he followed with great accuracy the details of her trial for witchcraft, he increased Joan's understanding of her religious role. He saw her as the first Protestant, the first to stand steadfast for freedom of conscience against the dictates of the Church. The play presents the episodes of Joan's betrayal, the trial, a touching Inquisition scene, Joan's disavowal of the voices, then her retraction and assertion of her own judgment, her own belief in the authenticity of the voices—which means her death. Shrewdly cynical pictures are given of the French prelates and the generals who for various political reasons desire that Joan shall be discredited and removed. In a dream of the year 1455, King Charles, whom Joan had crowned, rejoices that she has been cleared of the charge of witchcraft. An Epilogue dated 1920—the year of the Maid's canonization— permits Shaw to examine the meaning of her story to the world today. The ghosts of those that condemned her come each to sing her praise but, on the very grounds of his praising, to urge that she come not again to the world today. Joan, anguished, cries: "Oh God, when will the world be ready to receive Thy saints?"

The world premiere took place on December 28, 1923, in the New York Theatre Guild production with Winifred Lenihan. Dame Sybil Thorndike enacted Joan in London in 1924, where the Old Vic revived the play in 1934 with Mary Newcomb and Maurice Evans. Evans came to New York to act in a 1936 production, opening March 9, with Katharine Cornell. Elisabeth Bergner enacted Joan in Berlin. Luise Rainer played in a Piscator production in Washington, D.C., in 1940; Uta Hagen, in a New York revival, opening October 4, 1951.

Although in March 1924 the French Minister gave Winifred Lenihan the "Gold Medal of Jeanne d'Arc," the play was roundly attacked in Paris. In September 1936 "Catholic Action," by publishing a list of changes it felt should be made, broke off the project for filming Shaw's play; the story of the Maid was next screened after the stage success of Anderson's *Joan of Lorraine.* The best screening of the story remains *The Passion of Joan of Arc,* 1929, with Mme. Falconetti as Joan; in this, a series of close-ups of the faces of Joan, her judges, and her prosecutors, creates a tensely dramatic mood.

Shaw, interested in presenting Joan as taking the first steps of individualism, failed to make a theological distinction drawn by the church, between the claim to private judgment regarding the teachings of the Church in faith or morals, and the claim to private inspiration. The first claim, always disallowed, produces the heretics, as Wyclif and Luther. The second claim, when allowed, manifests the mystics, including Joan. Shaw's oversight of this distinction was probably deliberate, intended to press his thesis that Joan was a pioneer of the Reformation. How Shaw's own pressing of distinctions may be overlooked was shown in the comments of Percy Hammond (December 30, 1923): "just another example of Mr. Shaw's gift for interminable rag-chewing . . . some of this surplus conversation is none too good. Thus 'Are you an Englishman?' 'No, I'm a gentleman.'" . . . In his review of the 1936 revival, Percy Hammond repeated this quotation, and added: "George Kaufman might get away with a crack like that, but Howard Dietz or Moss Hart would be ashamed of it." Percy was less percipient than Shaw, for the dramatist meant the remark to help carry a basic point: Joan was both "protestant" and French; not only the sense of individual integrity but the spirit of nationalism was being born in those days.

The yeomen were developing a national consciousness, but the more conservative "gentleman" of the day still felt no sense of a nation, but held himself as in the feudal system. Joan thought of "God and I" without the Church intervening; this pointed to protestantism. She thought "the King and I" without the peerage intervening; this pointed to nationalism. One of Shaw's secrets, in truth, is the contemporaneousness with which he endows his characters. These figures of past ages are our neighbors, and ourselves.

In this play, Shaw had less need than elsewhere to inject his ideas; they flow naturally from the situation, they issue inevitably from the lips of prelate and protesting Maid. As a consequence, as Luigi Pirandello* said, in the *New York Times* (January 13, 1924): "In no other of Shaw's works have considerations of art been so thoroughly respected as in *Saint Joan*." Shaw's consideration for ideas is equally noteworthy, making Harold Hobson, of the *London Sunday Times,* exclaim of a December 3, 1947 revival: "I wish I had space to praise not only the skill and suppleness of Mr. Shaw's mind in this play, but also its generosity . . . Mr. Shaw believes in Joan; but he knows, not only that her enemies may have been good men, but that their ideas were not necessarily either foolish or wicked. One leaves the theatre in a mood of reconciliation, which is better than that of indignation, however righteous." The artist for once restrained the controversialist; at worst, Shaw had other fish to fry. He pictured a conflict of moral systems, a new good to supersede the old good, with honest intentions on both sides.

And Joan, his protagonist, is doomed by her own pride. "The old Greek tragedy is rising among us," the Archbishop foretells; "it is the chastisement of *hubris*." In a superbly constructed play, with swift scenes capped by miracles picturing Joan's rise, Shaw shows her at the peak of her power already set apart for denial and destruction. First the General, then the King, then the Archbishop, repudiate the Maid. "Her allies oppose her for little reasons, as her enemies, for big," William Irvine pointed out in *The Universe of G. B. S.* (1949). "Then, deserted, denied, and doomed in the midst of her triumph, she rises abruptly from despair to the full height of her lonely pride and inspiration. She will follow God and her voices to the end. The trial scene is a magnificent and beautiful irony on human politics. Never were reasons of state more eloquent, more lofty, more imperious, yet never did they lead to greater catastrophe." The deeper tragedy springs not from evil balanced against good, but from good intentions that tortuously pave the road to hell.

The Epilogue, bringing the play into our own time, was most vigorously challenged. Some critics felt that it was unnecessary, that the audience might have been trusted to make the application to today. "With regard to the play itself," said Irvine, "the epilogue is an anticlimax, a vulgarization, and a lengthy elucidation of the obvious. Even so, it is too irresistible to lose its place on the stage. "Defending the Epilogue, Pirandello declared that in this final part of the play "we may gather almost explicitly the reason why Shaw wrote it. This world, he seems to say, is not made for saints to live in. We must take the people who live in it for what they are, since it is not vouchsafed them to be anything else." Shaw might agree that we must take people for what they are; but he would hardly accept the implication that we should take them and keep them, be content with those to whom "it is not vouchsafed" to be better. The play rings challenge to authority, assertion of individual independence and integrity—demand that the better strive, in the hope that they will ultimately prevail.

The 1936 revival found the play accepted as a masterpiece, "increasing in popular stature," said Atkinson, "ever since it was first acted"—but left the Epilogue still in dispute. John Anderson (March 10, 1936) protested: "The point is not whether the play should have an epilogue showing Joan's final triumph, but whether this epilogue is the sort of epilogue *Saint Joan* needs. There are moments when it descends from the high veneration of sainthood to the brassy informality of showing the Girl Who Made Good, a sort of: P.S. She got the job." John Mason Brown, however felt that "its epilogue, which was widely condemned when the Guild first produced the play back in 1923, now seems to be a further demonstration of Shaw's wisdom. . . . It succeeds in giving a sad point and a great glory to this story of the Maid."

Brilliant as Shaw's talk may be, it was protracted beyond the concentration point of many hearers. A revised version (sent to America too late for the 1923 premiere) somewhat shortened the play; but even in 1936 Robert Garland enlisted himself among those "who, along with the Dauphin who is soon to be Charles VII, wish that Joan would keep quiet or go on home." After Shaw's insistence that his plays be uncut has died, they may be handled as freely as Shakespeare's. But remember that the uncut *Hamlet** still proves the most moving. *Saint Joan,* as it now stands, is a vivid portrait gallery in a drama that does not merely preach but lives a battle cry of personal freedom.

THE APPLE CART   *Bernard Shaw*

In 1929, four years after Shaw received the Nobel Prize, another honor came to him—the creation by Sir Barry Jackson of the annual Malvern Festival for the presentation of Shaw's plays. The first of his works to be performed there, on August 19, 1929, was his new "political extravaganza," *The Apple Cart.* The play delighted the conservatives and shocked the laborites. The latter saw in it a glorification of monarchy, although, as the play itself emphasizes, the monarch holds his power only by threatening to resort to the democratic polls.

The Apple Cart is loosely constructed; it consists of two dramatized political discussions separated by a frolic of the monarch and his "platonic concubine," which ends in a wrestling match because she wants him to stay and he wants to get home in time for dinner with his wife.

The monarch of the play is King Magnus of Great Britain, ruler in the 1960's. His wife is the prosaic and patient Jemima; his recreational lady, the romantic and effervescent Orinthia. Involved in the political discussion are various folk. There is the American Ambassador, whose suggestion that the United States seek readmission into the British Empire is received with considerable concern, since England would thus become a mere appendage to the United States. There are two women in the Cabinet: Amanda, with little education but sterling character, and a sense of humor that at most embarrassing moments pricks her colleagues' pretentiousness; and Lysistrata, a high-strung intellectual, with the best brain in the government but no sense of humor, and likely if hard pressed to take refuge in hysterics. Bonerges, the complacent "self-made" labor leader, is on hand. Such plot as the play has centers upon the efforts of Prime Minister Proteus to reduce the King's power and to wipe out the royal veto; and the King's countermove: "rather than be a cipher" (as Shaw put it in the Preface) "he will abandon his throne and take his obviously very rosy chance of being a popularly elected Prime Minister himself." In dismay at this proposal, the Cabinet yields.

The "apple cart" that seems to have been upset is democracy, which comes in for a thorough walloping in the play. On the one hand, government by the people, we are told, means government by those that can persuade the run-of-the-mill, low-level populace. On the other hand looms the tremendous monopolistic trust, Breakages, (un)Limited, which suppresses inventions and produces perishable objects, thus ensuring plenty of work, and profit. Lysistrata points out to the King that "it is not the most ignorant national crowd that will come out on top, but the best power station; for you can't do without power stations, and you can't run them on patriotic songs and hatred of the foreigner, and guff and bugaboo, though you can run nationalism on nothing else." Neither monarchy nor democracy is the danger, but big business.

The world premiere of the play, under the title *Vanity Fair,* was in Warsaw, June 14, 1929; it was the seventeenth Shaw play translated into Polish by Sobieniowski; his theatre had bid for the premiere of *Saint Joan,* * but Shaw, having promised that to the Theatre Guild, gave Warsaw *The Apple Cart.* The play was banned in Dresden in 1930 as reactionary; in the same year Reinhardt produced it in Berlin as *The Emperor (Kaiser) of America. Der Abend* remarked: "Shaw can still put all other wits into his pocket." The Theatre Guild produced the play on February 24, 1930, with Claude Rains. Richard Lockridge said that Shaw was returning to political themes "as a steam-roller might return to a daisy patch."

Politics, if not daisied, is indeed a patchwork. Henry Nevinson, in England, called the drama "a maliciously manufactured contrast between democracy and royalty to the disadvantage of the former." Shaw, in his Preface (1930), answered this by saying that there is no longer any battle between democracy and aristocracy: both have been bought by plutocracy. Indeed, "Democracy is no longer bought; it is bilked. Ministers who are Socialists to the backbone are as helpless in the grip of Breakages Limited as its acknowledged henchmen . . . I am going to ask you to begin our study of Democracy," he went on, "by considering it first as a big balloon, filled with gas or hot air, and sent up so that you shall be kept looking up at the sky whilst other people are picking your pockets." Those that are responsible to all—Shaw repeats the old argument—are responsible to none; hence he makes "a desperate bid for dictatorship," for sane and commanding leadership in an else doomed world. It was inevitable that such a demand would find sharp attack, as in Henry Hazlitt's words in the New York *Nation* (April 22, 1931): "Wouldn't it be lovely, the play says in effect, if final political power were in the hands of a man of charming manners, who would pay no attention to what the people wanted or demanded but would know infallibly what was good for them, and would provide it; who, though a member of a hereditary upper class, would appreciate fully the feelings and needs of workers and slum dwellers; who would never be subject to popular recall yet would never abuse his power; who—We need hardly go on. That is not a solution but a self-contradictory day dream." Even in the specific struggle of King Magnus and Prime Minister Proteus, Hazlitt found Shaw misdirected, "for democratic politicians are strong precisely where *The Apple Cart* makes them appear weak. A successful politician, especially a prime minister, may be a thundering ass so far as his knowledge of economics or his grasp of any abstract or complicated question whatever is concerned; but there is one direction in which he is extremely unlikely to be an ass, and that is in his ability to handle men, to flatter, impress, charm, cajole, bargain, negotiate, outwit." The continuing timeliness of such questions—the value and defects of democracy; the extent to which "benevolent despot" is a contradiction in terms—gives present interest to *The Apple Cart.*

Shaw's defense of the play, though less concernedly, carried over to the looseness of its form, specifically, to the playful interlude with the "romantically beautiful" Orinthia. Why may not he, Shaw queried, like a composer of music, introduce a slow second movement? The boudoir episode, he suggested, provides comic relief; and "Shakespeare understood what I understand; if you put humor into a play, it must be cheap humor." The Interlude, however, has a serious significance: "It completes the portrait of the King, who in the middle of the crisis is seen, not merely as a statesman, but as a human being with a domestic life." Shaw recognized that political discussions, especially onstage, must come in temperate doses; between them, he inserted the trifling of sex, which culminates, like a burlesque of the Greek *gamos,* in a roughhouse tumble of the man and woman on the floor. After this, one can take some more politics! There is, perhaps, a still deeper meaning to be found in the Interlude. Setting aside the autobiographical identification of Orinthia as Mrs. Patrick Campbell and Jemima as Mrs. Shaw—with Proteus poking at Ramsay MacDonald—one may see in the romantic lady the symbol of beauty and art. Shaw (or the King) amuses himself with these; he finds use for them; but he is not deeply tempted; society, the general good, the simple everyday person, come first. Thus, out of debate balanced with banter, Shaw maintains liveliness as through parable and paradox he pummels our minds and challenges our souls. If the cart be tumbling, here are at least tart apples to digest.

IN GOOD KING CHARLES'S GOLDEN DAYS   *Bernard Shaw*

A "true history that never happened," Shaw called *In Good King Charles's Golden Days,* 1939, an intellectual frolic set in the Restoration days of 1680. From the point of view of the theatre, the play consists of one long act of conversation in which a monarch, a scientist, a religious leader, and an artist cross verbal swords to the bywords of a trio of the king's mistresses, and a much shorter, wholly disconnected act of tender understanding, though still intellectualized, talk between the king and his wife. The two acts together present some of Shaw's finest foolery and some of his most challenging thought.

The main scene is the library of Isaac Newton. To the literal-minded but clear-headed philosopher come George Fox, founder of the Society of Friends, and Mr. Rowley—who is King Charles II in his incognito moments. On the monarch's trail arrive three lovely but possessive and quarrelsome vixens. Nell Gwynne, come for her king, is attracted by the Quaker Fox in his leather breeches. Lady Castlemaine bursts upon them in a rage; she has time to cool somewhat while Newton demonstrates mathematically that Charles could not possibly have been unfaithful to her, as she protests he has, a hundred thousand times.

The Duchess of Portsmouth, go-between for Charles and the French Louis XIV, the Sun King, comes to get a love potion from "Mr. Newton, the alchemist." Save for the darts of these women at one another, when jealousy bares the nails, almost the only physical action in the play is a wrestling match between Isaac Newton and the King's brother when, on James' refusal to leave, Isaac (whose "home is his castle") tries to throw him out of the window. (A wrestling match is always good theatre, especially when, as

Shaw manages to make them—see *The Apple Cart**—the opponents are of different rank or sex.) Newton has, in fact, at one time or another asked them all to leave. In spite of his formally restrained impatience, the conversation ranges widely through the issues of the day, with men who are worthy of the Shavian wit. Charles and James argue the theory of modern kingship as opposed to the older ideas; when James proposes the restoration of absolute rule, Charles drily observes: "This is a deuced foggy country for sun kings." And Charles with the scientist, the pastor, and the painter, combs out the case for Protestantism and the case for the Pope; science and art fight their battle. Shaw would have liked to use Hogarth as the artist, but the dates don't fit; he therefore brings in the painter Godfrey Kneller. The women make a gay, uncomprehending, but consciously delightful chatter all about.

Newton was right in resenting these intruders. For, if the play can be said to have any conflict, it springs accidentally out of the undirected conversation, as first a remark of the Quaker, and then a remark of the painter, upset two of Newton's basic conceptions, and the idle interruption of a day threatens to spoil the labors of a lifetime. Newton is working on a chronology of the world, based on its creation four thousand and four years before the birth of Jesus; Fox laughs him into the idea that God is not such a niggard of time. And Newton has been building his theory of gravitation on the concept that the universe is, "in principle," rectilinear; whereas Kneller, taking the ladies to witness, assures him that the basic drive—of beauty, and of space—is not a straight line but a curve. We leave the perturbed scientist, to watch King Charles in gentler but still wise talk with Queen Catherine. Some critics have lamented Shaw's picture of Charles the tender and loving husband as a distortion of history. In his Preface, Shaw upholds Charles as "the best of husbands": he used Louise to get money from Louis XIV of France; and "historians who confuse Charles's feelings for his wife with his appetite for Barbara Villiers do not know chalk from cheese biologically." Whatever the facts of history, in this scene between Charles and Catherine the playwright realized some of his tenderest moments. As the *London Times* (August 14, 1939) put it, "Mr. Shaw does not often achieve and sustain beauty so quiet." Even the matter-of-fact New York *Variety* (August 23, 1939) called the scene "a touching and fine piece of writing."

The various characters of the play, indeed, are deftly drawn and neatly differentiated. Richard Watts (December 13, 1942) comments on Shaw's handling of the women: "The simple earthiness of Nell Gwynne, the feminine guile of the French Duchess of Portsmouth, the heavy jealousy of the amorous Duchess of Cleveland, the motherly understanding of Queen Catherine—all are managed with humor and dexterity." Outstanding, however, is King Charles, seen more subtly by Shaw than by most writers. As the *London Observer* (May 12, 1940) noted, we watch "the pathos of a wry but very real talent for life which has been warped by historical accident. The potentially sage, and often sad, sovereign has been deflected by destiny into wearing the title of Merry Monarch." Throughout, it is a wise—wise more than witty, though not without wit—and a wistful king that we behold.

The play is not well constructed. It begins as a play about Newton. Then, for a long spell, it is a conversation piece wholly without plot or advancing action. "Mr. Shaw knows well enough," said the *Observer*, "that plays must have movement, but believes that an argument hurtling through the air is

as good a form of motion for an intelligent audience as the flash of a sword."
In the second act, it becomes a play about Charles, whose picture, Watts
adds, is "one of the most winning in all the playwright's portrait gallery."
Whatever his theme, through these vital personages Shaw argues with a
liveliness and brilliance that hold keen and delighted attention.

The title of the play is itself doubly satiric. The play *The Dame of Honor,*
by Thomas D'Urfey, 1706, used seriously, in a song, the refrain "In Good
Queen Bess's golden days." A bit later (1734) an anonymous religious and
political satire, the poem *The Vicar of Bray,* picturing a time-serving and
turncoat minister, used with satiric intent the refrain "In good King
Charles's golden days." Shaw took the refrain as a title, and twisted
the satiric intent by picturing a short but truly golden mean between the
extremes of two revolutions. While the manners in the play have the
intertangled roughness and politeness, bluntness and formality, of revolu-
tion-enclosed Restoration times, the ideas are sharply drawn to present
pertinence. Reading the play is a joy and exhilaration. Seeing the drama is
also a rich experience. Shaw wrote the play for the Malvern Festival, at
which it had its world premiere on August 12, 1939. James Agate wrote in
the *London Times*: "The body and bulk of it is the best warp and woof that
has come from the Shavian loom since *Back to Methuselah.** " After seeing a
performance in Dublin, Watts wrote (Dec. 13, 1942): "Here once more the
master is in his best vein. Here is Shaw at his mellowest and most charming. His lucid writing style has never seemed more winning and attractive."
"The critics unite," said Harold Hobson in the *Christian Science Monitor*
(September 9, 1939), "in praising the play's intellectual brilliance, its flashing eloquence, its inexhaustible vitality."

Shaw himself said in his Preface: "Anyone who considers a hundred and
fiftieth edition of *Sweet Nell of Old Drury* more attractive than Isaac
Newton had better avoid my plays: they are not meant for such. And anyone
who is more interested in Lady Castlemaine's hips than in Fox's foundation
of the great Cult of Friendship should keep away from theatre and frequent
worse places." Yet he gives us the ladies as a sauce to the intellectual
speculations. Three years after Charles died came the Bloodless Revolution.

A few recent revivals of Shaw's plays are here mentioned.

Mrs. Warren's Profession: London, 1956, also to New York. NT, thirty-four
times in repertory, 1970-1971.   New York Vivian Beaumont (then in
charge of Joseph Papp), 1975. Yale, 1981.

Arms and the Man: Greenwich, England, Festival, 1978, in honor of Miss
Horniman, who in 1984, unknown to Shaw, had financed the premiere of
the play. Felicity Kendal was the delightful Raina.

Candida: Roundabout, 1978-1979. Circle in the Square, 1981.

You Never Can Tell: Roundabout, 1977-1978.

The Devil's Disciple: Tyrone Power, 1956. ELT, 1963. Guilford, England,
1965. Asolo, 1972. RSC, August 7, 1976, with Zoe Wanamaker as Essie;
John Wood, General Burgoyne; T. P. McKenna, Rev. Anderson; Tom Conti,
Dick Dudgeon; Patience Collier, Mrs. D. Roger Butkin, who designed the
play, commented: "It is surprising, considering the length of Shaw's stage
directions, how inaccurate he is on visual details. Many items he describes
were simply not in existence in England, certainly not in America, in 1777."

Caesar and Cleopatra: New York, December 13, 1951, for sixty-seven
performances, with Laurence Olivier and Vivien Leigh. London Old Vic

1956; London again, 1961. With book, music, and lyrics by Ervin Drake, *Her First Roman* came OffBway October 20, 1968, with Richard Kiley and Leslie Uggams; Claudia McNeil as Ftatateeta. Songs included "Hail Sphinx," "Save Me from Caesar," "The Things We Think We Are," "In Vino Veritas"—but it lasted only seventeen performances.

Captain Brassbound's Conversion: London, 1956. Bristol Old Vic, 1958. Oxford, 1965, with John Turner as the Captain, Barbara Jefford as Lady Cicely. London's Cambridge Theatre, February 18, 1971, with Ingrid Bergman; New York and American tour, 1972. London Haymarket, June 6, 1982, with Penelope Keith and John Turner, and Charles Rea making a major triumph in a minor role, as the U.S. Navy Captain who presides at Brassbound's trial.

The Doctor's Dilemma: London, 1956, 1963, 1966.

Androcles and the Lion: New York, 1925, starring Henry Travers, with Romney Brent as the Lion; Clare Eames, Lavinia; Tom Powers, the Captain; Edward G. Robinson, Caesar. Fifty-four performances at London Mermaid, 1961. New York Phoenix, forty-eight performances with John Heffernan. London, 1966. Stratford, Conn., Festival, 1968.

Man and Superman: APA-Phoenix, 1964-1965. CSC, 1967, 1969, 1971. Roundabout played *Don Juan in Hell,* 1980-1981.

Major Barbara: London Old Vic, July 16, 1956, with Moira Shearer. New York, October 30, 1956, with Glynis Johns; Charles Laughton as Undershaft; Eli Wallach, Walker; Burgess Meredith, Cusins. London, August 28, 1958, with Joan Plowright. Asolo, 1967. RSC, 1970, its first Shaw play, with Judi Dench, Brewster Mason, Elizabeth Spriggs, forty-four performances in repertory.

Heartbreak House: New York Billy Rose, 112 performances, directed by Harold Clurman; Maurice Evans as Captain Shotover; Diana Wynyard, Mrs. Hushabye; Pamela Brown, Lady Utterwood; Alan Webb, Mazzini Dunn; Dennis Price, Hector; Sam Levene, Boss Mangan. Chichester Festival, 1967, then London for 116 performances with Irene Worth and John Clements. NT (Old Vic), 1975, highly praised, with (cast in the order above) Colin Blakeley, Eileen Atkins, Anna Massey, Alan MacNaughton, Paul Rogers. London, 1983, with Rex Harrison, Diana Rigg, Rosemary Harris.

Back to Methusaleh: NT, 1970. A two-act condensation by Arnold Moss opened March 26, 1958, Theatre Guild at the New York Ambassador, with Tyrone Power as Adam; Faye Emerson, Eve; Valerie Bettis, the Serpent— each player doubling along—and Arnold Moss as Shaw. Compare Shaw's play with Capek,* *The Makropoulos Secret.* London, in successive nights, 1984.

St. Joan: Phoenix, 1956-1957 with Siobhan McKenna. New York Lincoln Center, January 4, 1968, for forty-four performances with Diana Sands.

In Good King Charles's Golden Days: New York, 1957.

Pygmalion: Asolo, 1973. London, 1974, with Diana Rigg and Alec McCowen. London Young Vic, August 18, 1981, with Lorraine Chase and Richard Easton. Peter O'Toole at the London Shaftesbury, 1984.

With book and lyrics by Alan Jay Lerner, music by Frederick Loewe, directed by Moss Hart, *Pygmalion* was triumphantly transformed into *My Fair Lady* at the New York Mark Hellinger, March 15, 1956, the London Drury Lane on April 20, 1958. In New York Julie Andrews played Eliza; Rex Harrison, Professor Higgins; Cathleen Nesbit his mother; Stanley

Holloway, Doolittle; in London the same cast, save for Zena Dare as Mrs. Higgins. Harold Hobson called Rex Harrison's "the best performance ever given on the English stage in a musical." In Chicago, 1957–1958, *My Fair Lady* ran for six months. In the London revival, 1979–1982, the cast (in the same order): Jill Martin, Tony Britton, Anne Neagle, Peter Bayliss.

Doolittle sang "Wiv a Little Bit o' Luck" and—when, suddenly wealthy with the award for the most undeserving of the poor, he became lugubriously respectable and made a "good woman" of Eliza by taking her mother into matrimony—in highcockalorum Cockney costume he led his pals on a final spree, with the wedding-day lyric "Get Me to the Church on Time." Eliza has her gems: "Wouldn't It Be Loverly"; the transformation from Cockney "the Rine in Spine" to the King's English "The Rain in Spain Falls Mainly on the Plain"; the enthusiastic "I Could Have Danced All Night"; as well as the extravaganza of the spectacular gavotte and display of hats as the ladies let themselves be seen for the races at Ascot, and the resplendent aristocratic ball at which Eliza outmaneuvers the suspicious foreign linguistic expert, and proves herself fit mate for speechmaster Higgins. Higgins, bewildered by Eliza, wonders in song, "Why Can't a Woman Be More Like a Man?"

It is no wonder that New York enjoyed the musical for 2,212 performances; London, for 2,281. Shaw must have been smiling in the wings.

The film of *My Fair Lady,* with Rex Harrison and Audrey Hepburn, has been popular also on TV, as August 28, 1983, on BBC I; it revels in many ways impossible on the stage, as with the horses flying by the colorful crowd at Ascot, or at the early-morning open market where Eliza gets her flowers and to which, as the lady, she makes nostalgic return.

Despite his lack of poetry, Shaw's dramas may survive until the issues he argues with caustic and pungent prose in the plays have been settled in our lives.

OPERATION SIDEWINDER, ETC.   *Sam Shepard*

Sam Shepard (American, b. 1943), with fantasy, science fiction, satire, is still experimenting. The 1971 *Mad Dog Blues* has two men in a drug dream: Kosmos, a rock star who "leads with his cock," and Yahoudi. Kosmos conjures up Mae West; Yahoudi, Marlene Dietrich. They go treasure hunting with Captain Kidd; Jesse James and Mae West flee with the booty to the United States, where it turns out to be bottle-caps.

Operation Sidewinder opened at the New York Lincoln Center (Beaumont Rep) March 12, 1970, for 52 performances. Blazing eyes forerun an enormous sidewinder (rattlesnake). When Dukie and his Honey arrive, the snake entwines Honey. Dukie runs for help; Honey gradually pulses with the snake's undulations until she has an orgasm. Dukie comes upon a mechanic fixing a car; when he looks ready to help, the impatient young driver shoots Dukie and the mechanic. A Forest Ranger crosses the stage, oblivious to the car and the corpses. The young driver rescues Honey; soon they join sexually. Indians come, and behead the snake. Meanwhile we discover that the serpent is really a robot calculator, designed for the U.S. Army to communicate with UFO from outer space. The Indians use it in their ritual snake dance. Desert Tactical Troops shoot the Indians, who, immune to the shots, continue their chant. A Trooper snatches the sidewinder. Blue lightning flashes; hot then cold wind blows through the audience. Louder chanting; the Troops fall on their knees. Blackout. Lights: Only the huddled Troops remain. Curtain.

Shepard's best plays, says Ruby Cohn (*New American Dramatists,* 1982), "startle the eye, haunt the ear, tickle the funny-bone, and etch a deep impression on the mind."

Shepard's realistic plays, he calls his "family trilogy": *Curse of a Starving Class,* 1976; *Buried Child,* 1978. *True West,* 1980, dream-pictures the U.S. West. *Starving Class* opened at the OffBway (Public), February 14, 1978, for 62 performances, and won the Obie (OffBway) award. It shows a family on a tumble-down farm, ending with mother and son in a vision of cat and eagle clawing in midair and crashing, as (Cohn) "greedy America has seized its own killer." *Buried Child,* which opened OffBway (Circle), June 20, 1979, for 90 performances and the Pulitzer Prize, shows three generations in "a town like any other town. A town like Mama used to make with lace doilies and apple pie and incest and graft." It ends with Grandpa Dodge carrying off to bury the decayed infant corpse of such an incest—implying, some critics felt, the way the American family buries its youth.

In 1980, Shepard won an Obie "for sustained achievement." The 1981 *Best Plays* spoke of his current "indifferent offerings." His America has been compared to O'Neill's; but he shows shiftlessness, drugs, violence, and crime around, whereas O'Neill* exposes warped and anguished spirits within. Perhaps Shepard will come to probe more deeply and sympathetically into human lives.

THE RIVALS   *Richard Brinsley Sheridan*

Richard Brinsley Sheridan (1751-1816) is the only Englishman that has had a distinguished career as both playwright and politician. His fame as a playwright is based upon three comedies, written within a period of four years. As a young law student, Sheridan married the beautiful Elizabeth Linley of Bath and took her off the concert stage, thus leaving the couple without funds. The theatre always seems a get-rich-quick pathway; Sheridan tried it. His play *The Rivals; or, A Trip to Bath,* 1774, was accepted by Mr. Harris, manager of Covent Garden. Sheridan wrote to his father-in-law that Harris "and some of his friends also, who have heard it, assure me in the most flattering terms that there is not a doubt of its success. It will be very well played, and Harris assures me that the least shilling I shall get (if it succeeds) is £600 . . . I shall make no secret of it toward the time of representation, that it may not lose any support my friends can give it. I had not written a line of it two months ago, except a scene or two which I believe you have seen in a little farce." But the play opened January 17, 1775, was a failure the first two nights and was withdrawn. Blame has been placed upon the actor John Lee, the "boring player" who enacted Sir Lucius O'Trigger. The truth is that Sir Lucius was a boring part. The play was drastically cut and rewritten. It opened again on January 28, with Laurence Clinch as Sir Lucius, to instant and enduring success. The author won much more than his £600, and fame to boot.

The Preface to the printed play admits that *The Rivals* was withdrawn to "remove those imperfections in the first representation which were too obvious to escape reprehension, and too numerous to admit of a hasty correction." Contemporary judgment is recorded in the *London Evening*

Post. The Prologue spoke of the unnamed author as a law student who, "finding Coke, Littleton, Blackstone, etc., to afford but dull amusement, hath commenced poet, to grace his brow with a sprig of bay from Mount Parnassus." The *Post* (January 18, 1775) withheld that sprig of bay: "It [the play] requires much castigation, and the pruning hand of judgment, before ever it can pass on the town as even a tolerable piece. In language it is defective to an extreme; in plot outré, and one of the characters is an absolute exotic in the wilds of nature. Time will not permit a thorough investigation of this Comedy, but if *The Rivals* rests its claim to public favor solely on the basis of merit, the hisses of the Auditors on the first night of representation give reason to suspect a most fatal disappointment . . . the dulness of *The Rivals* lulled several of the middle gallery spectators into a profound sleep."

After corrections and cuts, the play became a favorite on the stage. Thus the *London Gazetteer and New Daily Advertiser* (January 17, 1777) observed: "This piece has a considerable share of merit. . . . The plot is interesting and ingenious, the characters natural and new, the sentiments noble and refined; there is a good deal of sterling wit and real humor in several scenes, without ever bordering on obscenities, or the mean subterfuge of a double-entendre, which we think reflects the highest honor on the Author. The whole play last night was received with the strongest marks of approbation by a very numerous and splendid audience." Down the years through the nineteenth and the twentieth century, *The Rivals* has continued to hold. A list of those who have played in it would include almost every star of the English and American stages. In The Players' revival in New York, opening June 6, 1922, were Tyrone Power, Pedro de Cordoba, and Francis Wilson. In the Equity Players' production opening in New York May 7, 1923, were Sidney Blackmer and Eva Le Gallienne. Later New York revivals came in 1936, 1941, and 1942. The last of these, with Mary Boland, Walter Hampden and Bobby Clark, had lyrics by Arthur Guiterman and music by Macklin Morrow. There was a musical version in London in 1935, with music and lyrics by J. R. Monsell and others, which W. A. Darlington, in the *London Telegraph* (September 17), called "a very bright and attractive show, excellently produced and sung."

The story is quite subordinate to the fascinating gallery of portraits drawn in the play. The plot is, nevertheless, a swiftly moving and continuously interesting tangle around the love of Captain Absolute and Lydia Languish, niece of Mrs. Malaprop. To win the romantic Lydia, the rich Absolute has pretended to be a poor ensign; his friend Bob Acres becomes his unwilling rival; Mrs. Malaprop will not consent to the match. Duels and elopements hang upon the event, until the lovely Lydia resigns herself to wealth and happiness. But how each character stands separately and clearly forth! Sir Anthony Absolute, though the angry father of whom he is a pattern may be traced to the old Roman comedy, is superbly drawn. Indeed, said J. Ranken Towse (June 7, 1922), "Sir Anthony must always be the dominant figure. If a trifle overdrawn, he is an extraordinary and consistent study." Sir Lucius O'Trigger is a furious fire-eater, a combination of the Roman braggart soldier and the Englishman quick with the challenge. Mrs. Malaprop has been called "a Dogberry in petticoats," but her "nice derangements of epitaphs" have given her enduring fame. Bob Acres is the most popular of comic good-natured simpletons. Lydia Languish is an absurd yet delightful, vapory flutter of romance and sweet simple daisy.

Mrs. Malaprop has a direct ancestor in Mrs. Slipslop of Fielding's *Joseph Andrews,* with predecessors in several of Shakespeare's plays.

It is to be noted that Mrs. Malaprop is not a fool. She is, on the contrary, quite a shrewd woman; but her desire to speak learnedly catches her often just short of the proper term. It is on the tip of her tongue, but, being a woman, she cannot wait, and a neighbor word (always with the same accent and number of syllables) darts out. "He is the very pine-apple of politeness." "Illiterate him, I say, quite from your memory." But the absurd inconsequencies of Mrs. Malaprop, the comic satire and amusing picture of life, are not all that one may find here. Thus Heywood Broun observed (May 8, 1923) that "the scene between Bob Acres and David just before the duel is as telling and as modern a plea for pacifism as anything Mr. Shaw will write the day after tomorrow." The *New York Journal,* a year earlier (June 7, 1922) had summed up the play's values: "The fine wit, the exaggerated sentiment, and the true humor and faithful characterization of this famous piece, embodied in a well-nigh perfect production, afford an evening of pure delight." Dickens, after Chaucer, comes nearest to giving us another such gallery of British characters, slightly overdrawn for our amusement but real enough for our insight, as Sheridan offers in *The Rivals.*

Among the many recent revivals: Chichester Festival, 1971, with John Clements director and Sir Anthony; Margaret Leighton Mrs. Malaprop; Angela Scoular, Lydia; Clive Swift, Bob Acres. The *London Times,* May 6, 1971, said the performances stressed "the gap between the wishfully brisk lusts of age in contrast to the romantic obstacles which youth places in its own path to the bedroom." Catholic University, Washington, October 9 to November 4, 1973. The new Royal Exchange, Manchester September 1976; Patricia Routledge as Mrs. Malaprop. Old Vic, September 9, 1978, Isla Blair, Lydia; Margaret Courtenay, Mrs. Malaprop. Stratford, Ontario; also ACT, 1981. NT (Olivier) into repertory April 12, 1983, with Sir Michael Hordern outstanding, a crochety, thumping Sir Anthony Absolute.

A musical *All In Love,* book and lyrics by Bruce Geller, music by Jacques Urbont, opened OffBway (Martinique) November 10, 1961, for 141 performances; in London March 16, 1964. Among its songs were "A More Than Ordinary Glorious Vocabulary," "The Lady Was Made to Be Loved," "The Good Old Ways," "To Bath Derry-O."

THE SCHOOL FOR SCANDAL   *Richard Brinsley Sheridan*

After the success of *The Rivals,** Richard Brinsley Sheridan led a busy life. In the same year, 1775, his comic opera *The Duenna* was produced, with music by his father-in-law, Thomas Linley. In 1776, Sheridan took over from Garrick the management of the Theatre of Drury Lane. "In you, Sir," said one of the staff to Garrick, "we have lost the Atlas of the stage." "Well, Sir," responded Garrick, "I have left you a young Hercules to supply my place." The first play presented under Sheridan's management justified the remark. It was Sheridan's own comedy, *A Trip to Scarborough,* 1777, which, in the days before copyright limitations, is a rewriting of *The Relapse; or, Virtue in Danger,* 1697, by John Vanbrugh.* Shortly after the success of *A Trip to Scarborough,* Sheridan presented at Drury Lane, on May 8, 1777, his most successful play, esteemed by many as the greatest English comedy, *The School for Scandal.* It was long in the writing; parts were handed the actors piecemeal, as they were rehearsing. Sheridan supervised the production himself; to prevent poor productions elsewhere, he withheld the play from print. Nevertheless, many pirated versions appeared. For example, the actor John Bernard, who had played in the authorized production, in seven days, for ten shillings a week increase in salary, copied out a version that ran for a season at the Exeter Theatre. The first authentic text of the play—which was printed in twenty-three editions from 1780 to 1799—was issued in America in 1786, from the copy given by Sheridan to John Henry. (Henry played Sir Peter Teazle in New York in 1786). The next authentic edition was issued in Dublin, in 1799.

Before its opening, the play had to hurdle obstacles. Moses, the moneylender in the play, was thought too close a portrait of one Hopkins, candidate for City Chamberlain of London; the censor refused the play a license because it reflected "seditious opposition to a court candidate." Through Sheridan's personal friendship with Lord Hertford, the Lord Chamberlain, the license was granted on the very day of the premiere. Thenceforward all was success. The Prologue was by Garrick, then at the height of his popularity. The journalist Reynolds, passing the theatre that evening, recorded that he heard such a noise and vibration that he ran for his life, lest the building fall: it was the applause at the final curtain. All London went to see the play.

Hazlitt has called *The School For Scandal* "the most finished and faultless comedy we have." "No other comedy in the language," said J. Ranken Towse, "contains so long an array of important and vividly contrasted characters."

In the play, Charles Surface is heedless, happy-go-lucky, but honest; his brother Joseph is a scheming hypocrite. The ward of Sir Peter Teazle, Maria, and Charles are in love; Joseph woos Maria for her fortune while also courting the young Lady Teazle. Lady Teazle is tempted to Joseph's room, where the arrival of Sir Peter forces her to hide behind a screen while the men converse—until the screen is thrown down and the Lady exposed. Meanwhile, Oliver Surface, the wealthy uncle of Charles and Joseph, unexpectedly returning from India, resolves, while still unrecognized, to test the character of his nephews. The hypocrisy of Joseph is made clear to all; Sir Peter gives Maria to Charles, and forgives Lady Teazle.

The first reviews of the comedy show as favorable a reception from the critics as from the public. Thus the London *Observer* (May, 1777) declared: "The chief satire of this piece is pointed against hypocrisy and scandal, in which the author displays great genius, wit, and observation. His characters are finely drawn with a masterly pencil, and have strong marks of originality." The *Lady's Magazine* (same date) called the play "an additional proof of that gentleman's great abilities as a dramatic writer. . . . The characters are drawn with a bold pencil, and colored with warmth and spirit. . . . The dialogue of this comedy is easy and witty. It abounds with strokes of pointed satire, and a rich vein of humor pervades the whole, rendering it equally interesting and entertaining."

Down the years, a list of great players attests the popularity of the play; its one drawback for staging is that it deserves a galaxy of stars for the many important parts. Among those that have played in it may be mentioned Charles Kemble; Ada Rehan and John Drew, in Daly's production in 1891; Junius Brutus Booth in 1892; Ben Greet and Edith Wynne Matthison in 1899. In 1923, in New York, The Players' revival used John Drew, Robert Mantell, Walter Hampden, Ethel Barrymore, and Violet

Kemble-Cooper. Ethel Barrymore—whose mother and grandmother had also played the part—acted Lady Teazle in 1931 and frequently for a decade thereafter. John Gielgud revived the play in London in 1937. An adaptation called *Lady Teazle* opened December 30, 1881, with Fanny Davenport. A musical version, also called *Lady Teazle,* with Lillian Russell in the title part, opened December 24, 1904, with book by John Kendrick Bangs, lyrics by Roderick C. Penfield, and music by A. Baldwin Sloane. This was hailed as the best musical comedy of the season; it followed Sheridan closely and added a number of lively songs.

If any scenes may be selected as outstanding in a play so consistently entertaining, there are: for sentiment, that in which Charles, selling the family portraits to his uncle in disguise, refuses to let go the portrait of "the ill-looking little fellow over the settee" who is his uncle; for satire, the gathering of the scandal-mongers, Sir Benjamin Backbite, Lady Sneerwell, and Mrs. Candor, who "strike a character dead at every word"; and for dramatic intensity, perhaps the most famous scene in English comedy, the exposure of Lady Teazle behind the screen.

Praise of the play has not been universal. On November 24, 1789, when President Washington in New York took the State's governor, the foreign ministers, and some Senators to see the play, one of the latter characterized it as "an indecent representation before ladies of character and virtue." Washington was with the majority who have enjoyed it. Among the dissenters has been Henry James, who reviewed a Boston production in the *Atlantic Monthly* (December, 1874): "In sentiment, what a singularly meagre affair it seemed! Its ideas, in so far as it has any, are coarse and prosaic, and its moral atmosphere uncomfortably thin. . . . The distinctly amusing scenes . . . are those in which Lady Sneerwell's guests assemble to pull their acquaintances to pieces. . . . To measure the difference between small art and great, one should compare the talk of Sheridan's scandal-mongers with that scene in Molière's *Misanthrope** in which the circle at Célimène's house hit off the portraits of their absent friends. In the one case one feels almost ashamed to be listening; in the other it is good society still, even though it be good society in a heartless mood." James allows, however, that the play wins popularity through wit that everyone can understand and think himself clever; as well as through "its robustness and smoothness of structure, and its extreme felicity and finish of style."

Many players have been singled out for their performance in this comedy. Horace Walpole praised Mrs. Fanny Abington (a former flower girl, the original Lady Teazle; Sir Joshua Reynolds selected her to sit for his painting of "The Comic Muse." For "The Tragic Muse," he chose Mrs. Sarah Kemble Siddons.) Charles Lamb sang the praises of Palmer as Joseph Surface; in Lamb's opinion, this actor "stole the play." The London *Examiner* (October 15, 1815) called Charles Kemble "the best Charles Surface we have ever seen"—and added, "Why can we not always be young, and seeing *The School For Scandal?*" Brooks Atkinson (January 11, 1931) gave garlands to Ethel Barrymore: "Few episodes in the British drama have greater prestige than the screen scene . . . Miss Barrymore has shown us why." The vitality of the play was attested (January 11, 1931) by John Mason Brown: "Not only does its fun still belong to it as they perform it, but it comes bubbling out so contagiously that an audience cannot resist it . . . still comes down the centuries as an irresistible comedy." Good fun, and smiling satire at the hypocrisy that we prefer to see in our neighbors, and at the vanity in ourselves that makes us its easy victims; a superb gallery of comic yet recognizable figures; and a dramatic story superbly told, sustain the freshness of *The School For Scandal*.

An outstanding production, London April 5, 1962, New York Majestic January 24, 1963, had John Gielgud as director and Joseph Surface; Ralph Richardson, Sir Peter Teazle; Geraldine McEwan, Lady Teazle; Margaret Rutherford, Mrs. Candour; Peter Massey; Anne Massey; John Neville. Also APA-Phoenix in repertory March 17, 1962, sixteen performances, director Ellis Rabb; Rosemary Harris, Lady Teazle; returning November 21, 1966, for forty-eight performances. NT (Old Vic), May 11, 1972. Hartford Conn., May 10, 1974, for eight weeks. Cincinnati Playhouse February 24, 1981, for a month. ART, Cambridge, Mass., June 12, 1983, "an antiphony of cynicism and sentimentality."

THE CRITIC   *Richard Brinsley Sheridan*

Originally presented on October 30, 1779, as an afterpiece, *The Critic* is the most successful play in the tradition of the dramatic burlesque. It satirizes not only the sentimental tragedy of Sheridan's day, but the supercilious and often malignant criticism of the time. Dangle and Sneer are the two critics; their easy victim is Sir Fretful Plagiary (a caricature of the dramatist Richard Cumberland, who had sneered at *The School for Scandal**). When Plagiary complains that the Drury Lane manager has stolen bits from his manuscript, Sneer suggests that Plagiary take a cruel revenge by declaring the manager the author of the whole piece! But the most amusing figure is Puff, "a Practitioner in Panegyric or a Professor of the Art of Puffing," whose analysis of the varieties of what we call ballyhoo and blurb is as fresh, as searching, and as pertinent today as when it was first spoken. Puff has written a tragedy, "The Spanish Armada"; he takes Sneer and Dangle to a rehearsal. This tragedy is an absurd burlesque, mingling actual historical figures at the time of the Spanish Armada—Sir Walter Raleigh, Sir Christopher Hatton, Lord Burleigh—with burlesque creations: Tilburina, daughter of the Governor of Tilbury Fort; and Don Ferolo Whiskerandos, a Spanish prisoner whom Tilburina loves. Among the characters are an Italian family with a French interpreter—all unintelligible. Dangle and Sneer tear the tragedy to tatters as we watch a spectacle of the English and Spanish fleets in fierce battle; the triumph; and a final procession and choral dance of English river gods.

When the play opened, the *London Gazeteer and New Daily Advertiser* (November 1, 1779) observed: "The audience were informed . . . that an affectation of sentiment and scrupulous virtue had destroyed the true spirit of comedy; and that modern tragedies were so very moral, pious, and dull, that they put the actors almost, and the audience quite, to sleep—that trick and situation were introduced instead of the wit and humor of comedy, and of natural feeling and genuine pathos in tragedy. To expose these errors has therefore become the proper subject of satire in the present day. . . . The purpose aimed at is effected by a kind of burlesque parody, of which there are several thousand lines extended through the greater part of two acts. These must have been a very tedious, laborious, and disgusting task; and the effect of this kind of ridicule is so very strong, that it soon grows tiresome and disagreeable. The public opinion of modern tragedy is already so very low . . . that the game is hardly worth the pursuit." The reviewer discerned some passages that seemed aimed at older playwrights; indeed, "some which seemed more applicable to Shakespeare than to any other writer." The play does, in truth, parody the obvious method of conveying information to the audience that Shakespeare employed in *As You Like It** and *The Tempest.**

Several reviewers found a different reason for objection. It was the practice, at that time, for persons in need to advertise their poverty and plead for assistance in the public press. Puff announces that he has supported himself for several months by advertising fictitious distresses. The *Spectator* at once cried that this satire was "too severe, and may be of dangerous tendency, in preventing the hand of benevolence being extended to real objects of distress. There are impostors of every class—but charity is already too cold to require further chill upon it." The *Universal* magazine of August 1781 brought up the point again, mentioning that the audience "expressed some displeasure at Puff's boast," and adding: "Nobody could suspect that the Author, in the Wantonness of Wit, could wish to divert the humane Attentions of the Benevolent from the real Objects of Charity; and Mr. King (who played Puff) converted their Displeasure into Marks of Approbation, by seizing a lucky Moment to assure Sneer that he did not mean to deaden his Feelings, or lessen his Humanity, but merely to awaken his Prudence."

A parody of contemporary foibles, such as *The Critic*, is likely soon to seem out of date; revivals continually interpolated jokes to keep the humor fresh; and Jack Bannister (the original Whiskerandos) told Charles Mathews (who played Puff for over thirty years) how Sheridan himself laughed at the new lines: "The style of tragedy it ridicules has passed away, probably elbowed out of existence mainly by the force of this very satire; and it is only by the plentiful interpolation of jokes referring to the present that the public is now entertained . . . Even the swallowing of the moustache by Whiskerandos, which has often been denounced as 'too broad,' was taken from an accident which really happened, on the first night of Leigh Hunt's play *A Legend of Florence,* to a Mr. Moore, who played the principal character, and who was obliged to leave the stage for some minutes, being totally unable to proceed with his part . . . I can safely assert that there is not one 'gag' introduced that I cannot, from my own experience, cap with an actual one even exceeding it in absurdity." *The Critic* survives, however, because most of what Sheridan caught on his comic barbs is lastingly rooted in human nature.

The play has been frequently revived. The *New York Times* (December 25, 1938) reported that a Harvard University production dressed Dangle and Sneer to resemble Alexander Woollcott and George Jean Nathan. A revival by the Old Vic company was brought to New York on May 20, 1946, with Laurence Olivier as Puff and Ralph Richardson as Lord Burleigh. All the reviewers felt the freshness and vigor of the piece; John Chapman called it "as wise to show business as tomorrow's drama page or next week's tradesheet. Wiser. It deflates the conceit of everybody connected with the stage. It hands the audience many laughs about critics—and then quite deftly deflates the audience. Its comments on playwrights cannot be bettered . . . And, as the company romps with abandon through the performance, it is a definite and utterly delightful example of dreadful acting. The play within the play is just bad enough to mirror all the sins of Actors' Equity and British Equity combined."

The Critic has scarcely anything in the way of plot, of situations, even of form; it achieves its uproarious effects through romping fancy and verbal ingenuity. It remains the freshest satire of the foibles and excesses of critics, playwrights, actors, and audiences, as it laughs at the ways of the theatre that it loves.

The Critic was played in Palo Alto, Calif., 1965. It was put on a Decca long-playing record, 1966. After a September 29, 1982, broadcast on BBC 1, the *Observer* declared: "It is impossible to imagine Sheridan's satirical farce being done better . . . with a droll wordless cameo from John Gielgud, made up to look like Dame Edith Evans."

JOURNEY'S END   *Robert Cedric Sheriff*

Undoubtedly the most successful, and in many minds the best, play about the first World War is *Journey's End,* by Robert Cedric Sheriff (English, b. 1896). It made its debut in London, January 21, 1929. On March 22, 1929, it opened in New York City for a run of 99 performances; in June it was revived. By March, 1930, it was being played by 56 companies in 22 languages. Between the two wars it was frequently revived; in Calcutta in 1931; at the University of Washington in 1937, and many places and times between. In 1941 it was performed by the 165th Infantry while in training in Georgia. It was shown again in London, opening October 5, 1950.

The play pictures the last four days in the lives of some dozen soldiers holding a short sector of the British front near St. Quentin against the German advance of March, 1918. Among the tense soldiers a few stand out. Stanhope, though a mere youngster, has had four years of the war; only constant drinking keeps his taut nerves from the break. Lt. Osborne, affectionately called "Uncle," walls himself against the strain with talk of flowers and good old *Alice in Wonderland*. Hibbert is on the edge of hysterical terror—saved from utter funk when Stanhope unveils his own agony of mind. The cockney Lt. Trotter is more fortunate, being gifted with a lack of imagination that leaves him comparatively calm. Raleigh is a rooky just up from training school. We watch this assorted group of soldiers through the nerve-crumbling monotony of standing guard, and through their routine hours. Occasionally a simple action attains swift poignancy— as when Raleigh writes home; or when they quickly don gas masks at Trotter's call, and what he smells turns out to be "a blinking May tree." Poignant, too, in the unspoken expectancy of doom, are the preparations for the daylight raid of Osborne and Raleigh. Raleigh returns with a prisoner—and horror. Stanhope, whom Osborne had been sustaining, breaks. But the next morning, when orders come to hold at all costs against the German advance, they pull together again. A shell sends Raleigh to die in Stanhope's arms. A second shell blasts the dugout. The group have come to their journey's end.

R. C. Sheriff had had more experience as a soldier than as a playwright, before setting hand to his play. He had written a few amateur plays for production by friends. Letters to the family during the war, which Sheriff tried to shape as a novel, grew into this play. It was rejected by most London managers. Bernard Shaw, reading it, was not especially enthusiastic; but a Stage Society production ensued with Laurence Olivier. Then Maurice Browne, who had done considerable work with little theatres in America, took the drama for his first London production. In it were Melville Cooper, Colin Clive, and Maurice Evans. Before bringing the play to the United States, Gilbert Miller opened the American company for a week in London. Both houses were sold out. In the American production were Leon Quartermaine and Colin Keith-Johnston, who also played in a 1939 New York revival.

The British Secretary of War, Sir Laming Worthington-Evans, called *Journey's End* "the finest play I have ever seen." The Prince of Wales (later Duke of Windsor) said it was "the most impressive play I have seen in all my life." In America the reviewers were equally stirred. Richard Lockridge called it "the finest play that tragic conflict has produced. Pity catches at your throat. Gallantry sends chills along your spine." Alexander Woollcott, in the *Ladies' Home Journal* (September, 1935) linked *Journey's End* with *The Green Pastures** as "the two finest plays evolved in the English-speaking theatre during the post-war era." R. Dana Skinner, in *Commonweal* (April 10, 1929), sought to explain the source of the play's power, as a revelation of men's souls on the brink of eternity. Contributing was the "awesome silence which pervades so much of it—a broken silence which fairly throbs, like the murmur of the earth itself before dawn. . . . But whether at the mists of dawn, or in the amber of an afternoon sun, or in the candle-lit gloom of night, there is always the feeling of last hours, of nature hushed before the summons of God, and of men bidding brave, unhurried goodbyes to the only existence which they have known." Breaks in the gloom and the stillness help to establish the mood; the characters themselves are revealed through constant action. There is no single drive of plot; but the incidents of the play, insignificant in themselves, are given meaning through the lens they form by which we see the various men, and are given depth by the imminence of doom we feel in ourselves and sense in them, the unspoken recognition, with each routine movement or simple act, that this may be the last time. *Journey's End* faithfully and poignantly conveys the fears and the devotion, the breaking yet controlled anguish, of steadfast service unto death.

The play proved stirring in revivals. Among them: New York, September 9, 1972, Ted Kalem in *Time* calling it "a season in hell . . . a spare, sharp, impeccable revival." February 1, 1979, Melbourne; the *Herald* emphasized "the wrath of the relationships of men under stress who come from a society sustained by old-established true-blue values." The OffOffBway (Classic) revival November 11, 1979, was closed by the transportation strike; it reopened January 11, 1980, to rave reviews. Hollywood June 5, 1982, for a six-week run.

Of a 1972 revival Irving Wardle in the *London Times* (May 19, 1972) declared: "It is abundantly clear that Sheriff was no war correspondent but an artist writing out of experience and meditation . . . within the natural circumstances of the front line, and using these singlemindedly to explore the nature of British behavior in a way which applies no less to peace than to war."

IDIOT'S DELIGHT   *Robert E. Sherwood*

"The world is playing Idiot's Delight. It is a game that never means anything and never ends." Such is the feeling, in *Idiot's Delight,* of Harry Van, once a "shill" with a carnival show, now a "hoofer" leading a group of American chorus girls seeking to enliven Europe with their dancing act. They are caught in a hotel in the south Tyrol, on the border of four counties, at Zero Hour in the next World War. We watch while a French Communist, a German scientist, and an English artist slip the cloaks of their ideals to become cogs in the war machine. More objective stands the munitions magnate, who "had the honor of promoting" the war; he moves off to safety, leaving behind his Russian mistress, Irene. Harry Van (who is sure, despite her evasion, that she is a girl he slept with in 1925 back in Omaha) gives up his chance to cross the border in order to stay and help Irene. Despite his apparent flippancy and his antic ways, Harry is basically serious, an earnest if somewhat superficial observer of human nature.

The play, by Robert E. Sherwood (American, 1896-1955), was warmly received. It opened in New York on March 24, 1936, running for 121 performances with Lynn Fontanne and Alfred Lunt, the latter especially amusing in his song and dance act with his blonde chorus girls. It was revived August 31, 1936, and ran for 179 performances more. In London, with Raymond Massey and Tamara Geva, it opened on March 22, 1938 for a run of 230 performances. Lenore Ulric has played it in the summer theatre; Clark Gable in 1939 starred in the film version. The play proved equally pert and pertinent when it opened, May 23, 1951, at New York's City Center, with Lee Tracy, Ruth Chatterton, and amusingly caricatured chorines.

The American reviewers hailed the comedy: "Idiot's Delight," said Gilbert Gabriel (March 25, 1936), "and yours and mine." "It causes you to shake with laughter and with fear," said Robert Garland, "to remain around and cry 'Bravo!'" It is, said the *Literary Digest* (March 28, 1936), "a thundering, contemptuous blast at nations that make war, men who make bullets, and the inarticulate, sheep-like humanity that allows itself to be in peonage to war." In Melbourne, Australia, the *Argus* (February 6, 1939) declared the play "touched off an explosion in the theatre . . . a farce with tragic cross-currents, a melodrama with a biting lesson, a tragedy with even a dash of musical comedy." In this play Sherwood most fully heeds the W. S. Gilbert* injunction that one must always gild the philosophic pill. The reviewers in England, though they liked the play, more soberly questioned its implications. "*Idiot's Delight* is not a masterpiece of argument," said James Agate in the *London Times* (March 27, 1938). "It is very nearly a masterpiece of light theatre with a core of thought." Even that core was challenged by Charles Morgan, writing from London for the *New York Times* (April 10, 1938): "To speak of war as an idiot's delight and to rail at mankind as fools because they suffer it, is a terrible arrogance. War is no one's delight; and men who are prepared to suffer for an idea are not idiots. . . . Because it fails to recognize this, Mr. Sherwood's piece, though a splendid piece of rhetoric, remains unsatisfying because it seems to have missed its aim as a criticism of contemporary life."

The English felt the wings of war too close to be content with the shallow optimism of Harry Van and the surface satire of Robert E. Sherwood; yet *Idiot's Delight* drives home, with laughter over wells of emotion, a basic sense of human decency and faith in the survival of human values.

Out of *Idiot's Delight,* the musical *Dance a Little Closer*, book and lyrics by Alan J. Lerner, music by Charles Strouse, is the second musical Lerner framed from another play; the first was *My Fair Lady,* from Shaw's *Pygmalion.** The first was a triumph; the second, a disaster. Opening May 11, 1983, it revealed, said Frank Rich in the *Times,* "a huge, extravagant mishmash . . . an initially shaky premise is steadily dismantled by errors of judgment on all sides." Set in "the avoidable future," the pre-World War II maneuvers were shifted to a Soviet confrontation with the West; but "it's the changes of structure, tone, and characterization that turn a light parable into a dour, nonsensical lecture with songs."

The American hoofer, Harry, is played by Len Cariou; his possible one-night partner, here called Cynthia, played by Liz Robertson, is the mistress of a diplomat, played by George Rose to remind us of Henry Kissinger. For good measure, a homosexual couple do an ice-skating number, then go through a marriage ceremony. A few good songs get lost in the mismatched evening. Its opening night also marked its closing. *Idiot's Delight* continues.

ABE LINCOLN IN ILLINOIS   *Robert E. Sherwood*

Dealing with what have been called the undramatic years of the Great Emancipator's life, *Abe Lincoln in Illinois,* 1938, richly reveals their spiritual seeding for the later harvest. The play shows the change in Lincoln from the hobbledehoy, shrewd but unambitious "artful dodger" whose chief desire was to be left alone, to the earnest man aroused for humanity, the vigorous embattled champion of human rights. Leaning heavily on Carl Sandburg's *Life of Lincoln,* the play takes us from the early days in Salem of 1830, when the six-foot-four Lincoln was a shy but determined lad of twenty-one, through the days of his love for Ann Rutledge, of his work as an attorney in Springfield, of his courting, dodging, and being courted by, Mary Todd—whose fanatical ambition was a whip to Abe's flagging will—on to that summer of 1858 when Lincoln stood up to Stephen Douglas on the planks of a country debating platform. The play ends as we watch the rear of a train on which the new president has embarked for the White House.

This drama was the first production of the new Playwright's Company, organized by dramatists Anderson,* Berman,* Howard,* Rice,* and Sherwood. After a premiere in Washington, October 3, 1938, with Raymond Massey, it opened in New York on October 15 for a run of 472 performances, to the highest critical acclaim. It won the 1939 Pulitzer Prize and has been widely performed throughout the country. Paris saw the play in 1948, called *Si je vis (If I Live).*

The importance of the theme of democracy to the present day did not escape, and indeed may have lent enthusiasm to, the critics. Thus Richard Watts declared (October 30, 1938): "Here is not only one of the finest and most stirring of American plays but one of the most glorious achievements of all that is best in the national spirit . . . shows us something of the soul and the genius of our best-beloved national hero, brings to us a sense of the greatness of the true democratic spirit, and makes the fierce struggle of the most ominous period in our history a burning contemporary issue. . . . Magnificently played by Raymond Massey in one of the finest performances of the modern theatre, *Abe Lincoln in Illinois* is the greatest of our patriotic dramas." *Stage* (November 1939) found the play equally pregnant: " Here is one of those rare occasions when the gifts of a playwright and an actor join to kindle a blaze which illumines a dark moment of history. In a time when what is happening in the world today cannot—apparently—be interpreted on the stage in terms of valid theatre, the overtone and implication of this play come like a searchlight beam cutting though a fog."

Like most plays that seek to cover a stretch of years, the drama depends upon chosen episodes to give the effect of continuous growth. The tender memory of one woman's love, and the persistent prick of another woman's urge that he take part in life, helped shape in Abraham Lincoln the understanding devotion and the resolve that gave course to our country's history and added decency to democracy. This clarion call for human decency, for democracy based on fellow-love, rings through *Abe Lincoln in Illinois*.

THERE SHALL BE NO NIGHT   *Robert E. Sherwood*

This drama about Finland's courageous stand against Soviet aggression sprang of a broadcast from Finnish trenches on Christmas of 1939.

Its story centers upon the reaction of a Finnish family to the Soviet invasion: the Nobel Prize winning neurologist Kaarlo Valkonen, his American-born wife Miranda, his son Erik, and Erik's fiancée Kaatri. As the play opens the neurologist is broadcasting to America, questioning the value of the elimination of pain: will not people then become pampered and stupid; do not pain and trouble quicken the mind? Their national problem intrudes upon the household. Kaarlo feels that the Russian people do not want to fight; Erik has faith in the Mannerheim line. Both prove wrong. Erik is killed on ski patrol; Kaarlo, rejecting a chance to leave the country, feels he must fight against a gathering world insanity. In a schoolroom near Viipuri Bay, Kaarlo and his comrades await the order to march to certain death. His wife prepares to burn their home; there shall be no surrender.

There shall be no night because men no longer talk of the glory of war; they accept it as a task that must be done. But individuals are awakening; more and more will ask "*Why* must it be done?" Then are the war-mongers and the tyrants doomed. This is the argument of the play, but the history of the play shows how far down the years fulfilment of such hopes must lie. After a premiere in Providence on March 29, 1940, the drama opened in New York on Arpil 29 with Alfred Lunt and Lynn Fontanne, for a run of 115 performances and the Pulitzer Prize. The Lunts toured in the play as a benefit for the brave but overwhelmed Finns. Then Hitler invaded Soviet Russia—and the program notes for the 1941 road tour were carefully worded: "In this development of Hitler's murderous career, the Finns have been compelled to fight and die on his side. . . . Since this play first opened, no important line of its text has been changed. . . . The purpose of this play was to set forth the tragedy of every civilized home in every civilized but unprepared free country which happened to lie in the path of the international assassins. It was and is obvious that this play, written by an American for Americans, was and is intended to say that this same tragedy may come upon us." That tragedy came with Pearl Harbor, after which, the *New York Post* reported (December 15, 1941) Mr. Sherwood decided that "the best interests of this country" would be served by closing the production. Two years later the play opened in London and ran for 220 performances—with the characters and situations altered to apply to the Italian invasion of Greece!

Despite—or because of—the failure of reality to match its ideals, the play struck a deep chord in many hearts. Most reviewers looked upon it as a dramatized sermon rather than as a drama. "I don't think *There Shall Be No Night* can be taken," said Wolcott Gibbs (May 11, 1940), "as much less than a plea for our immediate and total entry on the Allied side—only because he [Sherwood] knows no other way to preserve the kind of life that self-respecting men and women can live." That the intended message is correctly expressed by Mr. Gibbs may be seen from Sherwood's Preface: "There could be only one reason for America's reluctance to give any help to the Finns, and that was abject fear. And if we were in a state of abject fear, then we had already been conquered by the masters of the slave States, and we must surrender our birthright. So I decided to raise my voice in protest against the hysterical escapism, the Pontius Pilate retreat from decision, which dominated American thinking and, despite all the warnings of the President of the United States and the Secretary of State, pointed our foreign policy toward suicidal isolationism." This intention of the play, pressed by the author's earnestness, divides its power to the disadvantage of the other face of the play's coin—the ultimate hope of a rebellion for peace.

In London of 1943 reviewers were more wholehearted and more nearly unanimous in the play's praise. The *New Statesman and Nation* (December 25, 1943) gave it a Christmas gift of superlative: "the most moving war tragedy yet seen upon a London stage. . . . It is conceived in the spirit of that old Anglo-Saxon ballad of defeat, celebrating the Battle of Maldon, 991; also the spirit of Winston Churchill's speeches in our darkest hour." Adding to such comments more purely dramatic criticism, James Agate in the *London Times* (December 19, 1943) praised the skill and naturalness of the drama.

The idea behind *There Shall Be No Night* may today seem a trite thought in an insecure world, but the personal drama that embodies the thought remains vivid, poignant, and true.

The title is drawn from the promise in the Bible, Revelation 22:5: "And there shall be no night . . . for the Lord God giveth them light, and they shall reign for ever and ever." Amen.

BAREFOOT IN THE PARK   *Neil Simon*

Neil Simon (b. 1927) is the most amusing of current writers for the American theatre. In the years 1966-1967 he had four plays running concurrently on Broadway, a record surpassed only by Clyde Fitch,* with five plays in 1901. As Howard Taubman saw him, in the *Times*: "Mr. Simon evidently has no aspiration except to be diverting, and he achieves this with the dash of a highly skilled professional writer."

His most successful comedy, *Barefoot in the Park,* opening at the New York Biltmore October 23, 1963, attained 1,530 performances. It opened in London in 1965, to a much milder reception. The story is simple. Corie, married but six days to Paul Bratter, brings him to the apartment she's rented. It's a sixth-story walk-up, with no heat, no tub in the bathroom, no room for a double bed. A mad Hungarian lives in a loft over them; he takes them to an Albanian restaurant on Staten Island. They come home to a lovers' quarrel, so that hubby sleeps on the living room couch, and snow falls upon him through a hole in the skylight. Their fight, said Norman Nadel in the *World-Telegram*, "is an uproarious glory." Corie thinks her husband a "fuddy duddy" because he refuses to walk barefoot in Washington Square Park with the thermometer registering seventeen degrees. Of course, they kiss and make up.

The newlyweds were played by Elizabeth Ashley and Robert Redford; the neighbor, Kurt Kasznar. Mildred Natwick, as the bride's mother, added to the comic effect. Mike Nichols, in his first directional assignment, kept the action deftly moving.

"They're perfectly nice kids," said Walter Kerr in the *Herald-Tribune,* "she without a brain in her head, he without a penny in his portfolio (he is a young lawyer and he's just been awarded 6¢ damages on his first successful case). . . . The number of different laughs [Simon] is able to get out of the agonies of folk who have climbed six flights is astounding. . . . Mr. Simon is cheerfully equipped to produce, almost indefinitely, the back-handed lines needed to keep nonsense afloat." John McClain began his review in the *Journal-American*: "*Barefoot in the Park* is the funniest play I can remember. It's as simple as that."

Simon's humor, said Henry Hews in the *Saturday Review,* "is based upon our absurdly casual acceptance of and ways of dealing with contemporary civilization's enforced incongruities." Less casually, John Simon, in the summer of 1968 *Hudson Review,* called Simon's later play *The Odd Couple* "nothing much more than a joke book tossed upon the stage." (This play, opening March 10, 1965, ran for 965 performances; it showed the complications of a bachelor couple trying to live together. Simon is now planning a similar play with two women.) The playwright's deft presentation of the comic aspect of everyday situations has kept audiences throughout theatrical America eagerly expectant of a new Neil Simon play.

BRIGHTON BEACH MEMOIRS   *Neil Simon*

Neil Simon's first plays were followed by a cluster of equally successful comedies. His twentieth Broadway show, *Brighton Beach Memoirs,* opened at the Los Angeles Ahmanson Theatre on December 10, 1982, then came to the New York Alvin March 27, 1983. It presents a Jewish family in 1937, the time of the author's boyhood. The set shows the front yard and living-dining room of their Brighton Beach house, the stairway, and two bedrooms upstairs. There are seven in the Jerome family: Kate and her husband, Jack, holding two jobs in his struggle to sustain the household; their two sons, Stanley, eighteen and a half and Eugene, fifteen; Kate's widowed sister, Blanche, with her two daughters, coddled, sickly Laurie and blossoming beautiful Nora, in their teens.

Through Eugene, who talks to the audience and to his diary, we follow the constant "crises" of the family days. We laugh, sometimes at the author's expressions, sometimes at the triviality of the incidents that precipitate the excitement and the bickering; but beneath their oppositions we sense a basic family love, and we are drawn into their feelings, their little joys and major tribulations.

Eugene is wondering whether to become a baseball star or a writer, but he has begun to notice Nora's beauty and to be aware of sex. When he hesitatingly, questioningly, tells his brother of a nocturnal emission, Stanley explains that everybody indulges even in self-induced effusions— "even our father—of course, in his earlier days." Eugene wonders about women, and Stanley, the knowledgeable male—hasn't he spent $5 for a "pro"?—assures him that women indulge five times more than men.

But the family faces more serious storms. Jack, trying to hold two jobs, has a warning heart attack and is ordered to rest for three weeks. Stanley, hoping to increase the family funds, loses his whole week's salary ($17) in a poker game. Aunt Blanche, dressed in new finery and her sister's pearls for her first dinner date since her husband died, receives a note from her date's mother—Mrs. Murphy across the street, who has never spoken to the Jews. In formal but not unfriendly words, her own anguish showing through, Mrs. Murphy writes that her son is in the hospital, from an accident while driving drunk; when he recovers they are moving upstate, to relatives, where there is a chance of curing his addiction to drink.

Worried by her husband's ill-health and the financial problems, Kate, the family workhorse, explodes and pours her frustrated feelings upon her sister, who has been pampered and sheltered all her life. They make up and hug, but Blanche has awakened to the need for independence; they agree that she will stay until she finds a job and a place for her and the girls. Meanwhile Nora has had a chance to dance in a play headed for Broadway; when she is told to stay in school and get her diploma, she rebels and goes out with her sponsor. We never learn whether she will give her body or attain her goal, but that is how life flows. Then—this is 1937—word comes that the Jeromes' Polish cousins have escaped the anti-Semites and are soon to arrive. The family at once joins in planning how to receive them: cots in the dining room, and so on—all but one.

For Neil Simon is shrewd in ending the many crises with a surefire climax. As Eugene listens to his brother's description of Nora, whom he had seen nude in her shower, with breasts like "—yes, nectarines," the first act ends. And now, while the others are together, Eugene lingers in his room upstairs for a long look at the photograph his brother has given him, his first woman nude; and in his enthusiasm he cries, as he has imagined it before, on beholding "the golden gate of the palace of the Himalayas"—and the final curtain falls.

Sex thus rears its head, but more constant if not more important are the family interrelationships. There are touching moments of honest talk, elder sister to sister; father to son. Jack's response to Stanley's gambling is not anger, but "One of these days I'll teach you to play poker." Most of the verbal humor comes from Eugene's comments to the audience. At dinner: "The tension is so thick you could cut it with a knife, which is more than you could say for the liver." Eugene is constantly called upon by his mother, to run for groceries, to put out the garbage. "Write quietly, Eugene," she admonished him, as his exhausted father is resting. Yet, said Frank Rich in the *New York Times* of March 28, Simon looks upon "his less-than-rosy Depression adolescence with an affection that is too warm to be fake. Although there are some reservations among the reviewers—Clive Barnes in the *New York Post* of March 28, said, "Simon confuses the *Reader's Digest* with literature"—there is general agreement that this is Neil Simon's finest work.

Eugene's final words foreshadow not the baseball star but the writer. We are allowed to assume that the play is in part autobiographical. And Eugene's dream has come true: on June 29, 1983, the Alvin, where *Brighton Beach Memoirs* still holds enjoying crowds, was renamed the Neil Simon Theatre. One may recall that Owen Davis* wrote a hundred potboiling lurid melodramas before he grew into a serious dramatist and won the Pulitzer Prize. We may hope for further growth in Neil Simon.

ONE-WAY PENDULUM   *N. F. Simpson*

What author Norman Frederick Simpson (English, b. 1919) called "an evening of High Drung and Slarrit" left the audience equally amused and bemused. *One-Way Pendulum,* opening at the London Royal Court De-

cember 22, 1959, and moving in 1960 to the Criterion, was recognized by
Harold Hobson: It "has Lewis Carroll's gift of absurd logic, starting from
impossible premises and then, by impeccable steps, reaching ridiculous but
irrefutable conclusions."

Barnes is a genial neighbor, who chats with the audience about the
family. Head of the family is Mr. Groomkirby, who "earns a living" by
feeding sixpence into parking meters, then standing beside them so as not
to waste the hour's fee. He is also building a replica of the London Old
Bailey Criminal Court in his living room. His son does not talk throughout
the play, only murmuring, "Mi-mi-mi-mi-do-re-mi-sol-do," as he is training
a cluster of Speak-Your-Weight machines to sing the Hallelujah Chorus.
The daughter, whose boyfriend gave her a skull *memento mori,* goes with
him to the zoo, and worries that her arms are shorter than the gorilla's.
Mother Groomkirby has hired a neighbor to come eat the leftovers, so as to
avoid waste. Father Groomkirby has a series of profound thoughts, such as
"All this absurd, wasteful squabbling as to which side shall put the balls
through which goals—and when and how often—as if this weren't a matter
that could be settled in an adult and sensible manner around a table
beforehand." Having completed his court, Groomkirby of course must pre-
side at a trial.

The accused is Kirby, who admits to forty-three killings. A detective
complains: "They're piling up and down at the Morgue and after all it isn't
Albert Hall we've got." On the witness stand, Kirby's mother explains that
if a black child had been born, it would have been dressed in white; since
she had a white child, she dressed it in black. Grown up in black, he
naturally became a killer. But Kirby is a humane killer: he tells a joke; as
the victims laugh, he hits them over the head with an iron bar, and they
die happy. (During the trial Mother Groomkirby, hugging a hot-water bottle, maunders through the court on her way to bed.) And the judge refuses
to send the killer to prison, for then it would be impossible to punish him
for all the crimes he would commit if he were not confined.

Reporting from London to the *New York Tribune,* January 24, 1960,
comedian Joe Cook said: "It's no good saying it doesn't make sense. There
was not a frustrated or unhappy person on the stage or in the theatre. And
that makes more sense than a lot of things staged." The *New York Times,*
March 20, 1960, called the court scene "as brilliant a piece of fooling as
one could look for."

Presenting its outrageously eccentric situations as matter-of-fact and
normal, *One-Way Pendulum* challenges the audience to ponder to what
degree real "normal" things—such as riots after football games, or, for
that matter, bombings and wars—are sensible, and to leave the theatre
wondering when the pendulum—toward sense and sensibility, toward
peace—will swing back.

The play was shown OffBway, East 74th Street, September 18, 1961; in
1964 at the New York Hunter College and at the Sequoia Theatre, Calif.;
and it could be widely, wisely, and pleasantly viewed again.

THE DRUNKARD   *William Henry Sedley Smith*

A "domestic temperance drama by W. H. Smith and a gentleman," *The
Drunkard; or, The Fallen Saved* was presented in Boston in 1843 by P. T.
Barnum as an "illustrated sermon" on the evils of drink. Many respectable
people shunned the theatre in Barnum's day, but at his Museum the "ser-

mon" attained 144 performances. Written by William Henry Sedley Smith (American, 1807-1872) in four facts, the melodrama was played constantly for a score of years; in New York, opening June 17, 1850, it ran for 198 performances. At the Boston performances, we are told, "it was no uncommon sight to see scores of men and women weeping like children." Toward the end of the century productions dwindled. With the twentieth century advent of Prohibition in the United States, the fortunes of *The Drunkard* underwent a decided shift. It became a nostalgic drama: through its fifteen scenes the audiences hissed the villain, reassured the heroine, and cheered the hero, while thumping mugs of "near beer" on the tables. Later the liquor grew stronger but the amusement no less. The play was presented without sets in front of painted drops; between the acts there were vaudeville skits, songs and dances, singing waiters, and acrobats. Presented at the Provincetown Theatre, New York, December 30, 1929, during Prohibition, the play proved a persistent piece; on March 10, 1934, it reopened for 277 performances. London tried it in 1934 and 1942. Mary Pickford spent at the play "one of the gayest evenings I ever remember." The comedian W. C. Fields, who saw it some two-score times, called it "the greatest show on earth." In 1939 the play was presented in Sydney, Australia. In 1944 it was banned by Boston; Chairman Mary Driscoll of the Licensing Board declared: "The Board does not approve of the production of the play in connection with a place licensed to sell alcoholic beverages."

The story grows out of the machinations of the evil lawyer Cribbs, playing and preying upon Edward Middleton, a fine, honest fellow, but with an unfailing failing for drink. The play opens with an old-fashioned wedding in a cottage as Edward marries Mary. It moves deviously down the husband's drinking course—there is the famous saloon scene in which his innocent child, Julia, sings "Father, dear Father, come home with me now." As Edward, under the lawyer's plying, grows more besotted, "Be revenged on the world!" Cribbs cries, and seeks to induce Edward to forge the name of the philanthropist Adam Rencelaw on a check. Edward refuses, Cribbs himself signs Rencelaw's name. Meanwhile, Cribbs seeks to seduce Edward's wife Mary, who is starving in an attic; this failing, he forges a will, forecloses their home, and blames all their misfortunes on weak Edward. "Mother, do not cry!" Julia pleads. Mary's prayers are answered when Adam Rencelaw succeeds in foiling the plots of lawyer Cribbs and reunites with his family the repentant Edward, who has sworn off forever. Tangled in the plot are such persons as battling Farmer Stevens and wandering mad Margaret, and such happenings as a bottle's being handed to the drunkard by an arm reaching out of a hollow tree-trunk.

"When the West was new *The Drunkard* was old," said the *Los Angeles Times* (July 5, 1936); but it was to such audiences as the miners who crowded the West that the play made serious appeal. It belongs, like *East Lynne,* to a less sophisticated theatre age than that of Broadway, out beyond the towns touched by the touring companies. As sophomores gibe at the lowly freshmen, so those recently advanced beyond this play in theatrical sophistication find fun and complacent superiority in laughing at the husband who "came to swig and stayed to swoop." Other levels draw other diversion from the play. "Shakespeareans," said Ivor Brown (in the *London Observer*; December 2, 1934) "will observe that the author thought Ophelia worth stealing, and other scholars will welcome the Latinity with which the sinful lawyer can stiffen his plots and plans. Simpler folk will enjoy the persistence with which vice attacks and the punctuality with which virtue pops up to the defence."

The recent popularity of the play is a reminder of one value of the theatre unique among the public arts—the added emotional drive that rises from an audience's undergoing an experience together. There would be the thin lip of scorn pressed against *The Drunkard* by the few that might peruse it in the library; in the theatre, there is the open mouth of laughter, the shared gusto of the audience and the players. The villain leers defiance at those that hiss him; the heroine thanks them for taking her side. The spectators join the between-the-acts singing and now and again a star in the audience is persuaded to make her table the stage. The theatre comes into its own, fully though on the level of just good fun, as a home of shared experience. And one may question whether *The Drunkard* could be successful, even as a butt, if it did not have—beneath its crudity and simple sermonizing, its ink-well villain and white-wash heroine, its hustlings and poundings and heroics—a basic core of vitality and an upward surge of the spirit as with a Salvation hymn.

Do not imagine that *The Drunkard* has lost its appeal. Opening July 8, 1933, at the Los Angeles Theatre Mart, it ran for twenty years without music, and six more when a score was added, finally closing in October 1959 (now exceeded by Agatha Christie's *The Mousetrap**). The same year, it opened OffBway (the Gate). London laughed and was moved by it in 1961. It played there again at the New Lyric November 16, 1964, moving to the Vaudeville in February 1965, with David Holliday as the bibulous Edward. In England again June 1966, with music by David Ryall, book and direction by Peter Hahlo, retaining the time-honored "Father, dear Father, come home with me now."

It had forty-eight performances OffBway April 13, 1970, adapted by Bro Herrod to music by Barry Manilow. It reached Cedar Grove, N.J., August 1974 and Greenville, S.C., April 4, 1975. Los Angeles tried it again, at the Arena Theatre, February 21, 1975, as *The Wayward Way,* with music by Lorne Huycke, lyrics by Bill Howe, Jr. It may be viewed, with mixed feelings, as long as drink delights and debilitates mankind.

LIGHTNIN'   *Winchell Smith*

Bill Jones, a silver-haired tosspot, a latter-day edition of Rip Van Winkle, whom folk called "Lightnin'" as they call the town fat boy "Slim," was a favorite barnstorming figure of actor Frank Bacon (1864-1922). Bessie Bacon said: "For thirty years, under one name or another, Father played the role in vaudeville." Then, one day, Bacon and Winchell Smith (1871-1933) put the figure into a full-length play. Opening on Broadway August 26, 1981, *Lightnin'* ran for 1,291 performances. From New York, there was a parade to the station to launch its tour, led by Mayor John F. Hylan. *Lightnin'* played in Chicago for sixty-seven weeks; Frank Bacon died during the run. The play opened in London January 27, 1925, for 151 performances. It was revived in New York with Fred Stone, September 15, 1938. Will Rogers played in the film version.

Lightnin' Bill Jones could never be out-yarned. "I once did that," he would say, and follow with a prodigious story. Liar and lavish drinker, he is nevertheless a lovable harum-scarum with a head on his shoulders. He owns a hotel that straddles the Nevada-California line; lawyer Raymond Thomas and his crony Hammond come from San Francisco to swindle the Joneses out of it. They have bought the neighboring property of the Marvins, and are trying to evade detection by seeking to arrest John Marvin—

who escapes the Nevada sheriff by stepping across the hotel lobby into California.

Mrs. Jones falls for the suave ways of the city lawyer; when Lightnin' refuses to sell, she sues him for divorce. Lightnin' comes to court in a G.A.R. uniform; accused of lying, he defies anyone to disprove his statement that he once drove a swarm of bees across the plains in the dead of winter without losing a bee. The divorce case and the trickery of the two rascals from San Francisco grow intertangled; their double-dealing is exposed; Mrs. Jones goes back to Lightnin', and their daughter Mildred accepts John Marvin.

Lightnin' was well received in both New York and London. Burns Mantle (August 27, 1918) declared: "*Lightnin'* is compounded of some sense and a lot of heart . . . with amusing twists of dialogue and scene that save it from following a slavish formula." And the *Graphic* (London, January 28, 1925) stated: "From start to finish the play is crammed with breeziness and wit so clever and clean that a Lutheran censor could not take exception to one line."

These qualities of the play were emphasized in the Golden revival, on which John Anderson commented (*New York Journal,* September 16, 1938): "*Lightnin'* manages to strike twice in the same place, the vulnerable spot just abaft the funny-bone and right under the box-office . . . a piece of theatre-lore that has become a legend, and the triumph of soothing syrup over all objection."

Lightnin' Bill Jones moved slowly; he talked with a slow-time drawl; but his simple hold on the affections was sure. He belongs among the folk-fellows of our wide and sentimental land.

AJAX   *Sophocles*

During the youth of Sophocles (Greek, 497-405 B.C.), the theatre was dominated by Aeschylus.* Rivalry between the two playwrights soon developed as each quickly took advantage of the innovations of the other. Sophocles, who had a weak voice, discontinued the practice of having the dramatist perform his own plays. He added a third actor to the company. Aristotle states that Sophocles introduced scene painting. He increased the number and variety of stage properties. In his later works, he did not follow a single theme through a trilogy, but presented three plays on different subjects. Of some 123 plays that he wrote, seven survive, the earliest, *Ajax,* written when he was fifty.

Sophocles was very popular in his day and a devoted son of Athens. In the dramatic contests he won the first prize twenty-four times; all his other entries won second place. When first Sophocles and Aeschylus presented opposing plays in the dramatic contest in 468 B.C., public feeling ran high. To satisfy everyone of the impartiality of the ten judges, the archon did not select them by lot as usual. When the ten generals entered the theatre to make the opening libations to the gods, he named them judges; they gave the victory to Sophocles.

Ajax (*The Whip-Bearing Ajax*), 447(?) B.C., presents an episode of the ancient legends that falls between the *Iliad* and the *Odyssey.* When Achilles died, Ajax and Odysseus both desired the dead hero's armor. It was awarded to Odysseus; Ajax in his pride felt that he had been slighted, and resolved to kill the Greek leaders. At this point the play opens. The program of a New York production (March 24, 1904) sums it up: "Self-glory and scorn of the gods are punished by madness, during which Ajax commits acts unworthy of himself; acts which on the recovery of his sanity so overwhelm him with shame that he escapes only by death; acts which are so dreadful in the eyes of the Greeks that they are unwilling to give his body decent burial until Odysseus, who has learned humility and justice from Athena, intercedes in behalf of the dead hero and persuades Agamemnon to allow the sacred rites to take place."

Sophocles' style has a sweetness that earned him the nickname, "the Attic bee." His chief advance beyond Aeschylus is in his concern for character. In Aeschylus it is an external fate, a "curse," that works upon the mortals of the story; in Sophocles, there is a heroic attitude toward life, within the character, that drives him to his doom. Even the minor figures are carefully drawn. Tecmessa, the loyal concubine of Ajax, is one of the most appealing women in the Greek drama. Odysseus is no stock hero; he has natural, human traits: alarm when the madman Ajax is about to come from his tent; but magnanimity at the close, when his words win proper burial for his fallen rival. Only Menelaus the Spartan—Sparta was the foe of Athens, in Sophocles' day—is shown as consistently base. A further neat touch in several of Sophocles' plays is the introduction of silent characters, usually children—here, the young son of Ajax and Tecmessa—whose silent helplessness and bewildered sorrow add considerably to the emotional power of the drama. Euripides also uses such children, as in the *Medea.**

The chief character, Ajax, is most carefully drawn. His excessive pride (hybris) has set the madness upon him, so that he wreaks havoc upon the Greek flocks and scourges a ram he takes to be Odysseus. Yet he must be rehabilitated—perhaps, indeed, that was the basic reason for Sophocles' writing the play—because the most famous Athenians, Miltiades, hero of Marathon, Thucydides, and Alcibiades, claimed descent from Ajax, King of Salamis. With care and consummate skill Sophocles follows the mental anguish of Ajax from the time he recovers his reason and discovers his mad actions through the shame and the heroic resolve that lead to his suicide and "peace."

In the Ajax, as in Sophocles' plays thereafter, the gods are less external forces than symbols of the hero's own impulses. The temple of Zeus at Olympia showed a figure of Heracles straining every muscle to uphold the heavens, while the goddess Athena with one relaxed arm makes the deed possible. This interaction of the human and the divine becomes in Sophocles a manifestation of the divine within the human. The *theos,* the outer god, has become the *ethos,* the inner spirit. Ajax holds to his standards. His nobility leads to, but triumphs in, his death.

In two other important aspects the drama marks a growth in theatrical art. There is first a conscious increase in the use of dramatic irony, which raises the audience as it were to Mount Olympus, contemplating, with such prevision as the gods possess, the imminent plight of the unwitting mortals. When Ajax, for example, speaks of "peace" to come, the chorus sings a song of joy at his recovery; but allusions that the chorus fails to catch let the audience know that Ajax himself is looking forward to the peace of death. The second change is the bringing of direct, even violent, action onto the stage. Before *Ajax,* combats, murders, and other desperate deeds occurred out of sight, and were reported by messenger. Here, when Ajax is ready to die, he plunges on his sword in full view of the audience. This revolutionary change was not adopted for all subsequent Greek plays; but it is basic in the shift from a primarily lyric to a truly dramatic theatre.

Frequently produced in ancient Greece, the drama was enacted at Cambridge, England, in 1883. During rehearsals for a 1903 production by the Greeks in Chicago, the Athenian and the Spartan Greeks quarreled over the parts; all the Spartans stayed away from one rehearsal, and an Athenian remarked, "I guess the Peloponnesian War will never end." The first New York production, also in Greek, was in 1904.

"A day can humble all humans, and a day can lift them up." With beauty, dignity, and power Sophocles' *Ajax,* showing the hero fallen because he refuses to live with shame, lays bare for our beholding the deep impulses of human nature and the consequences our natures bring upon ourselves.

ANTIGONE   *Sophocles*

Sophocles' thirty-second play, *Antigone,* written in 442 B.C., was in ancient times considered his best work. Its theme is the still insistent conflict of the individual and the state, the question of the right of a person to reject a human edict that in his judgment violates a higher law. Its story is told nowhere else in ancient writings and may be Sophocles' invention.

As told in Aeschylus' *Seven Against Thebes,** the two sons of Oedipus have slain each other. In *Antigone,* King Creon orders Eteocles, the son that had defended Thebes, to be buried; but he denies to Polyneices, the son that had attacked the city, the funeral rites that were of final import to the Greeks. Antigone resolves that her brother shall be decently buried. In the opposition of wills that follows, Antigone is led to death; Creon's son Haemon, who loves her, kills himself; his mother then does the same in grief for him; and Creon is left to mourn the results of his obstinate pride.

The drama abounds in splendid passages and choral lyrics. Early in the play is a splendid eulogy of man; later, a rousing ode to love. Sophocles' contemporaries, in addition to the beauty and the forcefulness of the drama, may have discerned in some of Creon's specious arguments satiric shafts against the sophists, then becoming prominent in Athens. As a result of the play's success, tradition reports, Sophocles was appointed in 440 B.C. (along with Pericles) as one of the generals to conduct the Samian War.

The play has continued successful. In the nineteenth century, it was presented frequently in London. In 1846 it was done with music by Mendelssohn. Six years later Miss Vandenhoff made a tremendous impression as Antigone. The *Lady's Newspaper* (April 10, 1852) quotes the *London Times* as saying she "produced an effect perfectly electrical, and totally unlike anything else that we have seen," and the *Observer* as declaring her work "one of the most perfect impersonations on the English stage, or, it may be, in the whole compass of the English drama." From Covent Garden, London, a production of 1844 was brought the next year to New York. There the *Spirit of the Times* (April 12, 1845) commented that "*Antigone,* the concluding section of the Oedipus story, is the simplest, least mechanical, most sublime. . . . The language is assuredly sublime; the words of the chorus, in places light and graceful, at times measured and affecting." Within a week, however, in the vogue of the day, a burlesque of the play appeared.

In more recent years the drama has been reshaped to various purposes. Jean Cocteau wrote a version, with music by Arthur Honegger, which, translated by Francis Fergusson, was presented in New York by the American Laboratory Theatre, opening April 24, 1930. Cocteau declared that if one "photographs Greece from an airplane one sees it in quite a new light. It is in this way that I wished to translate *Antigone*. From a bird's eye view great beauties are lost; others emerge for the first time: new relationships, blocks, shadows, angles and reliefs are discovered." The critics recognized that in the Cocteau version great beauties were lost; his triumph, said John Mason Brown, "consists of robbing the original of both its dignity and its beauty and putting nothing in their place." Cocteau here failed as aviator, photographer, and playwright.

Political use has also been made of the play. Walter Hasenclever rewrote it in 1916 as a protest against World War I: "*Antigone* was for me the bearer of the ideal of emancipation and of human brotherhood in the desert of murder and violence." Creon and his marshal, in this version, resemble Kaiser Wilhelm II and Ludendorff. Hasenclever's version was adapted for Soviet Russia in 1929 by Gorodetzky; the director Tairov stated: "In our transcription of the play, *Antigone* is the tragedy of the insufficiently organized and therefore until now unsuccessful attempt of the European nations to cast off the yoke of imperialist Absolutism or Fascism, which reared its throne on the corpses of the fighters for a new life."

Such contemporary twistings and limitations of an eternal thought seem bound to make the play banal. Jean Anouilh rewrote it in Paris during World War II, and his modernized version, translated by Lewis Galantiere, was brought to New York on February 18, 1946, with Cedric Hardwicke as Creon and Katharine Cornell as Antigone. Although superb acting kept the play onstage for 64 performances, Anouilh, seeking both to placate the Germans who occupied Paris and to rouse the French, succeeded merely in boring Americans. He presented Creon not as a harsh tyrant, but as a calm worker for law and order, which are to him more important than any individual code of morals. When his son and his wife commit suicide Creon sighs and goes to a Cabinet meeting. Anouilh's product, said the generous George Jean Nathan, proved "less Sophocles than sophomore." In addition to these stage versions and perversions, the play has been translated by R. C. Jebb; by R. C. Trevelyan; by Dudley Fitts and Robert Fitzgerald—whose translation, said the *New York Times* (March 5, 1939), "brings the play measurably nearer to us than most"—and by Shaemas O'Sheel. The Fitts-Fitzgerald version was movingly directed by N. Bryllion Fagin at the Johns Hopkins theatre in Baltimore in 1949.

The superb and sensitive character-drawing of Sophocles is manifest in the play. The frail and feminine Ismene is effectively contrasted with her resolute and calm sister Antigone; yet for all her weakness Ismene is ready to die for those she loves—an emotional quality that is met with scorn by the deliberate and reasoning Antigone, sure both of her rectitude and her pathway. Without compromise or regard for consequences, she does what she feels is right, knowing it will bring on her doom. Creon, on the other hand, recognizes his error as he mourns over his son's body. Both were unalterable; he with the obstinacy of a tyrant; she with the firmness of a hero.

Among the technical devices that mark Sophocles' skill, two may be mentioned. He introduces comic relief into the tragedy (as later, Shakespeare*), making the guard over Polyneices' body a bit of a wag, with pity for Antigone as he arrests her, but not so much pity as he'd have had for himself if she had slipped by. And he makes effective use of silence to add to the dramatic intensity, as when, on hearing of her son's suicide, Creon's wife Eurydice steals wordlessly away to end her own life.

The beauty and the vibrant force of *Antigone* press through the well-knit drama. Its basic conflict of the individual judgment and will against the mandate of the state is as recurrent as its final thought is true: "Great words of prideful men are ever punished with great blows and, in old age, teach the chastened to be wise."

From the German of Friedrich Holbein, an adaptation by Bertolt Brecht was presented by the Living Theatre at the Dublin Festival, 1967, with Judith Malina as Antigone; Julian Beck, Creon.

Less austere than the Greek, the Anouilh version grew popular. At the Old Vic, 1949, Laurence Olivier was Chorus; Vivien Leigh, Antigone. A New York 1955 reading was by Luise Rainer and Albert Dekker. It was twice performed OffBway in 1959; again 1978. In London, 1959, classical Sophocles alternated with Anouilh in modern dress. A modern version in 1965 distributed copies of "The Theban Times," with headlines: "Death of Oedipus' Sons Ends Succession Fight—Creon, New Ruler, to Address Nation Today." In New York, 1971, there were two versions: a modern slangy translation by, and directed by, Leo Aylon; and the Fitts-Fitzgerald at Lincoln Center, with Martha Henry as Antigone, escorted by masked guards.

OEDIPUS THE KING   *Sophocles*

Most students of the drama consider *Oedipus Tyrannus* the masterpiece of the ancient stage. Aristotle mentions it more than any other play and calls it a model in the treatment of its plot. It is truly a superbly constructed play. Two important aspects of Greek and of much modern tragedy—the "recognition" scene and the peripeteia or reversal of fortune—are so deftly developed that they come together: Oedipus' awareness of his identity is also Oedipus' doom.

The play begins with Theban citizens pleading with their king, Oedipus, for relief from the pestilence that is devouring the city. Creon returns from the oracle with word that first the city must cleanse itself of the defilement within, and must avenge the murder of its former king, Laius, who has been killed in a roadside brawl. Step by step—with a skill unsurpassed in the neatest detective story of today—as Oedipus seeks the source of the pollution, we learn the fatal facts. It had been prophesied that the son of King Laius and Jocasta would kill his father and marry his mother; the infant, therefore, had been given to a shepherd to leave to die. Laius' widow, Jocasta, has married the hero Oedipus, who has saved Thebes by solving the riddle of the Sphinx. With gathering horror, as the inquiry goes on, Jocasta suspects the truth and tries to stop the investigation. Teiresias, the blind seer, bids Oedipus seek no further. But Oedipus, blinder than the seer, forces the inquiry on. Jocasta rushes away and hangs herself. Though the light begins to dawn in him, Oedipus takes the only honorable part, insisting that the inquiry proceed. In an awful moment, he wakens to the knowledge that he himself is that son of Laius, that the prophecy has been horribly fulfilled. Oedipus blinds himself, and goes forth a wanderer, leaving Creon to guide the recovery of Thebes. Silently Antigone and Ismene, the two little daughters of the incestuous union, stand watching and by their presence deepen the tragic grief.

The characters are developed with a skill that matches that of the play's structure. Creon is a temperate man; his response to Oedipus' charges that he is stirring trouble is restrained; his reasons for not wishing to be a ruler are measured, and pertinent today; his gentle firmness with the broken Oedipus makes him most sympathetic (quite unlike the side he reveals in the *Antigone**). Jocasta is a warm-hearted woman whose love does not blind her; she tries to calm Oedipus, to mediate between him and her brother Creon; she grows into a richly developed tragic figure. Oedipus himself is the criterion of tragic heroes, a great man doomed not through depravity but through the very excess of some good quality in him. It is his firmness on the proper path, in the quest of his people's good, that brings him down. The play ends with the maxim that opens *The Trachiniae*: "Count no man happy until he has crossed life's border free from pain."

Athens was devastated by a great plague from 430 to 427 B.C. Most scholars believe that the play was written at this time. Others, pointing out that the dramatist Phrynichus had earlier been fined for a play reminding the Athenians of misfortunes, believe that Sophocles produced his drama before the plague. The story was, indeed, most popular among the playwrights. All three of the great tragedians and at least ten minor ones wrote plays of Oedipus. Julius Caesar wrote one. Seneca's version, of about A.D. 60, survives. In modern times Sophocles' play continued popular. Racine called it "the ideal tragedy." Corneille wrote *Oedipe* in 1657; in his version, Oedipus is not a noble figure, but suspicious, designing, not heedful of his people's well-being but eager to keep his crown. The version by Dryden in 1679 introduces much new material, including a daughter of Laius and Jocasta for whom Creon incestuously hungers; it is ranting and bloody. Voltaire's version, in 1718, makes the most vigorous use of the story in modern times; it introduces Philoctetes as another suitor for Jocasta and emphasizes the cruelty of the gods. Voltaire's play was popular because of certain scandals in court circles of his day; similarly, Shelley's *Oedipus Tyrannus, or Swellfoot the Tyrant*, 1820, was a satire on the matrimonial affairs of George IV. (Oedipus means swollen-foot: when the infant was exposed, it was hung to a tree by a twig passed through its feet.)

The drama has been frequently revived. Oedipus was the greatest role of the French actor Mounet-Sully, around 1880; he played it in New York in 1894. The first American production was at Harvard University in 1881, in Greek, with a cast of a hundred and nineteen. In 1882 George Riddle produced the play in New York, Oedipus speaking Greek, the others English. The first wholly English performance was with John E. Kellard in 1911. *Oedipus* was played in New York in German with Rudolph Christians in 1914. In 1931 an elaborate production of Jean Cocteau's French version, with music by Stravinsky and Stokowski conducting the Philadelphia Orchestra, was given at the Metropolitan Opera House with Paul Althouse as Oedipus and Margarete Matzenauer as Jocasta. In May 1948 the Habima Players presented the drama in New York in Hebrew. It was played in Delphi, Greece, in 1951. A French version by André Gide was enacted by Jean-Louis Barrault in Paris and in London in 1951. The modern Greek version of the Greek National Theatre, with superb use of the chorus, was shown in New York opening November 24, 1952.

Several productions in English are memorable. In 1915 Augustin Duncan presented Margaret Wycherly as Jocasta, with the Chorus sung and danced by Isadora Duncan and her group. In 1923 Sir John Martin-Harvey brought to the United States a production that Max Reinhardt had supervised, in the vigorous Gilbert Murray translation. The *New York Times*

(October 26, 1923) declared that "*Oedipus Rex* came to life last night in its true Hellenic quality, as few modern productions of Greek tragedy have ever done." Of a later Reinhardt production in London, James Agate, in the *London Times* (October 4, 1936), observed: "The final exit through the audience is one of those colossal mistakes of which only your highbrow producer is capable." In Dublin in 1933 the Abbey Theatre produced a version by William Butler Yeats, a fiery poetic translation of the vivid Greek. This version was brought to New York by the Old Vic Company in 1946, with Laurence Olivier giving his best performance of the tour, as Oedipus. The presentation was grimly realistic, with the blood from the blinded Oedipus smearing the cheeks of his little weeping daughters. The production unfolded, said Howard Barnes (May 21, 1946) "with soaring imagination and artistry." Two recent versions in France call for attention. Both include the legend of Oedipus and the Sphinx. In the short and shocking play by André Gide (1931), all the characters are proud and corrupt; the sons of Oedipus' incest seduce their sisters. Gide makes his play banal with trivial puns and images, as he makes it perverse with added horrors; but he presses home the thought that sin is infectious. Jean Cocteau's *The Infernal Machine* (1934) rises to eloquence in the dialogue and is effectively imaginative in many moments. But in sum, where Gide made the story more horrid, Cocteau made it more sentimental. Even in its incestuous horror, the Greek original holds the chastity of art.

One reason for the perennial hold of *Oedipus* lies in the fact that its legend of the king that kills his own father follows the pattern of the primordial drama, the nature myth and ritual slaying of the Old Year by the New Year, which then marries the wife-mother Nature. This primordial pattern of incest, at once abhorrent and essential for the primitive renewal of a people's strength, still lurks in the fixations and the complexes—including the Oedipus complex—that modern psychology finds lurking within us all. However, the play needs no reenforcement from modern psychology; rather, it gives forcefulness of illustration to a basic human drive.

Through the ages the drama has lived, to deepen in our hearts and minds the sense of human suffering; of human dignity in the grip of great misfortune; of human power to bear. And out of such tragedy, through its truth and its beauty, wells an exaltation, a reaffirmation of human onward effort and human worth.

Recent productions of *Oedipus Rex* are too numerous to list. The Gilbert Murray version was done in New York in 1958 and 1962; the David Thompson in London, 1964; one by Paul Roche, Sheffield, England, 1968.

Our violent age seems to prefer the Seneca emphasis on horror and sex. Thus, the NT (Old Vic) production March 19, 1968, directed by Peter Brook, with Irene Worth all in black as Jocasta, John Gielgud as Oedipus, Colin Blakeley as Creon, and Frank Wylie as Tiresias, was vividly described by Harold Hobson: "There rises a huge and golden cube, which, when it revolves, hurls into the eyes of the audience shafts of brilliant and burning light that dazzle, and hurt. The earth is diseased, man is arbitrarily trapped and then tormented, and the shining sun is baleful. . . . Man's greatness is that the gods themselves cannot blast him. . . . Man is redeemed, not by god, but by man. The play ends with a ceremoniously unveiled gigantic golden phallus which I am sure Mr. Brook would not have introduced without some serious aesthetic purpose, but I cannot for the life of me guess what that purpose is."

Succeeding productions have no doubt informed him: to Seneca, the only one of the gods still powerful is Priapus. Sophocles has Jocasta hang herself; Seneca has her thrust her sword up into her womb, whence had come her son Oedipus and her incestuous children by this son-husband. At the 1970 production by HARPO (*Har*vard *P*roducing *O*rganization) the chorus closed with a frenzy of copulation: one couple removed their pale red robes, she with a pair of enormous rubber breasts, he with a gigantic rubber phallus, while the chorus watched with boisterous applause.

In Hollywood's Oxford Playhouse, 1973, a Sphinx (whom Oedipus had destroyed by guessing her riddle) loomed as a nemesis throughout the performance. There was an equally terrifying production by RADA November 11, 1975; also by two OffOffBway groups: the Performance Group, November 19, 1977, and Theatre Genesis, July 6, 1978, in the sculpture garden at St. Marks'. They seem to find zest in sinning with Seneca. One group mixed moods by ending with a Dionysian procession through the audience, led by a jazz band playing "Yes, We Have No Bananas." For another variation, see Cocteau's *The Infernal Machine.**

ELECTRA   *Sophocles*

The story of Electra survives in plays of all three of the great Greek tragic dramatists: the *Choephori** of Aeschylus, the *Electra,* 413 B.C., of Euripides, and the *Electra,* 414(?) B.C., of Sophocles. In all three, the basic plot is the same: Orestes, grown to manhood, returns to Mycenae, where his sister Electra has been awaiting him, and kills his mother Clytemnestra and her lover Aegisthus, the murderers of his father, Agamemnon, on his return from Troy. The minor variations in the plays show the different natures and purposes of the dramatists.

When Sophocles wrote his drama Aeschylus had been dead for forty years and his drama was a monument, the public's love of which Sophocles had to weigh and counterbalance to win approval of his different emphasis. Sophocles presents to the intellect a character-study of a woman pressed upon by grievous circumstance. He develops skillfully the high-spirited Electra, by contrast with her mother and with her weaker sister, driving with resolute sense of duty to the desperate deed as she "defends the right, and shows to godless men how the gods vindicate impiety." To strengthen this feeling, Sophocles neglects Clytemnestra's more legitimate motive for killing her husband, his sacrifice of their daughter Iphigenia, and emphasizes her lust for her lover Aegisthus. Electra urges her brother to the deed; when Clytemnestra shrieks inside the palace, Electra cries out "Strike again!" The play ends with a note of triumph, and the chorus concludes that the curse has fallen from the house of Atreus, "crowned with good by this day's enterprise." Sophocles alone has Clytemnestra die before Aegisthus; this order also keeps prominent the earlier crime and the justice of the present deed. But this is Electra's play, not Orestes'; its theme is endurance and the choice of adversity because of the soul's demands upon itself.

Euripides' *Electra,* which may be an answer to Sophocles,' tones down the horror and seeks to humanize the deed. It thus makes Electra a more sympathetic figure, and has proved the most appealing of the three dramas. Plutarch tells us that in 404 B.C., at the end of the Peloponnesian War, when Lysander was pondering whether to wipe the fallen Athens from the earth, a citizen of Phocis sang the opening chorus of Euripides'

Electra, "O Agamemnon's child, Electra, to thy humble cot I come": a gust of pity swept the assembled leaders, and Athens was spared.

American productions of Euripides' play include many by Mr. and Mrs. Coburn in the 1910s; one by Actors Equity in New York in 1924; at Carnegie Tech, Pennsylvania, in 1932; off-Broadway in 1951. But most recent revivals, like that of London's Old Vic on March 13, 1951, have used the starker *Electra* of Sophocles. The Greek National Theatre brought its modern Greek version to New York with Katina Paxinou in 1952. (For various adaptations of *Electra,* see Aeschylus' *Oresteia.**)

The role of Electra has lured many great stars. Mrs. Pat Campbell opened in New York on February 11, 1908, with Mrs. Beerbohm Tree as Clytemnestra, in a version translated by Arthur Symons from the 1904 German adaptation of Hugo von Hofmannsthal. This mixture of potent Greek and perfervid Freud produced, said the *New York World* "a performance true in every detail to a well wrought conception, plastic, picturesque, and horrid, with a now smothered, now outbursting lust of revenge, a kind of craze of blood . . . curious, sensually cruel—and fascinating." Margaret Anglin, beginning with an open-air performance in Berkeley, California, in 1915, returned to the role of Electra frequently. In 1918, in New York, she alternated the roles of Electra and Medea (for a comparison, see Euripides' *Medea**). John Corbin (February 17, 1918) observed: "It does take some little detachment of mind to enter into the mood of a heroine who rejoices in matricide as a religious duty. The greater credit, then, to Sophocles and to Margaret Anglin that the performance stood out in such glowing colors, had power to move us so deeply." Nine years later Brooks Atkinson (May 4, 1927) said that her performance held "all the majesty of Greek tragedy at its best . . . full austerity and frigid beauty. . . . She is an instrument rather than a personality; she is a sublimation of justice purging the house of Atreus." Margaret Anglin used the E. H. Plumptre translation; a less effective version by J. T. Sheppard was used in the 1932 production, with Blanche Yurka as Electra and Mrs. Pat Campbell this time as Clytemnestra. The *New York Herald-Tribune* (January 9, 1932) felt that the "treatment was marked by a Shakespearean robustness rather than that marble-like austerity commonly associated with the classic Greek."

No more recent American productions can match the work of Margaret Anglin, especially in the 1918 performances at Carnegie Hall, including music by Walter Damrosch. There was a production in Greek at Randolph-Macon College in 1943. Katina Paxinou, who with the Royal Theatre Company of Greece gave a Greek production at Cambridge, England, in 1939, with, said the *London Times* (June 19, 1939), "an effect not only of its natural power but of an extraordinary freshness," gave English readings of the play in New York in 1942. In French, Jean Giraudoux produced a version in Paris (June 17, 1937), which began with Electra unaware of her mother's misdeeds, and which slowed the action by many comments of the modern dramatist. Concentration of the action around the long steps and the central door helped give simple beauty and austere power to a production, in the translation of Francis Fergusson, in April 1948 by the Johns Hopkins Playshop in Baltimore. The best productions, indeed, have been made with vigorous translations, not modernized adaptations. "Euripides still appears to us," said Clayton Hamilton in *Vogue* (April, 1918), "as he seemed, long ago, to Aristotle, 'the most tragic of the poets,' but Sophocles is more august and monumental in the architecture of his plays." That "architecture" rears, in the story of Electra, a lofty tragic figure, still made most vivid and most touching in the telling of the ancient Greeks.

Among recent revivals of the Sophocles *Electra*: New York City Center, September 1961 and April 1972. OffBway (La Mama), November 1972. London (Mermaid), June 1967, prose translation by Jack Lindsay directed by Bernard Miles, in jackboots and jerkins, with flick-knives, and the head of the murdered king tossed like a football. In 1971, translated by David Thompson; Orestes frolics homosexually with Pylades, and walks up the aisle telling the audience he can recognize a good man. Electra's husband speaks the Prologue as a bawdy clown.

PHILOCTETES   *Sophocles*

Written when Sophocles was 87 years old, his *Philoctetes* won first prize in the contest of 409 B.C. It is the best presentation of a moral problem in the Greek drama.

The play is based upon an episode in the Trojan War. Long before the point at which Sophocles' drama opens, young Philoctetes, for having lighted Heracles' funeral pyre, was by that dying hero given his bow and arrows. When the Greeks set out against Troy, they had to stop to sacrifice at a shrine; Philoctetes, who guided them, was bitten by a serpent and afflicted with a loathsome, unhealing sore and stench. The Greek commanders thereupon ordered Odysseus to maroon Philoctetes on the uninhabited island of Lemnos. Now, after nine years of vain siege of Troy, it is prophesied that if Achilles' son Neoptolemus come to Troy, and if Philoctetes willingly bring Heracles' bow and arrows, the besieged city will fall. The play opens with Odysseus and Neoptolemus come to Lemnos for the arms. Odysseus remains the same throughout, the shrewd schemer with no moral qualms, justifying the means when the end is the glory of Greece. But each of the other two main figures works through a human problem. Neoptolemus, a noble, patriotic youth, is persuaded by Odysseus, whom Philoctetes would have recognized and spurned, to use guile to secure the bow and arrows essential to their victory. The youth's repugnance, then his yielding for his country's sake, are admirably shown. After winning Philoctetes' friendship and the weapons, however, Neoptolemus in honest revulsion finds the deceit too mean; he frankly tells Philoctetes who they are and what their needs and returns the bow and arrows. Philoctetes, the young man says, should freely accompany them to Troy. Now the moral conflict shifts to the breast of the older man. It is harder for him to be generous. Through long years on the lonely island he has nursed his hatred with his injury: what has his country done for him, that he should now strike for her? Neoptolemus recognizes the validity of the objection and agrees to go with Philoctetes back to Greece. This friendship wakens a responsive chord in Philoctetes. Then Heracles, who had given Philoctetes the bow and arrows, comes down onto the stage and bids him go to Troy. After he has held firm against guile, force, even friendly persuasion and the promise that his sores will be healed, then freely the will of Philoctetes himself (as Cedric H. Whitman, views it, in *Sophocles,* 1951), makes the fit choice, as a noble man must. Philoctetes beholds Heracles, and "suddenly his victory appears to him. There are few moments in drama more breath-taking than this one." The god makes manifest the divinity within the man. The "god from the machine" has become the voice of the spirit.

The story of Philoctetes was very popular; six lesser dramatists used it, as well as the great three. Only Sophocles' version remains; but the critic Dion Chrysostomus, of the first century A.D., has left us a comparison of the versions of Aeschylus, Sophocles, and Euripides. (Euripides' was presented in 431 B.C. along with the extant *Medea.**) According to Dion, Aeschylus' version was marked by simplicity, greatness of soul, power of thought and language; Euripides' by keen rhetoric and choral exhortations to noble deeds; Sophocles'—as we, too, can attest—by dignity and naturalness, truth to human nature. The farewell of Philoctetes to Lemnos, where he has long dwelt in fortitude, makes a rare and exalted close to the drama.

Philoctetes is without female characters. Its men are among the most complex in ancient drama, shrewdly studied, clearly portrayed. Their problems of the practical versus the decent action, of concern for one's own interests versus concern for the good of the state, of the endurance of injustice and many woes with unquenched nobility, are fundamental in every time and have had few more searching presentations in the drama.

Philoctetes was revived OffBway: at the Theatre de Lys, from the version by André Gide, January 1959; Sheridan Square, April 1961; Grand Street, August 1964. London, 1964.

OEDIPUS AT COLONUS   *Sophocles*

The longest extant Greek tragedy (1,779 lines), *Oedipus at Colonus,* possibly written in 406 B.C., is by many acclaimed as Sophocles' best. The last play of the aged dramatist, it was produced posthumously in 401 B.C. by his grandson, Sophocles the younger, and won the first prize. The work was highly esteemed throughout antiquity; Longinus, a critic of the third Christian century, remarked: "Magnificent are the images that Sophocles has conceived of the death of Oedipus, who makes ready his burial amid the portents of the sky."

We see here the last hours of Oedipus, twenty years after he has blinded himself. He has come, a beggar in rags, to Colonus in Attica, but still a figure of majesty and of portent. For it has been prophesied that the city where he is buried will have a future of peace and glory. Creon, King of Thebes, therefore comes to take Oedipus back to that city; he refuses to go and is protected by Theseus, King of Athens. Oedipus walks—as though sight had returned to him, or a god were his guide—to the place where he has to die and, in an awe-filled silence, disappears.

This is the only known play on the theme of Oedipus' final hours. Sophocles saw the dramatic possibilities in the subject; but also, Sophocles was born at Colonus, where Oedipus died, and the playwright was moved by a deep devotion to his native land. Colonus was a division of Attica just north of Athens; Sophocles' choral lyric (lines 668-719) in praise of the city, along with that in Euripides' *Medea** (lines 824-845), is the noblest tribute to Athens in the Greek drama. When Sophocles' son charged the nonagenarian playwright with incompetence, Sophocles' only defense was to recite in court this lyric, which he had just composed: he was at once acquitted. The poetry throughout the play is unsurpassed in Sophocles; another great speech is Oedipus' comment (lines 607-623) on the changes wrought by time. The conception of Oedipus in this play is richer and nobler than in Sophocles' earlier *Oedipus Rex*.* Beggar in body, the blind man is noble in spirit, He walks with his daughter as guide yet bears himself assured by an inner power. Time has dimmed the horror of his deeds, his killing his father and marrying his mother, and, as he has acted innocently, he is burdened with no sense of guilt. There still is vigor in the man, as shown in the vehemence with which he curses his undutiful sons, who for their own ends would have him return to Thebes. Oedipus rebukes them for their persistence on an ignoble way; but he himself has moved toward tranquility and peace, to the final calm that, all passion spent, marks the noble end of a great man.

Perhaps for some contemporary purpose that we cannot guess, Sophocles makes Polyneices not the younger but the elder son of Oedipus. King Creon of Thebes, Sophocles presents as an unscrupulous schemer who comes in guile and leaves in violence. King Theseus of Athens he shows as a just and beloved ruler and protector of the weak. Like a man of lofty character, Theseus has a democratic spirit; he welcomes the exiled and beggared Oedipus. As the Athenians had defeated a Theban detachment near Colonus in 407 B.C., the year before the play was written, it is obvious that Sophocles' deep love of his country and his desire to cheer it in the present crisis contributed to the power of the play. Athens was in desperate straits, her leaders incompetent, her armies crumbling, her citizens unfed; yet Sophocles speaks of Athens as inviolable. Time goes on, but remains the same; fortitude and knowledge, enduring, grow. The fortitude of Athens is embodied in Oedipus.

Recent productions include one in Berlin in 1929, another at the Greek Theatre of Syracuse, Sicily, in 1936. There are several English translations of the play: a rather literal one by R. C. Jebb: a poetic one by Yeats; one by R. C. Trevelyan. Reviewing the last-mentioned version, the *London Times* (June 22, 1946) declared that it "conveys, more certainly than any other Greek play, the sense of ultimate serenity." The play was performed in New York, OffBway, in 1955.

Certainly there is no easy optimism in this last play of the great dramatist, written in his ninetieth year, when a long war was moving toward disaster for his beloved city. Yet the final words are of courage and fair pride, for the chorus calls: "Come, cease lamentation, lift it up no more; for verily these things stand fast." Here, against the triumph of death, Sophocles erects the dignity and the will of man in one of the most beautiful and most exalting of all dramas.

At the NT, June 1966, Katina Paxinou alternated *Oedipus Tyrannus* and *Oedipus at Colonus,* in Greek. In English, ELT, February 1972.

LAMP AT MIDNIGHT   *Barrie Stavis*

There was a time when, across the wide continent beyond Broadway, an eager semiliterate audience enjoyed slapstick farce, fierce melodrama, and such pseudorealistic pieces as *Aaron Slick from Punkin Crick,* which showed the scorned hick, supposedly an easy mark, giving the city slicker his comeuppance. To such simple spectators radio and television have come as blessed anodynes. Meanwhile there has grown a nationwide serious audience, in college and community theatres, that is not content with Broadway trivia, the theatre of illusion, but seeks sound presentation of basic themes and problems of human life. For this serious audience, Barrie Stavis (American, b. 1906) is a most provident provider.

Working with a fluid stage that—like Shakespeare's—can move quickly and smoothly from scene to scene and across months or years, Stavis is, as the noted critic and stage-designer Mordecai Gorelik puts it, "intensely aware of the social, economic, and political problems of human society. . . . He writes about people who dare to take action against manifest evils, even at the risk of their lives." His major works, thus far, form a tetralogy: *Lamp at Midnight* (1947, Galileo Galilei, a searching for truth); *The Man Who Never Died** (1954, Joe Hill, of human dignity); *Harper's Ferry* (1967, John Brown, of freedom); *Coat of Many Colors* (1968, Joseph in Egypt, of power).

Lamp at Midnight moves with a quiet but intense dignity to its inevitable end, as Galileo presents the newly opened heavens and the idea of a revolving earth to a church grown around the age-old Aristotelian system of a motionless earth central to God's universe. There is especial agony in the scientist's heart because he himself is a devout Catholic, hoping that the Church will be flexible and wise enough to absorb the newfound facts. Cardinal Bellarmin mildly corrects him: "My son, no fact is a pure fact. The aura of attendant consequence can never be severed from the fact itself." Feeling its authority threatened—the story is familiar—the Church exacts from its anguished but accepting son his official recantation. After the Pope leaves, Galileo prays, not for himself but for the salvation of the Pope.

Galileo is too famous a scientist to be burned; he is ordered into silence and six months' exile. On his return his daughter—who had copied his findings as he dictated, and is now Sister Maria Celeste, weakening toward her own last days—encourages Galileo and wins his promise to continue his research. She recites his penitential prayer as he says: "You cannot change the fact, nor the truth of the fact, by one jot." He stamps on the earth. "It moves." (This was in 1634. Three years later, Galileo became physically what the Church officials were spiritually: blind.)

ANTA undertook to present *Lamp at Midnight* at one of its 1947 special matinees; finding Brecht's *Galileo* available, with Charles Laughton, it put that on instead, December 7, 1947. Two weeks later, *Lamp at Midnight* was presented by New Stages—the first production in what has grown to be the widespread OffBway theatre. With Paul Mann and Peter Capell, Stavis' play was recognized as far superior to Brecht's. As Brooks Atkinson, in the *Times,* December 22, 1947, put it: "In comparison with that pretentious piece of exhibitionism, Mr. Stavis' play is obviously superior." Harry Grannick in the London *New Theatre* of April 1948 called *Lamp at Midnight* "that unusual event, a dramatic masterpiece that moves the mind and the gut by coming to grips with the complex reality of man's most fateful conflict." Playwright Arthur Miller hailed it as "a mature and eloquent drama." John F. Matthews, critic and professor at Brandeis University, declared: "I should like to see it performed annually in all our universities as a regular part of the curriculum. I can imagine no better way to bring home to our students the meaning and dignity of that freedom of mind which is our noblest heritage." Herb Shore, of the Department of Theatre, University of South Florida, commented on the 1974 revised version of the play: "In an age that seems almost to deny reason and truth, to deny Man himself, Barrie Stavis has created a theatre with faith in man, committed to reason and perception, and exploring ideas with a power that raises them to the level of passion." Love of truth may be as passionate as any other love. As I said in my *New Leader* review: "*Lamp at Midnight* shines in the theatrical sky."

Tyrone Guthrie directed an American tour of the play in 1969, that visited fifty cities over six months, starring Morris Carnovsky. In 1966 it was shown on TV's *Hallmark Hall of Fame,* with Melvyn Douglas and David Wayne—released for cable television in 1983. *Lamp at Midnight* has been shown abroad in eighteen different languages; in English at the Bristol Old Vic in 1956, with Joseph O'Conor as Galileo, Peter O'Toole as the Pope, Robert Lang, and Rachel Roberts. It was sung as an oratorio, *Galileo Galilei,* music by Lee Hoiby, first at Huntsville, Ala., March 15, 1975. It remains a favorite of college and community theatres, an impassioned presentation of a broken life that bequeathed a fertile lesson to the world. An abridged version for TV was played at the Chicago Goodman Theatre in 1972, and printed in the May 1983 issue of *Dramatics.*

First seen in London in 1960, Brecht's *Galileo,* in revival at the NT (Olivier) August 13, 1980, roused Milton Shulman in the *Standard* to reminiscence. The story, he felt, "deserves mature analysis rather than condescending simplification. Michael Gambon, as Galileo, starts off like a hectoring physics master with a very dull class on his hands, and then dwindles without much reason into an abject gourmet, preferring delicacies to ideals." Shulman was moved to wider examination: "To be on Bertolt Brecht's dramatic wavelength one has to lower one's perception and expectations to the level of someone who has stopped reading at the age of 14. It is precisely the view that culture must never be far out of step with the lowest common denominator of mass receptivity that accounts for Brecht's appeal to Marxists and intellectuals. In the East Brecht* fits in perfectly with the ossification of Marxist art. . . . In the West, his banal prose and ponderous over-simplification of complex issues is hailed by liberals as a significant step towards egalitarian drama. . . . When I first saw it 20 years ago, it put me in mind of these Hollywood historical films starring Don Ameche with lines like 'Hiya, Newton. Watcha doing under that apple tree?'"

Brecht's victims of "supine adulation" point out that Shakespeare, too, freely borrowed most of his plots. Not mentioning Shakespeare's other qualities, one may note that he converted earlier stories into plays; Brecht converted earlier plays into propaganda pieces. To use a figure familiar to Brecht's admirers, one may say that the playwright's vogue has gone up like a rocket; one may expect it to fall like the stick. There is more illuminating substance in the work of Barrie Stavis. The continuing timeliness of the Stavis play was shown by the creation in April 1983, the 350th anniversary of Galileo's trial, of a papal commission, and also an international committee of scientists, to consider the current implications of "the case of *Church* v. *Galileo.*"

THE MAN WHO NEVER DIED   *Barrie Stavis*

Joe Hill, born Joel Hägglund in Sweden, 1879, became a Wobbly, an itinerant worker who composed songs of the laborers, their sorry lot, and their hope of rising from it through "one big union," the International Workers of the World, the IWW. "They call us the Wobblies," he says in the play, "but we don't wobble, we stand firm—like a rock." His best-known song is "The Preacher and the Slave," which begins:

> *Long-haired preachers come out every night,*
> *Try to tell you what's wrong and what's right;*
> *But when asked about something to eat*
> *They will answer with voices so sweet:*
> > *You will eat bye and bye*
> *In that glorious land above the sky (Way up high);*
> > *Work and pray, live on hay,*
> *You'll get pie in the sky when you die. (That's a lie.)*

Joe Hill has thirteen songs in the 1913 edition of the *Little Red Song Book*.

The play traces Joe's story from 1913, when he was in Salt Lake City, a center of copper mining and construction interests. A 1912 strike of unorganized miners in nearby Bingham Canyon had failed, but a 1913 strike in nearby Tucker, of some 1,500 men, organized by the IWW, was successful. High on the list of the copper police was Joe Hill, whose songs and jokes were drawing many into the Union. Joe has been living with Martha Weber, whose drunkard husband, Henry, had abandoned her. Tom Sharpe, planted provocateur, plies Henry with drink, gives him a gun, and leads him home to discover his wife with Joe, whom he shoots and wounds. The same night (January 10, 1914) a grocer and his son are killed by two masked burglars, one of whom is wounded as they flee. By an easy switch the wounded Joe is accused, and convicted, of the murder. The Webers had conveniently "disappeared." Despite appeals by the Swedish Ambassador, by the A.F. of L. (which bitterly opposed the IWW), despite President Wilson and appeals from many parts of the world, the Governor of Utah let the sentence hold, and on November 19, 1915, a firing squad took the life of Joe Hill. As he was being led to his execution, his friend Ed Rowan declared: "As long as there are people in this land who sing . . . who are ready to work, to fight, to risk death for the good of their fellowmen, Joe Hill will never die." As Joe's last poem is read, ending

> *Yes, blessed is work,*
> *And blessed is the man who works,*

the final lights dim and die.

The Man Who Never Died had its premiere in St. Paul, 1955. It ran for 150 performances at the Jan Hus House, OffBway, opening in November 1958. It has been heard in twenty languages; Soviet Russia, Japan, India, both sides of Germany; in 1983 at Ibadan, Nigeria. In 1967 it was played the same year with Jean-Louis Roux in Montreal. It has been played so often in Sweden that they've nicknamed it "the play that will not die." From it came the opera *Joe Hill*, music by Alan Bush, at the East Berlin Staatsoper, September 29, 1970; over England's BBC in July 1979 and April 1981. In 1979, the centennial of Joe Hill's birth, there were some twenty-five productions around the world.

The prevalence of strikes in our world today shows that the growing power of the unions, even with the widespread closed-shop system, has not resulted in labor-management harmony. As long as there is economic and social injustice, *The Man Who Never Died* will have both power and pertinence, and will deeply move all who desire fair dealing.

FIDDLER ON THE ROOF   *Joseph Stein*

Out of the stories of Sholem Aleichem ("Peace be with you": Solomon J. Rabinowitz, 1859-1916; early a rabbi, escaped the Russian pogrom of 1905—the date of the play's action) came the musical. It was set in the Czarist ghetto village of Anatevka, where the Jews had learned to endure their age-old poverty, where they even found ways to enjoy the petty coursing of their days: the men in their ritual dancing in the joy of the Lord, the couples in the joy of their mating—for Tevye, the dairyman and moving spirit of the folk there, had three marriageable daughters. Two of them became happily matched; but one—let it not be whispered in the dawnings, nor furtively told by dusk!—married a non-Jew and went away, and by orthodox tradition her name was spoken never more.

On the whole it was a tolerable life, with pains and pleasures mixed, with the olden melodies of the fiddler, with a helping hand to the needy, a sharing of hands and hearts in companionship and love. Tevye even had many one-sided chats with the Lord, as when he asked, on a wistful impulse, how hard it would be to make him a millionaire. So the community could face, with resignation but also with resolve, the news that their village was to be taken from them, they were to be evicted. Some of them planned to go to the land of the free and (as Robert Cushman noted in the London *Observer,* July 10, 1983) "among the things created by their descendants was the American musical, of which *Fiddler on the Roof* is a culminating achievement." From this, or a similar ghetto town, much of the sort is true.

Book by Joseph Stein, lyrics by Sheldon Harnick, music by Jerry Bock, choreography by Jerome Robbins, *Fiddler on the Roof* came to the New York Imperial September 22, 1964, with Zero Mostel as Tevye, and ran for 3,242 glowing performances. In London, at Her Majesty's February 16, 1967, the Israeli Topol carried Tevye through 2,030 rousing times. Rather young, then, for the part, Topol came back, to the Apollo Victoria June 28, 1983, and was hailed through 96 scheduled performances.

The play had a long run in Copenhagen, 1967, also in Japan, translated by Takeshi Kurahashi. Luther Adler played Tevye in Los Angeles; Herschel Bernardi succeeded Mostel on Broadway. Sydney, Australia, saw the musical in 1968. Among the remembered airs are "Tradition," keynote of the orthodox Jew, and the wedding song "Sunrise, Sunset."

The humor of the play is in no sense artificial, but rises naturally from the acts and reactions of the living persons. Out of events, characters grow.

Even in lands where Jews are not numerous—their East European ghettos now long gone—audiences were moved by the warmth and wonder of their ways, by details everywhere familiar in the daily rouse, by the smiles, the hidden tears, the laughter and the love of life, and the assured determination to keep on, that make *Fiddler on the Roof* one of the theatre's most enjoyable musicals, popular throughout the world. In Zero Mostel's Tevye, said Howard Taubman in the *Times,* "it has one of the most glowing creations in the history of musical theatre."

GAMMER GURTON'S NEEDLE   *William Stevenson*

Acted at Christ's College, Cambridge, for several years after 1553 and published in 1575, *Gammer Gurton's Needle,* by William Stevenson (died in 1575), is the first English comedy with a wholly native theme. *Ralph Roister Doister,** which preceded it by a decade, draws upon Roman themes and types, though it sets them in England; *Gammer Gurton's Needle* is native from the first stitch in the Prologue to the final prick. It is, furthermore, a folk play; the characters are not only English, but close to the English soil.

The story is scarcely more than a dramatized incident. Gammer Gurton loses her precious needle, supposes that it is stolen, and sets the village in an uproar on the hunt for it. "The crazy Diccon," as Allardyce Nicoll has described it, "the dull-witted Hodge, Dame Chatte the gossip, Doctor Rat the curate, and Master Baylye are all dragged into the storm, and just as its height seems nearing, the needle is found in the most unexpected of places. The comedy, perhaps, is a trifle rough; the scenes occasionally take on the coloring of mere horseplay; but there is a genuine breath of fresh air, a healthy breeziness, in situations and in dialogue, which mark out *Gammer Gurton's Needle* as a play not to be forgotten." Others might think that the place where the needle is found is quite the expected spot, but the play works up to it deviously, so that the discovery comes—as is proper in the theatre—with surprise followed by instant acceptance as natural. The long rhyming lines of the play carry a lively vernacular, much of it consists of the characters' mutual abuse.

There have been a number of recent revivals of the play, especially by college theatres. Brooklyn, New York, saw it in 1933; Westchester, New York, in 1937; Oxford, Ohio, 1939; New York University, and Alabama College, 1940. Recent performances in England include one set at the Malvern Festival of 1937 and one in London in 1940. Back in 1564, it was played before Queen Elizabeth on her visit to Cambridge.

The various incidents of the hunt for Gammer (Grandmother) Gurton's needle enliven the movement of the play while they enlighten us as to the mood and spirit of early English village life. Many of the characters are well caught, especially the simple Hodge with his long-drawn explanations—in one case twenty-four lines all ending "see now? . . . see now?"—that never explain. The humor is no less English and no less vigorous and fresh today for being rough-house and plain-spoken in the frank countryside way of calling a spade a dirty spade. This earliest English comedy has a new-mown-hay-and-manure savor of folk drama found in few plays since its time.

The needle is found when Diccon smacks Hodge hard on the buttock.

THE REAL THING   *Tom Stoppard*

Stoppard's *The Real Thing* opened at the London Strand November 16, 1982, with Felicity Kendal and Roger Rees, directed by Peter Wood. It was voted best play of the year, and is still running as I write. It manifests Stoppard's continuing interest in language. One of the men of the two interchangeably unfaithful couples is a writer, tangled both in his problems with words and his anguish at being a tolerant cuckold. Out of the verbalization of the continual protests of love within the infidelity, "the real thing" seems to me to lapse into a tricky imitation, made tolerable by Stoppard's delight in finding words for ideas—marred more than in his other plays by worn expressions: "Happiness is a warm puppy"; awkward "as a three-legged cow."

As *The Real Thing* opens, we look upon Charlotte coming back from a trip, while her husband Max tricks her into revealing her infidelity. In Scene Two, we discover that we have just watched an episode from *The House of Cards,* a play by Henry, who is the actual husband of Charlotte, Max being married to Annie. Whether Charlotte has been unfaithful to Henry we do not learn, but Henry has found other embraces, and he leaves Charlotte for Annie, for they are deeply in love.

In Act Two, two years later, the tables are turned. Still protesting her love for Henry, Annie gives herself to macho Brodie, a poor playwright but an antinuclear agitator, whose energy has swept her off her feet.

At least one of the two meetings of Annie and Brodie, alone in a railway compartment, is part of a TV play in which they are acting. They frolic a bit, but their houghmagandy takes place offstage. Annie admits it to Henry. Action is less presented than confessed and, of course, discussed. Henry, a man of words, talks himself into an acquiescent cuckoldry, preserving the bond of his and Annie's mutual love. "The subject matter," says Mel Gussow in the *New York Times Magazine* of January 1, 1984, "may shift from moral philosophy to modern marriage, but the voice is always that of the author [Tom Stoppard, not Henry] caught in the act of badinage, arguing himself in and out of a quandary."

Tom Stoppard at his best is the most sparkling writer of our day, with wit and wisdom, neat wordplay, teasing literary allusions. Clive Barnes in the *New York Post* (January 6, 1984) found the play "measurably funny, immeasurably clever, and unexpectedly moving . . . a terrific night out, gusty and cheerfully intellectual." Frank Rich in the *New York Times* of the same date called it "not only Mr. Stoppard's most moving play, but also the most bracing play that anyone has written about love and marriage in years."

Bracing, perhaps, but not embracing. For Stoppard has Henry reason out all his attitudes. Whereas in Pirandello the contrast between "reality" and fantasy grows into poignant emotional crises, in Stoppard the conflicts of "public posture and private soul" grow rather through talking and pondering into calculated response. Stoppard has stated that *The Real Thing* sprang from a line of Auden, which he paraphrased: "Public postures have the configuration of private derangement." Derangement, not despair.

Nor are all the author's verbal adventures at the same high level. Though the audience laughs at the moment, time reveals little wit or wisdom, for instance, in the remark: "What's free about free love is love." At one point, Annie asks: "What's a petar?" Sure enough, in her next sentence, she is "hoist!" Shakespeare (*Hamlet* III, 4) delved with a defter engineer. It seems as hard to stop Stoppard from wordplay as Samuel Johnson deemed Shakespeare. In life, Stoppard sometimes plays cricket with his sons and with fellow-playwright Harold Pinter. And in *The Real Thing,* swinging a bat, playwright Henry delivers himself of what Frank Rich calls "a glorious speech likening the sacred power of a writer's words to convey ideas to a cricket bat propelling a ball." I'd have called that one caught out.

After the Broadway opening at the Plymouth January 5, 1984, the play also received rave reviews, with tribute to director Mike Nichols, and to the cast, headed by Jeremy Irons as Henry and Glenn Close as Annie. There is a brief appearance, at the end, of Cynthia Nixon as Debbie, the beautiful and word-easy daughter of Charlotte and Henry, reminding us of the marital complications, and showing that, if love is not around the corner, sex is always on the alert. The problems of love and marriage are shown and talked about (mainly by "Henry" Stoppard) rather than deeply felt. The rouse is less emotional than intellectual. In fine, says Stoppard, "Happiness is equilibrium. Shift your weight."

The Real Thing has outlasted the New York season and has already won the Drama Critics Circle award.

For a fuller view of Stoppard's work, see *Rosencrantz and Guildenstern are Dead,* after *Hamlet*; and *Dogg's Hamlet, Cahoot's Macbeth.* Also see Nestroy, and *The House of Bernarda Alba.*

THE CHANGING ROOM   *David Storey*

The Changing Room, by David Storey (b. 1933), is perhaps the best example of the non-drama—in its extreme form called anti-drama—that has recently come upon the stage. It presents three periods of activity in the changing room of the "City" rugby team, on the day of a North of England game: the gathering of the team as they get ready to play; just before and during the interval, when one player, Kendall, a forward, with a broken nose, is taxied off to a hospital; and at the end of the game, which "City" has won.

The dialogue is almost a transcript of the conversation usual at such times, often bawdy, sometimes with antagonisms breaking through; and the characters are clearly distinguished. In addition to the seasoned players, some high-keyed, some nonchalant, and the two somewhat edgy youngsters on reserve, the non-players are also well etched. There is Harry, the cleaner, with his obsession that soon the Communists will take over England. Luke, the masseur, is perky and brisk, and looks at the players with non-committed eyes. There are also the two trainers with watchful ways and proffered counsel; Tallon the referee, friendly but objective; and the aristocratic Chairman Thornton with the obsequious Mackedrick, Club Secretary. Perhaps most significant, neat, crisp, friendly, but keeping his distance, is Danny Owens, stand-off half and captain of the team.

The play opens with Harry giving the room a last sweep before the players arrive—and ends with Harry sweeping after they've gone. There is no plot. We learn the aspirations of the younger players, feel the fears of the older ones that their seasons are nearly over; we listen to the interplay of the teammates; occasionally we hear the roars of the crowd outside watching the game. No connected story, only chitchat and isolated incidents, as when Kendall refuses to lie still, saying he'll go on with the game, before they pack him off to the hospital with his bloody nose. "Bloody" is perhaps the most frequent word in the dialogue. "Its reality," said Morton Gottfried, "is its own and only meaning."

The Changing Room was first presented at the London Royal Court Theatre, home of many unusual plays, November 8, 1971, with an all-male cast of twenty-two and moved on to the Globe. From the Long Wharf, New Haven, it came to the New York Morosco March 6, 1973, for 192 performances, and won the Drama Critics Circle award. Not often does one find oneself at such a session; it seems completely true, and the interest holds.

THE FATHER   *August Strindberg*

Perhaps the most widely read and performed of all the plays by (Johan) August Strindberg (Swedish, 1849-1912), *The Father* pictures the relentless struggle between a fairly intellectual man and a determined woman, with "a woman's intuitive unconscious dishonesty."

At first the disagreement between Cavalry Captain Adolph and his wife Laura seems not ominously important: they have different ideas as to the education of their daughter Bertha. Neither will yield, however; and the struggle grows into a fight for mastery. Laura intimates that perhaps Adolph has no right to speak, perhaps he is not Bertha's father. Adolph grows increasingly baffled, increasingly violent; Laura seizes upon a letter in which he says he thinks he's going mad as a pretext for locking him in a straitjacket; and in a fit of apoplexy Adolph dies.

The violence of the play, its almost naturalistic realism and overwhelming surge of unloosed passion, brought attacks from some critics, upon whom Strindberg promptly showered a counterblast. The play won wide attention throughout Europe. Zola, the father of naturalism, praised it highly; and in the next six years Strindberg wrote fourteen naturalistic dramas, almost all of them on the same central theme. It should be noted that Strindberg does not, as many wrongly suppose, blame the woman. He indicates that she is usually the more unscrupulous, the shrewder, therefore the more often successful, in the battle of the sexes; but the battle itself he sees as inevitably rooted in nature's ways.

In its juxtaposition of violence and sentiment, this drama bears resemblances to Shakespeare. In the drive of its action, the play observes the Greek unities of time and place. Yet in its sharp, bitter dialogue, ranging from quiet hate to apoplectic fury, and in its naturalistic presentation of human character and motives, the play is thoroughly modern and distinctively Strindberg's own. There is no more harrowing scene in the drama since King Lear's wandering in the storm, than the piercingly ironic moment in which the Captain's old nurse, believing she is acting for his good, croons childhood memories to him while, without his recognizing what she is doing, she slips on him and ties tight a straitjacket.

The American premiere in New York on April 9, 1912, won mixed reviews. The *New York Dramatic Mirror* (April 17) stated that "dramatically, the play abounds in striking characters and effective scenes," but added: "The trouble with introspective thinkers like Strindberg is that they question human minds and motives so much that either they don't know what they do believe, or they make themselves believe any fantastic things they wish." In 1928 Robert Whittier acted Captain Adolph in New York, in his own adaptation of the play, ill received. In London meanwhile (1927) a company including Robert Loraine played in it successfully, continuing in London and on tour for four years and bringing the play to New York on October 8, 1931. Robert Garland said that in comparison, "the depression seems bright and cheerful." John Anderson called the play "one of the most unpleasant and most fascinating of the modern classics, a cruel, obsessed, almost maniacal tirade aimed, from the top of its screech, at the conspiracy of women against men."

The play found vivid revival by the Studio-7 group in New York in 1949; less happily, with Raymond Massey on Broadway; but Munich the same year saw a production with Fritz Kortner which Ellis St. Joseph found "supremely alive, and charged with contemporary importance." Kortner gave the play a fresh and challenging interpretation, making its essence the overwhelming of high intelligence by the forces of stupidity. The Captain is an inquiring and accomplished scientist; he naturally desires to give his daughter the opportunity of free intellectual growth, away from the superstitious women now encompassing her. The play starts as high comedy; the Captain's wife is a beautiful woman using her sex to wheedle her way with him; only gradually, out of stupid determination not conscious will to power, does this complacently bourgeois woman rally to her aid the professional stupidities of the doctor, the minister, and the soldier, to break the spirit of the man that moves with conscious mind. The drive of the play intensifies ominously until the Captain is torn to fury and madness. Then the high intelligence, forced to recognize the power of stupidity in the world, accepts defeat; and calm in the straitjacket as a toga'd Senator, the Captain looks death in the face and passes judgment on his conquerors. His body, even his will, is broken; but at the final thrust he is again the captain of his soul. Here is the supreme tragedy of the play—as of the world today: creative intelligence doomed by blind stupidity, powerless save to know its own worth even as it dies. It was inevitable that the forces of reaction should seek to close Kortner's production; and it is a hopeful sign that it continued to run well into 1950.

This interpretation does not lessen, but sets a richer glow upon, the battle of the sexes in the play. Brooks Atkinson (October 9, 1928), calling it "one of the great works of modern drama," noted that "Strindberg writes like a demon possessed. There is nothing quite so cruel, pathetic, and remorseless as this living portrait of a man of intellect succumbing bit by bit to the cold fury of a voracious virago. All that he is becomes his undoing. The superiority of his intelligence is his vulnerable spot in this conflict with a woman. Although the father is the victim and the mother the treacherous aggressor, Strindberg takes pains to show that the strife is instinct in the nature of things. Being a genius, he turns his drama into a hurricane of the furies. It is a dance of death of the evil forces in the world." "What raises the play to greatness," said Alan Harris, in the Introduction to *Eight Famous Plays by Strindberg* (1949), "is those moments where Strindberg rises for an instant above his own frantic rancor and sums up the whole tragedy of life in a few words of sublime fairness." *The Father* is the clearest and most powerful of Strindberg's dramatic presentations of the universal need of adjustment between the sexes, of the time-long war in which some happy couples find truce, but which others wage unto their mutual destruction.

The Raymond Massey revival was with Mady Christians; in it Grace Kelly (later Princess of Monaco, 1956-1982) played the daughter, in her Broadway debut. *The Father* was revived by Roundabout 1966-1967 and 1973.

MISS JULIE   *August Strindberg*

After *The Father*,* Strindberg drove his dramas for a time more directly on naturalistic lines. Encouraged by a letter from Emile Zola, he wrote the two-act *Miss Julie* (also translated as *Countess Julia*), 1888, which Alrick Gustafson in *A History of the Modern Drama* (1947) calls "probably the best frankly naturalistic play ever written."

The story is simple. On Midsummer Eve Julie flirts with, then gives herself to, Jean, the valet of the Count her father. The valet then tries to assert himself as cock of the walk. Julie recognizes the essential vulgarity of the situation. When the Count returns and rings for his valet, Jean too feels that the situation is impossible. He hands Julie a razor, and she takes her life.

Beneath these surface events the dramatist examines the elements of heredity and environment that have made these two what they are. The static picture of many naturalistic plays—a "slice of life" that lies on a slab for our examination—Strindberg replaces with a dynamic growth of understanding and emotional intensity. The contrasted natures of the two vividly reveal them both: the conventional Jean, who builds the evening episode into plans for a permanent union; the aristocratic, bored Julie, who toys with the idea of going away with Jean, but cannot leave her bird behind—whereupon Jean chops off its head before her eyes. And her eyes open to the coarseness of the man, to see that simple human decency demands that the vulgar situation come to an end.

In his printed preface to what he declared was "the Swedish drama's first naturalistic tragedy," Strindberg suggested production devices that were startling novelties at the time, but have since become commonplace technique for realistic drama. He proposed side spotlights instead of footlights; very little make-up, and a simple, natural tone of speech and performance. Antoine distributed copies of this Preface to the Paris audience at the French premiere in January 1893. The play has been a favorite in repertory on the Continent. It was shown in New York for special matinees in 1913, and became popular with little theatre groups. London saw it in 1929; in 1933 in French, with Pitöeff; and in 1939. An American revival opened in Philadelphia January 20, 1947, with Elisabeth Bergner, who had played Julie in Berlin, Vienna, and Paris.

The drama rose partly from Strindberg's marriage in 1877 with Siri von Essen, which grew increasingly stormy until their divorce in 1891. But it had other springs as well. One of the continuous conflicts within the troubled Strindberg was the question of class. Son of an aristocratic father and a socially inferior mother, he never adjusted himself to any social stratum. His play, as Alan Harris said in the introduction to *Eight Famous Plays* (1949), "is saturated with class feeling, and Strindberg certainly saw himself in the valet, the coming gentleman, by virtue of his energy and ability, as against the 'degenerate' aristocrat." The Swedish working-class audience cheered when the valet triumphed.

Received by the public with combined repulsion and fascination, the play was called by the *London Era* (October 2, 1929) "a startling, almost a terrifying, experience . . . a midsummer nightmare. But although its theme is peculiarly repellent and concerns itself almost exclusively with human weaknesses and the baser side of man's nature, the technical skill with which the piece is constructed forces us to follow, with closest attention, the working out of the tragedy. Here is a masterpiece of playwriting; the sense of reality with which it is imbued is so strong that we feel inclined at times to turn our eyes away from a spectacle which seems so painful and so personal. . . . Decidedly this play is only for those who are able to do without illusions." The *London Times* (February 14, 1933) even more clearly pictured at least the Anglo-Saxon unwillingness to submit to the play's mood: "It has a fierce intensity peculiar to Strindberg's genius which has the effect, for many spectators, of carrying the action so far beyond their interpretation of nature that they defend themselves intuitively from its attack by attacking in return with an accusation of insanity. It is the play's quality of abnormal imaginative pressure, the core of its greatness, that stands in its way."

There is rich development of the figures in *Miss Julie,* which is a searing study of character, to be set beside Ibsen's *Hedda Gabler,** of boredom seeking distraction, yet preferring death to the dictatorship of vulgarity. Deep within its depressing drive, there is thus held clean the urge for decency within the human soul.

Miss Julie, adapted and directed by George Tabori, was revived 1955–1956. New York saw it again in 1981.

THE DANCE OF DEATH   *August Strindberg*

In the most hopeless and heavy-hearted of all his dramas, the two parts of *The Dance of Death,* 1901, Strindberg made his most pessimistic presentation of the endless war of man and woman. In the drama, after twenty-five years of marriage, a deep, ingrown hate has festered in the lives of Artillery Captain Edgar, of an island garrison, and his wife Alice. Edgar is a self-centered domestic tyrant, but Alice is strengthened by the power of her loathing. When their friend Curt, Alice's cousin, comes for a visit, each tries to use him as a weapon against the other. Alice for a time seems the victor, because she throws her body into the fight; but after her yielding, Curt flies from the witches' cauldron of seething hate. By superhuman will, Edgar pulls himself together after a heart attack; he will not accord Alice the satisfaction of his dying. Their fate is a drear continuance of horrid hate, in loathsome union. The second part of the drama carries on the dreary struggle to the dregs of Edgar's doom. It contains, however, a tender and hopeful episode of love between Allan, Curt's son, and Judith, Edgar's daughter, which, as Alan Harris remarks in the introduction to *Eight Famous Plays* (1949), "almost succeeds in transfiguring it by its poignancy and beauty."

Though gripping in performance, the play is too depressing to be often presented. In New York, it was shown May 9, 1922, in a special performance by the Theatre Guild, in a condensed version—the two parts together—by Henry Stillman, that piled on the horrors almost too horrendous. Yet it displayed, said the *New York Dramatic Mirror* (May 22, 1922), Strindberg's "uncanny gift of gripping dialogue." The picture of Edgar was especially impressive. The New York *Stage* (Midsummer issue, 1922) called his portrait "a supreme study in selfishness, demonstrating the devastating effect of a strong-willed egomaniac in his society, which terminates only with his death. It is, of course, all told in a minor key mordantly bitter, almost cynically repulsive, and yet so convincing in the telling that one's interest is perfectly sustained. His will for evil is as potent as the disasters wrought by the fates in the old Greek tragedies." New York also saw the play (Part I) in German, with Irene Triesch, opening December 16, 1923. The two parts were played in London in November and December 1925. The London *Stage* (November 27, 1925) said: "The two characters are intensely interesting, and the grip of the author all-powerful in spite of what appears to be an indifferent translation." Revived in Vienna in 1925, the play was hailed as Strindberg's "most famous work." It was shown again in London, in 1928, with Robert Loraine. The *New York Times* (February 5, 1928), reporting the London production, said that the play "has a spiritual power that makes all its structural weaknesses seem unimportant." These "weaknesses," indeed, are imperceptible in the fierce psychological drive of the drama.

This play differs from Strindberg's other works on the theme of the sex war in that here the man is the more active agent of evil. During his stroke the Captain has a vision of hope which leads him to seek a reconciliation; thus Strindberg presses the double irony of an illusion based on an illusion. This play, declared the *New York Herald* (December 17, 1923), is "the full sized canvas of a picture for which his more familiar *Miss Julie, Creditors* and *The Father* were merely preliminary sketches. If ideas rather than morals could ever excite the censors of the theatre, this play would undoubtedly be banished from every stage in Christendom, for it is a savage warning versus the holy state of matrimony, undermining the whole structure of family life. Ibsen's rebellious Nora, once so horrible an example of revolutionary ideas, is an amiable Pollyanna creature beside Strindberg's Alice."

[Strindberg's *The Dance of Death* is not to be confused with a play of the same name by the English poet W. H. Auden, staged in 1936 by Alfred Kreymborg in the New York Federal Theatre. This is a drama of the English middle class.]

The naturalistic presentation of the tortures of embattled souls can go no further than in Strindberg's play. He looks into the awful depths of "that yawning abyss which is called the human heart," and lifts for our beholding the monsters of the deep. "It is the normally suppressed, but not abnormal, life of thought breaking out into speech," said Alan Harris, "that gives *The Father** and *The Dance of Death* their peculiar horror, and, incidentally, makes the conventions of polite society, so easily assailable from many sides, suddenly seem infinitely precious." Infinitely precious, too, to Strindberg's tortured spirit, were thoughts of happy domesticity and peace; and Harris finds a personal yearning in remarks that dot the dramas. But the strains of his life did not relax. Continued pressure means explosion, the bursting of the bonds of reason into the distorted realm of phantasmagoria, nightmare, and the mad. Thus *The Dance of Death* is his last, and his most powerful, lucid and logical drama of human lives.

It was revived 1967, by NT, thirty performances in repertory, with Laurence Olivier. In New York, 1971, with Rip Torn and Viveca Lindfors; City Stage Co.,1984. The theatre of cruelty anticipated the theatre of the absurd.

THE DREAM PLAY   *August Strindberg*

With *The Dream Play,* 1902, Strindberg moved wholly into the irrational land of fantasy. With some half-hundred persons, through fifteen scenes, there flows a timeless spectacle of the miseries and evils of human life and the human spirit. There is no single story of embattled urgencies or hates, but a pageant of the agonies of humanity, the absurdities of human attempts at justice, the mockery of human endeavors to find the meaning of life or to imbue it with meaning. There is no objective analysis of a situation or of a character, but a threnody with the reiterate refrain: "Life is evil! Men are to be pitied!" And yet the whole arrives at the hopefulness of beauty.

In the vision of the Poet, the daughter of Indra comes to earth to see what life is like. With the incongruities, inconsequentialities, irrationalities, and sudden juxtapositions of a dream, she is exposed to the sufferings and the cruelties of mankind. She wishes to see with the eyes of a man, to hear with the ears of a man, to think with those curious convolutions that are the human brain. The grotto of one scene has the shape of the human ear. "The characters," said Strindberg, "split, double, multiply, vanish, solidify, blur, grow clear. But one consciousness reigns above them all—that of the dreamer; and before it there are no secrets, no incongruities, no scruples, no laws. There is neither judgment nor exoneration, merely narration. And as the dream is for the most part painful, rarely pleasant, a note of melancholy and of pity for all living things runs all through the wobbly tale. Sleep, the liberator, often plays a dismal part; but when the pain is at its worst, the awakening comes and reconciles the sufferer to reality, which, however distressful it may be, seems nevertheless happy in comparison with the torments of the dream." The daughter of Indra, in this phantasmagoria, meets the Officer (who may represent the body), the Lawyer (the mind), the Glazier, the Coal-heaver, and other human aggressors or victims; everyone is either an oppressor or oppressed; only the Poet (the heart) wins some measure of freedom from life's enslaving toils.

The play, which some critics have said will act best in the mind, was presented in Berlin in 1916 by Rudolph Bernauer, with Irene Triesch; even more successfully there in 1919 by Max Reinhardt. In 1919 in Vienna, Joseph Schildkraut played the Officer. *The Dream Play* was presented in New York, opening January 20, 1926, at the Provincetown Playhouse. London saw it in 1933 with Donald Wolfit. There was a very successful revival in Stockholm in 1935, with further symbolic touches: the Poet was made up to resemble the bust of Strindberg; the Officer, the portraits of Strindberg in his youth.

The critics in New York were, on the whole, baffled by the play. Thus John Anderson (January 21, 1926) protested: "Nothing is so palpably unreal as bogus unreality. . . There are, nevertheless, some startlingly beautiful moments in it." In the *Montreal Daily Star* the next week, Clifford Baker was moved to comment on the New York reaction: "The production of Strindberg's play by the Provincetown group was the signal for an avalanche of ridicule and invective. . . . It was a simple thing for the local wise men to accuse Strindberg of dire and distasteful pessimism. It never occurred to one of them that Strindberg was more optimist than pessimist, that not once did he miss an opportunity of pressing home the fact that the ills of humanity are humanity's own. A mind not devoid of imagination might deduce from this that humanity has the power of curing them." Indeed, out of these later, unrealistic plays of Strindberg there does rise the shimmering of human hope. The *London Times* (April 3, 1933) remarked that the play has "unity less in action than in thought, and less in thought than in spiritual impulse." The compassion in the daughter of Indra must find fruition in deeds, through the gathered wisdom of man; but the hopelessness that shrouds man's lot breaks with a faint glimmer as through a rift. The play is, despite the wretchedness it depicts, decidedly not sordid; much of it is tender, and it is full of lyric beauty. In setting, too, a production of *The Dream Play* lifts with beauty, opening with a glory of giant hollyhocks, behind which stands a castle crowned with a bud, which at the play's end blossoms as a great chrysanthemum. Certain features persist in various guises, like the door with the clover-leaf opening, like the linden tree that becomes a hat-stand in an office, a candelabrum in a church. Music as well plays a harmonious part in gathering the many dream symbols into a rich pattern of beauty.

The thought of the play similarly sifts through the crowded incoherencies of its telling, "richly interesting and alive," said the *New York Daily News* (January 21, 1926), "as viewed in the jumbled vision of the dreamer." "There are passages," said Gilbert W. Gabriel, "that hammer at your heart until they have battered it completely out of human shape or ordinary usefulness." Without the wilder eccentricities of *The Spook Sonata,** *The Dream Play* imposes its mood upon the audience, as for some years it imposed its technique upon the experimenters in the world theatre.

THE SPOOK SONATA   *August Strindberg*

In 1907, Strindberg and director August Falck opened The Intimate theatre in Stockholm. This was a "chamber theatre" seating fewer than 200 persons, dedicated to the plays of Strindberg, which were becoming too difficult for the wider public. The best of Strindberg's plays written during the four years of this theatre is *The Spook Sonata,* 1907.

Looking at the same world as in *The Dream Play,** Strindberg is in more savage mood. There is no pity here. With a great flail of mockery and satire, he strikes forth in all directions. The nightmare Life-in-Death gallops through the drama in the wildest conglomeration of evil, of decrepit, distorted creatures, who live in agony or madness or spring from beyond the grave. Most evil of the play's creatures is the vampirish octogenarian Hummel, who from his wheel-chair or his crutches pours grief and confusion upon the rest. He says he has saved the girl he killed—we see her wraith in Act I; finally he is strangled by the Mummy. The Mummy is a woman who lives in a cabinet sealed away from daylight, under a marble memorial to her own spent beauty; she dresses like a parrot, and when brought forth squeaks and squawks in parrot tones. She has a delicate daughter, a girl who cannot live without hyacinths. There is also a crippled and self-deified student who returns to claim the girl's child as his, only to be driven away. There are elaborate meals, yet everybody is starving; for the cook squeezes all the nourishment from the food before she serves. The decayed remains of a deceased milkmaid pass to and fro. Phantasmagorias multiply, a symbolic array of the greeds and lusts that prey upon the world; until at the end, when the girl dies, the student turns and warns those across the footlights that their sins, too, will find them out.

In a swirl of weird colors, masks, and bizarre stage effects, the drama was presented at the Provincetown Playhouse in New York, opening January 5, 1924, with Clare Eames and Walter Abel. Alexander Woollcott (January 7) called it "a sedulously eccentric, elliptical, and singularly baffling play," but added that it "holds the attention taut." Percy Hammond stated: "Strindberg again comes to the gloomy conclusion that the earth is a morgue and a madhouse. . . After attending *The Spook Sonata* I began to suspect that Strindberg's pessimism is not so terrible as is his manner of presenting it." The *Telegram* saw in the play "sudden flashes of that great light which the Illuminated Ones of all ages have cast on reality . . . close to the danger line where sheer inspiration lapses into sheer insanity." The *Drama Calendar* (January 14) more trenchantly declared that the play's mood is "so powerfully imagined and so poignantly expressed, it can hardly fail to exhilarate and grip an audience which looks for more than a pleasant time. The thrusts pierce with unerring skill, and the imagery is richly fantastic."

In Europe, where the drama was promptly and widely played, it came in the van of the "modern" modes, the successors to naturalism in the theatre. Thus by the time the play came to New York, Eugene O'Neill could say, in a program note for the Provincetown Playhouse: "Strindberg was the precursor of all modernity in our present theatre, just as Ibsen, a lesser man as he himself surmised, was the father of the modernity of twenty years or so ago ... Strindberg is the greatest interpreter in the theatre of the characteristic spiritual conflicts which constitute the drama—the blood of our lives today.... All that is enduring in what we loosely call 'Expressionism'—all that is artistically valid and sound theatre—can be clearly traced back through Wedekind to Strindberg's *The Dream Play, There Are Crimes and Crimes, The Spook Sonata.*" But the play found many of the New York critics unprepared for its nightmarish technique, unwilling to accord Strindberg the place O'Neill and Ibsen gave him. Thus Gilbert W. Gabriel (January 7, 1924) blandly surmised that Ibsen's remark "may have been a soft answer to turn away Strindberg's wrath, or simply the pleasant gesture of one who knew the world would safely contradict him ..." Americans, Gabriel went on to confess, "seem always to react to Strindberg with that antagonism which neurotics exhibit in the presence of the downright insane." It was not until its comment on the Stockholm revival of the play that the *New York Times* (December 8, 1935) hailed Strindberg as "the one blazing, flaming genius in the whole of Swedish literature."

In the whole of world drama, there are few playwrights whose hatred of the evil of life pours with such a black bile and vitriolic power. Certainly there is no other play so eerily compelling, in its maggoty, chimeric compounding of nightmare dreads, so Dantesque in its lightning-sear over human ills and human evils, as Strindberg's drama macabre. Such works as this mark Strindberg as exponent of an attitude caught in a character's words, that life is "horrible beyond all description"; mark him, as Alan Harris put it, in the introduction to *Eight Famous Plays* (1949), as "a name of power to the Western world, the representative man of an attitude toward life which will never be outdated so long as the human predicament remains." It should not be overlooked, however, that the playwright's bitterness rises from a hatred of the evils in the world; behind this there is an equally burning desire for human betterment. Gorki has compared Strindberg to the hero of a Danubian legend, who tore out his own heart and set it on fire to light his fellow-men on the way to freedom. *The Spook Sonata,* by its shimmering over the baleful aspects of morality, gives dramatic urgency to man's most horrid battle, the grim struggle against the forces of destruction within himself.

GUYS AND DOLLS   *Jo Swerling*

Out of the activity of Times Square habituées was fashioned the liveliest and most cheerful musical about Broadway, *Guys and Dolls.* Not the drug drifters and pornography pushers of the 1970s, but from a slightly earlier time, frequented by, as George Jean Nathan described them, "the cheesecake eating, crap-shooting, bookie-haunting, sartorially inflammatory riffraff of the bedizended highway of Runyan's fancy." Some of Damon Runyan's characters and episodes were shaped by Jo Swerling and Abe Burrows, with music and lyrics by Frank Loesser, into the musical, which, deftly directed by George S. Kaufman, opened at the New York 46th Street Theatre November 24, 1950, and ran for 1,200 performances.

Its exaggerations were in the spirit of John Gay,* whose *Beggar's Opera* did much the same thing for eighteenth-century London, laughing at the excesses of a city he loved. Before "I ♥ New York" was blazoned on buttons and printed on T-shirts the creators of *Guys and Dolls* wrote in that spirit.

Among the hangers-on are Nicely-Nicely Johnson, Harry the Horse, and Angio the Ox, but chief of the scroungers is Nathan Detroit, who earns a sort of living by arranging, mainly for eager out-of-towners come to enjoy the big city, "the oldest permanent floating crap game" in town. The game goes on, one night, in Save-a-Soul Mission while the Salvation Army is holding an all-night street revival; then it adjourns to a platform in a city sewer, where choreographer Michael Kidd sets one of his most hilarious dance numbers.

Nathan has been engaged for fourteen years to the Hot Box nightclub star Adelaide, but has never had cash and courage combined, to propose matrimony. Chief of his gambling friends is Sky ("the sky's the limit") Masterson. To make an easy thousand dollars, Nathan bets Sky there's one doll he cannot persuade to go to Havana with him, and he introduces him to Captain Sarah Brown of the Save-a-Soul Mission—and sets off the second love-tie of the evening. Sky wins the bet by promising Sarah a dozen sinners to attend her mission, and gets them as forfeits in the crap game. Kipling in his novel *Kim* says, "Good luck she is never a lady," but Sky sings "Luck, be a lady" and she smiles on him. He wins the game, and of course also Sarah.

There actually is a mission of the Salvation Army near Times Square (on Forty-ninth Street). Sky is drawn from the life of one Bat Masterson, "sheriff of Dodge City, who went east and playfully forgot to leave his gun behind"; and several other characters have been identified with underworld figures Damon Runyan knew. They have been worked into a hilarious swirl as the "permanent" crap game moves to the city sewer, where the Chicago gangster gets his comeuppance and Sky gets the dozen reluctant sinners. They all live, as Brooks Atkinson phrased it, "in a gaudy, blowzy world that is somehow warm and hospitable." The play ends with a double wedding, in a dreamful mist of swirling bridesmaids, and Sky in Mission uniform beating the big bass drum.

In the first cast, Vivien Blaine played Adelaide; Sam Levene, Nathan; Robert Alda, Masterson; Isabel Bigley, Sarah Brown. Among the lively songs were "Adelaide's Lament," "Take Back Your Mink" (on discovering the expected payment), "If I Were a Bell, I'd Ring"; "I Love You, a Bushel and a Peck," "I've Never Been in Love Before." Pat Rooney, Sr., who beat the big Mission drum, sang "More I Cannot Wish You"; the critics seemed to think "More I cannot wish you than that you see the show."

The dances, too, are noteworthy, ranging from the high kicks of the Broadway cuties to the bumps of the hot Havana beauties and the acrobatic crapshooters in the sewer.

Once its Broadway run was over, the musical ran all over the country. Among its productions: New York City Center, 1955 and again in 1956; Connecticut, Mahopac, N.Y., and Fort Wayne, In., 1956; Cleveland, 1957; Peoria, Rochester, Cohasset (American Theatre Wing), 1958; New York Theatre in the Park, Detroit, and Honolulu, 1958; Plattsburg and San Juan, 1961; St. Bart OffBway, 1974. The Broadway production opened in London (Coliseum) May 28, 1953, with Jerry Wayne and Lisbeth Webb as Sky and Sarah, and ran for 555 performances. It was filmed in 1955 with

Frank Sinatra and Vivien Blaine as Nathan and Adelaide; Marlon Brando and Jean Simmons as Sky and Sarah. It was played in New York by an all-black cast in 1976.

On March 9, 1982, *Guys and Dolls* became the first musical ever presented by the NT (Olivier), with Bob Hopkins and Julia McKenzie as Nathan and Adelaide; Ian Charleson and Julie Carrington, Sky and Sarah. With a high background of lighted advertisements that would do Times Square proud, and seedier shops below, the production was sparked with individual touches of comedy, as by the supercilious waiter at the Hot Box (played by Kevin Williams) and justified Irving Wardle's praise in the *London Times,* as "a genuine love match between the English classical stage and the greatest show ever created on Broadway." Its combination of lilting caricature and unexpected tenderness captivated the London theatre; several numbers literally stopped the show, and the play continued in the NT repertory in 1983. There is in *Guys and Dolls* a laughing yet loving capture of the continuing luminescence and lure of Broadway.

THE PLAYBOY OF THE WESTERN WORLD   *John M. Synge*

Sardonic humor, the most frequent mood of John Millington Synge (Irish, 1871-1909),is especially keen in his most famous work, *The Playboy of the Western World,* 1907.

This attack on the ignorance and crass hero-worship—really, bully-worship—of the Irish common folk pictures Christie Mahon, after slicing open the head of his tyrant father, accepted as a hero in a village far away. Pegeen, romantic daughter of the public-house owner, gives up her timorous Shawn Keogh for Christie boy; and the Widow Quinn angles for his favors. Suddenly the "slain" father appears. As the village folk turn against Christie, in desperation he tries to kill his father; but this is no far-off legendary slaying, this is near at hand, and murder. When the horrified villagers want to deliver Christie to the police, his father joins the boy in the fight to keep him free; and they set out for home again on equal terms. Christie has found his manhood and self-confidence. Pegeen alone is left lamenting the loss of the only Playboy of the Western World.

The chief target of Synge's satire is the habit of accepting appearances for reality, of taking things at their face value. Ironically, that is just how his play (like the earlier Irishman Swift's *Modest Proposal*) was taken. There were riots at its opening at the Abbey Theatre, Dublin, on January 26, 1907. There were even more boisterous riots among Irish-Americans when it was first played in New York, Philadelphia, and Boston. The *New York Dramatic Mirror* (November 29, 1911) reported the disturbance under the headlines: "Synge Play Greeted As No Other Play Has Ever Been Received in New York—100 Police Quell the Disturbance." The attack began, appropriately, with the hurling of an Irish potato. Among those arrested for creating the disorder were Barney Kelly, Patrick O'Connor, and Shean O'Callaghan. Attorney Spellisy, himself Irish, declared at the trial: "The sketch was the nastiest, vilest, most scurrilous and obscene thing I have ever seen. I don't blame them for hooting." A niece of the Irish patriot Robert Emmet testified she had seen O'Callaghan throw four eggs. He was fined $10.00. The excitement approaches that when riots in Paris greeted the mention of *handkerchief* in *Othello** and more lengthily Hugo's *Hernani.** Many of the protesting Irish were especially indignant at the author's picture of Pegeen; for, they said, no good Irish girl ever mentions her shift. As late as 1933, several Irish-American organizations petitioned the Irish Consul-General to have the Irish Free State cancel the subsidy of the Abbey Theatre because it continued to present the play, with its "filthy language, drunkenness, and prostitution," and its maligning of the Irish people.

After a time, however, convinced by others that they should be proud of the play, more of the Irish took it to their hearts. At the 1930 New York production Brooks Atkinson could say: "Out of the balcony, whence the vegetables and abuse came in 1911, chuckles and titters kept up a steady commentary on the play, and proved that the gallery gods, like many of the monarchs of the orchestra, knew the play by heart and needed only a suggestion or two from the stage." Later, Atkinson remarked (October 30, 1932) that "talk that 'kicks the stars,' like the prancing mule in Synge's own play, restores the theatre to its highest uses." John Mason Brown, called the play "one of the richest, most imageful, and full blown of all modern comedies." The play is a mixture of the comic, the sardonic, and the tender. The first two qualities are linked in Maxim Gorki's remark: "In it, the comical side passes quite naturally into the terrible, while the terrible just as easily becomes comic." The tender mood of the drama was best described by James Agate, in the *London Times* (October 29, 1939): "The scene after Christy's victory at the sports contains the best love-making since *Romeo and Juliet*.... In fact though it be heresy to say so, there are ways in which the Synge is better than the Shakespeare." With dramatic deftness, this romantic spell is broken—saved from sentimentality—by the arrival of Christy's bandaged father, furious to break his braggart son's bones. Nor, indeed, are the persons themselves in any sense romantic: Christy, as Agate said, "badly wants what the Army used to call delousing," and Pegeen is a girl "wi' the stink o' stale poteen."

The underling bitterness and sadness were emphasized by Edward Shanks in the London *Outlook* (August 13, 1921), who felt that "the play is extraordinarily bitter; it is perhaps the most bitter work of art that exists ... Synge's laughter is sad and his satire holds no liveliness.... His poetry is as depressing as it is impressive." Not one of the characters in the play, Shanks observed, is an upright, decent person.

Not merely the notoriety of its early productions, but its intrinsic qualities have made the play a favorite little theatre work. A professional New York performance opened October 26, 1946, with J. M. Kerrigan and Burgess Meredith. John Chapman said that "Synge's bubbling yet deep-thrusting comedy of a thin-witted exhibitionist is the perfect vehicle for its cast." George Freedley declared that "few plays in modern dramatic literature are as satisfying."

The dialect of the play calls for notice. Originally dialect in the drama was limited (as in Shakespeare's *Henry V**) to a character or a group for purposes of contrast, usually comic. In Synge's drama, we find what Allardyce Nicoll has called "the triumph of the new conception, where dialect (expressing a certain sphere of life removed by certain peculiarities from 'normal' city existence) is used, not to form a contrast with something else, but in and for itself."

The Playboy of the Western World demands pondering. Its rapid movement of comedy and satiric drama will otherwise speed one past its deeper riches, of tenderness and sadness, of pithy human joy, coarse human weakness, but earthiness touched with grandeur and with grace.

The original Dublin cast included Fred O'Donovan (Christie), Maire

O'Neill (Synge's fiancée and sister of Sara Allgood, who played the Widow Quinn) as Pegeen, Arthur Sinclair (who later married Maire O'Neill) as Pegeen's father. The last three were in the revival at London's Royal Court 1909 and 1921. Maire O'Neill, with W. G. Fay as Christie, was in the London premiere in 1907. Other London revivals: 1925 (O'Donovan, O'Neill); 1930 (O'Donovan, Natalie Moya); 1939 (Cyril Cusack, Pamela Gibson); 1960 (Siobhan McKenna, also in the film). NT (Old Vic) 1975, (Lyttleton) 1976, with Susan Fleetwood and Stephen Rae. Gregory Peck played it in New York, 1948.

In the old flyting tradition, Synge did not leave the protesters unanswered. Of one woman, he wrote:

> *Lord, confound this surly sister;*
> *Blight her brow with blotch and blister,*
> *Cramp her larynx, lung, and liver,*
> *In her guts a galling give her.*

> *Let her live to earn her dinners*
> *In Mountjoy with seedy sinners:*
> *Lord, this judgment quickly bring,*
> *And I'm your servant, J. M. Synge.*

DEIRDRE OF THE SORROWS   *John M. Synge*

"Till an Irish poet has killed his Deirdre," said the *Boston Transcript* (May 4, 1910), "he is like a brave who has not yet killed his man." The story of the doomed Deirdre has been told by Yeats (presented in London, 1908, with Mrs. Pat Campbell); by Lady Gregory (*Cuchulain of Muirthemne,* a telling of the whole cycle of legends); by James Stephens (London, 1923, a very sensitive dramatic recapture); by A. E. (George William Russell, 1929). The drama of Synge, all but complete when he died, is, said Allardyce Nicoll, "the most powerful of all the many efforts made to dramatize that most poignant of all Irish legends." Synge's play was performed at the Abbey Theatre in Dublin, January 13, 1910; in London, May 30, 1910; in New York, September 27, 1920. On the Canadian radio it was accorded a three-hour production in 1946 in opera form, with libretto by John Coulter and music by H. Willan. New York saw the Synge play again on September 5, 1936 with Jean Forbes-Robertson and Michael MacLiammoir.

The legend of Deirdre is in the Red Knights' Branch of the Ulster Cycle of Irish tales. Deirdre is a beautiful foundling raised by the Druids, who set a curse upon any that might marry her. Beloved of Conchubor, the aging king of Ulster, Deirdre flees with the young hero Naisi (also Naise, Naoise). They live in happiness until they are lured to return; Naisi is stabbed by Conchubor's men and Deirdre kills herself beside his grave.

It is a simple and familiar story, but it carries a widespread sadness, the grief that rises from the imbalance of youth and age, when power and love flash within different hearts. The pattern of the play follows the legend. Except for this simple structure, however, as the *Manchester Guardian,* (quoted in the *Boston Transcript,* May 4, 1919), pointed out: "everything in

Synge's play is wholly original. It is written in a prose . . . close to speech, and as musical, austere, and melancholy as natural sounds like the crying of curlews or the whistle of blown grasses, rhythmic plaintiveness which in this last play has more changes of melody than it ever had, thinning to a whine for the crazed spy Owen ('It's a poor thing to be so lonesome you'd squeeze kisses on a cur dog's nose') or swelling to a noble stateliness in Deirdre's dying descant on her own fate in life and in story. . . . In this last play, Synge not merely got back to his own balance; he perfected it, and was able, while keeping as fiercely clear of sentimentalism as ever, to achieve a tenderness and radiancy of beauty that he had not before reached. The ecstasy of the two lovers over their life together in exile, 'waking with the smell of June in the tops of the grasses,' has this quality, and so has the whole expression of their mood of surrender to the general consignment of lovers to death. . . . The impression left by the passages of exaltation was of a loveliness quite unembittered. . . . All that was Synge is expressed in this play, the sure ear, the instinct for idiom, the brooding joy in hard, strong lines of character, the disdain for artistic compromise, the energy of tragic imagination—as well as a new serenity of beauty."

A word more might be said of the language of the play. Deceptively simple, as peasants might speak—Owen says, of a girl he once had loved, "now she'd scare a raven from a carcass on the hills"—the accustomed words build into apt and vivid images, like country hands that cup the poetry of clear spring water, and the spring ripples on in many-shaded rhythm. Fragile but well nigh flawless, *Deirdre of the Sorrows* combines closeness to the Irish soil and tender telling of an olden legend into a drama of poignant loveliness and beauty.

MONSIEUR BEAUCAIRE   *Booth Tarkington*

The novelist Booth Tarkington (American, 1869-1946), with the help of Evelyn Greenleaf Sutherland, turned his tenderly sad romance of eighteenth-century England, *Monsieur Beaucaire,* into a play: a new play by a new author, opening a new season in a new century, with a new company at a new theatre. At the London Garrick October 8, 1901, Richard Mansfield scored a personal triumph as Monsieur Beaucaire. When the play came to New York, December 2, 1901, Alan Dale headed his review: "Mansfield is Pure Delight."

"There are old hands in the theatre," said the *Times* (London, November 17, 1931), "who speak of 'cast-iron situations,' and swear that before no audience and in no circumstances can these altogether fail. One of them concerns a traveler who comes to the wrong house without knowing it; another tells of a beggar maid who took the wrong turning and found that it was the right one; a third conceals a lady behind a screen; a fourth describes the adventure of a great or noble hero in humble disguise who, having been mocked by everyone except ourselves and the heroine, reveals himself—and our own superior wisdom—in the last act. It will be observed that all these legends give the audience an opportunity to hug a secret and to pat themselves on the back, which is among the chief purposes of popular drama. *Monsieur Beaucaire* belongs to Type 4."

Coming to England in the disguise of a barber, to escape a royally ordered marriage, the Duc d'Orléans catches the English Duke of Winterset cheating at cards, and has Winterset introduce him to Society as the Duc de Châteaurien ("Duke of Nocastle"). When Lady Mary Carlisle falls in love with the Duc, Winterset first has him set upon, then exposes him in public as an impostor. Thereupon the French Ambassador, in deep respect, introduces him as the Duc d'Orléans. In the book Lady Carlisle turns in scorn from the "impostor" and the Duc, a sadder but a wiser man, goes back to the bride the King has chosen. In the play (and the later musical) Lady Mary turns from Beaucaire not because he is a menial but because he has imposed upon society; this distinction enables them to marry "and live happily" at the end.

In New York, the play was revived in 1921 and 1934. In London, opening October 25, 1902, it ran for 430 performances, and was revived almost yearly until 1932. King Edward VII attended a command performance November 19, 1904. The February 23, 1924, revival lasted 102 performances.

A musical version of *Monsieur Beaucaire*, book by Frederick Lonsdale, lyrics by Adrian Ross, and tuneful music by André Messager, opened in London April 19, 1919, with Marion Green, Maggie Tyte, and Dennis King, for 221 performances; in New York December 11, 1919, for 143. Among its pleasant songs are "Philomel," "That's a Woman's Way," "I Do Not Know," and "Red Rose":

> *Oh fair be wind and weather!*
> *Let the sunlit ripples dance*
> *As the fairest rose of your England goes*
> *On the heart of a son of France!*

The musical has had several revivals, on both sides of the Atlantic.

On the screen, the story attracted Rudolph Valentino (1924) with Bebe Daniels, Lois Wilson, Doris Kenyon, and Lowell Sherman. With an equally prominent cast—Joan Caulfield, Constance Collier, Joseph Schildkraut— Bob Hope in 1946 played a travesty of the role, as actually the barber of Louis XV, changing places with the Duc, who wished to avoid a marriage.

Monsieur Beaucaire, with the quaint charm of an olden story, pleasantly rings the changes along the course of gallant gentlemen and lovely ladies toward love. Audiences saturated with violence and sex in the theatre today might find nostalgic pleasure in the daring and dalliance of *Monsieur Beaucaire*.

OUR AMERICAN COUSIN   *Tom Taylor*

Trenchard Manor, England, is the scene of this famous play by Tom Taylor (English, 1817-1880).

The wealthy estate has fallen upon evil days, for Sir Edward Trenchard has been tied up in mortgages and cast down by his tricky agent, Mr. Coyle, who will relent only if Trenchard's daughter Florence will marry him. Despite the family troubles, all are shaken with laughter at the odd speech and odder ways of their cousin Asa, just over from America. Asa is beneficiary, to the extent of $400,000, under old Mark Trenchard's will; Mrs. Mountchessington therefore casts her cap at him, but Asa falls in love with pretty Mary Meredith, the milkmaid. When Asa discovers that Mary is the natural linear heir of Mark Trenchard, he lights his cigar with the will. Meanwhile, with the aid of Coyle's clerk, Abel Murcott (who had proposed to Florence when he was her tutor and, rejected, had taken to drink), Asa finds a flaw in Coyle's mortgage. Florence is freed to marry her sailor, Harry Vernon; Asa is hitched to his Mary; and sundry other couples are fitly joined.

When *Our American Cousin* was first written, in 1858, among the minor characters was a frail miss, Georgina, who fell in a Victorian faint on the filmiest breath of a provocation. Also present—given only forty-seven lines in the original version—was a literal-minded Lord Dundreary with side whiskers and a habit of pronouncing "w" for "r." This comic role was entrusted to E. A. Sothern (1826-1881). In his entrance on opening night, Sothern stumbled over a tear in the carpet, recovered himself with a skip and a hop, and was greeted with howls of laughter. That skip and a hop, repeated nightly as the character's natural gait, his inane appearance, his literal interpretation of every remark, and his robust love-making with the delicate Georgina, made the part so popular that it grew until it became the most important in the play; and E. A. Sothern became one of the most famous figures on the American stage. Some productions of the play have been called *Lord Dundreary,* and the long side-whiskers Sothern wore in the part became known as dundrearies.

In the premiere production of *Our American Cousin,* the part of Asa Trenchard was played by Joseph Jefferson (1829-1905), seven years before his debut in Boucicault's *Rip Van Winkle.** *Our American Cousin* was first presented by Laura Keene (1826?-1873) at her own New York theatre; she played the part of Florence Trenchard. Influence of the play has been visible in the English theatre for some time, as in *The Silver King,* by Henry Arthur Jones* and Henry Herman (1882).

Our American Cousin established new long-run records on both sides of the Atlantic. Opening in New York October 15, 1858, it ran for 138 performances. The *Spirit of the Times* (October 8, 1859) was moved to comment: "Miss Laura Keene, with a perverseness that can be accounted for only on the grounds of sex and profession, has the most provoking way of always setting at naught the prognostications and wise auguries of the critics, as well as her own speculative anticipations, failing where success seems certain, and gaining triumphs from experiments that bode little but disaster. Look at *Our American Cousin,* tried almost as a desperate chance, when first-class pieces, cast better than they ever had before, under her management, wouldn't pay expenses. Miss Keene herself never expected it would go, and the critics, to a man, pooh-poohed the idea of its running through a week. Yet it brought her crowded houses nearly all the season." At a time when theatre was taboo in many respectable homes, the *Century* magazine (March 5, 1859) declared: "Parents may take their children to see it and they will be richly compensated by the amusement, without danger to their morals."

In Washington, D. C., *Our American Cousin* opened on January 31, 1861, for a record run of 35 nights. In London, at the Haymarket, the play reached 36 performances after its premiere, September 12, 1860; it played again in 1861; it opened January 27, 1862, for a record run of 314 performances; and it achieved almost a score more of revivals along the century. In New York City, Sothern's son, E. H. Sothern, played Lord Dundready in 1907 and after. In American life, the play became linked with a deeply tragic occasion. Laura Keene, who had played Florence Trenchard over 1,000 times, was giving a benefit performance, her last appearance in the role, at Ford's Theatre in Washington, on April 14, 1865. The play was interrupted by the assassination, in his theatre box, of President Abraham

Lincoln. The *London Illustrated Times* (May 6, 1865) tells how Laura Keene, "the leading lady of the stage . . . proceeded to the box and endeavored in vain to restore consciousness to the dying President. It was a strange spectacle—the head of the ruler of thirty millions of people lying insensible in the lap of an actress, the mingled brain and blood oozing out and staining her gaudy robe. In a few minutes Mr. Lincoln's unconscious form was removed to a house across the street, and here the soul of the President took its final departure."

Lord Dundreary has become almost a legend in the theatre. There is joy in watching the gradual gathering, then the bursting of an idea, as reflected in his urbane and inane countenance. The *Boston Transcript* (January 15, 1908) shrewdly observed: "Dundreary stumbles, but at bottom he is never stupid. Rather he takes everything with a wholly simple and innocent literalness and so finds what is really a new point of view. Such humor lasts because it is rooted in genuine human traits, which it exaggerates and travesties." The *New York Times* (January 10, 1908) called Dundreary "such a delightfully sincere idiot that we cannot but love him."

More sense, but just as amusing characterization, may be observed in Asa Trenchard. Said the *Times:* "The climax of the second act, which shows the wild and woolly American 'shooting up' the family armor just to see if his hand is 'still in,' is absolutely far funnier than anything in the comedy line that our modern stage can offer."

In these days of the conversion of plays into musicals, it is surprising that no one has yet transformed *Our American Cousin,* which is not only one of the most famous and successful comedies of the last hundred years, but still a vigorous and highly amusing play, with a lively story swept along by engaging characters.

E. H. Sothern gave a different explanation of the hop and skip he copied from his father: "The little skip he used in his gait originated simply from his trying to keep in step with my mother (who played Georgina) as they walked up and down back stage arranging their lines." Joseph Jefferson (with whom E. A. shared the expense of two riding horses) persuaded Laura Keene to let Sothern enlarge the originally forty-seven-line role.

A June 28, 1960, adaptation of *Our American Cousin* by Lowell Swortzell began with an old watchman at Ford's Theatre, with a flashback to 1865. It also, said the *Christian Science Monitor* (Boston, June 30, 1960), used "a free flow of slang that has salted the American literary tradition ever since." This version was used by the York Players OffOffBway November 18, 1975. A version called *The Lincoln Mask,* by V. J. Longhi, was directed by Gene Frankel at the New York Plymouth October 30, 1972, also starting with Ford's Theatre; the usually gentle and generous Clive Barnes said in the *Times:* "It was every bit as bad as you suspected." Taylor's play does not need the memory of Lincoln to maintain its hold.

THE TICKET-OF-LEAVE MAN *Tom Taylor*

If for no other reason, *The Ticket-of-Leave Man,* 1863, will be remembered because of the figure who, pulling off his disguise, exclaims "Who am I? Hawkshaw, the Detective!" Its main personalities, Bob Brierly and Hawkshaw, said the *London Times* (September 21, 1946) "have made *The Ticket-of-Leave Man* immortal. . . . By any standard other than that of the 'reformers' it is the outstanding play of the Victorian drama." Its facile author, Tom Taylor, wrote more than 100 plays.

The play centers around Bob Brierly, saved from a drunkard's grave by the power of love; then framed and sent to jail for forgery. His sentence served, Bob loses job after job as a jailbird, until the criminals, headed by "The Tiger," James Dalton, think they have forced him into working with them. Using the boy Sam Willoughby as their unwitting tool, the criminals, who have made their plans in a tea-garden, and slipped away during a public-house brawl, are now waiting in the churchyard near the office they intend to rob. Bob, whom they think they have forced to their purpose, reveals his honest intentions. The criminals close upon him, but before Jack Dalton can wreak his foul revenge, Hawkshaw the Detective steps forth, and gets his man. Bob in the meantime has won the heart of May Edwards, the fair heroine.

The Ticket-of-Leave Man continues to win high praise. Allardyce Nicoll, in A History of Late Nineteenth Century Drama (1946) stated that it "is one of the first melodramas to deal with the criminal life of London, to take as a hero a man who had suffered imprisonment for association with criminals, to introduce a detective on the stage, and to break away from the familiar domestic interior sets in an attempt (as in the restaurant scene) to treat of the teeming world of contemporary social life." The *Times* (date above) adduces earlier examples: a hero who had suffered through criminal associations in *The Heart of London; or, The Sharper's Progress,* by William Thomas Moncrieff (1794-1857); the teeming life of the day, in *The Bohemians of Paris.* The plot—which Taylor took largely from *The Return of Melun,* by Edward Brisebarre and Eugène Nus—was borrowed soon again, for Hazlewood's *The Detective; or, The Ticket-of-Leave's Career,* 1870. The *Times* agrees, nonetheless, that "when Professor Nicoll says that *The Ticket-of-Leave Man* 'has a quality of its own which must induce us to rate Taylor as one of the more noteworthy dramatic authors of the century,' the statement cannot be doubted." "To this day," said the *New York Herald-Tribune* on July 16, 1933, "Hawkshaw the Detective retains a vitality altogether thrilling to the gods of the gallery."

Opening in London May 27, 1863, *The Ticket-of-Leave Man* achieved the then remarkable run of 407 performances; in New York, November 30, 1863, it began a run of 102. The play was most popular throughout the century; W. J. Florence played Bob Brierly over 1500 times. *The Ticket-of-Leave Man* was presented in Provincetown, Mass., in 1933, with Richard Whorf as Dalton, and Kate Mayhew—who in 1869 had played the boy Sam Willoughby—playing Sam's grandmother.

A Victorian homily was read on October 13, 1863, when the *London Globe* reported: "It is to be feared, says Sheridan, 'that people go to the theatre chiefly to amuse themselves'; and it may be feared that such was the chief object of a certain absconding clerk in going to a theatre with £2,500 of his employers' money in his pocket, with which, 'in the ease of his heart,' as Wordsworth says, he had taken himself off from Liverpool. But the ease of his heart could not stand the pressure of Mr. Tom Taylor's play. *The Ticket-of-Leave Man* awakened three-fifths of a conscience in the clerk's breast—he was so affected that he went out of the theatre, got three envelopes, and sent £1,500 back to his employers. This clerk took his place in the theatre, if not a hardened, yet certainly an unsoftened and unchastened offender against social law and right. He went out of the theatre a striking example of instantaneous conversion from the error of his ways." If this be not the shrewd strike of an early press agent, it shows something of the effect produced by the dramatically rousing scenes, especially the sudden swoop of Hawkshaw.

The *London Illustrated Sporting and Dramatic News* (April 26, 1884) called *The Ticket-of-Leave Man* "a most welcome bill of fare." Early in an age of swift and spectacular melodramas, it held its own even against such ripsnorters as *Under the Gaslight* and thrilled generations of audiences such as now wait for "The Shadow" and other mystery shockers on the air.

George Coulouris played *The Ticket-of-Leave Man* in London, 1956. It was revived in Worthing, England, 1968. There was an OffOffBway production (at the Midway) beginning December 22, 1981, for thirty-one performances.

GODSPELL, ETC.   *John Tebelak, etc.*

In the April 1939 *American Mercury* an article of mine called "Broadway Tries God" surveyed the dozen or so plays of 1938 and 1939 that dealt with religious themes. These included *Murder in the Cathedral,* * *Many Mansions, Father Malachi's Miracle, On Borrowed Time,* and *The White Steed.* * The last act of *Our Town* * is in the next world; of *Outward Bound,* * on Judgment Day. One could not tell from the title the theme of Philip Barry's *Here Come the Clowns.*

A generation later the young, in their search for lost values, were rediscovering religion. Middle Eastern Muslim, Oriental Zen; and in various Christian offshoots even their elders were "reborn." But the enthusiasm of the adolescent gave swinging success to musicals that in 1971 brought Jesus live upon the stage.

The last seven days of Jesus of Nazareth frame the story of *Jesus Christ Superstar,* with lyrics by Tim Rice and music by Andrew Lloyd Webber. It was "conceived and directed" by Tom O'Horgan, who had performed the same service for *Hair**; its producer, Robert Stigwood, had earlier brought out *Oh! Calcutta!** and *The Dirtiest Show in Town**: sex and religion, the plays appealing to spectators of the same emotional age. Bernard Shaw said that "Fifty million Frenchmen can't be right"; this is equally true of fifty million adolescents as judges of art, but they assuredly make known what they like. Astutely, the producers of *Jesus Christ Superstar* put the records on sale before the show opened. The album fell flat in England, but elsewhere some two million copies were sold before the New York opening on November 2, 1971. (The total sales were over five million.) Chief of the songs are "Everything's Alright," "Could We Start Again, Please?", "What's the Buzz?", and "Jesus Christ Superstar."

At the Broadway opening three separate groups—of Catholics, Protestants, and Jews—protested outside the Mark Hellinger Theatre, but the show ran for 720 performances. In London, opening August 17, 1972, despite the *Times'* verdict it was "vulgar, pretentious, and painfully noisy," it was simpler than the New York production, and it ran until 1980, totaling 3,085 performances, London's longest-running musical. After *Jesus Christ Superstar* occupied the London Palace for eight years and two weeks, composer Webber on August 23, 1983, bought the theatre. In 1972, Roger Sullivan directed a long tour in Scandinavia. Webber also composed the music for *Cats.* * There was a New York revival at the Queens Theatre in the Park in 1983.

Because of the time of the story (A.D. 33), the hand mikes the players carried were disguised as hand mirrors, fans, and the like. Judas Iscariot's mike cord was within a rope; but the rope by which he hanged himself dropped from heaven; he handed his mike to one of the black-clad Furies that had been hounding him, and was hauled up into the hereafter. Jesus himself entered up from a golden chalice, in a shimmering white cloak. For his crucifixion, a fierce storm blows, a stage cloth writhes; when calm is restored the great backdrop eye opens to reveal Jesus outstretched within a golden triangle (base on top); this floats out of the eye to the front of the stage as the music roars crescendo—and the lights go out.

Before Rice and Webber turned to Jesus (and then to *Evita,* the story of Peron's wife and her power in Argentina, which opened in New York September 25, 1978, and attained 1,566 performances) they had been drawn to the most frequently dramatized Bible story, that of Joseph and his brethren, with of course the episode of Zuleika, Potiphar's wife. A dozen dramatists before them had tried this subject; one at the New York Chambers Street Theatre in 1856, with Edward Eddy as Joseph. The best of these earlier plays is *Joseph and His Brethren,* by Louis N. Parker, which opened January 11, 1913, at the New York Century Theatre, with James O'Neill (Eugene's father) as Jacob, Brandon Tynan as Joseph, and Pauline Frederick as Potiphar's wife. This was the first biblical play the Lord Chamberlain (then censor) permitted on the London stage, opening at His Majesty's September 2, 1913, with Herbert Beerbohm Tree as Jacob for 154 performances. The play develops a romantic attachment between Joseph and Asenath, daughter of the Egyptian priest of On (Heliopolis), who met Joseph when he was a slave in Potiphar's house, and whom he married. She is mentioned in only two verses in the Bible: Genesis 41:45 41:50. (The second is repeated at 46:20.)

Asked by London's St. Paul's School for a fifteen-minute sketch for the younger boys, Rice and Webber in 1968 wrote a piece that involved Joseph and his brothers, the twelve sons of Jacob, along with sundry camels and Ishmaelites. Doubled to thirty minutes, this was presented in 1972 at the Edinburgh Festival—to rave reviews. Expanded again, with Jacob's Journey, it was shown by the Young Vic at the London Albery, opening February 19, 1973, and *Joseph and the Amazing Technicolor Dreamcoat* was on its wide-swinging way. In Dublin, 1973, the Olympia Theatre roof fell in and the play was transferred to an old cinema house; it was revived in 1976 in a Dublin paddock, with real animals (except for the camels). The London production, directed by Frank Dunlop, came to the New York BAM in 1976-1977, with Cleavon Little as the Narrator, David-James Carroll as David, Virginia Martin as Potiphar's wife. Washington saw the play in 1978 (Catholic University) and at Ford's Theatre in 1980. It reached Manhattan (Entermedia) November 18, 1980, and moved to Broadway's Royale June 27, 1981, with a spirited female Narrator, Laurie Beechman; Bill Hutton played Joseph, and Randon Lo "Mrs. Potiphar." Despite mixed reviews, it proved appetizing, apple-pie to the general, and ran for 828 performances.

There is no spoken dialogue in the play; it is a sort of rock cantata. There are, said lyricist Tim Rice, "visual jokes and some wonderful outrageous rhymes." On its comic-strip level it is excellent fun, unpretentious and constantly amusing. As Rice admits, "*Superstar* aims higher, and doesn't quite get there." *Joseph* aims lower, and hits the target. Harold Hobson in the *London Times,* March 14, 1973, called it "one of the most joyous entertainments I have ever seen, not too complicated for children nor too simple for Nobel Prizewinners." At the beginning and at the end of the London production, a large JOSEPH in light bulbs spread across the stage. The characters were dressed as cowboys, or as straw-hat strutters, save one man in a dress shirt and black tie. Pharaoh makes a lightning change from ancient Egyptian imperial garb to the dress and deportment of a white-suited rock star; Joseph makes his final appearance in a golden Rolls-Royce.

In the New York production Jacob is played by Gordon Stanley with spectacles; he reads a Hebrew newspaper; he goes to Egypt, not on one of the camels on wheels, but on a scooter. His eleven other sons, who with Joseph founded the twelve tribes of Israel, romp around the stage, gesticulating to show their jealousy of their favored brother and his "dreamcoat" (snatched from him, but returned by Jacob at the end), gloating over his departure as a slave in chains; then illustrating the song "Grovel, Grovel" before he discloses his identity in the throne room of Egypt.

Mention should be made of Leonard Bernstein's *Mass*, libretto by Stephen Schwartz, which in 1971 inaugurated the Kennedy Center for the Performing Arts in Washington, D.C. On June 24, 1972, it came for a month to the Metropolitan Opera in New York, with a cast of over 150, and two onstage rock and folk bands in addition to the Metropolitan orchestra. Using the words of the Catholic Latin Mass as "a sort of skeleton," it embodies the plot of a Celebrant, a guitar player, who sings "a simple song," gradually becomes a doubter, goes mad, and smashes the religious symbols—a realistic iconoclast—leaps into the orchestra pit, and returns at the end as a spectator. During his metamorphosis, with songs including "Mass," "God Said," "Thank You," amid much sound and fury we watch the decline of religion, with alienated clergy, pagan and atheistical behavior—until the actors, singers, and dancers lying deeply depressed onstage, in a sort of spontaneous people's revival arise, kiss one another, and believe again.

Also in 1971 came the best of the Jesus plays, *Godspell*, written and directed by John Michael Tebelak, age twenty-two, with music and lyrics by Stephen Schwartz, age twenty-three. Tebelak, then a student at Carnegie Mellon University, long-haired and casually dressed, on coming out of an Easter morning service at St. Paul's Cathedral, Pittsburgh, was asked by an officer if he would permit himself to be searched for drugs. Meditation on this led not to anger but to the merriment of *Godspell*. The name is an early form of *gospel*, which means *good spell*, good tidings, and the play celebrates the earth-days of Jesus, according to Matthew. Without losing a holy simplicity, the story of Christ's coming is told with mime, magic, song, dance, charade, and clowning. Jesus appears in the guise of a clown. For the clown is always and all ways the butt, the human and humane scapegoat. He takes upon himself the follies of mankind (sins are but excessive follies); he is always and all ways buffeted; we laugh, and are the better for it.

Among the play's songs are "Tower of Babble," "We Beseech Thee," "Bless the Lord," "All Good Gifts," "All for the Best"—and "Long Live God," in the chorus of which the audience often joins. At the end, the crucified Jesus is borne up the aisle and out.

After a performance at Carnegie Mellon University *Godspell* went to Café La Mama in New York, then, in May 1971, to the OffBway Cherry Lane, where at intermission the audiences were offered free wine and matzoh. Moving in August to the Promenade, uptown but still OffBway, it finally went to the Broadhurst, completing 2,100 performances. It was by then the longest-running musical at Ford's Theatre in Washington, had played in Paris, London, various cities in Canada and Germany, and had two companies touring Australia. There were eight road companies in the United States. It had 103 performances, beginning June 18, 1974, by ACT. Boston gave the play a run of 652 performances. In 1978 it was presented at the John Jay College of Criminal Justice, C.U.N.Y. *Godspell* opened the first theatre in Maseru, capital of the Kingdom of Lesotho.

That the clown Jesus involved no loss of reverence is manifested by the church response. In New York the play and the company were blessed by the Reverend John Duffell of the Church of the Sacred Heart; in London, the blessing was by the Archbishop of Canterbury.

It was inevitable that the play be compared with the other Jesus shows that opened the same year. Thus, Richard Coe in the *Washington Post*: "If one thinks of *Superstar* as having the hard, sultry heat of a late August afternoon, and *Mass* the controlled temperature of a starry autumn night, *Godspell* has the cool, fresh air of a sunny May morning." The London opinion was more favorable still: *Godspell* has a genuine artistic idea, an illuminating essence; both *Mass* and *Superstar* have everything on their side—except this illumination, "a *sine qua non* without which anything on a stage is as sounding brass (in Bernstein's case, *very* sounding brass)." Thus the cynical and the sophisticated pall in the presence of the simple and sincere.

It may not be irreverent to mention Arthur Miller's unfortunate entry, *The Creation of the World and Other Business,* which came from Boston and Washington to New York November 16, 1972, lasting forty-one performances, the realistic playwright's sorry venture into the field of fantasy. George Grizzard, said Richard Watts, Jr., "made the Devil more attractive than God." Marjorie Gunner (president of the Outer Circle, so far the only woman president of any of the New York critics' groups) said that Miller's best line was "Am I my brother's keeper?" The London production, opening August 18, 1974, was greeted as "Miller's catastrophic comedy." When the play was shown in German in Vienna, 1974, *Die Presse* spoke of its "slovenly up-to-date accent, like borscht in the Garden of Eden."

The play did take a definite stand on one question that has engaged Christian theologians: Did Adam and Eve have a navel, that vestigium of nourishment within a mother's womb? Wearing skin tights, the couple in Miller's Eden were equipped with an obvious belly button.

After *Paradise Lost,* Milton wrote *Paradise Regained.* Arthur Miller, after his Paradise play, had similar thoughts. For eleven years, he pondered. Religious musicals were current hits; he tried a musical. After a "concert version" at the University of Michigan in 1973, and at the Washington Kennedy Center and the New York Whitney Museum in 1977, Miller's *Up from Paradise* came to the 100-seat Jewish Repertory Theatre OffOffBway October 25, 1983, and *Up from Paradise* sank down. As a lyricist Miller was not lively. The score (said Frank Rich in the *Times*) "often sounds like liturgical fragments that God had the good sense to eliminate from his sanctified repertory." Miller declared: "I reserve the right of my own exuberance." Perhaps he should read (*Paradise Lost,* III, 448) Milton's description of the Paradise of Fools, "all who in vain things/ Built their fond hopes of glory or lasting fame."

Your Arms Too Short to Box with God, a musical from the biblical book of Matthew, began with Vinette Carroll's Urban Arts Corps. music and lyrics by Alex Bradford with additional material by Micki Grant. It was presented at the Spoleto (Italy) 1975 Festival. Played without intermission, it came to the Ford Theatre, Washington; on December 22, 1976, to the New York Lyceum for 429 performances; then on a year's tour to sixty-six American cities. Among its songs are "Beatitudes," "We're Gonna Have a Good Time," "There's a Stranger in Town," "Do You Know Jesus? He's a Wonder," "Can't No Grave Hold My Body Down." Clive Barnes in the *Times* called the play "a black celebration . . . funny and fervent . . . the joyous sound of gospel singing . . . Miss Carroll has given her work something of the sublime simplicity of a medieval mystery play." It is set in a chapel, with the all-black cast in "vaguely liturgical" red and cream robes, from which they change to biblical garb to act out the story from Palm Sunday to the Resurrection, ending with a tribute to gospel singers of the past, from Mahalia Jackson to Louis Armstrong. The workmanship was uneven, but the audience enjoyed and joined in the hand-clapping songs.

Of all these, *Godspell* is illuminating in its basic conception, and ingenious in its theatrical growth. It is fresh and wholesome in its appeal, a sort of Christian circus. God is not forever solemn; he should be welcomed with jubilation, with joyous song and happy dance. One leaves the theatre ready to smile with God.

BECKET   *Alfred, Lord Tennyson*

In the year in which Alfred Tennyson was made a peer, his tragedy *Becket*, 1884, was published. Although it was not intended for the stage, Henry Irving saw theatrical possibilities in the drama and won Tennyson's approval for a production, though the poet died before his play was enacted. It opened in London on February 6, 1893, with Irving, and Ellen Terry as Rosamund for a run of 112 performances. Irving, who scored a personal triumph in the role of Thomas à Becket, frequently revived the play, and acted in it on the night of his death in 1905. (Alfred, Lord Tennyson, English, 1809-1892).

In the nineteenth century, *Becket* was occasionally presented at the homes of the nobility, as in 1886 at Wimbledon. It has been professionally revived several times, and was played annually at the Canterbury Festival until 1935, when it was supplanted by T. S. Eliot's drama on the same subject, *Murder in the Cathedral.**

Tennyson's play is based upon the life of St. Thomas à Becket (1118?-1170), intimate friend of King Henry II of England until he reluctantly accepted appointment by Henry, in 1162, as Archbishop of Canterbury. Thereafter, Becket felt obliged to oppose the King's measures against Church privileges. He spent seven years in exile. On his return, the disputes broke out again; and the King in passion spoke words that led four of his knights to Canterbury, where in the Cathedral they slew the Archbishop, on December 29, 1170. King Henry did penance there; and Becket's shrine became the most famous in Christendom. The poet Chaucer's *Canterbury Tales* presents a group on pilgrimage to Becket's shrine.

Tennyson added to the story of Becket himself the tale of his protecting fair Rosamund de Clifford, Henry's beloved, from the wrath of Henry's Queen, Eleanor of Aquitaine. The play begins dramatically and symbolically with a game of chess between Becket and Henry, in which the bishop mates the king, whereupon the impetuous King kicks over the chessboard. In these opening moments, Henry reveals his dissatisfaction at the independence of the clergy, particularly in regard to its holdings; he gives voice to his fears that Queen Eleanor may seek the life of Rosamund, for whom he has provided a secluded "bower" and now seeks Becket's protection, even though Becket disapproves of the amour; and he appoints Becket Archbishop of Canterbury. Later, Eleanor meets Rosamund's little son Geoffrey, and makes him innocently lead her to Rosamund's bower. Here, Eleanor and her henchman Fitzurse would kill Rosamund, but Becket arrives to save her. Fitzurse remembers the Archbishop's scorn; and, at the end, it is Fitzurse that stikes the first blow, before he, De Brito, De Tracy, and De Morville dash from the Cathedral while lightning flashes light the interior and reveal Rosamund kneeling beside Becket's body.

Henry Irving's acting version of *Becket* was well received in the United States. The *New York Tribune* (November 19, 1893) reported: "It has some moments in it that are divine, and it has also something of the mystery that many poets and playwrights fail to grasp. . . . The scene in the last act approaches the nearest to a passion play that has been done in our time. All through are a great nobility and a great purity." "Particularly effective," said the *London Times* (June 6, 1933) in reporting a perform-ance at Canterbury, "were the scenes between Eleanor and Rosamund, the feeding of the beggars by Becket, and the murder scene, after which Becket's body was borne through the audience by the monks." Clement Scott remarks, in the *Illustrated London News* (July 28, 1894), "It stands out as a very fine and bold piece of workmanship, interesting, dra-matic. . . . There are no dull or unnecessary moments in it. . . . *Becket,* in every respect, is a play of which English art can be justly proud."

Becket is written in prose and blank verse, with a few pleasant lyrics—a troubadour love song of Eleanor of Aquitaine; a pleasant love duet in Rosa-mund's bower. In Tennyson's version, without the Irving dramatic inten-sification, *Becket* is rather static until toward the end, with many passages of eloquent rhetoric; but it is vibrant with a deep integrity, and it posseses considerable strength and beauty. Setting loyalty to one's heav-enly and to one's earthly king in stark opposition, *Becket* keeps a stirring theme pulsingly alive.

THE WOMAN OF ANDROS   *Terence*

Born in Carthage, the slave Terence (Publius Terentius Afer; Roman, c. 195-159 B.C.) was educated and freed by the Roman senator Terentius Lucanus, whose name he took. He became a member of the learned circle of the time; some scholars think Scipio may have helped write his plays. Since all his comedies are adaptations (four of the six, from Menander*), they might have less prominent place if we possessed the originals. It is known, however, from various sources—including Terence's own Prologues, which he used not to tell the play's story, as was the ancient custom, but to defend his own dramatic practices—that Terence combined and otherwise altered the Greek dramas he drew upon.

The earliest of Terence's plays is *Andria (The Woman of Andros)*, pro-duced at the Megalensian Games in April, 166 B.C. by the actor-manager Lucius Ambivius Turpio and set to music by the slave Flaccus, "for flutes of equal size, right- and left-handed." These two men produced and com-posed the music for all six of Terence's plays. Five of these (*The Mother-in-*

Law is even shorter) are of about 1,000 lines; but their many scenes—they average twenty-five—indicate that Terence relied largely on stage action.

Terence invariably used a double plot; in this, his first play, rather simply. *The Woman of Andros* presents the usual New Comedy story of a young man, in love with a courtesan, whose father wants him to marry a citizen's daughter. Terence complicated the situation by having young Pamphilus promise to marry both his sweetheart (by whom he has had a child) and the citizen's daughter. Also, the playwright provided a second young man, in love with the second girl. The play moves to its happy solution when, after the usual number of complications, it is revealed that the supposed courtesan is a second daughter of the citizen.

This familiar plot Terence sparkles with a number of novel features. The father, instead of being the butt of the clever slave, himself plans the intrigue in the play, trying to catch his son by a pretended wedding; and it is by his being told the truth and refusing to believe it because he expects a lie, that the old man is self-deluded. While not telling the story of the play in the Prologue sacrifices some dramatic irony, it adds considerably to the suspense. And, while mention of the possibility that Pamphilus' sweetheart may be a citizen prepares the audience—despite the slave's rejection of the idea as nonsense—for such an outcome, the fact that she is the other girl's sister comes as a complete surprise. Finally, all those in the play are of good character, well drawn and effectively distinguished, likable persons.

Several remarks in the play became proverbial; especially the cautionary *Nequid nimis,* Nothing too much.

The style of *The Woman of Andros* marked Terence at once as a master. Replacing monologues with dialogue, he speeded up the movement of the drama. Disdaining the spirited and rude, at times crude, colloquial speech of Plautus,* he achieved naturalness without sacrificing grace. He used fewer lyrical meters than Plautus, and a simpler metrical construction. He used interjections and other devices of speech deftly; and (unlike Plautus) might open a scene in the middle of a metrical line, with a naturalness as though life were breaking in. Like all ancient writers of comedy, Terence uses the aside; but he has added a humorous effect, in using it as an interjection of the thoughts of one person while another is speaking. The breaking of dramatic illusion, however, by having a character step out of his part to address the audience—a frequent device in broad comedy— Terence does not employ; and, after *The Woman of Andros,* it is not an actor but the musician that at the close of the play requests the audience's applause.

Among plays that are based on *The Woman of Andros* are Steele's *The Conscious Lover,* 1722, and Bellamy's *The Perjured Devotee,* 1739. The novel by Thornton Wilder, *The Woman of Andros,* 1930, is a romantic handling of the theme.

The two lovers of the sub-plot, in Terence's play, present the first instance in comedy of a respectable young man wooing a respectable young woman of good family. *The Woman of Andros,* as a whole, within its comic framework of error, self-deception and intrigue, is the first instance of a friendly play about friendly people, entangled—as what good folk may not be?—in complications that can be ironed out with patience, good-will, and the gentle hand of the goddess of good luck. This is the only sense in which the gods come into the dramas of Terence. *The Woman of Andros* is an amiable, sympathetic picture of upper middle class society, simply and perennially human.

THE SELF-TORMENTOR   *Terence*

In *Heautontimorumenos (The Self-Tormentor)*, 163 B.C., Terence again proves his dramatic ingenuity by combining two familiar stories in a novel way. The play presents two young men who seek to deceive their fathers, for one needs money for a courtesan, and the other wishes to marry a poor girl to whom his father objects. Terence livens these trite motifs by concentrating attention on the two old men.

Menedemus, whose severity has sent his son off to the wars, has repented of his harshness, and is punishing himself by drudgery work on his farm. He is a conscious self-tormentor. His friend Chremes, a good-natured busybody, full of sound saws, is constantly giving out good advice that he does not follow, and tangling himself in the very difficulties he counsels others to avoid. He is an unconscious self-tormentor. Which of us is not one of the two?

While the two fathers provide the chief interest in the drama, several other aspects of the play are worthy of note. The usual surprise ending has in this play been moved into the body of the drama; the recognition that the girl Menedemus' son loves is his neighbor's daughter does not solve, but further complicates, the problem of the story. Once again Terence, but this time with the slave conscious of the trickery, used the device of having the slave deceive the old men by telling them a truth that they do not believe.

The Self-Tormentor is one of the few ancient plays in which the "unity of time" is violated: a night intervenes between Act II and Act III. The play also begins with a novelty, in that characters are in the midst of activity onstage at the start: Menedemus is working his farm as Chremes comes out to speak with him.

One of the most famous remarks of classical antiquity, frequently quoted in all ages since, is made by Chremes in this drama: *Homo sum; humani nil a me alienum puto:* "I am a human being; I consider nothing human foreign to me." This universality is embodied in the play itself. With a trickily complicated intrigue of interwoven plots, Terence has achieved searching and sound character study, of individuals through whom we all may see ourselves, in *The Self-Tormentor.*

THE EUNUCH   *Terence*

The most popular in ancient times of Terence's plays, performed twice on a single day, *The Eunuch,* 161 B.C., is his nearest approach to farce. Woven into the double intrigue are two stock figures, a boastful soldier and a parasite, who, along with the intriguing slave, add more horseplay and broad humor than usual in Terence.

The plot involves two brothers, one of whom is the soldier's rival for the affections of a courtesan. The younger brother, loving a supposed sister of the courtesan, disguises himself as a eunuch to gain access to her, and rapes her. When this girl is disclosed as a citizen, he marries her. And his elder brother, convinced that the courtesan prefers him, consents to let the soldier, while making a major contribution to her support, have a minor portion of her favors.

Terence is not content, however, to let the usual situations develop without novel variations. Many neatly turned details explain the play's great popularity. More basic are the character portrayals, some novel, all masterly. The boastful soldier, in *The Eunuch,* is prouder of word than of sword; it is his wit that he esteems—and his lack of wits that makes him easy mark. The parasite laughs at those he gulls into feeding him; readily and expertly he turns over his old host, the soldier, to the untender mercies of the two brothers, his hosts-to-be. The younger brother, Cherea, is especially well drawn. His youthful overbubbling excitement in love; the ardor with which he pursues his beloved; the self-satisfaction over his conquest, with which he is so transported that he must pour out his story—and that story of his ravishing the maiden after her bath is a gem of delicate restraint and pictured enjoyment: all these establish one of the most successful portraits in ancient comedy. The courtesan herself is quite a pleasant young woman, as fair to the young man she favors as her profession allows; as agreeable as charming. There is no vulgarity in the play, but even in its broadest moments a basic decency.

Episodes of farce are equally well handled, as the siege of the courtesan's house by the aggrieved soldier. Neatly farcical, too, are the rapidly moving last scenes of the play, with their swift alterations of feeling, from joy to sadness, from hope to despair, before the final reconciliation and general delight.

The style of *The Eunuch* is graceful, a bit more lively and exuberant than that of Terence's other comedies. Colorful figures of speech abound, as in the slave's opening reflections on love, which, knowing no reason, cannot be managed by rule; and as in the later exclamation: "Ruined like a rat, betrayed by my own squeak!", or the comment since adapted as motto by many a learned restaurateur: *animus est in patinis,* "my spirit's in my pans." Attracted by these features, but repelled by the broader and more farcical aspects of the play, Gilbert Norwood has called *The Eunuch* "a strange medley of qualities. Dull and brilliant, immoral and edifying, abjectly Plautine and spendidly Terentian—it is all these by turns." Within its basic decency, it is Terence's liveliest and bawdiest farce.

Among later plays influenced by *The Eunuch* are Udall's *Ralph Roister Doister,** Jean de Baif's *L'Eunuque,* 1568; Aristo's *The Supposes,** also Gascoigne's; Pierre Larivey's *The Jealous Ones,* 1580; Wycherly's *The Country Wife,** and Sedley's *Bellamira,* 1687. Cardinal Newman adapted *The Eunuch* for a performance at Westminster in 1880.

More farcical than Terence's other plays, *The Eunuch* nevertheless maintains his high standards, both of human dignity and of deft dramaturgy, and provides a lively picture of Roman exuberance and Roman commonsense, neat capture of the society of the day, in the frame of an amusing story.

THE BROTHERS *Terence*

Adelphoi (The Brothers), 160 B.C., is Terence's last play and his masterpiece. Again he takes the two most common motifs in the New Comedy—a young man who needs money for his mistress, and a young man hiding his involvement with a poor but respectable girl—joins these in an intricately but neatly woven plot, and out of the usual material makes an unusual play. In *The Brothers,* Terence's chief concern is the contrast between two elderly brothers, and particularly their different ideas on the bringing up of youth. With these characters and the consequent happenings, Terence built the shrewdest social problem play of ancient times.

Demea, a strict and stern parent, has brought up his son Ctesipho most rigidly. His son Aeschinus, he has left to his easy-going bachelor brother, Micio, who believes in kindness and trust. Both boys deceive their mentors. In the end, after numerous complications, each boy gets his girl. But the progress of their loves is wholly subordinate to the conflicting mental attitudes of the two elder men. The interest, M. S. Dimsdale has said, "is educational and ethical as much as dramatic"; but this is the dictum of a library scholar. *The Brothers* drives ahead as drama; the opposed educational theories are made manifest, in the young men and their old mentors, as impelling forces to living action.

Neatly, Terence holds the balance between the two educational points of view. The forbearing Micio shrewdly observes to his brother: "There are many signs in people's characters whereby you may easily guess, when two persons are doing the same thing, how it will affect them; so that you can often say: 'It will do this one no harm; it will harm that one'—not because what they are doing is different, but because their characters are different." The two boys are all right, Micio continues; let them have scope. And if they seem a bit extravagant, remember that as we grow older we grow wiser, except that we become "keener after money-making than we ought to be. Time will make them sharp enough at that."

The friendly, hospitable, beneficent ways of Micio seem to work out, and Demea decides to adopt them. Indeed, he reminds Micio that an old man should fight that money-loving impulse, should not merely preach but practice generosity. Micio is thus pressed into a reluctant marriage with the bride's mother; he is plagued until he gives away a farm, frees and establishes his slave—and recognizes that even along his gentle path of generous geniality, one may go to extremes. The turnabout of Demea, called by J. W. Duff "the drollest thing in Terence," paves the way for Micio's discomfiture, in a superb scene that is, as Gilbert Norwood put it, "the legitimate fruit of the whole play, the perfectly sound result of that collision between Micio and Demea which has created and sustained the whole wonderful drama." Demea has learned that severity must be tempered with tolerant understanding; Micio, that discipline must reenforce forbearance. The doctrine of the golden mean, "nothing too much," has been pressed delightfully home. And the two old men ruefully ponder the idea that Menander set down (preserved in a fragment of the original of *The Self-Tormentor**): "Every father is a fool."

All the men in *The Brothers* are excellently drawn and shrewdly contrasted. Micio, the easy-going city dweller, fond of ease, is guardian of the solid, responsible Aeschinus, who can make decisions: Aeschinus is firm in his desire to marry a poor girl; and, to shield his brother, he is ready to shelter his brother's music girl. And Demea, hardworking country fellow, has raised Ctesipho, who seeks the luxuries and extravagant pleasures of the city. The interplay of these four persons, on two age levels of contrasting natures and ideas, makes thought-provoking comedy. Behind them, even the two slaves are differentiated, the one scrupulous, the other dissolute. The sympathies of the author, despite his even-handed balancing of the concerns, perhaps were drawn toward the mild Micio. It is only in Micio, S. C. Sen Gupta observed, in *Shakespearian Comedy* (1950), "in the whole range of Latin drama, that we have a character who has not been dwarfed by the plot." "Micio's tolerance and wisdom," said George E. Duckworth, "his understanding of human nature, make him Terence's most attractive male character." *The Brothers* is the New Comedy's most attractive play.

After the success of *The Brothers,* Terence took a trip to Greece; there, with the manuscripts of further plays, he died the following year.

The Brothers has influenced many later playwrights. Terence was so popular in the tenth century that the nun Hrotswitha wrote six plays, with the pious intention of "moralizing" Terence. To us, his integrity, dignity, and moral earnestness are clear, and give his dramas a noble fervor.

Later works using situations from *The Brothers* include Giovanni Cecci's *The Unlike,* about 1580; Marston's *The Parasitaster,* 1606; Beaumont and Fletcher's *The Scornful Lady,* about 1609; Molière's *The School for Husbands,* 1661; Steele's *The Tender Husband,* 1705; Diderot's *The Head of the Family,* 1758; Colman's *The Jealous Wife,* 1761; Cumberland's *The Choleric Man,* 1774; and Fielding's *The Fathers,* 1778.

With its well-knit plot, lifting the usual farce motifs into a high comedy of character, and with searching analysis of the eternal problem of the education of youth, *The Brothers* combines intrigue with intellectual interest, and is the most richly stimulating of the Roman comedies.

CHARLEY'S AUNT   *Brandon Thomas*

Although he wrote two other plays, actor Brandon Thomas (English, 1856-1914) is remembered only for *Charley's Aunt,* one of the funniest farces of several generations. Its first run, opening in London on December 21, 1892, was for 1,466 performances. It was revived in London almost once a year from 1901 to 1938. In New York, the original run, opening October 2, 1893, was for 205 performances; among revivals, that of October 17, 1940, with Jose Ferrer, reached 233 performances. For a quarter of a century there were always one or more companies on tour with the play in England. *Charley's Aunt* has been performed in twenty-two languages, including Esperanto. Samuel French, play publishers, report that among 125,000 American amateur theatrical groups, *Charley's Aunt* is the most popular play. Lewis Funke, in the *New York Times* (October 10, 1948), recorded that the estate of Brandon Thomas was still doing $100,000 a year business, over the world, with *Charley's Aunt.* It proved still popular in the summer theatres of 1952, alongside the film version of *Where's Charley?* with Ray Bolger.

Charley's aunt is Donna Lucia d'Alvadorez, a widow, left a fortune by her husband in Brazil. She is about to visit Charles Wykeham, at St. Olde's College, Oxford—just in time, Charley figures, to be chaperon for the visit of his sweetheart, Amy Spettigue, and of Amy's friend Kitty Verdun, sweetheart of Charley's friend Jack Chesney. Jack's father, Colonel Sir Francis Chesney, pops up from India with a load of debts; Jack suggests that his widower father marry Charley's wealthy aunt. Then Charley's aunt wires that she's been delayed. Refusing to be without the girls, Charley persuades Babbs—Lord Fancourt Babbersly—who arrives dressed up for some theatricals as a Victorian old lady, to impersonate the missing aunt. Suspicious old Spettigue—Amy's uncle and Kitty's guardian—arrives; when he learns that the chaperon is the fabulously rich widow, he becomes an ardent suitor.

There is considerable comic confusion. "Aunt Lucia" kisses the two girls. The two boys try to get them away, so that each can propose to his sweetheart. The two men maneuver to be alone with the aunt, to snag her fortune—though Colonel Chesney is considerably relieved when the old hag rejects him. Further complications develop: Charley's actual aunt, Donna Lucia, arrives, a comely widow of forty, with a quick wit and a sense of humor; and a girl, Ela Delahay, also appears, who is the dream girl Babbs had once too briefly seen. Sensing something askew, Donna Lucia introduces herself as Mrs. Beverly-Smythe, to discover what plots are under way. Sir Francis prefers "the poor Mrs. Beverly-Smythe" to the millionaire aunt, and wins her. Meanwhile, Spettigue under the spell of his engagement to "the wealthy widow" has given permission for the girls to marry the boys. Charley, unwilling to accept happiness through fraud, reveals the deception; but the real Donna Lucia, taking the letter Spettigue addressed to her, reveals her identity, and four couples are made happy as the curtain falls.

Charley's Aunt requires deftly artificial playing. Then, the response is wholehearted. A typical comment is that, after a production in Polish, of the *Warsaw Weekly* (July 17, 1937): The play is "already classical in style, situations, and characterization; the humorous power is great and it excites laughter in the most earnest people, even when the stupidity or improbability of the situation is quite evident." It should be noted that criticism of melodrama or farce on the score of improbability shoots at the wrong target. These plays are not meant to be believed; the audience grants what Coleridge said art always requires, "the willing suspension of disbelief." No more did Elizabethan audiences believe the disguises and coincidences of their comedies; these were accepted because, without disturbing the mood of the play, they added to the audience's pleasure.

Babbs introduces himself to the girls as "Charley's aunt from Brazil, where the nuts come from"; the words have become a sort of trademark for the play. ("Nut," to Victorian England, was slang, not for a lunatic, but for an outlandish dresser.) As in most good farce, the fun in *Charley's Aunt* is in the main not verbal, but sprung out of the situations, which follow mistake with understanding in swift and errant succession. There is always a hearty burst of laughter, for instance, when that particular and prudish Victorian lady, "Charley's Aunt"— Babbs in a supposedly unseen moment—is discovered smoking a cigar!

In 1948 *Charley's Aunt* was converted into a musical, *Where's Charley?*, with book by George Abbott and music by Frank Loesser. The superb acting of that "cross of string bean and jumping bean," Ray Bolger, made this an effervescent delight. Opening in Philadelphia September 13, *Where's Charley?* came to the New York St. James October 14, 1948, for 792 performances, with another six weeks starting January 29, 1951. The musical complicates the fun by eliminating Babbs and having Charley himself impersonate his aunt.

Charley's Aunt, being free of any "timely" concern, and sufficiently artificial to make its Victorian concepts of chaperon and guardian's consent part of the frolic, continues to be a lively and a very entertaining farce of impersonation and the fun that rises from confused identity.

The play was revived at the London Aldwych, with Griff Rhys Jones, in 1983. The musical continues: Manchester, December 3, 1957, then London, February 20, 1958, for 404 performances. New York, 1964, for 792; again at the City Center for the regulation two weeks. ELT, March 10, 1983. Among the songs: "My Darling," "Make a Miracle," "Once in Love with Amy," and the title song.

The musical marked a turning point in the career of Frank Loesser, who had been a lyric writer until in the U.S. Army he put to music his own words "Praise the Lord and Pass the Ammunition." Harold Arlen was scheduled to do the music for *Charley's Aunt;* he withdrew, and Loesser took over. He moved along, with "Baby It's Cold Outside" winning an Oscar; then "Slow Boat to China," and in 1950 *Guys and Dolls.* *

HOOPLA!   *Ernst Toller*

After his release from prison, Ernst Toller (1893-1939) found himself in a world that left him dismayed. He set his impressions, sardonically, into the tragic drama *Hoppla, wir leben (Whoops, we're alive!)*, 1927, which was presented in England in 1928 as *Hoopla!* It has not yet had professional production in the United States.

Hoopla! is the story of Karl Thomas, a Communist agitator who, after the commutation of his death sentence, is confined in a mad-house. Released after ten years, he blunders about in a new world. His former comrade, Kilman, now a powerful Socialist minister with reactionary leanings, tries to brush him aside with platitudes. Thomas attends a party election, where all seems craven and fruitless. He gets a job as a waiter in a hotel; mankind seems contemptible, vile. Thomas goes out to shoot Kilman, but when he sees him again deems him too petty to be worth the powder. A Nationalist, however, does flash by and shoot Kilman; Thomas is arrested for the crime. Just before the news that the assassin has confessed, Thomas hangs himself in his cell.

In Toller's plays there seems a despair beyond which the playwright could not rise. It was a disillusionment rooted in weakness, without that summoned proud human strength which can look at hopeless evil and yet survive. In one drama, *Pastor Hall,* 1939, based on the experience of Pastor Martin Niemöller, Toller did picture a man who, despite persecution, holds steadfast to his faith. But in the same year, in New York, Toller committed suicide.

Hoopla! as produced in Berlin by Erwin Piscator, seemed a revelation in the theatre, a promise and at once a fulfillment of the effectiveness of the new technique. Between the acts of the play, motion pictures—newsreel shots of actual history—linked the personal events of the drama with world affairs around. The stage itself showed five rooms on various levels. As C. Hooper Trask described the production in the *New York Times* (December 11, 1927), "The backing of each of these sections is a white screen, on which is thrown from behind either a stereopticon picture or a film. Also, a good part of the time, a transparent scrim is let down over the front of the stage, and movies and captions are projected on this from another concealed machine. In the first scene in the prison, the figure of a sentry appears at the back, comes terrifyingly near, and fades away. As the prisoners attempt to break out of their cell, motion pictures of soldiers shooting are thrown on both sides of the scrim at the front. During the voting scene in the restaurant, moving pictures of election riots are thrown on several of the screens, while in the center photographed ballots come floating down in a never-ending chain. In the final scene the various prisoners are communicating with each other by telegraphic raps and their messages are flashed word by word on the scrim opposite their respective cells." The vividness of the presentation, and the sense of integration, widening the story of the one man to a capitulation of the era, constituted "a complete triumph of modern technique."

The documentary presentations of the American Federal Theatre, *The Living Newspaper,* are adaptions of the technique here developed by Piscator. The best of *The Living Newspaper* "editions," *One Third of a Nation,* gave protesting vividness and vehemence of illustration to President Roosevelt's concern over "one-third of a nation ill-clothed, ill-fed, ill-housed." Mingling actors and motion pictures, placarded processions, harangues, and snatches of drama, *The Living Newspaper* sought to use the theatre to present burning issues of the day. More deeply, but no less urgently, *Hoopla!* makes vivid the state of the Germany of its day, with the death of morale and the dearth of values that made empty and desperate spirits ready for a dictator's call.

THE REVENGER'S TRAGEDY   *Cyril Tourneur*

Long neglected on the stage, though constantly praised by critics in the reading, *The Revenger's Tragedy,* 1607, by Cyril Tourneur (English, c. 1575-1626) is a richly colored drama in which violent emotions course to equally violent ends. Couched in tempestuous broken blank verse, with occasional rhyming couplets and some prose, the play, as John Addington Symonds said in the Preface to the Mermaid Edition, "is an entangled web of lust, incest, fratricide, rape, adultery, mutual suspicion, hate, and bloodshed, through which runs, like a thread of glittering copper, the vengeance of a cynical plague-fretted spirit. Vendice emerges from the tainted crew of Duke and Duchess, Lussurioso, Spurio and Junior, Ambitioso and Supervacuo, with a kind of blasted spendour. They are curling and engendering, a brood of flat-headed asps, in the slime of their filthy appetites and gross ambitions. He treads and tramples on them all. But he bears on his own forehead the brands of Lucifer, the rebel, and of Cain, the assassin. The social corruption that transformed them into reptiles has made him a fiend incarnate. Penetrated to the core with evil, conscious of sin far more than they are, he towers above them by his satanic force of purpose." Vendice, properly executed at the drama's close for his own deeds, shows the unending pattern in which crime breeds crime.

The play's events justify Vendice's perturbation almost to frenzy. Knowing that the Duke's son Lussurioso covets their sister, Castizia, Vendice and Hippolito, disguised as his messengers, test their mother, Gratiana; and she seeks to persuade her daughter to the amorous meeting. The scene in which the two brothers reveal their identity and reproach their mother, who repents, is fraught with passion. "The reality and life of this dialogue," said Charles Lamb, "passes any scenical illusion I ever felt. I never read it but my ears tingle, and I feel a hot flush spread my cheeks, as if I were presently about to 'proclaim' some such 'malefactions' of myself, as the brothers here rebuke in their unnatural parent; in words more keen and dagger-like than those which Hamlet speaks to his mother. Such power has the passion of shame truly personated, not only to 'strike guilty creatures unto the soul,' but to 'appal' even those that are 'free.'" Lussurioso is killed for his passionate endeavors.

The Duke himself desired Gloriana, the beloved of Vendice, and when she repelled him had her poisoned. The play opens with Vendice, holding Gloriana's skull, watching the Duke go by. Later, Vendice puts clothes beneath that skull, in a darkened room, smears deadly poison on the grisly face, and entices the lecherous Duke to come for a kiss and die.

Played in London March 8, 1937, for the first time since Tourneur's day, *The Revenger's Tragedy* proved powerful indeed. The *Times* wondered whether the public of today could accept the "shameless intensity" of its passions, for now "appeal is rarely made, and response is usually wary, to what is histrionically appalling, prodigious, and extreme." Nevertheless, the *Times* praised the part of Vendice, "the largeness and . . . tormented grandeur of the half-insane figure who sees in the tainted ducal family the epitome of humanity and works upon it with abominable ingenuity a kind of rough justice;" and praised also "the forcible directness, the persistent urgency, and the fine gravity of the dialogue." The *Telegraph*, expressing the hope that the play will be more frequently performed, said that "the tremendous passion which inspires both theme and writing calls for dramatic expression," and found in Vendice a figure "that offers great possibilities for a really fine actor." The horrid circumstances of the play do not mitigate its present emotional power.

The story of *The Revenger's Tragedy* sounds like a fragment of Italian history, but there is no known source for Tourneur's plot. There is equal violence, save for a happy ending, in Tourneur's other play, *The Atheist's Tragedy*, 1611. He has, however, created no character more interesting than Vendice, who is one of the outstanding figures of our early drama.

Vendice is true to his sense of honor and of duty; yet he is cruel even to outrage in his revenge. This tempest of righteousness wreaking evil gives the grandeur of a stormy sunset to *The Revenger's Tragedy*, one of the most vivid, swirling revenge plays of Elizabethan times.

The play was shown again in England, Cambridge, 1959; by the RSC at Stratford-upon-Avon October 5, 1966, Trevor Nunn directing, with Patience Collier and Ian Richardson; Richardson again in 1969. In America: CSC, 1969; Yale, 1970; University of California at Berkeley, 1979.

Note the names: Vendice: vengeance; Castizia: chastity; Lussurioso: full of lust; Spurio: spurious, a bastard; and more.

Scholars today tend to attribute this play to Middleton, but it was still "by Tourneur" in the 1981-1982 OffBway (Jean Cocteau Rep.) production. This was directed by the English Toby Robertson, who, perhaps to show the continuing brutality of mankind, instead of having Vendice and his brother led offstage under guard, had them horribly killed before the audience, already steeped in horror.

MACHINAL   *Sophie Treadwell*

Although in 1936 Sophie Treadwell (American, 1890-1970) made the best of the several attempts to dramatize the life of Edgar Allan Poe, it is only in her *Machinal* that she rises to distinction. This "inescapably touching tragedy" (*Herald Tribune*, June 18, 1933) moves through the expressionist technique with no sense of strangeness, and with fine sensibility lays bare the soul of a troubled woman.

The play drew its surface facts from the notorious Snyder-Gray murder (New York, March 20, 1927), one of the first such cases to which newspapers assigned noted writers. Sophie Treadwell treated the material with a free hand. "From the sordidness of a brutal murder," wrote Brooks Atkinson (September 8, 1928), grew "a tragedy of submission. . . . Subdued, monotonous, episodic, occasionally eccentric in its style, *Machinal* is fraught with a beauty unfamiliar to the stage." The Young Woman (she is given no name) who struggles inarticulately to achieve happiness instead of embracing resignation is shown with tender but unerring scalpel. Her actions and words, commented a columnist of the time (Elsa McCormick, *World*, September 26, 1928), are "quite true to the usual psychology of the timorous husband-killer. Ruth Snyder, I may add, was one of the few that did not belong in this group."

In the play the Young Woman, burdened with a complaining mother, seeks comfort in marriage with the smug vice-president of the firm that employs her. Love strikes in the person of a Young Man, who impresses her with his masculinity and his tale of exploits in Mexico. To him, however, she is but a passing "frail." Back in her home, she kills her husband. The testimony of "Richard Roe," by affidavit from Mexico, helps bring her to the electric chair.

This movement, in *Machinal*, becomes (Gilbert Gabriel, the *Sun*) "a cruelly beautiful and affecting thing"; (Alison Smith, the *World*) "a stabbing, desperate, compassionate recital of a bewildered woman caught in life's machinery." The measure of the woman's agony and strain before the deed is shown in her answer to the Judge's question: "If you wanted to be free, why didn't you divorce him?" She cried out: "Oh, I couldn't do that! I couldn't hurt him like that!" There is a burst of laughter in the courtroom, and its echo in the audience; yet the remark is deeply true. The husband was a complacent fellow. Why shouldn't his wife be happy? Hasn't she a fine home, all the money she needs, and a—well, a splendid husband?—for whom death was more merciful than the shattering of his illusions.

That husband is superbly drawn, too, as is the woman's mother. *Theatre Magazine* (January 1929) saw him as "a pudgy individual with a sly and elephantine humor, given to reiterating platitudes accompanied by guffaws of uncontrolled laughter"; and the mother as "a heavy, slatternly woman of middle age, whose intellectual horizon is bounded by the frying-pan, the garbage pail, and the gossip of the window-sill." What wonder that a young girl, with aspirations toward a life not of dull ease but of quickening culture, should feel that she has flopped out of the frying-pan into the ashes!

Such a soul is condemned by its own sensitivity. It will flutter; it will be bruised; it may—like this young woman—strike out in violence. But it will always be bewildered by life, and always be a victim.

This sensitive and sobering picture is given colorful expressionistic staging. The *Herald-Tribune* called it "the last, and in some ways the most successful play of the late expressionistic movement in the American drama." The *Boston Transcript* (September 29, 1928) declared: "When expressionism seemed a dead dog in the American theatrical pit, Miss Treadwell unexpectedly galvanized it into a winner of blue ribbons. She has indeed; but for no other reason than the fitness of expressionistic procedure to the design and the matter of the play." The *World* felt that no play since "the unforgettable *From Morn to Midnight*"* had so fully realized the values of expressionism.

One of these values is the recurring use of sound, as background to the ten episodes of the drama. In the business office, the routine tap and clatter punctuate the soliloquy in which the young woman wonders whether the attentions of Vice-President Jones point the way to fulfilment and freedom. At home, street sounds, radio blaring, wailing of kids, all emphasize the drabness of the kitchen days with her mother. The raucous din of jazz music, outside her honeymoon hotel, jangles upon the tawdry disappointment of her marriage. The steel riveter clanking outside her hospital room pounds in the horror of childbirth in an unloving union. The irrelevant chatter of other couples in the speakeasy brings out the essentially casual and callous nature of the episode from which the still hopeful girl builds her dream. And, with grimmer irony, even the prayer of the priest in the death cell is a background noise, an awesome impotent irrelevance. For the girl still wonders and queries: "When I did what I did I was free. Free and unafraid. How can that be, Father? A mortal sin, for which I must die and go to hell; but it made me free. Tell me, how is that, Father?" For all answer comes the Latin drone of words that, like life itself, she cannot understand.

In Moscow, 1933, Alexander Tairov made a hit with *Machinal*. It is interesting to see how he built the play into an indictment of the western world. Elsie McCormick thought the play was basically the study of an individual: "The machine era was dragged in by its crackling and metallic hair. A girl who possessed as flaccid a backbone as the youthful heroine would have come to grief even in the early bronze age." Tairov (in the *Herald-Tribune,* May 28, 1933) saw it otherwise: "*Machinal* is undoubtedly a considerable event in the domain of western theatrical literature. It sums up the various efforts to represent in an effective and condensed form the mechanized life of a large capitalistic city, its soulless movement in a circle, its standardized existence, its empty dynamic, syncopated rhythm . . . the hypocrisy of its sacred institutions, the deathly grip of its blindly moving wheels . . ."

The play does, however, in a deeper sense, give dramatic expression to an attitude that underlies the Soviet system. *Machinal* presents, indeed, the strongest personal picture in the drama of a woman whose sufferings may seem to be no fault of her own, but due to her environment, to society. The Humanitarian point of view, that the fault lies not in the sinner but in the slums, is traceable from Marx into *Machinal* as well as into Russia.

This underlying attitude of *Machinal* was scored by the English critics. (The play, as *The Life-Machine,* was shown privately in London, July 18, 1931; then licensed and publicly presented. Advertisements noting it "For Adults Only" were castigated by the critics, who found the play itself a rousing drama, but who rose in defense of the notion of personal responsibility for one's deeds.) Thus, W. A. Darlington in the *Telegraph,* August 4, 1931, protested: "Throughout the play, the author throws all the sympathy, and tries to attract ours, onto the side of the girl. The husband has damp hands. It is enough. He must die. . . . The moral balance of this play is all wrong." The *Observer,* July 19, 1931, observed: "Really, young women cannot be allowed to despatch their husbands because they happen to dislike them, and my sympathies were wholly with the victim of the crime and not at all with the heroine of the play and victim of the law-courts and gaol."

Machinal opened at the New York Plymouth, September 7, 1928, for ninety-one performances. Zita Johann made her debut as the Young Woman; the Young Man was played by an unknown actor named Clark Gable. The reviewers praised the play highly, but the public, led to expect a Snyder-Gray murder melodrama, did not flock to the sensitive character study expressionistically conveyed.

Despite the lapse of expressionism, there have been revivals of *Machinal*. Dolores Sutton and Gerald O'Loughlin, directed by Gene Frankel, acted it in 1960 on a platform with girders, winning the Vernon Rice award. In 1978 the Encompass Theatre presented it in a staged reading, then in a production OffOffBway, where it was again revived by Theatre Ensemble, April 9, 1981.

Machinal is a superbly constructed study, a poignant drama of a woman's bewildered struggle for happiness, which rises to grueling horror in the closing scenes of the prison and the pitch-dark death house. Its final triumph is that it rises above the machine philosophy it seems to illustrate, and leaves us with the chastening thought that violence, even sought as a path to freedom, does not lead to freedom; freedom and peace reside within.

A MONTH IN THE COUNTRY   *Ivan Turgenev*

The one memorable play by the Russian novelist Ivan Turgenev (1818-1883), built, as Stanislavski said, "on the most delicate curves of love experience," is *A Month in the Country*, 1850. "For the lover of fine shades, of subtle approaches," the play—anticipating Chekhov* and Jean-Jacques Bernard's* "drama of the unexpressed"—is a touching comedy of boredom reaching out for love and closing fingers on frustration.

On the isolated estate of the practical Islaev, his wife Natalia (Natasha) Petrovna regrets her more glamorous past, and is fearfully conscious of her waning charms. Bored by the languid and polite attentions of her husband's friend Mikhail Rakitin, Natasha is roused to fresh love when the zestful young Aleksei Belaev arrives as tutor for her son. Aleksei is equally ready to flirt either with the twenty-nine-year-old Natasha or with her seventeen-year-old ward Vera (Veroshka); but Natasha's jealousy and ardor drive him back to Moscow. Rakitin, despite Islaev's pleading, also leaves. The observant and cynical Dr. Ignati Spigelski, the only one who has been getting what he wants, teaches the clumsy old neighboring landowner Bolshintsov how to propose, and thrusts the now bitter and lonely Vera, who had bloomed beneath the tutor's attentions, into the old man's arms. Natasha is left frustrated, more lonely and more bored than before.

A Month in the Country was at once recognized as a masterpiece. It has had frequent performance in many lands. In London it was first seen on July 5, 1926; again in 1936; in an adaption by Emlyn Williams, February 11, 1943, with Michael Redgrave as Rakitin, for 313 performances; and at the Old Vic opening November 30, 1949. In New York, the Theatre Guild presented the play, borrowing much from Stanislavsky's Moscow productions of 1909 and after, on March 17, 1930, with Alla Nazimova, Dudley Digges as the doctor, Henry Travers, and Alexander Kirkland. Ruth Gordon was in the Williams adaption in Westport, Connecticut, August 2, 1949.

The half-tones of *A Month in the Country*, its soft regrets, pale passions, and inexpressive sighs, are, said the London *Stage* (July 8, 1926), "infinitely less depressing than the dull, if more closely analytical, dramas of the ever boosted Chekhov." It is, as the *Chicago Journal* (August 19, 1926) declared, "a beautiful play all through; but its second act seems one of the most beautiful things in modern drama." It is hard to realize that this delicate drama, its effects wrought by suggestion and understatement, was written, as John Mason Brown pointed out (March 18, 1930), "when Turgenev himself, as a resident of Paris, was sitting nightly before the dramas of Scribe* and Musset*; in fact, when the playgoers of England and

America were still patronizing the claptrap of such ardent claptrappers as Sheridan Knowles and Dion Boucicault."*

The portrait of Natalia Petrovna is superb. On the isolated Islaev estate she still holds the stage, but with no significant lines to speak, no situation to command, no attitude to strike. She feels herself, as N. Bryllion Fagin put it in the *Hopkins Review* (Fall, 1949), drooping toward a settled age.

William Archer has compared Chekhov's plays to opera librettos: the performance fills in the music. This is even more true of *A Month in the Country*, wherein, as the *London Times* (October 1, 1936) stated, "the passions are implied, and actors are left a thousand eloquent omissions through which, if their insight and skill be equal to the extraordinarily difficult task, the heat of the invisible flames may be conveyed. There, to those that admire conscious art, the play offers exquisite pleasure." These reticences, however, in no wise lessen the sense of reality. The play is, indeed, the *Times* continued (October 4, 1936), "full of an astounding actuality, which persuades us that the actors when they have completed one scene retire not to their dressing-rooms but to some other part of the house to resume a life from which they have been momentarily snatched. Any scene presented to the audience is only a section of the stage, those sections out of view seething with life though we do not see it."

The picture of life in *A Month in the Country* is as rounded as reality. Pathetic it is, in Natasha's weak-winged and foredoomed flight from futility, and in the environing waste and misdirection. Yet always the touch of life's comedy comes as a timely leaven: just when the subtlety threatens to sink into flatness, the cynical observations of the doctor lift the mixture again, with wit and understanding that quicken the mind to companion the flow of the emotions. Turgenev has, with a mellowness unknown to Chekhov, written a masterly drama of waning lives.

Among many revivals: adapted by Emlyn Williams, April 5, 1956, directed by Michael Redgrave; Luther Adler as the doctor and—"best in our time"—Uta Hagen as Natalia, for 48 performances. She had competition. New York, February 28, 1963, Celeste Holm. Guilford, June 2, 1965, then London, September 23, with Ingrid Bergman, Fay Compton, Emlyn Williams, Michael Redgrave, for 172 performances; Ingrid Bergman had played Natalia in Paris. Chichester Festival, August 30, 1974, with Dorothy Tutin, Derek Jacobi as Rakitin, then the London Albery, November 20, 1975. New York Roundabout, 1975-1976, also December 11, 1979, with Tammy Grimes and Amanda Plummer. And NT (Olivier), February 19, 1981, with Francesca Annis.

Turgenev's model for Natalia was the actress and prima donna Pauline Viardit, whom Turgenev followed around Europe; she was the daughter of the great gypsy tenor Garcia. Turgenev told the actress Savina (who played Vera): "Rakitin is myself. Always in my works I depict myself as an unsuccessful lover." He found a wistful atmosphere in his play.

RALPH ROISTER DOISTER　　　　　　　　　　　*Nicholas Udall*

The first English comedy, *Ralph Roister Doister*, was written about 1540 by a scholar familiar with the Latin comedies of Terence* and Plautus.* Nicholas Udall (1505-1556) was headmaster of Eton; later, of Westminster School. Good Roman structure and good English figures and fun are fused; there are, said Allardyce Nicoll, "a series of excellent stage tricks, and a dialect which is moderately easy in spite of the fettering rime."

The character of Ralph is that of the *miles gloriosus,* the boastful warrior, which springs from Plautus' play of that name. Ralph is a boaster and a coward; he has money, but spends it foolishly. He is vain of his appearance, imagining himself what his fellows of later times would call a "masher" or a "lady-killer." Ralph is, at the moment of the play, drawn toward Widow Custance, and in the absense of her fiancé, the merchant Gawyn Goodluck, Ralph seeks to win her. He is about equally helped and hampered by his boon campanion, the parasite Merygreek, who flatters and bullies and bosses Ralph. The winsome widow, unable to get rid of the pair, determines to get what fun she can out of them. Gawyn, returning, is jealous; but an old friend, and Ralph's cowardly confession, clear the widow and the situation.

Although the intrigue of the play is typical of Roman comedy, the figures in *Ralph Roister Doister* are genuinely English. Ralph, for all the lengthy dramatic background of his type, speaks and acts like those in the audience around, fringed with the frank exaggeration of satire. Merygreek, Gawyn Goodluck, and the rest are native stock. The dialogue, too, is vernacular, and lively; with the movement of the play, it creates an atmosphere of urbanity, a merry mood of life among the comfortable middle class of old England. The play was long popular for performance in English schools. The essential elements of comedy as we know it today are all present: characters ridiculous and serious (some the more ridiculous for taking themselves seriously), incidents laughable in themselves, temporary misunderstandings that rise to a climax of bewilderment, and more.

The merriment of the play remains delightful entertainment. "Definitely farce," said the *London Times* (August 2, 1932) when it was produced at the Malvern Festival. Allowing for the change in mode of expression, there are still robust humor and amusing incident in *Ralph Roister Doister.* It had its "New York premiere" at the OffBway Parkside July 31, 1980.

FATA MORGANA   *Ernö Vajda*

Fata Morgana, 1914, by Ernö Vajda (Hungarian, 1887-1954), is perhaps the most tender and touching dramatic presentation of the ardor, and the anguished disillusion, of young love. Morgan le Fay—Fata Morgana—was the evil fairy, sister of King Arthur; because of her fair but false allure, her name is also used for the mirage. The seductress in this drama, who offers George but the mirage of happiness, is named Mathilde Fay.

Preparing to go to the annual village festival from their farmstead on the sand-swept Hungarian plain, three ladies (played in New York, 1924, by Armina Marshall, Josephine Hull, and Helen Westley) tear to tatters the reputation of the coming Mathilde. But confusion of messages brings Mathilde when all have gone save George, poring over his books for college. Making the best of a lonely evening, the city lady flirts with the trustful George—until the fire of his passion takes her in mutual flame. Next morning, when Mathilde's husband arrives with an unexpected check, and the prospect of a trip to Ostend at the height of the season hurries Mathilde to depart, George blurts out that Mathilde is planning to get a divorce and marry him. Horrified at the prospect of a life in poverty for a night's pleasure, Mathilde cries out that the boy is mad. Taking tense hold of his passion, to drown it in the dregs of shame and disillusion, George declares that he had spoken from a wild fancy—and Mathilde and her reassured husband go gaily off. Behind them they leave the ashes of George's youth.

Vajda has woven this moon-calf tragedy with tender understanding. The young and sensitive George is no more sympathetically drawn than the older Mathilde. "She who had begun in cool and tempting passion," the *Boston Transcript* (March 4, 1924) pointed out, "falls under the spell of romance. Her spring has come again. Feverishly, she fondles in him her youth returned; as eagerly he caresses in her the long-pent ideal of passion. . . . Here between romance and reality plays life." Robert Benchley (*Life,* March 27, 1924) called the play "full of little heart-breaking moments."

The play was first shown at the New York Garrick March 3, 1924, with Emily Stevens and Morgan Farley. London welcomed it September 15, 1924. It found frequent performance in summer and community theatre. At the New York Royale December 25, 1931, Douglas Montgomery played George; Ava Gerald, Mathilde; the *Times* declared: "Without sacrificing any of the poignancy of the role or the integrity of its emotion, he brings to his portrayal a certain robust quality that the frail Mr. Farley lacked." On August 4, 1933, the play went on tour, from Greenwich, Conn. It came to Australia in October 1936. The ELT, February 11, 1947, used a new translation by Clement Scott Gilbert. *Fata Morgana* was revived March 23, 1964, at Croydon, England, with David Hemmings and Sarah Churchill.

To a puritanical charge, the *Manchester Guardian* (back on September 19, 1924) declared: "This play of seduction may be called pornography. But it is the kind of pornography that would drive a man to a monastery." George Jean Nathan stated: "With the wit and humor of Sacha Guitry he combines a deep psychological sense, a full measure of reflection and tonic irony, and a nice gift of cultivated sympathy."

The attitude of the playwright toward the love-struck youth is in bright contrast to the complacent adult superiority of such plays as Booth Tarkington's *Seventeen,* wherein young love is seen as cause for laughter, and to the grimmer intensity of such dramas as *The Awakening of Spring,** wherein youth's questing finds disaster.

There are affection and awakened understanding within more than the central figures of *Fata Morgana.* George's mother is an excellent study of love and sympathy trying to break through her son's pride, which holds her at arm's length. His father also watches, mitigating authority with affection, reaching out to the heartbroken boy by indirection. When the Fays leave for Ostend, his father suggests that George take a holiday trip before college. George prefers to return to the study Mathilde had interrupted the night before.

In this sympathetic atmosphere, *Fata Morgana* presents a consummate dramatic picture of the development of a sensitive youth, to whom a mature woman brings love, then disillusion, rungs on the ladder of understanding. "Comedy of the very highest order," George Jean Nathan called it; comedy that stakes a smile on the worth of living, from over the brink of tears.

MON FAUST   *Paul Valéry*

Of two recent variants of the Faust story, the second is significant. The first, *Dr. Faustus Lights the Lights*—although given constantly flashing lights in the surrealistic setting of Julian Beck, in the New York Living Theatre production December 1, 1951, with a dog played by a woman, who instead of barking says "Thank you"—left the audience in the dark. The *Times* compared it to "a straight dive from the high board into a dry swimming pool."

Of a different order is the poetic *Mon Faust,* witty and crystal clear, by the outstanding French poet Paul Valéry (1871-1945), in which Faustus tries to convince Satan that the world no longer believes in him; it can go its own way to destruction without his help. Satan seeks to demonstrate that there is still a place for him, and thus for guilt and damnation, in the modern world.

My Faust is actually two unfinished plays: *Luste, or the Crystal Girl* (first three acts of four), and *Le Solitaire; ou, Les Malédictions d'Univers, (Féerie dramatique,* two-thirds complete).

In the first play, Faust is in his study, seeking a world divorced from reality, from body and mind—to rid them of trouble by a "gross convulsion": the convulsion of mind is laughter. His secretary, Luste, unwittingly tempts him from his abstractions. Mephisto comes; Luste curtsies, remarking: "It's odd, but you don't scare me at all." Mephisto replies: "If I scared people, I shouldn't be the Devil. But . . . I can, if I wish." A student comes to Faust for counsel; Faust bids him "beware of love." Mephisto: "He speaks for humanity, you know. Perhaps, for something beyond." Three devils in Faust's library, Belial, Ashtaroth, and Gongrina (a succuba), who gnaw, befoul, or copulate, are driven out by Mephisto, who tells the student: "In a word, I *serve.*"

Mephisto defines Faust as "a mind mastering the mind." The student falls in love with Luste; when she rejects him, he cries: "You are giving me back to the Devil!"

The Solitaire is lying flat and unnoticed when Faust and Mephisto come, in an exhausting climb, to the highest peak. Mephisto has "no head for heights" and at Faust's bidding goes down. Faust muses: "There's an enormous amount of nothingness in the Whole [*le Tout*]. The rest? A pinch of scattered dust." The Solitaire awakes: "My little eye offers itself this universe; one eye is enough for the infinite glory . . . I close it and become the power that denies." He bids Faust, "Go away, Filth . . . you exist." Faust: "And you . . . then you do not?" "No. Since there is only me, there is no one." The Solitaire continues (a sort of cynical Brand; see Ibsen*): "Thought spoils pleasure and increases pain. Prostitution is the basic principle of the mind; to whom, to what, does it not give itself? . . . Every work of the mind is an excretion, relieving it, in its way, of its excesses of pride, despair, lust, or boredom . . ." He hurls Faust into the abyss.

In what is called "Interlude" fairies appear, bringing Faust gradually back to consciousness. They offer him the world; he that knows everything should know the words that can bring the change [*metamorphose*].

Faust: Do I know one of these words?

Second Fairy: You know only to deny.

First Fairy: Your first word was No.

Second Fairy: Which will be your last.

Curtain

Valéry was seeking mind at its highest level of abstraction—knowledge beyond mind, toward absolute vacuum, leaving Mephisto helpless and superannuated.

Francis Fergusson declared: "The genre of this sample is intellectual comedy akin to that of Shaw or Giraudoux. Valéry masters its tone and movement with extraordinary ease. He weaves a texture which is both witty and delicately lyrical." T. S. Eliot asserted: "Valéry will remain for posterity the representative poet, the symbol of the poet, of the first half of the twentieth century—not Yeats, not Rilke, not anyone else."

Valéry himself gave readings of *Mon Faust* at Monaco, Villa des Charmettes, in July 1940; also November 1, 1940, March 1, 1941, and August 1, 1944. There were dramatic readings at the *Théâtre d'Essai*, Monte Carlo, April 6, 1946, April 25, 1952, and November 26, 1956. On April 28, 1945, a production at the Comédie Française; another at the Paris Théâtre Rochefort, July 29, 1946. Beginning January 10, 1947, the play had a week's run in Brussels, and one in French in March 1952 at the National Theatre, Helsinki. It was broadcast by the Madeleine Renaud—Jean-Louis Barrault Company October 31, 1951, and several times in 1953.

For three nights beginning February 10, 1967, the Theatre for Ideas, OffOffBway, presented an English dramatic reading of *My Faust,* with literary critic Leslie Fiedler playing Faust as an inflated pedant, and drama critic John Simon a hissing, disdainful Mephisto, "the devil incarnate." Baudelaire declared that if God did not exist, man would have had to create him; it is the fate of every Faustus that the Devil goes on and on.

THE SERPENT   *Jean-Claude van Itallie*

The Serpent, by Jean-Claude van Itallie, is perhaps the liveliest example of the "open theatre," which involves the audience and may give scope to spontaneous creation in the course of a performance's drive. The play tells the story of the Garden of Eden with an amusing admixture of primeval simplicity and modern comprehension. The snake consists of five interlocked men, writhing and twisting their way to the temptation. Like the two Gondoliers in Gilbert's play, each of the five actors, jauntily sinister, speaks one of the phrases that build into a sentence. When Eve eats the apple, crates of apples are shared with the audience.

Cain, wondering how to kill, tries various holds on Abel; Abel, not understanding that his end is near, makes no objection. The episode is chanted by a chorus as the actors mime; as "it occurred to Cain to kill his brother but it did not occur to Cain that killing his brother would cause his brother's death." (Does not this curious confusion persist? Cain obeyed an impulse many a person even today in a moment's anger expresses—"I could kill you for that!"—and then pushes aside. The play, indeed, begins with the assassination of President John F. Kennedy.)

Toward the end, fully dressed in tights, shifts, and T-shirts, with hands, feet, and faces bare, the actors experiment, seeking modes of procreation. They fumble; they succeed, and make beginning of the long line of "begats." Finally they begin to hum; the humming grows into the singing of "Moonlight Bay"; they drift up the aisles and away. The audience has eaten the apples; the serpent has sowed its seed.

The Serpent glided into Rome June 28, 1968; it toured Germany, Switzerland, Denmark; then the Spoleto Festival back in Italy. Its American première was at Cambridge, January 12, 1969. In New York it was shown beginning February 20, 1969, at the Open Theatre and weekends in May at the Public; again in June 1970. New Orleans saw it October 23, 1970; Channel 13 showed it on television. Berkeley, April 28, 1971. *The Serpent* is an amusing example of a new and lively aspect of theatrical presentation, with links to the commedia dell'arte and the ancient satyr play.

THE RELAPSE   *Sir John Vanbrugh*

Sir John Vanbrugh (1664-1726) was an architect, among his noted structures being Blenheim Palace, Oxfordshire. His few plays seem to have come almost incidentally. His first and most continuingly successful play was an avowed sequel (and part parody) of Colley Cibber's *Love's Last Shift*, 1695 (which won "first prize for mistranslation" in the French *La Dernière Chemise de l'Amour*). In Vanbrugh's *The Relapse; or, Virtue in Danger,* premiered at the Royal Theatre, Drury Lane, November 25, 1696, Vanbrugh has Cibber's Sir Novelty Fashion purchase promotion as Lord Foppington. The Lord has arranged a marriage with Miss Hoyden, daughter of the wealthy country squire Sir Tunbelly Clumsey. Young Fashion, piqued because his elder brother refuses funds for his overdrawn allowance, goes to the squire's, posing as the Lord, and succeeds in arranging a secret marriage with the girl. When the Lord arrives, Fashion flees. Hoyden, the nurse, and the parson keep mum until she and Lord Foppington are wed. Then Fashion pops up at Lord Foppington's home and claims his bride. The fact that he is the Lord's brother brings Hoyden back to him.

This story, given prominence in later productions, is actually subplot to the story of Loveless, a reformed libertine, and his beloved and loving wife, Amanda. Loveless, in London, is tempted by an old flame, the young widow Belinthia; Worthy, who wants Amanda, makes sure she knows of her husband's lapse; she is distressed but faithful. Berinthia, who wants Worthy, shames Loveless, who returns to his forgiving wife.

Vanbrugh was the last of the Restoration dramatists, in whom, said Allardyce Nicoll in *The History of the Drama,* volume 1, "fancy and carnal thought alternated or became confused, clashed and grew into what we know as the comedy of manners." Colley Cibber (1671-1757) made his reputation as an actor by his playing of Lord Foppington. In 1977 Sheridan* adapted *The Relapse* "for a more polished stage" as *A Trip to Scarborough,* toning down the language, explaining Berinthia's temptation of Loveless as from her desire to punish Worthy (now called Towneley) for turning from her to Amanda; and having shame, not exposure, send Loveless back to his wife.

Among many recent revivals of *The Relapse*: London Phoenix, 1948; Cyril Ritchard directed and played Lord F., with Madge Elliott; John Emery as Loveless; also 1950 with the New York Theatre Guild. Harold Hobson (January 3, 1948): "sparkles and flashes continually." RSC Aldwych, August 17, 1967, directed by Trevor Nunn; Donald Sinden, Lord F.; David Waller, Sir Tunbelly; Janet Suzman, Berinthia; Susan Fleetwood, Amanda. Again Harold Hobson (October 7, 1967): "This is a very funny play, stuffed with wit, nonsense and sheer buffoonery. It needs considerable skill and not a little moral courage to insist that an audience which is happily roaring its head off should suddenly pay attention to the very real emotional situation that unexpectedly flowers. Mr. Nunn, with the help of a most promising young actress, Susan Fleetwood, makes it true and touching." It had forty performances in repertory. Again in repertory (forty-five times) August 15, 1968, with Barry Ingham, Lord F.; Brewster Mason, Sir Tunbelly; Toby Robins, Berinthia. OffBway (Good Shepherd), 1974; OffOffBway (Meat & Potatoes Co.), 1980. Also April 16, 1980. Phoenix, University of Michigan.

Called *Virtue in Danger,* book and lyrics by Paul Dehn, music by James Bernard, the adaptation came from Oxford to the London Mermaid April 10, 1963, then June 3 to the Strand, with, said the *Stage* (April 16, 1963), "wit, charm, or bawdy bluntness." Patricia Routledge was Berinthia; John Moffat, Lord F.; Patsy Byrne, Miss Hoyden; Hamlyn Benson, Sir Tunbelly. Among the songs were "Fortune, Thou Art a Bitch!", "Stand Back, Old Sodom!", "Wait a Little Longer, Lover."

THE PROVOK'D WIFE   *Sir John Vanbrugh*

The Provok'd Wife may have been written in prison in Paris, the French being then at war with the English. Opening in 1697, it continued popular throughout the eighteenth century. Betterton and Mrs. Barry were in the original cast; others who have played in the comedy include Colley Cibber, Nance Oldfield, Peg Woffington, and David Garrick. There were London revivals in 1919 and 1936.

The play opens with Sir John Brute—a scold and a coward—regretting his marriage. Matrimony confines him, bores him, chafes him. His wife, naturally, seeks solace elsewhere. At Spring Garden, she is frolicking with Constant—whose friend Heartfree is there with Mrs. Brute's niece, his beloved Belinda—and Lady Brute is on the brink of yielding to Constant when jealous Lady Fancyfull arrives. The men and the ladies repair to Lady Brute's, but Sir John comes home unexpectedly. He had been arrested, while disguised in a parson's gown, for engaging in a street brawl, and been lectured and dismissed by the magistrate. Although Sir John finds the men concealed, he accepts the explanation that they are there because of Heartfree's hopes of Belinda. At the same time, his jealousy has been sufficiently aroused for him to find more value in his wife and to treat her with more attention and respect thereafter.

Vanbrugh was the most spontaneous, in creation, of the playwrights of his time, and *The Provok'd Wife* is written much as he might have talked. The result is that the dialogue remains surprisingly fresh and lively; and the characters, though put through situations similar to those in dozens of the dramas of the day, seem natural and hearty, quite humanly endowed with impulses and feelings. It is this quality that explains the complaint of the critic of the *London Chronicle* (October 7, 1758): "It is amazing to me that Mr. Garrick will attempt the part of Sir John Brute . . . in which he is absolutely prejudicial to the morals of his countrymen."

There were other complaints about the play's morals. As one small bow to these, the parson's gown in which Sir John Brute disguises himself was changed to a lady's dress. (A deeper obeisance was Vanbrugh's writing of *The Provok'd Husband.*) But the bluntness of the portrayals has helped keep them alive. Thus W. A. Darlington in the *London Telegraph* (October 6, 1936) found *The Provok'd Wife* "a gay and lively piece." And the *Times* (same date) felt that Vanbrugh wrote "fashionably, grossly, and amusingly.

. . . The comedy smilingly insists that laughter is not (whatever French psychologists say) incompatible with some degree of emotion." *The Provok'd Wife* remains one of the most alive of the seventeenth century comedies.

After Vanbrugh's death, Colley Cibber completed his friend's last play, *A Journey to London,* which Vanbrugh said he wrote as an apology for *The Provok'd Wife.* Cibber "cleansed" it further, and called it *The Provok'd Husband.* It opened in 1728, and was played frequently until (its last professional production) 1860. Cibber, acclaimed when the British Army in New York in 1782 performed *The Provok'd Wife* as "by Colley Cibber," was made Poet Laureate in 1730; for the years until his death in 1757, he was the worst poet ever to hold that office. His reputation rests on his vivid though protestingly moral description of Restoration and early-eighteenth-century drama in his 1740 *Apology for the Life of Colley Cibber, Gentleman.* For the 1722 production of *The Provok'd Wife,* Cibber recorded, Vanbrugh disguised Brute not as a clergyman but "unto the undress of a woman of quality. Now the character and profession of a fine lady not being so indelibly sacred as that of a churchman, whatever follies he exposed in the petticoat, kept him at least clear of his former profaneness, and were innocently ridiculous to the spectator."

Early in the play comes a typical sample of Vanbrugh's "genteel comedy":

Belinda: Ay, but you know we must return good for evil.

Lady Brute: That may be a mistake in the translation.

Later, Brute: "I married because I had a mind to lie with her, and she wouldn't let me." Lady Brute married him for his money.

The *London Chronicle* of October 7, 1758, declared that Garrick was "absolutely prejudicial to the morals of his countrymen. When he drinks Confusion To All Order, there is scarce a man in the house, I believe, who is not for that moment a reprobate in his heart." By December 2, 1980, Robert Cushman could state, of Geraldine McEwan's Lady Brute, that "her command to her swain, 'Into the closet!' in its sophisticated weariness, is worth the price of admission."

A few of the recent revivals, in England: Oxford to Richmond to the London Vaudeville, July 24, 1963, "first West End production in a century and a half:" still, said Richard Watts, Jr. (*New York Post,* reporting from London), "full of zest, and biting comment on men, women and manners." The *London Times* deemed "the gross pranks of Sir John diverting as well as deplorable." Greenwich, June 1973, Sheila Allen and James Grout as Lady Brute and Sir John, using the 1647 version, with Brute disguised as a parson; Fenella Fielding as Lady Fancyfull. NT (Lyttleton), October 28, 1980, directed by Peter Wood; John Wood and Geraldine McEwan, Sir John and Lady Brute; Dorothy Tutin, Lady Fancyfull; Lindsay Duncan, Belinda. This went to Paris May 28, 1981.

In America: spring 1950, Brattle Theatre Co., Cambridge, for seven weeks. January 1, 1965, San Francisco (Beech St.), Dean Goodman and Paula White as the Brutes. The Actors Touring Co. of London, after showing *The Provok'd Wife* there, brought it to the United States for the "Britain Salutes New York" festival, April 1983.

OUTWARD BOUND   *Sutton Vane*

The novelty of *Outward Bound* found producers reluctant; Sutton Vane (English, 1888-1963) produced it himself near London, September 18, 1923. It came to London October 15, with Cissie Loftus, for 227 performances, and was revived there in 1926, 1935, and 1940. New York saw the play January 7, 1924, with Dudley Digges, Leslie Howard, Alfred Lunt, Margalo Gillmore; it ran for 144 performances, and was revived in 1938-1939 with Florence Reed, Vincent Price, and Laurette Taylor, for 255; Morgan Farley and Helen Chandler played the young couple. It was filmed twice, in 1930 with Leslie Howard, and again in 1944, and is frequently presented by college and community companies; in 1971 OffBway, and by ELT with Garson Kanin as Scrubby; at New York Lincoln Center April 23, 1977; and by the Troupe OffOffBway July 8, 1982.

The play opens on board a ship. The only visible member of the crew is Scrubby, the steward; the passengers are a mixed lot indeed. Tommy Prior is a young but world-weary drunkard. Mrs. Cliveden-Banks is an aristocratic snob; the only passenger she accepts as an equal is the officious and obnoxious, purse-proud businessman, Mr. Lingley. Two young folk, Ann and Henry, close-bound in love; an earnest clergyman, the Rev. William Duke, and a motherly charwoman, Mrs. Midgett, complete the list. These folk gradually sense that there is something strange about their voyage. Act I ends with their discovery that they are sailing on "the Styx"—they are indeed "outward bound," being dead. Their destination? "Heaven, Sir," explains Scrubby, " —and Hell too. It's the same place."

The Examiner comes on board, and each is allotted the appropriate doom. The charwoman, who has supported her son through college while keeping him unaware of her lowly station, is allowed to go on secretly serving him—Tom Prior. Ann and Henry—whom the steward calls "halfways"—feel the breath of a different air, and at the end of the play escape from their suicide pact back to life. The intermittent drumbeat is soft as the curtain falls.

Outward Bound presents its characters with a mixture of sympathy and irony that raises them to genuine value, and persuades us to accept their unusual journey, in this modern morality. "Even to his favourite characters," said the *Spectator* (London, October 27, 1923), "he is malicious in a friendly way, and he has nothing worse than an acidulated irony for his cruel snob and his bullying businessman." The play has passages, said the *Times* (London, August 8, 1935), "remarkable at once for their imaginative boldness and their restraint, which have set *Outward Bond* apart from its competitors, and preserved it. . . . It has what is very rare in the theatre, the thrill of a poetic idea—and it has power to impregnate its audiences' minds and enable them to imagine for themselves." Eleanor Roosevelt, in her newspaper column, "My Day," January 30, 1939, called the play "among the finest in the theatre." On June 23, 1963, the *Herald-Tribune,* commenting on the author's death, ended: "The sunny fantasy about death is still alive."

The hereafter, onstage, may be shown from three points of view. It may be shown as the playwright imagines it; such is the hell of Shaw's *Man and Superman,** where one may do as one likes, and everything is permitted except intensity. It may be shown as the character involved imagines it; thus, in *Liliom** justice hereafter is dealt out in a court like a police magistrate's here and now. When several persons are involved in the trip to the next world, the problem is more complicated; and the playwright is likely—as does Sutton Vane—to fall back upon the audience's point of view, the conventional heaven and hell of reward and punishment. It is less, however, the dramatic justice of their final disposition than the naturalness of the characters and attitudes revealed upon the journey, and the thoughts aroused by the spectacle of that awesome trip, that give distinction and power to *Outward Bound*.

S.S. TENACITY   *Charles Vildrac*

Le Paquebot Tenacity (S.S. Tenacity), by Charles Vildrac (French, 1882-1971), is a simple play. Its lack of rousing action is counterbalanced by the deftly drawn portraits of its characters: Mme. Cordier, owner of the cheap seaport restaurant; Therese, her waitress; the garrulous and hard-drinking but kindly observer of life, Hidoux; and the two main figures, Bastien and Segard, printers and friends on their way from Paris to try their fortunes in far-off Canada.

Segard is a simple, stay-put sort of fellow; he is there because he has been swept along by the decisive Bastien, who prides himself on his firm will. The two men are attracted to the pleasant waitress; but while the dreamer Segard merely loves Therese, the practical Bastien takes her. Therese and Bastien go off together, leaving Segard alone to continue the trip to Canada—where he never wanted to go in the first place. The name of the ship bears cargo of irony.

Played at Jacques Copeau's Theatre in Paris in 1920, *Le Pacquebot Tenacity* was a warm success. London saw *S. S. Tenacity* June 15, 1920, with Basil Sydney; New York, January 2, 1922. Its gentle quality gave the play no lengthy run in English; but it was welcomed by the critics. "One of the most delicately written plays we have seen in a long time," the London *Era* called it. "The story is but the thread to string together three or four exquisitely conceived character studies. The whole thing is quite slight, and perfectly blended." In New York, Alexander Woollcott praised the "telling and convincing seduction scene." The *Evening World* commented: "Steering clear of theatrical claptrap, *S.S. Tenacity* is as staunch and true a play as has come to this port from France or any other country in many a day. . . . Seldom do we get a play that touches life so closely . . . the life of workaday people who have little more than they put on their back, yet take their lot uncomplainingly and get along as best they can." Segard is bewildered and buffeted by life, but moves humbly yet with innate dignity along the path life allows him. One cannot say that he is plushed along; others may spin him and point him, but he goes forward of his own motor force.

The simple yet searching study of human nature, of common folk moving through more or less ordinary days, involved in actions calling for no heroic resolution or tumultous roar of passion—the motivation and the deed done, even as you and I—give the play quiet distinction.

THE WESTERN CHAMBER   *Wang Shih Fu*

After China's conquest by the Mongols during the Yuan Dynasty (1280-1368), the scholars, excluded from government posts, found expression in the drama. Some 550 plays were written in about fifty years. Outstanding among these is *Hsi Hsiang Chi (The Romance of The Western*

Chamber), by Wang Shih Fu, which, according to Younghill Kang in the *New York Times* (August 15, 1937), is "considered by Oriental critics the best specimen of Mongol drama." *The Western Chamber* drew its plot from a play written in the vernacular about A.D. 800.

The play shows the young scholar Chang stopping at a Buddhist monastery while on his way to the capital to take the examinations. He encounters Lady Cheng, the widow of a minister, her daughter Ying-Ying, expert in embroidery and the classics, and their alert and intelligent maid, Hung Niang. Chang promptly falls in love with Ying-Ying. However, Ying-Ying is also desired by Flying Tiger, the leader of a bandit host. Lady Cheng promises her daughter to whoever drives off the bandits. Chang, with the help of "the General on the White Horse," accomplishes this; but the young couple learn that Ying-Ying's father had already betrothed her to another. They exchange love poems and vows; a friendly monk helps them; and finally their love seems so intense and so desperate that Lady Cheng feels forced to unite them.

Long popular in China, *The Western Chamber* was given its first performance in English, translated by Henry H. Hart, at Sacramento Junior College, March 10, 1938. A version by S. I. Hsuing was acted in London, in 1938-39.

The play has many beautiful lyric passages, and the characters are drawn with considerable charm, against the mild Spring background of the monastery in the hills. It lacks the swift pace of western drama, but flows with the almost untroubled tranquility of a gentle stream on a quiet evening. The pleasant country folk are well caught; there is a touch of mischief in the nimble-witted maid; and the fragrant breath of eternal romance keeps the two lovers fresh across the centuries.

THE WHITE DEVIL   *John Webster*

John Webster (English, 1580?-1625?) began his theatrical career by collaborating with other playwrights (Marston and Dekker), then in two great works established himself as the outstanding creator of the tragedy of blood. The preface, 1612, to *The White Devil* indicates the difference between Webster and most of his contemporaries; he compares his aims to those of Euripides,* declares that he writes slowly and carefully, and hopes for the judgment not merely of his time but of posterity.

The White Devil; or, The Tragedy of Paulo Giordano Ursini, Duke of Brachiano, With the Life and Death of Vittoria Corombona, the Famous Venetian Courtesan, based upon actual events in Italy from 1581 to 1585, was acted by the Queen's servants about 1608; it was revived in 1635, 1665, and 1672. A version by Nahum Tate, called *Injured Love; or, The Cruel Husband,* was produced in 1707. The play thereafter was largely confined to the library; but after Charles Lamb called attention to it, it became one of the best known of Elizabethan tragedies. A revival at Cambridge, England, in 1937 went on a widely successful Scandinavian tour. There were productions in London in 1935 and 1947; one in New York, by Equity Library, in 1947. The London *Theatre World* (May 1947) called the production "a notable theatrical event." The drama still holds great power in the playing, as was shown even in the modern dress, sweater-girl production of the New York Phoenix Theatre in March 1955.

Webster was concerned with the problem of evil in the world, more specifically, of sin; for he believed in free will and deliberate choice. He believed, also, that evil is predominant in the present life.

The characters of Webster fall into three general groups. There are the creatures of a single ruling passion, regardless of all others and all else in its fierce drive. Such are Vittoria and Brachiano in *The White Devil.* Then there are the cynics, who see all mankind as fools or knaves, amid whom they coldly calculate their own way to power. Such a one is Flamineo, Vittoria's brother. Finally there are the good, like Brachiano's wife Isabella and Vittoria's and Flamineo's mother Cornelia: noble, pitiful, courageous—and passive victims of evil passions not their own. In Webster's plays, the good folk are destroyed in body, but steadfast in soul; the evildoer also is destroyed, recognizing that he is a sinner. Flamineo has "felt the maze of conscience" in his breast. And the hope of a new period of moral order closes the tragedy.

In *The White Devil,* Flamineo, to promote his own fortunes, lays his eager sister Vittoria open to the adulterous passion of Brachiano, by effecting the murders of Brachiano's wife and Vittoria's husband. When his brother Marcello is horrified, Flamineo kills him; their mother Cornelia goes mad with grief. After a trial, Vittoria is imprisoned, but runs away and marries Brachiano. Avengers finally kill Brachiano, Vittoria, and Flamineo.

The power of Webster's play rises not from the succession of melodramatic incidents, but from the deep sense of human nobility that animates the author, despite his dark vision of human life. "Webster is a true tragic poet," said David Cecil in *Poets and Story-Tellers* (1948): "one who, facing the most dreadful and baffling facts of human experience in all their unmitigated horror, yet transmutes them by the depth and grandeur of his vision into a thing of glory." "No poet," said Swinburne, "is morally nobler than Webster."

There is, in *The White Devil,* not so much a direct progression of plot as a succession of dramatic moments: a poignant, then a passionate, then a delicate situation. "Each part," said John Addington Symonds in the preface to the *Mermaid Edition,* "is sketched with equal effort after luminous effect upon a murky background; and the whole play is a mosaic of these parts." Tableaux and processions, pageantry and related fantastic or symbolic dreams, irrelevant though they may sometimes seem to the progression of the plot, are nonetheless essential to Webster's purpose. They bring before us, in multicolored life, the crowding temptations and the devilish drives that press men into devious ways of evil. We watch, in dumb show, the death of Isabella, by kissing a poisoned picture of her husband Brachiano. In dumb show, too, we watch Flamineo's murder of Vittoria's husband, Camillo. Such scenes stir the emotions deeply as the words. Even grimmer is the scene in which Brachiano's enemies, disguised as monks come to comfort him when sick, proceed to strangle him. "This is a true love-knot, sent from the Duke of Florence," smiles one of them, as he slips the noose around Brachiano's neck. Here irony tightens horror.

Webster colors this dramatic flow with a dark beauty of language—a diction at once poetic and struck deep with the diseases Webster sees in life. Through his language we feel, as Clayton Hamilton has said, "flashes of poetic insight into the elemental emotions which throb in the heart of man, passages of awful grandeur which stir to the very core, touches of delicate tenderness relieving the gloom that hovers over a tale of human ruin." Webster's figures press his oppositions, as when Brachiano exclaims

"Woman to man Is either a god or a wolf." Even speaking of ordinary things, the metaphors seem a lightning flash that briefly illuminates the nether darkness: "You speak as if a man Should know what fowl is *coffined* in a baked meat Afore you cut it open;" and in more homely fashion, "They that sleep with dogs will rise with fleas." The most frequent motifs are of poison, which kills from concealment, and infection, which corrupts before 'tis seen.

The character of Vittoria Corombona is superbly drawn. She suggests the murders of her husband and Brachiano's wife, through a dream she tells of a yew-tree. By conceiving his scene thus, David Cecil has pointed out, Webster "turns an ugly episode of lust and treachery and assassination into a thing of sinister magnificence. The strangely precise images set the fancy mysteriously and sublimely astir: the ear thrills to the subtle muted music of the versification. Yet though he beautifies the horror of his scene, he does not soften it." At her trial, Vittoria stands splendid in intellect and courage, brazening it out like virtue itself, indignant. "This White Devil of Italy," declared Lamb, "sets off a bad cause so speciously, and pleads with such an innocence-resembling boldness, that we seem to see that matchless beauty of her face which inspires such gay confidence into her, and are ready to expect, when she has done her pleadings, that her very judges, her accusers, the grave ambassadors who sit as spectators, and all the court, will rise and make proffer to defend her, in spite of the utmost conviction of her guilt." This "diversivolent woman"—"fair as the leprosy." Hazlitt called her, "dazzling as the lightning"—is a true figure of tragedy.

The deftness and delicacy of Webster's language enable him to move from the arousal of horror to the evocation of tenderness and pity. The madness of Cornelia spills forth in a song that suggests the mad Ophelia's: "Call unto his funeral dole The ant, the field mouse, and the mole"—of which Lamb said: "I never saw anything like this Dirge, except the ditty that reminds Ferdinand of his (supposedly) drowned father in *The Tempest.** As that is of the water, watery, so this is of the earth, earthy. Both have that intenseness of feeling, which seems to resolve itself into the element which it contemplates."

This power over language, this nobility of soul, enabled Webster, "Shakespeare's greatest pupil in the art of tragedy," Symonds called him, to carry the tragedy of blood—begun by Kyd, developed by Tourneur, transformed in *Hamlet**—to its ultimate perfection. With Webster's death, the species died—though its ghosts roam through the realm of gory melodrama. In *The White Devil,* we see the tragedy of blood at its noblest and best.

The play has retained its grim power in recent revivals. Among them: State University of Iowa, May 1960. Circle in the Square, opening December 6, 1965, for 152 performances. London, 1969, 39 performances in repertory.

THE DUCHESS OF MALFI *John Webster*

The second of Webster's great tragic studies of the consequences of sin in the world, *The Duchess of Malfi,* 1613?, is based upon a story in Bandello's Italian *Novelle,* retold in Painter's *Palace of Pleasure,* 1566. The play was published in 1623, 1640, and 1678. A Spanish play based on the story was written in 1618 by Lope de Vega.

The Duchess of Malfi was revived in London in 1707; it was adapted as

The Fatal Secret in 1735 by Lewis Theobald (emendator of Shakespeare, and victim of Pope's *Dunciad*). Webster's play was produced again in 1850, 1859, 1864, 1869, and 1892; again in 1935, 1939; and in 1945 with John Gielgud; it was brought to New York in a modern version by W. H. Auden, opening October 15, 1946, with Elisabeth Bergner as the Duchess, John Carradine as the Cardinal, and Canada Lee as Bosola.

In the play, Bosola, servant of the Duchess, seeks advancement by betraying her to her brothers, Duke Ferdinand and the Cardinal. She is secretly married to her steward, Antonio; her brothers, desiring her duchy, have warned her not to remarry; at their instigation Bosola tortures and murders the Duchess and two of her children. Bosola has been corrupted by the evil world; he has followed its unscrupulous pattern. Now he repents, and warns Antonio. But by a bitter irony, seeking to kill the Cardinal, Bosola accidentally kills his new friend. Then Bosola attacks the Cardinal; Duke Ferdinand, now gone mad, interferes; and all three die.

Few Elizabethan dramas outside of Shakespeare's have been more highly praised than *The Duchess of Malfi*. Newspaper comments of the nineteenth century include that in the London *Lady's Newspaper* (November 23, 1850): "The plot of this play is simple to the last degree, but the author has filled it with horror, mental and physical, to its extreme complement." The *London Times* (April 14, 1868) declared: "*The Duchess of Malfi* is most admirably placed on the stage. . . . It is impossible to speak too highly of this magnificent production."

The use of devices of horror is greater in *The Duchess of Malfi* than in *The White Devil**: around the imprisoned Duchess rings the clamour of lunatics; the effigy of her murdered husband is displayed to her; the ingenious and perverse cruelty of her torturer summons before her on earth the hell to which, hereafter, not all their devilish will can make her fall. This scene rings with horrendous grandeur in Webster, and in the description of Charles Lamb: "All the several parts of the dreadful apparatus with which the duchess's death is ushered in are not more remote from the conceptions of ordinary vengeance than the strange character of suffering which they seem to bring upon their victim is beyond the imagination of ordinary poets. As they are not like inflictions of this life, so her language seems not of this world. She has lived among horrors till she is become 'native and endowed unto that element.' She speaks the dialect of despair; her tongue has a snatch of Tartarus and the souls in bale. What are 'Luke's iron crown,' the brazen bull of Phalaris, Procrustes' bed, to the waxen images which counterfeit death, to the wild masque of madmen, the tombmaker, the bellman, the living person's dirge, the mortification by degrees? To move a horror skilfully, to touch a soul to the quick, to lay upon fire as much as it can bear, to wean and weary a life till it is ready to drop, and then step in with more instruments to take its last forfeit—this only a Webster can do. Writers of an inferior genius may 'upon horror's head horrors accumulate,' but they cannot do this. They mistake quantity for quality, they 'terrify babes with painted devils,' but they know not how a soul is capable of being moved; their terrors want dignity, their affrightments are without decorum." This, agreed Hazlitt, "is not the bandying of idle words and rhetorical commonplaces, but the writhing and conflict, and the supreme colloquy, of man's nature with itself."

The Duchess of Malfi is a supreme example of the tragedy of blood. In fact, "considered *solely as a tragedy of blood*," said Clayton Hamilton, "the mechanism of *The Duchess of Malfi* is superior to that of *Hamlet*. While

Shakespeare clung to the clumsy figure of the ghost crying out for revenge, Webster wisely discarded an expedient so essentially mechanical.
While Shakespeare relinquished the stock villain, who had always been
one of the most interesting characters in the tragedy of blood, Webster
applied his genius to creating creatures of flesh and blood to replace the
one-sided figures of his predecessors, and gave us such admirable studies
as the contrasted Machiavellians, Ferdinand and the Cardinal, and the
heroic rogue, Bosola. The action of Webster's play is simpler and more
concentrated than that of the Shakespearean tragedy, and the climactic
development of the revenge and the counter-vengeance is magnificently
handled."

The simple and tender touch of Shakespeare is matched in Ferdinand's
words as he looks on the body of his twin sister: "Cover her face; my eyes
dazzle; she died young."

The Duchess and "the white devil" of Webster's other play are both
figures of intense dramatic power; as Swinburne aptly calls them, Webster's "two sovereign types of feminine daring and womanly endurance,
the heroine of suffering and the heroine of sin." Although the Duchess
(like Caesar in Shakespeare's *Julius Caesar**) is the early center of sympathy, Bosola (like Brutus) is the chief driving force in the play. Through the
fierce course of Bosola's sinning, and the belated ills of his repentance, as
well as through the Duchess's courage and faith, the noble moral fervor of
Webster combines with his poetic and dramatic power, to vivify and enrich, as lightning over a stormy landscape, the passion-torn pattern of *The
Duchess of Malfi.*

The plays of Webster, as the poet H. D. suggested in *By Avon River*
(1949), give us, "in a Renaisssance setting, parables that represented unbearable actuality." His was a tortured England, and his works "are outstanding examples of the black wave of terror and despair that swept over
the island as a result of the dissolution of the monasteries, and the seven
years spent by Mary in trying to restore them. Following the fires of
martyrdom and the reeking stench of the unburied was an aftermath or
after-birth of Hell." If England, then, what with plagues and persecutions,
took on the fetid air of a shambles, Webster's plays, for all their dark
thunder, are a stand of nobility amid the ruin.

The 1946 revival received mixed reviews. Brooks Atkinson called it
"Shakespeare without the magnificence." John Gassner, however, called it
"a timeless nightmare in which human beings are writhing grubs in
darkness." The acting may have been to blame: Canada Lee, a black in
"whiteface," was disappointing, and the coy Elisabeth Bergner made the
heroine a very—not veritable—arch Duchess.

By Shakespeare alone, said Swinburne, "have the finest scenes and passages of this tragedy ever been surpassed or equaled in pathos and passion, in subtlety and strength, in harmonious variety of art and infallible
fidelity to nature." After the Duchess is arrested, said Clayton Hamilton,
"there follows that magnificent symphony of terror which, with the single
exception of the third act of *Othello,* is the greatest single act in the
English language." James Russell Lowell added, of Webster's two plays:
"Aristotle's admirable distinction between the horrible and the terrible in
tragedy was never better illustrated and confirmed than in the Duchess
and Vittoria."

The play continues to win revivals. Among them: Phoenix (New York),
March 19, 1957, directed by Jack Landau. IASTA, 1966. In London, 1960,

with Max Adrian, Eric Porter, Patrick Wymark. RSC Stratford-upon-Avon, 1957 and 1971. Pitlochry Festival, 1967. OffOffBway, 1983.

THE AWAKENING OF SPRING   *Frank Wedekind*

Beginning as a German journalist, then a novelist and playwright, Frank Wedekind (1864-1918) organized a theatrical company and toured his native country. He acted in many of his own plays. As a dramatist, he was opposed to the naturalism of his time, "a mere copy of life"; his plays move with an intensified imagination, eerie and at times spectral, that makes him a forerunner of expressionism.

Two themes give force to Wedekind's dramas. Most pervasive is his picture of the sexual impulse as the driving force of life. Man refuses, as Wedekind sees it, to admit this fact, and with various forms of hypocrisy seeks to hide this basic urge. Civilization itself, indeed, seems to the playwright little more than the gloss men have set over the natural impulse of sex. The second theme is the inherent conflict he sees in man's striving for both integrity and happiness.

The most noted of Wedekind's dramas is *The Awakening of Spring*, 1891 (not produced until 1905, when Reinhardt's production ran for 325 performances). This drama pictures the sexual urge as it becomes manifest at puberty, and shows how the conventional educational methods may wreak havoc in the adolescent mind. In poetic, but quite natural and frank presentation, *The Awakening of Spring* carries us through fifteen scenes, that bring the inquiring minds and urging bodies of three children to disastrous consequences. Moritz, a serious, thoughtful lad, full of wonder about life, failing in his school examinations, commits suicide. Meanwhile, the mother of Wendla, one of the school girls, avoids Wendla's questions about the sister's new baby; and when a storm drives young Melchior and Wendla to seek shelter in a hay-loft, they discover for themselves the facts of life. Wendla dies in an attempted abortion. Melchior, escaping from the reformatory to which he is sent, comes upon Wendla's tombstone. Here, the spirit of Moritz and a masked man representing Life struggle for Melchior, who finally decides it is his obligation to live.

For all its frankness, *The Awakening of Spring* is a tender and deeply touching drama. The scene in the hay-loft is delicate and moving; it is played in darkness, faintly broken by lightning flashes. There is masterly irony in the faculty meeting scene, with the hide-bound teachers arguing more insistently over whether or not to open the window than over Melchior's behavior. There is a gruesome scene in the reform school to which Melchior is sent, that most hopefully misnamed of institutions! Building its power—in a technique the expressionists borrowed—through a succession of rapid scenes, *The Awakening of Spring* drives relentlessly home its picture of the effect of hypocrisy, of sex evasion, upon these adolescents. The play is, indeed, as the *New York Dramatic Mirror* said when it was presented here in German (March 22, 1912) "an intense and absorbing work."

The Awakening of Spring was presented in English in New York on March 30, 1917, with Fania Marinoff as Wendla, as a "membership" production under the auspices of the *Medical Review of Reviews*. License Commissioner Bell saw a rehearsal at noon, and forbade the play, but a court injunction enabled the matinee to begin at four o'clock. The reviews ranged from deepest moral indignation to high artistic praise.

Burns Mantle led the chorus of protest, calling the play "a purposeful but profitless drama that does not act. . . . All that it reveals to Anglo-Saxon minds, and particularly to Anglo-Saxon youth, is at once suggestive of hidden nastiness and a thoroughly unhealthy adolescence. . . . We naturally resent the assumption that we now stand in serious need of help from the outside. . . . We resent it particularly at this time and from this source, when a bloody war is each day proving that however materially efficient Mr. Wedekind's frankly-spoken and seriously philosophical people may have become, they still stand sadly in need of a spiritual rebirth to put them on so much as even terms with the civilized peoples of the earth. We resent it again when we note that practically every vice report that is published, and every degenerate tendency or crime that is traced to its source, is found rooted in minds and muck that are not native to this country. The task of clearing the scum from the melting pot is ours, for we are all in it; but we have a fixed notion that both the method and the manner in which the task shall finally be accomplished should also be ours. . . . As propaganda they like it in Berlin. Its creation there would indicate that they need it in Berlin. We are quite content that they should keep it in Berlin."

Without dragging in the World War to damn Wedekind, the *Times* also objected to the play: "Adolescent sexual perversions are discussed and acted in this drama with coarse freedom. That they are common enough in the United States to warrant the exploitation of such cases in the theatre is certainly open to question. . . . Scenes like the one showing flagellation among children cannot be anything but degrading unless before an audience of physicians and alienists." The *Globe* (April 3, 1917), on the other hand, expressed regret that this "powerful, masterly play" had to be seen under such untoward auspices: "No other work in literature so sympathetically interprets the storm and stress of youth at the age when it is torn between its desires and the dread of the unknown. . . . Instead of being invited to see it as a work of art by a distinguished author we were asked to submit our dull heads to instruction and homily. How Frank Wedekind would have grinned if he could have seen Henrietta Rodman informing us in tragic tones that this was an historical event second in importance only to the Russian Revolution—a piece of innocent blatherumskite to which we listened in respectful stupefaction not unmixed with explosive titters." The *World* thought the play limited in its appeal: "Indeed this is a play primarily for parents, and poor little pregnant Wendla, grown wise too late, strikes the keynote when she exclaims 'Oh, Mother, why didn't you tell me everything?'" The *Sun* felt that Wedekind had seen beyond the immediate situation: "He takes the fact, known to every parent in the world, that adolescence is beset with sexual difficulties, and builds on it a heart-breaking, sinister, and capricious tragedy."

The play proved still touching in an OffBway production opening October 9, 1955.

In numerous plays, Wedekind has dramatized the urgency and primacy of the sexual impulse. Other playwrights who have shown the moon calf, the early flush of new-found love, have, as George Jean Nathan compared them to Wedekind, taken us to Wedekindergarten. Seldom has there been a more tender, discerning, and poignant dramatic picture of the early rouse of sexual impulse and wonder in groping childhood than in the tragic movement of *The Awakening of Spring*.

Today's problems, including the question—now being argued in the English courts—as to whether the National Health Service may give contraceptive advice and devices to young girls without notifying their parents, indicate the continuing relevance of the play. Translated as *Spring('s) Awakening,* it has had two adaptations recently: by Bert Greene, 1955, in New York; in Britain, 1963; and by Thomas Osborn, London, 1965, York Festival (Cambridge University Mummers), 1966, and London, 1967.

MARAT/SADE   *Peter Weiss*

The Persecution and Assassination of Jean-Paul Marat, as Performed by the Inmates of the Asylum of Charenton Under the Direction of the Marquis de Sade (1963) is set in the communal bathroom of the asylum in France, 1808. (Marat was assassinated in 1793; Sade, 1740-1814, sent by Napoleon, spent his last thirteen years in the asylum.) The play is by Peter Weiss (1916-1982), son of a Swiss woman and a Czechoslovakian, born in Berlin, moved to Sweden in 1939. In German free verse, *Marat/Sade* combines intellectual interest with emotional shock.

Before a group of aristocratic spectators, the asylum director Coulmier presents the actor-inmates. Marat, whose painful skin condition keeps him always in a tub, cries for violence, for a bloodbath; the ragged chorus cries, "Revolution NOW!" In the turbulence Charlotte Corday enters, followed by the Girondist Duperret, who lusts for her. The Marquis de Sade has her flagellate him with her long hair, while the lunatics whistle to the rhythm of her blows. A demagogue writhes in a straitjacket as he rants a call for revolution; he is beaten by the guards. From a pile of guillotined heads, simulated by the inmates, a clownlike sweeper empties a bucket of blood. Sade declares that imagination is the only reality, and calls for a revolution that will impose uniformity. The herald announces Intermission.

When action resumes it is increasingly disorderly. A nude man climbs through a trapdoor and merges with the other excited inmates; Charlotte Corday reenters and kills Marat. The director, ordering the nuns and nurses to use their batons to subdue the patients, says: "Things are better now"; but it is the nuns and nurses who are overpowered; the inmates cry, "Napoleon! Nation! Revolution! Copulation!" as Sade stands on a chair grinning in triumph, and the asylum director orders the curtain down.

The play's premiere was at the West Berlin Schiller, April 29, 1963, with Ernest Schroder as Sade; Peter Mosbacher, Marat. Opening August 2, 1964, in an English version by Geoffrey Skelton, the verse by Adrian Mitchell, it was given 68 performances by the RSC, directed by Peter Brook, with Glenda Jackson as Charlotte Corday; Clive Revill, Marat; Patrick Magee, Sade. With Ian Richardson as Marat, the other two unchanged, the RSC went to the New York Martin Beck December 27, 1965, for 144 performances, and won the Tony and the Critics' Circle awards. Peter Brook tried to combine the total involvement of the audience, as in Artaud's theatre of cruelty, with "pouring cold water on the emotions so that the intellectual and critical faculties could have full rein," as in the epic theatre of Piscator and Brecht.

The Revolution came and went,
Unrest replaced by discontent.

A 1970 New Orleans production was raided by the police. The play was presented in 1970 in Manitoba, Canada; in New York by CSC, 1971-1972; in Stamford, Conn., 1975; at Tulane University, 1981.

Watching, pondering, the disorder and violence of a revolution in a madhouse, one may come to consider that in a mad world, however idealistic the dreamers of revolution, they will be stamped out by the mindless many fed on clichés and slogans, whose passions are controlled and propelled by the steel-hard bludgeoner and the equally cruel cunning conniver castoff—opportunists both, aware that attaining and maintaining power depends upon their subjection of the passive or grumbling obedient and elimination of the muttering or maneuvering resistant. The usual end of revolution is the substitution of a different form of tyranny. What must be changed is not a system of government but the impulses of human nature. As the sage Ananda K. Coomaraswamy put it, our future is metanoia or paranoia. Meanwhile we live in a mad merry world, my masters.

A play called *Madame de Sade,* said the author, Yukio Mishima (b. 1925; in 1970 he committed seppuku: ritual suicide), presents Sade as seen through women's eyes. Five women discuss his deeds. Chief are the antagonistic Mme. de Montreuil, his mother-in-law; Renée, his frightened but fascinated wife; and the dominating Comtesse de Saint-Fond, leather-clad and whip in hand, who relishes the story of her having served as a nude "table" in the celebration of a Black Mass. Renée adds to the details of her husband's orgies. In Japanese fashion, the play has long formal speeches; as in ancient Greek and French classical drama, it relates much of the action instead of showing it. Comte Donatien Alphonse François de Sade (he never was, though he called himself, Marquis) does not appear in this play. He knocks on the door at the end; the exclamations and expressions of the various ladies then reveal emotions ranging from disgust, through fear, frightened attraction, to anticipant lickerish delight with a snap of the whip, as the curtain slowly falls.

In translation by Donald Keene, *Madame de Sade* was produced October 30, 1972, in Lucille Lortel's matinee series at the Theatre de Lys, with Diane Kagan as Renée and Ruth Ford as the Comtesse, a fit female Sade. Shown at the King's Head, London, opening August 14, 1975, it was called by *Stage and Television Today* "interesting and at times fascinating." It pictures the man who gave the language the term *sadism* (sexual exultation in giving pain) from the more pertinent feminine angle, which is almost obliterated in the vivid social and political sweep of *Marat/Sade.*

GOAT SONG   *Franz Werfel*

The tragic *Bockgesang (Goat Song),* 1920, of Franz Werfel (Austrian, 1890-1945) probably roused more controversy than any other modern play since the dramas of Ibsen.* Not even those of Pirandello* are open to so many interpretations as this greatest play of the Austrian poet, dramatist and novelist—best known in America for his novel and motion picture, *The Song of Bernadette,* 1941.

The surface story of *Goat Song* is an eerie one. In a Serbian village, about 1790, there escapes from its secret prison a monster, half-human, half-goat, which its farmer-parents had been hiding for many years. The sight of its awful shadow across the sky bloodies the world, as peasants, gypsies, and Jews revolt against the landowners. Ikons and relics are smashed; the countryside is devastated. Stanja, betrothed to the monster's normal brother, Mirko, but led by the student Juvan to join the revolt, goes as a living sacrifice to the monster. The Turkish soldiers come and crush the revolt. Mirko and Juvan are killed; the monster's carcass is exhibited by the scavenger, a penny a peep. Despite the burning of their farmstead, for the first time the monster's parents, Stevan and his wife, discover peace. And beneath the breast of Stanja the child of the monster is coming to be.

Goat Song excited audiences all over Europe. In New York, the Theatre Guild gave it elaborate production (January 25, 1926), directed by Jacob Ben-Ami, with Edward G. Robinson, Albert Bruning, Blanche Yurka, George Gaul, Lynn Fontanne, Helen Westley, Alfred Lunt, and Herbert Yost, with a great cyclorama for the ominous signs in the heavens, above the background of the Serbian hills. Discussion meetings were held, to elucidate the drama's meaning.

Bockgesang, goat song, is a literal translation of the Greek word *trag-oedia,* which means, and gives us the word, *tragedy.* The early Greek tragedy may have sprung from rituals of the goat-god—perhaps linked with the meaning observed in the Biblical story of the scapegoat. Thus there is a literal binding of the monster, in Werfel's play, with the release of passions that, by their very explosion, leads to a release from passion, to a calm and peacefulness—within which the seeds of the next revolution brood. Thus the goat-monster represents the spirit of revolution, which through oppression bursts to violence, by that very violence defeats its ends, and slumps to weary acquiescence in which the cycle is renewed. But beyond these general meanings, the details of symbolic reference multiply, until, as the *New Yorker* (February 6, 1926) declared: "every hen and loiterer, housewife or gypsy, stands for a whole class, a nation at large, some force or foolishness in the human race." And beyond the political significancies, out of the apprehensions of the parents that led them to hide away their monster-son (as with the monster of Calderon's *Life Is A Dream,* in the world of symbols, and with the horned human of Crom-melynck's *The Magnificent Cuckold* *) rises the lesson that what we dread, we create: our greatest evils are the figments of our fears, which become the realities we have to face. The world today should take heed.

The atmosphere of *Goat Song* is given goulish intensity, through the media of expressionism, of which mode Werfel was a pioneer. His rework-ing of Euripides' *The Trojan Women,* * Wolfgang Paulsen in the *Columbia Dictionary of Modern European Literature* (1947) hailed as "a milestone in the history of the expressionist theatre." In *Goat Song* scenes drunk with excitement reel in and out amid scenes of tenderness and loving promise—the wild pagan orgy in the despoiled church, the deathlike quiet among the charred ruins of the farm, where the monster's parents discover peace. The goat-man itself is, as Alexander Woollcott stressed, "unseen save for one monstrous shadow thrown athwart the sun, unheard save for one dreadful cry out of the shadows (when the woman comes in to him), as mighty and as destroying a sound as ever I heard issue from a human throat." *Goat Song* is, Woollcott continued in the pamphlet *Second Thoughts on First Nights,* "a timeless, untethered play, of the stature, say, of *Peer Gynt.* *"

Neatly the development of the play draws us into its symbols. The whole of the first act is on the realistic level; we may suspect, but we need not seek, further heights of meaning. Werfel, said the *Boston Transcript* (Feb-ruary 16, 1926): "evokes the concentrating and intensifying word, the impinging image, the sustained speech, that are trait and emotion caught out of the moment, the personage—the impulses and deeds of humanity thick and deep behind. . . . A veracious realist might not better achieve the scene of the outcasts and the elders in petition and repulses. A poetic playwright might not better snare the supernatural promptings and stirrings through the vagabonds and visionaries of the inn." Thus out of the action wells the vision, in a tangled growth of beauty and horror like the flaming passage of mankind.

Werfel's other plays move out of the expressionist technique." Still using some of its devices is the "magic trilogy" *Mirror Man,* 1920, a fantastic drama of man's conquest over his evil self, as Thamal at last beats back the temptations of the "mirror man," who seeks to lead him into sin. *Juarez and Maximilian,* 1923, produced in New York in 1926, is in the form of a realistic historical play, but is rather a psychological study of the Austrian Archduke Maximilian, Emperor of Mexico, 1864-1867, who is presented as a true humanitarian, refusing all recourse to violence, who goes to his death gladly, rather than relinquish his ideals. *Paul Among the Jews,* 1926, picturing the moment of the breaking of Christianity from Judaism, and *The Kingdom of God in Bohemia,* 1930, a drama of the breakdown of ideals with the acquisition of power among the fifteenth century Hussites, and the disillusionment of their leader, Prokop, renew Werfel's earlier interest in religion. *The Eternal Road,* 1935, is less a drama than a great spectacle, a succession of episodes from the harried history of the Jews, in another dark hour of persecution. Indeed, all of Werfel's plays focus upon the deeper values of life. Most vivid and most searching of them is *Goat Song,* showing how both fear and oppression breed violence and how futile violence is. The eerie plot and bizarre effects of production make one feel as though one's mind were heaving in an atomburst; but dimly, on restoring foot to earth, one glimpses stars. There were revivals at ELT, 1953 and 1959.

A TRILOGY   *Arnold Wesker*

Arnold Wesker (b. 1932) drew attention with three separate but interlinked plays, presented in London in three successive years, then (June 7, 1960) shown together at the London Royal Court.

Chicken Soup with Barley opened in Coventry July 7, 1958, and came to the Royal Court the next week. Dominating mother Sarah, in 1936, is actively Marxist-Leninist. Her weak-willed husband, Harry, prefers to sleep. He does so most of the time in Act II, 1946, being usually out of work. By 1956, Act III, he has had a second stroke and is partly paralyzed. Daughter Ada, early a firebrand, has grown disillusioned, and moves to the country to seek a new life with her equally disillusioned husband, Dave. Younger Ronnie, still eager for life in 1946, ten years later is ready to follow his father. The last words of the play are Sarah's urging: "Ronnie, if you don't care, you'll die."

The play balances a sense of social responsibility against an individual growth of unconcern. On the personal level, the *Observer* commented: "the play's progress is circular; on the individual, it seems to move in a straight line. Personally, the play seems to be about the recurrent pattern of behavior from generation to generation; socially, it is about the working-class's loss of purpose with the arrival of a socialist government and the Welfare State."

Roots (1959), the action of which occurs within a fortnight, presents one personal response to the problem. Beatie Bryant, engaged to Ronnie in London, lives in Norfolk with her farm-worker parents. Her mother is stupid but savage, especially when Ronnie (who does not appear in the play) sends word that he's not coming to meet Beatie's family, as the marriage won't work. The mother feels that her anger is justified, but Beatie begins to think for herself. "We want to be third-rate—we got it! I'm beginning, on my own two feet. I'm beginning." The superb acting of Joan Plowright helped give the awakening of Beatie the ring of truth, wherein lies its value. *Roots* had seventy-two performances in a May 6, 1961, revival at the Mayfair.

I'm Talking about Jerusalem (1960) follows Ada and Dave, who in the second act of *Chicken Soup with Barley* had moved to the country, to seek a life away from the domination of the machine. After a first act in which Sarah and Ronnie help them unpack, the play proper begins. Dave is dismissed by his employer, a squire-figure of the old school, for a bit of petty pilfering "and, even more, lying about it." The Labour Government has in the meantime been voted out of office; the couple accept defeat in the countryside and move back to London. Dave recognizes that as an individual he is not important; and they recall father Harry's frequent remark about life: "It'll purify itself"—but the millennium will not take place in their lifetime. The age-old resignation but patient hopefulness of the Jew carries them on.

The program notes of the Royal Court June 7, 1960, bore comment by author Wesker: "My people are not caricatures, they are real (though fiction). And though the picture I have drawn of them is a harsh one, yet still my tone is not of disgust. I am at one with these people—it is only that I am annoyed with them and myself . . . *Chicken Soup with Barley* handles the Communist aspect. *Roots* handles the personal aspect, that is, Ronnie feels you can only teach by example. *I'm Talking About Jerusalem* is a sort of study in a William Morris kind of Socialism. If you like, the three plays are three aspects of Socialism, played through the lives of a Jewish family. These are not true life stories. They are distillations."

It is not his discussion of Socialism, but his sympathetic observation of his characters, that enlightens the trilogy of Arnold Wesker.

DIAMOND LIL   *Mae West*

As actress and author, Mae West (1892-1980) occupies in the American theatre a special niche that she carved for herself. She swaggers in it superbly, the tired businesss man's bosom friend. To establish herself as prime exponent of one aspect of our life, she had not only to develop her special type of performance, but also to write the plays to which that performance adds body and form. No picture of the American theatre would be complete without Mae West.

In the United States, women are the dominant sex. They own most of the property; they shape most of the mores. In the traditional eye, women fall into two categories: mistress or mother—sinner or saint. From this division flows man's attitude toward sex: it does not exist (saint), or (sinner) it must be hidden. It peeps through, for a wink or a leer, in "off-color" stories, in musical comedy skits and girlie shows. There are but flicks and flashes; in America, sex must hide.

Mae West, as actress and author, flaunts sex in bold bedizenment. She gives release to the greatest American inhibition. Yet—despite Comstockian protests and puritanical raids—we are not shocked, but delighted. For—and this is her subtlety and her success—Mae West adds just the touch of paraded effrontery that makes her marketing of her wares a superb self-parody; and sex becomes sexless. So caught are we in the touching-up of the performance, that the lass is no longer lascivious. Mae West alone, said Ellis St. Joseph, has made saltpeter glamorous. "Sexcess" is the secret of her success. Mae West alone has made us laugh at sex.

Of the three or four plays in which Mae West has bosomed herself to America, the best is *Diamond Lil.* I say three *or* four advisedly, because *The Pleasure Man,* which opened in New York October 1, 1928, seems to be a variation of *The Drag,* which, after various encounters with the censors and the police, closed before reaching Broadway. In both plays, the big scene is a wild party of homosexual carousing, but the "pleasure man" himself is abnormal only in the extent, not in the direction, of his desires.

Before this play, Mae West wrote under the pseudonym Jane Mast, and on April 26, 1926, opened in New York in a play called *Sex,* for which she spent ten days in jail. *Sex* is the story of Margie La Mont, a gay girl of a disorderly house, whose exploits carry her from Montreal to Trinidad, with one torrid love scene and with her introduction, seemingly a sweet society girl, as the fiancée of a young man of high society. It is after Margie recognizes this young man's mother as a woman who had come to the Montreal dive on a joy party, that Margie gives up the social whirl for her less complicated joys with a sailor. *Sex,* said the Telegraph (April 28, 1926) hits "the speed limit of suggestiveness"; the *American* declared that "a more flaming, palpitating play has not been seen hereabouts for some time." But the *New Yorker* critic averred that Mae West's pretending to be an innocent girl of wealth and refinement "I shall always cherish as one of my fondest memories in the theatre."

On April 9, 1928, *Diamond Lil,* the best of the Mae Westerns, came to New York for a run of 176 performances. The story of New York's Bowery in the 1890's was "suggested by Jack Linder," but the flavor of the dialogue and the overtone that gives the events their tang are wholly Mae West's. The play established the author-star in her unique and unassailable position in the American theatre. London was less hospitable in 1932; but in 1948 *Diamond Lil* ran there for ten months. Again in New York, opening February 5, 1949, it continued for 181 performances. *Cue* (February 12, 1949) hailed the return of "an indestructible American institution named Mae West. . . . She could read the budget, and make it sound erotic." After a long tour, the play came back to New York on September 14, 1951, but now with an overemphasis on its physical aspects, crystallized in the fact that on opening night detectives lurked about while Mae West wore over a million dollars' worth of diamonds. Then they were safely carted back to storage, where it is perhaps time that the play joined them.

Diamond Lil is set in the Bowery saloon of Gus Jordan, district boss and runner of white slaves to Rio de Janeiro. Flashiest of the fancy girls is his mistress Diamond Lil, who wears impossibly fabulous costumes, honey-colored ostrich plumes, and more diamonds than the Metropolitan horseshoe, and sleeps in a pink bed shaped like Leda's swan. Among the other men who look, with equal ardor but varying degrees of impetuousness and possessiveness, upon the luscious and lickerish Lil are a powerfully sexed Latin, a Bowery politician who is double-crossing Gus Jordan, an escaped convict—who comes dramatically into Lil's bedroom during a violent storm—and a Salvation Army Captain. Lil always loved a uniform. And neatly Lil plays upon these men so that one gets rid of another—except for the Salvation Army man, who turns out to be no other than "the Hawk," of the Secret Service. He arrests Gus Jordan, and salvages Diamond Lil for himself. The curtain falls on their embrace. Her last words are: "I always knew you could be had."

Through the scenes of this "lurid and frequently rousing melodrama" walk shoplifters and stagger drunks. In the saloon, we watch a floor show, with singing waiters, ancient yet agile acrobats, and Diamond Lil flaunting her charms in songs of the 1890's and a lively version of *Frankie and Johnny.* One scene sends genuine shivers along delighted spines. Rita, the procuress from Rio, jealous for her Latin lover, takes a stiletto from her stocking and steals upon Lil; watching in the mirror, Lil turns and pins her assailant to the couch—only to discover that the dagger has pierced Rita's back and killed her. (In the 1951 production, Lil viciously stabbed the dame.) A knock at the door; it's a policeman. And as the officer warns Lil that her convict lover has broken jail and may be expected to visit her, she combs the long tresses of the dead woman, and talks to her as though to a resting friend, until the policeman shuts the door and she is safe alone.

Diamond Lil is a woman of no uncertain pathway. When one of the girls exclaims: "Goodness, what beautiful diamonds!" her instant reponse flicks: "Goodness had nothing to do with it, dearie." While she may seem only a peahen in a gilded cage, she is really a shrewd and thoroughly competent woman, decent, too, by the dingy lights of the Bowery. When the Salvation Army Captain remarks that the cold gleam of her diamonds reflects the emptiness of her soul, Lil's thoughts for a spell turn to self-examination; and you may believe—if you are the sort of playgoer that looks beyond the final curtain—that the Captain's ethical teaching (combined with his lusty love) will keep Lil faithful to him. It is to the Captain that she speaks the line that became Mae West's trade-mark: "Come up 'n' see me some time!"

Diamond Lil, like a knife in a poison-bite that cuts deeper than the snake fangs, so digs into sex that it makes sex clean. The play is, said the *New York Times,* "amply if somewhat embarrassingly entertaining;" but the embarrassment is rather at our usual shamefast attitude than at its present purging. The story and color of the play, as the *New Yorker* on February 2, 1949, quoted its own review of 1928, capture "a certain flash brashiness that reached a climax in the underworld of New York in the 1890's, as few subtler playwrights could have done it." But *Diamond Lil* survives, not for its colorful background and eventful story, but for its unique and superbly extravagant presentation, at once exposure and exposé, of sex. But who will enact Mae West?

HÄNSEL AND GRETEL   *Adelheid Wette*

Hänsel and Gretel, by Adelheid Wette (German, 1858-1916), with music by Englebert Humperdinck, is the formal German operatic counterpart of the free and easy British pantomime *Babes in the Wood.** The story is retold from the tales of the brothers Grimm. Hänsel and Gretel, dancing about their cottage, are driven out by their mother Gertrude to pick berries in the wood. Their father Peter, a broom-maker comes home; Gertrude remembers that the Crunch Witch lives in the forest, and the parents are alarmed. Meanwhile, the children have been put to sleep by the Sand Man; in their slumbers a guard of angels descends from Heaven to watch over them. They awaken, nevertheless, to find themselves beside the Gingerbread Hut of the Crunch Witch; and when in their hunger they nibble at the house, the Witch seizes them. She decides to fatten Hänsel for her table; but Gretel is a plump enough morsel to enjoy at once. The Witch makes the children help her start the fire. When she wants Gretel to get into the oven, they ask her how; as she shows them, they shove her in and slam the door. Hänsel in joy sings out the Witch's charm; this brings to life the gingerbread figures beside the house; they are children the Witch has charmed. Just as the Witch is burned to a crisp, Peter and Gertrude arrive, overjoyed to find their children alive and safe.

In some productions, the oven with the witch inside explodes. The forest scene, especially the golden stairway of the Angels and the gingerbread hut of the witch, afford opportunity for colorful decoration. At the close come general festivity and a lively dance. *Hänsel and Gretel* is indeed a Grimm tale made gay.

Produced at Weimar December 23, 1893, and at Munich December 30, within two years *Hänsel and Gretel* was heard in England, Italy, Holland, Belgium, and America. New York saw the opera in English for a run opening October 8, 1895; also, in German, at the Metropolitan Opera House. In many cities it has become a traditional Christmas revival. It was presented over television in 1949, and has often been produced with puppets. It is in the New York Metropolitan repertory, 1982.

The music of *Hänsel and Gretel* is pleasantly accordant with the lighter aspects of the story. As H. E. Krehbiel has analyzed it: "Humperdinck has built up the musical structure of *Hänsel and Gretel* in the Wagnerian manner, but with so much fluency and deftness that a musical layman might listen to it from beginning to end without suspecting the fact. . . . The little work is replete with melodies which, though original, bear a strong family resemblance to two little songs which the children sing at the beginning of the first and second acts, and which are veritable nursery songs in Germany. . . . The prelude is built out of a few themes which are associated with some of the most significant elements of the play. . . . They stand for dramatic ideas and agencies; and when these are passed in review, it will be found that not the sinister but the amiable features of the story have been chosen for celebration in the overture." Among the more effective moments are the "Brother, come dance with me," the Sand Man's song "I send the children happy dreams," the Prayer theme that heralds the angels; the Witch's song, and the music of the final rousing celebration. There is the pleasure of childhood memories of fairy tale and wintry evenings, mingled with the pleasure of charming and surging music, in the fairy opera *Hänsel and Gretel*.

LADY WINDERMERE'S FAN   *Oscar Wilde*

With his aesthetic eccentricities and his bland admission of his superior tastes and talents, Oscar Fingall O'Flahertie Wills Wilde (Irish, 1856-1900) caught public attention early. Coming to America for a lecture tour, in 1882, he announced at the Customs House: "I have nothing to declare but my genius."

At once, with *Lady Windermere's Fan*, 1891, Oscar Wilde took London by delighted surprise. Many critics still think the play his most brilliant

social comedy. With a vividly dramatic plot, brilliantly satirized characters, and dialogue that scintillates with bon mot and paradox, *Lady Windermere's Fan* bred a swarm of imitators and excelled them.

The play presents Lady Windermere on the eve of her twenty-first birthday ball, learning that her husband has been most attentive to a Mrs.
Erlynne. When Lord Windermere asks his wife to invite Mrs. Erlynne, she
indignantly refuses; on his insistence, Lady Windermere declares that she
will break her fan across Mrs. Erlynne's face should she be bold enough to
come. Mrs. Erlynne, it happens, is really Lady Windermere's divorced
mother, long away; Lord Windermere, who alone knows her identity, is
trying to help her back into society.

When Mrs. Erlynne attends the ball, Lady Windermere in exasperation
goes to the rooms of her admirer, Lord Darlington. Mrs. Erlynne follows
her, and has persuaded her to go home—when the men, including Lord
Windermere, arrive. The women hide, but Lady Windermere's fan is
noticed; to avert scandal from her daughter, Mrs. Erlynne steps out, and
Lady Windermere slips away unseen. She changes her opinion about Mrs.
Erlynne—who once more beats retreat from England, but this time with
her daughter's esteem.

Announced as *A Good Woman*—its real title kept secret until the eve of
the opening—*Lady Windermere's Fan* came to London February 20, 1892,
for 156 performances. Marion Terry played Mrs. Erlynne; and again in
1904. There were London revivals in 1911 and 1930, and one opening
August 21, 1945, with John Gielgud and Isabel Jeans, for 602 performances. In New York, the play ran for eight months in 1893; it was shown
again in 1904; 1914; 1918, with Margaret Anglin; opening October 14,
1946, with Cornelia Otis Skinner, Estelle Winwood, Henry Daniell, Penelope Ward, and Cecil Beaton (who also designed the colorful costumes and
the sets); and in 1948 at the Provincetown Playhouse. The play has been
frequently produced in community theatres.

At the London premiere, the cordial reception prompted Wilde to say: "I
have enjoyed the evening immensely. The actors have given us a charming
rendering of a delightful play, and your appreciation has been most intelligent. I congratulate you on the great success of your performance, which
persuades me that you think almost as highly of the play as I do myself."

The plot of *Lady Windermere's Fan* took strong hold on the early audiences. For the first two nights, there was no relationship established
between Lady Windermere and Mrs. Erlynne. Then they were revealed to
the audience as mother and daughter, in the last act; but very soon this
revelation was shifted to Act I. This is, of course, its most powerful presentation; when Lady Windermere threatens to strike with her fan the
woman we know is her mother, the audience stiffens with tense expectancy. Brander Matthews exclaimed: "You couldn't have pried me out of my
seat with a crowbar!"

Later, however, the hold of the story weakened. Thus on November 21,
1904, the *London Telegraph* stated: "The play is perhaps not quite so great
as we thought it. It is very clever, very bright, very ingenious, a lightly-
told comedy which affords an excellent entertainment, a brief story which
is throughout interesting and at one moment positively absorbing. But its
figures do not always strike one as psychologically true or observed from
the life; its second act is not very effective—we do evening parties better
on the stage nowadays; there is never enough motive for the sudden lapse
of the heroine from the strict code of morals in which she has hitherto

brought herself up. . . . Despite all criticism, just or unjust, real or imaginary, it is still quite clear that *Lady Windermere's Fan* is a brilliant piece of work. Its dialogue is admirable in point and subtlety; the interest in the last two acts is sustained to the very end; the third act positively grips one by its vivid dramatic power. On Saturday night, when revived at the St. James's Theatre, the play came out as fresh, or almost as fresh, and entrancing as ever. The verbal fireworks had all their old scintillation. . . . We have rarely sat through a premiere in which the verdict of the audience was more unanimous and more overwhelmingly favourable." Another two score years, and we find John Mason Brown (November 9, 1946) turning Wilde's superior laugh back on the playwright: "'One must have a heart of stone to read the death of Little Nell without laughing' was Oscar Wilde's comment on *The Old Curiosity Shop.* Much the same kind of heart is needed nowadays not to laugh at the passages in *Lady Windermere's Fan* which Oscar intended us to take with the utmost gravity. These graver melodramatic interludes are among the funniest in the play. Indeed, among the many paradoxes in which *Lady Windermere's Fan* abounds, perhaps the final one is that all we can now take seriously in the text is its gaiety. If this is so, it is because what Wilde's people say remains wonderfully witty, whereas what they do has become patently absurd. . . . Yet surely there never was a more diverting bad play than *Lady Windermere's Fan*. Or one that has more shimmering virtures." The adverse comment is invariably qualified; and in truth, despite changing social conventions, the story still holds power. "It's true that it has aged," said the New York *Billboard* (February 6, 1932), "but not because of the years since it was written; merely because of the copies that have been made of it since. These copies have made stale and flat and profitless a plot that isn't nearly so bad as it may now seem."

It has also been pointed out that most of Wilde's characters utter Wildean epigrams, that they are artificial, unreal. Thus James Agate in the *Masque* (No. 3, 1947), while pointing out that Mrs. Erlynne is "very nearly the first example on the modern stage of the courtesan, or something of that sort, being treated sympathetically," added: "Mrs. Erlynne is redeemed by her wit, for if a character is witty enough nobody cares whether it is true to life or not. Whereas Lady Windermere is the complete goose." Agate, too, made amends, speaking in the *London Times* (August 26, 1954) of the play's wit: "This is superb throughout and inferior—may one think?—to Congreve and Sheridan only in this, that it does not grow out of the character, but is sprinkled indifferently over fool and fop, like a gross feeder with the pepper-pot."

Wilde's epigrams are often but inversions of a truism, and beneath the epigram lurks melodrama; but there is enough of both to keep the audience waiting for more.

At the close, Mrs. Erlynne goes with Lord Douglas, whom she has promised to marry if he will leave England:

Lord Windermere: Well, you are marrying a very clever woman.
Lady Windermere: Ah, you're marrying a very *good* woman.

Among other revivals: Dallas, Tex., November 1950, directed by Margo Jones. In 1958, with Dolores del Rio in Mexico City. London Queen's, October 13, 1966, with Isobel Jeans, Ronald Lewis, Coral Browne, Juliet Mills, for 146 performances, the costumes by Cecil Beaton outdoing those of *My Fair Lady** in color and daring. In 1973, Harvard. A lavish revival at Guilford, England, October 1978. Briefly, a 1960 musical, *A Delightful Season,* by Don Allan Clayton.

A WOMAN OF NO IMPORTANCE   *Oscar Wilde*

The wit of Wilde continues to sparkle in his dramatic examination of the "double standard," *A Woman of No Importance.* The play presents Lord Illingworth, meeting and liking young Gerald Arbuthnot, offering Gerald a post as his secretary. Gerald's mother insists that he refuse the post, without, however, giving her reason—Illingworth, who turned her away years ago, as "a woman of no importance," is Gerald's father; and she fears the playboy influence Lord Illingworth may have upon her son. Illingworth's nature pops out in his advances to Gerald's fiancée; Gerald is about to beat him, when the mother confesses their relationship. Lord Illingworth, repentant, proposes to marry her; now Mrs. Arbuthnot dismisses him as a man of no importance.

A Woman of No Importance opened in London, April 19, 1893, with Fanny (Mrs. Bernard) Beere, Julia Neilson, and Fred Terry; it ran for 113 performances. The play was revived there in 1907 and 1915. New York saw it on May 26, 1893, with Rose Coghlan and Maurice Barrymore; again in 1916, with Margaret Anglin and Holbrook Blinn. Despite its brilliance, the subject is not conducive to frequent revival, especially in conservative small towns. On its production in New York, the *Illustrated American* (May 27, 1893) declared: "The theme of *le fils naturel,* though long ago seized upon by the dramatic sociologists of France and Germany, is new to the modern English stage. Mr. Wilde has dealt with it daintily, gracefully, and refreshingly, but not masterfully. He has produced an hors-d'oeuvre, not a chef-d'oeuvre." To the charge that Wilde inserts epigrams anywhere, the critic continued: "Mr. Wilde's seemingly adscititious employment of brilliant dialogue, his constant recourse to epigram and aphorism, is not nearly so reprehensible as the circumstance that all of his wit, humor, and repartee have to do with but one subject—woman."

There is, however, more than wit in *A Woman of No Importance.* The play embodies an attack upon the conventional attitude that there is one law for men and another for women. James Agate, indeed, in the *Masque* (No. 3, 1947), stated that this point is too heavily pressed: "Not all the wit in Mayfair can sweeten that little tract called *A Woman of No Importance.* It was judged otherwise in performance. Charles Darnton (April 26, 1916) declared: "Stupid people who imagine themselves to be intelligent when they say merely that Oscar Wilde's plays are 'brilliant' have something to learn from Margaret Anglin, who makes *A Woman of No Importance* so human that clever, superficial tricks of speech leave no more lasting impression than a rainbow." The *New York Dramatic Mirror* (April 29) felt that "this story—of a woman who, betrayed and deserted twenty years before, fights to shield her illegitimate son from the influence of his father—effectively withstands the passing of the years. Its flashing wit still bites, its epigrams still strike home, it is still a keen-edged satire upon society." More probingly, the *Christian Science Monitor* (April 27) pointed out: "After a whole evening of assertion that the conventional right is always wrong, the right triumphs. The woman of no importance becomes of the greatest importance. The man of greatest importance, the man of mighty inverted truths, is revealed as of no importance whatever; his little house of epigrams tumbles about his head. And off toward the sunlit garden, one arm around the son who has chosen her in preference to his father, the other around the girl he has chosen for his wife, walks the woman who has thrilled her audience with a deeper understanding of mother love. Wilde dabbles in the mud till he is tired of it; then he picks a flower. Most of us forget the mud in remembering the fragrance of the flower."

Lord Illingworth, who has lived according to the principle that "nothing succeeds like excess," says of Society: "To be in it is merely a bore. But to be out of it is simply a tragedy." This flippancy—though many have thought it characteristic of Wilde himself—is flayed in this play of Wilde's. Wilde, indeed, can be both caustic and kind. To the critics that had declared *Lady Windermere's Fan* has too little action, he recommended the first act of *A Woman of No Importance*: "There is absolutely no action at all. It is a perfect act." The actress Mrs. Beere, in the London *Sketch* (April 26, 1893), testified: "Mr. Oscar Wilde is a delightful author. Most dramatists are very touchy about their work; but he seemed quite anxious to alter and cut down his play to suit stage purposes." The man must not be mistaken for his characters. Oscar Wilde is, nevertheless, neatly characterized through a remark of Flaubert, who said that a writer should be like God in His universe: present everywhere but visible nowhere. Wilde is visible—manifest—in all his creatures, in all his works.

Judged on the basis of his plays, Wilde is a moralist as well as a wit. Changing social conditions may render less urgent and less timely the theme of *A Woman of No Importance*; the basically tough moral fibre, and the surface of scintillant wit, endure.

It ran for 116 performances in London, opening December 28, 1967, with Tony Britton and Phyllis Calvert, borrowing lines from other plays of Wilde's.

AN IDEAL HUSBAND   *Oscar Wilde*

The many persons that accept Wilde as a trivial spinner of superficial wit, a mere polisher of epigrams, should more thoughtfully look beyond these at the core of his dramas. *An Ideal Husband*, 1894, strikes deep into the conventional codes, as Bernard Shaw pointed out in *Dramatic Opinions and Essays*, "in Sir Robert Chiltern's assertion of the individuality and courage of his wrongdoing as against the idealism of his stupidly good wife, and in his bitter criticism of a love that is only the reward of merit." But when the surface dazzles, few discern the depths.

Lord and Lady Chiltern, as the play opens, are holding a soirée. To this comes Mrs. Chevely, "a genius in the daytime and a beauty at night"; Lady Chiltern recognizes her as a schoolmate expelled for theft. Lord Chiltern, Under-Secretary of Foreign Affairs, discovers that Mrs. Chevely still holds a letter incriminating him in the giving of advance information on State policy, a score of years ago. With this, she attempts to force his hand in the current issue of an Argentine Canal. He wavers, then—when his wife protests his changing point of view—refuses. Mrs. Chevely reveals Chiltern's early act to his wife. Lord Goring, who had loved Lady Chiltern, and who once knew Mrs. Chevely "so little" that he got engaged to her, has in the meantime pinned a bracelet theft on Mrs. Chevely, and traded that secret for Lord Chiltern's incriminating letter. Goring, whom Chiltern's sister Mabel has promised to marry, helps Lady Chiltern to readjust her values; and Lord Chiltern moves on, with her richer love, to a post in the Cabinet.

The serious purpose of Wilde, hidden beneath his wit, did not escape all his critics—despite Shaw's prophecy: "The English critic, always protesting that the drama should not be didactic, and yet always complaining if the dramatist does not find sermons in stones and good in everything, will be conscious of a subtle and pervading levity in *An Ideal Husband*." The *London Press* (March 17, 1895) analyzed more deeply: "So far as we may estimate the peculiar excellence of this unconventional author, it would seem that Oscar Wilde derives his power from naturalism. He has an Ibsenistic quality.... Wilde holds the mirror up to the smart people in England as cleverly as Ibsen depicts the peasant folk of Norway. That, it seems to me, is the reason why his plays are enjoyable. They are bits of nature painted with masterly technique, with quick intuition, with local atmosphere, and with exact naturalness. *An Ideal Husband*, divested of its extravagant passages, which are put in to catch the general public and are irritating to those who know the real people and the real object of Oscar Wilde's study, is a very true picture of life in modern English society. Wilde's distinctive gift in comedy is naturalism." And in New York, the *Sun* (September 7, 1918) declared this "Wilde's most satisfactory play, as it has not only the wit and polish of high comedy, but also a solid substratum of good sense. Indeed, it has a sincerity that Wilde seldom allowed himself to express." The *Globe* remarked that "the scintillant flashes of humor, the playful gambolings with words, are beyond mere persiflage and repartee. They have a surer foundation in the keenest observation of men and manners."

The opposite tendency, to mock at Wilde as a man of ideas while hailing his wit, continued. It appeared in the *New York Times* (September 17, 1918): "Wilde's wit was never more luminous . . . it is possible his philosophy was never more profound. . . . The business of the play is to show the degrees by which the husband rises to the point where honor seems fairer than his career and reputation, and by which his lady realizes that it is better to be the wife of a real human being than to burn incense before an ideal. Nothing could be sounder than the 'message' of the piece. Mrs. Humphrey Ward could not do better. But it is hardly the forte of Wilde to act as messenger boy." Later, Ivor Brown in the *London Observer* (November 21, 1943), smiled at "this curious museum-piece whose bones had been dug out of the overworked goldfields of Sardoodledum by Fingal O'Flahertie Wills while the great Oscar Wilde titivated the corpse with the jewels of his wit. . . . The plot, it may be explained, discharges a lurid stream of compromising letters, ladies in bachelors' premises, stolen jewels, Cabinet secrets betrayed, and the faithful hearts of a Rising Liberal and his noble young consort, hearts beating as one until nearly riven asunder by la Femme Fatale." And James Agate, in the *Masque* (No. 3, 1947), declared that he would have great "difficulty in thinking that this wittiest of playwrights took the slightest interest in what emotions Lord X was feeling between paradoxes, or what Lady Y was meditating between *bétises*."

Wilde himself felt that the critics had missed the point of the play, had lost "its entire psychology," he said in an interview reported in the *Cleveland Plain Dealer* (February 3, 1895) "—the difference in the way in which a man loves a woman from that in which a woman loves a man; the passion that women have for making ideals (which is their weakness) and the weakness of a man who dares not show his imperfections to the thing he loves. . . . The critics really thought it was a play about a bracelet." The jewels of Wilde's wit make a sparkling cluster; but they are set in solid thought.

An Ideal Husband, opening in London, January 3, 1895, ran for 119 performances. Its revival of November 16, 1943, with Dame Irene Vanbrugh, Martita Hunt, and Esme Percy, ran for 266 performances. In New York, it played for five weeks at the Lyceum Theatre, opening March 12, 1895, with Herbert Kelcey, Isabel Irving, and Mrs. Thomas Whiffen— although the September 16, 1918, production with Norman Trevor, Constance Collier, Merle Maddern, and Julian L'Estrange called itself the New York premiere. This production announced itself as "modernized by George Alexander," which led Louis Sherwin to exclaim "Who in the name of greasepaint is Alexander, to presume to cut and edit the work of his betters?" Sherwin might, appositely, have quoted Lady Markby in the play itself: "You are remarkably modern, Mable. A little too modern, perhaps. Nothing is so dangerous as being too modern. One is apt to grow old-fashioned quite suddenly."—It is the modern attitude toward morality in *An Ideal Husband* that now seems, to some, "old hat" and trite. The surface is as glittering as ever, but we have made many soundings in its depths. Those depths of thought, however, though better known, remain sound.

An Ideal Husband played at the Pitlochry Festival, 1959. Manchester, December 1965, with Ursula Jeans. London, 1965-1966, for 189 performances, with Margaret Lockwood and Robert Stephens.

THE IMPORTANCE OF BEING EARNEST   *Oscar Wilde*

In *The Importance of Being Earnest*, 1894, Oscar Wilde is, for the first time in his dramas, completely playful. There is no underlying thesis in this play; its social satire plays lightly over the characters as—with integrity of taste and cultured poise, however absurd in conduct and paradoxical in speech—they breeze through the deft and rapid movements of a farce. In *The Importance of Being Earnest*, said James Agate in the *Masque*, Wilde has written "the wittiest light comedy in the language."

The Importance of Being Earnest opened in London, February 14, 1895, with Irene Vanbrugh. It was revived there in 1902; in 1909, opening November 30, it attained 324 performances; more recent revivals include one July 7, 1930, for 104 performances; an "Old Vic" production in 1934; John Gielgud and Edith Evans, January 31, 1939; another in August, another in December, 1929; and one in 1942. New York saw the play in 1902, with Margaret Anglin and William Courtenay; in 1921; 1939; with Estelle Winwood, Clifton Webb, and Hope Williams; with John Gielgud in 1947, "giving Wilde's finest play," said *Time* (March 17) "a wonderfully high-styled production . . . often farce at its most absurd. But it is also farce at its most elegant—as insolently monocled in manner and as killingly high-toned in language as mischievous tomfoolery can make it." "There couldn't be anything in the theatre," said Richard Watts (March 4, 1947), "much more delightful than John Gielgud's enchanting production of Oscar Wilde's masterpiece . . . if only for its zestful creation of that wonderful Wildean world of wit, beauty, charm, and grace, where every man is debonair and epigrammatic and every woman lovely—save the dowagers, who are witty and greatly enjoy their own paradoxes." There has been little save praise for *The Importance of Being Earnest*.

There has been, however, some analysis as well. Max Beerbohm, in the London *Saturday Review* (December 11, 1909), observed: "In *The Importance of Being Earnest* there is a perfect fusion of manners and form. It would be truer to say that the form is swallowed up in the manner.... The bare scenario is of the tritest fashion in the farce-writing of the period. Jack pretends to his niece, as an excuse for going to London, that he has a wicked brother whom he has to look after. Algernon, as an excuse for seeing the niece, impersonates the wicked brother. Jack, as he is going to marry and has no further need of a brother, arrives with the news of his brother's death; and so forth. Just this sort of thing had served as the staple for innumerable farces in the sixties and seventies and eighties—and would still be serving so if farce had not now been practically snuffed out by musical comedy. This very ordinary clod the magician picked up, turning it over in his hands—and presto! a dazzling prism for us. How was the trick done? Part of the play's fun, doubtless, is in the unerring sense of beauty that informs the actual writing of it. The absurdity of the situations is made doubly absurd by the contrasted grace and dignity of everyone's utterance. The play abounds, too, in perfectly chiselled apothegms—witticisms unrelated to action or character; but so good in themselves as to have the quality of dramatic surprise.... But, of course, what keeps the play so amazingly fresh is not the inlaid wit, but the humour, the ever-fanciful and inventive humour, irradiating every scene. Out of a really funny situation, Oscar Wilde would get dramatically the last drop of fun, and then would get as much fun again out of the correlative notions aroused in him by that situation."

The situations referred to by Beerbohm far from exhaust the absurdities of the play. Just as John (Jack) Worthing has invented a brother named Ernest as an excuse for going to London, so Algernon Moncrieff has invented an invalid named Bunbury as an excuse for going to the country. Jack is engaged to be married to Gwendolen Fairfax, daughter of Augusta, Lady Bracknell. Jack is also the guardian of Cecily Cardew, who is being wooed by Lady Bracknell's nephew, Algernon. Algernon gains admission to Jack's country house by pretending to be Jack's brother, Ernest. The deceit is uncovered; but so is Jack's past. Jack was the baby left in the hand-bag of Miss Prism at the Victoria Station, London; this means that he is really Algernon's long-lost elder brother—named Ernest. Miss Prism is relieved enough to accept the hand of the Rev. Canon Chasuble; Jack embraces Gwendolen; Algernon embraces Cecily; and Wilde embraces the opportunity for a final pun that gives the play its name.

In *The Importance of Being Earnest* Wilde maintains complete unity of cultured banter and farcical play. "Even in a jocular play," said Allan Monkhouse, in the *London Times* (February 5, 1939), "we expect the dramatist to steady himself occasionally and say something about the Union Jack or the sanctity of home, and in Wilde this austerity of art that never trifles with morals or realities, except in the sense that it is all trifling, is disturbing to respectable citizens.... The day may come when this country has deserted the Union Jack for a pair of crossed broomsticks and the sanctity of the home is held for an intolerable thing. And if it does, how will Wilde be concerned? Not at all. His masterpiece belongs to no time and no place."

Subtitled "a trivial comedy for serious people," *The Importance of Being*

Earnest sends its ripples afar. Appreciation of its range and power came from so polished a stylist as Walter Pater: "His genial, laughter-loving sense of life and its enjoyable intercourse goes far to obviate any crudity that may be in the paradox, with which, as with the bright and shining truth that often underlies it, Mr. Wilde startling his countrymen carries on, more perhaps than any other, the brilliant critical work of Matthew Arnold." Catching the savour of a society in its rippling flow, *The Importance of Being Earnest* is a joy to all that appreciate the theatre as art.

It has been said that wit consists in the truth, plus a surprise; for example: My lady's bosom is as white as snow—and as cold. Wilde knew the formula; thus Lady Bracknell: "I dislike arguments of any kind. They are always vulgar, and often convincing."

Among many revivals: 1955, opening night of English commercial TV, Margaret Leighton, John Gielgud, Edith Evans. London Old Vic October 13, 1959, Alec McCowen, Miles Malleson, Fay Compton, Judi Dench. OffOffBway (Madison Av.) February 25, 1963, 164 performances. Roundabout, 1967-1968. London, February 8, 1968; Daniel Massey, John Standing, Isobel Jeans, Flora Robson, over 130 performances.

Several musicals: *Oh Ernest,* May 9, 1927, 44 performances. *Half in Earnest,* by Vivian Ellis, Bucks County, Pa., June 17, 1957, and Coventry, England, March 17, 1958. *Ernest,* by Henry Burke, Farnham, England, May 18, 1959. *Ernest in Love,* book by Anne Croswell, music by Lee Pockriss, May 4, 1960, 103 performances. *Found in a Handbag,* by Allen Bacon, Eastbourne, February 1, 1968. The September 18, 1982, NT (Lyttleton) production with Judi Dench included Zoe Wanamaker as Gwendolyn; Elizabeth Garvie, Cecily; Martin Jarvis, Worthing; Nigel Havers, Algernon; Paul Rogers, Canon Chasuble. Francis King in the *Telegraph* compared Judi Dench as Lady Bracknell with the sixty-three-year-old Edith Evans in the same role—"so perfect that it must be laid up in heaven": Edith Evans "like some powerful mare"; Judi Dench "like some mettlesome pony." When they hear where Jack had been left as a baby, Edith Evans disapprovingly "brayed the famous 'A handbag!'; Miss Dench, hands trembling, hardly got it out." The play is more than a bagful of comic treasures. A musical, *The Importance,* was at the London Ambassador, 1984.

OUR TOWN   *Thornton Wilder*

Beginning his literary career as a writer of novels—*The Bridge of San Luis Rey* won the 1927 Pulitzer Prize for fiction—Thornton Niven Wilder (American 1897-1975) turned also to dramatic adaptations (Obey's *Lucrece** in 1932 for Katharine Cornell; Ibsen's *A Doll's House** in 1937 for Ruth Gordon; Nestroy's *He Will Have His Fling** as *The Merchant of Yonkers* in 1938) and to original plays. *The Merchant of Yonkers*, rewritten as *The Matchmaker,* was presented in London, then New York, in 1955, with Ruth Gordon in her liveliest comic role.

The most popular of Wilder's dramas and the most effective evocation of the spirit of American small town life is *Our Town.* Opening in New York February 4, 1938, with Frank Craven, it ran for 336 performances and won the Pulitzer Prize. London saw the play April 30, 1946. *Our Town* has been played constantly in various parts of the United States; it has already found a place in text-book anthologies of American literature. It was shown on television in 1950. Thornton Wilder himself has more than once (*e.g.,* Summer, 1950) enacted the stage manager in the play.

Suggested by the poem *Lucinda Matlock* (one of the pioneer group in Edgar Lee Masters' *Spoon River Anthology*), which the play quotes, *Our Town* presents life and death in Grover's Corners, New Hampshire. It moves by the simplest means, with no set scenery, just a few props. A "stage manager" saunters in and introduces the town and the people. He gives facts, statistics, shrewd observations, in a dry, matter-of-fact way that cuts to the heart of the topic, hence touches the audience's heart. Among those that we meet are Dr. and Mrs. Gibbs, with their children George and Rebecca, and their neighbors, the local editor Mr. Webb and his wife, with their children Emily and Wally. We watch the awakening of the town—the rouse of the milkman, the slink of the town drunkard—the chores of the day; and the drift toward evening, with the children's homework and the neighbors' chat. Three years later (in Act II), George is giving up his thoughts of college to marry Emily and settle on a farm. We watch the homey bustle before the wedding, the interchange of the family's chatting, the paternal talk to the son before his new responsibilities: all simple, natural, familiar yet touchingly roused to real emotion. Nine years later (in Act III), we watch the dead in the cemetery of Grover's Corners; they are sitting in chairs above the graves, commenting on the ignorant ways of life. Emily, who has died in childbirth, has just joined them; their lack of interest in the living folk perplexes her; she grieves when George throws himself on her grave; she wants to go back. Allowed to pick a day, Emily returns to the happy time of her twelfth birthday—to recognize how limited is the scope of living life, how hurried, how unseeing, are the folks on earth. Reconciled to her eternal future, Emily rejoins the dead; and life and death continue their pattern at Grover's Corners.

"Grover's Corners"—one of the children receives a letter addressed— "Sultan County, New Hampshire, United States of America, Continent of North America, Western Hemisphere, the Earth, the Solar System, the Universe, the Mind of God." The children are overawed; but Thornton Wilder is suggesting that the simple, kindly folk of Grover's Corners might indeed be moving along a line of hope for the destiny of mankind. The play speaks to the years ahead: "Well, people a thousand years from now, this is the way we were—in our growing-up, in our marrying, in our doctoring, in our living and our dying." Here is the humble, staunch backbone of the American way of life; here is democracy's cradle, and democracy's growth.

"In all my days as a theatregoer," said Alexander Woollcott, "no other play has ever moved me so deeply." "It captures the mind and the spirit of this country," said Robert Coleman, "as have few plays of our time." It is, said Brooks Atkinson, "one of the finest achievements of the current stage." It presents, said the *New York Sun,* "not the isolated experience of the day but the whole pattern of life from the ancient past into the depths of the future."

So simply is the story of *Our Town* presented, with the "stage-manager" Narrator, with plain folk in ordinary talk on the almost bare stage, that there seems nothing unusual in the gathering of the dead in the last act, their calm aloofness setting the face of the future against the ephemeral grief of the mourners. Though it shows the living as incapable of fully realizing life's gifts, *Our Town,* in the simplest dramatic form, is a moving reaffirmation of the values of living.

In my 1957-1958 year's trip around the world, lecturing in fourteen countries on American life as shown in the American theatre, I ended with Wilder's *Our Town*. The play was presented at the Pitlochry Festival April

19, 1968; by the University of Southern California at the Edinburgh Festival September 2, 1968; OffBway November 1969.

THE SKIN OF OUR TEETH   *Thornton Wilder*

This combination of slapstick and fantasy, of seemingly grab-bag and helter-skelter gathering and commingling from all times upon the earth, presents a picture of man's man-long struggle for survival and his wonderment as to why it is worth that trouble to survive. The picture of Mr. Antrobus (the name is from a Greek word meaning *man*) battling the forces of nature and of fellow-men, seeking to increase his understanding and improve his lot, striving to wrest a corner of contentment and peace from his troubled days, grows ironically yet tenderly through Thornton Wilder's kaleidoscopic play.

The audience is drawn into the play's action, as a military band marches, playing, down the aisles; newsreels and colored slides entertain the gathering crowd. There is a meeting of the Ancient and Honorable Order of Mammals, Human Division. A pretty girl, Sabina, repeats the cue lines and behaves like a burlesque of a maid in a parlor drama. In the first act, the world is being almost overwhelmed by the Ice Age. George Antrobus, of Excelsior, New Jersey, who has just invented the alphabet and the wheel, sends a singing telegram as a dinosaur and a baby mammoth shiver. He broadcasts a message to all mammals. Many of the audience laughingly agree when the maid Sabina looks across the footlights to say to them: "I hate this play, and I don't understand a word of it!" In the second act, which is a great convention—wide sideshows and fortune tellers and merry drinking and noise—Antrobus picks the blossoming Sabina as Miss Atlantic City, and Sabina (the eternal Lilith) picks Antrobus as her future mate. The more matter-of-fact Mrs. Antrobus (the eternal Eve) goes calmly on maintaining the family home. Indeed, after the great world conflict (it is now Act III), Mrs. Antrobus bustles everybody back to the business of home-building: "There's nothing to get emotional about. The war's over." Her son Henry returns from the War with the mark of Cain and a burning hatred. George Antrobus, who had sworn to kill the boy, merely makes him douse his head in cold water. Gladys Antrobus comes up from the cellar shelter with her baby. Sabina gives George the beef-cubes she has been hoarding—keeping one to pay her admission fee to the movies. She can stand this "crazy old world" if now and again she sees a movie. And the crazy old world goes on.

All of this time-leaping action occurs in settings as fantastic as the events. The scenery disappears when Sabina dusts it. After the war's devastation, Mrs. Antrobus pulls up the walls of their home again. As the ice moves nearer, we are told they are burning pianos in Hartford; Antrobus picks up some of the theatre seats to feed the fire. The telescoping of time—Ice Age and radios; dinosaurs and bathing beauties; refugees that include Homer, Moses and "the Muse sisters"—adds to the whirligig spin of the human span. The play's wide pattern was defended by the author in the *New York Times* (February 13, 1938): "The theatre longs to represent the symbol of things, not the things themselves. The theatre asks for as many conventions as possible. A convention is an agreed upon falsehood, an accepted untruth. When the theatre pretends to give the real thing in canvas and metal and wood, it loses something of the realer thing which is its true business." The true business of *The Skin of Our Teeth* is through man's unending struggle to ring a clear note of faith in man—in Eve's simple, clear-headed hold on essentials, in Adam's more roundabout, sometimes more pig-headed, but undaunted constant rebuilding. And an eye for the surplusage beyond living's need, of beauty, of peace, and of art.

Opening in New York, November 18, 1942, with Tallulah Bankhead and Fredric March, *The Skin of Our Teeth* ran for 356 performances, and won the 1943 Pulitzer Prize. It came to London May 16, 1945, with Vivien Leigh; again September 11, 1946, for 108 performances. Betty Field was in a summer production in 1948, at Westport. The play found the reviewers sharply divided. The *Baltimore Sun* (October 15, 1943) referred to the "stubborn groups of New York critics who mistook Mr. Wilder's sophomoric display of mental confusion for something arty"; but there were resignations from the Critics' Circle when the play did not receive the critics' award (no award was made, that year). The *New York Post* (November 21, 1942) said that Wilder "is now using the theatre chiefly as a medium to distract attention from the fact that he has nothing left to say of any particular significance. *The Skin of Our Teeth* is one of the emptiest dramas any modern philosopher ever turned out; but as a comic extravaganza, it has its points." *Variety* (February 24, 1943) estimated that "between ten and fifteen patrons" walked out of every performance. Balanced against these opinions are such comments as that of the *Herald Tribune* (November 22, 1942): "A play of cosmic and cockeyed proportions has come to town"; and Alexander Woollcott's hail: "Thornton Wilder's dauntless and heartening comedy stands head and shoulders above anything else ever written for our stage."

The controversy as to the value of *The Skin of Our Teeth* grew complicated when Henry Morton Robinson (poet, and senior editor of the *Readers' Digest),* Professor Joseph Campbell of Sarah Lawrence College, and others, attacked the play as "a bold and unacknowledged appropriation of a dead man's work," charging that its characters, philosophy situations, and language are thinly disguised borrowings from James Joyce's *Finnegan's Wake.* The tendency toward a combined simplicity and stylization, however, and blent symbolism and fantasy, is evident in Wilder's earlier plays and adaptations. And the theme of mankind's constant survival "by the skin of our teeth" was presented earlier in the drama by, among others, Edouard Dujardin, in *The Eternal Return,* 1932—Dujardin, from whom James Joyce acknowledged that he appropriated the interior monologue technique of his *Ulysses.* Such cross-currents of influences are less than reprehensible, being inevitable, and often fruitful.

The Skin of Our Teeth, with Helen Hayes and Mary Martin, was one of the two plays presented in Paris for the 1955 "Salute to France." Returning, it toured, then opened on Broadway, August 17. The clever trick of telescoping ages seemed less fresh, and lengthily labored. The breaking of the players from their parts, to discuss themselves or the play, seemed an unnecessary complication if not a confusion. But Atkinson called the production "perfect".

The mixed merits of *The Skin of Our Teeth* were well caught by Ivor Brown in the *London Observer* (September 15, 1946), who called the play a "clever-clever charade and sermon for all." Plays such as *The Skin of Our Teeth* remind us that out of the "proud and angry dust" may somehow be fashioned a shining star.

Wilder, in his Preface to *Three Plays,* acknowledged indebtedness to *Finnegan's Wake,* adding: "Literature has always more resembled a torch race than a furious dispute among heirs." Revivals of *The Skin of Our Teeth* include: Washington to New York August 17, 1955, with Mary Martin, Helen Hayes, George Abbott. Bristol Old Vic March 27, 1956. Pocket Theatre, Atlanta, Ga., directed by Mitzi Hyman, April 27, 1967. Chichester Festival, July 31, 1968.

THE CORN IS GREEN   *Emlyn Williams*

The Welsh actor Emlyn Williams (b. 1905) had already won attention by several plays, especially the two melodramas *A Murder Has Been Arranged,* 1930, and *Night Must Fall,* 1935 (a hit in London and in little theatres, though less heartily welcomed on Broadway), when his play *The Corn Is Green* established him as a considerable playwright. It was played superbly by Dame Sybil Thorndike and the author in London, in 1938. In New York Ethel Barrymore made it one of her best roles. Opening on November 26, 1940, with her and Richard Waring, Thelma Schnee, Sayre Crowley and Rhys Williams, it ran for over a year, then toured the country until it returned for another New York run, on May 3, 1943. It was presented in 1946, with Cherry Hardy, by Equity-Library. A film was made of it in 1945. The title is from an old English proverbial warning used in Kyd's *The Spanish Tragedy*:* You count your harvest when the corn is green.

The action of the play lies in an almost illiterate mining district of Wales, where the middle-aged English spinster Miss Moffat founds a village school, discovers a boy of genius, fosters his talent, and enlists the help of the at first hostile gentry to enter the boy for an Oxford scholarship. The boy, Morgan Evans, passes the examination. But earlier in a discouraged moment, he could not pass the tempting Bessie Watty; and now, in the moment of his triumph, Bessie returns with the demand that he support their baby. Miss Moffat saves him from disaster by adopting his illegitimate child, and sends him forth to enrich the world.

When the play opened in London, the *Times* (September 21, 1938) warned aspiring dramatists from venturing on such a theme, but admitted having had "an uncommonly well rewarded evening, to which the Welsh songs are a genuine and moving contribution. . . . The outstanding quality of Williams' work is its moderation. . . . All his play's background—the village school, the Welsh and the English, the rare feeling of humanity with which he endows his stage—is a recommendation of his central narrative so strong as to cloak its minor improbabilities."

Granted the boy's genius, the "improbabilities" are minor indeed; but it has been argued that the melodramatic episodes of the slut Bessie and her baby are extraneous to the main drive of the drama. Sex, however, does rear its head even in Welsh mining towns; and the final sacrifice of Miss Moffat is not only natural to her but integral to the play's movement. Miss Moffat, while she is a deftly differentiated individual, is also a born teacher: by faith, resolution, and self-denial, she passes the flame of enlightenment and beauty to a soul that will bear it farther.

Several of the scenes in the play are especially effective. Kronenberger (May 4, 1943) declared that "the most dramatic and exciting moment of the play is still the moment when Morgan Evans sits down to take his examination for Oxford." There is a tenderness even more moving in the scene where, on his first return from the University, Morgan sits by Miss Moffat and tells her of his thoughts as he walked up Oxford's High Street, how the subjects he'd be cramming then took pattern in his mind, and the world gathered beauty and meaning.

The assemblage of Welsh figures in the drama won Brooks Atkinson's praise (November 27, 1940): "His characters are glowing members of the human race—some of them comic, one of them supercilious, one of them slatternly, another dour but aspiring. Representing all sorts of pride, vanity, rebellion, coarseness, stubbornness, and good-will, they make an uncommonly attractive lot, and Mr. Williams keeps moving them in and out of his drama with intimate understanding."

The Corn Is Green is a superb theatre play. It has a heart-warming role for the star, and several excellent parts for other players. Its theme, of the teacher's, of the older generation's, sacrifice for the enrichment of those to come, is widely appealing. Its background is unusual and colorful.

All in all, *The Corn Is Green* has enough melodrama and sex to keep it exciting, enough devotion and struggle for good ends to keep it exalted. *Theatre,* 1941, called the play "tenderly tragic," but in 1947 Freedley, in *A History of Modern Drama,* called it "a tender comedy." It mingles tears and smiles as life itself, and—keeping its sentiment within the range of truth—presents some hardworking and humble persons of whom humanity may be proud.

The first London runs of *The Corn Is Green* were: the Duchess September 20, 1938, for 395 performances; December 19, 1939, Piccadily, for 205. Bette Davis played Miss Moffat in the film. A musical, *Miss Moffat,* closed in the tryout.

A STREETCAR NAMED DESIRE   *Tennessee Williams*

Broken spirits of the once fair South seem to be the specialty of Thomas Lanier "Tennessee" Williams (American, 1914-1983), both in his one-act and in his full-length plays. His first produced full-length play, *Battle of the Angels,* was accepted by the Theatre Guild, presented in Boston, 1943, and then withdrawn. *The Glass Menagerie,* 1943, was almost withdrawn in Chicago, but favorable criticism turned the tide and it went on to win the Critics' Circle Award as the best play of 1945. It has had numerous revivals, most recently at the New York Eugene O'Neill November 23, 1983, with Jessica Tandy and Amanda Plummer.

The promise of Tennessee Williams came nearer to fulfillment when on December 2, 1947, *A Streetcar Named Desire* won acclaim, and later gave Tennessee Williams the Pulitzer Prize, as well as his second Critics' Circle Award. It ran in New York for 855 performances, then toured the country, returning to New York May 23, 1950, for two weeks at the City Center. Again the play was favored with a superb production: the squalid living-room-bedroom-kitchen, with street and stairs to the left, had a rear wall of scrim so that lighting could make visible the street behind. Staged by Elia Kazan, the play showed Jessica Tandy, later Uta Hagen, as Blanche DuBois, Kim Hunter as her sister Stella Kowalski, and Marlon Brando as Stanley Kowalski, in their best roles.

In the play, Blanche DuBois, with the old family mansion overburdened with debts, has had to work for a living, teaching in the town school. She seeks to sustain her gentility by flaunting it, and thereby makes clear that it has gone. She seeks to preserve the vitality she no longer feels pulsing within her by pulsing in semblance of passion with every man. Become too notorious a harlot, she is told to leave town. *A Streetcar Named Desire* opens with her attempt to escape her past, at her sister's shabby home in New Orleans. But however far a bird may fly, it takes its tail along—and Blanche's is gaudy but faded plumage. Her sister Stella welcomes her; but Stella's coarse, rough-neck husband, Stanley Kowalski, sees right through Blanche's preening. He breaks up her attempt to lure his friend Harold into marrying her. When Stella goes to the hospital to have her baby, Stanley rapes Blanche. Stella, on her return, sizes up the situation, but refuses to admit the truth. The only way to make her relations with Stanley endurable is to have Blanche taken away to an insane asylum.

The picture that carries Blanche from the forced gaiety of her arrival to her final enforced confinement spares no details. Its very thorough-going detail won *A Streetcar Named Desire* mixed reviews. Richard Watts, for example, pointed out that "her downfall is studied with almost loving detail. The result is that the play has a painfull, rather pitiful quality about it." John Chapman, on the other hand, called it "throbbingly alive, compassionate, heart-warmingly human." George Jean Nathan said that the author "seems to labor under the misapprehension that strong emotions are best to be expressed strongly only through what may be delicately termed strong language . . . that theatrical sensationalism and dramatic substantiality are much the same thing." Whereas Brooks Atkinson declared that "although Blanche cannot face the truth, Mr. Williams does. . . . Out of poetic imagination and ordinary compassion he has spun a poignant and luminous story."

Only a few would disagree with Louis Kronenberger's opinion, that *A Streetcar Named Desire* marks "an enormous advance over that minor-keyed and too wet-eyed work, *The Glass Menagerie*." Yet, in two ways, the end of the play is disappointing. In the first place, the emphasis is shifted at the close. The play is concerned with the "harlot's progress," with the downward troubles of Blanche DuBois—but bearing her off to the asylum solves her sister's problem, not her own. Secondly, the exaltation of truly tragic art is replaced by a sniffling pity. Howard Barnes said of the final scenes: "They are truly touching, but they lack some of the nobility that defines high tragedy. These are minor defects." It is, rather, the play's major failing that it builds to no rouse of spirit at the end. Blanche goes off, not horror-stricken yet her own master, like self-blinded Oedipus; she is a whipped and frightened child. Her world ends not with a bang, but with a whimper. We leave depressed; not exalted, as after tragic surge.

Again the symbolism is left for the audience to develop. (We are told that there was actually, in New Orleans, a streetcar with the destination-sign "Desire"; this is of course immaterial.) Blanche, looking unbelievably at her sister's squalid home, explains: "They told me to take a streetcar named Desire, and then transfer to one called Cemeteries and ride six blocks and then get off at—Elysian Fields." Later on, Blanche confuses desire with life; but her opening words suggest that desire leads to death—if one ride on the car of desire only.

Nathan declared that the play, "making realistically dramatic such elements as sexual abnormality, harlotry, perversion, venality, rape, and lunacy . . . while unpleasant, is not disgusting, yet never rises to be enlightening." To which Ellis St. Joseph (whose astute and urbane observations should more often find print) retorted that when the unpleasant is not enlightening it is disgusting. St. Joseph declared of *Streetcar* that Williams "has insisted on making a tragedy out of a cartoon." The devices and the deeds are, in truth, from the stock-in-trade of the old, murky melodrama. Over in Paris Robert Kemp, quoted in the *New York Times* (October 30, 1949), called the play "a collection of scraps of old melodrama fixed up with sauce *à l'Americaine* and sprinkled over with alcohol. Nothing in it could less resemble what I like." Despite such reactions, *A Streetcar Named Desire* achieves a measure of distinction through the searching study it makes of a blasted soul.

The 1951 motion picture version of the play presents Blanche at the end as obviously insane; indeed, she is usually so presented, now, on the stage. The other interpretation—that she is near the breaking point, but must go to the asylum because her sister cannot face the truth—makes the characters more complex and the situation more poignant. In either case, there is climactic irony in the fact that Kowalski's rape of Blanche while Stella Kowalski is at the hospital having her child, the very act that sets the final teeter to the balance of Blanche's sanity, is the act that Stella must dismiss from the world of reality in order to live with her husband, and can dismiss by calling Blanche, who proclaims it, mad. And, however natural, it is a sinking betrayal that the coarse and ruthless Kowalski, whose one virtue is that he is straightforward, in this one test of his honesty stands silently by. He that cast the first stone has added the last straw. And their broken world is patched with an untold lie.

A Streetcar Named Desire was a hit both in London and in Paris. Both productions emphasized Blanche's sexual urge. In London, where it opened October 12, 1949, with Vivien Leigh, and ran for 333 performances, the play was nicknamed "The Bus Called Lust." In Paris, the play was produced with extra, ironic effects behind the transparent backdrop. For example, while Stanley is raping Blanche, beyond the scrim there writhes and pumps a black belly-dancer. "The latest sensation in Paris?" wrote Ellis St. Joseph: "*A Streetcar Named Desire*, adapted by Jean Cocteau—and directed as if it were Mae West in *The Madwoman of Chaillot.**" This tone of melodrama, hushed in the pathos of Williams' treatment, is nevertheless implicit in his story, which does not rise to the more universal tones, and the exaltation, of tragedy.

"*A Streetcar Named Desire*," John Mason Brown stated, "is more than a work of promise. It is an achievement of unusual and exciting distinction." Contrariwise, J. C. Trewin in *A Play Tonight* (1952) says Williams "has not persuaded us that Blanche's genteel-murky past, muddled present, or, dark future, can matter a stick of gum to anybody but Blanche."

The Glass Menagerie, with its frail spirit cherishing her glass animals for lack of human companionship, her one meeting with a young man a fiasco, has drawn greater attention. The faith of Laurette Taylor as the mother, drawing along Julie Haydon as the daughter, was justified. The play was shown at the New York City Center November 21, 1956; at Cambridge, England, February 6, 1961; at the New York Brooks Atkinson with Maureen Stapleton and George Grizzard May 4, 1965, for 175 performances.

A Streetcar Named Desire was the last play of the old New York Lincoln Center Rep., 1973.

CAMINO REAL   *Tennessee Williams*

In his one venture beyond realistic drama of sexual strain, Tennessee Williams with *Camino Real* aroused the greatest diversity of critical opinions. Critic and theatrical historian George Freedley called it "certainly the finest play by the outstanding American dramatist." Experienced critic Walter Kerr called it "the worst play yet written by the best playwright of his generation." Others, more baffled, called it an intellectual *Hellzapoppin,* a burlesque for Ph.D.s.

Camino Real means King's Highway, but the scene is the courtyard of a Mexican town, walled in from the outside world, with window dummies and shop signs. Within there is a confusion of citizens, along with real and fictional characters—Camille, Casanova, Don Quixote, the Golden Gloves champion Kilroy (of the ubiquitous "Kilroy was here" graffiti) and more; all frustrated, eager to leave but unable to get out. There are streetcleaners with the carts, shoveling and wheeling away the dead. There is a rush to embark in an airplane, of no announced destination— which doesn't matter, for it crashes and all aboard are killed. At a fiesta, there is a Crowning of the Cuckold (the tired old peacock Casanova); there is a Virginity Restored (the gypsy's seductive daughter).

Kilroy loses, then recovers, his heart of gold; then he trades it for dusty finery to give to the gypsy girl. At the end Kilroy—now a circus patsy with a fright wig and a bulbous, blinking nose—leads Camille and Casanova to climb the barrier wall. He flinches, then with tattered but jaunty grandeur Don Quixote reanimates him, and they go forth—into eternity.

As Whitney Bolton put it in the *Telegraph:* "He pays tribute to totalitarians, wasters, homosexuals, mountebanks, sadists, masochists, dopes and dreamers, but always with compassion." Brooks Atkinson, in the *Times* (March 20, 1953), added: "The performance moves lightly through a miasma of hopelessness, cruelty, and decadence—never literal, never dull or diffuse."

For the negative: Richard Watts, Jr., in the *Post:* "I fear he hasn't really the important and significant things to say he thinks he has." (Significance? That mankind, always boxed in by human weakness, always hopes to soar beyond.) Walter Kerr again: "From time to time an electrified sign flashes a sales message: Magic—Tricks and Jokes. The tricks and jokes are here in abundance. The magic never shows up."

Neutral: John Chapman in the *Daily News:* the play "may become the darling of self-conscious intellectuals."

For the positive: Atkinson continues: "The great mass of it is lucid and pertinent . . . Eli Wallach's good humored, colloquial portrait of Kilroy, the American boy, is excellent. Jo Van Fleet's pathetic Camille, Joseph Anthony's frightened Casanova, Frank Silvera's heartless, jeering landlord, Jennie Goldstein's raucous gypsy, Barbara Baily as her strumpet daughter, Hurd Hatfield as the poet [Byron] who still has a touch of purity in his soul—are beautifully acted character portraits." Hatfield also played Don Quixote, with a quiet dignity beneath his rags.

Camino Real, with incidental music by Bernardo Segall, directed by Elia Kazan, opened at the New York National March 19, 1953, for sixty performances. Its large cast of tricky personalities, and its difficult production devices, make it hard to present, but it has had other productions. San Francisco's Workshop, 1955; St. Mark's OffBway, May 16, 1960; New York's Beaumont, January 8, 1970, for fifty-two performances; Phoenix, 1976. London saw it April 8, 1957, directed by Peter Hall, with Diana Wynyard, and Denholm Elliott as Kilroy.

The same diversity of opinion continued. Clive Barnes in the *Times,* January 9, 1970: "There are people who think that *Camino Real* is Tennessee Williams' best work, and I believe that they are right. It is a play that seems to have been torn out of a human soul: a tale told by an idiot signifying a great deal of suffering and a great deal of gallantry . . . no story as such, even though it has as many fluttering incidents as an aviary has birds. 'Make Voyages! Attempt them! There's nothing else!' . . . a play of genuinely poetic vision." Walter Kerr, in the *Sunday Times,* saw no reason to change: "We cannot give ourselves over to the passion of a gummed label, a sticker, a baggage tag. . . . Emotion is play-acted; it is never communicated. It cannot be, because there is neither bone nor blood at the base of the dream . . . the vapors, the drifting insubstantial Naming, of *Camino Real."*

The play continues to present a challenge to directors, actors, and audiences, as the "best . . . worst" play of the most stimulating American playwright of his generation.

CAT ON A HOT TIN ROOF   *Tennessee Williams*

Another grim picture of Southern degeneracy is Williams' *Cat on a Hot Tin Roof,* set on a plantation in the Mississippi delta in the 1950's, on Big Daddy Pollitt's sixty-fifth birthday. Wealthy and domineering Big Daddy has two sons; his favorite is Brick, sinking into alcohol after an early athletic career left him with a broken ankle, a broken will, a crutch, and a dead crony, Skipper, to whom his attachment had been questionably emotional. Brick's frustrated wife, Maggie, having failed to seduce Skipper, is determined that the fortune of the ailing Big Daddy shall not go to the other son, Gooper, who has five children and a pregnant wife. Childless Maggie refers to the children as "no-neck monsters."

In a tense quarrel with his father, who says, "You can't stand the truth!" Brick counters, "Can you?" and blurts out the fact that the old man is dying of cancer. When Big Daddy and Big Mamma indicate that Brick might be the favored heir, if only he had a child, Maggie cries out that there is one on the way—and drags Brick out: "Tonight we'll make it come true, and then we'll get drunk together."

When the play was in rehearsal, director Elia Kazan persuaded Williams to write another ending. In the second version, Brick gives Big Daddy his birthday present: announcement of the coming child, "sired," says his wife, "by Brick, out of Maggie the Cat, and there's nothing more determined than a cat on a hot tin roof." Son Gooper tears up the trustee papers he'd expected his father to sign; Brick flings off his crutch and forswears liquor. Maggie says she loves him; he answers: "Wouldn't it be funny if that were true?" He accepts Maggie's hand caressing his cheek as the curtain falls. (Both endings are given in the printed edition of the play; producers may now take their choice.)

Cat on a Hot Tin Roof opened at the New York Morosco March 24, 1955, with Barbara Bel Geddes as Maggie, Ben Gazzara as Brick, Burl Ives and Mildred Dunnock as Big Daddy and Big Mama, and Pat Hingle as the elder son, Gooper. It attained 692 performances, to mixed reviews. When it opened in London, with Kim Stanley as Maggie, January 30, 1958, the Comedy Theatre was converted as a "club," to evade the censor. The *Guardian* declared: "It has a violence of utterance beyond anything else Mr. Williams has written, and it is about sawn-off, coarse, violent people, often seen with a savage veracity but not, as in some of Williams' other plays, winning much sympathy." The *Times* was even less sympathetic: "The characters behave with such animal ferocity that they cease to resemble human beings." Furthermore, it continued, "Mr. Williams is a slow writer in the sense that he writes about every idea several times before deciding that it is roughly the idea that he is looking for, and we have fully grasped many of his situations while he is still putting finishing touches on them." Among these ideas is Brick's worry that his fondness for Skipper might have been homosexual.

The play was a flop in Chicago in 1957; but an ANTA revival September 24, 1974, planned for eight weeks, was extended to twenty, with Elizabeth Ashley as Maggie the Cat. Mel Gussow in the *Times* called the play "a piercing, truthful drama by our finest living playwright." The new ending was used in West Springfield, Mass., November 10, 1973. A revival February 12, 1975, at the Kennedy Center, Washington, used frank expletives for earlier euphemisms. On October 3, 1970, Akiko Naruoka played Maggie in Japanese in Tokyo.

George Jean Nathan, quick with a quip, hailed Tennessee Williams as a "Southern Genitalman of Letters."

In his words after Tennessee Williams' untimely death, Frank Rich in the *Times*, February 26, 1983, said: "If his world was grotesque and nightmarish, it was nonetheless, as the famous Williams phrase had it, 'lit by lightning.' That lightning was provided by Mr. Williams's extraordinarily fecund and lyrical poetry, his mastery of dramatic moments and effects, and his ability to raise lowly characters to almost mythic size." There is no question that the coarse characters in *Cat on a Hot Tin Roof* generate tense interest. Many have considered it Williams' best play.

THE PLAIN DEALER   *William Wycherley*

Though critically well received when produced in March 1674, *The Plain Dealer*, 1666, was slower in winning popular favor than *The Country Wife,** and has not had so many revivals. It has a story of less immediate application to daily life—even the life of the London gallant—but its wit and its originality, and its character portraits, make it the fourth best of the comedies of William Wycherley (English, 1640-1716).

The "plain dealer" of the play is Captain Manly, who on going to sea entrusts his money to his beloved Olivia and Olivia to his friend Vernish. He has little faith in humanity else; but his faith here is sadly misplaced, for on his return Manly finds the two married, and Olivia unwilling to give back his funds. With the help of his servant Fidelia, with whom Olivia becomes enamoured and makes rendezvous, Manly hopes to expose the perfidious heartless woman. Vernish breaks in upon them; in the scuffle, Fidelia is wounded—and discovered to be a woman, who in love of Manly had disguised herself to be with him. The spell of Olivia broken, Manly gives Fidelia his love.

Other characters add to the satiric picture of the times. The Widow Blackacre is a litigious old woman, who teaches her son to go to court on every occasion and any pretext—until he turns the lesson upon her own estate. Novel and Plausible, two coxcombs of the town with hopes of Olivia's favors, open their eyes when her letters to them are exchanged; save for the name, the contents are identical. When Olivia, with affected prudery, and her cousin Eliza, with the candor of simple honesty, engage with Novel and Plausible in a critique of *The Country Wife* (written after but produced before *The Plain Dealer*, to which this scene is an addition) Wycherley's brilliant antitheses and sparkling fancy reach their height.

This scene was suggested by Molière's *Critique of The School for Wives,** as other parts of the play were suggested by his *Misanthrope*;* but Wycherley's handling of the situation is as original as his development of them is ingenious. As Voltaire said in the *Letters Concerning the English Nation* (1733), "All Wycherley's strokes are stronger and bolder than those of our *Misanthrope,* but then they are less delicate; and the Rules of Decorum are not so well observed in this play."

Some critics have felt that, while Molière's misanthrope reaches almost tragic intensity in his hatred of human hypocrisy, Wycherley's becomes almost odious in his sense of superiority to the hypocrites around. Molière, in truth, shows that excess of blunt frankness in Alceste, as well as excess of polite pretense in those about him, leads to social evils, whereas Wycherley seems to condone, if not to approve, the rude bluntness of Manly. There may, indeed, be something of the author in the man, for many of the playwright's contemporaries referred to him as "manly Wycherley."

The preface to the 1766 edition of *The Plain Dealer* states that the play "was one of the most celebrated productions of the last century; it acquired him the personal friendship of two of his sovereigns, and the praises of the learned both at home and abroad; and certainly we find in it the happiest combination of wit, humour, character and incident, that can be imagined. At the same time, it was remarked that propriety "could allow no charms in a tainted beauty"—and it was an expurgated version by Isaac Bickerstaffe that David Garrick presented, on December 7, 1765, and this sweeter-scented adaptation held the stage for the next half century. Nineteenth century productions were few. *The Plain Dealer* was shown again in London, November 15, 1925. In plot, the play is far-fetched; in morals, while it presents the laxity of its time, it excoriates the licentious in its satire and its story, and shows faith, love, and honesty triumphant. In fertility of invention, in richness of wit, while later surpassed by Congreve,* it gave him lessons. The dedication of the play to the aging but notorious procuress Mother Bennet is characterized by Steele in the *Spectator* (No. 266): "The ironical commendation to the industry and charity of these antiquated ladies, these directors of Sin after they can no longer commit it, makes up the beauty of the inimitable dedication to *The Plain Dealer,* and is a masterpiece of raillery on this vice." In this dedication, Wycherley remarked that objection had been made, not to the manners in the play, but to his satire of these manners: "'Tis the plain-dealing of the play, not the obscenity; 'tis taking off the ladies' masks, not offering at their petticoats, which offends 'em." *The Plain Dealer* is a deft portrayal of prudery masking prurience, a masterpiece in its satire of Restoration society.

THE GENTLEMAN DANCING MASTER   *William Wycherley*

The Gentleman Dancing Master is generally conceded to be the most entertaining of Wycherley's plays. It is in vivid prose dialogue, with amusing situations and a simple, unified action. Despite the dallying of Monsieur de Paris with Flirt and Flounce, "two common women of the town," the play has more of innocent fun and less of suggestive banter than Wycherley's other plays, or indeed most plays of the period. First acted in 1671, the play was revived in London December 20, 1925, full (as the *Boston Transcript* agreed, January 7, 1926) of "John Bullish humor."

The printed play bears a motto from the Latin *First Satire* of Horace:

" 'Tis not enough to make the listener laugh aloud, though there is some merit, even in this." Wycherley's picture of the times—the play includes mention of the first Punch and Judy show in England—is informative as well as amusing; there is enlightenment beneath the surface laughter.

The play opens with Hippolita protesting that her father, James Formal, keeps her shut from the pleasures a growing young woman should have. She is guarded by her aunt, Mrs. Caution, and is destined to be wife of her cousin Paris. Hippolita tricks Paris into allowing a friend, Gerrard, to visit her; naturally, the two fall in love. While they are together, Hippolita's father comes in; she introduces her swain as her dancing master. The father watches the lesson; there is an amusing scene, since Gerrard knows little of dancing. Mrs. Caution sees through the disguise, but Formal refuses to believe that he can be fooled. Before the exposure, the lovers find opportunity to marry.

There is neat satire in the portraits of Formal and Paris. The latter calls himself Monsieur de Paris and has assumed all the airs and affectations of a French fop. While wooing Hippolita, he is bargaining on the terms on which he shall keep Flirt as his mistress; he finds her more demanding than a wife. Formal has just returned from Spain; he has assumed Spanish costume and punctilio, and goes so far as to have himself called Don Diego. Much byplay and banter spring from these aping ways.

The play was revived at the London Gateway Club in 1950. In Croydon, England, April 17, 1961, Ronald Falk played Paris; Valentine Dyall, Formal; Athene Sayler, Mrs. Caution; Hazel Penwarden, Hippolita. From the Oxford New, September 30, 1963, it moved to London October 6, 1963: Jimmy Thompson, Paris; Fay Compton, Mrs. Caution; Mark Dignan, Formal; Catherine Feller, Hippolita. Ivor Brown wrote a new Prologue:

> *Your Sunday nights with Wycherley to spend*
> *Is asking British strictness to unbend;*
> *But if old art, new dressed in suit of jeans,*
> *Is not enough, why there's another means*
> *To win attentive audience: Everywhere*
> *This Christmastide one call is in the air:*
> *'Buy British Goods.' And though his plays are skittish*
> *Who can deny that Wycherley was British? . . .*
> *Raffish, perhaps, his laughter; rough his wit;*
> *'Tis native none the less, and should the pit*
> *Regard his good old days as passing bad,*
> *Remember that he was a Shropshire lad!*

Each time has its different reasons for deeming itself "passing bad," and of masking or exposing its foibles, as did Wycherley.

A few episodes in the play are drawn from *The Dancing Master* of Calderón,* such as the father's surprising the lovers and the daughter's saying the man is her dancing master. The father in Calderón's play is named Don Diego. But both the main movement of the story, and the satire and environing wit, are Wycherley's. The play, says W. C. Ward (in the Mermaid Series) is "fairly overflowing with wit and mirth." The picture is as lively and as neatly satiric as the story is amusing. After seeing James

Formal Don Diego, we can sympathize with Hippolita's protest: "I will no more take my father's choice in a husband than I would in a gown"—a sentiment that later in the play is expressed in a merry song, and that has not weakened along the years. Such thoughts, and the prank of its basic situation, help keep *The Gentleman Dancing Master* fresh. Today's taste might convert it into a delightful musical.

THE COUNTRY WIFE   *William Wycherley*

Popular in his person for a time, upon the Restoration scene, more lengthily popular in his dramas that mirror that licentious age, William Wycherley represents that period at its most typical range of gallantry and polite seduction. His first drama, *Love In a Wood; or St. James's Park,* acted in 1671, led him into the arms of the King's mistress, the Duchess of Cleveland. His second was *The Gentleman Dancing Master.* His third to be produced (though written after *The Plain Dealer**), *The Country Wife,* 1672, most extravagantly exploits the manners and attitudes of the time. In this play, Allardyce Nicoll has said, "the Restoration comedy of manners reached the acme of impropriety; yet this play contains some of the most brilliant scenes produced in an age when wit was sharpened upon wit and lightness of touch descended even upon dullards and dunces."

The play catches in its satiric net both excessive jealousy and excessive trust. Mr. Pinchbeck brings his artless country wife, Margery, to London, for the marriage of his sister Alithea. Alithea's fiancé, Sparkish, by his credulity, loses her to a rival, Mr. Harcourt. And Pinchbeck, by the very tricks and connivings of his jealousy (forcing her for a time to dress as a man; again, to send a disdainful letter to her pursuer) throws his wife into the arms of the libertine Horner, who takes what God sends him and justifies his name. At the end, Horner, who has given scope to a rumor that he is impotent so as to gain scope for his amours, persuades Pinchbeck that his wife is innocent; for the sake of family peace, Pinchbeck pretends to believe, and the play ends with a cuckolds' dance.

The Country Wife swept London with gales of laughter. It was constantly revived until 1766; then David Garrick presented an expurgated version he called *The Country Girl,* which held the stage throughout the nineteenth century. In 1884 there was a production with John Drew, Otis Skinner, and Ada Rehan. Of a later revival with Ada Rehan, the *Boston Transcript* (April 26, 1898) declared: "Even with the comedy in its present shape, *The Country Girl* is a play of abundant wit and sparkling intrigue. Its plot is both complicated and lucid; its turns and twists are made with startling rapidity, but the motives are all as clear as daylight, and the progress of the story is never obscure. The characters are lifelike, their doings are human and sensible, and the entire play is a thing to give infinite pleasure and satisfaction to audiences obliged to put up with our modern substitute for stage humor known as farce comedy." More recently, the expurgated version of *The Country Wife* ran in London, opening March 2, 1934, for 183 performances. The unexpurgated play ran there in 1936, with Edith Evans, Ruth Gordon, and Michael Redgrave; and in 1940. In New York, Ruth Gordon achieved 90 performances, opening November 30, 1936, with the full comedy. *Stage* (February 1937) said that the play, "packed with vivid duplicity, blatant with biological urge, tipsy with Wycherley's effervescent and fermenting dialogue, blunt, brilliant, magnificent, dumps verbal rough diamonds as from a burlap bag." Cambridge,

Massachusetts, saw a production of the play for seven weeks in 1950, with Madge Elliott and Cyril Ritchard.

The question of the morality of *The Country Wife* has engaged many critics. Macaulay called the play "a licentious intrigue of the lowest and least sentimental type between an impudent London rake and the idiot wife of a country squire . . . too filthy to handle and too noisome even to approach." This mid-Victorian attitude was countered in advance by Lamb: "They break through no laws or conscientious restraints; they know none. They have got out of Christendom into the land—what shall I call it?—of cuckoldry—the Utopia of gallantry, where pleasure is duty, and the manners, perfect freedom." Steele had earlier, in the *Tatler* (April 16, 1709), called the play "a good representation of an age when Love and Wenching were the only business of life." Hazlitt felt that Miss Peggy (the "country girl" substituted for Mistress Margery Pinchwife) "is a character that will last forever, I should hope . . . while self-will, curiosity, art, and ignorance are to be found in the same person, it will be just as good and intelligible as ever, because it is built on first principles and brought out in the fullest and broadest manner." The *London Times* (March 3, 1934) declared that "it is remarkable, considering what a subject Wycherley has to discuss, how little gross his language is; it is not decorous, but neither is it brutal or corrupt." The *Telegraph* (March 3, 1934) summed it up: *The Country Wife* is "a brilliant picture of an unsavoury period . . . one of the most amusing comedies in the language."

Although some of the situations in *The Country Wife* are borrowed from Molière's *The School for Wives** and *The School for Husbands,* they are handled with originality as well as ingenuity. Among the play's most brilliant scenes is that in which Pinchwife forces his wife to write a letter repelling Horner. Nowhere since Shakespeare, said James Agate in the *London Times* (October 25, 1936), is there "a more brilliant example of pure comedy than this famous letter-writing scene." "As innocent to behold as a snowdrop," as the *London Illustrated News* called her (March 1, 1924), "and as wily within as a flower of witching Oriental perfume," Margery is pressed by her husband's own insistence into taking what Alithea calls "the innocent liberty of the town," and actually has Pinchwife lead her (masked and in her sister's gown) to an assignation with her lover. Licentious as Wycherley may be, there is no denying the tart flavor of his dialogue, the bawdy fun in his situations, and the keen satire that shows excess of caution bringing on the very consequences that it feared.

A line Wycherley tucked into *the Plain Dealer* is: "Very fine! Then you think a woman modest who sees the hideous *Country Wife* without blushing or publishing her contempt for it." George Meredith 225 years later declared: "There can be no question that the men and women who sat through the acting of Wycherley's *Country Wife* were past blushing." John Evelyn in 1688 prophesied:

> *So long as men are false and women vain,*
> *While gold continues to be virtue's bane,*
> *In pointed satire Wycherley shall reign.*

His truth still holds. Among many recent performances of *The Country Wife*: 1956, Joan Plowright and Laurence Harvey, London Royal Court; George Devine directed and played Pinchwife. Julie Harris with Laurence

Harvey, Pamela Brown, Colleen Dewhurst at the Adelphi November 27, 1957. Of a Stratford, Ontario, production August 7, 1964, Howard Taubman said in the *New York Times:* "The language and costumes may be remote, but the false airs, affected manners, and elaborate insincerity of the characters describe large segments of any society, including ours." Judi Dench and Michael Craig at Nottingham, 1969; the same year Chichester Festival with Maggie Smith and Keith Baxter. Five weeks in Cleveland, opening January 16, 1970. Stratford, Conn., June 13, 1973, Carol Shelly as Mrs. Pinchbeck. New York Juilliard, December 9, 1976. NT (Olivier) November 29, 1977, Albert Finney as Horner; Elizabeth Spriggs, Lady Fidget. The Actors Co. at Cambridge, England, opened May 15, 1979, with the David Garrick version, which surprisingly omits Horner; Pinchwife (called Moody) hardly moves an inch from his eager-to-learn-about-love lady. Wycherley's play was performed again OffOffBway (Ensemble), June 7, 1979, and (City Gates) September 22, 1981. Also in San Diego (Old Globe) at the 32nd Shakespeare Festival, August 11, 1981.

There were two musical versions. *She Shall Have Music,* book by Stewart Bishop, music and lyrics by Dede Meyer, briefly OffBway, January 22, 1959, and at Asolo May 7, 1977. *My Love to Your Wife* with twenty-six songs by John Franceschina, including "Poor Harry Horner," "The Signs of Love," "What's the Use of Honor?", "Never Take a Wife to the City." It also introduced some actual persons of the time: the rakish Earl of Rochester; diarist Samuel Pepys; actress Nell Gwynn; playwright Aphra Behn. *Variety,* June 1, 1977, said, "The stimulating versatile score pleasantly propels the ribald plot." Susan Borneman and Bradford Wallace effectively played Mr. and Mrs. Pinchwife.

An entirely different play, *The Country Girl,* by Clifford Odets,* opened at the New York Lyceum November 10, 1950, for 235 performances. It shows an aging alcoholic American actor trying to make a comeback, aided by his wife (the girl from the country), with a jealous director. This had several revivals: at the Papermill, N.J., 1961, with Shelley Winters and Joseph Anthony; 1961, ELT; 1966, New York City Center, with Jennifer Jones, Rip Torn, and Joseph Anthony; 1972, the New York Billy Rose.

In London, 1958, with Michael Redgrave as the aging actor, to avoid confusion with the earlier title, the play's name was changed to *Winter Journey.* With John Stride at the London Apollo, 1983, the emphasis was shifted to a struggle between wife and director for the actor's "theatrical soul." Odets' *Country Girl* ran into 1984.

NAUGHTY MARIETTA   *Rida Johnson Young*

The most successful of the plays of Rida Johnson Young (American, 1875-1926), which include *Maytime, Little Old New York,* and *Brown of Harvard,* is *Naughty Marietta,* which is graced with the most popular music of Victor Herbert (1859-1922). With lively tunes, romantic mood, and turbulent action, *Naughty Marietta* swirls gaily with adventurers, intrigue, disguises, and swift amours in old New Orleans.

New Orleans about 1750 was a buzzing hive of international aspirations. In the play, the Lieutenant Governor is scheming to make Louisiana a republic. His son, the playboy Etienne Grandet, is trifling with his beautiful quadroon slave, Adah. Captain Richard (Dick) Warrington is in the city in quest of the notorious pirate Bras Pique. Both Dick and Etienne become smitten with a "casket-girl," Marietta. Marietta is really the Contessa d'Altena, run away from her convent and come to New Orleans with a shipment of girls, from decent middle-class families, each given a casket—"hope chest"—by the King of France, and sent to marry the virile and lonely men in the colony. The hoydenish Marietta persuades Rudolfo, the marionette man, to disguise her as his son; but at the ball, her reasserted beauty takes all hearts. Etienne auctions off Adah, to be free for Marietta; and when Dick buys Adah, Marietta misinterprets and in jealousy accepts Etienne. Then Adah reveals that Etienne is the pirate Bras Pique. The Lieutenant Governor refuses to order his own son's arrest; Etienne skips away, and what can Dick and Marietta do but embrace as the curtain falls?

Opening in New York November 7, 1910, with Emma Trentini and Orville Harrold, *Naughty Marietta* was an instant success. Indeed, Charles Darnton declared, in the *Evening Journal,* November 9: "A new standard for comic opera has been set on Broadway." The play was filmed in 1935, with Jeanette MacDonald, Nelson Eddy, and Frank Morgan. Its most elaborate Broadway production was in 1936, when, as the *Post* (September 3) recorded: "Hordes of lovely ladies wander in and out, in handsome period costumes. . . . The whole thing is designed to give you your money's worth. It does. Oh boy, and how!" Some of the comedy was freshened; but much of the 1910 vintage proved still sparkling. Thus, the comedian's old gag of swallowing a whistle and trying to talk but producing only little "peeps"— and being brought to the pump to wet his whistle—was still, as the *Post* said: "hilariously funny." The humor, being incidental, may keep changing; the basic rouse and rhythm remain.

Among many recent productions: New York at the Hotel Pierre, 1960; a short "café" version at the Astor Hotel, 1964. It entered the LOOM repertory in 1975, their first venture outside of Gilbert and Sullivan. Cyril Ritchard as Narrator and Lieutenant Governor headed an eight-week American tour in 1976; in the same year, a summer showing came to its "hometown," New Orleans. In 1978, in the repertory of the New York City Opera at Lincoln Center. In 1982 The Smithsonian made it the first full recording of a Victor Herbert operetta score.

Naughty Marietta is rich in remembered songs. Adah has a haunting song, " 'Neath the Southern Moon"; Marietta, as the marionette boy, an Italian street song. A vigorous march, "Tramp, Tramp, Tramp"; a sentimental solo, "The Sweet Bye and Bye"; a quartet, "Live for Today"; and the two most popular love songs, sung by Captain Dick: "Ah, Sweet Mystery of Life" ("Dream Melody"), and "I'm Falling in Love With Someone." These tender ballads or surging songs, the color of the setting, and the romantic love story amidst intrigue in the years of our country's forming, give laughter, delight, and long life to *Naughty Marietta*.

THE MELTING POT   *Israel Zangwill*

From early humorous writings Israel Zangwill (English, 1864-1926) turned in 1892 to a study of Jewish conditions in the novel *Children of the Ghetto*. This was dramatized in 1899, and with its wide popularity did much to improve the status of the Jew. Zangwill followed *Children of the Ghetto* with other novels and plays of Jewish life. The most successful and influential of these is a picture of the Jewish immigrant in America, *The Melting Pot*, 1908. The play received on the whole very favorable criticism. By many critics it was hailed as the drama that most fully captured the meaning of our expanding democracy; and the title of the play, until the First World War, was often used as a synonym for the United States.

The story of *The Melting Pot* entangles European memories with American hopes. David, a young Jewish composer, the only member of his family to survive the Kishinev massacre of 1903, has come to New York, where he falls in love with Vera Revendal, also from Russia but a non-Jew. The millionaire Quincy Davenport wants to divorce his wife and marry Vera; he brings Vera's father from Russia to prevent her marrying a Jew. David sees, in Baron Revendal, the leader of the Kishinev pogrom, and he turns from Vera. Then, on the Fourth of July, David's symphony "America" is played to an immigrant audience; David's faith in the melting pot of democracy returns, and he and Vera face the future together, as true Americans.

The Melting Pot had its premiere in Washington, October 5, 1908; it went to Chicago on the 21st, it reached New York September 17, 1909. Everywhere it kindled great excitement. In the play, David rails upon the millionaire, Quincy Davenport, as a blight upon America; from his box on opening night President Theodore Roosevelt exclaimed: "You're right; I've been warning the people against these Quincy Davenports." The President, however, objected to the immigrant's words, in the play, referring to the millionaire's desire for a divorce: "We are not native-born Americans; we hold our troth eternal." Zangwill declared that the President was no Czar and had no control over art, but he changed the line to "Not being members of the Four Hundred, we hold even our troth sacred." And, back in England (November 21), Zangwill wrote: "I am convinced that, in regard to the great mass of the American people, the married life is stabler and better than that of the English in many respects."

President Roosevelt called *The Melting Pot* "one of the best plays I've ever seen." Whereupon A. B. Walkley, in the *London Times,* exclaimed: "What a stupendous naiveté there is in such a statement as that! For, after all, what is this glorification of the amalgamated immigrants, this exaggerated freshness of the New World and staleness of the Old, this rhapsodizing over music and crucibles and statues of Liberty, but romantic claptrap?" To this, the American playwright Augustus Thomas* made rejoinder: "Having gone to the theatre with a constant enthusiasm for the last forty years, and having been professionally associated with the institution for twenty-five years, I am inclined to agree with Mr. Roosevelt."

The lawyer Clarence S. Darrow said: "This drama should mark a period in our upward ascent as a nation." The financier and philanthropist Jacob H. Schiff called it "a great play—a great human canvas—a feat of genius." The drama reviewer Burns Mantle declared: "The play's message should be driven deep into the heart of every foreign-born person in the country." The *Washington Times* said in an editorial (October 10, 1908): "Has it waited for a foreigner to write a great American play? *The Melting Pot* would indicate so. For in it finds expression the very genius of our national life." The *New York Telegraph* (September 19, 1909) called it "the most powerful and splendid play of modern times."

There were dissenters. Thus, after the New York opening, Alan Dale protested: "The Jewish 'tendency of mind' is impudently idiotic." The *New York Times* more objectively objected: "It is awkward in structure, clumsy in workmanship, and deficient as literature." But the play was even more provocative, in its day, than in recent seasons have been such motion pictures as *Gentleman's Agreement* and plays that have won awards, and that have roused protests like a recent one, similar to Alan Dale's, from a drama reviewer who referred to himself as a "pale-faced Protestant." (Alan Dale was the pen-name of Alfred J. Cohen.)

The *Chicago Daily News* (October 21, 1908) came nearest to the basic fault of the drama, pointing out that Zangwill "has swamped a magnificent theory in rhetorical excess, framed some vivid and tragic tableaux of Kishinev in anguish too torturing to be endured, and by his own luxurious genius for Yiddish hysteria, picturesque but ineffectual, he has nearly written a long Niagara of the woes and faults of Judea, instead of a startling American drama. . . . He does not clear the air of shocking reminders, nor does he put the young tempestuous Jew into the American melting pot with his Irish, Dutch, French, and English emigrant strugglers, but leaves him still the victim of the haunting face which ordered the butchering of the Jews that fatal Easter morning."

The original draft of *The Melting Pot* did not have the description of the Kishinev massacre. Walker Whiteside, who starred in the play, had read the manuscript and thought it would fail; George Tyler, the producer, felt that it would be a hit, but that it needed the picture of Kishinev to justify David's turning from Vera. Zangwill refused to make any change; Whiteside visited him in England, read the play aloud; and Zangwill added the emphasis on the massacre. This increased the pathos but lessened the universality of the drama.

The Melting Pot remains, nevertheless, despite its over-emotional presentation of the theme, the first and still the best dramatic plea for interracial understanding and picture of the United States as a crucible where people of all the earth are being fused into that new form, the democratic American. As the *Baltimore World* (October 13, 1908) declared, "*The Melting Pot* is a prophecy—a prophecy of life that may come, that has long been dreamed of, but has never been realized." Social conditions have in many respects changed since 1908, but the vision of *The Melting Pot* remains valid, and—unfortunately—remains a dream.

THERESE RAQUIN   *Emile Zola*

The novelist Emile Zola (French, 1840-1902), founder and chief of the naturalistic school of fiction, made several efforts to write for the theatre. His first venture, at the height of the naturalistic furore, was his one lasting success. this was the dramatization of his novel *Thérèse Raquin,* 1867 (also called *Thérèse).*

The story is one of crime wreaking its own revenge: murder will out. Thérèse Raquin has come to loathe her shiftless, consumptive nincompoop of a husband, Camille, and his doting mother. She eggs on her lover, the artist Laurent, until one day they drown Camille, but their story makes his old mother thank them for trying to save him. After a year, Camille's mother herself suggests that they marry. In the bridal chamber hangs a painting of Camille by Laurent. And beneath it the couple, soul-sick with gathered horror at their crime, reproach one another. Camille's mother overhears—and is stricken with paralysis. Only her eyes are alive; but they burn with scorn and fever for revenge. Thérèse and Laurent grow more and more unable to endure their burden, until they find release in a double suicide.

The production of *Thérèse Raquin* in Paris on July 11, 1873, divided the city. The champions of naturalism hailed the play as the first tragedy in the genre. The opponents admitted the play's power, but attacked its theme and its presentation of only mean folk in sordid situations. They asked why a "slice of life" must always slice through the viscera. When London saw the play, opening October 10, 1891, in an adaptation by George Moore, at J. T. Grein's Independent Theatre, its forcefulness was equally felt. The *Graphic* declared: "The play is one of great power, and produces a deep impression by apparently simple means. The characters seem very human, the dialogue is very natural, and the atmosphere of horror is wonderfully created. By simple, subtle touches one is caused to feel the coming horror and to understand and sympathize with the soul-quakings of the guilty pair. . . . As for morality, I can only say that the naturalists are the most desperately moral of all the schools." Basically, Zola in *Thérèse Raquin* presents the searching moral idea that crime brings its own punishment.

What shocked the more sensitive, in *Thérèse Raquin*, was not the moral to be extracted from the story, but the lack of moral fervor, of moral fibre, in the characters, their loathly level of ethical unconcern; and certain details of the action. Thus Boston audiences in 1892 were shocked when the murderess bride, beneath the slain man's portrait, undresses to receive the murderer lover-turned-husband.

Against such protests, the *New York American* (December 31, 1892) launched strong attack: "We are a nation of boys and virgins. It would shame our shrinking chastity, suffuse our lily-white natures with the pink of pudicity if we thought to discover in *Thérèse Raquin* something besides the frank brutalitay of Zola's theme, such as the unflinching methods of its treatment, the masterly development of effective details, the unswerving pursuit of the rational, inevitable end. . . . We see in *Thérèse Raquin* only a picture of lust, and bourgeois lust at that. . . . When, a twelve-month after the murder of the driveling, snarling invalid Camille, Thérèse and her lover meet in the intimacy sanctioned by marriage, we crane our necks to miss no part of a scene concerning which rumor has aroused our liveliest anticipations. To acknowledge to our selves that these are but the touches of an artist giving life, color, movement, atmosphere, the better to impress upon us his meaning—not his craft—would be to convict ourselves of an appreciation, an admiration of what we know in our sure simplicity to be unseemly, indecent. . . . To him who views the much blamed play of M. Zola in a spirit free from the hyperaesthesia of purity that afflicts the national temper, *Thérèse Raquin* cannot fail to present many of the characteristics of the mighty tragedies which embodied the lofty scheme of Greek morals. It lifts guilt above the fallible judgment of man, and submits its punishment to the unerring wisdom of Deity. That is the acme of human tragedy, and that is the acme to which the tragic lesson of *Thérèse Raquin* ascends."

After a 1934 London production, Charles Morgan also emphasized the power of the play, as viewed in the eyes of the mother: "Zola saw Madame Raquin as a mirror of conscience, a personification of avenging fate. . . . The audience is battered by horror and suffering. The analysis of character is elaborate and thorough. The dialogue has economy and spring."

Such qualities, combining in an onslaught upon audience emotions, have brought *Thérèse Raquin* frequent revival. London saw it in 1923, and in 1928 with Emlyn Williams as Camille. The 1934 London version was called *Thou Shalt not – – –*. A powerful New York production opened October 9, 1945, with Eva Le Gallienne, and with Dame May Whitty eerily vivid as the old mother. This version ended with the mother recovering from her paralysis sufficiently to start a message informing on the couple; she does not complete her story, but they confess to the police.

Zola, in his naturalistic zeal, wanted his characters not to be played but to "live" before the public. "I wanted," he said, "to make a purely human study, free from all extraneous interest; going straight to its goal: the action lying not in any story whatsoever but in the internal conflicts of the characters; there was no longer a logic of facts, but a logic of sensations and feelings; and the dénouement became a mathematical consequence of the given problem."

Lauded as *Thérèse Raquin* has been, and powerful as it still is, the play nonetheless lacks the exaltation of tragedy. The reason for this lack was set down by James Agate, in *At Half Past Eight* (1923): "Conceiving it his duty to protest against the Romantics with their glorified stories of changelings, their windy nursery-moralities and their *grands mots bêtes* —the protestor went too far for comomon sense and not far enough for high tragedy. What Zola's play lacks is nobility. But nobility to this realist was *vieux jeux,* the worn-out fashion of Aeschylus and Shakespeare, Racine, le père Hugo, the whole bombastic crowd. Ignobility was his theme, the bee in a very clever bonnet." *Thérèse Raquin* tramples powerfully in the mud; it holds us with the picture of the bespattered souls sinking deeper, until they are submerged. The play stamps us with their story. But, being in the mud, it cannot reflect the stars. It remains a grim picture of a passion-gripped couple, torn by their own emotions as the play tears at ours. *Thérèse Raquin,* the best naturalistic drama by the leading figure in the movement, thus illustrates at once naturalism's limitations and its potent force.

The play proved equally powerful in revivals: as unrelieved melodrama, in Edinburgh February 21, 1955. London Winter Garden, May 6, 1955, in a version by Juliet Mansel and Robin King called *The Lovers,* directed by Sam Wanamaker; Helen Hayes was the mother; the Hungarian film star Eva Bartok played Thérèse in her stage debut. Guilford, England, August 20, 1974, with Helen Ryan a last-minute Thérèse (replacing the ill Gayle Hunnicut), and Joan Miller as the mother. OffOffBway (Golden Fleece), May 26, 1978.

DON JUAN TENORIO   *José Zorrilla y Moral*

One of the most familiar figures in world literature is Don Juan, whose name has become the label of the reckless rake and triumphant libertine. There was, apparently, a Don Miguel Mañara in fourteenth century Seville, who seduced a trusting maiden, then killed her father, and spent his later days doing penance in a monastery. Out of his story grew the play *El Burlador de Seville (The Seducer of Seville)* by Tirso de Molina (pseudonym of the Spanish monk Gabriel Tellez, 1570-1648), the first dramatization of the Don Juan tale. In this telling, the statue comes into action. After Don Juan has seduced Dona Anna, he kills the Commandant Don Pedro, her father, who has come seeking vengeance. In the graveyard, the statue of Don Pedro warns Don Juan to repent and change his ways. Don Juan laughs, and in mockery invites the statue to a banquet—at which the statue plunges Don Juan down to hell. "Tirso de Molina did not invent the story of the Statue," declared the *London Times* (September 23, 1949), "nobody invented it. It is a symbol of the dominion exercised over the living by the dead, a dominion present in the human imagination since the earliest times. When Don Juan mocks the Statue he outrages a great taboo. In his amorous intrigues, he is a sinner at odds with society; in his dealings with the Statue he calls down on himself the wrath of God." This deep-rooted horror at the knight's blasphemy combines with the fascination of his conquests to give strong and wide appeal to the Don Juan story.

Just how Don Juan achieves his dominion over women, Molière* is the only dramatist to indicate. In his *Don Juan, ou Le Festin de Pierre (. . . or The Stone Feast)*, 1665, there is a superb scene in which Don Juan, caught between two women with whom he has been dallying, makes each believe she is his only love. After Molière, many other playwrights retold the story: Thomas Corneille, in French, in 1673; Thomas Shadwell, as *The Libertine*, in English, in 1676. With music by Mozart, and libretto by Lorenzo da Ponte, Molière's play was turned into the opera *Don Giovanni, or, The Marble Guest.* This, the most popular of all versions of the story, had its premiere in Prague, October 29, 1787. Its American premiere was in 1824. At the Metropolitan Opera House, New York, it marked the debut of Antonio Scotti in 1899; in Dallas, Texas, of Ezio Pinza in 1929. A Metropolitan performance, January 23, 1908, enlisted Scotti, Feodor Chaliapin (as Don Juan's servant, Leporello), Emma Eames, Johanna Gadski, and Marcella Sembrich, with Gustav Mahler as conductor. In the opera, Leporello, an impudent rascal and poltroon, sings to Dona Elvira a list of Don Juan's conquests—in Spain, 1,003; in Turkey, 91—to a total of 2,670 women fallen to his charms.

In addition to poems and stories (Byron, Merimée, Tolstoi) plays about the fabulous libertine continued. There was a burlesque of *Don Giovanni* by T. Dibdin (English, 1771-1814) played in New York in 1819. The German Christian Grabbe combined two great symbols of man's questing in his *Don Juan and Faust*, 1829. In 1830 the Russian Pushkin* followed Molière, in his "dramatic scene" *The Stone Guest*, but by making Don Juan sincere pointed toward the admiration of Baudelaire. The French Alexandre Dumas père in 1836 wrote *Don Juan de Mañara; or, The Fall of an Angel.* This has five acts, but in mood is like a medieval mystery, with good and bad angels accompanying Don Juan throughout the play, and struggling for his soul. It contains duels and deaths by the half-dozen, seductions, suicides, elopements, murders by sword and by poison, ghosts, and spectral visions. Thackeray, in his *Paris Sketch Book*, protested against Dumas' play as immoral, indecent in its effect. About fifty years later, Edmond Haraucourt made a four-act verse play of the Dumas version, and in 1937 *Don Juan de Mañara* became an opera, with English book by Arnold Bennett and music by Eugene Goossens. In the Dumas version and its followers, Don Juan repents and ends his years in a monastery.

Perhaps heeding Thackeray—at any rate, for Victorian taste—Richard Mansfield, on May 17, 1891, appeared in *Don Juan, The Sad Adventures of a Youth*, which, he declared, "avoided every incident or allusion that might be thought indelicate." He changed the reckless rake into a little Lord Fauntleroy gone wrong. More searchingly, the Spanish playwright Echegaray,* in *the Son of Don Juan*, 1892, showed the sins of the father visited upon the son: Don Juan stands by as his child Lazarus, dying, cries (like a ghost of Ibsen's *Ghosts*) "The sun—mother—give me the sun." Bernard Shaw, in his *Dramatic Opinions and Essays* (Vol. I, 81-89) quoted a long speech of Don Juan's from Echegaray's drama, concluding that Spain had produced "a genius of a stamp that crosses frontiers." Shaw's own *Don*

Juan in Hell [the vision of John Tanner (named from Don Juan Tenario) in the third act of *Man and Superman* *] marks a second step in the libertine's reclamation. The first step was taken by the superb poet of French decadence, Charles Baudelaire (1821-1867), in his dramatic poem *Don Juan,* in which a Byronic gentleman, leaning on his rapier in Charon's barge crossing the Styx, disdains to take notice of the pageant of his years translated into an infernal spectacle. Baudelaire's poem was enacted in Paris in 1948; the *London Times* (September 23, 1949) declared: "The impious libertine of a Counter-Reformation Seville became a martyr, one of the greatest saints in the romantic canon. . . . Damnation became apotheosis. . . . The arch-Romantic, Mr. Bernard Shaw, took matters to their logical extreme in *Man and Superman* by harrowing hell and sending Don Juan heavenward after Rembrandt and Mozart."

Recent years have seen no stay in the flood of Don Juan plays. Carl Sternheim wrote one in German, 1910; James Elroy Flecker, in English verse, 1911. Three French versions are noteworthy. Henri Bataille's *The Man With the Rose,* presented in New York, with Lou Tellegen, September 5, 1921, is a modernized version, sophisticated and cynical. Edmond Rostand's *The Last Night of Don Juan,* 1922, adapted by Sidney Howard and presented in New York in 1925, on the other hand, exalts the ideals of spiritual love and womanly virtue. André Obey's *Don Juan* (played by Pierre Fresnay in Paris; likewise in London opening February 26, 1934, in French) is written as a medieval morality. Don Juan in this play represents sinning, suffering humanity, struggling, blundering, groping for happiness in a life that leads to death. Don Juan hides from his fear of death by making love to women; conquest gives him a momentary sense of power, of security. When he is about to be condemned for his rape of Anna, Elvira—who has always loved him—seeks to save him by marrying him. Don Juan thanks her, puts a dagger to his breast, and by embracing a prostitute he had set on the downward path, presses the blade into his repentant heart.

The most widely popular of the dramatic retellings of the Don Juan story is *Don Juan Tenorio,* 1844, by José Zorrilla y Moral (Spanish, 1817-1893). This was the favorite play of Emperor Maximilian, who during Zorrilla's stay in Mexico (1855-1866) had the author direct private performances at Chapultepec Castle. In many Catholic cities and towns of Spain and Spanish America, after the visits to the cemetery on All Souls' Day (November 2), Zorrilla's play is presented every year, as a sort of horrible example and dramatic catharsis. Don Juan is really bad, the *New York Herald-Tribune* (November 3, 1929) reported after such a production. "He teaches a lesson, though, in the grand manner, and in beholding—for six or seven hours— his magnificent strut, his swordplay-and-satin wickedness, you can almost have your sin and abjure it too." Zorrilla's poetry is potent, the reviewer continued: "It soothes the ear, this stately verse, with its sonorous climaxes of rage, consternation, the very best *amor,* exaltation, and damnation." It is a richly surging drama, recapturing the power of the olden story.

The figure of Don Juan lends itself to many meanings. It has been viewed as embodying the constant impulse of man's body, as Faust represents the tireless impulse of man's mind. It has been viewed as showing the attempt of man to hide from his fears. It is best presented when the dramatist, like Zorrilla, presses no single symbol of his own, but shows within Don Juan qualities and urges that in lesser measure every man can recognize within himself, so that the universal human figure takes the unique and individual aspect of each one. Thus Don Juan Tenorio becomes another, a less Puritan and more catholic Pilgrim, on blundering, destructive, yearning, pathetic progress toward a goal he can only dream.

Molière himself played Sganarelle, the artfully subservient valet who (as Richard Eder pointed out in the *New York Times,* April 7, 1979) "is simultaneously bursting with ingeniously reasoned arguments against his master's nihilism, and choked with fear of him. His speeches begin as denunciations, change course in midstream, and end as fulsome flattery." Among the many revivals of the Molière play: in England: April 18, 1956, in London in French, Jean Vilar director and star. May 15, 1956, English by Ronald Duncan, with Keith Mitchell and Joan Plowright. December 4, 1958, at Oxford, translated and directed by Adrian Brine. London, October 28, 1958, by Théâtre National Populaire. Bristol Old Vic, 1958, adapted by Max Frisch as *Don Juan, or the Love of Geometry.* NT (Cottesloe), May 7, 1981; Eric Shorter declared: "Here are the passionate unbelief and eager amorality of the typical modern anti-hero."

In the United States: OffBway (Downtown), 1956. Yale, 1970, Alvin Epstein as Don Juan. *Time* magazine (June 15, 1970) said: "His only power is to destroy whatever he can touch . . . His obsessive sexuality is chillingly sexless." With a new subtitle, *Enemy of God,* the play had a Prologue and Epilogue, with a Black Mass wherein sinister cowled figures sacrifice a goat; important speeches are delivered from a pulpit, and Don Juan himself seems a sacrificial religious object. Phoenix, twenty-two performances beginning December 11, 1972. Goodman Theatre, Chicago, 1977. Arena Stage, Washington, 1979. CSC OffBway, January 20, 1980, translated by Christopher Martin. Tyrone Guthrie, 1981, in Minneapolis, with thunderous thumpings and organ claps.

Bertolt Brecht made an adaptation for the Berliner Ensemble.

The Zorrilla *Don Juan Tenorio* is still produced annually in Mexico City during All Souls Week, sometimes with as many as ten productions at the same time. The authorities have had to restrain modernized passages, with sexual indecency, or social and political emphases. In Madrid also, there may be three or four seasonal productions. Don Juan, from a desire to mock or secret envy, still holds a strong appeal.

THE CAPTAIN OF KÖPENICK   *Karl Zuckmayer*

An amusing and sharply pointed satire on unquestioning subservience, on the instant obedience a uniform commands, swept all of Europe with laughter in *The Captain of Köpenick,* by Karl Zuckmayer (German, 1896-1977). Based on an actual incident, the play depicts the plight of an old cobbler who cannot get a passport. (In much of Europe passports are required of every citizen, even within his own town.)

As a young man, cobbler Voigt was sent to prison for petty larceny, and for the rest of his life he finds himself a marked man. Unable to get a decent job, or to provide himself with a "clean" passport, he struggles more and more hopelessly until his fifty-seventh year. Then he steps forth. For he has noticed what unquestioning obedience is given a man in uniform; indeed, says the dealer in second-hand clothes: "If this uniform went for a walk without anyone in it, every soldier would salute it, it's so genuine!" In the railway station washroom of the town of Köpenick, the cobbler dons the captain's uniform. He then commandeers a troop of soldiers, marches them to the Town Hall, arrests the Mayor and sends him to Berlin, demands an accounting of the Treasurer, and accepts the town's current funds. Unfortunately, the suburban town does not have a passport office.

Voigt goes back to the Berlin slums; the hoax becomes a headline sensation. When everyone is seeking the impostor, Voigt walks into headquarters and says that, if they promise him a clean passport, he'll reveal the false captain's whereabouts. They do, and he does. The officials' mirth is so great that we are led to believe Voigt will be let off lightly. When one of them tells Voigt he was lucky, the old man retorts: "Luck is the first requirement in a commander, Napoleon said." They want to see the cobbler in the uniform and posture of command, and the play ends as Voigt gets a look at himself in a mirror and cries the notorious two words: "Im—possible!"

The Captain of Köpenick develops its story in a succession of rapid scenes. Some are soberly moving, touched with a bitter view of life, as when Voigt's brother-in-law welcomes him to stay and try to make a fresh start, though his sister fears that he may become a burden; and Voigt watches over the death-bed of their child. Most of the scenes are humorous, though even then with sober undertones, as in the attempt, in a cheap café, to bargain with a tart, who protests: "You can't ride me as though I'm a ten cent bus!" Voigt can't get work unless he is registered, and the police won't register him until he has a job. Out of his life-long quandary Voigt emerges by a process of self-hypnosis: "I put on the uniform and then I gave myself an order, and then I went and carried it out." He acts on the principle that "a man is looked upon as he makes himself look."

The Captain of Köpenick had its premiere in Berlin in 1928, with Werner Krauss. The play, and the motion picture made of it in 1931, were banned in Germany in 1933. The story was refilmed in America in 1941, with Albert Bassermann, and has come to the stage again since the War. Its capture of the human weakness of unquestioning obedience to an outer form combines with lively movement, with natural characters and dialogue, to give the play a continuing sober significance beneath its rollicking laughter.

The Captain of Köpenick was brought to New York November 24, 1964, by the Schiller Theater of West Berlin. It was played in English at the Keswick Festival, England, July 20, 1965. Paul Scofield played the Captain in London, 1971.

PLAYS BY UNKNOWN AUTHORS

THE BOOK OF JOB

"A philosophic religious dramatic dialogue of great intensity," as Leo Auerbach described it in the *Encyclopedia of Literature* (1946), *Job* has increasingly been presented in dramatic form. Some scholars believe that this book of the *Bible* was written about 400 B.C. by an Alexandrian Jew sufficiently Hellenized to be aware of the classical Greek theatre. As Richard Green Moulton showed by his arrangement in 1907, no changes in the text are needed—only in the format—to convert the poem into a great drama of Job's temptation and steadfastness under trial. "With great boldness," said the *New York Times* (March 8, 1918), "and with a frankness remarkable in the fifth or sixth century before Christ, it copes with the problem of the origin of evil and its persistent flourishing in this world. . . .

The final appeal is to God, who speaks in answer from the whirlwind, and bids men trust and revere His wisdom, though it passes understanding."

In an arrangement by Horace Kallen, *The Book of Job* was presented at Harvard University, May 8, 1916. It was presented in New York, March 7, 1918, with George Gaul as Job and Walter Hampden as Elihu; again in New York in 1922; in Los Angeles in 1932. Of the New York premiere, the *Times* stated: "What most deeply impressed yesterday's audience was not the profundity of the thought; it was the intense drama, the vivid struggle of wills, that underlies the poem. If the philosophic speculations of this Job lacked clarity and constructive development it was because he was one quivering agony of soul-suffering, and could only cry out to his friends and to his God to be consoled. His 'comforters' were likewise less remarkable as disquisitionists than as dramatis personae—saliently, if quite simply, characterized as pharisaical exponents of ancient wisdom that rides roughshod over present suffering. Even the Voice from the Whirlwind did not greatly impress one as accounting for evil and human woe; but it came as a stunning climax. Let those who can, enjoy *The Book of Job* as philosophy. To yesterday's audience it was high poetic drama."

We are told that the devil can cite Scripture for his purpose. In 1934, under the auspices of the German Ministry of Enlightenment and Propaganda, a production was given in Cologne of *The Play of Job the German*. This began, as does the *Bible* drama, with Satan's declaring that Job is devoted to God only because all is well with him, and God flinging His fateful challenge: on Job's response to Satan will hang the salvation of the world. But among Job's afflictions is an enemy's advance; his sons gird for war; and Job exclaims: "That is good! When the youth of a land ceases to be warlike and lusty in fighting, it lets its country go to ruin. Who will not fight shall not possess." And when, at the close, discomfited Satan retreats, the Choir sings: "Praised be the victory of the German."

The Book of Job, without such transmogrification, is a majestic and passionate dramatic poem, as Job, outside his village in the land of Uz, lifts up his voice in protest, in bewilderment, in wonder, and in joyous praise of his God. In the face of all his wretchedness, against the crude arguments of his harsh comforters, Job's exultant cry "I know that my Redeemer liveth" rings with dramatic triumph, with inner truth and shining beauty.

Various actors have adapted *The Book of Job* for presentation, such as Orlin Corey, for twelve performances OffOffBway (Methodist Christ Church), February 9, 1962.

In Prologue and eleven scenes, Archibald MacLeish told the story in the guise of J.B., a businessman who sits at Thanksgiving dinner with his wife, while God and Satan—Mr. Zuss, a circus balloon-vendor (God), and Nickles, a circus popcorn-vendor (the Father of lies)—don masks to make their mortal wager. J.B. is plagued by the death of his children in a car crash from drunken driving; in an air raid; then with personal pain, burned from atomic fallout. When he cries out, why?, feeble answers are proffered by priest and psychologist; he holds to his faith in God's final justice.

Produced first at Yale, April 1958, *J.B.* went to New York December 11, 1958, with Christopher Plummer as Nickles, Raymond Massey as Mr. Zuss, Pat Hingle as J.B., for 364 performances and the Pulitzer Prize.

Jean Dalrymple took the play to the September 1958 Brussels Exposition. It was played by Asolo OffBway in 1981. While the MacLeish version indicates that the problem of evil is forever pertinent, *The Book of Job* remains the stark yet resolute reminder that man may keep his faith beyond all suffering.

The futile or specious attempts of those around to lend support to the troubled man has led to the general ironic use of the term "a Job's comforter."

THE CIRCLE OF CHALK   *Unknown Author*

Out of a cycle of one hundred plays of the Yuan dynasty (1259-1368) in China, by way of a nineteenth century prose and verse French translation of Stanislaus Julien, *Hoei-Lan-Kin* (*The Circle of Chalk*) was adapted in 1924 in German by Klabund (pseudonym of Alfred Henchke, 1891-1928). Reinhardt's 1925 production, with Elisabeth Bergner, was a hit. The English version by James Laver, opening in London January 22, 1931, with Anna May Wong and Laurence Olivier, ran for over a year. New York, in 1933, saw a version by I. S. Richter. Erwin Piscator presented the play at his Dramatic Workshop, with Dolly Haas, in 1941 and in revivals through the next decade. From Klabund, Bertolt Brecht* drew his German *Caucasian Chalk Circle,* translated into English by Eric and Maja Bentley in 1947.

The circle is a symbol of personal integrity; and in *The Circle of Chalk* the steadfast heroine Hai Tang, subjected to many trials, sustains her integrity through all her suffering and her final elevation to the Imperial throne. When her father, oppressed by taxes, kills himself, the young Hai Tang is sold to a House of Joy. Thence, despite the bidding of Prince Po, she is bought by Ma, the tax official. Ma's first wife, the childness crone Yu Pi, poisons Ma, and declares that Hai Tang has not only committed the murder, but also stolen Yu Pi's baby, claiming it as her own. Through bribery and corruption Yu Pi presses hard upon Hai Tang. But at court the judge, disreputable and cynical drunkard though he is, subjects the two women to the traditional test of the chalk circle: the child is put within the circle and released to the two women; only the true mother can lead him out. Yu Pi tugs hard at the child; Hai Tang does not touch it. And with the wisdom of Solomon, the judge decides that Hai Tang, who would rather lose than hurt the child, is the true mother. Prince Po adds the crowning happiness when he admits that he is the father of Hai Tang's child.

When *The Circle of Chalk* was presented in Vienna, in 1925, its charm made "an impression to which the critical faculty readily surrenders." The London 1931 production showed girls in gilded cages in a House of Joy, guarded by a hideous unsexed headsman. In 1945, with more simplicity of décor, the play seemed "a pleasing piece of willow-waly." In New York the *Post* (March 26, 1941) praised its "quaintness and delicacy"; the *Christian Science Monitor* (March 27) found it "full of emotion, beauty, and vitality."

The Circle of Chalk is remarkable for the naturalness of the many characters, who seem to grow from the earthy movement of the story. There is a homely healthiness, too, in the comments of many of the figures, especially of the corruptible judge who unexpectedly (to Western minds; the Chinese knew that this style of play must have a happy ending) restores the child to its mother. There is also considerable humor in the play: sometimes this is just good fun, as when the palanquins (hobby-horse poles with a head on top) jostle for place on the Peking road; sometimes it is caustic against abuses of the times, abuses still found in many lands.

There is lyrical verse of considerable beauty in *The Circle of Chalk*. Part folk-tale, part realistic revelation of men and women urging toward good through all their weakness and evil, *The Circle of Chalk* brings simple beauty and friendly laughter and basic truths out of a far land and distant century. It is further evidence of the unchanging roots of human nature, and of the timelessness of art.

Recent popularity calls for further attention to Brecht's Chinese adaptations. He set *The Caucasian Chalk Circle* in Georgian Russia in 1945, where two groups—one of Caucasian goatherds who abandoned a valley on the Nazis' approach; one of fruit growers who have planted the valley— dispute the territory. It is granted to those who can make it bring forth fruit. (This seems a rather literal interpretation for egalitarian Brecht; are not goatherds doing good social service, too?) At a festival to celebrate their victory, the fruit growers enact "the old Chinese play" on the same theme. In the Brecht version, the old judge is hanged by rebellious soldiers, who make Azdak judge because he amuses them. He's a genial but unscrupulous judge, but he favors the poor. One poor fugitive whom Azdak has sheltered turns out to be the Grand Duke, and when the rebellion is crushed, the Duke saves Azdak from hanging and allows him to remain judge. It is then that he decides the case of the disputed child.

Elisbeth Bergner played Klabund's *Circle of Chalk* in Berlin, 1925, directed by Max Reinhardt. Klabund's play was shown in London, 1956, for one performance, followed by the Brecht version. Klabund, in translation by John Halstrom, was played again in London 1962.

Translated by Eric Bentley (Brecht's American champion), *The Caucasian Chalk Circle* was shown in 1948 at Carleton College; at the Hedgerow Theatre, Pa., in 1961; in 1977 at the Washington Arena Stage. It was given ninety-three performances at the New York Vivian Beaumont; Douglas Watt in the *News* (January 4, 1966) declared: "Brecht and his theatre are simply not for us." Brecht still has his followers: the RSC sent the play, directed by John Caird, for a 1979 tour of twenty-six English cities; and in 1982, adapted and directed by Michael Bogdanov, it was shown at the NT (Cottesloe) and on tour.

The Good Woman of Setzuan was adapted by Brecht while in exile in Scandinavia; its world premiere was in Zurich in 1940. It was played Off-Bway in 1949; and in 1956, translated and directed by Eric Bentley, was played by the Phoenix with Uta Hagen and Zero Mostel. The Bentley version went to London in 1956, with Peggy Ashcroft and Joan Plowright. A version by Ralph Manheim opened at the New York Lincoln Center November 5, 1970, with Colleen Dewhurst, for forty-six performances.

The play's ten scenes of prose and verse, with music by Paul Dessau, modernize the olden legend of three gods who come to earth, seeking one good person for whose sake they will spare the world. A poor prostitute, Shan Te, is the only one who takes them in. She says she's too poor to be good. The gods give her money and a tobacco shop; but when the poor flock in, she invents a ruthless male cousin to keep them off, and amasses the profits. She falls in love with an unemployed scoundrelly aviator, who, when he can't get her money (she's running the tobacco plant like a sweatshop), accuses her of murdering the cousin. The gods, incognito, sit as judges; Shan Te confesses her invention of the cousin; she pleads that to be good to herself she cannot be good to others. The gods float away, smiling at her: "Blessed be the good woman of Setzuan."

Brecht here seems to apply the old legend ironically to the current world. He, too, is having his day.

Addendum: The "chalk circle" is of course an Oriental variation of the sword of Solomon, Bible, I Kings 3:23-28. In early folk tales, of India and Tibet in the fifth century, the child was to be pulled across a straight line; the circle appears in the fourteenth century. The story was told in French in 1832; in German, 1876.

In the Brecht *Chalk Circle*, when the Governor of a provincial capital is killed and his wife flees helter-skelter without heed for their child, the Nurse hides it and lovingly rears it. Years later, the mother, needing an heir, reclaims the chld. The judge applies the test of the "chalk circle," and awards the child to the Nurse. Brecht's implication is that "truth" is socially conditioned.

THE PASSION PLAY   *Unknown Author*

Two themes of the medieval mystery play survive, in various modifications of the original forms, in current and widely played religious drama. One of these is in *The Passion Play,* the drama of the passion (suffering) of Jesus Christ. This presents episodes, varying from play to play, of the last days of Jesus. The play is enacted, in some communities, in annual remembrance of the lifting of a plague or other local disaster; or as a pious offering at Easter time or at the Feast of Corpus Christi. The other major surviving theme is in *The Shepherds' Play,** or some other enactment of the Nativity, the birth of Jesus, presented as part of the Christmas festival. (See *Everyman.**)

The best known drama of the passion of Christ is that which is enacted once every ten years at Oberammergau, Bavaria. This dramatic representation of the last days, the crucifixion and the resurrection of Jesus has been given by the villagers, interrupted only by the Franco-Prussian and the two World Wars, since 1634, to keep a vow made during an epidemic of the Black Death. In the early nineteenth century, miracle plays were banned in Bavaria, having become worldly, coarse, even immoral. *The Passion Play* of Oberammergau was then rewritten by Father Ottmer Weiss, of nearby Ettal Abbey, with music by Schoolmaster Rochus Dedler. Approved by the authorities, it became so popular that in 1870 the Oberammergau Burgomaster protested: "We do not wish the spectacle of our Lord's Passion, now represented here for 230 years, to be made a scheme for money-making by foreign speculators, and I enter an indignant protest against such a profanation of the intention of our play, which, descending to us as a solemn vow from our ancestors, aims at purifying the feelings from worldly thoughts." The attitude of the community has changed. The open-air theatre at Oberammergau now seats 4,000; and in 1934, at the 300th anniversary of the cessation of the plague, some 400,00 spectators attended *The Passion Play.* Performances were revived in 1950.

While the Oberammergau presentation is the best known, it is by no means the oldest of the many productions. The one at Freiburg was begun in 1264 and claims to have been shown without interruption since 1600. At Barzio, Italy, with a rather primitive text by a Genoese priest, *The Passion Play* has been presented since the early seventeenth century. A very interesting production, and perhaps the oldest continuous one, is that of the almost inaccessible town of Roquebrune, on the French Riviera. The scene in the Garden of Olives is performed under real olive trees; the company moves in solemn procession to the Stations of the Cross—and has done so annually, it is claimed, without missing a single year since the great plague of 1467. Other quite old productions are those at Bene-diktbeurn, Bavaria, and St. Gall, Switzerland. Other European cities have had annual performances for many years.

With variant details, and different degrees of elaboration—*The True Mystery of the Passion,* re-enacted in Paris in 1936, was a 34,000-line play in 1582 and took six days to perform—the passion plays follow the same general pattern. Most of them begin after Judas's betrayal, presenting the Agony in the Gardan, Christ before Pilate, the Condemnation, the Carry-ing of the Cross—at Oberammergau the most famous Christus, Anton Lang (who acted the role 1900-1930), carried a hundred-pound cross, and was suspended upon it for twenty-two minutes—the Crucifixion, the De-scent from the Cross, the Resurrection, and the Ascension. The whole is a sort of Divine Comedy; its theme is mankind's redemption. The dialogue is simple, devoted; it is often crude, and usually without literary distinction. The quality of the play rises from the earnest devotion of the performers and from the simple faith of the spectators, which makes them one with the soul-story enacted before their eyes.

The law of England until 1965 prohibited representations of Jesus in any place licensed for public performance. Almost every other land with nu-merous Catholics has its passion plays, varying according to the spirit and customs of the country. The most elaborate in the New World is probably that given in the village of Chinantis, Guatemala, every Good Friday for some 300 years. Judas is chased by the crowds, as he shakes his bag of silver; sometimes the actor has been given really rough treatment.

The United States also has its passion plays at the Easter season. The Black Hills *Passion Play* is an old one; others seem more sporadic. Two in the east were presented over thirty years. *Veronica's Veil* was enacted beginning 1915 at Union City, New Jersey—Veronica, wife of Caiaphas, wiped the blood from the face of Jesus as He carried the Cross: the veil thus used became miracle-working. And in Brooklyn, New York, from early in this century until 1942, the Redemptorist Fathers sponsored an-nual productions of *Pilate's Daughter.*

Simple or elaborate, but essentially of the folk, these passion plays throughout Christendom perpetuate not only the spirit and faith they ex-emplify, but the essential drama of the Christ story, and the eternal spirit of the theatre—the bodying forth of things unseen, the challenge to man's powers, the surge of man's resolve and exaltation—that took its birth in the church.

THE SHEPHERDS' PLAY   *Unknown Author*

Second only in popular interest to *The Passion Play** is the drama of the Nativity of Jesus. This was always well represented among the mystery plays of the tenth to the fourteenth centuries. And it is in the joyous celebration of the coming of the infant Jesus that humor seems first to have entered modern drama. "The hilarity of *The Second Shepherds' Play,*" as Freedley and Reeves remarked in *A History of the Theatre* (1941), "is still funny." A production of this play of the English Wakefield cycle, of the fourteenth century, was given with marionettes at New York Univer-sity, in 1938. Into the manger, where a cradle is awaiting the expected babe, comes a shepherd who has stolen a lamb. Fearful of pursuit, he looks for a place to hide it, and tucks it, covered all save the nose, into the cradle. The searchers, and others, come; all admire the new-born babe until, in the midst of the chorus of praise, it opens its mouth and says "Baa!"

Variations of *The Shepherds' Play* are still presented in many Catholic regions. In Mexico, at Christmastide, *Los Pastorales* (*The Pastoral Plays*) are enacted in the Sunday Schools, in a form tradition says was used by St. Francis in Umbria, in 1223. In the backyards, meanwhile, or in the village square, there is presented a play, *Los Pastores* (*The Shepherds*) passed down by word of mouth. Manuscripts of this do exist, some, it is claimed, set down in eleventh century Toledo; but in hundreds of Spanish-speaking towns and villages, daily for the twenty-four days from "the good night" (Christmas Eve) to Candlemas, the play is performed as in the oral tradition.

Hence there are many local variations on the basic biblical theme. Some details are widespread, such as the famous remark of the Shepherd who objects to following the Star of Bethlehem: "If Heaven wants to see me, let Heaven come to me!" This folk play contains further elements of humor, which the sober Passion Play lacks. The Devil tries to keep the angels and the shepherds from Jesus's crib. At the end, with the Devil sent howling to Hell—his tail perhaps popping with firecrackers—the shepherds raise the infant Jesus and sing a lullaby; then the cast begs the Holy Babe for His blessing.

Often the productions of these plays were decorated like the naive religious folk paintings, as as piously regarded. One in Spain was described in the London *Pictorial World* of May 22, 1880: "After the Magi had presented their gifts to Mary, who was seated beside a pasteboard manger, surrounded by pasteboard oxen, with a great deal of genuine straw about, at the tinkle of a little bell ballet girls in short skirts and pink tights darted from the side scenes and, pirouetting around the group, finally struck an attitude with their hands over the cradle and their elevated toes pointing to the audience. . . . It was deeply religious to the people, and many women wept." The mingled sobriety and fun, the jollity and reverence, of these occasions, draw the fullest audience participation, and are a rich continuance of folk dramatic art. (See *Everyman.**)

The spirit of such dramas still stirs in contemporary authors. There is tenderness and true simplicity in Claudel's *The Tidings brought to Mary.** The *Bethlehem*, 1902, of Laurence Housman* is a Nativity favorite; it has been produced annually at Kinosha, Wisconsin, for many years. Henry Ghéon (French, 1875-1944) and Henri Brochet (French, b. 1898) have given us such modern Nativity plays as Ghéon's *Christmas on the Square*, 1937 (translated by Sister Marie Thomas, O.P.), and Brochet's *Noel dans le hameau perdu*, translated by M. S. and O. R. Goldman as *Christmas at the Crossroads*. Mrs. Goldman has written such plays in America. These are intended for production by amateur religious groups and are presented in various parts of this country and Canada, as well as France, every Christmastide. They are deftly as well as reverently written, by intelligent, sensitive, and skilful hands; and they show that the basic drives of the theatre—its first, its fundamental and its highest appeal, that lifts the soul in exaltation—still gather power wherever the drama takes form.

EVERYMAN   *Unknown Author*

In the Middle Ages, when the church official with his poking-stick could not keep the peasants awake through the long sermons in Latin, some wise old priest decided to let the people, in their own language, know what was going on. And outside the church, on Sunday, was a sort of float, with a man holding a boy over a butcher-block; in the vernacular, the gaping crowd was told the story of Abraham about to sacrifice his son Isaac to the Lord. In this manner, the mystery play was born, with—as a modern press-agent might put it—"God's mysteries made manifest."

At first only Bible stories were shown. Later, episodes in the lives of saints and holy martyrs were pictured; some scholars call these miracle plays. The earliest known in England is the play of St. Katherine, performed about 1100 by the schoolboys of Dunstable. Such plays were popular for some 400 years. Many sections of England developed series of mystery and miracle plays; among the few of these extant are the York, the Wakefield, and the Chester cycles, of the thirteenth and fourteenth centuries. Dramatically effective episodes abound in them. In the Wakefield play of *The Crucifixion,* for example, there is a superb touch of heroic dignity in the complete silence of Jesus through the long dialogue of his four torturers.

The Church drew upon the assistance of the various guilds to present these plays; after a while, the guilds took them over; the Bakers' Guild, accustomed to roasting and boiling, put on *The Harrowing of Hell*; the Carpenters' Guild put on *Noah's Ark*. The York Cycle was probably developed by three poets with the aid of forty-eight guilds. Its plays run from Creation to Doomsday, including Adam's fall, the Passion, Resurrection, and Ascension, the fall of Lucifer, and Christ's harrowing of Hell. In an abridged and modernized form, the York Cycle was presented in 1951 at the Festival of Britain, its first performance since 1570.

There were often considerable tenderness and pathos, with occasional subtle character sketches, in the mystery plays. Thus, when little Isaac becomes aware that his father is preparing to sacrifice him to the Lord, he is overcome by fear; his pleadings that he be spared are pitiful; but gradually he senses his father's own struggle and anguish, until, mastering his fear of death, the boy not only accepts the situation but seeks to assuage his parents' grief.

As soon as the Guilds relieved the sober churchmen of the burden of presenting the mysteries, the introduction of another note was inevitable. Youth everywhere is irrepressible; with the entrance of the apprentices came horseplay and humor. Noah's wife, for instance, refuses to enter the ark without her neighbor gossips, and must be hauled aboard, kicking and squealing. While the empty cradle waits in the stable, for the soon-to-be-born Jesus, a boy hurries in with a lamb he has stolen. Shepherds are in quick pursuit; he tucks it into the cradle, and persons coming in bend over to admire the beautiful baby, until it bleats at them. Out of such episodes in the miracle and the mystery play, native comedy—as in the English *Gammer Gurton's Needle**—came to birth. (For further discussion, see *The Passion Play** and *The Shepherds' Play.**)

In the fifteenth century, another form of drama came into being. As the miracle and the mystery presented a religious story, the morality presented an ethical lesson, by means of an allegory in dialogue. The characters were such figures as Death, The World, Justice, Peace; most popular was Vice, played either as a devil or as a fool. These moralities were very popular in the reign of Edward IV of the house of York, of the white rose (king 1461-70, 1471-83) when England was torn asunder by the Wars of the Roses (1455-1485), with the Princes killed in the Tower, with intriguing, and fighting in France, with the introduction into England of printing and the silk industry—a turbulent, disorderly time, when a man might well think to his soul. And at the market-fairs, everyone eagerly awaited the covered wagon, atop which a platform was adorned with "stations," from Heaven's Gate at the left to Hell's Mouth gaping at the far right, through which the damned would be dumped to Hell (in the dressing room below). Between Heaven and Hell were the earthly stopping-places, church, home, tavern, of mankind's journey.

Far and away the best of these dramatized allegories is the English *Everyman,* c. 1450. It is probably from an earlier Dutch version; the pattern is that of a Buddhist parable told in *Barlaam and Jehoshaphat,* perhaps by John of Damascus, who died in 1090.

Left in the libraries for a couple of centuries, *Everyman* was revived in 1901 by William Poel, whose simple, moving production was joined in 1902 by Ben Greet, with Edith Wynne Matthison as Everyman. The latter gave the play its first American performance, in New York, October 13, 1902, and it is impossible to count the revivals since. *Theatre* magazine (November 1902) declared that the "naive allegory is rendered with simple reverence and strangely moving effect . . . its sombre morality far outweighs the occasional suggestions of pensive poetic charm. . . . Its fundamental lesson is effective now and always, since, with Death's inevitable summons awaiting us, 'this memory all men may have in mind.'"

The *London Times,* in 1939, exclaimed: "Curious how much better the play acts than it reads!" A little thought, however, makes this less strange. An abstract quality, on a printed page, may seem to have no more life than a wooden signpost moved mechanically. But on the stage, how present Slovenry, save like the town drab? How Drunkenness, save like the tavern toss-pot, with personal touches the watching villagers will recognize? On the stage, Death looms with a fearful actuality, and Greed and Friendship and the Five Wits come to life indeed. The morality play is thus the beginning of the satirical picture of everyday life in the drama.

Ben Greet continued his production of *Everyman* in England and America for some thirty-five years. It has also been played by college and community groups every year; for instance, in 1936, it was presented by the Barter Theatre, and by the WPA in special performances in churches on Sunday. After a 1929 performance at Columbia University, New York, Montrose J. Moses, in the *Columbia Institute Magazine* (November), praised its "permanence of human characterization, with clearness and definiteness of allegory . . . by far the best knit, the most clearly wrought morality of all time . . . in such a morality as this, we see the artist-playwright dominant over the ecclesiastic." Of an earlier New York performance, with Charles Rann Kennedy, Edith Wynne Matthison, Constance Bennett, and Pedro de Cordoba, the *New York Dramatic Mirror* (January 26, 1918) declared that "the vitality of this old play still endures." In 1955 it went on tour with college casts in California and in New England.

In the German town of Salzburg, in the open square before the cathedral, the lavish director Max Reinhardt, on June 11, 1913, gave a performance of a German version of *Everyman—Jedermann,* by Hugo von Hofmannsthal. The enthusiastic reception of this adaptation led to the holding of an annual festival at Salzburg, and to productions far and wide. An English adaptation of the German version, by Sir John Martin-Harvey, called *Via Crucis,* was presented at Stratford-on-Avon, December 15, 1922, and in London and New York in 1923. This was also played at the Hollywood Bowl, California, in 1936, with Ian Keith (and, later, Lionel Atwood) as Everyman, with Peggy Wood and Lionel Braham. In the meantime, the Reinhardt production itself came to the Century Theatre, New York, in 1927, with a German cast including Alexander Moissi as Everyman, Vladimir Sokoloff as Death, Arnold Korff, Maria Solveg, Harold Kreutzberg, Dagny Servaes, Lili Darvas, Hermann Thimig, and Hans Thimig.

The German *Jedermann* makes Everyman a wealthy burgher; Death interrupts him during a lavish banquet for his *belle amie*. The setting and the spectacular mode of presentation were on the grand Reinhardt scale that set the pace for Hollywood's most "stupendous" productions. They were far from the quiet earnestness and ominous sobriety of the English morality play. *Jedermann,* said Samuel Chotzinoff at Salzburg, August 22, 1936, "has everything but simplicity"—but it achieved, on its prodigal scale, a powerful and lasting effect. Brooks Atkinson, indeed, after a New York production by refugee actors, wondered (May 9, 1941) whether *Jedermann* doesn't go too far: "Taken out of its period, *Everyman* seems to modern ears uncomfortably like an immorality play. For Everyman manages to have a lot of cake and eat it, too. He is rich and sinful; he . . . holds iniquitous wassail with his mistress and revellers. Although an eleventh hour conversion gets him into heaven with enviable alacrity, it takes a keener eye than this theatregoer has to detect any improvement in his moral character."

About the Reinhardt production, however, there were few dissenting opinions, although Alexander Woollcott found himself "smouldering with resentment over the great wealth of the protagonist." There is, indeed, a change of emphasis, of values, from the English *Everyman* to the German *Jedermann*; instead of you or me receiving an awful summons, we watch the less immediately self-involving spectacle of a rich man trying to get into heaven. But, on its own terms, *Jedermann,* as Gilbert Gabriel said (December 8, 1927), "is crammed with splendors for the eye, largesse of bells and uplifting voices for the ear—when God the Invisible spoke out of the unplumbed blackness of the opening scene, it was as if He had torn a Vesuvius from the forehead of the earth, and were using it for a megaphone. And Death answered Him in cruel, feverish staccatos, his words splintering as jaggedly as bleached bones." Brooks Atkinson also found this production imposing: "Dr. Reinhardt's command of all the instruments of the theatre achieves two or three effects that are nothing short of miraculous. For instance, after the orchestra has sounded the opening bars of Einar Nilson's score, antiphonal choirs, dimly lighted, sing from opposite boxes just under the dome of the theatre. And nothing else anywhere in the performance communicates the supernatural mood of the legend as forcefully as the spirit cries of 'Jedermann!' 'Jedermann!' 'Jedermann!', some far off, some frightfully close at hand, while Everyman at his banquet table listens as though to the voice of Doom. They are dying words; they summon Everyman to the judgment of his Maker. Dr. Reinhardt has timed them and varied them with the stygian grimness of Death itself."

That the play is most effective when produced simply was evident in a Poel production in the open air, with Everyman at the end going down into an actually dug grave, while sparrows were twittering by.

Jedermann is a tremendous and a moving spectacle; *Everyman* is a tremendously moving play. Its very simplicity gives it a deeper impact, a wider import. The morality plays, said W. H. Haddon Squire in the *Christian Science Monitor* (September 18, 1943), "are as eloquent of those who made them, acted them, and listened to them, as are the cathedrals that gave them birth—Gothic was first and foremost a folk art." *Everyman,* he continued, holds its strength through the "vividness of its metaphor and imagery and the clean, square-cut vigor of its English." There is a quiet dignity in Everyman, as he finds his earthbound qualities (his companions) slipping from him, that marks man's noblest response to the one summons all men must heed. The journey of Everyman, simply told in dramatic form, bears a spell of beauty, and a challenge of conduct, for us all.

MASTER PIERRE PATELIN   *Unknown Author*

The farce of *Master Pierre Pathelin* (later printed as *Patelin*) is the earliest extant comedy of the modern theatre. It was probably written by a lawyer about 1464. Produced in 1469, it was published at Lyons in 1485. The farce has been played again and again, and altered down the ages. A lively New York production opened March 20, 1916, with Helen Westley, Roland Young, Glenn Hunter, and Edward J. Ballantyne of the Washington Square Players, which became the Theatre Guild. John Masefield directed the play in London in 1926. The play may be by Antoine de la Salle (c. 1398-1461); the original is in eight-syllable verses. The most requently used French version is that of Brueys (1640-1725) and Palaprat (1659-1721), called *Lawyer Pathelin.* The most frequently used adaptation in America is that of Moritz Jagendorf, in Federal Theatre productions of 1938, and in many little theatres since.

The play consists of two bits of amusing trickery, cleverly intertwined. Lawyer Patelin, after long bargaining with a draper, marches off with a roll of cloth, the draper to follow for payment. Come to Patelin's house, the draper finds Patelin in bed. Then follows a scene of which, said Henry James in the *Galaxy* (April, 1887), "the liveliest description must be ineffective. Patelin pretends to be out of his head, to be overtaken by a mysterious malady which has made him delirious, not to know the draper from Adam, never to have heard of the dozen ells of cloth, and to be altogether an impossible person to collect a debt from. To carry out this character, he indulges in a series of indescribable antics, out-Bedlams Bedlam, frolics over the room dressed out in the bed clothes and chanting the wildest gibberish, bewilders the poor draper to within an inch of his own sanity, and finally puts him utterly to rout." Patelin then dances triumphantly with his wife.

To lawyer Patelin comes a shepherd, accused of stealing a sheep. Patelin bids the fellow, no matter what is asked him, answer only "Baa!" Before the judge, Patelin argues that the shepherd has lived so long with his flock that he has become as simple and as innocent as the sheep themselves; he could not possibly have stolen one of them. But the owner of the sheep is the very draper Patelin has outwitted, and the lawyer is wearing a suit made of the draper's cloth. On seeing him, the draper begins to cry out for his cloth or his money. The judge tries vainly to keep the draper to the question of the stolen sheep, until in exasperation he dismisses the case, bidding the shepherd never again come before him.

Alone with his client, Patelin rubs his complacent hands. Congratulating himself on the cleverness with which he has saved his client, Patelin asks for his fee. The shepherd looks at him, and says "Baa!"

These intertwined anecdotes unite in an uproarious comedy. In current playing, directors usually shorten the scene of Patelin's pretended delirium, in which, railing in several dialects, he chases the draper as though trying to drive out the devil. The delight with which we see the cheater cheated makes us completely overlook the sorry state of the draper, who has been doubly duped.

The judge, confused by the draper's demanding his cloth, several times exclaims: "Revenons à ces moutons!" (Let's get back to these sheep!) This expression (reproduced by Rabelais as "Retournons à nos moutons") has become a proverbial reminder when someone slips away from the subject. *Master Pierre Patelin* is a vivid reminder of the escapades and trickeries of the Middle Ages. While it does have a bedroom scene, it is not only the first French farce, but almost the only one without emphasis on sex.

ARDEN OF FEVERSHAM   *Unknown Author*

Arden of Feversham, 1579?, like *Machinal** of recent years, draws its plot from a notorious murder. This one, recorded by Holinshed, took place in February, 1550-1. Since the characters are commoners, the play has been called the first middle-class tragedy. George Lillo, who later wrote the domestic tragedy *The London Merchant,* also wrote a play based on the Arden story.

Mistress Arden and her lover Mosbie—an emotional, quarreling couple, with Mosbie always softening to Alice Arden's allure—hire two ruffians, Black Will and Shakebag, to murder Arden. As Arden, with his friend Franklin, is returning home, he is attacked and killed. The plot being discovered, mainly through the detective work of Franklin, the guilty pair are put to death.

Published in 1592 by Edward White, who also issued unauthorized printings of Shakespeare's plays, *Arden of Feversham* is probably a revised version of *The History of Murderous Mychaell,* listed in the Revels Office as performed in 1579 at Whitehall by the Lord Chamberleyne's servants. Some have thought that *The Tragedy of Mr. Arden of Feversham*—to give the play its full title as printed—is an early work of Shakespeare. Its verse is of uneven quality, with some lines that give substance to such attribution.

Especially effective is the dramatic irony with which the play moves toward the murder. On the road, Franklin is telling Arden a story of a faithless wife, confronted with and trying to outface the clear evidence of her guilt. Franklin has a sick spell; his breath grows short, he cannot go on with the tale, which Arden is eager to have him continue—until, in a moment, the murderers put Arden beyond all further hearing.

Few plays of Tudor times deal with other folk than kings and nobles. The drama that finds importance in the lives of ordinary folk, through Lillo and Ibsen* to the domestic dramas of today, Tennessee Williams* and such popular probing as *The Death of a Salesman,** has had an early forceful forerunner in the tragedy of *Arden of Feversham.*

Its vitality was still clear when it entered the repertory of the RSC in 1982, with Bruce Purchase as Arden; Jeffery Dench, Franklin; Jenny Agutter, the guilty Alice. *Punch* called the play "superbly crafted, marvellously tense." The *Guardian* called "Terry Hands' bold and striking production a gripping piece of theatre." It was still playing at the Barbican RSC as of September 1983.

BABES IN THE WOOD   *Unknown Author*

Like Topsy, the British Christmas spectacle that is still called a pantomime "just growed" in the late nineteenth and early twentieth century. In part fairy tale, in part burlesque of current events and personalities, the pantomime employs dance and song, spectacular theatrical effects and tricky devices, comic lines and funny situations, pageantry, elaborate or fantastic costumes, characters drawn from the Bible, from British history, from continental folktale and legend—and mixes a madcap merry potpourri for the holiday season. A frequently revived pantomime is *The Forty Thieves,* and another favorite is the lovely pantomime based on the fairy tale of *Cinderella,* which, presented annually at the Christmas season, remained for more than a hundred performances in 1883, 1893, 1895, 1905, 1922, 1925, 1931, 1934, 1936, 1939, 1942, 1943, 1945. Drawn from a widespread folk story retold by Grimm, which was fashioned also into the opera *Hänsel and Gretel,** the most popular of these Christmas pantomimes is *Babes in the Wood.*

In Allardyce Nicoll's *Appendix B:* Catalogue of plays from 1850 to 1900, in his *History of Late 19th Century Drama,* there are two pages listing licensed plays called *Babes in the Wood,* as the Christmas pantomime was altered from year to year. The *Babes in the Wood* pantomimes were in blossom by 1875. Among the most popular of these annual extravaganzas have been the one opening December 26, 1888, which ran for 176 performances; that opening December 27, 1897, for 135; December 26, 1907, for 116; December 26, 1920, for 108; December 24, 1941, for 114; December 23, 1942, for 113. The 1938 production at Drury Lane had over 200 in the cast.

The two "babes" are usually Dorothy and Norman, or Marjorie Daw and Jack Daw. Their wicked and childless uncle (The Duke; Baron Hardup; Baron Bluster) sends them into the woods, with two ruffians who are to kill them. These ruffians (Tuff and Duff; Ta-ra-ra and Boom-de-ay) fight one another, and the children run off. The wood is Sherwood Forest; hence Robin Hood and Maid Marian appear. (Some versions use the title *The Babes in the Wood and Bold Robin Hood.*) With less excuse, Noah and the creatures of the ark parade; or a living alphabet; or the mantel-piece porcelains come to life in eighteenth century costumes. The Court of the Snow Queen spreads forth like a three-dimension Valentine, a gorgeous spectacle, with fairies flying in the snow; or Neptune's Grotto glitters in shimmering green, with mermaids and undersea sprites. Demons, fairies, gnomes, abound in elfin dances; and ever and anon a clown, or an assheaded oaf, or a mischievous spirit, sings a patter-song or a satyrical topical lyric. At some late hour, the lost boy blows his horn, Robin Hood comes to the rescue of the Babes, and Fairy Goodwill brings the bad Baron to proper repentance.

Dozens of authors, song writers, composers, and comic concocters of quips and cranks and wanton wiles have through the years had fingers in these Christmas puddings. Augustus Harris was responsible for productions of the 1890s. The 1905 version was mainly by A. A. Milne.* Horace Lennard wrote the 1940 book. Many of the comedians have supplied their own material. Some of the songs remain for successive versions; others are sung for a season, and replaced. There is constant freshness and variety, over a basic pattern that runs on through the years.

A wholly satiric travesty of *Babes in the Wood* was presented in London as a subscription production (thus avoiding the censor), in 1939, by Unity Theatre. The Queen said to King Useless the Useless: "All right, be huffy and abdicate." The wicked uncle carried an umbrella, looked like Chamberlain, and gave the Babes to the ruffians Hitler and Mussolini. The Fairy Wish-Fulfilment waved her wand. Lady Astor and the Cliveden set sang "England is made safe for our class"; but Robin Hood—the spirit of old England—arrived in time to save the Babes and their land. This political burlesque traded upon the popularity, but could effect no permanent distortion, of the Christmas pantomime. Fresh and in honest delight and love of living, the pattern is an ever popular one; for the 1950 Christmas season, the British on their tight little isle produced 150 pantomimes, with 20,000 performances.

Babes in the Wood is the most varied, the most spectacular, the most popular, and the most delightful, of the recurrent Christmas pantomimes. And the Christmas pantomime is a colorful and happy capture of the hopeful and ever resurgent free spirit of England, romping in the theatre to celebrate the eternal upward rouse of men of good will.

In June 1983 the daily theatrical listings carried the advertisement that reservations could now be made for the Christmas pantomime *Aladdin*, opening December 16. Others no doubt will follow throughout the land.

Late Addenda

NUMBER ONE
Jean Anouilh

Le Nombril (The Navel) had its premiere at the Paris Atelier in 1981, running for over a year. As *Number One,* opening at the London Queens, April 24, 1984, it proved noisier than most of Anouilh's comedies. For in his skylighted attic studio the successful playwright Leon Saint-Pé is aging, and plagued by gout; he bangs his cane on whatever is near; he literally twists the arm of his doctor to elicit a frank prognosis; with mingled malevolence and mischief, he rails at his sullen son who is demanding money. He is sweeter to his daughter, who also needs money but wants him to tell her husband to grant her a divorce.

"Is he unfaithful to you?"

"No. I'm unfaithful."

But the husband is a rigid scion of an old family that fends away the dust of scandal with the silent vacuum cleaner of respectability: never a divorce. Leon's visiting wife demands money, too, but rails upon him, and especially against "the whore" he is keeping—he bars her way as she rushes toward the bedroom door. There is also a novelist friend of Leon's, seeking further loans. The only one not directly asking him for money is his young mistress, who in their bedroom scene is clearly maneuvering for a stellar role in one of his plays. As he falls—or pretends to fall—asleep, she tells of the "chances" she has turned down, because of him, to dine with directors who have a role just for her.

Although Leon enjoys keeping everyone on tenterhooks, he passes out bountiful checks at the end. Every other character considers Leon caught by the title's implication of self-concern; none sees that it applies as much to him or her. A natural self-interest abides in all of us; it is only in our neighbors that it grows obtrusive. One's own mental mirror is obliging. Its variations give amusement and enlightenment to Anouilh's comedy.

The London production is still running as I write. Leo McKeon gives a lively picture of the likable old rascal; but we might wish that adapter Michael Frayn had given even the stereotype minor figures—rebellious son, "Hell hath no fury" wife, fussy physician, dumbbell tart—what motion picture magnate Samuel Goldwyn called "some fresh clichés."

THE CLANDESTINE MARRIAGE
David Garrick

David Garrick (1717-1779), theatre manager and playwright, was the greatest actor of his time, introducing an easy, natural manner of speech, which replaced the earlier lofty declamation. He made his first great success as Richard III (Shakespeare's) on October 19, 1741; but his best roles were in comedy, as of Abel Drugger in Jonson's *The Alchemist.** Among his leading ladies were Kitty Clive, Mrs. Colley Cibber, also Peg Woffington, who was his mistress for many years. Garrick became manager of Drury Lane (one of the two theatres with royal license) in 1747; when he retired in

1776, he sold his share in the Patent to R. B. Sheridan* (with Ford and Linley). He had in the meantime introduced several innovations, including barring the audience from sitting on the stage.

Among Garrick's adaptations is *The Country Girl* (1776) from Wycherley's *The Country Wife* * of 1675; Garrick's bowdlerization was popular well into the nineteenth century.

Garrick persuaded his friend George Colman the Elder (1723-1794) to try the theatre; he allowed Colman's play, *Polly Honeycomb*, to bear his name until the success of their collaboration, *The Clandestine Marriage*, 1766. This play, however, broke the friendship, for Garrick refused to play Lord Ogleby, giving the role to Tom King; and in spleen Colman took the lease of the royal theatre, Covent Garden, which for some years he had to struggle to maintain.

William Hogarth made a series of six oil paintings, *Marriage à la Mode*; the first of these, *The Marriage Contract,* suggested the Garrick-Colman play. Its prologue states:

> *Tonight, your matchless Hogarth gives the thought*
> *Which from his canvas the stage was brought.*
> *And who so fit to warm the poet's mind*
> *As he who pictured morals and mankind?*

The Clandestine Marriage is a mixture of the popular comedy of manners and a new breath of sentimentality. Mr. Sterling (Pounds sterling!) and his sister, the widow Heidelberg (an imperious and interfering woman), both see for his daughters no marriage not combining title and money. That is why his younger daughter, Fanny, and his clerk, Lovewell, must keep their four-month marriage secret—though circumstances make Fanny feel that it must soon be disclosed. Meanwhile, Sir John Melvil, Lord Ogleby's nephew, engaged to the elder Sterling sister, sees and falls in love with Fanny. Though Sterling is startled, the exchange of daughters seems no great obstacle to him; but, of course, Fanny is distraught. She seeks help with Lord Ogleby, a vain old fool whose name shows his nature; when Fanny confesses that another man than Sir John holds her heart, Ogleby assumes that she means him and swears to share his fortune with her. Then Fanny's sister and Mrs. Heidelberg attack the door of Fanny's bedroom, where they know a man is with her. Fanny comes out—and faints. Lovewell rushes out to her, and their relationship is revealed. Lord Ogleby, recovering his wits, says he has pledged his fortune to her; Sterling's eloquent countenance (wordlessly) inquires, confirms, accepts—and all is well.

The play, long popular, was revived by Anthony Quayle's "Compass," opening at the London Albery, June 7, 1984, with Quayle as Lord Ogleby, Joyce Redman as Mrs. Heidelberg, and Roy Kinnear as Sterling. Amusingly overacted, despite its many asides and the obvious opposition of sweet innocence and crude self-concern, "high manners and low intentions," the play remains thoroughly enjoyable, as well as a vivid presentation of the period (as the play's Prologue goes on)

> *Where titles deign with cits to have and hold*
> *And change rich blood for more substantial gold.*

Mutatis mutandis, much truth in the play still holds.

AMERICAN BUFFALO, ETC.   *David Mamet*

David Mamet (b. 1947, in Chicago) is the most varied of current American playwrights, in manner, mood, and choice of subject.

Duck Variations premiered at Goddard College, Vermont, in 1972; then OffBway (St. Clement's), 1975; OffBway (Cherry Lane), June 1976; London (Regent), December 1977. Emil Varec and George S. Aronovitz, "two gentlemen in their sixties" (named in the program but not in the play), sit on a park bench and in fourteen "variations" discuss the ducks on and over the lake nearby. Their talk is rambling, repetitious, with (says Ruby Cohn in *New American Dramatists,* 1982) "mastery of the speech of old men." Toward the end, George remarks that the old men in ancient Greece used to watch the birds all day. Emil closes the play: "Each with something to contribute. That the world might turn another day. A fitting end. To some very noble creatures of the sky. And a lotta Greeks."

Sexual Perversity in Chicago, first produced in Chicago (Organic Theatre) in 1974, was usually—as at St. Clement's, Cherry Lane, and the London Regent—presented with *Duck Variations.* In it, Dan Shapiro, Bernard Litko, and Deborah Solomon—who has left the consequently bitter and sarcastic lesbian Joan Webber to live with Danny—talk about sex in such detail as only the most permissive stages would allow, as when Deborah explains why she loves "the taste of come." (In all his plays, Mamet's favorite word seems to be *fuck,* in any of its forms, literally or as a casual epithet.) The two men go to a pornographic movie. They watch the women at a beach: "With tits like that, who needs—anything." Everywhere they talk sex, rather than perform it. They watch an imaginary woman go by; she makes no response to their greeting. Danny says "Deaf bitch!" and the curtain falls. But perhaps he was giving vent to his feelings at having broken with Deb.

In 1969, David Mamet worked in a real estate office. At the NT (Cottesloe) on September 21, 1983, appeared his *Glengarry Glen Ross,* picturing six real-estate salesmen, in groups of two in a Chinese restaurant, bitter rivals in a fly-by-night firm that uses psychological pressure on innocent buyers of dream homes in pseudoparadises, like Glengarry Glen Ross. Two of the salesmen plan to steal the list of leads— *leads* are appointments for interviews with potential purchasers, the best given by the bosses to their preferred salesmen. Mamet says "*lead,* in the same way that a clue in a criminal case is called a *lead*—i.e., it may lead to the suspect, the suspect in this case being a *prospect.*" The next morning (Act Two) in the office, the theft has taken place. Frustration and confusion mount, until the detective pulls the guilty salesman Levene into the inner office, and the younger and more successful Roma goes to lunch. Michael Billington in the *London Guardian* said: "You won't hear much better dialogue on the London stage than you get in *Glengarry Glen Ross.* The play is filled with spiraling obscenity and comic bluster . . . yet underneath there is fear and desperation . . . a chillingly funny indictment of a world in which you are what you sell."

At the New Haven Yale Rep in 1977 a new mood for Mamet was evoked in *Reunion,* given 33 performances at the OffBway Circle opening October 18, 1979. This pictures a father of fifty-three meeting his twenty-five-year-old daughter, whom he had long ago abandoned. Shown with this was the brief *Dark Pony,* also of a father and daughter, both plays with a tenderness and understanding unexpected in these unsentimental, often cynical, times. Mamet seems at his best with lovable little people.

In all his plays, perhaps most in *American Buffalo,* Mamet favors speeches of few words, often only "Yeah!" "No." "What?" Of *Buffalo's* last seventy "speeches," two are of nine words, the rest of fewer, twenty of only one. *Newsweek* said: "Mamet's ear is tuned to an American frequency."

Many are familiar with the American buffalo on the American five-cent piece, the old nickel; and in Don Dubrow's junk shop, Don and Walter Cole— a know-it-all fellow called Teach—are planning to steal a coin collection. Teach is confident he can crack the safe—by finding the combination the owner has hidden, in case he forgets it. "Action counts," says Don. "Action talks and bullshit walks." Bob, Don's gopher (current slang for one who will *go* on errands *for* others), being scarcely a half-wit, hinders rather than helps. The fellow-conspirator they are awaiting never gets there, being mugged on the way. But the others never get there either. Bob comes with a buffalo nickel he has bought, hoping to please Don; Teach cracks Bob viciously on the side of the head, and the play ends as Don tries to comfort Bob on the way to the hospital.

American Buffalo premiered at the Chicago Goodman, November 23, 1975. At the OffBway St. Clement's, February 1976; opening for 135 performances at the New York Ethel Barrymore, February 16, 1977, and winning the Obie award. It has been produced widely across the United States; thus twenty-one performances at Costa Mesa, Cal., and fifty at Long Wharf, New Haven in 1980; thirty-three at the Washington, D.C., Arena, 1981. It came to the NT (Cottesloe), June 1978, and was revived at the London Duke of York's, July 1984, where it is still running as I write. David Nathan in the *Jewish Chronicle* of August 10, said "Mamet uses speech as a probe to burrow deep into the lives of those that dream the American dream and cry out in pain in their sleep." Teach is a boastful but frustrated loser in a land that pays homage to the winners, praises and pays. Mamet (says Ruby Cohn) conveys "the problematics of personal relations in the most economical dialogue."

London criticism of *Buffalo* was divided, but there was unanimous praise for Al Pacino as the bossy but basically self-tormented Teach. It should be noted that Mamet's plays have little plot, and no climactic endings. As in life, there is more to come. We look for more to come from David Mamet.

Shakespeare—Personal

Two phantoms hovering over the Bard of Avon should be briefly exorcised. First, the eager search for the black lady—called the "dark lady" to win more pleasant acceptance (just as *diamorphine*—who wants to die o' morphine— was glibly called by the vendors *heroin*). The sonnets call the lady *black* ten times, dark only once, and that to avoid repetition:

> For I have called thee fair, and thought thee bright,
> Who art as black as hell, as dark as night. (Sonnet 147)

Note also—which the ardent woman-hunters ignore:

> In nothing art thou black save in thy deeds. (Sonnet 131)

First mentioned is the notion that all the sonnets are addressed to the Queen. Then came words about Jane Davenant (whose son the writer

William was content to have the rumor spread that he was Shakespeare's son); she was wife of the innkeeper, with whom Shakespeare may have stayed, between Stratford and London. Literal-minded hunters have not ceased to search. One suggestion claims "Lady Negro, Abbess of Clerkenwell," who, says the *Shakespeare Encyclopedia,* was unquestionably dark—without any mention that *abbess* was slang for a brothelkeeper, and Clerkenwell not a convent but the red-light district of London.

Several ladies of Queen Elizabeth's court have been put forward. Latest investigator to intrude into the fold has been historian Alfred L. Rowse, who advances as the black lady the wife of one of the Queen's musicians, seduced and described by astrologer Simon Forman in his Elizabethan diary, which Rowse unearthed. He rouses no more enthusiasm than the rest. It should be clear to poets and literary scholars that all the acts, moods, and attitudes attributed to the so-called dark lady are to be found in the many sonnet series in the two centuries from the Italian Renaissance into the Elizabethan; Shakespeare's "lady" seems more real simply because he was a greater artist. Except as the traditional sonnet-man (of his Sonnets 57, 58, 141), Shakespeare was never slave to any woman.

Second, sprung perhaps of the nineteenty-century bardolatry, is the notion that the poorly educated son of a provincial butcher could not have produced the Shakespearean masterpieces, with all their erudition and knowledge of courtly ways. As late as 1919, J. Thomas Looney advanced as author the seventeenth Earl of Oxford. He was properly squelched by the query: "Who is loony now?" Earlier, with a long list of believers—Lord Penzance, Lord Palmerston, William Henry Smith, Sir George Greenwood, Professor Lefranc—in his 1888 two-volume *The Great Cryptogram* Ignatius Donnelly with many ciphers claimed the plays for Francis Bacon. Though somnolent, this claimant still haunts the chambers of dream: as recently as 1984 a volume used modern scientific knowledge (eye color) to protest that Bacon's official parents could not have begotten him, and Elizabethan backdoor rumor to declare him the offspring of Queen Elizabeth and Leicester, as well as author of the plays. Bacon's "mother" was First Lady in Waiting to the Queen, so the secret could have been kept.

What all the Baconians have overlooked, however is that Shakespeare himself used their own weapons to destroy their story. For the significant title of his play *Much Adoe About Nothing*—so spelled in the first printing, 1600, and in the famous First Folio of the collected works, 1623—is an anagram of "Bacon? O, naught due to him." Leave Shakespeare to his plays.

The name, by the way, spelled in at least thirteen ways, was probably not warlike; it was presumably pronounced with a short *a.* The spelling Chacksper has led to the suggestion that it may have sprung from Jaques-Pierre, two common peasant names.

Incidentally, many gentlemen before Byron, who swam the Hellespont, might agree that "in bountiful air, bath is idiotic." This happens to be an anagram of Shakespeare's most famous nonce word, that long alternation of consonants and vowels: *honorificabilitudinitatibus,* in *Love's Labor's Lost,* V, i.

INDEX

Page numbers in <u>italics</u> refer to main discussions of plays.